The Bill James

HISTORICAL

Baseball Abstract

The Bill James

HISTORICAL
Baseball Abstract

Bill James

 VILLARD BOOKS
NEW YORK 1988

**This book is dedicated to the man
who has done more for baseball research
than anyone else living—L. Robert Davids.**

Library of Congress Cataloging in Publication Data
James, Bill, 1949–
   Bill James historical baseball abstract.

   Bibliography: p.
   Includes index.
   1. Baseball—United States—History. 2. Baseball—
United States—Records. I. Title.
GV863.A1J36   1988   796.357′0973   87-40570
ISBN 0-394-75805-6 (pbk.)

Photograph on page 234 courtesy of
the Bettmann Archive.

Photographs on pages 106, 153, 181, and
226 courtesy of Wide World Photos.

Text designed and illustrated by Mary A. Wirth
Manufactured in the United States of America

Book-of-the-Month Records® offers recordings on
compact discs, cassettes and records. For information and
catalog write to BOMR, Department 901, Camp Hill, PA 17012.

Contents

Acknowledgments

■ Behind every great man there is a great woman, and some of us ordinary Joes get lucky, too. My wife, Susan McCarthy, would do credit to a man of far greater accomplishments than myself. She has her own work to do (she is an artist), but this has never stopped her from putting in twenty or forty or sixty hours a week on my work as well, and each time a book deadline draws near, she begins to devote more and more time to it, and to assume more and more responsibility for seeing that it gets done. She is an accomplished typist, secretary, statistician, office manager, bookkeeper, proofreader, schedule-maker, and editor. She is patient of husbands who work until 4 o'clock in the morning, neglect their share of the household duties, grow irritable when their work does not go well, and make unreasonable demands on all who are around them. Without her help, this book would not be what it is.

I could say the same of many others:

• Jim Baker worked with me while I was writing the first edition of this book, and provided invaluable assistance in helping to develop the library necessary to research it, helping to research it, helping to write it, and taking care of other duties so I could work on this book.

• Neil Munro did most of the work of assembling the data on players' career records in categories which had not been published before, such as hit by pitch, caught stealing, and grounded into double plays.

• Pete Palmer, David Frank, Gordon Herman, Randy Lakeman, and Chuck Waseleski also provided information and research.

• Tom Heitz, Jeff Kernin and Donna Cornell of the Hall of Fame Library in Cooperstown were very generous with their time, and were invaluable in certain parts of the research, as well as in locating and getting copies of photographs.

• Jim Carothers contributed time and intelligence to his own project within these pages.

• Peter Gethers remains a supportive and helpful editor, who tries to get the book out the way I want it, rather than trying to get me to write the book that he wants. Other people at Villard and/or Random House who have put time and effort into trying to make this thing work include Laura Godfrey, Audrey Simon, Marc Jaffe, Melissa Browne, Kim Banks, Mary Wirth, Anet Sirna-Bruder, Linda Rosenberg, and, of course, the sales force.

• Liz Darhansoff continues to represent my interests in the publishing business, and to be an unfailing source of advice and good counsel.

Uncounted masses of people provided ideas, made suggestions, helped me to solve problems that I was having, or wrote articles that were used as background research. I have tried hard to acknowledge these throughout the book, as appropriate, and not to appear to take credit for the work that other people have done (baseball has one Joe Reichler; it doesn't need another). Still, I may have failed to credit someone who did original research from which I lifted certain facts. To those people I send my apologies, and I would ask, on a personal level, that if you feel that I borrowed some of your research and didn't properly credit it, you might contact me and let me know, because there is a good chance that this book would be re-issued in a few years, and I would want to correct that if I could. Thanks to all.

The people who form that indistinct and maligned mass known as "the media" have, without exception, been quite kind to me, most of the time on purpose, but failing that by accident. Thanks to all.

Stokely and Isadora are just dogs, and we will probably never be able to get them to understand that they were acknowledged here, but all the same, they are terrific dogs, and I appreciate the effort. Thanks to D, T, B, TB, C, I, LC, BH, the S and LF, as well as W, W and S. Thanks to Paul, Phyllis, Rosalie, Carol, Georgine, Nell, Craig, Chris, Dan and Dallas, and most of all to those who read. Without any of you, this book would not be the same, and without all of you, I wouldn't have any idea who I was writing to.

Introduction

■ Hi. My name is Bill James. I write an annual book about baseball called *The Baseball Abstract*. It's kind of a technical book, at times, and there are a couple of essays in it every year that are not real easy to understand; it's sort of like *Street and Smith's Baseball Annual,* only it's for adults. I invent all manner of different ways of measuring things, estimating things, describing relationships within the game, and I use these to analyze almost any question about baseball that comes up. Some people like it, some people don't. I was once described by a now defunct publication as "the guru of baseball statistics," and by Sparky Anderson as "a little fat guy with a beard . . . who

knows nothing about nothing." Actually, I'm seven inches taller than Sparky is, but what the heck; three out of four ain't bad, and it sure beats being described as the guru of baseball statistics.

Anyway, *The Baseball Abstract* is published by Ballantine Books. Ballantine has a sister named Villard Books, which publishes mostly hardcover stuff, and the people who run Villard Books were wondering if I could adapt the premises of the annual book to cover the history of baseball, since this would create a book that had a shelf life longer than a package of Oreos. I said I could, and I did, and in many ways I was surprised by the book—this book—that resulted.

In contrast to the annual entries, this is not a very technical book, and not a very serious book. I've done some of the same sort of stuff, the weighing and measuring of everything, that I do each year. But the basic premise of *The Baseball Abstract* is that I try never to tell the reader anything he already knows. The things that you as the reader already know about baseball history are much different than the things that you already know about the contemporary game—much more difficult to judge, for one thing. But whereas in writing about the present, one must occasionally retreat to some obscure statistical reference chart in order to find something to say about a player or team that has not already been booted about, I found that in writing about the past there was much less need for that, and much greater opportunity to discuss matters closer to the surface, such as personalities, strategies, parks and games.

Strategy in baseball never comes to rest; it is in constant search of an equilibrium that, the Lord willing, it will never find. The first section of this book, called "The Game," is, in a sense, about that search for an equilibrium, about how the game of each decade was different from the game of the one before. But if each decade is different in some ways, in many more ways it is the same, and the first section of the book is also about that, about the repeating patterns and habits of the game.

The second section of the book, called "The Players," could be described as the Who-Was-Better-Than-Whom section, and consists in the main of information and arguments about the relative merits of the few hundred best players in the history of the game. I'm an argumentative cuss by nature, and how much you enjoy that section of the book is likely to depend to a large extent on how much you like to argue about baseball players.

The third section of the book, called "The Records," is a reference section, and contains the most complete data ever published for about two hundred players, most of them great ones.

I have tried to make this book self-contained and self-explanatory. At the same time, the annual editions of *The Baseball Abstract* are, in essence, each part of a discussion continued from year to year, and this book is also very much a part of that discussion. If you're new to the discussion, welcome; you've come at a good time. If you've been here before, welcome back.

—Bill James

Section I

THE

Game

Oh-oh say, can you seee,
By the dawn's early light,
What so prou-dly we hailed
At the twi-lights last gleam-ing

Whose broad stripes and bright stars
Through the perilous fight
O'er the ram-parts we watched
Were so gallant-ly streaming

And the rockets' red glare,
The bombs bursting in air,
Gave prooof, through the night,
That our flag was still there.

Oh-oh say, does that star-spangled
          banner yet wa-ave
O'er the lan-and of the freee
And the home
Of the braaave?

PLAY BALL

Introduction

The first part of this book, comprising the bulk thereof, looks at the history of baseball as it has unfolded, decade by decade since 1870. There are eleven sections, one on each decade from the 1870s through the 1970s.

As I originally envisioned the *Historical Abstract,* this section of it would have been small, almost perfunctory, a quick look at the history of the game to set the table for Section II—a detailed analysis of the greatest players in the history of the game, who was greater than who and why, etc. But as I began to do research on the history of baseball (in order to discuss those questions more intelligently) I began to feel that there was a history of baseball that had never been written—a history of good and ordinary players, a history of being a fan, a history of games that meant something at the time but mean nothing now. I had read so many articles on Joe Di-Maggio and Cap Anson, and so few on Wally Moses and Tom Seats and Kirby Higbe and Buck Ewing and Bill Lange, that when I began to find out things about those players I felt that I was stumbling across a wilderness, fascinating—and I knew then that I would not be at ease writing more articles on Di-Maggio and Anson, but must write instead about Larry McLean and Henry Clay Pulliam.

It's a question, really, of what questions do you answer? Baseball histories usually try to answer the great questions. Who was the greatest player ever? Who was the greatest pitcher ever? What was the greatest team ever? What was the greatest team of the era? How did baseball develop? Who should be in the Hall of Fame? I decided, instead, to write a book that would discuss the small questions, and the small questions about each era—and to try, in that way, to give a sense of what it was like to be a baseball fan in 1885, or what it was like to be a baseball fan in 1925, or what it was like to be a baseball fan in 1940. Who was the best second baseman of the 1930s? What outfielder had the best throwing arm? How was the game changing at this moment? Why did it change? What were the passing news stories, the petty controversies? Who was the most admirable star player of the time? Who was the least admirable? Who was the best hitting pitcher? Who was the worst hitting pitcher? Who was the best looking? Who was the ugliest? What was the best World Series of the time? What was the best trade of the time? Whose death was in the newspaper, and what did he die of? Make up thirty more questions just like those, and try to find the answers to them.

Somewhere in there I went plumb crazy, and I began to believe that baseball history was as much a history of Carl Reynoldses and Bob Cervs and Boss Schmidts as it was a history of Ted Williamses and Tris Speakers and Duke Sniders. Somehow I completely forgot what baseball history was all about—the Homer in the Gloamin' and the one that Ruth pointed off Charlie Root and Branch Rickey telling Jackie Robinson that he wanted a man who had the guts not to fight back—and I started digressing into Albert Spalding's attempt to keep the identity of his official scorer secret, how nicknames changed from the twenties to the thirties, and what ballplayers did for a living after they retired.

The results of this delusion are broken down into three parts in each decade:

1) *How, Where, and by Whom.* How the Game Was Played, Where the Game Was Played, and Who the Game Was Played By.

This material is fairly basic, and much of what is in it will not be new to those of you who are knowledgeable about baseball history. Some of it seeks to correct misunderstandings about the period (such as the notion that a "lively ball" was adopted in 1920), and a certain portion of it is argumentative, but some of it is not even that. It is written first of all for the benefit of readers who do not feel that they have an understanding of the changes in how the game was played that have taken place over the course of the century, and second to create a reference framework for the rest of the material about the decade.

2) *The Decade in a Box.* Small questions with short answers. Who was the highest-paid player of the decade? What was the attendance during the period? That sort of thing.

I received some help in answering these questions. Jim Baker was assigned to find answers to many of these questions, and is occasionally credited with writing one of the answers. Many other times he found the answer or a reference with which the

question could be answered.

One question I asked about each decade was "What were the best baseball books written?" The answers to that question, and a few related comments about baseball writing during the period, were supplied by someone more knowledgeable than myself, Dr. Jim Carothers. Jim is a friend of mine who teaches English Lit. at the University of Kansas, and offers a popular class on the literature of baseball, which I gather is popular only because the little devils don't realize that he actually intends to make them work to gain control of the material, just like a regular class. No, I'm sure they do realize that, but anyway, it is a legitimate class, with no more than sporadic outbursts of football players enrolled in it, and Jim is a legitimate authority in the field.

The citations for the best-looking and ugliest players, again, were made by a qualified expert: my wife. Susie spent many hours poring over every photograph in my library, and emerged with a list of the handsomest and homeliest from each period (selections that are exactly as good as anybody else's), plus an introduction of her own, which follows this introduction.

While she was doing this, she also made notes on how baseball uniforms were evolving over time. This gets back to one of the basic things that we were trying to do with this section, which is to help you, working together with your own imagination, to visualize the game as it was played in that time. It relates to something that Jim Baker said early on in putting the book together:

I think it is important, when visualizing a game in the 1880s, not to have a man in the on-deck circle swinging a bat with a weighted donut.

Exactly. What were the details of the game? What was the man in the on-deck circle wearing? What was the uniform made out of? How was it fastened? *What was baseball like then?*

Susie feels the need to emphasize that she is not an expert on the history of uniforms or cloth or clothes in general; I've tried to tell her, as I've tried to explain to so many people, that when you write facts they are either true or they are false, and being an expert or not being an expert really has absolutely nothing to do with it. She worked hard to double-check the things she wrote and see that they were true, and while she might have bobbled a ground ball or two, I'm sure that for the most part she got it right.

Many of these selections are matters of opinion, or matters of best evidence, or matters of best guess on the available evidence. Sometimes the selections are as arbitrary as it's possible to be; there are a hundred players in any of the first eight decades who could be selected as the best unrecognized player.

One thing that it is important to note about citations such as "fastest player in the game," "slowest player in the game," "most aggressive baserunner," "best outfield arm" and "best athlete in the game" is that statistics played only the most minor role in making these selections; they are based almost entirely on comments about the players in the literature of the sport. If there are eighty selections like that in the book, there aren't more than two that are based on statistics; we did that only if (a) we could find absolutely no discussion of the matter in the literature, and (b) the statistical evidence was clear. Otherwise, statistics might have played a peripheral role in choosing among candidates; if we had three comments about outfielders having notoriously bad arms, but one of them averaged five assists a year and another one twelve, I certainly would not make a selection that flies in the face of the statistical evidence. I wouldn't pick a guy as the fastest runner of his time if he grounded into twenty double plays a year; that just doesn't make sense.

But I've always said that awards based on statistics are dumb; nobody needs a shoe company or an antacid tablet to tell them what somebody's statistics are. Although these are not awards, the same principle applies. Statistical selections only make sense when they tell you something that you can't immediately see for yourself. One of the operating assumptions of this book is that you either own Macmillan's *The Baseball Encyclopedia* or aren't interested in what it has to say; in either case, you don't need me to tell you what an outfielder's assists totals were. To use the 1920s as an example, there is an absolute consensus as to which outfielder had the best throwing arm of the time; I could show you a half-dozen books in which somebody just flat-out says that this guy had the best arm in baseball. In the previous decade, there are many comments about good-throwing outfielders, but there is no consensus as to whose was the best. But that's what we're looking for, and only secondarily at assists totals.

Sometimes an item in the decade box will be marked with an asterisk. The asterisk means that more information on the subject can be found in the headlines.

3) *Headlined Articles.* The headlined articles contain anything that doesn't fit in one of the other categories; for example, when an article about the best unrecognized player in the decade gets longer than

a couple of paragraphs, it gets pulled out of the box and a headline is put over it. It's like a newspaper form, a catch-all. You say what you're trying to say and make it fit.

Let's get to it. Susie's introduction follows, and then on to the section on the 1870s.

INTRODUCTION TO SUSIE'S SELECTIONS

Just before my study was complete, I stumbled across an article entitled "Baseball's Ten Handsomest Men" in the September 1957 issue of *Sport* magazine. The author talked about how women (giggly girls) swooned when the strikingly tall, dark and handsome Ted Williams walked to the plate. He was "all man," you know; she wrote about how women just love a strong, dominant man, and she went on (and on) about a particular "boy" being the one you would have wanted to carry your books, while another was the one you would have wanted to ask you to the prom, or the boy you would have wanted to marry. Some other classic lines: of Jerry Coleman, "Brown eyes that sparkle and dark brown curly hair make women's eyes roll like ball bearings." Of Vinegar Bend Mizell, "He flips female hearts with his masculinity." Of Eddie Mathews, "but with those beautiful muscles, he can make a girl believe anything."

Just for the record, I wanted to say that this study was not conducted to do any of the things that the *Sport* article seems to be about. I have yet to see a baseball card that made me want to marry anybody, and it would take me months to get the mothball smell out of my prom dress. Come to think of it, I don't have a prom dress.

This study was done, basically, just for the fun of it. We can't claim that there is any reason you should accept our findings. We could claim that we had to do it because nobody else would. Handsome players and ugly players are a part of every decade, just like minor leaguers and major leaguers, fast runners and slow runners and tobacco chewers. I got to pick them because I seemed to be of the appropriate sex for the task. For another thing, I come to the history of baseball with little knowledge, being largely unfamiliar with the players, their numbers or faces, and this ignorance should prevent me from making the "I know he's ugly but he sure could play second base" type of calls. On the other hand, no doubt I glanced quickly over some faces that I should have paid more attention to. Bill gave me only one hint about who he thought I ought to pick. Donald Mossi. I did have to scout around for a picture of him, but he was worth it.

—Susan McCarthy

The 1870s

HOW THE GAME WAS PLAYED

The national sport in the last century, having distinguished itself from rounders by an accretion of changes in the period 1830–70, has since fractured into any number of related games—baseball, softball, slow-pitch softball, tee-ball for small ones, stickball for the streets, work-up for the sandlot. Of those games, baseball in 1870 resembled fast-pitch softball more than any other, including modern baseball. The pitch was delivered underhand from a distance of 45 feet, 15 feet closer than now; the rules required a stiff arm so as to control speed, but the rules were not tightly enforced, and pitchers could move the ball in there pretty good with a flick of the wrist. The ball was not wound so tight as it would be later; it was a handmade ball of yarn with a cover on it, not terribly standard in size or shape, and to hit the thing 400 feet would probably have been impossible.

Basic play in other respects was largely then as now, much of which is common to the family of games. Bases were 90 feet apart and touched in the same sequence as now. The rule specifying a putout by hitting the runner with a thrown ball had disappeared from use during the 1850s. The rule allowing an out for a ball caught on one bounce was on the way out after 1863. The batters batted in order, as they do now.

In other small respects, the game was different, but it is important to understand that many features of the modern game were present despite somewhat different rules. "Anyone who searches through old records," wrote Harold Seymour in his classic history of the development of baseball *(Baseball: The Early Years),* "is bound to be impressed with how much was already known about the fundamentals of the game, playing the various positions, and 'inside baseball.'" Seymour insists that Charles Comiskey in the 1880s was not the first man to play off the bag at first, as others have written, and that "this method of play was familiar and commonly used back in the 1860s." (Another historian, David Voight, credits Joe Start with originating this play.) Seymour also ticks off the following list of developments prior to 1870:

- First basemen held the runner on first if needed, and played off the bag when the base was empty.
- Left-handed first basemen were regarded as having an advantage.
- The expression "long ball" was used, though, since few parks had outfield walls within reach, it rarely referred to the automatic home run that we know now.
- Pitchers changed speeds.
- The controversy about whether or not a pitcher could make a ball curve was already going.
- Teams in 1870 would put their most agile infielder at shortstop, and the infielder with the best arm at third base.
- Speed and throwing arms were valued in the outfield, and the fastest man on the team was often the center fielder.
- The system of relaying throws in from the outfield already existed.
- Outfielders shifted their positions to play the hitters.
- Sliding was becoming more common.
- Baserunners would tag up and advance after a play.

- Dickey Pearce, a shortstop, had invented bunting.

In other respects the game, of course, was not the same. A ball was fair if it bounced in fair territory, which effectively required the fielders to cover a larger area. (Ross Barnes hit .404 or .429 in the first season of the National League, 1876, by perfecting the "fair-foul bunt"—that is, landing the ball in fair territory so that it would roll foul. At the time, a batter who walked was charged with an at bat, thus creating the discrepancy between his batting average as it was then and as it is now.) The batter called for a high pitch or a low pitch, to his liking, which in some respects is like a football team calling for a run or a pass, but in another sense can be seen as an outgrowth of one of baseball's unique features: It is the only sport in which the team that has the ball is on defense.

Nine innings and three strikes antedate professionalism in baseball, but it took nine balls to walk somebody, so you didn't get too many of those. Not many walks, not many homers, but lots of singles and lots of errors. That's the one largest difference between the offensive constructions of 1870 and those of 1920—all those errors. The Boston Red Stockings in 1871 hit .295 as a team and probably did not hit a huge number of home runs (though the count

is not recorded), but they scored in excess of twelve runs a game because of the much greater number of errors. Fielding gloves were not introduced until 1875, and they had no padding then, so a fielder's hands would swell up something fierce; it wouldn't have been at all unusual for a team to make three, four, maybe more errors in an inning—and that made the innings long enough to get out of hand. Though stolen base records do not exist, base stealing does not seem to have been as common in the early days of the professionals as it had been in the amateur baseball of the sixties or as it would be later. George Wright confirmed that in his day they had never realized the potential value of base stealing.

Teams at the beginning of the 1870s played only about thirty games a year and used but one pitcher; as the decade progressed the schedules grew longer almost every year, and by 1879 all teams carried a spare to give their Number 1 pitcher an occasional day off (the Number 1 man might start seventy of eighty games, for example). Combining these two points, then, it is clear that the prevention of runs was essentially the responsibility of the defense, and much less so of the pitcher.

Another point with regard to the schedule is that the teams often played nonleague teams. In 1871, when the Association teams only played about thirty games each, they might well have played another fifty or sixty games or even more (I don't think anybody knows) against teams from other leagues—nonprofessional leagues, city all-star teams, anything. The season stretched until November 15.

It is very much an open question as to when the National League teams became distinctly superior to any other teams. Sportswriters often insisted that the so-called "major league" teams were no better than other teams until the mid-eighties. It would be a worthy study to go back and find a city that had good sports coverage in the era, like Louisville or Syracuse, and find out how many games the city's team did play against nonleague competition in this period, and what their record was. I'm sure that the Boston teams under Harry Wright regularly demolished their opponents, but I think it likely that some of the weaker teams in the National League in 1878 or so were really no stronger than a hundred other teams around the country.

When you arrived at a game in 1878, a player might take your ticket; this was still true as late as 1890. George Wright, who lived to be ninety, recalled the era in an interview with the *New York Sun* in 1915. "Youngsters who are accustomed to see 1 to 0 and 2 to 1 games may well wonder,"

he said, "how it was that the early Base Ball nines were able to score so many runs. The fact is that the pitchers in those days were not the skilled artists of the present and depended mainly on an underhand ball, which was easy to hit; and then again, the fielders did not gobble up the grounders so skillfully or try to stop with their bare hands the wicked liners that are 'speared' nowadays." Wright also said that "Batting was not done as scientifically in those days as now. The sacrifice hit was unthought of and the catcher was not required to have as good a throwing arm because no one had discovered the value of the stolen base. Long drives were more common than at present." The long drives would shortly return.

But it was baseball; you wouldn't have any trouble recognizing it. The games were a little long and the scores were a little high, but it was baseball. The skills in demand were the same, the personalities were the same, the arguments were the same. Baseball was baseball before it was professional baseball.

And with that blithe assurance, I'm going to have to warn you that the picture presented here of baseball in the nineteenth century is, of necessity, rather incomplete. Just to answer fully one of the questions that make up the data boxes on these first three decades could easily use up a

book. Team vs. team in the 1890s? There are volumes in that subject. Player vs. team (salary battles, player/management battles) of the 1880s? There could be books written on that subject. Overlooked stars of the nineteenth century? They're almost all overlooked—all your average fan knows about baseball in the nineteenth century is Willie Keeler and the Baltimore Orioles. How the game was changing from decade to decade? New strategies in use? New terms in use? You got a million words there.

It is far beyond the scope of this book to repair the common ignorance of baseball in the nineteenth century. If you are really interested in the subject, read Harold Seymour's book, mentioned earlier, or David Voight's *American Baseball: From Gentleman's Sport to the Commissioner System,* or join the Society for American Baseball Research and start collecting their stuff. I am neither competent nor at leisure to write the volumes that would be required to do this century justice.

WHERE THE GAME WAS PLAYED

We're talking about two leagues here. The first avowedly professional league, the National Association of Professional Baseball Players, which lasted from 1871–75, allowed whoever wanted to join in to do so, provided that they pay the entry fee and abide by the other rules of the league. The entry fee was initially $10, equivalent to about $150 today. The teams drew up their own schedules, agreeing only to play at least five games against each of the other teams. Initially, there were teams in the league from Boston, Chicago, Cleveland, Fort Wayne, New York, Philadelphia, Rockford, Troy (New York) and Washington, D.C. Some teams would drop out and others join in; before going out of business the league would include Baltimore, Brooklyn, Middletown (Connecticut), Elizabeth, Hartford, St. Louis, New Haven, and Keokuk. If you'll note that list carefully you'll see that it started out with a midwestern flavor, anchored around Chicago, and gradually moved east, anchoring around New York.

The National Association is to the National League precisely as the American states under the Articles of Confederation are to the United States. There were agreements but no provisions for enforcing them, no strong central authority. Teams would not schedule the games that they were required to or not play them when they were scheduled. There was no uniformity in umpiring, ticket pricing, or field conditions. Teams haggled over how the gate was to be shared between visiting and home teams; some stronger teams demanded and got inequitable relationships with the weaker teams. The association was plagued with "revolvers," players who jumped from one team to another. Eventually the stronger teams got tired of putting up with the tentative and ineffectual management of the Keokuk's and Middletown's of the league, and broke off to form the National League.

The National League transferred the power in the structure from the players to the financial backers, the "owners" as we would call them today. It was named the National *League* of Professional Baseball *Clubs*. They also created a structure for the league—a league president, secretary/treasurer, board of directors—and assessed each club $100 a year for the costs of doing business. This implied that that central organization had authority and would use it, and it did. The man who had organized this palace revolt, and would wield the power in the league until his death in 1881, was William Hulbert.

In 1876 the league started with teams in Boston, Chicago, Cincinnati, Hartford, Louisville, New York, Philadelphia and St. Louis—a good selection of the biggest and best baseball cities in the nation as it was then. But at the end of the 1876 season, New York and Philadelphia refused to make their final, western road trip, figuring they had already lost enough money on the year. For this, New York and Philadelphia were kicked out of the league. It was, to extend the parallel, the National League's Whiskey Rebellion, and authority was effectively asserted.

The wisdom of this action has been debated regularly over the course of the last century. On the one hand, it was necessary to establish respect for the rules of the league; on the other, it deprived the young league of the nation's two largest cities, eventually forcing the league back into cities like Syracuse and Troy, and endangering its position as the nation's strongest league.

Anyway, to resume the list of cities . . . Buffalo, Indianapolis, Milwaukee, Providence, Syracuse, and Troy.

WHO THE GAME WAS PLAYED BY

Entrepreneurs, Irish, and people from Brooklyn, Philadelphia, and Baltimore. The entrepreneurs were few in number but large in impact, for this was the era in which a young player with brains, ambition, and self-discipline could wind up owning his own team, as Albert Spalding did, and Alfred Reach, and John Montgomery Ward, and as a few more players from the next decade would (Comiskey, Griffith, Connie Mack). Many players, for as much as forty years later, would become the owners of minor league teams. Of course, players who combined brains, ambition, and self-discipline were in a distinct minority, and the entrepreneurial ambitions of many of the players involved fixing an appropriate price at which to sell the game to the gamblers. Harry Wright had trouble with alcoholism and poor training habits on the very first professional champions, and baseball players as a group would acquire an unsavory reputation with certain factions of the public within ten years of the beginning of professionalism.

In *American Baseball,* Voight commented on the large number of Irish names on the rosters of teams as early as 1871, and certainly there were many. The list of names in the National Association also included intriguing combinations like "Cherokee Fisher" and "Count Sensenderfer." There were several Jewish players, and a good many immigrants. Without tracing the ancestry of all the names, it doesn't seem to me that the Irish influence in 1870 was as strong as it was in 1890 or 1895.

The Philadelphia influence . . . well, that's another story. Going through the birthplaces of men who played in the National Association, it would seem that at least half must have been born in either Philadelphia, Brooklyn, or Baltimore. This is not nearly as true of the best players as it is of the ordinary ones, suggesting that the teams of this period still retained some of the flavor of small local organizations, in which a man brought his brother along and recommended a neighbor who was a good outfielder. The Middletown, Connecticut, team had several members who were actually from Middletown. But the best players were likely to come from anywhere. Spalding was from Byron, Illinois. Ross Barnes was from Mt. Morris, New York. Cap Anson was from Marshalltown, Iowa. Candy Cummings was from Ware, Massachusetts. Lip Pike was from New York City. Harry Wright was born in Sheffield, England.

Checking In

1870—Jesse Burkett, Wheeling, West Virginia
1871—Buck Freeman, Catasqua, Pennsylvania
     Orville Wright, Dayton, Ohio
1872—Willie Keeler, Brooklyn
1873—John McGraw, Truxton, New York
     Harry Davis, Philadelphia
     Jimmy Collins, Niagara Falls
1874—Honus Wagner, Carnegie, Pennsylvania
     Fielder Jones, Shinglehouse, Pennsylvania
     Bill Klem, Rochester, New York
     Robert Frost, San Francisco
1875—Nap Lajoie, Woonsocket, Rhode Island
1876—Mordecai Brown, Nyesville, Indiana
     Ginger Beaumont, Rochester, Wisconsin
     Rude Waddell, Bradford, Pennsylvania
1877—Frank Chance, Fresno, California
1878—Mike Donlin, Erie, Pennsylvania
1879—Miller Huggins, Cincinnati
     Josef Stalin, Tiflis, Georgia, Russia

Checking Out

1870—Robert E. Lee, 63
1872—Al Thake, 22
1875—Andrew Johnson, 67
1876—Bub McAtee, 31
1879—Jimmy Hallinan, inflammation of the bowels, 30

THE 1870s IN A BOX

Attendance Data: While systematic attendance data prior to 1900 is scarce, it is doubtful that many games played prior to 1880 drew as many as 5,000 fans. The 1875 Boston team had gate receipts of $34,987.74. This figure includes some shares of road attendance, but, of course the other side of that is that they gave away a portion of their home gate (though the Red Stockings usually demanded 60% of the gate even on the road). Assuming that they charged fifty cents a head, which was the figure encouraged by the Association, that would imply a season's attendance of about 70,000, and that probably included many nonleague games.

Most Home Runs:
> Charley Jones, 1879, 9
> Charley Jones, 18

All leaders in categories here are based on the totals for the National League only, 1876–79, unless otherwise noted.

Best Won/Lost Record by Team:
> Chicago, 1876, 52–14, .788
> Boston, 176–98, .642

Worst Won/Lost Record by Team:
> Cincinnati, 1876, 9–56, .138
> Cincinnati, 104–158, .397

The Philadelphia team, expelled after only one season, had a winning percentage for that one season of .237.

Heaviest Player:
> Though Cap Anson's listed weight of 227 pounds was probably not attained until later, he was probably the biggest man in the league almost from the day he entered it.

Lightest Player:
> Candy Cummings, who weighed only 120.

Most Strikeouts by Pitcher:
> Monte Ward, 1879, 239
> Tommy Bonds, 595

Highest Batting Average:
> Ross Barnes, 1876, .404
> Cap Anson, .352

As mentioned, Ross Barnes' 1876 batting average was .429 if walks are not counted as at bats. Barnes' batting average for the five years of the American Association was also .379, making him the true batting champion of the era.

As many of you probably know, Barnes was also a superb defensive second baseman, whose career was derailed after the fair-foul hit was disallowed in 1877.

Hardest-Throwing Pitcher: George Zettlein was reputed to be a very hard thrower at the start of the decade, though his record suggests that he had lost most of his speed by the time league play began. Al Spalding threw very hard, but Tommy Bond was probably the fastest.

Best Baseball Books: Henry Chadwick's *Beadle's Dime Baseball Player,* the first guide, began publication in 1860 and lasted through 1881. (The dime referred to the cost of the book; the ballplayer was much more.) The *Spalding Guide* began publication in 1877, edited by Lewis Meacham; Chadwick later came over and ran it, instead.

Best Outfield Arm: Jim Hatfield, a member of the famous Cincinnati team that is often described as the first professional team, threw a baseball 400 feet, 7½ inches on October 15, 1872, a record that was not matched for many years.

Most Runs Batted In:

> Jim O'Rourke, 1879, 62
> Charley Jones, 1879, 62
> Deacon White, 190 for the four years (1876–79)

Most Aggressive Baserunner: King Kelly

Fastest Player: Lip Pike

On August 27, 1873, Pike, a noted sprinter, beat a racehorse (a trotter) in a 100-yard dash to win a bet. The trotter was allowed to start 25 yards behind the line, and Pike took off when the horse reached him. They held even for most of the race, and when Pike began to pull ahead late in the race the horse broke into a run. But Pike still beat it by four yards (item based on note by Al Kermisch in 1979 *Baseball Research Journal*).

Slowest Player: Paul Snyder

Best Control Pitcher: No one stands out. With nine balls to work with, most pitchers could avoid walking too many people. Besides, as George Wright said in the 1915 interview, "This method of reaching base [the walk] was unusual because it was an unwritten law that the hitter should do his utmost to connect with the ball and he was not handicapped by any rule as to where he should step in order to hit it."

Most Stolen Bases: Unknown

Best-Looking Player: King Kelly

Ugliest Player: Charlie Gould

Clint Hartung Award: Steve King

Outstanding Sportswriter: Henry Chadwick

*Most Admirable Superstar: Deacon White

Least Admirable Superstar: George Hall

Franchise Shifts: A "franchise," as we know it now—a collection of contracts with players, stadiums, and fans—did not exist. Teams dropped out of the league or were dismissed and new ones came in, but there was no concept of doing business somewhere else.

*New Stadiums: Primitive parks

Best Pennant Race: 1871 National League

In 1871, the Chicago White Stockings were in the middle of an exciting three-team race with the Philadelphia Athletics and the Boston Red Stockings when their park was destroyed by the Great Chicago Fire. Despite losing their uniforms, their equipment, despite being without funds, the players saw the season through on the generosity of their competitors. They eventually lost the "pennant" to the Athletics in Philadelphia in the last game of the season.

Best World Series: No World Series

Best-Hitting Pitcher: Albert Spalding

Worst-Hitting Pitcher: Candy Cummings

*Best Minor League Team: 1878 Buffalo Bisons

Best Minor League Player: Pud Galvin

Best Negro League Player: No Negro Leagues. One of the best of the early black players was Bud Fowler, who played against white players in minor leagues from 1872 until the onset of Jim Crow practices in baseball during the 1880s.

Odd Couple: Albert Spalding and William Hulbert

Drinking Men: Cap Anson was arrested for being drunk and etc. in 1884, but he certainly didn't have a problem with it. A couple who did were Jim Devlin, the pathetic figure of the Louisville fix, and Asa Brainard.

*New Strategies:

Catcher moving close to plate—1875(?)

Fielders backing up one another

New Equipment:

1875—Catcher's mask

1875—First fielding gloves introduced

Chest protectors introduced for catchers (exact date uncertain)

1876—Turnstiles

The Association had no standard baseball. Some teams used red baseballs.

*Player vs. Team: Davy Force vs. the White Stockings

Team vs. Team:

Chicago (Hulbert) against Philadelphia

Chicago (Hulbert) against New York

Chicago (Hulbert) against Cincinnati

From Hulbert against Philadelphia (see comment on Force Case, if you haven't), it degenerated to Hulbert against the National League, and seemed to be headed for Hulbert against the World. New York and Philadelphia were kicked out of the new league in 1877 for not making a road trip. Louisville fell apart in 1878 during a gambling scandal. Cincinnati was expelled in 1881 for playing ball on Sunday and selling beer at the games. Not to be too harsh, but the death of Hulbert in 1882 was probably the best thing that could have happened to the league at that point. He was a strong man and a strong leader, but he had the league under too tight a rein.

Uniform Changes: Throughout the decades, my wife Susie will be making comments on the uniforms that were in use at the time. The introduction to these comments, as well as the comments on the uniforms of the 1870s, can be found in the longer comments after the box.

New Terms or Expressions: During a tour of England in 1874, Henry Chadwick drew up a lexicon of the game for the benefit of the British writers. It included such terms as assists, passed balls, balks, fungoes, grounders, pop-ups, double plays, overthrows, and whitewashed. Other terms are not now in use, such as muffed balls, daisy cutters, and line balls (which, of course, became line drives).

Most Wins by Pitcher:

Al Spalding, 1876, 47

Monte Ward, 1879, 47

Tommy Bond, 154

Spalding was *the* pitcher in the years of the Association, winning as many as 57 games in a season (he was 57–5 in 1875) and leading the Association every year. He won 207 in the Association, 48 in the league for a total of 255.

Highest Winning Percentage:

Al Spalding, 1876, .783

Tommy Bond, 154–68, .694

Best Unrecognized Player: Levi Meyerle

Highest-Paid Player: Probably Harry Wright, at $2,500 (Modern Equivalent: about $35,000)

New Statistics: Statistics made available by the National League in 1879 were games played, at bats, hits, runs, batting average, average runs per game, times reached first base (which apparently included reaching by an

error or forceout), on-base percentage, putouts, assists, errors, total chances, fielding average, passed balls for catchers, batters facing pitcher, runs allowed, average runs allowed (per game), hits allowed, opposition batting average, walks, average walks per game, and wild pitches. Some of this material, such as passed balls and batters facing pitcher, fell out of use —and will be noted when it returns. In many cases, I have changed to modern terminology—that is, "batting average" rather than "percentage of base hits per times at bat."

A Very Good Movie Could Be Made About: The 1871 Chicago White Stockings, fighting for a pennant and for survival at the same time.

I Don't Know What This Has to Do with Baseball, But I Thought I'd Mention It Anyway: Amateur teams of the 1860s and early '70s would often ride out to the park in decorated carriages, singing their team songs.

NICKNAMES OF THE 1870s

There were no rules for nicknames, to begin with, and a sportswriter, who might be the only one in town, could call a player whatever he wanted. Charlie Pabor was called "The Old Woman in the Red Cap," probably the only seven-word nickname ever; a similarly outlandish handle was "Death to Flying Things," assigned to the overbearing defensive wizard Bob Ferguson. Will White was called "Whoop-La," a forerunner of "Ee-Yah Jennings" and "The Say-Hey Kid." Hardy Richardson was called "Old True Blue," Billy Reilly "Pigtail Billy," George Bradley was called "Grin" and Jim O'Rourke "Orator Jim." Bob Addy was called "The Magnet," and Joe Gerhardt was called "Move Up Joe," a nickname which might presage that of a twentieth-century second baseman, Tony Lazzeri.

But as there was no rule as to what a nickname might be, there was also not such a strong feeling that a player had to have one. The game, remember, was still on a much more human level then; it is not unrealistic to think that a hard-core fanatic—a breed that existed from the very first day—might have known personally the players for whom he rooted. Players did talk to the fans (there were attempts made to prohibit this, but those attempts were still being made thirty years later, which suggests that they were not initially very successful). The cities were much smaller; the National League had a rule that a team must represent a city of at least 75,000, but several cities did not meet the standard. A fan probably knew where a player lived and who his wife or girlfriend was.

There was not the need, then, to give the player a human face by assigning him a name; nicknames probably were used more for opposition players than for the members of the home team. Nicknames didn't really get rolling until the late eighties, when the scale of the operation changed and the distance between the players and fans increased.

BEST MINOR LEAGUE TEAM OF THE 1870s

Joseph M. Overfield, writing in the 1977 *Baseball Research Journal,* makes a strong case for the prowess of the 1878 Buffalo Bisons of the International Association. They were a team with such established stars as Dave Eggler and Davy Force. There were players with great futures in the majors, like Pud Galvin and Joe Hornung. They won the International Association and a good many exhibition games, including a 10–7 record against National League opponents. In 1879 the Bisons moved into the National League with essentially the same team, and finished third.

In 1877, the *Louisville Commercial* printed a standing of the best clubs in America at the end of the season, sort of like a modern college football poll. The list made no distinction between the National League teams and teams in other leagues, which shows the position that the league held in public opinion of that time. It was a good league, but just another league; it later became the major league.

—Jim Baker

❧ THE LOUISVILLE SCANDAL ❧

In 1877, the Louisville Grays had built a large lead over Boston. With a quarter of the season to go (fifteen games), the Grays needed to win only half of their remaining games to clinch the flag, while Boston needed to take thirteen of their remaining fifteen.

Louisville was sparked by outfielder George Hall, sort of an early-day Hal Chase, who had developed a reputation for dishonesty while in the National Association. They also had star pitcher Jim Devlin, who boasted a pretty mean "drop" pitch.

With the pennant seemingly assured, the Grays began dropping games due to a variety of "bonehead" plays; strikeouts, pick-offs, and costly errors abounded. Louisville consequently blew its lead and finished second to Boston. Certainly this would have qualified as the pennant race of the decade except there was a foul stench in the air.

At the conclusion of the season, a Louisville paper, the *Courier-Journal,* made accusations that the team had gone in the tank. The primary culprit was alleged to be Jim Devlin, who was now, according to some reports, sporting a variety of fancy jewelry. After the season he pitched well in exhibitions after doing quite poorly in the stretch run. A league investigation followed and resulted in the lifetime expulsion of Devlin, Hall, shortstop Bill Craver and Al Nichols. Nichols was only a substitute, but it was said that he had key connections with seedy New York gamblers, so it was he who put together the swoon.

Devlin literally begged for reinstatement for a number of years thereafter. He was often seen hanging around the National League offices dressed in rags with a pleading look on his face. Devlin died in Philadelphia at the age of 33, reportedly working at the time as a police officer.

—Jim Baker

NATIONAL ASSOCIATION ALL-STAR TEAM
National Association operated, 1871–1875.
Records given are totals for tenure in league.

Pos	Player	Games	At Bat	Hits	Runs	Avg.
C	Deacon White	259	1316	456	287	.347
1B	Cal McVey	262	1319	477	326	.362
2B	Ross Barnes	266	1425	540	462	.379
3B	Cap Anson	262	1400	494	399	.353
SS	George Wright	245	1222	430	277	.352
LF	Andy Leonard	266	1334	424	350	.318
CF	Dave Eggler	260	1254	402	303	.321
RF	Lip Pike	286	1468	471	335	.321
U	Levi Meyerle	221	1093	386	245	.353
P	Al Spalding	284	1445	462	334	.320

Pitcher	Games	Won-Lost
Al Spalding	284	207–56
Candy Cummings	203	124–72

NATIONAL LEAGUE ALL-STAR TEAM
1876–1879
Records in seasonal notation, based on 75 games played.
Pitchers based on 60 starts.

Pos	Player	Years	Hits	HR	RBI	Avg.	Other
C	Deacon White	3.52	113	1	54	.343	61 Runs
1B	Joe Start	3.24	113	1	33	.320	
2B	Ross Barnes	2.20	114	1	43	.329	
3B	Cap Anson	3.14	119	0	53	.352	20 doubles
SS	Johnny Peters	3.52	104	1	40	.302	20 doubles
LF	Charley Jones	3.54	99	5	50	.307	9 triples
CF	Paul Hines	3.62	114	2	51	.334	
RF	Jim O'Rourke	3.62	109	1	39	.331	

Pitcher	Years	Won-Lost	SO	ERA	Other
Tommy Bond	3.77	41–18	158	1.97	535 Innings
Monte Ward	1.78	37–17	199	1.92	516 Innings

MOST-ADMIRABLE SUPERSTAR, 1870s

Deacon White, catcher–third baseman for several teams from 1876 to 1890. Henry Chadwick admired him because he was never known to complain, and wrote about him that "there is one thing in which White stands pre-eminent, and that is the integrity of his character." The *Cincinnati Enquirer* wrote that "Mr. White has few peers as a ballplayer and he has always been a gentleman in his professional and private life." He picked up his nickname from the strange habit of going to church.

White also got off the quote of the decade in 1889, when battling against the reserve rule. An excellent article about White was written by Joseph Overfield, and appeared in the 1975 *Baseball Research Journal;* most of these facts are taken from that article. In 1888 the Detroit franchise in the National League went out of business, and sold its players around the league. Deacon White and Jack Rowe were sold to Pittsburgh, but instead of reporting to their new team, that December the two of them purchased a team in Buffalo, New York, in the International League, intending to play for themselves. They weren't too happy about the fact that they had been sold for $7,000 and

JIM "DEACON" WHITE

were being asked to report to Pittsburgh for a fraction of that. Things didn't go well in Buffalo, and eventually they capitulated and reported to Pittsburgh, but they were paid $1,250 each plus good salaries, $500 a month.

White told a Buffalo reporter, "We are satisfied with the money, but we ain't worth it. Rowe's arm is gone. I'm over 40 and my fielding ain't so good, though I can still hit some. But I will say this. No man is going to sell my carcass unless I get half."

THE DAVY FORCE CASE

The National Association was a player-dominated outfit that had no reserve clause and no real protection against one team stealing players from another. The players who went from team to team were called "revolvers," and the most famous of them was Davy Force, a 5-foot-4-inch shortstop.

Force was described by Francis Richter as the greatest shortstop of his day, except for George Wright. It was defense he was talking about; though Force hit extremely well in the National Association (.412 in 1872), he never hit much after the National League was formed in 1876. He seems to have been hurt quite a bit by the rule allowing a pitcher to throw sidearm, as a small player might. He was built funny; "his legs," said Richter, "were muscular, but short and bowed, he being in these respects a miniature Honus Wagner . . . he had, like Wagner, a sort of awkward grace."

Force's contract problems were one of the keys to the alliance of powers that made the National League possible. During the winter of 1874–75, Davy negotiated with both Chicago, for whom he had played the previous year, and Philadelphia. This created no particular problem, there being no reserve rule, until he signed contracts with both teams, which a good many players in that time did. The prior contract was signed with Chicago, and on that basis the Association's Judiciary Committee awarded him to the White Stockings. However, there was another meeting of the Association later in the spring in Philadelphia, at which Mr. Spering, of Philadelphia, was elected president of the Association—and appointed a new Judiciary Committee. The new Judiciary Committee reversed the old one, and awarded Force to Philadelphia.

This reversal made William Hulbert, Chicago's financial backer, quite angry. Hulbert's anger resulted in the dissolution of the National Association and the formation of the National League. Hulbert generalized his own ailments, and concluded that the Association was not being run properly—too lax, too player-oriented, not enough protection for the "owners"—and he began drawing up a new set of by-laws and organizing the league's other financial backers. Further, Harry Wright, though not directly involved, felt that the Association had handled the matter badly by allowing Force to play for Philly. Wright was the most influential figure in baseball at this time, with the possible exception of Henry Chadwick, and his view of this issue may have led him to side with Hulbert in the ensuing battle.

INTRODUCTION TO THE UNIFORM COMMENTS

What men wore to play baseball in the early days now seems quaint and a little odd, but their dress reminds us of the great luxury of beginnings, the freedom from tradition. Not that baseball was the first organization of its kind to need a uniform. Baseball men undoubtedly looked to other sports, such as cricket and horseback riding, as a guide to appropriate dress, and were also influenced by military uniforms of the day. Once the form was established and accepted, though (as it was by about 1910), change came slowly through a series of gradual refinements—with a few exceptions.

This study is intended to be a general overview of changes in the baseball uniform. It is not meant to date precisely where something began or to include every change in uniforms, only to give a sense of what the uniforms of the time looked like. The study is based mostly on observations from photographs in guides, magazines, and books, plus occasional references to uniforms in texts. A SABR publication, *The National Pastime: A Special Pictorial Issue—The Nineteenth Century,* was very useful for examining the first thirty years, plus being a delight to marvel at, with photographs dating back to the 1850s. The text, by John Thorn and Mark Rucker, illustrates the photographs, not the other way around.

Small town teams or college teams of the 1850s dressed very simply and practically in long dark pants, with long-sleeved light-colored shirts. The club teams of the period seemed intent on designing a suit of clothes that designated the members as ballplayers, but was still stylish in the fashion of the day. With this in mind, they disregarded completely the fact that a close-fitting collar with a bow tie and a shirt with long sleeves and cuffs was just not very comfortable for playing ball.

A few examples: The Lowells of Boston wore what looked like leftover military trousers from the Civil War; a white, long-sleeved, bibbed shirt (that is, a large oval area on the shirt front extended from the collar down to the midsection, detachable, with button closures all round), a small bow or ribbon tie, high leather-top shoes and a cloth cap. The 1864 Mutuals of New York looked smashing indeed in all-white dress—long pants, long-sleeved and collared shirts, with a dark belt at midsection spelling out "Mutuals."

In contrast, the 1867 Niagaras of Buffalo were not a very homogenous group; it looks like they borrowed from each other's closets. A few wore ties, some wore long-sleeved shirts with bib closures, while others wore button-up shirts with no collar. Long trousers were common to all, but some were checked, while others have checked tops. The editors of *The National Pastime* noted that the first major league team to wear checked uniforms was the Brooklyn Robins (we'll keep an eye out for the first pinstripes).

Shown on the first baseball card in 1868, the Brooklyn Athletics were dressed in dark military-style pants with a white stripe up the side and pant clips around the ankles. In 1869 photographs we find the first appearance of true sports clothes, in the form of knickerbockers, which became widely accepted by ball teams in the seventies and be-came fashionable in public dress in the eighties. Knickers, a variation of the European breeches popular at the time of the French Revolution and before, were worn by hunters in the sixties and later adopted by golfers and cyclists. Members of the Red Stockings Base Ball Club of Cincinnati were photographed in knickers and long stockings, with the initial of their town embroidered on the bib of their shirts.

A historic note—the first uniform was officially adopted by the Knickerbockers of New York in 1849. It consisted of long blue trousers, white shirts and straw hats. The term "knickerbocker" originally referred to descendants of Dutch settlers in New York, and by extension meant any New Yorker.

—Susie McCarthy

SORRY

In 1877, the *Utica Herald* published a report of a game played there that had this appended to the summary: "Apologies by pitchers for hitting batsmen, Morgan 4, Neale 3."

UNIFORMS IN THIS DECADE

By 1875, the style was just about set for the rest of the century. Teams wore baggy knickers, long stockings, lace-up high-top leather shoes, long sleeves with cuffs; shirts had stiff-looking collars, which gradually relaxed and were often turned up to sort of fan the face. A tie was worn in the early years, but when incidents of players choking to death while trying to make plays increased, the custom soon faded. The bib was still around, but by the late seventies shirts began to appear with a different closure—the opening from the waist to the neckline was secured by lacing one side to the other. The team's city was usually spelled out across the chest. A wide, dark belt with rather fancy clasps was worn around the middle, and sometimes bore the team name.

The Ithacas, an independent team from New York, followed this general style but their stockings were striped and their caps were more like bowlers than baseball caps. Several club teams from this period looked remarkably modern in uniform, with round necks on shirts that were made of what looks like a stretch knit material. An early Harvard team even wore short sleeves, and their knickers were much more form-fitting. While wool or flannel (and even silk) were the fabrics commonly used, some of these tighter fitting pants would almost have to have been made out of some sort of jersey or other knit material.

Albert Spalding in 1876 put different-colored hats on the players to designate positions, making the team look like a "Dutch bed of tulips." The first instances I found of teams using a descriptive symbol on their uniforms, rather than the initial or name of the city, were the Skull and Bones team from Massachusetts and the Maple Leafs of Guelph, Ontario, both in 1876. The two teams later joined to form the Cemetery League.

—Susie McCarthy

Editor's Note: Susie is just joking about the player's choking to death with those neckties. Didn't happen.

NEW STRATEGIES OF THE 1870s

According to Voight, Deacon White in 1875 introduced the practice of the catcher standing right behind the batter to take the throw. This practice did not become standard for nearly another thirty years, but there is some doubt about when it started. The *New York Times* article on Nat Hicks at the time of his death (1907) states that Hicks was the first catcher to do this, at a date unspecified but apparently in the sixties, and further that after he did so the other catchers followed suit. So this practice may have had a vogue before 1875.

Harry Wright during this decade developed the practice of one fielder backing up another one. The first season tickets were sold by Cleveland in 1871.

PARKS OF THE 1870s

To state the matter without hyperbole, the finest ballpark in the U.S. in 1879 would today be considered inadequate for the Florida State League. The first enclosed ballpark was the Union and Capitoline Grounds, commonly known as the Union Grounds, in Brooklyn, built in 1864 by William Cammeyer. It seated about 1,500 people on long benches.

The "stadiums" where baseball was played in the 1870s would seem to be not too different from the accommodations at which I witnessed rodeos at small towns in Kansas in the late 1950s and early sixties—actually, the rodeo places might be closer to the parks of the late 1880s than the late seventies. The owners bought some wood and threw up fences and primitive bleachers and maybe a clubhouse or a dugout; the players often assisted in the construction. In a cou-

ple of years the thing fell down or burned down or rotted out, or they just got tired of it and built another one (the average occupancy of a park before 1890 was probably four to six years). These teams, remember, were not the only teams in town; the gentlemen's clubs that had dominated baseball in the 1850s and 1860s were still around, and frequently competed against the professionals. Though most teams probably owned their own parks, it was not unusual for a team to switch accommodations in mid-season, entering into or departing an arrangement with one of these clubs or with someone who rented a ballpark out as a business.

Under these circumstances, of course, if a team drew 4,000 people, it looked like an enormous number; people would be spilling off the bleachers and standing along the foul lines to watch the game. This

is still true into the twentieth century, that the crowd was not necessarily confined to the seats. For large gatherings as late as 1935, there might be ropes put up in the outfield and fans standing behind the ropes.

In the first edition of this book, I commented that to make a full accounting of all the parks that teams played in during this period would be a massive undertaking. That undertaking was undertaken by Philip Lowry, who produced the book *Green Cathedrals,* published by the Society for American Baseball Research in 1986. Lowry attempted to document and describe every park used in the major leagues from day one to the present, as well as some minor leagues parks and other miscellaneous information. It is a wonderful reference book.

The 1880s

HOW THE GAME WAS PLAYED

The 1880s were a time of extensive experimenting with the rules of the game, as the professionals now in charge began to adapt baseball to their own needs. The committee on playing rules accepted suggestions all summer, and every winter issued new rules. The number of balls required for a walk, which was nine before, was changed to eight in 1880, to seven in 1882, to six in 1884, back to seven in 1886, to five in 1887, and to four in 1889. This was done in an attempt to speed the game up, require the pitcher to get the ball in there where it could be hit. The pitcher's box was moved back from 45 feet to 50, and the dimensions of the box were changed twice (a pitcher at this time was allowed to take a short run before delivering the ball). The rules were changed several times on how high a pitcher could raise his arm, but by the end of the decade he was allowed to throw overhand. Flat bats were legalized for a few years. These experiments were conducted in the attempt to find the right balance between offense and defense. In 1887, the rule allowing the batter to call for a high pitch or a low pitch was eliminated, and a standard strike zone was defined. For one year a strikeout required four strikes. Batters were given first base if hit by a pitch.

With three leagues operating, rule changes were not always conducted in unison, so you would have widely different rules applying in different leagues, and some confusion about what they really meant. The scoring rules were fiddled around with continuously— what to count as a hit, what not to count as a hit, what to charge as an at bat, what not to charge as an at bat, when to charge an error and to whom —all that was in constant flux.

The number of runs scored jumped up and down, but wound up the decade around six per team per game in both surviving leagues. Fielding gloves received general acceptance during the decade, and errors consequently diminished. The stolen base was in its heyday, in part because catchers, with pitchers throwing overhand and from 50 feet away, were neither anxious nor able to deal with the pitched ball as they do today. (Stolen bases were counted beginning in 1887, but since players were credited with a stolen base whenever they took an extra base on the basepaths, such as in going from first to third on a single, it is difficult to know how many stolen bases there were in the modern meaning of the term. It is clear, though, that there were a lot.)

The game began to get rough. In the 1850s and sixties, baseball's ethics were set by the gentlemen's clubs which, as they developed more interest in won and lost records, gradually drew in the better athletes, providing that background for many of the first professional players. Respect for the umpires was the accepted norm, and leading citizens often served as volunteer umpires. With the coming of professionalism—and professional umpires—this quickly went out the window.

The center of rowdyism in the 1880s was the St. Louis team in the American Association, led by Arlie Latham (The Freshest Man on Earth) and manager Charles Comiskey. This great team—and many think them the greatest team of the nineteenth century—employed the strategy of driving the opponents off their

MIKE "KING" KELLY

game with constant verbal abuse. Since they won, others imitated them. Players acting as coaches ran up and down the baselines hurling insults and obscenities at the pitcher; this led to the coach's box being established in 1887. Latham was known for his talents and enthusiasm as an antagonist, leading to constant fights. The Association would fine them and Chris Von der Ahe, the owner, would pay the fines, believing such tactics to encourage attendance.

The fans got in the act. Visiting players had no dugouts to hide in, only a bench, exposed to the hostile fans who were sitting close enough to be heard, close enough to hurl, close enough to reach out and touch. And the way they treated umpires! Well, we'll deal with that in the next decade, when it was even worse, but many people felt that you just couldn't win in St. Louis; if the fans didn't get to you they'd get to the umpire.

King Kelly was noted for his innovative circumvention of the rulebook; someone said that half of the National League's rules were written to keep King Kelly from cheating people. When the rules were changed to allow in-game substitutions, all a player had to do was call himself into the game. This practice continued until one day when the third out of the ninth inning was popped up over the head of King Kelly, seated on the Chicago bench. Kelly stood up, called himself into the game and caught the ball (or so, at least, the story goes). Whether he actually did that or not, he certainly did, at times, cut across the infield (as a baserunner) when the umpire was distracted, and invented such tactics as limping to first base in great pain, then suddenly recovering to steal second, and dropping his catcher's mask where the baserunner would trip over it.

One could make too much of this element of the game in the 1880s. The rowdy behavior was far worse in the American Association, which charged twenty-five cents admission and sold beer, than in the National League, which preferred the fifty-cent admission and did not. But the average man in the 1880s, while rougher than today, was not a thug, nor was the average ballplayer helpless to defend himself. There probably were many games marked by the best of sportsmanship on all sides; the surprise at the time was to see so many which were not, so that's what people wrote about.

Another thing about baseball in this decade was the lengthening of the schedule. As teams began to play 90, 100, 120, 130 games a year, and as pitchers began to throw overhand, the one-man pitching staff died out; by 1889 most teams were using three pitchers, not exactly in a modern rotation, but alternating.

WHERE THE GAME WAS PLAYED

We're talking about three major leagues here—the National League, which was there for the duration, the American Association (1882 through the end of the decade) and the Union Association (1884). These are the cities in which each operated:

NATIONAL	AMERICAN	UNION
Boston	Baltimore	Altoona
Buffalo	Brooklyn	Baltimore
Chicago	Cincinnati	Boston
Cincinnati	Cleveland	Chicago
Cleveland	Columbus	Cincinnati
Detroit	Indianapolis	Kansas City
Indianapolis	Kansas City	Milwaukee
Kansas City	Louisville	Philadelphia
New York	New York	Pittsburgh
Philadelphia	Philadelphia	St. Louis
Pittsburgh	Pittsburgh	St. Paul
Providence	Richmond	Washington
St. Louis	St. Louis	Wilmington
Troy	Toledo	
Washington	Washington	
Worcester		

As you can see, there were three efforts to place major league baseball as far west as Kansas City, but none of the three took, in part perhaps because Kansas City's press at this time was too primitive to play the role that the press has always played in helping make a team go. Baseball, as

the population, remained concentrated in the northeast corner of the nation.

At the beginning of the decade, the National League had been forced into a number of smaller cities by William Hulbert's wars with other teams; indeed, Hulbert's oft-quoted remark that he would rather be a lamppost in Chicago than a millionaire in any other city, combined with his record of antipathy toward the teams in New York and Philadelphia, might suggest a personal bias against the big cities of the east. This enabled the American Association, opening shop in 1882, to move unchallenged into the nation's largest cities. Denny McKnight, first president of the Association, estimated that the Association drew from 2,370,000 fans, whereas the National served only 1,156,000. But following the death of Hulbert, the National League marched into the big cities of the east, and balanced the scales.

WHO THE GAME WAS PLAYED BY

One thing about the players of the nineteenth century that should be noted is their size. Few were over 6 feet tall.

The players were still mostly eastern, mostly Irish, and a little rough, though the stories about their having been unwelcome in the best hotels apparently are not true.

Pos	Player	Years	Hits	HR	RBI	Avg.	Other
C	Buck Ewing	5.92	157	7	72	.295	19 Triples
1B	Dan Brouthers	7.24	186	11	91	.348	37 Doubles
2B	Hardy Richardson	7.49	171	7	71	.307	114 Runs
3B	Pete Browning	8.14	185	6	74	.344	66 Stolen Bases
SS	Jack Glasscock	8.10	156	2	56	.296	
LF	Harry Stovey	8.22	170	11	73	.313	135 Runs
CF	George Gore	7.32	164	5	65	.308	67 Walks
RF	Sam Thompson	3.82	173	14	118	.319	
U	King Kelly	7.92	170	7	85	.314	78 Stolen Bases

MAJOR LEAGUE ALL-STAR TEAM
1880–89
Records in seasonal notation, based on 130 games played.
Pitchers based on 60 starts.

Pitcher	Years	Won-Lost	SO	ERA	Other
Hoss Radbourne	7.55	36–22	225	2.53	526 Innings
Tim Keefe	8.15	36–22	270	2.71	472 Innings
John Clarkson	5.46	40–18	276	2.54	523 Innings

Checking In

1880—Christy Mathewson, Factoryville, Pennsylvania
   Sam Crawford, Wahoo, Nebraska
   Joe Tinker, Muscotah, Kansas
   Addie Joss, Juneau, Wisconsin
1881—Branch Rickey, Lucasville, Ohio
   Ed Walsh, Plains, Pennsylvania
   Johnny Evers, Troy, New York
1883—Ed Reulbach, Detroit
   Hal Chase, Los Gatos, California
1884—Chief Bender, Brainerd, Minnesota
   Eddie Cicotte, Detroit
1885—George S. Patton, San Gabriel, California
1886—Ty Cobb, Narrows, Georgia
   Home Run Baker, Trappe, Maryland
1887—Eddie Collins, Millerton, New York
   Walter Johnson, Humboldt, Kansas
   Grover Alexander, St. Paul, Nebraska
   Joe McCarthy, Philadelphia
1888—Tris Speaker, Hubbard City, Texas
   Joe Jackson, Brandon Mills, South Carolina
   Eugene O'Neill, New York City
1889—Smokey Joe Wood, Kansas City, Missouri

Checking Out

1881—James Garfield, gunshot, 50
1882—William Hulbert, heart attack, 49
1884—Jim Devlin, 33
1885—Ulysses S. Grant, 63
1888—Asa Brainard, 47

1883: ZAP MAIL

A Philadelphia zookeeper named Jim Murray introduced in 1883 a system of relaying scores almost instantly all over the City of Brotherly Love by means of carrier pigeons. Homing pigeons would be released with the results of each half-inning, and the workers at the zoo would "know how the inning went before the men are out in the field for the next one." A few fans from other parts of the city heard about this and wanted in on it, so provisions were made for them, too. On some days as many as a half-dozen birds would be released at the end of each frame. (Item based on a note in the quite delightful book, *The Scrapbook History of Baseball,* by Deutsch, Cohen, Johnson and Neff.)

1882: THE SECRET SCORER

When Albert Spalding was president of the Chicago National League team from 1882 to 1891—the team that is now the Cubs—he felt that the official scorer should be independent, not subject to pressures for favors or subject to criticism. Most club presidents feel that way, but, being Albert Spalding, he did something about it. According to an article by Alex Haas, Spalding successfully kept secret the identity of his official scorer for the entire decade. Cap Anson, the team manager, did not know who it was. The league president, who received the scores, did not know who was sending them. The press had no idea who the official scorer was. The man who mailed them to the league office did not know what he was mailing; he was just dropping something off for his mother.

His mother was Elisa Green Williams, and she was the official scorer. She attended every game and sat between the wives of the teams two biggest stars, Cap Anson and Abner Dalrymple. She scored every play without ever tipping them off that hers was the official version.

THE 1880s IN A BOX

Attendance Data: Systematic data not available. Attendance grew rapidly during the decade; it was a very successful period on the field. Crowds of 10,000 or more were still unusual enough to draw comment, but there were many such crowds during the eighties. The Giants in 1886 drew a record crowd of 20,709, and by the end of the decade there were crowds near 30,000; the Giants' attendance in 1889 was reported as 201,662.

With the advantages of larger cities, Sunday ball, the twenty-five-cent admission, and beer sales at the game, it was the Association, not the National League, which was the attendance leader in the early part of the eighties. The *Cleveland Leader* reported that five of the six Association clubs drew larger crowds than the National League's best gate draw, the Chicago White Stockings with Cap Anson. This forced the National League to compete, by moving back into the larger cities and assuming gradually those features that gave the A.A. its advantages (though few, if any, N.L. teams of the 1880s charged admission of twenty-five cents).

Most Home Runs:
> Ned Williamson, Chicago, 1884, 27
> Harry Stovey, 91

Williamson's twenty-seven home runs were a fluke, a result of a short fence at Lakefront Park, which created inflated home run totals for the entire team. In all other seasons, balls hit over that fence were considered doubles.

Best Won-Lost Record by Team:
> St. Louis (U), 1884, 94–19, .832
> St. Louis (A.A.), 618–323, .656

Worst Won-Lost Record by Team:
> Wilmington (U), 1884, 2–16, .111
> Philadelphia (N.L.), 1883, 17–81, .173
> Washington (N.), 163–337, .326

Heaviest Player: Roger Connor, 220, or Cap Anson again
Lightest Player: Davy Force, 130
Most Strikeouts by Pitcher:
> Matt Kilroy, 1886, 513
> Tim Keefe, 2,195

Highest Batting Average:
> Tim O'Neill, 1887, .435
> Dan Brouthers, .348

O'Neill and Pete Browning, both in the American Association in 1887, were the only .400 hitters of the decade. They seem to have benefited quite significantly from the 1887 rule that a strikeout was four strikes. At the time, O'Neill's average was considered .492, as walks were considered hits for that one season.

Hardest-Throwing Pitcher: Charlie Sweeney
The 1924 *Spalding Guide* said that "Modern Base Ball enthusiasts would find it hard to realize the amount of speed that Sweeney could put into his work." Walter Johnson is called the "speed king," but he never pitched with more speed than Sweeney, and perhaps not as much. See note about Sweeney under "Negotiating Tactic."

Best Baseball Books: No classic books, but many important publications began in this period. *The Sporting News* began publication in 1886. The *Reach Guide* and *The Sporting Life,* both eventually edited by the incomparable Francis Richter, started in 1883 (Richter founded *The Sporting Life* and assumed the position as *Reach* editor later). *Casey at the Bat* first appeared in the *San Francisco Examiner* in 1888. Among the popular books of the period were *Mike Kelly's Play Ball: Stories of the Ball Field,* in 1888, and Fred Pfeffer's *Scientific Ball,* in 1889.

Best Outfield Arm: Jimmy Ryan

Most Runs Batted In:
 Sam Thompson, 1887, 166
 Cap Anson, 803

RBI records for this era are not complete. Early rules did not require the batting order to be announced prior to game time. Before this was changed in the early eighties, Anson would sometimes wait and see if the first two men got on in the first inning. If they did, he would bat; if not, he would wait and hit in the next inning.

Most Aggressive Baserunners:
 King Kelly
 Arlie Latham

Fastest Player: Billy Sunday

When he got old, Cap Anson said that Billy Sunday had been a greater player than Ty Cobb. The 1919 *Reach Guide,* conceding Sunday's greatness as a baserunner, found it necessary to rebut this at some length.

Slowest Player: Dick Buckley

Best Control Pitcher: Jim Whitney

*Nicknames: See notes

Most Stolen Bases:
 Hugh Nichol, 1887, 138
 Hugh Nichol, 321

Stolen base data available only for the years 1887–89.

Best-Looking Player: Billy Sunday

Ugliest Player: Grasshopper Jim Whitney

A reporter wrote that Whitney had "a head about the size of a wart with a forehead slanting at an angle of 45 degrees."

*Clint Hartung Award: Ebenezer Beatin

Outstanding Sportswriter: Oliver Perry Caylor

Most-Admirable Superstar: Bid McPhee

McPhee's record is remarkable not only because, as Voight pointed out, he played for many years with one team, but because he played for so many years at one position. In a time in which players were shuttled about to repair gaps in the small rosters opened up by injuries, no one except a catcher and perhaps a particularly immobile first baseman was left at one position. Yet McPhee played 2,135 games in his career, 2,125 of them at second base—a sure sign of a remarkable defensive second baseman.

Least-Admirable Superstar: Paul Hines, an outstanding offensive and defensive ballplayer, was castigated by William Hulbert in an open letter for his lack of hustle and poor attitude. In 1922 Hines was arrested in Washington as a pickpocket.

Franchise Shifts: Franchises constantly dropping in and out of the leagues. Exactly when the first team to "move" with its contracts, etc. was, I don't know. It could have been Worcester, which was moved to Philadelphia and became the Phillies in '83.

1885: THE GOOD PEOPLE OF THE EARTH VERSUS PETE SOMMERS

On May 28, 1885, Joseph Andrew Sommers, later a major league catcher, was arrested in Cleveland and charged with playing ball on Sunday, with the Cleveland team in a minor league. A jury trial was held. The team wished to admit evidence showing that baseball had been played on Sunday in Cleveland for several years without interference, and that other entertainments were permitted under the law. The judge would admit no evidence relating to those issues, but instructed the jury to consider only the question of whether Sommers had, indeed, played ball on Sunday. Since he acknowledged that he had, this simplified their work considerably.

The Cleveland club appealed, claiming that the law was unconstitutional in that it made no provisions for someone who might wish to keep a different holy day. They also argued that the law did not apply to Sommers, who was not "playing" the game, but merely following his avocation, as permitted under the law, and that the judge had erred in restricting the scope of the issues before the jury.

RECRUITING POSTER

In 1886 the owners of the two leagues agreed to hold salaries to a maximum of $2,000. More creatively, the owners decided to charge players for the use of their uniforms, and also to charge them 50 cents a day for expenses while on road trips.

John Montgomery Ward, a star player and a graduate of Columbia Law School, decided to form a union.

OUT

The only known case of a dishonest umpire in professional baseball was that of Dick Higham, fired by the National League in June 1882, after confessing to collusion with gamblers.

Higham was also the first umpire to wear a face mask.

*New Stadiums:
 1882—Exposition Park, Pittsburgh
 1883—Lakefront Park, Chicago (remodeled)
   Washington Park, Brooklyn
   Recreation Park, Philadelphia
 1884—Redland Park, Cincinnati
 1886—Capitol Park, Washington
 1887—Huntington Grounds, Philadelphia

Best Pennant Race: 1889 National League
 Giants won and Boston lost on the last day of the season to give Giants a one-game margin.

*Best World Series: 1886 Series, won by St. Louis over Chicago, 0–6, 12–0, 4–11, 8–5, 10–3, 4–3

Best-Hitting Pitcher: Guy Hecker
 In 1886, Dave Foutz won forty-one games and played the outfield when he wasn't pitching. In 1887 Foutz and teammate Bob Caruthers both played the outfield (fifty-four games for Caruthers, fifty for Foutz), and each hit .357 while Caruthers won twenty-nine games and Foutz twenty-five.

Worst-Hitting Pitcher: Cannonball Titcomb

Best Minor League Team: Dallas Hams, 1888

Best Minor League Player: Bill Krieg

Best Negro League Player: No Negro Leagues; outstanding black players included Fleetwood Walker, who played for a while in the majors.

Odd Couple: Cap Anson and King Kelly

Drinking Men:
 Charlie Sweeney
 King Kelly
 Jim McCormick
 Gid Gardner
 Lee Viau
 Mickey Welch
 Pete Browning
 Jack Farrell

*Best Unrecognized Player: Buck Ewing

New Strategies:
 Cap Anson extended Harry Wright's principle of backing up fielders to include a system of backing up throws in the infield.
 Pregame batting practice introduced by Harry Wright.
 Sacrifice hitting became commonly used.

New Equipment:
 Flat-sided bats legal, 1885–1893.
 Sliding pads introduced by Sam Morton.
 First made-to-order bats by Hillerich.
 Umpires' indicators invented.
 First night baseball game played at Hull, Massachusetts, September 2, 1880.

Player vs. Team: The reserve clause, developed in 1879, was submitted to a number of court tests during this decade and lost them all. In the first big test, the case of Charlie Bennett, the court ruled that the clause Bennett had signed was merely an agreement to execute a contract at a later date, and not a contract in and of itself; this implied that Bennett had a right to reject the later offer. This was merely the first of many courtroom defeats for baseball's reserve arrangement, which survived nonetheless for eighty-five years beyond the decade.

Team vs. Team: A Detroit owner named Frederick Kimball Stearns spent $25,000 between 1885 and 1887 to turn Detroit into a powerhouse team, knowing that the Detroit area at that time probably would not support such an effort. Stearns planned to get some of the money back by being a big draw on the road, where he was entitled to a percentage of the gate. Once the other owners in the National League realized this, they changed the rules so that instead of a percentage of the gate, Stearns would collect only the fixed sum of $125 a game, and thus would have no chance to recoup his investment.

*Uniform Changes: Position-coded uniforms

New Terms or Expressions: Fans at this time were called "cranks" or "kranks." Thomas Lawson wrote a little book, *The Krank: His Language and What It Means* (1888) which listed such terms as "willow" or "ash" for bat, "circus catches" for circus catches, "robber" or "tenth man" for umpire, as well as "butter fingers" and "back up" fielders.

Most Wins by Pitcher:
Old Hoss Radbourne, 1884, 60
Tim Keefe, 292

Highest Winning Percentage:
Fred Goldsmith, 1880, 21–3, .875
Jim McCormick, 1884, 21–3, .875
Bob Caruthers, 175–64, .732

Highest-Paid Player: One article says that Fred Dunlap received $10,000 late in the eighties. The salary would not be greatly out of step with the time, though I'm not sure the report is accurate or correctly placed in time. Charlie Comiskey received $8,000 in 1889 (equivalent to about $115,000 today).

New Statistics:
1883—Total bases
     Wild pitches
1884—Runs earned by opponents (earned runs) and earned run average adopted by National League
1886—Stolen bases
1888—Pitcher's walks
1889—Pitcher's strikeouts and hit by pitch

Wild pitches and walks were originally made a part of the pitcher's fielding record, later switched to part of his pitching record. The *Chicago Tribune* introduced RBI in 1880, but the concept didn't catch on until many years later. Existing RBI records for the period were figured later.

Best Athlete in the Game: Ed McKean

A Very Good Movie Could Be Made About: Baseball in St. Louis, 1883–86. It's got everything—great teams, unbelievable characters like Lucas, Von der Ahe, Comiskey, Sweeney and Latham, pennant races, World Series. Best material for a baseball movie ever.

I Don't Know What This Has to Do with Baseball, But I Thought I'd Mention It Anyway: The original "Louisville Slugger" was Pete Browning, the Louisville slugger who discovered the bat-making talents of Bud Hillerich. Pete Browning was the first man to have Ted Williams' love affair with his bats, and did a lot to change bats from crude nineteenth-century table legs into modern tools of the trade. Browning had over 200 bats, each of which had a name. He used names from the Bible if he didn't have anything else in mind.

Browning was released from an insane asylum in Louisville in 1905, and died in a city hospital later in the year.

NEGOTIATING TACTIC

Charles Sweeney was a pitcher; by July 21, 1884, he had a record of 17–8. That day Sweeney arrived at the park indisposed, and announced that he had been out drinking all night. His manager started him anyhow, but Sweeney was hitting the sauce between innings, with predictable effects. Since a substitution could not be made without the consent of the opposition, in the fifth inning Sweeney was asked to switch with the right fielder, a standby pitcher stowed away for such an occasion. Sweeney, however, refused to go to the outfield, and continued to pitch.

According to an article by Frederick Ivor-Campbell, the manager after a couple of innings became insistent, at which point Sweeney walked off the field, forcing his team to play a man short. Sweeney was released that evening.

Which didn't turn out badly. The emancipated Sweeney signed with St. Louis in the Union Association, earning a nice raise. It is suspected that the incident may have been planned to force his release.

BEST WORLD SERIES OF THE 1880s

The World Series of the 1880s, made possible by the peace of 1883, were not regular, prearranged events, but rather were set up by the participants to suit themselves. The 1886 series stands above the others for a number of reasons. Its format is easily the most familiar to the modern fan. It was a best of seven match, unlike later series that stretched to nine, ten, and fifteen games. It was seen through to the end, unlike that of the previous year, which was abandoned in dispute. It was the first time that all of the games would be played in the home stadiums of the combatants. Before this (and for two years after) the series was treated as a sort of traveling show, with the champion teams performing in a number of neutral parks. It was agreed before the series that the winning team would take the entire purse, which must have put an edge on the competition.

The series pitted the two premier teams in baseball at the time, and involved many or most of the great players of the eighties, including Charlie Comiskey, Arlie Latham, Tip O'Neill, Bob Caruthers and Dave Foutz of St. Louis, and Cap Anson, Fred Pfeffer, Jimmy Ryan, Ned Williamson, King Kelly and John Clarkson of the White Sox. The series was a re-match between the two teams which had won their leagues in 1885 (with much more impressive records than '86) but played to a

JOHN CLARKSON

draw in the series (although St. Louis fans have always regarded the Browns as having won the 1885 series.)

Despite having the edge over the other "World Series", it was not a classic contest. There is little evidence of great desire on the part of either side. The games, though in retrospect viewed as an early World Series, seem to have been treated like exhibitions. Several games were not played to their conclusion because of dark and cold weather, and Jimmy Ryan, primarily an outfielder, started Game Five to give Clarkson a day of rest.

The first three games were blowouts. Clarkson pitched a shutout for Chicago to win the first, 6–0; "Parisian Bob" Caruthers returned the compliment and Tip O'Neill hit two home runs to give the upstart Americans the second game, 12–0. Clarkson pitched again in Game Three—two days after his shutout, but that wasn't unusual then—while Caruthers came back with no rest for the Browns. Clarkson won, 11–4, being supported by home runs by Kelly and Gore. The game lasted eight innings.

Chicago up, 2–1, but the series now moved to St. Louis, and that meant moving in on the most notorious fans in baseball, egged on by Von der Ahe. In Game Four, Clarkson, obviously trying to prove something, pitched again and

JAMES "TIP" O'NEILL

got rocked, losing 8–5. This game lasted seven innings. The series was even. Jimmy Ryan started the fifth game— you tell me why—and was pounded, 10–3. This one was stopped by nightfall and disinterest after seven innings. St. Louis led, 3–2.

Game Six was the redemption. Interest in the series had mounted, despite the scores. The White Sox led in the seventh, 3–0; a light rain was falling and there was talk of calling the game off. The fans would have none of that. The Browns erased the 3–0 lead in

the bottom of the eighth, and went on to win with one out in the tenth on a legendary steal of home by Curt Welch. This was the most famous play in nineteenth-century baseball —the $15,000 slide, so-called because the Browns grabbed all the receipts, which actually totaled $13,910.20, on the strength of the play. Bob Caruthers was the winning pitcher for St. Louis—and the American Association could claim its only undisputed World Championship.

—Jim Baker and Bill James

NICKNAMES IN THE 1880s

One thing that is interesting to note about this first generation of baseball nicknames is what caught on and what did not. Nicknames with allusions to literature or the heroic past were used, but never caught on; Tony Mullane was "The Apollo of the Box"; Charles Comiskey, "The Old Roman"; Milt Scott "Mikado Milt" and Pete Browning "The Gladiator." But Jim Galvin became the first of dozens of hard-throwing pitchers to be likened to a train, when he was called "The Steam Engine," and Ed Morris served a like function in being called "Cannonball." Long nicknames disappeared quickly; Arlie Latham's five-word handle was one of the last. But Mickey Welch, being called "Smiling Mickey," set a pattern for hundreds of players, and for the first time animals came to be used (though infrequently) to suggest images. Pete Hotaling was called "Monkey," Jim Whitney was "Grasshopper Jim" and Willard Mains just plain "Grasshopper." Those particular animals, however, are not used anymore.

Two forms of nicknames that were popular were those that suggested places or movement, such as "Parisian Bob" Caruthers and "The Little Globetrotter" (Billy Earle). There were a few nicknames alluding to the player's voice, and a player named George Miller, who must have had one of the greatest voices ever, had three of them: "Doggie," "Foghorn," and "Calliope" (if that kid was growing up today they'd send him to a speech therapist). Tim O'Rourke was called "Voiceless Tim," and Mike Tiernan, a very quiet man, was "Silent Mike." George Tebeau was called "White Wings"; Jim Baker noticed in going through some 1890s newspapers that garbage workers of the time were called "White Wings," which probably is connected somehow (it is quite possible he could have done that in the off season). And the decade probably had as many great one-of-a-kind nicknames as any decade ever, of which I present a few:

> Sureshot (Fred Dunlap)
> Bloody Jake (Jake Evans)
> Scissors (Dave Foutz)
> Pebbly Jack (Jack Glasscock)
> Prunes (George Moolic)
> Dandelion (Fred Pfeffer)
> Peach Pie (Jack O'Connor)
> Bollicky Billy Taylor
> Razzle Dazzle (Con Murphy)

All deaf and dumb players were called "Dummy."

THE ALLENTOWN WONDER

In 1887 a twenty-year-old pitcher by the name of Ebenezer Beatin shamelessly signed contracts with several professional teams, including Detroit, Cincinnati, and Indianapolis of the National League. He was called "the Allentown Wonder" due to his pitching prowess in that city. The matter of his baseball polygamy was put up before the league, and decided in favor of the Detroit Wolverines, who used him in two games en route to the 1887 National League pennant. He put in a mediocre year there in '88, and moved on to Cleveland, where he was 20–15 in 1889 (of course, winning twenty games was not considered so highly when the league leader would win forty to fifty). This was to be the highlight of his career. The next year Eb was "Beatin" thirty-one times, and the fans were more impressed with an Ohio youngster named Cy Young. He departed in 1891 after an 0–3 record. The pitcher that everybody had wanted four years earlier had a final record of 48–57, making everybody wonder what was so wonderful back there in Allentown. He signed five contracts but was only allowed to dishonor one with his pitching.

—Jim Baker

BUCK EWING

EBENEZER BEATIN

Pete Browning hit a double in his home park in Louisville on May 5, 1882. He had this to say about the drive: "That would count a home run in St. Louis."

Buck Ewing is not what you would usually describe as an unrecognized player; he has been in the Hall of Fame since 1939, and his name would probably be vaguely familiar to anyone who is a deep baseball fan. But almost no one, anymore, remembers *how* great his contemporaries thought he was. No one would remember him now as being in a class with Ty Cobb, Honus Wagner and Babe Ruth—but that is where he was placed for thirty or forty years after he retired.

I'll give you a few examples. The *Reach Guide* in 1919 had an article entitled "Superlatively Great Players." The three greatest players in baseball up to that time, according to Francis Richter, were Ty Cobb, Honus Wagner, and Buck Ewing—and Richter went further: "It is a difficult, not to say ungrateful, task to select any one player as superior to all the rest, though we have always been inclined to consider Catcher-Manager William ('Buck') Ewing in his prime, from 1884 to 1890, as the greatest player of the game from the standpoint of supreme excellence in all departments—batting, catching, fielding, base running, throwing and base ball brains—a player without a weakness of any kind, physical, mental, or temperamental."

Though Richter was old by this time, he was never an old fogey; he stayed fresh, as is suggested by his other two selections (Cobb, then thirty-two years old, and Wagner, just retired). But he was not necessarily right.

Consider this. When the Hall of Fame preparations were being discussed in the late 1930s, the editor of the *Spalding Guide* (John Foster) chose his personal all-time all-star team, the greatest players ever. "The first to be picked, and the first who should be selected in this stretch of fifty years, is William Buckingham Ewing, better known as 'Buck.' He is to be the catcher. He has been called the greatest all-round player ever connected with the game. I think he was." By the way, note the middle name. The Macmillan *Encyclopedia* doesn't credit him with having one.

Again, the fact that a man—a very knowledgeable man—who saw all the greats from Anson through Gehrig *said* that Ewing was the best of them doesn't mean that he was. But the position of guide editor was a position of great respect in baseball's early days, and the fact that two men who between them edited guides for over eighty years both thought that Ewing was the greatest player ever is not something that can be lightly dismissed.

There are others. In a 1980 *Baseball Research Journal* article about Billy Sunday, I find this quote: "In 1934, in response to a reporter's question, he named his all-time baseball team. He included only two players from his own era—Buck Ewing as catcher and Larry Corcoran as one of the pitchers." Clark Griffith in 1915 named his all-time all-star team; Buck Ewing was the catcher. John Montgomery Ward stated that he regarded Ewing as the greatest player of his time. And on the first vote of the Old-Timers for the Hall of Fame, the first-place slot ended in a tie: 39½ votes for Cap Anson, 39½ for Buck Ewing. They were followed by Willie Keeler, Cy Young, and Ed Delahanty. (Incidentally, although everybody knows that the first five players selected for the Hall of Fame were Ruth, Cobb, Wagner, Johnson and Mathewson, almost nobody remembers that there were supposed to be ten initial selections, not five. Five players were to be named from after 1900, five from before 1900, and those ten were to go in together. The only reason Cy Young isn't in the original five is that he split his vote between the two groups. Anyway, the Old-Timers committee started quarreling among itself about who the five should be, and didn't come up with any selections to meet the 75% standard of the Hall, so the Hall of Fame opened with just the five "modern" players as the original inductees.)

Ewing's batting records won't bowl you over. They're awfully good, but they don't suggest a player who would be compared to Ruth or Cobb. From 1885 to 1893 he hit .304, .309, .305, .306, .327, .338, .347, .310, and .344; still, his lifetime average was only .303. He led the league in triples once (twenty) and home runs once (ten), and caught only 636 games in his career. He played in the day when catchers took a lot of punishment,

BILLY SUNDAY

WILLIAM BUCKINGHAM "BUCK" EWING

Hans Wagner, the super-excellent shortstop of the Pittsburgh club." Foster wrote: "As a thrower to the bases Ewing never had a superior. . . . Ewing was the man of whom it was said 'He handed the ball to the second baseman from the batter's box.'" In 1889, with his team short of pitching, the star catcher started two games on the mound and pitched complete-game victories two times. His team won the pennant by a single game.

Ewing became an unpopular man in 1890 when, depending on whose version of the matter you believe, he did or did not desert the Player's League. A lot of players *felt* that he did, anyway, and many of them would not speak to him for several years afterward. Monte Ward, the organizer of the league, apparently did not share the bitterness, but those bad feelings probably are the reason Ewing only tied Anson for first place in the first voting for Old-Timers in the Hall of Fame, rather than finishing a clear first. But the rule is that the further you get from a player's active career, the more important his statistics become in the public's evaluation of him. In his career, Ewing had only about half as many hits as Cap Anson; it would be a promotion for him now to be half as famous.

and was by far the best-hitting catcher of his time. He was a good base stealer, finishing among the top ten in the league in stolen bases three times, although he didn't come close to playing a full schedule. He hit a consistent fifteen triples and six home runs a year, playing a hundred games or less.

So his batting numbers, if you look carefully and you look at the context, are good —but to rate him as high as these people have rated him, a lot of points would have to be given for defense. What else did they say about him, and what did they say about his defense? Richter wrote: "I have seen all the players in the major leagues in action since 1868, and . . . Ty Cobb appears to me to be, with two exceptions, just a trifle superior to all the rest . . . these two exceptions are Buck Ewing, the greatest catcher that ever stood in shoe leather, and

BALLPARKS IN THE 1880s

There were some parks built in the 1880s that, if not successful as long-term domiciles for major league teams, at least had pretensions in that direction. With the great increases in attendance early in the decade, there was (1) a recognized need for larger parks, and (2) a new belief in the stability of the institution. One must remember that a National League owner in 1876 had no reason to believe that the National League would last another thirty years, and hence little incentive to build a permanent ballpark.

The palace of baseball in the 1880s was Lakefront Stadium in Chicago. Lakefront, built in 1877, benefited from almost constant improvements by Albert Spalding, and after a major renovation in 1883 it seated 10,000 fans, making it the largest baseball park in the country. Spalding's private box was equipped with a gong to call his help and (believe it or not) a telephone, so that he could conduct business and look like an earlier-day Bowie Kuhn. The park featured eighteen private boxes with armchairs and curtains to keep the sun out; it also had a pagoda built to accommodate a small brass band, which entertained before and after the game and between innings, but never, on any occasion, played anything like "Ring of Fire" when Tommy Burns came to bat, bullfight music for George Gore, or imitated the sound of popcorn popping for Fred Pfeffer.

The new ballparks of the decade . . . Washington Park in Brooklyn (1883) was a little 2,000-seater, built for a minor league team, that burned down in 1889. When Alfred Reach bought the Worcester, Massachusetts, team and moved it to Philadelphia in 1883, he built a small park called Recreation Park; the Phillies quickly outgrew this, so he built the Huntington Grounds in 1887. This park was perhaps the finest of the late part of the decade, a big double-decker seating 20,000 people, and no doubt Reach intended it to last a while. It burned in 1894, not completely, was rebuilt and collapsed in 1903, killing twelve. The park survived this, too, and eventually became the Baker Bowl. The American Association team in Cincinnati in 1884 threw up a jerry-built park in the month before the season opened; a section of the seats collapsed on opening day, killing one spectator and injuring many others. (In my hometown of Mayetta, Kansas, in the early sixties, there was an annual rodeo, ran for about a week. As the crowd was departing one day, a section of the bleachers collapsed, killing one woman and injuring several; this is probably why I think of these bleachers in terms of those.)

Henry Lucas, the enthusiastic millionaire who backed the Union Association, laid out a small but pretentious ballpark on his private estate in St. Louis, while crosstown rival Chris Von der Ahe spent $6,500 to convert old Sportsman's Park (built 1876) to the task of simultaneously accommodating baseball games, horse races, beer sales and fireworks shows. The Hewitt brothers built Capitol Park in Washington in 1886; it seated 6,000. The Giants from 1883 onward were playing at the first Polo Grounds, which would receive large crowds, if not necessarily seat them; they left in a Tammany Hall wrangle in 1890. When you add it all together, I doubt that any team except the White Stockings spent the entire decade in one park. But with crowds of 30,000 by the end of the decade, the day when that would change was drawing into view.

❧ UNIFORMS OF THE 1880s ❧

How about the ingenuity of the Detroit Wolverines in 1882? From the *National Pastime:* "each player's jersey, belt and cap were designated by position—1B, red-and-white stripes; CF, red-and-black; SS, brown; P, sky blue; and so on, with team colors reflected only in the stockings. The heavy silk 'clown' shirts were not only humiliating to the players but uncomfortable in the heat; the experiment was mercifully ended in June." (Can't you just see how this ended . . . about June the owner looked out there and said, "You know, I really think you can tell what position the man is playing just by looking at where he is on the field.") The Wolverines continued to wear stripes, as did the American League Detroit Wolverines in 1901, who then became the Tigers because of the black-and-yellow stripes on their stockings.

A few other notes . . . with no identification numbers on the uniforms, did you ever wonder how players kept track of their own? A photograph of Wee Willie Keeler's shirt provides an answer; "W. Keeler" was embroidered on the front shirttail, the part that would be tucked in. An up-close view of the shirt belonging to a member of the Baraboo Base Ball Club shows the detachable bib I've mentioned before, but also has long sleeves that could be detached just above the elbow.

More and more uniforms were going all-dark about this time, probably following the famous black uniforms of the New York Giants. The Chicago uniform, for instance, became dark pants and top, contrasting white caps, stockings, lace-up closure, belt, and lettering. One more little tidbit from the *National Pastime:* Will White was the only player of the nineteenth century to wear glasses.

—Susie McCarthy

❧ TERRY LARKIN ❧

This is not a pretty story, and you may not wish to read it. Terry Larkin was a pitcher with Hartford and Chicago in the National League from 1877 through 1879, winning eighty-nine games. One day in 1883 his wife, Catherine, got on him for coming home drunk, and he pulled a pistol from his hip pocket and shot her, afterwards a) threatening to kill anyone else who came near him, and b) cutting his own throat with a razor. He was arrested and held in a hospital, where, under the impression that his wife would die, he again attempted to commit suicide, this time by banging his head against a steam register, causing an ugly gash. Restrained, he begged a policeman to "For God's sake hit me in the head and put an end to my suffering."

His wife recovered, and his sufferings did not end then. Larkin returned to the majors in 1884, and returned to the crime section in 1886. Fired from a job as a saloon keeper in Brooklyn, Larkin showed up at the bar with two loaded pistols and insisted that the saloon owner fight a duel. The owner was unwilling to do this, but Larkin insisted, and forced him at the point of one gun to take the other. When they began marching their ten paces, the owner marched out the door and locked Larkin in, returning with a policeman, who then arrested the old ballplayer. "Larkin's examination," reported a local paper, "was adjourned for a week, so that he could get the liquor out of him."

According to Richard Malatzky "Larkin appeared in *The Sporting Life* periodically after his baseball career with regard to slashing police officers and other relatives." Mr. Malatzky searched for ten years for the time and place of Larkin's death, finally learning that Larkin's unhappy life ended in Brooklyn on September 16, 1894.

The 1890s

HOW THE GAME WAS PLAYED

Dirty. Very, very dirty.

The tactics of the eighties were aggressive; the tactics of the nineties were violent. The game of the eighties was crude; the game of the nineties was criminal. The baseball of the eighties had ugly elements; the game of the nineties was just ugly.

Players spiked each other. A first baseman would grab the belt of the baserunner to hold him back a half-second after the ball was hit. Occasionally players tripped one another as they rounded the bases. Fights broke out from day to day. Players shoved umpires, spat on them, abused them in every manner short of assault. Fans hurled insults and beer bottles at the players of opposing teams.

The great team of the time, and the team responsible for promoting this style of play, was the Baltimore Orioles, the team of John McGraw, Hughie Jennings and Willie Keeler. Writing about them in *The Ultimate Baseball Book,* Robert Creamer said that John McGraw "had a genius for making enemies. He had been knocked down in spring training by a rival manager after blocking a player on the basepaths. He did grab base runners' belts to slow them down as they passed, stood in their way deliberately to make them run around him, stepped on their feet as he took throws at the bag." McGraw himself recalled a game in which "the other team had a runner on first who started to steal second, but . . . spiked our first baseman on the foot. Our man retaliated by trying to trip him. He got away, but at second Heine Reitz tried to block him off while Hughie . . . covered the bag to take the throw and tag him. The runner evaded Reitz and jumped feet first at Jennings to drive him away from the bag. Jennings dodged the flying spikes and threw himself bodily at the runner, knocking him flat. In the meantime the batter hit our catcher over the hands with his bat so he couldn't throw, and our catcher trod on the umpire's feet with his spikes and shoved his big mitt in his face so he couldn't see the play."

Great fun, huh ... *The Sporting News* said that they were "playing the dirtiest ball ever seen in the country," and that they would maim an opponent if need be. One of my heroes, one of the finest and one of the sharpest men ever associated with major league baseball, was John Heydler, later National League president but at that time an umpire. Heydler said of the old Orioles that "they were mean, vicious, ready at any time to maim a rival player or an umpire, if it helped their cause. The things they would say to an umpire were unbelievably vile, and they broke the spirits of some fine men. I've seen umpires bathe their feet by the hour after McGraw and others spiked them through their shoes ... the worst of it was that they got by with much of their brow beating and hooliganism. Other clubs patterned after them, and I feel the lot of the umpire was never worse." David Voight said that "umpires were cursed, bombarded with beer bottles and rotten eggs, and subjected to beatings."

It was hell to be an umpire in the 1890s; it's a wonder anyone would do it. One of the best was Bob Ferguson, old "Death to Flying Things." But as nearly as I can figure out, the fans never actually did kill an umpire. They tried. There were countless incidents of umpires requiring police protection, and there was an incident in Minnesota in 1906 in which a crowd got hold of an umpire with apparent intent to do bodily harm, but was dissuaded from it by a local athlete. A good many umpires have been killed in on-field accidents, some of them in the minors. But if they didn't kill one in the 1890s, then it just wasn't destined to happen, because they sure tried.

The mess was preserved by a persistent myth that the fans liked this kind of thing. Many owners believed this, what we might call the Von der Ahe myth, after the St. Louis owner of the 1880s who deliberately encouraged rowdyism, and was largely responsible for giving it a toehold in professional baseball. Some fans, of course, did like it. In 1918, Christy Mathewson (of all people) said that baseball had gotten too tame, and that what it needed was "a real old-fashioned feud." Horrified, Francis Richter replied with an article entitled "The Cost of Rowdy Ball." A witness to the entire period, Richter wrote that "in the '80s there developed a spirit of rivalry which led to much abuse of umpires by players and of players by each other." He cited Anson and Comiskey, from the eighties, as being the worst offenders, but "the situation developed nothing more serious than an occasional riot." But then "the steady growth of rowdyism reached its apogee in the decade of the '90s, during the sole reign of the 12-club National League. Obscene and indecent language between players and to the umpires reached such a pitch that ... some of the magnates could not stand the raw work of the players, and protested continually against it. But the larger number of the magnates condoned and excused every act of rowdyism, no matter how flagrant."

As to offensive styles, many people have written that the baseball of the 1890s was the first "modern" baseball, a statement that I think reflects a fundamental misunderstanding about the game—namely, that the way in which it is played is defined largely by the rules. It isn't; the way in which the game is played is defined mostly by the conditions under which the game is played, with the parks as the paramount condition. It is defined no more by the rules than by the players, the ethics, the strategies, the equipment, or the expectations of the public. These people played seven-run-a-game baseball, and we could play seven-run-a-game baseball today or two-run-a-game baseball with the same basic rule structure; it all depends on how and when we fine-tune the game. But it is true that the rules attained essentially their modern form after 1893, when the pitching distance was moved back to its present 60 feet, 6 inches.

In the early nineties the

pitchers were in control; batting averages in 1891–92 were in the range of .250, though teams still scored in excess of five runs per game because an average team still committed over three errors a game. Still, five runs a game were regarded at that time as too few, and in 1893 the pitching mound was moved to 60 and 6. After that the hitters took over; league batting averages went up near .300 (.309 in 1894) and runs per team per game were around seven. Base stealing declined slightly throughout the decade (as it becomes easier to score a man from first base, it makes less sense to risk him in a steal attempt) but remained at levels that are historically high— very comparable to the present, in fact. A little higher.

WHERE THE GAME WAS PLAYED

The cities were Baltimore, Boston, Brooklyn, Buffalo, Chicago, Cincinnati, Cleveland, Columbus, Louisville, Milwaukee, New York, Philadelphia, Pittsburgh, Rochester, St. Louis, Syracuse, Toledo, Washington.

By 1890 the National League had occupied the larger cities of the east, but the American Association was doing all right for itself in the Midwest, in cities like St. Louis, Louisville, Columbus and Toledo. A reserve arrangement was in

place. The Players League opened (and closed) in 1890, going head-to-head with the National League in the big eastern cities, in several cases in ballparks separated by just blocks. By 1892 two of the three leagues folded, with the stronger American Association teams joining the National League.

This created a twelve-team National League monopoly, and one that should have provided good ammunition for Joe Cronin in 1968 when he was arguing for adoption of the division setup. His argument was "You can't sell a twelfth-place team." They sure couldn't. With the weakest teams in the leagues finishing forty-five, fifty, fifty-five, sixty games behind every year, the bottom of the league began to atrophy. Every year three teams opened the gates on opening day and died. Only the fans of Boston, Baltimore, and Brooklyn were entitled to dream of a pennant. Eventually, this led to the second abomination of baseball in the 1890s, syndicate ownership.

Baseball in the 1890s allowed a man to own stock in two different teams or for that matter several different teams, and by a series of trades, sales, and gambling debts, there arose a bizarre system in which the same men owned stock in different teams all over the league. When the weak teams in the league, losing by fifty games a year, grew weak enough, the

strong teams simply bought them. In modern terms, what was meant by syndicate ownership was that George Steinbrenner would, for example, purchase the Seattle Mariners and transfer all their best players to the Yankees. Seattle comes up with an Alvin Davis; the Yankees get him. Seattle brings around a Mark Langston, and pfft, he's in pinstripes. Seattle would continue to function in the American League, with a manager or GM doing the best he could under the circumstances, but every time he succeeds in coming up with a winner . . . well, there he goes again.

There were several of these diseased arrangements in the National League. As the decade wore on, it reached the point of absurdity, or obscenity, or both. The Robison brothers owned both the Cleveland and St. Louis entries. A cabal of the same people owned both Baltimore and Brooklyn. Barney Dreyfuss and company owned both Louisville and Pittsburgh. If one team had a chance to win, it got all the players—and it needed them, to compete against the other superteams. They had formed, in effect, a hybrid major/minor league, with teams competing against what would later be called their own farm teams.

To show the effect that this had on the leagues, let me present the records of the first-

and last-place teams in the National League from 1892 through 1899. The 1892 season, actually, was a split season, Boston winning the first half of the schedule and Cleveland the second; the records given below are the combined totals:

Year	First				Last				GB
1892	BOS	102–48	.680		BAL	46–101	.313		54.5
1893	BOS	86–43	.667		WAS	40–89	.310		46.0
1894	BAL	89–39	.695		LOU	36–94	.277		54.0
1895	BAL	87–43	.669		LOU	35–96	.267		52.5
1896	BAL	90–39	.698		LOU	38–93	.290		53.0
1897	BOS	93–39	.705		STL	29–102	.221		63.5
1898	BOS	102–47	.685		STL	39–111	.260		63.5
1899	BKN	101–47	.682		CLE	20–134	.130		84.0

Given the inequality between teams and the high-scoring game that was played, there must have been endless 12–1 and 16–3 games. Can you imagine what it was like trying to convince the Cleveland fans to support the 1899 Cleveland Spiders? Well, neither could anybody else. No one went to their home games, and eventually they stopped playing them, and wound up traveling from road game to road game, serving as virtually an automatic victory for their opponents—and, by acclamation, the worst major league team ever.

And baseball's greatest disgrace. The 1919 White Sox sold only one series; the Cleveland owners sold out the whole season.

Checking In

1890—Casey Stengel, Kansas City
Larry MacPhail, Cass City, Michigan
Stan Coveleski, Shamokin, Pennsylvania
Sam Rice, Morocco, Indiana
Dwight D. Eisenhower, Denison, Texas
1891—Dazzy Vance, Iowa
1893—George Sisler, Manchester, Ohio
1894—Harry Heilmann, San Francisco
Ford Frick, Wawaka, Indiana
Norman Rockwell, New York City
1895—Babe Ruth, Baltimore
1896—Rogers Hornsby, Winters, Texas
Oscar Charleston, Indianapolis, Indiana
1898—Frankie Frisch, Queens, New York
1899—Judy Johnson, Snow Hill, Maryland
Pie Traynor, Framingham, Massachusetts

Checking Out

1891—Larry Corcoran, 32
Jim Whitney, 34
P. T. Barnum, 81
1892—Alexander Cartwright, 72
Darby O'Brien (pitcher), consumption, 25
1893—Darby O'Brien (outfielder), 29
1894—Bob Ferguson, 49
King Kelly, typhoid fever or pneumonia, 36
Ned Williamson, liver and heart problems, 36
E. J. McNabb, murder/suicide, 28
1895—Harry Wright, pneumonia, 60
Pacer Smith, hanged, 42
1896—Cannonball Crane, accidental overdose of chloral, 34
1897—Old Hoss Radbourne, paresis, 42
1899—Minnie McGraw (wife of John), died following appendix operation, 23

WHO THE GAME WAS PLAYED BY

The Irish.

Baseball in the 1890s was dominated by Irish players to such an extent that many people, in the same stupid way that people today believe that blacks are born athletes, thought that the Irish were born baseball players.

Of course, people also associated the roughness and unruliness of the players with their ethnic background; the Irish have, indeed, always been known for that. But there is evidence that a good many of the players who were playing the game at this time were thoroughly disgusted with the way the game was being run. By the middle part of the decade, an educated element was filtering into the game; by 1900, there were a good many college players in the majors. When the Western League/American League went for major league status as a "clean" league, this element was very attractive to many players, and helped the league to acquire the quality players they needed to establish credibility.

It was in this period also that ballplayers developed an exaggerated reputation as unsavory characters. There is little doubt in my mind that the players must have been intelligent enough to realize that, because of the way the game was conducted on the field, they were losing respect, as men, in the eyes of the community. They couldn't have been very happy about that, but as professionals it would have been difficult for them to disdain these tactics and allow their opponents an advantage.

MAJOR LEAGUE ALL-STAR TEAM
1890–99
Records in seasonal notation, based on 154 games played.
Pitchers based on 50 starts.

Pos	Player	Years	Hits	HR	RBI	Avg.	Other
C	Chief Zimmer	5.67	157	4	86	.278	
1B	Roger Connor	5.95	182	12	106	.310	
2B	Cupid Childs	8.21	187	2	88	.316	109 Walks
3B	John McGraw	5.51	193	2	72	.336	116 BB, 153 Runs
SS	Hughie Jennings	6.49	191	2	107	.323	
LF	Ed Delahanty	8.25	226	10	131	.354	130 RBI
CF	Billy Hamilton	7.67	220	4	74	.357	176 Runs, 94 SB
RF	Willie Keeler	5.37	256	3	85	.387	

Pitcher	Years	Won-Lost	SO	ERA	Other
Kid Nichols	9.41	32–16	158	2.96	427 Innings
Amos Rusie	8.34	28–18	220	2.74	447 Innings
Cy Young	9.92	27–15	96	3.05	375 Innings

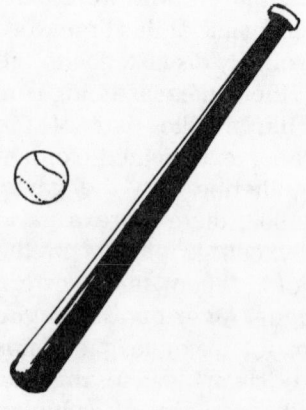

HUGHIE (EE-YAH) JENNINGS

THE 1890s IN A BOX

Attendance Data: No systematic data available. In 1890 it was reported that the Player's League drew 981,000 fans, the National League 814,000; there were eight teams in each league. That was with two teams going head to head, dividing the crowds, and was considered poor attendance at the time.

Throughout the decade, as you can imagine given the way in which the game was played, attendance apparently was awful, and declining. I would be very surprised if the average attendance for a National League team in the period 1896–99 was more than 180,000 a season—two to three thousand a game.

Most Home Runs:
> Buck Freeman, 1899, 25
> Hugh Duffy, 80

Best Won-Lost Record by Team:
> Boston, 1897, 93–39, .705
> Boston (N.L.) 869–508, .631

It is interesting to note that while the Orioles are universally thought of as the great team of this generation, the Beaneaters won more championships (4–3), and had the best one-year record and the best overall record of the decade. The Boston team, as we shall see, was the true offensive innovator of the period, and was noted for playing clean ball, at least by contrast. Boston was the only team in the decade to lead the National League in both runs scored and fewest runs allowed, which they did in both 1891 and 1897; Boston in the American Association also did this in 1891.

Worst Won-Lost Record by Team:
> Cleveland, 1899, 20–134, .130
> St. Louis (N.L.), 400–707, .361

Heaviest Player: Wilbert Robinson, 5′ 8½″ and listed at 215 pounds, but described in newspaper stories of the time as weighing more than that. Another candidate who should be mentioned, if only for his name, was Carlton Molesworth, who pitched briefly for the Washington Nationals in 1895. He stood just 5 feet 6 inches, but weighed 200. Carlton Molesworth is such a great name for a factotum. Can't you see this portly man in a butler's garb, waddling to the beck and call of an even more portly industrialist?

RICH FOP: Molesworth, draw my bath.
MOLESWORTH: As you wish, sir. Will there be anything else, sir?
RICH FOP: No, Molesworth, you are free to go after that task is complete. However, I do not wish you to "raid" the larder on your way out, as has been your custom of late.
MOLESWORTH: Very good, sir. Good night.

—Jim Baker

Lightest Player: Willie Keeler, 140
Most Strikeouts by Pitcher:
> Amos Rusie, 1890, 345
> Amos Rusie, 1,891

Highest Batting Average:
> Hugh Duffy, 1894, .438
> Willie Keeler, .387

Hardest-Throwing Pitcher: Amos Rusie

BASEBALL LANGUAGE IN THE 1890s

The term "fan" for what was earlier called "crank" is supposed to have been coined by Ted Sullivan, who preceded Charlie Comiskey as manager of the Browns. It existed in the 1880s but was rarely used.

It has been written that the term "Texas Leaguer" comes from the major league debut of Ollie Pickering, who got four hits in his first game after being called up from the Texas League; each one blooped just over the infield. The next day a reporter who missed a play saw Pickering on first base and asked what happened. "Oh, he just made another one of those Texas League hits," said another reporter. However, Robert McConnell looked up the game stories for Ollie Pickering's 1896 debut, and reports that the events will not support this story.

The "Baltimore chop," of course, owes its origin to Willie Keeler.

The term "big league" apparently referred originally to the size of the one major league, which had twelve teams in it. But the "big league" came to stand for the "major league," and "big leagues" became a synonym for "majors."

1899: GOD'S DOUBLE AGENT

On July 10, 1899, the Rev. Sherman Powell bought a ticket to a baseball game in Fort Wayne, Indiana, and began copying down the names of players, spectators, and ticket takers, apparently intending to use this evidence to convict the pagans of playing ball on Sunday. When he was discovered, a nasty crowd encircled him, took away his pen and notebook and made him fear for his safety. The police were called and escorted the reverend from the park, to his great indignation.

Mr. Powell issued a statement saying that the Good Citizen's League would continue its fight against violations of the Sabbath in Fort Wayne.

1890: WANTED: ONE SEXY SHORTSTOP

On August 26, 1890, a New York gentleman named W. S. Franklin announced his intention to form a Women's Professional Base Ball League. His help-wanted advertisement said that applicants "must be young, not over 20, good looking and good figure." Applicants outside of the city were requested to send photographs.

Best Baseball Books: The first Frank Merriwell story was published in *Tip Top Weekly* on April 18, 1896. There were eventually 986 Merriwell stories collected into 245 books, some written by Gilbert Patten under the pseudonym Burt L. Standish, some written by other people under Patten's supervision. Frank could make a curve break twice, regularly got the game-winning hit for Yale, and was the best and finest baseball player who ever lived.

—Jim Carothers

Best Outfield Arm: Lou Sockalexis
Worst Outfield Arm: Sliding Billy Hamilton
Most Runs Batted In:
    Sam Thompson, 1895, 165
    Hugh Duffy, 1,085
Most-Aggressive Baserunner: Patsy Tebeau

Tebeau, though not very fast, was Cleveland's John McGraw, a tough, aggressive player of no excess in manners. The 1919 *Reach Guide* says that "early in life [he] was given the name 'Pat' by his neighbors because of his fondness for shoveling sand and also carrying a dinner pail." Guess you had to be there . . . anyway, Tebeau managed in the majors for ten years, had a good record, though he kept finishing second. In 1894, he was involved in a confusing scandal in which he was drunk, beaten, robbed, and paid $250 blackmail to avoid a lawsuit. After his retirement in 1899 he ran a saloon in St. Louis until he shot himself, committing suicide, in 1918, aged fifty-four.

Fastest Player: Billy Hamilton
Slowest Player: Malachi Kitteredge
Best Control Pitcher: Cy Young
Best Minor League Player: Perry Werden
Best Negro League Players:
    Home Run Johnson
    Frank Grant
Drinking Men:
    Lou Sockalexis
    Jack McCarthy
    Marty Bergen
    Harry Decker
    Willie McGill
    Patsy Tebeau
Nicknames:
    Foxy Grandpa (Jimmy Bannon)
    Eagle Eye (Jake Beckley)
    Dodo (Frank Bird)
    The Crab (Jesse Burkett)
    Chewing Gum (John O'Brien)
    The Curveless Wonder (Al Orth)
    Tacky Tom (Tom Parrott)
    Little Eva (Bill Lange)
    What's the Use (Pearce Chiles)
    Derby Day (Bill Clymer)
Most Stolen Bases:
    Billy Hamilton, 1891, 115
    Billy Hamilton, 730

Stolen bases included things not now considered part of the category until 1898.

Best-Looking Players:
    John Clarkson
    Billy Nash

Ugliest Player: Fred Tenney
*Clint Hartung Award: Lou Sockalexis
Outstanding Sportswriter: Tim Murnane
Most-Admirable Superstar: Dummy Hoy
Least-Admirable Superstar: John McGraw
Franchise Shifts:

In the fall of 1891, two American Association teams, Louisville and Columbus, folded. The National League then persuaded Chris Von der Ahe, the power in the league and owner of the St. Louis team, to come into the National League; Von der Ahe did and brought Washington, Baltimore, and a resuscitated Louisville with him. The four teams finished ninth, tenth, eleventh, and twelfth in the National League in 1892, but after that the league was stable for the rest of the decade. In 1900, the National League contracted to eight teams by getting rid of three of the old Association teams (Washington, Louisville, and Baltimore), plus Cleveland.

New Stadiums:
1890—Manhattan Field in New York (became new Polo Grounds in 1891; seated 16,000).
1891—League Park in Cleveland (wooden structure).
1892—National Park, Washington (seated 6,500).
1895—Union Park, Baltimore (concrete and steel, but seated only 6,500).
1899—Robison Field, St. Louis.

The exciting new park of the decade was the Polo Grounds. A renovation of Redlands Park in Cincinnati also apparently made it into quite an attractive, modern stadium with some concrete and steel. Several parks, as usual, burned down during the decade, and at one point three parks burned in a few weeks, causing some to fear that there was a "baseball arsonist" at work.

*Best Pennant Race: 1897 National League
*Best World Series: None
Best-Hitting Pitcher: Jack Stivetts
Worst-Hitting Pitcher: Tully Sparks
New Strategies: Pitchers began to cover first base.

The practice of catchers signaling for the pitch became common in the 1890s, but had existed before.

The split season was tried for the first time.

The practice of chopping down on the ball—the Baltimore chop—was developed.

Brooklyn in the mid-nineties invented the cut-off play.

Philadelphia became the first team to use an illegal electric sign-stealing system.

Hit and run developed by Boston Beaneaters.

New Equipment:
Pitching machine
Cincinnati painted center field fence black to help hitters

Player vs. Team: Amos Rusie of the New York Giants was the dominant strikeout pitcher of the 1890s, leading the league in Ks in 1890, '91, '93, '94, and '95. He was a consistent winner, going 36–13 in 1894, and 22–21 with a bad team in '95. The Giants owner at this time was Andrew Freedman, who could best be described as George Steinbrenner on Quāāludes, with a touch of Al Capone thrown in. Mean sum' bitch. Rusie had had a number of run-ins with this madman, but when he drew his last paycheck in 1895, he found that Freedman had withheld $200—the most you could make for a season at the time was $2,500—for unspecified violations of training and indifferent pitching late in the season.

STATISTICS IN THE 1890s

The New England League, a good minor league, counted batter's strikeouts in the 1890s, twenty years before the majors did.

In 1898 one of the Washington owners, to quote Harold Seymour, "admitted getting the official scorer to add 40 base hits to infielder Gene DeMontreville's record, to bring his batting average above .300 so he could sell him to Baltimore for a higher price." He thought this was a legitimate tactic.

I think the Washington owner was probably stretching the truth a bit. If this was true, DeMontreville's average would probably have dropped about 70 points on joining Baltimore. It did drop 20, but not 70. I believe that he may have told the official scorer to give DeMontreville a break on any hit/error decision to make him look better in the stats, but baseball people have always greatly overestimated how much difference that makes, and I doubt seriously that the effect of this was anything like forty hits.

MEMORIES

Do you realize that there might still be people alive who saw Cap Anson play? Think about it—Anson played 114 games in 1897, when he was forty-six years old. If you were eight years old then, you'd be ninety-eight now (1988). There are people around who are ninety-eight. Some of them—at least *one* of them, surely—must have seen Anson play. Do you suppose any of them remember it, remember seeing him play? Do you suppose you could find one of those people if you tried? Jeez, it's all I can do to remember seeing Dick Stuart play for Lincoln in 1957.

MISTY WATER-COLORED MEMORIES

The only major league player who has lived to be a hundred years old was Ralph Miller, a pitcher for Brooklyn and Baltimore in 1898–99.

That was the last straw. Rusie knew that Freedman was simply lowering his salary without going to the trouble of negotiating it with him. He refused to report to the Giants in 1896 until the money was refunded. Freedman refused to give it back. Rusie held out. All year. The press supported him. The fans organized a boycott. Freedman would not relent.

With John Montgomery Ward representing him, Rusie appealed to the league. He lost. He sued. The other owners pleaded with Freedman to be reasonable. He refused.

Finally, the other owners got together and paid Rusie a reported $3,000 for the season that he had missed. Rusie rejoined the Giants.

Team vs. Team: Nothing dies without a lawsuit. When the American Association fell apart in 1891, the owners of two of the teams that were not involved in the settlement threatened to sue, as well they should have, having just been deprived of their property. The case would have been a perfect precedent for the case filed by the Baltimore Terrapins twenty-five years later, but the National League paid the two teams $131,000 (equivalent to about $2 million now) for their assets.

Best Baseball Movies: According to Jack Spears, "The first use of baseball as subject matter for a motion picture was in 1898 when the Edison Company released *The Ball Game,* a few disjointed shots of a Newark NJ amateur team playing an unknown opponent."

*Uniform Changes: How women dressed for baseball—see notes.

*New Terms or Expressions:
> Fan
> Texas Leaguer
> Baltimore Chop
> Big League

Most Wins by Pitcher:
> Bill Hutchinson, 1891, 43
> Kid Nichols, 297

Highest Winning Percentage:
> Jim Hughes, 1899, 28–6, .824
> Clark Griffith, 158–78, .66949
> Kid Nichols, 297–147, .66892

Best Unrecognized Players:
> George Davis
> Herman Long

Both shortstops, both outstanding offensive and defensive players for a long period of time.

Highest-Paid Player: Unknown, but surely someone in the first two years of the decade, before the National League monopoly. It was reported that salaries increased 100 percent in 1890–91 as opposed to the previous two years (because of the Player's League), which, if true, would have made salaries of $6,000 or more quite common. After 1892 a system of salary limits was in place, and unlike that of the late eighties, which was widely circumvented, was quite effective. Although some teams no doubt paid bonuses in excess of the $2,500 salary ceiling, that probably was only done for exceptional players, and the system (combined with declining revenues due to decreased attendance) effectively kept salaries low.

*New Statistics:
> 1893—Sacrifice hits. See notes.

Most Unpredictable Career: Lave Cross

STRATEGY IN THE 1890s

The sacrifice bunt, though still not universally accepted (it is not universally accepted even today) was by now old stuff. If you read the newspapers of the late eighties, it sometimes seems like the bunt is all that anybody wanted to talk about . . . it should be made illegal, it shouldn't be made illegal, the batter should be given credit for it, he shouldn't be given credit for it, he should be charged with an at bat, he shouldn't be charged with an at bat, it should be legal but it's a bad play, it's a good play . . . on and on. They changed the rules on how to score it a couple of times and talked about doing so the rest of the time. A lot of this was still going on in the early nineties.

Exactly when the hit and run play developed is a matter of some confusion, and I want to spend a minute here discussing that. During this decade the art of signaling was advanced. The Boston team and Tommy McCarthy in particular got a lot of credit for developing runner-to-batter signals, which is one of the key reasons McCarthy is in the Hall of Fame. (Almost anyone who writes an article explaining why some outfielder, particularly a nineteenth-century outfielder, should be in the Hall of Fame will do a comparison of his batting stats with those of Tommy McCarthy. Of course, it's irrelevant, because McCarthy isn't in the Hall of Fame because of his hitting.)

Anyway, Monte Ward, then manager of the New York Giants, said in 1893, "I have never, in my twelve years' experience on the diamond, seen such skillful playing. The Boston players use more head-work and private signals than any other team in the country, and that alone is the reason why they can win the championship with such apparent ease. McCarthy is the chief schemer. He is the man who has introduced this new style of play into the team and he has been ably assisted by Nash, Duffy, Long, Lowe and Carroll. . . . 'Team-work in the field' used to be a prime factor in a pennant-winning team, but now 'team-work at the bat' is the latest wrinkle, and the Bostons have it down fine."

These quotes are from the 1895 *Spalding Guide*, but were offered in 1893. Ward also added a surprising description of the sacrifice bunt. "Say, for instance, that they have a man on first and nobody out. *Under the old style*

---

*Best Athlete in the Game: Bill Lange
Most Lopsided Trade of the Decade: January, 1894, Brooklyn traded Dan Brouthers and Willie Keeler to Baltimore for Billy Shindle and George Treadway.
A Very Good Movie Could Be Made About: A great movie could be made about the 1897 pennant race, capped by the series that is described in some detail in the notes. It's good versus evil, clean baseball versus Mugsy and assorted thugs—and good triumphs. It's so easy to root for Kid Nichols and Jimmy Collins and Herman Long and Hugh Duffy against McGraw and Jennings and Reitz.
I Don't Know What This Has to Do with Baseball, But I Thought I'd Mention It Anyway:
The Designated Hitter rule was first proposed in the 1890s. The first serious discussion of it was about 1930; in both cases the advantages proposed for it had little to do with increasing offense.
I Don't Know What This Has to Do with Baseball Either, But I Thought I'd Mention It, Too:
A woman by the name of Elizabeth Stroud, playing under the name of Lizzie Arlington, played briefly in the Atlantic League in 1898.

WILLIE KEELER

of play a sacrifice bunt would be the proper thing. . . . The Bostons, however, work this scheme: The man on first makes a bluff attempt to steal second, but runs back to first. By this it becomes known whether the second baseman or the short stop is going to cover second for the throw from the catcher. Then the batsman gets a signal from the man on first that [he] is going to steal on a certain pitched ball. The moment he starts for second the batsman just pushes the ball for the place occupied only a moment before by the infielder who has gone to cover second base." (Italics mine.)

What Ward has described, of course, is the modern hit and run play. The fact that the extra element of deceit in the play would succeed suggests that the play is very new; later on, the play would be worked without the false start.

Two things happened after that to confuse the issue. Number one, John McGraw spent thirty years as the darling of the New York press corps, during which time he was able to effectively shift the credit for these innovations from Boston, which really developed them, to the Orioles. And number two, Harold Seymour wrote a classic history of baseball, in which he suggested that the hit and run play was used in the eighties. His evidence was that Cap Anson said the White Stockings were using it then.

Well, Cap Anson was a blowhard, and the older he got, the harder he blew. The fact that Cap Anson said, twenty or thirty years after the fact, that his team was using the hit and run play first—that just really does not mean vinegar to a rabbit.

Monte Ward was known as the smartest, most alert player of his time. It is very clear from his comments that he had never seen this play before. The best evidence is that Tommy McCarthy invented the hit and run play. Monte Ward picked up on it and taught it to Willie Keeler, and Keeler brought it to Baltimore. The term "hit and run" may have been used earlier—but if it was, I doubt very seriously that it applied to the play that we now know as the hit and run.

COME "A STRUTTIN"

Bill Lange was probably the greatest athlete to play major league baseball in the nineteenth century, and as a player has become one of the most thoroughly forgotten standouts in a largely forgotten era. The 1918 *Reach Guide,* writing one of those little asides that made Francis Richter's guides so marvelous, wrote that "on the ball field speed counts for more than actual physical power in the way of brute strength . . . still there have been a good many herculean players. . . . Such giants of the past

1897: THE GOOD OF THE EARTH VERSUS JOHN POWELL

John Joseph (Jack) Powell, pitcher for the Cleveland Spiders, was tried in June of 1897 on a charge of playing ball on Sunday. He was fined $5 and court costs, which came to a healthy $153. Stanley Robison, owner of the Spiders, announced his intention to appeal the issue, but Sunday ball in Cleveland was discontinued for the rest of the season—and, as it turned out, for the rest of the century.

were Ed McKean, shortstop of the old Cleveland club; Bill Lange, commonly known as 'Little Eva,' the old Chicago outfielder, who combined great strength with wonderful speed for so large a man."

Little Eva was 6′2″, 200 pounds, and he must have had some speed; he stole 399 bases in just 811 major league games. Of course, again we get into the problem of the changed definition of stolen bases, but only a handful of players in the era stole bases with the same frequency. The comments of writers of the time suggest that he may have been the fastest player of the 1890s.

This combination of size and speed leads to the one thing that Lange is sometimes remembered for, a play that he allegedly made in which he crashed through a wooden fence in a successful effort to make a game-saving catch. Arthur Ahrens in the 1980 *Baseball Research Journal* argues convincingly that this play never occurred, but was a confusion of events that took place on August 31, 1896, in which one player (Kip Selbach, also cited by Richter in the article on the greatest athletes ever to play the game) deliberately smashed through the fence, using a ladder as a battering ram, while help-

ing an injured player to the hospital, and Lange, just two outs later, fell down making a spectacular catch in the same area, one on which it was reported that "From the grandstand it looked as if Lange covered almost half the distance spanned by the ball. The crowd rose and cheered him lustily, the players on the [opposing] Washington bench joining in the applause." Several years later the story about his crashing through the fence first surfaced in a filler item in the *Chicago Tribune,* giving specific enough details to convince me that it was, in fact, a confusion of the incident discussed.

Anyway, while Ahrens was forced to conclude that this fabled catch never happened, he did find reference to many spectacular plays that Lange did make. In the 1981 *Research Journal,* William Akin was trying to identify the greatest defensive outfielders of the decade, and after mentioning several candidates and selecting a center fielder, he wrote, "In the absence of logically compelling statistical evidence, the impressions of contemporary observers must be given greater weight. The evidence points to Bill Lange of Chicago."

To digress for a paragraph, Akin goes on to say that "Contemporaries seldom rated Tommy McCarthy with Lange, but McCarthy is in the Hall of Fame." As a fielder, I think this is true, and as a hitter it is obvious. "McCarthy's fame rests on two fine seasons as one of Boston's 'heavenly twins' and his fielding ability." This, as I said above, is not correct. Hugh Duffy was the other of the "heavenly twins," and other writers have gone further, suggesting that McCarthy rode into the Hall of Fame on Duffy's shirttails. "Bob Quinn credits McCarthy with perfecting the trapped ball, which had players of his day standing on base after the ball was hit. If they ran, Tommy caught the ball and doubled them up; if they failed to run, he picked the ball on the short hop and made them run." Interesting, but less important, I would think, than inventing the hit and run play.

An article by James D. Smith in *The National Pastime* (fall 1982) discusses players who had outstanding seasons in their last major league campaigns. He says that "Bill Lange stands as the finest every day, all-around player to retire from baseball at the peak of his career." Smith writes about Lange's impressive physical tools, and says that he was regarded by some as "the greatest player of the era."

Although Akin credits Little Eva with "unequaled desire," Smith's article gives the impression that his dedication to his baseball career could have been improved upon in several ways. On the field, there is no doubt that he dashed around like a hurricane. But in 1897, apparently, Lange wanted to stay out west (he was a native of San Francisco) to see Jim Corbett fight in Nevada on March 5 (and to digress again, Jim Corbett's name comes up constantly while researching baseball in the 1890s). To delay his reporting, Lange demanded an extra $500 (this was the time of the salary limits, remember) and was surprised when the team met the demand, on condition of secrecy and immediate reporting. So Lange made up a twisted ankle and stalled another week or so, anyway. After finally reporting, he hit .340 and led the National League with seventy-three stolen bases.

He got married two years after that, and retired at age twenty-eight to go into business with his father-in-law. He left some impressive numbers. His career average was .330. He hit .389 in 1895, and was fourth in the league in slugging percentage. He was among the top five in the league in stolen bases four times, despite missing some games, and was often in the top twelve in the league in batting. He walked over fifty times a year and rarely struck out. His range and assists totals, while not exceptional, were quite good.

One gets the feeling, somehow, that he wasn't as good as they said he was. A nephew, George Kelly, is in the Hall of Fame; Lange can't be considered because he played only seven major-league seasons. A completely forgotten outfielder named Jake Stenzel, who also had good speed and a seven-year career ending in 1899, was a better hitter than Lange was, although not as good a center fielder. Albert Spalding named Lange to his all-time all-star team, over Tris Speaker, saying that "Both men could go back or to either side equally well. Both were lightning fast in handling ground balls. But no man I ever saw could go forward and get a low line drive like Lange." I don't know . . . somehow that sounds like a burst of Old Fogeyism. Tim Murnane's all-time all-star outfield was Ty Cobb, Joe Jackson and Bill Lange—but Murnane's picks were mostly from his youth; he also picked Cap Anson, Ned Williamson, Ross Barnes, Bob Caruthers, and Charlie Bennett. Francis Richter picked him to the all-decade team, but he picked six outfielders. The highest praise comes from Al Spink, one of the founders of *The Sporting News,* who considered Lange the equal of the young Ty Cobb.

Lange was an exceptionally good-looking man, and in many ways he could be described as a nineteenth-century Mickey Mantle, with a little more defense and a little less offense. But playing a game in which the home run was scarce, and in which, therefore, the walks would probably be not quite as common, how great would Mickey have been? And if he played it for only seven years, where would he rank? I'd like to know more about Bill Lange, because he may have been a great player, and he was certainly a unique one. But I don't think that the evidence exists at this time to rate him among the greatest.

1894: THE LAST REAL MAN RETIRES

The last position player who did not wear a glove in the field was Jerry Denny, the ambidextrous third baseman who retired from the Louisville team following the 1894 season. Though a right-handed batter and thrower, Denny could catch the ball with either hand, and if the pressures of time required would scoop up the ball and fire it with whichever hand it happened to be in.

Pitcher Gus Weyhing, who lasted until 1901, also did not wear a glove.

JEREMIAH DENNY

UNIFORMS IN THE 1890s

There was a time in the nineteenth century when all-women teams were in vogue as a small-time entertainment. And what did women wear to play baseball? A photograph of one such team, the "Young Ladies Base Ball Club No. 1" of 1890–91 has the team posed like any all-male counterpart. The women are wearing regular striped baseball caps, knee-length dark- and light-striped dresses, gathered at the waist and held there with a wide clasp belt. The sleeves are long and the neckline is tightly fastened shut with a big polka dot bow. They wear long, dark, heavy-looking stockings and pointed, ankle-high leather shoes with a small heel. (Smart to put those dress heels in the closet, ladies.) The team members look relaxed, with several holding bats and a ball in the foreground. Women who played baseball around this time were called "fair base ballists."

For the men, a photo taken at spring training in 1896 shows the New York Giants in their heavy woolen gear. Quilted knickers are worn along with hip-length wool sweaters, heavy stockings and baseball caps. One would think that wool uniforms in general would be more than warm enough, but quilted knickers can be seen at times other than just in spring training.

—Susie

Editor's note: Glad you brought that up. Baseball teams in the 1890s were big on the medicinal value of sweating. Sometimes before games they liked to do light workouts in heavy clothes, thus getting the juices flowing without wasting energy.

❦ PENNANT RACES OF THE 1890s ❦

Among its many shortcomings, the twelve-team league produced very few good pennant races. From an inauspicious start in 1892 with the idea of a split season, which was reviled by everyone, the "big league" never produced a three-team race. Third-place teams never got closer than eight games off the mark. For the years 1893–99, the National League's third-place teams averaged ten games out of first.

And there were only a few decent two-team races. The 1895 race, though decided by only three games, was not especially climactic, since, in the last ten days of the season, Baltimore played seven games, and runner-up Cleveland played only two. Kind of slows down the scoreboard watching. . . . Baltimore went six and one while Cleveland split, so that the half game lead of September 21 edged up by the day, with Cleveland powerless to do anything about it.

There was a great two-team race in 1897. On August 21, the defending champion Baltimore Orioles trailed the Boston Beaneaters by three games. On the twenty-eighth, they had pulled ahead by percentage points, but were still a half game behind because they had played fewer games:

	Won	Lost	Pct.	GB
Baltimore	69	32	.683	.5
Boston	72	34	.679	—

And then, for twenty-eight days, the margin between the two teams never grew larger than one full game. Baltimore won eleven in a row from September 4 through September 16; Boston answered with eight out of nine. By the twenty-third, things hadn't changed much:

	Won	Lost	Pct.	GB
Baltimore	87	36	.707	.5
Boston	89	37	.706	—

Another problem with the twelve-team league, familiar to fans of the 1980s, is the dilution of the schedule; the two teams rarely met. But on this date, Boston began a three-game set in Baltimore; they would have only one series left when the series was over. A crowd of 12,900 turned out to see Boston move into first place with a 6–4 victory; the crowd included 135 "Rooters" down from Boston under the leadership of John Fitzgerald, wearing Red Badges and armed with tin horns. The Orioles had the tying runs on base when Willie Keeler ripped a liner that was speared by Herman Long, the great Boston shortstop, who doubled off second the runner, "who had incautiously lit out for third when Keeler hit the ball."

On the twenty-fifth, Saturday, 18,750 people saw the Orioles come back, 6–3. The Orioles took a quick 3–0 lead, but the Beaneaters in the seventh had the tying run on third (Billy Hamilton) and another man on first (Bobby Lowe). When Lowe got caught in a rundown between first and second, Hamilton headed home, but Dirty Jack Doyle made a quick throw home and got him, with Wilbert Robinson landing hard on the tiny Hamilton, according to a newspaper report "almost

HERMAN C. LONG

crushing him with his two hundred and fifty pounds of solid flesh." The game was described as a "nerve destroyer," and it was said that the series so far had comprised two of the most exciting games in the history of baseball.

No Sunday ball. Game Three was played on Monday, September 27, and was attended by 25,375 cranks, bringing the three-day total to a remarkable 57,000. It was a wide-open slugfest, common in 1897; Baltimore scored five early off the great Kid Nichols, but Boston exploded for nine runs in the seventh, and won it 19–10. Baltimore's three top pitchers all worked in the effort, but Boston was in first place with three to play.

The Baltimore crowd seemed to enjoy the barrage; the papers reported them laughing good-naturedly at the onslaught. Billy Hamilton was cheered lustily when, "after being trampled upon and severely stunned by Jennings at second, he made a grand run for home on Lowe's single, collided with Baltimore's fleshy backstop and, falling heavily, pluckily crawled toward the base, almost fainting as he touched it." On-the-scene reports paint a pleasant picture, very different from the one we usually see of the period. When the game was over "ten thousand people congratulated the visitors with handshakes and cheers and told them what good fellows and fine players they were." Then again, the size of the crowd suggests that these were not the regular fans of the era, so much as some people who got caught up in passing excitement. The *Topeka Capital* lauded this demonstration of appreciation as "a fitting climax for the greatest spectacle Baltimore has ever seen."

In what was probably the greatest series in nineteenth-century baseball, Germany (Why-on-Earth-Aren't-You-in-the-Hall-of-Fame) Long had nine hits, three of them doubles, and scored four runs. Willie Keeler and Hughie Jennings had seven hits apiece for Baltimore, Wilbert Robinson six. There were twenty-two doubles in the three games, four by Jennings.

Baltimore was one and a half back with one series remaining, and, since Boston won two of its three, out of the race.

—Jim Baker

WILBERT ROBINSON

EDGAR McNABB

Edgar McNabb was a pitcher for the Baltimore Orioles in 1893. He posted an 8–7 record and an ERA of 4.12. Not asked to return to the team in '94, he had signed on with Grand Rapids.

Aside from pitching, McNabb was involved in other sport, namely an illicit affair with actress Louise Kellogg, a.k.a. Mrs. Louise Rockwell. She was a good-looking and "shapely" blonde who was married to R. E. Rockwell, a Seattle ice merchant. In his spare time he was president for the Pacific and Northwest League.

McNabb and Mrs. Rockwell had been carrying on their affair for "at least a year" when all bliss ended in Pittsburgh on February 28, 1894. There, at the Hotel Eiffel, the wages of sin caught up with the couple. Despite witnesses' testimony describing their manner that night as "gay . . . and . . . jolly," McNabb was apparently not in the best of spirits. They were staying at the Hotel Eiffel as "E. J. McNabb and wife," and at approximately eight in the evening went up to their room to prepare for a trip to the theatre. Once the door was closed, pistol shots were heard, as well as scuffling and screaming. The door was broken in by an L. Gilliland, a friend of McNabb's and for-mer minor league ballplayer.

Gilliland found Mrs. Rockwell on the floor in a pool of blood, shot twice through the neck. McNabb was down for the count and going fast, having shot himself in the mouth. Mrs. Rockwell survived for a time, paralyzed from the waist down by a bullet that had lodged in her spinal column.

The newspapers speculated that the couple was penniless and McNabb saw this route as an end to their problems.

—Jim Baker

LOU SOCKALEXIS

Unlike Hartung, who was said to be able to do it all but didn't, Lou Sockalexis did enough to suggest that the ballyhoo about him was deserved. His college record suggested he would be great, and in his rookie season he did well, hitting .338 with some power. He was fast and his arm was feared; he was supposed to be the direct descendant of Sitting Bull, which was quite remarkable in view of the fact that Sitting Bull was a Sioux and Sockalexis a Penobscot. But he had learned more than hitting in his time at Holy Cross and Notre Dame. He was expelled from the first school for drinking, a hobby that he pursued in earnest in his first year with Cleveland, 1897.

One account of his life attributes his failures after that to the treatment he received from the fans on account of his ancestry. Whenever he would come to the plate he was greeted with Indian war whoops. No doubt he did not enjoy this, being a rather refined-looking gent with schooling at two fine universities. In part, the fans probably gave him the works because he let it get to him.

In 1898 the effects of whiskey were showing up in his record. He ended up in the minors in New England, where he became a street person, fond of begging while wearing rags and the accoutrements we associate with Skid Row. His career ended in 1900, but his drinking was just getting into swing. He died in 1913, one of the great could-have-beens of all time.

Some sources say that the Cleveland Indians acquired their name in his memory.

—Jim Baker

WORLD SERIES OF THE 1890s

The championship series of 1890 between the A.A. champions of Louisville and Cincinnati of the N.L. ended in a draw. In 1892, there was a playoff between the first-half champions, Boston, and second-half champions, Cleveland; Boston won, five games to none.

Then there was the Temple Cup. The Temple Cup was a big, gaudy $800 trophy, given by William C. Temple of Pittsburgh. The Temple Cup series pitted the National League's first- and second-place teams, and it was a bust from the word *go*. Supposedly the winners would get 65 percent and the losers 35 percent, but there were persistent rumors that players on the two sides were making arrangements to split fifty-fifty, and then just playing exhibition games, with no real incentive. The results of the Temple Cups:

1894: New York over Baltimore

1895: Cleveland over Baltimore

1896: Baltimore over Cleveland

1897: Baltimore over Boston

This business about the first-place team playing the second-place team never worked too well, either. Bos-

NOTES ON A LEFT-HANDED SHORTSTOP

Often a baseball discussion will turn to the relative merits of using left-handers on the left side of the infield. Mike Squires' attempts at third base have rekindled speculation that a gifted glove man could handle chores that baseball has traditionally denied southpaws. Hall of Famer Willie Keeler played a number of games at third in his career, as well as a few up the middle. The legendary fielding genius Hal Chase saw action in thirty-six games as a second baseman. (Second base is the one base Squires insists that a lefty couldn't play, citing the difficulty of the pivot on the double play.) But these men are other position players, Squires and Chase first basemen and Keeler an outfielder.

In 1896, the Phillies used a left-hander named Bill Hulen as their shortstop in seventy-three games. He also played some second base, but never any other position in his brief major league career. (The Washington Nationals gave a brief trial to a nineteen-year-old left-handed second baseman named Kid Mohler in 1894. Although he never returned to the major leagues, he was reputed to be the best second baseman in the Pacific Coast League for a number of years after that.) Hulen's fielding record for the '96 season might give us some indication why he was just about the last of the left-handed shortstops. Below is a chart of the fielding records for the twelve most-used National League shortstops (one per team) in 1896. Their records are given on a per game basis so as to make for a better comparison than mere totals would give:

SHORTSTOP	G	PO/G	A/G	E/G	DP/G	F.A.	RF
Hugh Jennings	130	2.9	3.7	.51	.54	.928	6.56
Bill Dahlen	125	2.5	3.3	.57	.53	.915	6.13
Tommy Corcoran	132	2.4	3.6	.48	.52	.926	6.06
Herm Long	120	2.6	3.5	.69	.43	.897	6.05
Gene DeMontreville	133	2.3	3.6	.73	.40	.890	5.89
Joe Dolan	44	2.1	3.6	.36	.57	.940	5.70
Monte Cross	125	2.4	3.2	.67	.25	.892	5.54
Bones Ely	128	2.0	3.4	.48	.41	.918	5.39
Frank Connaughton	54	1.6	3.7	.65	.35	.892	5.33
Germany Smith	120	1.7	3.4	.41	.39	.926	5.12
Bill Hulen	73	2.0	2.8	.70	.45	.874	4.85
Ed McKean	133	1.6	3.0	.43	.39	.915	4.62

From this we can see that Hulen's range was severely lacking and the balls he did get to often resulted in an error. He had the worst fielding average and the second-worst range factor. His putouts per game rank eighth though, suggesting that perhaps he did have the quickness required of a shortstop. However, his assist totals were by far the worst going (more than half an assist

ton and Baltimore fought a terrific battle in September of 1897, but if they immediately turn around and play again, what are they playing for? The Temple Cup undercut the pennant race and was anticlimactic in itself. In 1895 the Giants felt that they should have been allowed to defend the Cup, which they had won the year before, although they were neither first nor second in 1895.

—Jim Baker

per game below the league average), which certainly suggests that he was having trouble making the half turn a lefty needs to make before he throws to first. It would be interesting to know how many of his errors were of the throwing variety. I also think it's safe to assume he lost a number of assists to speedy baserunners taking advantage of his slow release time.

His .45 double plays per game ranked him seventh, which at least indicates he didn't have as many problems making the short throw to second or making the relay to first after taking a toss from the second baseman (which, when visualized, would not appear that much more difficult for a lefty than a righty).

Hulen's play did not warrant a return to the Phils in '97. His fielding, coupled with the fact that his hitting ranked him ninth or tenth among shortstops, spelled the end of the last major left-handed shortstop experiment, although Hulen returned for nineteen games at short for Washington in 1899.

—Jim Baker

1893: RACE RELATIONS IN BASEBALL, CHAPTER SEVEN

George Treadway was an outfielder for the Baltimore Orioles and a couple of other teams from 1893 to 1896. He was apparently a man of dark features, and rumors started as soon as he entered the league that he had Negro blood. Treadway denied the rumors heatedly, and said that "nobody but a cur and a cutthroat would say such a thing about a man," and blamed them on the spite of a former teammate. "I will wait till I meet him," he added, "and then the world will know who is more worthy to associate with decent people—he or I."

In *American Baseball* David Voigt says that "players suspected of being Negroes . . . were hounded from the league," and adds that such was the case with Treadway, "a fine Oriole outfielder." Well, maybe. A lot of the problems of this fine outfielder had to do with hitting the ball. He hit .328 in 1894, but you must remember that among the other N.L. left fielders that year were players hitting .393, .349, .400, .358, .356, .330, and .386; the league average was .309. That was his good year; he hit .260 in 1893, when the league average was .280, and .257 in 1895, when it was .296. I suspect that every outfielder in baseball who didn't hit any better than Treadway did was hounded from the league just as quickly.

The 1900s

HOW THE GAME WAS PLAYED

Clean baseball finally arrived in 1901 with the emergence of the American League. Byron Bancroft "Ban" Johnson became president, in 1893 (other sources say 1894), of an established minor league known as the Western League. Through an aggressive investment strategy dedicated to acquiring the best players in the game and moving into the largest and most attractive cities, Johnson placed this league in the course of becoming a second major league. This was accomplished in 1901, under the name of the American League.

Johnson realized that baseball was suffering from the bad manners and offensive extremes of "Rowdy Ball," and he would not permit it in his league; in combating it, Johnson was high-handed, imperious, arbitrary and effective—all of the things that Landis would later be in controlling scandals of integrity. As the American League quickly became not only a major league, but clearly the better of the two leagues in the eyes of the public, the National League was forced to follow suit, and clean up its innings.

When the fists quieted down and the offenses went to work, the game, by the standards of the future, was still a baserunner's game. Stolen bases per team per season were in the range of 150 to 200, while home runs per team per season lay in the range of 15 to 30. At the time, this decline in baserunning was considered calamitous. In the 1906 *Spalding Guide,* Henry Chadwick was certain that baseball owners would take some action to restore baserunning once they saw in print just how few stolen bases there were. "By way of further illustration of the remarkable falling off in base running due to the foul strike rule, we give below the percentages of stolen bases made by all of the players of the National League clubs in 1905, who had a credit of not less than 20 stolen bases. The table in question will astonish the magnates of the leading

HENRY CHADWICK

of runs that were being scored. With runs becoming dear and outs comparatively cheap, one-run strategies dominated. With a runner on first and nobody out, a bunt was so automatic that many managers didn't even have a sign for it. The hit and run, popularized in the previous decade as an aggressive, big-inning tactic, now became a defensive, get-one-base-if-nothing-else maneuver. By 1915, traditionalists were complaining that the hit and run had ruined baseball.

WHERE THE GAME WAS PLAYED

After some experiments early in the decade, the major leagues settled by 1903 into the eleven cities that were to be privileged to have it for the next half-century. Major league cities during the decade included Baltimore, Boston, Brooklyn, Chicago, Cincinnati, Cleveland, Detroit, Milwaukee, New York, Philadelphia, Pittsburgh, St. Louis, and Washington.

WHO THE GAME WAS PLAYED BY

No other period has featured such a diverse, wide-ranging, nonhomogeneous cast of characters as the baseball of the first twenty years of this century. The Irish dominance of the previous two

clubs when they see by the figures what a comparatively poor record their crack players made in base running last season to that of four years ago." The "percentages" referred to show stolen bases as a percentage of games played, not as a percentage of stolen base attempts.

The rule change referred to there was probably the major defining force in play of the game during the decade. Prior to 1901, a foul ball was not a strike. This change, instituted in 1901 in the National League, 1903 in the American, shifted the balance of power dramatically toward the pitcher. Batting averages dropped from near .280 down to the .240–.250 zone for the rest of the decade. Strikeouts went up by more than 50 percent. Base stealing, as Chadwick notes, was reduced. Even power hitting, which then meant doubles and triples more than home runs, was curtailed as hitters became defensive with two strikes on them.

Errors continued to drop sharply throughout the decade as gloves, now free of the shame and ridicule originally given them, grew in size and padding. All of these things tended to reduce the number

decades was broken down by the emergence of the American League, which had been a midwestern league staffed heavily by midwestern players, many of whom remained when it reached major league status in 1901. The National League gradually began to shed its Irish flavor, though some of that was retained until about 1915.

This may be one of the keys to the booming attendance of the decade, for whereas baseball in the nineteenth century was in danger of becoming a game of the Irish, by the Irish, and for the Irish, it now began to appeal to a broader cross-section of the public. Ethnic identity was still very important in the United States at the turn of the century; when you knew a man, you knew where his family came from and when they got off the boat. Many of the game's biggest stars were the heavily accented sons of immigrants, and in particular German and French immigrants (though at that, I'd say at a guess that the immigrant population in baseball was smaller than throughout most of society). There were several Indian players, some of them big stars, and a few Jewish players—not many, but many more then than now.

Even more importantly, baseball was becoming a game for the educated. The college sports programs adopted a quasiprofessional outlook, and began fighting for the right to educate the young men who could run the fastest and throw the hardest. When these players became professional, baseball teams emerged as combinations of college-educated alcoholics and marginally literate or outright illiterate, but still self-disciplined, young men from the backwoods of nowhere; dapper dandies from state universities formed double-play combinations with street-toughened muscle men who carried razors and shoeless southern farm boys who carried handguns or Bibles or both. Players sometimes came straight out of the coal mines into the majors, and went straight back to the coal mines. Davy Jones commented directly on this in *The Glory of Their Times.* "The players were more colorful," he said, "drawn from every walk of life. We had stupid guys, smart guys, tough guys, mild guys, crazy guys, college men, slickers from the city and hicks from the country." No decade was ever richer in odd couples. Sam Crawford, an educated man of great dignity and varied interests, spent over ten years in the outfield with a tough young ruffian from the backwoods of Georgia who reportedly packed a pistol; they never did learn to get along. Tinker and Evers hated each other but played together like Tracy and Hepburn, and one cannot but wonder what kind of chill traced the spine of Christy Mathewson when he first learned that the salty John McGraw was to be the new manager of the Giants. Sometimes they all made it work, and sometimes the teams simply disintegrated, splitting into warring tribes. It was wonderful when it worked.

Baseball in the years from 1905 to 1919 was soaked in strategy as it never was before and never has been since, and it is possible to see a connection between that fact and the discordant nature of the roster. I have speculated before that the historical tendency of the Boston Red Sox to split into civil camps of stars and scrubs might be related to the park in which they play. Whereas the Houston Astros play in a park in which an offense consists by necessity of one man who gets on base, one who moves him along, and one who brings him around, Fenway Park rewards and thus encourages players who act as individuals, since they can create runs by their individual acts. Somewhat to my surprise, baseball men have generally reacted to this suggestion not as if it were a silly idea, but as if there might be something to it.

If there is, then one could draw a similar connection, going the other way, between the personnel and the strategies of the 1905–19 era. Strategies in baseball, whether wise or unwise, are *team* actions; they require two or more people to know about them in advance, and cooperate in their execution. Signaling among teammates, though it existed in the nineteenth century, was brought into full flower in this era. It is possible that the managers, sensing (even subconsciously) the constant danger that the team would disintegrate into fractious subcommittees, demanded of them more cooperation—and thus more strategy—than was really necessary. Or rather, that the strategy was necessitated not by the game situations, but by the personnel.

Checking In

1900—Lefty Grove, Lonaconing, Maryland
   Cal Hubbard, Ketesville, Missouri
   Louis Armstrong, New Orleans
1902—Charles Lindbergh, Detroit
1903—Charlie Gehringer, Fowlerville, Michigan
   Lou Gehrig, New York City
   Tom Yawkey, Detroit
   Cool Papa Bell, Starkville, Mississippi
   Carl Hubbell, Carthage, Missouri
   Mickey Cochrane, Bridgewater, Massachusetts
   Chuck Klein, Indianapolis
1905—Leo Durocher, West Springfield, Massachusetts
   Howard Hughes, Houston
1906—Joe Cronin, San Francisco
   Satchel Paige, Mobile, Alabama
1907—Luke Appling, High Point, North Carolina
   Jimmie Foxx, Sudlersville, Maryland

Checking Out

1900—Jack Taylor, Bright's disease, 28
   Marty Bergen, murder/suicide, 28
1901—William McKinley, gunshot, 58
1902—Pud Galvin, catarrh of the stomach, 36
   Fred Dunlap, 43
1903—Win Mercer, suicide by gas, 28
   Ed Delahanty, drowning, 35
   Twelve people killed in collapse of bleachers at Phillies game (200 injured), August 6
1905—Pete Browning, complications from mastoiditis, 44
1906—Susan B. Anthony, 86
   Buck Ewing, 47
1907—Chick Stahl, suicide by swallowing acid, 34
   Cozy Dolan, typhoid fever, 34
   (Stahl and Dolan, regular outfielders for the two Boston teams, died within a few hours of each other)
1909—Geronimo, 75
   Frank Selee, tuberculosis, 49
   John Clarkson, pneumonia, 47
   Foghorn Miller, kidney disease, 42
   Henry Clay Pulliam, suicide by gunshot, 40
   Herman Long, tuberculosis, 38
   Jimmy Sebring, "convulsions," 27

Henry Chadwick, the Father of Baseball, had a head cold but insisted on attending the Dodgers' home opener in wet, cold weather. He developed pneumonia and died April 20, 1908, at the age of eighty-three.

THE 1900s IN A BOX

Attendance Data:

Total: 50 million (49,880,718; 1901–1909)

Highest: New York Giants, estimated 910,000, 1908
           New York Giants, 4,977,481

Lowest: Philadelphia (N.L.), 112,066, 1902
           Boston Braves, 1,492,753

While no systematic attendance data is available prior to 1901 for the sake of comparison, it is agreed that attendance boomed during this period. Attendance in 1901 was 3.6 million, or about 230,000 per team. This increased every year except for a small decline in 1906, and by the end of the decade had more than doubled. The primary causes were the effective control of vulgarity and unseemly behavior on the field, a series of outstanding pennant races, and huge popular interest in the World Series.

Most Home Runs:

Sam Crawford, 1901, 16

Socks Seybold, 1902, 16

Harry Davis, 66

Best Won-Lost Record by Team:

Chicago (N.L.), 1906, 116–36

938–538, .636, by the Pirates

Worst Won-Lost Record by Team:

Washington, 1904, 38–113, .252

480–833, .366, by Washington

Heaviest Player: The heaviest weight listed is for Ed Walker, a 6-foot-5-inch, 242-pound pitcher who appeared in only four games. Harry Lumley, though his weight is unlisted, appears to have run up some pretty good tabs in the hotel coffee shops. Lumley led the league in triples and home runs as a rookie in 1904, and in 1906 he hit .324 with 35 stolen bases, and also led the league in slugging. A picture of him taken in 1908 reminds one of an unregenerate Dom DeLuise, and during that season he hit just .216 and stole only four bases in 127 games.

Lightest Player: Probably Sammy Strang. Johnnie Evers is the smallest player for whom a weight is listed, weighing but 125.

*Clint Hartung Award: Johnny Lush

Most Strikeouts by Pitcher:

Rube Waddell, 1904, about 349

Rube Waddell, 2,251

Exact 1904 figure is disputed.

Highest Batting Average:

Nap Lajoie, 1901, .422

Honus Wagner, .352

Hardest-Throwing Pitcher: Walter Johnson

Best Baseball Books:

1900—*A Ballplayer's Career* by Cap Anson
        The first baseball autobiography.

1907—*History of Colored Base Ball* by Sol White.

1908—*Baseball Magazine* begins publication.

Best Outfield Arm: Wildfire Schulte

Worst Outfield Arm: Duff Cooley

HARRY BAY

Most Runs Batted In:
>   Honus Wagner, 1901, 126
>   Honus Wagner, 956

Most-Aggressive Baserunner: Ty Cobb or Kid Elberfield

  The nickname "Kid" generally was used to refer to a small player noted for his aggressiveness. Wayne Tolleson, had he been active in 1903, might have been known as "Kid Tolleson."

Fastest Player: Harry Bay

  Ty Cobb wrote in his autobiography that there were "faster men around than me, like . . . Harry Bay, a 10-second man at 100 yards." Bay's electrifying speed also made him one of the first players to be captured in moving pictures.

Slowest Player: Piano Legs Hickman, late in the decade.

Best Control Pitcher: Cy Young

*****Nicknames:**   Animals and hometowns were the dominant themes of a decade full of classic nicknames like "Crossfire," "Yip," "Wagon Tongue," and "Little All Right."

Most Stolen Bases:
>   Ty Cobb, 1909, 76
>   Honus Wagner, 487

Best-Looking Player: Christy Mathewson

Ugliest Players:
>   Hal Chase
>   Addie Joss

*****Strangest Batting Stance:**   Possibly Cy Seymour, who hit with his weight very far forward, and his bat stuck over his shoulder, parallel to the ground.

Outstanding Sportswriter: Francis Richter, editor of *The Sporting Life* and the *Reach Guide*

Most-Admirable Superstar: Honus Wagner

Least-Admirable Superstar: Hal Chase

Franchise Shifts:
>   Milwaukee to St. Louis (American League), 1902
>   Baltimore to New York (American League), 1903

*****New Stadiums:**
>   1901—Huntington Avenue Grounds, Boston (for Red Sox)
>   South Side Park, Chicago (for White Sox)
>   Bennett Park, Detroit
>   Columbia Park, Philadelphia
>   American League Park, Washington
>   1903—Hilltop Stadium, New York (Highlanders)
>   1909—Shibe Park, Philadelphia
>   Forbes Field, Pittsburgh
>   League Park, Cleveland (concrete version)
>   Sportsman's Park, St. Louis (renovated)

*****Best Pennant Race:**   National League, 1908.

Best World Series: 1903, Boston with Cy Young and Bill Dineen rallying from a three games to one deficit to beat Pittsburgh in eight games, 3–7, 3–0, 2–4, 4–5, 11–2, 6–3, 7–3, 3–0, in a series that meant the same thing in its time as Super Bowl III (Joe Namath and the Jets against the Colts).

  Red Sox fans taunted Honus Wagner by singing an amended version of "Tessie" ("Honus, why do you hit so badly?" instead of "Tessie, you know I love you madly").

Best-Hitting Pitcher: Al Orth

Worst-Hitting Pitcher: Red Ames' inability to hit was a running joke with the New York press. A bat company once advertised that they had a bat that even Leon Ames could get a hit with. Red hit .123 for the decade.

*Best Minor League Team: 1900 Chicago White Sox

Best Negro League Players:
- Bingo DeMoss
- William S. Monroe
- John Henry Lloyd

Best Minor League Player: Emil Frisk, the "Wagner of the minors," who had 272 hits in the P.C.L. during one of their perpetual seasons in 1904, and had over 2,000 hits in his minor league career, despite spending several years as a pitcher.

The Odd Couple: Tinker and Evers

Drinking Men:
- Howie Camnitz
- Rube Waddell
- Bugs Raymond

   In discussing this question in *Pitching in a Pinch,* Christy Mathewson (or ghost writer John Wheeler) was shockingly frank and at the same time subtle. "Like great artists in other fields of endeavor," he wrote, "many Big League Pitchers are temperamental. 'Bugs' Raymond, 'Rube' Waddell, 'Slim' Sallee and 'Wild Bill' Donovan are ready examples of the temperamental type. The first three are the sort of men of whom the manager is never sure. He does not know, when they come into the ball park, whether or not they are in condition to work. They always carry with them a delightful atmosphere of uncertainty."

   You write that today, Christy, and you got yourself a lawsuit.

New Equipment: 1907—Shin Guards

Player vs. Team: On April 11, 1909, Johnny Evers stated that he desired to lay off for a season, and had completed correspondence with President Murphy of the Chicago team to that end. He said he wanted to take a complete rest for the 1909 season.

   On May 1, 1909, Evers signed a two-year contract, and rejoined the Cubs.

*Team vs. Team: Philadelphia vs. Philadelphia

*Best Baseball Movies:
- 1906—*How the Office Boy Saw the Ball Game*
- 1906—*Play Ball on the Beach*
- 1907—*How Jones Saw the Ball Game*

*Uniforms:
- High collars
- Blousy shirts
- Special undershirts for pitchers
- Handmade shoes
- Long stockings
- Team sweaters
- Sunglasses

*New Terms or Expressions: Yannigan

Most Wins by Pitcher:
- Jack Chesbro, 1904, 41
- Christy Mathewson, 236

Highest Winning Percentage:
- Wild Bill Donovan, 1907, 25–4, .862
- Sam Leever, 167–72, .699

YANNIGAN

The term "yannigan" was popular as the name for any rookie, replacement or second-line player. It has a certain negative connotation to it, like the modern "scrubeenie"; it just *sounds* derogatory. The term occasionally achieved a kind of official recognition; after the San Francisco earthquake in 1906, Brooklyn played a benefit game for the relief effort and split the squad into "Regulars" and "Yannigans." If you were a major league player, would you like to play on a team called the "Scrubs"? I think that would be the modern equivalent. Since rosters were smaller then, several pitchers started for the Yannigans, as well as Sammy Strang, a yannigan from the rival Giants, and manager Patsy Donovan. The Yannigans won, 3–2; 5,000 were on hand, and $12,000 was raised for the people of San Francisco.   —Jim Baker

*Best Unrecognized Players:
  Harry Davis
  Ed Reulbach
Highest-Paid Player: Probably Nap Lajoie
New Statistics: The basic pitching record took form in this decade. Innings Pitched first appeared in a *Guide* in 1910, reporting on American League innings pitched during 1909. It may seem curious that they did not appear sooner, but one must remember that (1) until 1890, virtually every game was a complete game, hence all one needed to know was how many games the pitcher had pitched, not how many innings, and (2) even today, official statistics do not give defensive innings at other positions.
*Most Unpredictable Career: Jimmy Sheckard
Best Athlete in the Game: Honus Wagner

Sam Mertes, the muscular second baseman–outfielder, was also recognized as a great all-around athlete. He was possibly the strongest man in the game after Bill Lange retired, and he was fast enough to finish second to fifth in the league in stolen bases every year.

Most Lopsided Trade of the Decade: In the winter of 1900–1901, Cincinnati acquired Amos Rusie, who had 243 wins behind him but none ahead of him, from the New York Giants in exchange for a minor league pitcher with an 0–3 record in the big time: Christy Mathewson.

A Very Good Movie Could Be Made About: The final days of the 1908 season.

I Don't Know What This Has to Do with Baseball, But I Thought I'd Mention It Anyway: The first congressional baseball game was played in Washington in 1909. The center of attention was Republican Representative John Tener of Pennsylvania, an Irish immigrant who had pitched for Cap Anson's Colts; he was the Vinegar Bend Mizell of his time. Despite Tener's presence, the Democrats squeaked out a 26–16 victory.

Tener later became governor of Pennsylvania and president of the National League. At the same time, no less.

❧ NICKNAMES OF THE 1900s ❧

Animals, always a staple of player nicknames, were in hot vogue in the first decade of this century, usually modified or described in some way. Mike Donlin was "Turkey Mike," Clark Griffith was "The Old Fox," Frank Isbell was "The Bald Eagle" and Jake Beckley "Eagle Eye," Davy Jones was called "Kangaroo," Lou Ritter was "Old Dog," Bill Shipke was "Muskrat Bill," Jimmy Slagle was called "The Human Mosquito" (a nickname that in later generations would have been shortened to "Skeeter"), Sammy Strang was "The Dixie Thrush," and Jesse Burkett and Johnny Evers were both called "The Crab."

We also see in this decade the emergence of the "hometown" nicknames. There were a few before this time (Amos Rusie was "The Hoosier Thunderbolt") but very few, because, for one thing, all the nineteenth-century players came from the same towns. A few of these included "The Duke of Tralee" (Roger Bresnahan), "Wahoo Sam" (Crawford), "The Goshen Schoolmaster" (Sam Leever), and "Wabash George" (George Mullin). Albert Schweitzer, who certainly did not need a nickname, was called "Cheese." A few others, from the time when people believed in good nicknames:

The Peerless Leader (Frank Chance)
The Tabasco Kid (Kid Elberfield)
Wagon Tongue (Bill Keister)
Little All Right (Claude Ritchey)
The Flying Dutchman (Honus Wagner)
Miner (Three Finger Brown)

Frosty Bill (Bill Duggleby)
Crossfire (Earl Moore)
Yip (Frank Owen)

All Indian players were called "Chief."

All players who could run were called "Deerfoot."

JOHNNY LUSH

An eighteen-year-old first baseman-pitcher for the Phillies in 1904, Johnny Lush was the youngest regular player of this century. He hit a respectable .276 as a rookie (the league average was .249), though he lost all six of his starts as a pitcher. Despite this, Lush was converted to a more-or-less full-time pitcher in 1906, winning eighteen games with a decent ERA, but faded after that. He wound up his career with a batting average of .249 (Hartung's was .238) and a won/lost record of 66–86.

MAJOR LEAGUE ALL-STAR TEAM
1900–1909
Records in seasonal notation, based on 154 games played.
Pitchers based on 45 starts.

Pos	Player	Years	Hits	HR	RBI	Avg.	Other
C	Roger Bresnahan	6.34	147	3	60	.285	79 Walks
1B	Frank Chance	6.72	158	3	75	.299	53 Stolen bases
2B	Nap Lajoie	7.95	210	6	100	.347	45 Doubles
3B	Jimmy Collins	7.14	175	4	76	.288	
SS	Honus Wagner	9.05	204	6	106	.351	54 Stolen bases
LF	Mike Donlin	5.22	200	7	107	.338	
CF	Ty Cobb	3.86	198	5	101	.338	49 Stolen bases
RF	Sam Crawford	9.16	183	6	88	.307	18 Triples

Pitcher	Years	Won-Lost	SO	ERA	Other
Christy Mathewson	8.23	29–14	218	1.97	361 Innings
Cy Young	8.64	27–15	182	2.12	Only 46 Walks
Three Finger Brown	5.01	29–13	159	1.63	

THE 1908 PENNANT RACES

To give a modern fan the sense of it, the National League pennant race in 1908 was like the American League race in 1967, only with one of the teams being in New York and another in Los Angeles, and with Fernando Valenzuela or Mark Fidrych being called up by another team in September so he could make four starts against one of the teams that was trying to win the thing, and with one of the key games suddenly erupting into a Pine Tar–type controversy, which necessitates New York making a special trip to Los Angeles for the 162nd game, which Sandy Koufax is to pitch against Bob Gibson, with a few odd death threats, riots, attempts to fix the game, and some loose talk about a strike thrown in for good measure. The world has never seen the like of it.

The American League also had a terrific pennant race the same year. On September first, four teams were separated by two and a half games (Detroit was in first, followed by St. Louis, Chicago, and Cleveland). Three of the teams (Detroit, Chicago, and Cleveland) would play better than .600 ball in September; St. Louis dropped off the pace and finished six and a half out. Cleveland had opened up a two-and-a-half game lead by

September 24, and when they staged a dramatic come-from-behind win on the twenty-sixth, the Cleveland crowd and three bands marched around the field for half an hour.

They thought they had it won, but the Tigers had just begun a ten-game winning streak that would put them a half game in front by the end of September. On October 2, the Indians and White Sox hooked up in one of the greatest pitchers' duels ever: Addie Joss threw a perfect game, and Ed Walsh struck out fifteen in eight innings, losing 1–0. The Tigers kept their streak alive that day, but lost the next despite Ed Killian's one-hitter.

The last day of the season opened with half a game separating the three teams, Chicago playing Detroit and Cleveland playing St. Louis. The Tigers had a rain-out that did not need to be made up under the rules of the time, and on that basis when they beat the White Sox they had it. No race has ever been closer.

The National League race of 1908 is now remembered as the greatest of all pennant races, and clearly, it merits consideration for that title. One thing that is not entirely clear, however, is whether it was recognized at the time as

something more spectacular than the American League race, or whether that is a simplification of the record with hindsight. Some unusually good journalism has been invested in the 1908 National League race. There is a chapter on the final game of the N.L. campaign in *Pitching in a Pinch,* which I swear is as fine a 5,000-word piece about baseball as has ever been

1905: VE KNOW VERE TO VIND CHEW, BROOKLYN PLAYERS

For several Sunday games in 1904 and 1905, the Brooklyn team evaded the blue laws by not charging admission. Instead, they sold scorecards (which usually cost a nickel at that time) for four different prices: a dollar, seventy-five cents, fifty cents, and a quarter. Describing a game of April 23, 1905, the *New York Times* reported that several dozen policemen were on hand, and the names of all players and scorecard sellers were taken down, but neither the police nor the Sabbath Observance Association attempted to stop the game. A crowd of 11,642 pagans was in attendance.

written. The Merkle incident and the Harry Coveleski scenario are center-stage items in the incomparable *The Glory of Their Times,* and there was a clippings book about the race done a few years ago which I haven't read but which I understand is pretty good.

Journalists of the time, however, tended to discuss the two races together, for years after the fact. Al Munro Elias, founder of the Elias Bureau but otherwise a reputable person, wrote in 1922 that "Whenever there happens to be a close race in either major league, or in both, comparison is always made with the pennant races of 1908, and the dope is dug up to show that for thrilling finishes base ball has never seen their equal. That is true, in the fact that in 1908 four clubs ran neck and neck in the American League, and three in the National for the last two weeks of the season." There follow two subsections of this article, entitled, in order, "Wonderful American Battle" and "National's Closest Race." There is nothing in the article that indicates, either directly or on the backhand, any inequality between the two.

In the 1925 *Reach Guide,* following the great races of 1924, Editor Richter observes that in the American League "a hard and close race was begun from the start and maintained to the end—in this respect almost duplicating the famous race of 1908, which was not decided until the very last day." Later on in the book, Stoney McLinn writes that "both of the major league races almost duplicated the great races of 1908, which were the closest in base ball history." Again, in a several-hundred word review of the 1908 season, there is no implied inequality of the races, and in fact McLinn writes that "the American League pennant quarrel in 1908 was even more bitterly waged than the one in the National League, with the exception that there was no protested game and play-off to enliven the proceedings." An interesting linguistic note there—the use of the term "play-off" to describe the 154th game of the National League season.

Anyway, as time went on, the American League half of the story tended to get buried behind the National. Hardly a man is now alive who remembers those famous races; it is only the memories created by words on paper that are keeping it alive. If it no longer warrants equal billing, still the American League race should be a part of the story simply because it enriches the story, and simply because it is a part of the true picture of baseball in the 1908 season.

〰️〰️〰️ DEAD HEAT 〰️〰️〰️

Perhaps the most identical seasons ever posted by two pitchers on the same club were the matched set turned in by Orvie Overall and Jack Taylor of the '06 Cubs. Both were acquired in trades—Orvie from the Reds and Jack from the Cardinals. Check out these similarities after they went to work for the Cubs:

	OVERALL	TAYLOR
Wins	12	12
Losses	3	3
Winning %	.800	.800
ERA	1.88	1.84
Games	18	17
Starts	14	16
Completions	13	15
Shut Outs	2	2
Innings Pitched	144	147
Hits Allowed	116	116

The only categories in which they differed greatly were walks and strikeouts, with Overall, at 51 BB and 94 SO, doing a bit more than Taylor (39 BB, 34 SO). Taylor was a nonstrikeout pitcher all of his career, yet was traded for rookie hurler Fred Beebe, who went on to lead the National League in strikeouts for the season.

—Jim Baker

THE 1900 WHITE SOX

The American League was not built in a day into a major league. When the National League contracted in 1900, shrinking from a twelve-team to an eight-team league, the American League, though still a minor league, took in many of the dispossessed players in preparation for their move on major league status the following season. It was already a strong league, and the addition of these players lifted it to a unique status among "minor" leagues.

The championship team in the American League that year, as it would be the next, was the Chicago White Sox.

They were a minor league team in name only; almost all of the White Sox players had played in the major leagues before and would play in the major leagues again, and were near their prime. Their every-day lineup was this:

1B—Frank Isbell
2B—Dick Padden
3B—Fred Hartman
SS—Frank Shugart
LF—Hermas McFarland
CF—Dummy Hoy
RF—Steve Brodie
 C—Joe Sugden
 P—John Katoll
 P—Roger Denzer
 P—Chauncey Fisher
 P—Roy Patterson

You may not recognize the names today, but a baseball fan of 1915 would have remembered them all, because they were all major league players. Charles Comiskey was the manager, and many other major leaguers, including Cy Seymour, played for the team during one part of the season or another. They finished with a record of eighty-two wins, fifty-three losses; an excellent article about the team by Arthur Ahrens appears in the 1978 *Baseball Research Journal.*

I'VE HAD THOSE SEATS . . .

The Baseball Writers Association of America was formed at the World Series in 1908, after out-of-town writers in Chicago were placed in the back row of the grandstand, while at Detroit they were asked to climb a ladder to the roof of the first base pavilion, and try to write their stories in the rain and snow.

The word "pavilion" is derived from the French word *papillon,* which means "butterfly." It originally referred to a canvas tent, with wings that flapped in the breeze, that was put up at a fair or carnival.

CHARLES COMISKEY

1909: THE MODERN BALLPARK ARRIVES

When the American League opened its turnstiles in 1901, it found itself several short in the ballpark department, and so it did, or its owners did, what owners had been doing for forty years: It threw up a bunch of them. Three American League teams moved into or remained in existing facilities, while the other five owners ordered some wood to be purchased and pointed down the line that way and the other and said, "Put up a ballpark here." As a digression: Bennett Park in Detroit was named after Charlie Bennett, a longtime National League

A PITCHER'S STATE

There were two leagues operating in Kansas at this time, the Kansas League and the Central Kansas League (plus the state had teams in a couple of other minor leagues). In the Kansas League, Larned had a team batting average of .155, and the league champion Lyons team hit .216. In the Central Kansas League, Salina hit .193, and Ellsworth won the pennant with a team batting average of .201.

catcher (Detroit Wolverines, 1881–88) whose legs were cut off when he fell under a train. The accident occurred in Wellsville, Kansas, just a few miles from Lawrence, when Bennett got off the train to speak to a friend. Within weeks of the accident, Bennett had written a letter to *The Sporting Life,* expressing thanks for the kindness he had received at the time of the accident, reflecting on all that he still had to be thankful for, and looking "forward to the time when I can stumble around with artificial limbs."

Anyway, in 1901 one team found itself without a park a month before the season, but they scrambled around, bought some property and got it built. It was not, you see, a "ballpark" in the modern sense of the word; the concept of the huge, permanent, sturdy, fireproof, grand, spacious, elegant thing that we now call a ballpark sprang into existence rather suddenly in 1907 or 1908. The first concrete-and-steel ballpark was Shibe Park, built in Philadelphia by one of baseball's great innovators, Benjamin Shibe, in 1909. The second was built in 1909, the third in 1909, the fourth in 1909, and by 1916 there was hardly anything else in baseball.

The dramatic increase in the popularity of the sport had rendered the old ballparks archaic in two ways. The larger crowds demanded more seating, and the fattened wallets of the owners could now undertake larger investments. This is not to detract from the vision of men like Shibe and Barney Dreyfuss, who were the first to conceive of the modern ballpark. Shibe Park opened on April 12, 1909, opening day. 30,162 paying customers and several thousand invited guests attended, and were filled with an appropriate sense of history: nothing like this had ever existed before. It had three decks. It would be hard to overstate the excitement that the occasion generated. It was the first time that people had experienced something that is special to each of us now, which we all share but feel individually, that experience of looking around a grand ballpark for the first time and saying helplessly, "This place is really something, isn't it?" Thirty thousand people were experiencing that together. The park "has inaugurated a new era in base ball," said *The Sporting Life.*

They did not exaggerate. Forbes Field in Pittsburgh opened on June 30 of the same year. Slightly smaller than Shibe—it seated 23,000—Forbes was regarded for many years somewhat the way Dodger Stadium is regarded today, as the crown jewel in the diamond tiara. It was never the biggest, but it seemed, somehow, the best—the sight lines were the best, it contained and expressed the enthusiasm of the crowd the best; it was just the best place to watch a baseball game. I'm not certain, but I think it was the first park (or stadium) to have the open walkway or promenade under the top deck. "Under the main seating area of the grand stand is a broad promenade, nearly as long as three city blocks and wider than most streets," reported the *Reach Guide.* The sense of grace and comfort that this imparted to the park was part of its charm, and found its way into modern stadium design.

League Park in Cleveland and Sportsman's Park in St. Louis, existing parks, were reborn in concrete and steel forms by the time the year was up. While they didn't have the same stature or the same impact, those parks with renovations would serve major league teams for many, many years, and become a part of the affectionate memories of millions of people. The early years of the next decade would see more of the same. The throw-'em-up and let-'em-burn-down era of ballparks was over.

JIMMY SHECKARD

Jimmy Sheckard played in the National League for seventeen years and was brilliant a little more than half the time. In his best years he was an awesome performer, and if he had had one of those years when playing for the Cubs in the 1906–10 period, they might never have lost a game. He hit as high as .353 and .332, but in two other seasons he hit in the .230s. He led the league in home runs (nine) and triples (twenty-one), but in one six-year stretch, playing regularly the whole time, he hit but nine home runs and thirty-six triples. Late in his career, he decided to draw more walks, and he drew 269 of them in a two-year period; his 147 walks in 1911 were a National League record for many years, and the record is now 148. In his last season, 1913, he hit .194 but with an on-base percentage of .366. For the rest of his career his walk totals were good, but ordinary. He stole as many as 77 and 67 bases, leading the league, and as few as 15.

After one of his so-so years (1905), the Cubs traded four players, all of whom had played regularly either in 1904 or 1905, to acquire him. He rewarded them by hitting in the .260s and going 0-for-21 in the 1906 World Series. He was apparently a terrific outfielder. He led the league in outfield assists several times, with a career total of 307, eighth highest in history. He was known as a smart player and an unselfish player, but he was never smart enough to have one of his good years when he was in a position to attract a lot of attention for it. He was certainly a greater player than Frank Chance and arguably greater than Tinker, Evers, or anyone else on those teams except Brown; indeed, an article about him by Gregg Dubbs in the 1980 *Baseball Research Journal* says that Ring Lardner once referred to him as "the greatest ballplayer in the world." And probably somebody, somewhere, once described him as the worst player in the world, and he wasn't that, either. But he had moments of lurching in both directions.

NOT THE STRANGEST BATTING STANCE

A lot has been said about Ty Cobb's split-handed grip, and it has been written many times that he was the only player to do that or that he and Wagner were the only ones to do it. In fact, the split-handed grip was the most common grip at one time in the nineteenth century, and there were still many players at this time who did not bat with their hands together. Roy Thomas batted with one hand about eight inches from the knob and the other about halfway up the bat, sort of a combination of Ty Cobb and Nellie Fox. The notion that Cobb was the only player to bat that way might have started because he was the last player to do it, hence the only one who was seen by the Dan Daniels generation of sportswriters; I don't know that he was the last, but I don't know of any others who lasted as long, and that would explain the misconception. There are thousands of existing photographs of players batting with their hands apart.

1909: HARRY'S COMET

Perhaps no pitcher in major league history began as well as Harry Krause, the Mark Fidrych of 1909. Krause made two starts and two relief appearances for the Philadelphia Athletics in 1908, pitching fairly well and splitting two decisions. He started the 1909 season on the Philadelphia roster, watching; he was twenty-one, like Fidrych.

The schedule was much different then; a team might play eight games in April and forty or more in September, or they might play as many in April as they did in September. It wasn't regular the way it is today; they'd let the double-headers pile up much higher. Krause relieved in a lost cause on May third at New York, pitching five good innings (two runs allowed) without a decision. His first start of the year was on May 8 in Philadelphia, against Washington. He pitched a three-hitter and won the game, 1–0. He had to wait nine days for his next chance, which came in Chicago on May 17. He hooked up in another pitcher's duel; it was nothing–nothing after nine, but he stayed in and eventually won it, 1–0 in twelve innings, striking out eight and allowing only five hits.

Still, on a staff with Eddie Plank, Chief Bender and Jack Coombs, there wasn't a lot of spare work around. Krause waited another twelve days until he pitched again. He struck out ten men, allowed only four hits and beat Boston, 6–2. That was the first game of a double-header and they had another one later in the series, so Krause got to pitch again on June first. He pitched another complete game, did not walk a man, struck out eight, and won again, 1–0.

How do you put this . . . I don't know where the statistics are, but I would bet that the average Hall of Fame pitcher probably wins about a dozen 1–0 games in his career. Krause now had won three one-to-nothing complete-game victories, one of them in twelve innings, in four starts. He relieved against Chicago two days later, pitching just an inning and a third, and then did not pitch again for fifteen days, starting against Detroit on June 18. He beat Detroit, 3–1.

That got him some work. He pitched against Washington on June 23, and beat them, 3–0. He worked in Boston on the twenty-ninth, and beat them, 9–0. Three days later, with the team still in Boston, he started again, against Smokey Joe Wood. He beat Joe, 1–0, his sixth shutout and fourth 1–0 victory in eight starts.

On July 8, he started in Detroit. He held Cobb, Crawford, and company to six hits (he hit Cobb with a pitch), and beat them, 3–1. Four days later he started against them again. This time he gave them four hits and one unearned run, winning 7–1. His record was ten wins, no losses.

He lost his next start after that, and though he pitched well the rest of the year the magic was gone. I did not find box scores with attendance data, but it seems a safe guess that the Philadelphia fans had to have reacted to him, at least a little. For the season, Philadelphia attendance was 675,000, up almost 50 percent from the previous season, and the highest for the franchise until 1925, higher even than the pennant-winning teams of 1910, 1911, 1913 and 1914. These are the line scores for his first ten starts:

HARRY KRAUSE

						IP	H	R	ER	BB	SO
May 8	vs.	Washington	W	(1–0)		9	3	0	0	4	5
May 17	vs.	Chicago	W	(2–0)		12	5	0	0	2	8
May 29	vs.	Boston	W	(3–0)		9	4	2	2	2	10
June 1	vs.	Boston	W	(4–0)		9	7	0	0	0	8
June 18	vs.	Detroit	W	(5–0)		9	8	1	1	1	5
June 23	vs.	Washington	W	(6–0)		9	5	0	0	2	6
June 29	vs.	Boston	W	(7–0)		9	5	0	0	1	4
July 2	vs.	Boston	W	(8–0)		9	4	0	0	0	9
July 8	vs.	Detroit	W	(9–0)		9	6	1	1	4	5
July 12	vs.	Detroit	W	(10–0)		9	4	1	0	3	4

For these ten starts he had a 0.38 ERA; for the rest of the 1909 season he was just 8–8, but had a 2.27 ERA, leading the league in this then-unused category, with a 1.39 mark. He was 18–8; Fidrych was 19–9.

Krause began to have arm trouble after that, and never was the same pitcher. He was 8–8 in 1910 (Fidrych was 6–4 after his big year), 12–8 in 1911, sent to the minors early in 1912. His career major league record was 38–26; Fidrych was 29–19. But unlike Fidrych, Krause had an option: the Pacific Coast League. His arm did eventually come back, and he pitched for sixteen years in the Pacific Coast League, winning 249 P.C.L. games. With fifty-one victories in other minors, he was a 300-game winner in the minor leagues.

1908: ED WHO?

Ed Reulbach is one of the Dangerfields of baseball history, a player whose name commands little respect today and, proportional to his accomplishments, drew little respect when he was active. In 1907 he won 17 games and lost 4, and Jack Ryder wrote about him in the 1908 *Spalding Guide* as if he were still in short pants:

The [Chicago] pitching staff did not look remarkably powerful at the getaway . . . Reulbach was effective at times but extremely wild and unreliable.

Much of the credit for the superlative showing of the Chicago twirlers was due to Manager Chance, who seldom let a man stay in the box too long when he was proving ineffective and who always had a substitute warmed up and ready to jump in the game at an instant's notice. The most possible use was made of Reulbach's skill, and the erratic fellow was allowed to lose only four games, being yanked out invariably at the first sign of weakness.

Damned big of Manager Chance, don't you think, to take such good care of his erratic fellow? Throughout his career, the erratic fellow was allowed to lose only 104 games, while his indulgent skippers suffered him to win 185 of them, a .640 career winning percentage. The year before this, the "extremely wild and unreliable" Reulbach had won 19 and lost 4, and the year after he would win 24

and lose 7, making him the only pitcher other than Lefty Grove to lead the league in winning percentage for three consecutive seasons.

The editors of the *Spalding Guide* seem to have had something almost personal about Reulbach. In the 1909 *Guide*—Henry Chadwick was now dead, and this is John B. Foster writing—they describe a June 18 game that the Giants won 7 to 2 "against Reulbach and Lundgren" and they add "the latter was much more effective than Reulbach." Yet in their lengthy analysis of that greatest of all pennant races, I can find no mention of Reulbach's remarkable pitching during the stretch run, although it was probably a larger factor in the outcome of the race than the infinitely rehashed hot streak of Harry Coveleski. With the Cub pitching staff in a bind after the Merkle game, Reulbach volunteered to pitch a double header September 26 against Brooklyn—and he pitched two shutouts, the only time that has ever been done. He also threw a shutout in his last start before that, and a shutout in his next start after that, and five innings of scoreless relief two days after that. Somehow, he managed to end his season with forty-four consecutive scoreless innings, smack in the middle of the

most-talked-about, most-written-about, most-remembered, and most-argued-about pennant race of all time—and have it forgotten about.

The *Reach Guide* of 1912 also spoke of "the erratic work of Reulbach and McIntire," thereby lumping Reulbach, who had won 16 games with an ERA under 3.00, in with a pitcher who had won 11 with an ERA over 4.00.

An article by my good friend Cappy Gagnon in the 1982 *Baseball Research Journal* quotes *Baseball Magazine* as describing Reulbach as "one of the brainiest players" and "possessor of the finest curve ball in either league." He came by these qualities the hard way; he spent three years at Notre Dame and a fourth at the University of Vermont, as an engineering student (in the summers he pitched professional baseball under the name of "Lawson"). After his playing days he would study law at Columbia University. He was one of the founding directors of the Baseball Fraternity, and served as its secretary in 1914 and 1915. One of his goals in this work was to make a pledge of abstinence a part of the standard player contract. He took a loss there.

Reulbach has not been seriously considered as a Hall of Famer, and perhaps he does not deserve that honor. His career record (185–104) is better than that of Chesbro (197–128), Walsh (197–126), Waddell (193–142), Joss (160–97), or Marquard (201–177), with all of whom he was contemporary, and all of whom are in the Hall of Fame. His career ERA, 2.28, is the eleventh best of all time.

The Ryder article raises some legitimate questions about his true effectiveness in relation to his statistics. It is difficult to put any of those questions to rest on Ryder's side. As to being yanked at the first sign of trouble, Reulbach completed 16 of 22 starts in 1907, and 20 of 24 in 1906. That's 78 percent of his starts, which is well above the league average, and would hardly be consistent with the notion of being yanked early and often even if it were well below the league average. As a starting pitcher he averaged 8.1 innings a game in 1906, 8.0 in 1907. He walked a few men, but he wasn't anywhere near the worst of the league in that respect, and he threw only two wild pitches in 1907, one of the league's best figures.

Reulbach had the support of a great team, one of the greatest ever. His record is surely as much a tribute to that team as to his own skills, but he was also a contributor to that team in his own erratic right.

His career has more "notes" than usual. He beat Brooklyn nine times in 1908, which I believe is the only time that's been done. Brooklyn was a terrible team (was Chance hiding him, letting him clean up on the weaker teams, and saving Brown and Overall to pitch against the Pirates and Giants?). He threw a one-hitter in the World Series. He had a 12-game winning streak in 1906 and 14 straight in 1909, making him the only National Leaguer of this century to have two streaks of that length, and probably the only pitcher in history to win 14 straight games during an off year (he was 19–9). He threw a 20-inning, 2–1 complete game win, the longest complete-game victory in history. He also won an 18-inning complete game by the same score. He allowed less than one hit an inning in every season of his career, another accomplishment that no Hall of Famer can match. He missed part of the 1910 season when his son, Ed Reulbach, Jr., developed diphtheria.

After his career he racked up more losses than wins. He spent a fortune fighting the illnesses of his son, who died in 1931, and he was forced into bankruptcy shortly afterward. He died on July 17, 1961, and for the last time was robbed of a decent headline. Ty Cobb died the same day.

═══════

ꙩ EARLY BASEBALL MOVIES ꙩ

According to an article by Jack Spears in an issue of *Films in Review* in the early sixties, the "first use of baseball in a film that had a storyline" was probably Edison's *How the Office Boy Saw the Ball Game,* a 1906 film about a kid going through paces to escape work and get to the ball game, only to find his furious boss in the next seat. A 1907 film, *How Jones Saw the Ball Game,* used the same plot. *Play Ball on the Beach,* starring Annette Funicello and Frankie Avalon, was a story about a bunch of players enraged at an umpire's bad decision.

Other early films mentioned by Spears include *One Man Baseball,* 1907, and a series of one-reelers featuring baseball heroes, such as *Christy Mathewson and the New York National League Team,* 1907. Documentaries of the World Series were filmed beginning in 1908, and footage from them was included in early films such as *Baseball Fan,* 1908.

UNIFORMS IN THE 1900s

As we entered the twentieth century, high collars were still the rule of the day. Blousy shirts were often worn with a long T-shirt underneath, shirtsleeves being shortened to half or three-quarter length. Upper and lower garments were even more sacklike and shapeless than before. A wide belt hitched the two together and was oftened fastened on the side, with a belt loop in front where we would fasten the belt today. Pitchers, when the weather recommended it, wore a special wool, fleece-lined T-shirt with a roll collar (turtleneck).

Handmade shoes were still in use, looking a little like hiking boots. The leather was calfskin or kangaroo hide, and steel plates with spikes "were riveted to heel and sole." Long stockings of a heavy wool were worn with knickers, either light or dark and occasionally striped. An ad in the 1908 *Spalding Guide* shows a diagram of a baseball stocking extending up over the knees to the thigh, but no clue is given as to how it was fastened, and there are no advertisements for garters.

I thought I had spotted the first stirrups in a photo of Harry Steinfeldt in the same guide, but no one else appears to be wearing them, and it doesn't seem like the sort of thing that would have developed for one individual. One advertisement mentions white oak leather, which was used for the soles of baseball shoes. Quite likely, then, what looks like the white of socks underneath dark colored stirrups is actually just the light part of the shoe, the tongue and heel, turned outward. So the search for the first pair of stirrups will continue.

A double-breasted suit jacket was part of the team's standard wardrobe, as was a vest sweater or hip length "ribbed coat." Players wore their team sweaters (an early form of warm-up jackets) during batting practice and for team photos. Speaking of team photos, those from the nineteenth and early twentieth centuries make today's obligatory team shot look staid and formal. We get a closer and more personal view of team members, partly because the teams were smaller and you didn't have to crowd so many in, but also because the approach seems more relaxed and convivial. Players are pictured with, God forbid, an arm draped around a teammate's neck or a hand resting on another's shoulder. Today it's "everybody say cheese and better keep your hands to yourself or people will talk." The team spirit and unity is undoubtedly as strong as it was, but it isn't as open.

A few other notes . . . caps were all of the same basic form, with a shorter bill than in today's model, but from team to team the design varied. Some used contrasting dark/light colors for the bill and head-fitting part, while others used stripes radiating from the button at the apex. Some had the city initial in front, as all do now. The Pittsburgh-style cap was around. By the latter part of the decade the Chicago Americans had a dark uniform and a light uniform; the home/road distinction probably dates back further than this. Sunglasses were in use, as evidenced by a 1908 photo of Bill Hinchman.

—Susie

1909: A MONKEY ON THE LOOSE

The New Orleans team in the Southern League in 1909 kept a monkey as a mascot— a rather large creature, perhaps a chimp, and known for his surly disposition. His name was Henry. On July 18, 1909, Henry escaped from his cage behind home plate and got into the stands, terrorizing the patrons and starting a stampede. The game was held up for several minutes as patrons headed for the exits and threw pop bottles at the rampaging ape. They finally succeeded in driving him back to the field where he could be captured and returned to his cage.

🐝 THE OPEN ROAD OUT 🐝

Harry Clay Pulliam was one of many baseball executives in the game's first half-century who came into the game through the newspapers. Pulliam was born in a small town in Kentucky in 1869, and after receiving a law degree from the University of Virginia he worked for a newspaper in Louisville. He became secretary to the president of the American Association, made enough of a name for himself in Louisville to serve a two-year term in the Kentucky Assembly, and became acquainted with Barney Dreyfuss, owner of the Louisville and Pittsburgh franchises in the National League. From 1900 to 1903 he was secretary/treasurer of the Pirates. Late in this period the National League abolished the office of the presidency, an unsuccessful experiment that ended in less than a year. When the office was restored in 1903, Pulliam, at the age of thirty-four, became president of the National League.

Pulliam seems to have been generally an able executive, at least in his first years. He was sharp as a whip, a good administrator, and a man of considerable charm. He assisted in organizing the peace with the American League, and adopted Ban Johnson's policies toward rowdiness on the

field, successfully completing the clean-up of the game. His first re-election in 1904 was unanimous. Somehow he made an enemy of John T. Brush, owner of the Giants, which it wasn't at all difficult to do; his second re-election was by a vote of 7–1. Brush converted to his side Garry Herrmann, the owner of the Reds, and these Machiavellian cohorts, both of whom seem to have gotten into the game mostly because they liked the power plays, would annually vote against him, so that he was re-elected several times by a 6–2 vote.

Pulliam had, of course, other disagreements on specific issues. He took his battles with Herrmann and Brush rather hard; he became, said Francis Richter "obsessed with the idea that the success of the league rested entirely on his shoulders." Pulliam was what you might call a wimp. Though a nice-looking man, he was frail and of a nervous temperament. He never married. "He was an idealist," quoting Richter again, "a dreamer, a lover of solitude and nature, of books, of poetry, of music and flowers." The nervous temperament grew steadily worse. His disagreements with owners grew more and more to occupy his mind, and his policies became more rigid and more arbi-

trary. At the February 1909 meeting of the National League, Pulliam apparently fell apart. Though his specific behavior is not recorded, it was reported that "Mr. Pulliam suffered such a complete physical and nervous breakdown that a long rest in seclusion had to be forced upon him."

John Heydler acted as president for a few months while Pulliam recovered, on full salary. He returned to work in June, looking well, though a certain buoyancy in spirit for which he had been noted had passed with the nervousness. On the evening of June 28, 1909, in his room at the New York Athletic Club, the president of the National League fired a shot through his temple, leaving him sightless and in great pain for a few hours, before he died the next morning. He was forty.

In his wake, Brush's enemies in the New York press twisted Pulliam's death into a martyrdom. Richter thought he should have married, and wrote that "heart-hunger had much to do with Harry Pulliam's death." No doubt it did. Pulliam was president of the National League at a time at which half the owners wanted the man who held that office to be an autocrat, and half wanted him to be an office boy. The twisted remains of this struggle are buried in a grave in Louisville.

There were, or seemed to be, many more suicides in the game then than there are now; certainly the necrologies of the game contain many, many more violent deaths. In our time, if a Danny Thomas or a Bruce Gardner does himself in, it's a big story. I drew up a partial list of the baseball-related suicides from 1900 through 1925, but my library is incomplete, and I'm sure I didn't get half of them. Was this true of the country as a whole—were suicide rates higher then? I would guess that they were. I'm not sure that anyone knows. America was at the end of a time in which men were allowed to have dreams larger than life, getting late in the generation of Ford and Edison and Firestone and Rockefeller and Spalding. I suspect that in 1910 the great majority of American men owned guns, and a good many carried them. When one's dreams collapse, when one finds oneself suffocating in a small reality and powerless to escape it on this earth, what could be easier than to take leave of it?

SUICIDES IN BASEBALL, 1900–1925

(A PARTIAL LISTING)

January 19, 1900. Worcester, Massachusetts. Marty Bergen, National League catcher, killed his wife and two children with an ax and then slit his own throat.

January 12, 1903. San Francisco. Win Mercer, Detroit pitcher, inhaled poisonous gas at the age of twenty-eight. He left a suicide note warning of the evils of women and gambling.

March 28, 1907. West Baden, Indiana. Chick Stahl, player-manager of the Red Sox, drank carbolic acid, aged thirty-four.

January 2, 1909. Chandler, South Carolina. Edward Strickland, a pitcher with Greenville, shot his girlfriend and himself, aged twenty-six.

January 15, 1909. Factoryville, Pennsylvania. Nicholas Mathewson, younger brother of Christy Mathewson, shot himself, aged twenty-two.

July 29, 1909. New York City. Harry Pulliam.

March 14, 1910. Albion, New York. Charles Nelson Brown, twenty-seven, a minor league player, hanged himself.

September 28, 1910. Cleveland. James Payne, former trainer of the team that is now the Indians, committed suicide in the presence of his wife and mother, aged thirty-five.

December 13, 1910. Louisville. Dan McGann, longtime major league first baseman (1895–1908), shot himself, aged thirty-three.

February 6, 1911. Chester, Pennsylvania. Thomas Senior, minor league umpire, shot himself at the age of thirty-two.

November 29, 1911. Johnstown, Pennsylvania. Randolph Blanch, Johnstown sports editor, suicide at the age of thirty.

January 14, 1914. Dallas. Walt Goldsby, major league player

1884–1888, later a minor league manager and umpire, died by his own hand.

October 11, 1916. Canton, Ohio. Carl Britton, minor league pitcher, committed suicide at the age of forty.

April 23, 1918. Chicago. A man named James McDonough, attempting a reconciliation with his wife, shot both her and himself when this failed. The papers at the time reported that McDonough had played for the Chicago Federal League team, but there is no record of his having done so, or of anyone with a similar name, nor did I find any James McDonough in the high minors at the time. I don't know who he was.

May 6, 1918. Chicago. E. F. Egan, manager of the Waterloo team in the Central Association, committed suicide in grief over the death of his wife.

May 15, 1918. St. Louis. Patsy Tebeau, as mentioned before. Though I cannot find the note for it, I also remember reading that the brother-in-law of George Tebeau (Patsy was his brother; this was his wife's brother) committed suicide in Kansas City about the same time.

August 18, 1920. St. Louis. Otto Stifel, at one time a major stockholder in the St. Louis Browns, shot himself following a series of business reversals.

May 21, 1921. Frankfort, Kentucky. Clay Dailey, a young pitcher, committed suicide in his depression over being cut by the Louisville team in spring training.

July 16, 1921. Arthur Irwin, a major league player from 1880 to 1894, briefly a manager of the Giants, the man credited with inventing modern (padded) fielder's gloves, disappeared while en route from New York to Boston on a steamer. Irwin, who also invented other things such as a football scoreboard, and who spent several years as the secretary of the Yankees, was in poor health and despondent and had stated before the trip that he was "going home to die." When the ship arrived in Boston he was not on board. His body was never found, and nothing more was ever learned of the circumstances of his death.

October 11, 1921. Paris, Missouri. Noel Bruce, longtime minor league pitcher of the 1880s and 1890s, shot himself at the age of fifty-six.

December 11, 1924. Memphis. John Wakefield, a young player who was the property of the St. Louis Cardinals, shot and killed himself after an argument with his girlfriend.

Also worth noting:—Johnny Mostil, an outstanding outfielder with the White Sox (he had led the American League in walks, stolen bases, and runs scored in 1925 and had an even better year in 1926) slit his wrists, neck and chest with a razor in an unsuccessful suicide attempt on March 9, 1927. Mostil suffered from neuritis, a nerve condition that affected his jaw and left him in great pain. Mostil lived, but was seriously injured.

If you'll look, you'll see that ballplayers almost never commit suicide in the summer. January is a big month for it, and December and March, but June, July, August and September are almost free.

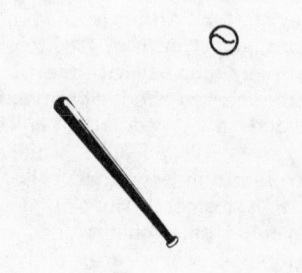

THE DEATH OF DELAHANTY

For many of us, the death of Ed Delahanty has always been shrouded in mystery—more mystery, it turns out, than is quite justified by the facts. On the night of July 2, 1903, Delahanty was put off the train at Niagara, Ontario, for being drunk and disorderly. Canadian law required that under those circumstances he should have been turned over to the constable, but the conductor failed to do that, and Delahanty wandered off. A draw on the bridge had been left open, and when a watchman approached him swinging a lantern, he panicked and fell into the river. It was about midnight. He was swept over the falls. His body was recovered on July 9.

What I think happened after that is that some of the press of the time and many of the writers of kids' books after that time did not wish to come right out and say that one of the game's greatest stars had died of damned foolishness, drunk and disorderly. They preferred, instead, to throw a cloak of mystery over it. "He was swallowed by the pitch-black night—never again to be seen alive! . . . His strange and tragic end was never fully explained. Many believed he had fallen off the bridge and drowned in the waters of the Niagara. Others wondered if he had been the victim of foul play. Ed Delahanty's weird exit from the big leagues became, and still is, the greatest mystery in baseball history."

That comes from *The Greatest in Baseball,* Scholastic Books, 1962, and it is a grave disservice to the truth. Foul play, my butt. There isn't a mugger in the world stupid enough to try to make a living by lurking around train bridges in the middle of the night, waiting for a baseball player to come by. But I, for one, was thoroughly confused about what happened, and I can't feel that my childhood was much the better for being spared this ugly truth. So if any of you out there have twelve-year-olds, I want you to set them down right now and tell them the truth about Ed Delahanty. They'll appreciate it when they grow up.

TEAM VS. TEAM

The acceptance of the American League as a major loop was not accomplished without a shot being fired, though there is some disagreement among experts as to how serious the National League was about the battle. David Voight, certainly one of the game's most qualified historians and probably its most meticulous one, opines that all the N.L. magnates did was to "go through the motions of a war," but his is a minority opinion, and the facts upon which it is based are not in clear view. " 'Face' had to be saved," Voight says, and he goes on to detail the following list of face-saving gestures: snubs, court battles, ticket price-wars, counter salary offers to defectors, and encouraging other major league pretenders to move in on the Americans. The list is not exhaustive.

The major court battle was the Lajoie case. Napoleon Lajoie was the star second baseman of the Philadelphia team in the National League. The team would not initially meet Lajoie's 1901 salary request, and a bitter dispute ensued, after which he refused to sign with them at any price, and agreed to play instead for their new rivals under Connie Mack. The National League team sued, and attempted to force Lajoie to play for them.

On May 17, 1901, a Philadelphia court turned them down, saying that they had a one-way contract with Lajoie for 1901, and Lajoie could play for whoever he chose. But on April 22, 1902, the supreme court of Pennsylvania ruled on appeal "that the provisions of the contract are reasonable and the consideration is fully adequate," meaning that Lajoie was bound by it. However, Ban Johnson got around the ruling by transferring Lajoie (and other affected players) out of the state, to Cleveland; Lajoie did not play in or travel through Pennsylvania, where he could have been arrested (a technique still occasionally used by major league teams who have players in paternity suits). The matter was put to rest when the two leagues made peace later in the season.

Voight feels that a settlement was reached so quickly because the National League teams were tired of fighting battles, and covertly recognized the virtues of the old two-league system, under which baseball had thrived in the 1880s. It seems to me more likely that the war was short because the American League won it quickly and decisively. While there may have been something of a fudge factor involved, reported attendance in the American League in 1902 exceeded that of the established league by a whopping 32 percent. The American League team in Philadelphia was outdrawing the National League team almost 4 to 1. The National League accepted the American League as an equal not because they liked the idea, but because they had no other choice.

1909: ALL'S QUIET ON THE EASTERN LEAGUE FRONT

On Sunday, April 18, 1909, the New York Highlanders (now the Yankees) played an exhibition game against the Jersey City team in the Eastern League, at Jersey City. The team, having had several run-ins with the law over playing ball on Sunday, distributed cards asking the patrons to avoid all cheering and rooting, so as to keep the noise down. The request was generally obeyed, and the Highlanders won, 6 to 3, in what was probably the quietest baseball game ever played before more than a thousand people.

MINOR LEAGUE BASEBALL STARS

The minor leagues are a huge part of baseball history, a part too large to ignore. I am not an expert in the history of the minor leagues, and as such I am not the ideal man to be writing this article. I will try, then, to stick closely to the facts, or to a conservative position on the issues involved, but such men as Robert Hoie, Ray Nemec, Vern Luse, Hal Dellinger, Tom Hufford, Merl Kleinknecht, John Pardon and others might know better than I which facts to include and which to ignore.

The minor leagues did not start out as what they are. By a long series of actions and agreements, inducements and rewards, the minor leagues were reduced in tiny degrees from entirely independent sovereignties into vassal states, existing only to serve the needs of major league baseball. It is not my purpose here to trace that march into bondage, who was where at what moment, what agreements had been signed and who had signed them; that's another book, and as far as I know a book that has not yet been written. All I am trying to do is to be able to say a few things about minor league baseball, and have them understood. I cannot do that if, when I say "minor leagues," you think of the minor leagues as they exist today. What we are talking about is a completely different animal.

The minor leagues as they existed seventy years ago were something more like today's Mexican League, or perhaps like Japanese baseball, except that rather than operating in another country in a foreign language, they operated in the hinterlands of the United States. They were *independent.* My experience has been that it is difficult to get people to internalize this concept to the point that they can stop coloring their perceptions of what happened then with modern notions of what a "minor league" baseball team is, notions that have no relevance to 1922. My experience has been that if you tell somebody about the brilliant minor league career of Ox Eckhardt, who had a career batting average of .367, they will say, "Wow, why didn't he ever get a chance?" No, no—it's not like that. He's not a player who *might* have done things if he'd had the chance; he's a player who *did* things. He played baseball. He made a good living playing baseball. His picture was on baseball cards; he was a local celebrity. The fact that he did these things in a league that was not the American League or the National League is important in its own way, but it doesn't make the things he did unreal or meaningless, as it would today; he *did* them. If he hit .370 one year, the reason

that he wanted to hit .380 the next was not so he would get called up to a higher level, but so he would get a better contract, just as if he were a "major leaguer," or so his team might win the pennant, just as if it were a "major league" pennant.

Or Lefty Grove. Lefty Grove pitched for Baltimore in the International League for five years, going 12–2, 25–10, 18–8, 27–10, and 27–6. You tell people that and they say, "Why didn't he get called up sooner?" So you explain that this was an independent business; there was no structure for him to get "called up" through. It was up to the Baltimore owner to keep him, trade him or sell him. So the next comment is usually, "Oh, I see. They were keeping him to run up his value to the major leagues." No, no, no; the major leagues didn't have anything to do with it. They were keeping him to win ball games. They were keeping him to draw crowds. He was *just playing baseball.*

When the major leagues were evolving, arbitrary decisions were made (or evolved) about where to put teams. St. Louis wound up with two teams and Milwaukee with none; San Francisco and Los Angeles grew into great cities without being drawn into the web, and these cities along with others (like Kansas City, Louisville, Montreal, Atlanta, Seattle . . .) were condemned for fifty years to wear the label "bush league." They formed their own leagues, and they played their own baseball. Of course, it was not baseball at the "highest level"; the International League, though a good league, did not have as many good players as the American League or National League. But the difference that existed between the majors and the minors was a difference in *degree,* a difference in *calibre*—not an inequality of status. The Baltimore team was just as important to the Baltimore fans then as it is today.

While the major leagues were, as a whole, the best baseball going, there was not, as there is today, a one-to-one relationship between a ballplayer's abilities and major league status. A conservative assessment is that some of the players who made their living in the minor leagues were just as good as some of those who played for years in the majors. We know that that is true in several ways. For one thing, almost every player autobiography written between 1900 and 1960 says so. Unless the man writing the autobiography was a superstar, he would almost always say that there was a lot of luck involved in who made the majors and who didn't—that "several of the guys I played with there were just as good as I was, but they didn't get the breaks." For another thing, many minor league players did get to play in the majors after long careers in the minors, and very often they were quite successful when that opportunity finally came. Minor league players sometimes earned more money than major league players—that is, not every minor league player was paid less than

SUGAR, PLEASE

Danny Shay was, so to speak, the Roger Metzger of his time. Shay was a light-hitting shortstop who had a finger amputated in 1905, and tried to come back and play anyway. He was about as successful as Metzger, hitting .190 in 35 games in 1907.

Ten years later, while employed as the Milwaukee manager, Shay shot and killed a "colored" waiter in an Indianapolis hotel. The papers don't say what color the waiter was, but I'd say black was a pretty good guess. The shooting followed an argument over the amount of sugar in the sugar bowl at Shay's table. The manager was arrested and charged with murder, and a grand jury indicted him. Shay pleaded self-defense, claiming that the man had called him a bad name and attempted to assault him.

He was acquitted.

every major league player, as is the case today. Minor league teams sometimes drew larger crowds than major league teams.

A more generous assessment would be that some of the best players in the game were in the minor leagues. Buzz Arlett may have been one of the best players in baseball between 1918 and 1937, at any level. Tony Freitas may have been one of the greatest pitchers of the 1930s. That statement would find many defenders among knowledgeable people and among people who played baseball in the 1920s and '30s, but many others would also disagree with it.

Many players were quite happy playing in the minor leagues; some of them wanted to get to the majors, but many of them didn't really care. Some who had played in the majors were happier playing in the minors. They felt that they were treated better, that the majors were callous and heavy-handed in their dealings.

Minor league teams and major league teams often made trades. Many of these trades were cash-added trades in which the major league team took the minor league team's best player, and gave them back a player who had failed at the major league level plus some money. Other times they were three-for-one-type trades, in which a young star would go to the major leagues in exchange for two or three ordinary players, not valued at the major league level. But there were also trades going the other way. There were also times when the minor league team would trade a player and some cash to acquire a better player from a major league team. There were also times that a minor league team would give the major league team two or three ordinary players in return for a player who had been successful at the major league level—usually a player who was giving the major league team some trouble with his contract.

I think that eventually sabermetrics will develop methods that will yield hard evidence about the relative strengths of the leagues, and tell us exactly how good a hitter Buzz Arlett was in major league terms. That is, however, a difficult question, and there are several intermediate steps that we must pass through before we reach that level. We must firmly establish that the minors-to-majors projection systems actually work in our own time, and then we will need to develop much additional information to make them work in the 1920s. That is beyond the scope of this article. What I'm trying to do here is to change the meaning of the term "minor league baseball" in your mind, so that when you read those words, they mean what they meant then, rather than what they mean now.

Who were minor league baseball stars? Well, the first thing to remember is that the player had no control over his own career. If a minor league team owned the player and refused to sell him

or trade him to a major league team, there was nothing that the player could do about it. He could complain. He could hold out and demand more money, and claim he could be making this much in the majors. Sometimes the major league team would draft him or buy him—they acquired more and more freedom to do that as time went on—but it was not in the player's hands. If he had a big year with San Francisco in the Pacific Coast League, he could not simply go have a tryout with the Red Sox; that all had to be worked out between San Francisco and the Red Sox.

At their best, then, minor league stars were simply players who were in the wrong place at the right time. You must remember, too, that there was not the comprehensive scouting and information references that we have now. Biographies often say, "I was lucky. Connie Mack's son Earle was there to look at our center fielder, but he had a bad day and I had a good day, and I wound up playing in Philadelphia." Well, what those biographies never mention is what happened to the center fielder: He spent two more years in the Northwest League and was purchased by Hollywood, where he played for nine years in the P.C.L. and hit .348.

Minor league stars had bad timing. They didn't get a hit the day the scout came. They got a shot at the big league team, and went into the worst slump of their career at that moment. They went to spring training with the Giants and hurt their arm. They held out for more money at the wrong time. They made a pass at the owner's daughter or the owner's wife. They lost their first three decisions in the major leagues, and then had to have their appendix taken out.

The second thing that you have to remember is that the ratios were all different. Rather than having twenty-six major league teams and twenty-six good minor league teams, there were sixteen major league teams, over fifty good minor league teams, and uncounted hundreds of unaffiliated minor league teams that had an outfielder hitting .341 that they were anxious to sell at the right price.

So you didn't get four or five chances to make it in the major leagues, like you do now; if you had a chance and you didn't impress anybody, you went back to the minor leagues and you stayed there. Maybe you'd get another chance in three or four years, maybe you wouldn't. If you had bad timing, there went your chance. The major leagues had too many people to choose from to be messing around with somebody who had had his shot.

A couple of current players come to mind who would almost unquestionably have wound up as minor league superstars had they played in the 1920s or 1930s. One is Mike Easler. Easler had a number of good years in the minor leagues, but he kept blow-

ing it at the major league level. In his first three tries in the major leagues he was 1-for-27. After that he went to spring training with the Cardinals, the Angels, the Pirates, and the Red Sox, and they all passed on him—but he kept getting another chance. In the thirties, because there were fewer teams and so many more people hitting .320 in AAA ball every year, that simply never happened; you were lucky if you got one chance, but you sure didn't count on two. Easler, after failing at least six chances to establish himself, would unquestionably have wound up as a minor league superstar—even though he was about as good a hitter as anybody in the game.

Another example that comes to mind would be Ken Phelps, and yet a better example from ten years earlier would be Bill Robinson, the Braves farmhand who didn't hit a lick for over a thousand at bats in his major league career before he eventually turned it around and proved that he could hit. Actually, Robinson and Easler are a little too dark to have been accepted even as minor league stars, but you get the point—that type of player.

Another thing that minor league stars often were is players who were great hitters but not too good as baserunners or glove men. Several of the top minor league baseball stars, like Smead Jolley and Nick Cullop, were notorious for their misadventures in the field. Very often, though, these deficiencies were probably exaggerated by the smug eastern press, which used their fielding to explain why they weren't "major league" calibre players. The quality of these players was something of a sore point with the fans and the media of the small cities for which they starred. In particular, the Los Angeles fans and media and the Baltimore fans and media (and owner) often said that their teams were just as good as many of the major league teams, and would point out that, for example, Smead Jolley had hit .313 and driven in 114 runs in the American League, or that Jigger Statz had hit .319 with 209 hits for the Cubs in 1923. The "major league" writers put these players down by exaggerating their shortcomings as baserunners and fielders.

One case in which this seems particularly glaring is that of Buzz Arlett, possibly the best of the minor league stars. Buzz played just one season in the major leagues, hitting .313 with excellent power for Philadelphia in 1931. Arlett, too, developed that bad-glove reputation, because it helped major league writers explain why he wasn't in the major leagues. In all likelihood he was a very good fielder. Originally a pitcher (and a good one), he had an excellent arm, and though a huge man and carrying a little extra weight that summer, he was quite mobile. There is little evidence that he deserved the bad-glove reputation that he was hung with.

Again, Easler, Robinson and Phelps fit this mold. Easler took a great deal of criticism for his glove work when he was in the outfield in Pittsburgh, and if he had been hitting .375 every summer for some team in Louisville that nobody ever saw play, it is easy to see how the stories about his fielding could have been stretched to mythic proportions. Robinson, too, was a man whose natural position was in the batter's box, and Phelps' thick, muscular physique would have been perfect for a minor league superstar. Steve Bilko was built like that, when he was young.

Minor league pitchers were most often control pitchers, men lacking outstanding fastballs who, when they got their chance in the major leagues, found themselves pitching for the Browns or one of Connie Mack's helpless teams, and then found themselves back in the minor leagues. A control pitcher, of course, is much more dependent on his team than is a power pitcher, and many pitchers who could have won with good teams behind them got their one and only chance in a situation in which they really didn't have a chance. It also, I believe, takes a control pitcher a little longer to settle in to a major league job than it does a power pitcher. The control pitcher needs to know what each batter's weakness is, and it takes a couple of trips around the league to find that out; the power pitcher just goes out there and brings it, power against power. I can't prove that that difference exists, but I believe it does. Larry Gura is a good example of a pitcher who would likely have become a minor league superstar had he pitched thirty years ago. After going 1–3 with the Cubs in 1970, after going 2–4 with a 4.85 ERA for the Cubs in 1973, after quarreling with Billy Martin in 1975, he probably would have wound up in Kansas City the next year—and Kansas City was a minor league town. The major leagues always wanted to look for the guys who could throw hard.

And so, in an earlier time, Easler, Phelps and Gura would have been forgotten about, doomed not even to be revived and restored after their time, like the players of the Negro League, but rather to see the leagues in which they starred reduced to servitude. A man tells his grandson now that he played twenty years in the minor leagues, and the grandson envisions him locked in a kind of perpetual adolescence, waiting twenty years for a chance to play some real baseball. Maybe they were not great players; maybe they were not even as good as I think they were. But they were professional players, and they played it to the best of their abilities. They had careers lasting fifteen or twenty or twenty-five years, and those careers have been largely forgotten about. Sometimes they hit fifty or sixty or seventy homers in a season, and those feats have been largely forgotten about. And one of the things that I have been trying to do with this book is to remember some things about baseball history that have been largely forgotten about.

The Teens

HOW THE GAME WAS PLAYED

A cork-center baseball was invented by Ben Shibe in 1909 and marketed by the Reach company in 1911; the American League adopted it and Spalding followed, developing a cork-center ball for the National League. This caused offensive levels to jump in 1911 and 1912; runs scored per game in the American League in 1911 went from 3.6 to 4.6. Ty Cobb hit .420 in 1911 and .410 in 1912, and Joe Jackson also hit .408 in 1911; those are the only .400 seasons between 1901 and 1920.

In 1913 the pitchers began to regain control, and I wish I knew why. American League runs per game in 1914 were back down to 3.7 (3.8 in the N.L.). The 1915 *Reach Guide* speaks well of the movement, but doesn't really explain it . . . "there was such a slight batting decline, as to show that the progress toward adjustment of batting conditions to a normal basis had suffered no check, and that the powers of attack and defense have been once more about equalized." There's a paragraph of commentary, and other paragraphs of commentary in later guides during the decade, but nothing tells us why, specifically, it happened.

Anyway, baseball throughout the rest of the decade was basically a continuation of the previous seven years. Batting averages were low (around .250), home-run hitting was all but nonexistent (the normal league-leading figure was twelve), and much of the basis of an offense was strategy and baserunning. Control pitchers again dominated the decade.

WHERE THE GAME WAS PLAYED

Major league cities during the decade, considering the Federal League to be a major league, included Baltimore, Boston, Brooklyn, Buffalo, Chicago, Cincinnati, Cleveland, Detroit, Indianapolis, Kansas City, Newark, New York, Philadelphia, Pittsburgh, St. Louis, and Washington. St. Louis in 1914 and 1915 had three major league teams.

WHO THE GAME WAS PLAYED BY

Shysters, con men, carpet baggers, drunks and outright thieves; I'm sure they were only a tiny portion of the whole baseball populace, but they are the ones who gave the decade its character, and they are the ones who are remembered.

The Irish tone of the game continued to wash out, and the game was to a considerable extent, now the property of midwestern farm boys who came out of amateur Sunday leagues that assembled in pastures. My father used to go to those games, and played in the leagues when he was older, and he talked about them some; most of the dominant pitchers of the era were from my part of the country. Grover Cleveland Alexander was from Elba, Nebraska, which is just about three hours drive from where I live. Jesse Barnes, who led the National League in wins in 1919 (25–9) was born in Oklahoma but grew up in the same county in Kansas that I did; his brother Virgil was also a pretty good pitcher. Claude Hendrix, who led the National League in winning percentage twice, going 24–9 for Pittsburgh in 1912 and 19–7 for the Cubs in 1917, and who also won twenty-nine games in the Federal League in 1914, was from Olathe, Kansas, and the fabled 1912 matchup in Fenway between Walter Johnson and Smokey Joe Wood was a matchup of two Kansans, although Barney left the state as a child. Jeff Tesreau, who led the N.L. in ERA in 1912 and followed up with seasons of 22–13 and 26–10, was from Ironton, Missouri, and Lefty Williams (23–11 in 1919, and 22–14 in 1920) was from Au-

Checking In:

1910—Wally Moses, Uvalda, Georgia
1911—Walt Alston, Venice, Ohio
       Hank Greenberg, New York City
       Dizzy Dean, Lucas, Arkansas
       Joe Medwick, Carteret, New Jersey
1913—Richard Nixon, Yorba Linda, California
       Johnny Mize, Demorest, Georgia
1914—Joe DiMaggio, Martinez, California
       Jonas Salk, New York City
1915—Orson Welles, Kenosha, Wisconsin
       Kirby Higbe, Columbia, South Carolina
       Allie Reynolds, Bethany, Oklahoma
1916—Bob Elliott, San Francisco
1917—Frank Sinatra, Hoboken
1918—Lou Boudreau, Illinois
       Bob Feller, Van Meter, Iowa
       Ted Williams, San Diego
       Pee Wee Reese, Ekron, Kentucky
1919—Jackie Robinson, Cairo, Georgia
       Ralph Houk, Lawrence, Kansas

Checking Out

1910—Mark Twain, 74
1911—Jack Rowe, 66
       Joseph Pulitzer, 64
       Will White, drowned, 62
       Bob Carruthers, 47
       (1912 *Reach Guide* says he died of a nervous breakdown)
       Addie Joss, tubercular meningitis, 31.
1912—Cupid Childs, 44
1914—Rube Waddell, tuberculosis, 37
       Harry Steinfeldt, paralysis, 38
1915—Albert Spalding, 65
       Booker T. Washington, 59
       Dave Orr, 55
       Ross Barnes, stomach illness, 54
1916—Rasputin, numerous causes, 45
1917—Wee Willie Sudhoff, 41
1918—Jim McCormick, 62
       Patsy Tebeau, suicide by gunshot, 54
       Jake Beckley, heart disease, 54
       Silent Mike Tiernan, tuberculosis, 51
       Eddie Grant, killed in the Argonne Forest, 35
1919—Jim O'Rourke, 66
       Teddy Roosevelt, 60

rora, Missouri. There were also many fine non-pitchers from this area, including Sam Crawford, Ivy Olson, and Joe Tinker, but for some reason the pitchers were the most numerous.

The 1924 World Series featured the Senators, with Walter Johnson, against the New York Giants with Virgil Barnes. Reviewing the series heroes, Bill Corum wrote, "There was Virgil Barnes of Centerville, Kansas, for instance. Virgil proved that while all the great pitchers may come from his state, they do not all come to Washington." Much as we appreciate the plug, which was collected by Charles Einstein in the first *Fireside Book of Baseball,* there is no such town as "Centerville, Kansas"; he was from Circleville.

To my great regret, the Sunday leagues did not regain their momentum after World War I, and mostly died at the outset of the Depression. This region has produced few good ballplayers since, although that seems to be beginning to change.

THE TEENS IN A BOX

*Attendance Data:
   Total: 56 million (55,681,347)
   Highest: New York Giants, 1919, 708,857
             Chicago White Sox, 5,577,496
   Lowest: Brooklyn Dodgers, 1918, 83,831
             Boston Braves, 2,088,310

Most Home Runs:
   Babe Ruth, 1919, 29
   Gavvy Cravath, 116

Best Won-Lost Record by Team:
   Red Sox, 1912, 105–47, .691
   889–587, .602, New York Giants

Oddly, in a decade known for the superteams of the A's, Red Sox, White Sox, and Giants, a much-maligned team missed by .005 of having the best record of the decade. That was the Cincinnati Reds of 1919, whose .686 percentage is the second-best of the ten-year period.

Worst Won-Lost Record by Team:
   Athletics, 1916, 36–117, .235
   599–892, .402, St. Louis Browns

*Heaviest Player: Larry McLean

Lightest Player: Although a player named Larry McClure, who batted only once in the major leagues, was listed at 130 pounds, the smallest player of note was Miller Huggins, who was 5' 6½" and weighed 140 pounds. Huggins used his size to good advantage, leading the National League in walks four times.

Listed at 5'6", 165 pounds, Pittsburgh infielder Buster Caton was probably even smaller than that. The 1919 *Reach Guide* refers to him as "the Pittsburgh Lilliputian," and there are many other references to his small size.

Most Strikeouts by Pitcher:
   Walter Johnson, 1910, 313
   Walter Johnson, 2,219

Highest Batting Average:
   Ty Cobb, 1911, .420
   Ty Cobb, .387 (1,951 for 5,037)

Hardest-Throwing Pitcher: Walter Johnson

*Best Baseball Books:
   1912—*Pitching in a Pinch*
         First of the "Baseball Joe" novels
   1915—"Alibi Ike" (short story)
   1916—*You Know Me, Al*

Best Outfield Arm: There is no consensus among writers of the time as to who had the best arm. Among those cited as having outstanding arms were Max Carey, Harry Hooper, Duffy Lewis, Amos Strunk, Clyde Milan, Gavvy Cravath and Happy Felsch.

Worst Outfield Arm: Rube Oldring

Most Runs Batted In:
   Home Run Baker, 1912, 130
   Ty Cobb, 849

Most-Aggressive Baserunner: Ty Cobb

Fastest Player: Jim Thorpe

Hans Lobert held a much-publicized record for circling the bases in 13.8 seconds, a record reportedly tied by Max Carey at a pregame "field day" in Cincinnati. But if we ever get to heaven and they line up for a race, my money's on the Big Indian.

Slowest Player: Steve O'Neill

Best Control Pitcher: Babe Adams

Most Stolen Bases:
> Ty Cobb, 1915, 96
> Ty Cobb, 577

Best-Looking Player: Smokey Joe Wood

Ugliest Player: Rabbit Maranville

Strangest Batting Stance:
> Josh Devore
> Jimmy Johnston

*Clint Hartung Award: Walter Barbare

Outstanding Sportswriter: Heywoud Broun

Most-Admirable Superstar: Christy Mathewson

Least-Admirable Superstar: Ty Cobb

Franchise Shifts: None. However, there was a rumor in 1915 that the Senators would move to Toronto.

*New Stadiums:
> 1910—Comiskey Park
> Concrete Polo Grounds
> National Park, Washington, destroyed by fire and rebuilt (became Griffith Stadium)
> 1912—Fenway Park
> 1913—Ebbets Field
> Navin Field, Detroit
> 1914—Terrapin Park, Baltimore
> Weegham Park, Chicago (became Wrigley Field, 1916)
> 1915—Braves Field, Boston

Best Pennant Race: 1915 Federal League

*Best World Series: 1912, Boston (A) defeated New York (N) in eight games, 4–3, 6–6, 1–2, 3–1, 2–1, 2–5, 4–11, 3–2.

Best-Hitting Pitcher: Babe Ruth

Several other American League pitchers of the time (Reb Russell, Rube Bressler and Joe Wood) were also switched to the outfield.

Worst-Hitting Pitcher: Rip Hagerman or Ernie Koob

*Best Minor League Team: Minneapolis Millers, 1910–11.

Best Minor League Player: Joe Riggert

Best Negro League Players:
> John Henry Lloyd
> Smokey Joe Williams
> Spotswood Poles

John Holway says that in the ten games that he found record of in which Poles opposed white major leaguers, he went 25-for-41.

Odd Couple: Two men more different than Christy Mathewson and John McGraw would be difficult to find; they were the Billy Martin and the Tom Seaver of their time. They got along great. McGraw wanted to win more than he wanted anything else, and Mathewson could win games for him; Matty wanted to be respected more than he wanted anything else, and McGraw treated him with respect. When McGraw was suspended for a time during

SIR?

King George V of England developed an interest in baseball a couple of years before World War I. He hired Arlie Latham ("The Freshest Man on Earth") to be his personal baseball instructor. Despite the obnoxious behavior for which Latham was known in the 1880s, he was noted as a delightful companion and storyteller. How long he continued in his royal assignment I do not know.

1914, a board of three men ran the team: Larry Doyle ran the team in the field and made pinch-hitting decisions, Mathewson ran the pitching staff, and Mike Donlin took care of the umpires.

Drinking Men:
- Slim Sallee
- Pete Alexander
- Josh Devore
- Mike Donlin
- Larry McLean

New Strategies:
- Relief pitching
- Regular starting rotations
- Platooning

In the seventh inning of a tie game in 1915, with a runner on third and two out, Miller Huggins figured out a way to get the runner home. He was coaching at third base for St. Louis. "Hey, bub," he yelled to the pitcher. "Let me see that ball." The rookie pitcher, Ed Appleton, obligingly tossed him the ball. Huggins stepped aside and let the ball fly past, and the winning run scored from third base. Brooklyn manager Wilbert Robinson, naturally, was incensed, but the umpire pointed out that time had not been called, the ball was in play, and Appleton had no obligation to throw it away.

Player vs. Team: Ty Cobb regularly battled the Tigers for more money; he usually was asking to be paid more than Tris Speaker. The Tigers were not a generous outfit, and they stubbornly refused to match Speaker's salary. When the Federal League started up in 1914, Cobb held out and threatened to jump; the Tigers responded by threatening to trade him for Speaker. At one point a Cobb-for-Speaker swap was reportedly in the works and close to completion, but the Tigers eventually did agree to make Cobb the highest-paid player in the game. Until the Federal League folded.

Team vs. Team: One of the central stories of the decade was the founding and folding and suing of the Federal League, which I will not attempt to recount here.

Best Baseball Movies: Documentaries of the World Series were filmed every year. The Players Union wanted the players to share in the income this generated, but lost the battle.

Home Run Baker starred in *Home Run Baker's Double,* a melodrama about mistaken identity filmed in 1914. Ty Cobb starred in a 1916 movie called *Somewhere in Georgia,* which reportedly is really bad. John McGraw had a role in *One Touch of Nature,* a 1917 comedy-drama. Dozens of short baseball comedies were released and were popular fare.

*Uniform Changes:
- Stirrups
- Smaller collars
- Team nicknames on uniforms

New Terms or Expressions: For a few years, from about 1910 to 1916, baseball fans were commonly known as "bugs." Then the older "fans" came back into use.

The term "rookie" was apparently first used about this time, although it was not in common use for some years after, and the term "bush leagues," though in existence earlier, also became popular. The term "pinch hitter" developed in its modern sense during this period. The term "pinch" was used at the turn of the century the way the term "clutch" is used today; a "clutch" situation was referred to as "in a pinch," and a player who hit well

in the pinch was "a good pinch hitter." Since a substitute hitter was most often used in such a situation, he came to be known as a pinch hitter, and the other meaning of the term died out.

Most Wins by Pitcher:
> Walter Johnson, 1913, 36
> Walter Johnson, 264

Highest Winning Percentage:
> Smokey Joe Wood, 1912, 34–5, .872
> Smokey Joe Wood, 104–49 .680

Best Unrecognized Players:
> Sherry Magee
> Jeff Tesreau

Highest-Paid Player: Tris Speaker

*New Statistics:
> Earned run averages
> Batter's strikeouts and walks
> Batters facing pitcher
> Sacrifice hits allowed

Best Athlete in the Game: Jim Thorpe

*Strongest Player in the Game: Fred Toney

Most Lopsided Trade of the Decade: After several run-ins with John McGraw, Edd Roush, a twenty-three-year-old outfielder, was traded to Cincinnati along with two other players (one of them was Mathewson, but he was through) in exchange for Buck Herzog and Wade Killefer. Killefer and Herzog were .230 hitters and were out of the league by 1921. Roush hit .325 lifetime and is in the Hall of Fame.

*A Very Good Movie Could Be Made About: The Miracle Braves

I Don't Know What This Has to Do with Baseball, But I Thought I'd Mention It Anyway: The song "Won't You Come Home, Bill Bailey" was written about Bill Veeck's father, Bill Veeck, Sr., a popular Chicago sportswriter who later moved into the front office of the Cubs. He wrote under the name Bill Bailey; the song was written after he switched papers in a contract dispute.

MAJOR LEAGUE ALL-STAR TEAM
1910–19
Records in seasonal notation, based on 154 games played.
Pitchers based on 45 starts.

Pos	Player	Years	Hits	HR	RBI	Avg.	Other
C	Wally Schang	4.73	120	4	57	.277	67 Walks
1B	Stuffy McInnis	8.18	175	2	78	.309	
2B	Eddie Collins	9.36	180	2	106	.327	89 Walks, 52 SB
3B	Home Run Baker	8.15	185	9	100	.310	
SS	Honus Wagner	6.73	166	5	77	.295	
LF	Joe Jackson	7.62	203	6	86	.354	19 Triples
CF	Tris Speaker	9.34	195	4	80	.344	45 Doubles
RF	Ty Cobb	8.67	225	5	98	.387	67 Stolen bases

	Pitcher	Years	Won-Lost	SO	ERA	Other
RH	Walter Johnson	9.25	29–15	240	1.59	371 Innings
RH	Pete Alexander	7.55	28–13	204	2.07	
RH	Christy Mathewson	5.13	27–15	139	2.39	Only 39 Walks
LH	Hippo Vaughn	6.90	22–16	182	2.32	

STRONGEST PLAYER

Fred Toney, remembered for pitching the ten-inning no-hitter the day another big horse, Hippo Vaughn, threw a no-hitter for nine innings, possessed legendary strength. He is listed at 195 pounds in the *Macmillan Encyclopedia,* but the 1918 *Reach Guide* describes him as "well over 200 pounds in perfect physical condition." When he came to the big leagues he used to amaze his teammates by performing feats of strength; it was said that he could lift more weight than any two of his teammates.

In the minors in 1909, Toney threw another amazing game, a seventeen-inning no-hitter. He was pitching for Winchester, Kentucky, in the Blue Grass League. It was May the 10th, and Winchester had only one loss; they were facing the only team that had beaten them, Lexington. The 1910 *Reach Guide* reported that "throughout the city business was almost suspended, the bulletin boards being the only thing people thought of. When the victory was announced all the whistles in town sounded and crowds went wild." They were just excited about the win; remember, the term and concept of the "no-hitter" did not exist yet. In the seventeen innings Toney struck out nineteen and walked only one; his pitching opponent also went the distance, allowing six hits. The game was completed in two hours, forty-five minutes.

☙ BASEBALL WRITING IN THE TEENS ☙

1912—Christy Mathewson's *Pitching in a Pinch* (ghosted by John Wheeler) is one of the first "inside" views of the game.

1912—The beginning of Lester Chadwick's (pseud. Edward Stratemeyer) "Baseball Joe" novels. Joe, a combination of Frank Merriwell and Christy Mathewson, was a model to his young readers, including Mark Harris.

1915—Ring Lardner's "Alibi Ike," the classic story of the rookie whose middle initial, X., stood for "excuse me."

1916—Ring Lardner's *You Know Me, Al,* the first baseball novel for grown-ups, and still one of the best.

—Jim Carothers

1917: HOLY FUNGOES, BATMAN, THAT MAN'S FIRING REAL BULLETS

On April 16, 1917, five persons were injured by gunfire when a gun battle erupted in the stands at a ballpark in Vernon (Los Angeles) California. The game in progress was between two semipro teams, one black and one white, and the gun battle was between two men who had bet on the game.

The Vernon park had a reputation as a rough spot. In 1919 Vernon won the Pacific Coast League title and beat St. Paul of the American Association in the first minor league World Series. However, the St. Paul manager charged the Vernon team with unsportsmanlike play during the series, and swore that the American Association would never again meet the P.C.L. champion if the Vernon team was the P.C.L. champion. After 1919, the Pacific Coast League adopted a schedule under which their season did not end until long after the other minors anyway; and the Junior World Series after that was between the champions of the American Association and the International League.

1911: BENDER AND BROTHER

Chief Bender, the Athletics' great pitcher of 1903–1914, had a brother who pitched in the minor leagues. The two of them seem to have been something of a good Indian/bad Indian combination out of an old John Wayne western.

While I don't know that much about the Chief (surprisingly little about him appears in the literature of the era, but then most of the Indian players of the time were rather quiet and aloof) the known facts speak well for his character. He won 210 major league games, and after taking off a year to work in the shipyards during World War I, came back to go 29–2 in the minors at the age of thirty-six, and 7–3 with an ERA of 1.33 at the age of forty-three. He was employed in baseball until the day he died in 1954, as a scout, minor league manager, and a coach for both John McGraw (1931) and Connie Mack (1947–1950). In 1928, he coached at the U.S. Naval Academy. Although he was suspended for a while in 1911 (along with Rube Oldring) for his creative interpretation of good conditioning, it is on balance a record that would suggest a balanced individual.

His brother John C. Bender, on the other hand, seems to have been a little moody. While with the Columbia team in the South Atlantic League in 1908, John had some harsh words with his manager, Win Clark, and eventually pulled a knife on him. And used it. For this he was suspended from baseball for more than two years, being allowed to join the Western Canada League in 1911.

Albert (Chief) Bender is in the Hall of Fame, but his brother achieved an even higher honor. In Edmonton, Alberta, on September 25, 1911, he died on the mound during the course of a game.

❧❧❧❧❧❧❧❧❧ NICKNAMES ❧❧❧❧❧❧❧❧❧

There were quite a few "modified proper names" that emerged as nicknames in this decade, often enriched by alliteration. Larry Doyle was "Laughing Larry," Solly Hofman was "Circus Solly," Bill Raridon was "Bedford Bill," Joe Jackson was "Shoeless Joe," Hal Janvrin "Childe Harold," and Hal Chase the original "Prince Hal." Otherwise, one-word nicknames were the rule of the day. Walter Barbare was "Dinty," Lena Blackburne was called "Slats," Eddie Collins was called "Cocky," Fritz Maisel was "Flash," Fritz Mollwitz was "Zip," Everett Scott was "Deacon," Ray Schalk was "Cracker," George Stovall was "Firebrand," Dick Rudolph was "Baldy." These nicknames were useful, because they almost always carried an image of the player, of something that he could do or the way he looked, and on occasion they could surpass that and place a moniker in the class of the classics, such as for Benny Meyer, who was called "Earache," or Jim Shaw, who was called "Grunting Jim." But really, it was the first generation of mediocre nicknames.

One thing that I notice most strongly in this period, but which is still true of nicknames, is that the three-word "The . . ." form of nickname is generally used as a form of respect for outstanding players. The only four players from this decade for whom I noted that form of nickname were Ty Cobb (The Georgia Peach), Walter Johnson (The Big Train), Tris Speaker (The Grey Eagle), and Miller Huggins (The Mighty Mite). This continues to be true, perhaps a little less noticeably, throughout history. Mickey Mantle was "The Commerce Comet," Ted Williams was "The Splendid Splinter," Joe DiMaggio was "The Yankee Clipper," Honus Wagner was called "The Flying Dutchman," Frankie Frisch was called "The Fordham Flash," Stan Musial was "The Donora Greyhound." Carl Hubbell was known as "The Meal Ticket." There are quite a few medium-level stars who have nicknames in that form, like Carl Furillo (The Reading Rifle) and Dom DiMaggio (The Little Professor), but very few poor or mediocre players do. The use of the "The" implies a certain uniqueness on the part of the player named, and the adjective (the second word) serves to enhance that uniqueness. If more than three words are involved the name tends to acquire a comic tone (The Freshest Man on Earth, The Wild Horse of the Osage).

⚜1910: GLAD YOU NOTICED⚜

For the first forty plus years of major league baseball, a no-hitter had no particular significance. When Lee Richmond and John Montgomery Ward threw perfect games just a few days apart in 1880, the press took no particular note of it. When Henry Porter of Kansas City threw a no-hitter at Baltimore in June of 1888, a Kansas City paper reported the game the next day without commenting on the uniqueness of the event; a week later they observed that when Porter had pitched the game without giving up a hit in Baltimore, this was "believed to be the first time all season" that it had been done. They were wrong; Adonis Terry of Brooklyn had hurled a no-hitter ten days earlier.

As late as 1907, the no-hitter still meant little. When Frank Pfeffer of Boston threw a no-hitter on May 8 of that season, the summary of the game in the *New York Times* read "Pfeffer shut out Cincinnati without a hit or a run today and Boston won easily, 6 to 0. Runs came through bunching hits in four innings." That, and the box score, was all there was; it was the briefest account given to any game played that day.

Within a few years this would change; when Miles Main threw a no-hitter in the Federal League in 1915, the Kansas City paper reported that he had knocked on the door of the Hall of Fame and been admitted, presenting the no-hitter as his credentials. Why, how, and yet more precisely when the recognition developed is an interesting question. There may have been a single game in there somewhere that grabbed the public's imagination and started the whole thing, but more likely there wasn't. The *Reach Guide* began publishing a list of the season's most memorable games about then, and in 1911 they inaugurated a special feature on low-hit games—a feature so successful that it is still a part of the modern guides. My guess is that that was the lens which focused attention on outstanding pitching performances in general, of which the no-hitter of course was the king.

From our vantage, the question seems to be not how it developed, but how it could have taken so long to develop. It's such a perfect diversion for the early innings; although I have been to hundreds of ball games and have never seen a live no-hitter, I still think about it almost every time I'm at the park. I think about it when the first batter gets out or when he gets a hit, I think about it when one side or the other goes in order in the first, and I think about it whenever I look up at the scoreboard and see that 0 0 0. Each day the pitcher plays Russian roulette with sudden immortality, and each day he loses, and after the fourth inning it is all forgotten.

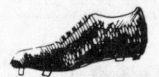

1911: JEFFS PFEFFER

The Pfeffer brothers, who pitched in the National League between 1905 and 1924, were named Francis Xavier Pfeffer and Edward Joseph Pfeffer, but they were both called "Jeff." Actually the older brother, Francis, was called "Big Jeff," and Edward, who was a huge man himself, was just called "Jeff." Big Jeff threw a no-hitter, but could never find his control and was never too successful. But Jeff was quite a pitcher, going 23–12, 19–14, 25–11, 17–13, 16–9, and 19–12 in various seasons.

THE CLASS OF ELEVEN

The 1911 season produced one of baseball's best rookie crops. It was led by Shoeless Joe Jackson, the only man to hit .400 as a rookie, and Pete Alexander, who led the N.L. in wins with twenty-eight without an inning of prior big-league experience, and it included some other pretty good players, such as Max Carey and Stuffy McInnis.

But that's nothing compared to the rookie crop that entered that year into the Baseball *Writing* Fraternity. It's really funny to look at the list of early members of the BBWAA. The charter members are, for the most part, a bunch of people whose names wouldn't mean a thing to you. They were joined in 1909 by several more people whose names don't mean anything, and in 1910 by a couple of guys named Harry Cross and Herman Wecke. Then seven people joined the association in 1911. Alphabetically, their names were Bill Brandt, Heywoud Broun, Sid Keener, Fred Lieb, Grantland Rice, Damon Runyon, and Irving Vaughan.

Wow.

∽BEST WORLD SERIES∾

The decade had two outstanding World Series, the 1911 World Series in which Home Run Baker earned his nickname by hitting two game-winning home runs, and the 1912 World Series, which was one of the greatest, and which I intend to recount here in unconscionable detail. The 1914 World Series, in which the red-hot Miracle Braves rolled over the supposedly unbeatable Athletics, was good in its own way, a series that is an excellent match for the 1969 Mets/Orioles matchup.

The 1913 *Spalding Guide* said that "No individual, whether player, manager, owner, critic or spectator who went through the 1912 World Series will ever forget it. There never was another like it . . . from the lofty perch of the 'bleacherite' it was a series crammed with thrills and gulps, cheers and gasps, pity and hysteria, dejection and wild exultation, recrimination and adoration, excuse and condemnation." Some of the bleacherites, actually, were not pleased, but more on that later.

In the first game, the Giants took a 2–0 lead in the third inning, the key hit being a double by Larry Doyle. Tris Speaker tripled and scored in the sixth to make it 2–1. But in the seventh, Doyle made a nice stop but couldn't recover his balance, in the process fumbling a possible double-play ball to set up a three-run inning and put the Red Sox up 4–2. The Giants had three straight hits (the last a double) with one out in the ninth, but Smokey Joe Wood, who was 34–5 that year, struck out the last two batters to preserve the 4–3 victory.

The Boston fans brought a band (the game was played in New York) and marched around the field in victory.

The second game was an eleven-inning, six–six tie, halted by darkness. The Giants made five errors and trailed 4–2 entering the eighth, when a routine fly ball bounced off Duffy Lewis' glove, setting up a three-run rally keyed by Red Murray's double. But in the bottom of the eighth, Lewis doubled—Red Murray crashed the fence trying to catch it, and lay inert on the field for some moments afterward—then scored to tie it up. Chief Meyers tripled and scored in the tenth to put the Giants back ahead, but in the bottom of the tenth Speaker tripled and scored—some writers insisted it should have been a home run—to even it up again. The game, *Spalding* reported, "was conspicuous because of the wonderfully good fielding of Doyle and Wagner. The former made two stops along the right-field line which seemed to be not far from superhuman."

How'd you like Game Two?

WALTER BARBARE

The 1915 *Reach Guide,* published after Barbare had played only fifteen major league games, said that several named observers "claim that Walter Barbare . . . is the best young infielder they have seen in years. [He] is a freak in build and endowed with nature's ball-playing weapons. He has abnormally long arms and wide hands, and possesses wonderful natural knowledge of batsmen. He never rests his hands upon his knees . . . but stands in a crouched position with his long arms swinging and his hands almost touching the ground. He reminds one of a gorilla and is remarkably fast in starting from this peculiar, but natural, position. He is a fast man on the bases and looks like a hard and natural hitter." Barbare hit .191 in 77 games that year, and played but 500 games in the major leagues, hitting .260 with only one home run.

Game Three was easy; the Giants scored two early and survived a ninth-inning charge to win 2–1. Josh Devore made a catch to end the game (with runners on second and third, mind you) that was the Sandy Amoros play of the pretelevision era, a play that many who saw it said was the greatest catch ever. Whether it was or wasn't, it turned victory into defeat for Boston, and knotted the series at one each.

Game Four was even easier, 3–1. It was 2–0 in the seventh when the Giants scored once and lost the tying run at the plate on a throw from right field. Smokey Joe Wood struck out eight, walked none, and won his second game of the series. Game Five was a pitcher's duel, Hugh Bediant beating Christy Mathewson 2–1. Game Six was a blowout, the Giants scoring five in the first to win, 5–2. Boston still led, three games to two.

There was an off day the day after that—the only off day of the series, which was played in nine days—and the Red Sox returned to Boston. They figured they had it. Smokey Joe Wood was ready to start. The Giants scored six in the first off Wood, and won it 11–4.

"No ingenuity of preparation, no prearranged plot of man," reported the *Spalding Guide,* "no cunningly devised theory of a World Series could have originated a finale equal to that of the eighth and deciding game . . . the New York players were champions of the World for nine and one-half innings. Within the next six minutes they had lost all the advantage which they had gained." The game was picketed, and successfully. A Boston executive, a warm human being, no doubt, and probably figuring it was going to be the last game of the year so who cared what they thought, decided to sell off the seats usually occupied by a group called the Royal Rooters, the same loud bunch who had sung "Tessie" to Honus Wagner a decade earlier. They organized a 300-man picket line of the game, holding the crowd for one of the greatest ball games ever played to 17,000 people (some say that Boston Mayor John Fitzgerald, "Honey Fitz," led the picket lines, but I don't know that that is correct).

The game was scoreless for two innings. There were men on in every frame, but none came across. In the third, Red Murray doubled with two out to drive home the first run; New York led, 1–0, In the fourth, Buck Herzog led off with a double that would have been a triple but for a special ground rule put in for the series, because of crowds that were supposed to be there but weren't. If it had been a triple he would have scored, and the Giants would have won the game. It wasn't. The score remained 1–0. In the fifth inning, Larry Doyle hit the ball into the seats, but Harry Hooper reached over and caught it. Bare-handed. It remained 1–0.

It was an odd pitcher's duel; there were men on base all over

the place. In the Boston seventh, Jake Stahl hit a pop fly ball that three New York players (Fletcher, Murray, and Snodgrass) let fall among them. He moved to second on a walk. With two out and two strikes on him, pinch hitter Olaf Henrickson ripped the ball right at third base. It hit the bag, bounded in the air and bounced back toward home plate, getting away so far that Stahl scored from second. Game tied, 1–1.

Smokey Joe Wood, kayoed the day earlier, entered the game for the pitcher, who had given way to Henrickson. No one scored in the eighth. No one scored in the ninth. With one out in the tenth, Red Murray doubled to left, and Fred Merkle singled him home. The Giants led, 2–1, in the tenth with Mathewson on the mound. Smokey Joe settled down to strike out Herzog, but Meyer smashed the ball back to the mound. Smokey Joe bare-handed it and threw him out at first, but the ball was hit so hard that Wood had to leave the game.

Key point: Smokey Joe Wood could hit. He hit .290 that year (.283 lifetime), with 13 doubles in 124 at bats. He was scheduled to lead off the bottom of the eleventh, and there was no way they were going to pinch hit Clyde Engle for him (Engle hit .234 with five doubles in 171 at bats). But Meyer's drive had blistered Wood's hand so that he couldn't hit, so Engle had to try it.

Engle hit a long fly to center field. Snodgrass played it perfectly until it hit his glove and bounced away. Engle wound up on second base. Harry Hooper then ripped an apparent triple to center field, but Snodgrass went back and robbed him, in a catch variously described as "magnificent," "miraculous," and "even better than the speedy play of Devore in the third game." Engle held second.

Mathewson, who had pitched brilliantly in the series but lost one and tied one, stayed in. He walked Steve Yerkes, the Boston second baseman. Tris Speaker came to the plate—and he got him. Speaker hit a high pop-up down the first-base line. Mathewson, Merkle (first base), and Meyers (catcher) converged on it, Mathewson screaming, "Chief! Chief! Chief!" Chief didn't hear him. The ball dropped, foul.

Speaker hit a single, tying the score and putting runners on first and third. Larry Gardner flied to left. Devore fired home, but too late. Yerkes had scored the winning run.

Within the nine days, every player on either team was perfectly positioned to be the goat of the series, or the hero of the series. Smokey Joe Wood, who six minutes earlier had been in a position to lose the last two games of the series, wound up as one hero, with three wins among the four Boston victories. Snodgrass wound up with goat horns, though he had done no more to earn them than a dozen other players; the music simply stopped when he didn't have a chair. For *the* hero of the series, the *Reach Guide* (which occasionally listed the heroes of each World Series) listed Hugh Bediant, who started against Matty in Games Five and Eight. He, too, could as easily have been listed as the goat; he left the final game trailing.

For the rest of the decade, the World Series weren't much. The American League just kept beating the National League teams severely about the head and shoulders, and after a while it ceased to be interesting. The Detroit teams had lost the World Series after winning the American League, 1907–1909, so it was a redemption of sorts when the Philadelphia A's crushed the Cubs in five games in 1910. The Giants were still the favorites in the 1911 contest, and it was still a surprise when the Athletics finished them off in six games, winning the last one 13–2. The American League won again in 1912, but they had their hands full. But then Philadelphia crushed the Giants again in 1913, the Red Sox took a quick (though tight) five-game series from the Phillies in 1915, and beat Brooklyn in five again in 1916. The White Sox beat the Giants in six in 1917, and the Red Sox beat the Cubs in six in 1918. Is it any wonder the White Sox were a heavy favorite in 1919?

QUISENBERRY 1

Ernie Shore made his major league debut in Boston on June 20, 1912, as a member of the New York Giants. John McGraw entered the ninth that day with a 21–2 lead, and he figured that was a safe time to find out what the kid could do. Shore surrendered eight hits and ten runs, reducing the lead to 21–12, but eventually got out of the inning and was released, not necessarily in that order. It was his only National League appearance.

When compiling the Macmillan *Baseball Encyclopedia* in 1968, the research group credited Ernie Shore with having saved the game.

QUISENBERRY 2

That was not to be the only strange save that Shore would have, among his career total of five. Shore survived that inaugural shellacking and resurfaced as one of the starters on the great Boston Red Sox staff of 1914–17. In 1917 Shore made two relief appearances, and his record shows fifteen relief innings, one earned run, one win, no losses, and one save. We know what one of those games was, right? Five years and three days after the auspicious, Shore took over for the ejected Babe Ruth with nobody out in the first, faced twenty-six batters and retired twenty-seven for a perfect-plus game. That means that in

1914: A BRIEF, SHINING MOMENT

The Boston Braves drew the smallest crowds of any major league team in the first decade of this century, but when they caught fire and won the World Series in 1914, the fans turned out. The Braves drew 383,000 that year, the highest in the National League; in fact, four of the other seven teams that year drew less than half as many. Even so, the Braves were second fiddle in Boston, where the Red Sox led all of baseball with 481,000 clicks of the turnstile. The Braves attendance stayed pretty good for two more years after that, but then collapsed; and for the decade as a whole, as well as for the last one and the next one, the Braves were baseball's least-watched team.

his other relief appearance that year, Shore pitched six innings, allowed one earned run, and was credited with a save.

Now here's the question for you:

How do you pitch six innings and get a save?

JOHNNY EVERS

🦀 1911: LIVE WIRE 🦀

Johnny Evers, the 125-pound middleman of Tinkers to Evers to Chance, was known as "The Crab" because of his intensity. He was a Billy Martin–type; many didn't like him, but nobody questioned his desire to win. He missed a good part of the 1911 season after having a nervous breakdown.

It was said of Evers that he was so full of electricity that he could not wear a watch. It was a common practice in this time to give watches in testimonial dinners, and he was given several fine timepieces, but when you put a watch on Johnny Evers' body it would not keep accurate time. So he'd always give the nice ones away and buy a cheap one, and throw it away after a few months. Even so, he often had to ask for the time.

1912: 36 TRIPLES

Owen Wilson's record of 36 triples in a season is one of the most remarkable standards in baseball, and one of the game's greatest flukes. Wilson played regularly in the major leagues for seven seasons, during which his triples totals read 7, 12, 13, 12, 36, 14, 12. The record for home runs in a season is 61, but other people have hit 60, 59, 58, 58, and 56. Eight minor league players have hit more than 61 home runs in a season (actually, seven; Joe Hauser did it twice). The record for doubles is 67, but other people have had 64, 64, 63, 62, and 60. The minor league record for doubles in a season is 100. The major league record for hits in a season is 257, but other people have had 254, 254, 253, 250, and 250. The minor league record for hits in a season is 325. But no player in this century has ever challenged Wilson's record for triples. The ten highest totals read 36, 26, 26, 26, 25, 25, 25, 24, 23, and 23. No other player in history, either in the minor leagues or the majors, either in this century or last, has ever hit 36 triples in one season.

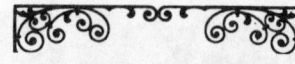

LARRY McLEAN

Although three pitchers who didn't pitch fifty innings among them are listed at 230, the biggest player of the time was a lean, mean, fightin' machine named (would I make this up?) Larry McLean. His legal name was John Bannerman McLean, and he was born in Cambridge, Massachusetts, and grew to be 6'5", 228 pounds give or take a few. He played thirteen years in the major leagues, hitting .262, and hit .500 (6-for-12) in the 1913 World Series.

According to the 1922 *Reach Guide,* "McLean was a man of great size, a convivial disposition and a bad temper when under the influence of liquor, which led him into many more or less serious rows during his baseball career . . . [after the] 1913 World Series, his habits were such that Manager McGraw was forced to release him." After that he was reportedly connected with the movie business for several years.

On March 24, 1921, McLean was shot and killed by a bartender in a near-beer saloon in Boston's South End. His friend Jack McCarthy, who also played in the National League for several years, was injured in the fracas. The bartender was given a light sentence, it being shown that McLean and McCarthy were the aggressors in the incident.

LARRY McLEAN, PHOTO BY CHRISTY MATHEWSON

❧ATTENDANCE: A DECADE OF NO GROWTH❧

Attendance had reached a high-water mark of 7,266,000 in 1909, but never got back to that level within this decade. Attendance started out well enough, averaging a little over 6 million a year from 1910 to 1913, which is acceptable in view of the fact that, following the terrific pennant races of 1908 and 1909, there were no pennant races of any merit during this period. But in 1914, attendance collapsed, dropping below 4.5 million. The 1915 *Reach Guide* gives two long paragraphs of reasons for the decline, one set of "internal causes of decline" and one of "external causes of decline." Many of the "internal" causes that Francis Richter cites seem petty and not particularly relevant to the question of why attendance was 6.36 million in 1913 and 4.45 million in 1914; he lists a "natural recession of interest and enthusiasm after a really wonderful continuous retention for nearly a decade . . . a disposition to change base ball from a gripping sport to a mere amusement in competition with more varied and cheaper amusements . . . the steadily increasing cost of base ball to its patrons . . . the gradual elimination of its staunchest friend, the 'sun-god' of the bleachers . . . squabbles over excessive player salaries . . . the mercenary spirit displayed by the players." The external causes are somewhat more convincing. These include "Political unrest and revolution in the nation . . . the constant harassment and depression of the country's big and little business . . . the competition of such cheap daytime amusements as the 'movies' furnish . . . the ticker-service to the saloons and pool rooms, where the games are read about and gambled upon, instead of being witnessed." There are many others, including the competition from the third league, the Federal League. One might be tempted to say that the Federal League was the key, but one should note that attendance declines were almost as severe in the cities that had no new competition as in those that had it, and also it was an equally disastrous year for the minor leagues, which should not have been thus affected. Attendance recovered somewhat after the collapse of the Federal League, but as it began to move back near the 7 million mark, World War I came and shortened the seasons. Attendance for the decade as a whole was up very slightly from the previous ten years, but it was 22 percent less than it would have been had the decade simply held the pace that had been established in 1908 and 1909.

1914: THE OLD FOG SCAM

The Memphis Park in the Southern League, like many parks of the era, minor and major league, had several signs painted on it: Hit this sign and win a suit, Knock it Here and win a quart of Red Eye, Bump this fence and get a dozen Never-Wear-Out socks, etc. Mickey Finn, who managed the Memphis team in 1914, claimed that one time a fog moved in so thick you couldn't see the outfield fence, and one of his outfielders hit a drive out there somewhere and collected a suit, two bottles of booze, the sox, a hat and a pound of coffee.

Many hitters of the time claimed that these outfield signs were distracting, and interfered with their hitting. This poem, unattributed, appeared in the 1915 *Reach Guide*:

The fence signs at the ballpark are yellow, green and red,
The fierce glare queers the hitting; the batting eye goes dead.
It seems to hurt the Giants even more than other nines,
But Cobb and old Sam Crawford—they just don't believe in signs!

NEW STATISTICS

Under the leadership of John Heydler, secretary and later president of the National League, the statistical picture of the game came into much greater focus in this era. Earned Run Average became an official statistic in the National League in 1912, the American in 1913; it was widely praised as the fairest way to evaluate a pitcher, and its acceptance was quick. I am, on the other hand, a little confused about a couple of points relating to it. For one thing, the *Spalding Guide* as early as 1883 had carried a category called "Runs Earned by Opponents," sometimes expressed also as a percentage ("Average Runs Earned by Opponent" in some cases, "Earned Run Average" in others). What was that earned run average? Was it total runs? Doesn't seem to have been; One Arm Daily, shown in the modern encyclopedias with an 1883 ERA of 2.42, is listed there with 1.36. What is it? Is it runs scored only with the aid of hits, which was a later definition of an earned run? Anybody know?

Another thing: *The Baseball Encyclopedia* has a note under "Changes in Playing and Scoring Rules" that says "1917 Earned Runs also include runs scored by the aid of stolen bases." When I noticed this I was delighted. I thought, "Aha. I can use that. I can use that to figure out how many runs were scored by the aid of stolen bases." As an aside, throughout much of this period, catchers were sometimes charged with errors by some official scorers for allowing bases to be stolen —that is, if the scorer felt that the catcher had time to make the throw, he would charge the catcher with an error if he didn't get the guy.

Anyway, if earned runs in 1916 did *not* include those stolen with the help of stolen bases, and those of 1917 did include them, then the percentage of runs that were earned should have increased in 1917 in proportion to the number of runs that were scored with the aid of a stolen base, right? Makes sense to me. If the change in the percentage of runs that were scored as "earned" was large, then it would indicate that many runs resulted from the stolen bases; if it was small, that would indicate that few runs resulted from stolen bases.

So I checked to see what those percentages were. Guess what: The percentage of runs that were scored as earned actually went *down* in 1917. In 1916, 76.5% of all major league runs were scored as earned by the ERAs listed in Macmillan (6800 of

8889); in 1917, this dropped to 74.9% (6707 or 8949).

This, of course, doesn't make any sense, and it suggests that there is something going on here that I don't quite understand. Even I don't think so little of the stolen base as to suggest that it would not even register on the percentage of runs that were earned. Does this mean that the editors went back and recomputed all those earned run averages? Doesn't look like it; the ERAs shown in the Macmillan for 1916 are the same as those appearing in the 1917 *Reach Guide*. Was the change effected in some other year, not 1917? The earned percentages from 1913 through 1919 read 75.4, 73.1, 74.5, 76.5, 74.9, 76.4, and 79.0; if there's a line drawn in there, I don't see it.

I have a copy of the 1916 *Spalding Guide* and the 1917 *Reach*. The rules as appearing in the 1916 *Guide* (which are the same as those appearing in a 1915 *Reach Guide*) offer no definition of an earned run, and indeed make no reference to earned runs that I can see. The rules as appearing in 1917 include a "Definition of Runs Earned Off Pitcher," and the definition does say that the runs scored with the aid of a stolen base are earned. But before that, they are silent on the issue, and nowhere that I can find does it say anything about the rules being changed in this regard. I suspect that what may have happened was that an oversight in an announcement about the earned run in 1913 or 1914 may have been misinterpreted later to mean that runs resulting from stolen bases were unearned—but they were never scored that way. Official scoring in this period is so lax that it is quite possible that some scorers were scoring it one way and some the other, both before and after the ruling was changed. Box scores from different newspapers sometimes scored the same plays differently. It wasn't like it is now.

Anyway, to return to the general subject of new statistics. From 1913 to 1916, the American League recorded runs scored by batters broken down into earned and unearned runs, a silly idea which was stopped after four years. Both leagues started figuring out how many batters a pitcher had faced, but this was done differently in the two leagues from about 1912 until the seventies. Counts of sacrifice hits allowed by pitchers—a truly minor statistic— appeared in the National League stats in 1916, and still do.

Another experiment in this era that didn't take was an attempt to sort errors into types of effect. The box scores of the 1912 World Series in the 1913 *Spalding Guide* contain the categories "First Base on Errors," "Fumbles," "Muffed Flies," "Muffed Foul Fly," "Muffed Thrown Ball," and "Wild Throw." "First Base on Errors" was given only for teams, not players. Only two things stuck from the attempt to detail defensive performance with more specific information: "Double Play" totals, and "Passed Balls." Both became official statistics in the early twenties.

I suppose that much of this strikes you as arcane and difficult to deal with, but I, for one, wish they had stuck with it. The basic idea of statistical records is that they are supposed to describe the action. I have many complaints about the concept of an error, but one of the main ones is that it does not describe what happens, even in terms of how it changes the game. A "single" can be a 40-foot bleeder or it can rocket off the wall in Fenway Park, but all singles have one thing in common: They all take a batter and put him at first base. That is the minimum expectation for a category, that it tell you what happened as a result. But an "error" can be a three-base misjudgment of an easy fly ball, and put a runner on third, or it can be a wild throw that moves a man from first to second. It can even do nothing at all; an error is often charged on a foul fly that leaves the batter standing at home plate. I once saw Willie Wilson charged with an error in Detroit for allowing a runner to go from first to third on a single; the official scorer thought he should have made a play there, so he handed out an error. "Muffed foul fly" is a far better description of a play than is "Error," and for that reason, if we had those statistics we would know far more than we do about the defensive skills of players, and about the role that defense plays in the creation or prevention of runs. That's what statistics are supposed to do.

Batters' strikeout and walk totals first appeared in the National League statistics for 1910. The *Reach Guide* passed these along with something less than great enthusiasm: "Secretary John A. Heydler . . . gave to the press an official tabulation of the number of bases on balls given to, and strikeouts by, each National League player," Editor Francis Richter wrote. "The figures are of no special value or importance—first, because the number of strikeouts affords no real line on the player's batting ability, especially under the foul-strike rule; and, second, because bases on balls are solely charged to the pitcher, beyond the control of the batsman, and therefore not properly to be considered in connection with his individual work, except as they may indicate in a vague way his ability to 'wait out' or 'work' the pitcher."

Judge him not too harshly; remember that many people

as recently as five years ago still took essentially the same view of walks as a hitter's statistic, even after there had been data available to the public for seventy years that showed it to be complete nonsense. Richter was writing as a man who had never seen statistics showing some players receiving 100 bases on balls in a season and others 20. When George Stovall drew 6 walks in 145 games (565 at bats) in 1909, no one other than perhaps Ernest Lanigan and Al Munro Elias was even aware of it. Remember also that people even today, and by "people" I mean statisticians and some of the brightest men in the game, often have very, very, fuzzy, ill-considered ideas about baseball statistics, and hold those ideas sacred. In the same way, you and I have fuzzy, ill-considered ideas about other subjects. (I always thought that you could make up a good series of books there, such as *The Political Vaporizings of Albert Einstein, The Complete Works of Sigmund Freud When Writing on Subjects About Which He Knew Absolutely Nothing and Would Not Shut Up, The Ruminations and Reflections of Tolstoy as a Crazy Old Man,* and *Isaac Newton's Stupid Experiments That Had No Basis in Reason or Common Sense.* Just with those four subjects you'd have about a hundred volumes.) History will find it easy to ignore them; you and I may have to work at it.

1917: ESCAPE FROM ST. LOUIS

On September 5, 1917, owner Phil Ball of the St. Louis Browns charged that the Browns' players were deliberately playing badly in an attempt to escape the Browns and their manager, Fielder Jones. "Every $1,000 I lose on the Browns this season will cost the ballplayers $100," he was quoted as saying. "Salaries will be cut next season. These fellows are all wrong when they think they will get away from the Browns by laying down on the job. Because they dislike their manager is no reason the Browns should not put forth their best efforts."

Three days later, Ball's double-play combination filed suit against him. Shortstop Doc Lavan (who, by the way, really was a doctor) and second baseman Del Pratt (who really was a ballplayer) filed separate suits, each asking $50,000, charging that Ball had slandered them by alleging "that the plaintiffs were unfaithful and dishonest in their profession of base ball."

Among what seems like hundreds of lawsuits in baseball that decade, this was surely the most justified. The other suits were all about money; Lavan and Pratt sued to defend their integrity. But it had a side benefit. Both players were traded that winter.

1917: ANOTHER BASTION OF CLEAN LIVING FALLS TO SIN

On August 21, 1917, Judge R. E. Blake of the circuit court in Tennessee refused a request by the state attorney general to issue an injunction against Sunday ball in Nashville. The judge declined to overturn the decision of a lower court, the magistrate of which had attended a Sunday ball game and concluded that the game was not a public nuisance, as the attorney general had asserted.

✂️ UNIFORM CHANGES, 1910–20 ✂️

The big news for this decade on the fashion scene is final confirmation on the stirrups issue . . . I think. A 1914 photo of Shoeless Joe Jackson (with shoes) in the *Ultimate Baseball Book* provides a close-up view, and you can definitely see the two distinct parts. The lower part of the stirrup matches the color of the socks underneath, while the uppers (from ankle to knee) are dark. It's possible with the smaller photographs from the guides that I could have missed stirrups galloping onto the scene earlier. But I think we can safely let this date stand as being close to the first time that stirrups were used. Most teams were still using the traditional dark solid stockings, or perhaps the striped variety. Stirrups were apparently adopted to help prevent a player from being spiked and losing a leg to blood poisoning in the days before tetanus shots.

Other developments came mostly in the form of refinements. The collars became smaller. Many more uniforms featured a short, stand-up collar, similar to that of a Nehru jacket. A contrasting band around the neck and sleeve was common, as well as a bit of trim work up the sides of the pants and around the neckline. An ad in one guide proudly offers a uniform with "Gusset Ventilated Sleeves," which allow the player greater movement and better ventilation. The belt loops on the left and right sides were elongated, called tunnel loops; the loops of today are much the same. Belts became narrower.

The basic style of the uniform was by now traditional, and much the same from team to team. The next area for experimentation was the team name. In 1908 the Cubs put "Cubs" on their uniform, putting an end to the time in which nicknames were informal and subject to change at the whim of a sportswriter. By the middle of the teens Philadelphia, the two Chicago teams, the Red Sox and the Pirates used their team nicknames on their uniforms; by the end of the decade the count was up to nine. In 1919, the Chicago Nationals displayed three variations of their name on different uniforms. On one, "Chicago Cubs" is spelled out in full; on a second there is a large *C* with a little cubbie inside; and on a third, a rectangular *C* encloses the letters *UBS*. Chicago seems to have been a hotbed for this kind of innovation, because the other team in town showed similar diversity. A big *S* on the left side of the shirt enclosed an *O* in the top loop and an *X* in the bottom. The big *S* is variously decorated with little balls or bats or socks. Flags on the sleeve denote either postwar patriotism or league loyalty. The Washington team also displayed an American flag on the left breast pocket, with a weak-looking *W* on the sleeve. The Philadelphia White Elephants attached a little elephant on the left breast pocket, and the Denver Bears used a bear symbol in the same place.

In 1911 the Yankees and the Athletics were given permission by the league to use for their home uniform a white flannel cloth with "fine stripes." But there were earlier instances of pinstripes—the Detroit Wolverines in 1888 wore white shirts with thin stripes, dark pants; St. Louis in 1910 and the Cubs about the same time did also. In the *Ultimate Baseball Book* a photo of Larry Lajoie shows him in a Cleveland pinstriped uniform; no date is given but a blurrier version of the same photo, much smaller, appears in the 1910 *Spalding Guide,* meaning that it was taken no later than 1909.

—Susie

BEST MINOR LEAGUE TEAM: MINNEAPOLIS MILLERS

The Minneapolis Millers of 1910–11 were the outstanding minor league team of this time. The star of the team was Gavvy Cravath, who then was at his peak, and was one of the finest players in baseball at any level, as he would clearly establish when he finally got back to the major leagues, in his thirties. Cravath was a star with the Los Angeles team in the Pacific Coast League as a youngster, and was sold to Boston (American) in 1908. He hit pretty well with the Red Sox, really; he hit .256 and slugged .383 in a season where the league marks were .239 and .304. But the Red Sox at that moment were an aggressive organization, buying a lot of young talent from all over the country, and they eventually had to make a choice among Cravath, Tris Speaker and Harry Hooper. Cravath got off to a slow start with the White Sox in 1909 and found himself back in the minors, at Minneapolis.

Cravath was the dominant player in a darn good minor league. In 1911 he won the batting title at .363, led the league with 53 doubles, and hit 29 home runs, the most of any player anywhere in organized baseball. He stole 33 bases. His teammates included two other big major

league stars. One was Rube Waddell, who had drunk himself prematurely out of the major leagues, but was still winning when he departed (15–14 with a very bad St. Louis team in 1909–10). Rube was 20–17 for Minneapolis in 1911, which was far below the average of the team, but he was second in the league in strikeouts. The other was Sam Leever, who the Pirates had decided was too old, but who had had the best winning per-

centage in the major leagues in the years 1900–1909, and had departed the majors with a streak of eleven straight winning seasons. Sam went 7–4.

The team was almost entirely composed of former and/or future major leaguers. The left fielder, second in the league in hitting in 1911 at .356, was Claude Rossman, thirty, who had hit .294 with 33 doubles and 13 triples for the American League champion Tigers in 1908 (he was sixth in

GAVVY CRAVATH, AFTER HE HAD RETIRED FROM BASEBALL AND BECOME A JUDGE

the A.L. in batting that year). At second base was Jimmy Williams, thirty-four, an outstanding player in both major leagues from 1899 to 1909, who left the majors after a below par season in 1909. At third was Hobe Ferris (same story, but not quite as good a player). Dave Altizer was the shortstop, and Otis Clymer the third outfielder. Most of these players were good, major league regulars in their mid-thirties; the poorest regulars probably were Warren Gill, the first baseman, and Frank Owen, the catcher.

The pitching staff also included Nick Altrock (three straight twenty-win seasons in the American League, 1904–1906), Pug Cavet, and Art Loudell.

That was the 1911 team. The 1910 team did not have quite as many big names, but had a better record. Cravath was there in 1910, though he didn't have quite as big a year, but Waddell and Leever weren't. The 1910 team got a big year out of Long Tom Hughes (31–12), who had gone 18–14 in the American League in 1908, and who then went back to the majors. They also had Jesse Tannehill on the staff for a while, and, given better years from Altrock, Altizer, Ferris and some others, finished 107–61, seven games better than the 1911 team (99–66).

The Minneapolis team, a middle-of-the-pack American Association team before 1909, had always collected players from the major leagues, which was not unusual at that time. About 1909, they started concentrating on getting the best of those available. While today it seems strange that a minor league team would have so many good players, the question of how they built their team is no different, really, than the question of how the Red Sox or any other major league team of the time built their strength. They made good trades and put out the money when they had to.

1916: OLD BALLPLAYERS NEVER DIE

"Base ball today is not what it should be. The players do not try to learn all the fine points of the game as in the days of old, but simply try to get by. They content themselves if they get a couple of hits every day or play an errorless game. The first thing they do each morning is to get the papers and look at the hit and error columns. If they don't see them, some sportswriter gets terrific panning, of which he never hears.

"When I was playing ball, there was not a move made on the field that did not cause every one of the opposing team to mention something about it. All were trying to figure why it had been done and to watch and see what the result would be. That same move could never be pulled again without every one on our bench knowing just what was going to happen.

"I feel sure that the same conditions do not prevail today. The boys go out to the plate, take a slam at the ball, pray that they'll get a hit, and let it go at that. They are not fighting as in the days of old. Who ever heard of a gang of ball players after losing going into the clubhouse singing at the top of their voices? That's what happens every day after the games at the present time.

"In my days, the players went into the clubhouse after a losing game with murder in their hearts. They would have thrown out any guy on his neck if they had even suspected him of intentions of singing. In my days the man who was responsible for having lost a game was told in a man's way by a lot of men what a rotten ball player he really was. It makes me weep to think of the men of the old days who played the game and the boys of today. It's positively a shame, and they are getting big money for it, too."
—Bill Joyce

As quoted in the 1916 *Spalding Base Ball Guide*. Joyce was a third baseman and manager in the 1890s.

A VERY GOOD MOVIE COULD BE MADE ABOUT

One is tempted to say that the Black Sox scandal, which is a fascinating story, would make a great movie; I'm not so sure that it would. It is engrossing to read about, and certainly a script about it would involve many scenes of great potential. The problem with making a movie of it is that of engaging the emotions of the viewer. Unlike a book, a movie is more something you experience than something you learn about, and as such, for a movie to work, one must, as a viewer, share in the experience of one of the characters. Since this story almost has to focus on the players who threw the games, that creates problems; it is difficult to ask an audience to share the feelings of the conspirators. One might view it from the standpoint of, say, Buck Weaver, who is trying to negotiate an impossible straight without breaking faith with anyone. From his standpoint, it is basically a fight to deal with what is happening to him and maintain his integrity. But this presents too many opportunities to distort and fictionalize the story, for it is not basically a story about Buck Weaver, and if you're not going to tell the story the way it happened, then why

not just have an honest work of fiction?

The scene of the 1918 World Series is similarly magnetic, but presents similar problems: Where do the viewer's sympathies lie, and how do you end it leaving him feeling that something has happened?

Perhaps an entertaining, quirky, off-beat movie could be made about the Boston Braves' fight to win the National League pennant in 1914 with a ragtag collection of nobodies and cast-offs. It is certainly much less of a story, but it is a story that the good guys win, and the problems are, for that reason, much more manageable.

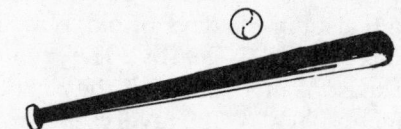

REACTION TO THE FIRST VOLLEY

When Babe Ruth hit twenty-nine home runs in 1919, the record was thought to be one that would stand for a long time. The 1920 *Spalding Guide* opined that "Perhaps, and most likely, Ruth will not be so successful in 1920. The pitchers will eye him with more than ordinary caution and they will twist their fingers into knots to get more curve and still more curve on the ball. They will give one another private little tips." The editor, John Foster, also penned this verse:

> King of the Realm of Swat,
>   Omnipotent in the Land of Slug;
> You surely set a mark
>   At which others will plug—and plug.
> To beat that "29"
>   Will take some breadth of shoulder,
> And when they put a "30" up;
>   Well—we'll most likely be some older.

Ruth had hit only seven home runs by the end of June that year, but hit twenty-two over the last three months, including fourteen after August 14.

NEW STADIUMS

The building of new and impressive stadiums continued apace as the decade opened. Comiskey Park opened in 1910, and was promptly declared "the finest Ball Park in the United States, which means the finest in the world" by the *Reach Guide.* It seated 48,600 people (36,000 stands, 12,600 bleachers) and was constructed at a cost of $750,-000. The new Polo Grounds, the old ones having been destroyed by fire, were rebuilt into the largest baseball stadium in the country in 1911, though at its opening it did not receive, or deserve, the same barrels of praise that were carried to the other new parks. The Yankees moved in with the Giants in 1913.

Boston had a park war. Fenway Park opened in 1912; John Fitzgerald, grandfather of JFK, threw out the first ball at its dedication. Fenway was not large when it was built (about 27,000), and would quickly become tiny. In 1914, when the Braves won the pennant, the Red Sox invited them to play their World Series home games in Fenway, which could accommodate larger crowds than the old South End Grounds, where the Braves played. The Braves accepted, but immediately began building the huge,

bland, Braves Field, which opened on August 18, 1915. (Legend has it that a dozen horses and mules were buried alive in a cave-in during construction, and lay beneath the third-base line as long as ball was played there.) The Red Sox then won the pennant in 1915, and the Braves invited them to come play the World Series in Braves Field, which seated 40,000 and would hold more. The Red Sox accepted.

National Park in Washington was destroyed by fire in 1911 and rebuilt in only eighteen days; with a number of remodelings, it stayed on the scene until the sixties. Crosley Field in Cincinnati was also destroyed by fire in 1911, and was rebuilt and rededicated May 18, 1912. As attendance declined, the parks became less ambitious. Ebbets Field, small but gorgeous, opened in 1913, as did Navin Field (now Tiger Stadium) in Detroit. When it opened it was a single-decked stadium seating 23,000. When the Federal League started in 1914 they had several new parks, the most important of which were Weegham Park in Chicago, which became Wrigley Field, and Terrapin Park in Baltimore, where the International League Baltimore Orioles, the greatest of minor league

teams, played until the 1940s.

And that was it. Baseball looked around at what it had done, and it was very, very proud. Though some were much less impressive than others, in 1916 every major league team except the Phillies was playing in a concrete-and-steel park less than ten years old. The teams were tied down then; you don't just walk away from a $750,000 investment. The parks not only stood but improved with age, and with a few exceptions there would be no more for forty years. Those parks defined baseball in that era. The Pirates played the way that they could play the best in spacious Forbes Field; the Dodgers and Giants built for power to accommodate the Polo Grounds and Ebbets Field. By the time they began to think about needing new parks, the investment involved in constructing one had become massive. (Can you imagine a city building two major league parks in three years today, as Boston did from 1912–1915?) Baseball had been living in apartments since the time it began; now each team had its own home. It would be many years before anyone in baseball was ready to leave home.

A DECADE WRAPPED IN GREED

There are three essential news stories of Ty Cobb's decade, in each of which there are buried many dollar signs. The first of these is the founding of the Player's Fraternity in the closing days of the season of 1912. This organization started well. President David Fultz, a religious man, gained respect from all sides for the professionalism with which he conducted his business, and in reviewing the 1914 season was able to report that the organization "has made remarkable progress, both in increased membership and in concessions gained for its members . . . a large majority of the sporting writers have given us very flattering notices." Players who were veterans of ten seasons or more gained the right to have an outright release when their teams were through with them, and could not be optioned to the minors without consent.

In the winter of 1913–14, Fultz declared an embargo on contract signing to gain leverage in one negotiation, and received the needed compliance. This, too, was unfortunate, for it gave the impression that the Fraternity had more muscle than it ever really did. Holding out is easy in the winter time, and it would soon become obvious that the Fraternity was carrying an unloaded weapon. The organization concentrated much of its work on trying to secure gains for players who were released, sold, traded, or optioned between teams, and thus had its largest impact at the minor league level. This was a deliberate strategy on the part of Fultz, who recognized that the structure of the game was a pyramid, with the largest numbers buried at the bottom. It was not an unwise strategy, but it was to prove an unfortunate one, for in the coming wars minor leagues dropped like tulips in a spring hailstorm, sending frightened minor leaguers scurrying peaceably into the arms of their employers.

The second news story was not a relative of the first, but the two quickly became friends. In 1914 the Federal League set up shop, attempting to compete as a third major. For two years salaries boomed and the National Commission—the forerunner of the Commissioner's Office —looked left and right and decided, with that unerring instinct for the physics of power plays that major league owners had from 1875 to 1969, that the threat from the left was one they could live with; they issued recognition to the Fraternity and began to schedule meetings with them.

The Federal League folded after two years, the National Commission stopped meeting with the Fraternity, and major league players realized suddenly that they were as powerless as before. In the end, the Federal League killed the Player's Fraternity, for as a player's salary went from $4,000 to $12,000 and back to $4,000, the infant Fraternity stood by, helpless to stop it, and was crushed by the scattering anger.

In the muck of this there were innumerable lawsuits. I should make an accounting of them, but I haven't the heart for it. On opening day, 1915, the Kansas City paper expressed relief that "the umpires have taken the indicators away from the Judges." It is a feeling which a fan of the 1970s could easily understand, and in the seventies we had but a taste of it; this decade got the full meal. There was the Hageman case, the Kraft case, the Terrapins case, the Johnson case (Cincinnati versus Kansas City) . . . players sued owners, owners sued players, players sued players, teams sued teams, leagues sued teams, Curly sued Moe, Moe sued Larry, Larry sued Curly and they all got together and sued the cameraman; Lord, it was an awful time, and then the war started.

World War I came about, I am told, because the expansionist dreams of the imperial powers reached the limits of the earth and began to crush against one another; when there were no more territories to be claimed and conquered, the great powers began to fight over the ones already in tow. It was a greedy time; there's no other way to put it. Remember how the decade started? In 1910 the Chalmer's company decided to give a car to the batting champion, and you would have thought it was made of gold, the things they did for it. The Browns' third baseman played ten feet behind third base while Nap Lajoie dropped seven straight bunt singles in front of him, trying to cheat Ty Cobb out of the automobile; Ban Johnson, seeking an essential truth in lieu of true facts, made up a couple of extra hits for Cobb and declared him the champion anyway, and Chalmer's gave them a car apiece. In discussing the decline of the Detroit team that year, the *Reach Guide* observed that "it is believed that factional troubles also existed, which were apparently augmented by rows growing out of Cobb's personal ambition and his desire to win an automobile offered as a batting prize." Of the ten greatest players in baseball history—you pick 'em—Ty Cobb was the only one marked by greed.

The *Spalding Guide*s of the period feature recurring headlines that, stumbled over in isolation, provoke a laugh:

Base Ball in France
Base Ball Booming in Australia
Base Ball in the Philippines
Base Ball Around the World
Base Ball in Yucatan
Base Ball in the Canal Zone
Base Ball in Guatemala

But Albert Spalding was quite in earnest about these headlines, for, having completed a virtual monopoly of the sporting goods market in the United States, he was quite intent upon spreading the game of baseball to every corner of the earth where a man might have two nickles to spend on a bat or a glove.

When attendance collapsed in 1914, these expansionist goals, in baseball, were suddenly focused on a diminishing universe. The 1970s in baseball were a greedy decade, but whereas baseball in the seventies was booming— the owners were unhappy because the players were consuming *marginal* revenues— baseball in the teens was collapsing, leaving the players (their appetites whetted by a brief, unilateral prosperity) and owners fighting over the pieces of a shrinking pie.

It was bound to get ugly, and it did. The third major story of the decade was a product of the unhappy marriage of the first two. The players started selling ball games.

It is not my intention—far from it—to make apologies for the dishonest ballplayers.

But there are two things that you have to see to understand what happened. Number one, there was a generation of players to whom baseball made a lot of promises, which it didn't keep. And number two, every baseball headline in the entire decade has a dollar sign attached to it. Every one. The great infield of the time was called the "$100,000 infield." The label was intended as a figure of speech, but Connie Mack took it literally, and the members of this great infield were priced and sold around the league. Marty O'Toole was called "the $22,000 beauty." Stars and superstars—the biggest stars in the game, including Babe Ruth, were auctioned from one set of fans to another for whatever they would bring, and then ordered to report to camp for a fifth or a tenth of that amount.

It is a hard thing to know that another man is making money off of your labor, and has no intention of dealing fairly with you. This is not to say that Joe Jackson or Happy Felsch or Heinie Zimmerman were not guilty of their own crimes, because they were. But the arch-villain of this villainous era was Charles Albert Comiskey. He had no reason in the world not to deal fairly with his players. The White Sox drew the largest crowds in baseball in this period— even larger than the Giants— yet the White Sox were one of the lowest-paying teams.

Comiskey held all the power in the relationship, and he had to rub their noses in it.

Other than the Black Sox, many or even most of the dishonest players—at least those who were exposed—were refugees from the Federal League. Heinie Zimmerman had been an officer of the Fraternity. It wasn't young, reckless ballplayers who got involved with the gamblers, but the sour veterans of the decade's bright beginnings. They all wanted the money, and they all wanted it all.

The game was saved by two men. One was Comiskey's one-time ally, now his bitterest enemy, Ban Johnson. The other was a man Comiskey could never have comprehended, a man with a great lust for everything *except* money. Put Joe Jackson in the Hall of Fame? How about if we kick Comiskey out? Bury them all in a common grave, and put up a marker with an eleven-word epitaph. They all wanted the money, and they all wanted it all.

A HISTORY OF PLATOONING

Who invented platooning? Where does it come from? When did it become common? What was said about it when it began? Who was the first manager to platoon extensively?

One of the things I had wanted to do with this book was to answer those questions. Platooning existed prior to 1910 but was rare; by 1920 it was common. It is curious that baseball has, really, not even a myth to explain the origins of platooning; its beginnings are not shrouded in a haze, but blanketed in utter darkness. This is atypical for baseball, for, as historian David Voight has pointed out, baseball men love myths of creativity, and have spun birth-in-a-thunderclap legends about the inception of almost everything connected with the game. Of platooning, though, one sees only an occasional suggestion that "some say it was John McGraw" who first realized that a left-handed batter might have an advantage against a right-handed pitcher, and vice versa.

It was not John McGraw who first realized this. For one thing, there is the matter of switch hitting. The fact that one would switch hit, bat right-handed against a left-hander and left-handed against a right-hander, implies clearly a recognition of the platoon advantage. The first man to switch hit—and thus, in one sense, the inventor of platooning—was Bob "Death to Flying Things" Ferguson, whom we have encountered several times in the early history of the game. Ferguson played in the major leagues from the time they were organized (1871; he was twenty-six then and a well-known "amateur" player) until 1884; he was switch hitting before McGraw was born. Ferguson was more noted as a glove man and manager, but he did hit .351 in 1878.

His experiment with switch hitting was not widely imitated at first, in part perhaps because nobody wanted to be like Bob Ferguson, but in the 1880s it became the fashion, and there were quite a number of switch hitters. Will White, the bespectacled pitcher, was a switch hitter (1877–1886). The first outstanding switch hitter was Tommy Tucker (1887–1899), who won the American Association batting title in 1889 with a .372 mark. After him there were a bunch of them. There were at least four outstanding switch hitters in the 1890s. John Montgomery Ward experimented with switch hitting in 1888, plus, of course, you have the famous switch pitcher, Tony Mullane. Actually, according to Al Kermisch, at least three right-handed pitchers of the 1880s pitched a few innings left-handed—Mullane, Larry Corcoran, and Icebox Chamberlain.

So the platoon advantage was something they were thinking

about, but when did they start platooning? In *The Glory of Their Times,* Al Bridwell (a left-handed batter) was discussing the play on which Merkle failed to touch second in 1908:

> I stepped back into the box. Jack Pfiester was pitching for the Cubs, a left-hander. We didn't platoon in those days. The fact that Pfiester was a lefty and I was too didn't bother anybody. I was supposed to be able to hit left-handed pitching just as well as right-handed.

Let us use 1908, then, as the back boundary of platooning; it started sometime after then.

The boundary of platooning on the other end is 1920, when the strategy had its first big vogue. I have heard a number of baseball people say in the last few years that Casey Stengel was the first man to platoon extensively. This is completely false; Tris Speaker platooned at four positions in 1921, and platoon arrangements at two or three positions were quite common at that time. A few years later, platooning fell out of favor, and was not widely used for many years until Stengel revived it—but by no stretch of the imagination did he initiate it, or even raise it to new levels.

If platooning was being done at three and four positions in 1920, then it must have begun sometime before 1920, but when? Jim Baker and I attempted to answer this question by "walking it backward," starting at 1920. Pardon me; I intend to describe that process here in some detail. In the 1920 World Series, both managers used platoon arrangements. In Game One, with Marquard (a left-hander) starting, Tris Speaker started Joe Evans in left field, George Burns at first base and Smokey Joe Wood in right field, all right-handed batters; when a right-hander (Al Mamaux) relieved Rube, the left-handed hitting Charlie Jamieson pinch hit for Evans, and left-handers Doc Johnston and Elmer Smith came into the game to play first base and right field. Speaker continued to make strict platoon moves with these six players throughout the series, in which Brooklyn split its innings almost equally between left-handed and right-handed pitchers. For his part, Brooklyn's Wilbert Robinson used the right-handed Bernie Neis in right field against the Duster Mails, the only left-hander to pitch for Cleveland, but Tommy Griffith (a left-handed hitter) against all the other pitchers.

What about 1919? In the 1919 World Series, Cincinnati's manager used Bill Rariden at catcher against Chicago's two left-handed pitchers (Williams and Kerr), but used Ivy Wingo against the right-handers. That's a platoon arrangement. For his part, Kid Gleason of the White Sox used Nemo Leibold in right field against Cincinnati's right-handers, and Shano Collins against the left-handers.

1916: AN OBVIOUS IMPOSTOR

Hughie Jennings got a letter from a pitcher from a small town in Michigan in 1916 who claimed he could strike out Ty Cobb anytime on three pitches. The guy said it would only cost $1.80—train fare to Detroit—for Jennings to find out. Hughie figured well, you never know, and sent the dollar-eighty. The pitcher showed up—great, big, gangly kid, 6-foot-4, and all joints. They let him warm up and called out Cobb.

Cobb hit his first pitch against the right field wall. His second pitch went over the right field wall. The third pitch went over the center field wall. Cobb was thinking they ought to keep this guy around to help him get in a groove.

"Well," said Jennings. "What have you got to say?"

The pitcher stared in hard at the batter's box. "You know," he said, "I don't believe that's Ty Cobb in there."

In short, platooning is strong in 1919; it's easy to find. In the 1918 World Series—I'm using World Series because the box scores are available—the Cubs did not platoon themselves, and started left-handers in all six games, so Boston didn't platoon either. In the 1917 Series, the White Sox again used the Leibold/Collins platoon arrangement in right field—sort of. All five of Leibold's at bats in the series did come against right-handed pitching, but Collins played all of the time against left-handers and half of the time against right-handers.

For his part, John McGraw did not have an option to platoon in that series, and that could be significant. Chicago had basically a five-man pitching staff, with two right-handers and three left-handers, but the two right-handers (Faber and Cicotte) did all the pitching in the World Series. If you look at the Giants' lineup, it's basically a right-handed hitting lineup—so that may imply that Pants Rowland, in 1917, was selecting his starters with recognition of the platoon advantage.

1916—Boston platooned Tilly Walker in center field with Chick Shorten. Brooklyn platooned Casey Stengel in right field with Jimmy Johnston.

1915—Philadelphia (National League) used only one left-hander in the series, Eppa Rixey, who was brought into the game in the third inning. When Rixey entered, the Red Sox made a response move, bringing Del Gainor off the bench to play first base instead of Hoblitzell. A trip to the microfilm room at the library to find some more box scores confirms that this was, indeed, a platoon arrangement. However, Philadelphia did not platoon; they used exactly the same lineup to face the left-handed Dutch Leonard in Game Three that they had used the first two games.

It's growing weaker; we're down to one team and one position here. The 1914 Series is the same cities—Philadelphia against Boston—but a switch of leagues. This is the Braves against the Athletics. Philadelphia started a right-hander in Game One and a left-hander in Game Two; Boston made two response moves, starting the right-handers Les Mann and Ted Cather in place of the left-handers Joe Connolly and Herbie Moran. In Games Three and Four, the A's went back to right-handers, and the Miracle Man, George Stallings, went back to Moran and Connolly. When a left-hander relieved in Game Four, Mann came back in, but Moran stayed in right field, as Stallings played to preserve the lead. Connie Mack did not platoon in the series.

Two things about this, I would later decide, were significant. Number one, it was the first time that a manager had platooned at two positions in a World Series. And number two, it was the first time that a National League manager had platooned in the World Series—and quite possibly the first time that a National League manager had platooned, period.

GEORGE STALLINGS, SR.

Let's continue to walk it back. In the 1913 World Series (Connie Mack versus John McGraw), neither team made any platoon changes, although both teams used both left-handed and right-handed pitching. In the 1912 World Series (Jake Stahl versus John McGraw), neither team made any platoon changes. In the 1911 World Series (Mack versus McGraw again), neither team made any platoon changes. Significantly, Connie Mack used a left-handed catcher and a right-handed catcher all year, but did not use them in a platoon arrangement, choosing instead to rotate them on some other basis. He started the left-handed Lapp against the left-handed Marquard in one game and the right-handed Thomas against the right-handed Mathewson in another.

Christy Mathewson put his name on a book written during that 1911 World Series, the book *Pitching in a Pinch*. On page 44 of that book, he says that Josh Devore "has improved greatly

against all left-handers . . . so much so that McGraw leaves him in the game now when a southpaw pitches, instead of placing Beals Becker in left field as he used to." This would be evidence of early platooning on the part of John McGraw, except for one thing. Beals Becker was also a left-handed batter. In taking Devore out against a left-hander, McGraw was not platooning, but reacting to a weakness on the part of the player—a weakness that many other players must have had before 1910.

With platoon combinations in the World Series drying up, I started looking for evidence of platooning in the rest of the league. If a manager platoons at a position and sticks with it, this is fairly easy to recognize in the statistics; you'll have a left-handed batter with 60 to 80% of the at bats (50 to 70% in our own time), and a right-handed batter who plays the same position with 20 to 40% of a full season's at bats. The problem, of course, is that with platooning in an embryonic state, you're not going to get that kind of commitment to it; a manager might platoon a man in left field for a few weeks, then play him regularly for a month at third base to cover an injury, then bench him entirely, or any number of other options. You can recognize possible platoon combinations, but you have to get into the box scores to know for sure whether they were or were not.

Jim Baker and I spent a good many hours checking out those possible platoon combinations. We found no evidence that any National League manager was platooning prior to 1914. This certainly does not mean that there isn't, anywhere between 1876 and 1914, any platoon combination in that league; there may well be. We didn't find it. With platoon combinations stopping sharply before 1914, it seemed appropriate to look more closely at what happened that year.

The account of the 1914 World Series in the *Reach Guide* runs to many thousands of words, but makes only two brief references to this matter. The first occurs in the discussion of Game Two, the second in the discussion of Game Four:

> In accordance with his season-long policy, Manager Stallings shifted his outfield to meet southpaw pitching, and Mann and Cathers acquitted themselves creditably. . . .
> When Pennock relieved Shawkey, Manager Stallings followed his season custom and substituted right-handed Mann for left-handed Connolly in the sixth inning, but allowed Moran to remain in the game when his turn at bat arrived in the seventh inning.

Stallings' handling of his outfield that year deserves an essay in itself. He used eleven outfielders in 1914, several of them interesting people but none of them terrific ballplayers, giving each of those at least two weeks in the outfield to impress him. It is not strictly true that he alternated on a left/right basis all season; for one thing, the right-handed hitting Mann had 389 at bats, and if you count the number of left-handed pitchers in the National League in 1914, you quickly realize that that ain't right. At one point in the season Boston went about three weeks without seeing a left-hander. But he did platoon when he saw a left-hander; one of the people he platooned with, incidentally, was Josh Devore.

Anyway, that is not this essay. For this essay, the key point is that Stallings was "The Miracle Man," the media hero of the 1914 season. As best you can tell, he deserved to be; what he did that season is like winning the pennant by coming up with a handful of Hurricane Hazles. His cleanup hitter for much of the season was Rabbit Maranville; Maranville led the team in RBI, too. The *Reach Guide* gave him a two-page spread: Boston's Miracle Man. So what you have here is a manager who is (a) following a new and experimental policy, (b) having remarkable results, and (c) receiving extensive praise. Although no one, that I can find, cited his platooning as the key to his accomplishment, it is a fact that the popularity of the strategy grew rapidly, as we have seen, after 1914. For example, the other Boston manager, Bill Carrigan, who was not platooning in 1914, began platooning in 1915.

George Stallings was a smart man. He graduated from the Virginia Military Institute in 1886 at the age of seventeen; whether or not that is unusual I don't know. He then began to study medicine, but Harry Wright, then managing the Phillies, saw him catching a game and offered him a contract. He went to spring training with the Phillies in 1887, but Wright cut him. Ten years later, Stallings was managing the Phillies. He was the bright guy who buried the wire into the third base coach's box.

But he did not, as best I can ascertain, invent platooning. He apparently imported it to the National League from the American. In 1911, Hughie Jennings, manager of Detroit, platooned in left field—not all year, but most of it—with Davy Jones and Delos Drake. Jones, also interviewed in *The Glory of Their Times*, makes no reference to this. But it happened, and for a time I thought this would stand as the first identifiable case of platooning. Note the distinction; we are down now to trying to find the first, isolated instance of platooning.

I missed one for a while because I was looking for left/right combinations. But because we knew that Hughie Jennings was platooning in 1911, I thought I'd better look a little more carefully at his earlier teams, particularly his pennant-winning teams of 1907–1909. In the 1909 World Series, I noticed that Boss Schmidt, a switch hitter, did not play in one game, the one game that a left-hander had started. In the 1908 World Series, again, there was one game that Schmidt had not played, and one game that a

JOSH DEVORE

CHARLES "BOSS" SCHMIDT

left-hander (Jack Pfiester, the man who just weeks earlier had surrendered the single to Al Bridwell, providing the back boundary for platooning) had started for the opposition. They were, again, the same game. In the 1907 series there was, again, one game started by a lefty—and again, it was the one game in the series that Schmidt did not play.

The three series games that Schmidt missed were started by Freddie Payne, Ira Thomas, and Oscar Stanage—all three of them right-handers. Though Schmidt was listed as a switch hitter, he was, in effect, a left-handed platoon player. The microfilm quickly confirmed this.

Schmidt was, obviously, a left-handed hitter who couldn't hit left-handed pitching, and tried to switch hit in desperation. But unlike McGraw, who replaced Devore with another left-hander,

McGraw's old teammate Jennings had evolved a series of platoon combinations—Schmidt and Payne, then Schmidt and Thomas, then Schmidt and Stanage. It is interesting to note that Thomas, as a platoon player in 1908, hit .307. He was traded to Philadelphia after that season, and in Philadelphia, not platooning, he hit .223.

These were the only platoon combinations I found that Jennings was using; I never found any instances of his generalizing the principle and platooning at another position. In the time that he was using this arrangement in Detroit, one of his rivals was the New York Highlanders, who were lifted briefly out of the basement and into the pennant race during a period in which they were, quite by coincidence, I'm sure, managed by George Stallings. Stallings had a bad New York club in the pennant race in 1910, and it is during that period that I find the first instance of platooning on any team other than Detroit. The Miracle Man experimented for a time with platooning Charlie Hemphill and Bert Daniels in center field.

It seems, in short, to have been Stallings who first formulated the idea of platooning as a weapon, rather than as a possible response to a player's weakness.

I wish that we could let it rest there, because that makes a creditable story. Hughie Jennings was a famous and successful (a) ballplayer, and (b) manager. He was a lawyer, an educated man, but also a part of the Old Orioles with McGraw and Wee Willie, a running mate and later a coach of little Napoleon. That's a good story—the lawyer/manager thought up the idea of platooning sometime while he was playing, implemented it when he became a manager in 1907, and immediately won a pennant with it. This spread the idea at least as far as George Stallings, and Stallings' success attracted the attention of others, and platooning became popular. That makes perfect sense; if Hughie Jennings didn't invent platooning, he should have.

It makes sense, and it fits. If you were to draw a schematic of baseball history, and you were to say, "Where *should* platooning begin?" you would come up with the answer that an American League team should have begun platooning at the catcher's position sometime about 1905.

Platooning should have begun at the catcher's spot, obviously, because that was the one spot at which few teams (very few teams) used regular players prior to 1920; almost every baseball team from 1876 to 1920 consists of a pitching staff, seven regulars and two or three catchers (sometimes the seven regulars change in a season, but rarely would any manager alternate). Platooning should have begun about 1905 because (a) we know it was common by 1920, and (b) it would have been very difficult to platoon prior to 1900.

There are two reasons why it would have been difficult to platoon prior to 1900. Number one, the rosters were too small. The National League teams in the 1890s used a varying number of people, but seventeen is about the median, and with the game under severe economic pressure, the crunch was to reduce it even lower. When baseball became popular again after the turn of the century, the rosters swelled rapidly in size, reaching twenty-five by the end of the decade. That makes it a lot easier to platoon.

Number two, there weren't enough left-handers. Of the fifty-two National League pitchers listed in the 1900 *Spalding Guide* (1899 season), only nine were left-handed. My guess is that that ratio represented a big increase from the earlier part of the decade. Let me ask you: If you were playing with a sixteen-man roster, in a twelve-team league with only nine left-handed pitchers in it, do you think you would platoon?

Platooning should have started in the American League because that's where the left-handers were. For some reason or probably no reason, the American League from 1901 through 1915 had many more left-handed pitchers than the National; a spot check of 1905 shows that American League left-handers accounted for 316 decisions, 26 percent of the league total; National League left-handers accounted for only 178 decisions, 15 percent of the total. You can start considering platooning at 26 percent; it's very difficult to do at 15 percent.

It's a good story, and it fits, but it isn't exactly true. We had walked it back now to 1907, before the Bridwell line, and I was ready to declare that the start of it. But I felt compelled to check out the rest of Boss Schmidt's career, and guess what. Jennings did not invent a platoon arrangement. He inherited it.

Schmidt came to the majors in 1906. I had Jim check out a forty-eight-game sample of the Tiger's schedule for 1906. Here's what he found:

Schmidt started:	19 games
Against left-handers	1
Against right-handers	18
John Warner started:	17 games
Against left-handers	5
Against right-handers	12
Freddie Payne started:	12 games
Against left-handers	10
Against right-handers	2

John Warner was a left-handed batter—and that's a platoon arrangement; the Tigers started the catcher who would give them the platoon edge (considering Schmidt a left-hander) in forty of the forty-eight games.

Well, what about 1905?

No major league team was platooning in 1905, at any position. I state this with some confidence, as we made a real effort to nail it down.

What I did is, I developed the idea of a "platoon scan." To make a platoon scan, you divide a team's starts into games against right-handed starters and games against left-handed starters. Then you go through that team's box scores, game by game, and you count the number of left-handed batters (or right-handed batters) in the lineup. If they have three left-handed batters in the lineup against a right-handed pitcher, you write down a "3" under "Right." Boston's platoon scan for one twenty-two-game sample in 1905 looks like this:

	Right	Left
Boston	3322223333333	432222233

Using this method, if a team is platooning, it very quickly becomes obvious, even if there is some shifting around in the lineup that might tend to disguise it. Full-scale platooning would look like this:

	Right	Left
Boston	3322223333333	321111122

While the inconsistent, spotty platooning that you might otherwise miss would look something like this:

	Right	Left
Boston	3322223333333	312211231

If they're *really* platooning, the average of the "Right" column and the average of the "Left" column will differ by 1.00 (or 2.00 if platooning at two positions). But even if they're just kind of experimenting, a separation of .40 or .50 should appear quickly.

We took samples of at least fifty games for every American League team in 1905, and quite simply, there was no platooning in that league. We didn't do the platoon scans in the National League, but we did do a thorough job of checking out player usage patterns that could have resulted from platooning, and I am 99 percent certain that no National League team was platooning in 1905.

It makes a terrible story, you see. The first known platoon arrangement was operated by some guy named Bill Armour, who nobody knows anything about, who thought it up and implemented it in his fifth and final season as a major league manager, had a poor year, and was fired?

I don't know that. I know this: No one was platooning in the major leagues in 1905, and Bill Armour was platooning in 1906. I still get the feeling, somehow, that somebody did platoon, sort of, sometime in the nineteenth century. It would have been awkward as hell, but they could have done it. I fully expect some other baseball researcher to take an interest in this subject and find an earlier platoon arrangement.

(After the first publication of this book in 1986, a gentleman named David Ball sent me a letter. "In 1887 the Indianapolis Hoosiers, playing out the string on a hopeless season, were carrying some extra men," Ball writes. The Hoosiers, a National League team, finished 37–89. "They started alternating Frank Gardner, a right-handed hitter, and Tom Brown, a left-hander, against different kinds of pitching, and doing the same with Henry Jackson and Otto Shomberg at first base. The newspaper reports make it clear that they were platooning in the the modern sense to take advantage of the lefty-righty differential." Mr. Ball also questions the evidence for citing Bob Ferguson as the first switch hitter, and suggests that the Chicago team in the late 1870s may have used a different batting order against a left-hander than a right-hander, with the same players.)

The other thing that we didn't find was the discussion of the issue. What I had expected to find, somewhere in this process of walking it backward—and what I still know must exist, somewhere—is a whole bunch of essays by journalists of the period discussing the issue, talking about who started it and what the idea is and who else is doing it and where's it all going to end. We never could find that article saying that "Alfred Smartguy has a new strategy this year of playing his left-handed hitters against right-handed pitchers." We could never find Fred Lieb telling us what he thought about the idea in the *New York Press,* with Grantland Rice answering the next day in the *Tribune* and Damon Runyon the third day in the *American.* Maybe that's why platooning has no myth of creativity, like everything else; it just sort of snuck up on everybody, and it was fifteen years old before anybody realized it was here to stay.

Well, let's go forward with it. Tris Speaker, like Jennings, inherited a platoon arrangement and improved upon it. In mid-season, 1919, he took over a Cleveland team that was platooning at two positions. He extended that arrangement to three positions in 1920 and occasionally to four positions in 1921, as discussed before, making him the first manager to use extensive platooning.

As platooning grew, John McGraw was never ahead of the pack at any time; he was not the first man to platoon, or the first to platoon at two positions or three or four or anything. He was never the last one to adapt, either, but so far as I can tell he never

A CAPSULE HISTORY OF PLATOONING

(For those of you who are too "busy" to read the whole thing.)

1871—First professional league opens with Bob Ferguson, the first switch hitter.

1887—First known platoon arrangement in Indianapolis.

1889—Tommy Tucker, first outstanding switch hitter, wins American Association bat title at .372.

1906—Detroit experiments with platooning their catchers.

1914—First known National League platoon arrangement; first platooning at more than one position helps Boston win World Series title.

1920—First extensive platooning, by Tris Speaker in Cleveland.

1930—Platooning falls into disfavor.

1949—Revived by Casey Stengel's success in New York.

1968—Earl Weaver hired by Baltimore, adds batter/pitcher record keeping and evolves personal style in platooning.

used a strict platoon arrangement. He used more of a platoon recognition in alternating players.

As the American League had more left-handed pitching, platooning as it developed was always more of an American League thing. The American League champions platooned at at least one position every year between 1915 and 1925, with the possible exception of 1922. The major proponent of platooning in the National League in this period was Bill McKechnie, who had extremely good success with platoon combinations at Pittsburgh, including his 1925 combinations of George Grantham (.326) and Stuffy McInnis (.368) at first base, and Earl Smith (.313) and Johnny Gooch (.298) behind the plate.

After about 1930, platooning fell into some disfavor. Even McKechnie, who had been so successful with it at Pittsburgh, abandoned the practice, though there were always a few who kept a candle burning for it. Casey Stengel, a player when platooning was in its heyday, was one of those—and if you look at his records as a player, it isn't hard to understand why. As a platoon player in 1922 and 1923, Stengel hit .368 and .339, the lower figure being 55 points above his career average.

Casey would eventually breathe new life into platooning. One reason for this was that he took some criticism for platooning through much of his career, and he became defensive about it; he spoke about it as "my platooning," particularly after his platooning was vindicated in New York. For those of us in my generation, Stengel stands at the border of our memory, and only records exist before him. But through those records, you can walk platooning backward a long, long way before 1949.

The 1920s

HOW THE GAME WAS PLAYED

The change between the baseball that was played in the teens and the baseball of the twenties is the most sudden and dramatic of this century. The Black Sox scandal and related scandals, coming on the heels of seven poor years of attendance, so terrified major league owners that they were willing to accept changes; desperate, indeed, to climb aboard any ship that looked like it might be heading to a safe port in any direction. From a structural standpoint, Judge Landis provided that ship; from an economic standpoint, Babe Ruth was the transportation.

The fans were galvanized by the Ruth phenomenon; his coming was unquestionably the biggest news story that baseball has ever had. Thus when the Black Sox story broke late in the year, major league magnates were faced with sudden prosperity on the one hand, and doom and disaster on the other. Under those unique circumstances, the owners did not do what they quite certainly would have done at almost any other time, which would have been to take some action to control this obscene burst of offensive productivity, and keep Ruth from making a mockery of the game. Instead they gave Ruth his rein, and allowed him to pull the game wherever it wanted to go. Baseball then moved forcefully in the direction in which it had been trying to move since the coming of parks with permanent seats in the outfield. Home run totals soared beyond anyone's imagination. Batting averages jumped 20 to 50 points as compared to the previous decade. The stolen base, the sacrifice bunt, and every other symbol of tyrannical strategy was sent scurrying for the portholes as baseball men, made suddenly more wealthy by the explosive popularity of the new baseball, lined up to draw arms in support of it.

This was, of course, in some measure a return to the form of baseball in the early 1870s, but no one except the baseball historians around—and there were fewer then than now—knew that. It was all new to them. Most baseball fans believe that there was a change of baseballs that was instituted in 1920, a "lively ball" that was adopted which made possible the home run explosion by Babe Ruth, who hit the unimaginable total of fifty-four in a season. There was no such switch in baseballs. A better quality of yarn was available after World War I, and this may have accidently increased the resiliency of the balls, but that was incidental, and its effect was not dramatic. The 1922 *Reach Guide* reported that "An attempt was made by many writers, during the greater part of the season, to blame the heavy batting on the ball, assuming that it had been changed so as to make it much more 'lively' than the old cork-center ball. This the manufacturers flatly denied, asserting that the ball was precisely the same as had always been used." Early in the 1921 season, National League president John Heydler launched an investigation to see if the league was being sold some "rabbit balls." He concluded that the balls in use were the same as always, and that the changes were due to the abolition of the spitball and other freak deliveries, plus the example of Babe Ruth, who had shown that it was possible to hit home runs with much greater consistency than was previously thought.

If there was an uninten-tional change in the manufacture of the balls, as has happened many other times in baseball history, it probably was not a major factor in the change in offensive levels. As Pete Palmer and John Thorn have pointed out, Ruth's fifty-four-homer explosion would have happened in 1919 had the circumstances been right for it. Ruth hit twenty-nine home runs in 1919, but there are two things to remember. Number one, it was a short season. The leagues decided that they were losing money on those early-April games, and cut the schedule back to 140 games (it was not a war-shortened season; it was an economic decision). The Red Sox played only 138 games, and Ruth played only 130. And number two, Ruth was playing in 1919 in Fenway Park, which at that time was an extremely tough home run park, whereas in 1920 he moved to the Polo Grounds, an excellent home run park. His home run total in neutral parks increased in 1920 only from twenty to twenty-five; his home runs at home increased from nine to twenty-nine in moving from Boston to New York.

More important than that, the *one-year* increases in offensive totals throughout the league were not extraordinary. In 1920, runs per game in the American League increased by .65, whereas in 1911 they had increased by .97; in the National League,

the increase was only .32, whereas in 1911 it was .39. But whereas in other years the increases in offense were resisted by baseball men, and consequently negated by subsequent changes in the game, the changes of 1920 were accepted around baseball, and later supplemented by other measures that emphasized the effect. The gap between offensive levels of the 1920s and the 1910s is remarkable—but the gap between the levels of 1920 and 1919 is not.

Of the increase in offense in 1920 alone, probably a more important cause than any change in baseballs was the limited ban of the spitball in the winter of 1919–20. One of the primary causes of the action against the spitball, apart from the fact that it was rather disgusting, was a fear that it could not be controlled and was dangerous. In a symposium on the spitball (Should it be banned?) in the 1909 *Spalding Guide,* most of the writers who responded expressed a dislike of the spitball, and several cited the danger of one getting away and someone being hurt as one of the reasons for their opinion.

In 1920, then, we get one of the real keys to the lively ball era. A pitch, probably not a spitball, did get away from a pitcher, Carl Mays, and killed the batter. Although a good many players had been killed in on-field incidents at the minor league level, the death of Ray Chapman was a consid-

CARL MAYS

erable shock to the baseball community. Chapman was killed by a dirty gray ball that he probably did not pick up as quickly as he could have. After that the league powers realized that simply banning the deliberate discoloration and abuse of the ball was not enough, and from then on there was much more of an effort made to keep a clean, fresh ball in play. In *The Glory of Their Times,* Fred Snod-

grass reflected that "We hardly ever saw a new baseball, a clean one. If the ball went into the stands and the ushers couldn't get it back from the spectators, only then would the umpire throw out a new one." He also remembered that all of the infielders would chew tobacco and licorice and spit into their gloves, to help make the ball as dark as possible for their pitcher. This ended in 1921, when

the spitball and the "emery ball" were banned, and clean balls kept in play. The pitchers complained that the new baseballs were difficult to grip. The 1922 *Reach Guide* reported that "the pitchers claimed that they were unable to curve the new balls, because they were not able to get a proper grip on them by reason of the excessive gloss upon them, and asked for permission to rub the gloss off with a small amount of rosin. *They also complained greatly of the number of new balls thrown constantly into the games by the umpires.*" In response to the complaints about the gloss, the practice of having the umpires "rub down" the game balls, a practice that continues to this day, was begun in 1921. The clean, new balls were incidentally much more "lively" than the old, soiled, battered and spit upon baseballs of the previous decade, but that was not initially the purpose of their use.

When the owners discovered that the fans *liked* to see home runs, and when the foundations of the game were simultaneously imperiled by disgrace, then there was no turning back. In 1925 a new "cushioned cork center" ball was introduced, perhaps more lively than those before it, and offense was allowed to dominate the remainder of the decade.

WHERE THE GAME WAS PLAYED

Major league cities during the decade included Boston, Brooklyn, Chicago, Cincinnati, Cleveland, Detroit, New York, Philadelphia, Pittsburgh, St. Louis, and Washington.

WHO THE GAME WAS PLAYED BY

Country boys. With the widespread development of the minors after the increased popularity of baseball around the turn of the century, baseball began to draw more and more of its personnel from the minor league teams, and less and less from the colleges. College-educated players, of whom there were scores in the first fifteen years of this century, now became rare. Second-generation immigrants and fourth-generation farm boys played Sunday baseball in the pastures or the parks of small cities, formed semipro alliances and caught the eye of the local press or the local manager, and thus found their way into the lowest levels of an increasingly structured system in which talent bubbled up from the bottom. The earlier the age at which an athlete entered that system, the more time he had to make it to the top. It did not behoove a young player to waste four precious years in college.

RAY CHAPMAN

MAJOR LEAGUE ALL-STAR TEAM
1920–29
Records in seasonal notation, based on 154 games played.
Pitchers based on 40 starts.

Pos	Player	Years	Hits	HR	RBI	Avg.	Other
C	Gabby Hartnett	4.60	137	18	79	.287	
1B	Lou Gehrig	4.98	185	29	127	.335	127 Runs
2B	Rogers Hornsby	9.29	225	27	124	.382	44 Doubles
3B	Pie Traynor	7.70	194	5	104	.322	
SS	Joe Sewell	9.12	186	3	90	.322	Only 11 Strikeouts
LF	Harry Heilmann	9.21	209	15	123	.364	43 Doubles
CF	Al Simmons	5.32	220	22	105	.356	.570 Slugging
RF	Babe Ruth	9.08	191	51	146	.355	136 Walks

	Pitcher	Years	Won-Lost	SO	ERA	Other
RH	Dazzy Vance	6.41	23–14	228	3.10	
RH	Pete Alexander	7.77	21–14	84	3.04	Only 45 Walks
RH	Burleigh Grimes	8.96	21–15	114	3.52	
LH	Herb Pennock	8.15	20–14	90	3.46	

Checking In

1920—Stan Musial, Donora, Pennsylvania
    Bob Lemon, San Bernadino, California
    Early Wynn, Hartford, Alabama
1921—Warren Spahn, Buffalo, New York
    Roy Campanella, Philadelphia
1922—Ralph Kiner, Santa Rita, New Mexico
1923—Bobby Thompson, Glasgow, Scotland
    Larry Doby, Camden, South Carolina
    Norman Mailer, Long Branch, New Jersey
    Hoyt Wilhelm, Huntersville, North Carolina
1925—Yogi Berra, St. Louis
    Malcolm X, Omaha, Nebraska
1926—Don Newcombe, Madison, New Jersey
    Duke Snider, Los Angeles
    Marilyn Monroe, Los Angeles
    Robin Roberts, Springfield, Illinois
1927—Nellie Fox, St. Thomas, Pennsylvania
1928—Billy Martin, Berkeley, California
    Whitey Ford, New York City

Checking Out

1921—Socks Seybold, car wreck, 51
    Larry McLean, gunshot, 39
1922—Morgan Bulkeley, 84
    Ben Shibe, 83
    Alexander Graham Bell, 75
    Cap Anson, 69
    Sam Thompson, heart attack, 62
    Austin McHenry, brain tumor, 26
1923—Jimmy Ryan, 60
    Pancho Villa, 45
1924—Candy Cummings, 75
    George Wood, 65
    Frank Chance, pulmonary trouble, 47
    Jake Daubert, complications following surgery for
    appendicitis and gallstones, 40
    Tony Boeckel, car wreck, 29 (Bob Meusel, a passenger in
    the car, was unhurt)
1925—Monte Ward, 65
    William Jennings Bryan, 65
    Christy Mathewson, tuberculosis, 47
1926—Cal McVey, 75
    Eddie Plank, 49
1927—Joe Start, 84
    Lave Cross, 60
    Hughie Jennings, 58
    Ross Youngs, Bright's disease, 29
1928—Al Reach, 87
1929—Miller Huggins, 50

THE 1920s IN A BOX

Attendance Data:
 Total: 93 million (92,652,885)
 Highest: New York Yankees, 10,527,508
 Lowest: Boston Braves, 2,499,518
 Attendance boomed. After a record-shattering 9 million plus in 1920 (5 million plus in the American League), attendance took a half-step backward in 1921, following the revelation of the fixing of the 1919 World Series. The damage was contained, however, and new attendance peaks were set in 1924 (9.45 million), 1925 (9.54 million), 1926 (9.8 million), and 1927 (9.9 million). The Yankees drew over a million almost every year, and the Tigers (1924) and Cubs (1927–29) also made it over the million mark.

Most Home Runs:
 Babe Ruth, 1927, 60
 Babe Ruth, 467

Best Won-Lost Record by Team:
 Yankees, 1927, 110–44, .714
 Yankees, 933–602, .608

Worst Won-Lost Record by Team: Philadelphia (N) 1928, 43–109, .283 566–962, .370, by the Phillies
 The two Boston teams ranked fourteenth and fifteenth among the sixteen teams in winning percentage for the decade. The Braves were 603–928, .394, and the Red Sox 595–938, .388.

Heaviest Player: Garland Buckeye, known as Gob Buckeye, was a left-handed pitcher in the American League, stood but 6 feet tall and weighed a reported 260 pounds. Another player who collected a few hits in the steak and potatoes league was Fats Fothergill, who was 5 feet 10 and a half inches and weighed 230, but hit .326 in a twelve-year career. Fats didn't live to see forty.

Lightest Player: Doc Gautreau, a 5′4″, 129-pound second baseman who played for Boston, 1925–28.

Most Strikeouts by Pitcher:
 Dazzy Vance, 1924, 262
 Dazzy Vance, 1,464

Highest Batting Average:
 Rogers Hornsby, 1924, .424
 Rogers Hornsby, .382

Hardest-Throwing Pitcher: Lefty Grove. Charlie Gehringer, who played against both, said that Grove threw "much harder" than Bob Feller. Joe Cronin, who also faced the two, said that no one threw harder than Grove.

*Best Baseball Books: None

Best Outfield Arm: Bob Meusel (without question)

Worst Outfield Arm: Glass Arm Eddie Brown

Most Runs Batted In:
 Lou Gehrig, 1927, 175
 Babe Ruth, 1,330

*Most-Aggressive Baserunner: Probably Ruth, again. Ruth or Frankie Frisch.

Fastest Player: Kiki Cuyler
 A minor player, Maurice Archdeacon, broke the record for fastest time circling the bases, getting around them in 13.4 seconds before a minor league game in 1921. Archdeacon was born ten years too late. He hit .333

in 127 major league games, but he had no power, and his speed, which would have been a valuable weapon in the previous decade, didn't match up against Babe Ruth's home runs.

Slowest Player: Johnny Bassler

Best Control Pitcher: Grover Cleveland Alexander

Best Minor League Player: Buzz Arlett

Best Negro League Players:
>Bullet Rogan
>Cool Papa Bell
>Martin Dihigo

Odd Couple: Babe Ruth and Lou Gehrig

Drinking Men:
>Pete Alexander
>Flint Rhem
>Paul Waner
>Phil Douglas

Nicknames:
>Union Man (Walter Holke)
>Poosh 'Em Up (Tony Lazzeri)
>Spinach (Oscar Melillo)
>The Sultan of Swat (Babe Ruth)
>The Crown Prince of Swat (Lou Gehrig)
>The Rajah of Swat (Rogers Hornsby)
>The Rabbi of Swat (Moe Solomon)
>Bucketfoot Al (Al Simmons)
>Big Poison (Paul Waner)
>Little Poison (Lloyd Waner)
>The Mississippi Mudcat (Guy Bush)
>Shufflin' Phil (Phil Douglas)
>Camera Eye (Max Bishop)
>Turkeyfoot (Frank Brower)
>Trolley Line (Johnny Butler)
>Governor (Frank Ellerbee)
>Slug (Harry Heilmann)
>Ol' Stubblebeard (Burleigh Grimes)

Most Stolen Bases:
>Sam Rice, 1920, 63
>Max Carey, 346

Best-Looking Player: George Pipgras

Ugliest Player: Joe Martina

*Strangest Batting Stance: Rogers Hornsby

*Clint Hartung Award: Moe Solomon

Outstanding Sportswriter: Ring Lardner

Most-Admirable Superstar: Lou Gehrig

Least-Admirable Superstar: Rogers Hornsby

Franchise Shifts: None

New Stadiums: 1923—Yankee Stadium

*Best Pennant Race: American League, 1920

Best World Series: Impossible to pick; there are too many good ones. The 1921 series was won by the Giants over their tenants, the Yankees (0–3, 0–3, 13–5, 4–2, 1–3, 8–5, 2–1, 1–0), and featured every kind of game and every kind of play you can imagine. The 1923 series, won by the Yankees 4–2, is remembered for Casey Stengel's two game-winning home runs, after the

JOE MARTINA

second of which he was reprimanded by Judge Landis for thumbing his nose at the pitcher as he rounded third base. The 1924 series featured four one-run games, was won by the Senators (3–4, 4–3, 4–6, 7–4, 2–6, 2–1, 4–3) and was regarded by some at the time as the greatest World Series ever played. The 1925 series, won by Pittsburgh over Washington (1–4, 3–2, 3–4, 0–4, 6–3, 3–2, 9–7), featured the controversial super-catch by Sam Rice and is one of the few times that a team has come from a 3–1 deficit to win. The 1926 series, won by St. Louis over the Yankees (1–2, 6–2, 4–0, 5–10, 2–3, 10–2, 3–2), featured the infinitely rehashed story of Grover Cleveland Alexander, thirty-nine going on seventy, coming in to strike out Lazzeri in the seventh game. Any of those can be called the greatest series of the time.

Best-Hitting Pitcher: George Uhle. Uhle's lifetime batting average, .288, is the highest of any pitcher with 500 or more at bats. Uhle hit .291 during the decade.

Worst-Hitting Pitcher: Win Ballou

THE 1920 AMERICAN LEAGUE PENNANT RACE

The American League pennant race was decided by a three-team race among the Indians (98–56), White Sox (96–58), and Yankees (95–59). There was enormous excitement around the league generated by Ruth's great season, which evolved into a pennant race worthy of its own book when a) Ray Chapman of Cleveland was killed by a pitched ball (the Indians replaced him with a Hall of Famer, Joe Sewell), and b) the story of the Black Sox broke in the last week of the season. Ranks with the 1908 National League race, 1978 American League East race and no more than one or two others as the greatest of pennant races, combining great baseball with human drama.

1920: A CLIMATE OF FEAR

In order to combat gambling on the games, Tris Speaker did not name his starting pitchers until game time during the 1920 World Series.

*Best Minor League Team: 1920–25 Baltimore Orioles

Player vs. Team: After leading the St. Louis Cardinals to the World Championship in 1926 as a player and manager, Rogers Hornsby broke into a feud with Sam Breadon, the owner of the Cardinals. Hornsby accused Breadon of being too concerned with the dollar signs and not enough with the players, and said that he had, among other things, scheduled too many in-season exhibition games. Hornsby, the best player in the National League, was traded to the Giants for Frankie Frisch and a pitcher.

Team vs. Team: The New York Giants, apparently jealous of the success of the Yankees, threw them out of the Polo Grounds in 1922.

Best Baseball Movies:
> 1924—*Battling Orioles*
> 1925—*Life's Greatest Game*
> 1927—*Casey at the Bat*
> 1927—*Slide, Kelly, Slide*

*Uniform Changes: Sanitary factories!

New Terms or Expressions: The term "General Manager" was first applied to William Evans, a former American League umpire who became General Manager of the Cleveland Indians in 1927.

Most Wins by Pitcher:
> Jim Bagby, 1920, 31
> Burleigh Grimes, 190

Highest Winning Percentage:
> Emil Yde, 1924, 16–3, .842
> Remy Kremer, 107–55, .660

Best Unrecognized Players:
> Earl Whitehill
> Wilbur Cooper
> Bing Miller
> George Grantham
> Buddy Myer

STRANGEST BATTING STANCE

Rogers Hornsby stood very far back from home plate. As Fred Lieb tells it in *The St. Louis Cardinals, a History of a Great Baseball Club* (1944), when he came to the majors "Hornsby was more or less of a choke and crouch hitter; at the 1916 training camp [Bob] Connery had Rog change his batting stance . . . it was from that position that he later leveled off at a pitched ball; it became one of the most famous and unusual stances in baseball. No other ranking star ever stood so far away from the plate." But Hornsby, in his autobiography, gave more of the credit for developing his hitting to Dots Miller, a Cardinal infielder of the time (with a lifetime .263 batting average).

Highest-Paid Player: Babe Ruth, $80,000 (equivalent to about $520,000 today)

New Statistics:

    1920—Caught Stealing

    1923—Double Plays

    1920 N.L., 1925 A.L.—Passed Balls

    1920–25, American League Counted Stolen Bases Against Pitchers

Most Unpredictable Career: George Harper

Best Athlete in the Game: Emil Yde, a star in track and boxing at the University of Wisconsin, was a successful outfielder as well as pitcher in the minor leagues. He only pitched in the majors.

    Rogers Hornsby was a great athlete. Andy High, speaking at a SABR convention in 1979, said that Hornsby used to offer to race anybody in the league for $500, and nobody ever took him up on it. Kiki Cuyler was a terrific athlete—one of those guys who could have been in the Ty Cobb, Babe Ruth class if he'd wanted it badly enough. Of course, Babe Ruth wasn't exactly a wimp, and Lou Gehrig was probably stronger in the upper body than anyone playing major league baseball today, even with weight training and all. And he could run, too.

Most Lopsided Trade of the Decade: In May 1927, the Senators traded Buddy Myer to Boston for an infielder named Topper Rigney, who was to play only forty-five more games in the major leagues. A year and a half later, they traded five players to get Myer back.

A Very Good Movie Could Be Made About: The life and times of the most fascinating individual ever associated with major league baseball: Ban Johnson.

I Don't Know What This Has to Do with Baseball, But I Thought I'd Mention It Anyway: Just for you, Guindon . . . Herman Pillette's middle name was Polycarp.

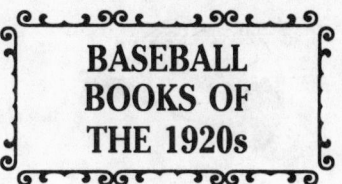

BASEBALL BOOKS OF THE 1920s

The breaking of the Black Sox scandal, ironically, coincides with the beginnings of hero journalism in American sports. Jim Carothers, asked to name the best baseball books of each decade, responds that "If I were writing the history of baseball literature, there would be few, if any, selections from the twenties and thirties, many more from the sixties and seventies." *Sport* magazine began publication in 1927.

REJUVENATION

T. Raymond Cobb, they said in May,
Has ceased to figure in the fray;
He's through; his batting eye is dim;
Why doesn't Navin pension him?

But lo, this ancient King of Swat
Once more doth bust 'em from the lot,
And come again the bleacher mob
Doth rave about T. Raymond Cobb.

Again he almost leads Ban Johnson's clan;
And yet, perhaps, there is a fan
From somewhere in this happy land
Who thinks Ty used a monkey gland.

1922 Reach Official American League Guide
                    —Author Unknown

TWENTY-TWO MEN OUT

Historians simplify impossibly complex realities into patterns of light and shadow, and the popular memory then reduces these to black and white. But few oversimplifications of memory are as bizarre as the notion that the Black Sox scandal hit baseball out of the blue, that there was just this one blight on an otherwise faultless record of integrity. In fact, of course, the Black Sox scandal was merely the largest and ugliest wart of a disease that had infested baseball at least a dozen years earlier and grown, unchecked, to ravage the features of a generation.

One thing that I have always wanted to see, and have never been able to find, is a complete list of all the men who were banned, officially or unofficially, in the various scandals that hit baseball in the 1917–1927 period. I don't think many people realize how many of them there were.

By my count, thirty-eight major league players were involved in the scandals of the era. "Involved" means either they were banned, or serious charges were made against them. Nineteen active major league players were either banned outright, or clearly unwelcome to continue in the profession, because of issues related to the integrity of the game; one more was banned but reinstated. Four retired players were seriously implicated in the scandals. One active player was banned for life and two others banned for two years or more in matters not relating to the integrity of the game. The other ten players were either cleared of the charges made against them, or allowed to stay in the game for lack of hard evidence. By no means do these counts include players who were approached about the possibility of throwing a game, or players who had incidental knowledge of a fix, or players who were alleged to have advance knowledge of a fix; that list would be enormous. Of the nineteen "hard core" of the list, not all were officially suspended, but there was no doubt about their eligibility. (For example, Bob Hoie's article in the *Baseball Historical Review* says that Chase was not formally banned from baseball by Judge Landis; however, the 1922 *Reach Guide* says that he was. Whether or not he was officially declared ineligible, Hal Chase was as welcome in baseball as a rat in a dark elevator.)

I'm not sure that I've got them all, but the ones I can find are given below, alphabetically:

Rube Benton Banned by National League, 1922, on a variety of charges including guilty knowledge of 1919 series fix, failing to report offer of $800 from Chase and Zimmerman to help fix Giants games in 1919, and counter-allegations ensuing from charge that Buck Herzog had attempted to bribe him to lose games in 1920. His story was one of the keys to breaking the scandals. Reinstated by Landis.

Bill Burns Though out of major league baseball for seven years before the scandal, Burns, a major league pitcher from 1908 to 1912, was the man who initially brought together the White Sox and the gamblers who fixed the series. Burns was discovered hiding in Mexico by Ban Johnson; Arnold Rothstein testified in court that all he knew of the fix was that Burns and Abe Attell had approached him about fixing the series.

Paul Carter National League pitcher, allegedly involved in attempt to fix Cub games, 1920. Persona non grata after 1920.

Hal Chase Involved in an endless series of gambling escapades; prominently mentioned as one of those constructing 1919 fix. Accused by his manager, George Stallings, of trying to throw a game in 1910. Charged by Christy Mathewson, his manager in 1917, with throwing games that year. Charged by Lee Magee with bribing him to lose games in 1918. Suspended by Giants for allegedly throwing games during 1919. Alleged by Rube Benton to have won $40,000 betting on 1919 series. Banned from Pacific Coast League parks in 1920 for trying to bribe an umpire. Presumably holds the all-time record for games fixed.

Eddie Cicotte World Series conspirator. His confession broke the wall of silence. Banned for life.

Ty Cobb Alleged by Dutch Leonard to have conspired with Tris Speaker to fix the final game of the 1919 season. Acknowledged writing of seemingly incriminating letter. Acquitted.

Cozy Dolan Giants' coach; alleged by Jimmy O'Connell to have been behind attempt to fix game in 1924. Gave evasive answers on examination by Landis; Banned for life.

Phil Douglas Wrote a letter to Les Mann in 1922 (he was drunk at the time) opaquely offering to desert the Giants, if rewarded, so that he wouldn't have to help McGraw win the pennant (he was mad at McGraw for chewing him out). Banned for life.

THE CALIFORNIA WINTER LEAGUE

One of the histories of baseball that should be written but never has been, as far as I know, is an account of the California Winter League, which operated for a couple of years (I think; maybe it was only one year) in the early twenties. The league included such stars as Rogers Hornsby and Ty Cobb, both of whom were player/managers.

The first time the two ever met was before a game in the California Winter League. Hornsby was introduced to Cobb and said, "Glad to meet you." Cobb said, "Nice to meet you." The next time they met was when Cobb came sliding into Hornsby at second base. Hornsby said, "Hey you, where do you get that stuff?" Cobb said, "Say you, watch your step if you don't want to get your legs cut off."

1921: THE ROWDY ELEMENT

About the time of World War I the throwing of pop bottles and beer bottles at players on the field became a serious problem. John Heydler helped to bring it under control by devising a plan wherein the concessioneers at the games, who sold the offending material, were asked to instruct their vendors to keep an eye out for the guilty parties; the league would prosecute and the vendors would serve as witnesses. It must have worked, because references to the problem declined rapidly after that.

Jean Dubuc National League pitcher. Involved with Chase and Zimmerman, 1919. Had advance knowledge of series fix. Banned for life.

Happy Felsch World Series conspirator. Banned for life.

Ray Fisher National League pitcher, banned from baseball, 1921, for alleged contract jumping. A respected gentleman and longtime baseball coach at the University of Michigan, Fisher got involved in a contract battle with August Herrmann, Cincinnati owner, at a time when Judge Landis needed Herrmann's support.

Frankie Frisch Alleged by Jimmy O'Connell to have known about attempt to fix game in 1924. Denied everything; acquitted.

Chick Gandil World Series conspirator; some have portrayed him as the real heavy, the man who set the whole thing up. Banned for life.

Joe Gedeon St. Louis second baseman. Friend of Swede Risberg. Served on the Ad Hoc Committee to Throw the World Series; banned for life.

Joe Harris American League first baseman/outfielder. Disqualified for two seasons (1920–21) for playing in outlaw league.

Claude Hendrix Apparently had agreed to throw a game that he was scheduled to start, August 31, 1920. Never officially banned, but persona non grata in baseball after 1920.

Buck Herzog Alleged by Rube Benton to have joined with Hal Chase in offering Benton $800 to lose a game in 1919. Allegedly involved in attempt to fix Cub game, August 31, 1920. No action taken; played in minors after 1920.

Joe Jackson World Series conspirator. Banned for life.

Bill James American League pitcher, 1911–1919. Name was brought up in two gambling incidents; charged with being a go-between in the 1917 business alleged by Swede Risberg, and with having knowledge of the 1919 Cobb/Speaker incident. Admitted to having collected $850 from Risberg and divided it among Detroit players, but claimed it was for bearing down harder to help beat Boston in earlier series. Acquitted.

Benny Kauff The Ty Cobb of the Federal League. Name was mentioned several times in connection with the investigation of the fixed series. Allegedly refused offer from Chase and Zimmerman of $500 to help throw games in 1919. Later banned from baseball after being charged in New York with auto theft and receiving stolen property. Sued Landis seeking reinstatement following his acquittal, but lost.

George Kelly Alleged by Jimmy O'Connell to have known about attempt to fix game in 1924. Denied everything; acquitted.

Dickie Kerr One of the "clean Sox"; suspended 1923–1925 for pitching against outlaw team (including a couple of the Black Sox) during contract dispute.

Dutch Leonard Incriminated self in the process of bringing charges against Cobb and Speaker, 1927. Never officially banned; persona non grata.

Fred McMullin Expressed an interest in helping to throw the 1919 World Series if they would let him play. Banned for life.

Lee Magee National League outfielder/infielder. Confessed in 1919 to having helped Chase and Zimmerman fix games in 1918. Stated at the time that if barred he would take some famous people with him "for tricks turned ever since 1906." Banned for life.

Billy Maharg Boxer; one major league game in 1912 and one in 1916; possibly same person as Peaches Graham, major league catcher, 1902–1912. Enlisted by Bill Burns to act as a go-between in negotiations toward fixing of 1919 World Series. Never officially banned; persona non grata.

Fred Merkle Of the famed boner in 1908. Rumored to be involved in fixing of Cub game, August 31, 1920. Retired following season; never banned or suspended.

Jimmy O'Connell Told Philadelphia infielder Heine Sand before a game in 1924 that "It will be worth $500 to you if you don't bear down too hard against us today." On whose authority he did this has never been ascertained. Banned for life.

Jimmy Ring Allegedly paid $25 by Chase after losing a game in 1918. No action taken.

Pants Rowland Chicago manager in 1917. Swede Risberg charged in 1926 that Rowland had participated in the fixing of four games between Detroit and Chicago in 1917, after the pennant race was decided. Acquitted.

Gene Paulette   National League first baseman. Accepted gifts from St. Louis gamblers, 1919. (One of the gamblers was Carl Zork, who was tried and acquitted with the Black Sox.) Banned for life.

Swede Risberg   World Series conspirator; banned for life.

Tris Speaker   Alleged by Dutch Leonard to have conspired with Ty Cobb to fix the final game of 1919 season. Acquitted.

Buck Weaver   Participated in meetings where the fixing of the World Series was discussed; banned for life for guilty knowledge.

Lefty Williams   0–3 with a 6.61 ERA during the 1919 World Series. Banned for life.

Smokey Joe Wood   Alleged by Dutch Leonard to have been the man who placed the bets for Speaker and Cobb. Acquitted.

Ross Youngs   Alleged by Jimmy O'Connell to have known about attempt to fix game in 1924. Denied everything; acquitted.

Heine Zimmerman   Outstanding National League third baseman, 1907–19; batting and home run champion, 1912. In 1919, Zimmerman and Hal Chase allegedly tried to bribe Benny Kauff, Lee Magee, Fred Toney, Rube Benton, Jean Dubuc and others to help them fix games. Banned for life.

The eleven active players who were thrown out of baseball, in addition to the Black Sox eight, were Paul Carter, Chase, Phil Douglas, Jean Dubuc, Joe Gedeon, Claude Hendrix, Benny Kauff, Lee Magee, Jimmy O'Connell, Gene Paulette, and Heine Zimmerman. The four retired players who were not invited to any old-timers games were Burns, Dolan, Maharg and Leonard.

There has always been speculation that the Cobb/Speaker matter was settled with a secret agreement, that Cobb and Speaker could stay in the game, but that neither would manage again. The record as it appears at the time is simpler, makes more sense, and is much more fair to all involved: They were acquitted. Richard Lindberg wrote an excellent history of the White Sox, *Who's on 3rd?*, but in a weak moment he complains that "Landis looked past the shady dealings of others, preferring to make scapegoats of the White Sox who had been judged not guilty by their peers." Nonsense. In straightening out the scandals of the time, Landis "looked past" the shady dealings of absolutely nobody. The recent notion that Joe Jackson, Lefty Williams *et al* were the victims of injustice is childish, an emo-

tional reaction to the story without respect for the facts. It only proves that no matter what proposition is put forward, somebody will find it necessary to take the opposite position. The only injustice that was done to Joe Jackson and friends is that the sons of bitches were allowed to walk the streets, rather than going to jail where they belonged. There is overwhelming evidence against Joe Jackson; there is no credible evidence against Tris Speaker, nothing. Landis was a poor judge, but he was a judge; he didn't ordinarily act against players unless there was evidence against them. Too many of his critics have confused "leniency" with a finding of "not guilty."

UNIFORMS IN THE 1920s

To lead off the twenties, a quote from an ad in the 1923 *Spalding Guide:* "All Spalding base ball uniforms are made by us in our own sanitary factories. They are so built and so maintained. Our employees receive the benefits that an abundance of light and air in the workrooms brings to them. When you put on your Spalding uniform, you have our assurance that it was made under clean and healthful conditions." Just thought you might like to see what kind of stuff was considered important back then.

The ad goes on to describe various styles of uniforms, from the "World Series" down to the "Amateur Special." Two styles of shirts are offered— one with a V-neck collar and the other with a "military" collar (what I've been referring to as a Nehru type). For length of sleeves, there was a choice between full, half, three-quar-

ter, or detachable. The big selection on baseball pants is between elastic or tape bottoms. There was a choice of block or fancy lettering. Colors of suits offered were mostly neutrals (white, pearl gray, brown), but a variety of stripe colors were available for the asking. The cost of the top-of-the-line uniform consisting of cap, shirt, pants, belt, and stockings was $25 to the club, $30 for one suit.

Baseball caps featured in another ad range from the solid-color "Philadelphia Style" to the "Boston Style," which has a solid-color visor but a pinstriped crown. The type of cap now worn by the Pirates was advertised as the "Chicago Style." All styles were fully equipped and ready to wear with "ventilated crowns, no lining . . . stitched visor and perspiration proof sweatband."

More movement on team

name representation. In 1921 the Cleveland Americans chose to identify themselves not by city or symbol but with "World Champions" ablaze across their shirts. The black letter Detroit "D," used in the nineteenth century, reappeared about 1922 and is still there today. The two Cardinals seesawing on a bat was in place by the same time. (Incidentally, the original nickname for the St. Louis team had nothing to do with birds. It referred to the cardinal red trimming on the uniform first used in the nineteenth century. They were called the "Cardinals" as earlier St. Louis teams had been called "Browns" and "Maroons.") The Boston Nationals had two designs to illustrate their name; one is a circular symbol on the left breast pocket that looks like an emblem of an Indian.

—Susie

THE BALTIMORE ORIOLES

	Won	Lost	Pct.	Position
1919	100	49	.671	1st (+ 8)
1920	110	43	.719	1st (+1½)
1921	119	47	.717	1st (+20)
1922	115	52	.689	1st (+10)
1923	113	54	.677	1st
1924	117	48	.709	1st (+19)
1925	105	61	.633	1st

The greatest minor league team of the 1920s, and indeed the greatest minor league team of all time, was the Baltimore Orioles of the International League from 1920 to 1925. The Orioles owner was a man by the name of Jack Dunn, who, while not the wealthiest, was the strongest, smartest, and most farsighted owner that a minor league team ever had. From the time he first owned the team, Dunn scouted the bushes and purchased the best young players that he could find, and he kept them as long as he could. He was aided by a strong baseball tradition in Baltimore, which produced several hometown players, and supported the team in the manner deserved.

When the Federal League brought major league baseball to Baltimore in 1914, Dunn complained loudly that he had a better team than the Federal League Baltimore Terrapins, but that the "minor league" label was killing his attempts to sell the team to the public. But since he couldn't sell the team, hard up for cash, he had to sell one of his most promising players, the nineteen-year-old Babe Ruth, to the Boston Red Sox. He always regretted that, and from then on swore that he would never sell a star player unless he could replace him. Dunn survived the Federal League challenge, and in time purchased their park.

As the years passed and the agreements were made that reduced the minor leagues more and more into a subservient relationship to the majors, Dunn always refused to sign. His concept of the minor leagues was that they were simply in smaller cities than the major leagues, but not in any other sense unequal, and he was not about to sign any agreement that might have required him, for example, to sell his best player to the major leagues in exchange for a fixed price, or to recognize territorial rights of the major leagues that they did not recognize for him. He felt that for the minor league teams to sell their best players to the majors would lead ultimately to the destruction of the minors. Though the wisdom of this view is now self-evident, it was not a popular opinion at the time. The 1922 *Reach Guide*

JACK DUNN

scoffed at the minor leagues' need for independence, and in discussing the refusal of the top minor leagues to agree to a draft agreement with the majors, argued that "to off-set this rather shadowy advantage, they cannot secure new blood from lesser leagues, and will be forced to purchase such players as they need." The editor also argued that "The Baltimore Club's idea that a AA League Club should not sell a star player at any price is all wrong, as the sale of real stars not only helps to equalize teams, but the money derived from sales to the major leagues amply compensates for possible lessened gate receipts."

Fortunately, Jack Dunn never accepted that nonsense, and by 1920 there was no doubt in anyone's mind that his team was as good as many of the "major league" teams. The same *Reach Guide* observed a few pages later that the "Baltimore team was universally regarded as of real major league caliber." Unfortu-

MOSES SOLOMON

In the fall of 1923, John McGraw paid $4,500 (equivalent to about $30,000 now) to acquire a player who had just established a new minor league record for home runs in a season. Four and a half thousand dollars wasn't a lot of money for a prospect even then—the A's would shell out $106,000 for another Moses a year later—but Moses H. Solomon came with special credentials, and became the immediate darling of the Big City press. He was christened the Rabbi of Swat, and he was supposed to hit home runs, and he was supposed to have a special appeal to the New York audience. He had hit forty-nine home runs that year at Hutchinson in the Southwestern League, and no one but Babe Ruth had ever hit that many. Anywhere.

Moe Solomon's lifetime major league batting average was .375—three for eight. Seems like he had a lot of trouble with the glove and a certain amount of trouble with the curve ball, and the Giants had a couple of other rookies in 1924 that they preferred to go with—Bill Terry and Hack Wilson. Moses was out of baseball in a few years; his forty-nine home runs in 1923 were over half of his career

nately, all the other minor league teams eventually did accept it, and thus ultimately the minor leagues shriveled up and knelt.

The Orioles star pitcher was Robert Moses Groves (Lefty Grove), who was only the greatest pitcher ever to heave a horsehide. Lefty's records with Baltimore were 12–2, 25–10, 18–8, 27–10, and 27–6 (or 26–6). He led the league in strikeouts from 1921 through 1924, with totals ranging from 205 to 330. Eventually, Dunn would relent and sell him to Philadelphia for $106,000 (or $100,600, depending on who you believe), surpassing the amount New York paid for Babe Ruth as the highest figure ever spent for a ballplayer, at any level. $106,000 then would be equivalent to about $700,000 today.

But Grove was merely the peak of the mountain; the 1922 Orioles probably had a better pitching staff than the 1927 Yankees. While Grove was 109–36 during those five years, a pitcher named Johnny Ogden was 118–45. Ogden was 27–9 in 1920, 31–8 in 1921, and generally accepted as the best pitcher in the minor leagues at that time. John McGraw wanted him for the Giants, Connie Mack wanted him for the A's, and Pat Moran wanted him for the Reds, but Baltimore had him, and Baltimore kept him.

Between Ogden and Grove came an eccentric named Rube Parnham. Parnham pitched briefly for the Philadelphia Athletics in 1916, the worst major league team of this century, and won two out of three starts. Parnham pitched eleven innings with Philadelphia in 1917 before being acquired by the Orioles, for whom he was 16–9 in 1917, 22–10 in 1918, and 28–12 in 1919. In 1920 he jumped the team after going 5–0 at the start of the season, not returning until 1922. In 1923, he was 33–7 (making Grove the number two pitcher on the staff at 27–10), and ended the season with twenty straight wins. (He had won eighteen straight games with a week left in the season when he jumped the team again. He showed up at the park on the final day of the season, and won both ends of a double-header to make it twenty straight.) He left baseball again in 1924, and his total record for the five years was 60–22.

When those three weren't pitching there was Jake Bentley, the regular first baseman, who would take a turn on the mound once in a while and went 16–3 in 1920, 12–1 in 1921, and 13–2 in 1922 before moving on to the New York Giants, for whom he went 13–8 and 16–5 the next two seasons, hitting .427 for good measure in 1923 (he was traded to Philadelphia in 1926, and the Phillies made him a first baseman again). Other pitchers who passed through included George Earnshaw, Tommy Thomas, and Clifford Jackson, the former two very successful starters in the major leagues later on. A pitcher named Harry Frank went 25–12 in 1920. In 1925, the first year without Grove, Tommy

Thomas won thirty-two games, George Earnshaw twenty-nine and Johnny Ogden twenty-eight.

The rest of the team was not as good as the pitching, but still the best lineup in a good minor league. Probably the biggest star was Bentley, the pitching first baseman, who in 1921 hit .412 with 47 doubles, 16 triples and 24 home runs in 141 games. When the Giants acquired Bentley in 1923 it was a surprise to most that he was made into a pitcher; the general feeling was that he was more valuable as a first baseman. Other stars included Fritz Maisel, Twitchy Dick Porter, Joe Boley, Maxie Bishop, Merwin Jacobson, Otis Lawry and Maurice Archdeacon.

In 1920 the Orioles won their last twenty-five games in a row, with an outstanding Toronto team hot on their heels and winning twenty of twenty-two, one of the greatest minor league pennant races. In 1921 the Orioles won twenty-seven in a row early in the season to make a shambles of the race.

As is often true of great pitching teams, the Orioles' performance in postseason play was a disappointment. In 1920 they crushed St. Paul, champions of the American Association, five games to one to win the Minor League World Series, the second to be played. In 1921 they were upset in the Junior World Series by a Louisville team managed by the young Joe McCarthy. It was a classic series. In Game One Louisville pasted Lefty Grove and won, 16–1, but Johnny Ogden shut them down in the second and evened it with a 2–1 victory. In Game Three Louisville exploded again off Tommy Thomas and Grove in relief, winning 14–8.

In Game Four in Louisville, Baltimore was ahead 12–4 in the seventh inning when a call went against the home team, and the crowd went wild, swarming the field and throwing objects at the police and umpires—a minor league Joe Medwick incident, I suppose. The game was forfeited, and the series even.

Play resumed four days later in Baltimore, and Baltimore went ahead three games to two with a 10–5 victory behind Johnny Ogden. But in Game Six, Louisville beat Lefty again, 3–0, to tie it up, and won the two final games 7–6 and 11–5 to emerge as champions. Joe McCarthy's teams were tough to beat in postseason play.

In 1922, St. Paul again won the American Association, and the Orioles again crushed them, four games to two. In 1923 they were upset by Kansas City, five games to four. In 1924 they were upset by St. Paul, five games to four.

The end of the Oriole dynasty was visible in the east after that season: The rest of the league was tired of getting beaten. Under the leadership of Dunn, the International League had been the last minor league to hold out against the major league draft arrangement, refusing to have its best players taken from it for

total in professional baseball. He had a successful post-playing career, investing in real estate. The pressure that was put upon him to become New York's Jewish superstar is something that no one, to this point, has been able to live up to. Though I chose not to cite him, the Hartung award for the 1970s would fit Ron Blomberg as well as it would fit anyone. (More details on the story of Moses Solomon can be found in an article by Howard Lavelle in the 1976 *Baseball Research Journal.*)

$5,000. But with the Orioles able to keep their best players, they were able to stay in control of the league, and the rest of the league began to tire of supporting this policy. In 1924 the major leagues agreed to modifications of the original draft arrangement (a team was allowed to hold a player for a few years before having him drafted), and the International League capitulated and signed the agreement. In fairness to the other owners, there may have been a conflict between what was good for the minor leagues in the long run and what was good in the short run. It probably was not too healthy for the International League to be dominated by Baltimore, and while it is no doubt true that they would have been better off in the long run to have emulated Dunn, and started developing their own stars, it is also true that many of them did not have the financial resources to seriously consider that option. Anyway, faced with the prospect of losing his star players for $5,000, Dunn was forced to start selling them to the major leagues, and the Oriole dynasty began to crumble. By 1927 the ashes of the great Oriole team were spread around the American League, and Baltimore was without its champions.

1923: 325 HITS

The minor league record for hits in a season was set in 1923 by Paul Strand, with Salt Lake City in the Pacific Coast League. Strand's complete record for the season appears below:

Year	G	AB	R	H	2B	3B	HR	RBI	SB	Avg.
1923	194	825	180	325	66	13	43	187	22	.394

Strand led the Pacific Coast League in 1923 in runs, hits, home runs, runs batted in, and batting average. Salt Lake City finished with a record of 94 wins, 105 losses.

1924: 100 DOUBLES

In the Western League in 1924, an outfielder named Lyman Lamb hit 100 doubles, one of the more remarkable of minor league records. No other player in organized ball ever hit more than 75 doubles in a season, even in the elongated schedule of the Pacific Coast League. Lamb's complete record appears below:

Year	G	AB	R	H	2B	3B	HR	RBI	SB	Avg.
1924	168	699	149	261	100	4	19	—	15	.373

The Western League did not count RBI at this time. Lamb led the league in hits, 261, but finished third on the Tulsa team in batting, behind someone named Lelivelt, presumably Jack, and somebody called Washburn, presumably not Ray. Washburn hit .375 with 53 doubles, 48 homers and 458 total bases. Tulsa finished third, with a record of 98–69.

1924: OKMULGEE TAKES IT APART

One of the more fearsome minor league teams at a lower level was the Okmulgee team in the Western Association in 1924 (the Western Association was not the same as the Western League, in which Lamb hit his hundred doubles). First baseman Wilbur Davis had 487 total bases, the most ever outside of the Pacific Coast League, and an outfielder named G. Davis, who was called Stormy, had 467 and scored 187 runs. The team scored 1,158 runs in 158 games. A few of their individual batting records follow:

Pos	Player	G	AB	R	H	2B	3B	HR	RBI	SB	Avg.
C	Miner	53	195	40	79	20	2	5	—	4	.405
1B	W. Davis	160	650	151	260	50	11	51	—	6	.400
OF	Bratcher	130	564	140	216	44	11	23	—	11	.383
OF	Stellbauer	154	631	151	233	44	7	32	—	0	.369
CF	G. Davis	160	687	187	246	48	10	51	—	9	.364
3B	Corgan	129	504	80	172	37	7	14	—	9	.341

1929: 553 TOTAL BASES

In the Pacific Coast League in 1929, Ike Boone had 553 total bases, a minor league record (Paul Strand in 1923 had 546, the second-highest total). Boone's complete record appears below:

Year	G	AB	R	H	2B	3B	HR	RBI	SB	Avg.
1929	198	794	195	323	49	8	55	218	9	.407

Boone had a lifetime minor league batting average of .370, and a major league batting average of .319.

They had some other features, too. Stormy Davis had thirty-three assists in the outfield. They had three twenty-game winners. A pitcher named Walkup was 23–3 with an ERA of 2.60, with 165 strikeouts and only 37 walks. (Two pitchers named Jim Walkup, both of whom were from Havana, Arkansas, later pitched in the major leagues. My guess is that this was Jim Walkup the elder.) Their other pitchers included Cantrell (21–7), Tauscher (12–4), Moore (17–6), and Lyle (23–13). Okmulgee won both halves of a split season, going 51–21 the first half and 59–27 the second.

1924: OLD BALLPLAYERS NEVER DIE

The 1924 *Spalding Guide* reported Joe McGinnity, the Iron Man of twenty years earlier (and still an active pitcher with Dubuque of the Missouri Valley League, where he was 15–12 in 1923) was of the opinion that "the pitchers of the present time are not as good as they were in other days . . . McGinnity calls attention to the faults of the present-day pitchers and is depressed by the fact that so few of them possess a good curve or try to acquire one. He thinks this is due to the fact that so many pitchers 'got by' in the past with a straight delivery because they pretended to have a spitball, or some other method of pitching that was out of the ordinary."

❦ AUSTIN McHENRY ❦

Austin McHenry was an outfielder with the St. Louis Cardinals who hit .350 with 37 doubles, 17 home runs and 102 RBI in 1921, developed a brain tumor in 1922 and died of it that winter, leaving an unfinished career that has been speculated about ever since. I decided to finish the career out with the Brock2 system, just to see what we would get:

Age	G	AB	Runs	Hits	2B	3B	HR	RBI	BB	Avg.
20	0	0	0	0	0	0	0	0	0	0
21	0	0	0	0	0	0	0	0	0	0
22	80	272	32	71	12	6	1	29	21	.261
23	110	371	41	106	19	11	1	47	19	.286
24	137	504	66	142	19	11	10	65	25	.282
25	152	574	92	201	37	8	17	102	38	.350
26	157	581	72	177	29	9	16	80	36	.305
27	154	572	86	191	33	8	19	90	43	.334
28	155	570	74	182	30	7	17	83	36	.319
29	158	580	69	176	30	6	16	80	41	.303
30	156	567	67	176	29	6	14	77	40	.310
31	156	561	64	173	29	5	13	74	41	.308
32	155	553	57	164	27	5	11	69	41	.297
33	154	541	53	157	26	4	10	65	45	.290
34	153	533	50	156	26	4	9	62	38	.293
35	152	525	46	148	24	3	8	58	42	.282
36	81	255	21	71	12	1	4	27	20	.278
37	31	77	6	20	3	0	1	8	6	.258
	2143	7636	897	2310	385	94	168	1016	532	.303

However, the Brock2 system bases projections on what the player has done over the three previous years, and in the case of McHenry this may be inaccurate, because that takes him back into the era of the dead ball, and he would have finished his career in the lively ball era. The 1921 record was compiled in a league that scored 5,632 runs, which at that time was an enormous number, but which continued to go up after that. To partially compensate for this, I substituted a 1920 season that was actually the average of 1920 and 1921, and derived a second set of projections from that. These projections, which are probably still conservative, call for a .310 career average, 2,576 hits and 190 home runs. It is certainly possible that McHenry could have been a 3,000-hit man if he had had the right combination of desire and luck.

I'll run a similar thing later for Lyman Bostock, and the parallels between the two are strong. It strikes me that there is something ironic in a society that wages war, and well, on every illness known, but allows thugs to roam the streets with handguns. Maybe instead we should try to eradicate handguns and license brain tumors; the results would probably be about the same.

Anyway, Bostock and McHenry were very similar types of offensive players; indeed, Bostock's 1977 season and McHenry's 1921 season could easily represent the efforts of the same man:

	G	AB	Run	Hit	2B	3B	HR	RBI	BB	SB	Avg.
Bostock	153	593	104	199	36	12	14	90	51	16	.336
McHenry	152	574	92	201	37	8	17	102	38	10	.350

Each player was twenty-six years old at the end of this season; each died at age twenty-seven. McHenry played part of one more season and hit .303; Bostock played most of one more season and hit .296. Bostock's great year was played in the shadow of Rod Carew, who hit .388, the highest average in the American League in twenty years; McHenry's year was played in the shadow of Rogers Hornsby, who hit .397, highest average in the National League in twenty-two years. For what it is worth, I will mention that Bostock was born on November 22 and died on September 23, while McHenry was born on September 22 and died on November 27. Both players were fast, and though neither was regarded as a great outfielder, each had been moved to center field in the season of his death.

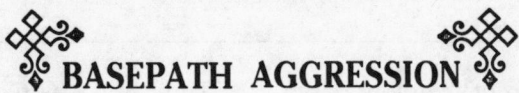

❖ BASEPATH AGGRESSION ❖

In selecting the most aggressive baserunner of the 1920s, we get into a problem of how to define "aggression"? Babe Ruth was rather vain about his speed, and he was probably allowed to get by with some things as a baserunner that any normal human being would have been admonished for. In 1923 he was seventeen for thirty-eight as a base stealer, and if you think he was probably running in throwaway situations, consider this: The 1926 World Series ended when Ruth was thrown out trying to steal second with the Yankees down 3–2 and Bob Meusel at bat. Even as late as the 1932 series, Ruth, as a gimpy thirty-seven-year-old, twice went from first to third on a single to left field (a runner goes from first to third on a single to left only about 10 percent of the time; an average player probably doesn't do it twice a season). In part that's a testimony to Riggs Stephenson's throwing arm, but it is also part of a pattern. We don't have data on how many times people were thrown out on the bases, but if we did, I think Ruth would be the leader during the 1920s.

Using another definition of an "aggressive" baserunner, a heads-up type of player who fights for every base he can get and spares no baseman who would deny it to him, we probably would pick Frankie Frisch.

The 1930s

HOW THE GAME WAS PLAYED

Following the 1930 season, in which runs scored rose to historic levels and any number of batting records were established, some action is supposed to have been taken to deaden the baseballs a little bit. I would tell you what that action was, but I was not able to find out. Anyway, the baseball of the 1930s was, from that point on, fundamentally a resumption of the baseball of the twenties. Batting averages and home run totals stayed high (to get technical, batting averages dropped a little and home runs continued to increase, as more and more players came into the game who had mastered the art of

the uppercut). Stolen bases and sacrifice hits continued to decline throughout the decade.

For some reason, a gap developed between the offensive levels of the two leagues; the American League offenses continued to rip, but the National League became more of a pitcher's league. The American League scored more runs than the National every year from 1931 to 1942, and in much of that period the differences are enormous. In 1933 American League teams scored almost five runs per game (4.96), and National League teams less than four per game (3.97). This is the only time in history until the late seventies that this kind of gap has developed.

The game was rich in characters but not particularly rich in strategy. Night baseball began to arrive late in the decade, but there really is no other decade in the history of the sport in which the game changed so little as it did between 1929 and 1939.

WHERE THE GAME WAS PLAYED

Major league cities during the thirties included Boston, Brooklyn, Chicago, Cincinnati, Cleveland, Detroit, New York, Philadelphia, Pittsburgh, St. Louis, and Washington. By 1939 the location of the major league teams was seriously out of whack with the nation's population distribution.

WHO THE GAME WAS PLAYED BY

By now the generation of players that Kirby Higbe accurately called the Babe Ruth generation was strongly entrenched. The ethnic identity of the players was still observable, and still more important then than it is now; many of these players are still second-generation or third-generation immigrants. The Italian population in baseball at this time has been much commented upon, in part perhaps because Italian names are easy to recognize, and there were a good many Italian stars (DiMaggio, Dolph Camilli, Ernie Lombardi), but in truth there were probably always more players of German descent than Italian. For the first time, the state of California became prominent as the garden of young baseball stars, with Joe DiMaggio (1936) and Ted Williams (1939) the most conspicuous California products. In terms of numbers, the South was probably the most productive region, and in particular the hill country of Arkansas, Tennessee, and Oklahoma. The number of educated players was probably at an all-time low.

Branch Rickey, one of the dominant figures of the era as mastermind of the strong St. Louis Cardinal teams, said, "I offered mill hands, plowboys, high school kids a better way of life. They rose on sandlots to big city diamonds. They earned more in a month than they could have earned in a year." That is according to *Branch Rickey: A Biography* by Murray Polner. Dizzy Dean was perhaps the quintessential player of the era. Dean would drop by Rickey's office, prop his feet up on the desk and "talk country." "If there was one more like him," Rickey said, "I'd get out of the game." He once said to his family that he wondered what a lawyer and educated man like himself was doing dealing with the likes of Dizzy Dean for a living. Yet curiously, though Rickey was an educated man who didn't drink, swear, or attend baseball games on Sunday, his teams both in St. Louis and Brooklyn were always the hardest-drinking, loudest-swearing, most raucous in the league. And in that as in everything else, all baseball men followed the leadership of Branch Rickey.

JOE DIMAGGIO

Checking In

1930—Earl Weaver, St. Louis
1931—Willie Mays, Westfield, Alabama
      Ernie Banks, Dallas
      Mickey Mantle, Spavinaw, Oklahoma
      Eddie Mathews, Texarkana, Texas
1932—Maury Wills, Washington, D.C.
      Ray Charles, Albany, Georgia
1933—Rocky Colavito, New York City
1934—Hank Aaron, Mobile, Alabama
      Roger Maris, Fargo, North Dakota
      Roberto Clemente, Carolina, Puerto Rico
      Al Kaline, Baltimore
1935—Frank Robinson, Beaumont, Texas
      Bob Gibson, Omaha, Nebraska
      Sandy Koufax, Brooklyn
      Harmon Killebrew, Fayette, Idaho
1937—Brooks Robinson, Little Rock, Arkansas
      Juan Marichal, Laguna Verde, Dominican Republic
1938—Willie McCovey, Mobile, Alabama
1939—Lou Brock, El Dorado, Arkansas
      Carl Yastrzemski, Southampton, New York

Checking Out

1930—William Howard Taft, 73
1931—Thomas Edison, 84
      Charles Comiskey, 72
1932—Dan Brouthers, 74
1933—Bill Veeck, Sr., influenza, 55
      Ring Lardner, 48
1934—Wilbert Robinson, 70
      John McGraw, uremia, 60
1935—Paul Hines, 80
      Hank O'Day, bronchial pneumonia, 74
      Billy Sunday, 72
      Len Koenecke, fire extinguisher, 29
1936—Deacon McGuire, 72
      Charles Stoneham, Bright's disease, 59
1937—John D. Rockefeller, 98
      George Wright, 90
      Harry Stovey, 80
      Ned Hanlon, 79
      Rube Benton, car wreck, 49
1938—Silver King, 70
      Bob Fothergill, 38
1939—Deacon White, 92
      Abner Dalrymple, 81
      Jacob Ruppert, phlebitis, 71
      Al Munro Elias, 67

THE 1930s IN A BOX

Attendance Data:

Total:	81 million (81,013,329)
Highest:	Chicago Cubs, 1930, 1,463,624
	New York Yankees, 9,089,953
Lowest:	St. Louis Browns, 1935, 80,922
	St. Louis Browns, 1,184,076

You sometimes hear it said that entertainment industries, such as the movies and baseball, thrive during a recession. Well, any idea that baseball thrived during the Great Depression is quite erroneous. After a good start, attendance during the years 1932–1935 was rolled back to the levels of twenty-five years earlier; it recovered somewhat after that, but never returned to the peaks of the mid- and late-twenties. Few industries in this country had a good decade; baseball certainly did not.

Most Home Runs:

Jimmie Foxx, 1932, 58

Hank Greenberg, 1938, 58

Jimmie Foxx, 415

Best Won-Lost Record by Team:

Philadelphia A's, 1931, 107–45, .704

970–554, .636, by the Yankees

Worst Won-Lost Record by Team:

Boston Braves, 1935, 38–115, .248

578–951, .378, St. Louis Browns

Heaviest Player: Jumbo Brown, a pitcher with the Yankees and Giants, was 6′4″ and dented the scales at 295. So far as I know, that is the grossest tonnage ever acknowledged by a major league player.

Lightest Player: Pat Ankenman, who played one game for the Browns in 1936, was 5′4″ and weighed 125. The smallest player of note was Charlie Dressen, who stood 5′6″ and weighed a little under 150.

Most Strikeouts by Pitcher:

Bob Feller, 1939, 246

Lefty Gomez, 1,337

Highest Batting Average:

Bill Terry, 1930, .401

Bill Terry, .352

Hardest-Throwing Pitcher: Bob Feller

Best Baseball Books:

1930—*Buck's Winning Hit,* by Elmer Dawson

1935—*Standing the Gaff,* by Steamboat Johnson (reminiscences of a minor league umpire)

1940—*Baseball, Individual Play and Team Strategy,* by John Coombs (Colby Jack tells "how to")

Best Outfield Arms:

Mel Ott

Chick Hafey

Worst Outfield Arm: Riggs Stephenson

Most Runs Batted In:

Hack Wilson, 1930, 190

Jimmie Foxx, 1,403

Most-Aggressive Baserunner: Pepper Martin
Fastest Player: Evar Swanson
Slowest Player: Ernie Lombardi
Best Control Pitcher: Red Lucas
*Nicknames: A mean streak emerges.
Most Stolen Bases:

Ben Chapman, 1931, 61
Ben Chapman, 269

Best-Looking Player: Hank Greenberg
Ugliest Players:

Ernie Lombardi
Suitcase Seeds

Strangest Batting Stance: Possibly Al Simmons (Bucketfoot Al), one of the few players ever nicknamed for his odd and supposedly incorrect batting style.

It's hard to say, to tell you the truth. These comments are based on one of two things—comments from the time or photographs, mostly from the Guides. For some reason, the fashion of the time was to photograph a player as he was completing his swing. What I mean by "fashion" is, if you look at a hundred photographs of players at bat in either the *Spalding* or *Reach* guides of the thirties, the odds are that all hundred will show the player finishing his swing. In the guides for 1932 to 1939, I doubt that there are ten photographs of players taking their stance, whereas there are thousands of photographs of players completing their swing. This makes it hard to answer the question.

Clint Hartung Award: Don Padgett
Outstanding Sportswriter: Grantland Rice
Most-Admirable Superstar: Charlie Gehringer
Least-Admirable Superstar: Hack Wilson
Franchise Shifts: None
New Stadium: 1931—Municipal Stadium, Cleveland (baseball, 1932) Indians played there only on weekends until 1948.
Best Pennant Race: 1930 National League

The National League had very good pennant races almost every year, while the American League had very bad pennant races almost every year. The Cardinals in 1930 were 13½ behind on August 8, in fourth place and only one game over .500 (53–52). They were 39–10 the rest of the way, a .796 percentage in the stretch, taking a three-game series against Brooklyn in Brooklyn, September 16–18 (remembered for the alleged kidnapping of Flint Rhem) to move into first place.

Best World Series: 1931 (Pepper Martin vs. Mickey Cochrane)
Best-Hitting Pitcher: Wes Ferrell
Worst-Hitting Pitcher: Johnny Broaca
*Best Minor League Teams:

1937 Newark Bears
1934 Los Angeles Angels

Best Minor League Player: Nick Cullop
Best Negro League Players:

Satchel Paige
Cool Papa Bell
Judy Johnson
Josh Gibson
Buck Leonard

WALTER "JUMBO" BROWN

Odd Couple: Joe DiMaggio and Lefty Gomez

Joe McCarthy assigned Gomez to room with DiMaggio when DiMag first arrived in 1936. The two men were personality opposites, DiMaggio shy and taciturn, Gomez gregarious and hyperactive. That's probably why McCarthy put them together, feeling that Gomez' good humor would help keep DiMaggio relaxed. Anyway, they became the best of friends, and it has been written that DiMaggio idolized the older, more sophisticated Gomez. That's been written, I say; personally, I find it difficult to conceive of Joe DiMaggio idolizing anyone, and most of the more sophisticated people that I know are not called "Goofy."

Residential Intellectual: Moe Berg

Drinking Men:

Jimmie Foxx (Ted Williams said in *My Turn at Bat* that Foxx regularly carried a flask of Scotch in his hip pocket.)

Hack Wilson

Len Koenecke

Bobo Newsome

Earl Whitehill

Paul Waner

LEFTY GROVE

New Equipment: After the 1933 season, the National League made a widely and deliberately publicized attempt to add more life to the baseball that they were using. National League runs per game did increase by 22 percent in 1934, but offense remained well below the levels of the American League.

*Player vs. Team: Joe DiMaggio vs. the Yankees

Team vs. Team: The essential battles of the 1920s and thirties were between major league and minor league teams. When Bob Feller was signed in 1936, his first professional activity was at the major league level, with Cleveland, and he was a seventeen-year-old sensation of the highest order. The Des Moines club in the Western League, which had been trying to sign Feller, protested that its rights in the matter had been violated, as, under the major-minor agreement of 1921, the major leagues had agreed not to sign players (other than college players) who were not already in organized ball. In a controversial and much-publicized case, Judge Landis allowed Feller to stay with Cleveland but awarded Des Moines $7,500 in damages.

Best Baseball Movies:
>1934—*Death on the Diamond* (a mystery melodrama starring Joseph Sawyer and Robert Young)
>
>1935—*Alibi Ike* (starring Joe E. Brown and Olivia de Havilland)

*Uniform Changes: Numbers on uniforms

*New Terms or Expressions: Base ball becomes one word

Most Wins by Pitcher:
>Lefty Grove, 1931, 31
>
>Lefty Grove, 199

Highest Winning Percentage:
>Johnny Allen, 1937, 15–1, .938
>
>Lefty Grove, 199–76, .724

Best Unrecognized Players:
>Sammy West
>
>Harlond Clift

Highest-Paid Player:
>Babe Ruth (about $80,000)
>
>Equivalent to about $650,000 today

New Statistics:
>1933—Hit into double play (N.L.)
>
>1939—Grounded into double play (both)

*Most Unpredictable Career: Wally Moses

Best Athletes in the Game:
>Joe Medwick
>
>Jimmie Foxx
>
>Joe DiMaggio

Most Lopsided Trade of the Decade: May 14, 1932; Cincinnati Reds acquired Ernie Lombardi as a throw-in in a three-for-three trade that was basically Babe Herman for Tony Cuccinello.

A Very Good Movie Could Be Made About: The Homestead Grays, the great Negro League team

I Don't Know What This Has to Do with Baseball, But I Thought I'd Mention It Anyway: In the Western Association in 1936, the top two hitters were named Arthur Rebel and Lynn South.

HARLOND CLIFT

MAJOR LEAGUE ALL-STAR TEAM
1930–1939
Records in seasonal notation, based on 154 games played.
Pitchers based on 40 starts.

Pos	Player	Years	Hits	HR	RBI	Avg.	Other
C	Bill Dickey	7.88	182	21	119	.320	
1B	Jimmie Foxx	9.53	193	43	147	.336	.652 Slugging
2B	Charlie Gehringer	9.31	200	16	108	.331	127 Runs
3B	Harlond Clift	5.79	162	21	114	.287	105 Walks
SS	Arky Vaughan	7.46	189	10	85	.329	Only 25 Strikeouts
LF	Chuck Klein	8.73	192	27	112	.326	
CF	Joe DiMaggio	3.60	220	38	155	.341	92 X-Base Hits
RF	Mel Ott	9.58	175	32	119	.313	100 Walks

	Pitcher	Years	Won-Lost	SO	ERA	Other
RH	Dizzy Dean	6.77	22–12	168	2.97	
LH	Carl Hubbell	8.77	21–12	146	2.70	Only 53 Walks
LH	Lefty Gomez	7.61	22–12	176	3.23	
LH	Lefty Grove	7.94	25–10	165	2.91	

TY COBB'S ALL-STAR TEAM

1B—George Sisler, 2B—Eddie Collins, 3B—Buck Weaver, SS—Honus Wagner, LF—Joe Jackson, CF—Tris Speaker, RF—Babe Ruth, C—Mickey Cochrane or Bill Dickey, Pitchers—Ed Walsh, Walter Johnson, Pete Alexander, Eddie Plank.

BABE RUTH'S ALL-STAR TEAM

1B—Hal Chase, 2B—Nap Lajoie, 3B—Jimmy Collins, SS—Honus Wagner, OF—Ty Cobb, Tris Speaker, and "X"; C—Ray Schalk, Pitchers—Walter Johnson, Christy Mathewson, Pete Alexander and Herb Pennock.

NICKNAMES

Nicknames in the thirties got nasty. There have always been a few less-than-complimentary nicknames around, sometimes more than a few, but in the thirties, under the pressure of economic catastrophy on the one hand and journalism as hero-worship on the other, nicknames in large numbers emerged as a way of defining the limitations of one and all. Harry Davis was called "Stinky," Frankie Hayes was called "Blimp," Red Lucas was "The Nashville Narcissus," Ernie Lombardi "Schnozz," and Eric McNair "Boob." Hugh Mulcahy, who lost seventy-six games in four years, was therefore called "Losing Pitcher Mulcahy," and Lynn Nelson was called "Line Drive Nelson" because everything he threw up there came rocketing back at him. Walter Beck, a pitcher with a career record of 38–69, was called "Boom Boom."

You didn't want to be fat in this climate, or it became part of your name. Freddie Fitzsimmons, a fine pitcher, was called "Fat Freddie," Babe Phelps was also called "Blimp," Walter Brown was called "Jumbo," and Alfred Dean was "Chubby" Dean. Bob Fothergill, of course, was called "Fatty," and a couple of players were called "Porky." Johnny Riddle was called "Mutt," and Bob Seeds was called "Suitcase" either because of his huge shoes or because he was traded or released so often. Nicknames, in this way, tended to call attention not to the player's strengths, but to his weaknesses. Leo Durocher was not "The Little General" or "The Peerless Leader," but "The Lip." Nick Cullop, whose face was beet red, was called "Old Tomato Face." Harvey Hendrick was called "Gink." Sammy Byrd, a defensive replacement for the Bambino, was called "Babe Ruth's Legs," a nickname which has no parallel that I know of (no one was ever called "Mark Belanger's Bat" or anything). Dom Dallessandro was called "Dim Dom," a play on sounds, and Bill Zuber was called "Goober Zuber," a terrific play on sounds but, again, not high on my list of things I should like to be known as.

In this context, even nicknames that were intended to be complimentary, or at least innocent, start to sound suspicious. Morrie Arnovich was "Snooker." Harry Danning was "Harry the Horse." Odell Hale was "Bad News." Dick Bartell was "Rowdy Richard." George Selkirk was called "Twinkletoes" (try hanging that on a major league player today, and see how it dances). Merrill May was called Pinkie, according to his son, because "he had the red ass." I'm sure no harm was intended, but would you want to have the nicknames assigned to Vernon Gomez (Goofy), Dick Porter (Twitchy), Alan Strange (Inky), Lloyd Brown (Gimpy), Atley Donald (Swampy), or Mel Harder (Wimpy)? Sounds like the Seven Dwarfs against Popeye the Sailor Man. Roy Mahaffey, by the way, was called "Popeye." Bill Dietrich, who wore glasses and was slightly pop-eyed, was called "Bullfrog Bill." Hazen Shirley Cuyler, who stuttered as a youth, was called "Kiki," because that was what he would say when attempting to pronounce his last name; at any odds, I'm sure he preferred that to being called Hazen Shirley. Another player, Johnny Tyler, was called "Ty Ty," but I don't know whether he had the same problem.

Great players were more fortunate, but not immune. How would a major league star react today if you called him "Bobo," like Buck Newsome, or "Dizzy," like Jerome Dean? Johnny Murphy, an outstanding relief pitcher, was called "Grandma" and "Rocking Chair Johnny." Al Simmons was called "Bucketfoot Al"—again, calling attention to his supposed weakness. Joe Medwick's name has been politely shortened to "Ducky" by future generations, because people today are reluctant to believe that a Hall of Famer was actually called "Ducky Wucky." But he was. Let's make up an all-star team to finish this off:

Left-handed pitcher	Gimpy
Right-handed pitcher	Wimpy
Catcher	Blimp
First base	Stinky
Second base	Inky
Third base	Pinkie
Shortstop	Rowdy Richard
Left field	Twitchy
Center field	Snooker
Right field	Ducky Wucky

IS THAT POSSIBLE?

Charlie Gehringer in 1936 led the American League in both errors by a second baseman (25) and fielding percentage by a second baseman (.974). The fluke occurrence happened because only four men played regularly at second base in the American League that year, and each of the four happened to make exactly 25 errors. Gehringer, with more total chances than the others, thus led in both errors (a four-way tie) and fielding percentage (by himself).

Frank Malzone in 1957 accomplished the same feat.

NEW TERMS AND EXPRESSIONS

"Baseball" was originally "base ball", two words. Beginning in the nineteenth century, but not really gathering momentum until the 1920s, it began to be written as one word. This seems odd to me, that a word in such common usage would change its spelling, as if "president" would somehow become "presadent" or "suburb" become "sub urb". I guess it happens sometimes. The guides were the last holdouts, using "base ball" until 1940.

ROGERS HORNSBY'S ALL-STAR TEAM

1B—George Sisler, 2B—Eddie Collins, 3B—Pie Traynor, SS—Honus Wagner, LF—Babe Ruth, CF—Tris Speaker, RF—Ty Cobb, C—Mickey Cochrane, Gabby Hartnett or Bill Dickey, Pitchers—Pete Alexander, Walter Johnson, Lefty Grove, Carl Hubbell.

WALTER JOHNSON'S ALL-STAR TEAM

1B—Hal Chase, 2B—Nap Lajoie or Eddie Collins, 3B—Jimmy Collins, SS—Honus Wagner, OF—Ty Cobb, Tris Speaker and Babe Ruth, C—Bill Dickey or Johnny Kling, Pitcher—Pete Alexander.

WALLACE MOSES

THANK GOD I'M A COUNTRY BOY

Kirby Higbe says in his autobiography that he developed his strong arm by throwing rocks at the Negroes. Satchel Paige says in his that he developed his arm by throwing rocks at white boys. Says he crippled up some of them pretty good.

WALLY MOSES

I remember Wally Moses from my childhood. He stayed in baseball after his playing days, as a batting instructor, among other things, and was famous for being able to drive a ball 325, 350 feet when he was pushing sixty. What people didn't understand is that he might have been at his peak then. Wally's career was a constant adventure, and taken at his best he was one of the best. When he first came up with the A's he hit .325 in half a season, and in his first full season (1936) he hit .345. He never hit higher than .320 again, and eventually slid as low as .245 and .239. He hit .345 in 1936 but without power, so he decided to add that in 1937, and he hit .320

with 48 doubles, 13 triples and 25 home runs—a total of 86 extra base hits. It was a campaign worthy of a Hall of Famer; he was never in double figures in home runs again, and never had as many as 60 extra base hits in a season again. He continued to hit .300 for four more years, though, before slipping to .270 and then .245. Realizing that if

he was going to hit that way he had to do some other things, Wally stole fifty-six bases in 1943—forty more than he had ever stolen before, and thirty-five more than he would ever steal again. Like Jimmy Sheckard, the one player in history who had the most similar career, he was a consistently good outfielder, had good range and an excellent arm.

1930: TEN MILLION, ONE HUNDRED AND THIRTY-TWO THOUSAND, TWO HUNDRED AND SEVENTY-TWO BASEBALL FANS CAN'T BE WRONG

What every baseball fan knows about the 1930 season is that it was a hitter's bacchanalia, a season-long batting binge featuring a 190-RBI campaign for Hack Wilson, the last .400 hitter in the National League, and flashy batting stats reaching all the way down to the basement, where the Philadelphia Phillies had two outfielders hitting over .380 and a team earned run average of 6.71. After the season, action was taken to take some of the pep out of the baseball, and return the game somewhat to its more natural form.

What nobody remembers about the season is that the fans loved it. Major league attendance in 1930 was 10,132,-272, the highest of any season between 1901 and 1945.

Fans like hitting. Fans have always liked hitting, and they always will like hitting. Throughout the history of the game, almost every significant increase in offense has been accompanied by an increase in attendance, and almost every decrease in offense has been accompanied by a decrease in attendance. With the sole exception of the 1930s, every hitter's era in baseball history has been a period of growth, and every pitcher's era has been a period of stagnation. When runs per game dropped from 4.5 in 1911 to 3.7 in 1914, attendance dwindled from 6.6 million to 4.5 million. Of course, competition from the Federal League was responsible for that. When runs per game jumped from 3.8 in 1919 to 4.4 in 1920, attendance exploded. Of course, Babe Ruth was responsible for that.

As attendance had stayed low in the dead-ball era, it continued to roar in the 1920s, reaching a peak in 1930. When

UNIFORMS OF THE 1930s

In 1883 the Cincinnati Red Stockings experimented with numbers on their uniforms, but the idea didn't catch on. In 1916 the Cleveland Indians used numbers on their uniforms, but the idea didn't catch on. But on April 18, 1929, the New York Yankees took the field with numbers on their uniforms, and it caught on. Within a few years, everybody had numbers. In early 1932, the Boston Braves wore numbers on their home uniforms, but some of the other clubs requested them not to wear them on their road games. But on June 22, 1932, the National League adopted a policy requiring that numbers be worn.

A few miscellaneous notes: All teams were identified by city and nickname now. About half used the nicknames on their uniforms, and half didn't. A note under "Base Ball Condensed Data," in the back of a *Spalding Guide* notes 1931 as the year glass buttons and polished metal on uniforms were forbidden (I knew you'd be anxious to hear when that happened). Knickers were stretching out to about mid-calf.

—Susie

the ball was deadened in 1931, runs per game dropped from 5.5 to 4.8 and attendance dropped from 10.1 million to 8.5. By 1933, runs were down to 4.4 per game, and attendance was down to. 6.1 million. Of course, the depression was mostly responsible for that. In 1943, runs per game dropped below four for the first time since 1918, and baseball suffered its worst attendance declines since 1931. Of course, that was mostly due to the war. In the late 1940s, runs per game were back up in the 4.7 range, and attendance shot up to over 20 million; in 1952, runs were down to a little below 4.2, and attendance was down under 15 million. Of course, that was mostly due to competition from television.

With the aid of four new teams, baseball finally broke its 1948 attendance mark in 1962, drawing 21.4 million people. Runs per game were at 4.5. Baseball owners, in one of their most puzzling moves ever, decided that there was too much hittin' goin' on, and expanded the strike zone, cutting runs per game below 4.0 for the first time since 1943. Eight hundred and ninety-eight thousand fans got up and left the ballpark. Attendance, while growing slowly, was largely dormant throughout the rest of the sixties, but it took the owners only six years to react to the problem.

In 1972, American League attendance was down to just 74 percent of what it was in the National League, and dropping lower every year. When the American League adopted the Designated Hitter Rule in 1973, the fans were, of course, horrified. But for some reason, American League attendance increased by two million that year, bringing them up to 81 percent of the National League, and within a few years the two leagues were virtually even. By the late 1970s, offense was at its highest levels in twenty years, and baseball was booming.

Fans like offense. Yes, I know there are dangers in overdoing it; if runs became so cheap that each run was meaningless, I doubt that the fans would like that. But there is a basic principle involved here. Offense is the art of making something happen. Defense is the art of preventing anything from happening. It is more exciting to see somebody make something happen than it is to see somebody prevent anything from happening. Baseball fans have always been of the opinion that it is more exciting to see somebody run around the bases than it is to see somebody keep everybody from running around the bases. They react more positively to seeing somebody hit a baseball hard than they do to seeing somebody try unsuccessfully to hit a baseball hard.

So often history counsels us in riddles. We should appreciate it when she speaks this clearly.

PLAYER VERSUS TEAM

Joe DiMaggio fought a series of bitter contract battles with the New York Yankees. After his first big year in 1937 (he hit .346 with 46 homers, 167 RBI) he asked for $45,000; Ed Barrow told him that Lou Gehrig was only getting $41,000 after twelve good years. Gehrig, said DiMaggio, was underpaid.

DiMaggio held out. The press fried him; he finally relented and signed for $25,000. Everywhere he went, he got booed. He said he felt like some places the only reason those people had come to the game was to give DiMaggio the works. He got hate mail; he said that the way some of the letters read, you would have thought he kidnapped Lindbergh's baby. It was, he said, the most unhappy period of his life.

——————1933: CHALLENGE——————

The 1933 Washington Senators, champions of the American League, were lifted to that perch by an odd series of straight-up trades—center fielder for center fielder, left-handed starting pitcher for left-handed starting pitcher,

1935: CUBS HAVE BIG EDGE AT HOME

The Cubs in the 1970s and '80s have had a consistently large home/road differential, which I had always tended to attribute to their exclusivity in playing all day games. There may be more to it than that. The 1935 *Spalding Guide*, written several years before the introduction of night baseball, contains this paragraph:

The Chicago team, as has been the case for the past three or four years, struck its hardest when playing on the home ground. It has always been a pronounced home winner. Other players attribute this superiority to the layout of the field, which is strongly in favor of those batters who can send long flies zooming into its furthermost limits or just over them.

The following summer the Cubs won the National League pennant by going 56–21 at home (44–33 on the road), and won 18 straight games at home in September.

that sort of thing—which might be called challenge trades (since, if the trade fails to work, it becomes glaringly obvious). Challenge trades have been relatively rare throughout most of baseball history; most trades are made to accommodate surpluses and shortages. But the Senators changed three lineup spots and three pitchers that winter, and in every case but one it is literally true that on balance they simply traded each player for the one other player in the league who was most nearly identical to him in terms of on-field abilities:

Roy Spencer, a thirty-two-year-old, right-handed-hitting, very well-regarded defensive catcher, was traded to Cleveland in exchange for Luke Sewell, a thirty-one-year-old, right-handed-hitting, very well-regarded defensive catcher. Spencer had batted 317 times in 1932, hitting .246 with 1 home run, 46 RBI; Sewell had batted 300 times, hitting .253 with 2 homers and 52 RBI.

The Senators swapped two outfield spots with St. Louis. Sammy West, a brilliant defensive center fielder who had hit .287 with 6 home runs and 83 runs batted in, was replaced with Fred Schulte, a very good defensive center fielder who had hit .294 with 9 homers, 73 RBI. In right field, Carl Rey-

nolds was replaced with Goose Goslin. Although Goslin over the course of his career was much the greater player, at that particular moment there wasn't a lot to choose from between the two. Reynolds had had a big year in 1930 (.359 with 18 triples, 22 home runs, 202 hits and 100 RBI), and in 1932 had hit .305 with 9 home runs, 63 RBI despite missing 45 games after Bill Dickey fractured his jaw during a brawl. Goslin had hit .299 with 17 homers, 104 RBI —your basic Goose Goslin year. West was four years younger than Schulte, but Reynolds was two years younger than Goslin, and each team gave up and received one left-handed hitting outfielder and one right-handed hitting outfielder.

A third player from each side was included in that trade. Lloyd Brown, a left-handed starting pitcher who had gone 15–12 with a 4.44 ERA, was traded for Lefty Stewart, who was 14–19 with a 4.61 ERA.

The one legitimate exchange was that Firpo Marberry, the outstanding starter/reliever (8–4, ERA of 4.00), was traded to Detroit in exchange for Earl Whitehill, another left-hander with stats almost identical to Brown's (16–12, 4.54 ERA). Marberry's relief work was taken over by

Jack Russell, acquired from Cleveland. (I'm not sure how. He may have been released after a poor 1932 season.)

The series of trades happened to hit just right; Whitehill and Russell had super years—by far the best of their careers, and Whitehill had a distinguished career. The pitching was significantly improved, Joe Cronin did good work as a manager, and with the help of another "career" year from Joe Kuhel, the offense held its own. The Senators improved by seven games, the Yankees declined by fourteen games, and the Senators won the pennant, plus an inordinate amount of praise for their astuteness in the flesh market.

Did they deserve the praise? It's hard to see; the trades were basically pointless, and if they worked for one year, one must also point out that a team which had been strong for several years collapsed suddenly in 1934. An intriguing question: What, exactly, were they trying to do? Why did they do it? Did they sense a staleness about the team? Did somebody say "We've got the talent to win it here, but we've just gone flat. Let's stir things up a little." Did they have a sense that the team was near the end of its run, and figure it was time to try to stretch for that little bit extra?

Or was it, as I see it, simply a cynical effort to drum up some off-season interest by changing the names without really changing the team—an effort which then became, after the fact, a brilliant sleight of hand due to good fortune. A seven-game improvement; that's nothing, really. It's well within the normal range of a team's fluctuation. They had won 92 to 94 games for three straight years before that, and in 1933 they became the first American League team in seven years to win the pennant without winning 100.

Whatever, it made its mark. The rest of the decade there were more "challenge" trades than normal. The Senators one year later would trade Goslin even-steven for outfielder John "Rocky" Stone. In 1938 the Cubs, having just won the pennant, traded shortstop Billy Jurges, outfielder Frank Demaree and backup catcher Ken O'Dea to the Giants in exchange for shortstop Dick Bartell, outfielder Hank Leiber and backup catcher Gus Mancuso. That would turn out to be one of those fabled trades that hurt both teams, but asked what he thought of it at the time, Bill Terry snapped, "What the hell do you think I think of it? I just made the trade."

That's the thing about challenge trades: They leave you nowhere to hide.

1931: FRANK SHELLENBACK, 27–7

Probably the best of the minor league pitchers was Frank Shellenback, who pitched for the Chicago White Sox of 1918 and 1919. Shellenback's major league career was respectable but not distinguished. In 1918 he was 10–12 with a 2.66 ERA, that figure ranking 27th among 55 American League starters. He got his chance that year when Red Faber was drafted and Claud Williams left the team early in the season. The White Sox had an off year, finishing sixth after winning the pennant in 1917, and when Faber and Williams returned and Shellenback started slowly in 1919, Frank was sent to Minneapolis. He was twenty years old.

Shellenback was a spitball pitcher, and he had the misfortune of being in the minor leagues at the time the spitball was banned. Although each league protected some pitchers who could continue to throw the pitch, so that they would not be put out of business, Shellenback, being in the minor leagues, was not among the major league's protected pitchers. Although Shellenback's effectiveness returned in 1920, he would never again pitch in the major leagues.

Shellenback would win 315 games in the minor leagues, which is very far from being a record (it is not one of the top ten minor league totals). There are several reasons for citing him rather than one of the other ten. His won/lost record, 315–192, is 123 games over .500 and a .621 percentage, both figures the best among minor league 300-game winners. His record was all compiled in the top minors; he was 9–6 in the International League, 11–8 in the American Association, and 295–178 in the Pacific Coast League. And, while he did pitch for some good teams, he also pitched for a lot of not-very-good teams. He was 18–10 in 1921 for a Vernon team that was a little under .500 when he wasn't pitching. In 1923 he was 19–19 for a terrible team (58–103 with other pitchers). In the following four years he was 14–7, 14–17, 16–12, and 19–12 with P.C.L. teams that were nowhere near .500 with other pitchers. When his teams were decent his records got better: 23–11, 26–12, 19–7, 27–7, 26–10, 21–12. The Hollywood Stars team for which he went 27–7 was only one game above .500 when he wasn't pitching. After 1934 it was back to pitching with bad teams.

Shellenback is best remembered today, if at all, as Leo Durocher's pitching coach.

BEST MINOR LEAGUE TEAMS OF THE 1930s

The two most celebrated minor league teams of the thirties were the 1937 Newark Bears, a farm team of the Yankees, and the 1934 Los Angeles Angels, who were the personal property of William Wrigley, who also owned the Cubs. The two teams make for an interesting contrast on several levels. The Bears, benefiting from exposure to the eastern media, are much the more ballyhooed, and are often cited as the greatest minor league team ever, which they clearly were not. Philip Roth wrote a great essay about them, and they were the subject of an informative and detailed book by Ron Mayer. The Angels, playing two thousand miles from New York, were, in my judgment, much the better team.

The '37 Bears were an impressive team. They won the league by 25½ games, going 109–43, cemented the title by winning two rounds of playoffs, 4–0 and 4–0, then met Columbus, led by Enos Slaughter, in the Little World Series. The Columbus Redbirds won the first three games of the series (in Newark) by scores of 5–4, 5–4, 6–3, only to have the Bears come back and win four straight in Columbus, 8–1, 1–0, 10–1, 10–4. Charlie Keller was the Minor League Player of the Year, hitting .353 with only 13 home runs but 61 extra base hits. (It is difficult to see how or why he was selected Minor League Player of the Year over Enos Slaughter, by the way. Slaughter hit .382 with 26 HR, 122 RBI, 42 doubles and 245 hits in the American Association; Keller had a fine year but wasn't close to any of Slaughter's standards.)

There were several other future major league players of quality on the Newark team, led by first baseman George McQuinn and second baseman Joe Gordon. Other major leaguers included Babe Dahlgren (who played third for Newark), Willard Hershberger, Buddy Rosar, and Bob Seeds. Seeds had a historic hot streak the following year in which he had nine hits, seven of them home runs, and drove in seventeen runs in two consecutive games. In 1937 Dahlgren and McQuinn hit .340 and .330 with doubles, triples and home runs aplenty. Gordon's stats were the same at Newark as they would be in a typical major league season for him, and both catchers (Rosar and Hershberger) hit well over .300, as they would in the majors.

The pitching staff listed a number of so-so major league pitch-

ers, good enough to win with the Yankees, but never rotation anchors; these included Atley Donald, Steve Sundra, Joe Beggs, Marius Russo, Kemp Wicker, and Vito Tamulis. Beggs, later the relief ace of the Cincinnati Reds, was a starter that year and was 21–4, while Atley Donald was 19–2.

To understand why I say that they were not the equal of the 1934 Los Angeles Angels, first of all you have to go back and take a look at what the minor leagues were at this moment. The minor leagues were at a crossroads. The major league owners and general managers, under the leadership of Branch Rickey, were fighting to turn the minor leagues into servants of the major leagues. Commissioner Landis was fighting a losing battle to keep them independent, existing for their own purposes.

There was a well-known incident in 1937 in which Landis freed ninety-one St. Louis Cardinal farmhands, ruling that the relationships between the Cardinals and the minor league teams were illegal. When this confrontation is discussed today, the idea usually comes across that the Cardinals had been guilty of some sort of covert shenanigans in signing and controlling minor league players. This is a most unfortunate misunderstanding, because what Landis in fact ruled was that the arrangements between the Cardinals and their minor league affiliates—arrangements that were, as Landis said, "Big as a house. Big as the Universe"—were in and of themselves illegal. Those same relationships, within ten years of Landis' death, became standard practice throughout baseball—and, indeed, were soon surpassed by new and even more restrictive arrangements that would have horrified the old judge even more.

Landis ruled that the Cardinal contracts had trapped the minor league teams in a relationship in which they were prohibited from taking actions that they might have needed to take to win the league championship—and thus, in effect, that they constituted a breach of faith with the team's fans, the same as surrendering the attempt to win the pennant in any other way. As I've tried to explain, once this breach of faith was complete, once the minor leagues no longer existed for their own purposes, they could no longer survive without subsidies. Let me quote from the exchanges between Rickey and Landis at the time, as released by the commissioner's office:

LANDIS: You have this arrangement which obligates Springfield to take optional players only from the owner of the Danville club, its competitor . . . suppose Springfield and Danville are in first and second positions, making a fight, and that Springfield can get an optional player who will strengthen Springfield. Have you a right under this agreement to say to Springfield, "You shall not take that player?"

RICKEY: I think we have.

LANDIS: Is that good?

RICKEY: It is not good for Springfield.

LANDIS: Is it good for that league? Is it good for the whole institution?

RICKEY: Many a club makes an agreement that is bad for itself. It is entirely a question of can a man make a deal for himself.

LANDIS: I am not dealing with the question of the selfish interest of Springfield in the deal. I am dealing with this question: *Here is a pennant race in the Three-I League that is, as far as the principle is concerned, just as important as if it were a pennant race in the National or American leagues.* They are fighting your club. You have the power to say to them: "This avenue of strength to your club we shut off." It is pretty plain that would be bad for the league, wouldn't it?

RICKEY: I get your point: Danville and Springfield are contending for the pennant in the same league. All right. Suppose . . . we withhold the benevolent hand and say, "You can't have any optional player from us, and other sources of supply are stopped; therefore, that will leave you in second place and Danville will win." . . . Yes, that is in it; you are right.

LANDIS: That is in this (the agreement with Springfield); isn't it?

RICKEY: Yes, that is in there.

LANDIS: Big as a house, isn't it?

RICKEY: It is not big as a house.

LANDIS: I think it is as big as the universe. *This is just as important in the Three-I League as it would be in the National or American leagues.* [my italics]

Regrettably, journalists interpreted this action, as they tend to interpret everything, on a personal level, as Landis against Rickey. The minor leagues decayed simply because the point that Landis was trying to make was lost—that a minor league team cannot survive if its fans are asked to support an outfit which is, in reality, an extension of a foreign power.

The minor leagues before Branch Rickey were a small war; after Rickey they were merely boot camp.

There was, in the 1930s, that tension between what minor league teams were and what they were to become. The Newark Bears were a vassal team. They may have been the strongest vassal team ever, a reflection of a time when the strength of the teams was imbalanced, but they were a vassal team in a vassal league—and to my mind, they could not possibly have been as strong as the strongest teams of the free minors. The 1934 Angels, while not entirely free as the Orioles had been a decade earlier, were more free than the Bears—and the league in which they competed was, from 1930 until 1955, the most independent of the minor leagues. The Pacific Coast League teams had their own stars, whom they kept for years.

Yet, ironically, this tends to work against the Angels in their evaluation by a modern fan. A modern fan, looking at the players involved, tries to figure out how good the guy was by looking at what he did in the major leagues. Because Charlie Keller and Joe Gordon and Babe Dahlgren later made names for themselves in the majors, they are good ballplayers—but because Marv Gudat and Jim Oglesby didn't, they weren't good ballplayers. Of course, this is nonsense. The Pacific Coast League was a good league— a better league, in 1934, than the International. The things those players did there did not need to be validated by major league performance in order to become real.

The Pacific Coast League had used a split schedule—first half, second half—for several years before 1931. They stopped in 1932. The Los Angeles Angels of 1934 were such an awesome team that they had to split the schedule again, or the Angels were going to win it by thirty-five games. Their first-half record was 66–18, winning by nineteen and a half games over Mission (or rather, they were nineteen and a half ahead when the rest of the league decided that they wanted to call it off and start over). It didn't help. In the second half the Angels were 71–32, beating Hollywood by twelve games. Their combined record was 137–50, a .733 percentage. The second-best combined record in the league was 101–85, by Mission. To make for a playoff, they chose an all-star team from the rest of the league. The Angels beat them, too, four games to two.

Who were those guys? The star of the team was Frank Demaree, who started the All-Star game for the National League in 1936 and 1937. Demaree had quite a season, hitting .383 with 45 homers, 173 RBI in the 187-game season. Demaree also had 51 doubles and 41 stolen bases, making this one of two 40/40 seasons (40 home runs and 40 stolen bases), that I am aware of, anywhere in the history of organized ball. The top pitcher was Fay Thomas, 28–4, who had the misfortune of being drafted by the Browns after the season, but who was a successful pitcher for many years in the minor leagues. That's what many of the Angels were—minor league stars. Center fielder Jigger Statz was a durable singles hitter who had nine straight .300 seasons in the Pacific Coast League; he was probably fairly comparable to the American League's Doc Cramer as a player. Third baseman Gene Lillard was an outstanding offensive and defensive player, who I think could have been a major league star with better luck. The names might not mean much to you, but they could play. The double play combination was Jimmy Reese (Babe Ruth's roommate) and Carl Dittmar, both longtime minor league stars. First baseman Jim Oglesby had a bout with blood poisoning in 1936, during the time that he was trying to establish himself in the major leagues (bad timing, Jim).

A book about the Angels by Richard E. Beverage was published by Deacon Press in Placentia, California, in 1981. The Angels probably were not as good as the Baltimore Orioles of a decade earlier, and quite possibly not even as good as the San Francisco Seals of 1922–25 or the Minneapolis Millers of 1911. By 1934 some of the structures were already in place to take all of the best players out of the minors and concentrate them in the majors. But I think they were the strongest team of their time.

HONORS

It is to the decade of the Depression that baseball owes its three preeminent honors, the Hall of Fame, the Most Valuable Player award, and the All-Star game. The BBWAA Most Valuable Player award was first given in 1931. The first All-Star game was played in 1933. The Hall of Fame was founded in 1936 and opened in 1939.

The psychological roots of this urge to honor in the midst of bleakness would make a study in its own field, but my intent here was to write about the honors, rather than the psychology of exaltation. The essential question of history is "How did things get to be the way they are today?" How did the awards get to be what they are today?

The first Most Valuable Player award came about as a result of the Cobb/Lajoie fiasco on the last day of the 1910 season, when the well-liked Lajoie was allowed to lay down seven bunt singles in an attempt to get his batting average higher than that of the hated Ty Cobb. Mr. Hugh Chalmers of Detroit, owner of the Chalmers automobile company, was going to give a car to the batting champion, and wound up giving two of them. After this it was realized that it was not advisable to make such an award contingent directly on player statistics, a principle still recognized today. Instead, the Chalmers company decided to base its award—the automobile—upon a poll of sportswriters as to who was the best player in the league.

The voting structure that they decided upon was, in general, very well thought out to begin with, and when it had problems those problems were corrected, so that it has evolved to be, as it is today, the best voting structure in baseball. Chalmers agreed to make the award on the basis of a committee decision, with the committee to be selected by Mr. Ren Mulford, who was the Cincinnati correspondent for *The Sporting Life*. Mr. Mulford se-

lected a committee that contained many of the best-known sportswriters of the day. The committee was composed of eleven men, one for each major league city. If the city had a team in each league, the writer would vote in each league; if it had only one team, he would vote only in that league, so that there were eight ballots for each league. The rules of the vote were formulated by the first committee, in conjunction with Mr. Chalmers, and since they did such a good job of it, let's mention their names:

Ren Mulford, Cincinnati, chairman
John B. Foster, *New York Telegram*
Charles B. Power, *Pittsburgh Gazette-Times*
I. E. Sandborn, *Chicago Tribune*
Joe S. Jackson, *Washington Post*
James C. Isaminger, *Philadelphia North-American*
Harry P. Edwards, *Cleveland Plaindealer*
Abe Yager, *Brooklyn Eagle*
Joe Smith, *Detroit Journal*
Tim Murnane, *Boston Globe*
M.F. Parker, *St. Louis Globe-Democrat*
Jack Ryder, *Cincinnati Enquirer*

The committee decided upon a secret ballot, with each ballot to have eight names on it. The first-place nomination was worth 8 points, the second-place worth 7. . . . the eighth-place worth 1. This, as you can see, is essentially the same structure that is used today, including the key points of a "weighted" ballot and equal representation for each team.

As a footnote, Ty Cobb cleaned up in the American League voting, winning first place on all eight ballots. The voting even after that was well-ordered; Ed Walsh was second with 35 points, Eddie Collins third with 32, Joe Jackson fourth with 28 and Walter Johnson fifth with 19. In the National League, however, the voting was wildly split, with eight men finishing in a group between 19 and 29 points. Wildfire Schulte won with 29 points, followed by Christy Mathewson (25), Larry Doyle, Honus Wagner and Grover Cleveland Alexander (all 23), Miller Huggins (21), and Fred Merkle and Rube Marquard (19 each).

At first the award was well received and well publicized, but over the next two or three years it seems to have lost most of its steam. It was argued about and awarded for four years and then discontinued, for reasons that I don't know.

The concept of a Most Valuable Player was revived eight years later (1922) by the American League. The American League offered an official award, selected, again, by an eight-man committee of newspaper reporters, using a structure identical to that of the Chalmers award—eight men voting, eight names on a ballot, with points being awarded in declining order. At this time no physical award was given. Instead, plans were made to erect a $100,000 Base Ball Monument in East Potomac Park in Washington, D.C., a gift to the government from the national sport. The names of the award winners were to be inscribed on the monument, the first name being George Sisler, who swept the initial vote decisively, earning 59 of 64 possible points.

This rather grandiose plan—I'd love to see sketches of the proposed monument—seems to have been something of a millstone to the League Award. A congressional resolution was introduced to approve the monument in 1924, and passed the House of Representatives but failed in the Senate; after that I lose track of it, and I assume it collapsed. It was to have been, said the 1925 *Reach Guide,* a "Hall of Fame for the game's great players."

The National League adopted its own League Award in 1924. The N.L. committee, chaired by Fred Lieb, decided on rules that were slightly different from the American League version. A look at the distinctions is useful to make us aware that the form into which the modern MVP award evolved was not inevitable; there were choices:

- The Chalmers Award had had a rule that a player, having won once, was no longer eligible. This rule made sense for them because they were giving away an automobile, and not that many people even owned one at that time. It wouldn't have made a lot of sense to give Ty Cobb another car every year, though I'm sure Cobb would have figured a way to clear a profit on the deal. The American League in 1922 had adopted this same rule, for no particular reason, as did, initially, the National League. But the National League committee soon realized that the *raison d'être* for that restriction had passed, and abolished it, so that a National League player was eligible to win the award year after year. Rogers Hornsby won the Award in 1925 and 1929, and finished second in the voting in 1927.
- The American League offered immortality; the National League offered cash. The National League gave a $1,000 bond and a trophy to its winner; the American League made plans to carve his name on the monument.
- A player-manager was not eligible in the American League, but was eligible in the National.
- The American League in 1923 adopted a system in which each writer named *one player from each team,* and then ranked these eight players one through eight as most valuable. This was a silly idea. For illustration, suppose that in the

National League in 1987 every sportswriter agreed that the two most valuable players in the National League were Ozzie Smith and Jack Clark, both members of the Cardinals, but were evenly split on which of the two was more valuable. Since each player would be totally excluded from half the ballots, it is likely that neither would win the award—even though there was unanimous consent that they were the league's best players. The National League, wisely, did not adopt this rule.

• The National League switched from the system of eight names on a ballot to the modern ten names.

So it was the American League which revived the idea, but, with the exception of the notion of giving cash, it was the National League which moved it forward, and made the more "modern" type of MVP selection.

Both awards died in the late twenties. It is my understanding that the American League award died in 1929 with the monument that was supposed to immortalize it; the National League award died of divisiveness and disinterest a year later. The $1,000 bonus tended to make the award look a little tacky, and by this time there were several National League owners who weren't too happy about paying extra money to Rogers Hornsby.

Or, apparently, anybody else. According to Gordon L. Herman of Spokane, Washington, "The baseball owners agreed among themselves to prohibit any Most Valuable Player Awards in 1930. They argued that any player voted MVP would demand a large pay hike in 1931. However, an AP story dated October 7, 1930 from Philadelphia reported that Hack Wilson had been voted unofficial Most Valuable Player in 1930. "Wilson was voted the award in a vote by a committee of the Baseball Writers Association of America, the identical committee that had voted Hornsby the official award in 1929. James Crusinberry, retiring president of the BBWAA, announced the following vote:

1. Hack Wilson, Chicago	70 of a possible 80
2. Frankie Frisch, St. Louis	64 of a possible 80
3. Bill Terry, New York	58 of a possible 80

End quote.

We have, then, two NL MVPs for 1930, inasmuch as *The Sporting News* gave its MVP award to Bill Terry. All existing record books show the BBWAA vote as having begun in 1931. This intriguing finding by Herman raises a question of whether perhaps an asterisk should be needed. Apparently, they voted the award in 1930 but didn't give out a trophy or anything, just a quick citation. In any case, I have adjusted the MVP Award Shares in Section III to reflect this data.

It was *The Sporting News,* in any case, that carried on the award. When the American League didn't give an MVP award in 1929, *The Sporting News* named Al Simmons the best in the league, using the same 8 × 8 vote. When the National League dropped it in 1930, *The Sporting News* picked up that league as well.

In 1931 the Baseball Writers Association of America came officially into the field, and started the award that was eventually to become the recognized MVP. It took better than a decade for that to occur, however; from 1931 through 1936 *The Sporting News* and the BBWAA gave separate MVP awards. The two were directly competitive, and in the early years *The Sporting News* award was probably the more respected and coveted honor. Today, Gabby Hartnett is recognized as the MVP in the National League in 1935, but that's really hindsight; in his time, Arky Vaughn, *The Sporting News* winner, was recognized as the MVP just as much as Hartnett was.

Mostly they used the same voting system. *The Sporting News* tried an experiment in 1932 with an eleven-man panel, one writer from each major league city, but with the writers voting on the players from both leagues, so that there was an 88-point ballot. They dropped that and adopted the system of eight ten-man ballots that was used by the BBWAA.

In 1937 an agreement was reached to unify the award. *The Sporting News* would recognize the BBWAA selection, and would provide a trophy for the winner. This would be known as *The Sporting News* trophy. This, however, reduced the number of voters who could participate in the balloting. In 1938, then, it was agreed to switch to a twenty-four-man (three writers from each team) panel, so as to reflect in the award the broader consensus that it now represented. At that time the point system was also changed, with the present method of counting 14 points for first place, 9 for second, 8 for third, etc, put in place.

This remained through 1943. In 1944, the BBWAA decided to make its own selection and to begin again issuing its own trophy, which was called the Kenesaw Mountain Landis Award. *The Sporting News* then resumed making its own selections. When Landis died and Happy Chandler became commissioner, one of his early acts was to request that *The Sporting News* cooperate in the effort to unify recognition—in other words, discontinue its selections, and allow the BBWAA vote to decide the honor. *The Sporting News* agreed, perhaps in part as a gesture of respect for Landis, for whom the award was named, and perhaps in part because their own selection had not really caught on. Anyway, the MVP award as it is today was finally in place.

Reference books often list the 1931 BBWAA vote as the first of

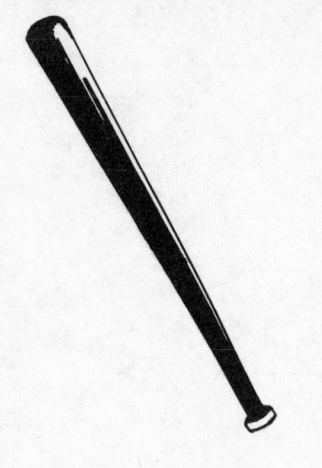

the series, although usually with a note about the earlier League and Chalmers awards. I wouldn't say, really, that that was terribly accurate; the list really should start with the Chalmers Award, pick up in 1922 and continue to the present, with just an explanatory note that the voting was not always conducted under the auspices of the BBWAA. It was the same people doing the voting, mostly. Jimmy Isaminger participated in the Chalmers voting in 1911, in the American League voting in 1922, in *The Sporting News* vote and the BBWAA poll in the early thirties. Jack Ryder was almost the same in the National League, and several other sportswriters voted in more than one of the polls. They used the same basic voting structure; a clear line of evolution can be traced from 1922 to the present without any gaps or any sudden changes in how the voting was done, and the 1922 vote was set up in imitation of the 1911–14 votes. The award given by the BBWAA was called "*The Sporting News* Award" for several years —yet the 1929 and 1930 *Sporting News* awards are somehow not considered to be a valid part of the line. You've got the same people, using the same basic voting structure, voting on the same award; the only thing that changes in 1931 is who is counting the votes and putting on the banquet. Wouldn't you say it was really the same award?

The All-Star game started in 1933. We'll let that one go by and hit it a lick in the fifties. It is not exactly accurate to say that the Hall of Fame, in contrast to the evolutionary development of the Most Valuable Player awards, was hatched full-fledged; it's not exactly accurate, but I'm going to say it anyway. The Most Valuable Player award started with a well-conceived voting structure and refined and improved what it had; the Hall of Fame started with a badly designed voting structure and, despite many attempts to reform it, has never addressed its substantive ills.

Let me offer first a mild defense of the Hall of Fame selections. No one is in the Hall of Fame who was not, at the least, a good ballplayer, and probably no one is in who could not have been described as a very good player. You could pick a team of the worst players in there—catcher Roger Bresnahan, first base Frank Chance, third base Fred Lindstrom, pitcher Jesse Haines, outfielders Earl Averill and Tommy McCarthy, etc.—and if you played a season with them, the odds are you'd win the pennant. So while there are many things wrong with the Hall of Fame selections, and while there is no question that the institution has failed in its responsibility to identify and honor the greatest players from each era, let's not get hysterical about it. I don't mean to minimize their errors; there are players in the Hall of Fame who were no better than Rico Petrocelli, Jason Thompson or Bob Boone. But Rico, Jason and Boonie are good players, if

LOU GEHRIG AND JOE DIMAGGIO

not qualified immortals; it hasn't reached the point, yet, of honoring ordinary players.

The Hall of Fame is a self-defining institution that has manifestly failed to define itself. A case can be made that the Hall of Fame selections have been so bad, so arbitrary and capricious, that the institution has lost the capacity to honor anyone. When Carl Yastrzemski becomes eligible for the Hall of Fame vote in a couple of years, he will go in, on the first ballot, but with 95 or 97 percent of the vote. And you know what the story will be? "Three percent of Hall of Fame voters don't vote for Yaz." One pompous but extraordinarily well-qualified candidate a few years ago was actually quite offended that he failed to win unanimous selection.

And when that happens, what does it mean? It means that the Hall of Fame has lost the capacity to honor Carl Yastrzemski. It

can only insult him. An honor that is expected is not an honor, only a paycheck, demanded when due. If Carl Yastrzemski does feel honored to be selected by the Hall of Fame, it can only be because he has no understanding of how many players have stood there before him, who didn't have half of his credentials. The Hall of Fame now can honor the Rick Ferrells and the George Kells. It can honor them by putting them in a class with the Yogi Berras and the Brooks Robinsons. But once they have sufficiently devalued the place, they'll lose the ability to do even that.

Suppose, however, we reach the end of that road, and there is a sudden general recognition that the public has lost respect for, and thus interest in, the Hall of Fame selections. What then? Can anything still be done to reverse the field, and restore an interest in the process?

To answer that, we have to understand what went wrong with the process. The best way to do that is to compare the Hall of Fame voting system, which doesn't work, with that of the Most Valuable Player award, which does. The differences between the voting systems are enormous, but I'm going to try to avoid reciting them point by point, and concentrate on the four things that I think most delineate the nature of each vote:

1) The Most Valuable Player voting was designed with a small, limited, balanced voting panel, the selection of which was covered with inherent safeguards designed to see that the voters were qualified and competent. The Hall of Fame ballots are distributed with a generous and well-intentioned assumption of competence on the part of all ten-year members of the BBWAA.

2) The Most Valuable Player voting allows for the expression of degrees of opinion. A voter who has a particular fondness for a Garry Templeton, a Glenn Hubbard or a Larry Parrish can vent that fondness by placing the player sixth, seventh, or third on his ballot; the number 1 man is going to win no matter what, and it's not going to be Glenn Hubbard. The Hall of Fame vote asks only one question: Is this guy in or out?

This forces the votaries of the lesser Gods to defend and in the process exaggerate the qualifications of their favorites. It's reached the point that to say a player "belongs in the Hall of Fame" is simply the language that we use to say that he was a great player. It would be very useful to us all if the partisans of Enos Slaughter or Jimmy Sheckard or Phil Rizzuto or whoever could find an effective way to say that their man was a great player without implying in some way that he was on an equal footing with Cobb and Ruth and Mantle and the other people that the Hall of Fame was really set up to honor.

3) The Most Valuable Player vote is unified and complete; twenty-four or twenty-eight ballots are cast at a specified time,

and that's it. Each MVP selection is a separate award, with no connection to any others. The Hall of Fame balloting is sprawling and polyglot, the work of unrelated committees and conventions spread over a period of time, and all Hall of Fame selections go into a common pool, each reflecting the standards of the whole.

And 4), and most importantly, the Most Valuable Player award is well-defined; everyone has a pretty clear idea of what it is supposed to represent and what type of player is supposed to receive it. The Hall of Fame was intended to be self-defining. A Hall of Famer is any player who is of the type and quality of those elected to the Hall of Fame, and that's really the only definition anybody has. But the selection process was set up so that the honor could never define itself, with the result being that after a half a century there is no hint of a consensus among us as to what a Hall of Famer is and what he is not.

I should emphasize that when I say "definition," it is not statistical standards that I have in mind. But more on that later . . . the question that then confronts us is, how could these virtues, these advantages that the MVP vote has, how could they be incorporated into the selection procedure for the Hall of Fame?

The best answer, to me, is by the creation of a yet higher honor, an "inner circle" within the Hall of Fame, to borrow a term from the Baseball Maniacs, in which the greatest of the greatest would go, or perhaps to bracket the present meaning of the term with both a lower and a higher distinction. Mistakes have been made in the past; I think that no knowledgeable person would quarrel with this. Many mistakes have been made. We can't kick those people out; we can't have Hall of Fame honorees wondering if the selection was temporary.

But what we can do is raise above the run-of-the-mill Hall of Famers (what an expression, and yet it fits) a special caste, a table reserved for the Musials and the Ruths and the Hornsbys, the people that you are supposed to think of when you hear the term "Hall of Famer." The Hall of Famers have plaques; these guys will have statues. The Hall of Fame adds five people a year; the inner circle will add one every five years.

And at the same time, we can add a lower rung as well, a place in the Hall of Fame for the Hank Bauers, the Davey Lopeses, the Sammy Wests. I can see a good case for that; those players and their contributions to our pleasure in this game should be remembered and immortalized, at some lower level. I'm all for that.

The inner circle, however, is no solution if it comes to be as poorly selected as the outer. How, then, to avoid that?

Simple. Do the things that the Hall of Fame should have done

when it opened its doors in 1939. Think through the selection process.

1) Limit and balance the voting board. Make sure that everybody who is voting is knowledgeable about the subject. Select, for example, a twenty-member board, representing the distant past, the not-so-distant past, and the recent generation, sportswriters, baseball officials, the National League, the American League, the institution of the Hall of Fame, and, most importantly, the fans.

I don't mean to pick on journalists, because in general they have done a good job of selecting from among the recently active players; it's the Veterans Committee that has done most of the sloppy work. But baseball journalists are not, as a group, exceptionally knowledgeable about baseball history. I would make a bet with you that if you polled the eligible voters for the Hall of Fame, at least a fourth would not be able to identify, for example, Joe Gordon. If you phrased the question this way:

> I played second base for the New York Yankees in the late thirties. I hit twenty to thirty home runs a year, and was regarded as perhaps the greatest defensive second baseman of my time. I played in six World Series and for five World Championship teams, four with the Yankees plus the Cleveland Indians of 1948. I played on a minor league team that many regard as the greatest ever. I hit as high as .322, and won a Most Valuable Player award. I managed in the major leagues in the fifties and sixties. Who am I?

I know of hundreds of baseball fans who would know the answer to that question by the end of the second sentence—but I would bet that over half of the eligible voters for the Hall of Fame would not be able to identify the speaker.

The BBWAA cherishes the right to elect Hall of Famers, and they're not about to share that right with the fans. But the notion that everybody who had paid ten years of dues to the BBWAA was therefore a qualified expert on the history of baseball was not well-considered, and the mischief that has grown from it is inherent therein.

2) Allow for the expression of degrees of opinion. This we accomplish by creating levels of distinction within the Hall of Fame; it would still be useful to provide for it in the voting.

3) Unify the vote. This idea of a 12-man committee making the selections on the left hand, and a 300-man body of opinion making the selections on the right hand, that just doesn't work. The idea of one body picking up and reviewing the qualifications of the players rejected by the first body is absurd; it sets up an inevitable downward spiral in the qualifications of those elected. It's like the Senate picking up and reviewing the legislation rejected by the House of Representatives. And if the Senate passes it, that's the end—no review, no veto, no appeal.

Bring the voters together, and sit them down in one room. Get them to talk, and have a chance to agree about what they are doing.

And 4), and most importantly, define what you are looking for.

Here's the deal: I don't know what a Hall of Famer is. Are there too many people in the Hall of Fame, or too few? I don't know. I know it's one or the other. I know that if Ed McKean doesn't belong in there, Freddie Lindstrom sure as hell doesn't.

But what is a Hall of Famer? A Hall of Famer is anybody that somebody elects to the Hall of Fame. It was supposed to be self-defining—and yet it was set up with separate and unequal committees, with unequal attention to different eras, using obviously and structurally unequal standards of entry. What is a Hall of Famer? Is Dave Bancroft a Hall of Famer? Then why isn't Bert Campaneris? Campy was a better player than Bancroft. Is Jesse Haines a Hall of Famer? Then why isn't Jim Bunning? Bunning was a better pitcher than Haines, by a comfortable margin. If Joe Sewell is in, why isn't Bill Dahlen, who was twice the player that Sewell was?

People ask me all the time if I think that some player should be in the Hall of Fame, and I always answer the same way: I haven't any idea. This is a self-defining institution that has manifestly failed to define itself. How in the name of Ruth am I supposed to know what the correct definition is?

I can only propose definitions; I have no idea how to pick the right one. Let me, then, propose some possible definitions of a Hall of Famer.

Definition A: A Hall of Famer is any player who could reasonably be argued to be the greatest ever at the position he played. Babe Ruth, Willie Mays and Walter Johnson would be typical Hall of Famers at this level.

Definition B: A Hall of Famer is a player who is one of the greatest ever at the position he played. Such a player should be the dominant player at his position at the time that he is active, with the exception of the relatively rare occurrence of talent doubling up at a position, such as Mantle and Mays. A Hall of Famer should be the biggest star on the field at almost any time. Such a player would ordinarily be the biggest star on a pennant-winning team. This definition would let into the Hall of Fame such players as Joe Morgan, Willie McCovey, Al Kaline and Joe Cronin.

Definition C: A Hall of Famer is a player who is consistently among the best in the league at his position. Such a player would ordinarily be the biggest star on his team unless it was a pennant-winning team, in which case he would be regarded as one of the most valuable members of the team. This definition would make room in the Hall of Fame for such players as Billy Williams, Willie

Stargell, Billy Herman, Fred Clarke, Johnny Evers and Harry Heilmann.

Definition D: A Hall of Famer is a player who rises well above the level of the average player, a player who would be capable of contributing to a pennant-winning team, and would be one of the outstanding players on an average team. This definition would include such players as Joe Rudi, Wally Schang, Lloyd Waner, Eppa Rixey and Tommy McCarthy.

I could offer an even more demanding definition along the same line, but if followed there would only be about five or eight players eligible for the Hall of Fame, or an even more liberal one, which would make perhaps a thousand eligible. (I would estimate that if the Hall of Fame were to induct all of the players who rise above a line described by the poorest already honored, its roster would include about five to seven hundred players.) Many other definitions could be offered, making distinctions such as those between players who rise briefly to a level and those who sustain that level, between players who combine offensive and defensive excellence and those whose abilities are but in one direction, etc.

I will be using these definitions in Section II, when discussing the greatest players ever at each position. But perhaps a better solution—another that should be considered, at least—would be not to try to agree upon a written definition, but to devise and rely instead upon a voting system that would make it possible to develop a *de facto* definition, a definition that is felt and understood, but never actually written down. Only one thing is really needed to make this come about: permanent rejection of certain candidates. The problem with the basic Hall of Fame argument right now is that it only works one way. People argue that if Pee Wee Reese is in the Hall of Fame, Phil Rizzuto should be in there, too. They say that if Tommy McCarthy is in, Pete Browning should go in. But it never works the other way. Nobody ever says that if Bob Johnson isn't in the Hall of Fame, Ted Kluszewski shouldn't go in either, or that if Harry Stovey isn't in, we shouldn't even be talking about Richie Ashburn.

It doesn't work that way because the Hall of Fame never makes a permanent, final rejection of anyone; there's always a thought that maybe he'll go in next year. Nobody argues, much, that because Jeff Burroughs won the MVP award Tony Armas should win it too. Last year's mistakes are sealed and shut, and it's for the good of everyone that they are.

Another way to achieve effective definition is by specifying the number of players that will be honored for a particular era or within a particular span of time. At this point, no one knows and there is no consistent pattern by which to estimate whether the Hall of Fame in the year 2025 will contain 300 players or a

thousand. If a limited number of players are to be honored, then the best will tend to come forward from the group, and form, again, an effective, though unwritten, definition.

This is the first time I've written about the Hall of Fame in years. I gave up writing about it because, as I said, I dislike howling into the wind. It's not like me to write an air castle article, which says how things could be done in a more perfect world; it's not something I often do. But I've done it here because I believe that over the next five to ten years there will be a growing recognition of the deficiencies in the Hall of Fame voting as we know it now, and thus a growing discussion of the alternatives for change. At the conclusion of that process the Hall of Fame selection procedure will be radically revamped. That is what the arguments about the Hall of Fame must center on in the next decade—not who belongs in the Hall of Fame and who doesn't, but how we can revise the Hall of Fame voting to create an honor that is worthy of the game's greatest players.

The 1940s

HOW THE GAME WAS PLAYED

In 1941, as you probably know unless you failed a number of history classes, America went to war. During wartime the quality of the baseballs used was inferior, as there was something in regular baseballs that was needed to make explosives or O.D. green paint or something, and the ball became rather dead. The quality of the play wasn't too good, either, but more than enough has already been said about that. Anyway, with most of the good players in the service, a collection of old men and children and men with one arm and seven dependents gathered regularly and battered around a dull spheroid, and this was called "major league baseball" for four years.

This baseball was characterized by low batting averages, low home run totals, and an unusual number of bases being stolen by anyone aged thirty-seven or younger. Strategy came to the fore, as it always does when talent is in short supply, plus there were some terrific pennant races and an unlimited supply of fresh human interest stories. On that basis the baseball of the war years was probably, in its own way, as enjoyable as any before or since.

The game that the Williamses, the DiMaggios and Fellers and Musials returned to in 1946 was somewhat different from the game they had departed from four years earlier. There was night baseball, and for that reason or some other, batting averages were lower. Thirty-five regular players had hit over .350 in the ten years before the war (1932–41); only eight would do so in the ten years after (1946–55). The offensive philosophies of Babe Ruth, as espoused by Ted Williams, dominated the latter part of the decade: Get a pitch you can hit and upper-cut it. Batters declined to swing at any pitch they couldn't hit into the seats; walks per game reached astonishing levels. A team in 1949 had one starting pitcher who walked 179 men in 196 innings, another who walked 123 in 214 innings, and a third who walked 138 in 275. Their ace reliever walked 75 men in 135 innings, and other pitchers had such totals as 57 walks in 95 innings, 48 walks in 49 innings, 29 walks in 58 innings, and 43 walks in 52 innings. That team used 14 pitchers, of whom only one allowed less than 4.5 walks per 9 innings. That team was the New York Yankees, and they were the World Champions. And in 1950, they issued even more walks than that (three of their four starters averaged 138 walks apiece) and they were World Champions again.

The definitive player of the era was Pat Seerey, who in 1948 hit .231 with 102 strikeouts in 105 games, but also drew 90 walks and drove in 70 runs in the 105 games. I could recite funny-looking combinations such as those for paragraphs, but instead I'll just recommend that you look up Eddie Joost, Eddie Lake, Eddie Stanky and Ed Yost in the *Encyclopedia* sometime. Multiply the results by Tom, Dick and Harry, and you'll get the idea.

Baseball boomed in the late forties, but this kind of baseball would drive a purist nuts —in fact, after a while it would even start to drive me nuts. Run production was high, but they were doing it all wrong. At its best, it was the baseball of the ticking bomb, the danger building up and up and up until somebody finally put one in the seats. At its worst it was station-to-station baseball run amuck, baseball with no threat except the threat of the long ball.

After 1950, home runs became even more plentiful but the walks became much more scarce; it's hard to say why. The strike zone was redefined in 1950, but the change went the other way. Perhaps what happened is that baseball moved from the Bob Feller generation of pitchers to the Robin Roberts generation— that is, toward a reliance on control pitchers, rather than on pitchers who tried for the strikeout. A manager in 1949 could reasonably have said to himself, "Look, if these guys are going to stand there and wait for my pitcher to get himself in a hole and make a mistake, I'll just go looking for the

EDDIE STANKY

kind of pitchers that don't make those mistakes. If they take the first two pitchers they'll be 0 and 2." Whatever, the basic trends both of this generation and of the next were in line with those of the entire period beginning in 1920 and not ending until the late sixties—more home runs, more strikeouts, and lower averages.

WHERE THE GAME WAS PLAYED

S.O.C. (same old cities).

WHO THE GAME WAS PLAYED BY

At a guess, about 40 percent of the major league players of the wartime period were truly of major league quality. Of the sixty-four National League regulars of the 1945 season, only twenty-two played a hundred or more games in the majors the next year (1946) and only eleven played a hundred or more games in the majors four years later (1949). As a control, I checked the same figures for the 1950 season. Of the sixty-four National League regulars of 1950, forty-four played a hundred or more games the next year, and twenty-nine played a hundred or more games four years later.

The biographies of the time

Checking In

1940—Ron Santo, Seattle
Tony Oliva, Cuba
1941—Pete Rose, Cincinnati
Bill Freehan, Detroit
Bob Dylan, Minnesota
1942—Muhammad Ali, Kentucky
Campy Campaneris, Cuba
1943—Joe Morgan, Texas
1944—Tom Seaver, Fresno, California
1945—Rod Carew, Panama
1946—Reggie Jackson, Pennsylvania
1947—Nolan Ryan, Texas
Johnny Bench, Oklahoma
1949—Mike Schmidt, Dayton, Ohio

Checking Out

1940—Sliding Billy Hamilton, 74
George Davis, 70
Willard Hershberger, suicide, 29
1941—Tommy Bond, 84
Mickey Welch, 82
Lou Gehrig, amyotrophic lateral sclerosis, 37
1942—Amos Rusie, 71
1943—Jimmy Collins, 73
Joe Kelley, 71
1944—Tony Mullane, 85
Kenesaw Mountain Landis, 78
Roger Bresnahan, 64
1945—Adolf Hitler, 56
291,557 American servicemen were killed in World War II. This accounted for a little less than 2% of the total combat deaths for all countries in the war.
1946—Gertrude Stein, 72
Walter Johnson, brain tumor, 59
Tony Lazzeri, 41
Nine members of Spokane team in Western International League, killed when their bus careened off a mountain road, June 24
1947—Jack Glasscock, 87
Jimmy Scheckard, 68
Johnny Evers, 66
Hal Chase, 64
1948—Henry Ford, 84
Mordecai Brown, 71
Joe Tinker, 68
Babe Ruth, throat cancer, 53
Hack Wilson, 48
Five members of the Duluth team in the Northern League were killed when the team bus collided with a truck, July 24
1949—Buck Freeman, 77
Wildfire Schulte, 67

give the impression that alcoholism in baseball was probably at an all-time high. Baseball may not have been great in the forties, but there have probably been more good books written *about* baseball in the forties than about baseball in any other time. Bill Mead's *Even the Browns,* Kirby Higbe's *The High Hard One,* and Leo Durocher's *Nice Guys Finish Last* all make good reading, as do the spate of recent books on the breaking of the color line, such as *The Year All Hell Broke Loose,* and a couple on baseball during the war years. These books portray a generation of rough, boozing, poorly educated but thoroughly trained ballplayers, many of them southerners, who helped to fight a war and returned to find a game and a society that were changing on them in ways that many of them found threatening and difficult to deal with. They faced the horrible challenge of the war with great courage, and the bright challenge of the future with great confusion.

THE 1940s IN A BOX

*Attendance Data:
  Total: 135 million (134,853,739)
  Highest: Cleveland, 1948, 2,620,627
          New York Yankees, 14,391,690
  Lowest: St. Louis Browns, 1941, 176,240
          St. Louis Browns, 3,330,861
Most Home Runs:
  Ralph Kiner, 1949, 54
  Ted Williams, 234
Best Won-Lost Record by Team:
  Cardinals, 1942, 106–48, .688
  Cardinals, 960–580, .623
Worst Won-Lost Record by Team:
  Phillies, 1941, 42–109, .278
  Phillies, 584–951, .380
Heaviest Player: Johnny Hutchings, a National League pitcher, stood 6'2" and weighed 250.
Lightest Player: Barney Koch, who played second base for Brooklyn briefly in 1944, weighed but 140.
Clint Hartung Award: Who else? Clint Hartung.
Most Strikeouts by Pitcher:
  Bob Feller, 1946, 348
  Hal Newhouser, 1,579
Highest Batting Average:
  Ted Williams, 1941, .406
  Ted Williams, .356
Hardest-Throwing Pitcher: Bob Feller
*Best Baseball Books: See Longer Comments at end.
Best Outfield Arm: Willard Marshall
Worst Outfield Arm: Pete Gray (sorry)
Most Runs Batted In:
  Ted Williams, 1949, 159
  Vern Stephens, 1949, 159
  Bob Elliott, 903
Most-Aggressive Baserunner: Jackie Robinson
Fastest Player: George Case
Slowest Player: Ernie Lombardi
Best Control Pitcher: Ernie Bonham
Most Stolen Bases:
  George Case, 1943, 61
  George Case, 285
Best-Looking Players:
  Whitlow Wyatt
  Lou Boudreau
Ugliest Player: Ewell Blackwell
Strangest Batting Stance: Stan Musial
Outstanding Sportswriter: Red Smith
Most-Admirable Superstar: Stan Musial
Least-Admirable Superstar: Joe Medwick

Least-Interesting Superstar: Joe DiMaggio

Franchise Shifts: None

New Stadiums: None

*Best Pennant Race: The best decade ever for pennant races.

Best World Series: 1947 Series, won by the Yankees over the Dodgers, 5–3, 10–3, 8–9, 2–3, 2–1, 6–8, 5–2.

Series featured Bevens' one-hitter and Gionfriddo's catch. 1946 Series is still much remembered (Pesky's late throw to the plate), but had only two close games.

Best-Hitting Pitcher: Schoolboy Rowe. Schoolboy hit only .253 during the decade but had 72 RBI in 474 at bats; led National League in pinch hits with 15 in 1943.

Worst-Hitting Pitcher: Preacher Roe

*Best Minor League Teams:

> 1941 Columbus (American Association)
> 1946 San Francisco (P.C.L.)
> 1948 Montreal (International League)

Best Minor League Players:

> Bill Thomas
> Frank Kelleher

Best Negro League Players:

> Monte Irvin
> Buck Leonard
> Ray Dandridge

*Odd Couple: Leo Durocher and Branch Rickey

*Drinking Men:

> Sig Jakucki
> Tex Shirley
> Tom Seats
> Kirby Higbe
> Jim Tabor

Player vs. Team: The most celebrated salary wrangle of the decade involved Hank Greenberg, a threat to retire, a desire to play for the Yankees, a trade, and a racehorse. Sketchy details are given with the data for Greenberg in Section III.

Team vs. Team: Yankees/Dodgers Feud, Spring of 1947.

Best Baseball Movies:

> *Pride of the Yankees,* 1942
> *It Happened in Flatbush,* 1942
> *The Stratton Story,* 1949
> *It Happens Every Spring,* 1949

*Uniform Changes: Nothing changing much.

Most Wins by Pitcher:

> Hal Newhouser, 1944, 29
> Hal Newhouser, 170

Highest Winning Percentage:

> Freddie Fitzsimmons, 1940, .889
> Tex Hughson, 96–54, .640

Best Unrecognized Player: Bob Elliott

Highest-Paid Player: Bob Feller

New Statistics: None

Most Unpredictable Career: Mickey Vernon

Best Athlete in the Game: Jackie Robinson

JOE DiMAGGIO SQUARED

Joe DiMaggio's batting streak ended on July 17, 1941. That same day, numbers were being picked out of a fishbowl in New York City to see who would be drafted into the U.S. Army. Each number picked, unlike the Vietnam era draft that you may remember, represented just one young man. The second number chosen, number 90, belonged to a twenty-one-year-old kid named Joe DiMaggio. You can imagine the resulting publicity; the media just loves that kind of thing. The kid loved the publicity, but he said he felt awful bad that Joe's streak had come to an end.

Most Lopsided Trade of the Decade: Billy Pierce for Aaron Robinson, November 10, 1948

A Very Good Movie Could Be Made About: The breaking of the color line. Actually the movie—*The Jackie Robinson Story,* with Jackie playing himself—was made in 1950. Somebody should try again.

I Don't Know What This Has to Do with Baseball, But I Thought I Would Mention It Anyway: Sitting around the house with nothing to occupy the devil's workshop, I decided that I would go through the entire 1947 *Sporting News Guide* page by page and find out which pitcher, in all of organized baseball, had hit the most batters with pitches. The answer turned out to be Bob Schultz, a pitcher in the Class D Kitty League, who apparently threw hard as hell. In 221 innings he hit 29 men with pitches, threw 22 wild pitches, allowed only 111 hits and struck out 361 batters. He finished 19–10.

Schultz never conquered his control problems, but he did eventually make the majors. He pitched for the Cubs from 1951 through 1953, posting a 9–13 record but walking 123 men in 181 innings. In 1951 he walked 51 men in 77 innings, but succeeded in hitting only two batters with pitches, thereby proving that there is one big difference between major league hitters and Class-D hitters. Reactions.

NICKNAMES

After a decade of use as instruments of torture, nicknames became almost apologetically pleasant again in the forties. Players of ordinary skills were bestowed such mildly flattering nicknames as "Mercury" if they ran well, "Scrap Iron" if they were tough, or "Old Reliable" or "Steady Eddie" if they were there everyday and put on a good show. Of the few derogatory nicknames of the forties, most were bestowed on players who didn't go to the war. It was hard to say anything bad about a man who had risked his life for you; you just didn't do that in the forties. A few nicknames, more or less at random:

Ding-a-Ling (Dain Clay)
Bow Wow (Hank Arft)
The Gay Reliever (Joe Page)
Fiddler (Eddie Basinski)
Buckshot (Tommie Brown)
The Little Professor
 (Dom DiMaggio)
Four Sack Dusak (Erv Dusak)
Slats (Marty Marion)
The Man (Stan Musial)
Foghorn (George Myatt)
Swish (Bill Nicholson)
Burrhead (Joe Dobson)

L'il Abner (Paul Erickson)
Old Folks (Ellis Kinder)
The Mad Monk (Russ Meyer)
Country (Enos Slaughter)
The Brat (Eddie Stanky)
Mountain Music (Cliff Melton)
Abba Dabba (Jim Tobin)
The People's Cherce
 (Dixie Walker)
The Mad Russian (Lou Novikoff)
All Jewish players were
 called "Moe."

ARGUMENTS ABOUT ALL-STAR SELECTIONS

MAJOR LEAGUE ALL-STAR TEAM 1940–49

	Player	Years	AB	Hit	2B	3B	HR	Run	RBI	BB	SO	SB	Avg.
C	Walker Cooper	5.71	536	154	27	5	19	68	96	32	35	2	.287
1B	Johnny Mize	6.16	572	174	29	6	35	106	121	80	42	4	.304
2B	Joe Gordon	7.59	568	153	26	5	24	90	94	75	70	8	.270
3B	Bob Elliott	9.45	567	165	31	8	12	85	96	77	44	6	.292
SS	Lou Boudreau	9.25	569	171	37	6	7	82	75	76	29	5	.299
LF	Stan Musial	6.96	594	206	43	16	21	117	101	81	29	6	.346
CF	Joe DiMaggio	6.02	592	192	32	11	30	114	131	75	30	2	.325
RF	Ted Williams	6.72	544	194	40	7	35	142	133	148	46	2	.356

	Pitcher	Years	G	GS	IP	W	L	Pct.	H	ER	SO	BB	ERA
S	Bob Feller	6.63	42	37	301	22	13	.626	244	97	222	131	2.90
S	Hal Newhouser	8.71	43	35	282	20	14	.590	244	89	181	123	2.84
S	Mort Cooper	5.79	42	36	277	20	12	.626	249	90	133	80	2.92
S	Spud Chandler	3.99	41	38	304	21	9	.714	261	90	136	97	2.67
R	Joe Page	4.07	59	11	178	13	10	.563	159	66	119	94	3.31

Records for the decade presented in seasonal notation, with players based on performance per 154 games, pitchers on performance per 40 starts, 67 relief appearances or equivalent combination.

Cooper's only real competition is Lombardi, but Lombardi's stats for the decade aren't as good (5.21 seasons of .294, with 17 HR, 80 RBI a season; only 16 doubles, 1 triple, and 47 runs scored), plus Cooper was a good catcher and much more mobile. Ernie's better years were the thirties. First base and the outfield are easy; only regret is that Kiner can't be included. Boston's DP combination of Stephens and Doerr have stats as good as the two selected—Stephens actually has better numbers than Boudreau—and they were terrific players, but Gordon clearly would have had a whole lot better stats than Doerr if they had played in the same park, plus he was an acrobat at second base. Jackie would be there except that he only had three years.

A half-dozen players could be picked at shortstop—Marion, Rizzuto, Reese, Appling—and Boudreau is virtually a dart-board selection. Elliott isn't remembered very much, and he probably wouldn't win a poll over Keltner, Kell, and Hack. But Elliott drove in more runs than any other player during the decade, was the only third baseman to win

an MVP award in the forties, was a good defensive player and would have far better statistics if he played in any park but Forbes. He was Stan Hack with more power or Keltner with more consistency, and he hit more home runs in a year than Kell hit in the decade. I feel sure I've got the right man there.

Feller and Newhouser are the only sure starters; Mort Cooper, Harry Brecheen, Bucky Walters and Rip Sewell are pick 'em for the other two. This is the hardest decade to choose from; everyone's career was chopped up by the war, so you've got fragments of the careers of two distinct generations of players. Chandler was always hurtin', but he was just *soo* effective when he was healthy—an MVP one year, 20–8 another, 16–5 a third and an ERA champion a fourth. Sewell won 133 games

in the forties, third best behind Newhouser (170) and Feller (137), and he did it without a lot of help from his teams. I don't know that he was ever as good a pitcher as Cooper or Brecheen at their best, but I don't know that he wasn't, either.

Hugh Casey or Johnny Murphy could be the relief man; none of them had more than a couple of good years in the decade.

 BLOCKING AND TACKLING THE PLATE

The modern method of blocking the plate is, quite simply, illegal. If you read the rule book (Rule 7.06 B), it is quite clear that the catcher is not allowed to block home plate in any way, shape or form without having the ball in his hand. Period.

The rules say that, and until about 1940 that is exactly what they meant. In the "Knotty Problems of Baseball" in the 1938 *Spalding Guide,* there occurs this exchange:

Q: I would like your opinion on a play where the catcher squats in front of the plate to prevent the runner from touching it. The runner cannot go around the catcher and does not want to slide into him to reach the base for fear of injuring him.

A: The position occupied by the catcher is illegal unless he has the ball in his hand ready to touch the runner.

Note, first of all, the tone of the inquiry. He doesn't ask "What do the rules really say about the catcher blocking the plate?" He doesn't ask "How far can the catcher legally go in blocking home plate?" He discusses a catcher who "squats" in front of home plate, and goes on to explain the unique purpose of this action. And his baserunner, having gone to the Darrell Porter school of aggressive baserunning (cf. 1980 World Series, games one and five) maintains a scrupulous interest in seeing that no harm should come to the squatting catcher.

Next, consider the response: He can't do that. Not "The rules really say that he's not supposed to do that, but we all know they do." Not "A technical interpretation of the rules would hold the catcher to be obstructing the baserunner." Just "That's illegal. You can't do it."

And when you consider, finally, that this exchange occurs in the knotty problems of baseball, a typical paragraph of which concerns itself with what happens when a ball in play lodges in the pocket of a passing marsupial, I think we can conclude that this was not, at that time, a common practice.

That got me started, and so I started looking through the guides of the twenties and thirties, looking for home-plate collisions. There aren't any, that would register by modern standards. There are plenty of photographs of plays at home plate, and sometimes they run into each other, but not like now.

Basepath obstruction, as you may know, was a major problem in the 1880s and nineties, when baseball was in danger of becom-

ing a contact sport. In 1897 the rules on obstruction were tightened up, and the principle of free access to the bases met with general acceptance at the other three positions. There was always something of a problem with catchers blocking the plate, but there were always limits. In 1922 two games were protested because of the intractability of catchers. National League president Heydler ruled against the protests, writing that "the unpopular practice of 'blocking off' runners at the plate . . . has always been the cause of dispute, ill-feeling among and serious injury to players, but against which no practical rule remedy has been found." However, it is, again, quite clear that what was meant by "blocking off" the plate then was tame indeed by the standards of the eighties. Heydler continues, "The decisions to be made by the umpires in this regard are usually the most important of the game, but they are decisions based solely upon the umpire's judgment *as to whether or not the runner beats the ball*" (emphasis mine). In other words, the principle that you were not to block the plate until you actually had the ball was still taken seriously at that time. And what did they mean by "blocking off" the plate? "Umpire Moran reports that catcher [Earl] Smith's left knee was in front of the corner of the plate nearest the left foul line, the imprint of his shin guard being plain on the rain soaked ground; but that there remained considerable uncovered plate for Schmandt to touch."

And that is, more or less, the position the catcher occupies in all of the shots of home-plate collisions that you will see from that era; there are *no* pictures of collisions occurring several feet up the line. Now, of course, the catcher sets up eight foot down the third-base line and wrestles the runner until help arrives, and Mike Scioscia occupies a position that will allow a runner to ramble all over Los Angeles and touch anything he pleases so long as it doesn't show up on the scoreboard. No one is expected to leave part of the plate open.

So when did the rule fall into disusetude? There isn't any moment at which it began, of course; they didn't just wake up one morning and say, "Let's start letting the catchers obstruct the baserunners." Thinking about it, I think it has changed a lot just in the last fifteen or twenty years. Maybe my memory is fooling me, but I don't remember Elston Howard or Bill Freehan doing some of the things that they do now.

To end with a digression, it is in principle most dangerous to have rules on the books which are not enforced, or to have one set of rules written down and another acted out. That is exactly how many of the game's controversies have erupted, including the Pine Tar incident and Merkle's Boner. The Giants have always claimed that what Merkle did (he failed to touch second to ceremonially complete the play) was common practice at the time. I have always felt that if, in fact, it was common practice, then O'Day (the umpire) used very poor judgment in deciding to commence enforcement of the rule at that particular moment. My friend Mike Kopf says that has nothing to do with it; a rule is a rule, and the rule says he's supposed to touch second.

Perhaps, but would you want to lose the pennant on a rule that hadn't been enforced for years? In the army, or in any fascist or totalitarian state, they have laws against most everything, laws that are never enforced so long as you behave yourself. Then you make somebody mad, or the captain wakes up on the wrong side of the cot, and *whammo.* You just broke fifteen laws. Having laws on the books that are not enforced puts every policeman in the robes of a judge, empowered to decide who the guilty are today. In a free society, since the law cannot be arbitrarily or selectively enforced, a statute that is not enforced is not enforceable. That was the principle affirmed by MacPhail in *Brett* vs. *Brinkman,* 1983. What we have here is another situation of which no good can arise.

THANK YOU, MA'AM

The Las Vegas team of the Sunset League in 1947 hit .338 for the season, with 271 home runs in 140 games. The statistics for the team's regulars are given below:

Pos	Player	G	AB	H	2B	3B	HR	Run	RBI	BB	K	SB	Avg.	Runs created
C	Castro	129	539	191	34	1	28	101	121	25	69	2	.354	119
1B	Myers	135	459	139	13	2	33	118	121	136	54	3	.303	118
2B	P Godfrey	118	509	163	26	7	14	93	103	32	65	5	.320	88
3B	Gregory	102	366	120	28	0	17	83	75	51	50	1	.328	82
SS	Kelly	126	508	170	33	2	33	153	99	93	114	7	.335	134
OF	R Godfrey	134	571	183	28	4	32	111	123	26	118	5	.320	110
OF	Felix	140	610	236	35	8	52	173	182	76	105	18	.387	201
OF	Zaby	133	531	213	47	7	18	158	132	104	78	22	.401	164

The team scored 1,261 runs, nine a game, but allowed 1,235 to finish with a record of 73–67.

THE CLEVELAND FENCES

Baseball lore has it that Bill Veeck in '48 was playing games with the fences, that he had them mounted on movable standards, and would move them back when the Red Sox or Yankees came to town, and in the rest of the time. After the league found out about it they made a rule against changing the fence distances in-season.

Since the pennant race ended up in a tie (the Indians won the playoff), I had always kind of discounted this as a phony championship, with the margin of victory provided by underhanded methods. But actually, it doesn't seem that the Indians derived much benefit from their shenanigans. In fact, the Indians home-park record that year (48–30) was seven games worse than the Red Sox in Fenway (55–23) and 2½ worse than the Yankees in New York (50–27). They won the pennant with a 49–28 record on the road. MVP Lou Boudreau hit .403 on the road, with 12 homers, 62 RBI and 74 runs scored in 76 games in front of hostile fans.

❀ ATTENDANCE: THE GREAT LEAP FORWARD ❀

The great leap forward in baseball attendance came in the year 1946, and not any other. After staggering through the war years with attendance a little below the levels of the late thirties, the crowds picked up in 1945 after the war was decided, and 1945 set a new high of 10.8 million. In 1946, attendance jumped to 18.5 million, an inconceivable 71 percent above the previous high. Earlier and subsequent surges in baseball attendance have led to new records 10 percent, maybe 20 or even 25 percent, above the previous record; there is no other such dramatic increase on record.

Why did it happen? This is a question capable of sabermetric analysis, but in lieu of that my guess is that three factors acted together. Number one was the acceptance of night baseball. Baseball had been toying with the idea of playing games at night since the 1870s, and in the process of resisting it had developed an almost impenetrable network of interlocking reasons for playing baseball in the day, when most of the audience was at work and unable to attend. The attendance declines of wartime forced a gradual acceptance of night baseball, which made it possible for many more people to attend the games after the war—and

might, incidentally, have set the stage for the attendance declines and franchise hopping of the following decade. But that's another story.

The end of the war marked the end of a fifteen-year nightmare for much of America, and perhaps it is remarkable that attendance held up as well as it did during that period. There was, economists might say, a "pent-up demand for baseball," which then broke loose in the relief of economic normalcy following the war. A nation suddenly more urban and suddenly more mobile was anxious to get out and move around, and a baseball game seemed an appropriate place to get out and move to. The power of these other two factors was greatly enhanced by the series of outstanding pennant races that baseball enjoyed during the decade.

UNIFORMS IN THE 1940s

We have reached the deadpan era. From 1920 until 1960, there just doesn't seem to be much to report in the way of significant changes in uniform style. I mentioned to Bill that I was having trouble finding many things of interest in here, and he said that during this period the game in general doesn't change quickly—slow evolutionary movement is more the speed. Likewise in baseball fashions.

From team to team, uniforms in the forties and fifties look very much alike—all white home suits, road uniforms usually gray. The form is still boxy and baggy; shirts have round necks, either button or zip up, with half-length sleeves and a T-shirt worn underneath. Some teams are a little heavy handed with the trim work up the sides, outlining the front button flap of the shirt, running several times around the neck and down the sleeves. Other clubs seem to prefer the stark simplicity of a plain white suit with no decoration save for the team name.

One historic note—the first batting helmet was used experimentally by the Brooklyn Dodgers in 1941. Originally made of fiberglass, it was later replaced by a stronger plastic. More about that next decade.

—Susie

THAT'S WOMEN FOR YOU

In 1941 and 1942 the Brooklyn Dodgers went to Cuba for spring training. Ernest Hemingway used to hang around with the ballplayers some, and he and Hugh Casey became good friends. They used to go to a dove-shooting club every day after practice, seven days a week. Sometimes afterward, and after spending some hours in a casino, Ernest would take a few of the ballplayers to his house up in the hills for a little boxing. Hemingway and Casey would put on the gloves and beat hell out of each other and the furniture until Hemingway's wife couldn't stand it anymore and would make them leave.

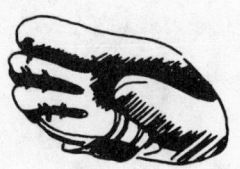

GERKIN'S CRUEL FATE

Steve Gerkin lost twelve games without a win for the '45 A's. First of all, why wasn't this man called "Pickles," like Pickles Dillhoefer? Or how about "Baby" Gerkin (except for the fact that he was twenty-nine years old). Instead they called him "Splinter". And second of all, how could he not win at least one game with an ERA about the same as that of the league average?

1945 was not a vintage year for pitching in Philadelphia. Both the Phils and A's finished in last place (with a combined total of 206 losses) and between them trotted out eleven pitchers who didn't win a game but lost at least one. The combined record for this group was 0–36. Not only that, but famous losers Bobo Newsom (twenty losses for the American League lead) and Hugh "Losing Pitcher" Mulcahy were in town. Some theorize that Philadelphians became famously adept at booing during this period. Makes sense to me.

In the middle of all this was Steve Gerkin, a right-handed rookie who was given twelve starts and nine relief jobs by Connie Mack. Gerkin posted an ERA of 3.62 (3.97 as a starter and 2.21 in relief), which was good enough for fifth on the staff and not much worse than the A.L. average of 3.36. He seemed to have picked exactly the right circumstances in which to lose. He gave up five earned runs in relief and that netted him three losses. Sure, the A's were last in the league in runs scored (3.29 per game), but hell, couldn't Gerkin have lucked out just once? Certainly other men on his team didn't pitch nearly as well and yet they managed to win a few:

1945 A's

	W	L	Pct.	ERA	Hits per 9	Walks per 9	Baserunners per 9
STEVE GERKIN	0	12	.000	3.62	9.88	2.38	12.26
Lou Knerr	5	11	.313	4.22	9.83	5.12	14.95
Don Black	5	11	.313	5.18	11.09	4.97	16.06
Charlie Gassaway	4	7	.364	3.74	8.69	4.19	12.88

Was he not bearing down? Did he antagonize the A's with nasty locker room pranks to the point that they purposely did not score for him or field any balls behind him? This just doesn't seem fair. What is especially not fair is that he did not get another chance to post a major league win.

Each of these other three hurlers were given other shots. Black went to Cleveland and posted more miserable ERAs, including 5.37 in the pennant year of 1948. Gassaway (now is there ever a man destined to win the Rolaids Relief award) joined him in Cleveland for 1946 and was dismissed after two decisions. Gassaway was from Gassaway, Tennessee. (Estel Crabtree, an outfielder with the Cardinals and Reds in the thirties and forties was from Crabtree, Ohio. Are there any others who hailed from a town bearing their names?) Knerr continued to pitch for the A's and led the American League in losses in 1946 when he posted a 3–16 record. Gee, Gerkin could have done *that*. Mack gave Knerr another twenty-two starts in '46, even with his 5.40 ERA (5.54 as a starter) and yet he couldn't give a pitcher with Gerkin's control another shot? Shameful.

—Jim Baker

BEST MINOR LEAGUE TEAMS OF THE 1940s

The 1941 Columbus Redbirds, a Cardinal farm team, included on their roster Lou Klein, who had an outstanding rookie season in the National League in 1943 but lost the best years of his career to the double whammy of wartime and expulsion from baseball after he signed to play in the Mexican League in 1946, plus Murry Dickson, Ray Sanders, George Myatt, Harry the Hat (Walker), Augie Bergamo, Tommy Heath, Bert Haas, Frank Gabler and Preacher Roe. Their top pitcher was Johnny Grodzicki, who was the Cardinals "other" late-season sensation in 1941, winning two games with a 1.35 ERA (at Columbus he was 19–5). The Redbirds finished 95–58, and won a four-team playoff easily.

The 1946 San Francisco Seals were led by two outstanding major league pitchers, Larry Jansen (30–6 that year, 21–5 in the National League the next year) and Cliff Melton (17–12). Melton, a star with the Giants in the late thirties, was only thirty-four years old in 1946, and had left the majors in a salary dispute after the Giants tried to cut his pay in 1945; though he had a sore arm much of 1944, his ERA for his last two major league campaigns (250 innings) was 3.35. There were several other major league players on the team, the best of whom was first baseman Ferris Fain, a two-time American League batting champion.

The 1948 Montreal Royals were perhaps the best of a long series of outstanding Dodger farm teams in that city. The 1948 team was led by Duke Snider, Sam Jethroe and Don Newcombe, and also included Jimmy Bloodworth, Al Gionfriddo, Bobby Morgan, Bud Podbielan, Jack Banta and several other major league players. They won the pennant by thirteen and a half games, won two best-of-seven series for the league championship, and cremated St. Paul in the Junior World Series.

UTILITY MAN

With Houma of the Evangeline League in 1948 (the same team that Bill Thomas had won thirty-five games for two seasons earlier), Roy (Tex) Sanner won the league's triple crown, hitting .386 with 34 homers and 126 RBI. He also hit 35 doubles, giving him a slugging percentage of .669. When not playing the outfield, Sanner pitched, winning twenty-one games and losing only two, striking out a league-record 251 batters in 199 innings and posting a 2.58 ERA.

DUROCHER AND RICKEY

Leo Durocher was the manager and Branch Rickey the general manager in Brooklyn between 1942 and 1946. Whenever Leo strayed from the reasonably straight and something approaching narrow, Branch Rickey would call him in and recite the parable of the Prodigal Son, always ostensibly when discussing someone else. "Through our many years together," wrote Leo in *Nice Guys Finish Last,* "Mr. Rickey recited the parable of the Prodigal Son to me many, many times . . . always about some other sinner or wastrel, but always at a time when I knew he looked on me as something less than the leading candidate for secretary of the YMCA." Rickey was a religious man, but he understood that ballplayers had their ways, and he never took it upon himself to reform them or to straighten out Leo. "It would have been impossible for him," said Durocher, "to come right out and say that he disapproved of sleeping with loose women on the Sabbath." Leo's value system was largely structured around loose women. Durocher said he was always afraid to lie to Rickey because he always figured Rickey had the answer before he asked the question.

TOM SEATS

TOM SEATS

Same subject. One time when Leo almost pushed it too far was in the matter of Tom Seats. This was 1945, and Seats, a thirty-three-year-old journeyman, had a good year in the low minors in 1944, and suddenly found himself in the major leagues. He was getting hammered regularly early in the season. Durocher called him in for a conference before his next start, during which it was decided that the problem was nerves, and that a couple of fingers of brandy before each game was just the thing to settle him down. Seats got settled down and finished the year with a 10–7 record, but when Rickey found out about it he was apoplectic. "You . . . gave . . . a . . . man . . . in . . . uniform . . . whiskey?" inquired the Mahatma.

"Yes, sir," Leo replied.

Rickey thought about it a while and said, "He will never pitch again for Brooklyn," and added that he should fire Leo as well.

Leo responded with a terse, defensive comment that is a perfect summary of the thinking of every good manager. "There is a 'W' column and an 'L' column," he said. "I thought when I signed my contract . . . it was my obligation to put as many as I could under that 'W' column." But Tom Seats never pitched in the major leagues again.

THE GREAT FEUD, 1947

Leo Durocher, chapter three. During the winter of 1946–47, Larry MacPhail of the Yankees engaged in a kind of "publicity feud" with his good friends Leo Durocher and Branch Rickey of the Dodgers. The feud got serious and then a little nasty, but Durocher and MacPhail remained friends, and the matter was within control until it began to get tangled up with allegations that MacPhail had invited gamblers into his box at a spring training game in Havana in March 1947. With the sudden revelations of a game-fixing scandal in college basketball and the Evangeline League scandal at the same time, pressure was being put on Happy Chandler to do something to prove himself an iron-fisted opponent of gambling's influence on baseball, rather than just a fat, silly-looking politician with a cushy job. There had been a series of unpleasant news stories involving, among other things, Durocher's reported friendships with people like George Raft and Bugsy Siegel and an incident of a man claiming to have been cheated in a dice game at Durocher's apartment (Durocher was not there at the time). Durocher was eventually suspended for the entire 1947 season "as a result of the accumulation of unpleasant incidents in which he has been involved."

KIRBY HIGBE AND LEO DUROCHER

1946: LIFE BEGINS AT HOUMA

Bill Thomas won 383 games in the minor leagues, and never threw a pitch at the major league level. His won/lost records for most of his career aren't very good—a seemingly endless series of 15–18 and 20–17 seasons—but he was one of those guys who had a talent for picking losers. He went 16–17 with Charleroi in the Middle Atlantic League in 1927, but you have to understand that the rest of the pitchers on the Charleroi team were 26–58, so he was almost 200 points better-than-team. It took him several years to reach the good minor leagues (he took the 1930 season off, for some reason) and when he did it was with Indianapolis, a middle-of-the-pack American Association team, and later he pitched for several years with Portland and Hollywood, then the weak sisters of the Pacific Coast League. His records in what would now be called Triple A baseball total up to a little below .500. He was 17–9 for Mobile in the Southern League in 1944, and the team still finished eleven games under .500.

In 1946 he was forty-one years old, and he was pitching for Houma, which emerged as the powerhouse of the Evangeline League. Houma played 131 games that year. Thomas won 35 games and

lost 7. Now granted, that wasn't much of a league, but 35 wins are a bunch. No other pitcher, anywhere in organized baseball, at any age, has won 35 games in any other season since 1922.

What happened then I have never been exactly able to figure out. The 1947 *Baseball Guide* contains a one-paragraph note "Five Banned in Gambling Probe," and says that on January 25, 1947, five players were placed on Organized Baseball's Ineligible List after an investigation of allegations involving thrown games and association with known gamblers. Thomas was one of the five. He was suspended for "conduct detrimental to baseball"—something which, apparently, extended beyond winning thirty-five games at the age of forty-one.

An article by George Hilton in the 1982 *Baseball Research Journal* discusses the Evangeline League scandal, which was the only one of its kind to hit organized baseball since 1919. It began when the owner of the Abbeville franchise, Mr. I. N. Goldberg, alleged that the players of Houma and Alexandria had conspired to fix the outcomes of three playoff games (the league had one of those consarned multitiered playoff systems, which beg to be abused). The allegation

against Thomas was that he had been in contact with gamblers who had asked him to throw games; he testified that he had, indeed, been approached by one such gambler, but had categorically refused any such involvement, and had not gone even so far as to learn the man's name. Unfortunately for Thomas, Judge Landis had established the principle of expulsion for guilty knowledge.

As Jim Baker points out, this raises some fascinating questions, such as "Where do you go to place a bet on the Evangeline League?" I mean, do you just walk into a Las Vegas casino one afternoon and say, "I'd like to put down ten grand on Thibodaux to beat New Iberia next Saturday." How many bets do you think you can win like this before they find you hanging from the nearest cactus? Apparently, illegal gambling was then flourishing in Louisiana, and the primary beneficiary of these dark deeds was an Alexandria bookmaker.

Clearly, some seedy things were going on down there; charges extended as far as money being handed into the dugout from the stands during and after games. It is not clear whether or not any games were successfully thrown; a Houma player, years later, said that all of the games that were supposed to be thrown were won by mistake, as the would-be Rothsteins were carrying insufficient protection, and one player accidently hit a double while attempting to strike out.

Anyway, for associating with these ne'er-do-wells, Thomas was banned from baseball. It is clear that Bill Thomas had not thrown any games; for one thing, he was 5–0 during the playoffs. He was angry and defiant about the banishment. Out of baseball, he worked as a roustabout in Texaco's refinery at Houma, and alternately threatened to sue and petitioned for reinstatement, which eventually was granted. Almost three years later. The next time he broke camp he was forty-five.

In 1950 Thomas went 23–8 for two teams in the Evangeline League. Then he moved on to the Rio Grande Valley League, where he pitched nine more games and pushed his season's record to 26–12. After that season, though, he was to win only twenty-three more games in the minor leagues.

Thomas was basically a control pitcher, and control pitchers (a) don't win with bad ball clubs, and (b) are always the last ones to catch a break. In almost 6,000 innings of minor league baseball, he walked less than two men per nine innings. Thomas would now be about eighty, and he may still be alive; it is not known where he lives or where he was buried. He was probably not a major league pitcher or at the least not very much of a major league pitcher, but at any level it doesn't seem right to let the memory of such a remarkable career drop entirely from sight. How many games he might have won with good minor league teams, and if he had had the four missing seasons of his career, it is impossible to imagine. It was a great service of Ray Nemec, Robert Hoie and the other SABR members who compiled the book, *Minor League Baseball Stars,* which traces the statistical outline of Thomas' career, and allows us to envision a memory of him.

BEST PENNANT RACE, 1940s

The decade of the forties was rich in great pennant races, at least in the American League. With twenty pennant races in the decade, there were at least ten outstanding ones, which I have ranked below:

1. 1940 American League
2. 1944 American League
3. 1948 American League
4. 1946 National League
5. 1949 National League
6. 1949 American League
7. 1942 National League
8. 1941 National League
9. 1945 American League
10. 1945 National League

The 1940 American League race is recounted in Dick Bartell's recent autobiography, *Rowdy Richard.* It was a five-team race with three teams hanging in until the last weekend, a race filled with controversy and heroics. The 1944 AL race is immortalized in Bill Mead's classic, *Even the Browns,* a book that I love but Bill, for heaven's sake stop changing the name of that thing. The 1948 race ended in a Cleveland/Boston tie, with the Yankees breathing on their necks.

With one exception, all of the close National League races in the decade involved only two teams—Brooklyn and St. Louis. Both were formidable teams. The 1942 Dodgers, I believe, were clearly the greatest second-place team ever, and also may have been the only team in baseball history that was above average at every positon.

1948: 254 RBI

Playing for Amarillo in the West Texas–New Mexico League in 1948, Bob Crues drove in 254 runs, thirty more than any other player in the history of organized baseball. His complete batting record for that season follows:

Year	G	AB	R	H	2B	3B	HR	RBI	TBB	Avg.
1948	140	565	185	228	38	3	69	254	90	.404

There were five small-time leagues down there, the West Texas–New Mexico League, the Big State League, the Arizona-Texas League, the Lone Star League and the Longhorn League. They were all hitter's leagues. Lots of people hit .380, hit 50 home runs. Just that season, someone named S. V. Washington in the Class B Big State League hit .384 with 29 HR, 129 RBI in 124 games for Texarkana, while Gainesville's Les Goldstein hit 58 doubles. In the Arizona-Texas League, which was Class C, Gene Lillard hit .364 with 20 homers, 92 RBI in 90 games, while Pete Hughes hit .347 with 21 homers and 118 RBI, and also drew 207 walks to give him an on-base percentage of .566. Lillard and Hughes were teammates, and the team finished fifth in a six-team circuit.

The Lone Star League was also Class C. Their batting champion, Joe Kracher, hit .433 to help Kilgore win the pennant. In the West Texas–New Mexico League, also Class C, in addition to Crues there was Herschel Martin, who won the batting title at .425 with 61 doubles (as well as managing the pennant-winning Albuquerque team), and Ed Carnett, who hit .409 with 59 doubles and 33 homers, and Virgil Richardson of Lubbock, who hit .397 with 196 RBI. And in the Longhorn League, Frank Stacey hit .389. By my count, these five regional leagues in 1948 produced seventy-two players who drove in 100 runs, and eleven who drove in 150 runs.

Bob Crues began his career as a pitcher, and went 20–5 in the same league in 1940. Then he hurt his arm and the war came, and he sort of got derailed, wound up as an outfielder. He had some mobility and a good arm. In his big year in 1948, he played fifty-seven games in center field (the WT-NM league maintained separate statistics for each outfield position, as every league should do). When he wasn't in center he was in right; he had sixteen outfield assists altogether. Crues spent most of his career in the West Texas leagues, and never played in the majors. His highest exposure was four games as a pitcher in the Eastern League in 1941.

A HISTORY OF RELIEF PITCHING

No question in baseball history is more impossible to answer than the question of when the role of the modern relief pitcher developed. From 1880 to the present, the role of the relief pitcher on a ball club has never reached an equilibrium; it has been in constant flux, different in each decade than in the one before it. The differences, though they may become subtle if you get far enough away from them, were perceived as significant in each generation, so that every generation of managers since 1920, if asked how the game had changed in the last fifteen or twenty years, has been inclined to say that one of the largest changes has been the development of modern relief pitching. I still hear people say that whereas ten or twenty years ago relief pitchers tended to be old, broken-down starters, now the bullpen is one of the keys to a team—and in a sense, that statement is still true. But people also said exactly the same thing twenty years ago and thirty years ago and forty years ago—and it was just as true then as it is now.

Who was the first modern relief pitcher? That question has a dozen correct answers. You know who invented relief pitching? Napoleon. No joke. Napoleon believed that every battle tended, for reasons of its own, to resolve itself into immobile, equal positions; he believed, in essence, in the Law of Competitive Balance as applied to a battle. So on the day of a battle he would take two or three regiments of crack troops, and sequester them a distance from the shooting, where they would eat and sleep in comfort. Over the course of a day or several days, the troops in the field would take positions and lose them and retake and relose them, growing ever more and more weary, their provisions in shorter and shorter supply, and their positions ever more and more inflexible. Finally, at a key moment in the battle, with everyone else in the field barely able to stand, he would release into the fray a few hundred fresh and alert troops, riding fresh horses and with every piece of their equipment in good repair, attacking the enemy at his most vulnerable spot. He did this many times and with devastating effect—and if that's not relief pitching, I don't know what is.

In 1880 the rules did not allow lineup changes to be made. The rules permitted a substitute to enter the game only when there was an injury, and it was up to the opposition to decide whether the injury was serious enough to warrant the change. In the gentleman's game of the 1850s and 1860s, this was viable, but as the professionals began to take over the game, the ethics of the situation changed, and teams would generally refuse to recog-

nize any injury as serious enough to allow a substitution, so that people sometimes had to finish games with broken arms and/or serious cuts.

The rules were changed in the 1880s to allow one "unchallenged" substitute. In 1891 it was decided to allow unlimited one-way substitution within the roster. Let's look at the role of the relief pitcher as it has been at the midpoint of each decade since, asking in each case how the role of the reliever differed from what it was ten years earlier:

1895: Starting pitchers still expected to finish the game. About 80 percent of games were complete games, most of the exceptions being one-sided games in which the fourth or fifth pitcher on the staff—the one with the least credentials—would be called upon to work.

1905: Good pitchers still expected to finish most of their games. Outstanding starters were now occasionally called into close games in the late innings. John McGraw was one of the first to do this; in 1904 his Giants won the National League despite finishing last in the league in complete games, and Giants pitchers almost annually led the league in saves, though all that it took to accomplish this was maybe four saves a season. Clark Griffith, whose Senators were to be a step ahead in relief pitching for many years, was player-manager of the Senators in 1905, and used himself as a kind of early relief ace, relieving in 18 games in 1905 and 15 in 1906, and he was effective in the role.

The practice of "star relief" grew more common over time; by the late twenties and during the thirties every ace of a staff was expected to make ten to twenty key relief appearances during the year as well as starting, and the practice did not entirely die out until 1957. Ed Walsh and Three Finger Brown, the pitching stars of the two Chicago teams, set the trend in this respect; each led the league four times in saves, and Brown in 1911 made almost as many relief appearances (26) as starts (27). *The Baseball Encyclopedia* lists Brown with 13 saves in 1911, which would have been a record, though of course no one was counting saves at that time.

By the thirties, as I said, this was the rule, rather than the exception. Lefty Grove saved 55 games in his career. In 1930 and 1931 he was 23–3 and 26–3 as a starting pitcher, but over the two seasons made an additional 27 relief appearances, saving 14 games and winning another 9. (The fact that he had a win, loss or save in almost every one of his relief appearances shows that the situations in which he was being used were the crucial situations; the A's used Grove at the times that in the seventies we would call for Goose Gossage.) Dizzy Dean, while winning thirty

games in 1934, worked 17 times in relief and saved as many games as any pitcher in the league except Carl Hubbell.

The last manager to do this, to expect his ace starter to double as a reliever, was Casey Stengel, who used Allie Reynolds that way with great success, and who in fact cited Reynolds over Whitey Ford, in his biography, as the greatest pitcher that he had managed, specifically because Reynolds could start or relieve. The practice of "doubling up" effectively ended in 1958, when Ryne Duren became Stengel's relief ace.

1915: By 1915 there were a few pitchers who pitched mostly in relief. Probably the first relief pitcher who should be mentioned was Doc Crandall. Crandall was a heck of a hitter, and he could pinch hit and play second base as well as relieve. As a pitcher he had no "stuff" at all—he was basically a junkballer at the age of twenty (Christy Mathewson wrote about this in *Pitching in a Pinch*). He was used for the most part as what would now be called a middle reliever. But he could pitch; he was not by any means some broken-down old starter. He was 17–4 in 1910 (10–3 as a starter, I would guess making most of his starts against tail-end teams, and 7–1 as a reliever). He was 15–5 in 1911, won 21 games in the Federal League in 1915, and had good earned run averages.

The *Reach Guide* took cognizance of this development in 1912 with the article " 'Relief' Pitcher a New Fad." "Indication of the growing extravagance in major league circles," this article began, "is the fact that in addition to carrying assistant managers, major league clubs are actually anxious to find pitchers who can be used for relief purposes only." Despite their disdain, they conceded that both Crandall and Charlie Hall of the Red Sox had "saved their teams many games by stopping rallies in the nick of time." Note that the word "save" was associated with relief pitchers from the very beginning; the current notion that it was not until the 1950s that relievers got the ball with the game on the line is very wrong. But these relief pitchers and others of this time, like Allan Russell of the Yankees and Roy Mitchell of the Browns, were still expected to start when the need arose.

1925: By 1925 there were true, full-time relief pitchers. Dave Danforth, a dentist (and alleged by some to have invented the slider, though that is usually attributed to Blaeholder) with the White Sox in 1917 had the best year to that point by a relief pitcher. Danforth still started occasionally and well; he made 9 starts and won 6 of them. But he made 41 relief appearances, many of them in key situations, to help the White Sox win the pennant. The 1918 *Reach Guide* reported that Danforth had been "called upon many times last season to save games apparently lost. Several times last season he went in with none out and the bases filled and yet won."

Allan Russell, never more than a fair pitcher, was kicking around as a starter/reliever from 1915 through 1922. In 1923 he worked 46 games in relief, and made only 6 starts as a member of the Washington Senators—another step toward the role of the full-time relief pitcher. Some feel that Russell represented a landmark in the development of relief pitching; I'm more inclined to dismiss him as a footnote.

Firpo Marberry was a landmark. Marberry was the first truly outstanding pitcher to be used primarily in relief over a period of several seasons. As a rookie in 1924 he started 15 times and relieved 35 times, saving 15 games and helping the Senators win the pennant. In 1925 he made 55 relief appearances without a start, saving fifteen more, and in 1926, he relieved 59 times with five starts, saving 22.

Firpo Marberry was not a good pitcher. He was a great pitcher. Whether or not his career had the longevity that is expected of a Hall of Famer, this I don't know—but for an eleven-year period of time, 1924 through 1934, Marberry was as valuable to his team as any pitcher in baseball except Lefty Grove. His records are deceptive because, in several of his best years, he split his work between starting and relieving. Take half of Jack Morris' record this year and half of Steve Bedrosian's and add them together, and you'll see what he was up against; he couldn't win 20, and he couldn't save 30. He started 187 times in his career, and his record as a starter was terrific (94–52). How many pitchers in the Hall of Fame do you think won more than half their starts? I don't know, either, but I know a lot of them didn't. In 1929 he made 26 starts and was 16–8 as a starter for a 71–81 team; in 1930 he started 22 times and was 15–2. In 1931 he started 25 times and was 13–3, in 1932 fifteen times with a 7–3 record. As a reliever, he was clearly the Number 1 man of his time, leading the league in saves (retroactively) in 1924, '25, '26, '29, and '32. He had a career winning percentage of .623, and that without pitching for either the Yankees or the A's, the two dominant teams in the American League through most of his career.

Wilcy Moore had a pretty fair year as a reliever for the 1927 Yankees, not in any sense a precedent-setting year, but remembered because of the team for which he pitched. Jack Russell had a very similar year for the Senators in 1933.

1935: By 1935 the bullpen was being used as a refuge for old starters. Starting with Jack Quinn and Eddie Rommel in Philadelphia, it became the practice to load the bullpen with veterans no longer up to 250 innings a year, but who still knew how to pitch. The bullpen was a way station on the road out for

most of the outstanding pitchers of this era, including Dolf Luque, Dazzy Vance, Herb Pennock, and Waite Hoyt.

The next outstanding career reliever after Marberry was Johnny Murphy of the Yankees. Murphy, a control pitcher, was consistently good for the Yankees from 1935 through 1943, when he was drafted. Unlike Marberry, he rarely started—only 20 times in his career after 20 starts as a rookie in 1934. He never relieved in as many as 40 games in a season, but the expectation that a quality starter would finish most of his games was still strong in 1935, and Murphy was probably the first regular reliever who was never used in a mop-up role—and in that sense, the first relief "ace."

Let's recap where we are here. There is, in 1935, no expectation that a team will have a full-time relief pitcher. Some teams have one, some don't. A few pitchers pitch 50 games a year without starting, but not many and they're not real good. The key saves are made by the starters, and the ace reliever, if the team has one, is often brought in with the score tied. Though there has been one outstanding career reliever, the assumption still is that your best pitchers go into the rotation.

1945: The war years were years of experimenting in the bullpen, and there were any number of almost spectacular two- or three-year successes, such as Ace Adams of the Giants, Joe Heving of the Red Sox and Indians, Gordon Maltzberger of the White Sox and Joe Berry of the Athletics. All of these men were relief pitchers from the day they reached the major leagues, and all of them had truly outstanding seasons. None had terrific stuff; all were mostly control pitchers. These players are comparable to more familiar recent players, such as Joe Hoerner, Jack Aker, Rawly Eastwick and Randy Moffitt—outstanding for a brief period of time.

More famous than these, though little if any more successful, was Hugh Casey of the Dodgers. Casey was the first flame thrower to be a successful reliever. He was a huge man who threw very hard, in that sense a forerunner of Dick Radatz, Ryne Duren and Goose Gossage, but he doesn't seem to have had an outstanding breaking pitch. He was a fairly successful starter/reliever from 1939 through 1941 (his career record as a starter was 34–22), then moved into the bullpen full time in 1942. He had three good years as a reliever—1942, '46, and '47.

1955: After Casey comes Joe Page. Joe Page was not a great pitcher, or if he was, it was only for a brief period of time, 1947–49. He could accurately be described as a failed starter. Yet Casey and Page, between them, are a very important marker in

the history of relieving, for several reasons. For one thing, they were stars, legitimate names. Unlike Johnny Murphy, who had a better career, Page worked 55 to 60 times a season, and through him the idea developed that a reliever could be not merely a valuable member of the staff, like Murphy, but a key performer. Casey saved 18 games in 1947—the most anyone had saved other than Marberry's 22 in 1926—and Page saved 27 games and won 13 in 1949 (Stengel's first season in New York), making him the first pitcher to be used day-in and day-out in key, game situations—in that sense, the first modern reliever. They both did it in New York and they both did it for championship teams and they were both impressive as hell to watch, and those facts, while they might be irrelevant to their greatness as pitchers, were important because of the impact they had on the game around them.

After 1950, everybody felt that he had to have a relief ace. Jim Konstanty, basically a one-year wonder, won the Most Valuable Player award in 1950. Joe Black in 1952 was Wilcy Moore all over again. The Red Sox took Ellis Kinder, who was an outstanding starter (23–6 in 1949), out of the rotation and put him in the bullpen, where he was an outstanding reliever. It is important to note this: It wasn't that Kinder failed and then was taken out of the rotation and then exiled to the bullpen, where he was rejuvenated. Not at all. It wasn't that the Red Sox had more starters than they could use. It was the climate of the time; it was Joe Page and Jim Konstanty and Joe Black and Hoyt Wilhelm: Everybody had to have one.

Relievers in this period usually pitched 60 to 70 games, and their role was not nearly so sharply defined as it is today. The idea that the starter should finish his work decayed so, so slowly; by 1930 it was still strong, by 1940 it was still strong, by 1950 it was still strong, by 1960 it was still very much alive, by 1970 it was still very much alive—yet in each year, in each decade it was weaker than the one before. But in 1955 there was still a great reluctance to take out a Bob Lemon or a Warren Spahn or a Whitey Ford (who completed 18 of 33 starts that year), and since there was that reluctance, a relief pitcher's job was still defined, in part, by what was left over for him.

It is in the mid-fifties that we finally encounter the first generation of professional relievers. There were three men of this group most worth noting—Hoyt Wilhelm, Elroy Face, and Lindy McDaniel. All were basically one-pitch pitchers. All were successful for periods of fifteen years or more, though all had up years and down years. All regularly worked 60 to 70 games a year. All started a little—McDaniel started the most (74 games) and Face the least (27). All had spectacular seasons. They were, in those respects, the first modern relief pitchers.

1965: Between 1960 and 1974, the trend was to ask the relief pitcher to work more and more. As the notion that the starter should finish decayed further, the relief ace assumed an ever-increasing share of the last innings, and new records for games pitched in a season were set in one league or the other almost annually. Significantly, none of the pitchers who set these records displayed the longevity of a Face, a Wilhelm, or a McDaniel.

Every year, there was a new relief sensation or two or three or five new relief sensations. Every team had one now—Arroyo and Radatz, Perranoski and Baldschun, Regan and Fisher, Aker and Ellis, Wyatt and Woodeshick. Radatz was certainly the most impressive of them; Stu Miller may have been the best. Or maybe he wasn't; maybe the best was Perranoski or Don McMahon. Ted Abernathy was darned good. Even a team's Number 2 or Number 3 reliever now, a man like Dick Hall or Harvey Haddix or Billy Hoeft, was liable to go 9–1 with an ERA in the ones. I haven't mentioned half of their names.

What these pitchers had in common was what they were not. Some threw hard and some threw soft and some threw screwballs—but none had more than two good pitches. Most only had one. None of the relief aces of the sixties was your basic fastball-curveball-slider type of pitcher. Some of them were great from age thirty-two through thirty-five, and some of them were great from twenty-two through twenty-five, and some of them were great from twenty-two through twenty-four and again from thirty-two through thirty-four—but none of them just came up at twenty-five and went on. Many of them, like Ron Kline, Mike Marshall and Hal Woodeshick, had washed out as starters—but many of them also had not. Few, if any, were recognized as among the organizations' prime assets at the time that they were asked to go to the bullpen—but all of them were recognized as among the most valuable men on their team at the time that they were on top of the world.

1975: In the seventies people began to realize two things. First, they realized that they were asking relief pitchers to do more than was humanly possible. The 90-game, 150-inning seasons came to a stop. The relief ace's role was defined as stopping comebacks. They stopped asking the ace to pitch when his team was behind. They stopped expecting even the best starters to finish their games, providing regularity to the workload of the relief ace.

Second, a connection was made between the caliber of the athletes assigned to relief—failed starters and second-line prospects—and the inconsistency of the performers. After this the great career relievers began coming—Sparky Lyle, Rollie Fingers, Goose Gossage, Bruce Sutter, Kent Tekulve, Dan Quisenberry—men who had great years and good years, as spposed to great and useless.

As was true before, most of these men were basically one-pitch pitchers—but there were two differences. Number one was the age at which they established themselves as relief aces. They started as relievers, developed as relievers, and reached stardom as relievers. And number two was the quality of their "other" pitches. They tended to be one-pitch pitchers by choice —not by force. Many of them could have been outstanding starters.

The question, for the future, is whether we have finally reached an equilibrium, or are we still in motion? I'm inclined to think we're still in motion. Save totals are now being pushed up year after year, and that means, to me, that the job is still subject to some redefinition. I think that if we look back at it again from 1995, we're going to be saying the same things then that we say now—that the role of the relief pitcher is different than it was a generation ago, that this is the first generation of "modern" relievers. But this is a book about the history of the game, intended largely to help people to stop saying silly things about the game's past, and not so much to speculate on its future. There is nothing more false than the notion of "contemporary history," for the advantage of historical perspective is that of knowing how things turn out. It is not the same to speculate about how they will turn out, and call that history.

BASEBALL BOOKS OF THE 1940s

Although no individual title had great significance, the Putnam series of team histories were collectively important. Other publishing events of note:

1940: *The Kid from Tompkinsville* introduces Roy Tucker, a worthy successor to Frank Meriwell, and a precursor, of sorts, of Malamud's Roy Hobbs.

1941: "You Could Look It Up," James Thurber's story of the pinch-hitting midget, is published in *The Saturday Evening Post,* ten years before Bill Veeck produces Eddie Gaedel.

1942: *Baseball Digest* begins publication.

1949: *Bill Stern's Favorite Baseball Stories.* A treasure-trove of legend, myth, and anecdote. Individual stories in this collection can be trusted about as far as you can throw the average piano.

—Jim Carothers

I'll throw in *Judge Landis and Twenty-five Years of Baseball,* by J. G. Taylor Spink, an authoritative 1947 book about baseball in the Landis years. The Putnam books, which were done in the late forties and early fifties, were done by some of the finest sportswriters of the time, and they were terrific. Frank Graham wrote the history of the Giants, Lee Allen did some of them, Fred Lieb some. Terrific series.

Within a year of his death, three biographies of Lou Gehrig were published and a movie made about his life.

Bill Stern in the 1940s wrote books of apocryphal baseball stories, which he presented as gospel truth. Today his name is synonymous with the worst in journalism—grand disregard for the truth or even likelihood of his stories, a lack of original research, sweeping interpretations of events based on limited knowledge. This is fair in some ways, for Stern was certainly guilty of the offenses charged, and on one level the truth is always fair. But Stern's standards were accepted in sports journalism at the time. Other people, Sam Molen and Mac Davis to name a couple, wrote the same kind of books. They're not subjected to ridicule today not because they were more accurate but because they weren't as successful at it as Stern was. Like Norman Rockwell and Edgar Guest and many others, Bill Stern has given his name to the failings of his genre.

—Bill James

The 1950s

HOW THE GAME WAS PLAYED

The baseball of the 1950s was perhaps the most one-dimensional, uniform, predictable version of the game that has ever been offered for sale. By 1950, the stolen base was a rare play, a "surprise" play. In the first seven years of the decade, no team stole a hundred bases in a season. In 1920, or arguably even earlier, powerful trends had gone into motion, trends toward an offense based more and more around the home run, and less and less around anything else. Batting averages, which had jumped early in the lively ball era, began dropping after 1930, for reasons about which we will speculate in the next

decade. In the early part of the 1950s, every team approached the game with the same essential offensive philosophy: get people on base and hit home runs. Every team, whether one of the best or one of the worst, featured players in the class of Gus Zernial, Ralph Kiner, Hank Sauer, Roy Sievers, Jim Lemon, Luke Easter, Eddie Robinson, Bob Niemann, Gus Triandos, Vic Wertz, Bobby Thomson, Roy Campanella, Sid Gordon, Willie Jones, Rocky Colavito and Ted Klusewski, muscular men not long in grace nor noted for acceleration, but men who commanded large salaries by their proficiency at the art of long hitting.

I wouldn't state it for a fact, but it is possible that the at-

tendance problems of the early fifties were in some measure attributable to this. Since every team's offense was so much the same, a baseball game was not, as it is today and has been throughout most of baseball history, a clash of opposing philosophies or unlike skills, but rather was reduced to a simple test of quality, a day-to-day worry about which pitcher had his control and which one would slip a pitch into the wheelhouse of the other's behemoth, and how many men would be on base at the time. Perhaps this was exciting baseball if your team was the Yankees or the Dodgers or (early in the decade) the Giants, and you figured each day that yours would be the fortunate team; besides, those three teams—the Yankees, Dodgers and Durocher's Giants—truly did play an exciting, aggressive game of baseball, as did a few other managers.

Another point on which baseball drew heavy criticism from the media in the fifties was the length of time that it took to play the games. The average length of a major league game rose from two hours, twenty-three minutes in 1951 to two hours, thirty-eight minutes in 1960, and the number of games played in less than two hours dropped in those years from 166 to 41. This engendered criticism that baseball had become too slow, and in the early sixties a series of steps was taken to speed up the games. It was at this time that the rule was enacted requiring a manager to remove his pitcher if he went to the mound more than once in an inning. This was done to stop repeated, and time-consuming, visits to the mound.

The game evolved slowly. Strikeouts, on the rise since the early thirties, continued their incline throughout the decade, with batting averages consequently in decline, and doubles and triples declining with batting averages. The trends in motion did not break during the decade— they did not break until 1969 —but they did bend into a new shape. The stolen base began to make a comeback. A

new breed of power pitcher was emerging.

Perhaps even more than the *games,* the stifling effect of this baseball of so few dimensions was felt upon the *races,* and thus upon the imagination of the fans. People tell me that baseball should never change, that it should remain forever locked the way it was the moment that they first discovered how wonderful it was. I shake my head, and I cannot understand how people can think that way. Baseball didn't change much between 1920 and 1960; it crept forward on a steady path like a scout on his knees, but it admitted no revolutions and no upheavals. They kept playing in the same parks in the same cities as long as they could, and they kept playing by the same unwritten rules and the same strategies, testing and retesting the same already proven theories about the game, and the same teams just kept winning. It sure doesn't seem to me like much of a way to greet the morning.

The decade ended on an optimistic note for fans who were growing weary of the reruns. In 1959 every team in baseball hit at least a hundred home runs *except* the American League champion White Sox, who hit but ninety-seven and were considered at the time to have a "running" offense.

WHERE THE GAME WAS PLAYED

In 1953, major league baseball broke from the east coast and headed for the Midwest; in 1958, it made it all the way to the coast. Major league cities included Baltimore, Boston, Brooklyn, Chicago, Cincinnati, Cleveland, Detroit, Kansas City, Los Angeles, Milwaukee, New York, Philadelphia, Pittsburgh, St. Louis, San Francisco and Washington.

WHO THE GAME WAS PLAYED BY

With the breaking of the color barrier, other ethnic identities ceased to have much meaning. Second-generation immigrants became third-generation became fourth-generation, and the accents ceased to be of languages and became the accents of regions. While some players still grew up in Little Italy or Fisherman's Wharf or Germantown, Illinois, more grew up in places with names like McAllister and Houston. But the difference between black and white was still deeply felt, and where the Blacks were, everybody else was just White.

There weren't that many blacks, really—about 8 percent. There were probably more Polish players in the fifties than blacks (Klusewski, Mazeroski, Kubek and Musial were some of the good ones; the Polish population in baseball was at its all-time high). A myth has developed that for a time each team could have two blacks, the star and his roommate. No such pattern ever existed, but there were no black-and-white roommates during the fifties. It's funny—Latins could room with blacks, and Latins sometimes could room with whites. There were quite a few more Latins as the decade wore on.

It's often written that the National League got integrated a lot quicker than the American League, which is how they finally caught and passed them after forty-five years as the weaker league. There is some truth in this, but it was much more of a team-by-team thing than a difference between the leagues; it just happened that more of the most open teams were in the National League. But Cleveland in the American League was well integrated by 1951, whereas the Cardinals did not have a black regular until Curt Flood in 1958. (Charlie Peete, who would probably have been their first black regular in 1957, was killed in a plane crash while returning from playing winter ball.)

As to regions, the South and California still produced a disproportionate share of the talent. Willie and Mickey were southerners, the Duke was from California (I consider Oklahoma southern because

Checking In

1951—Dave Winfield, St. Paul, Minnesota
1952—Fred Lynn, Chicago
1953—Dan Quisenberry, Santa Monica
George Brett, West Virginia
Keith Hernandez, San Francisco
Jim Rice, South Carolina
1954—Gary Carter, California
1955—Robin Yount, Danville, Illinois
1956—Dale Murphy, Portland
Eddie Murray, Los Angeles
1958—Rickey Henderson, Chicago
1959—Ryne Sandberg, Spokane
Tim Raines, Florida

Checking Out

1950—Kiki Cuyler, 50
Pete Alexander, alcoholism and epilepsy, 63
1951—Eddie Collins, 63
Joe Jackson, 63
Harry Heilmann, 56
Bill Klem, 77
1952—Arlie Latham, 93
Arky Vaughan, boating accident, 40
1953—Jesse Burkett, 84
Kid Nichols, 83
Josef Stalin, 74
Jim Tabor, 36
1954—Hugh Duffy, 87
Chief Bender, 70
1955—Cy Young, heart failure, 88
Honus Wagner, 81
Harry Agganis, pneumonia and pulmonary embolism, 25
1956—Connie Mack, 93
Al Simmons, 56
1957—Sen. Joseph McCarthy, 48
1958—Tris Speaker, heart attack, 70
Chuck Klein, 52
Mel Ott, head-on collision, 52
1959—Frank Lloyd Wright, 89
Nap Lajoie, 83
Ed Walsh, 78
Jim Bottomley, 59

they talk funny). Educated players began slowly to filter back into the game. The Yankees, in particular, had a number of players among the educated minority, including Moose Skowron, Bobby Brown, Jerry Lumpe, Andy Carey, and Bob Cerv.

THE 1950s IN A BOX

*Attendance Data:
>*Total:* 165 million (165,067,231)
>*Highest:* Milwaukee Braves, 1957, 2,215,404
>New York Yankees, 16,133,658
>*Lowest:* St. Louis Browns, 1950, 247,131
>Washington Senators, 5,598,081

Most Home Runs:
>Mickey Mantle, 1956, 52
>Duke Snider, 326

Best Won-Lost Record by Team:
>Cleveland, 1954, 111–43
>Yankees, 955–582, .621

Worst Won-Lost Record by Team:
>Pirates, 1952, 42–112
>Pirates, 616–923, .400

Heaviest Player: Ted Klusewski is the heaviest player listed, at 235, with Steve Bilko at 230. Both estimates are conservative. Oddly, there was no one in the decade who would admit to a weight over 235, although baseball in the fifties probably had more 250-pound players than at any other time.

Lightest Player: Eddie Gaedel, 65 pounds

Lightest Real Player: YoYo Davalillo, 140

Clint Hartung Award: Billy Consolo

Most Strikeouts by Pitcher:
>Herb Score, 1956, 263
>Early Wynn, 1,544

Highest Batting Average:
>Ted Williams, 1957, .388
>Ted Williams, .336

Hardest-Throwing Pitcher: Steve Dalkowski

Hardest-Throwing Major League Pitcher: Herb Score

*Best Baseball Books:
>1951—*The Official Encyclopedia of Baseball* by Hy Turkin and S. C. Thompson
>1952—*The Natural* by Bernard Malamud
>1953—*The Southpaw* by Mark Harris
>1954—*The Year the Yankees Lost the Pennant* by Douglass Wallop
>1955—*Fear Strikes Out* by Jim Piersall and Al Hirshberg

Best Outfield Arm: Carl Furillo

An outfielder named Glen Gorbous established a record in 1957 when he threw a ball 445 feet, 10 inches on the fly. Gorbous could throw but not hit; for the Phillies in 1955, he had ten assists in just sixty-two games, but hit only .244. He was playing for Omaha at the time the record was set.

Worst Outfield Arm: Ralph Kiner

Most Runs Batted In:
>Al Rosen, 1953, 145
>Duke Snider, 1,031

Most-Aggressive Baserunner: Minnie Minoso

Fastest Player: Mickey Mantle

Pedro Ramos, a pitcher for the Senators, was often used as a pinch runner, and always insisted he was the fastest player in baseball. In an attempt to prove this, he repeatedly challenged Mickey to a footrace, but it never came off.

Slowest Player: Gus Triandos

Best Control Pitcher: Lew Burdette or Robin Roberts

Most Stolen Bases:
> Luis Aparicio, 1959, 56
> Willie Mays, 179

Best-Looking Players:
> Eddie Mathews
> Mickey Mantle

Ugliest Player: Don Mossi

Outstanding Sportswriter: Arnold Hano

Most-Admirable Superstar: Ernie Banks

Least-Admirable Superstar: No one

Most-Lovable Superstar: Roy Campanella

Franchise Shifts:
> Boston (N) to Milwaukee, 1952
> St. Louis (A) to Baltimore, 1953
> Philadelphia (A) to Kansas City, 1955
> Brooklyn to Los Angeles, 1958
> New York (N) to San Francisco, 1958

New Stadiums: Two of the cities' that attracted teams, Baltimore and Milwaukee, built new stadiums to help them do that. Memorial Stadium in Baltimore was built in 1950, and the upper deck was added in 1953. Milwaukee's County Stadium, also completed in 1953, was the first stadium to be built with public money. The other teams that moved did so initially into old parks, and no new parks were built for other teams. However, Minneapolis and St. Paul got together in 1957 to construct Midway Park, to which a major league team was attracted in 1961.

Best Pennant Race: 1951 National League

*Best World Series: 1952, Yankees over Dodgers, 2–4, 7–1, 5–3, 0–2, 5–6, 3–2, 4–2

Best-Hitting Pitcher: Don Newcombe

Worst-Hitting Pitcher: Bob Buhl

*Best Minor League Team: 1954 Indianapolis Indians

*Best Minor League Players:
> Ray Perry
> Al Pinkston

Odd Couple: Yogi Berra and Dr. Bobby Brown were roommates and best of friends, although at a glance they seemed to have nothing in common.

Resident Intellectual: Jim Brosnan

Drinking Men:
> Ryne Duren
> Don Newcombe
> Ellis Kinder
> Don Larson

New Equipment: Batting helmets were a pet project of Branch Rickey. He required all of the Pirates to wear them in 1952, so that these valuable young stars who went 42–112 that year wouldn't get hurt and leave him with a bad team. The National League adopted them in 1955, the American League in 1956, with a grandfather clause that if you hadn't worn them before you didn't have to wear them.

Best Baseball Movie: *Damn Yankees,* 1957

Most Wins by Pitcher:

    Robin Roberts, 1952, 28

    Warren Spahn, 202

Highest Winning Percentage:

    Elroy Face, 1959, 18–1, .947

    Whitey Ford, 121–50, .708

Best Unrecognized Players:

    Larry Doby

    Al Smith

Highest-Paid Player: Ted Williams, $125,000, 1959

New Statistics:

    1954—Sacrifice flies

    1955—Intentional walks

Most Unpredictable Career: Walt Dropo

Best Athlete in the Game: Mickey Mantle

Most Lopsided Trade of the Decade: Nellie Fox for Joe Tipton (trade actually made October 19, 1949)

A Very Good Movie Could Be Made About: A day in the life of Casey Stengel

I Don't Know What This Has to Do with Baseball, But I Thought I Would Mention It Anyway: Joe McCarthy liked to claim that he once had a dream that he had died and gone to heaven, and the Old Man called him up and told him to assemble a baseball team. He looked around, and he had Christy Mathewson, Walter Johnson, Babe Ruth, Lou Gehrig, Tris Speaker, Cy Young, Honus Wagner, and most of the other superstars. He was thrilled; he figured it would be the greatest team there ever was.

Just then the phone rang, and it was Satan calling up from below, asking if he'd like to get together for a game. "But you don't have a chance," protested Marse Joe. "I've got all the ballplayers."

"I know," said the devil. "But I've got all the umpires."

MAJOR LEAGUE ALL-STAR TEAM 1950–59
Records in seasonal notation, based on 154 games played. Pitchers based on 40 starts.

Pos	Player	Years	Hits	HR	RBI	Avg.	Other
C	Yogi Berra	9.06	165	26	110	.287	Only 29 Strikeouts
1B	Stan Musial	9.45	187	28	103	.330	38 Doubles
2B	Jackie Robinson	6.03	161	16	79	.311	
3B	Eddie Mathews	7.62	160	39	103	.281	99 Walks
SS	Ernie Banks	5.99	176	38	110	.295	
LF	Ted Williams	6.46	165	35	113	.336	131 Walks
CF	Willie Mays	6.92	187	36	103	.317	26 Stolen bases
RF	Mickey Mantle	8.09	172	35	123	.311	110 Walks
U	Duke Snider	9.21	174	35	112	.308	

	Pitcher	Years	Won-Lost	SO	ERA	Other
RH	Robin Roberts	9.78	20–15	155	3.32	308 Innings
RH	Early Wynn	9.00	21–13	172	3.28	
LH	Warren Spahn	9.34	22–14	157	2.92	
LH	Whitey Ford	5.76	21–9	159	2.66	
R	Clem Labine	6.55	11–8	70	3.59	13 Saves

1951: WHERE IS EARL WEAVER WHEN YOU NEED HIM?

Bobby Thomson's pennant-winning home run against Ralph Branca, who was called into the game to pitch to him, was his third home run that season off of Branca, and teammate Monte Irvin had hit five home runs off of Branca. Altogether, the Giants that year hit eleven home runs off of Branca, and beat him six times, one less than the record.

THE FIFTIES NOBODY TALKS ABOUT: BASEBALL IN TROUBLE

The early fifties witnessed alarming declines in attendance. It was often written that baseball was in trouble—that television, which was usually blamed for the decline, was threatening the very existence of the game (somehow, this always gets left out of those nostalgic books about how great baseball was in the golden fifties). "TV Must Go . . . Or Baseball Will" screamed the headline article in the November 1952 issue of *Baseball* magazine, and then that venerable publication itself bit the dust (*Sport* magazine wrote much the same story, but survived it). The Negro Leagues died. Minor leagues were folding up as fast as one could count them, and major league attendance, after a peak just short of 21 million in 1948, dropped to 17.5 million in 1950, and was still fading (16.1, 14.7, 14.4 million in 1953). The teams felt helpless. They felt the need for better facilities—almost everyone at this time was playing in a park built between 1909 and 1915 —but the costs involved in constructing a new stadium had become prohibitive.

Finally, in a mood near general panic, the teams began to pick up and go to the fans. The Braves, after drawing just 281,000 fans in Boston in 1952, moved the team to Milwaukee, where they drew the largest crowds in all of baseball (even bigger than the Yankees) for the remainder of the decade. This held the 1953 attendance decline, which was 13 percent for the other fifteen teams, to a less omi-

VIC RASCHI

nous 2 percent. Baseball's other "weak sister," the Browns, followed suit in 1953, and met with similar, though less impressive, results, and then Philadelphia picked up and went to Kansas City.

Before the Kefauver Congressional Committee in 1958, Commissioner Ford Frick predicted that major league baseball would be out of existence within ten years if baseball could not get control of indiscriminate television broadcasting.

Buoyed by the attendance gains of the new cities, baseball refused to sink, and attendance began to grow slowly late in the decade, back to 18.3 million by 1959 (aided by two terrific pennant races). I have great sympathy for the fans of the Giants and the Dodgers, and the attendance of those teams was still at levels at which the owners possibly could have made a profit —but they, too, were in serious decline. The Dodgers, who drew 1.8 million in 1946 and 1947, put out a great team for ten years after that and suffered ten years of box office reversals, dropping to 1.03 million by 1957. The Giants, after reaching a peak of 1.6 million in 1947, suffered catastrophic reverses for most of the next ten years, down to 629,000 in 1956 and 654,000 in 1957. Think about that. In the biggest city in the nation, a team with an unparalleled wealth of tradition, boasting uncounted millions

of loyal fans who still wail and lament for their lost team, a team featuring one of the greatest and most exciting players who has ever played this game—was drawing 9,000 people a game.

Perhaps I should make this a separate article, called "Sympathy for the Devil," but consider honestly the position of Walter O'Malley in 1957. After purchasing a property in receivership, historically mismanaged and with more failures than successes behind it, after having built that team, through his own hard work and astute judgment, into the strongest franchise in the league, he continues *for ten years* to produce outstanding baseball teams—yet he watches that position of leadership slip away from him, as the attendance of his team falls to fifth in the league and less than one-half of that enjoyed by the owners in Milwaukee, who had the courage to seize new territory. His protests about inadequate parking and facilities are ignored, merely lame complaints of a pampered businessman. What is he then to do?

The cities were dying. The slums were clinging to the walls of the ballparks, and eating their way toward the core of the city. People were afraid to go to them; the crime rate was smaller but the fear was the same. Perhaps night baseball, the economic godsend of the forties, was responsible for that. Perhaps night base-

ball killed the neighborhoods which the teams then discarded. I don't know. They didn't intend to, but (with the exception of Mr. Wrigley) they didn't worry about it.

This does not make it right that the Dodgers in 1958 abandoned a city that loved them, but the true story of baseball in the 1950s is not a story about greedy men who betrayed the trust of loyal rooters, and brought the golden age of sport crashing to a close as they foraged for even greener pastures. It is a story about fear and urban decay, about a panic-stricken industry scrambling for survival. It is a story about old ballparks that had come to symbolize the rotting neighborhoods in which they stood, and were smashed apart so that something new and full of promise could be put in their place. We know now that that was a mistake, and we wish now that they had saved the old ballparks. But we must also hope that history will have compassion in surveying our mistakes, and for that reason we must try to understand those of the generation before us.

1952: WASTED DAYS AND WASTED NIGHTS

On July 2, 1952, Art Edinger, with Crowley in the Evangeline League, made seven plate appearances in a game without being credited with an official at bat.

THE BEST BASEBALL BOOKS OF THE 1950s

1951—Hy Turkin and S.C. Thompson, in *The Official Encyclopedia of Baseball,* produce the first modern compendium of individual player season and career statistics. Unique and invaluable B.M. (Before Macmillan).

1952—Bernard Malamud's *The Natural,* a satiric fantasy baseball novel on the theme that nobody ever really learns anything. Malamud's book, which owes much to Eddie Waitkus and T. S. Eliot, bears occasional resemblances to the 1984 Robert Redford vehicle.

1953—With *The Southpaw,* Mark Harris begins the saga of Henry Wiggin, left-handed pitcher and tale-teller extraordinaire.

1954—Douglass Wallop, *The Year the Yankees Lost the Pennant,* reworks Goethe's *Faust* into *Damn Yankees.*

—Jim Carothers

1955—*Fear Strikes Out* is my own addition to the list.

—Bill

THE BEST WORLD SERIES OF THE 1950s

The 1952 Series is probably the least remembered World series of the fifties—just another in a series of Yankee victories—but nonetheless it was one hell of a duel. The most remembered contests of the decade are the 1955 World Series, which is the one Brooklyn finally won, and the 1956, in which Larsen pitched a perfect game. The '54 series is remembered for Willie's catch on Wertz, and the '53 series as the one that Billy Martin hit .500. The 1957 series, also not much remembered, was also terrific. But the '52 series . . . well, with the exception of Game Two, a 7–1 contest (2–1 through five innings), any of the other games could easily

have gone the other way several different ways. If you're interested, let's wallow in the details of the series for a while:

Game 1: Brooklyn won, 4–2. But in the Yankee fourth, Rizzuto led off with a single, and Mantle beat out a bunt to put two men on with nobody out. With one out Rizzuto was on third, and Joe Collins lined to right field, but Carl Furillo fired a strike to home plate, and Rizzuto had to hold; the Yankees didn't score. Then in the fifth inning, Gil McDougald led off with a walk and Billy Martin singled, but Andy Pafko threw out McDougald trying for third. Then with two

❖❖ 1954: 72 HOME RUNS ❖❖

The minor league record for home runs in a season was set by Joe Baumann with Roswell in the Longhorn League in 1954, when he hit 72. Baumann's complete record is below:

Year	G	AB	R	H	2B	3B	HR	RBI	TBB	Avg.
1954	138	498	188	199	35	3	72	224	150	.400

As I said (see 1947: 254 RBI) the Longhorn League was a hitter's league, but this was a season. Hitting .400 with 150 walks and being hit by pitches nine times, Baumann had an on-base percentage of .545, a .916 slugging percentage, and created about 246 runs for Roswell. Roswell finished second with a record of 87 wins, 51 losses.

Baumann was an enormous man, 6'5" and 235 pounds. He ran a Texaco station in Roswell, pumped gas during the day and hit home runs at night. In his minor league career, which lasted only 1,019 games, he hit .337 with 337 home runs.

out Pafko made a diving catch, and the Yankees again did not score.

Game 2: Yankees won, 7–1. Sixth-inning explosion after Hodges dropped double play ball.

Game 3: Dodgers won, 5–3. Yankees loaded the bases in the fourth but didn't score; got two more on in the fifth and didn't score. Yanks later got two solo home runs, but Dodgers scored two runs in the ninth with the aid of a Reese/Robinson double steal and a passed ball charged to Yogi.

Game 4: Yankees won, 2–0, but Dodgers had more than enough chances. With one out and one on in the first, Billy Martin stumbled while fielding a ground ball and then threw it away, putting runners at first and third. Allie Reynolds struck out Robinson and Campanella to get out of it. In the third inning, Reese singled but was caught stealing.

In the fifth inning of Game Four, Pafko led off with a single, Hodges walked and Furillo sacrificed, so there's one out and two men in scoring position. (Furillo was batting eighth after his worst season.) On a suicide squeeze, Black missed the ball and the runner was out at the plate; Yankees got out of it.

Game 5: One of the greatest World Series games ever, won by Brooklyn, 6–5. Pafko in the second inning and Furillo in the eleventh inning both made sensational leap-

ing catches of balls at the right field wall—both of which were certain home runs if they got by the glove. (Dressen switched his defense in the outfield after scoring three in the fifth, which is how come both men happened to be playing right field.) Other plays of note: With Robinson on second in the second inning, Campy faked a bunt. McDougald broke to cover the bunt and Robinson stole third, which was momentarily unprotected. Later on in the inning, Carl Erskine made a good bunt down the first-base line with the bases loaded, but Ewell Blackwell (for the Yankees) fielded it and flipped it backhand to Yogi for the force. But in the fifth inning, Blackwell set up a three-run explosion with our old friend, the unsuccessful attempt to make the play at second on a sacrifice bunt. Cox lined a single off McDougald's glove to start the winning rally in the eleventh.

Game 6: Yankees won, 3–2, despite two home runs by the Duke. Cox led off the first with a double, but Reese popped out trying to bunt, and Dodgers failed to score.

Game 7: Yankees won, 4–2. In the fourth inning, Snider led off with a single, and then two straight Dodgers (Robinson and Campanella) bunted for base hits down the third-base line. Bases loaded, nobody out. Allie Reynolds was brought in in relief, making his fourth series appear-

ance (he pitched a shutout in Game Four, then relieved in Games Six and Seven). Allie got out with just one run scoring.

In the seventh inning, the Dodgers loaded the bases with one out and Snider and Robinson coming up. Bob Kuzava, the fourth Yankee pitcher of the afternoon, got them out of it.

A few other notes on the series. It was a Monday morning quarterback's dream, abounding in crucial managerial decisions on both sides. *The Sporting News* review of the series said that it was "packed with strategy which was contrary to the book, but . . . both Stengel and Charley Dressen profited by the moves. Dressen went an unusually long way with his starters—sometimes too long." Dressen's affection for the sacrifice bunt knew no boundaries. He *always* bunted when he had the opportunity, no matter who was up. The Dodgers lost several runners on the bases, but mostly in games that they won. Gil McDougald played very, very badly in the series —four errors, a couple of baserunning blunders; he hit .200 and the Dodgers kept dropping bunts in front of him. I don't know if Gene Woodling had a bad arm or something, but the Dodgers really took advantage of him, too. Johnny Mize was the hero of this series—he's not mentioned here because I'm focusing on what could have happened but didn't, rather than on what did.

Stan Baumgartner, reviewing the series for *The Sporting News Guide* the next year, called it one of the most thrill-packed series in history. The description seems accurate; the outcome of the series hung in doubt from beginning to end, with little relief. The Yankees had to win the last two games at Ebbets Field to remain the champions, and they did it.

BEST WINTER LEAGUE TEAM OF THE 1950s, PRESUMABLY

In the winter of 1953–54, the Santurce team in the Puerto Rican League had an outfield of Bob Thurman, Willie Mays and Roberto Clemente. Willie led the league in hitting at .395; Clemente, then nineteen years old, was fourth at .344. Toothpick Sam Jones went 14–4 for the team; Ruben Gomez was 13–4.

They won the pennant.

BEST MINOR LEAGUE TEAMS OF THE 1950s

The Indianapolis team of 1954 finished 95–57, winning the league by ten and a half games, and defeated Minneapolis in the first round of the playoffs before losing four out of five to Louisville. I'd still take my chances with them. The team featured three outstanding major league players, Herb Score (22–5, 330 strikeouts), Rocky Colavito (.271, 38 homers, 116 RBI), and Toothpick Sam Jones (15–8, second in the league in strikeouts with 178). It's safe to say that nobody was digging in on them; in the following two years Score led the American League in strikeouts (245 and 263), while walking 154 and 129, while Jones led the National League both years in both strikeouts (198 and 176) and walks (185 and 115). There were some other people on the team who could play a little—Suitcase Simpson, Hank Foiles, Billy Harrell, Joe Ginsberg, Joe Caffie, Owen Friend, Hurricane Hazle, a pitcher named Bob Kelly who had a good year.

The 1952 Milwaukee team, a farm club of the Braves, was also outstanding, particularly in the pitching staff, which was led by Gene Conley (the only man ever named Minor League Player of the Year twice), Dick Donovan, Don Liddle and Murray Wall. Wall, a so-so major league pitcher, had an outstanding minor league career, and turned up on several of the best minor league teams of the decade. Milwaukee also had some decent everyday players, including Bill Bruton, Gene Mauch, Billy Klaus and Johnny Logan and George Crowe for part of the year. The best minor league eight-man lineup of the decade was the Kansas City Blues lineup of 1953, which included Bill Skowron, Elston Howard, Vic Power, Bob Cerv and Bill Virdon, among others. That team had no pitching, but finished second in the American Association and won the playoffs anyway. Another Yankee farm team that was very similar was the Denver team of 1956. They had a double-play combination of Kubek and Richardson, surrounded in the infield by Woody Held (.276, 35 homers, 125 RBI) and Marv Throneberry (.315, 42, 145). Their outfield was pretty fair, but they had only one pitcher (Ralph Terry). The consistently strong Montreal teams of 1951–56 should also be mentioned.

THE MAN WHO INVENTED WINNING UGLY

I always kind of identified with Don Mossi. Don Mossi had had two careers as a major league pitcher, one as a reliever and one as a starter, and he was pretty darn good both times. No one who saw him play much remembers that, because Mossi's ears looked as if they had been borrowed from a much larger species, and reattached without proper supervision. His nose was crooked, his eyes were in the wrong place, and though he was skinny he had no neck to speak of, just a series of chins that melted into his chest. An Adam's apple poked out of the third chin, and there was always a stubble of beard because you can't shave a face like that. He looked like Joe Torre escaping from Devil's Island.

One of the problems with choosing ugliest and handsomest players is that a player who looks little short of grotesque in one pose or one photograph will look fine in another. Susie showed me a picture of Hoyt Wilhelm in which he looked positively handsome; I assured her that it was just a bad shot.

You never have that problem with Don Mossi. Don Mossi was the complete ugly player. He could run ugly, hit ugly, throw ugly, field ugly and ugly for power. He was ugly to all fields. He could ugly behind the runner as well as anybody, which made him a great ugly-and-run man. And you talk about pressure . . . man, you never saw a player who was uglier in the clutch.

Normally, I might be reluctant to write about this, but Don knows he's ugly. Don was so ugly that the broadcast media's rule of two Negroes applied. A sportscaster will ordinarily never say that two black men look alike, but there is an exception, if you have two players who look *so much* alike that you ruin your credibility if people think you haven't noticed. Ordinarily, sportswriters will seem not to notice a jagged tooth or a creative nostril, but Don was so ugly that people talked about it freely. He was a kind of public service, the ugly man's hero.

DON MOSSI

RUTHSRECORD

I had been a baseball fan but a year or two before Maris impounded it, yet I think I had always been aware of Ruth's record. That Ruth held a zillion records was immaterial and, in the dead zone after he retired and before the Macmillan *Encyclopedia* was published, not even widely understood by the upcoming generations. When Roger Kahn wrote in *Sport* magazine in 1956 that Willie Mays could be the man to beat Ruth's record, everyone understood that this didn't mean he could slug .848 for a season or .691 for a lifetime, or that he might score 178 runs or get 458 total bases or have 120 extra base hits or draw 171 walks or hit 715 home runs lifetime or pitch 31 scoreless innings in the World Series. The phrase "Ruth's record" is as much a part of the fifties as Jimmie Dean, sock hops, Hank Williams and Marilyn Monroe, and it was buried with more ceremony than any of them; Kahn meant only that Willie might be the man to hit sixty-one home runs.

I mention this first as a linguistics point, and second to call attention to this curious identification of Ruth with just one record, when he had so many. Was there ever anything called Cobb's record?

In part, of course, it was the category itself: home runs, season. The basic unit of power in the basic term of performance. But as much as that, the record drew so much attention simply because it was so vulnerable, so constantly under attack. Which is the more important standard, a .400 batting average or the all-time record for batting average? Yet if you asked people on the street, fifty times as many would know who was the last man to hit .400 as would know who holds the record. How many people know who holds the record for hits in a season?

Tommy Holmes was momentarily resurrected as Pete Rose charged by him in 1978, and what warmer sports story was there ever than the rediscovery of Doc White just before his death in 1969, when Drysdale broke his record? The sixty-home-run standard was often exposed because it was often threatened, and gradually it consumed the rest of Ruth's accomplishments. When Hack Wilson hit fifty-six homers in 1930, sportswriters wondered whether he might break Ruth's record for home runs in a season. When Foxx hit fifty-eight two years later, they wondered whether he might break Ruth's record for

homers (in a season). When Greenberg hit fifty-eight in 1938, they wondered whether he might break Ruth's record (for home runs). When Kiner hit fifty-one and then fifty-four, they wondered whether he might eventually break Ruth's record.

Roger Maris seems to have been a pleasant enough young man, yet as far as the public was concerned, his charm was cooked that summer by an experience such as no other sports figure has ever been asked to endure. Ruthsrecord was supposed to be broken by Willie or Mickey or at least somebody *impressive,* like Frank Howard. The manifestation of Ruth's memory in that one standard charged the man who would break the record with the responsibility to possess greater talents than Maris was given, and he was to be often reminded of his shortcomings.

This may come as a bit of a shock, but did you realize that in just a few years, Maris' record will be as old as Ruth's? It's been twenty-seven years, and the sixty-one figure has never been challenged, protected by the dimensions of modern stadiums. In the end, Ruth benefited from the effort. With the shattering of this record and that one, Ruth's image escaped from the prison of one or two numbers, and we all began to appreciate the breadth and scope of his accomplishments. There is no Ruthsrecord anymore, but there is still Ruth's record, and there is still none better.

RAYMOND LAWRENCE PERRY

My favorite minor league baseball star of all was a 5-foot-7-inch third baseman named Ray Perry. In the Far West League in 1950, Perry hit .366 with 44 home runs and 170 RBI in 138 games. Despite hitting .366, Perry had more walks than hits, 179–169, giving him an on-base percentage for the season of .547, by dint of which he scored 162 runs. Speed? He stole 23 bases, putting him among the league's top ten. His slugging percentage was .734. As a glove man, Perry led the league's third basemen in fielding percentage and was second in range factor. He filled in at second base in sixteen games, making only one error there (he didn't play any shortstop that year). In his spare time, Perry managed the Redding team, which finished 86–54, a game and a half out of first. It was, all things considered, not one of Perry's best seasons.

The Far West League was a Class D League, and Perry at this time was in his prime, at the age of twenty-nine. Even so, his domination of the league across the board was remarkable. The Far West League was not, like the Longhorn League or the West Texas–New Mexico League or the Sunset League, a hitter's paradise in which sluggers regularly cranked out 50 or 60 home runs and hit .400. With 44 home runs, Perry led the league by 10, and with 170 RBI he led by 28. In batting average he was second, behind a singles hitter named Joseph Borich. And Perry was not, like Joe Baumann or many of the other players who compiled these spectacular numbers, a slugging behemoth, a two-dimensional offensive player; he led the leagues in which he played in almost everything—and he did it for several years.

Ray Perry began his minor league career at the age of nineteen with Salt Lake City of the Pioneer League. The Pioneer League was not then, as it is today, a "rookie" league. I had always assumed that that was what was meant by the name "Pioneer" (it was for players who were just starting out) but that is not true; the Pioneer League has a long and honorable history, dating back before the modern farm system. The Pioneer League in 1939 was just a low-level league.

Anyway, Perry hit .295 with 17 homers, 94 RBI, scored 115 runs in 130 games and led the league with 41 doubles—a good year. In 1941 he moved up to Tacoma in the Western International League, where he had pretty much the same season, hitting .313

with 41 doubles, 12 homers and 88 RBI. He did not have the super strike zone judgment then—he drew only 49 walks—but he led the league's third basemen in fielding percentage and putouts, and finished second in assists and double plays. Late in the year he was purchased by San Francisco in the Pacific Coast League, and he had the look of a man who would be in the majors in a couple of years.

He didn't have a great year in his first year in the PCL. He hit 12 homers and drove in 75 runs, but his average was just .256. He split his playing time between third base (eighty-four games) and second (eighty-three games) and was decent at either position. As a twenty-one-year-old who had proven he could play in the P.C.L., Perry remained a good prospect. The most similar player in the league that year would have been Wally Westlake, an outfielder across the Bay in Oakland:

	Westlake	Perry
Born	Nov. 8, 1920	Dec. 23, 1920
Games	169	167
At bats	593	536
Runs	57	70
Hits	159	137
Doubles	26	27
Triples	6	7
Home Runs	7	12
RBI	74	75
Walks	47	50
Strikeouts	108	91
Batting	.268	.256
Slugging	.368	.399

Westlake grew from where he was to be a successful major league hitter, hitting in the .280s with over 20 home runs a year.

The first of Ray Perry's misfortunes was that of his entire generation: the War came. If you chart the number of players having successful major league careers by year of birth, you'll see a sharp dip in the years 1919–1922; Perry was right in the middle of that. At the ages of twenty-two and twenty-three, when he should have been sharpening his skills and earning his first serious looks from the big league scouts, Perry was out of baseball. Had it not been for the war, quite possibly he would have been in the majors by the end of 1944.

He returned to baseball, with the Seals, in 1945. He played only 135 games of San Francisco's 184. He hit .271 with 5 home runs, 58 RBI. With the soggy baseballs of wartime, only one player in the P.C.L. hit more than 14 home runs. He was becoming a more patient hitter, taking 70 walks. Only twenty-five, he was still in position to fight for a role in postwar baseball as the season opened in 1946.

On April 21, 1946, Perry was hitting .346 in the infant season

(9 for 26). He fractured his leg on that date, so severely that he was out for the rest of the year. And the next.

That finished him as a prospect. He was twenty-seven years old when he joined Redding of the Far West League in 1948 as a player/manager, and nothing he could do after that would ever restore his chance to play in the majors. He had been able to play baseball only one of the previous five years.

In the Far West League in 1948, Perry hit .411. A loud .411. He hit 36 home runs in 122 games, drove in 163 runs and scored 138. He drew 139 walks. He led the league in batting average by 63 points, in runs batted in by 48, and hit five more home runs than any other two players combined. His on-base percentage was .549, his slugging percentage .727. He stole 18 bases and played first base, second base, third base, the outfield and catcher as well as managing.

This was to become a fairly typical Ray Perry season. In 1949 he hit .404 with 45 homers, 155 RBI in 120 games. He drew 169 walks, giving him a career-high on-base percentage of .600, and scored 135 runs. He stole 20 bases, had a slugging percentage of .846, managed, and played second base, third base and short-stop, with the best fielding percentage in the league at third. I mentioned 1950 at the outset—.366, 44 homers, 170 RBI, 179 walks. In 1951 he slumped to .349 with 18 homers, 128 RBI, though he still led the league in home runs and RBI, and with 180 walks his on-base percentage remained a respectable .554. He still moved around well enough to steal 19 bases.

In 1952 Perry went back to the Pacific Coast League—briefly. Conceivably, Perry might still have advanced in his profession if he had gotten hot at the start of the season. But he was past thirty. He didn't get hot. Playing just occasionally, Perry went 3 for 27 at the start of the season and was optioned to Little Rock of the Southern League. He wasn't much better off there, going 7 for 37 before finding himself with El Dorado in the Cotton States League. He arrived there just in time to play 84 games and lead the league in home runs, drawing 79 walks and hitting .307. In 1953 he was in the California State League, hitting .337, leading the league in doubles (41), home runs (36), and runs scored (120), plus, of course, walks (142). In 1954 he hit .341 with 37 homers, 128 RBI, marking the seventh consecutive season he had led his league in home runs, a minor league record. That year he drew a career-high 184 walks and served as the first professional manager for Don Drysdale.

He began to fade a little after that. He hit just .268 in the Three-I League in 1955, with 23 homers and 82 RBI in 112 games; he was, for the first time in years, not the dominant player in the league. In the California League the next two seasons, he hit .316 and .350

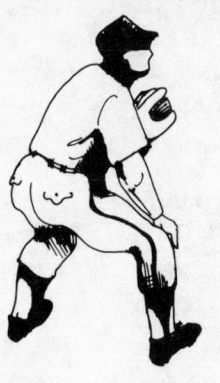

and drove in over a hundred runs a year. In 1958, aged thirty-seven, he retired in mid-season after hitting .293 and driving in just 50 runs in 77 games. He continued to manage in the minor leagues for several seasons after that. I don't know exactly when or why he drifted out of baseball, but he died in 1973 in Fremont, California at the age of fifty-two.

Was Perry capable of playing major league baseball? If you ask a hundred people you'll get a hundred different answers, but my answer is "of course he was." I know that the leagues that Perry dominated weren't very good leagues, and that there is all the difference in the world between playing major league baseball and having a low minor league roped and tied. But even in the low minors, the man played against any number of future or past major leaguers, and his offensive winning percentage was always about 100 or 150 points higher than their's. Vince DiMaggio, in his mid-thirties, played and managed in the Far West League in Perry's time. (Actually, there were two Vince DiMaggios in the league at that time, the real Vince DiMaggio and a pitcher named Vincent S. DiMaggio.) Although DiMaggio was also far above that league, he was never as good as Perry. In 1954, Perry was a teammate of the nineteen-year-old Don Demeter. Demeter hit .267 with 26 homers, 89 RBI; Perry hit .341 with 37 and 128. Chuck Essegian was one of the big stars in the league that year, hitting .319 with 31 homers and 118 RBI. He was twenty-two years old, twelve years younger than Perry, and his performance doesn't match Perry's in any respect. Among other players that Perry played against were Al Gionfriddo, Eddie Lake, Ron Hansen, Albie Pearson, Marty Keough, Gene Green, and Johnny Callison. He was always a better hitter than they were, usually a whole lot better. If they all went to the majors together, what was going to happen to make them better than he was all of a sudden? There is a reasonably predictable relationship between what players do in the minors and what they do when they reach the majors. For Perry to have missed as a major leaguer, given a hundred-game shot, he would have had to be miles away from that normal relationship.

Perry missed four key years in youth, due to wartime and injuries. In the years that he should have moved from the good minors to the majors, he moved from the good minors back to Class-C ball. Who could miss four key years out of his youth, and still make the majors? Ted Williams, maybe. Sal Maglie did. Like all minor league stars, Perry's timing was terrible. My guess is that as a player, he was somewhere between Eddie Yost and Stan Hack. As a hitter he was probably not a *lot* better than Don Demeter, Wally Westlake or Vince DiMaggio—but he *was* probably better. At the same age, he probably would have about matched them in power, hit for a little better average and had a far better strikeout-to-walk ratio. I think eventually sabermetrics will develop methods that can express minor league records in terms of major league equivalents with a high degree of reliability, and then we'll know exactly where he stands. But we'll never know what he would have done if he hadn't lost those four years.

ANIMAL HOUSE

Animals, for the second time, enjoyed a major vogue as a source of nicknames (although unlike the earlier period, the nicknames are generally not modified or expanded upon). One could probably make up an entire all-star team (or an entire zoo) of players whose nickname was simply that of a beast. Harry Brecheen was known as "The Cat," Harvey Haddix as "The Kitten," and Don Hoak as "Tiger," which about covers the felines; Frank House was called "Pig," Tom Sturdivant was called "Snake," Roy Sievers was called "Squirrel," Don Bessent "The Weasel," and Charlie Peete and Frank Lary were dubbed "Mule" (Lary was also called "Yankee Killer," making him, I think, only the third player nicknamed for his ability to defeat one other team. Jack Pfiester and Harry Coveleski were called "Giant Killers.") Jim Owens was called "Bear" and Mike Garcia "The Big Bear"; Johnny Schmitz was "Beartracks." Dick Farrell was called "Turk," although that may have been a family nickname rather than a baseball nickname, as was true of Moose Skowron, whose nickname actually was a shortened form of "Mussolini," a nickname he was given as a baby by his grandfather, who thought he bore a resemblance to Il Duce. Somebody is always called "Bull," and in this case it was Brooks Lawrence, as well as "The Baby Bull," Orlando Cepeda. A few animals were modified. Duke Snider was among several players to be called "The Silver Fox," and Joe Frazier was called "Cobra Joe."

Other nicknames:
The Nervous Greek (Lou Skizas)
The Chairman of the Board (Whitey Ford)
The Rope (Bob Boyd)
The Say Hey Kid (Willie Mays)
The Walking Man (Eddie Yost)
The Barber (Sal Maglie)
The Sphinx (Don Mossi)
The Little Potato (Camilo Pascual)

All very blond players in the fifties were called "Whitey."

MITTYS

The year 1954 saw two men, who appeared to be in the ballpark for other reasons, enter ball games and acquit themselves quite well.

In the Class-B Tri-State League, a groundskeeper started and won a game for the pennant-bound Asheville Tourists on September 5. Charles "Bud" Shaney was a groundskeeper at the Tourists' McCormick Field, but had been a pitcher for some twenty-two minor league seasons ending in 1942. The fifty-three-year-old former hurler went five innings and gave up four hits and no runs. He was credited with the 4–0 victory over Knoxville. Asheville had already clinched the pennant, as this was the next to last day of the season. Knoxville finished second in the six-team league.

The South Atlantic League's (Class A) Columbus Cardinals had one of their paying customers smash a grand slam for the team on April 24. Joe Carolan bought a ticket to the game that day against Macon. He also purchased a scorecard so as to learn the manager's name. Once he found out that the Columbus manager was George Kissel, he asked for a try-out. Some hasty pregame batting practice produced a number of long drives and ended with an instant contract for the

STEAMED

The Hot Springs, Arkansas, team in the Cotton States League was known as the Hot Springs Bathers. The Bathers took the plunge into the twentieth century on April 6, 1953, when they signed a pair of brothers as pitchers, Jim and Leander Tugerson.

Jim Tugerson was a big nice-looking kid, and no darker than, say, Juan Marichal; all the same, you could tell. The Cotton States League was not ready for this, and they kicked Hot Springs out of the league, declaring the franchise forfeit (it was probably worth about thirty to forty thousand dollars). George M. Trautman, the head of the minor league structure, overruled the league and let the Bathers back in the water, but they yielded to pressure and optioned the Tugerson brothers to an even lower league.

Hot Springs had some injuries to their pitching staff, and by May 19 they were down to four pitchers. Jim Tugerson could pitch a little; at Knoxville he went 29–11 with 286 strikeouts (no other pitcher in the league came within 8 wins or 60 strikeouts of him), and for good measure played some first base and pinch hit, hitting .308 with five homers and 35 RBI in 182 at bats. Hot Springs recalled him, and on May 20 he was listed as the starting pitcher for the Bathers. The umpires, acting on instructions from the league, declared the game forfeit. Tugerson was returned to Knoxville.

twenty-one-year-old, 230-pound Carolan. He started the game in the outfield and bashed the grand slam in his first at bat, which came in the second inning, which leads us to believe that the manager had enough confidence to sign him up, but still put him at the bottom of the order. At the time, it gave Columbus a 4–3 lead, but they eventually lost the game, 7 to 5, in 13 innings.

We'd like to report that Joe Carolan went on from there to demoralize Sally League pitchers with his potent bat,

but such was not the case. Carolan played in another thirty-two games. He hit four more homers and registered a .231 batting average. Four of his 13 RBI came in that first at bat. He did play errorless ball in 27 outfield appearances, but registered a range factor just over one. His total of 97 plate appearances in 33 games suggests that he was used as a pinch hitter a number of times. Columbus finished last in 1954, 30½ games out of first.

—Jim Baker

1957: THE FAILURE OF DEMOCRACY

The 1957 National League All-Star team, as selected by the fans, consisted of Ed Bailey of Cincinnati at catcher, Stan Musial of St. Louis at first, Johnny Temple of Cincinnati at second, Don Hoak of Cincinnati at third, Roy McMillan of Cincinnati at short, and Wally Post, Gus Bell and Frank Robinson of Cincinnati in the outfield. Cincinnati was destined to finish fourth that year, but with the help of broadcaster Waite Hoyt and a newspaper that printed ballots already filled out and the address of where to send them, their players did right well in the All-Star voting, so well in fact that the commissioner (Ford Frick) stepped in and ordered Post and Bell to leave the room. Hoak and McMillan were dismissed from the game after one plate appearance, and the match eventually began to resemble an All-Star game, rather than Cincinnati versus the American League.

The fans by then had been selecting the teams for years, but after that they decided the simpletons couldn't be trusted to vote on something as important as an All-Star team, so they gave the privilege to the players for a few years. The logical short-circuit involved here boggles the mind. You design and implement a system which has no controls, no guidelines, no checks or balances, no appeals or redress, in short no protection of any sort against every kind of abuse imaginable, a system that allows ballots to be published in the newspaper and dropped into the ballot box by the bushelful, and you put that system in the hands of the fans, and when it goes astray you blame . . . the fans?

Logically, this is equivalent to simply leaving an open ballot box in the middle of the street on the second Tuesday in November, waiting for the inevitable voting abuses to occur, and then announcing triumphantly that democracy does not work. Giving the vote to the players has the advantage of implementing a couple of automatic controls. You know who the players are; there's no problem with keeping track of who has voted and who hasn't. The votes are automatically balanced in that way, an equal number from each team.

We are back to fan voting now, and with a system that has a few, but only a few, more controls than the earlier form. The system is still heavily liable to abuse, but at least the ballots are now centrally printed and distributed, so that the league knows where the ballots go; the basic theory of the current controls is uniform opportunity for abuse of the ballot.

I have another that I would like to propose: voting by precinct. What they should do is, consider each of the twelve cities in the National League to be a separate local precinct. If you finish first in your precinct, that's twelve points toward the All-Star team; if you finish second, that's eleven, and so on. You could either count only the votes which are deposited at a ballpark, or you could make mail-in votes into a thirteenth precinct, considered as the at-large vote.

This would incorporate into fan voting the two basic advantages of the alternative, advantages which are also inherent in the structure of the MVP balloting, which (as I've said many times) is the best-designed voting structure in the game, and thus the best award in the game. Those are: one, the vote is under control, and two, the vote is regionally balanced.

What one might assume would happen, at least in the first year, would be that all of the hometown boys would finish first in each precinct. OK, fine; you all get twelve points each, so now let's get on with the serious voting. A San Francisco voter wants to

NATIONAL LEAGUE GROUP, TOP, LEFT TO RIGHT: FRANK ROBINSON, REDS, LEFT FIELD; JOHNNY TEMPLE, REDS, 2ND BASE; ED BAILEY, REDS, CATCHER; ROY MCMILLAN, REDS, SHORTSTOP. BOTTOM: DON HOAK, REDS, 3RD BASE; HANK AARON, BRAVES, RIGHT FIELD; STAN MUSIAL, CARDS, 1ST BASE, WILLIE MAYS, GIANTS, CENTER FIELD.

fill out 728 ballots for Bob Brenly? Fine; let him do it. Brenly wins San Francisco by an extra 728 votes. Precinct voting contains the impact of local-favorite voting within the precinct, and thus creates a cycle in which it all cancels each other out. The fact that there are more Dodger voters than San Francisco voters no longer means anything.

Since the idiot vote all cancels itself out, that leaves the intelligent voters to decide who gets to make the All-Star team. For several reasons, this should tend, over time, to encourage more intelligent and considered voting. Let's say that in Pittsburgh there are 200,000 votes cast. If 70 percent of those are local-favorite votes, that leaves the other 60,000 voters to decide who finishes second, and gets eleven points, and who finishes twelfth, and gets one.

That tends to encourage intelligent voting; you can either waste your vote in the R. J. Reynolds pile, or you can put it in with the 30 percent that do the effective work of the precinct. You split 60,000 votes eleven ways, and there are going to be some spots in there that are decided by just a few votes. Each vote, rather than being lost in an indistinct mountain of ballots, would have the potential to make a difference in where some-body ranks. That, again, tends to encourage intelligent voting. I confess that I cast several votes annually for Jerry Narron as the American League catcher, even when Jerry Narron is not in the majors; I wouldn't do that if I felt the vote had the potential to make any difference.

But since the idiot votes would all cancel each other out, would people continue to cast them? The teams, which make the situation worse by openly encouraging idiot voting, would have less incentive to do so. In subtle ways, the ethics of fan balloting would, I think, be improved. Ballot-box stuffing, which now is done openly, might not be looked at so favorably. Now, the Pirate fan is supposed to look at the man with sixty ballots in his hand and say, "Oh, good. He's really helping us get R. J. Reynolds on the All-Star team." But since *his* votes only have an impact on the same pool that *my* votes are going into, do I really want him to be doing that? If he's got sixty ballots there for R. J. Reynolds, then he's just a harmless fool—but if those aren't local-favorite votes, then I'm voting once and he's voting sixty times, and I'm not going to like that too well. It's even possible that the voters in a city, knowing that their collective ballot would become a matter of record, might start to take pride in their reputation as fair and intelligent voters, rather than taking pride in their ability to help elect local heroes.

On the other hand, I don't like ballot-box stuffing now, and that doesn't stop anybody. No, I don't mean to overstate the advantages of the idea. The essential point is that fan voting failed, and might well fail again, not because fans are not competent voters, but because the structure of the election was not well thought out. Precinct voting—or possibly some other alternative—would make it quite possible to keep the advantages of fan involvement, and control the effects of irresponsible voting. I would hope that would be considered before they give up on us again.

The 1960s

HOW THE GAME WAS PLAYED

As the decade commenced, baseball showed the promise of opening up into a new generation of exciting, multi-faceted offense. The use of speed as an offensive weapon, which had all but disappeared ten years earlier, began to reemerge in the late fifties, and by 1962 was a headline story, as Maury Wills stole 104 bases. Batting champions hit in the range of .350, and home run totals were at historic levels. Best of all, the expansion of 1961–62 counteracted somewhat the blurring effects of the ever-increasing competitive balance of the leagues, and allowed a few outstanding players to stand out from the crowd in a bolder relief.

On January 26, 1963, the Baseball Rules Committee voted to expand the strike zone. Previously defined as extending from the armpits to the top of the knee, the strike zone was then redefined to include the area from the shoulders to the bottom of the knee. Several things about this should be noted. First, this was not an action taken by baseball as a whole; the teams had no input into the decision. It was taken by a small, semi-private committee that had been established primarily to clear up small gray areas in the rules, and which never, at any time, intended to effect significant changes in the way the game was played. Second, the Rules Committee members apparently thought that they were, in taking this action, returning the strike zone to what it had been prior to 1950; that, at least, is what they announced at the time. If so, they overshot the mark just a little; the definition used prior to 1950 was from the player's *knees* to his shoulders; the new definition said from the *bottom of the knees* to the shoulders.

The effect of this redefinition was sudden, dramatic, and unexpected. The action was taken, quietly, because there was a feeling that runs (and in particular home runs) had become a little too cheap. The thinking was, apparently, that by giving the pitchers a few inches at the top and bottom of the strike zone, they could whittle the offense down just a little bit.

The action cut deeper than anyone had anticipated. Home run output in 1963 dropped by 10 percent and total runs dropped by 12 percent, from 4.5 per game to 3.9. Batting averages dropped by twelve points. The second dead-ball era had begun.

The question which puzzled people at the time was how this apparently minor redefinition of the strike zone could have had such a dramatic impact on the levels of offense, when basically the same redefinition thirteen years earlier, in the opposite direction, seemed to have only a small, temporary impact. I would answer that this way: Suppose that, in a period of small but consistent inflation, a man is given an 8 percent raise. The impact of this upon his purchasing power would seem to be small and temporary, as the inflation would quickly erode the gains. Thirteen years later, however, the 8 percent advantage is taken away from him, and he is cut back to 97 percent of his original salary, while the inflation continues unabated. The impact of this reversal upon his purchasing power would be dramatic, and would seem to grow more severe with each passing year.

The hitters were in a period in which the tide was running against them. From 1931 to 1968, long-range trends against the hitter and in favor of the pitcher were in motion, resulting in constant increases in the number of strikeouts, and steady (though fluctuating) declines in batting average. As batting averages dropped, sequential offense became more difficult to sustain, and it became more and more profitable to attempt to hit home runs. There were several causes for this trend, each of which could be evaluated by sabermetric analysis, but most of which have not been.

The most important cause, I believe, was an evolution in stadium architecture, creating parks in which the fans were further away (hence more foul territory), the mounds tended to be higher and the visibility worse. I think that if the issue were studied, we would find that almost every change in ballparks in this period took hits out of the league. Almost every time a team moved, they moved to a worse hitter's park than the one they left behind. When the Indians moved from League Park in Cleveland, one of the great hitter's parks ever, to cavernous Memorial Stadium, a huge number of hits went out of the league. (This move was gradual, 1933–48; for several years they played weekend games in Memorial Stadium, but weekday games in League Park.) When the Browns moved from Sportsman's Park in St. Louis to Memorial Stadium in Baltimore, again, a huge number of hits went out of the American League. The Dodgers moved in stages from cozy Ebbets Field to the pitcher's best friend, Dodger Stadium; the Giants went in two steps from the comfort of the Polo Grounds to the cold of Candlestick. The Braves in 1953 moved from one bad hitter's park to another.

That, I believe, was the largest cause of the drift in the direction of lower batting averages. Contributing factors were increased night ball on the schedule, and a predisposition on the part of the Rules Committee to permit those innovations and developments which favored the defense, while prohibiting those which favored the offense (for example, fielder's gloves were allowed to grow larger and larger, but corked bats were prohibited).

Anyway, batting averages dropped in 1963, and they were to drop lower. With a large, accommodating strike zone, unregulated pitching mounds being built up higher and higher, and hitters still swinging for the fences, the power pitchers were in complete command of the game. Every team had them, the Bob Veales, the Jim Maloneys, the Dick Radatzes and the occasional Bob Gibson. With the rules all stacked their way, they made sequential offense —four singles in an inning— almost impossible, and thus further encouraged an offense built around the home run. Stolen bases continued to creep back into the game, but the pace of the increase slowed down after 1962.

I've written some less than complimentary things about baseball in the 1960s, and I suppose that some people have gotten the idea that I didn't like it. Well, I loved it. I grew up in the sixties, and this was the only baseball that I knew, and I thought it was great.

But now that I've seen it, I don't particularly know that I want to see it again. I think that the baseball of the seventies and the eighties, honestly, is a lot more exciting. If the only baseball that was available was that pitcher-dominated game of the sixties, with day-in, day-out 2–1 games and offenses mostly consisting of waiting for somebody to hit a home run, I'd take it; there are a lot of exciting things that can happen in sixties-style baseball. But given a choice, I'd choose eighties-style baseball. And I think most fans would agree with me.

Checking In

1960—Mike Marshall, Illinois
Chili Davis, Jamaica
Tony Gwynn, Los Angeles
Steve Sax, Sacramento
Kent Hrbek, Bloomington
Cal Ripken, Maryland
Mel Hall, New York State
Fernando Valenzuela, Mexico
1962—Darryl Strawberry, Los Angeles
Eric Davis, Los Angeles
Don Mattingly, Evansville, Indiana
Roger Clemens, Dayton, Ohio
1964—Dwight Gooden, Tampa

Checking Out

1960—Fred Clarke, 87
Stuffy McInnis, 69
1961—Ty Cobb, cancer, 74
Ernest Hemingway, suicide, 63
Dummy Hoy, 99
Eddie Gaedel, 36
Dazzy Vance, 69
1962—Mickey Cochrane, 59
1963—Rogers Hornsby, heart attack, 66
Home Run Baker, 77
John F. Kennedy, gunshot, 46
1964—Fred Hutchinson, cancer, 45
Ken Hubbs, plane crash, 22
1965—Winston Churchill, 91
Paul Waner, emphysema, 62
Branch Rickey, heart attack, 83
1966—Charlie Dressen, cancer, 67
1967—Jimmie Foxx, choked on food, 59
1968—Sam Crawford, 88
Babe Adams, 86
Heine Groh, 78
Vern Stephens, 48
1969—Heine Zimmerman, 82

WHERE THE GAME WAS PLAYED

On both coasts and in the middle: Atlanta, Baltimore, Boston, Chicago, Cincinnati, Cleveland, Detroit, Houston, Los Angeles, Kansas City, Milwaukee, Minnesota, Montreal, New York, Oakland, Philadelphia, Pittsburgh, St. Louis, San Diego, San Francisco, Seattle, Washington. The Southwest (Phoenix) and much of the deep South including Florida still had no major league ball.

THE 1960s IN A BOX

Attendance Data:
- *Total:* 224 million (224,199,594)
- *Highest:* Los Angeles Dodgers, 1962, 2,755,184
  Los Angeles Dodgers, 21,781,262
- *Lowest:* San Diego Padres, 1969, 512,970
  New Washington Senators, 5,834,745 (figure covers only nine years, but would still have been the lowest in baseball if the tenth year had been their best ever)

On the basis of games played, attendance per game was slightly higher for the 1960s as a whole than for the 1950s as a whole. Attendance averaged 13,400 per game played in the 1950s, 14,050 in the 1960s. This figures to a growth rate of slightly less than one-half of one percent per season, as opposed to an average for the entire 1901–84 period of 2.5 percent per season. But attendance per game was higher in the late fifties than in the late sixties. On the basis of games played, the best attendance year of the decade was 1960, with an average of 16,162 per game played; on the basis of total attendance, the best year was 1969, with 27,225,765 (14,005 per game played).

Best Won-Lost Record by Team:
- New York, 1961, 109–53, .673
- Baltimore, 1969, 109–53, .673
- Baltimore, 911–698, .566

Worst Won-Lost Record by Team:
- 1962 Mets, 40–120, .250
- New York Mets, 494–799, .382

Heaviest Player: Frank Howard, given at 6'7" and 275, is the heaviest listed and went heavier; Dick Radatz, though listed at only 235, must have been close to 300 by the end of his playing days.

Lightest Player: Albie Pearson, 5'5", 140-pound American League center fielder

Clint Hartung Award: Mike Epstein

Most Home Runs:
- Roger Maris, 1961, 61
- Harmon Killebrew, 393

Most Strikeouts by Pitcher:
- Sandy Koufax, 1965, 382
- Bob Gibson, 2,071

Highest Batting Average:
- Norm Cash, 1961, .361
- Roberto Clemente, .328

Hardest-Throwing Pitcher: Sudden Sam McDowell

*Best Baseball Books:
- 1960—*The Long Season* by Jim Brosnan
- 1963—*Eight Men Out* by Eliot Asinof
- 1966—*The Glory of Their Times* by Lawrence S. Ritter
- 1968—*The Universal Baseball Association, Inc.: J. Henry Waugh, Prop.* by Robert Coover
- 1969—*The Baseball Encyclopedia*

*Best Outfield Arm: Roberto Clemente

Worst Outfield Arm: Tito Francona

WHO THE GAME WAS PLAYED BY

As I said, the game was dominated by power pitchers. The number of black players continued to increase throughout the decade, as did the number of Latin players. It will probably always be true that most star athletes come from the bottom of the economic spectrum.

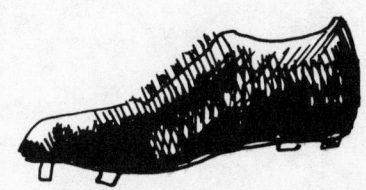

YOU'D HAVE A HECK OF A TIME PROVING HE WAS WRONG

In 1960 Jackie Robinson went to visit both of the presidential candidates, Richard Nixon and John F. Kennedy. He endorsed Nixon. In 1964 Robinson worked for Barry Goldwater. He felt that Lyndon Johnson, by politicizing the race issue, would ultimately undermine support for civil rights, that civil rights gains could not continue without the support of both parties. "It would make everything I worked for meaningless," Robinson told Roger Kahn, "if baseball is integrated but the political parties were segregated."

Most Runs Batted In:
>Tommy Davis, 1962, 153
>Hank Aaron, 1,107

Most-Aggressive Baserunner: Frank Robinson

Frank suffered a number of serious injuries in his career while in the process of combating basepath obstacles, most often fielders. The obstacles fared no better.

Fastest Player: Willie Davis
Slowest Player: Boog Powell
Best Control Pitcher: Juan Marichal
Most Stolen Bases:
>Maury Wills, 1962, 104
>Maury Wills, 535

Best-Looking Players:
>Bill Mazeroski
>Bob Gibson

Ugliest Players:
>Bill Skowron
>Dick Donovan

Strangest Batting Stance: Frank Cipriani
Outstanding Sportswriter: Jim Murray
Most-Admirable Superstar: Brooks Robinson
Least-Admirable Superstar: Denny McLain
Franchise Shifts:
>Washington to Minnesota (A.L.), 1961
>Milwaukee to Atlanta (N.L.), 1966
>Kansas City to Oakland (A.L.), 1968

New Stadiums:
>1960—Candlestick Park, San Francisco
>1962—Dodger Stadium, Los Angeles
>1964—Shea Stadium, New York
>1965—Astrodome, Houston
>   Atlanta-Fulton County Stadium, Atlanta
>1966—Anaheim Stadium, Anaheim
>   Busch Stadium, St. Louis
>1967—San Diego Stadium (baseball, 1969)

Best Pennant Race: 1967 American League

The 1964 National League pennant race is remembered because of its wild finish, but the whole thing was only interesting for about eight days. The American League was having a terrific pennant race that year, which no one remembers because the Yankees won it again, and the Phillies were in complete command of the 1964 race until the last two weeks. The 1962 N.L. race was kind of a west coast version of the 1978 A.L. East.

Best World Series: I guess I'd have to go with the 1960 series, but there were a number of great ones—1960, 1964, 1965, 1967, 1968; 1962 and 1969 were pretty good in their own way. Unmatched decade for World Series.

Best-Hitting Pitcher: Earl Wilson, who hit thirty-three home runs during the decade (684 at bats)

Worst-Hitting Pitcher: Hank Aguirre

*Best Minor League Team: Birmingham, 1967

Best Minor League Player: Joe Hicks

The Odd Couple: Danny Murtaugh and Roberto Clemente

Drinking Men:

   Sam McDowell

   Pumpsie Green

New Equipment:

   Weighted donut on bat

   Batting glove

   Outsized catcher's mitt for handling knuckleballs

*Player vs. Team:

   Throneberry vs. the Mets, 1963

   Koufax and Drysdale vs. the Dodgers, 1966

Best Baseball Movies: None

*Uniform Changes:

   Silly logos

   Sleeveless Tunics

   Year-to-year alterations gather speed

Most Wins by Pitcher:

   Denny McLain, 1968, 31

   Juan Marichal, 191

Highest Winning Percentage:

   Whitey Ford, 1961, 25–4, .862

   Sandy Koufax, 137–60, .695

Best Unrecognized Player: Bill Freehan

Highest-Paid Player: Probably Willie Mays (1969, about $145,000)

New Statistics: Saves (unofficial)

Most Unpredictable Career: Tommy Harper

Best Athlete in the Game: Bob Gibson

Most Lopsided Trade of the Decade: Lou Brock and two other players for Ernie Broglio, Bobby Shantz, and Doug Clemens

A Very Good Movie Could Be Made About: The life and times of Leo Durocher

I Don't Know What This Has to Do with Baseball, But I Thought I Would Mention It Anyway: In 1962, when Joe Pepitone was a rookie, he liked to hang around at the Copacabana with a lot of "rackets" guys. He recalled in an autobiography that some of them were pretty upset with Moose Skowron because he was playing ahead of an Italian. "We're gonna help ya out with that little problem ya got with Skowron," one of them said one night. "He's gonna have a little accident," explained another. Pepitone protested, and talked them out of it. But he still insists they were serious.

PLAYER VERSUS TEAM, 1960s

After his legendary season in 1962, in which he hit .238 with 49 RBI and led the league in errors, Marv Throneberry held out in the spring of 1963. The Mets responded by sending Marv to Buffalo, a technique now called "reality therapy."

The most publicized contract battle of the decade occurred in the spring of 1966. After a 1965 season in which Sandy Koufax went 26–8 and obliterated the modern record for strikeouts and Don Drysdale went 23–12 and doubled as one of the team's top pinch hitters, hitting .300 with 7 home runs, Sandy and Don staged an unprecedented joint holdout, reportedly asking for a three-year, $1.05 million contract to be divided evenly. That comes to $175,000 a year, which would have been a record at the time. It was described as the most celebrated salary dispute in history, albeit probably by someone whose knowledge of the history of the game was his memory. Koufax eventually settled for $125,000, Drysdale for $110,000.

KIRBY HIGBE

After his playing days, Kirby Higbe had trouble making a living, and eventually he wrote some bad checks and was sentenced to sixty days in the Richland County Jail in South Carolina. He made the acquaintance and won the trust of the warden, and wound up working as a guard there. From that he moved to working as a guard at the state pen.

Higbe started smuggling sleeping pills—at least he says they were sleeping pills—into the penitentiary. Appropriately, he got the pills in there by concealing them inside a baseball. The judge who heard his case said that Kirby had been one of his heroes, and Higbe was sentenced to three years' probation. While on probation he wrote an honest autobiography, *The High Hard One,* published by Viking in 1967. He does not emerge from his own book as a very likable man, or as a man of much intelligence or fiber, yet somehow the book is likable, intelligent, and excruciatingly honest. Higbe had a seventh-grade education and a hell of a fastball, and he did the best he could with both.

MAJOR LEAGUE ALL-STAR TEAM 1960–1969
Records in seasonal notation, based on 154 games played. Pitchers based on 40 starts.

Pos	Player	Years	Hits	HR	RBI	Avg.	Other
C	Elston Howard	6.62	149	17	76	.272	
1B	Willie McCovey	8.16	146	37	101	.279	
2B	Pete Rose	6.57	202	11	66	.309	103 Runs
3B	Brooks Robinson	9.74	174	19	86	.278	
SS	Maury Wills	9.30	187	2	40	.286	58 Stolen bases
LF	Frank Robinson	9.06	177	35	112	.304	86 Walks
CF	Willie Mays	9.25	177	38	114	.300	114 Runs
RF	Hank Aaron	9.51	191	39	116	.308	

Pos	Pitcher	Years	Won-Lost	SO	ERA	Other
RH	Juan Marichal	8.12	24–11	227	2.57	314 Innings
RH	Bob Gibson	8.06	20–13	257	2.74	
LH	Sandy Koufax	6.27	22–10	305	2.36	6 Shutouts
LH	Whitey Ford	6.10	19–9	171	2.83	
R	Hoyt Wilhelm	8.51	9–8	103	2.16	65 Games, 18 Saves

FRANK HOWARD AND MAURY WELLS

✦ NICKNAMES ✦

Nicknames in the sixties started to get nasty again. Although by no means as common nor as harsh as those of the thirties, less than flattering nicknames of the decade included a number of somewhat sarcastic handles given to players who had sudden hot streaks during undistinguished careers (Marv Throneberry was called "Marvellous Marv," Jose Azcue was tabbed "The Immortal Azcue" after a two-month hot streak in 1963, Willie Smith was called "Wonderful Willie" when he made his unexpected pitcher-to-hitter transformation at the major league level), plus a number of out-and-out uncomplimentary monickers, such as "Dr. Strangeglove" (Dick Stuart), "Motormouth" (Paul Blair), and "Iron Hands" (Chuck Hiller). Yankee pitcher Hal Reniff was probably the last player called "Porky." Other nicknames of note:

Moonman (Mike Shannon)	The Creeper (Ed Stroud)
No Neck (Walter) Williams	Daddy Wags (Leon Wagner)
Superjew (Mike Epstein)	The Toy Cannon (Jimmie Wynn)
Hoover (Brooks Robinson)	
Hondo (Frank Howard)	Mudcat (Jim Grant)
	Roadblock (Sherman Jones)
Stretch (Willie McCovey)	The Monster (Dick Radatz)
Honey (John Romano)	The Vulture (Phil Regan)

The best nickname of the decade, for my money, belonged to Sam McDowell—Sudden Sam. The nickname was original, sounded good, worked well in print or voice, and described the abilities and the career of the player, whose fame and fastball both arrived very suddenly. Terrific nickname.

Many players before Willie McCovey had been called "Stretch," but, as Ruth had done with "Babe," Willie redefined the name and made it his own. A writer today is reluctant to call a young player "Stretch" because it implies a comparison to McCovey, and there aren't many people who warrant the comparison.

YEAH, BUT DON'T FORGET THEY HAD TO PAY FOR THE PARKING ATTENDANTS

Don Drysdale was paid a reported $35,000 in 1962, when he went 25–9 and pitched 314 innings. In court proceedings resulting from an appeal on the evaluation of Dodger Stadium, the Dodgers reported a profit for the season of $4,347,177.

THE BEST BASEBALL BOOKS OF THE 1960s

1960: In *The Long Season,* Jim Brosnan provides the only baseball diary ever to be written by the ballplayer whose name appears on the title page.

1963: Eliot Asinof's *Eight Men Out.* A careful study of the 1919 Black Sox scandal.

1966: In *The Glory of Their Times,* Lawrence S. Ritter pioneered and perfected the technique of oral history of baseball. Often imitated, never excelled.

1968: *The Universal Baseball Association, Inc.: J. Henry Waugh, Prop.,* by Robert Coover.

1969: *The Baseball Encyclopedia,* published by Macmillan and Information Concepts, Inc. containing individual season and career statistics for all players, summaries of each season, and much more. *The Baseball Encyclopedia* marked the beginning of advanced statistical analysis of the game. If the last library in the world were on fire, this is the baseball book that would be most desirable to save.

—Jim Carothers

REMIND ME AGAIN NOT TO SAY THAT

Writing about Ty Cobb in *The Greatest in Baseball* (Scholastic Books, 1962), Mac Davis stated that "his career record of 892 stolen bases is not likely to be broken." Lou Brock was then in his rookie season.

UNIFORM STUDY

Was there something in the atmosphere of the giddy, disturbed sixties that gave birth to cutesy logos? Probably not, but the logos began to sizzle—from the sweet-faced Cubbie on the left sleeve of the Chicago uniform to the smiling Oriole bird logo on hat and sleeve to the fiercely grinning feathered Indian on Cleveland's uniform and the laughing Indian on the Braves' sleeve. Perhaps the most unusual logo signifies the Twin Cities of Minnesota with two cartoon musclemen shaking hands in front of a huge baseball. Pity the team whose nickname doesn't lend itself to a descriptive character; they usually come up with something. But silly logos didn't add much distinction to the player or the sport, and so they quieted down for a decade or so, only to reappear in their present form as theatrical mascots.

Shirt-sleeves, which started out full-length and had been getting progressively shorter, finally disappeared altogether from certain uniform styles in the late fifties. The Pirates, Reds and Indians all adopted sleeveless button-up tunics. With a T-shirt or sweatshirt underneath it, the new style apparently allowed more freedom of movement, something further facilitated a decade later by a change in fabric.

By this time, most teams made at least minor changes in design from year to year—a change in the lettering, or some additional trimwork. As color began to dominate in the next decade, the changes became more dramatic. (The rules committee gave the Kansas City A's permission to wear colored uniforms, rather than the traditional home white, in January of 1963.) Historically, though, a few teams have resisted the impulse to alter, and kept the same basic design from year to year and decade to decade. The Dodgers, Yankees, Reds and Royals are among those who do little to tamper with the traditional style.

—Susie

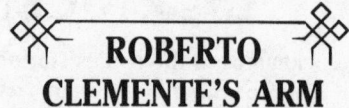

ROBERTO CLEMENTE'S ARM

I've been trying a little experiment, asking baseball fans that I meet who had the best throwing arm they ever saw. It's very rare that anybody who is old enough to remember seeing him play doesn't immediately say "Clemente." For younger fans, you just can't believe what it was like; I hope we see another one like it, or you'll never believe that it was possible. His throws combined strength, accuracy, and speed of release in whatever proportions were necessary to get the job done. Freddie Patek told me he saw Clemente throw people out at the plate from the warning track at Forbes Field, over 350 feet away. I never saw him do that, but I saw him grab a double in the gap and fire it to second base to make it an oops/single, when the entire transaction was so lightning fast that even having seen him do it four or five times, you still couldn't believe that it was possible.

∾ GRAMPS ∾

On September 10, 1963, Stan Musial hit a home run off of Glen Hobbie on his first at bat after becoming a grandfather.

BEST MINOR LEAGUE TEAM, 1960s

By the 1960s the free minor leagues were gone. The major leagues had taken their liberty, television had taken their audience, and expansion had taken their territory. The form remained alive, but no life remained in the form.

By this time the minor leagues were tightly structured; there was no possibility of some rebel league trying to get better ballplayers, upgrade itself and rise in stature, as the uppity Pacific Coast League had tried to do in the fifties. Everything was fixed; each player was an A player, a AA player, or a AAA player (or, early in the decade, a B player, a C player, or a D player). And yet, ironically, the strongest teams of the decade were not AAA teams, but teams from the lower classifications. Triple A baseball teams had become holding companies for players just one step away from the majors; when a player showed promise early in the season, up to the majors he went. AAA rosters sheltered largely indistinguishable veterans who had failed at the major league level, but whom the teams wanted to keep at hand in the event of an emergency. Even in the heat of a pennant race, the major league teams would now relieve their minor league "affiliates" of their best players, even when those players filled but a minor role on the major league scene. Under these circumstances, it was rare for a AAA team to play even .600 baseball, and the best AAA winning percentage of the decade (.642) was by a veteran Tulsa team which produced no future major league players of any quality.

In the lower minors, however, organizations usually had four to six AA and A teams, and they often played favorites, loading up the roster of one team with all of the organization's hot prospects, so that they would get acquainted, learn to play together, and establish a winning atmosphere. Some of these teams were pretty good.

If you're not really interested in the question of what was the best minor league team of the 1960s, you should stop reading this now, because I am, and I'm going to discuss the details of the subject for several paragraphs. One candidate is the Reno team in the California League (then called Class C) in 1961. Reno won ninety-seven games and lost forty-three, blowing the league apart. This team featured eye-popping numbers, but the nagging question of "Who were they?" There are only four names on the team that are meaningful today. Third baseman Ken McMullen hit .288 with 21 homers and 117 RBI, making him clearly the weakest of the four Reno infielders that season, though he was the most successful in the major leagues. First baseman Dick Nen had a monster season. Hitting .351 with 32 homers and 144 RBI, and also stealing 25 bases in 28 attempts. But he was a marginal major league player, remembered for one big home run.

Other than those two, probably the most memorable name on the roster was that of Bruce Gardner, the pitcher who shot himself on the mound at USC a few years later. He was the ace, going 20–4 and leading the league in ERA; he was probably a major league pitcher at that time, but he hurt his arm before he had a chance to prove it. Another sensational pitcher on the staff was Joe Moeller, who looked like he was going to be outstanding. Moeller was a big man (6′5″) with a good fastball and a huge, sweeping curve that had the minor leaguers completely overmatched; he was 12–3 with a 1.82 ERA and 162 strikeouts in 119 innings before moving on. He had equally sensational stats in two or three other minor league stops, and when Koufax was out in '62 he took

Koufax's place in the rotation, but his major league record was 26–36.

The real puzzle is the shortstop. This guy couldn't possibly have missed as a major leaguer. He led the league in hitting, at .363. He hit 18 homers, drew 66 walks, stole a few bases, drove in 97 runs and scored 132 and led the league's shortstops in assists, fielding average and double plays. But who was he? His name was Don Williams, and he never played in the major leagues. What happened to him? Did he kill himself, too, and if not why not?

Perhaps the best AAA team of the decade was assembled that same year at Tacoma, an outpost of the San Francisco Giants farm system. The Giants pitching staff featured several players who had major league careers, led by a future Hall of Famer, Gaylord Perry; others included Eddie Fisher, a successful major league reliever, Ron Herbel, a major league reliever for several years, and Jim Duffalo, a reliever. Two major league catchers helped to handle this staff, Tom Haller and John Orsino, and several other players behind them had major league careers and are still around somewhere as coaches, including Chuck Hiller at second base and Manny Mota in center field. The team featured no awesome stats, but won the league by ten games.

I settled, finally, on the Bir-mingham team in the Southern League in 1967. Charles O. Finley was a Birmingham boy, and when he got the chance he decided to pool most of his best minor league talent and put on a show for the home folks; the show included Reggie Jackson, Joe Rudi, Dave Duncan and Rollie Fingers, among others. Actually, the star of the show that summer was a nineteen-year-old Cuban-born right-hander named George Lauzerique, who went 13–4 with a league-leading 2.30 ERA. Lauzerique kept flirting with no-hitters. On May 11 he pitched no-hit ball for seven innings, but was taken out of the game because the A's had a rule in their farm system against young pitchers throwing more than a hundred pitches. On June 8, facing the major league A's in an exhibition, Lauzerique allowed only one hit in seven innings before being lifted for the same reason. Finally, on July 6, Lauzerique pitched a seven-inning perfect game, using only eighty-five pitches. Their record, 84–55, was not as impressive as their talent, but they weren't pushed.

1962: A WARM CUP OF COFFEE

Of all of the thousands of players who have been called up late in the season and given a brief chance to show what they can do, probably the most impressive argument was made by a giant named Walter Franklin Bond in September of 1962. Bond got into twelve games with the Cleveland Indians that year, and had nineteen hits good for a forty total bases; he hit .380 with six homers and 17 RBI. It's arbitrary, but my list of the greatest late-season smashes by young players follows (I used a 20-game limit and made an exception for Merv Connors):

Player: Year	G	AB	Run	Hit	2B	3B	HR	RBI	BB	Avg.	Sl Pct
Walt Bond, 1962	12	50	10	19	3	0	6	17	4	.380	.800
Gil Coan, 1947	11	42	5	21	3	2	0	3	5	.500	.667
Stan Musial, 1941	12	47	8	20	4	0	1	7	2	.426	.574
Elmer Valo, 1941	15	50	13	21	0	1	2	6	4	.420	.580
Jim Greengrass, 1952	18	68	10	21	2	1	5	24	7	.309	.588
Joe Jackson, 1910	20	75	15	29	2	5	1	11	8	.387	.587
Lou Gehrig, 1923	13	26	6	11	4	1	1	9	2	.423	.769
Charlie Reilly, 1889	6	23	5	11	1	0	3	6	2	.478	.913
Fred Lynn, 1974	15	43	5	18	2	2	2	10	6	.419	.698
Merv Connors, 1938	24	62	14	22	4	0	6	13	9	.355	.710
Monte Cross, 1894	13	43	14	19	1	5	2	13	5	.442	.837
TOTAL	159	529	105	212	26	17	29	119	54	.401	.679

There are maybe four, five other players who could go on the list—Piano Legs Hickman in 1899, Bob Nieman in 1951, George Puccinelli in 1930—but I think those eleven are the best. All of those players except Bond, Connors and Gehrig played regularly in the majors the next year, and most turned out to be pretty good players. Connors, who had a three-homer game in his try, was a no-third-baseman moved to first, where he was blocked behind Joe Kuhel. He was sent back to Shreveport and wound up hitting 400 home runs in the minor leagues. Gehrig waited one more year to get his shot.

Walt Bond was not destined to be a great player, and destiny in his case was unusually forceful. Bond was 6'7" and fairly mobile for a big guy; his natural position was first base but the Indians had him playing the outfield. He had hit .320 at Salt Lake City, fourth in the Pacific Coast League, with only eleven homers but 12 triples. The Indians had finished under .500 in '61 and '62, and you might think that a 6'7" guy who could run and hit baseballs out of sight would make an impression on them, but the Indians have never been the kind of organization that would let itself be intimidated by common sense. Joe Adcock was, like Walt Bond, a great big guy who could hit home runs and play first base, and he had the advantage of being thirty-five years old whereas Bond was only twenty-five, so that winter the Indians traded two young outfielders and a pitcher to acquire Joe Ad-cock. Bond was assigned to Jacksonville for the 1963 season, and told to work on his grammar or something.

Well, to make a long story short, Walt Bond would be dead of leukemia in five years. He finally got a chance to play, with Houston in 1964, in the worst hitter's park in baseball, and when he seemed in danger of succeeding anyway, they built a park that was even tougher. In 1964 he hit .254 with 20 home runs and 85 RBI—not outstanding numbers under any conditions, but you might note that his teammates Rusty Staub, Jimmie Wynn, Pete Runnels and Joe Morgan hit a combined .215. Of his twenty-seven home runs as an Astro, only nine were hit in Houston. I can't quite remember what it was, but I vaguely recall that he was involved in some kind of unseemly incident there in '65. Whatever, he hit .316 with Denver in '66, got a brief shot with Minnesota in '67, and died in Detroit on September 14, 1967.

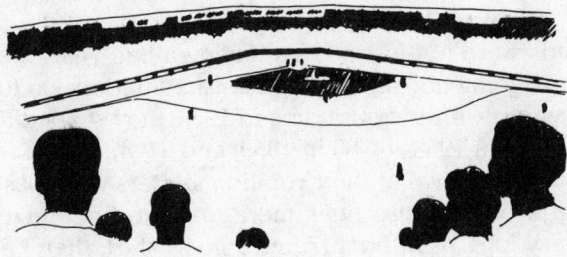

THE MIRACLE ON WESTERN AVENUE

Most of us, as baseball fans, are enrolled in a persistent fantasy that, if we were running the show, if we just had the chance, we could take over a bad team, execute a series of deft maneuvers, make this trade and that trade, move that fellow to third base and this one back to left field, and transform the team into a champion. For a general manager to actually do that—take a bad team, make a series of trades, and immediately come out of it with a championship team—is something which has actually happened, in all of baseball history, exactly once. That one time when somebody actually did it was in Cincinnati in the winter of 1960–61, and on that basis the moves that were made there deserve a closer look.

Bill DeWitt became general manager of the Cincinnati Reds on November 2, 1960, succeeding Gabe Paul. DeWitt had departed a sticky situation in Detroit, accused by the outgoing manager, Joe Gordon, of interfering with his running of the team, and asked by the incoming owner, John Fetzer, to accept a vice presidency. This would have been an honor for many executives, but DeWitt, who was already the club president, declined and asked to be paid for the two years remaining on his contract.

Gabe left him a few pieces, but he didn't leave him much of a ballclub. The Reds in 1960 had finished 67–87, a .435 percentage. They were 28 games out of first place, 15 games out of the first division. By comparison, the 1968 Mets had a better winning percentage (.451), were closer to first place (24 games behind) and much closer to the first division (8 games). The same is true of the 1966 Red Sox, a .444 team, 26 games behind and 9 out of the first division. The 1913 Braves were a .457 team, 31½ behind but only 10 out of the first division.

The Reds were not just a team having a bad year; they were a bad team, going down. They had finished under .500 for three straight seasons. After contending in 1956, they slipped to 80–74 in 1957, 76–78 in 1958, 74–80 in 1959, and 67–87 in 1960. Four of their regulars and two of their rotation starters were past thirty, and several others were near there. In that time, few players played very long past thirty. After a good start, they had gone 45–67 (.402) from June 1 to the end of the season. This was what the team looked like on paper:

CINCINNATI REDS, 1960

Pos	Player	G	AB	Hit	2B	3B	HR	Run	RBI	BB	K	SB	Avg.
C	Ed Bailey	133	441	115	19	3	13	52	67	59	70	1	.261
1B	Frank Robinson	139	464	138	33	6	31	86	83	82	67	13	.297
2B	Billy Martin	103	317	78	17	1	3	34	16	27	34	0	.246
3B	Eddie Kasko	126	479	140	21	1	6	56	51	46	37	2	.292
SS	Roy McMillan	124	399	94	12	2	10	42	42	35	40	9	.236
LF	Wally Post	111	333	94	20	1	19	47	50	37	75	4	.282
CF	Vada Pinson	154	652	187	37	12	20	107	61	47	96	32	.287
RF	Gus Bell	143	515	135	19	5	12	65	62	29	40	0	.262

	Pitcher	G	GS	IP	W	L	Pct.	H	SO	W	ERA
S	Bob Purkey	41	33	253	17	11	.607	259	97	59	3.59
S	Jim O'Toole	34	31	196	12	12	.500	198	124	66	3.81
S	Jay Hook	36	33	222	11	18	.389	222	103	73	4.50
S	Cal McLish	37	21	151	4	14	.222	170	56	48	4.17
R	Jim Brosnan	57	2	99	7	2	.778	79	62	22	2.36
R	Bill Henry	51	0	68	1	5	.167	62	58	20	3.18

It might be a good idea for you to make a mental note of who you would keep out of that list and who you would get rid of, because DeWitt's moves, in that light, will be coldly logical. A few more details on the team . . . the infield, in fact, was not as settled as it looks here. Frank Robinson, an outfielder spending the year at first base because of an injury-related throwing problem, had actually returned to the outfield late in the year, and Gordy Coleman, a twenty-five-year-old who had won the Southern League triple crown in 1959, had played quite a bit of first base. The second-base position was split among Billy Martin (97 games), Elia Chacon (43 games), and Eddie Kasko (33 games). The third-base job was divided among Kasko, Willie Jones (a thirty-four-year-old survivor from the Whiz Kids), and Cliff Cook (another minor league home run champion).

The only infielder to play a hundred games at a position for them—and he qualified only by frequent use as a defensive sub—was Roy McMillan. McMillan was the Mark Belanger of his day, the premier defensive shortstop in baseball but not much of a hitter. When the first Gold Gloves were given in 1957, he won the nod at short over Aparicio, Kubek, Willie Miranda and everybody else; they only gave one. They split it into A.L. and N.L. awards in '58, and McMillan won it again in '58 and '59, though in 1959 he had played in only seventy-nine games. I mention this because it explains one of the later trades, explains why Milwaukee would give up two kid pitchers to get him. They also traded for Frank Bolling; *Sport* magazine wrote an article, "Can Bolling and McMillan Bring Milwaukee the Pennant?"

DeWitt's first player transaction, on December 3, 1960, was to sell Billy Martin. On December 15, at the close of the winter meeting, he engineered a three-cornered deal among the Reds, Braves, and Chicago White Sox. That trade was to provide one of the two keys to the 1961 miracle. Milwaukee gave up two young pitchers, Juan Pizarro and Joey Jay, and acquired McMillan. Jay went to Cincinnati, Pizarro to Chicago. Chicago gave up a third baseman, Gene Freese, and acquired Pizarro from Chicago and Cal McLish from Cincinnati (McLish had won nineteen games in the American League in 1959). The Reds sent McLish to Chicago and McMillan to Milwaukee and acquired Freese and Jay.

At this point, the Reds on paper looked like this:

CINCINNATI REDS, 1961

Pos	Player	G	AB	Hit	2B	3B	HR	Run	RBI	BB	K	SB	Avg.
C	Ed Bailey	133	441	115	19	3	13	52	67	59	70	1	.261
1B	Frank Robinson	139	464	138	33	6	31	86	83	82	67	13	.297
2B													
3B	Gene Freese	127	455	124	32	6	17	60	79	29	65	0	.273
SS	Eddie Kasko	126	479	140	21	1	6	56	51	46	37	10	.292
LF	Wally Post	111	333	94	20	1	19	47	50	37	75	9	.282
CF	Vada Pinson	154	652	187	37	12	20	107	61	47	96	32	.287
RF	Gus Bell	143	515	135	19	5	12	65	62	29	40	0	.262

	Pitcher	G	GS	IP	W	L	Pct.	H	SO	W	ERA
S	Bob Purkey	41	33	253	17	11	.607	259	97	59	3.59
S	Jim O'Toole	34	31	196	12	12	.500	198	124	66	3.81
S	Jay Hook	36	33	222	11	18	.389	222	103	73	4.50
S	Joey Jay	32	11	133	9	8	.529	128	90	59	3.25
R	Jim Brosnan	57	2	99	7	2	.778	79	62	22	2.36
R	Bill Henry	51	0	68	1	5	.167	62	58	20	3.18

Among the 232 writers polled by *The Sporting News* in the spring of 1961, not one picked the Reds to win. Powel Crosly, longtime owner of the Reds, died during spring training. No articles were written asking, "Can Freese and Jay bring Cincinnati the pennant?"

When play started, Gordy Coleman was at first base, Chacon at second, Frank Robinson in right. Gus Bell was platooning with Post in left. Jay Hook was getting hammered, and Chacon was a disaster at second. Ed Bailey hit .302 in April but drove in only two runs. The Reds had an eight-game losing streak on the way to a 6–10 April record.

Ed Bailey was a big left-handed hitting catcher who blocked the plate as if a landmine was buried under it, and he was regarded as having a good arm when he was young and there were no base stealers in the league anyway. By 1961 the Dodgers had Maury Wills and Willie Davis in the lineup, and with the additions of Coleman and Freese, the Reds basepaths were getting seriously clogged. Bailey turned thirty in April, and Bill DeWitt never liked to keep a player past thirty. On April 27, Bailey was traded to San Francisco in exchange for second baseman Don Blasingame, catcher Bob Schmidt, and a pitcher.

When Jay Hook was sent to the bullpen and Ken Hunt inserted in his place, the restructuring of the team was complete. DeWitt,

in sum, simply kept everyone who hit better than .265 or had an ERA under 4.00, and got rid of everybody who didn't. Only one regular, Vada Pinson in center field, was still in his 1960 position. With Coleman, Freese and Robinson projected to 600 PA, this is what the team on paper now looked like:

CINCINNATI REDS, 1961

Pos	Player	G	AB	Hit	2B	3B	HR	Run	RBI	BB	K	SB	Avg.
C	Bob Schmidt	110	344	92	12	1	8	31	37	26	51	0	.267
1B	Gordy Coleman	151	573	155	23	2	14	59	73	27	73	2	.271
2B	Don Blasingame	136	523	123	12	8	2	72	31	49	53	14	.235
3B	Gene Freese	154	564	154	40	7	21	74	98	36	81	12	.273
SS	Eddie Kasko	126	479	140	21	1	6	56	51	46	37	9	.292
LF	Wally Post	111	333	94	20	1	19	47	50	37	75	0	.282
CF	Vada Pinson	154	652	187	37	12	20	107	61	47	96	32	.287
RF	Frank Robinson	153	510	152	36	7	34	95	91	90	74	13	.297

	Pitcher	G	GS	IP	W	L	Pct.	H	SO	W	ERA
S	Bob Purkey	41	33	253	17	11	.607	259	97	59	3.59
S	Jim O'Toole	34	31	196	12	12	.500	198	124	66	3.81
S	Joey Jay	32	11	133	9	8	.529	128	90	59	3.25
S	Ken Hunt										
R	Jim Brosnan	57	2	99	7	2	.778	79	62	22	2.36
R	Bill Henry	51	0	68	1	5	.167	62	58	20	3.18

And that's what they did. There were some small surprises, good and bad:

- Vada Pinson had the best year of his career, hitting .343.
- Bob Schmidt, the new catcher, was a disaster, hitting .129 in 27 games. This opened up a hole behind the plate that the Reds were never really able to close. Jerry Zimmerman, listed in the encyclopedias as the regular catcher, hit .206 with no home runs and 10 RBI in 76 games. Finally, Johnny Edwards was rushed prematurely to the majors; he hit .186 but at least had the defensive tools to contribute something.
- Frank Robinson won the MVP award, but his season really was not out of the context of his career—no better than his '59 season, and not a lot better than 1960.
- Don Blasingame, who had been a .270 hitter and would be again later, had the worst year of his career.
- Gordy Coleman hit a few more home runs, 26, than projected, though Coleman had been a good minor-league power hitter.
- Jim O'Toole developed.
- Jim Maloney didn't.

But when you add it all up, the Reds were *not* particularly lucky that year. Their lineup projected to hit 124 homers, and hit 128. These are the actual statistics of the Reds regulars in 1961:

CINCINNATI REDS, 1961

Pos	Player	G	AB	Hit	2B	3B	HR	Run	RBI	BB	K	SB	Avg.
C	Jerry Zimmerman	76	204	42	5	0	0	8	10	11	21	1	.206
1B	Gordy Coleman	150	520	149	27	4	26	63	87	45	67	1	.287
2B	Don Blasingame	123	450	100	18	4	1	59	21	39	38	4	.222
3B	Gene Freese	152	575	159	27	2	26	78	87	27	78	8	.277
SS	Eddie Kasko	126	469	127	22	1	2	64	27	32	36	4	.271
LF	Wally Post	99	282	83	16	3	20	44	57	22	61	0	.294
CF	Vada Pinson	154	607	208	34	8	16	101	87	39	63	23	.343
RF	Frank Robinson	153	545	176	32	7	37	117	124	71	64	22	.323

	Pitcher	G	GS	IP	W	L	Pct.	H	SO	W	ERA
S	Bob Purkey	36	34	246	16	12	.571	245	116	51	3.73
S	Jim O'Toole	39	35	253	19	9	.679	229	178	93	3.09
S	Joey Jay	34	34	247	21	10	.677	217	157	92	3.53
S	Ken Hunt	29	22	136	9	10	.474	130	75	66	3.97
R	Jim Brosnan	53	0	80	10	4	.714	77	40	18	3.04
R	Bill Henry	47	0	53	2	1	.667	50	53	15	2.21

It was real improvement; neither the .435 won/lost percentage of 1960 or the .604 of 1961 was an illusion. (The Reds played .605 ball in 1962, and stayed well over .500 for years.)

Was that the greatest *immediate* improvement in baseball history? Well, no other team ever moved from a .435 won/lost percentage to a championship in one season. Several other teams have bettered the twenty-six-game improvement in one season.

Most of the GLF (Great Leaps Forward) in baseball history have come about because of some combination of three things, with a heavy emphasis on the A factor:

A. The development of young talent
B. A change of managers
C. A real change in ability emphasized by luck—that is, bad luck one year followed by good luck the next, or very bad luck one year or very good luck the next.

The 1967 Red Sox, for instance, brought Reggie Smith and Mike Andrews out of the minors, and were aided by sudden improvements from Yastrzemski (age twenty-seven), George Scott (twenty-three), and Jim Lonborg (twenty-five), plus they benefited from the impact of the considerable managerial talents of Dick Williams. The 1969 Mets brought along suddenly a group of young pitchers, plus they were severely lucky—they were never really a .600 ballclub.

In retrospect, two of the moves that DeWitt and Fred Hutchinson made were the keys to the pennant. One was the decision to shift two players rightward along the defensive spectrum. Any team deals with limited resources; the collection of players that you have can only do so many things. To use a player who has the speed and the arm to play right field at first base is an inefficient utilization of resources. You can't just "find" a right fielder who can hit as well as a marginal first baseman, because you have to find someone who can also run and throw. The Reds shifted Frank Robinson from first base to right field, and replaced the right fielder who hit .262 with 12 HR with a first baseman who hit .287 with 26 HR. They also moved Eddie Kasko from third base to shortstop, and replaced a shortstop who hit .236 with 10 HR with a third baseman who hit .277 with 26 HR. More efficient utilization of their resources made that possible.

The other key was the acquisition of Joey Jay from the Reds. Jay went 21–10 in 1961, whereas he had gone just 9–8 with Milwaukee in 1960, and so there is a temptation to think that the Reds were simply lucky in that regard. But Jay's ERA was 3.25 in 1960 and 3.53 in 1961; indeed, his career ERA for 414 innings dating back to 1953, when he was an eighteen-year-old bonus boy, was 3.39. His hits/innings and K/W ratio were those of a good pitcher. He was in a tough situation in Milwaukee, fighting a fling of young pitchers for an occasional start behind an entrenched big three of Spahn, Burdette, and Buhl. DeWitt recognized that and took advantage of it.

Obviously, the Reds weren't *un*lucky in 1961. Their biggest break was that they were healthy. They weren't a great team, just a bad team that *suddenly* became a good team. If they had gotten lucky with their young talent, which included Leo Cardenas (who developed in '62) and Jim Maloney (who came around in '63), then they would have been a great team. They got a fantastic season from Jerry Lynch as a pinch hitter and part-time outfielder, and Fred Hutchinson deserves far more credit for his role than I have given him here.

But Hutchinson's work was done in the daily view of the press, and they recognized it, and they gave him credit for it, and he is remembered. DeWitt's remarkable accomplishment somehow glanced off the skull of the nation's press. Don Topping won *The Sporting News* award as the major league executive of the year in 1961. He earned it by shaping the Yankees into a team capable of winning their eleventh pennant in thirteen years. Bill DeWitt, too, is well remembered in Cincinnati. He's the guy who traded Frank Robinson to Baltimore.

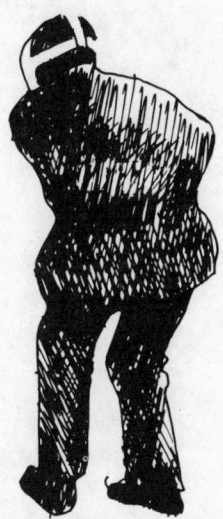

1969: GATES BROWN, .205

Pinch hitters are rarely successful for more than one season. Gates Brown is widely remembered for his sensational pinch hitting in the Tigers pennant-winning effort in 1968, when he was 18-for-39, or .462, off the bench. Actually, he drove in only six runs as a pinch hitter that year, but it was a good year. But he hit only .154 as a pinch hitter in 1967 (4 for 26), and only .205 in 1969 (8 for 39). Jerry Lynch, whom I regard as the greatest pinch hitter of all time, pinch hit just .238 in 1962 after a tremendous season in 1961, and Dusty Rhodes had a career pinch-hitting average of .186 except for his memorable performance in 1954 (his averages in the role read .111, .172, .333, .250, .179, .152, .188). Joe Frazier had a big year the same season as a pinch hitter for the Cardinals, going 20 for 62; the next year he was 4 for 45. The following chart lists all the players who have had twenty pinch hits in a season, and their performance as pinch hitters in the following year:

	That Season			Next Season		
	AB	H	Avg.	AB	H	Avg.
José Morales, 1976	78	25	.321	52	10	.192
Dave Philley, 1961	72	24	.333	28	4	.143
Vic Davalillo, 1970	73	24	.329	27	9	.333
Rusty Staub, 1983	81	24	.296	66	18	.273
Peanuts Lowrey, 1953	59	22	.373	53	7	.132
Sam Leslie, 1932	72	22	.306	6	3	.500
Red Schoendienst, 1962	72	22	.306	5	0	0
Smoky Burgess, 1966	66	21	.318	60	8	.133
Merv Rettenmund, 1977	67	21	.313	15	2	.133
Frenchy Bordagaray, 1938	43	20	.465	11	0	0
Jerry Turner, 1978	50	20	.400	28	5	.179
Doc Miller, 1913	56	20	.357	35	12	.343
Thad Bosley, 1985	60	20	.333	51	16	.314
Ed Coleman, 1936	62	20	.323			
Joe Frazier, 1954	62	20	.323	45	4	.089
Smoky Burgess, 1965	65	20	.308	66	21	.318
Ken Boswell, 1976	65	20	.308	53	14	.264
Chris Chambliss, 1986	68	20	.294			
	1171	385	.329	601	133	.221

The 1970s

HOW THE GAME WAS PLAYED

Baseball started to move a bit in the 1950s, and by the 1970s those changes had reached maturity. From naturalists we learn that there are three basic defensive reactions in nature: to freeze, to fight, and to run like hell. Men, being complex organisms, will sometimes use any of the three, and baseball, being run by men, is, when confronted by any threat, split among groups who want to freeze, those who want to fight, and those who want to run.

Well, baseball from 1920 through 1950 was dominated by men who wanted to freeze. In the 1950s, the balance shifted to those who wanted to run. When the Dodgers and Giants ran for the coast in the 1950s, they set into motion a chain of events that resulted, eventually, in the baseball of the 1970s. Stadium architecture, as I must have written somewhere else in this book, is the one largest dynamic of change in baseball; if you put the baseball players of today in the parks of the 1920s, with all of the other differences— the racial composition of the players, the schedule differences, the expansion, the different strike zone—with all of those, in three months they would be playing baseball pretty much the way it was played in the 1920s.

Baseball had been played in the same parks, and maybe they were wonderful parks, from 1922 to 1952. The fences had been moved around a lot, but it was the same parks. When baseball teams moved into new cities they moved into new parks, and that changed the game. I wouldn't say that I like what happened, but at least something happened in baseball in the sixties. The teams mostly moved into pitcher's parks, and that helped to make it a pitcher's decade.

But more than that, there was a change in the attitudes of a whole lot of people who were peripherally involved with baseball. When the Dodgers left Brooklyn, the cities realized that baseball men were dead serious when they talked about the need for better facilities—and that, if you didn't pay attention to them, they might just walk out the door. That touched off a new round of stadium building, and the new stadiums defined a new brand of baseball.

And a great brand of baseball it was. Don't get me wrong; I do not like artificial turf. I like the game that artificial turf creates. The stadiums built in the years 1965 through 1976 featured 330-foot foul lines (most parks of the fifties had one fence or the other 310 feet away or less) and artificial turf, and that meant speed. Speed was a necessity on defense; speed could also be used on offense. With the home run harder to come by, the focus shifted to hitting for average.

A speed-based game could very well be a pitcher's game. The fact that it didn't emerge as such is attributable solely to the fact that club owners did not desire for it to do so. Two rules changes implemented in 1969 started the ball rolling. One made the strike zone smaller, giving an edge to the hitter. The other reduced the height of the pitcher's mound, and also provided an enforcement mechanism to control what had become a common practice for some teams, making the mound higher than the rules allowed. A third rule to favor an offensive game, the designated hitter rule, was added in one league in 1973.

But it wasn't the rules that made it more of a hitter's game, and it wasn't the parks; it was the attitude. Most teams simply decided that they did not want any more batting champions hitting .301. One specific thing that I suspect was very important, but which has not been properly studied, is the actions that were taken to improve the background visibility for the hitters. In the 1960s, many major league stadiums had seats in center field, so that the white baseball was coming to the hitter through a sea of shirts. The effect that this had on hitting was known as early as 1906, but in the sixties no one was really worried about it. In the seventies, almost all of those teams blocked off the seats in center field, and painted them a solid green color. I think in some places, particularly Busch Stadium in St. Louis, this action may have had a very significant impact on the number of runs that were scored.

There were other actions. The Dodgers, proprietors of one of the two or three best pitcher's parks in baseball, moved home plate out toward center field in 1977, making it a better home run park, and thus a better hitter's park. Some teams have moved fences out in recent years; some have moved them in. Some have put up higher fences, some lower. It's an individual question; the teams don't all act in concert, and for that reason the drift in baseball today is slow, barely measurable, unlike the forceful shift toward more offense that took place from 1968 through 1977.

But baseball boomed in the 1970s for one basic reason: We had a great game. On one field at one time, baseball fans in the seventies could see players who hit over .350, players who hit 40 home runs, and players who would steal nearly 100 bases. Every team's offense was different, and thus every game regained that sense that it had had so many years earlier, the sense of being not merely an exhibition, but a trial of offensive philosophies, speed against power, big-inning offense against one-run offense. Not in many years had baseball fans been treated to such a diverse, varied spectacle on the field, and they responded to it with great enthusiasm.

WHERE THE GAME WAS PLAYED

Baseball by the late 1970s had gotten significantly behind the population again. The South and Southwest had grown great metropolises, such as Tampa/St. Petersburg, that had no baseball. The additions of baseball to Seattle and Toronto served the North a little better, and baseball (better late than never) arrived in the Dallas/Ft. Worth area in 1972. A full list of cities:

Anaheim, Atlanta, Baltimore, Boston, Chicago, Cincinnati, Cleveland, Detroit, Dallas, Houston, Kansas City, Los Angeles, Milwaukee, Minnesota, Montreal, New York, Oakland, Philadelphia, Pittsburgh, St. Louis, San Diego, San Francisco, Seattle, Toronto and (briefly) Washington.

WHO THE GAME WAS PLAYED BY

By 1970, the suburban generation of players was pretty much in place. Playing in organized leagues from the time they could walk, the players of the seventies possessed highly developed skills but a casual attitude toward the game that was difficult for some of the aging stars to accept. The impact of black athletes on the game reached its peak in the mid-seventies and began to decline very slowly; at first this change, like all change, was regarded by baseball men as evil per se and potentially catastrophic, and a number of silly editorials were written about baseball's need to keep the flow of black players coming. Soon the realization sunk in that it really doesn't make any difference whether the best players are black or white. Latin America continued to produce more than its share of the top stars in the game.

Checking In

Ask me in ten years.

Checking Out

1970—Chick Gandil, 83
Ray Schalk, 77
1971—Igor Stravinsky, 89
Carl Mays, 79
Goose Goslin, 70
Heine Manush, 69
Spike Eckert, heart attack, 62
1972—Zack Wheat, 83
Pie Traynor, 72
Gabby Hartnett, 72
Jackie Robinson, 53
Gil Hodges, heart attack, 47
Roberto Clemente, plane crash, 38
1973—George Sisler, 80
Frankie Frisch, automobile accident, 74
Lyndon Johnson, 64
1974—Sam Rice, 84
Dizzy Dean, heart attack, 63
1975—Casey Stengel, 86
Larry MacPhail, 85
Swede Risberg, 81
Lefty Grove, 75
Joe Medwick, 63
Nellie Fox, 47
Don Wilson, carbon monoxide poisoning, 29
1976—Red Faber, 88
Tom Yawkey, 73
Bob Moose, auto accident, 29
Danny Thompson, leukemia, 29
1977—Del Pratt, 89
Phil Wrigley, 82
Ernie Lombardi, 69
1978—Joe McCarthy, 90
Steve Bilko, 49
Lyman Bostock, murdered, 27
1979—Walter O'Malley, 75
Stan Hack, 70
Luke Easter, shot during holdup, 63
Thurman Munson, plane crash, 32

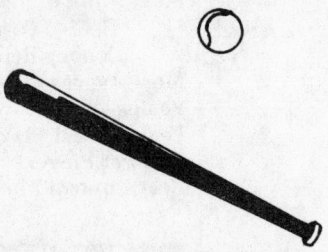

THE 1970s IN A BOX

*Attendance Data:
    Total: 330 million (329, 778, 984)
    Highest: Dodgers, 1978, 3,347, 845
              Dodgers, 24,480,796
    Lowest: Oakland, 1979, 306, 763
              Oakland, 7,646,599

Most Home Runs:
    George Foster, 1977, 52
    Willie Stargell, 296

Best Won-Lost Record by Team:
    Cincinnati, 1975, 108–54, .667
    Baltimore, 1970, 108–54, .667
    Cincinnati, 953–657, .592
    Baltimore, 944–656, .590

Worst Won-Lost Record by Team:
    Toronto, 1979, 53–109, .327
    Toronto, 166–318, .343
    San Diego, 667–942, .415

Heaviest Player: By the end of his playing days in 1977, Boog Powell's weight was probably around 275.

Lightest Player: Freddie Patek, about 147 pounds. Joe Morgan, two-time National League MVP, weighed but a few pounds more.

Clint Hartung Award: David Clyde

Most Strikeouts by Pitcher:
    Nolan Ryan, 1973, 383
    Nolan Ryan, 2,678

Highest Batting Average:
    Rod Carew, 1977, .388
    Rod Carew, .343

Hardest-Throwing Pitcher: Nolan Ryan

*Best Baseball Books:
    1970—*Ball Four* by Jim Bouton and Leonard Schecter
    1971—*The Boys of Summer* by Roger Kahn
    1972—*The Summer Game* by Roger Angell
    1973—*The Great American Novel* by Philip Roth
    1974—*Babe* by Robert W. Creamer
    1975—*Nice Guys Finish Last* by Leo Durocher

Best Outfield Arm: Ellis Valentine

Worst Outfield Arm: Don Baylor

Most Runs Batted In:
    George Foster, 1977, 149
    Johnny Bench, 1,013

Most Aggressive Baserunner: Hal McRae

Fastest Player: Herb Washington

Fastest Real Player: Willie Wilson

Slowest Player: Elrod Hendricks

Best Control Pitcher: Ferguson Jenkins

Nicknames:
      Sugar Bear (Larvelle Blanks)
      Downtown Ollie Brown
      Pudge (Carlton Fisk)
      Dirty Al (Alan Mitchell Edward George Patrick Henry Gallagher)
      Rojo (Doug Rader)
      The Rooster (Rick Burleson)
      Chicken (Fred) Stanley
      The Bird (Mark Fidrych)
      Bigfoot (Bob Stanley)

Most Stolen Bases:
      Lou Brock, 1974, 118
      Lou Brock, 551

Best-Looking Players:
      Carlton Fisk
      Ken Singleton

Ugliest Player: George Foster

Strangest Batting Stance: John Wockenfuss

Outstanding Sportswriter: Peter Gammons

Most-Admirable Superstar: Willie Stargell

Least-Admirable Superstar: Reggie Jackson

Franchise Shifts:
      1970—Seattle to Milwaukee
      1972—Washington to Dallas

New Stadiums:
      1970—Three Rivers Stadium, Pittsburgh
      1970—Riverfront Stadium, Cincinnati
      1971—Veterans Stadium, Philadelphia
      1973—Royals Stadium, Kansas City
      1976—Renovated Yankee Stadium Opened
      1977—Olympic Stadium, Montreal
      1977—Kingdome, Seattle

Best Pennant Race: 1978 American League Eastern Division

Best World Series: 1975, Cincinnati over Boston, 0–6, 3–2, 6–5, 4–5, 6–2, 6–7, 4–3

Best-Hitting Pitcher: Ken Brett

Worst Hitting Pitcher: Dan Spillner

Best Minor League Team: None

The Odd Couple: Earl Weaver and Jim Palmer

Drinking Men:
      Bob Welch
      Darrell Porter
      Roger Moret

New Equipment:
      Neck guard for catchers (invented by Steve Yeager)
      Sliding gloves

Player vs. Team: On December 28, 1975, arbitrator Peter (Abie Babie) Seitz freed the slaves and fed the Mercedes market.

Best Baseball Movies:
      1973—*Bang the Drum Slowly*
      1975—*The Bad News Bears*
      1976—*The Bingo Long Traveling All-Stars and Motor Kings*

*Uniform Changes:
>   Synthetic fabrics
>   Bright colors
>   Stretch waistbands
>   Many experiments

Most Wins by Pitcher:
>   Steve Carlton, 1972, 27
>   Jim Palmer, 186

Highest Winning Percentage:
>   Ron Guidry, 1978, 25–3, .893
>   Don Gullett, 109–50, .686

Best Unrecognized Player: Bobby Grich

Highest-Paid Players: In the late seventies new salary levels were reached every year. The highest-paid player of 1979, and therefore of the seventies, was probably Dave Parker, who became baseball's first million-dollar player that year.

New Statistics: None

Most Unpredictable Career: Ruppert Jones

Best Athlete in the Game: Dave Winfield

Most Lopsided Trade of the Decade: December 10, 1971, Mets traded Nolan Ryan, Don Rose, Leroy Stanton and Francisco Estrada to the California Angels for Jim Fregosi.

A Very Good Movie Could Be Made About: Dick Williams and the Oakland A's, 1971–1973. Williams came into a talented but chaotic system, and rendered enough order out of it to make it the best team in baseball.

I Don't Know What This Has to Do with Baseball, But I Thought I Would Mention It Anyway: Reggie Jackson has written two autobiographies, one done with Bill Libby for Playboy Press in 1975, and the other with Mike Lupica for Villard in 1984. Both books are named *Reggie,* and the jacket of each is entirely covered by a facial picture of Reggie, sans glasses, against a blue-gray background.

Don't be fooled by cheap imitations. Lupica's book is the one you want.

SOME ADDITIONAL SELECTIONS
FROM THE LOVED ONE

Special Wally Moon Eyebrows Awards:
>   Sammy Stewart
>   Happy Chandler
>   Andy Etchebarren
>   Gary Gentry
>   Joey Jay
>   Pete Browning

Browning's eyebrows were reportedly so bushy that people used to tell him he'd be able to see the ball better if he'd get them trimmed. He wouldn't do it. Said he figured God made them that way for a reason.

Special Selection for the Most Distinguished and Handsomely Aged Baseball Star: Joe DiMaggio

Special Selection for the Most Distinguished-Looking Nonplaying Baseball Man: Judge Kenesaw Mountain Landis

Special Citation for a Continually Smiling Face: Frank White

Special Selection for the Most Clownish Looking: Nick Altrock

BEST BASEBALL BOOKS OF THE 1970s

1970—*Ball Four,* called "detrimental to baseball" by Bowie Kuhn; but praised as being "just like junior high" by a Kansas City teenager. Leonard Schecter edited Jim Bouton's tape-recorded musings. Overrated.

1971—*The Boys of Summer.* Roger Kahn's bittersweet encounters with the Brooklyn Dodgers of 1952–53. Overrated.

1972—Roger Angell's *The Summer Game,* a gathering of his elegant *New Yorker* pieces, set a new standard for baseball journalism.

1973—Philip Roth, *The Great American Novel.*

1974—Robert W. Creamer, *Babe*, is the best of baseball biographies.

—Jim Carothers

Nice Guys Finish Last is my own addition to the list. Done with Ed Linn, Leo Durocher's version of his side of fifty years' worth of controversies is the best baseball autobiography that I have ever seen, by far. Sometimes what he is writing about is still interesting, and sometimes the subject has curled up and died in the years since it all happened. But from page one to page 364, the use of the language is astonishingly good, the pace is right, and all the right details are in place. There are no gaps; the book follows a complex, tumultuous life year by year and day by day, giving both the sense of the time and the sense of the event.

I also don't really endorse Jim's assessment of *Ball Four* and *The Boys of Summer;* I like both books. Jim Baker likes *Ball Four* more than I do, and filed his own recommendation.

—Bill James

I wonder if baseball historians a hundred years from now will appreciate the research possibilities of Jim Bouton's *Ball Four.* I'm serious about this. Ignoring the hype and reputation that the book has for being scandalous, it remains a great book about *baseball.* It is first and last a baseball book; even when Bouton is giving his opinions about the war in Vietnam and long hair (historians will need to be reminded that it was controversial at the time), he does it as it relates to baseball.

But why is it a good research tool? First, because it was written in a unique context. Second, Bouton was the ideal person to do a diary because he was (a) a nonconformist, hence outside of what was happening, (b) a relief pitcher, hence sitting and watching most of the time, and (c) a very funny man, but also honest and insightful. Historians who dust off this book a hundred years from now will get an account of:

• The only season of a team called the Seattle Pilots. Wouldn't you love to read a first-person account of the 1901 Milwaukee Brewers?

• The nature of a mid-twentieth-century expansion team. The instability of the rosters, the human side of the constant changes in personnel.

• Personal recollections of a man who was a member of the latter end of the great Yankee dynasty, 1921–64, and was on the scene during the breakup of that dynasty. Accounts of what it was like to play with Mantle, Maris, Ford and Berra.

• Insights into the psychological makeup of a pitcher. No one else has given such a good account of the constant assaults on the ego that a pitcher (particularly a marginal pitcher like Bouton) must undergo, nor described so well the emotional roller coaster ride that goes with living a few days from being put out of your chosen profession. What was lost on a lot of people was that the bizarre behavior Bouton described was often the result of pressures that ordinary people in the ordinary workworld never encounter. The beaver-shooting and the greenies and the foul language are not simply childish exploits, but rather a childish reaction to that extraordinary pressure.

• The unstable life of a ballplayer. Bouton changes teams three times in 1969, creating the same difficulties for his wife and family that it would create for your wife and family.

• The growth of the labor movement in baseball. Although the Player's Association's successes didn't really start to roll until years later, Bouton describes in fine detail where the movement was in 1969, where it was going, and how far it had come over the previous decade.

• The story of a pitcher with a new pitch. Although diaries don't have plots, the ongoing struggle in the book is the development and progress of Bouton's knuckleball.

• Conversations with coaches. You know, I've always wondered what all those guys with the pot bellies did for a living aside from hitting fungoes. Good coaches and bad coaches; Bouton talks about them all.

• The times in which Bouton lived. Unlike many baseball books, which can be dated only by checking the players involved, Bouton emerges as very much a prisoner of a specific time and a specific place, a place in which anybody who questioned authority was suspect, and a man who stops to think once in a while about the war going on in Vietnam is automatically a member of the counterculture. *Ball Four* brought the attitudes of the day to baseball.

—Jim Baker

AN UNLUCKY NUMBER

I figure that the absolute, theoretical minimum number of batters that a pitcher can face and be credited with pitching a complete game is thirteen. That can come about if a pitcher loses a 4½-inning game by a score of 1–0 and doesn't allow any other runner to reach base—and it has happened. In Baltimore on July 30, 1971, Dick Drago of the Royals faced thirteen batters and got them all out except Frank Robinson, who homered. Jim Palmer pitched a 5-inning 2-hitter to get the win.

1978: OLD BALLPLAYERS NEVER DIE

Observing the 1978 World Series, Joe Sewell offered the opinion that only two members of the '78 Yankees would have been able to make the Yankee team in 1932. And he thought those two, Thurman Munson and Ron Guidry, would both have been in the bullpen.

MAJOR LEAGUE ALL-STAR TEAM 1970–1979
Records in seasonal notation, based on 162 games played. Pitchers based on 40 starts.

Pos	Player	Years	Hits	HR	RBI	Avg.	Other
C	Johnny Bench	8.86	158	33	114	.267	
1B	Willie Stargell	7.75	163	38	117	.287	33 Doubles
2B	Joe Morgan	9.00	161	19	80	.282	119 Walks, 54 SB
3B	Mike Schmidt	6.69	142	35	100	.255	103 Walks
SS	Bert Campaneris	8.28	155	6	49	.255	41 Stolen bases
LF	Jim Rice	5.72	197	34	117	.307	
CF	Amos Otis	9.02	172	18	83	.284	33 Stolen bases
RF	Reggie Jackson	8.89	159	33	104	.275	
U	Pete Rose	9.90	207	8	59	.314	40 Doubles

	Pitcher	Years	Won-Lost	SO	ERA	Other
RH	Jim Palmer	8.85	21–12	176	2.58	310 Innings
RH	Tom Seaver	8.67	21–12	266	2.65	
RH	Catfish Hunter	8.21	21–12	160	3.17	
LH	Steve Carlton	9.18	19–14	228	3.18	
R	Rollie Fingers	9.89	8–9	98	2.89	21 Saves

ATTENDANCE IN THE 1970s

Attendance per game played throughout the seventies averaged about 16,600, up from 14,050 during the sixties, a handsome 18 percent improvement. The improvement from 1969 to 1979 is more striking: 1969 attendance totaled 27,225,765, or 1,134,407 per team, or 14,005 per game; attendance in 1979 totaled 43,550,398, or 1,675,015 per team, or 20,679 per game, an improvement of 48 percent.

As I've said, I think the biggest reason for the upsurge was simply the quality of the baseball that was played. Other contributing factors might include, as I would gauge their importance:

1) The improved accessibility of the new stadiums.

2) The maturing of the baby boom generation, which reached an age at which interest in baseball often returns.

3) A generally good series of pennant races.

4) Publication of the Macmillan *Encyclopedia* in 1969, a book which facilitated and thus encouraged baseball mania.

5) The 1975 World Series, which showed millions of Americans how good baseball had become, and annihilated forever the feeling that the game had become passe.

6) The split into divisions in 1969, which increased the number of teams that were perceived as having a chance to win.

7) The collapse of the Yankee dynasty in 1964, which opened up the American League races and restored interest in the Junior circuit.

Perhaps this last item should be higher; I honestly cannot visualize the return of baseball's popularity as occurring in the face of continued Yankee domination.

UNIFORMS OF THE 1970s

With the adoption by many teams of synthetic fabrics in the early seventies, dress became even more informal, and style and comfort became the aims of uniform selection. Doubleknit fabric is well suited to form fitting garments that produce a streamlined look, which is fine in some cases but knits tell all; no more hiding excess flab under loose, baggy suits. Bright colors marched back into the game on the backs of synthetic knits, and teams scrambled to adopt appropriate color schemes.

Styles swung widely within some organizations, while those with traditionalist sympathies simply adapted the new fabrics into their old style. The Tigers, Yankees, and Dodgers stuck with the old reliable basic white uniform—no flashy colors, no fancy stretch waistbands. The White Sox at one point tried a modernized throwback to the early days, with dark pants just below the knees and a pullover shirt with an open collar, not tucked in. This looked sloppy and disappeared after a few years; the Pirates' old-style hat caught on and looked modern again.

There were new looks around most of baseball— wide stripes here, thin stripes there, here a button-up, there a zip-up, everywhere a V-neck. Horizontal scales of bright yellow and orange blared out "Astros," and both the Pirates and Padres tried out combinations of black and gold. There were styles that looked just alike except for slight variations in color and border stripes. The stretch waistband closures became popular for a while, but by the eighties the novelty had worn off, and quite a few teams were returning to belts.

—Susie

FOUR ADDITIONAL LISTS FROM JIM CAROTHERS

ISLANDS IN THE MAINSTREAM (IMPORTANT AMERICAN NOVELS WITH BASEBALL ALLUSIONS)

E. L. Doctorow, *Ragtime* (1975)
John Dos Passos, *1919* (1932)
William Faulkner, *Sanctuary* (1931)
F. Scott Fitzgerald, *The Great Gatsby* (1925)
Ernest Hemingway, *The Old Man and the Sea* (1952)
Ken Kesey, *One Flew Over the Cuckoo's Nest* (1963)
Sinclair Lewis, *Babbitt* (1922)
Philip Roth, *Portnoy's Complaint* (1969)
J. D. Salinger, *The Catcher in the Rye* (1951)
Mark Twain, *A Connecticut Yankee in King Arthur's Court* (1889)
Larry Woiwode, *Beyond the Bedroom Wall* (1975)
Thomas Wolfe, *You Can't Go Home Again* (1940)

CARLTON FISK

GOOD RECENT BASEBALL BOOKS (NOT ONE OF THEM A WHINING, TAPE-RECORDED, FAMOUS-NAME RIPOFF)

Roger Angell, *Late Innings: A Baseball Companion* (1982)
Thomas Boswell, *Why Time Begins on Opening Day* (1984)
David Carkeet, *The Greatest Slump of All Time* (1984)
Robert W. Creamer, *Stengel: His Life and Times* (1984)
Barry Gifford, *The Neighborhood of Baseball* (1981)
Donald Hayes, *The Dixie Association* (1984)
W. P. Kinsella, *Shoeless Joe* (1982)
Lowell Reidenbaugh and Amadee, *The Sporting News Take Me Out to the Ball Park* (1983)
Jules Tygiel, *Baseball's Great Experiment: Jackie Robinson and His Legacy* (1983)

NO, BUT I SAW THE MOVIE (BASEBALL FICTION ON THE SILVER SCREEN)

William Brashler, *The Bingo Long Traveling All-Stars and Motor Kings* (1976 movie with James Earl Jones and Billy Dee Williams)
Valentine Davies, *It Happens Every Spring* (1949 movie with Ray Milland)
Mark Harris, *Bang the Drum Slowly* (1973 movie with Michael Moriarty and Robert DeNiro)

I'M WAITING FOR THE MOVIE (SOME GOOD BASEBALL BOOKS NOBODY TALKS MUCH ABOUT)

1973: DH RULE INCREASES STRATEGY

One of the complaints that baseball traditionalists have about the Designated Hitter Rule is that it drains the game of strategy, eliminating the need to make a series of crucial decisions and allowing a manager to cruise through the last few innings or to concentrate on something else. In response to this, I wrote in one of the annual *Abstracts*—I'd tell you which one except that I don't have any idea—that strategy can exist only when a manager has options. What the DH rule actually does, I suggested, is to eliminate from the game a series of forced, obvious moves, which involve in fact no option on the part of either manager, and thus no strategy. You've got a .113 hitter at the plate, a runner on first and nobody out in the fourth, and you have to bunt, don't you? Where's the strategy? With a DH up there at least you can *do* something. You're down four runs in the seventh with the pitcher leading off, and you have to pinch hit for him, don't you? What's strategic about that? The DH rule saves the pinch hitters, and thus in effect makes the roster larger. As such it creates, not eliminates, strategic options for American League managers.

It recently occurred to me that there was a way of checking to see whether or not that was true. Do you know the meaning of the term "standard deviation"? The standard deviation of a series of numbers is a measure of whether they are all pretty much the same, or whether they differ widely. Take two lists of numbers, one going 19–21–20–20–21–21–18, and the other going 13–34–41–6–11–22–13. The average in both cases is the same, 20, but because all of the first set of numbers are between 18 and 21, and the second set range freely from 6 to 41, the standard deviation of the second list is far, far higher than the standard deviation of the first.

If all of the managers in a league tended to bunt in the same circumstances, then the standard deviation of sacrifice bunt totals in that league would be low, since all the numbers (of sacrifice hits per team) would be about the same. If there were, within the league, a considerable difference of opinion as to when you should bunt and when you should not bunt, then the standard deviation of sac bunts would be much higher. The standard deviation of bunt totals within the league is a measure of the degree to which the managers in that league are predictable in when they will bunt and when they will not.

Certainly the DH rule decreased the numbers of bunts; there's no question of that. But if it diminished the strategic options of the managers, it would also have decreased the standard deviation of sac bunts; if it increased options, as I suggested, it would also have increased the s.d. (Generally speaking, if you take two lists of similar things, but one of which is at a higher level than the other, then the one which operates at a higher level will also have a higher standard deviation. If you list the weights of a group of people who weigh an average of 200 pounds, and the weights of a group of sixth graders who average 75 pounds, then the standard deviation of the weights of the 200 pounders will likely be much larger. In the absence of any countervailing force, then, we would expect the standard deviation of sacrifice bunts to be larger in the National League.) This chart gives the sacrifice bunt averages and standard deviations for both leagues since 1968:

STANDARD DEVIATIONS OF SACRIFICE HITS 1968–86

Year	American League Average	Standard Deviation	National League Average	Standard Deviation
1968	71	11.85	79	12.10
1969	65	8.81	74	14.63
1970	68	19.94	68	14.97
1971	74	15.21	77	14.55
1972	74	10.73	72	16.42
1973	49	11.18	80	16.84
1974	63	11.73	82	14.67
1975	66	14.36	90	20.20
1976	68	14.85	81	19.55
1977	66	22.43	71	11.28
1978	73	21.28	81	23.05
1979	68	23.70	79	18.36
1980	65	20.74	81	10.29
1981	40	7.46	57	10.88
1982	54	20.68	82	12.80
1983	46	10.76	77	7.51
1984	44	11.87	72	14.35
1985	46	18.56	75	15.23
1986	46	16.54	72	16.97

As you can see, the standard deviations of sacrifice bunt totals in the two leagues were fairly comparable in the five years before the Designated Hitter Rule was adopted. In the first few years of the DH rule, the rule did, indeed, eliminate strategy from the game, as managers, deprived of their ordinary bunting opportunities, just pretty much stopped bunting. Then, however, they began to recognize new situations in which the bunt might be useful, and differences of opinion began to develop about when one should bunt and when one should not. Since 1977, the standard deviation of sacrifice bunts has been higher in the American League than in the National in six of ten seasons.

Another category that measures the strategic decisions of managers is the number of pinch hitters used. The Designated Hitter Rule does, again, decrease the total number of pinch hitters used. But does it also decrease the essential difference in which strategy lies, the difference between when one manager

will bunt and another won't? This chart gives the averages and standard deviations of pinch hitters used in the two leagues since 1968, excepting the 1973 season for which I could not find data:

STANDARD DEVIATIONS OF PINCH HITTERS USED 1968–86

| Year | American League | | National League | |
	Average	Standard Deviation	Average	Standard Deviation
1968	204	36.51	176	19.99
1969	205	36.92	190	26.42
1970	212	40.53	201	39.87
1971	190	37.09	188	24.10
1972	182	24.26	173	35.56
1973	(data not available)		202	30.87
1974	105	26.42	220	25.46
1975	99	23.95	219	23.66
1976	112	22.10	213	21.80
1977	116	31.12	228	26.69
1978	112	39.00	201	29.56
1979	116	51.97	205	23.77
1980	134	41.24	217	40.73
1981	86	24.39	153	22.67
1982	124	49.30	222	31.00
1983	126	40.14	223	29.06
1984	148	41.40	272	41.74
1985	141	42.61	274	27.70
1986	121	44.97	287	37.72

Since 1974, the standard deviation of pinch hitters used has been higher in the American League in twelve of thirteen seasons. The pattern at its extreme is best illustrated by the data from the 1979 season. The National League managers used an average of 205 pinch hitters apiece, whereas the American Leaguers used an average of only 116. Both figures are very typical of season averages since 1973. But whereas in the National League, every manager used between 169 and 243 pinch hitters, the American League totals range from only 46 pinch hitters used by the Milwaukee manager (48 for Oakland, 52 for Toronto) on up to 218 pinch hitters used by Gene Mauch in Minnesota, and 189 in Texas:

PINCH HITTERS USED, 1979

AMERICAN LEAGUE		NATIONAL LEAGUE	
Milwaukee	46	Chicago	243
Oakland	48	San Francisco	228
Baltimore	132	Atlanta	205
New York	106	Montreal	169
Texas	189	St. Louis	181
California	65	Los Angeles	190
Seattle	147	Houston	191
Boston	93	Pittsburgh	192
Chicago	162	Philadelphia	218
Toronto	52	Cincinnati	180
Cleveland	102	New York	228
Minnesota	218	San Diego	237
Kansas City	156		
Detroit	106		

In the National League in 1980, every team used between 69 and 100 sacrifice bunts. In the American League, the totals ranged from 34 to 106.

A third area in which the impact of the Designated Hitter Rule shows up in the statistics, and a third area in which it has been alleged to impinge upon the strategies of the game, is in the use of relief pitchers. This shows up in the statistics in the "complete games" category; American League pitchers get to stay in the game even when behind, and thus get to complete more contests.

Again, though, the moves that are made are forced moves, rather than true option moves. Again, the standard deviation of complete games is higher, not lower, in the American League:

STANDARD DEVIATIONS OF COMPLETE GAMES 1968–86

| | American League | | National League | |
| | | Standard | | Standard |
Year	Average	Deviation	Average	Deviation
1968	43	13.15	47	14.29
1969	38	10.84	44	15.88
1970	32	10.37	39	10.75
1971	45	14.43	46	11.58
1972	42	12.25	42	9.71
1973	51	11.36	37	8.04
1974	54	8.22	37	8.69
1975	52	12.74	36	7.42
1976	49	11.87	37	8.70
1977	42	10.78	27	8.08
1978	46	12.29	32	10.25
1979	39	10.33	30	9.48
1980	39	16.37	26	6.24
1981	24	12.18	15	7.09
1982	32	8.35	24	9.59
1983	34	8.84	23	7.26
1984	28	11.27	19	6.34
1985	26	7.93	22	9.05
1986	25	8.28	19	8.04

I'm not an advocate of the Designated Hitter Rule; I'm only an advocate of seeing the truth and telling the truth. What the truth comes down to here is, a question of in what does strategy reside? Does strategy exist in the act of bunting? If so, the Designated Hitter Rule has reduced strategy. But if strategy exists in the decision about *when* a bunt should be used, then the DH rule has increased the differences of opinion which exist about that question, and thus has increased strategy. Does strategy exist in every use of a substitute batsman? If so, the DH rule has decreased strategy. But if strategy is an argument, then I would argue that there is *more* of a difference of opinion, not less, in the American League.

Answering Jim Baker's rhetorical question (see "Gerkin's Cruel Fate"), Ed Tassinari submits the following list:

John Townsend was from Townsend, Delaware
Thomas Jefferson Raub was from Raubsville, Pennsylvania
King Bader was from Bader, Illinois
Slim Love was from Love, Missouri
John Ogden was from Ogden, Pennsylvania
Curly Ogden was from Ogden, Pennsylvania
Verne Clemons was from Clemons, Iowa
Roger Clemens was not
Flint Rhem was from Rhems, South Carolina
Estel Crabtree was from Crabtree, Ohio
Beau Bell was from Bellesville, Texas
Charlie Gassaway was from Gassaway, Tennessee
John Goetz was from Goetzville, Michigan
Fred Cambria was from Cambria Heights, New York

Thanks, Ed; I'll stop holding my breath now. On a hunch, I checked all the players named "York." Tom York was from Brooklyn and died in New York, but more intriguing is Lefty York, who was born in West Fork, Arkansas and died in York, Pennsylvania. Elston Howard was born in St. Louis, but didn't he grow up in Howard, Oklahoma or something? Just a hazy memory—seems like the town he grew up in was named after his father or some such thing.

Peter LeClair sent along a similar list. In addition to many of those listed above, Peter informs us that George Turbeville was from Turbeville, South Carolina, Julius Green was from Greensboro, North Carolina, Syd Smith was from Smithville, South Carolina, Valmy Thomas was from St. Thomas, Virgin Islands, and Ron Willis was from Willisville, Tennessee. He also asked me not to mention that Joe Bean was from Boston, and pointed out that Ray Murray, a catcher from 1948–1954, was from the great baseball town of Spring Hope, North Carolina.

ROOK FOR A BLEAKING BALL

In 1976 Mark Fidrych became a sensation by hopping around on the mound like (as Richard Belzer said about Mick Jagger) a rooster on acid, mowing down hitters and, most notably, talking to baseballs. On June 28 Fidrych was facing the Yankees on national TV. When Fidrych began talking to the ball, Graig Nettles stepped out of the box and began talking to his bat. "Now don't you listen to that ball," said Nettles. "When it comes in here you hit it right up in that upper deck up there," and Nettles pointed to the upper deck.

Nettles popped up. "Goddamn," he said. "I just realized I was using a Japanese bat. Doesn't understand English."

THE ANGEL LYMAN BOSTOCK

Lyman Bostock, Sr. was a star in the Negro Leagues. Lyman Bostock, Jr. was a graceful outfielder who came up with the Minnesota Twins in 1975. Through three seasons with the Twins he compiled a batting average of .318, being among the league's best hitters in 1976 and 1977. In 1977, when he hit .336 for the Twins, with 199 hits and 104 runs scored, Bostock reportedly earned $20,000. He moved to the California Angels as a free agent in the winter of 1977–1978, signing a five-year, $2.25 million contract.

Bostock opened the 1978 season in a terrible slump, getting only 2 hits in his first 39 at bats. For the month of April 1978, he hit just .147. Feeling badly about getting all this money and not hitting, Bostock tried to give his month's salary back to the team. When the Angels wouldn't take the money, Bostock gave it to charity instead.

Bostock got hot after that, hitting about his usual .320 the rest of the year to get his season average up to .296. An exuberant, rambunctious fellow, he was called "Abdul Jibber Jabber" by his teammates. Bostock did not smoke or drink and was reportedly devoted to his wife, Yuovene. In the last two weeks of the season he was trying to get to .300 when, visiting friends in Gary, Indiana, on a trip to Chicago, Bostock was riding in the back seat of a car driven by his uncle, Thomas Turner. Another car followed them for several blocks until they stopped at a streetlight, at which point a man in the other car fired a shot through the back window of Turner's car, killing Bostock. The murderer turned out to be the estranged husband of one of two women in the car. He had intended to kill his wife.

The murderer, Leonard Smith, received a light sentence because, as I understand it, he was able to prove that he didn't ordinarily kill people, but just happened to be in a particularly bad mood that day. Bostock, if he were alive, would be 37 now, in the twilight of his career. The loss to his family and friends can never be known, but as I did with Austin McHenry in the 1920s, I thought I would project out the rest of his career with one of the Brock systems, just to provide a hint of what might have been lost to the baseball fan. Bostock's actual lifetime batting average was .311.

Year	G	AB	R	H	2B	3B	HR	RBI	BB	Avg.
1975	98	369	52	104	21	5	0	29	28	.282
1976	128	474	75	153	21	9	4	60	33	.323
1977	153	593	104	199	36	12	14	90	51	.336
1978	147	568	74	168	24	4	5	71	59	.296
1979	157	625	100	195	32	8	10	77	63	.312
1980	158	614	88	184	28	6	8	69	64	.300
1981	107	404	53	118	19	4	7	53	45	.292
1982	157	620	88	193	30	6	9	73	66	.311
1983	158	603	61	166	23	4	8	61	65	.275
1984	116	434	52	127	19	3	6	47	48	.293
1985	144	561	62	162	24	3	7	59	62	.289
1986	117	442	48	123	17	3	6	45	50	.278
1987	63	234	24	63	9	1	3	22	27	.267
1988	93	355	41	100	15	3	4	38	37	.282
1989	50	187	20	50	6	1	2	17	22	.265
1990	12	45	5	12	1	0	0	4	5	.256
16 yrs	1858	7128	947	2117	325	72	93	807	724	.287

THE MESSERSMITH CASE

One of the pivotal moments in the economic history of baseball occurred on December 23, 1975, when arbitrator Peter Seitz ruled in favor of the players in grievances filed by Dick Moss on October 7, 1975, on behalf of Dodger pitcher Andy Messersmith and retired Expo Dave McNally.

It is important to understand some things here. Mr. Seitz did not find that the reserve arrangement was illegal. It is perfectly legal for management and unions to negotiate reserve arrangements if they want to. Since the Supreme Court had found just three years earlier that the reserve arrangement was legal, it would have been quite remarkable for an arbitrator in a civil matter to overrule the Supreme Court and decide that it was illegal.

Mr. Seitz did not find that the reserve clause was invalid. The clause that was under dispute is, in fact, still a part of the basic agreement, and is still in effect.

Mr. Seitz's ruling had nothing to do with baseball's position as a monopoly.

It was assumed throughout the entire proceeding that the clause under dispute was legal and valid. What they were arguing about was what it meant. The clause in question reads:

If prior to March 1, the Player and the Club have not agreed upon the terms of the contract, then on or before 10 days after said March 1, the Club shall have the right by written notice to the Player to renew this contract for the period of one year.

The clubs argued that this meant one year, and then the next year, and then the next year—in other words, that the contract could be renewed in perpetuity. The players argued that one year meant one year. The arbitrator ruled simply that the players' interpretation would prevail.

During the period of the hearing, the public largely assumed that the players could not win. The argument made by the owners, relayed to the public by the sportswriters, was that organized baseball could not survive without the reserve clause. That argument was irrelevant to the issues of the case and insulted the intelligence of the arbitrator. If GM designs a defective automobile and finds itself facing hundreds of lawsuits as a result, can they defend themselves by arguing that if they lose the suit they will be driven out of business? Of course not. The consequences of losing the suit were not the issue. The contractual arrangement was the issue. And besides that, it's preposterous to argue that if the players won the issue they would use their power to destroy the institution, since it obviously was not in the players' interest to do this.

The arguments made by the owners in front of the arbitrator were not quite the same as the arguments made before the microphones, but they weren't a lot better. They filed a suit to prevent the issue from going before an arbitrator. The judge told them to arbitrate. They argued that to allow free agency would destroy competitive balance, another obviously irrelevant issue. They argued that they had to have the right to reserve players in order to defray the costs of operating a farm system.

"I am not unmindful," wrote Seitz in his decision, "of the testimony of the Commissioner of Baseball and the Presidents of the National and American Leagues . . . that any decision of the arbitration panel sustaining the Messersmith and McNally grievances would have dire results, wreak great harm to the reserve system and do serious damage to the sport of baseball."

You have to understand that an arbitrator is a professional skeptic. He hears self-serving arguments every day. Every day he faces people who are trying to get him to focus on something other than the issues of the case. Very often someone tells the arbitrator about the terrible consequences that will follow for all of us if you rule against me. After a while an arbitrator is not a trusting soul. He recoginzes a self-serving argument. He carefully distinguishes between relevant and irrelevant issues. The owners served the arbitrator a steady diet of the same stuff they had been feeding the media for a hundred years. The arbitrator didn't swallow it.

For several years afterward, I wondered if perhaps the owners hadn't lost a case that might have been won by a better argument. Sam Reich eventually convinced me otherwise. Sam Reich is Tom Reich's brother, a sharp attorney from Pittsburgh. Whenever we have a break while working on arbitration cases, Sam and I start arguing about stuff like how old Fritz Ostermueller was in the late forties, whether the Expos or Cardinals have a better pitching staff, and how the Messersmith case should have been presented. Sam recalls that when Tom first told him that the Players Association wanted to try this apporach, Sam scoffed at the idea. Tom got Sam a copy of the basic agreement, and Sam read it over a couple of times. "I took it back to Tom," Sam recalls, "and said 'Where is it?' I thought I just couldn't find it. I had heard so much all my life about this reserve clause that I assumed they *had* a reserve clause—you know, some good strong language spelling out what their rights were. I couldn't believe that the owners' entire case hung on this one sentence about renewing the contract for the next year."

But, I argued at first, regardless of the vagueness of the words, hadn't it always been assumed that this meant that the player was bound in perpetuity? Couldn't the owners easily have proven, I argued, that this clause had been around forever, and that both management and labor had always assumed that it meant that the player was bound from year to year? You could demonstrate a million ways that that was what it had always been assumed to mean —for example, that assumption underlies all of the arguments in the Flood suit. Couldn't they have argued that the clause had to be found to mean what both sides had assumed that it meant when they entered into the contract?

"Well," said Sam, "you can try that. But it's a very important principle of contract law that when the language is not specific, the contract will be interpreted against the party that drew up the contract, or against the party that drew up the disputed language. Obviously, it wasn't the players who put this clause in the contract. If the owners intended to retain the player in perpetuity, they had a responsibility to spell that out. You can't expect an arbitrator to read more into the contract then what is there. When Tom finally convinced me that there wasn't anything more than this in the contract, I knew that the owners were in serious trouble."

The reason the owners used the arguments they did, then, is probably not because they thought they were good arguments. They used the arguments they did becasue they were desperate. They had to try to do again what they had successfully done in the Federal League case a half-century before: to get the arbitrator to put aside his logic and his training and the facts of the case, and decide the issue on his emotions as a baseball fan. "You can't rule against us," they argued. "We're baseball."

Seitz had no alternative but to find for the players.

The 1980s

HOW THE GAME WAS PLAYED

Baseball brought into the 1980s a mixture of styles as diverse as the game has had at any point in over a half a century. Just in the first season of the eighties, 1980 itself, baseball had three players who hit over .340 and one who hit .390, ten players who stole 50 or more bases including three who stole 96 or more, three players who hit 40 to 48 home runs, two pitchers who won 24 or more games and one who struck out 286 batters, a player who hit 49 doubles, four players who drew over a hundred walks, a pitcher who completed 28 games and three pitchers who saved 30

or more games. There have been few ten-year periods in baseball history which presented players succeeding dramatically in so many different ways.

This could not last—or, since the wealth and diversity of the game has not completely dissipated, let me say that it can not last. Baseball is normally dominated by a relatively few strategies or approaches to the game; only in transition periods do you tend to have very successful players of many different types. Over time power drives out speed, power pitching drives out power hitting, strong bullpens drive out strong starting pitching or vice versa.

The baseball which returned from the strike in 1982

was perhaps a little lacklustre. Most Valuable Players and Cy Young Award winners were difficult to identify for a couple of years, 40-homer seasons were all but extinct and reliable starting pitchers scarcer than normal. There was a transition period between generations of stars, with the Roses and Reggies and Ryans and Carltons fading slowly away, and the Boggses and Mattinglys and Tim Raineses and Tony Gwynns not yet fully established. Only a few superstars, Dale Murphy and Robin Yount being the obvious ones, bridged the gap. George Brett and Jim Rice, though still of an age to be dominant players, did not dominate.

By 1985 the new generation

THE 1980s IN A BOX
(Covers the Years 1980–1987)

Attendance Data:
    Total: 351 million (350,770,108)
    Highest: Dodgers, 1982, 3,608,881
                   Dodgers, 24,972,807
    Lowest: Minnesota, 1981, 469,090
                   Cleveland, 7,447,141

Baseball attendance throughout the 1980s has shown outstanding growth, with new records being established almost every year, capped by an astonishing 52 million fans in 1987—4.5 million more than the previous record. The new record is a 9 percent boost in one year. Attendance for the years 1980–1987 already exceeds that for any other decade. Attendance per team per season for the eighties is 26 percent higher than it was in the seventies, without any adjustment for the 1981 strike. The Dodgers total for the eighties is already a record for a team in a ten-year period.

Most Home Runs:
    Mark McGwire, 1987, 49
    Andre Dawson, 1987, 49
    Mike Schmidt, 295
Best Won-Lost Record by Team:
    Mets, 1986, 108–54, .667
    Yankees, 695–545, .560
Worst Won-Lost Record by Team:
    Pirates, 1985, 57–104, .354
    (Blue Jays, 1981, 37–69, .349)
    Mariners, 532–711, .428
Heaviest Player: Terry Forster, about 285
Lightest Player: Jerry Browne, 140
Clint Hartung Award: Al Chambers
Most Strikeouts by Pitcher:
    Mike Scott, 1986, 306
    Nolan Ryan, 1,638
Highest Batting Average:
    George Brett, 1980, .390
    Wade Boggs, .354
Hardest-Throwing Pitcher: Nolan Ryan
Best Baseball Books:
    1981—*The Ultimate Baseball Book,*
    Edited By Dan Okrent, Harris Lewine
    1982—*Shoeless Joe,* Novel by W.P. Kinsella
    1987—*Voices of the Game,* by Curt Smith
Best Outfield Arm: Jesse Barfield
Worst Outfield Arm: Willie Wilson

of stars had taken over the game. From 1985 through 1987, baseball has wrestled with an unannounced, *de facto* redefinition of the strike zone, making the strike zone smaller and lower than it was. As the players have adjusted to the shrinking strike zone we have seen each year more walks, more strikeouts and more home runs than we saw the year before. The games get longer each year, which gives the media something to complain about although the fans don't really mind. The 1987 season was a hitters' year, and the fans responded to that the same way they always have. They packed the seats.

WHERE THE GAME WAS PLAYED

Baseball has entered its second era of remarkable stability. Though rumors of franchise moves continue to be heard, no major league franchise has moved now for sixteen years, since the Senators became the Rangers. There has been no expansion now for eleven years, the longest period without expansion since the expansion era began in 1961. Alphabetically, the twenty-three major league cities are Atlanta, Baltimore, Boston, Chicago, Cincinnati, Cleveland, Dallas Ft. Worth, Detroit, Houston, Kansas City, Los Angeles, Milwaukee, Minneapolis St. Paul, Montreal, New York, Oakland, Philadelphia, Pittsburgh, St. Louis, San Diego, San Francisco, Seattle, and Toronto.

WHO THE GAME WAS PLAYED BY

Every generation has certain types of players who excell. In the sixties we had a dozen of the finest power pitchers in the history of the game. Now we have several of the greatest leadoff men in the history of baseball, including probably the two greatest of all time in Tim Raines and Rickey Henderson. The American League is very strong in shortstops who can hit as well as shine on defense; the National League has a bunch of top power speed combination players, like Darryl Strawberry, Howard Johnson, Eric Davis and Barry Bonds.

Most Runs Batted In:
Don Mattingly, 1985, 145
Mike Schmidt, 839
Most Aggressive Baserunner: Alfredo Griffin
Fastest Player: Vince Coleman
Slowest Player: Mark Bailey
Best Control Pitcher: Dan Quisenberry
Nicknames: (Chris Berman has this one under control)
Most Stolen Bases:
Rickey Henderson, 1982, 130
Rickey Henderson, 668
Best-Looking Players:
Scott Sanderson
Ryne Sandberg
Dwight Gooden
Ugliest Players:
John Candelaria
Doyle Alexander
Strangest Batting Stance: John Kruk
Outstanding Sportswriter: Thomas Boswell
Most Admirable Superstar: Dale Murphy
Least Admirable Superstar: Dave Parker
Franchise Shifts: None
New Stadiums: 1982—Metrodome, Minnesota
Best Pennant Race:
1980 National League West or
1987 American League East
Best World Series:
1986, New York over Boston, 0–1, 3–9, 7–1, 6–2, 2–4, 6–5, 8–5 and 3–2.
Best Hitting Pitcher: Rick Rhoden
Worst Hitting Pitcher: Len Barker
*Best Minor League Team: 1980 Denver Bears
The Odd Couple: Steve Garvey and Jay Johnstone
Drinking Men:
Dennis Martinez
David Green
Rod Scurry
New Equipment:
Sliding Gloves
Bats with dimples in the end
Player vs. Team:
Goose Gossage vs. the Padres
In the summer of 1986, Gossage was suspended by the Padres after he alleged that his owner was poisoning the world with her hamburgers.
Best Baseball Movies: 1984—*The Natural*
Uniform Changes: See Susie's note
Most Wins by Pitcher:
Steve Stone, 1980, 25
Jack Morris, 141

Highest Winning Percentage:
Orel Hershiser, 1985, 19–3, .864
John Tudor, 94–58, .618
(Dwight Gooden, 73–26, .737)
Best Unrecognized Players:
Phil Bradley
Bo Diaz
Tony Gwynn
Highest-Paid Player: Jim Rice, approximately $2.4 million.
New Statistics: 1981—Game-Winning RBI
Most Unpredictable Career: Hubie Brooks
Best Athlete in the Game: Bo Jackson
Most Lopsided Trade of the Decade:
October 21, 1981, Yankees traded Willie McGee to the Cardinals in exchange for Bob Sykes.
I Don't Know What This Has to Do with Baseball, But I Thought I Would Mention It Anyway:
In a 1980 dress rehearsal for the 1981 strike, the players voted 967–1 to authorize a strike. The lone player to vote against the strike was Jerry Terrell of the Kansas City Royals, now a manager in the Royals minor league system.
Terrell was the Royals' player representative.

DENVER BEARS

Most people, if asked to name the outstanding minor league team of the 1980s, would choose the 1981 Albuquerque team. The Albuquerque team was indeed outstanding, led by first baseman Mike Marshall, who won the triple crown (.373, 34 homers, 137 RBI). The team also featured Jack Perconte, Rudy Law and Candy Maldonado, all of whom played regularly that summer and hit .335 or better, and all of whom would have good seasons in the major leagues. Several other people on the team have played some major league ball, including Ron Roenicke, Tack Wilson and Ted Power, who was 18–3 that year. The team won 94 games and lost only 38, winning both halves of a split season by huge margins.

I am somewhat more impressed by the Denver Bears of 1980. While the Bears record was slightly less awesome (92–44), the Bears had two players who were distinctly better all-around talents than any of the young bluebloods, those two being Tim Raines and Tim Wallach. Raines was the American Association batting champion and the Minor League Player of the Year, hitting .354 with 77 stolen bases in 108 games. Wallach hit 36 homers and drove in 124 runs, and Randy Bass, who never broke through in the big time, hit .333 with 37 and 143. Also on the team were Jamie Easterly, Roberto Ramos and Dave Hostetler. The Bears leading pitcher, Steve Ratzer, was a finesse pitcher whose major league career lasted only 21 innings, but who that summer went 15–4 and walked only 29 men in 166 innings.

MAJOR LEAGUE ALL-STAR TEAM 1980–1987

Records in seasonal notation, based on 162 games played. Pitchers based on 38 starts.

Pos	Player	Years	Hits	HR	RBI	Avg.	Other
C	Gary Carter	6.99	161	28	106	.269	
1B	Don Mattingly	4.40	210	28	117	.331	45 Doubles
2B	Ryne Sandberg	5.69	186	16	71	.288	36 SB, 101 runs
3B	Mike Schmidt	7.22	161	41	116	.283	104 Walks
SS	Ozzie Smith	7.16	150	2	53	.258	39 SB, 74 BB
LF	Tim Raines	6.27	192	10	61	.308	81 SB, 116 runs
CF	Ricky Henderson	6.75	176	18	63	.292	99 SB, 132 runs
RF	Dale Murphy	7.57	170	35	101	.284	17 SB
DH	Wase Boggs	5.38	219	10	76	.354	41 2B, 97 BB

	Pitcher	Years	Won-Lost	SO	ERA	Other
RH	Jack Morris	7.21	20–13	187	3.53	16 Complete Games
RH	Dwight Gooden	3.26	22–8	273	2.46	
RH	Ron Guidry	6.16	18–11	178	3.64	
LH	Fernando Valenzuela	6.32	18–13	232	3.08	
R	Dan Quisenberry	8.23	6–5	36	2.50	28 Saves

Per 162 games, Ozzie Smith struck out only 36 times, even less than Boggs (47). Raines had 81 stolen bases with only 12 caught stealing, 89 walks and 55 extra base hits (34–10–11) per season. Henderson had 112 walks to go with his 99 stolen bases, 18 homers and 132 runs scored. Quisenberrys's normalized season shows only 15 walks in 104 innings, 63 games.

SUSIE'S COMMENTS ON UNIFORMS OF THE EIGHTIES

At this point, the wacky stuff appears to be behind us. The eighties have seen a return to the uniforms traditionally styled in subdued and classic colors. The synthetic knits introduced in the late sixties and seventies are still the fabric of choice given their qualities of comfort, fit and durability. But the double knits no longer carry a mandate for a bright and gaudy color combo or a look unmistakably reminiscent of a leisure suit. Instead many jerseys have button-down fronts (although there are still pullover blouses with V necks) with the name spelled out across the chest and the club insignia on the sleeve. Sleeves are set-in or of the raglan, sometimes called shoulder-saddle, type. There seem to be a lot of players pulling at their shirt sleeves as they get set to hit, making one wonder if the jerseys are worn too tight or poorly designed for movement.

Pants come variously with built-in elastic waistbands in a self-belting style or in the standard beltloops-and-belt routine. Pants often have stripes down the side and are worn to lower calf lengths. Player numbers always appear on the jersey back and may also be found lurking just under the rib cage or near the front pocket. Most clubs put player names on uniform backs. Those who don't must be bound by tradition, just assume everybody knows who plays first base for them or are trying to sell extra scorecards.

Section II

THE

Players

I. Introduction to Section II

■ In the fashionable salons of the East, where baseball history is discussed each evening over appetizers and wine, no general topic is favored more than that of who is better than whom. Who was the greatest player ever? Who was the greatest catcher ever? The greatest pitcher? The greatest left-handed pitcher? The greatest relief pitcher? The greatest left-handed relief pitcher? Who really belongs in the Hall of Fame? Who were the 100 greatest players of all time? Which active players are among the greatest ever, and exactly where do they rank? How does George Brett compare to Eddie Mathews? Who do you like, Ozzie Smith or Luis Aparicio? What is your All-Time All-Star lineup?

There have been many books written on these subjects, and as I had originally envisioned the text part of this book, this was to have been another one. Once I got involved in doing the research, I began to feel that that was not the best or most interesting thing that I could do with the effort, and so I didn't; there is only this one section on the subjects.

In the second article in this section, I will offer a brief discussion of some of the other books which have dealt with these matters. I do hope that, if I have not discussed these issues as much as you might have wished, I have at least contributed a few fresh facts and explanations with which to fuel the discussion. Many's the time I have heard Babe Ruth's home run total discounted because he was "favored" by playing in Yankee Stadium, and Aaron's because he "got" to play his best years in "big home run parks," while Mays was supposed to have been damaged by the parks in which he played. The next person to write a book on the subject will have the reference section of this tome to disabuse him of these misunderstandings, and so, in time, they will decay.

The difference between my approach and the approach of a sports journalist is that while the journalist would leap directly to the argument for or against the player, I begin by setting up systems of analysis which apply not only to the player under discussion, but potentially to all players or all similar players. This I will do in the pages that follow.

With regard to an offensive player, the first key question is how many *runs* have resulted from what he has done with the bat and on the basepaths. Willie McCovey hit .270 in his career, with 353 doubles, 46 triples, 521 home runs and 1,345 walks—but his job was not to hit doubles, nor to hit singles, nor to hit triples, nor to draw walks or even hit home runs, but rather to put runs on the scoreboard. How many runs resulted from all of these things? How does this total compare with that of Rod Carew, whose average is much higher but who has hit only a fraction of 500 home runs? How does one compare the two players?

This concept of attempting to measure run production, attempting to express all other offensive performance in terms of the number of runs resulting, will be very familiar to those of you who have read annual editions of the *Baseball Abstract.* What will not be so familiar to you is the exact formulas that are needed to deal with the evolving data bank of baseball history. The formulas that work best today cannot be used to evaluate the players of the 1910–40 period or before, sometimes because the information used in them does not exist, and sometimes because the formulas make assumptions about the value of performance, assumptions that operate well in our own time, but not so well in other periods. Article III of this section will detail the series of formulas that are used to make the runs created estimates that appear in Section III, and which form the basis of much of the discussion of particular players in this section.

Creating runs is the essence of offense, but it is not the whole of the game. The value of a run is not a constant; it is not the same in 1922 as it is in 1968, nor the same in Yankee Stadium as it is in Wrigley Field. Offense is but half the game; the other is defense. How the creation of runs fits into the larger kaleidoscope of player evaluation is discussed in the fourth article of this section.

Finally, there is certain other evidence about the skills of players which, while different in kind than the statistical evidence, is no less valuable or less meaningful for the accurate assessment of historical talent. I speak here of awards, observations, the recognition of contemporaries and posterity; I will speak of good awards and bad ones in the fifth article of this section.

After running this five-course minefield of evaluation methods, we will get into the discussion of specific players. After that, there are a couple of other articles, which go in this section because I don't know where else they would go. Section II, in general, deals with the greatest players in baseball history, and all topics relating to the evaluation thereof.

II. Reference Points

■ In discussing the greatest players ever, it is useful to have specific reference points for the discussion, so that each of us can know how his own opinion matches what might be called the popular opinion or the prevailing opinion. I've never liked the terms "overrated" and "underrated," never use them. Who knows where the players are "rated"? If you say that Steve Garvey is overrated, what does that mean? Does that mean that he is not as good as Eddie Murray? Does it mean that he is not as good as Lou Gehrig? Does it mean that he is not as good as Jason Thompson? What? Where is he rated?

In writing the player comments which will follow here, I have used a number of specific reference points to help outline how players are viewed. In this article I wanted to list and describe some of those briefly, so that in the following comments you will know what I am referring to when I write that "Palmer ranks him . . ." or "Allen says that . . ."

1. Pete Palmer. Pete Palmer is a friend of mine who, with John Thorn, wrote a book a few years ago called *The Hidden Game of Baseball.* That book contained an intensive statistical analysis of the greatest players in baseball history, and a ranking of those players one through three hundred. Although I don't always agree with the conclusions or even the methods, it is useful to have another intelligent look at the statistics, as an objective reference for how much credit should be given to various statistical accomplishments.

2. Maury Allen's *Baseball's 100.* This 1981 book picked the 100 greatest players of this century in order, from Willie Mays as number one through Roger Maris as number 100, and contained a brief article about each.

3. *The 100 Greatest Baseball Players of All Time,* by Lawrence Ritter and Donald Honig, was published the same year and did the same thing, only without putting the 100 players in order.

4. Faber's Rankings. In 1985 Charles F. Faber published a book called *Baseball Ratings,* which presented lists of the fifty greatest players in each league, along with many other lists.

5. McCaffrey's Choices. In 1987 Eugene and Roger McCaffrey compiled a listing of the greatest in baseball (best fastball, best defensive catcher, best umpire) by contacting hundreds of retired players and collecting and studying their opinions. This research was published in the book *Players' Choice.*

6. The Hall of Fame. The Hall of Fame is the most basic "rating" of great players. All players who are in the Hall of Fame can be said, in a sense, to have been "rated" by history as great players, and to have been honored by history more highly than all others. This reference point, however,

has many problems, for it represent not anyone's opinion, but the opinions of many diverse groups, operating over a period of years and with no consistent standards or guidelines, so that no one could believe that, in selecting 180 players or whatever it is now, they happen to have selected the 180 greatest of all time.

Each of these gentlemen or committees has a different view of the game of baseball—the view of a journalist (Maury Allen), the view of historians (Ritter and Honig), the view of stat analysts (Palmer, Faber), the view of players (edited by the McCaffreys), the view of committees entrusted with the responsibility to select and honor fairly. Although I don't agree with any of these gentlemen straight down the line, the opinions or research of all of them deserve respect, and, I hope, will be treated with such in the following discussion.

III. Runs Created

*In which it is revealed how the runs created estimates
in Section III of this book are derived.*

■ A hitter's job is to create runs for his team. A hitter is not at the plate attempting to compile a high batting average, or a high slugging average, or a high total average, but rather to create runs for his team.

The number of runs that a player has created with any combination of singles, doubles, triples, etc., can be measured with a fairly high degree of accuracy. Of course it is true that a player who hits well with men on base or in certain other conditions will create more runs than another player with the same statistics who does not hit well with men on base, and thus we are missing that part of the complete data picture that would allow us to make runs created estimates even more accurate. It may be true that some hitters can create a small number of unmeasured runs by the ability to move runners along with an out.

But if any of those problems was serious, then runs created formulas would not work—and it can be clearly shown that they do work. The number of runs that any team will score in a year is a highly predictable outcome of its offensive statistics, with only a minor variation created by unmeasured or "intangible" skills such as those cited above or any other, including team speed. A team that has 1,450 hits in a season of 5,500 at bats, draws 600 walks and has 2,100 total bases is going to score about 706 runs. It might easily be 686 or 726. It might, on rare occasion (one time in fifty), be 656 or 756, and thus those fabled "things that don't show up in the box score" might, on occasion, explain a significant portion of a team's success. But there are very predictable relationships between those things that *do* show up in the box score, and wins and losses. Those relationships will hold the great majority of the time.

In each annual edition of the *Baseball Abstract,* I introduce three versions of the runs created formula. The first, which is called the "basic runs created" formula, uses only four categories of statistical information (hits, walks, total bases and at bats) and requires only four mathematical steps—yet even at that very simple level, the basic runs created formula is quite accurate in our own time; if it says a team will score 700 runs, they ain't going to score 800. For any group of teams as large as a league, the basic runs created formula is virtually always accurate within 2 percent, and usually within 1 percent. The basic runs created estimates for all fourteen American League teams for the 1984 season appear in the chart below:

BASIC RUNS CREATED FORMULA
Applied to American League, 1984

	H	W	TB	AB	Runs Created	Actual Runs
Baltimore	1374	620	2134	5456	700	681
Boston	1598	500	2490	5648	850	810
California	1363	556	2084	5470	664	696
Chicago	1360	523	2177	5513	679	679
Cleveland	1498	600	2166	5643	728	761
Detroit	1529	602	2436	5644	831	829
Kansas City	1487	400	2211	5543	702	673
Milwaukee	1446	432	2038	5511	644	641
Minnesota	1473	437	2140	5562	681	673
New York	1560	534	2289	5661	774	758
Oakland	1415	568	2204	5457	725	738
Seattle	1429	519	2128	5546	683	682
Texas	1452	420	2097	5569	655	656
Toronto	1555	460	2395	5687	785	750

The standard error of the formula in this particular group is 21.8, which is normal.

The form of the runs created formula, at all times, will be the same. There are three factors. The first is the on-base factor, or the A factor. In the basic version of the formula, the A factor is simply (Hits + Walks). The second is the advancement factor, or the B factor. In the basic version of the runs created formula, the B factor is simply total bases. The third is the opportunity factor, or the C factor. In the basic version of the formula, the C factor is simply (At Bats + Walks). The form is, and will always be, A times B, with the product divided by C.

$$\frac{(H + W) \times (TB)}{(AB + W)}$$

All abbreviations used are the abbreviations of statistical categories; if you don't recognize one, they are listed at the conclusion of this article.

The form is constant because it describes an offense. In order to score runs, an offense must do two things: get people on base, and advance runners. The opportunity factor measures the space in which these activities occur. As we add information to the formula, the measurement of each factor will become more complex and detailed, but the relationship among the factors, and thus the essential shape of the formula, will remain exactly the same.

The second version of the runs created formula is the stolen base version. The stolen base version of the formula makes two adjustments. The on-base factor is adjusted downward because of the runners taken off base by being caught stealing:

A Factor: (H + W) becomes
              (H + W − CS)

While the advancement factor is adjusted upward to allow for the value of the stolen bases:

B Factor: (TB) becomes
              [TB + (.55 × SB)]

So that the formula becomes—and this is the last time I am going to do this:

$$\frac{(H + W - CS) \times [TB + (.55 \times SB)]}{(AB + W)}$$

The runs created estimates for all twelve National League teams for the 1974 season are given below:

RUNS CREATED FORMULA, STOLEN BASE VERSION
Applied to National League, 1974

	H	W	CS	TB	SB	AB	Runs Created	Actual Runs
Atlanta	1375	571	44	2011	72	5533	639	661
Chicago	1397	621	73	2032	78	5574	651	669
Cincinnati	1437	693	49	2183	146	5535	756	776
Houston	1441	471	65	2075	108	5489	661	653
Los Angeles	1511	597	75	2227	149	5557	763	798
Montreal	1355	652	49	1872	124	5343	634	662
New York	1286	597	23	1801	43	5468	560	572
Philadelphia	1434	469	58	2052	115	5494	654	676
Pittsburgh	1560	514	31	2232	55	5702	744	751
St. Louis	1492	531	62	2049	172	5620	683	677
San Diego	1239	564	45	1786	85	5415	539	541
San Francisco	1380	548	51	1963	107	5482	629	634

The standard error of the formula in this particular group is 18.3, which is normal, perhaps slightly better than average.

The third version of the formula that is used in each annual edition of the *Abstract* is called the technical version, and it attempts to deal with all known information about the offense, and to make tiny adjustments for things like the "advancement value" of a walk. These are the changes that are made in forming the technical version of the runs created formula now in use:

A Factor: (H + W − CS) becomes
(H + W − CS + HBP − GIDP)

B Factor: [TB + (.55 × SB)] becomes
{TB + [.26 × (TBB−IBB+HBP)] + [.52 × (SH+SF + SB)]}

C Factor: (AB + W) becomes
(AB + W + HBP + SH + SF)

As I said, in the annual *Abstract*s we deal with three versions of the formula. In this book, we will have to deal with sixteen versions of the formula —the basic version, the stolen base version, and fourteen technical versions. The reason that we have to do this is that the data set changes and evolves rapidly throughout the century, or at least up until 1955, when the progress of evolution in statistical information came to a temporary halt (it stopped moving forward until Bill James and Pete Palmer came around, about twenty years later). In 1900 we have no data for how many times a player grounded into a double play, how many times he was hit by a pitch, how many of his walks might have been intentional, how many times he was caught stealing, or how many sacrifice flies he hit. This data was added sporadically in the years 1900 to 1955. Sometimes we have caught stealing but no hit by pitch; sometimes we have hit by pitch but no caught stealing. Sometimes we have a category called "sacrifice hits," but what is meant by sacrifice hits is what would now be called sacrifice hits or flies. Sometimes it means something else entirely; at one time players were credited with sacrifice hits whenever they advanced a runner with an out, without regard to intention.

As this crazy quilt of information changes, we will have to adjust our runs created formulas to make maximum use of what is there—in other words, devising a separate runs created formula to accommodate each data set. The technical version that was introduced above (and has been used in the 1984–1988 *Baseball Abstract*s) requires eleven categories of information— hits, walks, intentional walks, caught stealing, hit by pitch, grounded into double plays, sacrifice hits, sacrifice flies, total bases, stolen bases, and at bats. This will from now on (in this book) be known as the TECH-1 version of the formula.

All of this information exists, going backward in time, through 1955. During all of that period of time, the TECH-1 version of the formula works great; there is no need to make any adjustments to it. The chart below presents the runs created estimates, by the TECH-1 version of the formula, for all ten American League teams in 1964.

RUNS CREATED FORMULA, TECH-I VERSION
Applied to American League, 1964

	H	W	CS	HBP	GIDP	TB	SB	IBB	SH	SF	AB	Runs Created	Actual Runs
Boston	1425	504	16	28	144	2294	18	43	35	26	5513	725	688
Detroit	1394	517	27	40	105	2178	60	40	71	42	5513	707	699
New York	1442	520	18	31	117	2206	54	64	68	34	5705	705	730
Minnesota	1413	553	22	44	120	2395	46	43	74	37	5610	775	737
Baltimore	1357	537	38	27	126	2112	78	55	69	47	5463	671	679
Cleveland	1386	500	51	49	112	2130	79	63	63	42	5603	666	689
Chicago	1356	562	39	52	100	1938	75	58	96	45	5491	643	642
Los Angeles	1297	472	39	26	145	1843	49	40	78	37	5362	552	544
Kansas City	1321	548	20	42	152	2093	34	32	53	25	5524	645	621
Washington	1246	514	30	28	119	1876	47	34	66	33	5396	566	578

The standard error of the formula in this particular group is 22.0, which is normal, perhaps slightly worse than average.

That's about enough of that. The purpose of running charts of runs created data is to enable you to see for yourself, without undertaking heroic efforts such as a trip to the library, that the formula does, in fact, predict the number of runs that will result from a given combination of offensive incidents. We should have established that by now; the estimates are usually off by an average of about 20. If you don't yet believe that the formulas can do this, you're probably never going to believe it, but I'm not going to run thirteen more charts to show the same basic thing. Anybody who is that interested can go to the library.

For the runs created formulas that were used for seasons prior to 1955, let me explain them to you more or less as I developed them. What I did was to start in 1955 with the TECH-1 version of the formula. Then, working backward in time, as data became unavailable I would make whatever adjustments to the formula that seemed reasonable to allow for the changes in the data bank. If a formula was only going to be used for two league/seasons, I would test one of them; if it was going to be used for three or four leagues, I might test two; if it was going to be used for a decade in one league, I would test about three of them, etc.

I had it in mind that I would try to maintain the accuracy of the formulas within 30.0 runs per team. My assumption was that as we moved backward in time and lost information, it would become more difficult to develop accurate formulas. But in fact, I never had any trouble keeping the standard error below 25.0, and usually it was below 20.0 in the samples that I tested.

TECH-2

USED IN: BOTH LEAGUES, 1954

In 1955 we start with eleven categories. As the statistics of the two leagues prior to that time evolved independently of one another (though in the same ultimate direction), I will work backward in one league at a time, starting with the American.

We lose the first one of those eleven categories in 1954. Before 1955, neither league counted intentional bases on balls separate from other walks. This requires an adjustment to the "advancement" factor of the equation:

B Factor:
TB + [.26 × (TBB−IBB+HBP)] + [.52 × (SH+SF+SB)] becomes
TB + [.26 × (TBB+HBP)] + [.52 × (SH+SF+SB)]

A Factor remains: H + W + HBP − CS − GIDP
C Factor remains: AB + W + HBP + SH + SF

All we have done here is simply eliminated the intentional walk adjustment from the advancement portion. The second unit of the B factor (the part that is multiplied by .26) is an adjustment for the small advancement value that a walk has. A player doesn't get many RBIs on walks, but occasionally a walk will move a runner into scoring position or something, so its advancement potential cannot be totally ignored. Since an intentional walk almost never advances a runner who could score a meaningful run, I decided in drawing up TECH-1 to allow no credit for it in the advancement portion of the formula.

But this is such a tiny adjustment that its elimination does not require another, off-setting correction in some other part of the formula. It only changes the runs created estimates by something less than one-half of one percent. The accuracy of the formula with no other correction remains within the specified limits.

TECH-3
USED IN: BOTH LEAGUES, 1951–1953
AMERICAN LEAGUE, 1940–1950

The modern sacrifice fly rule was adopted in 1954; prior to that we are missing data on how many sacrifice flies each player and team delivered.

The absence of this data causes the advancement portion of the formula to be too small. We can offset the loss by increasing total bases by $2\frac{1}{2}$ percent. Also, since SF no longer exist, they can no longer be a part of the opportunity factor. Since sacrifice flies are now scored simply as at bats, the opportunity factor remains, in fact, the same, although it is written differently:

B Factor:
TB + [.26 × (TBB+HBP)] + [.52 × (SH+ SF+SB)] becomes
(1.025 × TB) + [.26 × (TBB+HBP)] + [.52 × (SH+SB)]

C Factor:
AB + W + HBP + SH + SF becomes
AB + W + HBP + SH

A Factor remains: H + W + HBP − CS − GIDP

Although the loss of this data probably creates some decrease in the accuracy of the formula, it is doubtful that that decrease would be large enough to be detected by a study of the 128 teams for which the TECH-3 version of the formula must be used. The formula retains essentially the same accuracy as before.

TECH-4
USED IN: AMERICAN LEAGUE, 1939

That adjustment gets us back, in the American League, to 1940. In 1940 the sacrifice hit was redefined (in both leagues); prior to 1940 a player was credited with a sacrifice hit (SH) on either a sacrifice bunt, as he is now, or a sacrifice fly. In other words, in 1939 we have (for the American League) exactly the same data that we have in 1954, except that both SH and SF (sacrifice hits and sacrifice flies) are included in the one category called SH. So the 2½ percent adjustment to total bases is no longer needed, and we have:

B Factor:
$(1.025 \times TB) + [.26 \times (TBB+HBP)] + [.52 \times (SH+SB)]$ becomes
$TB + [.26 \times (TBB+HBP)] + [.52 \times (SH+SB)]$

A Factor remains: $H + W + HBP - CS - GIDP$
C Factor remains: $AB + W + HBP + SH$

TECH-5
USED IN: AMERICAN LEAGUE, 1931–1938

The American League adopted the GIDP (grounded into double play) statistic in 1939; prior to that we have no such data in the American League. Since double plays take men off base, they are included in the runs created formula in the on-base factor, or A factor. Without this data, we now have too many people on base, and to adjust for this we must multiply the number of people on base by .96, adjusting the runs created estimates downward. This creates:

A Factor:
$H + W + HBP - CS - GIDP$ becomes
$.96 \times (H + W + HBP - CS)$

B Factor remains: $TB + [.26 \times (TBB+HBP)] + [.52 \times (SH+SB)]$
C Factor remains: $AB + W + HBP + SH$

This probably creates the first measurable decrease in the accuracy of the formula, as applied to the American League. However, on a test of three leagues, the decrease in the accuracy of the formula is not readily apparent; its standard error is still far less than 25.0 runs per team.

TECH-6
USED IN: AMERICAN LEAGUE, 1928–1930 AND 1920–1926
NATIONAL LEAGUE, 1920–1925

Prior to 1930, the major leagues used a different and yet more liberal criterion for sacrifice hits. A sacrifice hit was also credited on a fly ball which moved a runner, whether from second to third, first to second, or whatever. This change requires that we decrease ever so slightly the value of the event, so as to maintain the accuracy of the formula:

B Factor:
TB + [.26 × (TBB+HBP)] + [.52 × (SH+SB)] becomes
TB + [.26 × (TBB+HBP)] + [.51 × (SH+SB)]

A Factor remains: .96 × (H + W + HBP − CS)
C Factor remains: AB + W + HBP + SH

Although this definition of the sacrifice hit was not actually adopted until 1926, I have chosen to leave the reduced value of the sacrifice hit in place prior to that time. The formula still meets the required standards of accuracy in that period, and it seemed preferable not to introduce yet another version of the formula.

TECH-7
USED IN: AMERICAN LEAGUE, 1927
NATIONAL LEAGUE, 1926–1930

To approach this one from the other end, both leagues adopted the statistic "out stealing," which is now called "caught stealing," in 1920—ironically, in the very year in which the running game moved into its accelerated decline. The National League, after counting caught stealing from 1920 to 1924, abandoned it, but the American League carried on—with the exception of the 1927 season. For 1927, there is no official CS data.

This is a major loss, and it requires the development of a significantly altered runs created formula. In our own time, base stealing is more or less a break-even gamble for the league as a whole; some teams help themselves by stealing bases, while others hurt themselves by trying to. When we eliminate SB and CS from the runs created formula as applied to our own time, then, the formula becomes less accurate but not off-center; the league as a whole still scores about as many runs as it is projected to.

But in the 1920s, this is not true. The major leagues, applying the strategies and tactics of the dead-ball era to the conditions of what is called the lively ball era, were actually scoring *fewer* runs because of their base stealing efforts than they would otherwise have scored. This conclusion could also be inferred from the trends of the period, in which stolen base attempts were declining sharply in number. If the teams were not learning that the stolen base attempts were hurting the offense, then why did they stop running? The strategy adjusted to the reality. Casey Stengel specifically said that that was what had happened (see comment on Max Carey).

In the game of the twenties, then, when we eliminate SB and CS from the formula, we wind up with too many runs being projected—that is, because the stolen base attempts are lowering runs scored below the levels that would otherwise have occurred, the projections of runs created without stolen base data are too high. We need, therefore, to lower them in some other way. I have found that the best way to do this is to make small downward adjustments to both the on-base and the advancement factors:

A Factor:
$.96 \times (H + W + HBP - CS)$ becomes
$.93 \times (H + W + HBP)$

B Factor:
$TB + [.26 \times (TBB+HBP)] + [.51 \times (SH+SB)]$ becomes
$TB + [.26 \times (TBB+HBP)] + (.46 \times SH)$

C Factor remains: $AB + W + HBP + SH$

TECH-8
USED IN: BOTH LEAGUES, 1913–1919
             EXCEPT AMERICAN LEAGUE, 1916

Until now we have been adjusting the runs created formula to accommodate only changes in the available statistics. There is every reason to believe that, if the data that was required existed, the technical version of the runs created formula as it is used in the 1980s would work as well in the early 1920s. We have adapted it only to cover the missing information.

Prior to 1920, we must adapt the formula to react to the changes in the game of baseball itself. The baseball of the 1900 to 1919 period is much more of a baserunner's game than that which follows. There were many, many more stolen bases—even more than today, and far more than throughout most of the post-1920 era. And unlike today, when baserunning competes with other forms of advancement (like power hitting), baserunning and strategy were the dominant methods of advancing runners. For that reason, unlike today, there is a clear relationship between the number of bases stolen by a team and the number of runs scored. Between 1910 and 1919, thirteen of the twenty teams that led the league in stolen bases finished either first or second in the league; today, the team that leads the league in stolen bases is about as likely to finish last as first.

It wasn't only base stealing, but baserunning that was important. Players took many, many more chances on the basepaths, going from first to third on a single, tagging up at first and advancing to second on a fly ball, that sort of thing. Many more players were thrown out on the bases attempting to do this. Many more players reached base on errors, and it should be assumed that speed was a factor in a player's ability to do that.

At the same time, there is an unfortunate loss in data. Prior to 1920 we lose caught stealing, which we also did not have in the TECH-7 formula, the last one I explained, but which we did have in 1920. These changes require a radical revamping of the runs created formula.

A Factor:
.93 × (H + W + HBP) becomes
H + W + HBP − (.02 × AB)

B Factor:
TB + [.26 × (TBB+HBP)] + (.46 × SH) becomes
TB + [.85 × (SH + SB)]

C Factor remains: AB + W + HBP + SH

I have decided to reduce the on-base factor (A factor) by a percentage of at bats, rather than a percentage of runners known to be on base. I have decided to (or rather, I have found through experimentation that I should) reduce the on-base factor (to account for the loss of runners on the base-paths) by a percentage (.02) of at bats, rather than a percentage (.07) of times reaching base. This change really makes very little difference, but it works slightly to the advantage of a great hitter or a good team. For example, Joe Jackson in 1913 had 197 hits, 80 walks, and was hit by pitches 5 times, a total of 282 times known to be on base. Multiplying this by .93, as we did before, this would give him an A factor of 262.26. Subtracting .02 of his 528 at bats, however, leaves him with 271.44 in the A space. A lesser hitter would be affected differently by the change.

The B factor, the advancement factor, was more thoroughly overhauled. Early on in the process of developing this version of the formula, I was not using stolen base data, because I had no caught stealing data to balance against it. But I was having trouble getting the formula to work, and I decided eventually to try using the stolen base category. The results then were much better, and I decided to go with it.

Remember, this was not a game, as it is today, in which base stealing was a peripheral or optional attachment. Everybody stole bases in 1915; there's only a difference between those who were good at it, and those who weren't. The teams that stole the most bases were also the teams that were best at going from first to third on a single, the best at tagging up and scoring from second after a fly ball, and the best at avoiding the double play. Those were essential elements of the offense, much more so than they would be later. So we wind up with a runs created formula that puts a much higher value on the stolen base.

TECH-9
USED IN: AMERICAN LEAGUE, 1916

Neil Munro, who compiled much of the data that appears in Section III of this book, somewhere came up with caught stealing data for the American League in 1916 and occasionally other seasons. I believe the credit for this is due Bob Davids, scouring an old newspaper. Anyway, since we have it, we'll use it. We'll subtract caught stealing from the on-base factor, rather than .02 × At Bats:

A Factor:
H + W + HBP − (.02 × AB) becomes
H + W + HBP − CS

B Factor remains: TB + [.85 × (SH + SB)]
C Factor remains: AB + W + HBP + SH

TECH-10
USED IN: BOTH LEAGUES, 1908–1912

As we go further back in baseball history, there are progressively more errors, and thus a progressively increasing relationship between actual runs scored and runs as projected by the runs created formula. That is, as more runs result from errors or other things not measured by the statistics, the relationship between actual runs scored and the runs created formula changes; actual runs increase relative to runs created by any constant formula. A team was more likely to create a run with just two singles, for example, because there might be an error in there, or if not the team would pick up a base somehow. Stolen bases become even more important.

So we need to adjust the runs created formula to reflect this. First we'll make the adjustment to the advancement factor:

B Factor:
TB + [.85 × (SH + SB)] becomes
[1.025 × (TB + SB)] + (.75 × SH)

A Factor remains: H + W + HBP − (.02 × AB)
C Factor remains: AB + W + HBP + SH

TECH-11
USED IN: BOTH LEAGUES, 1900–1907

Prior to 1908, this trend continues, and the runs created formula again makes projections which are too low. This time we'll adjust the on-base factor upward, by eliminating the downward adjustment of 2 percent of at bats:

A Factor:
H + W + HBP − (.02 × AB) becomes
H + W + HBP

B Factor remains: [1.025 × (TB + SB)] + (.75 × SH)
C Factor remains: AB + W + HBP + SH

I did not attempt to derive runs created formulas that worked for the nine-teenth century. For those players whose careers began before 1900, I used the TECH-11 formula to estimate how many runs they had created, but appended a note saying that these estimates were of indeterminate accuracy. Now let's go back and catch up with the National League.

TECH-12
USED IN: NATIONAL LEAGUE, 1939–1950

We lost the National League in 1950. The National League did not record caught stealing from 1926 through 1950. You may remember that in 1951 we were using the TECH-3 version of the formula, the elements of which are:

A Factor: $H + W + HBP - GIDP - CS$
B Factor: $(1.025 \times TB) + [.26 \times (W + HBP)] + [.52 \times (SH + SB)]$
C Factor: $AB + W + HBP + SH$

The National League at this time was still in a position in which the base stealing was hurting the offense, so when we eliminate stolen bases and caught stealing from the equation, the result is a few too many runs being scored. We can adjust for this by eliminating the extra weight on the total bases:

A Factor:
$H + W + HBP - GIDP - CS$ becomes
$H + W + HBP - GIDP$

B Factor:
$(1.025 \times TB) + [.26 \times (W + HBP)] + [.52 \times (SH + SB)]$ becomes
$TB + [.26 \times (W + HBP)] + (.52 \times SH)$

C Factor remains: $AB + W + HBP + SH$

TECH-13
USED IN: NATIONAL LEAGUE, 1933–38

From 1933 through 1938, the National League recorded double plays but not GIDP, as today. They counted HIDP, which included all double play balls. There is also the redefinition of the sacrifice hit, which came in 1939, which throws the formula a little off. The runs created estimates are now a little too low; we can adjust for this by restoring the 1.025 weight to total bases.

B Factor:
$TB + [.26 \times (W + HBP)] + (.52 \times SH)$ becomes
$(1.025 \times TB) + [.26 \times (W + HBP)] + (.52 \times SH)$

A Factor remains: $H + W + HBP - HIDP$
C Factor remains: $AB + W + HBP + SH$

TECH-14
USED IN: NATIONAL LEAGUE, 1931–32

Prior to 1933, we lose hit into double play information, as we did in the American League in 1938. We adjust for this in the same way as we did there, by lowering the on-base factor by a fixed percentage to account for the difference. In the American League the figure that worked was .96; here it is .95:

A Factor:
H + W + HBP − HIDP becomes
.95 × (H + W + HBP)

B Factor remains: (1.025 × TB) + [.26 × (W + HBP)] + (.52 × SH)
C Factor remains: AB + W + HBP + SH

Until 1930, the National League is served by one or another of the same formulas that we have already introduced. From 1926 through 1930, when the National League has no stolen base data and the ultraliberal sacrifice hit rule, we use the TECH-7 version of the formula, also used in the American League in 1927. From 1920 through 1925, we use TECH-6, which is used in the American League from 1920 through 1930 except for '27. Prior to 1920, we use the same forms in the National League as we did in the American League, except for 1916.

Let's put all of those formulas in chart form, so you can find which formula to use for what year if you take the notion:

YEARS	AMERICAN LEAGUE	NATIONAL LEAGUE
1900–1907	TECH-11	TECH-11
1908–1912	TECH-10	TECH-10
1913–1915	TECH-8	TECH-8
1916	TECH-9	TECH-8
1917–1919	TECH-8	TECH-8
1920–1925	TECH-6	TECH-6
1926	TECH-6	TECH-7
1927	TECH-7	TECH-7
1928–1930	TECH-6	TECH-7
1931–1932	TECH-5	TECH-14
1933–1938	TECH-5	TECH-13
1939	TECH-4	TECH-12
1940–1950	TECH-3	TECH-12
1951–1953	TECH-3	TECH-3
1954	TECH-2	TECH-2
1955–1984	TECH-1	TECH-1

As I said, I believe that all of these formulas maintain an accuracy within 25 runs per team per season. However, one must remember that this is a first effort to find runs created formulas that maintain a high degree of accuracy throughout the century, and it should be assumed that none of these represents the highest level of the art. It is my expectation that if sabermetrics survives, other people are going to find ways of improving on these. Even the TECH-1 formula, the one in use for the present time, is not the end of the road; somebody is going to come along within a couple of years and point out some way in which it could be made more accurate. I fully expect other people to come along, do more extensive testing, and find out that where I have used 1.025, I should have used 1.03, and where I have weighted SH and SB evenly, I should have treated them separately. I look forward to learning those things. But these are the most accurate ways known at this moment to assess the offense of any player from any time in this century.

ABBREVIATIONS USED

AB	At Bats
CS	Caught Stealing
GIDP	Grounded Into Double Play
H	Hits
HIDP	Hit Into Double Play (includes all double plays, rather than simply ground ball double plays)
HBP	Hit By Pitch
HB	Hit Batsman (same as HBP)
IBB	Intentional Bases on Balls
SB	Stolen Bases
SH	Sacrifice Hits (bunts)
SF	Sacrifice Flies
TB	Total Bases
TBB	Total Bases on Balls (same as walks)
W	Walks (exactly the same as TBB; used interchangeably)

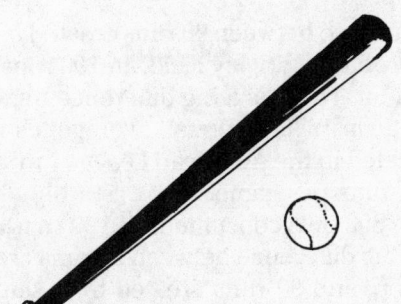

IV. Beyond Runs Created

Other considerations in the statistical evaluation of a player.

■ Knowing how many runs a player has created is the first essential step toward understanding what all of those statistics really mean. It is not the last step. A player who creates 100 runs for his team is not necessarily a more valuable player than another who creates 95, 90, 75, or even (conceivably) 50. There are two other things that we must gain control of in order to make a good assessment of the player's value on the field. Those two things are (a) the context in which the runs were created, and (b) the player's defensive contribution.

At the end of the rainbow here, rather than runs created we will have expressed the player's offensive contribution as a number of "wins" and "losses." Wins and losses have two advantages over runs created: constancy and importance. The totals of runs scored go up and down for many different reasons, and thus the value of each run goes up and down—but wins do not. Winning percentage is the one constant statistic; it stays at .500000 in every decade, in every park, in every season, in every game, and on every pitch. Everything that happens is good for one team precisely in the degree to which it is bad for the other.

But more important than that, wins and losses are what the game is all about. A player is at bat trying to create runs—but only because, in creating runs, he is helping to create wins. As singles and doubles and walks and stolen bases are but the bits and pieces of runs, runs are but the bits and pieces of wins. What we ultimately must do to understand the contribution that a player has made afield is to understand how many wins and how many losses he has been responsible for.

A. OFFENSIVE CONTEXT

There is a big difference between 90 runs created in the best hitter's park in baseball, which is probably Wrigley Field, and 90 runs created in the worst, which is Dodger Stadium. There is a big difference between 90 runs created in the American League in 1936, where an average team scored 5.7 runs per game, and 90 runs created in the American League in 1968, where an average team scored only 3.4 runs per game. There is a big difference between 90 runs created with only 300 outs consumed, and 90 runs created with 450 outs consumed. There is a big difference between 90 runs created by an outstanding defensive shortstop, and 90 runs created by a sluggish left fielder.

Context, then, is everything; 60 runs created can be an outstanding figure in one context, and 100 can be an inadequate contribution in another. The choices that one makes in placing a player's offense in an appropriate context are the most important choices to be made in understanding how the player fits into a winning or losing pattern, and thus the most important decisions to be made in player evaluation. And there are a zillion options, and it will be years before sabermetricians can state with any sense of certainty which are the best of those options.

If we cannot march directly to the best possible option, we can at least start out confidently in the right direction. The first decision to be made is in what ratio to state the player's production. The standard method is to state what the player has done per at bat or per plate appearance; 25 home runs in 600 at bats are a home run percentage of 4.2, etc. This method has evolved from the habits established by batting average, slugging average and other such raw percentages. For such simple ends the choice is correct or at least acceptable, but the method is clearly and unmistakably the wrong choice for any sort of comparative evaluation among a group of players; on this issue we are on very firm ground. Individual at bat totals are an individual category, and have no significance to the team for which the man plays.

What is significant, and what should always be used for stating ratios of productivity in baseball, is the number of outs that the player has been responsible for. Outs are the form in which opportunities are presented to the team; the team is given three outs each inning, 27 outs each game. It is not given 35 or 40 at bats in which to win the game. A player who bats 600 times and makes 350 outs and a player who bats 600 times and makes 450 outs have not had the same "opportunity" in any meaningful sense. Even if they have created the same number of runs, the impact that they have had upon the teams for which they play is quite different.

The number of at bats that a player has can be seen, in a sense, as being like dollars borrowed from the team's bank with the intention of earning a profit on them (the profit being, of course, the runs that he puts on the scoreboard). If two players each borrow 600 at bats from the team's bank, they are even at that point. But if the player reaches base, if he does not make an out, then he has returned those at bats immediately to the bank. There is obviously a difference between a player who borrows $600, but returns $250 to the team, using the other $350 to earn his run-profit, and a player who borrows $600 but returns only $150. Even if the profit earned is the same, there is an obvious difference to the bank (the team) between losing $350 to earn a profit of 80 runs, and losing $450 to earn a profit of 80 runs.

So stating productivity in terms of at bats is simply a bad habit, a leftover from the level of figuring batting averages and slugging percentages and stuff. It should never be done.

This is the last time that I will speak so confidently about the subject of placing a player's offensive contributions in an appropriate context. The next step in the progression that I have chosen is to express the ratio between runs created and outs as "runs per game." Let us say that a player, whom we will call Jim Rice, has created 119 runs while making 410 outs as a hitter, 7 outs while attempting to steal bases, 1 out with a sacrifice bunt, 9 with sacrifice flies, and 32 additional outs on ground ball double plays. Rice would then be responsible for 459 total outs, which happens to be 27 times 17.

I consider each 27 outs to be a game. It is not an absolute necessity that a team average 27.00 outs per game; there are such distractions as errors that can give a team extra outs, extra-inning games, rain-shortened games, and home teams that don't bat in the bottom of the ninth. By a fortunate coincidence, these factors have a strong tendency to balance one another, so that for a group of teams as large as one league, you will usually wind up with just about 27.0 outs per team per game. Here; I'll present the data for both leagues for 1982 and 1983:

	'82 A.L.	'82 N.L.	'83 A.L.	'83 N.L.
Hits	20,566	17,085	20,662	16,781
At Bats	77,886	66,263	77,821	65,717
Caught Stealing	795	822	744	870
Sacrifice Hits	762	978	640	921
Sacrifice Flies	641	580	708	548
GIDP	1797	1350	1870	1417
Total Outs	61,315	52,908	61,121	52,692
Team Games	2270	1944	2270	1948
Outs Per Game	27.01	27.22	26.93	27.05

So then, I figure how many runs the player has created per out, multiply that by 27, and call that runs per game. Jim Rice, in this example, has created 7.00 runs per game. These are the "runs per game" estimates that are used to figure the offensive winning percentages in Section III of this book.

Another small problem here is that, while we have the data to account for 27.0 outs per game now, we don't have it for all of baseball history. We don't have double play data or caught stealing data for many seasons, and the ratio between errors and extra innings has not been constant over the century. So we can't allow the player 27 outs per game for the entire century; if we did, the offensive winning percentages that we will figure later would not total .500 for many leagues, as logically they must.

For the seasons up to 1915, the records account for about 25.5 outs per game, and so this figure is used instead of 27. From 1916 to 1932 in the National League, 1916 to 1938 in the American (that is, before we have double play data), a "game" is considered to be 26 outs. From that time until the present, we can account for 27 outs per game.

There is nothing inevitable about the choice of expressing offensive totals on a per-game basis; you could leave Rice's figure at runs per out (.259), change it to runs per 1,000 outs (259), or express it as runs per team/season (119 runs in 459 outs is a rate that would produce 1,134 runs for a team in a season). I choose runs per game because, to me, it's a meaningful figure; an average fan, hearing the figure seven runs per game, knows that that's a good figure. He knows intuitively that an average team scores four or five runs a game, not seven.

But how you state that relationship between player and league, technically, is a troublesome problem, presenting many options, each of which has clear disadvantages. A player who creates 7.00 runs per game in a league that scores only 3.4 runs per game, like the 1968 AL, is obviously far more valuable than a player who creates 7.00 per game in a 5.7-run league, like the 1936 AL. But how best to state that? What I have done here, and what I have done in the past, is to attempt to express the runs per game ratio as a winning percentage.

A team that scored 7.0 runs per game and allowed only 3.4 runs per game would have a winning percentage of about .809. We know that this is true because the ratio between a team's wins and its losses will be about the same as the ratio between the square of its runs scored and the square of its runs allowed; this is what is called the Pythagorean approach to winning percentage. That is a consistent, reliable pattern; the chart below presents the runs scored and runs allowed for each major league team in 1984, and projects the won/lost record that should result from this combination. As you can see, most teams win almost exactly the number of games that they could be expected to win given the number of runs that they have scored and the number that they have allowed.

	Runs Scored	Runs Allowed	Projected Winning Percentage	Projected W-L	Actual W-L
Baltimore	681	667	0.510	83–79	85–77
Boston	810	764	0.529	86–76	86–76
California	679	697	0.487	79–83	81–81
Chicago	696	736	0.472	76–86	74–88
Cleveland	761	766	0.497	80–82	75–87
Detroit	829	643	0.624	101–61	104–58
Kansas City	673	686	0.490	79–83	84–78
Milwaukee	641	734	0.433	70–91	67–94
Minnesota	673	675	0.499	81–81	81–81
New York	758	679	0.555	90–72	87–75
Oakland	738	796	0.462	75–87	77–85
Seattle	682	774	0.437	71–91	74–88
Texas	656	714	0.458	74–87	69–92
Toronto	750	696	0.537	87–75	89–73
Atlanta	632	655	0.482	78–84	80–82
Chicago	762	658	0.573	92–69	96–65
Cincinnati	627	747	0.413	67–95	70–92
Houston	693	630	0.548	89–73	80–82
Los Angeles	580	600	0.483	78–84	79–83
Montreal	593	585	0.507	82–79	78–83
New York	652	676	0.482	78–84	90–72
Philadelphia	720	690	0.521	84–78	81–81
Pittsburgh	615	567	0.541	88–74	75–87
St. Louis	652	645	0.505	82–80	84–78
San Diego	686	634	0.539	87–75	92–70
San Francisco	682	807	0.417	67–95	66–96

As you can see, seventeen of the twenty-six teams came within three games of the number of wins projected for them, and twenty-three of the twenty-six within five games, the three exceptions being Pittsburgh, Houston, and the New York Mets. It can also be shown that teams that exceed their Pythagorean projection (winning more games than expected) will tend to decline in the following seasons, while those which win fewer than expected will tend to improve in the following seasons, suggesting that deviations from these ratios occur in part because of luck.

In comparing the player to the league, then, I treat the league average of runs per game as the player's "runs allowed," and project his winning percentage in the same way. This is what I have done in annual *Baseball Abstract*s through 1984, though it is not exactly what I have done here.

There are many options now, and I've never had any real confidence that I was selecting the right one. What Pete Palmer does in this situation is to compare the player to the league by figuring + or − runs. Let's say that the Jim Rice example before, that of the player who created 119 runs at a rate of 7.00 per season, was in a league which averaged 4.50 runs per game, which is a normal American League average. I would figure his offensive winning percentage, which would be .708, and show Rice with an offensive won/lost record of 12–5. Pete would figure the number of runs that would be created by an average player in the same opportunity space, which would be 76.5, and show Rice as +42.5 runs.

I have no strong feelings about which method is preferable to the other, and at this point it makes very little difference. It begins to make a difference, however, when you start to adjust for other factors of context, such as the position at which the man plays.

What Pete Palmer would do, and what is not a bad option in his structure, would be to compare Rice not to an average American League hitter, but to an average American League left fielder as a hitter. Whereas an average hitter might create 76.5 runs in that number of outs, an average left fielder might create 95, so that Rice would be +24, rather than +42.5.

I have always elected to leave defense out of the issue at this point. The problem I have always had with that is this: Nobody hits as a shortstop. I have been to hundreds of baseball games, and I have yet to see anybody collect a single hit while playing shortstop. Everybody hits as a hitter. All of the runs go into a common pool. If you create 100 runs, those 100 runs will create a given number of wins, which is not any different if you are a shortstop than it is if you are a first baseman.

This is not, however, an inevitable choice, nor have I any real sense that it is the best choice. What we are attempting to do here, in a sense, is to construct a mathematical image of the game that represents the game in the truest, most accurate possible way. Is it more accurate to say that Jim Rice is competing with the league, or that he is competing with the opposition left fielder? Is his value that margin by which he is greater than the league, or only that margin by which he is greater than the league's left fielders? And which of those assumptions will serve us better when dealing with the other problems in the image that we will encounter later? This I do not know.

The next problem is what to do about the ballpark. Ballparks tend to increase or decrease the number of runs that are scored by the team and by the team's opponents. The extent to which they do this can be measured and factored into the assessment of the player's value.

On this issue, I have chosen a different road this time than that which I have traveled in the past. What I have done in the past is to start with the league, and adjust the league for the park. What I have done this time is just to ignore the league and place the player in a "team" context. In the past, for example, I would have reasoned this way with regard to the Rice example:

a. The average American League team scores 4.5 runs per game; the initial context, then, is a 4.5-run-per-game context.

b. The Red Sox play half their games in Fenway Park, which inflates offense (and thus reduces the value of each run) by about 14 percent.

c. The value of Rice's runs must be reduced by 7 percent to compare him to the rest of the league.

What I have done this time is simply ignore the league and start with the team. The Red Sox played 162 games and scored 830 runs; their opponents scored 790. That is 1,620 runs in 162 games, or 5.00 runs per team per game; that is the context in which Rice contributed his 7.00 runs per game.

I started this, initially, because it seemed preferable to facing the incomprehensible task of figuring accurate "park effects" for every team for the entire century; it's hard enough to keep track of all that stuff for the last five or six years. Who knows what the "park factors" were for Wally Berger the year he hit 34 homers and drove in 130 runs for the last-place Braves? Who knows exactly how Del Pratt's batting record in 1916 was influenced by the park in which he played?

My original thinking was that by using team data, rather than league data, we would be approximating the effect of the park illusions. If the park in which Del Pratt played in 1916 tended to diminish offense, then Pratt's team would tend to score or allow fewer runs than the league average; if it was a hitter's park, they would tend to score and allow more. So I would just place Del Pratt for 1916 in the context not of the American League, but in the context of the St. Louis Browns.

But after I had been doing this for a few hundred players, I realized that it was not only an acceptable substitute, but actually a preferable alternative. Why? Because the team is the only thing that is truly relevant to the player.

Remember, what we are trying to do here is to figure out how many wins the player has contributed to his team's effort, and how many losses to hold him responsible for. Suppose you take two teams, both of which have scored exactly 700 runs and allowed exactly 680 in 162 games, an average of 4.26 runs per team per game. However, one of them plays in the National League, where the average team scores only 4.00 runs per game, but plays in a hitter's park which raises that figure. The other team plays in the American League, where teams average 4.50 runs per game, but plays in a pitcher's park. What I would have done before would have been to place the National League players in a 4.00-run-per-game context and reduced their productivity to adjust for the park illusion, and to place the American League players in a

4.50-run-per-game context, and given them a bonus because of the park in which they labored.

But isn't that, really, just a roundabout way of getting to the team figure? Yes, it is. And isn't it, really, quite irrelevant whether the player is in a hitter's park in a pitcher's league or the other way around? Yes, it is. A player creating 100 runs in 380 outs for a team that scores and allows 4.26 runs per game has exactly the same impact on his team's ability to win in either case. The construct of the "league," in fact, has nothing at all to do with the value of what this player has accomplished. The "league" is simply some other teams playing some other games that are utterly unconnected with the activities of this particular player.

Though those games may be important to him, they should not be used to inform the evaluation of what he does. If Tony Pena is in St. Louis driving in three runs in a game in the attempt to help St. Louis win the pennant, he might be vitally interested in the score of a game in Chicago—but whether the score of that game is 1–0 or 16–12 has nothing at all to do with the won/loss impact of Tony Pena's performance in St. Louis.

The offensive winning percentages and won/lost records that appear in Section III of this book are based, then, on player-to-team context comparisons. If Jim Rice creates seven runs a game and the Red Sox and their opponents average five runs a game, his offensive winning percentage will be .662, regardless of what the league averages are.

This now becomes a digression into the theoretical options in player evaluation, rather than an explanation of the information which appears in this book. But what we could do is to consider the "league" to be the average of the left fielders (in the case of Rice) in the league. The 5.00 is used in the Pythagorean formula to represent what the player has "allowed" his oppositions. I have problems with saying that what Rice has allowed is represented by the average runs per game in the context in which he plays. It might make more sense to say that what he has allowed is represented by his own individual defense—in other words, that his allowance rate is related to his defensive position. We might find, then, that left fielders over a period of time tend to average about 20 percent more runs created per out than other players. We could, then, apply that 20 percent adjustment to the Red Sox "context," and consider Rice to be creating his runs in a 6.00-run-per-game (5.00 times 1.20) context. Seven runs a game in a six-run-a-game context creates an offensive winning percentage of .576.

We could go one step further. We could say that since Rice is a pretty decent left fielder, at least in Fenway Park, we will assign him a "runs allowed" rate that represents a pretty decent left fielder. That a might be 5 percent lower than 6.00, or 5.70, and thus Rice's offensive winning percentage might be .601 (7.00 against 5.70). I haven't chosen this option, but I might at some other time.

That's another book. To summarize what we have done for the approximately 200 players listed in Section III of this one, for each season I have applied to the player's offensive statistics one of fourteen formulas to estimate how many runs the player has created for his team. This was then translated into a "runs per game" figure, based on one game for each 25.5, 26.0, or 27.0 outs that the player had made. The runs per game figures do not appear in print. The runs per game were then translated into a winning percentage, using as the context for each player the number of runs scored per game and runs allowed per game by the player's team. The winning percentage was then applied to the "games" for which the player was held responsible, one for each 25.5, 26.0 or 27.0 outs. The result was each player's individual won/lost record.

B. DEFENSE

I have not attempted, in writing this book, to set up a formal methodology to deal with defensive statistics. It is my feeling about defensive statistics that they are, while seriously (and annoyingly) flawed, still in general meaningful, in the same way that won/lost records and RBI counts are generally meaningful, while undoubtedly polluted.

What I have tried to do with defensive statistics is not to analyze them, but simply to present them in a form that makes sense. The most important thing that I have done here is to not do something that almost all other encyclopediasts have done, which is to mix together defensive statistics from different positions. I honestly don't know why they do this, but anyway, I didn't: I present defensive statistics for each player at only one position.

I once wrote that I thought that if some encyclopedia or reference book would just do that, it would destroy forever the notion that defensive statistics were meaningless. While that statement might have been overoptimistic, the point is that there are consistencies within defensive statistics which show that they are not random or meaningless events. A player who has a high range factor one year will have a high one the next, most of the time. Almost every player's range will decrease as he grows older, with the exception of the outfielders from the Babe Ruth generation, who were playing in a time in which more players began to uppercut the ball. Players who turn a lot of double plays one year or have a lot of assists one year will tend to do so again the next, and while range declines as the fielder ages, fielding averages tend to increase. Fielding records tend to hold their shape when a player moves from one team to another. These things would not happen if fielding records were truly meaningless.

I'll discuss fielding statistics and the role they play in the evaluation of a player's career more in the next article, and again periodically throughout this section.

C. GROSS VALUE

Other than the runs created estimates, the major statistical method that I have used to evaluate the players in this section is the calculation of what I call gross value. A player's gross value is the sum of his approximate values for all the seasons of his career.

Approximate values are simply a "count" of the number of positive things the player has done for his team—three points for hitting .300, two points for a slugging percentage over .400, one point for 20 stolen bases, that sort of thing. Unlike runs created, which have a specific one-to-one relationship to runs scored in baseball games, approximate values are meaningful only in relation to other approximate values. An approximate value for an average season might be 8 to 10; for an outstanding season, an MVP-type season, 16 to 18.

I used to call this simply "Career Approximate Value," or even shorten that to "Career Value," but I decided to switch to gross value in the process of answering a couple of readers' questions.

The foremost questions were, in essence, "How can Bobby Doerr have a greater approximate value than Billy Herman (182–153) when Herman has a better offensive won-lost record than Doerr (128–85 vs. 116–85)?" "How can Richie Ashburn have a greater career value than Duke Snider when Snider has a better offensive won-lost record?"

The general answer is that we use different methods to measure different things. There are many differences between the two methods. Offensive won/lost records are difficult to figure but attempt to be precise; approximate value is easier to figure but much less precise. Offensive won/lost records deal only with the offensive records of players; approximate values deal with everything a player does—hitting, fielding, pitching, all measured along the same scale. Offensive won-lost records are adjusted for context; approximate values are not.

The next question was "How can you rate Bill Terry sixtieth in your list of all-time greats and Fred Clarke seventieth when by your own estimates of approximate value Terry has 147 and Clarke 201?"

The answer to that question, and the more specific answer to the preceding ones, is the same: Career approximate value measures gross value. What we are trying to measure, in ranking players, is *net* value, not gross value. Net value is a much, much more difficult thing to measure, and I don't have a detailed statistical methodology to evaluate it—nor, indeed, do I believe it would be appropriate to develop one. In the rankings of Pete Palmer and Charles Faber, the statistical methods dictate the conclusions; indeed, it is not an overstatement to say that the results of the statistical methods *are* the conclusions. If their method says that Darrell Evans is a better player than Ernie Banks (Palmer) or that George Foster was a better player than Willie Stargell (Faber), they salute and say "Yes, sir," and that's what goes in the book.

I don't use statistics that way. I think baseball statistics are tremendously useful in understanding the game and in guiding conclusions—but they *guide* conclusions; they don't, standing independent of all other forms of analysis, dictate conclusions. Well, there are times when sabermetric analysis seems to leave only one possible conclusion, and thus it might be said that the method dictates the conclusion, but certainly not on this issue, not on who is better than whom. Statistical methods can only determine with certainty which of two players is better if two conditions apply—first, that the statistics considered evaluate accurately every aspect of the player's ability, and second, that the method employed to combine those statistics perfectly models the baseball universe. At present, no statistical analysis can meet either of those conditions—indeed, it is farcical, virtually obscene, to believe that we can meet either condition. There simply are too many things that we cannot know.

So we cannot truly measure net value. We can measure gross value; we can count all of the things that a player does. Those counts are not perfect, but they're not bad. Gross value and net value are related in the same way that gross income and profit (net income) are related. A company that has a gross income of a million dollars might show a profit of $250,000, or they might show a profit of $80,000, or they might show a profit of $5,000. They might even, in a rare situation, if there are serious miscalculations made, have a gross income of a million dollars and lose money. At the same time, gross income and profit are certainly very highly correlated among companies. IBM might lose money next year and Ed's Market might make money, but certainly the odds are overwhelming that IBM will make more profit than Ed's Market. Big companies not only take in more money than small companies, they also make more profit.

In looking at gross values, then (what I used to call career approximate value) you have the same relationships. A player with a gross value of 100 might have a net value of 25, or he might have a net value of 8, or he might even, in a rare situation, if there were serious miscalculations made, have a net value that is negative. In general, the greater the gross value, the greater the net value—but there are exceptions, limitations.

Net value is that portion of a player's contribution to the team which is a unique contribution toward winning the pennant, above the level of replaceable performance. Approximate values are set up so that two players who have 2000 hits apiece and 250 home runs apiece will tend to have about the same gross value, even if one player accomplished this in a ten-year period, and the other requires fifteen. The gross contributions of the two players would be the same, even though their value in the effort to win pennants would obviously be different.

If gross value isn't profit, you might ask, what is it?

It could be different things. It could be opportunity cost. It could be statistical illusion. It could be timeline bias or bias of many other sorts. Suppose that you have a player who bats 600 times. If the player gets 140 hits, does that have value? Certainly, yes; many of those 140 hits would contribute to victory. But does it have any *net* value? Probably not. If you took those 600 at bats and gave them to a AAA ballplayer off the street, he would probably get about 140 hits (a .233 average). What the player has done has value, but it is replaceable value. Hitters like that aren't going to win the pennant for you.

Compare him to a player who has 600 at bats, but 200 hits. He has only 43 percent more hits (200/140), but (assuming that the net value of the first player is zero) he has infinitely more net hits (60/0). Gross value, like approximate value, is unadjusted value. Or suppose that you have two players who have the same stats, but one of whom plays in Dodger Stadium and the other of whom plays in Wrigley Field, where compiling flashy batting stats is vastly easier. If their defensive skills and their baserunning abilities are the same, their approximate values would be the same—but their net value, their value once you let the air out, would be different.

It might be that baseball was a tougher game in the 1950s than it was in 1900. The approximate values of the players would not reflect this. These problems don't make the method useless; the method is still very useful. All statistics, like all ballplayers, have limitations. The Value Approximation Method is tremendously useful for some other issues, unrelated to what we are doing here. In comparing players, it is still a useful signpost. A player who has a gross value of 200 *probably* has a greater net value than a player who has a gross value of 150.

How much of gross value is net value? I might make a guess, though it is strictly a guess, that for an average player net value is 20 percent to 30 percent of gross value. For a great player, net value is probably 40 percent to 50 percent of gross value. So if Fred Clarke's net value is 35 percent of his gross value of 201 and Bill Terry's is 50 percent of his gross value of 147, who is more valuable?

We're *guessing*. We don't *know* who was actually a more valuable player than whom; I don't, you don't, Pete Palmer don't, Whitey Herzog don't and Bill Mazeroski don't, neither. Bill Mazeroski might use his playing experience to inform his judgment, but of course he didn't play against 90 percent of the players that he must rate. I use statistical analysis to inform my judgments, but I try to integrate that into a broader evaluation. Gross value is one of the things that I consider.

V. An Unavoidable Concern

■ There is, finally, one more question that must be answered before any evaluation of a player's greatness, whether mathematical or subjective, can be attempted. It's an obvious question, a roadblock of a question, and yet most of the people who have written about great players have not dealt with the question.

The question is this: When you ask who is a greater player than whom, do you want to know which one was more valuable at some moment in his career, or do you want to know which was more valuable over the course of his career? You absolutely, positively have to answer that question before you select your list of the greatest players ever. There is no standard or consensus answer to the question; some people mean one thing, some mean the other. The answer that it's some of one and some of the other won't do;

you have to decide. Because if you don't decide, you've got two correct answers to every question.

We can form models to answer either question. If you graph a player's career as a line, like this:

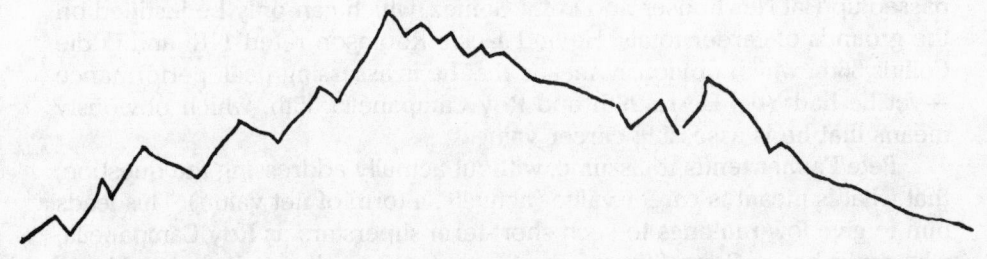

the two questions are 1) What is the highest point on the line? and 2) What is the total area under the line? We can find any number of ways to draw a line representing the career of any player—and on that basis, sabermetrics can answer either question for you, and develop methods that will yield ever more accurate answers. In answering the first question, "value" reaches a peak and remains there; in answering the second, value mounts up and up, as long as the player is active.

But you have to decide which answer you want. Take a few examples. Who was a greater left-handed pitcher, Warren Spahn or Sandy Koufax? If you want to know which was the more valuable pitcher at some moment in his career, it is absolutely clear that the answer is Koufax. If what you want to know is which pitcher was more valuable to his teams over the course of his entire career, it is equally clear that the answer is Spahn. Spahn won 198 more games than Koufax, and lost 158 more—meaning that he was, over his career, roughly as valuable as Koufax and Drysdale combined (Spahn was 363–245; Sandy and Don combined were 374–253).

Who was the greater third baseman, Al Rosen or Ron Santo? If you mean who was the greater at his best, obviously it was Al Rosen; if you mean who was the greater over the course of his career, obviously it was Ron Santo. Who was the greater reliever, Hoyt Wilhelm or Dick Radatz? Can't answer it unless I know which meaning is intended by the question. It doesn't do any good to say that it's both, because I don't know how to combine the two. You've got to decide which you're asking before you can hope to reach an answer.

And I'll give you another one, more argumentative, that puts you in the same position. Mantle and Mays. Over the course of his career, certainly Mays was a greater player than Mantle—yet it is just as clear that, at his best, Mantle was not only a greater player than Mays, but a *much* greater player than Mays. We'll argue about that later.

And yet, strangely, none of the people who compiled the lists of greatest players described in "Reference Points" showed any recognition that this problem existed. None stated explicitly that they were measuring career value, or that they were measuring peak value. All of them made selections which suggest that it is not clear in their own minds which meaning they intend. Allen had Koufax rated higher than Spahn, making it clear that, in that case, he was thinking of peak greatness, not career greatness. Yet on the other hand, he had Jim Kaat and Don Sutton among his top 100, while he passed up Hal Newhouser and Lefty Gomez, which can only be justified on the grounds of career totals. He had Jackie Robinson rated 11th and Eddie Collins 36th, which obviously means that he is assessing peak performance —yet he had Yogi Berra 29th and Roy Campanella 55th, which obviously means that he is assessing career value.

Pete Palmer tends to assume, without actually addressing the question, that what is meant is career value (actually, a form of net value). This leads him to give low rankings to such short-term superstars as Roy Campanella, who ranks below Gene Tenace, and Sandy Koufax, who ranks below Murry Dickson. Unfortunately, Pete made a critical mistake in defining career value, which also leads his career value lists to be skewed in a somewhat opposite fashion, resulting in truly eccentric listings. Charles Faber also aims toward career value (actually a form of gross value, career production with no attention to costs or context.)

Hitter and Ronig's standard is whatever the hell they feel like at the moment—career value, peak value or unadulterated whimsy. The Hall of Fame and the McCaffrey lists use either standard on occasion.

Which do I prefer, peak performance or career performance? I can't answer it. It's not like blondes or redheads, where you have a preference one way or the other. It's more like height and weight, where there is an absolute answer one way and an absolute answer the other, only our yardsticks and our scales have fuzzy digits, hard to read. I will give you the best answers I can give to both questions. I think it's silly to try to put them together.

VI. A Subjective Record

■ You possess, about each successful player of our time, an enormous fund of information, information that in twenty years' time it would be almost impossible to reconstruct. I have heard several people say that they have gotten so involved in the baseball of another era that they know more about the players of that era than the players of our own. I've found that that is almost never so, and indeed I wonder if it is even possible.

Pick a player—say, Mickey Rivers. You know so many things about Mickey. You probably remember how fast he was when he came up; that was all you heard about him for the first two years. You know how he walked on the field, with that pained, almost crippled gait, suddenly exploding into a blaze of speed when it was time to run. You know they called him "The Chancellor," and you probably know why. You know about his throwing arm, and can visualize him picking the ball off the wall in right-center and whirling, flapping like a goose and propelling the ball feebly in the direction of a cutoff man, with the throw most likely coming to earth fifteen feet short of target and a little to one side. You know the way he chopped down on the ball; you can probably call up the image of him fouling one off his foot, as he often did. You certainly remember him flipping the bat like a baton as he completed his swing. You remember Pete Rose staring down his throat, 25 feet in front of third base in the 1976 World Series. You know about the malapropisms for which he became famous late in his career, and could probably quote three or four of them from memory. You know about his fondness for the horses, and probably remember the stories about his placing bets between innings from the bullpen phone. You probably remember his minor conflicts with Billy Martin when Martin came to New York, trying to get him to work on his throwing. You may know how much Whitey Herzog thought of him as a player when he was young. You could probably call up a hundred things that you have seen him do on the field. One thing I remember is that he used to go back to the dugout a lot and get a rag to wipe his bat with.

So many things . . . so many mannerisms, witticisms, confrontations, friendships, habits, accomplishments, failures and customs—and yet he means nothing special to you; just another player. That you know what his playing skills were—that he could hit .300 and had great speed but little power, didn't walk very often—that goes without saying. Those things, the statistics, are but the merest fraction of what you know about him. And you know as much about two hundred other players—about Gary Matthews, Carlton Fisk, Steve Garvey, Darrell Porter, Joe Morgan, Bobby Grich, Don Baylor, Garry Templeton, Steve Carlton. About a few, such as Reggie Jackson and Pete Rose, you know far more.

To reconstruct that enormous library of information about the players of another era would be all but impossible; to reconstruct just the sense of one man would require that you read a biography of him—as, indeed, you have probably read a biography of Phil Niekro, a few words at a time, a biography splattered across twenty years of interviews and short blurbs in *The Sporting News*.

That is why I believe that, in evaluating players, much respect should be given to the opinions of the player's contemporaries, both afield and in the press box (or, for that matter, in the seats). It's not that they're always right; they're not. The sportswriters of the 1920s were as prone to misjudgments, mistaken impressions about the relative values of different accomplishments, and outright partisanship as are we today. But they knew so much more about those players than we do today, or than we ever can. If the sportswriters of his own time did not regard Bill Dickey as a great player—and they did not—we must assume that they had some reason for that. If the players who played against Buck Ewing and the sportswriters who reported about him regarded him as the greatest player of his time—and they did—we are not bound to agree with them, but we must respect the fact that they possessed far more knowledge than we can ever hope to obtain about him, about his contemporaries, and about the game they played.

The problem is that the way in which players are regarded changes so radically after they are retired; the way the players of the fifties or even the sixties are remembered even now is not exactly the way they were regarded while they were active, and it has but begun to shift. Some players, in retirement, continue to ascend to ever higher peaks of accomplishment, while others, regarded much more favorably in their time, begin to lose favor, and to see their talents reduced after they are no longer around to display them.

That is why I have tried, in writing this book, to pay careful attention to how players were regarded, not after the fact, but in their own time. I have tried to restore somewhat the image and reputation of the player as it existed when his sun was overhead.

One thing that is very helpful in this respect is award votes. Too many of us, in writing about award votes, are inclined to write about what is wrong with them—and indeed, there is always something wrong with them. But with that in mind, the value of awards has been too often understated. The value of awards is that they form an objective record of subjective judgments. I'm not talking about the Hall of Fame selections, which are mostly made twenty or thirty years (at least) after a player's best years, and by a badly designed voting system at that. I'm talking about the annual selections, which flash across the horizon, provide wire service copy for a few days, but tend to be forgotten as soon as the player retires. A careful look at how a player performed in the voting for these awards, I think, can tell us a lot about how he was regarded in his own time—and thus can do a lot to help restore an accurate picture of the player's reputation at the time when people were in the best position to evaluate him.

In compiling Section III, the player records, I have tried to draw up a history of the player's performance in award voting, to say what major awards he won, and to record in particular his position in the voting for the Most Valuable Player award. I have tried to make the player's performance in award voting a part of his permanent public record.

The Most Valuable Player votes are summarized in the notion of an Award Share, which I will explain in a moment. Most of you probably have in your library already a record of who *won* all of the Most Valuable Player votes. My notion was to make a record not only of what awards the player won, but of when he finished second, when he finished third, and when he drew no support at all. Why? Because I am trying to use the awards to form a clearer picture of how the player was regarded by the writers of his time. Whether he won the *honor* is not the question; the question is whether he won the respect of his contemporaries.

A couple of players who provide a good example of what I mean are two guys with the initials J. B. You may never have heard of either of them. One was a catcher for the Detroit Tigers in the early 1920s. His name was Johnny Bassler. Bassler played in the major leagues for only nine years, batting 2,319 times in his career. He never batted 400 times in a season. His lifetime average was .304, but he played in a time in which the good hitters hit .350. For example, in 1924 when Bassler hit a career-high .346, Rogers Hornsby hit .424, Babe Ruth .378, Zack Wheat .375, Charlie Jamieson .359, Ross Youngs .356, Kiki Cuyler .354, Bibb Falk .352, Eddie Collins .349, Edd Roush .348, and Harry Heilmann .346. Bassler's .346 average in 379 at bats didn't knock anybody's socks off, and it was by far the best of his career. He had no power (one career home run) and was known as the slowest player of his time, so that it was considered a phenomenon when he once stole home (October 1955, *Baseball Digest*).

Now look at the American League MVP votes for 1922 through 1924:

1922
1. George Sisler (59)
2. Eddie Rommel (31)
3. Ray Schalk (26)
4. Joe Bush (19)
5. Eddie Collins (18)
6. JOHNNY BASSLER (13)

1923
1. Babe Ruth (64)
2. Eddie Collins (37)
3. Harry Heilmann (31)
4. Joe Sewell (20)
   Wally Gerber (20)
6. Charlie Jamieson (19)
7. JOHNNY BASSLER (17)

1924
1. Walter Johnson (55)
2. Eddie Collins (49)
3. Charlie Jamieson (25)
4. Herb Pennock (24)
5. JOHNNY BASSLER (22)

Bassler played regularly in only two other seasons: 1921, for which there was no MVP award, and 1925, for which I was not able to find award voting. I don't know much else about Johnny Bassler—no mannerisms, no quotes, no memories; only this, and the statistics, and the statistics don't impress me. I believe he became an executive in the Pacific Coast League, and Cappy Gagnon says his strikeout and walk data are among the best ever. But I'll tell you: that man could play some baseball. The MVP selections for the American League at that time used basically the same form they do now, although there was just one voter for each team and there were some other rules. But for three straight years, a panel of presumably knowledgeable sportswriters, watching him play, reading his box scores and talking to his teammates, thought that Johnny Bassler was one of the best players in the American League. You've got to be impressed by that.

A similar case is Jimmy Brown, an infielder with the Cardinals from 1937 through 1943. Brown hit .279 lifetime with only nine home runs. He never really had a regular position, even for one year; he moved around every year between second base (392 games), third base (273), and shortstop (235). He wasn't a base stealer, he certainly wasn't an RBI man, and he never scored 90 runs in a season.

In 1939, hitting .298 with 3 homers and 51 RBI, Brown finished sixth in the MVP voting for the National League, just ahead of Joe Medwick (.332, 14, 117). In 1941, with about the same numbers, he finished fourth, ahead of all of his teammates, including Johnny Mize, Marty Marion, Enos Slaughter and Terry Moore. In 1942, hitting just .256 with one home run, Brown still finished thirteenth in the league's MVP balloting, ahead of the likes of Medwick, Moore, Bill Nicholson and Stan Hack, with far better statistics.

Whatever the reason for it, the people who saw Jimmy Brown play thought that he was something special. Maybe they thought that he hit well in the clutch. Maybe they thought he was a leader on the field or in the clubhouse. Maybe they thought he was a great fielder or a great baserunner, or both. You can look at his numbers and make some pretty good guesses, but it's not easy to know at this distance what it was about him that they liked. Maybe they were right, and maybe they were hallucinating. But there was sure something there that impressed people.

Sometimes there wasn't something there. There are other players who finished surprisingly poorly in MVP voting, despite good statistics. This too, I think, should be a part of the record. I'm taking a step here toward making it a part. Maybe sometime I'll publish the complete history of MVP voting.

For the explanation of Award Shares, let's use Mickey Mantle. The first time Mantle was mentioned on an MVP ballot was in 1952, at the age of twenty, when he drew 143 points in the balloting, finishing third. The maximum number of points possible in that vote was 336. Since 143 is 43 percent of 336, this is recorded as ".43 Award Share."

In 1953 Mantle drew only 4 points in the MVP voting; that's an Award Share of .01, and lifts him to a total of .44. In 1954, despite having his best statistics to that point (he led the league in runs scored, drove in 100 runs for the first time, and set a career high in homers with 27), Mickey was not in the top ten in the voting, which is all that I could find record of. He stays at .44 (if he was the eleventh man, his Award Share would have been no higher than .08). In 1955 he finished fifth in the voting with 113, an Award Share of .34. This brings him to .78. From then on:

Year	Pos.	Pts.	Possible	Share	Cumulative
1956	1st	336	336	1.00	1.78
1957	1st	233	336	.69	2.47
1958	5th	127	336	.38	2.85
1959	17th	13	336	.04	2.89
1960	2nd	222	336	.66	3.55
1961	2nd	198	280	.71	4.26
1962	1st	234	280	.84	5.10
1963		(No votes)			
1964	2nd	171	280	.61	5.71
1965	25th	3	280	.01	5.72

You probably know that Mantle was one of the few players to win three MVP awards; what you may not know is that he also finished second three times, third once, and fifth twice. In 1960 and 1961, he finished second to Roger Maris in what were, to that point, the two closest votes in the history of

American League voting. He missed the award by only three points in 1960, and by only four in 1961 (Dizzy Trout also missed by four in 1944).

This performance in MVP voting, while certainly quite impressive, is not the strongest showing in history. Who did draw the strongest support in the history of Most Valuable Player balloting? The answer was a surprise to me, and I'll wait a while to spring it on you. Of course, the history of award voting only completely covers a little less than half of baseball history; the MVP vote covers only a small portion of the careers of Ty Cobb and Babe Ruth, and does not completely cover players as recent as Lefty Grove. Still, surprisingly, several players have done better in award voting than Mickey. And a whole lot have done worse.

It's just evidence, that's all; it bears a certain weight. I wish there had been Gold Glove awards about twenty-five years sooner than there were. I'd love to know how the voting would have gone among Joe Gordon, Bobby Doerr and Jimmy Bloodworth, among Arky Vaughn, Billy Jurges and Dick Bartell.

I find that defense is one area in which subjective opinions, in the absence of the most careful and meticulous statistical analysis, simply have to be given a degree of weight. Pete Palmer, in assessing the greatest players in history, had Sam Crawford ranked surprisingly low (80th among non-pitchers). He would express the reason for this differently, but what it comes down to is that while Crawford is one of the greatest hitters ever (Pete has him ranked 24th), his range factors were not very good. From 1910 through 1916 he never made more than 1.54 plays per game.

Well, I put a certain weight on that. I certainly would like to know why Crawford's range factors were so low. But I can't justify, on the basis of such evidence, charging him a huge defensive penalty. All of the reports of the time—all of the people who saw him play—said he was a good outfielder, an outstanding outfielder when he was young. If there had been Gold Glove awards, and if he had failed to win one, then I might feel differently about that. But given a choice between the statistical evidence, in this case, and the evidence of the subjective record, I would have to give more credence to the subjective comments.

Sabermetrics is not numbers; sabermetrics is the search for better evidence. If subjective judgments can be drawn into the web of evidence, then we should welcome the aid. I would hope that, in ten years, we would know more than we do about many subjects as ancient as Sam Crawford's defense.

In ranking the 100 greatest players of all time, the first step will be to discuss and identify the greatest at each position. At each position we will begin by considering a group of twentieth-century players defined by (a) those in the Hall of Fame, (b) those in Maury Allen's *Baseball's 100,* (c) those in Ritter and Honig's *The 100 Greatest Baseball Players of All Time,* (d) those listed among the top 100 players or top 50 pitchers in Thorn and Palmer's *The Hidden Game,* and (e) those included in Section III of this book. That should pretty much cover it, but if there's anybody else that I particularly wanted to say anything about, I'll throw him in. The introduction to each player will contain his status within those various lists and honors.

There are three repeating references to things which appear in other parts of the book that I should cue in here for those of you who haven't yet read the whole thing. The descriptions of players as "Definition A" or "Definition D" Hall of Famers refer to an article that appears in the sub-section on the 1930s, in which I proposed some specific definitions that could be used to help determine whether a man should or should not be in the Hall of Fame. The comments about "peak value" and "career value," if not of self-evident meaning, are discussed in more detail in Article III-A of this section. At other times the analytical comments might refer to Articles II and III of this section. The offensive won/lost records are those which appear in Section III with the player data, except in a few cases.

There are two categories of players to whom we owe our regrets. Those are 1) players from the nineteenth century, and 2) players from the Negro Leagues. This section of the book is about the greatest players in baseball history, but it is also about how we distinguish among the greatest players in baseball history, as to who was greater than whom. There is no question that some of the players from each of those two excluded groups were greater players than many of those included here; my guess is that the top ten, if it could be completely reconstructed, would include Oscar Charleston, Satchel Paige and Buck Ewing. But much of the evidence that is needed to evaluate these players is not available, and it would be very difficult to reconstruct it. So we just have to consider those players, like the great stars of Japan or some other country, to be off the charts, not below these players but beside them on some other list.

We will deal with the candidates at each position in alphabetical order.

CATCHER

JOHNNY BENCH

HALL OF FAME? Not Eligible
DATA IN SECTION III? Yes
OFFENSIVE WON-LOST RECORD:
 137–84, .621
GROSS VALUE: 190 (highest of any catcher)

I once wrote that Johnny Bench was the greatest catcher in baseball history. I didn't write that, of course, in the context of a systematic effort to figure out who was

the best in baseball history, and in doing this I can't be worried about justifying what I wrote before.

YOGI BERRA

HALL OF FAME? Yes
DATA IN SECTION III? Yes
OFFENSIVE WON-LOST RECORD:
 134–74, .643
GROSS VALUE: 182
COMPARABLE RECENT PLAYERS:
Gary Carter. Berra is sort of a combination of Gary Carter and a dwarf.

Yogi Berra, and not Bill Dickey, was the greatest catcher in the history of the Yankees. Most of the opinions about the order in which the players rate that I will offer throughout this section are not firmly settled in my mind; there's some evidence on this side, there's some on the other. If I re-issue this book in a few years it seems likely that new evidence and new methods will have been developed that will lead to different conclusions with respect to many player rankings. But Yogi Berra *was* better than Bill Dickey; that is an absolutely clear verdict, supported by the overwhelming bulk of the evidence, and it is not likely that anyone will ever convince me otherwise.

The prevailing opinion, it is clear, is that Dickey was not only the greatest catcher in the history of the Yankees, but possibly the greatest in the history of the American League.

- Maury Allen, in picking the 100 greatest players, listed Dickey 19th, making him the greatest catcher of the century.

- Though not placing their 100 greatest players in order, Ritter and Honig wrote that "Until Johnny Bench came along to muddy the waters, the choice for the greatest all-time catcher lay between Dickey and his fiery contemporary, Mickey Cochrane."

- Palmer's methods assessed Gabby Hartnett as the greatest catcher of all time, with

Cochrane second, Dickey third and Berra fourth, although the four of them (and Bench, in fifth place) are drawn in a rather tight knot between 35.8 (meaning that they believe Hartnett to have been 35.8 games better than an average major league catcher over the course of his career) and 31.2.

- When major league baseball was celebrating its centennial in 1971, all-time all-star teams were selected for each team. Bill Dickey was selected as the Yankees' greatest catcher.

- *Sport* magazine has brought out a book several times called *Sport Magazine's All-Time All-Stars,* which contains articles about each of the twenty-two players regarded as the greatest at each position for each league. Bill Dickey is considered by the editors of this publication as the greatest catcher in American League history.

- In a 120-man poll of the BBWAA in 1958, Bill Dickey was selected as the greatest catcher in American League history.

- The players polled by the McCaffreys in "Players' Choice" chose Johnny Bench as the greatest catcher of all time, followed by Dickey and then Berra.

To confront the undivided opinion of so many knowledgeable men requires an

unusually heavy burden of proof; that, at least, is the only justification I can offer for writing a 3,000-word article on the subject. The proof that I offer divides into three categories and seeks to establish three essential points:

1) Berra's statistics, in the context of their time and place, are clearly superior to Dickey's. Berra was the greater hitter.

2) The men who saw him play, *at the time when he was active,* were far, far more impressed by Berra than they were by Dickey.

3) The careful consideration of such unmeasurable and elusive values as "defense" and "contribution to winning teams" weighs heavily on the side of Berra, rather than Dickey, as the greatest catcher that the Yankees have had.

1) Offensive Performance

Dickey's statistics are impressive, and there is no doubt that he was a fine hitter. He hit .313 for his career, hitting over .300 from 1929 to 1939 except for one year, and he hit with power, 202 career home runs. His triple crown statistics from 1936 through 1939 are loaded:

YEAR	HR	RBI	Avg.
1936	22	107	.362
1937	29	133	.332
1938	27	115	.313
1939	24	105	.302

But, of course, we must then face the question of what those statistics mean in their own time: In the time and place at which the player was active, how many wins and how many losses would likely result from these statistics?

You can get an idea of where each player stands among the best players of his own time by looking at the categories in which the player led the league or came close to so doing. I'll use the lists of league leaders that appear in Macmillan's *Baseball Encyclopedia,* which contain the top five in the league for major categories and the top three for minor categories, as a convenient reference:

CATEGORIES IN WHICH PLAYER WAS AMONG LEAGUE LEADERS:
Bill Dickey
    1936, Batting Average, third
    1936, Slugging Percentage, fifth
    1937, RBI, fourth

Yogi Berra
    1949, Slugging Percentage, fifth
    1950, RBI, third
    1950, Runs Scored, fourth
    1950, Total Bases, third
    1951, Home Runs, fourth
    1951, Total Bases, fourth
    1952, Home Runs, third
    1952, RBI, fifth
    1952, Home Run Percentage, third
    1953, Home Runs, fourth
    1953, RBI, fourth
    1953, Slugging Percentage, third
    1953, Total Bases, fourth
    1954, Batting Average, fifth
    1954, RBI, second
    1954, Total Bases, third
    1955, Home Runs, fourth
    1955, RBI, third
    1956, Home Runs, third
    1956, Slugging Percentage, fourth
    1956, Total Bases, fifth
    1956, RBI, fourth

Bill Dickey played in a time in which teams scored many more runs than they did in Berra's era. The most explosive offensive season in which Berra was active was 1950, when the average American League team scored 5.04 runs per game. In Dickey's years, the league exceeded that average nine times. In 1936 the average American League team scored 5.67 runs per game.

But in his own time, Dickey was never one of the leading offensive players. Bill Dickey never led the league in any offensive category; neither did Yogi Berra. But Dickey finished third in one category, fourth in one, fifth in one. Berra finished third in nine categories, fourth in nine, and fifth in four. Year in and year out, Berra was among the top players in the league in the most important offensive categories.

That's an informal approach; the formal approach, of course, is to calculate the number of runs that the player has created, and then to place that in the context of the league by expressing it as a number of offensive "wins" and "losses." Dickey's career offensive winning percentage was .626, which is good. Berra's was .643. Further, Berra sustained that effort over a longer period of time— 331 more games, 1,255 more at bats. In the context of his own time, Berra was clearly a greater hitter than Dickey.

2) The Impressions of Contemporary Observers

The Most Valuable Player awards, and the voting that goes with them, are important to us for one reason: They provide the best record—indeed, the best possible record —of the value that players are perceived as having at the time they are active. It is a subjective record, compiled by on-the-scene, informed observers. It is not always right, but it deserves respect.

Bill Dickey never won an MVP award. Yogi Berra won the award three times. Not once, not twice, but three times a group of the most qualified observers in the country watched him play a season and said, "Yogi Berra is the best player in the American League." Think about that.

And he won those three awards when he was having seasons that were not any better than the rest of his career. He won the MVP award in 1951, when he hit .294 with 27 homers and 88 RBI, but he didn't win it in 1950, when he hit .322 with 28 and 124, or 1953, when he hit .296 with 27 and 108. He didn't win, but he didn't miss by much, either; he finished third in the voting in 1950 and second in 1953. In addition to winning the vote three times, Berra finished second twice, third once, and fourth once. He finished in the top four in the MVP balloting for seven straight seasons, 1950–1956, and even in 1959 and 1960, when he was hitting less than 20 homers and driving in less than 70 runs, he still drew significant support in the MVP balloting.

Then you take a look at the MVP support for Bill Dickey, or lack thereof. In 1931, the year of the first BBWAA poll, Dickey hit .327. He did not finish in the top ten of the voting, which was all I could find record of, and did not draw a single vote in the *The Sporting News'* competing MVP poll. Two American League catchers figured in the voting. Mickey Cochrane finished eighth in the *TSN* poll and tenth in the BBWAA. Roy Spencer of the third-place Senators, who hit .275 with one home run and 60 RBI, drew 6 points—a 9 percent share of the vote.

In 1932 the Yankees won the pennant, their first pennant in four years. Dickey hit .310 with career highs in home runs (15) and RBI (84). Rick Ferrell, who hit .315 with 2 homers and 65 RBI for a sixth-place team, finished seventh in *The Sporting News* vote for the Most Valuable Player, with sixteen points. Bill Dickey, again, was not mentioned.

I have the 1933 BBWAA vote. Dickey hit .318 with 14 homers, 97 RBI for the second-place Yankees. He drew 9 points in the balloting, finishing in a tie for twelfth. He tied with Rick Ferrell, who hit .290 with 4 homers and 77 RBI and was traded in mid-season from the team that finished last in the league to the team

that finished next-to-last.

In 1934 Dickey hit .322 and led the league's catchers in home runs (12). The Yankees again finished second. Mickey Cochrane was the MVP. Dickey was not mentioned on any ballot. In 1935 Dickey had an off year, hitting .279 but leading the league's catchers in home runs (14) and RBI (81). Two catchers finished in the top ten in the MVP voting, and a third was mentioned. Dickey was not mentioned.

In 1936 Dickey had a great season, hitting .362 with 22 homers and 107 RBI. The Yankees won the pennant. He finished fifth in the MVP voting, ten points behind Charlie Gehringer, who hit .354 with 15 homers, and two points ahead of a first baseman who hit .321 with 16 homers and a pitcher with a 4.63 ERA. In 1937 he had perhaps his greatest statistical season, hitting .332 with 29 homers and 133 RBI. He finished in a fifth-place tie in the voting, with a catcher named Luke Sewell. Sewell had hit .269 with one home run for a third-place team. Think about that one a while.

After that Dickey did start to draw some respect in the MVP voting. Driving in 115 runs in 1938, he finished second in the MVP balloting. In 1939 he finished sixth again.

Dickey had an off season in 1940, and was not mentioned in the voting. In 1941, he had a decent comeback, and finished thirteenth in the voting. In 1942, as a half-time

player, he finished seventeenth in the MVP vote, and in 1943, as a half-time player in a war-depleted league, he hit .351 and finished eighth in the MVP voting.

But for their careers as a whole, there just isn't any comparison. Berra was regarded as one of the great players of his time, at the time that he was active; Dickey had to out-hit Luke Sewell by 60 points just to break even with him in the MVP voting. He simply was not regarded by the observers of his own era as a great player.

Berra played in fifteen All-Star games including two in 1960; Dickey, granting that the All-Star game did not start until Dickey's fifth year in the league, played in only eight. And read between the lines of this passage from *Sport Magazine's All-Time All-Stars* (which, by the way, is a pretty good book; better than it has any right to be). Remember, the writer is explaining to us why Bill Dickey should be considered the greatest catcher in American League history:

After New York had beaten the Cincinnati Reds four straight in the World Series, losing pitcher Paul Derringer reversed protocol and asked a writer who he thought was the most valuable Yankee. "Joe DiMaggio," the writer said, well aware of Joe's batting averages (.313 for the series and .381 for the season) and fielding proficiency. "Nope, not for my money," Derringer said, shaking his head. "From what I've seen in this Series, I'll take Bill Dickey."

Dickey had beaten Derringer with a ninth-inning single in Game One and had homered off of him in Game Four, which helps explain the sentiment. But first of all, who is the writer calling here as his expert witness? Joe McCarthy? Nope. (McCarthy, Dickey's manager for most of his career, was quoted as saying that the greatest catcher he ever saw was Mickey Cochrane.) Connie Mack? Nope. Ted Williams? Bob Feller? Red Ruffing? Nope. A National League pitcher, who probably had not seen Bill Dickey catch ten games in his life.

And second, note that this comes as a complete surprise to the writer, who (later) asks why he would make such a selection. Suppose that this was the 1976 World Series, rather than 1939. If you were asking a passing writer who he thought was the most valuable member of the Redleg juggernaut, and you were trying to prove it was Johnny Bench, don't you think you could find somebody who would get it in less than three guesses? Would you quote Ed Figueroa as your expert witness?

The point isn't that Dickey wasn't a fine player. He was. The point is that strange things happen to the reputations of players after they are retired. Yogi was always kind of a funny-looking little guy; he looked like if he was a piece of furniture you'd sand him off some. After he was retired, Joe Garagiola spent all

those years telling funny stories about the kind of dopey stuff Yogi used to say and do. Of course he didn't mean to do Yogi any harm, and he didn't, directly. But gradually the image of Yogi as a kind of short, knobby comic-book reader grew larger and larger, and the memory of Yogi Berra as one hell of a catcher kind of drooped into the background. As for the quiet, distinguished Bill Dickey, well, as soon as he was retired the league bat batting averages dropped about twenty points, and his statistics began to look much more awesome than they really were. But the evidence on how they were regarded by their contemporaries is very, very clear.

3) Other Contributions to the Winning Effort

"Perhaps the most significant statistic next to Bill Dickey's name," wrote Maury Allen, "is the eight World Series teams that he played on." Well, yes, but Yogi Berra played on almost twice that many.

Yogi Berra played for the most dominant team in baseball history; that is a fact. The Yankees were so dominant for so long that there is a tendency to let it all run together and say that they won almost every year from 1920 through 1964. But they didn't. From 1947 through 1963, seventeen years, they failed to win the pennant only three times. By contrast, in the ten years that

Gehrig and Ruth played together, the Yankees won only four pennants. In the six years that Gehrig, Ruth, and Dickey were together, they won but two pennants. Let's make a little chart out of that. Not counting seasons in which the player played 10 games or less:

Berra	14 of 17	82%
Dickey	8 of 16	50%

And yet, strangely, the talent of the fifties doesn't seem nearly as impressive. The Yankees of Bill Dickey's time had Ruth, Gehrig, DiMaggio, Ruffing, Gomez, Pennock, Waite Hoyt, Combs . . . so many Hall of Famers. The Yankees of Berra's time had only Mantle, Berra and Ford—yet they won with much greater consistency. And they had this habit of winning the pennant with a bunch of pitchers like Bob Grim, Johnny Kucks, Bob Turley and Ryne Duren, who weren't even any good except when they pitched for the Yankees.

Why is that? You tell me. Had the game gotten easier? Was there less talent around? The big differences between the eras are the breaking of the color line in 1947, the establishment of the organized farm systems (which few teams had until the forties), and night baseball. I don't really figure that any of those made the game easier, and I don't really think any of them made the level of talent in the leagues any weaker. In fact, I figure the game that Berra, Mantle, Stengel and Ford dominated in the fifties was as tough a competition as there ever was. But Yogi's team was the only team, ever, to sustain dominance for so long a period.

Defense? Neither Yogi nor Dickey played at a time when there was a great emphasis on the running game, as Johnny Bench did. Probably neither would have been the Gold Glove catcher of his time, if Gold Gloves had been awarded. Jim Hegan was the outstanding defensive catcher in the American League in the fifties, Rick Ferrell and Luke Sewell were the best in the thirties. But both were recognized as outstanding handlers of the pitching staff.

Pete Palmer has dredged up some data on opposition stolen bases in the years 1931 to 1934. That data (unpublished) shows that Roy Spencer of Washington and Cleveland was the most difficult catcher to run on at that time, with Luke Sewell close behind; Dickey was a little better than average. At a SABR convention a few years ago, I asked Roy Hughes, an American League base stealer of the late thirties, who he remembered as the toughest catchers of his time to steal against. The first man he mentioned was Rollie Hemsley, then Ferrell, Sewell; when I threw out Dickey's name he said, "Oh, sure. Dickey was tough, too."

From whence, then, comes the notion that Dickey was a greater player than Berra? A lot of it is simply a misunderstanding of the statistics, being captivated by those gaudy batting averages. Let me put it this way: You either have to adjust the batting performances of 1921–1939 downward, or else you have to conclude that all of the greatest players who ever lived played between 1921 and 1939.

Palmer's method? Palmer rates Berra ahead of Dickey on the sum of batting, baserunning and fielding, but behind him by a hair on the basis of a "position bonus," which I think means that the catchers of Dickey's era were, as a group, worse hitters than the catchers of Berra's era. I don't buy the reasoning, and besides, how seriously can you take a system that rates Gene Tenace thirty-five notches ahead of Roy Campanella? The statistical method for evaluating catchers defensively is so bad that the authors are forced to acknowledge three times that it doesn't really work.

Whatever, I think the evidence is overwhelming. Yogi Berra may not be the greatest catcher of all time, but he is certainly the greatest in the history of the Yankees.

ROGER BRESNAHAN

HALL OF FAME? Yes
DATA IN SECTION III? Yes
OFFENSIVE WON-LOST RECORD:
82–48, .633
GROSS VALUE: 99
COMPARABLE RECENT PLAYERS:
Manny Sanguillen

Roger Bresnahan was a catcher in the first decade of this century, elected to the Hall of Fame a few weeks after his death in December of 1944. This has been a controversial selection, but then few men's careers were ever more blessed with controversy. To recount briefly the highlights, Bresnahan first appeared in the major leagues as an 18-year-old pitcher on August 28, 1897, pitching for the Washington Senators in the National League. He pitched a six-hit shutout, and showed "a speedy shoot, an outcurve, an inshoot and a drop ball." Veteran catcher Deacon McGuire was impressed, and said that Bresnahan was made of "the right stuff." He won four games without a loss for Washington that fall, then was released the next spring in a dispute over how much money such a phenom should be paid. That should give you an idea of Roger's temperament, and also why the Senators were so terrible, and terrible they were.

Anyway, Bresnahan resurfaced as one of John McGraw's men on the Orioles, and then the Giants, in the first years of this century. A 5'9", 200-pounder who was fast and strong and agile and aggressive, Roger became one of McGraw's best friends, and played every position on the field for him. He caught in 1901, then moved to the outfield, primarily center, from 1902 to 1904. In 1903 he hit .350. In 1905 he became the Giants' catcher, apparently at the urging of Christy Mathewson.

During 1907 and the fabulous sustained pennant race of 1908, Bresnahan introduced two new pieces of equipment in an effort to stay in the lineup and catch more games than the 85–100 that were normal for a catcher at that time. One was the shin guards, which, like all developments in baseball from the curve ball to sabermetrics, was widely ridiculed and universally adopted within a few years. The other was a padded face mask, which also caught on. He caught 139 games in 1908, while George Gibson of Pittsburgh, also adopting the equipment, caught 140, astonishing figures at the time.

That winter Stanley Robison, the owner of the St. Louis Cardinals, moaned during a National League meeting that his manager, John McCloskey, had finished last in 1908 with the best pitching staff in the league. He let it be known that he was looking for a new man, and word of this got to John McGraw. McGraw, knowing that Bresnahan wanted to manage (what Bresnahan really wanted, one suspects, was

to be John McGraw), and perhaps sensing that Roger's workload had taken a toll on his legs, set up a meeting between Bresnahan and Robison. When the two of them reached an agreement, McGraw then extorted three players from St. Louis (Red Murray, Bugs Raymond and Admiral Schlei) in exchange for Bresnahan, who became player/manager of the Cardinals.

As manager he took over a 49–105 team that had traded its two best players, Murray and Raymond, to acquire him. He brought the team slow progress, to 54–98 in 1909, 63–90 in 1910, and 75–74 in 1911.

Bresnahan was a throwback to the Irish nineties. Almost every paragraph written about him seemed to include the adjective "fiery." He was one of those guys that if you were on his team and played hard he was as nice to you as could be, but if you got on his bad side you'd think he was the Breath of Hell. The 1910 *Reach Guide* reported that "Bresnahan's numerous disputes with, and ejections by, the umpires, in their cumulative effect, caused his team much loss in prestige and possible victories. In all other respects Bresnahan . . . scored a decided success, as he infused aggressiveness and ambition and kept the team keyed up to its best efforts nearly all season." In 1911 the same publication reported

that the St. Louis catching "was inefficient when Bresnahan was off duty, and he was off a great deal due to frequent suspension for umpire-baiting." A 1910 order from the league office to control vile and unbecoming conduct toward the umpires cited Bresnahan, and only Bresnahan, by name. At the winter meetings that year he became involved in a loud argument with President Murphy, of the Chicago club, in the lobby of the Waldorf Hotel, after which he asserted that Murphy had impugned his honor and gone so far as to call him a liar. This incident was argued about in the public presses for a year following, and was of such proportion that at the league meeting the next year Garry Herrmann, chairman of the National Commission, spoke about it in his address. "I refer to the accusations of Manager Bresnahan, of the St. Louis National League Club, that President Charles W. Murphy, of the Chicago Nationals, openly impugned his motives in the performance of an official act and branded him as a liar in a hotel lobby. Such incidents serve to discredit those in control of clubs and to bring the league with which they are associated into disrepute," Herrmann said, and went on to propose a system of reviews and punishments to follow any such future incident. Yet in spite of this record, Bob O'Farrell in *The Glory of Their Times* remembered Bresnahan kindly, and said that "aside from Bresnahan, nobody helped me any."

In the spring of 1911 Robison died and Lady Bee Britton, remembered as the prettiest young woman ever to own a baseball team, inherited the Cardinals. In the inimical manner of owners of all gender and appearance, Lady Bee began to criticize Bresnahan's managing, in public, and when he confronted her about this relations between the two of them deteriorated quickly. Apparently he used much the same selection of his vocabulary to address the lady that he used on the field. Bresnahan and Britton feuded, the team foundered, and Bresnahan was fired.

This involved him in a monstrous salary hassle, when he insisted, of all things, that the Cardinals honor his contract and pay him both as a player and on the managing contract. He had signed a five-year contract with Robison shortly before Robison's death, and had four years left on it. He refused to report until he was traded, couldn't clear waivers, was shipped to Chicago and continued the battle from there, supported by the infant Player's Union. He eventually won a $20,000 settlement, equivalent to about $230,000 in the late eighties. He later managed the Cubs for a year, but they had an off year, and he was not destined to be John McGraw, after all.

Was he a great player? He was a very good player. He was built like a tank, but nimble on his feet, strong and fast and smart, with a terrific arm. He caught 100 games only the one time, but in his era that wasn't unusual. He led the league in only one offensive category (walks, 1908) and wasn't too close in many others, yet his offensive winning percentage, .633, is in the same range as the other Hall of Fame catchers. Three things helped him get into the Hall of Fame—the shin guards, the timing of his death, and a comment that Fred Lieb wrote about him in *The St. Louis Cardinals, the Story of a Great Baseball Club*, published in 1944, which accentuated the normal emotional support that follows the death of any player. Lieb wrote that "Bresnahan was a great catcher, one of the greatest of all time. Roger was really an all-around player, who could have starred at any position." He made several other complimentary references to Bresnahan in that book, and none of them was exactly false. John B. Foster in 1938 named Bresnahan as the second-greatest catcher of all time, behind Buck Ewing.

But Bresnahan was never regarded, while active, as the outstanding catcher of his time. Johnny Kling was. I tend to think that that was an injustice, and that Bresnahan really was the better. He was one of those players, like Bill Dickey and Joe Sewell, whose star ascended after his retirement. He coached for John McGraw in the twenties and was a popular figure with the New York press, which no doubt aided the cause. He was outstanding offensively and defensively, but only for about five years. He was an innovator, and he was a presence. As a player he was no better than Wally Schang, Duke Farrell, Bob O'Farrell, Deacon McGuire, Charlie Bennett, Joe Torre or many others, yet neither was he the absolute bottom of the Hall of Fame barrel. Whether that should put him inside or outside, I don't know how to tell you.

ROY CAMPANELLA

HALL OF FAME? Yes
DATA IN SECTION III? Yes
OFFENSIVE WON-LOST RECORD:
72–48, .602
GROSS VALUE: 122

If Roy Campanella had been healthy for three or four more years, there would be no dispute about who was the greatest catcher of all time. And you know what? You can say the same about two or three other catchers, at a minimum —Bench, Cochrane, possibly Hartnett. They all had terrific seasons, but they all were dragged down by injuries. It's a tough position.

GARY CARTER

HALL OF FAME? Not Eligible
DATA IN SECTION III? No
OFFENSIVE WON-LOST RECORD:
120–68, .638
GROSS VALUE: 160

With the sole exception of Yogi Berra, no catcher in baseball history can match Gary Carter in terms of year-in, year-out offensive and defensive performance. Other catchers were greater. Johnny Bench had better years than Carter. Roy Campanella and Mickey Cochrane had better years. But all of those players had good years, and then they had bad years. Only Carter and Berra were among the best players in the league year-in and year-out for a period longer than three years.

Carter's career totals, as a hitter, are already impressive. As a power hitter he will match up with any catcher except Bench and Berra. As a defensive player he owes no apologies, although he can no longer throw. He has played for six teams that won 90 or more games. He is one of few catchers in baseball history who has led the league in a major offensive category.

MICKEY COCHRANE

HALL OF FAME? Yes
DATA IN SECTION III? Yes
OFFENSIVE WON-LOST RECORD:
97–45, .683
Offensive winning percentage is highest among catchers.
GROSS VALUE: 154

Cochrane was beyond any doubt a Definition-A Hall of Famer. He was a complete offensive player. He hit for average with tremendous secondary averages (career average of .320, secondary average of .336). He hit over .330 several times, slugged over .500 several years in a row, drew 100 walks twice, almost never struck out and had excellent speed. He was an outstanding defensive player and a great on-field leader. He was voted the Most Valuable Player in the league twice, by the league panel in 1928 and by the BBWAA in 1934. I think it unlikely that many observers of the era would have considered Bill Dickey to be his equal. Competing against Dickey and Hartnett, Cochrane was selected *The Sporting News* All-Star in 1925, 1928, 1929, 1930, 1931, 1934, and 1935 (1925 was his rookie season, 1935 the last season in which he was healthy).

Cochrane's offensive winning percentage was the highest of any catcher, but that could be misleading for two reasons. One was the decentralization of batting statistics that takes place in a high-average era. As conditions for hitting become more favorable, different players have unequal abilities to take advantage of the conditions, with the result being that, while the league offensive winning percentage will stay at .500, that of the best players will move higher and that of the worst lower. The other reason is that Cochrane's career was shortened by injuries, thus removing the statistics of his decline phase from the picture. Yogi Berra's career offensive won/lost record through 1956 was 92–46, similar to Cochrane's record, but Berra continued to play for several years after that, with declining effectiveness.

In 1936 Cochrane, to quote the 1937 *Reach Guide,* "broke down in health in mid-season and had to leave the team and go to Wyoming to recuperate." When he returned he resumed the stressful player/manager position, just a couple of months after the departure, which seems strange. Anyway, the next spring Cochrane suffered health problems that were even more serious. In late May he was hit square in the head by a fastball from Bump Hadley of the Yankees. There had been hard feelings in the series between the Tigers and the Yankees, and it has always been whispered that Hadley was throwing at him. For several days afterward Cochrane lay unconscious and near death; an operation had to be performed to relieve the pressure within his skull. He survived, but the doctors told him another beaning, even if far less serious, could well be fatal. He wanted to play baseball again anyway, but the Tigers' owner would not hear of it. He attempted to manage, but without the old enthusiasm, and he retired in mid-season in favor of a long vacation in Europe, which was said to do him much good.

BILL DICKEY

HALL OF FAME? Yes
DATA IN SECTION III? Yes
OFFENSIVE WON-LOST RECORD:
  106–63, .626
GROSS VALUE: 171

Another misunderstanding about Dickey has to do with his power. Throughout most of his seventeen-year career, Dickey hit with little power, totaling 100 home runs in thirteen of those seventeen years. From 1936 through 1939 he became adept at jerking the ball down the short right-field line at Yankee Stadium, and he hit 102 home runs in those four years—77 of them at home. In 1938, he hit .357 with 23 homers, 83 RBI in 64 games at Yankee Stadium, but .274 with 4 homers, 32 RBI in 68 games on the road, one of the most phenomenal home/road differentials in history. Throughout his career Dickey hit for a higher average on the road (.316) than in Yankee Stadium (.309), but two-thirds of his home runs were hit at home.

RICK FERRELL

HALL OF FAME? Yes
DATA IN SECTION III? No
OFFENSIVE WON-LOST RECORD:
  Approximately 82–91, .474
GROSS VALUE: 123
COMPARABLE RECENT PLAYERS:
Bob Boone

Recently elected to the Hall of Fame. An outstanding de-fensive catcher, but the number three catcher in the A.L. in his own time. His election implies that Definition D of a possible Hall of Famer is in use by the Veterans' Committee.

CARLTON FISK

HALL OF FAME: Not Eligible
DATA IN SECTION III? No
OFFENSIVE WON-LOST RECORD:
  114–87, .568
GROSS VALUE: 164

Let me point out a curious thing to you. Through the whole history of baseball, the workload that pitchers were expected to carry has declined steadily, being less in every generation than in the previous one. In early baseball pitchers were expected to pitch every day, and then four times a week, and then three and then there was a four-man rotation. For several generations, there was a gradual attrition in the number of complete-game pitchers, pitchers expected to finish their work most of the time. That trend eventually reached maturity, there being no pitchers left who completed most of their games, but just in the last fifteen years we have seen a gradual shift from four- to five-man rotations. The workload expected of outstanding pitchers has declined from the first day of professional baseball, and is still declining.

At the same time, the workload expected of catchers has increased with the same implacability, being in every generation ever so slightly more than in the previous. Did any catcher catch a hundred games in a season in the nineteenth century? Certainly not often, if at all. In the twentieth century we have seen the development of equipment, like shin guards, better face masks, better chest protectors, gloves with extra padding, shoes with metal toes, all intended to protect the catcher even more, and thus keep him in the lineup more and more.

Other things have contributed to these changing expectations. One is the disappearance of double headers. Catchers used to get an automatic off day every week when the team played a double header. Another is free agency. When the team owned the player's career, it was in the best interest of the team not to overwork a star catcher, not to destroy his knees. Now, since the team is paying for every bit of talent that it takes from the player, it has no paternalistic interest in protecting his future.

The case of Carlton Fisk, I think, provides evidence that the current generation of catchers may be overworked. Remember, Carlton was hurt a lot early in his career, playing only 52 games in 1974, only 79 in 1975, only 91 in 1979. Carlton Fisk, Johnny Bench, Thurman Munson, Bob Boone and Ray Fosse were all born in 1947. Their career totals in major league games caught by

1975 were Bench, 1,130; Munson, 808; Fosse, 706; Fisk, 398; and Boone, 392. The catchers who were worked hard as young men have long since been gone. OK, Munson was struck by a random fate, but even then, even in 1979, Munson's knees and back were hurting him. A lot. And he had lost a great deal of his offensive value over the previous two years. In my opinion his best years were unquestionably behind him. Fisk and Boone, the catchers who weren't overloaded when they were young, have had the longest careers among the group.

I think you've really got to wonder if perhaps we aren't asking our catchers to do too much these days. There aren't that many good catchers around, you know? Terry Kennedy played for the American League in the All-Star game last year. Would it really hurt the Cubs that much, when they are playing, let's say, Atlanta—which is a bad team and in the other division and doesn't have much speed—to give Jody Davis a day off, and maybe put a left-handed hitter in? If they think Jody Davis is going to catch 150 games a year for 15 years, they're kidding themselves.

BILL FREEHAN

HALL OF FAME? No
DATA IN SECTION III? Yes
OFFENSIVE WON-LOST RECORD:
  102–74, .580
GROSS VALUE: 128

A power hitter, a five-time Gold Glove catcher, recognized as a leader on the Tigers of the sixties, Freehan was third in the MVP voting in 1967 and second in 1968. He would be in the Hall of Fame if Definition D was applied, and would be marginal under Definition C. A better player than Ferrell, Schalk or possibly Bresnahan.

GABBY HARTNETT

HALL OF FAME? Yes
DATA IN SECTION III? Yes
OFFENSIVE WON-LOST RECORD:
  117–62, .654
GROSS VALUE: 169

Generally recognized as the greatest National League catcher before Johnny Bench.

ERNIE LOMBARDI

HALL OF FAME? Yes
DATA IN SECTION III? Yes
OFFENSIVE WON-LOST RECORD:
  99–63, .610
GROSS VALUE: 135
COMPARABLE RECENT PLAYERS: Joe Torre

Ernie Lombardi was a huge man, with huge, oak-trunk legs and huge feet and huge hands and a promontory with nostrils that protruded from a lumpy face. He had huge arms and wrists like giant power cables that snapped around an unnaturally large bat, the

heaviest used by any player of his time, and flicked the ball effortlessly wherever he wanted it to go. As he got older he acquired a huge belly, which he lugged around with a huge effort.

His knees were too low to the ground, and his center of gravity was four feet behind him, so that he was never endowed by nature with adequate speed. As he got older he slowed down, becoming surely the slowest player ever to play major league baseball well. The slowest player today is probably Butch Wynegar, and my guess is that if they raced three times around the bases Butch would lap him.

Ernie Lombardi was born in Oakland on April 6, 1908. He attended Cole Elementary School through the eighth grade, closing the books on his education at that time, which must have been in 1922. His Italian parents ran a family grocery store, where Ernie helped out for the next several years when not playing baseball on the corner lot or at Bayview Park, where he spent hour after hour working through games with a childhood friend named Abe Rose. In 1926 he played a few games with the Oakland Oaks of the Pacific Coast League, whom he joined for real the next year. Being regarded as a little raw for this powerful minor league, Lombardi was dispatched to Ogden in the Utah-Idaho league, where he hit .398 for 50 games, earning a

ERNIE LOMBARDI

ball circles and a .370 batting average."

Introduced to Uncle Robbie (Mgr. Robinson), the big man with the big nose said, "I'm Lombardi, from Oakland." He said this in a tone that, according to Reynolds, seemed to announce as well that he would lick any man in the house for two dollars. "He weighs 220 pounds right now but he isn't fat. He stands six foot two and his hands are like two enormous hams hanging at the end of his arms. He totes a 42-ounce bat, the heaviest on the club, and as far as any of the players could recall the heaviest in the league . . . (the other players) raised incredulous eyelids at the strange apparition."

Less impressed, Uncle Robbie told him that he would never remember a name like Lombardi and that from now on he was Lumbago, and asked him where his golf clubs were. Lombardi sneered at the idea of a ballplayer playing golf. He and Uncle Robbie were quick friends.

In the minors he had been called Bochy Lombardi, after a game he played as a kid ("It's something like bowling," he said), but his rebirth as a major league player required, in those days, a rechristening with a new name. The fact that Lumbago was a tremendous line drive hitter was immediately apparent, and drew much comment in the papers before he even played in an

quick recall to his hometown of Oakland. In three full seasons in the Pacific Coast League, Ernie hit within a few points of .370 each year, hitting over 20 homers and driving in over 100 runs in 1929 and 1930.

Lombardi was sold that winter to the Brooklyn Dodgers, for $50,000 (about $350,000 in today's terms). The Dodgers, who were managed by a huge old catcher (Wilbert Robin-son), were apparently of the school of thought that you can never get enough catching, but more on that later. Ernie reported to the Dodgers training camp on March 7, 1931. "Ernest Lombardi travels light," reported Quentin Reynolds the next day to the *World-Telegram*. "He carries nothing but a blue serge suit, a well-worn cap, a small leather bag, the biggest schnozzola ever seen in base-

intra-squad game. He also "snapped the ball to second base with a whiplike motion that brought a look of respect to Al Lopez's eye." (Quote also from *World-Telegram*, March 8, 1931.) Al Lopez was the Dodger's starting catcher. That whiplike throw to second was to become one of Ernie's trademarks, something that he was famous for, along with the nose, along with the slowness afoot, along with the heavy bat, along with the fingers intertwined on the bat.

Oh, the fingers—I should mention that. At some point in Lombardi's years with Oakland, the precise moment lost in history, Lombardi sustained an injury (or, according to one source, had a blister) on one of his fingers. To help protect the sore pinkie, he began interlocking the fingers of his two hands in his grip. He liked the effect that this had on his bat control, and after the injury had healed he continued to do it, as shown in the photograph on page 319. The sportswriters sometimes called it a golf grip (or the Gene Sarazen grip) although that isn't where it comes from.

As impressive as Lombardi was as a hitter and thrower, and as much as Uncle Robbie liked him, there just wasn't a place for him. The Dodgers' catcher was a defensive wizard and field general named Alfonso Raymond Lopez, who is also listed here. Lopez was four months younger than

Lombardi, who at that time was only twenty-two. As a rookie the year before, Lopez had hit .309 in addition to his exceptional defensive skills. Other than Lopez and Lombardi, the Dodgers had in camp Val Picinich, a respected veteran backup who would play a total of eighteen years in the majors, and Paul Richards, another youngster born in the same year as Lombardi and Lopez, also a highly regarded prospect. They had more catchers than a good team could have used, and they weren't a good team. At first base was Del Bissonette, one of the team's best hitters, and the idea of moving Lombardi to the outfield, given his speed, was out of the question. Playing little, Lombardi "won a big following among many fans" (*World-Telegram*, March 14, 1932).

What, then, to do with him? In September of his rookie year, Robinson hit on the solution: make him a pitcher. Robbie had had Lombardi pitching batting practice a few times, and he liked what he saw—a crackling fast ball, an easy motion, excellent control. He didn't have a breaking pitch, but the Dodgers were desperate for pitching, and Robbie figured he would learn that. Some sportswriters were so indiscreet as to compare Lombardi's fastball to that of Walter Johnson.

Robinson's eighteen-year reign at the helm of the Dodgers ended at the end of the

season, and the idea of moving Lombardi to the mound died with it. Max Carey was managing the Dodgers in the spring of 1932, and he wanted more of a sleek, aggressive team. During spring training in 1932, Lombardi was thrown in with Babe Herman, a big star, and Wally Gilbert in a three-for-three trade with Cincinnati.

At first the trade didn't seem to work out for Cincinnati. "With his club in the basement," wrote Charles L. Parker that summer, "you might figure that the manager would be ready to admit certain mistakes in assembling such a team, especially when players he yielded in his big trade of the year are making a pennant contender of another outfit. But not so with Dan Howley, of the Cincinnati Reds, who last March gave Joe Stripp, Tony Cuccinello and Clyde Sukeforth to Brooklyn for Babe Herman, Ernie Lombardi and Wally Gilbert."

"It was not the falling down of any of my three men that caused my team to tumble," responded Howley. Lombardi, though charged with a league-leading 17 passed balls, hit .303 and drove in 68 runs in 118 games. He also hit nine triples, evidence that his mobility at that point was not the problem it later became.

In a few years there would be no doubt about who won the trade. The legend of Lombardi was growing in Cincinnati. On May 8, 1935, he hit four doubles and a single in a game (reportedly, he hit four doubles against four different pitchers in four consecutive innings, although I haven't seen the box score). Hitting .300 every year, he landed home runs on the roof of a laundry beyond the left field fence at Crosley Field. It was a tough home run park, and probably cost him about five to seven homers a year. He was such a character, stronger than life. He became, according to many reports, the most beloved player ever to play in Crosley Field. In 1937 he drilled a pitch back at the mound, breaking three fingers on the hand of Cub pitcher Larry French. His strength was legend. His slowness afoot was legend. His disrespect for coaching strategy was legend (he swore that in one game he told the opposing hitters what was coming on every pitch, and the Reds still won the game). His snoring was legendary. His roommate, Chick Hafey, tried everything imaginable to stop him from snoring—tied his big toe to the foot of the bed, tried to get him to sleep with an ice pack on his tummy. His nose poked out through his face mask, and it was said that at times he would skin his nose on a foul tip.

Sportswriters, trying to capture this amazing image in words, gave him nicknames by the bushel—Schnozzola, the Schnozz, Lumbago, Bocci, Muss, Dogs (after his aching feet) and (my particular favorite) the Cyrano of the Iron Mask. He was loved by the fans, welcomed by the sportswriters, respected by opponents, on good terms with umpires. His relationships with teammates were no doubt more varied, but he had the personality of the gentle giant, the man whose sheer physical presence made him feel unthreatened and magnified any threat that he might happen to project. The world calls upon such men to put on a benevolent face, and Lombardi, like most such men, responded to those expectations. He was quiet, taciturn, yet fully engaged in the clubhouse give and take, handing out vaguely insulting nicknames and accepting them with grace. Dick Bartell reports that he was often the butt of practical jokes, a kind of clubhouse equivalent of schoolkids teasing the elephant. He hated to be shown up, though.

In *Rowdy Richard,* Dick Bartell's recent recreation of the National League of the thirties, he says that Tony Cuccinello once pulled the hidden ball trick on Ernie, catching him off second base. When he showed him the ball, Lombardi said "You tag me and I'll punch you right in the nose." Cuccinello, naturally, did not tag him, and Ernie walked off the field. He would show this dominant character trait many times over the next forty years. He hated to fail. He hated to fall on his face, and he hated to be shown up.

Lombardi was not equally beloved by the Cincinnati management. Beginning in about 1936, Lombardi was a holdout every spring. He just didn't care for spring training, on the one hand, and then on the other he never cared for the Cincinnati salary offers. Every spring he held out, and every spring there were rumors that he was as good as traded, usually to the Giants, where Bill Terry was one of his admirers. He held out in 1936, in 1937, in 1938. In the spring of 1938 the rumor had him going to New York with Harry Craft for Gus Mancuso and two other players.

Fortunately for the Reds, they didn't make that trade. Bill McKechnie was hired to manage the Reds in 1938, and Lombardi blossomed under his guidance. He made the All-Star team for the first time. Johnny Vander Meer pitched his two no-hitters, Lombardi catching both of them; this feat improved his defensive reputation immeasurably. Going into the last day of the season Ernie led Johnny Mize by two points in the race for the batting title. McKechnie offered him the day off, but Lombardi, as Ted Williams would three years later, refused to earn the title sitting on the bench. He played and got two hits to win the title, hitting .342. Although the Reds finished fourth, he was named the Most Valuable Player in the league. He was given an expensive shotgun as part of the prize for his MVP Award. As a reward for his performance and to avoid another holdout, Cincinnati General Manager Warren Giles (later NL President) gave him a $3,000 bonus. His salary for the season had been $13,000 —almost exactly $100,000 in 1987 dollars. He signed for 1939 for $17,000.

I believe that it was following the MVP year that the defenses began to get really weird against him. The infielders, realizing that they had extra time against Ernie, had always played him deeper than they played anybody else. Now, however, they recalculated the risks and backed up even more. Third basemen and shortstops played several feet onto the outfield grass, as deep as their throwing arms would allow them to play. Sometimes they played deeper than their arms would allow; if the ball was hit toward them they would get the ball and run several steps toward first before throwing. Ernie told Pee Wee Reese that "You had been in the league for five years before I learned you weren't an outfielder." That Ernie could continue to hit .300 by firing bullets between the five outfielders nourished his legend. Arthur Daley wrote that "When you look back on . . . his 17 years in the majors, you almost come to the conclusion that he was the greatest hitter of all time." Bill McKechnie said

later that he always thought that Lombardi was the only man who could have beat Hugh Duffy's record .438 batting average if the defenses had had to play honest with him.

The 1939 season was to be, for Lombardi, a painful, glorious, wretched year. On June 11, following a double header in Brooklyn, Lombardi stepped on a broken board in the shower room at Ebbets Field, and ran a splinter into the ball of his left foot. He was out of the lineup for about two weeks. He slumped on his return, but recovered in time to make the All-Star team, again catching the entire game for the National League. The Reds were driving toward the pennant. In a crucial game against the Cardinals in September, Ernie's snap throw to second caught Johnny Hopp, a rookie, off second base and stopped a rally. Hitting far below his average following the injury, he hit .343 in September and reached a career high in home runs of 20 along with a respectable .287 average, the lowest of his career to that point. The Reds won the pennant for the first time since 1919.

In the fourth and final game of the 1939 Series, Lombardi's career was struck by the kind of malevolent media lightning which flashes suddenly across the landscape sometimes, scarring a random target—a George Romney here, an Ernie Lombardi there—and

slashing on. It was the tenth inning and there were men on first and third when DiMaggio singled to right. Ival Goodman fumbled the ball a moment before throwing home, and the throw arrived just ahead of Charley Keller, the runner from first base. Keller hit Lombardi and knocked the 230-pound receiver flat on his back. While he lay on his back a few feet from home plate and the ball on the ground beside him, DiMaggio raced home.

Ernie's Snooze. Lombardi's Sit-down Strike. The Schnozz's swan dive. The play grew to have as many names as the player. His selection as the series goat was absurd. The Yankees won the series in four straight games. Ival Goodman made an error on the same play. Billy Myers had made an error (bobbled a ground ball) to put Keller on base moments earlier. The run scored by DiMaggio only changed the score from 6–4 to 7–4. Bucky Walters, the pitcher, faulted himself for not backing up the play. Anyone could have been the goat; the series was a rout. Nonetheless, the image of the behemoth catcher lying on his back, making no effort to resist the fate that was overpowering his team, became the dominant image of the series, and would haunt Lombardi for the rest of his life.

"It was an awful hot day in Cincinnati," Lombardi remembered years later, "and I was feeling dizzy. . . . When

Keller came in, he spun me around at the plate and I couldn't get up." (*New York Times,* September 28, 1977.) "I was kind of knocked senseless," he told another reporter, "Keller really whacked me."

Keller, oddly, insisted that not only had he not "really whacked" Lombardi, but that in fact he went by him without touching him. Keller was a rookie, perhaps lost in the excitement of the moment. Films are choppy but suggest that there was a collision. One of the ironies of his career was that Lombardi was famous, among so many other things, for his toughness and for blocking the plate better than any other catcher.

Lombardi was now the Bill Buckner of the 1930s, even more innocent than Buckner, and Buckner has plenty of people who should be holding up their hands to share his disgrace. Lombardi, a sensitive, avuncular man, was deeply hurt by the attacks. When Warren Giles used his misfortune against him in contract negotiations in 1940, Lombardi again balked at signing. Giles offered him $14,000, seeing this as a reasonable $3,000 cut for a player who had dropped 55 points from his MVP season the year before. Lombardi, counting the $3,000 bonus following the 1938 season as part of his 1939 income, saw this as an attempt to cut him $6,000 for setting a career high in home runs and getting

his team in the World Series, all based on this stupid World Series error. Rumors were that he would be traded to Brooklyn for a young player named Babe Phelps.

Most of the press supported Lombardi in his battles with Giles. A Cincinnati paper took a poll on keeping or trading Lombardi. They got 945 letters saying "Keep big Schnozz", and 23 saying "trade him."

Eventually Lombardi and the Reds worked it out. Lombardi reported determined to redeem himself, and was, according to contemporary reports, hustling as he never hustled before. The Cincinnati fans forgave him completely by early May. Once more he made the All Star team. On July 17 he split the middle finger of his right hand, causing him to miss several weeks, but Willard Hershberger filled in for him very well, and once again, the Reds were driving to the pennant. In the last days of July, though, the Reds blew a big lead in a game at the Polo Grounds. Some of the Reds players felt that the comeback would not have happened had Lombardi been in the lineup, and said so. On August 2, with Hershberger catching again, the Reds lost to a poor Boston team in the twelfth inning. Hershberger killed himself the next day, slitting his wrists and throat with a razor in the bathroom of a Boston hotel.

Lombardi was nearly ob-

sessed by the notion of getting back into the World Series, setting things right. On September 15, chasing a foul ball hit by Joe Gallagher of the Cardinals, Ernie twisted an ankle. He went to the hospital for X rays. He would not be able to leave the hospital for at least ten days. The ankle was badly hurt. He batted only three times in the series. Jimmie Wilson, a forty-year-old emergency catcher, was the star of the series, won by Cincinnati in seven games. The Reds voted a winner's share for the series, about $6,000, to Hershberger's mother.

Once more, in the spring of 1941, Lombardi held out. This time it was serious. They finally settled for a reported $18,000 (equivalent to $135,000 now) plus, reportedly, a bonus if he hit .300. When he finally did report, he showed "a noticeable limp as a hangover of the sprained ankle he suffered near the end of the 1940 season." The sportswriters, less sympathetic this time, alleged that he had not worked out all winter, so that the ankle injury naturally flared up as soon as pressure was put on it.

"Lombardi isn't the best catcher in baseball, but he hits the long ball that breaks up games," wrote Joe Williams that March. "Apparently, he did nothing to condition his ankle during the winter, and as soon as he started to bounce around in the spring his limp came back. Don't ask us why these high-salaried fellows who would be driving trucks if they couldn't hit a baseball are so indifferent to their physical soundness."

McKechnie insisted that Lombardi would be ready to open the season as his catcher.

"Lombardi is probably the greatest magnate *(sic)* for rumors in the history of the Cincinnati Club," wrote Gabe Paul, then traveling secretary/publicist for the Reds. "Many times during his Cincinnati career he was rumored to have been killed or seriously injured in auto accidents, while he was snoozing peacefully in his apartment. This past winter the report came in that he weighed 300 pounds. Then he was supposed to have hardening of the arteries, etc.

"Meanwhile, Ernie goes about his business, saying nothing. He knows that time will prove everything, and that as soon as he appears in the lineup, there will have to be a new angle to the rumors about him."

Appear he did, but in 1941, for the first time in his career, Lombardi did not play well. On a road trip in April, $300 was stolen from his hotel room while he was at the game. Overweight, his ankle aching, his feet killing him, Lombardi hit just .264 in 1941. Following the 1938 season there had been a banquet in Cincinnati honoring some of the players. A radio reporter stuck a microphone in front of

Lombardi, who had had a few too many, and asked if he had anything to say. Lombardi responded with a few ill-chosen words about the no good Warren Giles, and—at least as he told it—passed out on the air. From then on, he felt that Giles was just waiting for a chance to get rid of him. "As soon as I had a bad year," he said, "I was gone."

At the time it was reported that he had been traded to the Boston Braves for two players to be named later. In the new Macmillan *Encyclopedia,* which lists trades, the transaction is shown as a sale.

The war was on now. In March 1942 Lombardi was reported as working at a war-related job on the coast, unable to report. At thirty-four, coming out of a poor season, many assumed that his career was over. In late March, to the astonishment of the critics, he reported to the Boston Braves in shape and ready to go. He had eaten spaghetti only once or twice all winter. "I weigh only 220 pounds," he said. "That's because I stayed away from spaghetti. If you knew how much I love that stuff, you'd realize what a sacrifice I made to get myself in shape. I now weigh less than at any time in the last seven years." He announced that he intended to make the Reds sorry for trading him.

He returned to the All-Star team. He hit .330. It was the highest average in the league. However, he had suffered a

split finger trying to catch a "flutterball" thrown by Jim Tobin (with whose family he was boarding, incidentally), and so missed several weeks. He played in only 105 games, batting 309 times. The season ended with speculation as to whether he or Enos Slaughter, at .318, would be recognized as the batting champion. At the time of the Debs Garms fuss in 1940 (Garms won the batting title with 358 at bats) it had been announced that in the future batting champions would have to have at least 400 at bats. Hadn't it? Lombardi finished nearly 100 at bats short of the standard adopted a few years earlier. NL President Ford Frick ruled that catchers were entitled to special consideration, and annointed Lombardi the batting champion. "We did not announce a specific at bat rule at that time . . . because we had the catchers in mind particularly. A first-string catcher may not play 100 games and he seldom reaches 400 times at bat, even though he does all the work his job entails. To bar such a man from the hitting title would be an injustice." This generosity made Lombardi the only catcher in baseball history to win two batting titles, and the last catcher to win the batting title.

In the spring of 1943, Lombardi again declined to report to spring training. Once more there was talk of his probable retirement. The health of his father was a concern to him.

Lombardi, who was a bachelor at this time, lived with his sister, his sister's family, and his father, who was partially paralyzed. Unmarried, he would have been liable to be drafted, but he was listed as the sole source of support for his father and sister. In March the word appeared that his father's health had improved, but he was unhappy with the Braves' offer. He wanted to be traded. There were allegations of a "sinister influence" on Lombardi's decision—specifically, that another National League team had whispered to him that he could get more money from them than he could from the Braves.

In any case, he finally signed in early April 1943, reportedly for more than the $10,000 of the previous year. Despite these eternal salary battles, Dick Bartell says that Lombardi loaned money to players all over the league, and never pressured anyone to pay it back. A few days after signing he was traded to the New York Giants. At the time he was reported as going in exchange for $40,000 (several times his salary); later reports were that he went in exchange for Connie Ryan and Hugh Poland. In May, his father died. Shortly thereafter he was called in for re-examination by the draft board. A sportswriter wrote that it was "well known that the Schnozz has the worst feet in baseball," but he didn't know if that would be enough to keep Lombardi

out of the Army. Playing day to day, the remarkable Lombardi once more made the National League All-Star team. In September it was announced that he had failed his physical. He finished his first season with the Giants hitting .305.

In the winter of 1943–1944, Lombardi worked as a sheet metal artisan. In the spring of 1944, he held out again. He finally reported on April 5, weighing about 245 pounds. He always looked larger than he was.

"Ernie hasn't touched a bat all winter," said Hank DeBerry on April 8. "He is overweight, yet he can rifle pitches to the outfield as if it were mid-July. He laces out those line drives like clay pigeons winging out of a trap. . . . He still has one of the best arms in the business."

He started the season well. In mid-April he was hitting .450. Late in the month, though, he hit into three double plays in four games, two of them with the bases loaded. His average dropped to the mid-.220s by early June. The New York crowd was on Ernie badly. His arrival in New York had been heralded as making the Giants a pennant contender. Instead, they found him a slow, fat old catcher going through the motions for a second-division team.

Cincinnati still loved him. On August 14, 1944, the *World-Telegram* reported that "Ernie Lombardi still is Rhineland's greatest hero. He is

cheered here more vociferously than all the Reds put together."

On June 4, 1944, Ernie was cut in the middle of his forehead by the spikes of Pittsburgh outfielder Jim Russell. He had to leave the game. The next day he was married to an Oakland woman name Berice Ayres. He was thirty-six; her age was given as forty-three. His batting rallied. On August 21 he hit two line-drive home runs and a game-winning single, driving in all four runs in a Giant win. On September 10, 1944, there was an odd play in which a ball bounced away from Lombardi with a man on base. The umpire, Bill Stewart (apparently forgetting that there was a man on base) chased down the ball and flipped it to Lombardi. "Maybe that's what Ernie's longed for all along," suggested a writer, "an umpire-retriever."

By the spring of 1945 Ernie was thirty-seven years old. In late April he astonished the crowd by beating out a bunt. He'd do that once in a while; the rule was that if he bunted it was the pitcher's job to field it, no matter where it was. On May 2, 1945, Ernie beat out a bunt again, and once on base moved from second to third on a fly ball to center field, then scored on a foul pop to the second baseman. Two innings later, he scored from second base on a single. Continuing his aggressive play and hitting well, he won the fans over. On May 9 Joe King wrote that "The folks for the first time have taken him in lock, stock and proboscis." In early May he was leading the league in home runs.

He became a story. He told sportswriters that he was embarrassed about his performance of the previous season, and determined to do better. "Lom is unbelievably sensitive," said Mel Ott on May 19. "This year he seems determined to prove he couldn't possibly have been as bad as he was last year." On May 28 he hit his eleventh home run, one more than he had hit in 1944, and still the most in the league.

In the giddiness over Lombardi's recovery, it seems to have been totally forgotten that he was still thirty-seven. With 11 home runs in late May, it was a forgone conclusion that he would beat his career high of 20. One sportswriter thought he was a candidate to win the triple crown. Mel Ott let him catch 48 of the Giants first 53 games. By July he had fallen into a slump. On August 20 a foul tip off the bat of Roy Johnson whacked him in the middle finger, driving the nail back into the flesh. He was out about ten days.

The rest did him good. After his return his hitting surged again. He finished the year at .307 with 19 home runs, 70 RBI in 368 at bats. The Giants still finished fifth.

On January 5, 1946, the Giants purchased Walker Cooper from the Cardinals. Lombardi was no longer the number-one catcher. On April 15, 1946, he hit a home run in the first inning on opening day, the same inning in which Mel Ott hit the last of his 511 home runs. On May 9 it was reported that he was "doing a grand job while Cooper is shelved." June 18, 1946, was Ernie Lombardi day at the Polo Grounds.

The Giants (and the other New York teams) at this time had a problem with kids stealing their caps as they walked to the clubhouse after games. On September 5, 1946, a twelve-year-old kid swiped Lombardi's hat off his head. Lombardi, who had had enough of this, took off after the kid and, to the astonishment of everybody, caught up with him near the subway entrance. The kid had handed off the cap by the time the Schnozzola caught him, but Ernie picked him up and hauled him back to face the security force. The Giants did not press charges. "They simply hope that police confrontal will halt the thriving practice of stealing caps and sometimes gloves from the players."

Lombardi finished the year with a .290 average and 12 home runs in 238 at bats. The Giants finished last. In the spring of 1947 Lombardi again held out. Walker Cooper had a big year that year, and there were fewer at bats for Ernie, who still hit well (.282 with 21 RBI in 110 at bats). He was released at the end of the season, free to make his own deal with another team.

Lombardi signed to play the 1948 season with Sacramento in the Pacific Coast League. In April, however, his wife became ill, and Lombardi asked for voluntary retirement so that he could go home to Oakland and stay near her. His request was granted, but then Casey Stengel, who was managing the Oakland Oaks that summer, asked him to come back and play for Oakland, where he had begun his career so long before. Lombardi agreed and worked out the details with Sacramento. Oakland won 114 games, helping to propel Casey back to the major leagues. As Stengel went to the Yankees, Lombardi retired from baseball.

As we reach the end of his career, let us pause a moment and evaluate him as a ballplayer. He must have been an amazing hitter.

Harry Craft said "Ernie was the best right-handed hitter I ever saw, and he was an exceptional player in every department except running."

Carl Hubbell said "I thought he might hurt me, even kill me, with one of those liners." Hubbell many times chose Lombardi as the most difficult player in the league for him to get out, and claimed that when Lombardi was at the plate, Bill Terry would plead with him to pitch Lombardi inside and the third baseman would plead for him to be pitched outside. Neither one wanted to be shot with a line drive.

It was routinely written that he would have hit .400 many times if he could just run.

Arthur Daley wrote that "When Lom would grasp a bat with that interlocking grip of his, his bat looked like a matchstick. And the ball would ricochet off it like a shell leaving a howitzer."

Kirby Higbe said that "He was the best hitter I ever saw, including everybody."

Lombardi almost never struck out. He hit the ball hard, time after time after time. We should not, however, confuse the questions of how great a hitter Lombardi would have been other things being equal and how great a hitter he was. A baseball hitter must not be evaluated by how often he hits the ball hard. He must be evaluated by the good that he does for his team. He couldn't run. He grounded into double plays far more often than any other player in history—about once every twenty trips to the plate. The cost to his team was enormous.

Arthur Daley said that "he couldn't outrace a snail, even with a head start."

Lombardi himself, though sometimes sensitive about his speed, told a story about once being thrown out at first base after rocketing a ball off the *left* field wall at the Baker Bowl. He told the story in self defense; he wanted to explain that he just wasn't running because he was sure it was out of the park. Dick Bartell, in *Rowdy Richard,* says that this happened several times, but I doubt that it did.

Though a catcher's speed is usually considered irrelevant defensively, Lombardi was so slow that his speed was a problem on defense even at catcher. If the ball bounced away from him even a couple of feet, a runner was likely to advance before he could pounce on it.

He had other defensive shortcomings. He could not field a bunt. Foul popups dropped a few feet from home plate because he could not spring out of a crouch. However, he blocked the plate well, threw exceptionally well and had good hands.

Upon his acquisition by the Dodgers, the Brooklyn paper reported that "He is said to be only a fair catcher with a rather amazing throwing arm."

In July 1937, Gabe Paul wrote in a press release that "Ernie Lombardi is a changed ball player. He has improved himself in other departments and today he ranks as a fine catcher who is particularly adept at nipping runners off first base." But in January, 1939, Gabe was still singing the same song. "Until last year," Paul wrote, "He was generally regarded throughout baseball as just a hitter,

and not as a crack receiver. His 1938 performance altered the complete situation, for the manner in which he handled the youngsters on the Cincinnati staff, and a newly found attitude for his job . . ." But Dan Daniels, not in the employ of the team, wrote that, "In the National League Mel Ott . . . was a more valuable player than the slow-footed Lombardi, who drove in only 96 runs. Gabby Hartnett, who did not match Schnozz in batting effectiveness, did a great job as a catcher and a manager and in the minds of many experts deserved the top honor over Lombardi. Why, even Johnny Mize rated the nomination ahead of the Cyrano of the Rhineland." Remember, though, that Daniels was espousing a minority opinion. Lombardi did win the award.

Later in his career, and particularly after the Vander Meer no hitters, Lombardi developed the reputation for being able to help young pitchers. What veteran catcher doesn't develop such a reputation?

In the Hall of Fame dispute that developed later, Lombardi's leading proponents among former players were Bucky Walters, who successfully made the conversion to the mound and became the 1939 NL MVP with Lombardi as his catcher, and Harry Craft, another teammate who stayed in baseball for decades afterward as a coach, scout and manager. Craft claimed that at times Vander Meer, who was wild, would throw a ball two feet to the right of Ernie, and Ernie would just reach out and catch the ball bare-handed. Dick Bartell also says that every player in the league had seen Lombardi do this, although I know of no contemporaneous documentation for this remarkable skill. Craft also claimed that if Ernie's finger was split or broken by a pitch, he'd just rub some dirt on it, stuff his mitt under his arm, walk back to the dugout and not say a word. This, of course, is an exaggeration. Though Lombardi prided himself on staying in the lineup, there were many times in his career when he was forced to the bench with finger injuries.

Out of baseball, Ernie operated a liquor store in San Leandro, California, for several years. In 1953 he became seriously depressed, seemingly unable to go on. His wife decided to take him to a sanitorium in Livermore, California. Ernie agreed to go. En route to the sanitorium on April 8, 1953, they stopped to stay overnight with Ernie's sister. Ernie went into a bathroom and found a razor. He slit his throat from ear to ear. His wife found him and screamed. He pleaded with her not to save him, to let him die. He fought with the hospital attendants who tried to save him.

Although the papers described him as "clinging to life," apparently his injuries were not critical. He was transferred to the sanitorium two days later. The hospital stated that it was a private matter, but acknowledged that they would not have transferred him had his health been unstable.

I did not know Lombardi, and I would not speculate too freely on the causes of his pain. Athletes, losing their skills to time and removed from the athlete's world, are stripped of a central part of their identity, and are forced to fall back on the other elements of their selves, to identify themselves as husbands and fathers and grandfathers or businessmen or sportsmen or whatever. It is difficult for many of them. Lombardi had no children, no father or mother. As a ballplayer he had no hobbies to speak of. He wasn't a sportsman or interested in politics. He wasn't a reader. He wasn't cut out to be very successful in business, and he was many years too late to be a successful tradesman. Baseball was his world.

Beyond that, one cannot help but notice the similarities between the suicide of Willard Hershberger in 1939 and the attempted suicide of Ernie Lombardi fourteen years later. Did Ernie invent guilt for himself over the tragic death of Hershberger? At the very minimum, he must have said to himself that if he had just been in there playing instead of Hershberger, this would never have happened. For him not to have done that would not be human. Nobody dies without guilt. No one will ever pass from your life without leaving you feeling that you should have done something you didn't do and said something you didn't say. Suicides carry more guilt than anything, except maybe the death of a child. Look at the situation: It's a goddamn guilt factory. Lombardi *always* felt that he was supposed to be in the lineup, that he was letting the team down if he had to miss a few days with an injury. He was famous for being tough. He was out of the lineup, and the kid had to play, and the kid couldn't handle it. How much of this did Lombardi bury in the dark corners of his mind, where he would find it fourteen years later in his own black hours?

Following the 1957 season the New York Giants, for whom he had played ten years earlier, moved to San Francisco. Ernie was given a job as press box attendant in Candlestick Park. He continued in that job for six years, 1958 to 1963. Though well liked, his personality was not ideal for press relations. He tended to answer questions with a grunt, rarely said very much unless he'd had a couple of beers. When a young sportswriter insulted him in 1963, he quit in anger and embarrassment. For several years he dropped from sight.

One day an Oakland sportswriter stopped to fill up his car. A huge man about sixty years of age came to pump his gas. "Look at that nose," he must have said to himself. He recognized the man as Lombardi.

Interviewed at this point, Lombardi lashed out at the Veterans Committee of the Hall of Fame. "If they elected me now, I wouldn't even show up," he told one reporter. "That sounds terrible but I'm bitter. All anybody wants to remember about me is that I couldn't run."

"They can take the Hall of Fame and you know what they can do with it," he told another. "Even if they voted me in now, I wouldn't accept. It doesn't mean anything to me anymore."

Berice Lombardi died in Oakland on July 1, 1973. In 1975, in poor health, Lombardi moved to Santa Cruz. A Hall of Fame bandwagon began to get moving for him. On September 26, 1977, Lombardi laid down the mask in a hospital in Santa Cruz, California. Al Lopez, his National League rival of so long ago, had been inducted into the Hall of Fame just weeks earlier. *The Sporting News* chose

to turn his obituary into a Hall of Fame case.

In February 1986, the Veteran's Committee selected Ernie Lombardi and Bobby Doerr for the Hall of Fame.

AL LOPEZ

HALL OF FAME? Yes, as manager
DATA IN SECTION III? Yes
OFFENSIVE WON-LOST RECORD:
    73–94, .437
GROSS VALUE: 111
COMPARABLE RECENT PLAYERS:
Bob Boone

Al Lopez held the record for games caught in a career, 1,918, until passed by Bob Boone in late 1987. Boone, helped a little by the fact that he caught for only one season in the minor leagues, may push that record over 2,000, but that's still far less than the record for games played in the outfield, which is over 3,000.

It is important for the baseball fan to understand this, because the human body just will not take the kind of abuse the catching position hands out for more than maybe 1,500 games in most cases, maybe 2,000 tops. When a player catches 1,300, 1,400 games, the odds in favor of a precipitous decline go way up. Gary Carter, who has caught about 1,600 games, has already suffered a large loss in value due to the strain of the position. So if you're in an APBA League or a rotisserie league or something, you should never give up anything of value to acquire a catcher

who has caught more than 1,300 games.

LANCE PARRISH

HALL OF FAME: Not Eligible
DATA IN SECTION III? No
OFFENSIVE WON-LOST RECORD:
    73–64, .534
GROSS VALUE: 108

I've never been a great admirer of Parrish's, but certainly when you look at catchers in historical context, you've got to admit that he's got some of the elements of the All-Time greats. He has the size, strength and plate blocking of Ernie Lombardi, while being more mobile defensively than Ernie. In a four-year period he hit 27 to 33 homers a year and drove in 87 to 114 runs a year, a feat few catchers could match. His throwing arm is, or was, as good as anybody's that he played against.

Parrish has some weaknesses. Unlike Lombardi, he never seemed to trust his great strength to make good things happen if he put the bat on the ball. He is a wild swinger who will chase any pitch, and in consequence his batting averages have never been real good. He has never developed the reputation of being a good handler of pitchers. In the context of discussing him as a contemporary, these weaknesses don't amount to much. He's one of the best catchers available. In historic context, compared to the greatest who have played the game, they mean a lot.

WALLY SCHANG

HALL OF FAME? No
DATA IN SECTION III? Yes
OFFENSIVE WON-LOST RECORD:
94–61, .607
GROSS VALUE: 111
COMPARABLE RECENT PLAYERS:
Manny Sanguillen

See Jim Baker's article on Ray Schalk (below), which is really on the two players together. A couple of other notes on Schang. He was a good hitter. He hit over .300 six times, and when his averages dropped toward the end of his career he became one of those players who would have as many walks as hits. As an offensive player he was about equal to Lombardi, and as a fielder he wasn't chopped liver, either. The 1915 *Reach Guide* described him as "one of the most sensational catchers in recent years. Manager Mack obtained him by the draft route . . . after nearly every club in the two major leagues had put in a draft for him. He is a remarkably fast runner, a good hitter and a strong thrower." The 1914 *Spalding Guide* also described him as "sensational." The 1918 *Reach Guide* said that "Schang . . . gave the [Boston] pitchers excellent support" throughout the season. The 1922 *Reach Guide,* in reviewing the World Series, said that "of the catchers, Schang played the most consistent ball throughout the Series and yielded the Yankee pitchers valuable support, although he had a tendency to order too many waste balls to catch baserunners. His batting, too, was hard and timely, his throwing fast and accurate."

In 1923 he was seriously hurt when hit in the head by a pitch, and was out for several weeks. Jim (below) is curious about why Schalk is in the Hall of Fame and Schang is not. According to Bill Gleason in the Chicago *Sun Times*, February 9, 1976, "Chicagoan Ray Schalk made the Hall of Fame in 1955 because Chicago columnist Warren Brown campaigned for Schalk."

RAY SCHALK

HALL OF FAME? Yes
DATA IN SECTION III? Yes
OFFENSIVE WON-LOST RECORD?
75–87, .467
GROSS VALUE: 106
COMPARABLE RECENT PLAYERS: Jim Sundberg, but with better speed.

I can never think of Ray Schalk without also thinking of Wally Schang. I'm sure somebody who lived through their era does not have the problem, but the mind compresses the past; I'm convinced that in a few hundred years the words *Waterloo* and *Watergate* will mean the same thing.

WALLY SCHANG

These two men had even more in common than Waterloo and Watergate. First, obviously, is their names, Schalk and Schang. They appear on the same page of the Macmillan *Encyclopedia*. Second, both were catchers in the American League at the same time. Schalk came up in 1912 and played until 1929; Schang came up in 1913 and lasted until 1931. They finished with 5,306 at bats apiece, which must have taken years of planning.

Schalk is in the Hall of Fame and Schang is not. I'm not going to say that this is an injustice, because I really don't think either of them should be there, but it is fun to speculate on what keeps Schang out or what put Schalk in. Schang was much the better hitter. He hit for a higher average, had more power and drew more walks. Given the identical at bat totals in the same league in the same years, comparisons are simplified; Schalk struck out less and stole more bases, and Schang was better in every other category. Most of the differences are large. Schang hit five times as many homers, almost twice as many triples, many more doubles, drew 200 more walks. Schalk was a good base stealer, and held most of the base-stealing records for catchers, since broken by John Stearns and John Wathan. Schang was a fair base stealer himself, one of the few catchers to steal more than 100 bases in his career.

John Wathan and John Stearns are probably not going to get into the Hall of Fame, and that brings us back to the question of why Ray Schalk did. Schalk batted eighth for the great White Sox teams of 1917 and 1919, and still batted eighth for them when they weren't so great in 1927. I wonder how many Hall of Famers were career eighth-place hitters?

Schalk was probably the better defensive player. He led the league in fielding percentage a record eight times, and his career percentage is fourteen points higher than Schang's. He had a few more assists and double plays per game. More important, he and Steve O'Neill were the first catchers who had long careers and regularly caught more than 100 games a year. When Schalk retired he had caught more games than any other man (1,726); he is now seventh on the list of games caught. Schang's career was in the more traditional catcher's mold of the time; he caught over 100 games only five times, missing a couple of other times because of injuries, and often played other positions to keep his bat in the lineup (Ray Schalk never played a game at any other position). Schang's handling was common at the time. The concept of the "battery" was much stronger then; papers would announce a game's starting pitcher *and* catcher. Teams usually split the catch-

ing chores among two or three players. Schalk, who in 1920 became the second man to catch 150 games in a season, helped to break that mold.

I've often wondered if Schalk is in the Hall of Fame because he was one of the few White Sox not to go in the tank in 1919. Of the principal members of that team, eight were banned for life and three were put in the Hall of Fame (Eddie Collins and Red Faber were the other two). Only Nemo Leibold (did his mother read Jules Verne, or what?) and Dickie Kerr avoided either fate. In accounts of the the Black Sox scandal, Schalk comes out sounding like a martyr, the innocent protagonist doing his best to win despite some pretty fishy goings-on. He recounted for reporters how he called for pitches only to be ignored by Cicotte and Williams.

Whatever, he is in, and Schang is largely forgotten. The surprising thing about Schang's lack of recognition is that he played on great teams and with great pitchers. He played on seven pennant-winning teams, with the Yankees, the Red Sox and the A's of two different eras (1913 and 1930). In fact, he helped put each of those organizations over the top. The A's finished third in 1912, but got back to first in Schang's rookie season of 1913; Boston finished second in 1917, but first after they acquired Schang in 1918; the

Yankees won their first pennant ever in 1921, which was Schang's first season with them. He caught a remarkable number of gifted pitchers, including Chief Bender, Eddie Plank, Bullet Joe Bush, Herb Pennock, Bob Shawkey, Urban Shocker, Carl Mays, Babe Ruth, Waite Hoyt and Lefty Grove. Sometimes a player who has hobnobbed with such celebrity will acquire the status himself, but it didn't happen for Wally.

Another neat thing about Schang is how closely his World Series stats parallel his regular season stats. He batted .287 in six World Series, .284 in the season, and slugged .404 in the Series as opposed to .401 in the season. I don't know of anybody else who came as close in more than one series. Jimmie Foxx slugged .609 in both Series and season, and Charlie Gehringer hit .320 and .321, but neither was real close in both categories.

—Jim Baker

TED SIMMONS

HALL OF FAME? Not Eligible
DATA IN SECTION III? No
OFFENSIVE WON-LOST RECORD:
  142–101, .584
GROSS VALUE: 184

A great offensive player who caught for the Cardinals in the seventies, Simmons' throwing arm and overall defensive skills were not good, and the decision to make a catcher of him can be questioned. Simmons probably would have had 3,000 hits in his career had he not been a catcher.

HOW THE CATCHERS RATE

How, then, do we put them in order?

I will offer two lists at each position, the greatest players as they would appear in order of career value, and the greatest as they would appear in order of peak value. We don't have time, obviously, to discuss every player-to-player comparison, as I did on Berra and Dickey, so I will concentrate on picking the correct number one man.

I'll start with career value here because it's easier. Yogi Berra was more valuable to his teams, over the course of his career, than any other catcher. He was never as great a catcher at any moment as Johnny Bench was in his best years, or as Mickey Cochrane was or Roy Campanella, his contemporary. But Yogi's record of sustained excellence over a period of a decade is without parallel by any catcher in the history of baseball. From 1948 through 1959 he was never out for a great length of time with an injury, never had one of those sudden off years to which all catchers are prone, and caught 130 or 140 games a season, while performing at a level that is only an inch below the highest levels of performance ever attained by a catcher, a level that made him the greatest player in the American League in his time. Yogi is a very easy choice for the number one spot on the "career value" list.

Three catchers of this century, I think, reached peaks of performance that were higher than that attained by Lawrence Peter. Those were the three named above. They won a total of seven Most Valuable Player awards. It is very difficult to choose among them. We can start with the comparison between Bench and Campanella, because the two of them are so very similar. Bench in his best statistical season hit .293 with 45 homers and 148 RBI; Campy hit .312 with 41 and 142. They were similar at those moments in strike zone judgment and foot speed. Each had probably the best throwing arm of his generation, though each had one rival for that distinction. Each mixed together good years and bad years in an iambic pattern; Campanella, in the year following his best season, hit .207 with 19 homers and 51 RBI, while Bench, in his next season, hit .238 with 27 and 61. Each was the anchor of a great team with an indifferent pitching staff.

Bench had more years that were close to his peak than did Campy, and on that basis he will rate higher on the career value list. But under microscopic analysis, I have to choose Campanella as the greater player at his peak. One of the problems with Bench is that he didn't put his best offensive and his best defensive seasons together. When he had the super offensive seasons in 1970 and 1972, he was an unfinished defensive player, of awesome tools but just a little bit rough in the finishing. When he had his best defensive seasons in the mid-seventies, he had lost just a little as an offensive player.

Campanella's top three offensive winning percentages were .748, .744, and .735. Bench's were .739, .721, and .707. Campy had value approximations of 20, 17, and 15; Bench's best were 17, 16, and 16. Although there is a tendency to think of Campanella as being "favored" by Ebbets Field, he hit only 22 of his 41 home runs at home; Bench hit 30 of 45 in Cincinnati.

The comparison to Cochrane is a comparison to a significantly different type, and therefore even more difficult. Cochrane did not have power comparable to Campy's; he was basically a twelve-to-twenty-home-run-a-year man. He hit for a better average and took more walks, and he did these things in a game in which more runs were required to win. His best offensive winning percentages, (.754, .751, and .737) are infinitesimally better than Campanella's, but this is offset by the fact that Campanella was catching a few more games (140, 140, 127 were his top figures) than Cochrane (137, 135, 130). In fact, the offensive percentages for Hartnett and Dickey were higher than for either, but usually when they were catching 110 or 115 games a year, which is not the same thing.

It comes down to this: I think there is better evidence to say that Campanella was a great defensive catcher than there is to say that for Cochrane. If one of these players was worth a million dollars a year, then the other was worth $999,999.99 and the third worth $999,999.98. But I get the sense, just vaguely, that the observers of Campanella's time were a little bit more knocked off their feet by his defensive skills than were those of Cochrane's. That is the only thing I can find to make a choice on.

I think that an argument can be made for Gary Carter as being the equal of any catcher in terms of career value. Carter is active now and no one says this, but then that isn't unusual; when Brooks Robinson was thirty-three, no one said he was the greatest third baseman ever, either. Carter hasn't won any MVP Awards, isn't really a star of the magnitude of Mattingly or Boggs or several other active players. It is difficult to compare a hot pizza on the table in front of you to the fried chicken you had last week. It is difficult to put our contemporaries in historical context, and in this case I decided to err on the side of caution, to give Carter's career a few years to grow cold and then hold it up beside the other cold careers.

PEAK VALUE	CAREER VALUE
1. Roy Campanella	1. Yogi Berra
2. Mickey Cochrane	2. Johnny Bench
3. Johnny Bench	3. Mickey Cochrane
4. Yogi Berra	4. Gary Carter
5. Gary Carter	5. Carlton Fisk
6. Gabby Hartnett	6. Gabby Hartnett
7. Thurman Munson	7. Bill Dickey
8. Carlton Fisk	8. Ernie Lombardi
9. Bill Dickey	9. Roy Campanella
10. Bill Freehan	10. Ted Simmons

❧ FIRST BASE ❧

JIM BOTTOMLEY

HALL OF FAME? Yes
DATA IN SECTION III? Yes
OFFENSIVE WON-LOST RECORD:
130–75, .633
GROSS VALUE: 146
COMPARABLE RECENT PLAYERS:
Steve Garvey, Al Oliver

Bottomley is the first of a group of three first basemen who have been elected to the Hall of Fame. The three are Bottomley, Terry and George Kelly. All were active in the National League at the same time (Bottomley's years were 1922–1937, while Terry's were 1923–1936 and Kelly's were 1915–1932). All three hit for average with medium-range power (15–25 home runs a year, with a good many doubles and triples), and all three were RBI men. Many of their seasons are pretty nearly interchangeable; the list below contains three seasons from each player, and I doubt if you can tell which season belongs to who:

G	AB	R	H	2B	3B	HR	RBI	BB	SB	Avg.
150	580	101	189	32	13	20	121	46	1	.326
149	568	100	185	36	11	17	101	64	7	.326
153	602	109	213	30	6	8	83	60	0	.354
137	528	87	167	31	12	14	111	35	5	.316
134	523	79	194	34	14	8	94	45	4	.371
152	574	95	174	31	15	19	124	74	8	.303
149	587	95	181	42	9	23	122	40	4	.308
151	592	96	194	33	8	17	107	30	12	.328
147	577	73	169	45	9	5	103	33	7	.293

If you're curious, the top three seasons were Terry's, the next three Bottomley's, and the bottom three were Kelly's.

Terry was a Definition-B or Definition-C Hall of Famer. He was not the best first baseman of his time—Lou Gehrig and Jimmie Foxx were—but he was probably the best in the league. He had only a couple of seasons, if that, as the dominant star on his own team. In the early part of his career, that distinction would have been claimed by Frankie Frisch, with Irish Meusel and Ross Youngs rating as bigger stars than Terry. For one season the biggest star on the Giants was Rogers Hornsby, and as soon as Hornsby was gone there were a couple of kids named Mel Ott and Carl Hubbell. Terry was the biggest star on the Giants for a moment before Ott and Hubbell came into their own.

He was good. He got 200 hits a season regularly, hit over .340 six times. His lifetime average was .341, and almost 30% of his hits were for extra bases. His strike zone judgment was fair, and of course he once hit .401. He was a regular for only eleven seasons, ten of them consecutive, but he did enough in that period to clearly place him among the ten greatest ever at his position.

Behind Terry comes Bottomley. He got 200 hits in a season once. He hit over .340 three times, hitting as high as .371. His lifetime average was .310. He had as much power as Terry and his strike zone judgment was slightly better. He probably was not quite the defensive player that Terry was.

Bottomley was never the biggest star on his team. He came up to the Cardinals with Hornsby, and when Hornsby was gone there were Frisch and Hafey and Pete Alexander. If he was ever the best first baseman in the league, it was just for a couple of years, and not by a decisive margin. He played regularly for thirteen seasons, but for the last four he was probably a below-average player, hitting between .250 and .298 with less than 15 home runs a year. His qualifications for the Hall of Fame are not overpowering.

And then there is Kelly. Kelly was a fine defensive first baseman who led the league in RBI twice and home runs another year. Having said that, you have said all there is to say in support of his qualifications as an immortal. He hit but 148 home runs in his career. His best average, .328, is hardly an impressive mark in the National League of the 1920s. He never had 200 hits in a season. He never drew 50 walks in a season, and he struck out quite a bit, once leading the league. He was a good player, but to the Giants in the twenties, he was never anything but one of the guys who could also play some ball; he was to them what Tony Perez was to the Reds in the seventies, or what Carl Furillo was to the Dodgers of the fifties; indeed, both Perez and Furillo must be regarded as significantly greater players than Kelly. He played regularly but nine years, which includes a three-year decline phase. For whatever reasons, the Veterans' Committee of the Hall of Fame chose to subpoena him.

NORM CASH

HALL OF FAME? No
DATA IN SECTION III? Yes
OFFENSIVE WON-LOST RECORD:
   Approximately 136–61, .690
GROSS VALUE: 153

Norm Cash in 1961 turned in what is probably the greatest fluke season in baseball history—that is, the one season most out of context in the player's career. This, and other things, make his career as a whole difficult to get a sense of. He was never regarded, while active, as a great player. His career average was only .271, and with the exception of the 1961 season he never led the league in any important offensive category or drove in or scored 100 runs.

It is these statistics which cast an aura of ordinariness over Cash's memory, and yet for some reason, on any systematic analysis of the statistics Cash comes out looking surprisingly good. Barry Codell points out that his career base-out percentage is higher than Roberto Clemente's, while Palmer's methods, total average and his career offensive won/lost record all place him among the top 100 or so players of all time.

What it comes down to is that there are an unusual number of legitimate "buts" about Cash's career. While he hit only .271, he hit .271 in a league which often hit under .250. Cash's .263 average in 1968 is 33 points better than the league average. George Kelly, a lifetime .297 hitter, had only two seasons in which he exceeded the league average by 33 points. While Cash never led the league in home runs, he was a consistent home run threat over a fourteen-year period, finishing among the top five in the league in 1962, 1965, 1966, 1968, and 1971. Over 20% of his career hits were home runs.

Cash drove in 100 runs only once, but he drove in far more runs per at bat than Steve Garvey or Ted Simmons or his longtime teammate Al Kaline. He walked a lot and would miss about twenty games a year with injuries, so that he usually wound up in the mid-400s in at bats, which makes all of his numbers look less impressive than they are (83 RBI in 479 at bats, 82 RBI in 467 at bats, 91 RBI in 452 at bats). The public perception of him was dimmed by the contrast to Kaline, dimmed by the low averages of his time, dimmed by the contrast to his own 1961 season, dimmed by the missing 100 at bats a year, dimmed by the fact that nobody in his time paid much attention to the walk column, and dimmed by his own self-effacing humor. He was not a greater player than Clemente or Pete Rose or Al Simmons, as some analysts have tried to make him, but he was a very fine player for a long time.

ORLANDO CEPEDA

HALL OF FAME? No
DATA IN SECTION III? No
OFFENSIVE WON-LOST RECORD:
Approximately 152–79, .659
GROSS VALUE: 154

Up until 1964, when his knees started giving him trouble, Cepeda's offensive statistics are closely parallel to Hank Aaron's at the same age. Each broke into the major leagues at the age of twenty:

	CEPEDA			AARON		
AGE	HR	RBI	Avg.	HR	RBI	Avg.
20	25	96	.312	13	69	.280
21	27	105	.317	27	106	.314
22	24	96	.297	26	92	.328
23	46	142	.311	44	132	.322
24	35	114	.306	30	95	.326
25	34	97	.316	39	123	.355
Total	191	650	.310	179	617	.323

Through age twenty-four (1962) he was 17 home runs ahead of Aaron's pace, which I think (without thoroughly checking) makes him the last man to be significantly ahead of Aaron's home run pace at any age. The knee injuries ruined his career stats; he had only two outstanding seasons after the age of twenty-five.

Another interesting thing about Cha Cha's career is the unanimous MVP selection in 1967. Cepeda hit .325 that year with 25 home runs, 111 RBI; Roberto Clemente hit .357 with 23 and 110, plus of course he was Clemente in the outfield. One would think that, if nothing else, the similarity of their stats would have divided the votes, with Cepeda's infectious enthusiasm, contributions to a first-place team, and glovework at first being balanced off against Clemente's 32-point edge in batting and awesome defensive skills. But a committee of twenty men was entrusted with the responsibility to name the best in the league, and all twenty of them said it was Cepeda, something which had never before happened in the National League. You've got to respect that.

HAL CHASE

HALL OF FAME? No
DATA IN SECTION III? No
OFFENSIVE WON-LOST RECORD:
102–82, .556
GROSS VALUE: 97
COMPARABLE RECENT PLAYERS: Vic Power

Could he really have existed, or was he perhaps invented by Robert Louis Stevenson, along with the Master of Ballantrae, Long John Silver and the good Dr. Jekyll? Hal Chase is remembered as a shining, leering, pock-marked face, pasted on a pitch-dark soul. There is some evidence to say that he appeared in the flesh, but I lean more toward the invention theory. What mother, if he was real, what Rosemary could have given birth to such a creature? He was an attractive figure, of this there is no doubt (Susie, knowing nothing of his character, selected him the ugliest player of the decade, and he was that, too). His parentage is not much discussed in the literature, but he should have been, I would say, the bastard son of a bishop, by way of a woman down on her luck.

Within days of arriving in the majors in 1905, Hal Chase was acclaimed a star. No one ever saw him play without being left gasping for adjectives, and though his statistics may not explain why, he was routinely described as a great player. "His range was incredible," said Fred Lieb. "No other first baseman played so far off the bag. As a man charging in on a bunt he was fantastic. He was speed and grace personified." According to an article by Robert Hoie in the 1974 *Baseball Research Journal,* a year before he came to the majors the *Los Angeles Examiner* wrote that "If Chase isn't a great natural ballplayer, then Los Angeles never saw one." Within two years of his reaching the major leagues, *The Sporting Life* said that "a more brilliant player does not wear a uniform" and he was "perhaps the biggest drawing card in baseball."

That was in 1907. He was then in the middle of one of his early controversies, seeking to get more money out of the New York Highlanders. In 1908 the first charges appeared that Chase had been "laying down," the terminology of the day for throwing games. Chase, accusing the team of slander, jumped the New Yorkers and went to play in an outlaw league in California. He was suspended for this, but applied for reinstatement, paid a $200 fine and was eligible to begin the 1909 season.

In the spring of 1909 Chase developed smallpox. Some have attributed Chase's later disrepute to this untimely disfigurement, that he felt cheated of his youth and became bitter and greedy thereafter. Chase, in truth, was greedy and disagreeable before this, but never mind . . . reading his life as a work of fiction, we see the pox to have been an external manifestation of the rotten pulp at Chase's center, a clue to the other players and to the readers, if you will, that a wary eye should be kept upon him.

But there was a powerful magnetism within him. In trying to research something else that happened in the 1909 season, Jim Baker noted that it seemed the only thing the New York papers would report about the Highlanders was the status of Hal Chase. "Chase reported in Albany . . . Chase set to rejoin team next Tuesday . . . Chase reported on train . . . Chase in camp." Chase, who had departed the team in a huff the previous September, was presented a loving cup by his teammates when he rejoined them in May of 1909.

George Stallings was now the manager of the Highlanders. He was the second man to have gotten the job after Chase felt it should have been his. The team did remarkably well; an outfit that had lost 103

games in 1908, the year before Stallings took over, finished near .500 in 1909 and in 1910 improved to 88–63, second in the American League. There were printed charges, however, that Chase was unhappy —indeed, that he was so unhappy that he was laying down, trying to lose games so as to get Stallings fired. In mid-season Stallings accused Chase of trying to throw a game. The two nearly came to blows. Chase began to be mysteriously absent from the team. In late September Stallings said that he would resign if Chase was not replaced.

A half-century later, when interviewed by Lawrence Ritter for *The Glory of Their Times,* Jimmy Austin, a member of the team, was still somewhat astonished by what had happened then. Describing Stallings as "a fine manager—one of the best," he recalled that Chase "had gone to Mr. Farrell, the president of the club, and complained about Stallings and a lot of other things. Mr. Farrell supported Chase, so Stallings quit, and Chase was made the new manager. God, what a way to run a ball club!"

Gabby Street, a catcher with the club under Chase, told about standing behind Chase once at a poker game. With a big pot on the table, Chase was raising each round, so Street, not playing, glanced at Chase's hand and saw three kings. He looked away for a moment and then glanced

again, and Chase had four kings. As he stared at the hand, a low card disappeared as if by magic.

This sort of thing must have been great for morale. Chase was a dismal failure as a player/manager, and resigned after one year.

In 1913 Frank Chance, then managing the team (by now known as the Yankees), approached the sportswriters covering his team and charged that Chase was throwing games on him. The sportswriters let it pass once but then printed the charges. Chase was traded to the White Sox shortly after that, and a year later jumped to the Buffalo team of the Federal League, his right to do so becoming the subject of one of the decade's many lawsuits. Rumors were heard of peculiar events surrounding Buffalo's games, which complicated the difficult task of keeping the league alive, but again, nothing was proven. When the Federal League folded, their players were auctioned off to the other teams, Chase going to Cincinnati.

His first two years in Cincinnati were the most productive seasons of his career, but in time there again began to circulate charges reflecting on the integrity of Chase's efforts. In August of 1918, Christy Mathewson (manager of the Reds) suspended Chase for the balance of the season, and charged him with violations of National League Rule 40, which related to "Crooked-ness and Its Penalties," and specified that "Any person who shall be proven guilty of offering, agreeing, conspiring or attempting to cause any game of ball to result otherwise than on its merits under the playing rules, shall be forever disqualified..." Chase immediately filed a civil suit, demanding payment of his salary for the balance of the season, and issued a sweeping denial of the charges against him. National League President John Heydler was assigned by the league to conduct a trial of the issue, and to render a judgment based on the law and the evidence.

This was the third time that a matter of baseball treason had been heard by the National League, the first relating to the Louisville incident in 1877, and the other a comparatively trivial clearing up of unsubstantiated charge against Jack Taylor, a Cubs pitcher. The trial of Chase was conducted at Heydler's office in New York on January 30, 1919. Chase was present, and arrived armed with three lawyers, a clerk and a stenographer. The Cincinnati team sent no one; an attorney from New York represented the interests of the National League and cross-examined some witnesses. Christy Mathewson was with the United States Army in France, and was unable to attend. New York pitcher Pol Perritt, who had alleged that Chase had offered

to make it worth his while to bear down extra hard in a game against the Reds, was working on his plantation in Louisiana, and was also unable to attend.

This left Greasy Neale, a Cincinnati outfielder, as the leading witness against the infidel. Neale reported several conversations that Chase had had with other members of the Cincinnati team, each leaving the impression that Chase was betting against his own team. Chase argued that Neale was the head of a clique of Cincinnati players who had it in for him. Pitcher Mike Regan appeared and alleged that Chase had offered him a bribe; Chase denied it and charged that Regan was a part of the clique. He entered into evidence his batting and fielding records of the previous three seasons, during one of which he had led the National League in hitting, at .339.

John McGraw appeared, supposedly as a witness to incriminating conversations, but damaged the case by testifying as to Chase's good character, and offering the opinion that the Cincinnati club had no proper basis for their charges. Chase argued that the charges were absurd, that he had been a major league regular longer at that time than any other player, and that he had never before been charged with such dishonesty. When the prior indictments were brought up, Chase "explained previously unknown

circumstances in connection with troubles he had had in the American League, particularly while he was with the Yankees" (1919 *Reach Guide*). He had the advantage of being the only person present who was a party to those incidents.

Chase was publicly acquitted. Although John Heydler told friends that he was privately convinced of Chase's guilt, he had in front of him no evidence that would stand up in a court of law, and so he felt that his hands were tied.

Chase was free, then. It had all been brought out into the open, and he had gotten by with it. This seems to have had a liberating effect on Chase's activities, or perhaps it was not that but the fact that as the end of his career grew nearer, he had less to lose and became more reckless. Or perhaps he was just drinking too much. Anyway, John McGraw, to Heydler's irritation, signed Chase to play for the Giants in 1919. Back in New York, where the gamblers were easy to communicate with, Chase enlisted the help of a couple of teammates (Heine Zimmerman and Jean Dubuc), and between them they seem to have approached almost everyone on the team to see who was interested in making a little money on the side. He was free then, free to bring the gamblers right into the locker room if he chose, free to play his role in arranging the outcome of the World Series.

Heydler, however, had not let the matter drop. He continued to investigate the Chase affair, traveling to Boston to collect information about a gambler there with whom Chase had a connection. Eventually Heydler obtained a signed affidavit from the Boston gambler, as well as a copy of a $500 check given Chase for throwing a game in 1918. In late 1919, almost a year before the the revelation of the Black Sox scandal, Heydler banned Chase from the National League. In 1921 Judge Landis made the ban permanent and universal. Even this did not end Chase's career in dishonesty, but at least it kept it out of organized ball.

Chase's methods in throwing games apparently included bribing teammates, paying bonuses to opponents for bearing down harder, and a variety of on-field maneuvers. He collected hits at meaningless times to cover himself, and it has been suggested that opposing pitchers who were co-conspirators may have allowed to him to fatten up his average. A favorite trick was to break late in covering first, thus failing to make the catch while seeming to make a good effort, often causing the third baseman or shortstop to draw an error on a perfectly good throw.

His methods in arranging a fix are less well documented, and though the destination of his career is well known,

much of the scenery of the trip has been forgotten. It is my belief, though no one could claim to prove such a thing, that Hal Chase's personality is one of the keys to the corruption of the era, and that had Chase been a butcher, a baker or a candlestick maker, it is quite possible that the whole thing would never have happened—the "whole thing" including the series fix, all of the other scandals, and the arrival of Kenesaw Mountain Landis and the commissioner system to sort it out. I suggested this theory in the first edition of this book and convinced no one, but I later learned that Fred Lieb had expressed a similar thought. "How many good young ball-players," Lieb asked in *Baseball As I Have Known It,* "may have said, 'Chase gets by with it, year after year, so why shouldn't we pick up a little extra money when the chance is offered us?'" Visiting a SABR convention in the early seventies, Lieb reportedly said that he thought that all of the trouble started with Chase, and he didn't know if any of it would have happened without him.

As ugly as Chase was, something wonderfully masculine and persuasive drew men to him and compelled them to believe not only that he was honest but that he was *right,* that he was something more than ordinary. How else to explain it? The most astonishing thing is that *it all went on so*

long. There were printed charges that he was laying down in 1908, *twelve years* before he was expelled from baseball. Fred Lieb said that there was talk among the writers about crookedness when he arrived in New York in 1911. Lee Magee, one of the players that he took with him, charged that the business began in 1906. Three of baseball's most respected managers (Frank Chance, George Stallings and Christy Mathewson) charged Chase with dishonesty—yet he stayed in the game. Something about him made wrong shine as it were right and evil smell like good. If it seems incredible that any one man could so alter the ethics of the sport, remember that it was a smaller sport then, and consider too the rank improbability of what he is known to have done. He played in the major leagues for over a decade during which the cloud of suspicion returned to him again and again and again.

With the greatest of effort, personalities cannot be photographed and preserved. Chase's lost charm is something which can be forever speculated about, but it seems to me that Chase was one of those people—you may have known one or two yourself— to whom lies and truth are all the same, and who eventually was not always certain in his own mind when he was lying and when he was telling the truth. When it was alleged that

HAL CHASE

he paid a teammate $25 after the teammate (Jimmy Ring) had lost a game, he said it was just a gift. And he made people believe that. Was that how he did it—did he come bearing gifts?

He was known as a generous man. Bob Hoie writes that "He apparently would befriend the young players, was one of the few veterans to invite them home to dinner, etc. Many of them were almost worshipful of him. This appeal carried over to his days of outlaw ball in Douglas, Arizona, where men whose wives and girlfriends were seduced by Chase were still in awe of him 50 years later." (Quote from private letter.)

There is an evil, a smallness, lust and greed that lives inside of each of us. The secret of Hal Chase, I believe, was that he was able to reach out and embrace that evil. And he had so much class, don't you see? He was a man of such dignity and bearing, such wit, charm and grace, that he made you feel that it was all right to have that in you. It's OK; it's just the way we are. We're all professionals, aren't we? We're in this game to make a living, aren't we?

How good a player was Hal Chase? Walter Johnson in 1924 named Chase the greatest first baseman of all time. *Baseball* magazine, choosing an all-time team in July 1930, did the same. In Babe Ruth's autobiography, *The Babe Ruth Story* with Bob Considine (1948), Ruth chose as the greatest first baseman of all time not Lou Gehrig or Jimmie Foxx or George Sisler or Bill Terry or any of the other great first basemen who were his contemporaries, but Hal Chase, saying that some people "will feel that I should pick Lou Gehrig over Chase, (but

Chase) was so much better than anybody else that I ever saw on first base that—to me —it was no contest."

There is no doubt that his defensive skills were astonishing, and that you might fully share that conviction, but let me give you a couple more quotes. One, which I find in Hoie's article, was from a June 1913 issue of *The Sporting News.* "That he can play first base as it never was and perhaps never will be played is a well-known truth," said *TSN.* "That he will is a different matter."

The other quote is a poem from the 1915 *Reach Guide,* entitled "You Can't Escape 'Em." It goes:

"Sometimes a raw recruit in spring
Is not a pitching find.
He has no Walter Johnson's wing,
Nor Matty's wondrous mind.
He does not act like Harold Chase
Upon the fielding job,
But you will find in such a case,
He hits like Tyrus Cobb."

Lawrence Ritter and Donald Honig chose Chase as one of the top 100 players in baseball history. I would not choose him among a thousand. Okay, so he was the greatest defensive first baseman ever, and he once led the league in homers, and he once led the league in batting. He led the Federal League in home runs with seventeen, but that was playing in a tiny park in a marginal major league. With the exception of that one season, his career

high in home runs was five. He was no real power threat. He hit .339 in 1916, and he was a lifetime .291 hitter. But he was an impatient hitter, drawing less than 20 walks a year, and that combination—no walks, no power—makes for an empty .291 average. Chase never drove in or scored 100 runs in a season, or even 90. His on-field talents were essentially the same as those of Vic Power. Each player was the best defensive first baseman of his time. Each hit for a pretty good average and had excellent speed for a first baseman. Each had a little power but not much, and each was an excellent contact hitter, but not one to take a walk. I would guess that Power's career offensive winning percentage would be quite similar to Chase's .556.

But what greatness as a player comes down to is "What did he do to help his teams win?" If you were trying to win a pennant, how badly would you want the guy? Hey, this is not Joe Jackson that we are talking about here. This is not the corrupted. This is the corrupt. No matter what his skills, I would not want Hal Chase around, period, and I find it extremely difficult to believe that he ever helped any team, at all, period. He never played for a championship team. Most of the teams that he played for declined precipitously when he joined them and improved dramatically after he was gone.

The Highlanders/Yankees declined by twenty games in Chase's rookie year, and improved by eleven the year after he was traded. The White Sox claimed the pennant when they acquired Chase, but in fact they dropped from fourth to fifth, and improved by twenty-three games in their first full year without Chase. Chase's Federal League teams finished fourth and sixth. Cincinnati declined by ten games the year that Chase joined them and improved by twenty-two games the year after he left. That he was manipulator nonpareil is clear; that he was a great player is not.

FRANK CHANCE

HALL OF FAME? Yes
DATA IN SECTION III? Yes
OFFENSIVE WON-LOST RECORD:
  90–33, .733
GROSS VALUE: 82
COMPARABLE RECENT PLAYERS:
Keith Hernandez

The most famous, individually, of the Tinkers to Evers to Chance combination, Chance was probably the least qualified of the three for Hall of Fame selection (though, oddly, he is often cited by poorly informed historians as the best of the three). Unlike Tinker, who was an everyday player for thirteen seasons, and Evers, who was a regular when healthy for twelve seasons, Chance played regularly for only six seasons and never batted 500 times in a year, making his one of the shortest careers for a Hall of Famer. During those six seasons he was quite a player, hitting .300 consistently with excellent speed, fine defense and very good strike zone judgment, in addition to which he was a highly regarded player/manager.

CECIL COOPER

HALL OF FAME: Not Eligible
DATA IN SECTION III? No
OFFENSIVE WON-LOST RECORD:
  119–84, .587
GROSS VALUE: 129

JACQUES FOURNIER

HALL OF FAME? No
DATA IN SECTION III? No
OFFENSIVE WON-LOST RECORD:
  Approximately 95–47, .669
GROSS VALUE: 103
COMPARABLE RECENT PLAYERS:
Pete O'Brien

To the group of three National League/Hall of Fame first basemen discussed under the heading of Jim Bottomley, Jacques Fournier is the missing fourth. Active at about the same time (1912–27), Fournier was a similar type of player except that he was a more patient hitter, whose career statistics were hurt by the fact that he was in mid-career before the lively ball era arrived.

Jacques Fournier was born in Au Sable, Michigan—one guesses that it was a French community—in September of 1892. He entered organized baseball at the age of fifteen, playing in the Northwestern League in 1908. In 1911 he hit .377 in the Western Canada League, leading the league in runs scored, hits, doubles and triples, and was purchased by the Chicago White Sox. At the age of nineteen, he started the 1912 season as the White Sox first baseman, but started slowly and was dispatched to Montreal, where he hit .309 to earn a return to the major leagues. As a twenty-one-year-old in 1914, he hit .311 and had the best home run percentage in the American League, with 6 in 379 at bats. In 1915 he hit .322 and, with the help of 18 triples, led the American League in slugging percentage, edging Ty Cobb (who had led in the department in seven of the eight previous years), .491–.487.

At that point he was en route to immortality, but in 1916 he skidded to .240, and the White Sox, making probably the worst mistake in their history, acquired Chick Gandil from Cleveland and sent Fournier to the Pacific Coast League. Fournier had two outstanding seasons in the PCL and earned a look from the Yankees, for whom he hit .350 in 27 games while Wally Pipp was in uniform.

Pipp was a fine player. The evidence that he was a better player than Fournier does not survive, but the Yankees thought he was, and Fournier went back to Los Angeles for the 1919 season.

In 1920 Branch Rickey acquired Fournier, now twenty-seven, to play first base for the Cardinals. The lively ball era, as it is called, arrived that same season, and Fournier's trials were over. In the next six years he hit .306, .343, .295, .351, .334, and .350. His best season is difficult to pick. He hit triples (14, 9, 9, 13, 4, 16). He hit homers, leading the National League in home runs with 27 in 1924, and finishing second, third and fifth in other seasons. He drew walks, leading the league in 1925 (86) and finishing second in that category in 1924. He had good speed and was regarded as a decent first baseman. In a three-year stretch with the Dodgers, he drove in 348 runs. Though he never played for a pennant winner, he played for many teams that were in the thick of the pennant race.

After his playing career, Fournier was the coach at UCLA for a couple of years, and then spent a quarter of a century as a scout for the Browns, Cubs, Tigers, and Reds. His ranking by history has been hurt by the comparatively brief period of his uninterrupted excellence, 1920–25. His ranking in his own time was hurt by his inability to get into the World Series. He was essentially the same type and quality of player as Terry, Bottomley, and Kelly, and it is probably a fair summation of his career to say that if they belong in the Hall of Fame, he belongs in the Hall of Fame, and if they don't, he doesn't.

JIMMIE FOXX

HALL OF FAME: Yes
DATA IN SECTION III? Yes
OFFENSIVE WON-LOST RECORD:
165–53, .758
GROSS VALUE: 234 (highest among first basemen)
COMPARABLE RECENT PLAYERS: Jim Rice

If Jimmie Foxx were growing up today, he would probably end up as a linebacker in the NFL. A man of enormous upper-body strength, Foxx was light on his feet and had a fearsome throwing arm (he caught 109 games in his career and had a 1.52 ERA in ten games as a pitcher). His best seasons are quite comparable to Gehrig's or even Ruth's, and it is only by careful analysis that one can be sure that he was not, indeed, the greatest first baseman who ever lived.

STEVE GARVEY

HALL OF FAME? Not Eligible
DATA IN SECTION III? No
OFFENSIVE WON-LOST RECORD:
132–87, .603
GROSS VALUE: 153

LOU GEHRIG

HALL OF FAME: Yes
DATA IN SECTION III? Yes
OFFENSIVE WON-LOST RECORD:
168–42, .799
Gehrig's offensive winning percentage of .799 is the highest ever for a first baseman.
GROSS VALUE: 233
COMPARABLE RECENT PLAYERS: Don Mattingly

According to the research of John Tattersall, Lou Gehrig hit 23 grand slams, 73 three-run homers, 166 two-run homers, and 231 home runs with the bases empty, for a total of 874 RBI on home runs. The ratio, 1.77 RBI per home run, is the highest among players with 300 or more home runs.

HANK GREENBERG

HALL OF FAME? Yes
DATA IN SECTION III? Yes
OFFENSIVE WON-LOST RECORD:
108–32, .772
GROSS VALUE: 143
COMPARABLE RECENT PLAYERS: None

Hank Greenberg played regularly in the major leagues for only nine and a half seasons, during seven of which he was one of the dominant figures in the game. In 1934 (1) he helped get the Tigers to the top of the league by hitting 63 doubles and driving in 139 runs; in 1935 (2) he drove in 170 and was a unanimous MVP selection. In 1936 he had driven in 16 runs by April 17 (!) when he broke his wrist and was out for the season, but he came back in 1937 (3) to challenge the American League RBI record, finishing with 183 to miss by one. In 1938 (4) he challenged Ruth's home run record, and missed that by two, with 58. After an off season in 1939, he moved to outfield in 1940 (5) so that Rudy York could play first, hit 50 doubles, 41 homers, led the Tigers back to the championship and won the MVP award. He was drafted for training early in 1941, the first player to go, and was released on Saturday, December 6, 1941, only to be immediately recalled.

Coming out of the army for the second half of the 1945 (6) season, Greenberg drove in 60 runs in half a season to lead the Tigers to the World Championship. In 1946 (7) he led the American League in home runs and RBI, after which he got involved in a nasty salary hassle that was the major baseball news story of the winter of 1946–47.

Such intensive domination of the events of his time may have no parallel—and yet he was but the third-best American League first baseman of his time, sharing the spot (1932–38) with Foxx and Gehrig. That is probably the most remarkable concentration of talent at one position in one league that there has ever been.

Greenberg lost four and a half seasons to the war, missed one with an injury and retired early. My estimate by the Brock2 system is that had it not been for these events, he would have hit about 611 home runs in his career. That estimate seems conservative, for it calls for no more than 36 home runs in any of the missing seasons, while Greenberg in fact exceeded 36 home runs in four of his nine healthy campaigns. The projection also calls for 653 doubles, 2,097 RBI (projecting no season of more than 113; Greenberg in fact drove in more runs than that almost every year), and just short of 3,000 hits.

KEITH HERNANDEZ
HALL OF FAME: Not Eligible
DATA IN SECTION III? No
OFFENSIVE WON-LOST RECORD:
  128–56, .678
GROSS VALUE: 129

GIL HODGES
HALL OF FAME? No
DATA IN SECTION III? Yes
OFFENSIVE WON-LOST RECORD:
  126–74, .629
GROSS VALUE: 153
COMPARABLE RECENT PLAYERS:
Tony Perez

You ever notice how many outstanding first basemen were converted catchers and third baseman? Hodges came to the majors as a catcher, as did Rudy York and Frank Chance, and Foxx was tried as a catcher and third baseman (actually, Hodges' first major league game was also at third base). Garvey was originally a third baseman; Cap Anson was originally a catcher/third baseman. Tony Perez, of course, was a third baseman. Hodges hit .273 lifetime with 370 home runs, while Perez hit .279 with 379 home runs.

GEORGE KELLY
HALL OF FAME? Yes
DATA IN SECTION III? No
OFFENSIVE WON-LOST RECORD:
  Approximately 95–78, .548
GROSS VALUE: 115
COMPARABLE RECENT PLAYERS: Bill Buckner

See article on Jim Bottomley. In truth, Bill Buckner is a better player than George Kelly was.

TED KLUSZEWSKI
HALL OF FAME? No
DATA IN SECTION III? Yes
OFFENSIVE WON-LOST RECORD:
  104–57, .646
GROSS VALUE: 122
COMPARABLE RECENT PLAYERS:
John Mayberry, Willie McCovey

Rivals Hodges and Vic Wertz as the outstanding first baseman of the fifties if Musial is considered an outfielder. He had only four years as an outstanding player (1953–56), plus perhaps the 1950 season, but was one of the best for those four years. The fifties were packed with first basemen who were outstanding for a few years, like Eddie Robinson, Roy Sievers, Walt Dropo, and Joe Adcock, but none was consistently strong throughout the decade.

WILLIE McCOVEY
HALL OF FAME? Yes
DATA IN SECTION III? Yes
OFFENSIVE WON-LOST RECORD:
  165–67, .712
GROSS VALUE: 186

McCovey is probably the only truly great player in history to have been platooned for several years at the start of his career. It was an unusual situation, when the Giants came up with Cepeda in 1958 and McCovey in 1959, and neither one of them, really, could even do a passable job in the outfield (they had also come up with Bill White in 1956). The 1962 Giants scored more runs than any other team between 1954 and 1981 anyway, even with McCovey on the bench most of the time. If the National League had had the Designated Hitter Rule in 1962 it is frightening to think how many they would have scored.

STUFFY McINNIS
HALL OF FAME? No
DATA IN SECTION III? No
OFFENSIVE WON-LOST RECORD:
  Approximately 120–97, .553
GROSS VALUE: 133
COMPARABLE RECENT PLAYERS:
Mike Squires is the same type of player, except that his batting average is about 50 points lower. Rod Carew would be comparable.

An interesting comparison to Hal Chase, who Honig/Ritter chose among the 100 greatest, is Stuffy McInnis, a contemporary. Originally a middle infielder (like Chase), McInnis was regarded as the best defensive first baseman of the time other than Chase. He was the inventor of what was called the "knee reach"— in other words, he was the first first baseman to do a full, ground-level split in reaching for the throw, which is the one thing that he is remembered for other than being a member of the famed $100,000 infield. As an offensive player he was similar to Chase and about even. He had even less power than Chase, hitting only twenty career home runs and few doubles and triples, and Chase was faster, but McInnis out-hit him .308–.291 in his career and drew a few more walks. But whereas Chase never drove in or scored 90 runs in a season, Stuffy drove in more than 90 four times (more than 100 once), and whereas Chase never played for a championship team, McInnis played for five World Champion teams (the Athletics of 1910, 1911, and 1913, plus the Red Sox of 1918 and the Pirates of 1925) and a sixth league champion.

DON MATTINGLY

HALL OF FAME? Not Eligible
DATA IN SECTION III? No
OFFENSIVE WON-LOST RECORD:
    53–19, .732
GROSS VALUE: 57

JOHNNY MIZE

HALL OF FAME? Yes
DATA IN SECTION III? Yes
OFFENSIVE WON-LOST RECORD:
    130–40, .767
GROSS VALUE: 161
COMPARABLE RECENT PLAYERS:
McCovey

A left-handed slugger whose career is comparable to Hank Greenberg's, Johnny Mize was known as "The Big Cat," and thus is the big star on the feline all-stars. Mize lost three prime years to the war, without which he would have hit almost 500 home runs. His career offensive winning percentage, .767, is close to Greenberg's (.772) and higher than Foxx's (.758). He was an ordinary defensive player, but as a hitter very comparable to DiMaggio, and truly one of the least-remembered greats. He hit for an outstanding average with awesome power and excellent strike zone judgment, and that doesn't leave out too much.

EDDIE MURRAY

HALL OF FAME? Not Eligible
DATA IN SECTION III? No
OFFENSIVE WON-LOST RECORD:
    116–55, .678
GROSS VALUE: 113

TONY PEREZ

HALL OF FAME? Not Eligible
DATA IN SECTION III? No
OFFENSIVE WON-LOST RECORD:
    169–111, .604
GROSS VALUE: 178

GEORGE SISLER

HALL OF FAME? Yes
DATA IN SECTION III? Yes
OFFENSIVE WON-LOST RECORD:
    144–79, .646
GROSS VALUE: 177
COMPARABLE RECENT PLAYERS:
Rod Carew

George Sisler is probably the only player other than Gehrig who can reasonably be considered the greatest first baseman ever in terms of peak value. The reason I say that is that the other top contenders, most notably Foxx and McCovey, were the same type of players that Gehrig was, and thus they can be directly compared to him, a comparison that they clearly lose. But Sisler was a different type of player; he didn't have the home run pop, but he hit for a higher average, was faster and a better defensive player than Gehrig, and the comparison between the two is not easy.

George Sisler came to the American League as a left-handed pitcher in 1915, the first full season of another left-handed pitcher, George Ruth, who would also be shifted from the mound. As a pitcher Sisler had a career ERA of 2.35 in a little over a hundred innings, ranking him just below Ruth (2.28) on that account. Unlike Heilmann and to a lesser extent Hornsby, who became batting terrors after they began keeping fresh balls in play in 1920, Sisler was a great hitter in the dead-ball era, posting averages of .353, .341, and .352 (with a .530 slugging percentage) in the years 1917–19. In 1920 he was about as great a player as you can be, collecting 257 hits with a .407 average, with 49 doubles, 18 triples and 19 home runs among the hits, and stealing 42 bases. With the retirement of Chase he became recognized as the game's top glove man at first base, and he had 140 assists in 1920, the fourth-highest total ever at that time. His 1922 season, when he hit .420 with 51 stolen bases, is almost as awesome.

He was, at that moment, probably the best player in baseball with the exception of Ruth, and it was not hard to find people who felt that he was better than Ruth. In early September 1922, Sisler had a forty-game hitting streak, and the Browns were in the center of a pennant race when Sisler suffered a painful shoulder injury in a game against Detroit. The injury hurt Sisler both at bat and in the field, and he missed five games. When he returned he hit in one more to stretch the streak to 41, but then fell into a slump. The injury probably cost the Browns the pennant, which they lost by a single game.

Sisler missed the 1923 season with an infection affecting the optic nerve. After that he was never the same, never even close. The Brock2 system projects that, absent the injury, he would have collected about 3,800 hits in his career and finished with a career average of .357. I think that estimate's a little low; I think he would have gotten over 4,000 hits and hit about .362. Harry Heilmann came up in 1916, and in the years 1916 to 1922, Sisler out-hit Heilmann every year except 1921, and usually out-hit him by 30 points or more. Rogers Hornsby came up in 1915, the same year (and in the same town) as Sisler; Sisler out-hit Hornsby every year 1915 to 1922 except 1916 and 1921. Hornsby and Heilmann were just beginning their most productive years; I think that Sisler would have continued to out-hit them had he been healthy. Through 1922, his offensive totals will even stand the comparison to the Bambino, remembering of course that Ruth was not a full-time player until 1919. The categories in the chart below are runs created (RC), offensive wins (W), offensive losses (L), and offensive winning percentage (Pct.):

	SISLER			RUTH		
Year	RC	W-L	Pct.	RC	W-L	Pct.
1914				1	0–0	.201
1915	33	4–4	.530	19	2–1	.800
1916	94	12–5	.699	19	3–1	.678
1917	104	11–3	.788	22	3–1	.801
1918	92	10–2	.828	75	7–1	.866
1919	112	11–2	.817	128	10–1	.885
1920	186	13–2	.848	211	11–1	.934
1921	138	11–4	.739	238	12–1	.913
1922	173	12–2	.857	120	9–2	.854
Total	942	84–24	.778	833	60–8	.881

The point is not that he was as good as Ruth, of course, but that if you can stand next to Ruth and not look ridiculous, you're pretty good. Sisler's offensive winning percentage was comparable to Ruth's in four of the eight seasons.

Though his statistics after he came back look good by today's standards, in the 1920s he was just another player. The questions of history are not ultimately questions about what might have been, and Sisler receives no extra credit in my book for the career that he would have had; it is difficult enough to make sense of what *did* happen. But the peak of performance that he did reach before the illness marks him as arguably the greatest first baseman of all time—and, on that basis, Definition-A Hall of Famer.

Among the people who felt that Sisler was the greatest first baseman of all time are baseball's two leading hitters, Ty Cobb and Rogers Hornsby. Ty Cobb chose his all-time All-Star team in a letter to the Hall of Fame; his infield was Sisler, Eddie Collins, Honus Wagner and Buck Weaver. Hornsby chose his in his autobiography; his infield was the same except that he put Pie Traynor at third base.

BILL TERRY

HALL OF FAME? Yes
DATA IN SECTION III? Yes
OFFENSIVE WON-LOST RECORD:
119–49, .708
GROSS VALUE: 147
COMPARABLE RECENT PLAYERS:
Cecil Cooper is an excellent comparison in almost every respect.

See article under Jim Bottomley.

MICKEY VERNON

HALL OF FAME? No
DATA IN SECTION III? No
OFFENSIVE WON-LOST RECORD:
148–97, .603
GROSS VALUE: 151
COMPARABLE RECENT PLAYERS:
Keith Hernandez, Pete O'Brien

Not many first basemen in major league history could do all of the things that Mickey Vernon could do. He could do everything that Keith Hernandez could do, and in the main did most of them about as well. He hit for average (.353, .337, two batting titles). He had line-drive power, hitting 172 career home runs despite playing his career in terrible home run parks (career totals of 55 home runs in his home parks, 117 on the road. Most of his career was spent in massive Griffith Stadium). Three times he led the league in doubles. He was exceptionally mobile for a first baseman, twice stealing over 20 bases in a era which did not emphasize the stolen base. He hit almost as many triples in his career as Willie Mays, including 14 triples when he was 36 years old. This mobility contributed to making him a superb defensive player. He was a selective hitter who drew a good many walks. He drove in over 80 runs eleven times despite spending most of his career with poor teams. He was a respected man in the clubhouse. He was regarded as an intelligent, alert player on the basepaths and in the field. He had a long career, collecting just short of 2,500 hits despite missing two prime seasons to World War II. He hit .293 at the age of 40.

The one thing he was not, unfortunately, was consistent. After having a monster season in 1946 (.353, 207 hits, 51 doubles) he had an undistinguished year in 1947 and a miserable year in 1948 (.242, 3 homers and 48 RBI in 150 games). At age 34 he hit just .251 with 10 homers; the next year he hit .337 with 43 doubles, 205 hits, 115 RBI. Had Vernon been even reasonably consistent at the level of his best seasons, he would be not simply a Hall of Famer, but one of the inner circle, somebody you would compare to Stan Musial or George Sisler. He was there every year, playing 150 games a season. It's just that he wasn't good every year.

Generally speaking, we see baseball statistics as describing personalities on some level. We see inconsistent players as being inconsistent people, undependable. In the case of Mickey Vernon this perception just doesn't sit. He was such a dependable person, as I understand it, that it seemed very odd to me that he was not a consistent player. On that basis, in the first edition of this book I speculated that Vernon "must have spent about a third of his career playing hurt." He was, I suggested, the strong, silent type, of an age to have been nurtured on the legend of Lou Gehrig. Maybe he just had an injury that he never told anybody about.

A gentleman named Phil Wood, who writes for the *Towson Times,* saw that comment and happens to be a friend of Mickey Vernon's, so he decided to check out the guess. "Vernon told me," Wood reported, "that he suffered from back trouble off and on for several years, and finally one off-season was operated on for a troubled appendix." After the operation the pain in the back disappeared.

In the competitive environment of major league baseball at that time, with only sixteen major league teams and a dozen minor league sluggers like Steve Bilko and Rocky Nelson battering AAA pitching and waiting for a shot at the majors, Vernon simply never told the ballclub that he was having trouble.

"Another time," according to Wood, Vernon "imbedded a fishhook in his posterior, and the resulting infection caused him to alter his swing enough to upset his season at the plate." Again, Vernon told no one about it. But you should have seen the expression on the face of that fish. . . .

HOW THE FIRST BASEMEN RATE

In terms of career value, Gehrig is a comparatively easy choice for the number one spot, for not only did he reach a peak of performance that is as impressive as that of any first baseman of this century, but he sustained that peak for a decade of astonishingly consistent greatness. Only his contemporary, Foxx, can be considered in the same class.

As to peak value, the choice between Sisler and Gehrig is not so simple, but the basic assumption of sabermetrics is that you respect the conclusions of the best available methods unless you have some reason to suspect that the conclusion is invalid. The best available methods show Sisler creating 173 and 186 runs with offensive winning percentages of .857, .848, and .828, while Gehrig created 195 or more runs four times with offensive winning percentages of .884, .883, and .847. It is possible that given a more careful consideration of defense and baserunning, given that it might later be established that Gehrig's superhuman RBI totals were a natural outcome of his productivity and position in the lineup, I might switch to Sisler.

We have at present a tremendous crop of active first basemen, including Eddie Murray, Keith Hernandez, Cecil Cooper, Steve Garvey, Kent Hrbek and Don Mattingly as well as many young players who could develop into the class of all-time greats. Cooper, exceptional as he was from 1979 through 1983, petered out before qualifying to make the top ten. Garvey isn't my type of player. He's close to being among the top ten, and I'm sure that most people would put him ahead of Norm Cash, but this is my book and I have very good reasons to think that Cash was a better player. Eddie Murray and Keith Hernandez are magnificent players and have had enough good years that I have decided to make a place for them on the lists below, while admitting that I may be rushing it just a little bit. Don Mattingly obviously deserves a place among the greatest in terms of peak value and I have given him one, but again I have decided to err on the side of caution. If we ever re-do this book it would be easy to explain why I moved him up; it would be more difficult to explain how his peak value declined if he had to be moved down. The lists:

PEAK VALUE	CAREER VALUE
1. Lou Gehrig	1. Lou Gehrig
2. Jimmie Foxx	2. Jimmie Foxx
3. George Sisler	3. Willie McCovey
4. Willie McCovey	4. Hank Greenberg
5. Hank Greenberg	5. Johnny Mize
6. Johnny Mize	6. Bill Terry
7. Don Mattingly	7. George Sisler
8. Frank Chance	8. Keith Hernandez
9. Ted Kluszewski	9. Eddie Murray
10. Bill Terry	10. Norm Cash

❦ SECOND BASE ❦

ROD CAREW

HALL OF FAME? Not Eligible
DATA IN SECTION III? Yes
OFFENSIVE WON-LOST RECORD:
    163–82, .665
GROSS VALUE: 231

Placing him correctly among the greatest ever is difficult. He is certainly one of the greatest hitters ever to play second for a large portion of his career, and the complaints about his defense could easily be overdone. It was always said that he was not very good on the double play, and that's true; he wasn't. He wasn't very good on the double play when he came up, and he seemed to be making good progress until his injury in 1970, but not after that. But his range at second was pretty good and he didn't make a lot of errors, and I'd think you could give up a few double plays to get a second baseman who hits .350. As a first baseman he was less of an offensive plus, but compensated by hitting as high as .388, as well as being an exceptionally mobile defensive player in his first few years at the position. Ultimately, I'd rate him higher as a second baseman than a first baseman, and that's why he's here.

EDDIE COLLINS

HALL OF FAME? Yes
DATA IN SECTION III? Yes
OFFENSIVE WON-LOST RECORD:
    209–73, .742
GROSS VALUE: 262
Collins' gross value is the highest among second basemen.
COMPARABLE RECENT PLAYERS:
Willie Randolph is very comparable except that Collins' average was about 50 points a year higher. Nellie Fox is similar.

With apologies to Rogers Hornsby, the contest for the greatest second baseman of all time (career value) basically comes down to Collins against Joe Morgan. Collins' best season may not be any better than an average MVP season, but the thing is that his best season is impossible to locate. You've seen those lists of people who played in four decades? I wonder how many people hit over .340 in four decades? Collins hit .346 in 1909 (153 games), hit .365, .348, .345, and .344 in the 1910s, hit .369, .360, .349, .346 and .344 in the 1920s and .500 (1 for 2) in 1930. When he didn't hit .340 he hit .330 or .320. He stole 67 bases in 1909, and led the American League fifteen years later with 42. Drawing 60 to 119 walks a year, he had an on-base percentage over .400 (as a regular) thirteen times; his on-base percentage was over .400 in 1909, and over .450 in 1927.

Collins had no power, but he played a game in which power was basically no factor for most of his career. Batting second almost his entire career, he drove in over 70 runs many times, over 80 five times. He is to position players what Warren Spahn is to pitchers, the one player most remarkable for interchangeable high-performance seasons over a period of many years.

BOBBY DOERR

HALL OF FAME? Yes
DATA IN SECTION III? Yes
OFFENSIVE WON-LOST RECORD:
    116–85, .578
GROSS VALUE: 182
COMPARABLE RECENT PLAYERS:
Bobby Grich

I used to think, at a time when I knew less about these things than I know now, that Bobby Doerr was one of the unrecognized greats of history. He was recognized as a fine defensive player, graceful and quick on the double play, and his offensive stats speak for themselves—.325 in 1944, six 100-RBI seasons lead by 1950 (27 homers, 120 RBI, .294).

Doerr is no longer unrecognized, having been selected to the Hall of Fame in 1986. I think he is a worthy Hall of Famer. I think it would have shown better judgment to have asked Joe Gordon in first. The two players were direct competitors, like Reese and Rizzuto; they played the same position for the same years. Gordon was a better second baseman than Doerr, quicker and more active. Gordon did far better in the voting for the MVP Awards, totalling 1.57 Award Shares to Doerr's 0.47. Although Doerr's batting stats are superficially better than Gordon's because he played his whole career in Fenway Park, when the two players were not in their home parks, Gordon was a much better hitter, as is recounted in the Joe Gordon comment.

Of course some people simply dismiss the MVP votes because Gordon played for slightly better teams, but first of all, I don't think the contributions that one makes toward winning teams are supposed to be ignored, and second, Doerr's teams were very good. The Red Sox finished first or second in seven of Doerr's fourteen seasons. Okay, it was usually second, but even so the MVP voters' complete lack of interest in Doerr, if he was a legitimately great player, seems puzzling to me. Here's a second baseman driving in 100 runs a year for a contending team—yet he finished in the top ten in the MVP voting only once, that being a seventh-place finish one year when DiMaggio, Williams, Feller, Rizzuto and Joe Gordon were off at war. If he was as good as his numbers I can't understand why

that would have happened. He was a Definition C Hall of Famer—a player who was consistently among the best at his position. Joe Gordon was a definition B Hall of Famer: he *was* the best at his position.

LARRY DOYLE

HALL OF FAME? No
DATA IN SECTION III? Yes
OFFENSIVE WON-LOST RECORD:
123–65, .653
GROSS VALUE: 123
COMPARABLE RECENT PLAYERS: Jim Fregosi

Laughing Larry Doyle was the outstanding National League second baseman between Johnny Evers and Rogers Hornsby. As an offensive player he hit between .300 and .330 five times in a pitcher's era, led the National League in hits (172 in 1909, 189 in 1915), doubles (40 in 1915), triples (25 in 1911) and batting (.320 in 1915). He drew 60–70 walks a year, stole 30 or more bases for five straight years, and hit .290 in his career. Though his defensive statistics are just good, he was a well-regarded glove man. Heywood Broun once wrote that "it may be true that a person can only do one thing at a time but this rule does not hold for Larry Doyle on his good days" (*New York Times,* August 13, 1914). There were only two seasons during his career in which he could have figured in MVP voting—1911, when he finished third in the Chalmers voting, and 1912, when he won it, after which he

was not eligible. He was the Giants' on-field leader through three pennants, and often ran the team after the umpires ran McGraw. An easy Definition-C Hall of Famer.

JOHNNY EVERS

HALL OF FAME? Yes
DATA IN SECTION III? Yes
OFFENSIVE WON-LOST RECORD:
112–74, .602
GROSS VALUE: 113
COMPARABLE RECENT PLAYERS: Willy Randolph

It has been stated so often and with such authority that Joe Tinker, Johnny Evers and Frank Chance were elevated to Hall of Fame status by a bit of Franklin P. Adams doggerel that this wisdom itself might now be said to have attained the status of baseball myth. "Of the three," wrote David Nemec in *The Ultimate Baseball Book,* "only Chance was much of an offensive threat, and the poem's message to the contrary, the trio was far from being the era's top double-play combination or even its best infield unit." As once it was a part of baseball lore that these three men were the greatest of all double play combinations, now it is traditional knowledge that their double play totals would be considered poor marks indeed by the standards of today, and as for hitting, well, Johnny Evers sure didn't get into the Hall of Fame based on his .270 career batting average with 12 home runs.

To begin with, to judge the

fielding statistics of 1908 by the standards of 1985 is exactly the same as judging the batting statistics of 1930 or the pitching statistics of 1968 by the standards of today. In 1908 Johnny Evers turned only 39 double plays, which is, indeed, a microscopic total by the standards of today, when a good second baseman turns 120. But consider the game that Tinker and Evers were playing. The National League batting average in 1908 was .239, as opposed to the averages today around .260. The average National League team in 1983 had 1,399 hits; in 1908 it was 1,198. In the absence of power, an average team's pitchers issued about 400 walks a season, as opposed to about 530 now. Considering this and even allowing that there were more errors, there were a lot less players on base to begin with than there are now.

An average National League team in 1908 stole 172 bases. Although stolen bases are up quite a bit—and double plays down—over the last twelve years, the N.L. stolen base average is only around 150 per team. And, at least on the best available evidence, these people were not good percentage base stealers; whereas an average National League team now loses about 70 runners a year to unsuccessful base stealing attempts, my guess is (they didn't keep the statistic) that in 1908 it was 120 to 150.

Then there are sacrifice hits. Whereas an average National League team today lays down between 75 and 80 sacrifice hits, in 1908 the average was 172 (not counting sacrifice flies in either case).

And when the players of this era were not out-and-out sacrificing, they were bunting for a base hit, or they were using the hit and run probably two times in three. Let me ask you—you've got a league in which the league average is .239, and in which people don't walk much. Any time a runner is on first early in the inning, the manager either bunts, or he steals, or he calls for a hit and run; *it is automatic.* You've got 50% more stolen base attempts than today, and more than twice as many bunts, not to mention the fact that you've got long grass and soggy gray baseballs. How in the hell are you supposed to turn 100 double plays a year?

Now look at Johnny Evers. In a league in which the average man hit .239, Evers hit .300 —fifth in the league, and 61 points above the average. In a league in which the slugging average was .306, Evers slugged .375. Tinkers, Evers and Chance or *somebody* on that team played the field well enough that the Cub pitchers allowed only 1,137 hits, the lowest total in the league, and committed only 205 errors, the lowest total in the league. In addition, Evers stole 36 bases, placing him among the

league leaders. He had eight sacrifice flies, which was third in the league. Despite missing thirty-two games with injuries, Evers drew 66 walks, the third-highest total in the league, giving him a .379 on-base percentage. His offensive winning percentage was .786, which was a career high for Evers and would be a heck of a year for Eddie Murray. The team for which he did this won 99 games and its third consecutive pennant, plus the World Series; Evers was their leading hitter as well as playing an outstanding second base. The 1909 *Spalding Guide* described him as "one of the youngest and still the most brilliant of the Cubs."

Now I would say that the man had had a pretty fair season, wouldn't you? Was it an extraordinary year for him? Not really.

Let's look at 1910. In 1910 the N.L. average was up to .256, and Evers out-hit that only a little, at .263. In 125 games (Evers, who weighed only 125 pounds, was not durable) he stole only 28 bases, not a good year for him and not among the league leaders. But he drew 108 walks in those 125 games, making him second in the league in that category, and scored 87 runs. Striking out only 18 times, Evers drew six walks for each strikeout, whereas the league average was less than even (more strikeouts than walks). His walk-to-strikeout ratio was by far the best in the league;

Hans Lobert was second, at 30–9 or barely better than 3–1. The team for which he played second base won the pennant by thirteen games.

I'd have to say, wouldn't you, that he'd done his job pretty good? I mean, his offensive winning percentage was only .663, which was his lowest in three years, but I'd take that season.

Well, how about 1912? In 1911 a cork-center ball was introduced, and for a couple of years batting averages shot up. Johnny Evers hit .341, the fourth-highest average in the league. His slugging percentage, .441, was 72 points above league and 30 points away from being among the league's top five. His on-base percentage was .421. Whereas the league ratio was eight walks for each ten strikeouts, Evers drew 41 walks for each ten strikeouts—a ratio that was, again, the best in the league by a mile. He was and the Cubs were second in the league in double plays, Evers turning 71 and the Cubs 125. I'd say that year was all right, wouldn't you? The Cubs finished a mere 91–59 and in third place, but I'd say a Hall of Famer shouldn't be ashamed of that season.

Well, how about 1914? Before the season Evers was traded from the Cubs to the Boston Braves, a down-at-the-heels (69–82) ballclub, which —coincidentally, I'm sure— got hot and won the National League pennant. Evers hit a

mere .279, 28 points better than league, and drew only 87 walks (fourth in the league). He led the Miracle Braves in runs scored, but he had only 81 so you can't really count that. True, he did lead the league in fielding percentage at second base, .976, but that's nothing by today's standards, although the N.L. record at that time was .978 (Bid McPhee, 1896). The Braves did turn 143 double plays, which was 24 more than any other team in the league and the highest total since the turn of the century, but so what if they did? Rabbit Maranville helped set that mark, too. And lots of people have had better strikeout-to-walk ratios than 87–26, although it was the best in the majors that year. And true, they did give Evers the Chalmers award as the most valuable player in the league, but you know how MVP voters are.

I'd like to ask something of the people who dismiss Evers as a Hall of Fame impostor. On what season and on what analysis is it, exactly, that you do this? As a rookie in 1903, Johnny Evers hit .293 and the Cubs, 68–69 the year before, finished in third place at 82–56. In 1904 he hit .265 (league average: .249), led the league in putouts, assists and range factor, and the Cubs won 93 games. In 1905 he was injured and played only 99 games, but hit .276 (21 points over league), and had the

league's second-best range factor, while his team went 92–61. In 1906, when he played 154 games for the only time in his career, he was among the league leaders in stolen bases, led the league in putouts, beat the league batting average by eleven points and the Cubs won 116 games. In 1907 he had an offensive winning percentage of .650, was second in the league in stolen bases, led the league in assists and the Cubs won 107 games. 1908 we hit. In 1909 he had an offensive winning percentage of .707, was third in the league in walks despite missing 28 games, and the Cubs won 104 games to finish second. 1910 we hit. In 1911 he had a nervous breakdown; 1912 we hit. As a player/ manager in 1913 he hit a more-than-respectable .284; in 1914 he was the MVP. As an injury-prone part-timer in 1915, he still out-hit the league by 15 points and had the league's best strikeout-to-walk ratio, playing second for a second-place team.

As a double play combination, perhaps Tinker-to-Evers-to-Chance was overrated. The combo was together from 1903 through 1910. I figured for each of those years the percentage of opposition baserunners removed by the double play for each National League team (that is, double plays divided by the sum of the team's hits and walks allowed and errors). What follows is that data (in 1903, their first year together, the Cubs removed 4.4 percent of opposition baserunners by double plays; the league average was 4.9 percent and the Cubs ranked 7th in an eight-team league):

PERCENTAGE OF OPPOSITION
BASERUNNERS REMOVED
BY DOUBLE PLAY
Chicago and Rest of National
League, 1903–10

Year	Cubs	League	Rank
1903	.044	.049	7th
1904	.051	.047	2nd
1905	.059	.052	3rd
1906	.063	.051	2nd
1907	.069	.056	1st
1908	.044	.042	3rd
1909	.058	.052	3rd
1910	.061	.059	5th

When they removed 6.9 percent of opposition baserunners in 1907, that was the highest figure not only of that year, but of the entire period; still, they were usually the second- or third-best in the league, and not the best. They were better-than-league every year except their first year together.

Should Johnny Evers be in the Hall of Fame? Johnny Evers was more of an offensive force in his own time and place than Bobby Doerr was in his, a more valuable offensive player than Nellie Fox, Frankie Frisch, Billy Herman or Tony Lazzeri. He played at a time when runs were extremely hard to come by, and he put more than his share on the scoreboard. He had no power, but then there wasn't much power in the league. His averages were better-than-league every year, his strike-out-to-walk ratios were the best in the league every year, and he was one of the league's better base stealers. He was the premier defensive second baseman of the decade.

Besides that, Tinker, Evers and Chance were the guts of a great team, maybe the greatest team ever. Between 1906 and 1910 they won 530 games and lost only 235, the best five-year won-lost record of this century. In 1906 they had the best one-year won-lost record of this century. They went into the Hall of Fame together because they were always thought of together; they were a team. What's wrong with that? The Franklin P. Adams poem did not have one damn thing to do with their being selected to the Hall of Fame. When Whitey Ford and Mickey Mantle went into the Hall of Fame together, everybody thought that was cute; couldn't have worked out better. Nobody says there is anything wrong with Gehrig, DiMaggio, Dickey, Gomez and Ruffing all being in the Hall of Fame. If the players who are the core of a great team are not worthy of Hall of Fame selection, then who is?

FRANKIE FRISCH

HALL OF FAME? Yes
DATA IN SECTION III? Yes
OFFENSIVE WON-LOST RECORD:
   149–103, .591
GROSS VALUE: 207
COMPARABLE RECENT PLAYERS:
Rick Burleson

Meaning no disrespect to any of them—everyone listed here was a great player—Frisch, Gehringer and Traynor are classic examples of players whose value has been inflated in the eyes of history because of the inflated offensive totals of their era. Apart from the injury that prematurely diminished him, Burleson was an excellent comp for Frisch—a fiery on-field leader, a splendid defensive player, a good line-drive hitter and good baserunner. But not one of the leading offensive players of his time. (Frisch was a little better than the Roosta, but not much, and of course his career was three times as long.)

NELLIE FOX

HALL OF FAME? No
DATA IN SECTION III? Yes
OFFENSIVE WON-LOST RECORD:
   139–123, .531
GROSS VALUE: 167

Career offensive won-lost record is somewhat misleading because his defense was so good that he was able to play several years before and after his prime offensive seasons. From 1951 through 1960 his offensive won-lost totals were 101–69 (.594), and I suspect that as more sophisticated runs created methods are developed, he will probably be moved up some. A popular player, Fox is basically a modern Eddie Collins except that Eddie was much faster and played in an era which suited his talents better. . . . Had six years in the top ten in the MVP voting, got 187 or more hits eight times and, like Collins, won an MVP award when he wasn't even having a particularly good season.

CHARLIE GEHRINGER

HALL OF FAME? Yes
DATA IN SECTION III? Yes
OFFENSIVE WON-LOST RECORD:
  155–85, .646
GROSS VALUE: 224
COMPARABLE RECENT PLAYERS:
Lou Whitaker

In his time, Gehringer was much admired as a gentleman. When he won the MVP award in 1937, the *Spalding Guide* wrote that "no player is more modest and more deserving of such a compliment." As an offensive player he was quite comparable to Carew, though he was not quite as much a force in his own time as Carew was in the seventies. One thing he has in common with Carew is that both players kept pushing their offensive limits higher and higher throughout their careers. Gehringer hit .277 as a rookie in 1926, pushed his career best to .317 in 1927, .320 in 1928, .339 in 1929, to .356 in 1934 and .371 in 1937. In home runs he started out at one as a rookie, then pushed

that to 4, 6, and 13 in the next three years, to 16 in 1930, to 19 in 1932 and again in 1935, and finally to 20 in 1938. His doubles total started out at 19, went up to 29, 45, 47, 50 and finally hit 60 in 1936. His strike zone judgment started out fair and was outstanding by the end of his career (112 walks, 21 strikeouts in 1938, 101–17 in 1940). Carew is one of the few other players who showed the same broad-based, sustained growth for a period of a decade or more.

JOE GORDON

HALL OF FAME? No
DATA IN SECTION III? Yes
OFFENSIVE WON-LOST RECORD:
  102–63, .619
GROSS VALUE: 133
COMPARABLE RECENT PLAYERS:
Grich

In 797 road games in his career, Joe Gordon hit .279 with 134 home runs. In 911 road games in his career, Bobby Doerr hit only 78 home runs and averaged .261. Gordon's slugging percentage in road games was .482; Doerr's was .389, not even in the same league. Gordon's on-base percentage was .367; Doerr's was .327.

Unlike Doerr, Gordon drew great respect from MVP voters. He was mentioned in the vote every season of his career when he played 120 or more games except in 1949. He won the MVP Award in 1942 despite leading the league in strikeouts, errors and grounding into double

plays. Not that his stats were bad—he drove in 100 runs four times, scored 100 twice, was frequently in the nineties if not over a hundred. He could steal some bases, drew as many as 98 walks. He led the league often in range factors, assists and double plays turned at second, turning as many as 123. His teams were tremendous. He finished in the top ten in the MVP vote five times, once when playing with a team that finished fourth.

One thing that puzzles a lot of people is the performance of the Yankees in the years 1936–1939, when they won four straight pennants. In the first two of those years, Lou Gehrig was tremendous, hitting over .350 each year, driving in over 150 runs each year and whacking 86 home runs. In 1938 he dropped below his standard, and in 1939 he was forced to the sidelines—yet the Yankees got better without him, finishing 106–45 in 1939, without Gehrig. I've heard a lot of people wonder how they could have gotten better with Babe Dahlgren at first base, hitting .235 with 15 home runs.

Part of the answer is Gordon. Tony Lazzeri played second base for the Yankees in 1936 and 1937, and Gordon forced him out in 1938. Lazzeri was a fine player and would be a deserving Hall of Famer himself—but Joe Gordon was a better player than Lazzeri. They were comparable as hitters, but Gordon had more power and was a much better second baseman.

BOBBY GRICH

HALL OF FAME? Not Eligible
DATA IN SECTION III? Yes
OFFENSIVE WON-LOST RECORD:
120–71, .628
GROSS VALUE: 160

An old favorite of mine. A great offensive and defensive player who lacks any one statistic by which his skills are easily recognizable.

BILLY HERMAN

HALL OF FAME? Yes
DATA IN SECTION III? Yes
OFFENSIVE WON-LOST RECORD:
128–85, .601
GROSS VALUE: 153
COMPARABLE RECENT PLAYERS:
Dave Cash, Glenn Beckert are similar in type, though not quite of the same quality.

National League players of Herman's time often felt he was as good as Gehringer. Kirby Higbe wrote that "Billy Herman stood out at second base over any other second baseman I ever saw. He played the hitters better than any second baseman—or infielder, for that matter—that I ever saw. He was the greatest hit-and-run man in baseball, then or now." Leo Durocher wrote that "Billy Herman had been the premier second-baseman in the National League for nine years" (meaning nine years before Leo acquired him to play for the Dodgers). "He had be-

come universally accepted as the classic #2 hitter in baseball, an absolute master at hitting behind the runner. A smart player who would be able to give Pee Wee Reese just the kind of help that he needed."

The selection of Herman to the Hall of Fame in 1975, along with the failure to select an American League contemporary, Buddy Myer, illustrates the difficulty of drawing a line across the bottom of the Hall. They are probably the two best-matched Hall of Fame candidates that one could name. Herman played 1,922 games in the major leagues from 1931 to 1947; Myer played 1,923 from 1925 to 1941. Herman hit .304 lifetime; Myer hit .303. Herman's slugging percentage was .407, Myer's was .406. Myer scored 1,174 runs, Herman 1,163. Myer drove in 863 runs; Herman 850. Herman led his leagues in three categories but no "majors" (no triple crown categories), the three being hits and doubles (1935) and triples (1939). Myer led his league in stolen bases in 1928 and batting average in 1935. Herman scored 100 runs five times (113, 111, 106, 102, 101); Myer scored 100 runs four times (120, 115, 114, 103). Herman drove in 100 runs once—exactly 100—and Myer drove in 100 runs once—exactly 100. Both players played on championship teams (Herman four, Myer two); neither won an MVP award. In 1935

Herman led the National League in putouts, assists, double plays, range factor and fielding percentage. Myer the same year led the American League in assists, and had a better range factor (6.18–6.08) and fielding percentage (.979–.963) than Herman, though not leading the league, plus he set a major league record for double plays with 138 (still one of the highest totals ever). How in the world can you put one of those people in the Hall of Fame and leave the other one out?

ROGERS HORNSBY

HALL OF FAME? Yes
DATA IN SECTION III? Yes
OFFENSIVE WON-LOST RECORD:
166–46, .784
Offensive winning percentage, .784, is the highest among second basemen.
GROSS VALUE: 248
COMPARABLE RECENT PLAYERS:
George Brett

In the first edition of this book, probably the most controversial argument that I made was that Rogers Hornsby was the fourth greatest second baseman of all time, behind Joe Morgan, Eddie Collins and Nap Lajoie. The controversy was not over his being fourth rather than eighth; it was over his being fourth rather than first. I was very surprised by this. I expected controversy over the argument that Mantle was distinctly superior to Mays at his best. I expected controversy about all of the arguments concerning players of the post-war period. Many of my readers saw those people play more than I did, and naturally feel that they know more about it than I do. I expected that. But few people around now saw Hornsby play, and I really did not expect to be fired upon with so many guns merely because I interpret Hornsby's record differently than so many other people have interpreted it.

There is, as I wrote then, no way you can knock the numbers. Hornsby's batting records are all around terrific. He hit for incredible averages, with tremendous power. He had home-run power, doubles power and triples power. He walked a lot and didn't strike out much. His speed was good.

My concerns about Hornsby were threefold. On one issue, I was wrong. I speculated that his batting records may have been seriously inflated by the parks that he played in. Gordon L. Herman figured his home/road records for a couple of seasons, and those records, which are presented on Hornsby's page in Section III, do not support the belief that Hornsby's home parks were inflating his batting records. He was probably helped some; of the 84 home runs hit in the seasons located so far, about 60 percent were hit at home. That's not a Mel Ott or Chuck Klein-type advantage.

I also made a flat-out mis-take in the Hornsby comment, unrelated to the discussion of his relative value. I wrote that Hornsby managed Ted Williams at Minneapolis in 1938. If you read Ted Williams' *My Turn at Bat,* you would swear that that was what he was saying, but anyway he didn't; Donie Bush managed Williams that summer, and Hornsby never managed Teddy. I thank those of you who called this to my attention.

But on another issue, I may have bent over backward too far to be fair. I wrote that he was a better second baseman than some people have given him credit for. I wonder now if he was. Ty Cobb said in a letter to E. J. Lanigan that "Hornsby couldn't catch a pop fly, much less go in the outfield after them, could not come in on a slow hit." In *Veeck as in Wreck,* I note that when William Wrigley bought Rogers Hornsby from Boston for $120,000 and five players, Bill Veeck Sr. was so incensed that he quit immediately, coming back to work only when Wrigley promised never to meddle again. Dick Bartell says that Hornsby "couldn't come close to filling Charlie's (Gehringer's) shoes at second . . . I laugh when I see some of these how-to-play books with Rogers Hornsby writing the chapter on second base." Bartell says that Hornsby couldn't go back on a pop fly, and adds that with Hornsby playing second, the shortstop had to take the throw on any attempted steal, no matter what, apparently because Hornsby didn't want to risk getting spiked.

I look at how many pop flies there are around second base, how many times a good second baseman will go into the outfield pick off a looper, and I've got to think that was more of a problem than I originally allowed for. He was just fair on the double play. Although he led the league in double plays in 1922, the only reason for that is that he was the only second baseman in the league who played more than 122 games, and the Cardinals just missed by one of being last in the league in twin drillings. He did have better years in this respect, but this is a defender's position. Isn't that a lot of negatives for a guy who is supposed to be the best ever at the position? If Ted Simmons had hit another eight or ten homers a year he would be the best-hitting catcher of all time, but would you choose him as your all-time catcher?

On the third point, I remain unconvinced. I got a letter from one guy (writer rummages around in file cabinet, but cannot find letter) who said I was too hard on Hornsby for being an asshole. "He was just ahead of his time," the fellow suggested. "He was an asshole when players were supposed to be Jack Armstrong. Nobody would think anything about his being an asshole today."

Well, that's funny but it's not right; that's not what I was saying. I don't care if he was an asshole. My problem with Hornsby is the same as my problem with Dick Allen: that he said things and did things that made it more difficult for his teams to win. Dick Allen was a nice guy and a lot of his teammates thought the world of him, but he did things that disrupted the team at times when they really didn't need the disruption. And so did Hornsby.

So what do you have? You have a great hitter and a fine baserunner who is a bad defensive second baseman and a pain in the butt. I come back to the same thing I came back to before: Too many people had him and just couldn't wait to get rid of him. Nobody ever wanted to get rid of Willie Mays. Nobody ever wanted to get rid of Mickey Mantle. Nobody ever wanted to get rid of Stan Musial. Hornsby was traded year after year, and they didn't trade him because they wanted Frankie Frisch or they wanted Shanty Hogan or they had to have Bruce Cunningham and $200,000. They traded Hornsby because they wanted to get rid of Rogers Hornsby. The teams that traded Hornsby didn't get any worse, and the teams that got him didn't get any better. Everybody has their own idea of what is arrogance, but to me, to march back into history and tell Sam Breadon or John McGraw that "No no no; you

shouldn't have traded him. His numbers were too good" —well, that's true arrogance. A good player, yes. But I just can't reconcile the record of his career—the whole record, not just the statistical record —with the idea that he was the greatest second baseman who ever played.

MILLER HUGGINS

HALL OF FAME? Yes, as manager
DATA IN SECTION III? Yes
OFFENSIVE WON-LOST RECORD:
  99–60, .588
GROSS VALUE: 110
COMPARABLE RECENT PLAYERS:
Willie Randolph

A tiny man remembered only as a manager, Huggins led the National League in walks four times, was a good base stealer and was regarded as one of the smartest players of his day.

NAP LAJOIE

HALL OF FAME? Yes
DATA IN SECTION III? Yes
OFFENSIVE WON-LOST RECORD:
  181–76, .703
GROSS VALUE: 244
COMPARABLE RECENT PLAYERS:
Robin Yount

John Thorn has an odd comment in *The Hidden Game* that "Nap Lajoie, who is viewed today as an overlarge, out-of-position defensive liability who made his name with the bat. . . ." I didn't know that he was viewed that way, though I'm sure John must have had specific references in mind when he wrote that, but anyway, if he is, it's crazy.

As is reflected in his statistics, he was a great fielder. The 1919 *Reach Guide* wrote that "he was a superb fielder at first base, second base and in the outfield. He was . . . the personification of a peculiar grace, in the expression of which he made the hardest plays look easy."

As a hitter, Lajoie's greatness may have been overstated by some observers. Playing a game in which there was a heavy emphasis on baserunning, Lajoie was not blessed with great speed. He was an impatient hitter, drawing only ten walks in 102 games in 1900 and usually less than 30 a year. His great 1901 season, .422 with 13 homers and 125 RBI, was accomplished in a league that had been a minor league the year before, and is out of the context of his career. From 1902 to the end of his career in 1916, he never scored 100 runs and drove in 100 only once, 102 in 1904. He never played with a championship team, and rarely with a contender. He would probably have been a more valuable offensive player in the 1920s or '30s than he was in his own time.

Charles F. Faber, in the book *Baseball Ratings*, evaluates Lajoie as the greatest player of all time, by a rather comfortable margin. His top five are Lajoie, 3,196 points; Babe Ruth, 2,869; Honus Wagner, 2,842; Ty Cobb, 2,853; and Tris Speaker, 2,638.

TONY LAZZERI

HALL OF FAME? No
DATA IN SECTION III? Yes
OFFENSIVE WON-LOST RECORD:
104–75, .582
GROSS VALUE: 144

In the same general class of players as Grich, Gordon, and Doerr, Lazzeri doesn't seem to have been quite the equal of these men as a defensive player.

BILL MAZEROSKI

HALL OF FAME? No
DATA IN SECTION III? Yes
OFFENSIVE WON-LOST RECORD:
99–127, .439
GROSS VALUE: 143

Bill Mazeroski's defensive statistics are probably the most impressive of any player at any position. He led the league in thirty-five positive defensive categories (assists nine times, range factor ten times, putouts five times, double plays eight times and fielding average three times). Many of the assists, of course, stemmed from his wondrous pivot on the double play, the like of which no one living has ever seen. As a hitter he was severely damaged by a 365-foot left-field foul line in Forbes Field. In his first full season, 1957, he homered 3 times in 11 games in Philadelphia, twice in 11 games in Chicago, and also homered in three of the other five parks, but did not hit any home runs in Pittsburgh. In 1961 he homered seven times in nine games in Los Angeles, but only four times in 81 games in Pittsburgh. He hit most of his home runs on the road every year of his career except 1964 (5 at home, 5 on the road) and 1968 (2 out of 3 at home), and his career totals were 93 home runs on the road, only 45 in Pittsburgh.

JOE MORGAN

HALL OF FAME? Not Eligible
DATA IN SECTION III? Yes
OFFENSIVE WON-LOST RECORD:
181–74, .711
GROSS VALUE: 225

The most multifaceted player among the great second basemen. As a base stealer, only Collins can compare to him; as a power hitter, only Hornsby; in strike zone judgment only perhaps Miller Huggins. As a defensive player he won five Gold Gloves.

An address was given at a SABR convention a few years ago by a longtime baseball man, a man now in his seventies or eighties, who had had the pleasure of working with Joe Morgan early in Joe's career. An outstanding player in his own right, he felt a strong affection for Joe, and said that he thought Joe did as much to help his teams win as any player he had ever seen. "He's the smartest," he said, searching the room and finally locating John Holway in a far corner with some players who were stars in the Negro leagues, "he's the smartest black ballplayer I've ever seen. He's just always working to pick something up, and he knows what to do with it when he does." Where he thought Joe would have fit in along an IQ scale had he been a white man was not made entirely clear.

Pitching out when Joe Morgan was on first base was one of the most foolish things that any manager could do, and yet nobody could resist it. Why? He *always* read the pitchout. With absolute confidence. He would stand patiently at first with his hands on his hips, not breaking, not bluffing, not even ready to run, since the pitch was obviously a pitchout and would not be put in play. I always got the feeling that some people would pitch out against him just to watch him do it. An announcer asked him about it one time—this was years ago, and I'm paraphrasing the answer as I remember it—but as I recall he said that somebody would always give it away, and usually you could pick up three or four clues. The pitcher would not throw over to first like he usually would, or he'd look at you a little bit different, or he'd rush his delivery home, or the first baseman or second baseman would try to cheat toward the bag, or the catcher would look down at you right before giv-

ing the signal, or would set himself a little different so he could get up and throw. He said once you picked up one thing you'd start looking for the others, and you'd see them, too. I used to play cards with a guy like that. He'd read your eyes and know what you had. Drive you crazy.

DEL PRATT

HALL OF FAME? No
DATA IN SECTION III? Yes
OFFENSIVE WON-LOST RECORD:
117–81, .593
GROSS VALUE: 128
COMPARABLE RECENT PLAYERS: No one

I first began to take Del Pratt seriously as an outstanding player about 1976, when I was doing a rather pointless study to find out who had led the league in the percentage of his team's runs driven in. Pratt in 1913 drove in 87 runs for a team that scored only 528, and accounted for 21 percent of his team's RBI, a feat unmatched by many of the game's greatest RBI men. In 1915 he drove in 78 of his team's 521, in 1916 103 of 591. After the lively ball era began he was no longer a contender to lead the league, but he was second on the Yankees in RBI in 1920 with 97. He was traded that winter and retired to become the baseball coach at the University of Michigan (Branch Rickey nominated him for the position), but was talked out of his retirement and joined the Red Sox in time to drive in 100 runs in 135

games. In 1922 the Red Sox scored only 598 runs; Pratt hit .301 with 44 doubles and drove in 86. With Detroit in 1924 he drove in 77 runs in 121 games.

An All-American back at the University of Alabama, Pratt was known for his temper, and that being the case it was the custom of the day to work on him from the bench, get him riled up. During the St. Louis city series in 1913 (a post-season matchup of the Cardinals and Browns) Pratt became so upset at something said to him that he reportedly charged off the field into the Cardinal dugout and punched out a Cardinal rookie named Zinn Beck. Whether this was an act of extraordinary courage or extraordinary shortsightedness is a judgment call, but in either case he was then set upon by the twenty-four Cardinals who remained conscious and in condition to fight, and in the end received bruises and was kicked out of two games, it being the first of an exhibition double-header.

Buried on bad teams most of his best years, Pratt hit .292 lifetime with excellent doubles and triples power and good strikeout-to-walk ratios. In his early years he was one of the top ten base stealers in the league, stealing 37, 37 and 32. He led American League second basemen in putouts and range factor in 1913 and again in 1914, in putouts and double plays in 1915, in putouts, assists and range factor

in 1916, in range factor in 1917, in putouts and double plays in 1918, in assists in 1919, in assists and double plays in 1920. He was durable, consistent, and talented.

WILLIE RANDOLPH

HALL OF FAME? Not Eligible
DATA IN SECTION III? Nope
OFFENSIVE WON-LOST RECORD:
94–86, .523
GROSS VALUE: 127

JACKIE ROBINSON

HALL OF FAME? Yes
DATA IN SECTION III? Yes
OFFENSIVE WON-LOST RECORD:
94–40, .700
GROSS VALUE: 127
COMPARABLE RECENT PLAYERS: Joe Morgan

It has become one of the compulsory events of a baseball history to acknowledge that Robinson was a far better player than his statistics show. I have no reason to believe that he was not; his statistics themselves are pretty good. He was a multidimensional offensive player, hitting over .325 four times, leading the league in stolen bases twice, hitting with consistent medium-range home run power (12, 12, 16, 14, 19, 19, 12, 15) and drawing 80 to 106 walks a year. He was older when he played his first major league game than Kent Hrbek is on Opening Day, 1988, and Hrbek's been around forever. He was older than Darryl Strawberry will be on Opening Day, 1990. Jackie stayed good long enough to collect over 1,500 hits in the major leagues. Had he started at twenty-one, he would have been in the 2,500–3,000 range.

If Robinson possessed skills that go beyond what shows on paper, he was in this hardly unique; the same can be said for almost every player on this list. One thing I intended to get done for this book, but didn't, was an analysis of the role of baserunning in the World Series of 1947, '49, '52, '53, and '55 and '56, to see if I could document some portion of that supposed extra dimension. Because so much attention was focused on him, those skills in his case may have been driven more deeply into the public's mind than the quiet skills of a Red Schoendienst, a Nellie Fox. That is fair, too, for with that attention came a kind of pressure that perhaps no other major league player has had to contend with. Jackie Robinson consumed that pressure and was nourished by it.

RED SCHOENDIENST
HALL OF FAME? No
DATA IN SECTION III? Yes
OFFENSIVE WON-LOST RECORD:
123–113, .521
GROSS VALUE: 163
COMPARABLE RECENT PLAYERS:
None

After Robinson, the premier N.L. second baseman of his time. Schoendienst and Piano Legs Hickman (1902) are the only men to lead the league in hits while being traded in mid-season. A solid Hall of Famer if Definition C were applied.

FRANK WHITE
HALL OF FAME? Not Eligible
DATA IN SECTION III? No
OFFENSIVE WON-LOST RECORD:
83–117, .415
GROSS VALUE: 147

HOW THE SECOND BASEMEN RATE

In rating the second basemen in terms of their value at some moment in their careers, I am reasonably comfortable in selecting Joe Morgan as the number one man. There are two other men who I think could be given the nod. It could be that the greatest second baseman ever was Jackie Robinson, but for me to say that just places too much of a load on intangibles that I didn't see and that I couldn't specifically identify. Rogers Hornsby, in a good mood, in the best shape of his career, in the years 1921–25, was probably as devastating a player as you could want, and maybe better than little Joe. But his records don't prove that he was, and on the basis of everything that I know about the two of them, if they were standing in front of me it would not be a gut-wrenching decision to pass up Hornsby and all the baggage that comes with him for a player who walks more, runs the bases better and plays a superior second base.

Morgan and Hornsby are distinctly better offensive players than anyone else who has played second base, with the arguable exception of Lajoie. If Lajoie had concentrated his best years rather than spreading them out here and there, if his best season hadn't come in a suspect league, he might be the number one man. No one else was the same quality of offensive threat.

As to the greatest second baseman in terms of career value, I am by no means as comfortable in selecting Eddie Collins. Eddie Collins and Joe Morgan played far more games at second base than anyone else. This is not a coincidence; longevity is, in and of itself, an excellent indicator of the quality of play. I am certain that the greatest ever was Joe Morgan or Eddie Collins; I am not certain which. Morgan was the kind of player who could adapt to any game of baseball and take advantage of what it offered, and thus there are some conditions of the game under which he would be my favorite. But Collins *did* adapt. Whereas Morgan, while always a fine player, had about a six-year run as a truly great player, Collins sustained a remarkable level of performance for a remarkably long time. He was past thirty when the lively ball era began, yet he adapted to it and continued to be one of the best players in baseball every year.

While there is no one key to identifying the greatest player ever at a position, there are two things that I place a heavy weight on: the offensive won/lost record, and the respect of contemporaries. Collins rates the edge on both accounts. While Morgan's career won/lost record is superb, at 181–74, it does not match Collins', at 209–73. And while Morgan won two MVP awards and the impressive total of 3.14 Award Shares, Collins actually beat that performance even though there was no MVP award for most of his career. In the voting for the Chalmers Award, Collins finished third in 1911, third in 1913 and first in 1914. I don't have the voting for 1912, but since Eddie hit .348, swiped 63 bases and scored a career-high 137 runs, I'd reckon he was probably in there somewhere. When the voting for the MVP Award resumed under the auspices of the American League in 1922, Collins was still among the very best players in the league, finishing fifth in the vote in 1922, second in 1923 and second again in 1924. I credit him with 3.53 Award Shares, giving him nothing for 1909, 1910, 1912 or 1915–1921. Collins was one of the few men to win an MVP Award while just having his normal season, and the vote was barely short of being unanimous, Collins placing second on one ballot.

Eddie Collins probably had as many outstanding World Series as any player. He played in six of them, and hit .429 in 1910, .421 in 1913 and .409 in 1917. At one time he held a virtual stranglehold on World Series records; he still holds several of them. I am forced to conclude that his was the most valuable career that any second baseman ever had:

PEAK VALUE	CAREER VALUE
1. Joe Morgan	1. Eddie Collins
2. Jackie Robinson	2. Joe Morgan
3. Rogers Hornsby	3. Nap Lajoie
4. Eddie Collins	4. Rogers Hornsby
5. Nap Lajoie	5. Charlie Gehringer
6. Rod Carew	6. Rod Carew
7. Johnny Evers	7. Frankie Frisch
8. Charlie Gehringer	8. Jackie Robinson
9. Larry Doyle	9. Bobby Grich
10. Joe Gordon	10. Tie: Billy Herman
	Buddy Myer

❧ THIRD BASE ❧

HOME RUN BAKER

HALL OF FAME? Yes
DATA IN SECTION III? Yes
OFFENSIVE WON-LOST RECORD:
113–54, .676
GROSS VALUE: 132
COMPARABLE RECENT PLAYERS:
George Brett

Frank Baker's career is interesting, among other reasons, as a study of the impact that missing a season has on a player's hitting ability. From 1911 to 1914 he had established himself as a .700+ offensive performer, with offensive winning percentages of .711, .797, .764, and .706. He held out and missed the 1915 season in a kind of salary dispute. Well, it wasn't exactly a salary dispute. He was a member of the Philadelphia A's, one of the great teams of the time. A couple of his teammates jumped to the Federal League, and Connie Mack, fearing the loss of others, sold Eddie Collins and Jack Barry to help pay the salaries of those remaining. Baker refused to play with the decimated Athletics, and played semi-pro ball instead, forcing Connie Mack to sell him to the Yankees.

Anyway, when he returned he was a .600-range offensive player, with offensive winning percentages of .685, .638, .657 and .612 from 1916 through 1919. Then his wife died, in the winter of 1919, and he retired from baseball. He returned a year later, and by then was a .500-range offensive player, with offensive winning percentages of .501 and .536.

Baker was a great player, from 1911 through 1914; he and Eddie Collins were the biggest stars on a formidable team. He was much the greatest third baseman of his time, and probably the greatest hitter of those years other than Ty Cobb and Tris Speaker. He led the American League in RBI by margins of 24 in 1912 and 36 in 1913. On that basis I make him a Definition-B Hall of Famer, a player who was best of his time at the position he played.

BUDDY BELL

HALL OF FAME? Not Eligible
DATA IN SECTION III? No
OFFENSIVE WON-LOST RECORD:
134–112, .544
GROSS VALUE: 168

Buddy Bell's career has traced a long, slow path of growth, from a .260-hitting youngster playing right field so that Graig Nettles could play third base, to the .280–.300 hitter with 20 homers a year, Gold Glove third baseman with Texas and the Reds in the 1980s. Originally a player who struck out little and walked less (Bell had more strikeouts than walks every year from 1974–1979), Bell has become a more disciplined hitter, showing steadily improving strikeout/walk ratios. His K/W ratio has been better than even every year since 1980, with his best figures coming in 1986 (49–73) and 1987 (39–71). Though slow afoot and not a particularly good baserunner, Bell can count among his positives hitting for average, hitting for power, making contact, strike-zone judgment and all of the elements of defense—range, arm, consistency. His year-to-year consistency as a hitter is the equal of any third baseman in history. He could be the first true third baseman to get 3000 hits in his career, although he will be thirty-seven this August (1988) and is still about four years away from that goal. Buddy's father was a fine player—but Buddy has been a better one.

KEN BOYER

HALL OF FAME? No
DATA IN SECTION III? Yes
OFFENSIVE WON-LOST RECORD:
130–80, .619
GROSS VALUE: 155

An outstanding offensive and defensive player for nine years, 1956–64. A 1963 *Sport* magazine article rated Boyer over Eddie Mathews as the top National League third baseman, and a year later he was voted the Most Valuable Player. He was the *TSN* All-Star at third base every year, 1961–64, and with those references solidly qualifies as a Definition-C Hall of Famer. Substantially identical in terms of on-field skills, position and career pattern to Ron Santo, except that Santo was a somewhat more patient hitter.

WADE BOGGS

HALL OF FAME? Not Eligible
DATA IN SECTION III? No
OFFENSIVE WON-LOST RECORD:
  66–19, .778
GROSS VALUE: 74

GEORGE BRETT

HALL OF FAME? Not Eligible
DATA IN SECTION III? No
OFFENSIVE WON-LOST RECORD:
  135–58, .699
GROSS VALUE: 162

See comment on Mike Schmidt.

RON CEY

HALL OF FAME? Not Eligible
DATA IN SECTION III? No
OFFENSIVE WON-LOST RECORD:
  131–75, .637
GROSS VALUE: 140

I think that Ron Cey, like Norm Cash and Harlond Clift, was probably a significantly better player than he was given credit for being while active. I think there are three primary reasons for this. First is his peculiar body structure, which makes it difficult to think of him as being a great ballplayer. Second, he had his best seasons playing in Dodger Stadium, which is not a good park for a hitter. Third, his career ran parallel to that of the greatest third baseman in the history of the game, Mike Schmidt—not only parallel in time and place, but in the occasions of recognition. When Cey played for the National League West champions in 1977 and 1978, Mike Schmidt played for the NL East champions. He had to beat out Mike Schmidt to win a Gold Glove award, which he could never do; he had to beat out everybody else to win a spot on the All-Star team, assuming that there were two slots and that Schmidt would get one of them.

Cey's offensive won-lost record and gross value are among the best ever at third base—better than Jimmy Collins or Larry Gardner or Heine Groh or Fred Lindstrom; comparable to Stan Hack, Pie Traynor and Ken Boyer. That seems surprising, but then you start looking at how many runs he scored and drove in (over 2000 total), at how many championship teams he was a key part of, and you've got to admit that he has earned a place among the all-time top men at the position.

HARLOND CLIFT

HALL OF FAME? No
DATA IN SECTION III? Yes
OFFENSIVE WON-LOST RECORD:
  100–63, .612
GROSS VALUE: 125
COMPARABLE RECENT PLAYERS:
Darrell Evans

(The following comment on Harlond Clift is primarily the work of Jim Baker.)

It was Harlond Clift's business to play third base for the St. Louis Browns for the better part of the thirties and early forties. This was not a glamour position in Clift's profession; it was roughly equivalent, let us say, to teaching astronomy at the Colorado School of Mining, or if you were a chef this would be the equivalent of working in the kitchen at a fat farm. Not only was he a Brown, but he was a Brown when the ebb and flow of fortune had reduced them to an all-time low.

The Browns then were worse than any team would be allowed to get in this modern and civilized era. Only twice in his tenure as third baseman did the team break the 200,000 mark in season's attendance. This was counter-balanced by their two years under 100,000. From 1934 to 1942 (his seasons as a regular) they averaged just under 120,000 fans a year, or 2,000 a game. Clift played on teams whose pitchers were of the most dubious nature. From 1936 to 1939 they posted ERAs over 6.00 three times. The fourth season they got it down to 5.80. In 1937 they al-

lowed the opposition to score ten runs or more in a game 28 times. Of course, that and the fact that they were last in striking out batters twice and seventh once during that period certainly helped Clift's range factor, but this was small consolation for a bequest of anonymity in your own ballpark and in your own league, particularly since no one paid any attention to Harlond Clift's impressive range factors.

In fact, no one paid any attention to anything Harlond Clift did. Harlond was one of the new breed of third sackers who made large offensive contributions. Until the early part of the thirties, third base was not considered the domain of sluggers and high-average men. Defense was the only quality requested of a third baseman. This is reflected in the presence of so few third basemen in the Hall of Fame; the old joke was that third basemen should pay their way into the ballpark because nobody knew who they were. Clift was one of the men who helped change that image.

He was the first third baseman to hit 30 home runs in a season. He did that with 34 in 1938. The year before he had set the record for most homers by a third baseman, when he belted 29. (Mel Ott, a part-time third baseman for that one season, also hit 36 home runs in 1938. He played 113 games at third and 37 in the outfield, so it is doubtful that

he hit 30 home runs as a third baseman and extremely doubtful that he hit as many as Clift while playing third.) In addition to hitting home runs Clift hit doubles (40, 39, 36), walked over 100 times almost every year and hit around .300.

Aside from his standing as the primeval Mike Schmidt, Clift was also a helluva fielder, by reputation and by statistical performance. In 1937 he was the first third baseman to start 50 double plays in a season; his record was not broken until 1971, when Graig Nettles flipped 54. That same season he handled 603 clean chances, which is the best mark ever at that position. His career total of 309 double plays is the best for any third sacker who finished his career before the 1950s.

No one paid any attention. Through a variety of tricks of fate, Harlond Clift remained obscured from present recognition; the man was doomed to play baseball in a dark shadow. Legend has it that at a tryout for the Brownies in 1931, Clift moved for a ball while keeping his glove low. He stepped on the glove and catapulted himself skyward. He landed hard and broke his collarbone. Despite this, the Browns signed him, and he became the best third baseman in the major leagues. I conclude this, although he never made the All-Star game and was never named to the post-season All-Star team cho-

sen by *The Sporting News;* no alternative conclusion seems reasonable. Even in his spectacular 1937 and '38 seasons, they were always putting somebody like Red Rolfe or Pinky Higgins on the All-Star teams. I have no idea why they voted for Higgins in 1936, but the most reasonable explanation would seem to be something like chronic halitosis:

Category	Clift	Higgins
At Bats	576	550
Runs	145	89
Hits	174	159
Doubles	40	32
Triples	11	2
Home Runs	20	12
Runs Batted In	73	80
Batting Average	.302	.289
Slugging Average	.514	.420
Stolen Bases	12	7
Walks	115	67
Strikeouts	68	61
Games at 3B	152	145
Putouts	158	151
Assists	310	266
Errors	24	26
Double Plays	27	24
Fielding Average	.951	.941
Range Factor	3.08	2.88

The Browns even finished ahead of the A's, for whom Higgins played that season. From 1937 to 1939 the Yankees' Red Rolfe was named to all the honors. In 1937, Clift out-hit Rolfe by 30 points, stole twice as many bases, hit seven times as many homers, drew more walks, drove in about twice as many runs and set the record for double plays. They put Rolfe on the All-Star team.

In 1940 Clift could have gotten a reprieve from all of this. The Tigers were in the heat of the pennant race with Cleveland and New York and were interested in the Brownie third baseman. (Their man at third was the aforementioned Pinky Higgins.) The Tigers offered $200,000 for Clift, first baseman George McQuinn and pitcher Hillbilly Bildilli. Here was Clift's chance to play for a contender with decent men around him on the field and in the batting order. Browns owner Donald Barned turned them down. The Tigers went on to win it, and Clift remained in St. Louis.

In 1942 another chance for Clift (and the rest of the Browns) to escape St. Louis was beaten back by the coming of World War II. A planned move of the franchise to Los Angeles (where at least they would be losing in nice weather) had to be canceled because the extensive use of trains to get to and from the Coast would interfere with the war effort. By this time Clift wasn't slugging as much as he had been, but he was still getting on base almost 40 percent of the time and scoring constantly. Manager Luke Sewell was not fond of his play, though, and in 1943 said Clift was "no good in the clinches" and that he had been a part of the Brownie losing tradition for so long that he didn't know how to win. (Basically all the sort of things that managers say when they don't like a

player but can't prove he's no good.) In the middle of that '43 season, one year away from the season in which the Browns would hit paydirt, Clift was sent to the Senators for $35,000 and Ellis Clary.

The Senators weren't so terrible that year. They chased the Yankees for a while and ended up in second. But Clift was not around to enjoy the rarefied air of second place. Soon after joining the Senators, he returned to St. Louis on a road trip and caught the mumps from his daughter while visiting. When they worsened and spread to his testicles, he had to be hospitalized. So ended his '43 season.

That winter he was riding a horse on his farm in Washington and was thrown on his right shoulder. So went 1944. In 1945 the Senators were actually in a pennant race, but Clift did not perform well, due to his accumulated maladies. When the soldiers returned home the following year his career was over.

—Jim Baker

JIMMY COLLINS

HALL OF FAME? Yes
DATA IN SECTION III? No
OFFENSIVE WON-LOST RECORD:
107–88, .549
GROSS VALUE: 128
COMPARABLE RECENT PLAYERS:
Terry Pendleton

Collins is probably the best player for whom data is not presented in Section III, Col-

lins or Lou Brock. He was generally regarded as the greatest third baseman before Pie Traynor and indeed for some years after Pie Traynor. After an outstanding year at the age of twenty-one with Buffalo in the Eastern League, possibly the best minor league of the time, Collins was purchased by Boston. In his first eleven games with Boston, Collins hit .211 and played poorly in the field, for which he was torn apart in the Boston press, and the Boston owners (there were three of them, called the triumvirs) wanted to get rid of him. Manager Frank Selee fought for Collins and refused to release him, and arranged instead to loan him to Louisville, another National League team, for the balance of the season, where Collins proved that he could, indeed, play third base.

Playing a game in which people bunted incessantly, Collins was regarded as the best of his time at fielding the bunt. John B. Foster in the 1938 *Spalding Guide,* explaining why he had named Collins the greatest third baseman of all time, wrote that "Few bunts were made so skillfully that Collins could not make a play on the ball. . . . With a swoop like that of a chicken hawk Collins would gather up the ball and throw it accurately to whoever should receive it. He could pick off the runner at second with the same ease that others would get the batter at first. The beauty about

Collins was that he could throw from any angle, any position, on the ground or in the air. . . . the unstudied grace of the professional dancer characterized Collins' every movement while in pursuit of the ball. He could not bend ungracefully if he made an effort to do so."

His hitting was not ungraceful, either. He hit .346, .328, .332, and .322, with a lifetime average of .294. He led the National League in homers in 1898 with 15, and drove in 132 runs the year before that. According to some sources, he still holds the National League record for clean chances in a season, 601 in 1899 (the Macmillan *Encyclopedia* shows him with 593 that year). Whatever, it was hardly more than an ordinary year for him; he led the N.L. and later the A.L. in range factor almost every year, and holds four of the top ten marks of all time in that category.

DARRELL EVANS

HALL OF FAME? Not Eligible
DATA IN SECTION III? No
OFFENSIVE WON-LOST RECORD:
  155–86, .644
GROSS VALUE: 168

Most of the things I could say about Darrell Evans, I have already said about Norm Cash and Ron Cey. A tremendous defensive third baseman for many years, Evans spent most of his career playing for poor teams. An interviewer once asked me if I were a general manager, what kind of

player would I try to acquire. I told him the model would be Darrell Evans—a player with a low average, but good defense and a good secondary average. The low average will make such a player available; the high secondary average and the defense make him more valuable than a lot of players who would be considered untouchable.

LARRY GARDNER

HALL OF FAME? No
DATA IN SECTION III? Yes
OFFENSIVE WON-LOST RECORD:
  114–83, .579
GROSS VALUE: 125
COMPARABLE RECENT PLAYERS:
Buddy Bell

Basically the same player as Pie Traynor, except that he played most of his career in the dead-ball era and consequently his batting stats are not superficially as good. He was thirty-four years old when the spitball was outlawed, but he hit .310 with 118 RBI that year, .319 with 115 RBI the next before time caught up with him; in 1921 he drew 65 walks and struck out only 16 times. Both Traynor and Gardner hit for a good but not great average, had little home run power but good doubles and triples power. Each ran fairly well and had a good strikeout-to-walk ratio. Traynor may rate a slim edge on defense, batted right-handed while Gardner batted left, and was four inches taller.

Born in Vermont of English parents, Gardner reportedly

never played baseball until he entered the University of Vermont in 1904. A natural athlete, he became the star of the Vermont University team, received a degree from that institution, and was tendered offers from several teams, selecting the Red Sox as any good New Englander would.

He played third base for four American League champions, the Red Sox of 1912, 1915 and 1916, and the Indians of 1920. The 1916 *Spalding Guide* wrote that "he is a splendid fielder and an excellent batsman, besides being fast on the bases."

HEINE GROH

HALL OF FAME? No
DATA IN SECTION III? Yes
OFFENSIVE WON-LOST RECORD:
  107–68, .613
GROSS VALUE: 119
COMPARABLE RECENT PLAYERS:
Pete Rose (as a player only; Groh was a very different type of person)

One of the finest hitters to play third base before 1935, Groh led the league in walks in 1916, in hits and doubles in 1917, in doubles and runs scored in 1918, and was among the top five in the league in batting in 1917, 1918, and 1919. In the early 1920s he got involved in a nasty salary/tampering hassle with Reds owner August Herrmann, who by this time was in the Calvin Griffith stage of his career, intent on finding out how little he could pay his players without having an out-and-out revolt on his hands. (Groh's problem, which ended up in front of Judge Landis, is recounted briefly in the notes in Section III.) Heine played in five World Series (with the Reds, 1919, Giants, 1922–24, Pirates, 1927), and was the big star of the demolition of the Yankees in 1922, hitting .474 (he got the license plate number 474 every year for the rest of his life). Jim Baker filed the following comment on him . . .

When your analyst wants to play word associations with you and he says "Heine Groh," chances are you'll say "bottle bat." It seems that everybody knows that somebody named Heine Groh used a bottle-shaped bat at some point in baseball history, but that is the full memory outlay for Mr. Groh. Nobody seems to know what he did with the bat or why he even had it.

According to Lee Allen, Groh adopted the bat (which was 41 ounces with a six-inch handle) because he was having trouble with the curve ball. He needed more meat to hit the ball. To help himself further against the curve he would stand way up in the batter's box.

—Jim Baker

STAN HACK

HALL OF FAME? No
DATA IN SECTION III? Yes
OFFENSIVE WON-LOST RECORD:
   132–64, .674
GROSS VALUE: 141
COMPARABLE RECENT PLAYERS: A high-average hitter who would draw 90–99 walks a season, Hack was an outstanding lead-off man, comparable to Rickey Henderson or Tim Raines except that his speed was not so electrifying. He led the N.L. in stolen bases twice, but with totals of 16 and 17.

It seems very odd that Hack has not received more serious consideration as a candidate for the Hall of Fame. Clearly the outstanding National League third baseman of his time, Hack fits Definition C of a potential Hall of Famer, and arguably qualifies under Definition B. He was enormously popular, and he played in an era from which the Hall of Fame has honored many and slighted few.

GEORGE KELL

HALL OF FAME? Yes
DATE IN SECTION III? No
GROSS VALUE: Unknown
COMPARABLE RECENT PLAYERS: Carney Lansford

A five-time member of *The Sporting News* Major League All-Star team, Kell would probably be as good a candidate as any for the nomination as outstanding third baseman of the years 1920–1955.

FRED LINDSTROM

HALL OF FAME? Yes
DATA IN SECTION III? No
OFFENSIVE WON-LOST RECORD:
   Approximately 89–65, .578
GROSS VALUE: Unknown
COMPARABLE RECENT PLAYERS: Bill Madlock

A regular for only seven season, Fred Lindstrom compiled flashy batting stats in the high-scoring seasons of 1928 and 1930, and was selected to the Hall of Fame in one of their dizzier moments in 1976. Lindstrom is best remembered for three things, two of which were ground balls that hopped over his head in the seventh game of the 1924 World Series, leading to the defeat of his Giants. The third thing for which he is remembered is that he thought he was in line for John McGraw's job when McGraw retired. When the job went to Bill Terry instead, Lindstrom asked to be traded, and was. As an offensive player he was by no means one of the top players of his time, and as a defensive player he was so outstanding that he was shifted to the outfield in midcareer. His selection to the Hall of Fame, while it ignores players like Ken Boyer, Ron Santo, Ed Yost and Stan Hack, was a bad joke.

EDDIE MATHEWS

HALL OF FAME? Yes
DATA IN SECTION III? Yes
OFFENSIVE WON-LOST RECORD:
   173–67, .721
GROSS VALUE: 211

One rarely sees Eddie Mathews nominated as the greatest third baseman of all time, and it is difficult to put a finger on the reasons for this. As an offensive player he was Mike Schmidt, Sr. He hit over 40 home runs in a season four times despite playing in a poor home run park (in his career he hit 38 more home runs on the road than at home, making his home-park share, at 46 percent, the lowest of any 500-homer man). He led the league in walks four times, hit over .300 three times and was close three other times. He played on three league champion and two World Champion teams. Schmidt's only edge over him would be defense, but Mathews was a good third baseman.

One suspects that his regard has been dampened by two things. Number one, he had his best years very early, was projected as a man who could hit 700 home runs (he hit 47 at the age of twenty-one), and then not only did not do so, but was thrust into the shadow by the man who did. As great as he was, he spent most of his career as a mild disappointment. And number two, he never won an MVP award. He never put his best seasons together with his team's championship runs—indeed, the 1957 and 1958 years, when Milwaukee won the pennant, were his two worst seasons between 1953 and 1962, though he hit over 30 home runs each year. Had he had a 1958 season equal to his 1953 season, or had the Braves won one more game in 1959, he might well be regarded today as the man Schmidt must displace to achieve recognition as the greatest.

GRAIG NETTLES

HALL OF FAME? Not Eligible
DATA IN SECTION III? No
OFFENSIVE WON-LOST RECORD:
   150–108, .583
GROSS VALUE: 168

	GRAIG NETTLES'
IF HE HAD	NICKNAME
PLAYED IN	WOULD HAVE BEEN
1885	California Graig
1895	Gotcha
1905	The Leaping Octopus
1915	Emperor
1925	The Sultan of Leather
1935	Flatnose
1945	The Glove Man
1955	The Gnu
1965	Uppercut

BROOKS ROBINSON

HALL OF FAME? Yes
DATA IN SECTION III? Yes
OFFENSIVE WON-LOST RECORD:
   169–140, .547
GROSS VALUE: 185

In Pete Palmer's *The Hidden Game of Baseball*, Brooksie is listed as the 108th greatest non-pitcher of all time, behind such players as Ron Cey, Amos Otis, Fred Tenney, Miller Huggins, Art Fletcher and Jim Wynn. Assuming that many of the people who read that book will also read this one, you may have wondered what it was, exactly, that went awry with the rating system to create that ranking.

What happened is that all of the problems with Pete's analysis are concentrated in the examination of Brooks Robinson. Pete's park adjustments are inadequate, founded upon the rather silly assumption that only hitters' performance (and not pitchers) should be used to adjust for park illusions. This causes players in hitters' parks, like Bobby Doerr, to rate too high, and those who played in pitcher's parks, like Brooks Robinson, to rate too low. Second, while defense can be evaluated somewhat by defensive statistics, defensive statistics are less precise in evaluating individual performance than are offensive statistics, and Robinson's defensive statistics, while they are brilliant, probably do not give him full credit for his glovework, no matter how they are interpreted. Third, Pete's system for interpreting defensive statistics gives too much weight to the double play, and too little weight to other kinds of defensive achievement. Fourth, Pete used an analytical structure that considers an average player to be of no value and a below-average player to have negative value. Robinson spent a couple of years at the start of his career and several at the end as a below-average player, which (in Pete's system) reduces his career value. This is irrational, since it assumes that the player is being used by a team for several seasons although he has negative value, not to mention that Robby was being used for several seasons by a team that was winning 95 games a year. If a team is willing to play a player, then by definition that player must have some value.

All rating systems, as I have written, are liable to those kinds of problems. I don't believe that I could design a system that would avoid all of them, which is essentially why I don't rate players by statistical formulas. In other cases, most of those problems cancel one another out—one discrepancy moves the player down, another one moves him up. But there are a few cases, like Robinson on one end or Bobby Doerr on the other, where the flaws in the system conspire to create rankings that are frankly ridiculous.

AL ROSEN

HALL OF FAME? No
DATA IN SECTION III? Yes
OFFENSIVE WON-LOST RECORD:
   74–32, .697
GROSS VALUE: 93
COMPARABLE RECENT PLAYERS:
Bob Horner, in some respects; Rosen was a better fielder. Doug DeCinces is very comparable, except that Rosen hit for a better average.

A great player for a brief period of time, Al Rosen's 1953 campaign was probably the greatest season that any third baseman ever had. He hit .336 with 43 home runs, 145 RBI, drew 85 walks, led the league in RBI by 30, led the league in assists, double plays and total chances per game. He lost the triple crown on the last day of the season, becoming the first man to be unanimously chosen MVP by twenty-four voters.

Al Rosen was seventeen years old when World War II started, got trapped behind Ken Keltner in the farm system and was finished at thirty because of injuries. But for five years in between, he was as good a third baseman as you could want.

RON SANTO

HALL OF FAME? No
DATA IN SECTION III? Yes
OFFENSIVE WON-LOST RECORD:
   150–83, .642
GROSS VALUE: 176

I've written the Ron-Santo-for-the-Hall-of-Fame bit before (see 1982 *Baseball Abstract,* pages 182–85). Fits Definition C, possibly Definition B, of a

Hall of Fame candidate. His records are good enough that they eventually will earn recognition.

MIKE SCHMIDT

HALL OF FAME? Not Eligible
DATA IN SECTION III? No
OFFENSIVE WON-LOST RECORD:
   167–57, .746
Schmidt's career offensive winning percentage is the best among third basemen with ten seasons or more.
GROSS VALUE: 211
His career gross value is also the highest among third basemen.

Two of the greatest third basemen of all time, George Brett and Mike Schmidt, are now rolling toward the end of their brilliant careers. I have never seen a player who could dominate a baseball game, or a series, or month of series, the way that George Brett can dominate. Brett is an amazing hitter—strong, with tremendous bat control, excellent command of the strike zone. His swing is a thing of beauty. He is a study in balance, in concentration, in grace. He seems to be able to hit the best pitchers in the league as well as the weakest, and that makes him deadly in big games. No matter who the pitcher is—a Jack Morris, a Roger Clemens, a Ron Guidry or Goose Gossage, one always feels, as a Royals fan, that the pitcher is overmatched, that whether or not he makes a mistake George is going to hit the ball hard somewhere.

Brett has other virtues as a ballplayer. He is an alert defensive player and baserunner, quick to take advantage of any opposition oversight. He was a fine defensive third baseman, not a defensive wizard, but a player who would make more unexpected good plays than unexpected bad ones. His qualities as a team leader are splendid. He works hard and plays hard. He has more interest in the team than in the team politics. Whitey Herzog has said that George is the only player he ever had who did not need a manager. I have never seen any other player do as much to *make* a team win when they had every opportunity to lose.

That being said, George Brett is not the greatest third baseman of all time. Mike Schmidt is. As an offensive force over a short series, Mike Schmidt may not be the equal of Brett—but over the course of a season, he is every bit his equal, and over the course of a lifetime, he has been more than his equal. Schmidt's lifetime batting average is only .270, and it takes a lot of other positives to turn a lifetime .270 hitter into the greatest offensive player ever at his position. Schmidt has them. They are:

1) Power. 530 home runs speak for themselves.

2) Walks. Schmidt has walked 1,437 times through 1987, meaning that he has been on base over 3,500 times, and he has scored 1,435 runs. Schmidt's 1,437 walks have probably yielded about

480 runs for his team.

3) Consistency. Consistency may be the least noted of Mike Schmidt's assets. While most power hitters are noted for swings from high to low, Schmidt has had only one off season (1978) in a fourteen-year stretch. Among the roughly 200 players listed in Section III of this book, only perhaps a half-dozen could match that record.

4) Durability. Schmidt has played 89 percent or more of his team's games every year since 1974. Only a handful of third basemen in history has been as durable over a long period of time.

Brett has power, but not power in Schmidt's category. Brett draws walks, but not nearly as often. Brett hasn't been consistent at his own best standards, and he hasn't been durable. When you add those things together and throw in the speed that Schmidt had when he was young, giving him a career secondary average of .472, you have to reach the conclusion that Schmidt has put more runs on the scoreboard for his teams than any other third baseman ever, with only Eddie Mathews being close.

Whether Schmidt as a defensive player is of historic magnitude, or merely a superior defensive player in his own time, is debatable. It would be difficult to argue honestly that he has redefined play at his position, as Frank White has or as Brooks

Robinson did in his time. But if Mike Schmidt had hit .320, he would have been the best *player* who ever lived. Even fifty points lower, he is the best third baseman.

PIE TRAYNOR
HALL OF FAME? Yes
DATA IN SECTION III? Yes
OFFENSIVE WON-LOST RECORD:
   119–89, .570
GROSS VALUE: 161
COMPARABLE RECENT PLAYERS:
Carney Lansford

Thirty years ago Pie Traynor was generally recognized as the greatest third baseman of all time. A superb third baseman, a lifetime .320 hitter and a fast runner, Traynor played in a park that did not yield home runs, but he was always in double figures in triples and drove in 100 runs seven times.

With the flood of high-quality third basemen of the postwar era, Traynor can no longer be considered near the top at the position, and with the development of better understanding about the significance of offensive statistics, there have arisen serious questions about whether he belonged there at the time. He hardly ever struck out, but he didn't walk a lot and didn't have the extra-base power of his teammates Kiki Cuyler, George Grantham, Glenn Wright and Paul Waner, all of whom easily exceeded his career isolated power of .115, as did other teammates. The only category in which he ever led the league was triples, and that only once.

An interesting question is when Traynor began to be recognized as the best ever. An article in the 1938 *Spalding Guide* (see Jimmy Collins) says that there are many candidates for the number one man at the position, and names Ned Williamson, Jerry Denny, Bill Bradley, Art Devlin and Joe Dugan, but fails to mention Pie Traynor's name. In the January 1946 Hall of Fame vote, in competition with players from across the century, he received less than 35 percent of the vote, hardly suggesting a player regarded as the greatest ever at his position. The voting structure was redefined then, with the players from pre-1920 put into a different pool, and in 1947 Traynor finished fifth in the balloting behind Hubbell, Frisch, Cochrane and Grove, before entering in 1948.

ED YOST

HALL OF FAME? No
DATA IN SECTION III? Yes
OFFENSIVE WON-LOST RECORD:
  130–85, .605
GROSS VALUE: 128
COMPARABLE RECENT PLAYERS:
Toby Harrah would be the closest

Ed Yost got a shot at the major leagues when he was seventeen years old. There was a war on, and good talent being scarcer than wool suits at a Fourth of July picnic, Yost and a good many other high school kids were given a look in what was then called the major leagues. He was overmatched, hitting just .143 in seven games and just .080 in eight games the next year, but when he got out of the Army he went straight to the major leagues without benefit of a minor league education, becoming the regular third baseman for the Washington Senators in 1947.

At first he was still a little over his head. In 1947, at age twenty, Yost drove in only 14 runs in 428 at bats, one of the lowest ratios in history. From that point he grew rapidly and steadily, hitting .295 in 1950 with increasing numbers of doubles, triples and homers. In 1951 he led the league in doubles with 36. In 1948 he hit 11 triples. He hit 11 or 12 home runs in 1950, 1951, 1952, 1954 and 1956. He was a good third baseman, not exceptionally quick but steady with a fine arm.

What he is known for, however, is his walks. He was a leadoff man, and his specialty was getting on base by the walk. He led the league in walks with 141 (1950), 129 (1952), 123 (1953), 151 (1956), 135 (1959) and 125 (1960). He also drew 126 walks in 1951 and 131 in 1954, as well as having comparable ratios in several injury-shortened seasons. He was known as, and still is known as, The Walking Man. He scored a hundred or more runs five times, once leading the league.

Yost played most of his career with poor Washington Senator teams, poor teams in a poor hitter's park, a prescription for historical anonymity. When he was traded to the Tigers in 1959 he surprised the league with 21 home runs. Whereas for most of his career he had hit 3 home runs at home and 9 on the road—12 total—in 1959 he hit 12 at home and 9 on the road, 21 total. The Tigers didn't win, however, and Yost was easing toward the end of his career, which came with the expansion Los Angeles Angels in 1962.

Yost is still around, coaching with the Boston Red Sox for many years now. I see him out there coaching and wonder if he wouldn't have wanted to manage, and if it isn't too late for him now, at sixty-one. His career must have had so many disappointments, playing all of those years with bad teams, never getting into a World Series as a player, having a fine career which still falls a little short of being a Hall of Fame career, never getting to manage. I think perhaps we are luckier to have our disappointment concentrated into a childhood discovery that we simply can't play, rather than living a lifetime so close to our dreams. But Yost has taken a lot of paychecks out of the game, and I'm sure he, too, thinks of himself as a lucky man.

HOW THE THIRD BASEMEN RATE

It has often been written that third base has produced fewer great players than any other position. This may be part of a truth. Before 1930, third base was a fielder's position, like shortstop; third basemen were expected to have the quickest reactions on the team, and among the best throwing arms on the team. In a game in which bunting was far more common than it is today, they were expected to eliminate the bunt on the left side of the pitcher's mound. If they met this responsibility and hit .260, like shortstops, it was considered that they were doing the job. If they did the job and hit .290, they were stars.

Then came Harlond Clift and Eddie Mathews and Pinkie Higgins and George Kell, and the image of a third baseman shifted. It became impossible for people to understand that Willie Kamm and Larry Gardner and Ossie Bluege had been considered stars in their own time, stars of the glove rather than the bat. The Hall of Fame came along too late to honor the oldtime third basemen while their memories were fresh, and their stats were not good enough to force their enshrinement after the memories got cold. The Hall of Fame almost from day one had fewer third basemen than players at other positions.

In the last twenty-five years there have been as many outstanding third basemen as players at any position, perhaps more than any other position. I have tried throughout this book to be fair to the players of each era, favoring neither the present nor the past, looking at what each player meant to his own time. I find it very hard, in looking at the third basemen, to overlay the two types of players and know how they fit, to evaluate how much defense has been given up to gain offense. Maybe it isn't any; maybe it's a lot. Maybe it's a whole different position now.

But from 1911 through 1963, third basemen won only two MVP awards. Even shortstops did much better, winning eight. Ultimately, I must reach the conclusion that most of the greatest third basemen of all time are in the post-1960 era. Do I really believe that Darrell Evans was a better player than Pie Traynor?

The answer is yes.

PEAK VALUE	CAREER VALUE
1. Mike Schmidt	1. Mike Schmidt
2. George Brett	2. Eddie Mathews
3. Eddie Mathews	3. Brooks Robinson
4. Wade Boggs	4. George Brett
5. Brooks Robinson	5. Jimmie Collins
6. Home Run Baker	6. Ron Santo
7. Al Rosen	7. Buddy Bell
8. Ron Santo	8. Ken Boyer
9. Jimmie Collins	9. Stan Hack
10. Harlond Clift	10. Craig Nettles
	or Darrell Evans

SHORTSTOP

LUKE APPLING

HALL OF FAME? Yes
DATA IN SECTION III? Yes
OFFENSIVE WON-LOST RECORD:
  153–88, .635
GROSS VALUE: 211

AND

LUIS APARICIO

HALL OF FAME? Yes
DATA IN SECTION III? Yes
OFFENSIVE WON-LOST RECORD:
  138–163, .458
GROSS VALUE: 198

Between these two men of the oddly similar names, whom we will call the Lu Aps, the White Sox had shortstop in the hands of a Hall of Famer most of the time between 1930 and 1970. Luke Appling represented a type of offensive player that was common at one time and has all but disappeared today, a small man who didn't often hit the ball hard, but made an offensive contribution by slap-hitting .300—actually, he once hit .388, but that was kind of flukey—and working the pitcher for 85 to 120 walks a season. Others of the type included Richie Ashburn, Johnny Pesky, Dom DiMaggio, Ferris Fain, Bob Dillinger, Stan Hack, Harry Walker, and Elmer Valo, among many others. The player usually played a key defensive position, such as shortstop or center field, and ran well enough but

didn't make a fetish of it. He would score a hundred runs consistently, and if he chanced to land in the middle of an offensive juggernaut and stayed healthy and had a good year, would lead the league with 130 or thereabouts.

This type died out abruptly after 1950, with the exception of an occasional Matty Alou. It's hard to say why. A number of teams pulled their fences in about then, which probably reduced the distance between the infield and the outfield, and took away many of the dying quail hits that were a staple of the profession. The similar hitters who did exist after that tended to hit .260 or .270 and rarely played a key defensive position.

After them came the speed merchants, the little leadoff men who did not hit for quite the same average, walked less than half as much, and tried to make their offensive contribution by stealing bases, getting into scoring position. Luis Aparicio was the prototype of such a player.

That Luis Aparicio was the outstanding leadoff man in the American League was one of the unchallenged assumptions of my youth, and I find to my surprise that I approach the debunking of that myth was considerable trepidation, far more than I would feel in

challenging the credentials of an Omar Moreno or a Marvelle Wynn, a comparable offensive player of the eighties. The evidence that Aparicio was not a successful leadoff man is nonetheless clear, and with relish or without, the point must be made in the context of an effort to assess accurately his value.

Luis Aparicio was an outstanding shortstop and an outstanding baserunner. He stole 506 bases in his career and was a 79 percent base stealer, a much better percentage runner than Maury Wills. That was all that it took to convince the announcers of my youth —in Kansas City we had a different set every year—that he was the ideal leadoff man, and, being too young to know better, I always assumed that the announcers knew of what they spoke. They didn't. Aparicio reached scoring position under his own power an average of 68 times per 162 games, including 5 home runs. That ability to get into scoring position, while a positive thing in itself, was by no means significant enough to outweigh Aparicio's comparative inability to get on base.

I will spare you the math at this moment, but the number of runs that a leadoff man will score, given the number of times he reaches base, the number of times he reaches second base, etc., can be estimated quite accurately—and a player with a .306 on-base percentage is *not* going to score very many runs, no matter how many bases he steals. A Luke Appling–type of hitter will score more runs batting leadoff for the worst hitting team in baseball than a Luis Aparicio–type would score batting leadoff for the 1927 Yankees. Look at the facts. Aparicio never led the league in runs scored, which is the basic goal of a leadoff man. He never scored 100 runs in a season.

Maybe the offenses behind him could have been better. But Campy Campaneris, whose offensive skills were exactly the same as Aparicio's, never scored 100 runs in a season, either—and the offenses coming up behind him included Joe Rudi, Sal Bando and Reggie Jackson. Maury Wills scored 100 runs in a season only twice, and never led the league. Rarely even did Aparicio lead his own team in runs scored; often his total was bested by plodders like Curt Blefray (1965), Joe Cunningham (1962) and George Scott (1971), who had a superior ability to get on base. And for a leadoff man, that's inexcusable.

For a decade or more, baseball was held in the grip of the Aparicio/Wills generation of leadoff men. If it seems strange that all of baseball could have fallen victim to the delusion that forty or fifty stolen bases could compensate for a comparative inability to reach base, I would ask you to consider that all of the institutions of our society—our educational systems, our criminal justice system, our entertainment industry, our military—get entangled in strange, illogical, self-defeating practices and habits, and for a decade or more not a single state nor district nor individual will find the courage, wisdom and perspective to escape; indeed, whole countries go quite mad from time to time. Is it stranger that American baseball men became convinced that they had to use a type of player that analysis or simple reasoning can quickly show is not productive, or that American architects constructed an ethic that made an outcast of anyone who did not want to design glass boxes?

Delusions pass, and men do come to their senses. There is no doubt in my mind that by the year 2000, the Jerry Remy, Damaso Garcia type of leadoff hitter will be extinct, and of the two types of leadoff men—Appling and Aparicio—will develop a synthesis, a player who combines the speed and base stealing ability of Aparicio with the pesky patience of a Luke Appling. Rickey Henderson and Tim Raines are the harbingers of this new type.

While he was not a great leadoff man or even an adequate leadoff man, Luis Aparicio was a great shortstop. A winner of nine Gold Gloves, Aparicio's defensive statistics may be the best of any shortstop ever. Once, looking for the "Mazeroski of shortstops," the player who most dominated the defensive statistics of the position, I counted the number of "positive categories" in which each and every shortstop had led the major leagues. While there was no Mazeroski of shortstops, I found—no shortstop at least before Ozzie Smith has ever really dominated the defensive statistics of the position—Aparicio was the leading man, leading the league in twenty-three positive categories (fielding percentage eight times, assists seven times, putouts four times, double plays twice and total chances per game twice). That, combined with the fact that he did make an offensive contribution, albeit not as substantial a one as many people of his time believed, fully justifies his 1984 selection to the Hall of Fame.

DAVE BANCROFT

HALL OF FAME? Yes
DATA IN SECTION III? Yes
OFFENSIVE WON-LOST RECORD:
 119–99, .529
GROSS VALUE: 143
COMPARABLE RECENT PLAYERS:
Don Kessinger

Bancroft is the first of a number of shortstops that we will encounter of substantially identical contributions, shaped differently, perhaps, by the time and place at which the man played. I suspect that if you studied the issue, almost all experts would place Wagner at the top of the shortstop list, but after that there would be less agreement on the appropriate rankings than at any other position. These players were decent offensive performers, average or a little better than average, but their primary job was defense. Since the evaluation of defense has always been more of a personal thing, and more dependent on observation than is the evaluation of offense, who you think the greatest shortstops were is heavily colored by who you saw play, when you saw them play, and what you have read about them. Defensive statistics, while meaningful, are imprecise, and our ability to deal with the illusions and prejudices in them is not nearly as well developed as our ability to deal with those of offensive statistics. There is much in the evaluation of shortstops that we must take on faith.

ERNIE BANKS

HALL OF FAME? Yes
DATA IN SECTION III? Yes
OFFENSIVE WON-LOST RECORD:
  166–103, .615
GROSS VALUE: 211

From the beginning of the consecutive National League MVP awards in 1924 until 1958, two things were true. First, no one had ever won the award while playing on a team that finished under .500. The award, even in the twenties, was usually given to a member of the championship team, and there was a strong preference not to honor an individual from a team that finished near the bottom. And second, no one had ever won the award in consecutive seasons. Chuck Klein won the triple crown in the National League in 1933, after having won the MVP award the year before; he still did not repeat as MVP.

Imagine the force of the impression that Ernie Banks had to make on the observers of his time to shatter both of those barriers at the same time, winning the MVP award in 1958 with a team that finished 72–82, and again in 1959 with a team that was 74–80. In 1959 Henry Aaron had his greatest season, hitting .355 with 46 doubles and 39 homers, becoming the only National League player in the last thirty-five years to have 400 total bases. Banks still won the award.

It can reasonably be argued that the peak of performance reached by Ernie Banks in the late fifties was as high as anyone has ever seen—in other words, that Ernie Banks in the late fifties was the most valuable player there ever was. I don't know that I buy the argument, but you've got a Gold Glove shortstop here who hits over .300 with well over 40 home runs a year, driving in more runs than Don Mattingly.

The exact quality of Banks' defense is a matter of some debate. I think it is true to say that most semi-serious fans think of him today as a sluggish shortstop who really belonged at some other position, and played short mostly because the Cubs were a poor team and didn't have anybody else. I think that that is clearly a case of confusing after-the-fact images with the player's skills as they were perceived at the time. Banks' memory as a shortstop was severely damaged by the years that he played at first base, which created a strong image of him that was not consistent with that of an outstanding shortstop. Three points:

1) Banks' defensive statistics as a shortstop are quite good. In 1959, his second MVP year, he led in assists (519) and set a major league record for fielding percentage (.985), finishing behind only Dick Groat in double plays (97–95) and range factor (5.34–5.13). In 1960, when he again led the majors in home runs with 41 (although the Cubs won only 60 games, he finished fourth in the MVP voting, won by Groat), he led the N.L. in putouts, assists, double plays and fielding percentage. In 1961, his last year as a shortstop, he led the National League in total chances per game. The statistical image of Banks as a shortstop is that of a steady player with an A-quality shortstop's arm and adequate to good mobility at the position.

2) Though Roy McMillan was the great defensive shortstop of the time, Banks was voted the Gold Glove in 1960, which is clearly inconsistent with the idea that he was perceived, while active, as a stopgap shortstop.

3) Banks was moved to first base in 1962 not because of his defense, but because of injuries. The 1962 *Sporting News Guide* reported that Banks "fell victim of physical troubles. An ailing knee ended his five-year, 717-game playing streak, June 23, and later he was bothered by impairment of depth perception in his left eye." He was moved to first base the next year to take pressure off the knee.

These facts, combined with the remarkable MVP votes of 1958 and 1959, convince me that Banks was a good-to-excellent shortstop, and was regarded as such while active.

It might have been as well had he retired then. Though Banks had several comebacks after 1961 and drove in 100 runs in 1962, 1965 and 1969, his value to his team in the sixties (as Leo Durocher has observed many times with unnecessary meanness of spirit) was questionable. Playing first base in Wrigley Field and batting behind Santo and Billy Williams, a player can be expected to drive in a few runs.

Anyway, this is not about Banks the first baseman; this is about Banks the shortstop. Certainly it is true that his batting statistics were helped somewhat by playing in Wrigley Field. In 1958 and '59, he hit 54 home runs in Chicago and "only" 38 on the road. For his career, his home-park home run share was larger than any comparable star except Mel Ott. Certainly there are legitimate questions about why the Cubs failed to play .500 ball with such an awesome performer in the lineup.

But I think it is generally true that all power-hitting shortstops get a bad rap as defensive players. In our own time, Cal Ripken, Roy Smalley and Robin Yount have all been, in my opinion, far better defensive shortstops than they got credit for being. There is something about these power-hitting shortstops, from Joe Cronin to Glenn Wright to Alvin Dark to Vern Stephens and including Arky Vaughan, Dick McAuliffe and Granny Hamner, that they always seem to have better defensive statistics than reputations. They don't have a lot of putouts, generally, but they seem to do real well in assists and double plays, and often fielding percentage as well— the characteristics of a shortstop with a strong throwing arm. They're not spectacular, but they're effective, often better able to make the play from the hole than are the Ozzie Guillens and the Alfredo Griffins, who look more like shortstops.

People think in terms of images; I do, you do, everybody does. That's how we make sense of an overpowering world; we reduce impossibly complex and detailed realities to simple images that can be stored and recalled. People have trouble reconciling the image of the power hitter— the slow, strong muscleman with the uppercut—with the image of the shortstop, who is lithe, quick, and agile. When confronted with incontrovertible evidence that a man is a slugger—no one *really* doubts the validity of batting statistics—there is a subconscious dissonance with the idea that he was also a good shortstop. The image of him as a shortstop, being not locked in place by a battery of statistics, gets pushed aside so that it can accommodate the image of him as a slugger. Education is not eliminating images, but building more complex, detailed images that better represent the realities.

DICK BARTELL

HALL OF FAME? No
DATA IN SECTION III? Yes
OFFENSIVE WON-LOST RECORD:
114–105, .521
GROSS VALUE: 158
COMPARABLE RECENT PLAYERS:
Don Kessinger

Bartell is statistically a near twin of Dave Bancroft, a Hall of Famer. Bancroft hit .279 lifetime; Bartell .284. Bancroft played shortstop for the Phillies (1915–19), Giants (1920–23) and two other teams before ending up his career back with the Giants. Bartell played shortstop for the Phillies

(1931–34), Giants (1935–38) and three other teams before winding up his career back with the Giants. Bancroft was listed at 5′9½″, 160 pounds; Bartell was listed at 5′9″, 160. The biggest difference between the two seems to be their initials.

Although Bancroft is in the Hall of Fame and Bartell is not, there does not seem to be any real consensus about who was the greater player. Pete Palmer's methods rated Bancroft somewhat higher than Bartell, but put both well within the range of the all-time greats. Charles Faber's statistical method, however, ranks Bartell as the sixth greatest shortstop in National League history, Bancroft as the ninth greatest. The players surveyed by the McCaffrey's for *Players' Choice* had never heard of either one of them. Neither Maury Allen nor Ritter and Honig included either Bartell or Bancroft among their 100 greatest players.

Bartell is the author of a recent biography, *Rowdy Richard,* with Norman L. Macht, available from North Atlantic Books. It's a hefty work, not one of these three-hour reads that players come out with while they're active. It contains a considerable amount of extraneous information that would have been better left out, but I enjoyed reading it, and if you enjoy this book you probably would enjoy that one, too.

MARK BELANGER

HALL OF FAME? No
DATA IN SECTION III? No
OFFENSIVE WON-LOST RECORD:
  Unknown
GROSS VALUE: Unknown

Mark is listed here because Maury Allen, one of our reference points, listed him here as one of the 100 greatest players of all time. While he was no doubt a helluva glove man and is as good a guy as you could want to have on your side during an arbitration case, the idea of Mark Belanger as one of the 100 greatest players of all time is not intended to be taken seriously. Maury Allen put him there not for his unique accomplishments, but rather because "he carries the banner for all the weak-hitting infielders who made pitchers look good." Jeez, I didn't even know we were having a parade. . . .

LOU BOUDREAU

HALL OF FAME? Yes
DATA IN SECTION III? Yes
OFFENSIVE WON-LOST RECORD:
  110–61, .641
GROSS VALUE: 148
COMPARABLE RECENT PLAYERS: See comment on Luke Appling

The outstanding shortstop of the forties, Boudreau hit almost .300 lifetime, hit 45 doubles in a season four times and once drew 98 walks in a season with only 9 strikeouts. In his thirteen years with the Indians, he hit only 16 home runs in Cleveland, as opposed to 46 on the road. As a defen-

sive player he led the league in seventeen categories (fielding average seven times, double plays five), while Rizzuto, perhaps his strongest rival, counted only ten (and most of those after Boudreau was out of the league).

RAY CHAPMAN

HALL OF FAME? No
DATA IN SECTION III? Yes
OFFENSIVE WON-LOST RECORD:
  72–48, .601
GROSS VALUE: 85
COMPARABLE RECENT PLAYERS:
Willie Randolph

Remembered only as the man who was killed by the pitch, Chapman was a tremendous offensive and defensive player, probably destined for the Hall of Fame had he lived.

Chapman won what was possibly the toughest fight for a job that any rookie ever had to go through before Jackie Robinson. When he arrived with the Indians in 1912 they had three other major-league calibre shortstops on the roster:

1) Terry Turner. The Indians' shortstop from 1904 to 1910, Turner had been moved to third base in 1911 to make room for Ivy Olson, but he was by no means finished as a player. He hit .308 in 1912, played regularly for the Indians at third and second until 1916, and was in the league for three years after that.

2) Ivy Olson. Olson, who had done a good job at short with the Indians in 1911, hitting .261 and scoring 89 runs,

later re-emerged as a quality shortstop for the Dodgers, leading the National League in hits in 1919 and playing regularly until 1922.

Olson, who went to grade school in Kansas City with Casey Stengel, was remembered by him in *Casey at the Bat.* "I entered the Woodland School at the age of six," said Casey, "and as I went along I found out that the big bully there was Ivy Olson . . . he was tough.

"In the big leagues he was also tough. . . . He was an arm tagger. Some men, like Dave Bancroft, were hand taggers. They'd tag you so quick you couldn't hardly tell whether they'd touched you or not. . . . If a man came with his spikes high, Ivy would say 'The next time you come in like that, I'll put this ball down your throat.'" Casey added that Olson wasn't a great shortstop, but he was one of the brightest players of the era, and was a tremendous man at catching runners off base.

3) Roger Peckinpaugh. Beaten out of the job by Chapman, Peckinpaugh established himself as the shortstop for the Yankees and was one of the best of the era, scoring 128 runs in 1921 and winning the American League Most Valuable Player award with the Senators in 1925.

When Chapman arrived in Cleveland, Olson was nursing some minor injuries, Turner was playing third and Peckin-paugh, also a rookie, was struggling with the bat. Chapman got a chance to play a few games, and hit .312 in 31 late-season contests. The Indians, 54–71 on September first, went 21–6 in September and October. Withstanding challenges within the next couple of years from Walter Barbare and Billy Wambsganss, Chapman was not to leave the lineup alive.

Though his statistics are not eye-catching, he was the best-hitting shortstop in the American League. Hitting .270 with 70 walks, 36 stolen bases and 17 triples, he scored 101 runs in 1916. In 1917, when the American League average was .248, he hit .302, stole 52 bases, missing the league lead by three, and was third in the league in runs scored with 98. In 1918 he led the league in runs scored and walks; in 1919 he hit .300. At short he led the league almost every year in range factor, and the 1918 *Reach Guide* reported that the Indians "possessed a fast infield, in which shortstop Chapman and third baseman Evans shone."

In mid-August 1920, he had scored 97 runs in 111 games. On August 16, 1920, he was knocked unconscious by a pitch from Carl Mays, and died the next day. Known as a hitter who would not give ground, he seems to have frozen up on the pitch; a player standing nearby said that "he seemed to be hypnotized." The 1921 *Spalding Guide* said that "Chapman not only was the idol of Cleveland and of thousands of fans in other cities, but was one of the most popular and beloved players. . . . His rare personality, in addition to his brilliant ability, had won him the friendship of all who knew him and millions who did not."

That sounds more like a eulogy than a balanced assessment, and it probably is, but it is not on such reports that I base the statement that he would probably have made the Hall of Fame without Mays' interference. In the years following Chapman's death, batting averages jumped as much as 50 points higher than they had been during most of the period of his career—ironically, in part because of Chapman's death. I believe that Chapman was the kind of player who could have taken maximum advantage of the new era, and that had he lived he would have hit .300 regularly for several years thereafter, lifting his lifetime batting average to the .290 range.

There were, by a coincidence fortunate to the present analysis, five longtime major league shortstops who were born in 1891. Two of them were Hall of Famers, Bancroft and Maranville. The others were Peckinpaugh, Wally Gerber, and Chapman. Their career records through 1920 are given in the top chart at the bottom of this page.

"Through 1920" gives the other three an extra 40 games on Chapman, who was killed in mid-August, 1920, and, though Peckinpaugh nosed past him in career hits late in September, as you can see none of these players was comparable to Chapman as a hitter. Yet subsequent to 1920, Bancroft scored 121 and 117 runs, had 193 and 209 hits, and hit .319, .321, .318 and .311, and made his way into the Hall of Fame. Peckinpaugh scored 128 runs in a season, hit .288, .294 and .295 and won an MVP award. Maranville scored 90 and 115 runs, had 198 hits in a season, played regularly until 1933 and was taken in by the Hall of Fame. Even little Gerber hit over .270 several times, and scored 81 and 85 runs. The post-1920

records of the four survivors are given in the other chart at the bottom of the page.

It can very safely be assumed, I think, that Chapman would have continued to outhit these fine players by a wide margin, that he would have played at least a thousand more games in the major leagues and averaged well over a hit per game. That, plus the 50 hits that he is missing in 1920, would put him in the neighborhood of 2500 hits in the major leagues. Combined with his defensive skills, which were the equal of any of these players except possibly Maranville, that would have put him in the Hall of Fame. He had always been the best of the shortstops of '91; there is no reason to think he would not have continued to be.

DAVE CONCEPCION
HALL OF FAME? Not Eligible
DATA IN SECTION III? No
OFFENSIVE WON-LOST RECORD:
 113–148, .432
GROSS VALUE: 173

An outstanding player of our time, and like all such, difficult to evaluate accurately. I see little difference, at a glance, between Concepcion and Pee Wee Reese.

JOE CRONIN
HALL OF FAME? Yes
DATA IN SECTION III? Yes
OFFENSIVE WON-LOST RECORD:
 132–77, .631
GROSS VALUE: 197
COMPARABLE RECENT PLAYERS:
Robin Yount

Cronin is one of the few Hall of Famers to be flat-out given up on as a youngster. Cronin, at the age of twenty, spent the 1927 season on the bench for the Pirates, who had a very similar player, Glenn Wright, playing short for them. A powerful hitter with a powerful throwing arm, Cronin won an MVP award and was named to the *TSN* post-season team at short seven times. A Definition-B Hall of Famer.

RECORDS THROUGH 1920

	G	AB	R	H	2B	3B	HR	RBI	SB	AVG.
Chapman	1050	3785	671	1053	162	80	18	364	233	.278
Bancroft	789	2965	410	766	118	27	14	193	71	.258
Maranville	1047	3928	444	986	133	72	21	347	157	.251
Peckinpaugh	1156	4259	562	1063	153	47	29	384	155	.250
Gerber	437	1454	138	362	48	10	3	121	14	.249

RECORDS AFTER 1920

	G	AB	R	H	2B	3B	HR	RBI	SB	Avg.
Bancroft	1124	4217	638	1238	202	50	18	398	74	.294
Peckinpaugh	856	2974	444	813	103	28	19	355	52	.273
Maranville	1623	6150	811	1619	247	105	7	537	134	.263
Gerber	1085	3645	420	947	124	36	4	355	27	.260

ART FLETCHER

HALL OF FAME? No
DATA IN SECTION III? Yes
OFFENSIVE WON-LOST RECORD:
 82–80, .505
GROSS VALUE: 105
COMPARABLE RECENT PLAYERS:
Garry Templeton

Another in the general class of shortstops with Bartell and Bancroft, Fletcher qualifies for inclusion here because Pete Palmer's methods like his fielding stats. While not unmindful of this information, I can't regard his nomination among the greatest as anything other than an idiosyncratic choice, not unlike Allen's selection of Mark Belanger, Honig and Ritter's fondness for Herb Score and the Hall of Fame's vote for Travis Jackson.

TRAVIS JACKSON

HALL OF FAME? Yes
DATA IN SECTION III? Yes
OFFENSIVE WON-LOST RECORD:
 90–83, .522
GROSS VALUE: 130
COMPARABLE RECENT PLAYERS:
Leo Cardenas

See previous comment.

RABBIT MARANVILLE

HALL OF FAME? Yes
DATA IN SECTION III? Yes
OFFENSIVE WON-LOST RECORD:
 134–169, .443.
GROSS VALUE: 178
COMPARABLE RECENT PLAYERS:
Mark Belanger, Ozzie Smith

Maranville had an interesting career. Though he was regarded as an outstanding defensive shortstop, he lived something of a nomad life, playing for almost every National League team and in fact being sent to the minors for a season in mid-career (he played 135 games for Rochester in 1927, resurfacing when Tommy Thevenow had an off year). This seems a most odd condition for a great player to find himself in—Mickey Mantle, Willie Mays and Roberto Clemente, after all, were neither sent wandering around the league nor returned to the minors in mid-career—but there are some considerations that argue in Rabbit's behalf as a great player. One is the mere truth that he was able to play regularly in the major leagues at the age of forty-one while hitting .218, with no homers, for a contending team. This fact seems to be consistent only with the most formidable of defensive skills; even playing regularly when he was thirty-nine and hitting .260, given the averages of the day, is impressive. In 1920, after hitting .266 with one home run, he was traded for three players and $15,000, and the fans were outraged.

Second, he did do well in MVP voting. In 1924, hitting .266 for the Pirates, he finished seventh in the National League's MVP vote. In 1931, a thirty-nine-year-old shortstop whose offensive totals were nothing, he finished tenth in the first BBWAA MVP voting, with 15 points, and also drew about the same level of support in *The Sporting News* MVP vote. In 1932, moved to second base and hitting .235 with no homers, he finished eighth in *The Sporting News* MVP balloting, and in 1933, hitting .218 as mentioned before, he finished thirteenth in the MVP voting. He broke his leg in spring training the year after that, and sure enough the team that lost him, though replacing him with a .276 hitter, saw its team ERA balloon by over a run, and dropped five games in the won-lost category. Anyway, the perception that he was an extraordinarily valuable defensive player, whether accurate or inaccurate, was the perception of his own time, and not something that was created after the fact.

MARTY MARION

HALL OF FAME? No
DATA IN SECTION III? No
OFFENSIVE WON-LOST RECORD:
 Unknown
GROSS VALUE: Unknown
COMPARABLE RECENT PLAYERS:
Ozzie Smith

One of the few players to win an MVP award almost entirely with his glove, Marion belongs somewhere in the Bancroft-Bartell-Jackson-Reese-Rizzuto line, and I haven't the foggiest idea where.

PEE WEE REESE

HALL OF FAME? Yes
DATA IN SECTION III? Yes
OFFENSIVE WON-LOST RECORD:
   126–107, .541
GROSS VALUE: 164
COMPARABLE RECENT PLAYERS:
Concepcion

AND

PHIL RIZZUTO

HALL OF FAME? No
DATA IN SECTION III? Yes
OFFENSIVE WON-LOST RECORD:
   85–85, .500
GROSS VALUE: 122
COMPARABLE RECENT PLAYERS:
Bowa

Reese and Rizzuto, the third and final pair of "initial twins" among the shortstops, were linked so often while active that the election of Reese to the Hall of Fame has created a widespread assumption that Rizzuto must follow. While Rizzuto might well have been a great player, strong evidence for this does not survive in the statistics; the case for Reese is much better. Rizzuto won an MVP award, but that was in part because he had one season, the 1950 season, that was way above his head. Reese never had any such season, but finished among the top ten in the MVP voting eight times, which to me is a much more impressive accomplishment. Reese's defensive stats are a little better. It's kind of a B+ against a B, actually, with Boudreau and Marty Marion being the A students. Reese's offensive stats are quite a bit better.

JOE SEWELL

HALL OF FAME? Yes
DATA IN SECTION III? Yes
OFFENSIVE WON-LOST RECORD:
   113–88, .563
GROSS VALUE: 159
COMPARABLE RECENT PLAYERS:
Nellie Fox

If not striking out were the condition of excellence as a hitter, Sewell would be the most excellent of all. Joe Sewell is one of those players whose image has a hook that is always easy to find, but he was more than a man who never struck out. He was a good offensive and defensive player, scored and drove in quite a few runs and led his league in fourteen defensive categories at shortstop. A Definition-C Hall of Famer.

ROY SMALLEY

HALL OF FAME? Not Eligible
DATA IN SECTION III? No
OFFENSIVE WON-LOST RECORD:
   87–79, .525
GROSS VALUE: 108

Smalley is listed here because Pete Palmer's list in *The Hidden Game of Baseball* ranked him as one of the 100 greatest non-pitchers of all time.
He wasn't.

OZZIE SMITH

HALL OF FAME? Not Eligible
DATA IN SECTION III? No
OFFENSIVE WON-LOST RECORD:
   71–101, .411
GROSS VALUE: 117

ALAN TRAMMELL

HALL OF FAME? Not Eligible
DATA IN SECTION III? No
OFFENSIVE WON-LOST RECORD:
   82–72, .532
GROSS VALUE: 124

JOE TINKER

HALL OF FAME? Yes
DATA IN SECTION III? Yes
OFFENSIVE WON-LOST RECORD:
   107–90, .545
GROSS VALUE: 128
COMPARABLE RECENT PLAYERS:
Larry Bowa

Though not quite as good as Johnny Evers, Joe Tinker was a quality offensive and defensive player for a sustained period of years. As an offensive player he is in the same class as most of the other Hall of Fame shortstops, and better than several of them. He hit for a decent average and he had excellent speed. He was recognized as an outstanding defensive player—Adams' poem was setting down something that was in the air, not creating a myth from whole cloth—and his defensive statistics justify that respect (led National League in chances per game, 1904; double plays, 1905; fielding percentage, 1906; assists and fielding percentage, 1908; fielding percentage, 1909; putouts, assists, total chances per game and fielding percentage, 1911; putouts and chances per game, 1912; and fielding percentage, 1913; led Federal League in total chances per game, 1914).

When the first National League MVP vote was conducted in 1911, Tinker, not having an especially good season, was tenth in the voting. He played on five pennant-winning teams. His credentials for the Hall of Fame are as good as, and no better than, those of Pee Wee Reese, Dave Bancroft and Maury Wills.

ARKY VAUGHAN

HALL OF FAME? Yes
DATA IN SECTION III? Yes
OFFENSIVE WON-LOST RECORD:
  124–51, .710
GROSS VALUE: 161
COMPARABLE RECENT PLAYERS:
Alan Trammell

Vaughan became a popular Hall of Fame candidate about six or seven years ago and was inducted in 1985. I began the research for this book as a skeptic of his cause. If there is one thing certain about the Hall of Fame, it is that too damn many players from Vaughan's era are already in there. But I am now quite convinced that, while probably not ranking as high as Pete Palmer placed him on his list (29th among non-pitchers), Vaughan was indeed a great player.

Though his nickname might not suggest this, Joseph Vaughan was a very quiet man, a man who carried himself with considerable dignity; in this respect, he was sometimes compared to an American League contemporary, Charlie Gehringer. This, and playing in Pittsburgh during a decline phase for the Pirates, did not draw attention to him. At the time of his death in a drowning accident in 1952, Arthur Daley wrote that "More has been written about the colorful Willie Mays in one year than was said of Vaughan in a lifetime." Whereas it is true and worthy of note that Vaughan's performance in award voting was not impressive, this should be kept in mind. While Vaughan did not win the BBWAA MVP award in 1935, when he had the awesome stats (.385, 19 homers, 97 walks, .607 slugging percentage), he did win *The Sporting News* MVP award, of nearly equal prestige at the time. While it is true, and odd, that he made the *TSN* All-Star team only once, it is also true that Joe Cronin was better copy.

Vaughan's offensive statistics do not wilt under the closest of scrutiny; they are just flat impressive. He had a lot of good years, and they were mighty good. He led the National League in triples three times, runs scored three times, walks three times, stolen bases once, batting once and slugging once; he led in one thing or another seven different years. He hit .300 monotonously in what was not a great hitter's league or a great hitter's park; he hit .318 lifetime and had doubles, triples, a few homers and excellent speed. He walked an enormous amount and hardly ever struck out. His career defensive statistics are good.

And, like Enos Slaughter, Arky's missing about 550 hits that he ought to have. Late in the season in 1943, a Dodger team flap developed when Mickey Owen made a remark, apparently to a newspaperman, about Bobo Newsome throwing a spitball. Bobo was offended by this, and lashed out at Owen. Leo Durocher charged in trying to straighten it out, and wound up having words with Newsome, who he then suspended for no particular reason. After the next game, Vaughan took off his uniform and handed it to Durocher and said, in essence, "Here, if you're going to take his uniform you can have mine, too." Durocher, flabbergasted that the reserved, respected Vaughan would instigate this rebellion, began to backtrack immediately, and the matter was cleared up without any fines, suspensions, or direct repercussions. But it left an awkward relationship between Vaughan and Durocher, and Arky, who apparently didn't care too much for Leo anyway, retired following the season, rather than create a problem in the clubhouse.

He could still play. In 1943 he had hit .305, leading the N.L. in runs scored with 112 and stolen bases with 20, and had returned to shortstop after a season at third base. He was only thirty-one years old, and had collected over 2,000 hits; he was an excellent candidate to get 3,000. Had he been able to avoid the draft, he was also an excellent candidate to become the National League's MVP during the war years. Instead he worked at a wartime job and played semi-pro ball.

When Durocher was suspended in 1947, Vaughan returned to the Dodgers after a three-year layoff, and hit .325 in a utility role.

I see no evidence, in the end, that he was any less a player than his statistics show. "Run down the list of Vaughan's contemporaries at shortstop," wrote Daley (*New York Times,* September 3, 1952), "and you'll find that only the flamboyant Leo Durocher could outrank him as a fielder. None could outrank him as a hitter."

HONUS WAGNER

HALL OF FAME? Yes
DATA IN SECTION III? Yes
OFFENSIVE WON-LOST RECORD:
   213–70, .752
Wagner has the highest offensive winning percentage of any shortstop in history, by a comfortable margin. The only man within 100 points of him is Arky Vaughan, in a much shorter career.
GROSS VALUE: 289
Wagner's gross value is by far the highest of any shortstop.
COMPARABLE RECENT PLAYERS:
None

You sure do read a lot of weird stuff about Honus' con-tract negotiations. Honig and Ritter wrote that "Incredibly, Honus had little interest in money. In 1908 he signed a contract for $10,000 a year and until the end of his career kept earning the same amount, never asking for a raise." On the other hand, an article in a November 1984 issue of the *Sports Collectors Digest* says that Wagner's salary battles with Barney Dreyfuss were well known, and that they eventually culminated in a holdout. The 1969 edition of the Macmillan *Encyclopedia* does, indeed, list Wagner as a 1917 holdout.

A note in Curt Flood's fine book *The Way It Is* (with Richard Carter) retells a familiar anecdote in which Wagner "rejected a $2,000 contract offered by the club owner, Barney Dreyfus [sic].

"'Not on your life,' bellowed the shrewd Honus. 'I won't play for a penny less than *fifteen hundred* dollars.'"

Sure. I wouldn't wager that any of these gentlemen had gotten the straight poop on Wagner's salary negotiations, but to clear up the smallest misunderstanding, Honus did not hold out for more money in 1917. He retired after the 1916 season, but when the Pirates started losing in earnest —not to mention in Brooklyn, Philadelphia, St. Louis, etc.— there were calls from fans, press and players for Honus to come back. He got back into the game, forty-three years old, without benefit of spring training, and led the Pirates in hitting for a good part of the season, finishing at .265. It didn't help; the Pirates finished last, anyway.

Honus Wagner was not a fool or a buffoon. Beyond the extent to which all great athletes are sad figures after that which has set them apart from ordinary men has departed them, he did not wind up as a pathetic old wretch, bumming drinks from strangers. He was a cheerful, good-natured man, always ready to have a drink with an admirer and never short of admirers. One recent book, choosing up a "Chubby" all-star team, included Wagner along with Mickey Lolich, Smokey Burgess, etc., which has got to be the most ill-informed and frankly stupid selection for which I am not personally responsible. Wagner was built funny; he had an enormous barrel chest, short legs and huge, thick hands, arms, and all other features— but any suggestion that he was "chubby" is preposterous. He was the greatest athlete in baseball.

Among the great players in the game there are all kinds of men—smart alecks, tough guys, driven men and heavy drinkers. As gentlemen, there are many who seem worthy of admiration, including Musial, Mathewson, Gehrig, Johnson and Schmidt. None seems more worthy than Wagner. He was a gentle, kind man, a storyteller, supportive of rookies, patient with fans, cheerful in hard times, careful of the example that he set for youth, a hard worker, a man who had no enemies and who never forgot his friends. He was the most beloved man in baseball before Ruth. He couldn't manage, not because he wasn't intelligent enough, but because he wasn't hard enough. Those qualities are part of the reason why, acknowledging that there may have been one or two whose talents were greater, there is

no one who has ever played this game that I would be more anxious to have on a baseball team.

BOBBY WALLACE

HALL OF FAME? Yes
DATA IN SECTION III? Yes
OFFENSIVE WON-LOST RECORD:
131–124, .514
GROSS VALUE: 185
COMPARABLE RECENT PLAYERS:
Ozzie Smith, but his bat was better

Probably the most faceless member of the Hall of Fame as far as the public is concerned, Wallace was a premier defensive infielder who had some good seasons with the bat. He was a mild-mannered player, known as a bit of a dandy, a sharp dresser and popular with the fans. Late in his playing career his house burned down and a day was held in

his honor, at which he was given home furnishings and such.

MAURY WILLS

HALL OF FAME? No
DATA IN SECTION III? Yes
OFFENSIVE WON-LOST RECORD:
111–108, .508
GROSS VALUE: 140

While active, I think it was generally assumed that Wills was a Hall of Fame–calibre player. Damaging his chances with a variety of post-career embarrassments, Wills is still young enough to restore his image if he gets his act together. He was a smart player, and, as a Gold Glove winner, .300 hitter and base stealing champion on an outstanding team, a player with too many positives to be lightly dismissed.

HOW THE SHORTSTOPS RATE

The selection of the greatest one ever is easier at this position than at any other; after that it is desperate work. I will no doubt be criticized for overrating the good-hitting shortstops and underrating the glove men, but then I have enjoyed that criticism for many years concerning the rankings in the annual *Baseball Abstract*s, and I don't see why I should give it up now. The greatest shortstops ever, as I see them:

PEAK VALUE	CAREER VALUE
1. Honus Wagner	1. Honus Wagner
2. Ernie Banks	2. Luke Appling
3. Arky Vaughan	3. Ernie Banks
4. Lou Boudreau	4. Joe Cronin
5. Joe Cronin	5. Luis Aparicio
6. Robin Yount	6. Bobby Wallace
7. Ozzie Smith	7. Rabbit Maranville
8. Glenn Wright	8. Lou Boudreau
9. Maury Wills	9. Pee Wee Reese
10. Luke Appling	10. Dave Concepcion

❧ LEFT FIELD ❧

LOU BROCK

HALL OF FAME? Yes
DATA IN SECTION III? Yes
OFFENSIVE WON-LOST RECORD:
    180–110, .620
GROSS VALUE: 183

Historical revisionists of today, not satisfied with trying to turn Thomas Jefferson into a tyrant, convert Dwight Eisenhower into an intellectual and wash the blood from the hands of Robespierre, have begun arguing that Lou Brock was a good outfielder. This, gentlemen, is going too far. There are too many of us still alive who saw the man play. Lou had no arm and a tendency to freeze up on balls hit right at him.

Lou Brock represents an offensive player of a type with which I am not enamored. He represents, however, the best of the type and as such a very fine player. He hit .300 many times, drew some walks, hit doubles and triples and as many as 21 home runs. Combined with stealing more bases than anyone before Rickey Henderson, this put him in scoring position constantly, so that he scored 100 runs seven times, twice leading the league. He was the greatest World Series performer of my lifetime, rivaled only by his teammate, Bob Gibson, and a fellow named Reggie. When he became eligible for the Hall of Fame he slid in without a throw, as indeed he should have.

FRED CLARKE

HALL OF FAME? Yes
DATA IN SECTION III? Yes
OFFENSIVE WON-LOST RECORD:
    162–77, .678
GROSS VALUE: 201
COMPARABLE RECENT PLAYERS:
Curt Flood

A natural center fielder, Clarke played primarily left field and managed the outstanding Pittsburgh Pirate teams of 1900–1911.

Clarke is one of the few people in baseball history who had a Hall of Fame career as a player and a Hall of Fame career as a manager. As a player, he could hit (.315 lifetime, 2,708 hits), run (223 triples, 506 stolen bases) and field. A fanatic about conditioning and known for both determination and shrewdness on the field, Clarke became manager of the Louisville franchise at the age of 24. Shifted to Pittsburgh when the league contracted in 1900, he assumed the helm of the Pirates and led them to their first pennant ever in 1901. In 1902 his team went 103–36, winning the pennant by 27 and a half games, an all-time record. In 1903 they won again. From 1904 through 1908 they didn't win, but every year finished more than 20 games over .500. In 1909 they took the flag with 110 wins, with the thirty-six-year-old Clarke leading the league in outfield putouts as well as fielding percentage. For three more years after that the Pirates never finished less than 16 games over .500, completing a twelve-year run in which the team went 1123–672, 451 games over .500. Going head to head with McGraw's Giants and the Cubs of Frank Chance, they may be the least known among the great teams of history.

Early in his career, Clarke bought a ranch in central Kansas (see comment about Rube Waddell). Oil was discovered on his property, and it was widely written that Clarke had become a millionaire. Clarke denied this but lived comfortably. Called out of retirement by the Pirates in the mid-twenties, he served as a coach on the World Champion Pirates of 1925 and a vice-president of the team in 1926. He had apparently grown cranky with age, as happens to too many of us, and his career ended with less distinction than was perhaps deserved (see Max Carey). He died in Winfield, Kansas, in 1960.

GOOSE GOSLIN

HALL OF FAME? Yes
DATA IN SECTION III? Yes
OFFENSIVE WON-LOST RECORD:
155–82, .655
GROSS VALUE: 196
COMPARABLE RECENT PLAYERS: Al Kaline

One of the really good ones; one of the few stars of his era who was every bit as good as his numbers. He turned in 100-RBI seasons like clockwork for fifteen years, had outstanding speed, a powerful arm, and good strike zone judgment. In what should have been his best years, the years 1923–1929, he played in Griffith Stadium in Washington, an impossible home run park, which probably kept him from driving in 150 runs a year. (In 1926 he hit 17 home runs, all of them on the road, and his total for those seven years was 22 home runs at home, 82 on the road.)

Goslin played regularly on five American League champion teams, which is remarkable in view of the fact that he never played for either of the dominant teams of the time, the Yankees or Athletics. He played for the Senators in 1924–25, was traded away but rejoined them in 1933, when they won it again, and then was traded to the Tigers, where he had a couple more 100-RBI seasons to help the Tigers get where they needed to go.

Goslin had the skills that we would usually associate with an outstanding right fielder, and played that position later in his career. He played left field most of his life for two reasons: (1) The Senators had another Hall of Famer in right, Sam Rice, and (2) It was 401 feet to left field in Griffith Park.

All the markers are positive. He did everything well, he was consistent at it for a long period of time, and he helped his teams win. He has to be one of the top 100.

CHICK HAFEY

HALL OF FAME? Yes
DATA IN SECTION III? No
OFFENSIVE WON-LOST RECORD:
Approximately 85–41, .675
GROSS VALUE: Unknown
COMPARABLE RECENT PLAYERS:
Dave Parker, Rocky Colavito

An impressive player, Hafey had one of the greatest throwing arms of all time. Hafey had very poor vision, wore big, thick glasses (bifocals, no less); Andy High, a teammate, recalled that even with them he sometimes couldn't read the signs in the train depot. High said that it was astonishing that Hafey could hit at all as blind as he was, but hit he did. His power stats in his years in St. Louis, though somewhat inflated, are eye-popping.

He was the first batting champion to wear glasses, in 1931, and the 1932 *Reach Guide* commented that "Hafey had always been a heavy hitter, and when he was afflicted with sinus trouble a few seasons ago it was feared that his playing days might be over. . . . Perhaps Hafey's achievement will remove the prejudice against players wearing glasses in the future . . . more than one player flashes glasses in the privacy of his home when he wants to read."

MONTE IRVIN

HALL OF FAME? Yes, as Negro League star
DATA IN SECTION III? No
OFFENSIVE WON-LOST RECORD:
Unknown
GROSS VALUE: Unknown
COMPARABLE RECENT PLAYERS:
Ken Singleton

Among the people who were involved in or followed the Negro Leagues, it was unanimously assumed that if the color line was to be broken, Irvin would be the first man to go. Irvin was a consummate gentleman of great poise as well as great talent, sort of the Sidney Poitier of baseball, and some people were quite upset that he was not chosen to be The One.

But anyway, he wasn't exactly what Rickey was looking for, so Irvin, who was the same age as Jackie (within a month), didn't reach the majors until he was thirty. His career from age thirty-one on compares favorably to that of many or even most Hall of Famers, including (to name just a few) Medwick, Hafey, Klein, Bottomley, Kiner and Jackie Robinson.

GEORGE FOSTER

HALL OF FAME? Not Eligible
DATA IN SECTION III? No
OFFENSIVE WON-LOST RECORD:
  126–73, .633
GROSS VALUE: 126

Selected by Maury Allen as the 72nd greatest player of all time.

FRANK HOWARD

HALL OF FAME? No
DATA IN SECTION III? Yes
OFFENSIVE WON-LOST RECORD:
  128–57, .691
GROSS VALUE: 134

JOE JACKSON

HALL OF FAME? No
DATA IN SECTION III? Yes
OFFENSIVE WON-LOST RECORD:
  105–26, .804
GROSS VALUE: 135
COMPARABLE RECENT PLAYERS:
Tony Oliva

His offensive winning percentage, .804, is the third-highest of any player, behind only the immortals Ruth and Williams. I was surprised to discover this, but I realize that it does make sense. His career batting average, .356, is the third-highest ever, and since he compiled that in a low-average era and hit with power, he's got to be right up there. He edged ahead of Cobb, of course, only because he had no decline phase to his career. Had he not been thrown out of baseball as a crook, his batting average would have remained as high and perhaps even edged a point higher, but the relationship between him and the league would have flattened out rapidly. He was thirty-three years old, entering the phase of rapid real decline.

One of the roaringest of Hall of Fame debates centers on this man, dead now for many years. There can be no dispute about the quality of his play; he was one of the greatest. I have read everything I can find about the matter—accounts of the series, accounts of the trial, *Eight Men Out*—and I can get no firm sense of the degree of his guilt. The basic defense for him seems to be that he was too stupid to know exactly what was going on, and that he didn't *really* intend to help throw the games, but only to position himself to take a share of the cut. I do not find the defense convincing or ennobling. It is clear to me that the money men behind the fix orchestrated a cover-up that successfully prevented the whole story from ever becoming known. The signed confessions of Jackson, Williams and Cicotte, along with their immunity waivers, were stolen from the office of the assistant state attorney, and the stories of those for whom they were missing were conveniently changed. Jackson is among those who may have lied under oath to help confuse the issue. As to the charge that Landis dealt harshly with him, two points:

1) Jackson was suspended from baseball before Landis became commissioner. Landis' decision was only not to readmit him after the Illinois jury found insufficient evidence that a crime had been committed.

2) The policy stating that a player involved in the fixing of games was to be banned for life was not Landis' creation. It had been a part of baseball law for over forty years prior to the Black Sox scandal.

My own opinion as to whether or not Joe Jackson should be put in the Hall of Fame is that of course he should; it is only a question of priorities. I think there are some other equally great players who should go in first, like Billy Williams, Herman Long, Minnie Minoso and Elroy Face. Then, too, the players of the nineteenth century have never really gotten their due —Ed McKean, Pete Browning, Harry Stovey and several others have been waiting a long time. The players of the Negro leagues committed no crime except their color; I think we would need to look closely at the credentials of several of those before we decide where Jackson fits in. You wouldn't want the great stars of the thirties and forties, who are still living and can enjoy the honor, to pass away while waiting for the Hall of Fame to get done with the Black Sox, would you? And then I think there are some other players who should be considered strongly—Ron Santo, Ken Boyer, Larry Doby, Al Rosen, Roy Sievers, Vic Wertz, Lefty

O'Doul, Sadaharu Oh; there should probably be better provisions made for people whose contributions to the game were not made on the field, like Grantland Rice, Barney Dreyfuss, Harry Pulliam, maybe Mrs. Babe Ruth and Mrs. Lou Gehrig, the guy who wrote *Take Me Out to the Ballgame,* Harry Caray. And, too, we do not want to forget the many wonderful stars of the minor leagues, who brought baseball to most of the country before television and expansion—men like Ray Perry, Larry Gilbert, Jack Dunn and Nick Cullop. When they are in we can turn our attention to such worthwhile players of our own memories as Roger Maris, Buddy Bell, Fred Hutchinson, Larry Bowa, Bill North, Omar Moreno and Duane Kuiper. And then, at last, when every honest ballplayer who has ever played the game, at any level from Babe Ruth ball through the majors, when every coach, writer, umpire and organist who has helped to make baseball the wonderful game that it is rather than trying to destroy it with the poison of deceit, when each has been given his due, then I think we should hold our noses and make room for Joe Jackson to join the Hall of Fame. It is only right.

BOB JOHNSON
HALL OF FAME? No
DATA IN SECTION III? Yes
OFFENSIVE WON-LOST RECORD:
129–62, .677
GROSS VALUE: 174
COMPARABLE RECENT PLAYERS:
Jack Clark

You know, what I could never understand was how come Bob Johnson was "Indian Bob" but his brother Roy wasn't called "Indian Roy." He was only half Indian; I guess that explains it . . . outstanding player for a decade; Clark is an excellent comparison.

RALPH KINER
HALL OF FAME? Yes
DATA IN SECTION III? Yes
OFFENSIVE WON-LOST RECORD:
108–37, .747
GROSS VALUE: 129
COMPARABLE RECENT PLAYERS:
George Foster

It has become the custom, since his election to the Hall of Fame in 1975, to downgrade Kiner's skills, and to portray him as a one-dimensional slugger who at that hit "only" 369 homers for bad teams and with the help of a fence that was pulled in for him. Enos Slaughter said that he could score on a fly ball to Kiner 30 feet behind third base.

Great, Enos, but look at the facts. Slaughter's career high in runs scored was 100 even; this included runs scored tagging up on a fly ball to Ralph Kiner, runs scored from first base on a single, all those flashy things. Kiner scored, in consecutive seasons, 118, 104,

116, 112, and 124. Who you gonna take?

Ralph Kiner was, in terms of an established ability at a given moment, the second-greatest home run hitter of all time. Only Ruth dominated the home run hitting business the way Kiner did in his best seasons. OK, his park helped him a little, and his defense was nothing great. But he hit .300, drew a huge number of walks (112, 117, 122, 137, 110, 100 in consecutive seasons) and hit home runs. It's a simple combination, but it's extraordinarily valuable.

And nobody thought, when he was active, that it wasn't. Take a look at the outfields on *The Sporting News* All-Star teams from 1947 through 1951. In 1947 it was Williams, DiMaggio and Kiner. In 1948 it was Williams, DiMaggio and Musial, in 1949 Williams, Musial and Kiner, in 1950 Musial, Kiner, and Doby, in 1951 Musial, Williams, and Kiner. Musial, Williams, DiMaggio and Kiner—those were the great outfielders of that period.

There is one specific comparison that I just love, because it's such a perfect statement of the way that ballplayers' skills change after they are retired and people have talked about them a while. Late in his career, Warren Spahn's name appeared on an article "My Nine Toughest Batters," which appeared in the March 1961 issue of *Sport* magazine. Spahn named Kiner as the number four man, behind Musial, Mays and Ernie Banks, and wrote that "every time Ralph came up he endangered any lead that you had." Twenty years later, the imaginations of sportswriters being what they are, a journalist approached Spahn for an interview and wrote the same article for *The Baseball Digest* issue of October 1982—"Warren Spahn Recalls His Toughest Batting Foes," by George White.

Somehow, Kiner had entirely disappeared from the list. He had been surpassed by people like Jackie Robinson and Roberto Clemente, who were not even mentioned by Spahn in the 1961 article. But in the 1982 article, it is Kiner's name which is not mentioned.

SHERRY MAGEE

HALL OF FAME? No
DATA IN SECTION III? Yes
OFFENSIVE WON-LOST RECORD:
   151–65, .698
GROSS VALUE: 159

The slugging left fielder for the Phillies from 1904 through 1914, later played center for the Braves. A consistent power hitter, Magee led the N.L. in runs batted in 1907, 1910, 1914 and 1918, though it was not an official statistic the first two times . . . erroneously labeled as "Declared ineligible" by the 1969 Macmillan *Encyclopedia*. It was a clerical error; Lee Magee was the one thrown out. . . . Same book

also says he was "suspended for abusing umpire" in 1911. Actually, it was more in the nature of an assault (see notes in Section III).

JOE MEDWICK

HALL OF FAME? Yes
DATA IN SECTION III? Yes
OFFENSIVE WON-LOST RECORD:
   135–66, .671
GROSS VALUE: 170
COMPARABLE RECENT PLAYERS: Hal McRae

A good line-drive hitter and the most aggressive, physical player of his time, Medwick was not, with the sole exception of the 1937 season, an offensive force in his own time to be compared with Joe Jackson, Musial, Williams, Kiner, Stargell or Yastrzemski. He was an impatient hitter who hit a lot of doubles and triples and 18–23 home runs a year. He was a good left fielder, but then most of these fellows were.

MINNIE MINOSO

HALL OF FAME? No
DATA IN SECTION III? No
OFFENSIVE WON-LOST RECORD:
   Unknown
GROSS VALUE: Unknown
COMPARABLE RECENT PLAYERS:
Vada Pinson, Bobby Tolan

Much of the argument that has been applied to Enos Slaughter, and with merit, could also be applied to Minnie Minoso. But for a very brief trial, he didn't play in the major leagues until the age of twenty-eight, in large part be-

cause of his color—yet, since he played in the major leagues so long, few people think about the fact that his best years may have been behind him before he ever got a chance, and that his entire career was spent in what is ordinarily a player's decline phase. His highest batting average, .326, was in his rookie year in 1951.

As a player, he was tightly similar to Slaughter, a fast, hustling, line-drive hitter with medium-range power. They were about the same size, both very popular players. Their batting and slugging averages are virtually identical (batting averages are .300 and .298, edge to Slaughter; slugging averages are .459 and .453, edge to Minoso. Carl Furillo is in the same group, at .299 and .458). Like Slaughter, Minoso played in the major leagues until he was well past forty, as a hustling, aggressive player of this quality often will. Then he went and played in the Mexican League for another ten years. A comparison of Minoso and Slaughter in seasonal notation gives Minoso a few extra at bats, since Slaughter's last few years were as a pinch hitter; see the table at the top of the next page.

I ran an experiment with Minoso, reversing the Brock2 system to try to project what his career stats might have been had he been called up earlier. The Brock2 system is a complex method that at-

	Years	AB	R	H	2B	3B	HR	RBI	SB	BB	Avg.
Minoso	11.4	580	100	173	30	7	17	91	18	73	.298
Slaughter	14.7	541	85	162	28	10	12	89	5	69	.300

tempts to project a player's final career statistics, given his performance up to a certain point in time. What I did in the case of Minoso was to try to plug into the formula a combination of accomplishments at an earlier age which would create the projection that the player would later do exactly what Minoso later did. In other words, instead of asking: "Given these records up to age twenty-seven, what will the player's statistics be for the rest of his career?" I asked it: "What kind of a player would produce these statistics after the age of twenty-eight?" The method estimates that, if he had come up at the age of twenty-two, Minnie Minoso's career statistics would be those shown below:

Games	AB	R	H	2B	3B	HR	RBI	BB	Avg.
2863	9974	1970	3079	534	168	318	1429	1272	.309

The projection produces exactly the same totals after the age of twenty-eight that he actually had.

STAN MUSIAL

HALL OF FAME? Yes
DATA IN SECTION III? Yes
OFFENSIVE WON-LOST RECORD:
   228–58, .798
GROSS VALUE: 295
(Highest among left fielders)
COMPARABLE RECENT PLAYERS:
Carl Yastrzemski

The image of Musial seems to be fading quickly. Maybe I'm wrong, but it doesn't seem to me that you hear much about him anymore, compared to such comparable stars as Mantle, Williams, Mays and DiMaggio, and to the extent that you do hear of him it doesn't seem that the

image is very sharp, that anybody really knows what it was that made him different. He was never colorful, never much of an interview. He makes a better statue.

What he was was a *ballplayer*. He didn't spit at fans, he didn't get into fights in nightclubs, he didn't marry anybody famous. He hustled. You look at his career totals of doubles and triples, and they'll remind you of some-

thing that was accepted while he was active, and has been largely forgotten since: Stan Musial was one player who always left the batter's box on a dead run.

One of the major goals of this book, as you have likely noticed, has been to distinguish accurately between that which was written and said about the player's skills while he was active, and that which came along later. I have concluded, in that effort, that Stan Musial, while active, was probably the most respected player, by press, fans and other players, of the postwar era—more so than Mays, Mantle, Williams, Rose or anyone else.

One thing that I have tried to do, in that line, is to pay attention to award voting—MVP awards, *The Sporting News* post-season All-Star teams, regular All-Star teams, rankings and comments by contemporary press, anything like that. What player, I wondered, had done the best of any other in voting for the MVP award?

I thought that the answer would be "Mantle." It isn't. The men who have had 3.00 or more MVP Award Shares are:

1.	Stan Musial	7.47
2.	Ted Williams	6.42
3.	Willie Mays	5.97
4.	Mickey Mantle	5.72
5.	Hank Aaron	5.50
6.	Joe DiMaggio	5.46
7.	Lou Gehrig	5.15(a)
8.	Mike Schmidt	4.88(b)

9.	Frank Robinson	4.86
10.	Yogi Berra	3.95
11.	Jimmie Foxx	3.80(a)
12.	Brooks Robinson	3.69
13.	Pete Rose	3.68
14.	Hank Greenberg	3.62
15.	Eddie Collins	3.58(a)
16.	Charlie Gehringer	3.39
17.	Willie Stargell	3.30
18.	Reggie Jackson	3.28
19.	Harmon Killebrew	3.23
20.	Frankie Frisch	3.20(a)
21.	Jim Rice	3.15(b)
22.	Joe Morgan	3.14
23.	Carl Hubbell	3.13
24.	George Brett	3.08(b)
25.	Dizzy Dean	3.05
26.	Dave Parker	3.05(b)

NOTES:

a) MVP votes not available for entire career.

b) Includes votes through 1986 season.

Eddie Murray through 1986 has 2.97 Award Shares, a record for a player who has never won the award.

A side point here is that Williams, who I had always thought did not do well in MVP voting, actually did very well; he lost a couple of close races, but it simply is not true that the sportswriters of his time were not impressed with him. They were, by this one measurement, more impressed with Williams than with Willie Mays.

Anyway, as the total suggests, Musial's performance in MVP voting is the most impressive in the history of the award. Musial won three awards; so did Mantle, Berra, Campanella, and DiMaggio. But Musial also finished second in the voting four times,

meaning that he had seven years in which he was regarded by on-the-scenes observers as one of the two best players in the league. He finished as runner-up to Jackie Robinson in 1949, drawing five first-place votes. He was the (distant) runner-up to Konstanty in 1950 and to Campanella in 1951. In 1957, when Henry Aaron won his one MVP award as a twenty-three-year-old right fielder hitting .322 with 44 homers and 132 RBI for the league champions, Musial almost beat him as a thirty-six-year-old first baseman, hitting .351 with 29 and 102. The count was 239–230 in Aaron's favor.

Musial also finished fourth in the MVP voting in 1944, fifth in 1952, eighth in 1953, sixth in 1954, eighth in 1955 and ninth in 1956. Even when his statistics were not impressive, he still drew support in the MVP balloting. In 1958, hitting .337 but driving in only 62 runs, he still drew a 12 percent share of the MVP vote (39 points). In 1960, thirty-nine years old and not a regular (he hit .275 in 331 at bats), he drew a 6 percent share of the vote, finishing ahead of Maury Wills, who hit .295 and led the league with 50 stolen bases, and Frank Robinson, who hit .297 with 31 homers.

Musial made *The Sporting News* major league All-Star team eleven times. One reason for this remarkable performance in award voting is suggested by this selection

from Curt Flood's *The Way It Is,* an often bitter and uncomplimentary book, which does, indeed, tell things exactly the way they happened. Discussing his struggle to learn to hit the major league curve, Flood says that "Musial also helped —mainly by working as hard as he did on his own perfect swing. If this immortal felt the need for frequent extra practice, how could I hope to prosper on less effort?"

Unlike many of the players of his generation, Musial was always in shape; his one notable injury, that which moved him from the pitcher's mound to the outfield, occurred in an off-season gymnastics workout. I think you will find it a general principle of life that players who hurt themselves while working out in the off-season have long and successful careers, while those who hurt themselves running the bases do not.

LEFTY O'DOUL

HALL OF FAME? No
DATA IN SECTION III? No
OFFENSIVE WON-LOST RECORD:
  Approximately 67–30, .687
GROSS VALUE: 80
COMPARABLE RECENT PLAYERS:
Tony Oliva

O'Doul was an outstanding player in the Pacific Coast League for several years, hitting .392 and .375 for Salt Lake City in 1924–25 and .378 for San Francisco in 1927, with power. As a pitcher he also went 25–9 for San Francisco in 1921. O'Doul was a San Francisco hero; he was born and died there, and spent seventeen years there as a manager. There is still a restaurant in downtown SF called Lefty O'Doul's, or at least there was the last time I was there, about ten years ago. . . .

Anyone who thinks that O'Doul might have been a Hall of Fame–calibre star is advised to review the record of the major league transactions in which he was involved. In 1922 he was sold on waivers from the Yankees to the Red Sox. In 1928 the Giants traded O'Doul *and cash* to acquire an outfielder named Fred Leach. In 1930 O'Doul and Fresco Thompson were sent from Philadelphia to Brooklyn in exchange for Hal Lee, Clise Dudley, a minor league outfielder, and cash. After he won the batting title in 1932, the Dodgers packaged him together with their top pitcher to acquire a first baseman named Sam Leslie. If that's a great player, it's the story of the century.

TIM RAINES

HALL OF FAME? Not Eligible
DATA IN SECTION III? No
OFFENSIVE WON-LOST RECORD:
81–43, .652
GROSS VALUE: 90

JIM RICE

HALL OF FAME? Not Eligible
DATA IN SECTION III? No
OFFENSIVE WON-LOST RECORD:
130–78, .625
GROSS VALUE: 164

Jim pretty much put himself in the Hall of Fame in his twenties. In his thirties he has continued to post some impressive numbers—100 RBI seasons, 200 hits in 1986—but his value, except for the 1986 season, has been very questionable.

WILLIE STARGELL

HALL OF FAME? Yes
DATA IN SECTION III? Yes
OFFENSIVE WON-LOST RECORD:
160–60, .726
GROSS VALUE: 180

A couple of years ago, I went around asking people I met who were in baseball who they considered to be the best human being in baseball, and the worst human being in baseball. I thought it would make an interesting magazine article, or pair of articles— that is, 1,000 words on the best human being in baseball, 1,000 on the worst.

I never did the article, but anyway, there was virtual unanimity as to who was the worst human being in baseball, a general manager famous for lying, cheating, swindling, bullying and bragging during contract negotiations, trade talks, job interviews and sometimes just for the heck of it. Everyone in baseball will know to whom I refer as soon

as they read the description, and unfortunately I cannot tell the rest of you. There was no such agreement as to who was the best human being in baseball, but several people did think of Willie Stargell.

A power hitter, Willie's power totals were held down for years by playing in Forbes Field. In 1965 and 1966 he hit only 19 home runs in Pittsburgh, as opposed to 41 on the road. When the Pirates shifted to Three Rivers he broke loose with a couple of monstrous years, hitting 48 homers in 1971 and becoming the only player in many years to hit forty doubles and forty homers in the same season. Even in those good years, 1971–73, he hit more than half of his home runs (64 of 125) on the road.

He hit over .290 eight times with terrific power, and you can't argue with that kind of offense. As a defensive player his arm was good, excellent when the play was in front of him, but his range was never good. I don't care for the combination; I'd rather have the range than the arm, but combined with his offense and his leadership, Stargell has earned a mention as one of the greatest of left fielders.

RUSTY STAUB

HALL OF FAME? Not Eligible
DATA IN SECTION III? No
OFFENSIVE WON-LOST RECORD:
 Unknown
GROSS VALUE: Unknown

A productive player for a long time; a Definition-D Hall of Famer.

ZACK WHEAT

HALL OF FAME? Yes
DATA IN SECTION III? Yes
OFFENSIVE WON-LOST RECORD:
 170–79, .682
GROSS VALUE: 186
COMPARABLE RECENT PLAYERS:
Al Oliver

When the lively ball era began, some players were helped by the change a great deal, and others not so much. Wheat was one who was helped a lot, as was Tris Speaker, who was a similar type of hitter. Wheat was thirty-two years old in 1920 and his previous career high in hits was 177, but he then ripped out 191, 182, 201, 131 (injured), 212, and 221, his career high, at the age of thirty-seven. I always wondered why he was helped so much. Casey Stengel explained it in *Casey at the Bat,* saying that Wheat "was the most graceful left-handed hitter I ever saw. With the dead ball, many of his line drives were caught, but they were just shot out of a cannon almost every time up." Casey named Wheat the greatest N.L. left fielder he had seen except for Musial.

BILLY WILLIAMS

HALL OF FAME? Yes
DATA IN SECTION III? Yes
OFFENSIVE WON-LOST RECORD:
 178–80, .689
GROSS VALUE: 189

His offensive totals were unquestionably inflated by playing in Wrigley Field, as is shown by his home/road home run breakdown and his offensive decline in moving to the Oakland Coliseum. As time passes, I become more sold on his credentials as a great player. I still think Ron Santo was a more valuable player.

KEN WILLIAMS

HALL OF FAME? No
DATA IN SECTION III? Yes
OFFENSIVE WON-LOST RECORD:
 93–45, .675
GROSS VALUE: 129
COMPARABLE RECENT PLAYERS:
Bobby Bonds

Pete Palmer has him rated way too high (119th greatest player of all time among non-pitchers). While he is an interesting player, his credentials to be called a great one are shaky at best. His offensive totals were all compiled in his home park for a team that didn't win. For his "outstanding" 1922 season, when he had a power/speed number of 38.0 and drove in 155 runs, he was not mentioned on any MVP ballot. Granted, the rules of the time did not allow voters to list both Williams and his teammate Sisler, yet that still seems an odd reflection on a great season.

TED WILLIAMS

HALL OF FAME? Yes
DATA IN SECTION III? Yes
OFFENSIVE WON-LOST RECORD:
 168–28, .858
Williams' .858 career offensive winning percentage is the highest of all time, at any position.
GROSS VALUE: 280

The race for the distinction of being the greatest hitter of all time as measured by formal analysis is between Ruth and Williams, and it is so close that any revision of the method, however small, is likely to reverse the outcome. Using state-of-the-art methods, Williams' career offensive winning percentage is .858; Ruth's is .851. The last time I printed the comparison was in the 1982 *Baseball Abstract,* and at that time I had it Williams, .841–.836. The method has taken several steps forward since then, and there have been intermediate points at which Ruth seemed to be the number one man. There will be many changes to the method filed in the next ten years.

As mentioned in the Musial comment, Williams actually did extremely well in MVP voting throughout his career. I cannot agree with those who feel he should have done better. While everybody knows that Williams lost the 1947 MVP vote by one point because a Boston writer named Mel Webb (Williams called him in his autobiography "a grouchy old guy, a real grump") left Williams entirely off his ballot, what nobody remembers about that balloting was that *three* voters left DiMaggio entirely off their ballots, and three others had him eighth, ninth and tenth on the ballot—whereas no one except Webb had Williams lower than seventh. Williams lost that vote because only three people out of the twenty-four-man panel thought he was the Most Valuable Player—and the only reason it was close at all was that the Yankee vote was split among DiMaggio (eight firsts), Page (seven firsts) and George McQuinn (three firsts).

In 1957 a furor erupted and there were cries for reform of the voting because two A.L. voters placed Williams, who hit .388, ninth and tenth on their ballots. But even if they both placed him second, Mantle would still have won the award. For my part as a statistical analyst, I would like to say that anyone who thinks Ted Williams in 1957 was a better player than Mickey Mantle is a lunatic. You've got a huge difference in defensive value, you've got Mantle drawing 146 walks and driving

in and scoring more runs than Williams, you've got all the difference in the world in baserunning speed, you've got the difference between Fenway Park and Yankee Stadium, and you've got the fact that the Yankees won the pennant. There's no way you can seriously hold up a 23-point difference in batting average (Mantle hit .365) as being equal to all of Mantle's advantages.

CARL YASTRZEMSKI

HALL OF FAME? Not Eligible
DATA IN SECTION III? Yes
OFFENSIVE WON-LOST RECORD:
 220–118, .650
GROSS VALUE: 266

Yastrzemski and Musial were extremely similar in build, and there are some other parallels between the two of them. Their skills were vaguely similar, though Musial's were pitched a little higher; both were batting champions who hit around 40 home runs in a top season. Yastrzemski's best years

would fit in with Musial's career without sticking out too badly. Both had some speed, though Musial was much faster, and both had pretty decent arms, though Yastrzemski's was far better. Both are of Polish descent. Both used very unorthodox batting stances, stances that I would guess an ordinary athlete could not adapt successfully.

Their career progressions are more similar than their talents. Each arrived in the majors at the age of twenty-one (Musial had 12 games at age twenty), and each led the league in hits, doubles and batting within a few years. Both Yastrzemski and Musial had sudden power surges at the age of twenty-seven. Through age twenty-six Musial's career high in home runs was 19 and his career high in RBI was 103. Through age twenty-six Yaz's career high in home runs was 20, and his high in RBI was 94. At age twenty-seven Musial jumped to 39 and 131, while Yastrzemski set marks of 44 and 121. Neither player ever matched those totals again.

HOW THE LEFT FIELDERS RATE

I have tried, in rating the greatest, to avoid any quirky or idiosyncratic selections, and to respect a valid consensus where it exists—in other words, to respect the evidence rather than indulging myself with oddball selections. But to the extent that a consensus has developed that lifts Williams over Musial as the greatest left fielder of the forties, and thus the greatest left fielder of all time, I cannot agree with that consensus.

Look, I am not saying anything at all negative about Ted Williams. The further we go in the analysis of batting statistics, the closer we come to being forced to accept the conclusion that Williams, not Babe Ruth, was the greatest hitter who ever lived. I think he was the second-greatest left fielder who ever lived. That's not criticism.

But if I had to choose between the two of them, I'd take Musial in left field, Musial on the basepaths, Musial in the clubhouse, and Williams only with the wood in his hand. And Stan Musial could hit a little, too.

PEAK VALUE	CAREER VALUE
1. Stan Musial	1. Stan Musial
2. Ted Williams	2. Ted Williams
3. Ralph Kiner	3. Carl Yastrzemski
4. Carl Yastrzemski	4. Goose Goslin
5. Joe Jackson	5. Zack Wheat
6. Jim Rice	6. Billy Williams
7. Goose Goslin	7. Fred Clarke
8. Joe Medwick	8. Lou Brock
9. Willie Stargell	9. Willie Stargell
10. Tie: Billy Williams	10. Joe Jackson
Sherry Magee	

 CENTER FIELD

RICHIE ASHBURN

HALL OF FAME? No
DATA IN SECTION III? Yes
OFFENSIVE WON-LOST RECORD:
  148–77, .657
GROSS VALUE: 180

Richie Ashburn has the best defensive statistics of any outfielder ever to play major league baseball. It isn't close. He made over 500 plays as an outfielder six times in his career, 495 plays another time. All of the other outfielders in the history of baseball have only done this altogether, five times. In addition to the incredible range factors, he had excellent assists totals (178 in his career, 13 per 162 games) and good fielding percentages.

I have always argued that fielding records were generally meaningful. Like batting records, however, fielding records are subject to outside influences which can create statistical illusions. Since Ashburn's defensive stats are the best of any outfielder ever, I suggested in the first edition of this book that it might be appropriate to undertake some research into what kind of outside influences there might be on his statistics.

Well, somebody did. Bruce H. Garland, in an excellent article for the *Baseball Analyst,* examined a variety of factors which could have influenced Ashburn's defensive stats. His conclusions:

1) The ballpark probably helped him. It was 460, 468 feet to center field in Connie Mack Stadium, the deepest center field in the National League except for the Polo Grounds, with Forbes Field being close. The center fielders in the largest center field areas, at least in the National League in that period, tended to have the highest range factors. This, of course, might be either cause or effect. The larger the center field area to be covered, the greater the need to have a center fielder who can run. But from 1948 through 1954, Ashburn's first seven years, the park was occupied by two teams, the Phillies and also the A's. In six of those seven years, reports Garland, the A's center fielder also had a range factor above 3.0—and three times the Athletics center fielder had a higher range factor than Richie Ashburn. When Ashburn made 3.09 plays per game in 1948, A's center fielder Sam Chapman made 3.19. Chapman caught 450 flies in 1949, many more than an average center fielder, although 64 less than Ashburn. In 1950, when Ashburn made 2.81 plays per game, Chapman made 3.14.

Chapman was a fine ballplayer, but he wasn't Willie Mays and by 1948 he was into his thirties. In 1952, when Ashburn made 2.93 plays per game, A's center fielder Dave Philley made 3.05. One would have to suspect that the ballpark was a factor in shaping these statistics.

2) During this period, the Phillies teams were generally below average in both strikeouts and double plays turned, possibly allowing the outfielders more opportunity to make plays.

3) The other Phillie outfielders, Del Ennis and whoever, were not significantly below average in terms of putouts made—indeed, they were slightly above average—and did not influence Ashburn's opportunities.

Garland did not examine the issue of whether the Phillies pitchers tended to have fly-ball or ground-ball tendencies, although I have developed a method to do this and am sure it will get done eventually. Anyway, while it cannot be confidently asserted that Ashburn's defensive statistics prove him to have been the best defensive outfielder who ever lived, it can safely be said that they are clear proof that he was a very good center fielder. He was also the only leadoff man ever to lead his league in batting and walks in the same season. Jim Baker

wrote the following comment about him . . .

At the beginning and middle of the century, the Phillies had two very similar players patroling center field. In 1900 it was Roy Thomas; in 1950, Richie Ashburn. Both were strong defensively, both were good at getting on base, neither had much power and both had decent speed.

Actually, Ashburn was sort of a "new, improved" Roy Thomas. He did everything Thomas could do, only better, and he did a few things that Thomas couldn't. Ashburn didn't have much power, Thomas didn't have *any* power. Thomas had good range and a good arm; Ashburn had his arm but even better range. Ashburn is known among those who like freak show stats for his unusual ratios of runs scored to runs batted in, such as in 1959 when he scored 86 and drove in only 20 (4.3–1). Thomas was even more im-

balanced; in 1906 he scored 81 and drove in only 16 (5.1–1), and his career ratio was 3.38–1, while Ashburn's was only 2.25–1. They stole about the same number of bases (Thomas, 244; Ashburn, 234) but Ashburn did his running in an era when few other players ran, whereas everybody stole bases in 1900.

Ashburn didn't have home run power, but he did occasionally hit a double or a triple, twice leading the league in the latter category. Thomas came into the majors and immediately began walking a lot; Ashburn was into his prime before he started producing league-leading walk totals.

Ashburn was originally signed by the Cubs and then the Indians, but was declared free of both teams by the commissioner. Fred Lieb once called him a "modern reincarnation of the famed Dode Paskert," which may have made more sense at the time than it does now; anyway, Paskert was another similar player, who was the center fielder on the Phillies first pennant winner in 1915, not as good as either Ashburn or Thomas.

—Jim Baker

EARL AVERILL

HALL OF FAME? Yes
DATA IN SECTION III? Yes
OFFENSIVE WON-LOST RECORD:
118–53, .689
GROSS VALUE: 161
COMPARABLE RECENT PLAYERS:
Fred Lynn and Chet Lemon

The outstanding American League center fielder in the years just before DiMaggio, he is in some ways similar to DiMag. He had the even balance of skills, could hit .350 with 30 home runs, a graceful if unspectacular center fielder. Like DiMaggio, he began his minor league career with the San Francisco Seals (although, since he was twenty-four years old when he joined the Seals and seems to have been a fairly accomplished ballplayer, I've always been curious about what he was doing up to that time). Averill benefited from a fairly large home-park advantage, hitting .343 lifetime at home (.292 on the road) and with 144 home runs at home (94 on the road). Not overpoweringly qualified for the Hall of Fame, but a better player than Manush, Combs and some others; about even with Kiki Cuyler.

MAX CAREY

HALL OF FAME? Yes
DATA IN SECTION III? Yes
OFFENSIVE WON-LOST RECORD:
171–103, .623
GROSS VALUE: 198
COMPARABLE RECENT PLAYERS:
Brett Butler

Max Carey played left field and later center field for the Pirates from 1910 through 1925. Forbes Field until the time of Kiner had an enormous left field area, and when they were good the Pirates always had two center fielders in the outfield, one in center and one in left. When he came up Carey played left for several years with Owen Wilson and others in center field. In 1916 Carey moved to center and led the National League in putouts (419), assists (32), double plays (10) and chances per game (2.93). These figures remained high for a number of years afterward; in 1917 he ran down 440 fly balls, threw out 28 runners and handled 3.06 chances per game. His defensive statistics remained remarkably good from then through 1925, when he was 35 years old. The Pirates finally got in a World Series that year, and Carey hit .458 (11 for 24), reaching scoring position seven times and scoring six runs in seven games.

Carey's talents were quite similar to those of Brett Butler today—a switch hitter, a fine center fielder with an above-average arm, a hustling player, a leadoff man who would hit for a decent average (.285 lifetime), draw some walks (led the league twice) and steal bases. Two things lift Carey's career out of the ordinary-but-good, out of the Brett Butler class, and into the Hall of Fame. One is the exceptional duration of his period of effectiveness. He scored 114 runs in 1912, and was still one of the best leadoff men in the league in 1927. The other is his success as a base stealer. He began stealing bases in 1911, when everyone stole bases, and he continued to steal bases until the late twenties, by which time he had become an anachronism. He led the league in stolen bases ten times with figures ranging from 36 to 63, and he was a terrific percentage base stealer in an era in which base stealing was declining in use primarily because so many base stealers were poor percentage runners. As Casey Stengel wrote, "A base stealer is a valuable man for the club only when he makes it almost every time—the way Max Carey used to for Pittsburgh."

Before Lou Brock, when you talked about the greatest leadoff men of all time, Carey was one of the men you would have to talk about. He held the National League record for stolen bases, and he could do the other things a leadoff man is supposed to do fairly well, and he did them for a long time. After Brock and Rose and Raines and Henderson and all the other exceptional leadoff men of the last two decades, one can no longer consider Carey as possibly the greatest ever, but he was certainly a good one.

Carey's career as a Pirate ended in the summer of 1926 amid a storm of controversy. Carey was in a bad slump when, according to Dick Bartell's recent biography, Pirate General Manager Fred Clarke made an offhand remark to manager Bill McKechnie that if he couldn't find anybody else to play center he ought to put in the batboy, who couldn't be any worse than the fellow he had. The remark was repeated to Carey—a high-class fellow, to quote Bartell—and triggered a bitching contest that eventually led the owner to clean house, Carey going to Brooklyn, where he played for several years and later managed. Carey tried to install a running game with the Bums, but the game had changed too much, and it was easier to teach his youngsters to run often than to teach them to run successfully.

TY COBB

HALL OF FAME? Yes
DATA IN SECTION III? Yes
OFFENSIVE WON-LOST RECORD:
236–63, .790
GROSS VALUE: 351
(Highest of any center fielder)

Ty Cobb and Christy Mathewson, taken at the third World Series games in New York, October 17, 1911.

In photographs (make it a point to notice) Ty Cobb is often shown hiding one hand or both, twisting an arm behind his back or burying it in an article of excess clothing. One photograph of him with which I am particularly taken shows him posing with Christy Mathewson in the dugout before the third game of the 1911 World Series. Mathewson, as always, looks poised and confident, staring out toward right field. Cobb is peeking out of the corner of his eye at some unseen distraction—another photographer, probably —but what makes the photograph remarkable is that, to begin with, Cobb is wearing a suit that doesn't look as if it could possibly fit any of his relatives. Cobb was a big man, for his time (he is usually listed at 6'2", 180), yet this suit has got to be four sizes too large for him—it is hard to believe that a reputable haberdasher would have let him leave the store with it. He is holding what looks like an expensive overcoat, and he appears to be dragging it on the ground. His hat is jaunty and his smile is decidedly nervous, and he looks frankly a little bit crazy.

There was such a contradiction in that dugout. Cobb was then a five-time American League batting champion, with more or less seven seasons under his belt—and yet he was also a twenty-four-year-old hick from Nowhere, Georgia, a little in awe of Matty, of the photographers, of the crowd. He had no weapons, at that moment, to defend himself against his inadequacies—no spikes, no bat, no glove. He was so crude and unpolished that he must have felt that whenever they took those things away from him, he became nothing; his shortcomings glowed like a hot piece of iron in the dark. And whenever he saw them glowing, he got angry. You can see it in his face, I think, that if he could just put on a uniform and go out on the field it would be such a relief to him, out where manners and taste and style were all defined by bases gained and bases lost. And everyone else, for a change, would have to apologize to him.

EARL COMBS

HALL OF FAME? Yes
DATA IN SECTION III? No
OFFENSIVE WON-LOST RECORD:
Unknown
GROSS VALUE: Unknown
COMPARABLE RECENT PLAYERS:
Mickey Rivers

Were he not a member of the 1927 Yankees, Combs would not be remembered today. He was almost identical to Rivers on the field—a fast man, no arm, no power, hit for a good average. He walked a little more than Mickey. The 1924 *Spalding Guide,* reviewing Combs' season at Louisville, which was his springboard to the Yankees, said that "Combs was the second-best batter in the circuit and an outfielder of average ability, but not a player of the fast, hard-throwing type that has made the outfield famous in the major leagues." His .325 average (in a short career) is, in its time, no more impressive than Rivers' .295 average today. He was a good player, but there are twenty others as good who are twenty forgotten.

DOC CRAMER

HALL OF FAME? No
DATA IN SECTION III? Yes
OFFENSIVE WON-LOST RECORD:
118–136, .465
GROSS VALUE: 149
COMPARABLE RECENT PLAYERS:
Curt Flood

KIKI CUYLER

HALL OF FAME? Yes
DATA IN SECTION III? Yes
OFFENSIVE WON-LOST RECORD:
128–66, .660
GROSS VALUE: 162
COMPARABLE RECENT PLAYERS:
Willie Davis

A good line-drive hitter with exceptional speed, Cuyler is similar to a couple of American League contemporaries named Ben Chapman and Gee Walker, though he was the best of the three. Cuyler was once benched in mid-season for not hustling (as was Walker), and was traded after the 1927 season for virtually nothing. His offensive statistics are good, probably a little better than Willie Davis' and a little more consistent, but close. (Davis' statistics are really unfair, since he played in a terrible hitter's park at a time when batting averages all over were at a fifty-year low. Davis would have been a consistent .300 hitter in the seventies.)

JOE DiMAGGIO

HALL OF FAME? Yes
DATA IN SECTION III? Yes
OFFENSIVE WON-LOST RECORD:
134–44, .751
GROSS VALUE: 201
COMPARABLE RECENT PLAYERS:
Andre Dawson

Let's lay aside the question of Joe DiMaggio the ballplayer for a moment and focus on the analytical and philosophical questions that his evaluation involves. To begin with, there is the park problem. Di-

Maggio's offensive stats were cut severely by playing in Yankee Stadium. Playing in neutral parks, he out-hit Ted Williams lifetime (.333–.328) and had far more power than he had at home (213 home runs as opposed to 148). When you combine this with the three years he is missing for the war, it can be safely and accurately stated that his offensive statistics don't represent his true abilities.

But how to repair the damage, correct for the illusions? That DiMaggio was uniquely hurt by Yankee Stadium is interesting but not, as I see it, ordinarily germane to the assessment of his abilities. Why? Because the "real" standard against which we measure illusions is wins and losses. If a player has a unique ability to take advantage of the characteristics of a park, such as Wade Boggs' ability to dump doubles against the left-field wall in Fenway, then real wins will result from that ability. One must not, in adjusting for illusions, adjust those wins out of existence. Similarly, if a player is uniquely unable to take advantage of what the park will give him, then real losses (or in DiMaggio's case, fewer real wins) will result from that condition, and we must, again, respect that.

On the level of ordinary players, of helping to win pennants and the like, I have no problem with that; when the discussion turns to the evaluation of the immortals, then I do. Why? Because somehow the question turns a little bit; when comparing players of different eras who played substantially different games, one must become interested in the question of the adaptability of the skills of each to the game of the others.

I sense that there is a difference between one's ability to dominate the game at a specific time and a specific place, and one's rank among the greatest; I cannot exactly define what that distinction is. To discuss specifics, suppose that you are comparing a Harmon Killebrew season—let us say 1961, when he created 138 runs and had an offensive winning percentage of .801 with a won/lost record of 12–3—with an equivalent Honus Wagner season, which would be 1901, when he created 136 runs with an offensive winning percentage of .800 and the same won/lost record, 12–3. (Both seasons, incidentally, were expansion years.) If their careers ran so nearly parallel for their entire duration, one will still have to say that Wagner was the greater player. Why? Because, possessing as he did enormous physical strength, great speed and King Kong's hands, Wagner could unquestionably have adapted to the baseball of the post-1920 era, and hit a great many home runs. Killebrew, given his innate physical skills, could not likely have adapted as well to the baseball of Wagner's time. That Kille-

brew was as great an offensive force in 1961 as Wagner was in 1901 does not *exactly* make Killebrew as great a hitter as Wagner.

We return, then, to DiMaggio. True, he didn't steal bases. In his career he stole 30 bases in 39 attempts. Yet there seems to be no reasonable doubt that, had he played the game of the sixties, the seventies or the teens, he could have stolen about as many bases as anybody else. This seems, in this particular dispute, to be relevant.

Similarly, we take the gap in DiMaggio's career, three years he missed for the war. There can be no doubt that, given back those three years (not to mention the time it took him to get back into peak condition), DiMaggio would have accomplished much more, and had more "value" to his team, than he did. Dealing with players from within a particular time, the approach to this gap is easy: It's irrelevant. We're not talking about what he *could* have done or *might* have done or *should* have done, but what he did done. Pete Reiser's injuries are an inevitable consequence of his skills; they are, as such, a part of his skills and they help to define his value, just like Harmon Killebrew's foot speed. He gets no slack at all. Herb Score is not a great player because he might have been a great player.

But somehow, the war is different. It is in no way

related to the skills or habits or even the luck of the player; it is a condition of the time. I guess what I am suggesting is that when you compare players between eras, you must, in some sense, remove each from his niche on the time/space continuum. When you do this, you get inevitable absurdities—yet in entering the discussion, we agree to deal with those. My way of dealing with them, which I grant you is not entirely satisfactory, is to say that the conditions of the specific time and place remain extremely important, because what greatness as a baseball player is, primarily, is the ability to deal with the problems of the time and place and help your team overcome them—and yet consideration also must be given not only to the degree to which a player *did* help his team win and avoid defeat, but to the degree to which he would likely have done so at another time and another place. In giving DiMaggio back those three missing seasons, we are only following through logically on the premise of our debate.

As great as DiMaggio was, he likely would have been greater at most other times and in many other places. Playing in Willie's time, he almost certainly would have hit 450 to 500 home runs; playing in Fenway Park it would have been over 600. I think, in this case, that those are considerations germane to the issue.

LARRY DOBY

HALL OF FAME? No
DATA IN SECTION III? Yes
OFFENSIVE WON-LOST RECORD:
 108–41, .724
GROSS VALUE: 137
COMPARABLE RECENT PLAYERS:
Reggie Smith

A classic example of the type of broad-based talent that will never achieve much recognition, but which saber-metricians just love. Doby hit for average, hit for power, had speed, drew walks, and played a key defensive position for a championship team. His average went as high as .326, he led the league in homers twice, drew 90 or more walks six times, slugged over .500 four times. Very comparable to Earl Averill, the Indians' center fielder of two decades earlier; I rate Doby a slight edge on peak value, Averill the nod on career value.

RICKEY HENDERSON

HALL OF FAME? Not Eligible
DATA IN SECTION III? No
OFFENSIVE WON-LOST RECORD:
 88–63, .583
GROSS VALUE: 110

FRED LYNN

HALL OF FAME? Not Eligible
DATA IN SECTION III? No
OFFENSIVE WON-LOST RECORD:
 109–59, .650
GROSS VALUE: 138

Paul Izzo told me that he once happened to be sitting next to an octogenarian at Fenway Park, and in the course of a few innings learned that the gentleman had been sitting there watching the Red Sox since the time of Joe Wood. He asked the man who the greatest player he ever saw was, and the man said without hesitation, "Fred Lynn." Fred Lynn? Not Ruth? Not Speaker? Not Teddy? "Fred Lynn. Don't think much of him now, but for a few years there he was the best."

MICKEY MANTLE

HALL OF FAME? Yes
DATA IN SECTION III? Yes
OFFENSIVE WON-LOST RECORD:
 178–40, .815
Mantle's offensive winning percentage, .815, is the highest of any center fielder.
GROSS VALUE: 249

Mickey Mantle was, at his peak in 1956–57 and again in 1961–62, clearly a greater player than Willie Mays—and it is not a close or difficult decision. While there is no doubt that there are many unanswered questions in the analysis of baseball records, while there is room for legitimate difference of opinion on many issues among men who have studied the matter and who accept the same basic logical

premises for the debate, this is not such an issue. It is an issue upon all forms of analysis and all indicators within each form agree, and distinguish among the two players by such a margin that what I call the swamp—the morass of unknowns and unanswered questions—could not reasonably reverse the decision. Because even if Mays is given every conceivable break on every unknown—defense, base running, clutch hitting—his performance still would not match Mantle's.

First of all, let us compare offense, as that is the one most important part of an everyday player's ability as well as the one area in which the best information exists. We can, as you know, estimate quite accurately the number of runs that any player has created for his team in any season. Throughout his best years, Mantle created quite significantly more runs than Mays did. Their three best years are compared below:

MANTLE		MAYS	
	Runs		Runs
Year	Created	Year	Created
1956	188	1954	157
1957	178	1955	157
1961	174	1958	152

Mantle created 17 more runs for his team in his third-best season than Mays did in his best; Mantle's three best years average twenty-five runs better than Mays' (180–155).

However, Mantle created

these runs while using up far fewer outs than did Mays. Compare the number of batting outs (that is to say, at bats minus hits) plus caught stealing, sacrifice hits, sacrifice flies, and double play balls for which each was responsible in these years:

MANTLE

Year	AB-H	CS	SH	SF	GIDP	Total Outs
1956	345	1	1	4	4	355
1957	301	3	0	3	5	312
1958	351	1	1	5	2	360

MAYS

Year	AB-H	CS	SH	SF	GIDP	Total Outs
1954	370	4	0	7	12	391
1955	395	10	0	7	12	424
1958	392	4	0	6	11	413

Mantle was using, on the average, 67 fewer outs a year to create his runs. The value of an out can be estimated, conservatively, at .15 runs (that is, given 27 outs, a team in this time would score more than .15 × 27, or 4.05 runs runs per game). On this basis, we must charge Mays about ten runs a year (67 × .15) for the extra outs that he is taking away from his teammates. This puts Mantle 35 runs ahead.

I would also like to point out that any other offensive rating scheme that you could recommend would achieve a similar result. Pete Palmer, in *The Hidden Game,* evaluated Mantle's three seasons at +83.3, +88.9, and +76.3, meaning that he was a total of 248.5 runs (or 83 runs a year) better than the league's average hitter (with park adjust-

ments he would increase this estimate to 259.0). Mays' three seasons are evaluated at +61.8, +62.3 and +55.3, or a total of 179.4, which would be 179.9 with park adjustments. So Palmer's methods evaluate Mantle at 23 to 26 runs a year better than Mays as an offensive player.

By Thomas Boswell's Total Average or Barry Codell's similar Base-Out Percentage, the results would be similar. The comparison for the three seasons:

MANTLE

Year	Total Bases	Total Outs	Total Average
1956	500	355	1.408
1957	472	312	1.513
1961	494	360	1.372

MAYS

Year	Total Bases	Total Outs	Total Average
1954	458	391	1.171
1955	486	424	1.146
1958	447	413	1.082

The complete totals are 1.427 for Mantle and 1.133 for Mays. Projected into a 350-out season, that's a difference of a little more than 100 bases, which would put us in the same range of difference as the earlier methods.

Thomas Cover of Stanford University developed something called the "offensive earned run average." He rated Mantle's 1957 season as the greatest season of all time, and his 1956 and 1961 seasons among the top fifteen. Mays never made the top twenty. I find no way to dispute the

conclusion that Mantle was much the better hitter.

Turning our attention to other matters, we have:

1) Baserunning. Mays' supporters claim he was a faster runner than Mantle, while Mantle's supporters claim that he was faster than Mays. There are two measurable indicators of baserunning ability—stolen base percentage, and the frequency of grounding into doubles. In both respects, Mantle is superior. He was a sensational percentage base stealer, stealing successfully 80 percent of the time throughout his career, while Mays was close behind at 77 percent. During the three years in question Mantle was 38 for 43 as a base stealer, which is 88 percent, while Mays was 59 for 72, which is 82 percent. Mays grounded into double plays far more often, 251 in his career as opposed to 113 for Mantle.

In the three years in question, Mantle grounded into only 11 double plays, as opposed to 35 for Mays. There is no reasonable basis for giving Mays a bonus as a baserunner. In the 1987 *Baseball Abstract,* I introduced a method to evaluate a player's speed by examining a variety of speed indicators—stolen bases attempts as a percentage of times on base, stolen base percentage, runs scored as a percentage of times on base/not home run, frequency of grounding into double plays, triples hit, and defensive position and range. The analytical method agrees that Mantle was probably slightly faster than Mays.

2) Clutch performance. No one ever suggested that Mantle did not hit well in the clutch nor, so far as I know, that Mays was especially good in the clutch. Mantle played in twelve World Series and hit .257 with a .535 slugging percentage, and his team won eight of the twelve; Mays played in four, and hit .239 with a .282 slugging percentage, and his team lost three of the four. However, Mays was a better RBI man, probably because he batted fourth while Mantle batted third, but, anyway, let's award Mays an arbitrary five runs a year as a better hitter with runners on base. That leaves Mantle thirty runs ahead.

3) Defense. Defense is the big item. On the basis of what we know about the issue, statistics and reputation, Mays seems to have been clearly the better center fielder of the two. The question of the moment is, how many runs do we allow for that?

In an ordinary year, the difference between the team allowing the fewest runs in baseball and the team allowing the most runs in baseball will be somewhere around 220 to 240 runs. Think about what goes into creating that 240-run separation:

1) Pitching. That includes the difference between having the best pitching staff in base-

ball and having the worst.

2) Defense at nine positions. That includes the difference between a catcher who can throw and one who can't, the difference between a first baseman who can scoop out a low throw and one who watches it go by, the difference between a second baseman who can turn the double play and one who doesn't, the difference between a short-stop who can go in the hole and . . . you finish it. 240 runs.

3) Park effects. Nine times in ten the team which allows the most runs in baseball will play in a hitter's park, while the team which allows the fewest will play in a pitcher's park.

4) The DH rule. The team allowing the fewest runs will usually be a National League team, while the team allowing the most will usually play in the American League.

Two hundred and twenty, 240 runs, that's about what it will all come to. How much, then, to allow for the defense of a center fielder? Twenty runs? Thirty runs? Of course, no team is a collection of optimal or minimal parts, and thus, though the separation between teams rarely sums up to larger than 240 runs, the differences between the best and worst individuals would add up to much more than that.

But Mickey Mantle was a *very good* center fielder. He had blinding speed, made the play when the ball was hit to

him, and he had a good arm before the injury in the late fifties. How large, then, is the difference between a very good center fielder, and a very, very, very good center fielder?

Well, I don't know—but it isn't thirty runs. It's probably five or seven runs a season, at most. And that leaves Mantle twenty-three to twenty-five runs ahead.

There are other, nonstatistical things that could be considered. Leadership? But Mantle led his team to far more pennants than Mays did—indeed, the Yankees of Mantle won the pennant more consistently than *anybody* did, including DiMaggio's Yankees and the Ruth/Gehrig Yankees. Inspiration? Same argument; Mantle played brilliantly with great pain.

The opinion of contemporaries? Between 1955 and 1964 Mantle finished first or second in the MVP voting six times; Mays in his career was first or second four times over a less concentrated period of time. It was only after the fact, when the final statistics were in the book, that people began to say that Mays was the greater player.

And in terms of career value, he was; that decision is equally clear. Though Mantle's career offensive winning percentage is .815, the third-highest of all time and .047 ahead of his rival, Mays sustained a comparable level of greatness for a significantly longer period. But at his peak, Mantle hit for a better average than Mays, had more power, got on base much more, and was probably faster. His teams won more often, and his performance in MVP voting was more impressive. Mickey Mantle was the greatest player of the fifties.

HEINE MANUSH

HALL OF FAME? Yes
DATA IN SECTION III? No
OFFENSIVE WON-LOST RECORD:
  Approximately 130–90, .591
GROSS VALUE: 159
COMPARABLE RECENT PLAYERS:
Jose Cardenal

Not a great player; probably no greater, in the context of his time, than Cardenal. I probably should have listed him as a left fielder; he played some center, but he was marginal as a center fielder. He didn't walk, didn't have great speed, had doubles and triples power in a game in which the real hitters had home run power. His one credential is that he had six seasons among the top five in the league in batting.

WILLIE MAYS

HALL OF FAME? Yes
DATA IN SECTION III? Yes
OFFENSIVE WON-LOST RECORD:
  229–70, .766
GROSS VALUE: 301

I purchased his career home/road stats from David Frank, who figured them from box scores, and says that they might contain a few minor er-

rors. They don't show much; neither Mays nor Mantle was moved much off-center by the parks in which they played. But there are comments from time to time that Mays was hurt by Candlestick, so I thought I'd find out.

DALE MURPHY

HALL OF FAME? Not Eligible
DATA IN SECTION III? No
OFFENSIVE WON-LOST RECORD:
  107–54, .665
GROSS VALUE: 150

AMOS OTIS

HALL OF FAME? Not Eligible
DATA IN SECTION III? Yes
OFFENSIVE WON-LOST RECORD:
  125–83, .601
GROSS VALUE: 162

Not meant to be taken seriously as one of the all-time greats. A favorite of mine, I thought I would compile his complete stats and pass them along. Is at or near the top of the all-time lists in fielding percentage, stolen base percentage and frequency of sacrifice flies delivered.

Charles Faber rated Amos the 27th best player in the history of the American League. It's always nice to have somebody who rates your favorite player higher than you do.

VADA PINSON

HALL OF FAME? No
DATA IN SECTION III? Yes
OFFENSIVE WON-LOST RECORD:
  161–109, .595
GROSS VALUE: 184

PETE REISER

HALL OF FAME? No
DATA IN SECTION III? Yes
OFFENSIVE WON-LOST RECORD:
  Unknown
GROSS VALUE: Unknown
COMPARABLE RECENT PLAYERS:
Fred Lynn

Reiser was an idiosyncratic selection as one of the greatest of all time by Ritter and Honig. Reiser was a great player, if only for a moment, and I might even place him near the top of the peak value list if he had won the MVP award in 1941. His failure to make enough of an impression on the voters of that time to claim the award suggests to me that the impact he had on those who saw him has been overdrawn just a little.

EDD ROUSH

HALL OF FAME? Yes
DATA IN SECTION III? Yes
OFFENSIVE WON-LOST RECORD:
  134–70, .655
GROSS VALUE: 170
COMPARABLE RECENT PLAYERS:
Matty Alou

Better defense than Alou, sustained his performance for a longer period, and was more valuable then because his offense was not buried under the home run barrage. But the same basic model.

AL SIMMONS

HALL OF FAME? Yes
DATA IN SECTION III? Yes
OFFENSIVE WON-LOST RECORD:
  153–78, .661
GROSS VALUE: 223
COMPARABLE RECENT PLAYERS: Al Oliver

Al Simmons was born Aloysius (or Alois) Szymanski in a Polish section of Milwaukee. When he was a teenage ballplayer a Milwaukee sportswriter got tired of trying to straighten out his name in box scores and accounts of top amateur games, and shortened it to Al Simmons.

Al Simmons was determined to break into baseball. He wrote a letter to Connie Mack asking for a tryout with the Athletics. Connie didn't answer. Mack got hundreds of letters like that every year.

In 1922 Simmons was offered a contract including a small bonus to sign with the Milwaukee team in the American Association. The farm systems at this time were just getting organized, and Simmons preferred to get into a farm system. The New York Giants wanted him to join the Toledo team, but he asked the Giants to match the bonus, reportedly $150. Roger Bresnahan, then managing business affairs for the Giants, refused to pay the $150, and Simmons signed with Milwaukee. (See Arthur Daley's *Inside Baseball.* Daley describes the $150 as train fare to Toledo, but obviously it did not cost $150 to take a train from Milwaukee to

Toledo in 1922.) Milwaukee optioned him to Aberdeen in a low league, where he hit .365 in 1922, and then sent him to Shreveport in the Texas League in 1923.

Simmons's manager at Shreveport, whose name I have not been able to find, took one look at Al's batting stance, with his famous foot in the bucket, and told him he would never make it as a hitter. Simmons hit .360. Shreveport finished last, at 50–99. He returned to Milwaukee in the American Association, where he hit .398 in 24 games. He was purchased by Connie Mack for the Philadelphia Athletics.

Mack intended, apparently, to sit on Simmons for a year or two. Over the same winter he had purchased Paul Strand from the Pacific Coast League, where Strand's phenomenal batting totals (325 hits, .394 average with 187 RBI) had made him a hot property. Connie Mack had scouted him personally late in the 1923 season, decided he was for real, and negotiated a $70,000 deal with the Salt Lake City team. Simmons was purchased from Milwaukee for a fraction of that. When they opened spring training you know who the hot prospect was—the guy with the 325 hits and the $70,000 price tag. The number-two rookie in spring training was Maxie Bishop, the second baseman who had been purchased from Jack Dunn's great Baltimore team for a reported $50,000. The writers

felt that Simmons would have trouble hitting major league pitching with his foot in the bucket. Simmons did not agree, established himself as a regular early in the year and wound up the season with a .308 average and 102 RBI.

Simmons at this time was a center fielder. He was not a great outfielder, but he could hold the job. The A's were acquiring young players at a tremendous pace, purchasing Lefty Grove from Baltimore the next year, buying out the Portland team in the Pacific Coast League because they had a catcher named Mickey Cochrane that the A's liked. Another Milwaukee youngster named Joe Hauser seemed on his way to establishing himself as one of the game's great power hitters.

In 1925 Simmons blasted out 253 hits, with a .384 average and 129 RBI. Let us try to call up an image of the ferocious young man who could compile such ferocious numbers. His odd stance belied the fact that he was a passionate student of hitting. "I've studied movies of myself," Simmons said later in life. "Although my left foot would stab out toward third base, the rest of me, from the belt up, especially my wrists, arms and shoulders, was swinging in a proper line over the plate." Before facing a pitcher, wrote Wilfred Sheed, he worked himself into a homicidal rage. "I was a fighting, snarling player on the field," said Simmons. "I am proud, not ashamed, of that reputation. I played to win." He was cocky, nice looking in his own way, powerfully built, arrogant. For a contact hitter he had a relatively long, looping swing of great force, a lot of arm action but a level swing, no uppercut. About six feet tall and solid as a rock, he weighed near 200 pounds, ran with long, loping strides that ate up the ground in large chunks once his momentum was established.

Connie Mack was an eternal optimist; he often thought he was closer to his goals than he really was. In 1925, with this assemblage of young talent, he thought he would win the American League, and indeed his A's held a five-game lead in early August. Joe Hauser's career was wrecked by a freak injury that spring, however, and as young teams often do the Athletics collapsed, losing 12 games in a row and 17 of 19 at one point to finish a distant second.

When the team again failed to win the pennant in 1926, Connie decided to educate the young stars about what was needed to win championships by surrounding them with old stars. In 1927 and 1928 he added to the roster Ty Cobb, Tris Speaker, Zack Wheat, Eddie Collins, Jack Quinn and Bullet Joe Bush. "An interesting but not highly valuable collection of antiques," observed James Harrison in the *New York Times*.

Simmons apparently enjoyed having Cobb around, a rare man whose intensity and interest in hitting equalled his own. At times they roomed together on the road. On May 5, 1927, Cobb and Simmons were both ejected from a game against Boston by umpire Red Ormsby, who had ruled a home run hit by Cobb a foul ball. Cobb and Simmons screamed at the umpire and Cobb bumped him while hitting. When the A's lost the game by a single run a near-riot ensued, and league President Ban Johnson suspended both Cobb and Simmons indefinitely. Johnson at this time was involved in—and losing—a power struggle with Judge Landis and several American League owners; grasping at straws, he leapt irrationally upon any opportunity to assert his authority, which of course only further weakened his reign. He had tried the previous winter to expell Cobb from baseball; this, to him, was merely further evidence of Cobb's insidious influence. However, there were plans for a big Ty Cobb day in Detroit on May 10 (five days after the bumping incident), and the fans and Detroit management applied tremendous pressure to get the suspensions lifted. Johnson was obliged to yield once again. Cobb and Simmons were fined $200 apiece. Johnson was forced out of office later in the summer.

In late July of that year Simmons tore a groin muscle and missed about six weeks. The A's got hot with him out of the lineup, though they were out of the race behind the great Yankee team. Simmons, who had missed the batting title by only a few points in 1925, lost the title on the last day of the 1927 season when Harry Heilmann had seven hits in a double header to finish at .398. Simmons hit .392 in 106 games. Cobb felt a paternal interest in both Heilmann and Simmons.

"Since both were my pupils and finished one-two," said Cobb modestly, "I felt that my theories on batting remained as valid in the jack-rabbit-ball era as they seemed to be in 1906." No doubt it is a tremendous aid to a batting instructor to work with a pupil who gets 253 hits in a season even before you appear on the scene. (Quote is from *Ty Cobb: The Greatest*, by Robert Rubin.)

As much as he may have enjoyed Cobb's advice, by spring training in 1928 it was obvious that the outfield of Cobb, Simmons and Speaker had to be the slowest in the league. "Cobb can't come in," wrote Richards Vidmer, "and Speaker can't go back." "If this keeps up," remarked Simmons, perhaps thinking back to the groin injury of the previous year, "I'm going to be an old man myself by the end of the year."

On opening day of the 1928 season, Simmons was in the hospital with tonsillitis and swollen ankles, which it was eventually decided were caused by rheumatism. The ankles pretty much ended Simmons's career as a center fielder, forcing Bing Miller into center field and (once Simmons returned) Speaker and Cobb into part-time roles. With Simmons playing 119 games, the Athletics pushed the Yankees to the wire, losing by three games. In the spring of 1929 the old guys were gone, and that summer the A's exploded, burying the Yankees—and everybody else— with a record of 104–46. They won the pennant by 18 games. Simmons again lost the batting title by just four points, but this time he drove in a league-leading 157 runs and was named the Most Valuable Player.

Before the first game of the 1929 World Series, Simmons asked Mack rather truculently "Are you going to let that guy pitch?" Mack did, and "that guy," Howard Ehmke, justified this historic gamble by striking out 13 Cubs—fairly remarkable when you consider that he had struck out only 20 men all year. In the fourth game of the series the Cubs led 8–0 in the seventh when Simmons hit a lead-off home run, triggering the immortal ten-run rally. Simmons hit .300 in the series and drove in six runs, most of any player.

The A's won in five. A week later the stock market collapsed. Like most of the top players of the era, Simmons

lost some money. Perhaps feeling the pinch, he held out the next spring, not reaching agreement with Mack until the stands were filling up on opening day. Because of injuries, that was the first time in three years he had been in the opening-day lineup.

On Memorial Day in 1930, Simmons performed another of his most famous heroics. In the thirteenth inning of first game of double header, Simmons had to stop suddenly rounding third base. His knee popped, and he could immediately feel the knee swelling up under his uniform. In a half-hour he could hardly walk, but rather than going to the hospital he stayed in uniform to pinch hit in the second game if need be. He was needed, and pinch-hit a fourth-inning grand slam home run, rallying the A's from behind; they eventually won 14–11. He was out for a time but returned to enjoy perhaps his finest season, wrestling the batting title from Lou Gehrig on the last day of the season, .381 to .379. He drove in 165 runs. The A's rolled to another pennant. According to Connie Mack, Simmons in 1930 hit 14 home runs in the eighth or ninth innings of close games.

During the 1930 World Series Burleigh Grimes, as intimidating a figure as Simmons himself, figured out gestures to infuriate each Philadelphia hitter, a sort of an earlier-day Joaquin Andu-

jar. His schtick for Simmons was to brush imaginary dust off his uniform, mimicking a Simmons gesture. Unimpressed, Simmons homered off Grimes in the fourth inning of the first game. The Athletics took the series in six. Simmons was the leading hitter, at .364. Following the 1930 season, Simmons signed a three-year contract for $100,000 ($33,333 per year). That was the most that Connie Mack had ever paid a player.

"A man is never a real champion unless he repeats," Mack told Simmons in the spring of 1931. Battling his swollen ankles, Simmons repeated as batting champion in 1931, hitting .390, driving in 128 runs in 128 games. On August 23, 1931, there occurred the famous incident in which Simmons, nagged by injuries, took a day off, only to see his replacement (Jim Moore) misplay a line drive to bring an end to Lefty Grove's 16-game winning streak, precipitating one of baseball's most famous temper tantrums on behalf of the great left-hander. Lefty screamed at everyone in general and Moore, Mack and Simmons in particular for reducing his season's record (at that point) to 26–2. After his first loss he had bolted the team for a few days. The 1931 A's rolled to another pennant with a record of 107–45, though they were upset by the Cardinals in the series. Simmons hit .333 in the 1931 series and was the only player to homer more than once in the seven games, connecting again off of Burleigh Grimes.

At the close of the 1931 series, several of the A's players were scheduled to go on the first of the All-Star tours of Japan. For convenience, some of them stuck their World Series shares into the Bank of America in Philadelphia. While they were on the boat to Japan the bank panic occurred. The Bank of America folded. Unable to join in the nationwide epidemic of pulling their money out of banks, several players also returned home to find that other banks had folded and their money was gone. Simmons, again, was among those who lost money.

In 1932 Simmons was healthy for the first time in years, and played 154 games for the only time in his career. He had 216 hits, 35 homers, 151 RBI, 144 runs scored. On June 3, 1932, Simmons made a leaping catch of a drive off the bat of Lou Gehrig, who hit four others that day; Simmons's catch prevented Gehrig from being the only man to hit five in a game.

The A's, however, failed to win that year. Connie Mack loved Al Simmons, but he also loved the dollar bill, and with the depression on he was running short of the latter. He had on hand a young outfielder named Lou Finney, who in his optimistic way he thought might be as good as Simmons and who certainly would play

a lot cheaper. On September 28, 1932, Simmons, Mule Haas and Jimmie Dykes were sold to the Chicago White Sox for $150,000.

The deal marked the beginning of the end for both Al Simmons and the Philadelphia A's. Finney didn't cut it. The Athletics declined by 13 and a half games. Their attendance, 839,000 in 1929, dropped to 297,000 in 1933. Mack was forced to sell more players. The A's dropped under .500 in 1934, and never again saw the good side of the city until 1947.

In 1933 the first true All-Star game was played. Simmons, probably helped by playing in Chicago, where the whole thing had been organized, was the highest vote-getter in either league, totalling 346,291 votes. He finished the season with 200 hits, becoming the last American Leaguer until Wade Boggs to have five consecutive 200-hit seasons. His stats, however, were not quite so brilliant as they had been in Philadelphia. In 1935, after slumping to .267, he was sold to the Detroit Tigers for $75,000. A year later, despite hitting .327 and driving in 112 runs for the Tigers, he was sold to Washington for $15,000. After two years in Washington, his stats still good (21, 95, .302) he was sold to the Boston Braves for an unreported price, and then the next year he went on waivers to the Cincinnati Reds. He had become a baseball

nomad. He got into one final World Series game that fall, hitting a double in four at bats.

At the end of the 1939 season he was released by the Reds, and signed on with the now-destitute A's as a player-coach. Late in the 1941 season Ted Williams was driving toward .400, and everybody was rooting for him—everybody, perhaps, except Al Simmons. Trying to put extra pressure on him, Simmons offered to bet Ted that he wouldn't hit .400. "The only guy who tried to put me down was Al Simmons," wrote Williams in *My Turn at Bat*. "Simmons had a kind of swaggering way about him. The kind of guy who when somebody else was in the batting cage would say, 'Buy him a lunch. He's going to be in there all day.' Simmons wouldn't win any popularity contests."

Simmons, perhaps, couldn't quite believe that he had gotten old so quickly. By 1942 he was a full-time coach. In 1943, with Williams gone to the war, the Red Sox signed Simmons to play left field for them. The comeback was ill-fated; he hit just .203 in 40 games. He went back to coaching with Philadelphia; coaching, at least. He was the third base coach and perhaps the *de facto* manager of the A's during the late forties. Connie was in his eighties. "When he signals for an obviously wrong move these days," wrote Bob Considine, "Al Simmons turns his back a bit sadly on the old man, as if he did not detect the signal, and calls for the right move."

"You used better judgment than I did, Al," Mack would say at the end of the inning. It was not much of an accomplishment. (Quotes are from *The Fireside Book of Baseball.*) Between losses Simmons carried on a full-fledged feud with Ted Williams, explaining to anyone who would listen that Williams would be a much better hitter if he would be more aggressive at the plate, claiming that the Williams shift would finish Teddy as a hitter because he wouldn't adjust, arguing that Williams' batting theories were ruining the game.

After the 1949 season Simmons left the A's. He coached a year in Cleveland. The Indians were a better team. He thought perhaps a managerial opportunity would come his way. It didn't. He retired from baseball following the 1950 season. He began to drink heavily. In 1953 he was named to Hall of Fame. He died of a heart attack in his hometown of Milwaukee on May 26, 1956, just days after his 54th birthday. Connie Mack had passed away earlier in the year.

Simmons was a valuable contributor to a great team. He developed into a fine left fielder, and probably, had his ankles been better, would have developed into a fine center fielder. He was by reputation one of the greatest clutch hitters of all time.

Though I take Earl Weaver's attitude toward the subject of clutch hitting—sportswriters make entirely too much of it—one would not have difficulty finding evidence to support his clutch reputation. Certainly he had many big, big hits.

That being acknowledged, I cannot see Simmons as one of the greatest players of all time. Almost everything that one could say in characterizing Simmons' play would also apply to Al Oliver—an exceptional line-drive hitter, a man of great strength, a marginal center fielder but a good left fielder who contributed to championship teams, a batting champion but not the dominant offensive force of his time, an arrogant man, difficult to live with, a free swinger, a man who didn't draw many walks, a man who led the league in a few offensive categories (but just a few). That's Al Simmons; it is also Al Oliver. His numbers are superficially better than Oliver's, but no serious person can doubt that had Oliver played in the 1920s and thirties, he would have hit .380–.400 in his best seasons. Perhaps, at the very best, Simmons was Al Oliver raised to the power of George Brett or Jim Rice, but I doubt that he had the same impact on his own time that those two players have had on our time. He was a fine player.

REGGIE SMITH

HALL OF FAME? No
DATA IN SECTION III? Yes
OFFENSIVE WON-LOST RECORD:
Approximately 142–59, .706
GROSS VALUE: 162

Very similar to Larry Doby. Never really gets credit for being a "winner," yet in his rookie year the Red Sox were a miracle team, and it was in his first year with the Dodgers that they finally got over the big red hump. In 1974 he was traded from the Red Sox to the Cardinals; the Red Sox declined by five games and the Cardinals improved by four and a half. I think his record justifies the high ranking that Palmer gave him (52nd greatest non-pitcher of all time).

DUKE SNIDER

HALL OF FAME? Yes
DATA IN SECTION III? Yes
OFFENSIVE WON-LOST RECORD:
139–59, .704
GROSS VALUE: 176
COMPARABLE RECENT PLAYERS:
Dale Murphy

In 1954 the three New York center fielders averaged 36 homers, 114 RBI and .327. In 1955 they averaged 43 homers, 121 RBI and a .312 average. In 1956 they averaged 40 homers, 105 RBI and a .314 average, and in '57 36 homers, 94 RBI and a .324 average. Those were the only four years they were all three there; Snider led them in home runs (165) and runs batted in (449), Mantle in average. Duke was also the leading home run and RBI man for the decade as a whole.

He didn't receive a lot of help from Ebbets Field. From 1953 through '57 he hit 23 to 25 home runs every year at home, 17 to 19 on the road. How much help he got from being the only left-handed bat in the lineup, which kept the other teams from pitching left-handers, would be interesting to know. There weren't too many good left-handers in the N.L. in those days—Spahn, Simmons, Johnny Antonelli. My memory is that Spahn hardly ever pitched against the Dodgers, and they used to rowdy him up pretty good.

Well, hell, I'll do a little research. . . . Spahn through 1961 had 49 career decisions against the Dodgers, the fewest of any N.L. team, and a record against them of 17–32, whereas he was over .600 against every other N.L. team except the Giants, 50–36 against them. It looks like what happened was that they did beat Spahn so consistently that the Braves hardly ever pitched him against the Bums, and that some other teams followed suit and also avoided pitching left-handers against them. In 1953 Spahn was 0–2 against the Dodgers, 23–5 against the other six teams. In 1954 and 1955, when he was 21–12 and 17–14, he had no decisions either year against Brooklyn, and in 1956 he lost his only decision to them, winning 20 of 30 against other teams.

Antonelli fared better. Be-

ginning in '53 his records against Brooklyn were 1–1, 1–2, 0–1, and 3–0 (total, 5–4) while against the other six teams he was 11–11, 20–5, 14–15, and 17–13 (total, 62–44). Simmons pitched OK against them in '53 but then didn't face them much; in the same years he was 3–2, 1–1, 0–0, and 0–1, while going 13–11, 13–14, 8–8, and 15–9 against other teams (totals are 4–4 and 49–42). Really, he was more effective against them than Roberts, who was 1–6, 2–3, 4–4, and 3–4 against Brooklyn (10–17) while going 22–10, 21–12, 19–10, and 16–14 against the rest of the league (78–46).

TRIS SPEAKER

HALL OF FAME? Yes
DATA IN SECTION III? Yes
OFFENSIVE WON-LOST RECORD:
 212–62, .775
GROSS VALUE: 309
COMPARABLE RECENT PLAYERS:
Well, if you can imagine George Brett playing center field like Cesar Geronimo, you'd be pretty close.

It was not a unanimous agreement among the observers of Speaker and Cobb's time that Cobb was the better player. Cobb was a better hitter and a more prolific base stealer, but Speaker was a better outfielder, had a better arm, was probably faster, was a great hitter himself and seemed to wind up on winning teams more often.

I think the key words for Speaker are "intelligence" and "adaptability." When the

lively ball era came he was past thirty, but he adapted spectacularly well, and in 1923, aged thirty-five, hit .380 with 59 doubles, 11 triples, 17 homers, 130 RBI, 93 walks, 15 strikeouts and was second in the league in assists, with 26. He basically reinvented center field play, challenging the traditional idea that a center fielder should play deep and keep the ball in front of him. He made, in essence, exactly the same decision in center field that Graig Nettles made at third base (see Boswell's *Why Time Begins on Opening Day,* pages 172–75)—to risk an occasional double or triple to cut down on the number of singles falling in front of him. He was a natural right-hander, but fell off a horse at the age of ten and had to learn to do things left-handed with a broken right arm, and ever after threw left but was basically ambidextrous, like many of the great glove men. As a manager he was the first man to platoon extensively that I could find record of, with the arguable exception of George Stallings, and had a darn good .542 winning percentage in eight years as a player/manager. Intelligence, adaptability; that seems to be the common thread that runs through his career.

ROY THOMAS

HALL OF FAME? No
DATA IN SECTION III? Yes
OFFENSIVE WON-LOST RECORD:
  96–58, .623
GROSS VALUE: 129
COMPARABLE RECENT PLAYERS:
Richie Ashburn

(The following article is the work of Jim Baker.)

Roy Thomas is one of the many fine outfielders the Phillies had grace their pastures in the 1890–1905 period; others included Sam Thompson, Billy Hamilton, Ed Delahanty, Elmer Flick, Sherry Magee and, for a while, Nap Lajoie. All but Hamilton and Thompson broke in with the Phillies

Thomas was a sort of real life "Kid Who Batted 1.000." (*The Kid Who Batted 1.000* is a kid's book about a teenager who could hit foul balls at will, consequently drawing only walks and never making outs. He gets a big league contract on the basis of this talent and, as it must happen in all baseball books, the big hit at the end of the season.) According to Fred Lieb, Thomas "could drive a pitcher crazy by standing at the plate and fouling off balls as long as it suited his fancy. He once fouled off 22 balls before working the pitcher for a walk." Lieb states that it was primarily because of the skill of Thomas and John McGraw at doing this that the foul strike rule was adopted by the National League in 1901. Thomas' impressive walk totals dropped only slightly after that, which

may show that if you have the ability to foul off twenty-two pitched balls, calling two of them strikes isn't going to make much difference.

Thomas has to have been one of the weakest hitters ever, yet he still managed to define and carry out an offensive role. His isolated power of .019 in 1900 is the lowest mark ever by a full-time player; he had 4 doubles and 3 triples in 531 at bats. He had other seasons in which he had 4, 5, and 6 doubles in more than 550 plate appearances. But with Flick, Lajoie, et al. coming up behind him, he was just trying to get on base, and he did; his on-base percentage was over .400 the first seven years that he was in the majors, making him heir to McGraw's crown as the on-base king. He was not as good a base stealer as McGraw.

Thomas was the only Philly of quality who did not jump to the American League in 1902; without bats behind him, his skill was of little use. But he remained and played an outstanding center field, and made a unique and somewhat valuable contribution during a thirteen-year major league career.

—Jim Baker

LLOYD WANER

HALL OF FAME? Yes
DATA IN SECTION III? No
OFFENSIVE WON-LOST RECORD:
  Approximately 115–98, .540
GROSS VALUE: 149
COMPARABLE RECENT PLAYERS:
Willie McGee

There has always been a rumor that Lloyd Waner was elected to the Hall of Fame in 1967 because somebody made a mistake and gave the Veterans' Committee the statistics of his brother Paul. I don't know if this is true or not, but I maintain that it probably isn't. If it was, it would be the only time in history that the Veterans' Committee paid any attention to the statistical evidence.

SAM WEST

HALL OF FAME? Yes

DATA IN SECTION III? Yes

OFFENSIVE WON-LOST RECORD:
 93–77, .549

GROSS VALUE: 141

COMPARABLE RECENT PLAYERS:
Garry Maddox

HACK WILSON

HALL OF FAME? Yes

DATA IN SECTION III? Yes

OFFENSIVE WON-LOST RECORD:
 92–39, .705

GROSS VALUE: 124

COMPARABLE RECENT PLAYERS:
Jimmie Wynn

I will guarantee you that if any scout working today saw Hack Wilson playing college ball, he would write the guy off as no prospect.

JIMMIE WYNN

HALL OF FAME? No

DATA IN SECTION III? Yes

OFFENSIVE WON-LOST RECORD:
 Approximately 132–80, .620

GROSS VALUE: 145

Good player, like Joe Morgan; hit for power and drew many walks in a run-scarce environment.

ROSS YOUNGS

HALL OF FAME? Yes

DATA IN SECTION III? No

OFFENSIVE WON-LOST RECORD:
 Approximately 85–54, .611

GROSS VALUE: 106

COMPARABLE RECENT PLAYERS:
Pete Rose

A hustling, popular player, the case for him is better than I thought it was when I began writing this book. Though he wasn't elected to the Hall of Fame until 1972, he drew strong support in the early balloting. In 1938, when the Hall was still trying to clear all the generals off the shelf, he drew 40 votes for the honor, placing him ahead of Eddie Plank (38), Herb Pennock (37), Joe McGinnity (36), Chief Bender (33), Home Run Baker (32), Hugh Duffy (32), Joe Tinker (16), Harry Heilmann (14) and Sam Crawford (11), as well as many other people who made it long before he did. Though he didn't hit with much power, he was a valuable offensive player on a great team.

HOW THE CENTER FIELDERS RATE

I wanted to say, as a postscript to the Mantle comment, that I see the obvious parallel between the Mantle/Mays comparison and the Musial/Williams comparison, on which I chose the other way, at least as to peak value. Many of the arguments that I advanced in defense of Mantle you might also put forward in support of Williams. And it might be that you'd be 100 percent correct if you did, but anyway, to extend the parallel to the summation, I can't see any advantage for Mays over Mantle on the basepaths or in the dugout (if there is an edge, it's Mickey's), so we are left with Mantle at bat against Willie in the field, and in such a contest I have consistently preferred the hitter.

However surprising the selection of Mantle over Cobb as the greatest ever in terms of peak value, it is a selection entirely consistent with 1) careful statistical analysis (Mantle's offensive winning percentages are higher), 2) the opinions of contemporaries (Cobb was subject, while active, to many of the same type of doubts that dogged Ted Williams), and 3) the performance of their teams. As such it is not a particularly difficult or close call; indeed, since Cobb was no better center fielder than Mantle, it may be an easier selection than Mantle over Mays. The top ten as I see them:

PEAK VALUE	CAREER VALUE
1. Mickey Mantle	1. Ty Cobb
2. Willie Mays	2. Willie Mays
3. Joe DiMaggio	3. Joe DiMaggio
4. Ty Cobb	4. Tris Speaker
5. Tris Speaker	5. Mickey Mantle
6. Dale Murphy	6. Al Simmons
7. Duke Snider	7. Duke Snider
8. Al Simmons	8. Max Carey
9. Larry Doby	9. Richie Ashburn
10. Hack Wilson	10. Dale Murphy

RIGHT FIELD

HANK AARON

HALL OF FAME? Yes
DATA IN SECTION III? Yes
OFFENSIVE WON-LOST RECORD:
252–87, .744
GROSS VALUE: 319

I used to write that Henry Aaron was the one player in history whose best five-year home run period began when he was thirty-five years old. Now there are two, with Darrell Evans being the other. As you can see by the home/road home run totals (Section III), to a considerable degree Aaron's late-in-life resurgence is a statistical illusion created by moving from a very poor home run park, County Stadium in Milwaukee, to a very good home run park, Fulton County Stadium in Atlanta. At his peak, Aaron would have hit 50 home runs, and probably more than once, had he been playing in an average home run park; playing his best years in Atlanta (or Wrigley Field) he absolutely would have hit more than 60 home runs in a season. In 1957, he hit 26 home runs on the road (18 in Milwaukee), in 1962 27 on the road, in 1963 25 on the road. If you add his home run totals into two-year groups so that you have a full season of home games and a full season of road games, you get this:

YEARS	HOME	ROAD
1954–55	15	25
1955–56	29	24
1956–57	33	37
1957–58	28	46
1958–59	30	39
1959–60	41	38
1960–61	40	34
1961–62	37	42
1962–63	37	52
1963–64	30	38
1964–65	30	26
1965–66	40	36
1966–67	44	39
1967–68	40	28
1968–69	38	35
1969–70	44	38
1970–71	54	31
1971–72	50	31
1972–73	43	31
1973–74	35	25
1974–75	15	17
1975–76	10	12

The "road" total traces a fairly normal progression, reaching the peak about where the peak should be; the "home" total was generally lower than the "road" total as long as he was in Milwaukee, and then went in front of it after the move to Atlanta in 1966 (going back under it when Aaron returned to Milwaukee in 1975). According to the research of John Tattersall, Henry Aaron drove in 1,240 runs with his 755 home runs, an average of 1.64 RBI per tater. That would mean that he drove in 1,057 runs on other hits, which makes him the only man to drive in 1,000 runs on home runs and 1,000 on other hits. Only two other players, Ruth and Mays, drove in 1,000 on home runs; several dead-ball era players cleared a thousand the other way, and Cobb probably drove in 1,750–1,800 on non–home runs.

Ruth's data, actually, is quite similar to Aaron's— 1,209 RBI on home runs, 995 on other hits, 1.69 RBI per home run. Aaron drove in 54 percent of his RBI on home runs, Ruth 55 percent.

Among the top ten home run hitters of all time, Jimmie Foxx got the most RBI mileage out of his HR, with 944 RBI on 534 home runs, or 1.76 per home run. Willie Mays got the least, with 1,039 RBI on 660 home runs, or 1.57 apiece.

BOBBY BONDS

HALL OF FAME? No
DATA IN SECTION III? Yes
OFFENSIVE WON-LOST RECORD:
 134–71, .654
GROSS VALUE: 149

In some respects a modern Chuck Klein or Pete Browning, a player whose statistics are so outstanding that they won't allow him to be forgotten for a long time. I always thought Bobby was most effective as a leadoff man. In his years of doing that job he scored 120, 134, 110, 118, 131 and 97 runs, and the reason he only scored 110 in 1971 is that they moved him out of the leadoff spot for about half the season. In 1974, he was way off his numbers, at .256 with 21 home runs, and he still scored only eight fewer runs than Lou Brock did while stealing 118 bases. And before you get to that, the Cardinals scored 43 more runs than the Giants did, 677–634, and out-hit them .265–.252; the top hitter coming up behind Bonds was Gary Matthews (16 homers, 82 RBI, .287) while Brock was supported by Reggie Smith (23, 100, .309) and Ted Simmons (20, 103, .272). Anyway, they could never leave him alone and let him do what he was good at, and combined with some other problems, his career degenerated.

ROBERTO CLEMENTE

HALL OF FAME? Yes
DATA IN SECTION III? Yes
OFFENSIVE WON-LOST RECORD:
 169–85, .664
GROSS VALUE: 204

The word *barbarian,* as you probably know, comes from the Greek word meaning "foreigner," and is derived from the bleating of sheep—that is, the Greeks were saying that people who didn't speak Greek were making a sound like the "baa baa" of a sheep. The English got even by saying of any kind of unintelligible gibberish or nonsense that "It's Greek to me."

A couple of years ago a guy from the Elias Bureau, while going through the traditional explanation of why fielding statistics are meaningless, used Roberto Clemente as an example of an outstanding defensive player who didn't have good defensive statistics. He cited Clemente's fielding records as undistinguished because he never led the league in fielding percentage. You know what's funny about that? Clemente probably has the best defensive statistics of any right fielder ever to play the game. It's like using Babe Ruth as an example of a player who was a great hitter but didn't have great hitting statistics, because he led the league only once in batting average.

You get the point? You can never know that something is meaningless, whether it is sounds, letters, charts, data.

All you can possibly know is that it is meaningless *to you.* The line below means nothing to you:

ce v t.e RFmk keco e rw smsnagJ bo-eoaJegaaioef nnist

But if unscrambled by a very simple pattern it says "Reggie Jackson was not a member of the Jackson Five." You very often hear someone who talks about baseball statistics say that this is meaningless or that is meaningless. Whenever you hear that, you should realize that the man is asserting something which he cannot possibly know to be true.

ROCKY COLAVITO

HALL OF FAME? No
DATA IN SECTION III? No
OFFENSIVE WON-LOST RECORD:
 Unknown
GROSS VALUE: Unknown

A popular player, a world-class home run hitter with a powerful throwing arm; idiosyncratic selection of the Palmer method as one of the greatest players ever.

SAM CRAWFORD

HALL OF FAME? Yes
DATA IN SECTION III? Yes
OFFENSIVE WON-LOST RECORD:
  185–84, .687
GROSS VALUE: 206
COMPARABLE RECENT PLAYERS:
Roberto Clemente

Very comparable to Clemente. As I may have mentioned, his range factors are low although he was a fast runner—he holds the all-time record for triples, 312—was one of the best-conditioned athletes of his time, and was by reputation a good fielder. I suspect a statistical illusion of some sort. The man who followed him as right fielder of the Tigers, Heilmann, also had range factors consistently in the ones.

ANDRE DAWSON

HALL OF FAME? Not Eligible
DATA IN SECTION III? No
OFFENSIVE WON-LOST RECORDS:
  110–74, .598
GROSS VALUE: 134

DWIGHT EVANS

HALL OF FAME? Not Eligible
DATA IN SECTION III? No
OFFENSIVE WON-LOST RECORDS:
  131–76, .635
GROSS VALUE: 167

ELMER FLICK

HALL OF FAME? Yes
DATA IN SECTION III? Yes
OFFENSIVE WON-LOST RECORD:
  112–41, .733
GROSS VALUE: 118
COMPARABLE RECENT PLAYERS:
Tony Oliva

A line-drive hitter, a fast runner, he had a distinguished career cut short by three straight years' worth of injuries.

CARL FURILLO

HALL OF FAME? No
DATA IN SECTION III? Yes
OFFENSIVE WON-LOST RECORD:
  102–75, .578
GROSS VALUE: 131

HARRY HEILMANN

HALL OF FAME? Yes
DATA IN SECTION III? Yes
OFFENSIVE WON-LOST RECORD:
  147–63, .702
GROSS VALUE: 192
COMPARABLE RECENT PLAYERS:
Tommy Davis, if healthy

A big, strong, right-handed batter, Heilmann was probably the one player most helped by the changes in the game that took place about 1920. With a career offensive won/lost record of just 44–31 through 1920, he exploded after the spitball was banned in 1921 and was 74–20 in the next seven years.

An odd point about his defense . . . Heilmann is generally not regarded as a good defensive outfielder. Ken Smith wrote that he "was not a good fielder or . . . thrower, and there were several faster

players in every game he played" (quoted from *The Ultimate Baseball Book*). His career range factor, 1.87, is consistent with this evaluation, though he threw well enough to play right field for many years, while a couple of people whose arms were supposedly better, like Manush, were moved to left to accommodate him, and he also had 31 assists in 1924. Anyway, the odd point is that the Reds made him their center fielder for a large part of the 1930 season, when he was thirty-five years old. Can you imagine? That must have been some defensive outfield. No wonder the league hit .303 that year.

BABE HERMAN

HALL OF FAME? No
DATA IN SECTION III? Yes
OFFENSIVE WON-LOST RECORD:
  109–40, .731
GROSS VALUE: 128
COMPARABLE RECENT PLAYERS:
Dave Kingman

A notorious fielder and baserunner, he had the worst or next-to-worst range factor in the league every year he was a regular except one. He was an effective offensive player for a few years, at a time and place when high averages and impressive power totals were common. Pete places him 208th—and that's way too high. I doubt seriously that he is one of the game's one thousand greatest players. Buzz Arlett was a better player.

HARRY HOOPER

HALL OF FAME? Yes
DATA IN SECTION III? No
OFFENSIVE WON-LOST RECORD:
Unknown
GROSS VALUE: Unknown
COMPARABLE RECENT PLAYERS:
Jimmie Piersall, Paul Blair

A glove man with a decent bat; idiosyncratic selection of the Hall of Fame.

REGGIE JACKSON

HALL OF FAME? No
DATA IN SECTION III? No
OFFENSIVE WON-LOST RECORD:
190–93, .671
GROSS VALUE: 224

Whatever the controversies that surround him, there can't be any serious doubt that he was a great player. The one rap on him is that he only hit .300 the one time, which is the reason that Ritter and Honig, who are hung up on batting averages, didn't rate him. But even that's phony. If he hadn't played his best years in the Oakland Coliseum, the worst "average" park in the league, he'd probably have hit .300 several times. In 1973 he hit .321 on the road, but only .259 in Oakland. Through 1982 his career average in road games was *fifteen points* higher than Carl Yastrzemski's (.279–.264), and I'll bet anything if you check his career stats in the good hitter's parks in the league, like Detroit, Minnesota and Fenway, you'll find he's hit over .300 in them. Early in his career he was fast; late in his career he was as smart a baserunner as you'd

ever see. I've never thought that there was any significant evidence that he was a good clutch hitter, but he doesn't need any bonus points to be called a great player.

AL KALINE

HALL OF FAME? Yes
DATA IN SECTION III? Yes
OFFENSIVE WON-LOST RECORD:
194–87, .691
GROSS VALUE: 236

Clemente and Kaline were both born in late 1934, and were similar players. The career high in home runs was twenty-nine for each, and each was a batting champion, though Kaline was only champion once and Clemente was champion annually. One starts with the assumption that Clemente was a greater player than Kaline, and when everything is known about the subject we might come back to that conclusion. Clemente's career average is quite a bit higher, .317–.297, and I think it is accurate to say that the consensus of opinion while they were active was that Clemente was greater. Maury Allen placed Clemente 12th and Kaline 33rd; Ritter and Honig didn't include Kaline at all.

The best analytical methods available right now don't show that. With a big edge in home runs (399–240) and walks (1,277–621), Kaline created far more runs (1,848–1,557), a conclusion that is supported by the fact that he also scored more (1,622–

1,416) and drove in more (1,583–1,305). His on-base percentage was higher, and his slugging percentage was higher. If you adjust it for outs made, he's still ahead.

Defensively, Clemente was spectacular and Kaline, as Maury Allen said, was near perfect. Their range factors are the same, 2.09. In voting for the MVP awards, though Clemente won one and Kaline did not, Kaline edged Clemente in career performance, with 2.92 Award Shares to Clemente's 2.80.

Clemente's peak value was, no doubt, higher. But Kaline was a great player at age twenty, and Clemente didn't become one until age twenty-six. I have to rank Kaline higher in terms of career value.

CHARLIE KELLER

HALL OF FAME? No
DATA IN SECTION III? Yes
OFFENSIVE WON-LOST RECORD:
80–23, .774
GROSS VALUE: 94
COMPARABLE RECENT PLAYERS:
Steve Kemp

In DiMaggio's shadow, but a great player in his own right until stopped by a back problem that, as I understand, involved the deterioration of the discs in his back. A muscleman, he hit .286 lifetime but had the Ted Williams kicker to his batting: He hit 30 homers a year and drew 100 walks, plus he was faster than Williams. He came up the same year as Williams, actually, and out-hit him .334–.323 as a rookie, though without the power. His slugging percentage was over .500 his first eight years in the major leagues.

A son, Charlie Keller, Jr., was a bright star in the Yankee chain until stopped by the same back problem, which is congenital. He had a season in the Eastern League in 1961 that could be fit in with his father's career, and you'd never know it wasn't his. He led the league in hitting at .349 with a slugging percentage way over .600, and drew 95 walks in 139 games.

I would probably pick the outfield of Keller, DiMaggio, and Henrich as the greatest ever, at least before the Toronto outfield of the eighties. Keller's on-base percentage, lifetime, was .408, and he grounded into only seven double plays a year.

CHUCK KLEIN

HALL OF FAME? Yes
DATA IN SECTION III? Yes
OFFENSIVE WON-LOST RECORD:
115–55, .676
GROSS VALUE: 149
COMPARABLE RECENT PLAYERS:
Dave Parker, Dick Allen

Formerly the subject of a raging HOF dispute, which was quieted when they took him in in 1980. Dan Okrent's view of Klein, which always made a certain amount of sense to me, is that "there's just too much." You can't ignore *that much* statistical evidence. Yes, I know the Baker Bowl was a hitter's park. A

whole lot of other people played there, and they didn't hit .386. If you ignore the .386 you've got the triple crown year to deal with, or the time he hit 59 doubles, or the two straight seasons of 40 home runs, or the 170 RBI. He had hit totals of 219, 250, 200, 226, and 223; you knock off 20 a year for the park and you've still got 199, 230, 180, 206, and 203. Klein had 44 assists in 1930, a modern record, and people would say, "Oh, yeah, but see, in the Baker Bowl he could play so shallow that sometimes he'd throw people out at first," so we have to ignore that, too. And then, didn't he lead the league in stolen bases one year. . . .

You just can't ignore *that much* statistical evidence. It's just in the last year or so that I've become convinced that Klein was significantly over what we might call the Bonds line, the level of unquestioned excellence but marginal greatness. One reason is that it is obvious from the literature of the time that Klein *was* regarded, while active, as a great player; maybe not as great as Ott and Waner, but in the same group. He was one of those players, like Richie Allen, who was always the focus of attention wherever he went. The headline over every team he played for at the end of the season was always going to read "Klein has great season" or "Klein doesn't have great season."

Another reason is a note in

The Hidden Game, on page 95. See, the key question here is, "How much of Klein's productivity is a park illusion?" Granted, his statistics are a knockout, but you have to remember that he played for some teams that allowed seven runs a game and lost 100 games with statistics that are knockouts. Might it not be that, with the helium-inflated baseballs of the 1930s and a tiny park, the statistics of the time and place are just insanely out of whack? How much of it was really good hitting/bad pitching, and how much of it was a park illusion?

The chart on page 95 of *The Hidden Game* lists the all-time leader in runs allowed per game, home park, one season. It's the 1930 Phillies, 8.36. It also lists the all-time leader in runs allowed per game, road games, one season. That, too, is the 1930 Phillies, 7.03. Park illusion or no, those pitching staffs were just *bad*.

ROGER MARIS

HALL OF FAME? No
DATA IN SECTION III? Yes
OFFENSIVE WON-LOST RECORD:
  95–50, .656
GROSS VALUE: 103

The interesting thing about Roger Maris is that almost everything that people say about him is false. People say that he was a one-year wonder, but how can you be a one-year wonder if you win two Most Valuable Player awards? People say that he was a one-dimensional player, but after he lost that one dimension, he was still good enough to play right field for two National League champion teams. People say that Maris was a dead pull hitter who took advantage of Yankee Stadium, but the fact is that in 1960 he hit only 13 home runs in Yankee Stadium, as opposed to 26 on the road, and in 1961 he hit 30 at home, 31 on the road.

That's the really strange one, because looking at his records, which show the big jump in power in 1960, it is something easier than a natural assumption that, as a left-handed pull hitter, he was taking advantage of Yankee. My guess is that what must have happened is that when he moved to New York, either someone showed him or he figured out for himself that, if he was going to hit any home runs at all in that park, he would have to learn to pull the ball right down the line. One can think of a number of peo-ple on the Yankee scene who would have been qualified to help him learn how to do that. Once he did learn to pull the ball right down the line, then it helped him not only in Yan-kee, but in every park. So in a sense the park did "help" him, but only by forcing him to learn something, and not by giving him cheap home runs.

TONY OLIVA

HALL OF FAME? No
DATA IN SECTION III? Yes
OFFENSIVE WON-LOST RECORD:
  115–58, .665
GROSS VALUE: 119

Knee injuries cut short and diminished the brilliance of a career that would likely have been one of the greatest. Pal-mer/Allen consensus seems fair.

MEL OTT

HALL OF FAME? Yes
DATA IN SECTION III? Yes
OFFENSIVE WON-LOST RECORD:
  197–56, .779
GROSS VALUE: 258
COMPARABLE RECENT PLAYERS:
Well, let's see . . . Leon Wagner used to lift his leg when he swung. Joe Morgan was a little guy who hit homers and drew lots of walks. Reggie has hit about the same number of home runs and plays right field. Add on Andre Dawson's throwing arm, and you've about got him.

Craig Wright notes the fol-lowing about Mel Ott and Sadaharu Oh: Besides both lifting their front leg knee high as a way to keep their weight back, there are a number of remarkable similarities be-tween their careers. Both had short names beginning with *O*; both were in the "majors" as teen-agers and played 22 seasons all with the same team. Their teams were both nicknamed the Giants. Both were left-handed and extreme pull hitters. Their career totals in games, plate appearances and stolen bases are nearly identical. Both retired with ca-reer averages just over .300. Both were very disciplined sluggers who retired with their league's career records in homers and walks.

Craig once said that inside of every good manager was the soul of a sabermetrician. I wouldn't go that far, because I think that there have been good managers who were all sorts of different people, and besides that I've known some sabermetricians whose souls should not be wished upon a wolfhound, but anyway . . . Pie Traynor, who was good enough to manage in the major leagues for six years with more wins than losses, displayed the soul if not the methods of a sabermetrician when he was explaining why Mel Ott was the best player he had seen in the National League in all his years there as a player and manager. "My logic is simple," he said. "The best players are those who win the most games, and I can't name a player who has exerted as strong an influence upon so many games" (quoted from *Under Coogan's*

Bluff, by Fred Stein). Kirby Higbe said that he never saw Ott make a mistake in playing the right-field wall at the Polo Grounds, and named him the cleanup hitter on the his National League All-Star team. Casey Stengel was less impressed, and named Waner.

Ott was the one player among the all-time great home run hitters whose totals were seriously inflated by the park that he played in, hitting 323 home runs in New York and only 188 in other parks. But between the two of them and throwing in Chuck Klein, as likable and quotable as Paul Waner was, I have to go with Ott. The performance of the two in MVP voting was almost even, Waner drawing 2.58 Award Shares and Ott 2.66. Hitting 30 or 35 homers a year, hitting over .300 and drawing 100 walks a year, playing right field to perfection, it just seems likely to me that what Traynor said about him was true. He did more to help the other team lose than almost anybody else.

DAVE PARKER

HALL OF FAME? Not Eligible
DATA IN SECTION III? No
OFFENSIVE WON-LOST RECORD:
 134–72, .650
GROSS VALUE: 156

SAM RICE

HALL OF FAME? Yes
DATA IN SECTION III? No
OFFENSIVE WON-LOST RECORD:
 Unknown
GROSS VALUE: Unknown
COMPARABLE RECENT PLAYERS:
Willie Wilson

You probably know that Rice wound up his career with 2,987 hits, which happened because no one really paid any attention to career statistics at that time. Three thousand hits didn't mean anything; when Ty Cobb got his 4,000th hit in 1927 it was probably a big day in the life of Ernest Lanigan, but some of the newspaper reports of the game didn't even mention it.

FRANK ROBINSON

HALL OF FAME? Yes
DATA IN SECTION III? Yes
OFFENSIVE WON-LOST RECORD:
 211–68, .758
GROSS VALUE: 252

One of Maury Allen's odder choices was placing Robinson, who turned in some stupendous seasons in a long career, as low as he did (63rd). His commentary gives no hint as to why he viewed Robby as less of a player than, say, Rube Marquard or Richie Allen.

A 1963 player ratings article in *Sport* magazine picked Robinson as the number one right fielder in the National League, over Aaron and Clemente. Aaron's RBI totals in the four years previous to that were 123, 126, 120 and 128. Though perhaps he did not sustain the production quite as long, Robinson as a hitter was quite comparable to his contemporaries Mays and Aaron.

BABE RUTH

HALL OF FAME? Yes
DATA IN SECTION III? Yes
OFFENSIVE WON-LOST RECORD:
 188–33, .851
Ruth's offensive winning percentage, .851, is the highest of any right fielder.
GROSS VALUE: 382 (Highest of any player at any position)

I reckon you probably already know about this fellow; I have nothing much to add. I would have three minor disagreements with what I take to be the consensus picture of Babe Ruth that exists today. Number one, I think that few people have understood, despite some qualified attempts to help them understand, the extent to which Ruth was a mythic figure even before 1920. Number two, I think that some writers have overstated just a little the extent to which Ruth dominated the league in his own time, the extent to which he dominated home run hitting, for example. It's not a serious overstatement; it's an overstatement by selected facts, which is not like just making stuff up. Yes, it is true that Ruth hit 54 home runs in 1920 when nobody else in the league hit more than 19, and that he hit more home runs than any other American League *team* that season. But it's also true that everything that Ruth did, somebody else almost duplicated within a few years. For example, Ruth's 1923 season, when he hit .393 with 41 homers and 131 runs batted in, is essentially duplicated by Hornsby's 1922 season, when he hit .401 with 42 homers and had 152 RBI, and even Ruth's 1921 and 1927 seasons are almost matched by Hack Wilson's campaign in 1930 and Jimmie Foxx in 1932. Ruth was the first person to reach these levels and the most consistent at maintaining them, but the fact that other people were able to do basically the same things he had done shows that he achieved these levels not because he was some kind of superhuman athletic freak, but because he was a trail blazer, a man who had the courage to escape the fictions and falsehoods that constrained other men's talents, and show them what could be done.

And third, I think that some people including myself have overstated just a little bit the extent to which Ruth, by himself, changed the game of baseball. If you think that Ruth played a major role in destroying the old strategies and reshaping the game of baseball, you're right; if you think that it was mostly Ruth that was responsible for the change in baseball that took place about 1920, you're dead wrong. Napoleon said that "Without the revolution, I am nothing." Like Napoleon,

Babe Ruth was a remarkable man who came along at one of the gates of history, when the old ways had been destroyed and men were anxious to be shown the way to a safe new place. With the breaking of the gambling scandals and the death of Ray Chapman coming in less than a month, the old baseball was dead, and that had little to do with Ruth. Like Napoleon, Ruth's role was in leading the way to and defining the rules of the new order.

WILDFIRE SCHULTE
HALL OF FAME? No
DATA IN SECTION III? Yes
OFFENSIVE WON-LOST RECORD:
  117–83, .586
GROSS VALUE: 106

JIMMY SHECKARD
HALL OF FAME? No
DATA IN SECTION III? Yes
OFFENSIVE WON-LOST RECORD:
  144–84, .631
GROSS VALUE: 157
COMPARABLE RECENT PLAYERS:
Somewhere between Roy White and Joe Morgan

See article on Sheckard in Section I, under "Most Unpredictable Career," Decade 1900–1909.

ENOS SLAUGHTER
HALL OF FAME? Yes
DATA IN SECTION III? Yes
OFFENSIVE WON-LOST RECORD:
  147–68, .684
GROSS VALUE: 165
COMPARABLE RECENT PLAYERS:
Pete Rose, Lloyd Moseby

Fits Definition C of a potential Hall of Famer absolutely to a T—consistently among the best in the league at his position. People say that he might have had 3,000 hits in his career if it had not been for the war, which is, of course, silly. His career high in hits was 193. If he had matched that all three years that he was missing, he still wouldn't have had 3,000, and as to prolonging his career to get there, he played as it is until he was forty-three years old and hit .171, which is about as far as you can push it. But while he wouldn't have had 3,000 hits, he would have had 2,900, and that would put him in the Hall of Fame. I personally find the idea of excluding someone who otherwise would clearly be in because his numbers are a little short because he was in the service of his country to be rather offensive.

But we heard far more about him and his accomplishments when he was a Hall of Fame candidate than we will hear now that he is in. Not being in the Hall of Fame was keeping his memory alive.

PAUL WANER

HALL OF FAME? Yes
DATA IN SECTION III? Yes
OFFENSIVE WON-LOST RECORD:
174–75, .699
GROSS VALUE: 220
COMPARABLE RECENT PLAYERS:
None

There really hasn't been a similar offensive player in several years. Like Ott, his rival as the outstanding N.L. right fielder of the time, he was a small man. Whereas Ott had the advantage of short fences and took advantage of them by learning to pull the ball right down the line, Waner played in Forbes Field, where he became the all-time master at shooting for the foul lines, as Hal McRae did in the seventies, thereby spreading the outfield and making maximum use of the big green pastures. Besides, as he explained, if you hit a line drive to straightaway left, it either lands for a single or you're out; if you hit the same ball down the line, it's either a double or a foul ball, and you're still hitting. It was an ingenious and effective adaptation to a difficult situation.

I've always doubted, somehow, that Waner drank as much as people say he did. It doesn't seem to fit; he was too much a durable, consistent type of player, never had an off year until he was past thirty-five. . . . Casey Stengel named him as the greatest National League right fielder that he saw.

DAVE WINFIELD

HALL OF FAME? Not Eligible
DATA IN SECTION III? No
OFFENSIVE WON-LOST RECORD:
145–82, .637
GROSS VALUE: 172

Let me ask the questions here, and you make up your own answers. There are 28 right fielders listed here. How many hit for as much power as Dave Winfield? How many ran as well? How many had better throwing arms? How many hit for better batting averages? How many were more selective hitters? How many were better RBI men? How many were as durable over a period of years? How many were as consistent?

On almost every count, I think you'll find he ranks no worse than the middle of the pack—among the all-time greats.

HOW THE RIGHT FIELDERS RATE

Right field seems to be the one position at which all of the indicators of formal analysis are pretty much in agreement, and that being the case I will abide by the systematic evidence, with a minimum of interpretation:

PEAK VALUE	CAREER VALUE
1. Babe Ruth	1. Babe Ruth
2. Hank Aaron	2. Hank Aaron
3. Frank Robinson	3. Frank Robinson
4. Mel Ott	4. Mel Ott
5. Roberto Clemente	5. Reggie Jackson
6. Charlie Keller	6. Al Kaline
7. Reggie Jackson	7. Paul Waner
8. Tony Oliva	8. Sam Crawford
9. Dwight Evans	9. Roberto Clemente
10. Roger Maris	10. Harry Heilmann

MULTI-POSITION STARS

DICK ALLEN

HALL OF FAME? No
DATA IN SECTION III? Yes
OFFENSIVE WON-LOST RECORD:
   132–45, .745
GROSS VALUE: 149

HARMON KILLEBREW

HALL OF FAME? Yes
DATA IN SECTION III? Yes
OFFENSIVE WON-LOST RECORD:
   166–71, .702
GROSS VALUE: 186

TOMMY LEACH

HALL OF FAME? No
DATA IN SECTION III? Yes
OFFENSIVE WON-LOST RECORD:
   136–101, .574
GROSS VALUE: 151
COMPARABLE RECENT PLAYERS:
Bill Almon, though Leach was much
better

PETE ROSE

HALL OF FAME? Not Eligible
DATA IN SECTION III? Yes
OFFENSIVE WON-LOST RECORD:
   228–126, .644
GROSS VALUE: 242

There are four outstanding players for whom I could not comfortably find a position; they would rate higher as players than they would as first basemen, third basemen, or at any other position. Those are the four listed above. Three of them are modern players, and thus not in need of much introduction; the fourth was interviewed in *The Glory of Their Times*.

All four played third base for a good part of their careers (Leach, 44 percent; Allen, 37 percent; Killebrew, 31 percent; Rose, about 18 percent). All four of them also played the outfield, although two played more games in the outfield than at third (Rose and Leach) and the other two less. Three of the four, all except Leach, played some of their careers as first basemen. The two who played more out-field were primarily right fielders; the other two were primarily left fielders, and spent the rest of their games at first base.

Allen and Leach were outstanding baserunners, though not big base stealers; the other two were not blessed with speed. Defensively, they are impossible to compare except in effort, where Rose and Leach were both known as men who would give it their all, and Allen was not. Allen is probably the most gifted baseball player that I have ever seen; Rose is probably the least gifted great player ever. Three of the four were MVPs; the fourth played before the MVP awards, but would have been a marginal MVP candidate, had such an award existed, in 1902, 1903, and 1909. The multi-position stars, as I would rank them:

PEAK VALUE
1. Harmon Killebrew
2. Dick Allen
3. Pete Rose
4. Tommy Leach

CAREER VALUE
1. Pete Rose
2. Harmon Killebrew
3. Dick Allen
4. Tommy Leach

PITCHER

RIGHT-HANDED STARTERS

As I see them, the thirty greatest right-handed starters of all time are:

	PEAK VALUE		CAREER VALUE
1.	Walter Johnson	1.	Walter Johnson
2.	Christy Mathewson	2.	Cy Young
3.	Dizzy Dean	3.	Christy Mathewson
4.	Denny McLain	4.	Tom Seaver
5.	Bob Feller	5.	Pete Alexander
6.	Juan Marichal	6.	Bob Feller
7.	Tom Seaver	7.	Jim Palmer
8.	Dazzy Vance	8.	Juan Marichal
9.	Pete Alexander	9.	Bob Gibson
10.	Robin Roberts	10.	Gaylord Perry
11.	Bob Gibson	11.	Robin Roberts
12.	Dwight Gooden	12.	Mordecai Brown
13.	Joe Wood	13.	Early Wynn
14.	Mordecai Brown	14.	Don Sutton
15.	Ed Walsh	15.	Ferguson Jenkins
16.	Jack Coombs	16.	Phil Niekro
17.	Ed Cicotte	17.	Red Ruffing
18.	Catfish Hunter	18.	Ted Lyons
19.	Wes Ferrell	19.	Burleigh Grimes
20.	Don Drysdale	20.	Chief Bender
21.	Urban Shocker	21.	Nolan Ryan
22.	Cy Young	22.	Catfish Hunter
23.	Jim Palmer	23.	Bob Lemon
24.	Roger Clemens	24.	Stan Coveleski
25.	Jack Chesbro	25.	Dazzy Vance
26.	Addie Joss	26.	Urban Shocker
27.	Ferguson Jenkins	27.	Don Drysdale
28.	Red Ruffing	28.	Ed Walsh
29.	Joe McGinnity	29.	Lon Warneke
30.	Jim Maloney	30.	Dutch Leonard

There are two other active pitchers who might appear on one of these lists, those being Jack Morris and Mike Scott. The decision not to include them at this time is not intended to detract from their credentials, but merely to err on the side of caution; I can always revise the list later. Some hint of the reasoning behind these selections may be provided by the following notes on the pitchers.

GROVER CLEVELAND (PETE) ALEXANDER

HALL OF FAME? Yes
DATA IN SECTION III? Yes
CAREER WINNING PERCENTAGE:
.642
CAREER WINS ABOVE TEAM: 81.6
PERCENTAGE OF LEAGUE RUNS ALLOWED: 73%
COMPARABLE RECENT PITCHERS:
Marichal

Basically a control pitcher, Alexander threw a sinking fastball as his bread and butter pitch his entire career.

CHIEF BENDER

HALL OF FAME? Yes
DATA IN SECTION III? Yes
CAREER WINNING PERCENTAGE:
.621
CAREER WINS ABOVE TEAM: 16.2
PERCENTAGE OF LEAGUE RUNS ALLOWED: 84%

See the article "Bender and Brother" in the comments on the 1900–1909 decade.

THREE FINGER BROWN

HALL OF FAME? Yes
DATA IN SECTION III? Yes
CAREER WINNING PERCENTAGE:
.648
CAREER WINS ABOVE TEAM: 23.0
PERCENTAGE OF LEAGUE RUNS ALLOWED: 75%

Matty's Chicago rival, used to match up against him every time they got together. A unique and wonderful pitcher.

JACK CHESBRO

HALL OF FAME? Yes
DATA IN SECTION III? Yes
CAREER WINNING PERCENTAGE:
.606
CAREER WINS ABOVE TEAM: 23.9
PERCENTAGE OF LEAGUE RUNS ALLOWED: 92%

Jack Chesbro pitched in the major leagues for only eleven years, during five of which he was something less than an ordinary pitcher, posting won/lost marks of 6–10, 14–13, 9–10, 14–20, 0–4. It is to the other six seasons that he owes his place among the immortals. Five of those were twenty-victory seasons, which would be a more impressive accomplishment had twenty victories been a meaningful standard of excellence in his time. With pitchers winning thirty games more seasons than not, seasons such as 21–15, 19–13, and 24–16 were, in truth, more the level of a good journeyman, a Jerry Koosman type, than a certified immortal.

His fame, in essence, rests on one year, his 1904 season in which he set a "modern record" with forty-one wins—and that is the phoniest record in the books. In the context of its time, it was an outstanding season, like Carlton's year in 1980 (24–9), but it was nothing more than that. Nobody went around yelling, "Oh, my God, the man won forty-one games!" Bill Hutchison had won forty-three games just thirteen years earlier, and Ed Walsh would win forty just four years later.

In the beginning of baseball history, pitchers were not allowed to wind up, and did not throw nearly so hard as they later would. For that reason, there was nothing like the same strain on the arm that there would be in later years, and pitchers worked, literally, every game. By 1925, the four-man rotation was fairly well established—but in between there there is no magic line where the "modern" conditions suddenly begin. Mathewson and Alexander threw hard, but they threw hard fifteen, twenty times a game, as the situation demanded it, not every pitch. Walter Johnson threw hard, but the stunning impact that he had on all who saw him resulted from the fact that he threw much harder, every pitch, than anyone else did. If you look at his windup and his follow through, it is quite obvious to me that he could not have thrown as hard as modern pitchers. If you threw a 90-mph fastball with that motion, your arm would come off. The fact that they didn't need to work as hard the whole nine innings is the reason, and the only reason, that these pitchers were able to work 400 innings in a season and win a phenomenal number of games.

There is no moment at which the wins totals suddenly drop, and therefore what you recognize as the "modern" record is entirely a function of where you draw the line. If you draw the line in

1880, the record for wins in a season is 60, set in 1884. If you draw the line in 1885, the record is 53, set in 1885. If you draw the line in 1890, the record is 43, set in 1891. If you draw the line in 1900, the record is 41, set in 1904. If you draw the line in 1905, the record is 40, set in 1908. If you draw the line in 1910, the record is 36, set in 1913. If you draw the line in 1915, the record is 33, set in 1916.

Jack Chesbro became the "record holder," many years after the fact, because they drew a line behind him. And there is no reason to draw a line right there. Nothing happened in 1900 to suddenly create a "modern" game or "modern" conditions for the pitcher.

The irony of the story is that Chesbro became—and that was unfair, too—the goat of the 1904 season. Chesbro threw a wild pitch on the last day of the season, by way of which the Highlanders lost the pennant. The press of the day, which had crucified Honus Wagner the year before for a poor World Series and would within a few years turn on Snodgrass, Merkle and Heine

Zimmerman, blew this up and made it the biggest wild pitch that ever was, so much so that as late as 1928 the *Reach Guide* said that John Miljus' wild pitch, which decided the final game of the 1927 World Series, was "the wild pitch of wild pitches, the only parallel for a game of importance being the time early in the century when Jack Chesbro released a wild pitch that transferred a pennant from the New York Highlanders . . . to Boston."

Chesbro died just a few years after that. It's a pity. Had he lived another five years, he would have seen himself become the "modern" record holder for wins in a season.

EDDIE CICOTTE

HALL OF FAME? No
DATA IN SECTION III? Yes
CAREER WINNING PERCENTAGE:
   .587
CAREER WINS ABOVE TEAM: 12.6
PERCENTAGE OF LEAGUE RUNS ALLOWED: 80%

Another crook, but a great pitcher, threw a knuckleball, spitball. It was his confession, later recanted, that broke the story.

STAN COVELESKI

HALL OF FAME? Yes
DATA IN SECTION III? Yes
CAREER WINNING PERCENTAGE:
   .606
CAREER WINS ABOVE TEAM: 18.9
PERCENTAGE OF LEAGUE RUNS ALLOWED: 79%

For some reason, his name was spelled "Coveleskie" for his entire career, and the "e" was dropped after he retired. I've never really understood that.

DIZZY DEAN

HALL OF FAME? Yes
DATA IN SECTION III? Yes
CAREER WINNING PERCENTAGE:
   .644
CAREER WINS ABOVE TEAM: 24.8
PERCENTAGE OF LEAGUE RUNS ALLOWED: 78%
COMPARABLE RECENT PITCHERS: Denny McLain

I have him ranked third in peak value; his career value is not among the thirty. Was 82–32 over a three-year period; never had a losing record in the majors or minors.

DON DRYSDALE

HALL OF FAME? Yes
DATA IN SECTION III? Yes
CAREER WINNING PERCENTAGE:
   .557
CAREER WINS ABOVE TEAM: 4.8
PERCENTAGE OF LEAGUE RUNS ALLOWED: 82%

I probably put more work into deciding where Drysdale ought to rate than I did for any other player. There are two negative points that have been made regarding him as a pitcher, and both have consid-

erable merit. Number one, his career winning percentage is only a tiny bit better than that of the teams for which he pitched. Number two, he pitched in a situation—in Dodger Stadium in the mid-sixties—which heavily favored the type of player that he was, hence his terrific earned run averages (2.84, 2.63, 2.18, 2.74, 2.15) and strikeout-to-walk ratios (246–72, 251–57, 237–68, 196–60, 155–56) do not have the value that one would ordinarily associate with such accomplishments—as is reflected in his won/lost records (15–14, 19–17, 18–16, 13–16, 14–12; same five seasons are used for all three lists).

The criticism of Drysdale for not winning started early. In a September 1962 issue of *Sport* magazine, Steve Gelman reflected that "going into the 1962 season, Drysdale had 1,004 big-league strikeouts and a career earned run average of 3.30. His won/lost record was only 79–64, however, and everybody had a theory about why it wasn't better." This was three years before he went 18–16 with an ERA barely over 2.00.

I have concluded that, while there is some validity to these concerns, it is more a case of Drysdale suffering from the nearness of Koufax. Drysdale's won/lost record, for his career, is fairly close to what it could be expected to be in view of the offense of his team and the number of runs that

he allowed—which is a way of saying that his earned run averages are a true indicator of his ability to win, and thus significant.

The first study that led me to this conclusion was a comparison of Drysdale's offensive support as projected from two sources. One was the offense of his team, and the other was his won/lost record. The theory is that if a pitcher doesn't win for one season with the consistency expected in view of his runs allowed and probable offensive support, then that's something that can happen; maybe they didn't score many runs for him. If it happens consistently over his career, then it's probably him.

In 1956, for example, Drysdale allowed 35 runs to score and was a .500 pitcher, with as many wins as losses. This being the case, his "effective offensive support" is 35 runs—that is, regardless of how many runs the Dodgers actually scored for him, he won with the frequency that would have been expected had they scored 35 (in this case, as a .500 pitcher, the calculation is obvious; in other cases, we figure his effective offensive support by use of his won/lost record, runs allowed and the Pythagorean method).

The Dodgers in 1956 scored 4.68 runs per nine innings, while Drysdale pitched 99 innings. That being the case, they would have been expected to score 51 runs in

those 99 innings—and thus, in this case, it is true that his won/lost performance was not what could be expected. The Dodgers should have scored about 51 runs in those 99 innings; he allowed only 35 runs. If you've got 51 runs to work with and you allow 35, you shouldn't be a .500 pitcher. His "run effectiveness" that year is quite low, 35/51 or 69 percent (1.00 would be a normal figure).

He had some other years when it was low. In 1960 he should have been supported by about 128 runs, yet he won with the frequency of a pitcher supported by only 97 runs—76 percent. In 1964 he should have been supported by about 134 runs, yet he won with the frequency of a pitcher supported by only 97 runs—73 percent.

But for his career as a whole, he didn't do that badly. In 1965 he went 23–12 despite allowing 3.30 runs per game for a team that scored only 3.75 per game—that's 1.26. In 1962, going 25–9 while allowing 3.49 runs per nine innings, he won 20 percent more games than could have been expected (run support 214/178, 1.20). For his career, his "effective run support" was 96 percent of his "probable run support"—that is, he won only 4 percent fewer games than should have been expected (1,499/1,554). Even for a good hitting pitcher, receiving offensive support that much below what was expected is something that could easily happen.

As a matter of curiosity, I also ran these checks for some other pitchers. Warren Spahn, who nobody ever said didn't win as much as he should, came out lower than Drysdale, at 95 percent (2,504/2,625). Given the number of runs he allowed to score and the offenses of his team, Walter Johnson made effective use of only 92 percent of the runs that he should have had to work with (2,400/2,599). The best pitchers that I found in this regard were Juan Marichal (1,857/1,712, 1.09), Lon Warneke (1,522/1,470, 1.04), Catfish Hunter (1,701/1,633, 1.04), and Sandy Koufax (1,139/1,088, 1.05).

That gets us to the core of the problem, for not only was Sandy Koufax allowing less than two runs per game to score against him, standing right there beside Drysdale, but he was actually *winning* more often than he ought to have for that team, even given those sensational ERAs. There's an assumption, you see, that if Koufax goes 19–5 with a 1.74 ERA, a pitcher on the same team who has a 2.18 ERA should do better than 18–16. But what's unfair about that is that Koufax, even with his 1.74 ERA, really shouldn't have been 19–5. He was 19–5 only because he won *all* the close games.

As we shall see. Another thing I did was to go through the scores of the games for

1963 and 1964, which are the seasons at the heart of the complaint, trying to see if there was a pattern of Drysdale's losing the close games or anything. What fans will often say about certain pitchers is that "the guy's a loser. You give him three runs, he allows four. You give him one, he'll give up two."

Drysdale in 1964 did have a poor record in one-run games (2–7). That's a little unfair, because he lost four games 1 to 0, but there you have it; he pitched well when the other guy—usually Juan Marichal, who used to pitch against Drysdale a lot—was pitching a shutout. He was 5–3 in one-run games in 1963, so for the two seasons as a whole he was 7–10 in one-run games. He was also 3–8 in games decided by two runs, so that's not an illustrious record for those two seasons, even though he was 27–15 in other games—but remember, those were seasons in which he was "underefficient," whereas in other seasons he was "overefficient." It must be assumed that he probably won most of his close games in 1962 and 1965.

But really, he won, even in those seasons, about as often as you could reasonably expect given his offensive support. Given five or more runs to work with, Drysdale's record over those two seasons was 23–1, which is pretty near perfect. Given four runs to work with, he was 7–5, which

is so-so. Given three runs to work with, he was 4–6, which is pretty decent. Given two runs to work with, he was 3–6, which is excellent. Here's the full chart:

Offensive Support	Wins	Losses	Pct.
0 runs	0	7	.00
1 run	1	8	.11
2 runs	3	6	.33
3 runs	4	6	.40
4 runs	7	5	.58
5 runs	8	0	1.00
6 runs	4	1	.80
7 runs	3	0	1.00
8 runs	1	0	1.00
9 runs	3	0	1.00
10 or more runs	4	0	1.00

He won all the games that he should have won, and he split the ones that he should have split.

But here's the thing. While I was doing Drysdale, I figured I might as well do Koufax, too. Read these figures carefully. Given five or more runs to work with, Koufax was 18–1, about the same as Drysdale. Given four to work with, he was 8–2. That's sensational—you get four runs and win 80 percent of the time, you're doing the job.

Given three runs to work with, Koufax was 9–0. Given just two runs to work with, Koufax won six and lost three. And given only one run to work with, Sandy Koufax won three out of four decisions.

Think about it. Over a two-year period, given one, two, or three runs to work with,

Sandy Koufax was 18–4. That's an unbelievable accomplishment.

So Drysdale couldn't match that. Well, who could? How many pitchers can win 80 percent of the time given five runs to work with, let alone two?

And the same applies to the fact that Drysdale was only a little bit better than the teams he pitched for. The "team" is one-fourth Sandy Koufax, and when it's not Sandy Koufax it's Don Sutton, or it's Johnny Podres, or it's Claude Osteen, or it's Ron Perranoski. How much better than those guys do you have to be to be a Hall of Famer?

Was Drysdale famous? He was one of the most famous pitchers of his time. Did he have an impact on pennant races? Many. Did he help his teams win? They won, anyway. It seems to me that if you define the essential characteristics of a Hall of Famer, he should 1) be famous, 2) have an impact on pennant races, and 3) help his teams win. I think Drysdale qualifies.

BOB FELLER

HALL OF FAME? Yes
DATA IN SECTION III? Yes
CAREER WINNING PERCENTAGE:
  .621
CAREER WINS ABOVE TEAM: 34.3
PERCENTAGE OF LEAGUE RUNS
ALLOWED: 78%
COMPARABLE RECENT PITCHERS:
Nolan Ryan

In rating him as high as I did, I'm a little bothered by two things—his comparative lack of control, and the fact that he never led the league in ERA (with the exception of the disputed 1940 championship). His ERAs are not real good, despite pitching his career in a good pitcher's park (career ERA was 2.84 at home, 3.71 on the road; normal home-park advantage is 20–30 points). I could be convinced, I think, that I have him rated way too high.

But he won. Even when he walked 208 men as a nineteen-year-old, he won (17–11). When he walked 194 men in 1941, he still won (25–13). And that was an off year; the two years before that he was 24–9 and 27–11.

WES FERRELL

HALL OF FAME? No
DATA IN SECTION III? Yes
CAREER WINNING PERCENTAGE:
  .601
CAREER WINS ABOVE TEAM: 35.0
PERCENTAGE OF LEAGUE RUNS
ALLOWED: 94%

To my mind, clearly the better of the Ferrell brothers. As a pitcher he went 21–10, 25–13, 22–12, 23–13, 25–14, and 20–15; as a hitter, I think he would be in the Hall of Fame had he become an outfielder, and he is the one pitcher I would say that about. *Daguerreotypes* doesn't show it, but after he was through he went down to the minors and turned in some years as a hitter. In the Bi-State League in 1941 he hit .332 with 20 homers, 70 RBI in 74 games, and

still threw well enough to have 11 outfield assists in 64 games. In 1942 he led the Virginia League in home runs (31) and batting average (.361). . . . A third brother, George Stuart Ferrell, was a minor league outfielder for twenty years, hitting .321 lifetime with power.

BOB GIBSON

HALL OF FAME? Yes
DATA IN SECTION III? Yes
CAREER WINNING PERCENTAGE:
  .591
CAREER WINS ABOVE TEAM: 31.7
PERCENTAGE OF LEAGUE RUNS
ALLOWED: 80%

BURLEIGH GRIMES

HALL OF FAME? Yes
DATA IN SECTION III? Yes
CAREER WINNING PERCENTAGE:
  .560
CAREER WINS ABOVE TEAM: 20.5
PERCENTAGE OF LEAGUE RUNS
ALLOWED: 99%
COMPARABLE RECENT PITCHERS:
Don Sutton

The leading winner of the twenties . . . the question arises as to whether it should be kept in mind that Grimes was allowed to use a weapon, the spitball, that other players of his time were not permitted, and as to how much we should discount his accomplishments because of that advantage. The answer, to my mind, is clear: not one little bit. Grimes took the advantages that he had and used them to win, just like Mordecai Brown learning to throw strange curve balls with a damaged hand, just like Joe

Morgan using his small size to his advantage to get on base 300 times a year. Do you penalize Walter Johnson because he could throw harder than anyone else of his time? That's what the game is about: you all start out unequal, and you use what you've been given to try to win.

CATFISH HUNTER

HALL OF FAME? Not Eligible
DATA IN SECTION III? Yes
CAREER WINNING PERCENTAGE:
.574
CAREER WINS ABOVE TEAM: 16.2
PERCENTAGE OF LEAGUE RUNS ALLOWED: 90%

Hunter and Jenkins are both members of what I call the Robin Roberts family of pitchers, who share the following defining characteristics:

1) Outstanding control.
2) Medium-range strikeouts.
3) Very high number of home runs allowed.
4) Ability to pitch a large number of innings without arm damage.

Among their nondefining characteristics, these pitchers are generally right-handers with good fastballs and just fair breaking pitches. They never get cute; they never try to hit the corner on a 1–0 or 2–1 pitch; they just bring it in there. Such a pitcher can win twenty games very consistently. The records of these three pitchers—Hunter, Jen-

kins and Roberts—are virtually interchangeable. There are many other peripheral characteristics that I suspect these pitchers share; for example, I suspect that they usually aren't as effective against outstanding opposition as a comparable power pitcher would be. I suspect that their career progression is fairly predictable, with a peak about age 25–27 and a long, slow slide downward.

FERGUSON JENKINS

HALL OF FAME? Not Eligible
DATA IN SECTION III? Yes
CAREER WINNING PERCENTAGE:
.560
CAREER WINS ABOVE TEAM: 30.4
PERCENTAGE OF LEAGUE RUNS ALLOWED: 90%

See comment above.

WALTER JOHNSON

HALL OF FAME? Yes
DATA IN SECTION III? Yes
CAREER WINNING PERCENTAGE:
.599
CAREER WINS ABOVE TEAM: 96.0
PERCENTAGE OF LEAGUE RUNS ALLOWED: 67%

On either count, I have some reservations about picking him as the greatest ever. The teams for which he pitched, while not good, were not as bad as many writers assume they were, and his career winning percentage, .599, is quite a ways from the range of Matty and Grove. But in his best years, he had records as good as anybody for teams that weren't as good as anybody's, and he had so many

good years that it would be strange indeed to pick him first in peak value but not in career.

To those of us growing up in the Midwest twenty years ago, Walter Johnson was exactly what Matty was to Easterners. He was not only a legendary pitcher, but the incarnation of the athletic virtues of decency, charm, and style. When I was fifteen years old, Christy Mathewson was just a name and a dimly understood record to me, like Bill Hutchison or Red Ruffing, but I could have told you twenty stories about Walter Johnson. When I first began to read more widely about baseball, I was quite astonished to learn that some people thought that Mathewson, not Johnson, was the hero of the era—and to a considerable extent, I still think the Mathewson aura has been distorted and overblown. If you studied the impact that these two players had on attendance when pitching, I would bet that you would find that Johnson was a bigger star than Mathewson, at the very least in the Western cities.

ADDIE JOSS

HALL OF FAME? Yes
DATA IN SECTION III? Yes
CAREER WINNING PERCENTAGE:
.623
CAREER WINS ABOVE TEAM: 28.0
PERCENTAGE OF LEAGUE RUNS ALLOWED: 74%

BOB LEMON

HALL OF FAME? Yes
DATA IN SECTION III? Yes
CAREER WINNING PERCENTAGE:
 .618
CAREER WINS ABOVE TEAM: 9.6
**PERCENTAGE OF LEAGUE RUNS
ALLOWED:** 84%

DUTCH LEONARD

HALL OF FAME? No
DATA IN SECTION III? No
CAREER WINNING PERCENTAGE:
 .513
CAREER WINS ABOVE TEAM: 27.7
**PERCENTAGE OF LEAGUE RUNS
ALLOWED:** About 81%

This is Dutch Leonard II, the one from the thirties and forties, not the guy with the 1.01 ERA. We'll call the other guy Dutch Leonard, the Accuser, and this one Dutch Leonard, the Knuckler.

Leonard is a classic unrecognized pitcher. He had no impressive skills, just a fluttering knuckleball to drive people crazy and a little slip pitch with a mediocre fastball to use when he was in danger of walking somebody. Pitching for wretched teams most of his career, he had little chance

of winning twenty. But once in a while he'd slip in a 17–12 record with a 62–92 team (1947) or an 18–13 record with a 70–84 team (1941).

TED LYONS

HALL OF FAME? Yes
DATA IN SECTION III? Yes
CAREER WINNING PERCENTAGE:
 .531
CAREER WINS ABOVE TEAM: 43.3
**PERCENTAGE OF LEAGUE RUNS
ALLOWED:** 89%

I still think the use of an older pitcher on a regular once-a-week basis makes all the sense in the world. If you've got a pitcher who knows enough to get by without beating himself, if you give him a couple of extra days to come back from the last outing and get ready for the next one, there's no reason he shouldn't be able to give you fifteen good outings out of twenty starts . . . the teams that Lyons pitched for were much worse than Walter Johnson's, over the course of his career.

JUAN MARICHAL

HALL OF FAME? Yes
DATA IN SECTION III? Yes
CAREER WINNING PERCENTAGE:
 .631
CAREER WINS ABOVE TEAM: 36.7
**PERCENTAGE OF LEAGUE RUNS
ALLOWED:** 84%

I know a lot of people are probably going to disagree with me for rating Marichal over Gibson, but I don't see how I could help it. If you compare their records from 1960 through 1969, it seems strange that anybody thought Gibson was better:

Year	Gibson	Marichal	
1960	3–6	6–2	+3½
1961	13–12	13–10	+1
1962	15–13	18–11	+2½
1963	18–9	25–8	+3½
1964	19–12	21–8	+3
1965	20–12	22–13	+ ½
1966	21–12	25–6	+5
1967	13–7	14–10	−1
1968	22–9	26–9	+2
1969	20–13	21–11	+1½

Of course I know about the World Series, which is probably the explanation; a few good games on national TV, sufficiently rehashed, made Gibson unbeatable. But what the hey; Marichal's career ERA in post-season play was 1.50 (two runs in twelve innings). . . . The most amazing thing about Marichal is that if you add together his 1963, '64, '66 and '68 seasons, his *overall* record is better than that of the four Cy Young Award winners. His record for those four years is 97–31; their record totals 94–32. Yet he won not a single award. . . .

I used to hear it said that Marichal would run up his record against the weak teams in the league, like Houston and New York, but didn't pitch much or well against the good teams. I thought I'd check that out, and it turns out to be one of those myths that develop, as they so often do, directly into the teeth of the facts. Marichal in fact pitched a disproportionate share of his games against the toughest teams in the league, and pitched extremely well against them, much better even than should be expected from his outstanding won/lost records. The Dodgers were his favorite drum. His lifetime record against LA was 37–18, which is more than 40 points better than his career winning percentage, plus he had about fifteen more decisions against the Dodgers than against any other team. And at that, his record against the Dodgers in years when they were under .500 was just 5–3; when they were over .500 it was 32–15. In the key years 1962–66 his records against the dread rival were 3–1, 4–2, 4–1, 3–1, and 3–0—a total of 17 wins, 5 losses.

A few other notes from that study . . . against the Cubs he was 23–8 lifetime, which was 13–5 (.722) in years when they were under .500, 10–3 (.769) when they were over .500 (also note that he had only 31 decisions lifetime against the Cubs, who were down and out for his prime years). Against

the Cardinals he did not pitch well, 18–21 lifetime, but even that breaks down as 16–16 when they were a winning team, and 2–5 when they were a sub-.500 ballclub. Against the Braves he was 21–17 lifetime—20–11 in years when the Braves were over .500, but just 1–6 in their years under .500. His record against Houston, which was always a loser, was just 20–12, a few points under his career winning percentage. The only bad team that he regularly defeated was the Mets, against whom he was 26–8. Marichal in fact was a pitcher who pitched his best baseball against the league's toughest teams.

CHRISTY MATHEWSON

HALL OF FAME? Yes
DATA IN SECTION III? Yes
CAREER WINNING PERCENTAGE: .665
CAREER WINS ABOVE TEAM: 59.5
PERCENTAGE OF LEAGUE RUNS ALLOWED: 75%

Mathewson is much admired as the Tom Seaver of his time, a polite, photogenic gentleman whose honesty was so respected that umpires reportedly would sometimes ask for his help on a close play. (And by the way, I believe that that probably did happen. With only one umpire working the game, as was true when Matty came into the league, the umpire was often out of position or blocked from the play. It

wouldn't have been unusual for a gentleman of his time to put the principle of honesty above that of team loyalty.)

Anyway, I chose him as the most admirable superstar of the time, and that's not what I was thinking of. What I admire Matty for is his guts. Matty was one of the very few men, and maybe the only one in baseball, who would say at the time that he thought the White Sox were throwing the 1919 World Series. When everybody else in baseball wanted to pretend that it wasn't happening, Mathewson was the one who wanted to bring it out in the open and get rid of it. He was the one who tried to have Hal Chase thrown out of baseball *before* the World Series was fixed. If there had been a couple more like him, it would never have reached the level it did.

CARL MAYS

HALL OF FAME? No
DATA IN SECTION III? Yes
CAREER WINNING PERCENTAGE: .623
CAREER WINS ABOVE TEAM: 16.2
PERCENTAGE OF LEAGUE RUNS ALLOWED: 81%

Great pitcher; started with Ruth on the Boston team of 1916–1918 and had a better record than Ruth for those years; later went 26–11, 27–9 for the Yankees, 20–9, 19–12 for Cincinnati. Threw underhand, real hard . . . one thing you might note is that he always hit a lot of batters, before and after the Chapman incident. His fourteen hit batsmen in 1917 led the American League, and with eleven in 1918 and ten in 1919 he missed leading the league each year by only one. His hitting Chapman is not the sole reason he is not in the Hall of Fame. He was involved in several other controversies, which I don't have time to recount here.

IRON MAN McGINNITY

HALL OF FAME? Yes
DATA IN SECTION III? Yes
CAREER WINNING PERCENTAGE:
 .630
CAREER WINS ABOVE TEAM: 27.7
PERCENTAGE OF LEAGUE RUNS ALLOWED: 89%

PHIL NIEKRO

HALL OF FAME? Not Eligible
DATA IN SECTION III? Yes
CAREER WINNING PERCENTAGE:
 .537
CAREER WINS ABOVE TEAM: 39.6
PERCENTAGE OF LEAGUE RUNS ALLOWED: 94%

JIM PALMER

HALL OF FAME? Not Eligible
DATA IN SECTION III? Yes
CAREER WINNING PERCENTAGE:
 .643
CAREER WINS ABOVE TEAM: 26.5
PERCENTAGE OF LEAGUE RUNS ALLOWED: 76%

I ranked him 22nd on peak value, which is too high if anything. A lot of people, like Don Newcombe, have had better years than Palmer's best season. But not many people ever had so many of them.

GAYLORD PERRY

HALL OF FAME? Not Eligible
DATA IN SECTION III? Yes
CAREER WINNING PERCENTAGE:
 .542
CAREER WINS ABOVE TEAM: 23.1
PERCENTAGE OF LEAGUE RUNS ALLOWED: 86%

Did you know that on September 22, 1975, Gaylord's and Jim Perry's career records were identical, 215–174. . . . Gaylord's book, *Me and the Spitter,* is pretty good for what it is, tells about the time one of the baseball scouts was trying to act country, feeding sugar to the Perry's mule, and the mule bit off his finger.

ROBIN ROBERTS

HALL OF FAME? Yes
DATA IN SECTION III? Yes
CAREER WINNING PERCENTAGE:
 .539
CAREER WINS ABOVE TEAM: 33.4
PERCENTAGE OF LEAGUE RUNS ALLOWED: 86%
COMPARABLE RECENT PITCHERS: Ferguson Jenkins, Catfish Hunter, Dennis Leonard

One of the puzzles of history is Robin Roberts' failure to win the Most Valuable Player award in 1952, when he went 28–7, leading the National League in wins by a margin of ten, which if memory serves me is an N.L. record. His 28 wins that year is the most in the National League in the last fifty years, and in those pre–Cy Young days, pitchers often won the MVP award—in fact, Bobby Shantz of the crosstown rival Philadelphia Athletics won the American League award that same year with a 24–7 mark. The N.L. vote went to Hank Sauer, a sluggardly slugger who led the league in RBI, at 121, and who, while a certified hitter, is often cited as one of the worst all-around players to win the award. Robin's team finished 87–67, ten games better than Sauer's team and eight games better than Shantz's, and on top of that he had a 6–0 record against the team the Phillies were trying to catch, the Dodgers.

A leader in the Major League Baseball Players Association in its days of ineffectuality, Roberts was one of the most respected players of his time. Curt Flood wrote that "in an era of social unrest, the manager might well be chosen among former players qualified by intellect to deal not only with God and the press but with the team. . . . To name only four, Jackie Robinson, Bill White, Robin Roberts and George Crowe are eminently capable of overcoming the benightedness and confusion that wreck so many clubs."

EDDIE ROMMEL

HALL OF FAME? No
DATA IN SECTION III? Yes
CAREER WINNING PERCENTAGE:
.590
CAREER WINS ABOVE TEAM: 32.8
**PERCENTAGE OF LEAGUE RUNS
ALLOWED:** 86%

Another knuckleballer, was 27–13 on a terrible team in 1922, and remained effective until the end of his major league career.

RED RUFFING

HALL OF FAME? Yes
DATA IN SECTION III? Yes
CAREER WINNING PERCENTAGE:
.548
CAREER WINS ABOVE TEAM: Minus 2.8
**PERCENTAGE OF LEAGUE RUNS
ALLOWED:** 89%

Probably the only pitcher I ranked whose career record was worse than that of the teams he pitched for. Notwithstanding that, he was pretty good in the late thirties, winning 21 of 28 starts in 1939, and won two-thirds of his starts over a four-year period (1936–1939). (Even Koufax didn't win two-thirds of his starts from 1963 to 1966.) Another intriguing puzzle is the degree of Ruffing's improvement in moving from Boston to New York in 1930. Common sense tells you that if you're a .300 pitcher on a .400 team, which is what Ruffing was in Boston, you're not going to be a .650 pitcher on a .600 team, are you? If you drag down the level of a bad pitching staff, how can you possibly raise the level of a good pitching staff? If you were to find that a pitcher who pitches .400 baseball on a .400 team tends to pitch .600 baseball on a .600 team, then what that would show is that the record of the pitcher was essentially merely an expression of the ability of the team—in other words, that baseball was 0% pitching. I have yet to hear an explanation that would explain an even more extreme case, such as Ruffing.

NOLAN RYAN

HALL OF FAME? Not Eligible
DATA IN SECTION III? Yes
CAREER WINNING PERCENTAGE:
.516
CAREER WINS ABOVE TEAM: 15.1
**PERCENTAGE OF LEAGUE RUNS
ALLOWED:** 87%

One of a kind.

TOM SEAVER

HALL OF FAME? Not Eligible
DATA IN SECTION III? Yes
CAREER WINNING PERCENTAGE:
.603
CAREER WINS ABOVE TEAM: 61.1
**PERCENTAGE OF LEAGUE RUNS
ALLOWED:** 77%

Has the same basic credentials as Walter Johnson, .600 winning percentage on sub-.500 teams for a period of many years, great ERAs with a little help from the parks in which he has pitched.

URBAN SHOCKER

HALL OF FAME? No
DATA IN SECTION III? Yes
CAREER WINNING PERCENTAGE:
.616
CAREER WINS ABOVE TEAM: 28.0
**PERCENTAGE OF LEAGUE RUNS
ALLOWED:** 84%

The vagaries of history . . . the best pitcher on the 1927 Yankees, in terms of either peak value or career value, was Urban Shocker, this fellow; the second-best pitcher on the team is hard to pick, but in terms of peak value it was probably Bob Shawkey (although Shawkey was finished by 1927). However, two other starters on the team, Herb Pennock and Waite Hoyt, are in the Hall of Fame.

Though his career was shortened by illness and stopped by death, Shocker was 71 games over .500 lifetime, and his career winning percentage (.616) and ERA (3.17) compare very favorably to Pennock (.598 and 3.61), Hoyt (.566 and 3.59), and Shawkey (.569 and 3.09). Shocker with the Yankees was "just" 19–11 and 18–6, but he won twenty games four straight years with the St. Louis Browns, reaching a peak of 27–12. By contrast, Pennock won twenty only twice, with his best effort being 23–11, and Hoyt won twenty only twice, with his best being 23–7. (Shawkey, on the other hand, also won twenty four times, his best being 23–14.)

Also, whereas Pennock and

Hoyt won twenty only with the awesome Yankee lineups behind them, Shocker had two of his 20-win seasons with losing teams, and another with a team that was only over .500 because of his own efforts (Shawkey's best year was also with a less outstanding Yankee team in 1916).

Winning 27 games with a bad team may convince an analyst that you're a great pitcher, but winning 23 games with a great team will make you more famous. In truth, probably none of the four should be in there. It's the old question of standards: Tommy John was clearly a better pitcher than any member of the 1927 Yankees. Is that your idea of what a Hall of Famer is?

But since two of them are, why is it the wrong two? Three things: their careers were longer, their careers were later, and you could keep their names straight. Shocker and Shawkey both pulled up just short of 200 wins lifetime; Pennock and Hoyt got on the good side of it (although,

since Hoyt had 49 more wins than Shocker and 65 more losses, this is an addition of dubious value). Also, S & S were both done by 1927 (though Shocker won 18 games that year), so that by the time the Hall of Fame opened ten years later and finished inducting all of the Ruths and Mathewsons and such like a few years after that, they had been shoved back into the huddled masses with Home Run Baker and Tinkers to Evers to Chance. In terms of career value, Shawkey probably was not as good as Hoyt or Pennock, and by 1948 Shocker had been dead for twenty years. After that, the only time anybody gave him a thought was when they thought he was Shawkey.

DON SUTTON

HALL OF FAME? Not Eligible
DATA IN SECTION III? No
CAREER WINNING PERCENTAGE:
.562
CAREER WINS ABOVE TEAM:
Unknown
PERCENTAGE OF LEAGUE RUNS ALLOWED: Unknown

DAZZY VANCE

HALL OF FAME? Yes
DATA IN SECTION III? Yes
CAREER WINNING PERCENTAGE:
.585
CAREER WINS ABOVE TEAM: 36.3
PERCENTAGE OF LEAGUE RUNS ALLOWED: 81%
COMPARABLE RECENT PITCHERS:
Mike Scott

A weird career; became an awesome power pitcher in his thirties after struggling with his control for what should have been his best years. Few, if any, pitchers had greater careers after the age of thirty.

ED WALSH

HALL OF FAME? Yes
DATA IN SECTION III? Yes
CAREER WINNING PERCENTAGE:
.607
CAREER WINS ABOVE TEAM: 31.2
PERCENTAGE OF LEAGUE RUNS ALLOWED: 71%

With his durability and willingness to start or relieve, this very intelligent man was often said at the time to be the most valuable player in baseball.

LON WARNEKE

HALL OF FAME? No
DATA IN SECTION III? No
CAREER WINNING PERCENTAGE:
.615
CAREER WINS ABOVE TEAM: 17.5
PERCENTAGE OF LEAGUE RUNS ALLOWED: Approximately 84%

Turned in ten straight good-to-outstanding seasons in the thirties and forties . . . later spent seven years as a National League umpire.

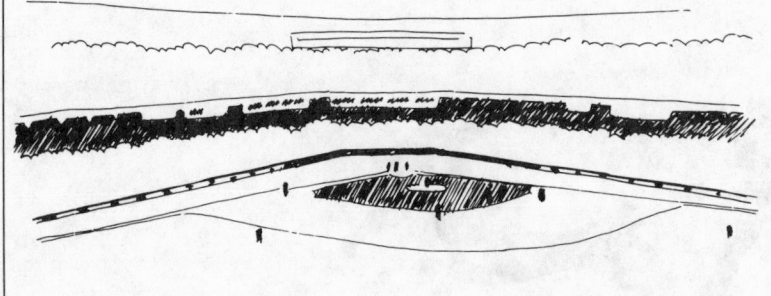

SMOKEY JOE WOOD

HALL OF FAME? No
DATA IN SECTION III? No
CAREER WINNING PERCENTAGE: .671
CAREER WINS ABOVE TEAM: Unknown
PERCENTAGE OF LEAGUE RUNS ALLOWED: Unknown

If what was meant by "peak value" was only the player's greatest season, Wood would rank even higher than he does. That isn't exactly it. Peak value refers to the highest level of ability that is clearly established, which would usually mean the player's second- or third-best year, unless his best years were widely scattered. In the case of Wood, that "clearly established level" is harder to see than in almost any other; he had no two seasons that are about the same. But if you add up 1911, 1912 and 1915, you've got 72 wins, 27 losses and an ERA well below 2.00, and that has to rank up there someplace.

EARLY WYNN

HALL OF FAME? Yes
DATA IN SECTION III? Yes
CAREER WINNING PERCENTAGE: .551
CAREER WINS ABOVE TEAM: 5.5
PERCENTAGE OF LEAGUE RUNS ALLOWED: 91%

CY YOUNG

HALL OF FAME? Yes
DATA IN SECTION III? Yes
CAREER WINNING PERCENTAGE: .620
CAREER WINS ABOVE TEAM: 103.1
PERCENTAGE OF LEAGUE RUNS ALLOWED: 78%

Young is basically a right-handed, 1890–1911 version of Warren Spahn. He was never generally accepted as the greatest pitcher in baseball at any time; there was always Hutchison or Rusie or McGinnity or Mathewson or somebody. But, like Spahn, he was right there among the best for roughly three generations of competitors. He threw hard and didn't beat himself; he had by far the best control records of his time, leading the majors in fewest walks per nine innings many times, beginning in 1893 and not ending until 1910.

LEFT-HANDED STARTERS

The ten greatest left-handed pitchers of all time:

PEAK VALUE	CAREER VALUE
1. Lefty Grove	1. Lefty Grove
2. Sandy Koufax	2. Warren Spahn
3. Carl Hubbell	3. Steve Carlton
4. Steve Carlton	4. Carl Hubbell
5. Vida Blue	5. Whitey Ford
6. Ron Guidry	6. Eddie Plank
7. Lefty Gomez	7. Sandy Koufax
8. Whitey Ford	8. Jim Kaat
9. Hal Newhouser	9. Tommy John
10. Rube Waddell	10. Billy Pierce

After the first publication of this book, several readers wrote to me expressing surprise that Warren Spahn was not among the list of the greatest ever in peak value. My response to this is that if you could even imagine that Warren Spahn should be on the list of the greatest ever in terms of peak value, then you don't understand the concept of peak value. Spahn was certainly a very great pitcher—but he quite certainly was not the domineering force, even in his best years, that pitchers like Hal Newhouser and Rube Waddell were. He would not be eleventh on the list, nor even twentieth. His peak value was roughly the same as that of Tommy John or Frank Tanana —a very good pitcher, but nothing more.

But how can you say that, these readers implore, when Spahn had thirteen seasons that were all but indistinguishable from his best? The answer is that that is simply irrelevant to the issue of peak value. Peak value is like height; career value is like weight. If a guy is 6'3" and weighs 450 pounds, that doesn't make him taller than another guy who is 6'4" and weighs only 180. Warren Spahn is the guy who was 6'3" and weighed 450—one of the "heaviest" players ever, certainly—but still not one of the tallest. It wouldn't matter if he had had that best season a hundred times. The breadth of his career is enormous—but the height is not.

STEVE CARLTON

HALL OF FAME? Not Eligible
DATA IN SECTION III? Yes
CAREER WINNING PERCENTAGE: .575
CAREER WINS ABOVE TEAM: 35.4
PERCENTAGE OF LEAGUE RUNS ALLOWED: 89%

WHITEY FORD

HALL OF FAME? Yes
DATA IN SECTION III? Yes
CAREER WINNING PERCENTAGE: .690
CAREER WINS ABOVE TEAM: 35.1
PERCENTAGE OF LEAGUE RUNS ALLOWED: 73%

When won/lost records are compared to the won/lost record of the pitcher's team, the most difficult thing that it is possible to do is to rise above the level of a great team. Few pitchers have ever done that consistently. Lefty Gomez, though a Hall of Famer, basically just matched the level of his team. Johnson and Young towered above their teams, but they were not very good teams. Only a few, including Grove, Mathewson, and Whitey Ford, were able to rise thirty or forty games above the level of a great team.

LEFTY GOMEZ

HALL OF FAME? Yes
DATA IN SECTION III? Yes
CAREER WINNING PERCENTAGE: .649
CAREER WINS ABOVE TEAM: 3.9
PERCENTAGE OF LEAGUE RUNS ALLOWED: 78%

One of my favorite baseball stories is about the time Lefty Gomez expressed concern to Joe DiMaggio, as a rookie center fielder, about how shallow he was playing some of the opposition hitters, particularly Greenberg. "Don't worry," said DiMaggio, "I'm going to make them forget Tris Speaker." Next time up Greenberg drove a triple to dead center field. "Roomie," said Gomez, "you keep playing Greenberg shallow and you're going to make them forget Lefty Gomez."

Like Carlton, Gomez was not particularly consistent; he mixed ordinary years and even rather poor years with years that are among the greatest ever. After going 26–5 with a 2.33 ERA in 1934 (the league ERA was 4.50) he dropped to 12–15 in 1935, but came back to post another 2.33 ERA in 1937, when the league ERA was even higher. Unlike Carlton, Gomez's career was not very long. Between 1931 and 1938, he had four twenty-victory seasons and two other outstanding years. His won/lost records got a lot of help from the teams that he played with, and his ERAs got a lot of help from Yankee Stadium, where his ca-

reer ERA was 2.89 (as opposed to 3.88 on the road).

But he was 87 games over .500 lifetime, probably a greater margin than your average Hall of Famer. He was 6–0 in World Series play. He was the greatest All-Star game pitcher of his time, and is the only pitcher to win three All-Star games. In 1932, when the Yankees ended the three-year reign of the Philadelphia Athletics, Gomez beat the runner-up Athletics seven times. At a guess, that may be the only time in history that any pitcher ever beat the team which his team *had* to beat seven times in a season. He also beat them three times in his first full season, 1931, when the A's lost only 45 games. On that basis, he was not only a great pitcher but, like Ford, one of the few pitchers in history who can be shown by a variety of evidence to have been a big-game pitcher.

LEFTY GROVE

HALL OF FAME? Yes
DATA IN SECTION III? Yes
CAREER WINNING PERCENTAGE: .680
CAREER WINS ABOVE TEAM: 52.6
PERCENTAGE OF LEAGUE RUNS ALLOWED: 71%
COMPARABLE RECENT PITCHERS: Koufax

The greatest pitcher of all time, period. The one best indicator of a pitcher's ability is his ERA, and Lefty Grove led his leagues in earned run average nine times. That, to me, is the most impressive credential claimed by any major league pitcher. No one else approaches it. These are the leaders in most times leading the league in ERA:

Grove 9
Koufax 5
Johnson 5
Mathewson 5
Alexander 5
Spahn 3
Seaver 3
Vance 3
Hubbell 3

Grove did this despite pitching his entire career in hitters' parks. As a thirty-eight-year-old left-hander in Fenway Park, he had won 14 games by July 14 (read that sentence carefully) when an injury stopped him for the year; he wound up the season 14–4 with a league-leading 3.07 ERA. And he was still striking people out—99 in 164 innings in a league where people didn't strike out much. Though nagged ever after by arm injuries, he still came back the next year to go 15–4, and led the league again in ERA, 2.54, as a thirty-nine-year-old left-hander in Fenway Park. Whereas an average pitcher has an ERA 20–30 points lower at home, Grove's career ERA was 3.09 at home, 3.07 on the road.

The second-best indicator of a pitcher's ability is his winning percentage. Guess what? Grove also led the league in that more times than anyone

else. The leaders from this century:

Grove 5
Ford 3
Chesbro 3
Reulbach 3

His career winning percentage, .680, is the highest among pitchers who had long careers, with only Christy Mathewson being close. Pitchers like Dean and Koufax have gotten into the Hall of Fame with winning percentages 25 to 40 points lower on careers little more than half as long.

How, then, can anyone doubt that he was the greatest ever? What argument, if any, could be presented against the proposition that Lefty Grove was the greatest pitcher who ever lived? He won "only" 300 games? Apart from the inherent absurdity of saying that someone won "only" 300 games, there are two problems. Cy Young and Walter Johnson were able to pitch a great many more innings in a season than was Grove because of one essential characteristic of their time: no home runs. Because the home run was so rare, a pitcher in the dead-ball era could afford to throw 70, 75 MPH fastballs most of the time, and "save" his good stuff for those moments when there was a runner on base and thus a danger of a run being scored.

This "pacing" or "saving" was a major part of pitching

science in the dead-ball era, and I could show you a hundred quotes from the time that tell about pitchers doing it. Christy Mathewson in *Pitching in a Pinch* reflected on a game early in his career that he lost by surrendering four runs in the ninth inning. After the game George Davis, his manager, told him, "Never mind, Matty. It was worth it. The game ought to teach you not to pitch your head off when you don't need to." Matty added that "Many spectators wonder why a pitcher does not work as hard as he can all through the game, instead of just in the pinches." Forty years later, Ty Cobb struck up a friendship with a high school boy who turned out to be a marginal major league pitcher named Barry Latman. He wrote Latman several letters, giving him advice about the game, and one thing he wrote about was this need to "save your stuff" for the key moments of the game.

After 1920, there was the danger of a run being scored *at any moment,* and the amount that any pitcher could pitch was thereby reduced. Many pitchers prior to that time won more than 300 games; since then, only Spahn and now Carlton have moved significantly beyond that point.

But besides that, what Grove's "career" record doesn't show is that he was a great pitcher—and I mean a great pitcher—for five years before he reached the majors. Is Grove to be deprived of the distinction of being the greatest ever because Jack Dunn wanted to keep him at Baltimore? What if Dunn had *never* sold him to Philadelphia. Would he just be nothing, then? Sure, Grove had to make some adjustments once he reached the major league level, but he had gone as far as he could go in the minors, and he obviously had the ability to make any adjustments that he needed. If you're comparing career length, Grove in my book has to be given some significant credit for those five years that he was a great pitcher before he came to the majors. That puts him around 370, 380 wins —and that's as impressive a win total, in its own time, as anyone ever had.

CARL HUBBELL

HALL OF FAME? Yes
DATA IN SECTION III? Yes
CAREER WINNING PERCENTAGE:
 .622
CAREER WINS ABOVE TEAM: 31.8
PERCENTAGE OF LEAGUE RUNS
ALLOWED: 76%

Another way to see how good Grove was is to compare him to Hubbell. Now, Hubbell was a great, great pitcher on a great team. He won two Most Valuable Player awards, a feat matched by only one other pitcher (Newhouser, and that during the war). Their careers match up very nicely; Grove was born in 1900 and was active 1925–41, while Hubbell

was born in 1903 and was active 1928–43, so if you start in the rookie season of each you are comparing pitchers at the same age. Grove had a better record almost every year, as you can see in the chart at right. That's exactly how good Lefty Grove was. He was thirty games better than great.

Year	Pitcher	W	L	Pct.	GB
1928	HUBBELL	10	6	.625	..
1925	Grove	10	13	.435	3½
1929	HUBBELL	18	11	.621	..
1926	Grove	13	13	.500	3½
1927	GROVE	20	12	.625	..
1930	Hubbell	17	12	.586	1½
1928	GROVE	24	8	.750	..
1931	Hubbell	14	12	.538	7
1929	GROVE	20	6	.769	..
1932	Hubbell	18	11	.621	3½
1930	GROVE	28	5	.848	..
1933	Hubbell	23	12	.657	6
1931	GROVE	31	4	.886	..
1934	Hubbell	21	12	.636	9
1932	GROVE	25	10	.714	..
1935	Hubbell	23	12	.657	2
1936	HUBBELL	26	6	.839	..
1933	Grove	24	8	.750	2
1937	HUBBELL	22	8	.733	..
1934	Grove	8	8	.500	7
1935	GROVE	20	12	.625	..
1938	Hubbell	13	10	.565	2½
1936	GROVE	17	12	.586	..
1939	Hubbell	11	9	.550	1½
1937	GROVE	17	9	.654	..
1940	Hubbell	11	12	.478	4½
1938	GROVE	14	4	.778	..
1941	Hubbell	11	9	.550	4
1939	GROVE	15	4	.789	..
1942	Hubbell	11	8	.579	4
1940	GROVE	7	6	.538	..
1943	Hubbell	4	4	.500	½
1941	Grove	7	7	.500	
GROVE		300	141	.680	...
Hubbell		253	154	.622	30

TOMMY JOHN

HALL OF FAME? Not Eligible
DATA IN SECTION III? Yes
CAREER WINNING PERCENTAGE:
 .562
CAREER WINS ABOVE TEAM: 17.3
PERCENTAGE OF LEAGUE RUNS
ALLOWED: 95%

I made an off-the-cuff remark that he was better than Pennock. The major indicators by which he was better than Pennock are career wins, earned run average, number of times won twenty games, career wins above team and number of categories in which led league.

JIM KAAT

HALL OF FAME? Not Eligible
DATA IN SECTION III? Yes
CAREER WINNING PERCENTAGE:
 .544
CAREER WINS ABOVE TEAM: 7.2
PERCENTAGE OF LEAGUE RUNS
ALLOWED: 99%

SANDY KOUFAX

HALL OF FAME? Yes
DATA IN SECTION III? Yes
CAREER WINNING PERCENTAGE:
 .655
CAREER WINS ABOVE TEAM: 27.8
PERCENTAGE OF LEAGUE RUNS
ALLOWED: 73%

The choice between Koufax and Grove as the greatest in terms of peak value is not an absolutely clear decision. You're talking about two men who threw extremely hard, had big breaking pitches, had good control and knew what they were doing on the mound. The first two things to look at in comparing pitchers are won/lost records and

ERA. The two are a split decision. Grove's 59–9 record over a two-year period is easily better than Koufax's best, as is his 79–15 record over a three-year period and his 103–23 record (or 108–27) over a four-year period. After that there is no comparison. Still, Grove did pitch for great hitting teams, and while the Dodgers of the sixties were championship teams, they were teams that scratched for runs and won the pennant with pitching and defense.

Grove's 1931 ERA of 2.06 is less than half the American League norm that year, a feat that Koufax matched in '64 and '66. Including earned and unearned runs, Koufax allowed runs at a rate 49% of league in 1964, 50% in 1966, and 52% in 1963. Grove's best were 51% in 1931, 56% in 1937 and 57% in 1939. However, whereas Koufax worked in a park that had a big built-up mound and distant fences, Grove worked his career in hitters' parks. If adjustments were made for this, I'm not sure who would come out ahead.

Well, let's do some research . . . I got out the guides covering the 1965 and 1966 seasons,

and added up the scores of games played in Dodger Stadium. This is the data:

RUNS SCORED

Dodgers at Home, 1965	268
Dodgers on Road, 1965	340
Dodger Opponents in L.A., 1965	218
Dodger Opponents on road, 1965	303
Dodgers at Home, 1966	286
Dodgers on Road, 1966	320
Dodger Opponents in L.A., 1966	220
Dodger Opponents on road, 1966	270

The consistency of the data seems to leave little doubt that the Dodger pitchers during this time benefited (and the Dodger hitters suffered) from a park illusion of a fairly massive nature, probably larger than any similar influence in baseball today. The Dodgers' reputation as a light-hitting team with great pitching was, to a considerable extent, the product of a statistical illusion created by Dodger Stadium, which seems to have reduced offensive production by about 21%. I will also note that there were only 67 home runs hit in Los Angeles in 1965, the fewest of any park in baseball except the Astrodome.

With a park adjustment, then, Koufax's best runs allowed rates would be about .55 or .56 of league, rather than .49 or .50. (I figure that this way: Sandy pitched half of his games on the road, where the park factor was 1.00, and

half in Los Angeles, where it was .79; that's a total of 1.79. His best two runs allowed rates were .49 and .50, which is a total of .99. We can estimate his park-adjusted share of league runs allowed, then, as .99/1.79, which is .553.)

The *Reach Guide* for 1931 does not carry home-park scores, so we will have to substitute the 1932 and 1933 seasons, for which it does. Fortunately, all four of these teams played the same number of home games as road games, so we don't have to worry about that:

RUNS SCORED

Athletics at Home, 1932	572
Athletics on Road, 1932	409
A's Opponents in Philadelphia, 1932	405
A's Opponents on Road, 1932	347
Athletics at Home, 1933	414
Athletics on Road, 1933	461
A's Opponents in Philadelphia, 1933	387
A's Opponents on Road, 1933	466

Here the data is more confusing. It seems to have been a fabulous hitter's park in 1932, but a poor hitter's park in 1933, which happens sometimes—it takes more than a season for the data to stabilize. Anyway, taking it together, it would seem to be a park that inflated offenses by about 5%. A note in the 1934 guide says that in the 1933 season, the one in which Shibe Park seemed to favor the pitcher, more home runs were hit there (132) than in any other major league park. Anyway, using the same method applied to Koufax, Grove's rate of runs allowed would be about 52% of league.

That would put Grove ahead on both counts. Both pitchers had fabulous strike-out-to-walk ratios; Grove's, in the context of their time, are better. Grove had strikeout-to-walk ratios between 3–1 and 4–1 when the average pitcher in the league was less than even; Koufax was in the area of 4–1 or 5–1 in the time of Dick Allen and Donn Clendenon, when the league average was more than 2–1.

Of course, as pointed out in the Drysdale comment, Koufax was actually *better* than his runs allowed rates. Both pitchers were deadly in the World Series, Koufax being just 4–3 but with an 0.95 ERA and 61 strikeouts, 11 walks in 57 innings, while Grove was 4–2 with a 1.75 ERA, 36 strike-outs and only 6 walks in 51 innings. Grove was a pretty decent hitter, hitting 15 home runs in his career; Koufax was not a hitter, but was a much better basketball player than Henry Aaron. There really isn't a dime's worth of difference between them in terms of peak performance, but my nickel goes to Grove.

HAL NEWHOUSER
HALL OF FAME? No
DATA IN SECTION III? Yes
CAREER WINNING PERCENTAGE: .580
CAREER WINS ABOVE TEAM: 18.2
PERCENTAGE OF LEAGUE RUNS ALLOWED: 81%

I cut him quite a bit because of the calibre of competition that he was facing, but his performance in 1946 and 1948 would put one through some fairly hefty contortions to show that he was not a worthy pitcher.

BILLY PIERCE
HALL OF FAME? No
DATA IN SECTION III? Yes
CAREER WINNING PERCENTAGE: .555
CAREER WINS ABOVE TEAM: 5.2
PERCENTAGE OF LEAGUE RUNS ALLOWED: 82%

GETTYSBURG EDDIE PLANK
HALL OF FAME? Yes
DATA IN SECTION III? Yes
CAREER WINNING PERCENTAGE: .630
CAREER WINS ABOVE TEAM: 33.4
PERCENTAGE OF LEAGUE RUNS ALLOWED: 78%
COMPARABLE RECENT PITCHERS: Spahn

A small man with a face of many freckles (the Macmillan says he was 5′11½″, but I doubt that he was), Plank was a noted "dawdler" on the mound, used to try the patience of the press by his slow pace as a workman. His stuff was not great, and for most of his career he was not Connie Mack's first choice to pitch a

big game. But he had the ability to "puzzle" the hitters, keep them off stride, which he did for the better part of two decades, at eighteen to twenty-six wins a year.

WARREN SPAHN
HALL OF FAME? Yes
DATA IN SECTION III? Yes
CAREER WINNING PERCENTAGE: .597
CAREER WINS ABOVE TEAM: 43.2
PERCENTAGE OF LEAGUE RUNS ALLOWED: 80%

The bottom four pitchers on the list of the greatest career left-handers are Sandy Koufax, Jim Kaat, Tommy John, and Billy Pierce. Warren Spahn won twenty games more times than all four of them combined. Until 1983, Warren Spahn had won twenty games in a season as many times as all of the left-handed pitchers in the history of the New York Yankees combined, including Herb Pennock, Lefty Gomez, Ed Lopat, Whitey Ford, Fritz Peterson, Ron Guidry and Tommy John. Guidry's 1983 twenty-victory season put them as a group ahead of Spahn, 14–13. Spahn had as many twenty-victory seasons as Jim Palmer and Tom Seaver, combined. His career won-lost record is about the same as Don Drysdale's and Sandy Koufax's—added together. And there are many nine-man pitching staffs which, added together, will not approach his career win total.

He did not do this on some

dusty shelf of forgotten history, in circumstances of reduced strain and imbalanced teams. He went head-to-head with Musial, Mays, Snider, Koufax; there were players still active until the mid-eighties who played against him. Before he started this work, he had to fight a war; he was twenty-five years old before he won a major league game.

RUBE WADDELL

HALL OF FAME? Yes
DATA IN SECTION III? Yes
CAREER WINNING PERCENTAGE:
.576
CAREER WINS ABOVE TEAM: 16.2
PERCENTAGE OF LEAGUE RUNS ALLOWED: 77%

A big, strong man/child with a blazing left-handed fastball and the best curve of his day, Rube Waddell would have been as great a pitcher as Walter Johnson if only he had had the sense God give a rabbit. It is sad to realize that Rube Waddell could not exist today, that in the eyes of modern men he would be given an appropriate label and properly taken care of, his competition limited to heaving a rubber-tipped javelin in the Special Olympics. Was Rube Waddell what you would call "retarded"? Well, I don't know, but Sam Crawford recalled in *The Glory of Their Times* that manager Hughie Jennings "used to go to the dime store and buy little toys, like rubber snakes. . . . He'd go to the first-base coaches box and set them down on the grass and yell, 'Hey, Rube, look!' " Mathewson told a story about Fred Clarke of Pittsburgh throwing Waddell completely off his game by inviting him out to his ranch in Kansas to do some hunting after the season. He had a bird dog that he offered to give Waddell if the dog took a liking to him, and Waddell got to thinking about the dog and forgot about the ball game. He didn't draw a regular salary because he didn't know what to do with it; he'd just go to the manager and get $5 or $10 as he needed it. One manager said if you gave him $25 you might not see him again for a week. He was irresistibly attracted to fire engines, and on the day that he was pitching a teammate or more was always assigned to make sure he got to the ballpark all right, and didn't go off chasing any fire engines. This just really does not sound to me like anybody who could fit into the commercial mold of the modern ballplayer.

Perhaps it was just an emotional problem, and could be controlled with the appropriate drugs. In the cruder times of 1900, Waddell's life was probably painful and his demise was quick, as there were no institutions to shelter him from the ends of his own actions. But he lived a real life, like anybody else's only with more adventure. We are not so adventurous anymore.

Honorable mention: Johnny Antonelli, Harry Brecheen, Wilbur Cooper, Mike Cuellar, Noodles Hahn, Ken Holtzman, Jerry Koosman, Mickey Lolich, Ed Lopat, Rube Marquard, Dave McNally, Sam McDowell, Mel Parnell, Herb Pennock, Howie Pollet, Eppa Rixey, Preacher Roe, Babe Ruth, Curt Simmons, Hippo Vaughn, Doc White, Earl Whitehill.

RELIEF PITCHERS

Relief pitching is a recent enough development that there should be no need to introduce you to the men or their credentials, since, with a couple of possible exceptions, they all pitched in the last few years. The greatest relief pitchers, as I see them:

PEAK VALUE	CAREER VALUE
1. Bruce Sutter	1. Rollie Fingers
2. Goose Gossage	2. Hoyt Wilhelm
3. Dan Quisenberry	3. Goose Gossage
4. Dick Radatz	4. Bruce Sutter
5. Rollie Fingers	5. Elroy Face

The 100 Greatest Players of This Century

■ Not everyone who has pondered or studied the issue has drawn the conclusion that the greatest player who ever lived was Babe Ruth; not everyone, but certainly most. There is an attraction, that being so, to the insistence that it was someone else. That insistence dovetails nicely on many occasions with the desire to make some particular point. Maury Allen chooses Willie Mays as the greatest player of the century because he wishes to make the point that the conditions of the game were not as tough in Babe Ruth's time as in Willie's. He puts Ruth behind Mays and Aaron, and explains that "The modern factors . . . have made the game more difficult. [Ruth's] feats were heroic. So were theirs. They simply did them under tougher conditions." Other people have argued that Cobb was greater than Ruth because the things that Cobb did—hitting line drives, stealing bases, etc.—are more important than the things that Babe Ruth did. Many of the old-timers of his day would not recognize Ruth as the greatest ever, but held to the position, as old-timers are wont, that it was Buck Ewing, and then, too, others have held out for Walter Johnson or Cy Young because baseball is 75% pitching.

The problem is that if one does not wish to assert some particular point, but one wishes only to identify the greatest player who ever lived, one is drawn almost unavoidably to the conclusion that it was George Ruth. He was a greater hitter than anyone with the possible exception of Williams, and a better fielder, baserunner and pitcher than Williams. I think it is safe to say that, of the men who saw both play, probably 80% felt that Ruth was a better defensive player than Ty Cobb, not even counting the "defensive" value of his pitching. I haven't any idea whether baseball was tougher in the fifties than it was in the twenties, and to tell you the truth, I seriously doubt that Maury Allen has any idea, either. I don't know how you could know unless you played in both eras, and nobody did. The assertion that hitting singles and doubles and stealing bases is more valuable than hitting home runs and drawing walks is provably false, and the assumption that baseball is 75% pitching is silly. If it was true, Babe Ruth, who was a great pitcher, would not have become an outfielder. If one wishes not to enlist the selection of the number one man in the cause of one argument or another, but only to make a selection that accommodates the evidence, one must make Babe Ruth that selection.

My rules for selecting the greatest ever call for an even blend of eras and positions. I've tried, in rating players at each position, to treat each era of the game's history since 1900 with equal respect, with a bias neither toward the past nor the present, neither toward the low-average era of the dead-ball days, nor the pretty averages of the twenties and thirties, the era from which so many players have been so badly overrated. In putting those other twelve lists together into one, I followed three basic rules:

1) Each group of players should consist of twelve to fourteen members, one for each position. In other words, one "team" should be completed before the next is begun.

2) Each "team" should consist of eight position players and four starting pitchers, which should include at least one left-handed pitcher and at least one right-handed pitcher. The relievers and multiposition stars can be mixed in as seems appropriate.

3) Don't get too carried away about the other two rules. Nobody makes up rules for the Almighty. If he chooses to make three right fielders who are greater than any catcher, you can't tell him not to.

The greatest players of this century are:

PEAK VALUE	CAREER VALUE
1. Babe Ruth	1. Babe Ruth
2. Honus Wagner	2. Honus Wagner
3. Mickey Mantle	3. Lefty Grove
4. Lefty Grove	4. Stan Musial
5. Sandy Koufax	5. Hank Aaron
6. Lou Gehrig	6. Ty Cobb
7. Walter Johnson	7. Lou Gehrig
8. Joe Morgan	8. Willie Mays
9. Stan Musial	9. Ted Williams
10. Ted Williams	10. Warren Spahn
11. Willie Mays	11. Joe DiMaggio
12. Christy Mathewson	12. Walter Johnson
13. Joe DiMaggio	13. Mike Schmidt
14. Ty Cobb	14. Cy Young
15. Roy Campanella	15. Eddie Collins
16. Mike Schmidt	16. Yogi Berra
17. Ernie Banks	17. Christy Mathewson
18. Jimmie Foxx	18. Pete Rose
19. Jackie Robinson	19. Tris Speaker
20. Mickey Cochrane	20. Mickey Mantle
21. Dizzy Dean	21. Jimmie Foxx
22. Tris Speaker	22. Joe Morgan
23. Denny McLain	23. Frank Robinson
24. Ralph Kiner	24. Tom Seaver
25. Bruce Sutter	25. Eddie Mathews
26. Johnny Bench	26. Grover Cleveland Alexander
27. Carl Hubbell	27. Luke Appling
28. George Sisler	28. Johnny Bench

PEAK VALUE	CAREER VALUE
29. Bob Feller	29. Bob Feller
30. Rogers Hornsby	30. Mel Ott
31. Juan Marichal	31. Willie McCovey
32. George Brett	32. Steve Carlton
33. Hank Aaron	33. Hank Greenberg
34. Tom Seaver	34. Jim Palmer
35. Frank Robinson	35. Brooks Robinson
36. Arky Vaughan	36. Nap Lajoie
37. Dazzy Vance	37. Carl Hubbell
38. Eddie Mathews	38. Ernie Banks
39. Mel Ott	39. Juan Marichal
40. Steve Carlton	40. Carl Yastrzemski
41. Grover Cleveland Alexander	41. Harmon Killebrew
42. Yogi Berra	42. Mickey Cochrane
43. Goose Gossage	43. Bob Gibson
44. Carl Yastrzemski	44. Rollie Fingers
45. Vida Blue	45. Joe Cronin
46. Dale Murphy	46. Rogers Hornsby
47. Wade Boggs	47. Reggie Jackson
48. Robin Roberts	48. Goose Goslin
49. Harmon Killebrew	49. Johnny Mize
50. Roberto Clemente	50. Gaylord Perry
51. Bob Gibson	51. Charlie Gehringer
52. Charlie Keller	52. Al Kaline
53. Joe Jackson	53. Whitey Ford
54. Dwight Gooden	54. Robin Roberts
55. Duke Snider	55. Paul Waner
56. Eddie Collins	56. Hoyt Wilhelm
57. Joe Wood	57. Rod Carew
58. Brooks Robinson	58. George Brett
59. Willie McCovey	59. Three Finger Brown
60. Gary Carter	60. Gary Carter
61. Napoleon Lajoie	61. Zack Wheat
62. Hank Greenberg	62. Luis Aparicio
63. Jim Rice	63. Early Wynn
64. Lou Boudreau	64. Carlton Fisk
65. Johnny Mize	65. Dick Allen
66. Mordecai Brown	66. Jimmy Collins
67. Rod Carew	67. Don Sutton
68. Ron Guidry	68. Bill Terry
69. Joe Cronin	69. Eddie Plank
70. Ed Walsh	70. Gabby Hartnett
71. Don Mattingly	71. Ron Santo
72. Gabby Hartnett	72. Sam Crawford
73. Lefty Gomez	73. Ferguson Jenkins
74. Home Run Baker	74. Bill Dickey
75. Al Simmons	75. Roberto Clemente
76. Robin Yount	76. Billy Williams
77. Al Rosen	77. Goose Gossage

PEAK VALUE	CAREER VALUE
78. Jack Coombs	78. Al Simmons
79. Eddie Cicotte	79. Fred Clarke
80. Johnny Evers	80. Sandy Koufax
81. Reggie Jackson	81. Bobby Wallace
82. Ozzie Smith	82. Frankie Frisch
83. Charlie Gehringer	83. George Sisler
84. Catfish Hunter	84. Bruce Sutter
85. Wes Ferrell	85. Buddy Bell
86. Thurman Munson	86. Ernie Lombardi
87. Goose Goslin	87. Duke Snider
88. Frank Chance	88. Phil Niekro
89. Don Drysdale	89. Eddie Murray
90. Whitey Ford	90. Red Ruffing
91. Larry Doby	91. Jackie Robinson
92. Dick Allen	92. Eddie Murray
93. Jimmy Collins	93. Rabbit Maranville
94. Urban Shocker	94. Roy Campanella
95. Glenn Wright	95. Ted Lyons
96. Dan Quisenberry	96. Bobby Grich
97. Hal Newhouser	97. Lou Boudreau
98. Pete Rose	98. Lou Brock
99. Cy Young	99. Ken Boyer
100. Tony Oliva	100. Pee Wee Reese

CAREER HOME AND ROAD BATTING

TY COBB

HOME

Year	G	AB	Run	Hit	2B	3B	HR	RBI	BB	Avg.
1905	15	52	4	14	2	0	0		3	.269
1906	53	189	26	67	3	6	0		10	.354
1907	78	304	42	112	16	7	1		12	.368
1908	74	274	50	91	21	5	0		16	.332
1909	78	294	67	116	19	6	6		20	.395
1910	70	237	50	94	17	6	4		32	.397
1911	76	297	81	124	27	12	5		24	.418
1912	72	280	55	113	15	12	1		18	.404
1913	60	197	38	85	12	7	0		27	.431
1914	48	172	30	72	9	5	1		29	.419
1915	76	261	73	103	17	8	1		67	.395
1916	71	254	57	91	13	6	2		40	.358
1917	74	281	45	98	21	13	1		28	.349
1918	49	180	38	64	13	10	0		17	.356
1919	63	252	45	100	19	5	0		18	.397
1920	57	201	45	67	18	4	1	30	37	.333
1921	62	240	61	95	18	8	5	41	23	.396
1922	73	269	55	109	23	11	1	58	30	.405
1923	72	280	47	101	21	5	2	47	33	.361
1924	78	306	61	100	22	6	0	36	46	.327
1925	59	190	39	63	12	9	2	46	36	.332
1926	41	97	18	25	5	5	0	26	9	.258
1927	65	236	54	82	15	4	2	47	34	.347
1928	53	200	33	66	18	0	1	20	20	.330
	1517	5543	1114	2052	376	160	36	351	629	.370

TY COBB

ROAD

Year	G	AB	Run	Hit	2B	3B	HR	RBI	BB	Avg.
1905	26	98	15	22	4	0	1		7	.224
1906	45	169	19	46	10	1	1		9	.272
1907	72	301	55	100	13	8	4		12	.332
1908	76	307	38	97	15	15	4		18	.316
1909	78	279	49	100	14	4	3		28	.358
1910	70	269	56	100	18	7	4		32	.372
1911	70	294	66	124	20	12	3		20	.422
1912	68	273	64	114	15	11	6		25	.418
1913	62	231	32	82	6	9	4		31	.355
1914	49	173	39	55	13	6	1		28	.318
1915	80	302	71	105	14	5	2		51	.348
1916	74	288	56	110	18	4	3		38	.382
1917	78	307	62	127	23	11	5		33	.414
1918	62	241	45	97	6	4	3		24	.402
1919	61	245	47	91	17	8	1		20	.371
1920	55	227	41	76	10	4	1	33	21	.335
1921	66	267	63	102	19	8	7	60	33	.382
1922	64	257	44	102	19	5	3	41	25	.397
1923	73	276	56	88	19	2	4	41	33	.319
1924	77	319	54	111	16	4	4	39	39	.348
1925	62	225	54	94	19	3	10	56	29	.418
1926	38	136	30	54	13	0	4	36	17	.397
1927	68	254	50	93	17	3	3	47	33	.366
1928	42	153	21	48	9	4	0	20	14	.314
	1516	5891	1131	2138	347	138	81	373	620	.363

BABE RUTH

HOME

Year	G	AB	Run	Hit	2B	3B	HR	RBI	BB	Avg.
1914	5	10	1	2	1	0	0		0	.200
1915	18	41	8	15	4	1	1		3	.366
1916	34	66	10	14	5	1	0		6	.212
1917	26	57	8	21	4	1	1		9	.368
1918	48	145	28	45	14	8	0		32	.310
1919	63	200	47	65	19	6	9		52	.325
1920	66	204	77	81	21	6	29	71	61	.397
1921	78	255	94	103	24	7	32	81	79	.404
1922	53	195	40	58	7	5	14	45	36	.297
1923	76	246	74	101	26	7	19	63	92	.411
1924	78	260	70	99	18	4	24	71	66	.381
1925	56	203	35	59	8	1	11	34	35	.291
1926	75	241	68	88	13	2	23	76	74	.365
1927	73	253	82	94	10	4	28	70	62	.372
1928	77	260	76	86	8	4	29	70	59	.331
1929	60	218	50	72	7	3	21	66	36	.330
1930	72	244	72	91	13	5	26	75	65	.373
1931	75	267	72	96	11	0	24	78	63	.360
1932	72	239	62	78	6	2	19	69	71	.326
1933	68	214	51	68	9	1	22	56	63	.318
1934	69	190	47	56	11	2	13	50	62	.295
1935	11	25	6	6	0	0	2	4	11	.240
	1253	4033	1078	1398	239	70	347	979	1037	.347

BABE RUTH

ROAD

Year	G	AB	Run	Hit	2B	3B	HR	RBI	BB	Avg.
1914	0	0	0	0	0	0	0	0	0	0
1915	24	51	8	14	6	0	3		6	.275
1916	33	70	8	23	0	2	3		4	.329
1917	26	66	6	19	2	2	1		3	.288
1918	47	172	22	50	12	3	11		25	.291
1919	67	232	56	74	15	6	20		49	.319
1920	76	254	81	91	15	3	25	66	87	.358
1921	74	285	83	101	20	9	27	90	65	.354
1922	57	211	54	70	17	3	21	54	48	.332
1923	76	276	78	104	19	6	22	68	78	.377
1924	75	269	73	101	21	3	22	50	76	.375
1925	42	156	26	45	4	1	14	32	24	.288
1926	77	254	71	96	17	3	24	70	70	.378
1927	78	287	76	98	19	4	32	94	76	.341
1928	77	276	87	87	21	4	25	72	76	.315
1929	75	281	71	100	19	3	25	88	36	.356
1930	73	274	78	95	15	4	23	78	71	.347
1931	70	267	77	103	20	3	22	85	65	.386
1932	61	218	58	78	7	3	22	68	59	.358
1933	69	245	46	70	12	2	12	47	51	.286
1934	58	175	31	49	8	2	9	34	41	.280
1935	17	47	7	7	0	0	4	8	9	.149
	1252	4366	1097	1475	269	66	367	1004	1019	.338

Source: Pete Palmer

LEON GOSLIN

HOME

Year	G	AB	R	H	2B	3B	HR	RBI	BB	Avg.
1921	10	33	5	6	0	0	1	2	5	.182
1922	49	158	21	48	8	3	1	27	19	.304
1923	78	313	46	95	15	11	1	48	18	.304
1924	79	278	49	90	14	14	1	59	39	.324
1925	76	285	55	92	19	12	6	57	30	.323
1926	69	255	41	83	19	9	0	43	27	.325
1927	75	295	56	105	19	11	7	60	16	.356
1928	63	195	34	68	15	5	4	38	19	.349
1929	71	261	31	72	14	4	3	34	35	.276
1930	27	106	23	35	8	5	3	23	10	.330
1930	49	196	39	63	12	4	14	48	20	.321
1931	75	286	60	97	27	4	15	59	51	.339
1932	74	270	49	82	13	4	12	56	50	.304
1933	67	264	39	82	15	6	4	31	24	.311
1934	77	294	43	82	17	2	4	47	36	.279
1935	75	286	46	89	17	5	1	53	33	.311
1936	75	289	67	79	13	0	12	54	41	.273
1937	46	99	20	25	5	0	3	24	21	.253
1938	16	17	3	3	2	0	0	2	7	.176
	1151	4180	727	1296	252	99	92	765	501	.310

LEON GOSLIN

ROAD

Year	G	AB	R	H	2B	3B	HR	RBI	BB	Avg.
1921	4	17	2	7	1	1	0	4	1	.412
1922	52	200	23	68	11	4	2	26	6	.340
1923	72	287	40	85	14	7	8	51	22	.296
1924	75	301	51	109	16	3	11	70	29	.362
1925	74	316	61	109	15	8	12	56	23	.345
1926	78	313	64	118	7	6	17	65	36	.377
1927	73	286	40	89	18	4	6	60	34	.311
1928	72	261	46	105	21	5	13	64	29	.402
1929	74	292	51	87	14	3	15	57	31	.298
1930	20	82	11	16	3	0	4	15	9	.195
1930	52	200	42	66	13	3	16	52	28	.330
1931	76	305	54	97	15	6	9	46	29	.318
1932	76	302	39	89	15	5	5	48	42	.295
1933	65	285	58	81	20	4	6	33	18	.284
1934	74	320	63	105	21	5	9	53	29	.328
1935	72	304	42	83	17	1	8	56	23	.273
1936	72	283	55	101	20	8	12	71	44	.357
1937	33	82	10	18	6	1	1	11	14	.220
1938	22	40	3	6	1	0	2	6	1	.150
	1136	4476	755	1439	248	74	156	844	448	.321

Source: Pete Palmer

MICKEY MANTLE

HOME

Year	G	AB	R	H	2B	3B	HR	RBI	BB	Avg.
1951	51	174	37	46	2	2	7	33	26	.264
1952	69	264	42	77	14	1	11	41	37	.292
1953	69	241	50	68	12	3	8	35	42	.282
1954	73	267	64	77	4	8	14	51	51	.288
1955	75	255	67	86	15	7	19	57	58	.337
1956	77	268	67	99	14	3	27	67	54	.369
1957	73	230	51	89	13	6	14	44	61	.387
1958	74	246	65	77	9	0	21	43	73	.313
1959	73	274	47	84	10	1	18	38	44	.307
1960	77	260	58	73	8	2	23	49	51	.281
1961	74	230	64	76	8	6	24	59	66	.330
1962	54	165	39	54	6	0	16	37	48	.327
1963	30	72	19	23	2	0	8	17	23	.319
1964	72	234	55	78	16	2	16	57	49	.333
1965	67	200	23	47	7	1	9	25	51	.235
1966	61	177	20	53	8	1	11	28	35	.299
1967	72	209	29	50	9	0	10	31	51	.239
1968	71	202	29	53	6	1	10	31	47	.262
	1212	3968	826	1210	163	44	266	743	867	.305

MICKEY MANTLE

ROAD

Year	G	AB	R	H	2B	3B	HR	RBI	BB	Avg.
1951	45	167	24	45	9	3	6	32	17	.269
1952	73	285	52	94	23	6	12	46	38	.330
1953	58	220	55	68	12	0	13	57	37	.309
1954	73	276	65	86	13	4	13	51	51	.312
1955	72	262	54	72	10	4	18	42	55	.275
1956	73	265	65	89	8	2	25	63	58	.336
1957	71	244	70	84	15	0	20	50	85	.344
1958	76	273	62	81	12	1	21	54	56	.297
1959	71	267	57	70	13	3	13	37	49	.262
1960	76	267	61	72	9	4	17	45	60	.270
1961	79	284	68	87	8	0	30	69	60	.306
1962	69	212	57	67	9	1	14	52	74	.316
1963	35	100	21	31	6	0	7	18	17	.310
1964	71	231	37	63	9	0	19	54	50	.273
1965	55	161	21	45	5	0	10	21	22	.280
1966	47	156	20	43	4	0	12	28	22	.276
1967	72	231	34	58	8	0	12	24	56	.251
1968	73	233	28	50	8	0	8	23	59	.215
	1189	4134	851	1205	181	28	270	766	866	.291

Source: Pete Palmer

STAN MUSIAL

HOME

Year	G	AB	R	H	2B	3B	HR	RBI	SB	Avg.
1941	6	22	1	12	4	0	0	3	1	.545
1942	71	230	48	77	17	1	8	45	2	.335
1943	81	302	52	105	29	7	7	41	9	.348
1944	73	266	50	86	25	9	5	53	4	.323
1946	78	303	66	112	24	10	10	56	4	.370
1947	76	298	48	100	12	7	5	55	0	.336
1948	77	293	56	98	17	9	16	55	1	.334
1949	79	299	69	104	28	7	13	64	1	.348
1950	73	273	53	101	22	5	15	56	0	.370
1951	79	295	66	105	18	7	19	62	4	.356
1952	77	275	49	82	21	3	10	41	5	.298
1953	78	293	75	112	32	5	15	62	2	.382
1954	76	295	61	102	22	6	19	62	1	.346
1955	77	280	55	94	13	3	22	64	3	.336
1956	78	293	49	102	20	4	14	57	0	.348
1957	68	246	36	75	19	2	12	40	0	.305
1958	67	226	28	77	18	0	13	43	0	.341
1959	59	177	20	42	7	2	10	29	0	.237
1960	58	174	33	48	7	0	10	35	0	.276
1961	61	169	30	58	15	2	11	43	0	.343
1962	68	210	28	67	14	0	10	46	2	.319
1963	64	183	23	56	9	1	8	41	0	.306
	1524	5402	996	1815	393	90	252	1053	39	.336

STAN MUSIAL

ROAD

Year	G	AB	R	H	2B	3B	HR	RBI	SB	Avg.
1941	6	25	7	8	0	0	1	4	0	.320
1942	69	237	39	70	16	9	2	27	4	.295
1943	76	315	56	115	19	13	6	38	1	.365
1944	73	302	63	111	26	5	7	42	4	.368
1946	78	320	57	116	25	10	6	46	3	.363
1947	73	290	65	83	18	6	14	40	3	.286
1948	78	318	78	132	29	9	23	76	6	.415
1949	78	312	59	103	13	6	23	58	2	.330
1950	73	282	52	91	19	2	13	53	5	.323
1951	73	283	58	100	12	5	13	46	0	.353
1952	77	303	55	112	21	3	11	49	2	.370
1953	79	300	50	88	20	4	15	52	1	.293
1954	77	296	60	93	20	3	16	64	0	.314
1955	77	284	42	85	17	2	11	44	2	.299
1956	78	301	38	82	12	2	13	52	2	.272
1957	66	257	46	101	19	1	17	62	1	.393
1958	68	247	36	82	17	2	4	19	0	.332
1959	56	164	17	45	6	0	4	15	0	.274
1960	58	157	16	43	10	1	7	23	1	.274
1961	62	203	16	49	7	2	4	27	0	.241
1962	67	224	29	76	4	1	9	36	1	.339
1963	60	154	11	30	1	1	4	17	2	.195
	1502	5574	950	1815	331	87	223	890	40	.326

Source: David Frank

WILLIE MAYS

HOME

Year	G	AB	R	H	2B	3B	HR	RBI	SB	Avg.
1951	60	230	35	66	10	4	13	40	3	.287
1952	16	57	9	15	0	3	2	14	2	.263
1954	76	279	67	96	16	4	20	48	5	.344
1955	79	298	60	98	13	8	22	55	11	.329
1956	75	284	49	85	13	5	20	37	20	.299
1957	75	278	53	95	8	10	17	54	11	.342
1958	77	289	64	94	15	6	16	54	9	.325
1959	77	284	55	82	20	1	16	55	11	.289
1960	75	280	48	84	16	4	12	45	14	.300
1961	77	275	59	80	17	0	21	61	11	.291
1962	82	309	68	102	21	1	28	83	8	.330
1963	76	286	58	92	20	3	20	47	1	.322
1964	78	270	57	85	11	3	25	57	6	.315
1965	78	272	63	87	13	1	24	48	4	.320
1966	74	251	47	73	15	2	16	42	2	.291
1967	71	233	42	60	9	1	13	39	2	.258
1968	74	244	43	72	13	0	12	37	5	.295
1969	55	175	30	48	7	0	7	25	3	.274
1970	69	219	39	61	7	0	15	42	3	.279
1971	65	193	39	55	11	3	9	27	13	.285
1972	44	113	19	30	2	1	3	7	1	.265
1973	37	117	14	23	1	0	4	15	0	.197
	1490	5236	1018	1583	258	60	335	932	145	.302

WILLIE MAYS

ROAD

Year	G	AB	R	H	2B	3B	HR	RBI	SB	Avg.
1951	61	234	24	61	12	1	7	28	4	.261
1952	18	70	8	15	2	1	2	9	2	.214
1954	75	286	52	99	17	9	21	62	3	.346
1955	73	282	63	87	5	5	29	72	13	.309
1956	77	294	52	86	14	3	16	47	20	.293
1957	77	306	59	100	17	10	18	43	27	.327
1958	75	311	57	114	18	5	13	42	22	.367
1959	74	291	70	98	23	4	18	48	15	.337
1960	78	314	59	106	14	8	17	58	10	.338
1961	77	294	70	96	15	3	19	62	7	.327
1962	80	312	63	87	15	3	21	58	10	.279
1963	81	310	57	95	12	4	18	56	6	.306
1964	79	308	64	86	10	6	22	54	12	.279
1965	79	286	55	90	8	2	28	64	5	.315
1966	78	301	52	86	14	2	21	61	3	.286
1967	70	253	41	68	13	1	9	31	4	.269
1968	74	254	41	72	7	5	11	42	7	.283
1969	62	227	34	66	10	3	6	33	4	.291
1970	70	259	55	78	8	2	13	42	2	.301
1971	71	224	43	58	12	2	9	34	10	.259
1972	44	131	16	31	9	0	5	15	3	.237
1973	29	92	10	21	9	0	2	10	1	.228
	1502	5639	1045	1700	264	79	325	971	190	.301

Source: David Frank

PETE ROSE

HOME

Year	G	AB	R	H	2B	3B	HR	RBI	SB	BB	Avg.
1963	80	307	56	84	10	5	2	19	10	36	.274
1964	66	244	28	62	9	0	3	22	1	18	.254
1965	81	333	62	100	19	2	7	42	4	32	.300
1966	75	312	53	100	14	2	11	43	2	20	.321
1967	75	302	50	96	19	2	7	48	5	27	.318
1968	72	306	49	107	27	3	6	25	1	22	.350
1969	77	308	61	118	22	6	10	44	3	41	.383
1970	81	327	64	105	17	5	7	25	6	39	.321
1971	79	308	44	97	13	0	8	23	7	31	.315
1972	76	309	47	90	17	10	1	22	4	32	.291
1973	79	328	53	118	16	5	3	33	6	29	.360
1974	82	312	57	93	30	4	2	29	1	58	.298
1975	81	328	58	106	21	3	3	41	0	45	.323
1976	81	330	65	111	23	4	7	30	7	39	.336
1977	81	314	47	101	22	3	3	29	10	37	.322
1978	79	317	52	101	25	2	2	28	6	29	.319
1979	81	293	46	99	15	5	1	26	13	59	.338
1980	81	313	49	89	27	1	0	34	5	43	.284
1981	55	218	44	76	11	5	0	21	4	25	.349
1982	81	307	29	79	12	1	2	28	3	27	.257
1983	76	241	26	63	8	3	0	21	2	24	.261
1984	59	177	18	47	8	0	0	10	1	18	.266
1985	60	196	27	50	5	2	0	23	2	47	.255
1986	36	121	8	31	6	1	0	13	2	12	.256
	1774	6851	1093	2123	396	74	85	679	105	790	.310

PETE ROSE

ROAD

Year	G	AB	R	H	2B	3B	HR	RBI	SB	BB	Avg.
1963	77	316	45	86	15	4	4	22	3	19	.272
1964	70	272	36	77	4	2	1	12	3	18	.283
1965	81	337	55	109	16	9	4	39	4	37	.323
1966	81	342	44	105	24	3	5	27	2	17	.307
1967	73	283	36	80	13	6	5	28	6	29	.283
1968	77	320	45	103	15	3	4	24	2	34	.322
1969	79	319	59	100	11	5	6	38	4	47	.313
1970	78	322	56	100	20	4	8	27	6	34	.311
1971	81	324	42	95	14	4	5	21	6	37	.293
1972	78	336	60	108	14	1	5	35	6	41	.321
1973	81	352	62	112	20	3	2	31	4	36	.318
1974	81	340	53	92	15	3	1	22	1	48	.271
1975	81	334	54	104	26	1	4	33	0	44	.311
1976	81	335	65	104	19	2	3	33	2	47	.310
1977	81	341	48	103	16	4	6	35	6	29	.302
1978	80	338	51	97	26	1	5	24	7	33	.287
1979	82	335	44	109	25	0	3	33	7	36	.325
1980	81	342	46	96	15	0	1	30	7	23	.281
1981	52	213	29	64	7	0	0	12	0	21	.300
1982	81	327	51	93	13	3	1	26	5	39	.284
1983	75	252	26	58	6	0	0	24	5	28	.230
1984	62	197	25	60	7	2	0	15	0	22	.305
1985	59	209	33	57	7	0	2	23	6	39	.273
1986	36	116	7	21	2	1	0	12	1	18	.181
	1788	7202	1072	2133	350	61	75	635	93	776	.296

Source: David Frank

TED WILLIAMS

HOME

Year	G	AB	R	H	2B	3B	HR	RBI	BB	Avg.
1939	75	277	74	95	22	5	14	68	52	.343
1940	76	297	69	101	28	5	9	60	47	.340
1941	75	243	72	104	21	2	19	62	80	.428
1942	75	261	73	93	21	3	16	68	64	.356
1946	76	266	74	98	21	4	18	69	73	.368
1947	81	277	67	92	24	6	16	63	84	.332
1948	66	239	57	88	23	1	9	66	66	.368
1949	77	272	87	95	27	2	23	86	91	.349
1950	43	160	50	57	13	0	16	56	41	.356
1951	73	268	69	108	22	3	18	81	64	.403
1952	4	6	1	3	0	0	1	3	1	.500
1953	19	47	10	17	4	0	8	18	10	.362
1954	58	186	48	69	12	0	19	39	72	.371
1955	54	172	48	67	11	1	15	47	52	.390
1956	72	205	39	74	19	2	10	43	59	.361
1957	63	206	42	83	19	0	12	36	52	.403
1958	66	207	47	68	14	2	10	41	57	.329
1959	52	134	14	37	10	0	3	21	20	.276
1960	60	164	32	54	8	0	15	38	47	.329
	1165	3887	973	1403	319	35	248	965	1032	.361

TED WILLIAMS

ROAD

Year	G	AB	R	H	2B	3B	HR	RBI	BB	Avg.
1939	74	288	57	90	22	6	17	77	55	.313
1940	68	264	65	92	15	9	14	53	49	.348
1941	68	213	63	81	12	1	18	58	65	.380
1942	75	261	68	93	13	2	20	69	81	.356
1946	74	248	68	78	16	4	20	54	83	.315
1947	75	251	58	89	16	3	16	51	78	.355
1948	71	270	67	100	21	2	16	61	60	.370
1949	78	294	63	99	12	2	20	73	71	.337
1950	46	174	32	49	11	1	12	41	41	.282
1951	75	263	40	61	6	1	12	45	80	.232
1952	2	4	1	1	0	1	0	0	1	.250
1953	18	44	7	20	2	0	5	16	9	.455
1954	59	200	45	64	11	1	13	50	64	.320
1955	44	148	29	47	10	2	13	36	39	.318
1956	64	195	32	64	9	0	14	39	43	.328
1957	69	214	54	80	9	1	26	51	67	.374
1958	63	204	34	67	9	0	16	44	41	.328
1959	51	138	18	32	5	0	7	22	32	.232
1960	53	146	24	44	7	0	14	34	28	.301
	1127	3819	825	1251	206	36	273	874	987	.328

Source: Pete Palmer

JOE DI MAGGIO

HOME

Year	G	AB	R	H	2B	3B	HR	RBI	BB	Avg.
1936	67	288	51	90	18	8	8	53	14	.313
1937	77	306	83	105	16	8	19	80	42	.343
1938	74	296	67	104	23	8	15	75	30	.351
1939	64	237	46	83	16	1	12	50	22	.350
1940	63	234	40	84	12	6	16	67	32	.359
1941	76	292	60	101	21	6	16	69	40	.346
1942	77	305	51	89	15	6	8	55	29	.292
1946	66	254	37	66	8	6	8	35	26	.260
1947	70	252	49	77	18	5	9	51	41	.306
1948	77	294	54	92	10	8	15	70	30	.313
1949	37	127	25	41	7	3	5	23	28	.323
1950	65	242	48	67	11	6	9	47	35	.277
1951	67	233	37	61	11	2	8	45	29	.262
	880	3360	648	1060	186	73	148	720	398	.315

JOE DI MAGGIO

ROAD

Year	G	AB	R	H	2B	3B	HR	RBI	BB	Avg.
1936	71	349	81	116	26	7	21	72	10	.332
1937	74	315	68	110	19	7	27	87	22	.349
1938	71	303	62	90	9	5	17	65	29	.297
1939	56	225	62	93	16	5	18	76	30	.413
1940	69	274	53	95	16	3	15	66	29	.347
1941	63	249	62	92	22	5	14	56	36	.369
1942	77	305	72	97	14	7	13	59	39	.318
1946	66	249	44	80	12	2	17	60	33	.321
1947	71	282	48	91	13	5	11	46	23	.323
1948	76	300	56	98	16	3	24	85	37	.327
1949	39	145	33	53	7	3	9	44	27	.366
1950	74	283	66	91	22	3	23	75	45	.322
1951	49	182	35	48	11	2	4	26	32	.264
	856	3461	742	1154	203	58	213	817	392	.333

Source: Pete Palmer

CARL YASTRZEMSKI

HOME

Year	G	AB	R	H	2B	3B	HR	RBI	BB	Avg.
1961	73	287	30	91	18	5	6	41	24	.317
1962	79	316	64	108	27	5	11	52	32	.342
1963	74	282	50	89	24	2	6	36	35	.316
1964	75	286	40	83	20	7	6	39	36	.290
1965	74	266	51	88	30	2	16	53	40	.331
1966	80	305	48	99	25	1	11	53	39	.325
1967	81	286	66	95	16	1	27	74	47	.332
1968	80	264	48	75	15	1	11	42	66	.284
1969	81	297	48	83	16	1	21	55	51	.279
1970	81	272	62	96	15	0	22	61	72	.353
1971	75	257	47	72	15	0	7	42	50	.280
1972	69	247	46	71	15	2	5	41	39	.287
1973	74	247	40	70	12	3	8	46	58	.283
1974	77	256	48	83	13	1	5	43	61	.324
1975	77	274	56	75	16	1	8	43	46	.274
1976	74	255	37	81	17	1	10	56	41	.318
1977	78	282	58	99	16	0	14	67	37	.351
1978	72	265	37	77	14	1	7	39	40	.291
1979	75	262	34	79	15	1	15	55	32	.302
1980	54	176	19	47	8	1	5	21	24	.267
1981	46	158	20	46	11	1	3	33	25	.291
1982	66	224	27	69	10	1	7	36	33	.308
1983	61	184	18	46	14	1	6	35	31	.250
	1676	5948	994	1822	382	38	237	1063	959	.306

CARL YASTRZEMSKI

ROAD

Year	G	AB	R	H	2B	3B	HR	RBI	BB	Avg.
1961	75	296	41	64	13	1	5	39	26	.216
1962	81	330	35	83	16	1	8	42	34	.252
1963	77	288	41	94	16	1	8	32	60	.326
1964	76	281	37	81	9	2	9	28	39	.288
1965	59	228	27	66	15	1	4	19	30	.289
1966	80	289	33	66	14	1	5	27	45	.228
1967	80	293	46	94	15	3	17	47	44	.321
1968	77	275	42	87	17	1	12	32	53	.316
1969	81	306	48	71	12	1	19	56	50	.232
1970	80	294	63	90	14	0	18	41	56	.306
1971	73	251	28	57	6	2	8	28	56	.227
1972	56	208	24	49	3	0	7	27	28	.236
1973	78	293	42	90	13	1	11	49	47	.307
1974	71	259	45	72	12	1	10	36	43	.278
1975	72	269	35	71	14	0	6	17	41	.264
1976	81	291	34	65	6	1	11	46	39	.223
1977	72	276	41	66	11	3	14	35	36	.239
1978	72	258	33	68	7	1	10	42	36	.264
1979	72	256	35	61	13	0	6	32	30	.238
1980	51	188	30	53	13	0	10	29	20	.282
1981	45	180	16	37	3	0	4	20	24	.206
1982	65	235	26	57	12	0	9	36	26	.243
1983	58	196	20	55	10	0	4	21	23	.281
	1632	6040	822	1597	264	21	215	781	886	.264

Primary Source: Pete Palmer

JIM RICE

HOME

Year	G	AB	R	H	2B	3B	HR	RBI	BB	Avg.
1974	12	31	2	9	1	0	1	7	1	.290
1975	71	275	46	86	17	2	12	56	20	.313
1976	76	291	34	87	17	4	12	51	16	.299
1977	79	312	57	100	16	8	27	76	26	.321
1978	82	335	69	121	12	7	28	75	32	.361
1979	79	301	69	111	19	4	27	79	32	.369
1980	61	239	40	73	11	4	11	45	15	.305
1981	53	215	28	66	10	0	10	35	18	.307
1982	77	306	51	101	11	4	9	49	29	.330
1983	81	329	50	107	21	0	16	62	27	.325
1984	79	330	58	95	15	3	17	71	23	.288
1985	69	274	44	96	13	3	11	64	20	.350
1986	81	312	50	105	25	2	10	48	28	.337
	900	3550	598	1157	188	41	191	718	287	.326

JIM RICE

ROAD

Year	G	AB	R	H	2B	3B	HR	RBI	BB	Avg.
1974	12	36	4	9	1	1	0	6	3	.250
1975	73	289	46	88	12	2	10	46	16	.304
1976	77	290	41	77	8	4	13	34	12	.266
1977	81	332	47	106	13	7	12	38	27	.319
1978	81	342	52	92	13	8	18	64	26	.269
1979	79	318	48	90	20	2	12	51	25	.283
1980	63	265	41	75	11	2	13	41	15	.283
1981	55	236	23	62	8	1	7	27	16	.263
1982	68	267	35	76	13	1	15	48	26	.285
1983	74	297	40	84	13	1	23	64	25	.283
1984	80	327	40	89	10	4	11	51	21	.272
1985	71	272	41	63	7	0	16	39	31	.232
1986	76	306	48	95	14	0	10	62	34	.310
	890	3577	506	1006	143	33	160	571	277	.281

Primary Source: *Annual Baseball Abstracts*

REGGIE JACKSON

HOME

Year	G	AB	R	H	2B	3B	HR	RBI	BB	Avg.
1967	23	75	8	14	3	4	0	5	6	.187
1968	78	270	33	65	9	1	9	37	27	.241
1969	78	288	61	80	20	1	26	55	56	.278
1970	74	201	24	40	7	0	8	25	27	.199
1971	74	262	39	68	13	0	17	40	31	.260
1972	72	262	40	71	11	0	16	38	31	.271
1973	73	243	39	63	11	0	18	54	43	.259
1974	71	233	39	70	9	0	14	43	34	.300
1975	77	288	40	73	21	1	18	50	29	.253
1976	67	247	34	63	15	0	12	42	21	.255
1977	73	247	48	70	17	2	11	42	42	.283
1978	71	257	43	74	4	5	17	53	33	.288
1979	67	235	39	71	8	1	15	50	32	.302
1980	71	256	43	70	3	4	16	46	35	.273
1981	43	145	12	30	1	1	7	22	22	.207
1982	76	267	46	76	7	1	21	53	40	.285
1983	57	192	22	37	8	0	7	23	27	.193
1984	71	246	34	52	5	0	15	48	25	.211
1985	70	225	30	49	10	0	15	44	38	.218
1986	67	195	33	54	6	2	11	32	51	.277
	1353	4634	707	1190	188	23	273	802	650	.257

REGGIE JACKSON

ROAD

Year	G	AB	R	H	2B	3B	HR	RBI	BB	Avg.
1967	12	43	5	7	1	0	1	1	4	.163
1968	76	283	49	73	4	5	20	37	23	.258
1969	74	261	62	71	16	2	21	63	58	.272
1970	75	225	33	61	14	2	15	41	48	.271
1971	76	305	48	89	16	3	15	40	32	.292
1972	63	237	32	61	14	2	9	37	28	.257
1973	78	296	60	95	17	2	14	63	33	.321
1974	77	273	51	76	16	1	15	50	52	.278
1975	80	305	51	77	18	2	18	54	38	.252
1976	67	251	50	75	12	2	15	49	33	.299
1977	73	278	45	80	22	0	21	68	33	.288
1978	68	254	39	66	9	0	10	44	25	.260
1979	64	230	39	67	16	1	14	39	33	.291
1980	72	258	51	84	19	0	25	65	48	.326
1981	51	189	21	49	16	0	8	32	24	.259
1982	77	263	46	70	10	0	18	48	45	.266
1983	59	205	21	40	6	1	7	26	26	.195
1984	72	279	33	65	12	2	10	33	30	.233
1985	73	235	34	67	17	0	12	41	40	.285
1986	65	224	32	47	6	0	7	26	41	.210
	1352	4894	802	1320	261	25	275	857	694	.270

Primary Source: Pete Palmer

Section III

THE

Records

Take me out to the ball game
Take me out to the crowd
Buy me some peanuts and crackerjack,
I don't care if I never get back
Oh we'll root, root-root for the home team
If they don't win it's a shame
For it's one, two, three strikes you're out
At the Old
        Ball
          Game.

Introduction

■ This now becomes a reference book. There are three basic reference sources for information about players from the past, *The Baseball Encyclopedia,* from Macmillan; the *Sports Encyclopedia: Baseball,* from Grosset and Dunlap; and *Daguerreotypes,* from the *The Sporting News.* The Macmillan *Encyclopedia* contains every player who has ever played in the major leagues, but presents only a bare statistical skeleton of each. The *Sports Encyclopedia: Baseball* presents basically the same data, but organizes it by years and teams rather than by players, plus upholding a higher standard of accuracy than the Macmillan and providing a synopsis of each season in a few hundred words. This is probably the one reference book in the field that I use the most, and would recommend the most wholeheartedly. *Daguerreotypes* focuses on a limited set of players—about 400—but presents more information about them, such as when they were traded and who for, any records they hold or unusual feats they accomplished (hit three homers in a game, July 29, 1957; that sort of thing), plus it has little pictures of them and tells you who they married.

What this section of the book proposes to do is to focus on an even more limited group of players (about 200) and provide even more information about each. A lot more. Macmillan presents a seventeen-column line about each player/season; this book presents a thirty-five-column line, plus notes. It is, beyond any doubt, the most complete data source ever made available for those 200 players. I'll start explaining what those columns are in just a moment, but in principle I tried to avoid duplicating or repeating information that was already available in one of the other references, except for repeating the essential data. For example, I didn't list birth and death dates because all three of the other sources already provide that; I didn't give pinch hitting stats because Macmillan does that; and I didn't list trades because *Daguerreotypes* does that. You may or may not find this to your liking, depending upon the capacities or limitations of your present library, but it has always been my position, in preparing each *Abstract,* to assume that I was writing to an audience which already owned the basic materials in the field, and wanted still more information. In transferring that to a historical subject, that's how it came out.

In almost all cases, extending the player's record into new areas means extending it into areas in which it cannot be made complete, at least at this time. What the other major references have done is to concentrate on building data sets *where they can be completed;* indeed, among them they have used up about every category of information that is systematically and uniformly available throughout the century. What I have done is to try to present whatever information exists or whatever information I could get about other aspects of play.

It was a maddening business, trying to figure out what was available, and how to get it. Neil Munro, a serious baseball researcher who lives in North Bay, Ontario, did most of the work of locating career information; without his help, this section would be much less complete than it is—yet even with him, it is far from complete. I wrote about the shifting sands of baseball record-keeping in Sections I and II; here's where you can go to see the effects. Obviously, I would like to have this information available more systematically, and not to have all the gaps in this section. If this book is ever reissued, we will have been able to fill in some of the gaps—but we will never come close to filling all of them. But while *complete* information about things like caught stealing and home/road home run breakdowns does not exist, a great deal of information does exist, but has never been gathered and made available. This book does that—it accepts the gaps in the evidence and assembles what evidence exists.

The categories presented in the records of non-pitchers are:

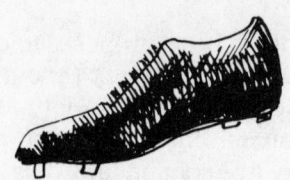

A. BATTING

1) G—Games Played
2) AB—At Bats
3) H—Hits
4) 2B—Doubles
5) 3B—Triples
6) HR—Home Runs

Just basic stuff, already available.

7) Hm—Home
8) Rd—Road

These two, in parentheses, refer to home runs hit at home and on the road. This may be the most significant new information in the section; it bears upon a subject about which there is much misinformation floating around. Not to repeat the comments of Section II, but it is important to put this material on record, because you hear it said so often that Willie Mays would have hit more home runs if he hadn't played in Candlestick Park, which is not true, or that Aaron and Mathews were taking advantage of cozy County Stadium, which is absurd, or that Ruth of course was helped a lot by Yankee Stadium, which is not so. My goal here was to create a reference for park effects on home runs that would be available, and hopefully would help to improve the information content of the discussion a bit.

I was surprised and pleased by how much of this information I was able to come up with. The primary sources for this information were

1) Pete Palmer, who has spent much time at Cooperstown studying park effects on American League batting, and who provided the totals for most of the American Leaguers, and

2) *The Sporting News Guide* since 1951, which carry annual breakdowns of home runs by parks, providing the basis of the material for the last thirty-five years.

There are a few distracting errors in the early Palmer data; don't know why, as Pete's usually very accurate. Anyway, these were supplemented by occasional home/road data in earlier guides, data from David Frank on Musial, and we wound up with most of the data for anybody who was a real power hitter. I believe the top home run hitter for whom we are missing some data is Johnny Mize, with 359 home runs, meaning that we have complete data for all of the top 35 home run hitters in history as well as most of the rest.

The most serious gaps in this category are that we have very little information concerning Rogers Hornsby and Chuck Klein. The data on Klein does exist; it was reportedly compiled by a man named Dave Hewson about ten years ago as a part of an attempt to dissuade the Veterans Committee from electing Klein to the Hall of Fame. However, I was not able to locate Mr. Hewson or to obtain the data, which so far as I know has not been published.

Probably all of this data, from Day 1, can still be recovered. I could figure Hornsby's complete home/road records if I wanted to spend a week in the library. I would expect that much more complete information in this category will become available over time.

9) TB—Total Bases

No big deal; you can figure it yourself if you want to. It's kind of fun to see all those "400s" lined up for Lou Gehrig.

10) R—Runs Scored

11) RBI—Runs Batted In

12) BB—Bases on Balls (also known as walks)

This, again, is just basic information.

13) IBB—Intentional Bases on Balls

Intentional Walks became an official statistic in both leagues in 1955; there is no information about them prior to that time that I am aware of.

14) HBP—Hit by Pitch

Hit batsmen have been a part of the records for as long as there have been official statistics, and dating back to the days when the only available statistics were not compiled by the leagues, but by independent guides or other publications, just as the *Abstract* does now. The guides began regularly publishing HBP totals between 1900 and 1910, and there may exist spotty data before that. Since box scores sometimes carried HBP notes before that, it may still be possible to reconstruct this information even further back, and I think there have been some attempts to do that.

Neil Munro assembled this data for me, and I'm not completely sure what the original source for some of it was. In a few cases, Neil included estimates for players whose totals were not available. These estimates are mostly zeroes, representing sac hit or hit by pitch totals for players with ten or fifteen at bats, and are always marked with an asterisk.

15) SH—Sacrifice Hits

Sacrifice Hits have been counted since the 1890s, and are almost uniformly available, with occasional exceptions such as the Federal League and maybe somebody who only played a few games and was left out of the guides.

What the category includes, however, has been redefined many times, as is discussed in Section II, so when you read these totals you should keep in mind that what you are looking at does not always represent what would be considered a sacrifice hit (sac bunt) today. If a player is averaging eight sacrifice hits a year and suddenly goes to fifteen or twenty, it is much more likely that they changed the rules on what constitutes a sacrifice than it is that he started bunting more.

16) SF—Sacrifice Flies

Sacrifice Flies were separated from other sacrificial acts beginning in 1954. Very little, but a little, data exists before then.

B. BASERUNNING

1) SB—Stolen Bases

Stolen bases have always been counted, and have not been redefined, with two minor exceptions, since 1898.

2) CS—Caught Stealing

Caught stealing have one of the more varied histories. The American League counted them for one season just before World War I, started counting them again in 1920, stopped counting them in 1927, started again in 1928, and has counted and published them ever since. The National League also started in 1920, but stopped in 1926 and did not resume until 1951. There is, in addition, some sporadic information available during the dark periods—notes in guides, that sort of thing—and Pete Palmer has organized an effort to assemble complete data for the American League for 1927, although I don't know what kind of success he's had. Caught stealing are not hard to recognize, and thus the scoring of them when available has been fairly uniform; however, it was not until the last fifteen or twenty years that scorers became consistent in charging a runner with a caught stealing when he broke for second after being picked off first.

3) SB%—Stolen Base Percentage

4) GIDP—Grounded into Double Play

The first GIDP data comes from the National League in the early thirties. It was originally HIDP, or hit into double play, and included also instances of players lining into a double play or hitting a fly ball that became a double play. This was figured for six seasons, 1933–1938, when both leagues adopted the modern GIDP stat. The 1940 Spalding/Reach Guide did not publish the new stat, so the 1939 data is difficult to come by. HIDP are shown as GIDP in this section.

In terms of the potential impact on the assessment of the player's value, this is the one most important category which was not previously available. Altogether, we have added six basic categories to the career records that were previously available —that is, six categories which are neither breakdowns of other records, like home/road breakdowns of home run totals, nor something you could figure from the available information like total bases or runs created. Those six are intentional walks, hit batsmen, sacrifice hits, sacrifice flies, caught stealing and grounded into double plays.

How important are those six categories? The additional information makes it possible to estimate more accurately how many runs the player has created. Suppose that you take two players, Ralph and Willie, who have identical totals in all of the Macmillan categories:

	Ralph	Willie
At Bats	550	550
Hits	150	150
Total Bases	240	240
Walks	50	50
Stolen Bases	30	30

Each player would have a basic runs created estimate of 80; each would have made 400 known outs, and thus each would be creating about 5.00 runs per game (25 outs).

However, the collection of categories that we have added to the record all tend to increase the estimates for Willie and decrease them for Ralph (except for the sacrifice categories, which don't really change anything very much):

	Ralph	Willie
Hit by Pitch	1	12
Sacrifice Hits	5	5
Sacrifice Flies	8	8
Caught Stealing	16	4
Grounded into Double Plays	24	5
Intentional Walks	12	3

The differences here are not extreme or unusual; no records are broken and none are threatened. Using the new information and the technical version of the runs created formula, we would now estimate that Ralph created 71 runs, and Willie 90. That's a very significant difference—about two games difference in the wins column of the teams they play for. But Willie has created his 90 runs while consuming only 422 of his team's outs; Ralph created 71 runs while consuming 453 outs. In a league averaging 4.50 runs per game, Ralph would be a below-average offensive performer, while Willie would have an offensive winning percentage of .616.

So in a case where all of the peripheral information is positive (Joe Morgan), or one where it is predominantly negative (Ted Simmons), the new information can significantly alter the evaluation of the player's total offensive contribution. In most cases, if one statistic is negative another will be positive, and the player's rank among the greatest will not jump appreciably or fall dramatically, but at least the picture that you can form of the player's offensive capabilities will be made more complete and more accurate.

C. PERCENTAGES

I presented the three most basic percentages—batting average, slugging percentage, and on-base percentage. Two of those were available from the other sources; on-base percentages were not. On-base percentage, as figured here, is walks + hits + hit by pitch, divided by total plate appearances (including at bats, walks, hit by pitch, sacrifice hits and sacrifice flies).

On-base percentage and slugging percentage, as I suppose you know, are the two offensive categories which provide the best indication as to how many runs a team is likely to score.

D. VALUES

These five categories are the only ones which represent my formulas, the only ones on which I have any impact. The five are:

1) Runs—Runs Created

As explained in Section II, it was necessary to derive a series of runs created formulas to take maximum advantage of the evolving data sources of the game's history.

2) Win—Offensive Wins

As explained in Section II.

3) Loss—Offensive Losses

As explained in Section II.

4) Pct—Offensive Winning Percentage

This process places the player's runs created estimate in the context of the number of outs that he has used and the offensive levels of the time and place in which he plays, and thus creates a constant reference point—a .500 offensive performer is always average, a .600 player is always good, a .700 figure is always excellent and an .800 percentage is always great.

5) AV—Approximate Value

Not a precise way of looking at any one season, but a reasonably effective way of comparing groups of seasons and delineating patterns within a career on the simplest possible level.

E. FIELDING

I presented defensive statistics for each player at only one position. The reason for this is that the understanding of defensive statistics requires the development of an extensive array of intelligible performance standards. What is a good fielding percentage for a second baseman? What is a good range factor for a shortstop on artificial turf? When dealing with a historical subject, we add an additional level of complexity: What is a good double play total for a shortstop in 1912? What is a good fielding average for a third baseman in 1933? Fielding statistics are not meaningless; they're just rather intractible. They are subject to all of the illusions and outside influences that batting statistics are subject to, but, fractured nine ways by the diverse nature of the nine defensive positions, not capable of developing the magic numbers (.300 averages, 100-RBI levels, and 20-win seasons) that we use to guide us through the understanding of other statistics.

When you mix together the unlike statistics from different positions and start adding (as almost every reference book in the field does), you further obstruct the development of those sensitive mental calipers that we need to make sense of the data. If you put Ernie Banks' records as a first baseman together with his records as a shortstop, the .996 fielding percentages and the 1,100 putouts at first base are disorienting, and make it more difficult to find a frame of reference for the .985 fielding percentage and 519 assists as a shortstop in 1959. And as to adding together fielding statistics from different positions in the same season—man, that's preposterous; those numbers don't mean anything at all. That's like adding together a player's scoring and assist totals in twenty-six games of basketball, eight games of hockey and five games of football. No one in the world can look at one of those combined records that represents twenty-six games in the outfield, eight games at first base, and five at third base and tell you whether the guy can play first base, third base, the outfield or spin-the-bottle. Yet almost every publication in the field insists on doing that.

Anyway, the fielding records that I present are just the basic defensive categories—games played at the position, putouts, assists, errors, double plays and fielding percentage, plus range factor. In most cases the position selected was the one at which the player played the most games in his career. In a few cases, such as Ernie Banks, I chose the position that he was playing in his best years, rather than the one where he played the most. There are two reasons for this. Number one, I'm more interested in the Ernie Banks of 1958 than I am in the Ernie Banks of 1968. And number two, the defensive statistics of shortstops are more descriptive and more informative in principle than are those of first basemen, who are usually the victims of the play rather than the perpetrators. First basemen and catchers have no range factors; passed balls are given for catchers.

F. NOTES

Notes are included on five types of things. The first just tell you what team the player was with in which seasons, and would be in the data block in the usual place except that we were pressed for space in the charts.

The second is an accounting of the player's performance in voting for the Most Valuable Player awards. As noted in Section II, I wanted to provide a better record of how players have fared in the balloting for this award, which I regard as having by far the best-designed balloting system in baseball. I was able to come up with an accounting of most of the votes, and I developed the notion of an Award Share to summarize the player's performance in the voting. Of course, to make sense of that with players whose careers begin before 1930, you have to keep in mind when there is an award and when there is none, plus some idea of when there was an award but an account of the voting is not available. If I had no data I left it blank in the notes; a "0" for the year means that I have complete data and he didn't draw any votes. After the publication of the first edition of this book, about a dozen people contacted me with additional information about MVP votes; those people are acknowledged in the back of the book in "Notes on the Second Edition." In chart form, the awards for which I was not able to locate complete voting are:

VOTING UNKNOWN; WINNER IS ALL THAT IS KNOWN
Chalmers awards, both leagues, 1912
League awards, both leagues, 1925, 1928; N.L. 1929

WINNERS TOTAL KNOWN; REST OF VOTING UNKNOWN
TSN awards, both leagues, 1930; A.L., 1929
BBWAA awards, both leagues, 1931, 1932

VOTING KNOWN FOR TOP FINISHERS
BBWAA, A.L., 1939 (top 19)
BBWAA, N.L., 1939 (top 18)
BBWAA, A.L., 1954 (top 10)
BBWAA, A.L., 1955 (top 12)
BBWAA, A.L., 1956 (top 10)
BBWAA, A.L., 1957 (top 10)
BBWAA, N.L., 1961 (top 11)

I found a complete voting record for *The Sporting News* awards in 1931 and 1932, and substituted those for the BBWAA voting, which I was not able to locate for those two years. For any award not listed above, including the Chalmers awards in 1911, The American League Awards of 1922, 1923, and 1924, the League Awards in both leagues in 1926 and 1927, and all other BBWAA awards since 1933, I was able, with the generous assistance of the Hall of Fame staff, to obtain a full record of the voting.

The third group of notes given pass along any reports that I happened to see on the player's salaries. I wasn't attempting to do a comprehensive study here, just to put together enough of these things that you see in autobiographies and articles about players to help them make sense of one another. Everything with a dollar sign in front of it changes so much over time that to know that a player was receiving $42,000 in 1934 is not really very meaningful unless (a) you are old enough to remember 1934, or (b) you can check somewhere and find out about what somebody else was making that year. I made it a point not to see too many salaries from the last ten years or so.

The fourth group of notes is the most ambitious. When you look at a player's record and you see that he hit .336 in 141 games one year, and .247 in 53 games the next year, you usually figure that something happened to him. I always wonder what it was. If he hurt himself, how did he hurt himself? When did he hurt himself? If he missed forty games, which forty games? If he was in the military, which branch? If he was suspended, what for? I decided to try, within the limitations of my time and my library, to answer those questions, to make that kind of specific information a part of the player's record. In some cases, I just could not find out what happened. When I could, I put it down where you can find it.

The fifth category of notes, which are called "Notes," was designed to contain small, specific bits of performance or award information wherever it happened to be available. If I found that somebody hit .347 against left-handed pitching in 1947, I'd make a note.

I also noted here whenever the player had won the Gold Glove award or been named to *The Sporting News* post-season All-Star team. I was interested in this, for reasons discussed in Section II. Sometimes *The Sporting News* All-Star selections were entered as "Named outstanding major league catcher of 1925 by *The Sporting News.*" Don't be confused; *The Sporting News* does not have a separate award for "Major League Left Fielder of the Year."

Most of the same notes are entered about pitchers, the exception being that I did not attempt to explain all of the gaps in the pitchers' careers. Pitchers' careers have many gaps, many more than everyday players, and if you looked up what caused them you'd wind up with a whole lot of notes saying "1926—Sore arm." I could not see this as a wise investment of my time.

A pitcher's record, as presented here, might contain as many as twenty-six categories. The first group of these describes what we might call his workload:

A. HOW MUCH HE PITCHED

This contains seven categories:

1) G—Game Appearances
2) GS—Games Started
3) CG—Complete Games

Routine stuff, already available, but necessary to provide a framework for the other information.

4) GF—Games Finished

Games finished were a part of the records almost from the turn of the century, but there are a lot of gaps in the data. Pitcher records in general were slower to develop than batting records, and throughout this section we will have a bunch of little gaps to deal with. In 1905, the American League batting records in the *Spalding Guide* include games, at bats, runs, hits, stolen bases, sacrifice hits, and batting average, and the fielding records contain everything that they have now except double plays—but the pitching records contain only wins and losses.

The National League always had games finished in the main body of the pitcher's record, but the American League until just a few years ago always displayed them in a separate chart, which would on occasion get left out of a guide. Also, the guides as recently as the 1940s often didn't bother to give complete information about players who played in less than fifteen games—including pitchers, for whom fourteen games is a third of a season's work. This makes it impossible to complete this part of the record for many pitchers.

5) ShO—Shutouts
6) IP—Innings Pitched

More basic information. Shutouts don't really help to answer the question "how much," but I didn't know what else to do with them.

7) BFP—Batters Facing Pitcher

This also has many gaps for pitchers with few games in a season. The National League has long figured batters facing pitcher, or "total batters faced," including all plate appearances against the pitcher. The American League for many years presented "opposition at bats"—that is, only the official at bats against the pitcher. This split in the records existed for over sixty years, until finally they were unified in the 1970s. Rather than presenting a patchwork of BFP, TBF and OAB, I converted OAB (opposition at bats) into BFP (batters facing pitcher) by adding the pitchers walks, hit batsmen, and sacrifices allowed to his OAB. I believe that the two are exactly the same with the exception of the relatively rare event of batters reaching base on catcher's interference, but I wouldn't want to swear that there isn't some other little distinction.

B. WHAT HE GAVE UP

There are twelve categories in this section of the pitcher's record:

1) H—Hits Allowed
2) R—Runs Allowed
3) ER—Earned Runs Allowed
4) HR—Home Runs Surrendered
5) SH—Sacrifice Hits Allowed
6) SF—Sacrifice Flies Allowed
7) HB—Hit Batsmen
8) TBB—Walks
9) IBB—Intentional Walks
10) SO—Strikeouts
11) WP—Wild Pitches
12) Bk—Balks

All of which are pretty much self-explanatory, and if you're really interested in when something became available all you have to do is check the data.

Throughout most of the pitchers' records, because there are so many gaps, I did not provide column totals unless the column was complete or almost complete. The standard used was "danger of deception." If I felt that showing a column total in batters facing pitcher created a deceptive idea of the relationship between BFP and innings, which are right next to it, then I didn't present the total. If the column total was of some interest, and if I felt that either (a) the column, while missing a few, was substantially complete, or (b) the column was so obviously incomplete that no one would misunderstand what the total represented, then I presented a column total. Because of the importance of the category, I did generally try to present the total of home runs allowed, reasoning that your average intelligent reader would want to know what that total was, and could look up the column to see whether it was complete or not.

C. WHAT THE RESULTS WERE

The end products of the things the pitcher has allowed are summarized in seven categories in the third part of the pitcher's record. The first three are wins (W), losses (L) and winning percentage (Pct.).

The fourth is "rest of team." The idea involved here is becoming familiar enough that most of you probably already know what this is, but I'll explain it just in case. Steve Carlton in 1972 won 27 games and lost 10; the rest of his team was 32–87, a winning percentage of .269. (However, in 1973 he was 13–20, a winning percentage of .394, while the rest of the Phillies were at .450.) Multiplying the .269 winning percentage times the 37 decisions, we come up with 9.9, and we thus conclude that Carlton in 1972 was 17.1 wins above the level maintained by the rest of his team. (In 1973 he dropped to 1.8 wins below the rest of the same team.) This is shown in the next category, Above Team, which means wins above team. Cy Young over his career was 103 wins better than the teams for which he pitched.

The sixth category in this subsection, runs per game, is the pitcher's average of runs allowed per nine innings. This is like Earned Run Average, except that all runs count. As I have written before, I think that the distinction between earned runs and unearned runs is silly and artificial, a distinction having no meaning except in the eyes of some guy up in the press box. But even if that were not my attitude toward earned run averages, I probably would have chosen to present the total run average anyway, on the grounds that of the two, it is the one which is not already available.

The final category, Percentage of League, divides the pitcher's run average by the league average that season of runs per game. Anything below 1.00, obviously, is good; anything above 1.00 and you'll probably have more losses than wins. A figure of ".82" in this category is roughly equivalent to a winning percentage of .600; a figure of ".66" should translate to a winning percentage of about .700; while a pitcher allowing only one-half as many runs as the league average (.50) should have a winning percentage of about .800 and a contract for about a million a game and all the redheads he can carry. Only the great ones ever get near .50.

The bottom line of each player and pitcher data chart presents the player's record in seasonal notation. This will be familiar to those of you who read the annual *Abstracts*; the line restates the player's career record, but in a more understandable form. Tyrus Raymond played 3,033 games in his career, which is the same as playing 162 games a year for 18.7 years; so the first note there is "18.7 years." For each 162 games that he played, he averaged 611 at bats; so he is shown as having 611 at bats a season, etc. Of course, Cobb never played a 162-game schedule, but the 162-game schedule is the frame of reference that is most meaningful to a modern baseball fan, and "meaningful" is the key word here. Saying that Cobb scored 120 runs a season is easier to comprehend than saying that he scored 2,245 runs in 3,033 games. (By the way, I used the *Daguerreotypes* version of Ty Cobb's records in 1910 and 1906, about which there is some disagreement.)

In most cases of incomplete data, I did not present seasonal notation for the affected column; in a few cases I did. For example, Cobb is shown with 19 caught stealing in his seasonal notation line. This means that for each 162 games for which we have records, Cobb was caught stealing 21 times (196 CS in 1,510 games). The .65 in the stolen base percentage column means that in the nine seasons for which we have the necessary data, Cobb was a 65% base stealer (364 of 560).

For pitchers, the seasonal notation assumes a "season" of 40 starts, with each relief appearance counting as 6/10 of a start. Warren Spahn in his career made 665 starts and 85 relief appearances; that is the equivalent of 716 starts, or 40 starts a season for 17.90 seasons. For each of those 17.9 seasons, he pitched 293 innings, struck out 144 men and walked 80, won 20 games and lost 14. A remarkable number of the pitchers in this group were twenty-game winners in their typical season, although few of them maintained the pace for as long as Warren Spahn.

Finally, in selecting these 200 players, there was absolutely no attempt to select the 200 greatest players of all time. I wanted to present the records of the games greatest stars, but I also felt it was necessary to balance that with some players who were a little closer to the league norms, and who would provide a better context for the Ruths and Aarons. I intended

1) to include everyone who was one of the *100* greatest players of this century, or could well be argued to have been so, and

2) to balance the list of players across the century, by position and league.

The players who are here are all very good players, but the fact that Hippo Vaughn is here and Catfish Hunter is not does not mean at all that I think Hippo Vaughn was a better pitcher than Catfish Hunter. Catfish Hunter was a great pitcher, but he is from an era in which there are a number of pitchers who won more games than he did and had better earned run averages; Hippo Vaughn won "only" 176 games, but he represents an era in which there is room for him. In a few cases I included players just because I liked them or was particularly interested in them. But Dave Winfield is certainly a greater player than Roy Thomas was, and if this book is ever reissued I will certainly take some note of those things, and make the appropriate adjustments.

Catcher

Roger Bresnahan
Ray Schalk
Wally Schang
Gabby Hartnett
Mickey Cochrane
Bill Dickey
Al Lopez
Ernie Lombardi
Yogi Berra
Roy Campanella
Bill Freehan
Johnny Bench

PLAYER: ROGER BRESNAHAN

				BATTING														BASERUNNING					PERCENTAGES				VALUES			
Year	G	AB	H	2B	3B	HR	(Hm	Rd)	TB	R	RBI	BB	IBB	HBP	SH	SF	SB	CS	SB%	GIDP		Avg.	Slug	On Base		Runs	Win—Loss	Pct.	AV
1897	6	16	6	0	0	0	(	)	6	1	3	1		0	0		0					.375	.375	.412		3	0—0	.547	0
1900	2	2	0	0	0	0	(	)	0	0	0	0					0					.000	.000	.000		0	0—0	.000	0
1901	86	295	79	9	9	1	(	)	109	40	32	23			4		10					.268	.369	.317		39	3—5	.402	4
1902	116	413	116	22	9	5	(	)	171	47	56	37			10		18					.281	.414	.333		66	7—5	.594	8
1903	113	406	142	30	8	4	(	)	200	87	55	61			12		34					.350	.493	.424		106	9—2	.824	13
1904	109	402	114	21	8	5	(	)	166	81	33	58			3		13					.284	.413	.371		69	8—3	.708	8
1905	104	331	100	18	3	0	(	)	124	58	46	50			7		11					.302	.375	.387		54	6—3	.678	8
1906	124	405	114	22	4	0	(	)	144	69	43	81			5		25					.281	.356	.397		70	8—3	.728	12
1907	110	328	83	9	7	4	(	)	118	57	38	61			6		15					.253	.360	.365		50	7—3	.693	7
1908	140	449	127	25	3	1	(	)	161	70	54	83			24		14					.283	.359	.378		71	9—4	.689	13
1909	72	234	57	4	1	0	(	)	63	27	23	46	1		7		11					.244	.269	.361		28	3—4	.450	3
1910	88	234	65	15	3	0	(	)	86	35	27	55	2		8		13					.278	.368	.408		42	5—2	.649	5
1911	81	227	63	17	8	3	(	)	105	22	41	45	3		6		4					.278	.463	.395		43	5—2	.677	5
1912	48	108	36	7	2	1	(	)	50	8	15	14	2		0		4					.333	.463	.419		22	2—1	.715	2
1913	68	161	37	5	2	1	(	)	49	20	21	21	2		4		7					.230	.304	.319		18	2—3	.392	2
1914	86	248	69	10	4	0	(	)	87	42	24	49	2		12		14					.278	.351	.386		41	5—3	.656	4
1915	77	221	45	8	1	1	(	)	58	19	19	29	0		4		19	3	.86			.204	.262	.291		22	3—4	.410	4
8.8 yrs	1430	4480	1253	222	72	26	(	)	1697	683	530	714	12		112		212	3	.86			.280	.379	.372		744	82—48	.633	99
	508		142	25	8	3				192	77	60	81					24					.280	.379	.372					

Teams: Washington (N), 1897; Chicago (N), 1900; Baltimore (A), 1901–1902; New York (N), 1902–1908; St. Louis (N), 1909–1912; Chicago (N), 1913–1915.
Points in MVP Voting: 1911, 0; 1913, 0; 1914, 6 (.09).
Explanation for Gaps in Career or Sudden Changes in Productivity: 1909— No record of major injuries; was player-manager in 1909, and apparently just chose to share playing time with another catcher.
1912—Held out well into season; involved in bitter dispute over termination of contract.

FIELDING CATCHER

Year	G	PO	AS	Err	DP	PB	Pct.
1900	1	1	0	0	0	2	1.000
1901	69	199	63	23	3	14	.919
1902	38	152	44	10	8	4	.951
1903	11	46	11	5		1	.919
1905	87	492	114	19	15	18	.970
1906	82	407	125	14	6	16	.974
1907	95	483	94	8	11	11	.986
1908	139	657	140	12	12	17	.985
1909	59	211	78	12	3	0	.960
1910	77	295	100	16	11	12	.961
1911	77	323	100	13	9	11	.970
1912	28	138	49	5	4	3	.974
1913	58	194	67	10	2	7	.963
1914	85	365	113	11	6	10	.978
1915	68	345	95	8	9	3	.982
	974	4308	1193	166	99	129	.971

Assists per 154 Games: 189

PLAYER: RAY SCHALK

Year	G	AB	H	2B	3B	HR	(Hm	Rd)	TB	R	RBI	BB	IBB	HBP	SH	SF	SB	CS	SB%	GIDP	Avg.	Slug	On Base	Runs	Win−Loss	Pct.	AV
1912	23	63	18	2	0	0	(	)	20	7	8	3		4	3		2				.286	.317	.342	8	1−1	.526	1
1913	128	401	98	15	5	1	(	)	126	38	38	27		3	13		14				.244	.314	.288	40	6−6	.508	6
1914	135	392	106	13	2	0	(	)	123	30	36	38		8	21		24	11	.69		.270	.314	.331	51	7−5	.610	9
1915	135	413	110	14	4	1	(	)	135	46	54	62		3	17		15	18	.46		.266	.327	.354	55	7−5	.558	10
1916	129	410	95	12	9	0	(	)	125	36	41	41		6	15		30	13	.70		.232	.305	.301	45	6−7	.475	8
1917	140	424	96	12	4	3	(	)	125	48	51	59		7	17		19				.226	.295	.320	47	7−7	.494	8
1918	108	333	73	6	3	0	(	)	85	35	22	36		3	15		12				.219	.255	.289	29	4−7	.369	5
1919	131	394	111	9	3	0	(	)	126	57	34	51		2	14		11				.282	.320	.356	50	6−6	.508	10
1920	151	485	131	25	5	1	(	)	169	64	61	68		2	21		10	4	.71		.270	.348	.349	67	7−8	.482	12
1921	128	416	105	24	4	0	(	)	137	32	47	40		7	9		3	4	.43		.252	.329	.322	47	4−8	.360	7
1922	142	442	124	22	3	4	(	)	164	57	60	67		3	22		12	4	.75		.281	.371	.363	68	8−6	.572	11
1923	123	382	87	12	2	1	(	)	106	42	44	39		4	17		6	4	.60		.228	.277	.294	35	3−9	.285	6
1924	57	153	30	4	2	1	(	)	41	15	11	21		2	6		1	5	.17		.196	.268	.291	13	1−4	.177	2
1925	125	343	94	18	1	0	(	)	114	44	52	57		3	14		11	5	.69		.274	.332	.369	49	5−6	.460	7
1926	82	226	60	9	1	0	(	)	71	26	32	27		2	8		5	1	.83		.265	.314	.338	27	3−4	.449	4
1927	16	26	6	2	0	0	(	)	8	2	2	2		0	1		0				.231	.308	.276	2	0−1	.291	0
1928	2	1	1	0	0	0	(	)	1	0	1	0		0	0		1	0	1.00		1.000	1.000	1.000	1	0−0	1.000	0
1929	5	2	0	0	0	0	(	)	0	0	0	0		0	0		0				.000	.000	.000	0	0−0	.000	0
	1760	5306	1345	199	48	12	(	)	1676	579	594	638		59	213		176	69	.63		.253	.316	.329	633	75−87	.465	106
10.9 yrs		488	124	18	4	1			154	53	55	59		5	20		16				.253	.316	.329				

Teams: Chicago, A.L. 1912–1928; New York, N.L. 1929.

Points in MVP Voting: 1913, 3 (.05), 1914, 13 (6th, .20); 1922, 26 (3rd, .41); 1923, 0; 1924, 0; 1926, 0; 1927, 0. TOTAL: .66 Award Shares.

Reported Salaries: No information available.

Explanation for Gaps in Career or Sudden Changes in Productivity: Can't help you. Must have had some kind of injury in 1924, but the 1925 *Reach Guide* discusses several other injury problems on the team, and does not mention Schalk.

FIELDING CATCHER

Year	G	PO	AS	Err	DP	PB	Pct.
1912	23	115	40	14	4		.917
1913	125	599	154	15	18		.980
1914	124	613	183	21	20		.974
1915	134	655	159	13	8		.984
1916	124	653	166	10	25		.988
1917	139	624	148	15	13		.981
1918	106	422	114	12	15		.978
1919	129	551	130	13	14		.981
1920	151	581	138	10	19		.986
1921	126	453	129	9	19		.985
1922	142	591	150	8	16		.989
1923	121	481	93	10	20		.983
1924	56	176	55	10	8		.959
1925	125	368	99	8	15	5	.983
1926	80	251	45	7	6	3	.977
1927	15	24	8	0	1	0	1.000
1928	1	4	0	0	0	0	1.000
1929	5	7	0	0	0	0	1.000
	1726	7168	1811	175	221	8	.981

Assists per 154 Games: 162

PLAYER: WALLY SCHANG

				BATTING													BASERUNNING				PERCENTAGES			VALUES			
Year	G	AB	H	2B	3B	HR	(Hm	Rd)	TB	R	RBI	BB	IBB	HBP	SH	SF	SB	CS	SB%	GIDP	Avg.	Slug	On Base	Runs	Win−Loss	Pct.	AV
1913	77	207	55	16	3	3	(0	3)	86	32	30	34		9	2		4				.266	.415	.389	34	4−2	.606	3
1914	107	307	88	11	8	3	(3	0)	124	44	45	32		9	7		7	7	.50		.287	.404	.363	47	6−3	.633	7
1915	116	359	89	9	11	1	(0	1)	123	64	44	66		14	12		18	3	.86		.248	.343	.375	53	6−5	.517	5
1916	110	338	90	15	8	7	(6	1)	142	41	38	38		10	13		14				.266	.420	.346	54	7−4	.649	6
1917	118	316	90	14	9	3	(1	2)	131	41	36	29		9	12		6				.285	.415	.350	49	6−3	.644	5
1918	88	225	55	7	1	0	(0	0)	64	36	20	46		2	9		4				.244	.284	.365	26	4−3	.558	3
1919	113	330	101	16	3	0	(0	0)	123	43	55	71		5	7		15				.306	.373	.429	58	7−3	.717	8
1920	122	387	118	30	7	4	(1	3)	174	58	51	64		7	8		7	7	.50		.305	.450	.406	75	8−3	.710	9
1921	134	424	134	30	5	6	(5	1)	192	77	55	78		5	6		7	4	.64		.316	.453	.423	88	8−4	.664	12
1922	124	408	130	21	7	1	(0	1)	168	46	53	53		6	23		12	6	.67		.319	.412	.386	72	8−4	.651	10
1923	84	272	75	8	2	2	(1	1)	93	39	29	27		9	7		5	2	.71		.276	.342	.352	36	4−4	.478	4
1924	114	356	104	19	7	5	(2	3)	152	46	52	48		4	13		2	6	.25		.292	.427	.371	59	6−4	.585	8
1925	73	167	40	8	1	2	(0	2)	56	17	24	17		0	7		3	1	.75		.240	.335	.298	18	2−3	.359	2
1926	103	285	94	19	5	8	(7	1)	147	36	50	32		4	11		5	5	.50		.330	.516	.392	59	6−2	.697	8
1927	97	263	84	15	2	5	(3	2)	118	40	42	41		2	4		3				.319	.449	.410	51	5−2	.652	6
1928	91	245	70	10	5	3	(2	1)	99	41	39	68		4	8		8	2	.80		.286	.404	.437	52	5−2	.689	7
1929	94	249	59	10	5	5	(5	0)	94	43	36	74		7	4		1	4	.20		.237	.378	.419	46	5−3	.623	6
1930	45	92	16	4	1	1	(0	1)	25	16	9	17		1	6		0	0	.00		.174	.272	.293	10	1−2	.233	1
1931	30	76	14	2	0	0	(0	0)	16	9	2	14		0	1		1	0	1.00		.184	.211	.308	6	1−2	.229	1
	1840	5306	1506	264	90	59	(36	23)	2127	769	710	849	107	160			122	47	.62		.284	.401	.383	895	94−61	.607	111
11.4 yrs		467	133	23	8	5			187	68	63	75		9	14		11				.284	.401	.383				

Teams: Philadelphia (A), 1913–1917; Boston, 1918–1920; New York, A.L. 1921–1925; St. Louis, 1926–1929; Philadelphia (A), 1930; Detroit, 1931.

Points in MVP Voting: 1913, 11 (8th, .17); 1914, 10 (10th, .16); 1922, 7 (.11); 1923, 0; 1924, 7 (.11); 1926, 0; 1927, 3 (.05). TOTAL: .58 Award Shares.

FIELDING CATCHER

Year	G	PO	AS	Err	DP	PB	Pct.
1913	71	317	97	14	9		.967
1914	100	498	154	30	11		.956
1915	26	110	46	9			.945
1916	36	136	67	14			.935
1917	79	260	102	17	11		.955
1918	57	188	49	9	4		.963
1919	103	359	131	14	15		.972
1920	73	285	76	16	8		.958
1921	132	500	101	19	13		.969
1922	124	456	102	14	12		.976
1923	81	292	60	11	6		.970
1924	109	423	89	15	9		.972
1925	58	172	55	6	8	6	.974
1926	82	224	75	10	7	7	.968
1927	75	213	73	7	10	7	.976
1928	82	263	46	5	5	1	.984
1929	85	268	56	4	6	5	.988
1930	36	126	18	4	2	4	.973
1931	30	91	20	4	6	2	.965
	1439	5181	1417	222	142		.967

Assists per 154 Games: 152

PLAYER: GABBY HARTNETT

					BATTING												BASERUNNING				PERCENTAGES			VALUES			
Year	G	AB	H	2B	3B	HR	(Hm	Rd)	TB	R	RBI	BB	IBB	HBP	SH	SF	SB	CS	SB%	GIDP	Avg.	Slug	On Base	Runs	Win–Loss	Pct.	AV
1922	31	72	14	1	1	0	(	)	17	4	4	6		0	4		1	0	1.00		.194	.236	.244	5	0–2	.144	1
1923	85	231	62	12	2	8	(	)	102	28	39	25		3	4		4	0	1.00		.268	.442	.342	37	4–3	.582	5
1924	111	354	106	17	7	16	(	)	185	56	67	39		5	9		10	2	.83		.299	.523	.369	72	7–3	.717	9
1925	117	398	115	28	3	24	(	)	221	61	67	36		2	7		1	5	.17		.289	.555	.345	75	7–4	.652	10
1926	93	284	78	25	3	8	(	)	133	35	41	32		2	7		0				.275	.468	.345	46	5–3	.652	7
1927	127	449	132	32	5	10	(	)	204	56	80	44		3	13		2				.294	.454	.352	73	8–5	.607	9
1928	120	388	117	26	9	14	(	)	203	61	57	65		2	9		3				.302	.523	.397	83	8–3	.761	12
1929	25	22	6	2	1	1	(	)	13	2	9	5		0	1		1				.273	.591	.393	5	0–0	.686	0
1930	141	508	172	31	3	37	(	)	320	84	122	55		1	14		0				.339	.630	.394	125	10–4	.707	19
1931	116	380	107	32	1	8	(	)	165	53	70	52		1	5		3				.282	.434	.365	63	6–4	.588	9
1932	121	406	110	25	3	12	(	)	177	52	52	51		1	4		0				.271	.436	.351	64	7–4	.616	9
1933	140	490	135	21	4	16	(10	6)	212	55	88	37		0	8		1			17	.276	.433	.321	67	9–6	.606	13
1934	130	438	131	21	1	22	(	)	220	58	90	37		3	9		0			15	.299	.502	.351	77	8–4	.669	13
1935	116	413	142	32	6	13	(	)	225	67	91	41		1	6		1			13	.344	.545	.399	91	8–3	.765	12
1936	121	424	130	25	6	7	(	)	188	49	64	30		6	8		0			12	.307	.443	.355	68	7–4	.637	10
1937	110	356	126	21	6	12	(	)	195	47	82	43		0	6		0			9	.354	.548	.417	85	7–2	.787	12
1938	88	299	82	19	1	10	(	)	133	40	59	48		3	3		1			8	.274	.445	.377	53	6–3	.684	7
1939	97	306	85	18	2	12	(	)	143	36	59	37		1	7		0			11	.278	.467	.350	50	5–3	.612	8
1940	37	64	17	3	0	1	(	)	23	3	12	8		0	1		0			3	.266	.359	.342	8	1–1	.477	1
1941	64	150	45	5	0	5	(	)	65	20	26	12		1	2		0			5	.300	.433	.352	23	3–2	.610	3
	1990	6432	1912	396	64	236	(	)	3144	867	1179	703		35	127		28	7	.70	93	.297	.489	.363	1170	117–62	.654	169
12.3 yrs		524	156	32	5	19			256	71	96	57		3	10		2				.297	.489	.363				

Teams: Chicago, N.L. 1922–1940; New York, N.L. 1941.

Points in MVP Voting: 1926, 0; 1927, 12 (10th, .15); 1931, 0; 1932, 0; 1933, 5 (.06); 1934, 0; 1935, 75 (1st, .94); 1936, 6 (.10); 1937, 68 (2nd, .85); 1939, 61 (10th, .18); 1940, 0; 1941, 0. TOTAL: 2.28 Award Shares.

Explanation for Gaps in Career or Sudden Changes in Productivity: Missed most of 1929 season with extremely sore arm.

Other Notes: Named top major league catcher by *The Sporting News,* 1927 and 1937.

FIELDING CATCHER

Year	G	PO	AS	Err	DP	PB	Pct.
1922	27	79	29	2	0	0	.982
1923	39	143	24	1	2	0	.994
1924	105	369	97	18	12	12	.963
1925	110	409	114	23	15	5	.958
1926	88	307	86	9	6	12	.978
1927	125	479	99	16	21	12	.973
1928	118	455	103	6	14	7	.989
1929	1	4	0	0	0	0	1.000
1930	136	646	68	8	11	10	.989
1931	105	444	68	10	16	8	.981
1932	117	484	75	10	8	11	.982
1933	140	550	77	7	17	4	.989
1934	129	605	86	3	11	9	.996
1935	110	477	77	9	11	5	.984
1936	114	504	75	5	8	5	.991
1937	101	436	65	2	7	8	.996
1938	83	358	40	2	8	6	.995
1939	86	336	47	3	3	8	.992
1940	22	69	9	4	2	1	.951
1941	34	138	15	1	1	3	.994
	1790	7292	1254	139	173	126	.984

Assists per 154 Games: 108

PLAYER: MICKEY COCHRANE

						BATTING											BASERUNNING				PERCENTAGES			VALUES			
Year	G	AB	H	2B	3B	HR	(Hm Rd)	TB	R	RBI	BB	IBB	HBP	SH	SF	SB	CS	SB%	GIDP	Avg.	Slug	On Base	Runs	Win—Loss	Pct.	AV
1925	134	420	139	21	5	6	(1 5)	188	69	55	44		2	8		7	4	.64		.331	.448	.390	76	7—4	.663	13
1926	120	370	101	8	9	8	(5 3)	151	50	47	56		0	26		5	2	.71		.273	.408	.347	60	6—6	.518	8
1927	126	432	146	20	6	12	(6 6)	214	80	80	50		2	23		9				.338	.495	.391	86	9—3	.754	13
1928	131	468	137	26	12	10	(6 4)	217	92	57	76		3	21		7	7	.50		.293	.464	.380	89	9—5	.619	12
1929	135	514	170	37	8	7	(6 1)	244	113	95	69		2	21		7	6	.54		.331	.475	.398	103	10—4	.701	15
1930	130	487	174	42	5	10	(6 4)	256	110	85	55		1	18		5	0	1.00		.357	.526	.410	111	10—3	.751	17
1931	122	459	160	31	6	17	(10 7)	254	87	89	56		3	2		2	3	.40		.349	.553	.421	108	9—3	.737	15
1932	139	518	152	35	4	23	(12 11)	264	118	112	100		4	3		0	1	.00		.293	.510	.410	115	10—4	.734	15
1933	130	429	138	30	4	15	(8 7)	221	104	60	106		3	4		8	6	.57		.322	.515	.456	109	8—3	.729	16
1934	129	437	140	32	1	2	(0 2)	180	74	76	78		4	5		8	4	.67		.320	.412	.424	83	7—4	.627	12
1935	115	411	131	33	3	5	(1 4)	185	93	47	96		4	11		5	5	.50		.319	.450	.443	91	8—3	.694	13
1936	44	126	34	8	0	2	(0 2)	48	24	17	46		0	6		1	1	.50		.270	.381	.449	27	2—2	.599	3
1937	27	98	30	10	1	2	(1 1)	48	27	12	25		1	2		0	1	.00		.306	.490	.444	23	2—1	.691	2
	1482	5169	1652	333	64	119	(62 57)	2470	1041	832	857		29	150		64	40	.58		.320	.478	.409	1082	97—45	.683	154
9.1 yrs		565	181	36	7	13		270	114	91	94		3	16		7				.320	.478	.409				

Teams: Philadelphia (A), 1925–1933; Detroit, 1934–1937.

Points in MVP Voting: 1926, 4 (.06); 1927, 18 (4th, .28); 1928, 1st (won award—voting totals unknown); 1931, 14 (8th, .22); 1932, 0?; 1933, 5 (.06); 1934, 67 (1st, .84); 1935, 24 (7th, .30); 1937, 0. TOTAL: 2.56 Award Shares.

Reported Salaries: No information available.

Explanation for Gaps in Career or Sudden Changes in Productivity:
1934—Tiger Stadium was poor home-run park before it was remodeled in 1937. 1936 and 1937—See comments about him in Section II.

Other Notes: Selected by *The Sporting News* as the outstanding catcher in the major leagues, 1925, 28, 29, 30, 31, 34 and 35. In 1928 he won the MVP award, but I couldn't locate the voting, so I credited him with an .80 share in tabulating the total; also missing data from two of his other best seasons. In 1932, the voting summary for *The Sporting News* award shows him receiving no votes although he had career highs that year in home runs and RBI.

FIELDING CATCHER

Year	G	PO	AS	Err	DP	PB	Pct.
1925	133	419	79	8	9	12	.984
1926	115	502	90	15	9	8	.975
1927	123	559	85	9	11	7	.986
1928	130	645	71	25	8	8	.966
1929	135	659	77	13	9	9	.983
1930	130	654	69	5	11	7	.993
1931	117	560	63	9	9	6	.993
1932	137	652	94	5	15	11	.993
1933	128	476	67	6	8	6	.989
1934	124	517	69	7	7	3	.988
1935	110	504	50	6	6	6	.989
1936	42	159	13	3	1	4	.983
1937	27	103	13	0	1	0	1.000
	1451	6409	840	111	104	87	.985

Assists per 154 Games: 89

PLAYER: BILL DICKEY

					BATTING												BASERUNNING				PERCENTAGES			VALUES			
Year	G	AB	H	2B	3B	HR	(Hm	Rd)	TB	R	RBI	BB	IBB	HBP	SH	SF	SB	CS	SB%	GIDP	Avg.	Slug	On Base	Runs	Win–Loss	Pct.	AV
1928	10	15	3	1	1	0	0	0)	6	1	2	0		0	0		0	0	.00		.200	.400	.200	1	0–0	.192	0
1929	130	447	145	30	6	10	5	5)	217	60	65	14		1	11		4	3	.57		.324	.485	.338	73	7–6	.548	11
1930	109	366	124	25	7	5	3	2)	178	55	65	21		0	9		7	1	.87		.339	.486	.366	67	5–4	.541	8
1931	130	477	156	17	10	6	4	2)	211	65	78	39		0	7		2	1	.67		.327	.442	.373	80	7–6	.538	13
1932	108	423	131	20	4	15	7	8)	204	66	84	34		0	2		2	4	.33		.310	.482	.359	72	6–5	.566	11
1933	130	478	152	24	8	14	9	5)	234	58	97	47		2	5		3	4	.43		.318	.490	.378	89	8–5	.607	13
1934	104	395	127	24	4	12	6	6)	195	56	72	38		2	3		0	3	.00		.322	.494	.381	74	7–3	.674	9
1935	120	448	125	26	6	14	11	3)	205	54	81	35		6	2		1	1	.50		.279	.458	.338	70	7–5	.569	11
1936	112	423	153	26	8	22	14	8)	261	99	107	46		3	0		0	2	.00		.362	.617	.428	111	8–2	.771	15
1937	140	530	176	35	2	29	21	8)	302	87	133	73		4	1		3	2	.60		.332	.570	.416	128	10–3	.760	19
1938	132	454	142	27	4	27	23	4)	258	84	115	75		2	1		3	0	1.00		.313	.568	.412	111	9–3	.748	16
1939	128	480	145	23	3	24	19	5)	246	98	105	77		4	4		5	0	1.00	9	.302	.513	.400	104	9–4	.723	16
1940	106	372	92	11	1	9	5	4)	132	45	54	48		3	1		0	3	.00	7	.247	.355	.335	46	5–6	.445	7
1941	109	348	99	15	5	7	5	2)	145	35	71	45		3	1		2	1	.67	10	.284	.417	.370	56	6–4	.602	9
1942	82	268	79	13	1	2	1	1)	100	28	37	26		1	0		2	2	.50	12	.295	.373	.359	34	4–3	.538	4
1943	85	242	85	18	2	4	2	2)	119	29	33	41		0	1		2	1	.67	5	.351	.492	.444	57	5–1	.851	7
1946	54	134	35	8	0	2	0	2)	49	10	10	19		1			0	1	.00	6	.261	.366	.353	17	2–2	.541	2
	1789	6300	1969	343	72	202	(135	67)	3062	930	1209	678		31	51		36	29	.55	49	.313	.486	.379	1193	106–63	.626	171
11.0 yrs		570	178	31	7	18			277	84	109	61		3	5		3	3			.313	.486	.379				

Teams: New York, A.L. 1928–1943; 1946.

Points in MVP Voting: 1931, 0; 1932, 0; 1933, 9 (.11); 1934, 0; 1935, 0; 1936, 29 (5th, .36); 1937, 22 (6th, .28); 1938, 196 (2nd, .58); 1939, 110 (6th, .33); 1940, 0; 1941, 18 (.05); 1942, 12 (.04); 1943, 58 (8th, .17); 1946, 0. TOTAL: 1.92 Award Shares.

Explanation for Gaps in Career or Sudden Changes in Productivity: Suspended July 4 to August 4, 1931, and fined $1,000 for breaking Carl Reynolds' jaw in a fight after a home-plate collision.

Other Notes: 1936—5 HR off LHP, 17 off RHP.
1938—5 HR off LHP, 22 off RHP.
1939—3 HR off LHP, 21 off RHP.
Selected as outstanding catcher in the major leagues by *The Sporting News*, 1932, 1933, 1936, 1938, 1939, 1941.

FIELDING CATCHER

Year	G	PO	AS	Err	DP	PB	Pct.
1928	6	6	2	0	0	1	1.000
1929	127	476	95	12	13	4	.979
1930	101	418	51	11	5	5	.977
1931	125	670	78	3	6	0	.996
1932	108	639	53	9	6	7	.987
1933	127	721	82	6	15	10	.993
1934	104	527	49	8	13	7	.986
1935	118	536	62	3	7	8	.995
1936	107	499	61	14	10	6	.976
1937	137	692	80	7	11	5	.991
1938	126	518	94	8	7	7	.987
1939	126	571	57	7	8	6	.989
1940	102	425	55	3	9	5	.994
1941	104	422	45	3	11	2	.994
1942	80	322	44	9	7	1	.976
1943	71	322	37	2	5	2	.994
1946	39	201	29	3	4	0	.987
	1708	7965	974	108	137	76	.988

Assists per 154 Games: 88

PLAYER: AL LOPEZ

	BATTING																BASERUNNING				PERCENTAGES			VALUES			
Year	G	AB	H	2B	3B	HR	Hm	Rd	TB	R	RBI	BB	IBB	HBP	SH	SF	SB	CS	SB%	GIDP	Avg.	Slug	On Base	Runs	Win–Loss	Pct.	AV
1928	3	12	0	0	0	0			0	0	0	0		0	0		0							0	0–0	.000	0
1930	128	421	130	20	4	6			176	33	57	33		2	10		3				.309	.418	.354	62	5–6	.474	10
1931	111	360	97	13	4	0			118	38	40	28		1	3		1				.269	.328	.321	39	4–6	.417	6
1932	126	404	111	18	6	1			144	44	43	34		0	6		3				.275	.356	.327	50	5–6	.467	8
1933	126	372	112	11	4	3	2	1	140	39	41	21		0	10		10			9	.301	.376	.330	47	6–4	.588	8
1934	140	439	120	23	2	7			168	58	54	49		2	14		2			15	.273	.383	.339	60	6–6	.516	10
1935	128	379	95	12	4	3			124	50	39	35		1	10		2			8	.251	.327	.308	41	4–7	.390	7
1936	128	426	103	12	4	8			147	46	50	41		2	1		1			15	.242	.345	.311	45	5–7	.391	7
1937	105	334	68	11	1	3			90	31	38	35		1	8		3			15	.204	.269	.275	25	2–8	.228	5
1938	71	236	63	6	1	1			74	19	14	11		2	7		5			9	.267	.314	.297	22	2–4	.352	3
1939	131	412	104	22	1	8			152	32	49	40		0	11		1			10	.252	.369	.311	49	5–6	.464	8
1940	95	293	80	9	3	3			104	35	41	19		0	5		6			11	.273	.355	.312	32	4–4	.446	5
1941	114	317	84	9	1	5			110	33	43	31		0	6		0			10	.265	.347	.325	36	4–5	.479	6
1942	103	289	74	8	2	1			89	17	26	34		2	6		0			10	.256	.308	.332	31	4–4	.480	6
1943	118	372	98	9	4	1			118	40	39	49		0	12		2			6	.263	.317	.339	45	6–5	.536	8
1944	115	331	76	12	1	1			93	27	34	34		1	5		4			7	.230	.281	.299	30	3–6	.331	5
1945	91	243	53	8	0	0			61	22	18	35		0	2		1			5	.218	.251	.314	23	2–5	.343	4
1946	56	150	46	2	0	1			51	13	12	23		0	4		1			4	.307	.340	.390	21	3–1	.642	3
1947	61	126	33	1	0	0			34	9	14	9		0	1		1	1	0.50	1	.262	.270	.309	11	1–2	.319	2
	1950	5916	1547	206	42	52			1993	586	652	561		14	121		46	1		137	.261	.337	.321	668	73–94	.437	111
12.0 yrs		491	129	17	3	4			166	49	54	47		1	10		4			137	.261	.337	.321				

Teams: Brooklyn, N.L., 1928, 1930–1935; Boston, N.L. 1936–1939; Boston–Pittsburgh, N.L. 1940; Pittsburgh, 1941–1946; Cleveland, A.L. 1947.

Points in MVP Voting: 1931, 0; 1932, 0; 1933, 18 (10th, .23); 1934, 1 (.01); 1935, 0; 1936, 5 (.08); 1937, 0; 1938, 5 (.01); 1939, 0; 1940, 9 (.03); 1941, 8 (.02); 1942, 0; 1943, 0; 1944, 0; 1946, 0; 1947, 0. TOTAL: .38 Award Shares.

Explanation for Gaps in Career or Sudden Changes in Productivity:
1938—Groin injury.
1940—Injured when hit by pitch.
1946—Broken hand.

Other Notes: Was never selected to *The Sporting News* major league All-Star team.

FIELDING CATCHER

Year	G	PO	AS	Err	DP	PB	Pct.
1928	3	9	0	0	0	0	1.000
1930	126	465	66	9	9	5	.983
1931	105	390	69	11	6	6	.977
1932	125	456	82	13	10	5	.976
1933	124	449	84	5	14	2	.991
1934	137	542	62	11	4	9	.982
1935	126	472	65	11	8	7	.980
1936	127	447	107	14	9	1	.975
1937	102	342	83	7	5	3	.984
1938	71	240	42	3	4	3	.989
1939	129	424	72	7	0	5	.986
1940	95	343	62	4	11	2	.990
1941	114	345	54	8	5	0	.980
1942	99	327	53	2	14	3	.995
1943	116	378	66	4	9	1	.991
1944	115	372	52	7	6	10	.984
1945	91	326	38	3	7	4	.992
1946	56	173	30	3	4	0	.985
1947	57	144	28	0	1	0	1.000
	1918	6644	1115	122	126	66	.985

Assists per 154 Games: 90

PLAYER: ERNIE LOMBARDI

Year	G	AB	H	2B	3B	HR	(Hm Rd)	TB	R	RBI	BB	IBB	HBP	SH	SF	SB	CS	SB%	GIDP	Avg.	Slug	On Base	Runs	Win–Loss	Pct.	AV
1931	73	182	54	7	1	4	( )	75	20	23	12		0	2		1				.297	.412	.337	25	3–2	.567	3
1932	118	413	125	22	9	11	( )	198	43	68	41		4	0		0				.303	.479	.371	74	8–3	.720	10
1933	107	350	99	21	1	4	(1 3)	134	30	47	16		4	3		2			26	.283	.383	.319	36	5–6	.464	6
1934	132	417	127	19	4	9	( )	181	42	62	16		3	0		0			24	.305	.434	.335	53	6–6	.501	10
1935	120	332	114	23	3	12	( )	179	36	64	16		3	0		0			11	.343	.539	.379	65	6–2	.738	9
1936	121	387	129	23	2	12	( )	192	42	68	19		7	0		1			15	.333	.496	.375	69	7–3	.668	9
1937	120	368	123	22	1	9	( )	174	41	59	14		2	0		1			12	.334	.473	.362	60	7–3	.690	8
1938	129	489	167	30	1	19	( )	256	60	95	40		0	0		0			30	.342	.524	.391	91	9–4	.708	14
1939	130	450	129	26	2	20	( )	219	43	85	35		3	6		0			24	.287	.487	.338	69	8–5	.595	11
1940	109	376	120	22	0	14	( )	184	50	74	31		7	0		0			18	.319	.489	.382	66	7–3	.725	10
1941	117	398	105	12	1	10	( )	149	33	60	36		0	0		1			19	.264	.374	.325	45	6–6	.503	7
1942	105	309	102	14	0	11	( )	149	32	46	37		1	0		1			17	.330	.482	.403	56	6–2	.755	9
1943	104	295	90	7	0	10	( )	127	19	51	16		1	1		1			18	.305	.431	.342	38	5–4	.552	6
1944	117	373	95	13	0	10	( )	138	37	58	33		1	1		0			23	.255	.370	.316	38	4–7	.347	6
1945	115	368	113	7	1	19	( )	179	46	70	43		5	1		0			12	.307	.486	.386	69	7–3	.708	10
1946	88	238	69	4	1	12	( )	111	19	39	18		3	3		0			8	.290	.466	.344	37	4–2	.634	4
1947	48	110	31	5	0	4	( )	48	8	21	7		0	1		0			4	.282	.436	.322	15	1–2	.452	2
11.4 yrs	1853	5855	1792	277	27	190	( )	2693	601	990	430		44	18		8			261	.306	.460	.357	906	99–63	.610	134
		512	157	24	2	17		235	53	87	38		4	2		1				.306	.460	.357				

Teams: Brooklyn, N.L. 1931; Cincinnati, 1932–1941; Boston, N.L. 1942; New York, N.L. 1943–1947.

Points in MVP Voting: 1931, 0; 1932, 2 (.02); 1933, 0; 1934, 0; 1935, 8 (.10); 1936, 1 (.02); 1937, 0; 1938, 229 (1st, .68); 1939, 0; 1940, 38 (9th, .1); 1941, 0; 1942, 24 (.07); 1943, 0; 1944, 0; 1945, 0; 1946, 0; 1947, 0. TOTAL: 1.00 Award Shares.

Reported Salaries: 1938—$13,000; 1939—$17,000; 1941—$18,000; 1943—$10,000.

Explanation for Gaps in Career or Sudden Changes in Productivity: Discussed at length in article in Section II.

Other Notes: Although he took part in five All-Star games, Lombardi was never named to *The Sporting News* major league post-season All-Star team—even in 1938, when he was the NL's Most Valuable Player.

FIELDING CATCHER

Year	G	PO	AS	Err	DP	PB	Pct.
1931	50	218	23	4	5	3	.984
1932	108	288	76	14	6	17	.963
1933	95	223	52	8	3	9	.972
1934	111	383	61	5	8	8	.989
1935	82	298	49	6	4	10	.983
1936	105	330	54	15	10	7	.962
1937	90	333	58	11	3	13	.973
1938	123	512	73	9	8	9	.985
1939	120	536	63	10	7	6	.984
1940	101	397	46	5	5	7	.989
1941	116	496	70	10	9	16	.983
1942	85	251	41	6	3	9	.980
1943	73	296	36	10	8	6	.971
1944	100	350	47	13	11	9	.968
1945	96	425	49	8	8	9	.983
1946	63	272	36	7	7	4	.978
1947	24	86	11	2	2	1	.980
	1542	5694	845	143	107	143	.979

Assists per 154 Games: 84

PLAYER: YOGI BERRA

							BATTING											BASERUNNING				PERCENTAGES			VALUES			
Year	G	AB	H	2B	3B	HR	(Hm	Rd)	TB	R	RBI	BB	IBB	HBP	SH	SF		SB	CS	SB%	GIDP	Avg.	Slug	On Base	Runs	Win–Loss	Pct.	AV
1946	7	22	8	1	0	2	(2	0)	15	3	4	1		0	0			0	0	.00	0	.364	.682	.391	6	0–0	.897	1
1947	83	293	82	15	3	11	(6	5)	136	41	54	13		0	0			0	1	.00	7	.280	.464	.310	41	5–4	.565	5
1948	125	469	143	24	10	14	(9	5)	229	70	98	25		1	2			3	3	.50	9	.305	.488	.340	77	8–5	.616	9
1949	116	415	115	20	2	20	(14	6)	199	59	91	22		6	0			2	1	.67	6	.277	.480	.323	65	7–5	.595	9
1950	151	597	192	30	6	28	(14	14)	318	116	124	55		1	0			4	2	.67	11	.322	.533	.380	123	11–5	.703	14
1951	141	547	161	19	4	27	(12	15)	269	92	88	44		3	0			5	4	.56	16	.294	.492	.350	92	10–5	.638	13
1952	142	534	146	17	1	30	(18	12)	255	97	98	66		4	1			2	3	.40	8	.273	.478	.357	95	10–4	.704	14
1953	137	503	149	23	5	27	(13	14)	263	80	108	50		3	1			0	3	.00	7	.296	.523	.363	96	10–4	.715	14
1954	151	584	179	28	6	22	(15	7)	285	88	125	56		4	1	7		0	1	.00	9	.307	.488	.367	107	11–5	.706	15
1955	147	541	147	20	3	27	(20	7)	254	84	108	60	6	7	2	5		1	0	1.00	13	.272	.470	.348	90	10–5	.646	13
1956	140	521	155	29	2	30	(19	11)	278	93	105	65	7	5	1	5		3	2	.60	8	.298	.534	.377	108	10–4	.713	16
1957	134	482	121	14	2	24	(17	7)	211	74	82	57	10	1	1	4		1	2	.33	11	.251	.438	.328	69	8–6	.592	13
1958	122	433	115	17	3	22	(13	9)	204	60	90	35	5	2	0	6		3	0	1.00	6	.266	.471	.319	67	8–5	.615	11
1959	131	472	134	25	1	19	(10	9)	218	64	69	43	5	4	0	2		1	2	.33	6	.284	.462	.347	77	8–4	.656	12
1960	120	359	99	14	1	15	(9	6)	160	46	62	38	6	3	0	4		2	1	.67	11	.276	.446	.347	55	6–4	.592	9
1961	119	395	107	11	0	22	(12	10)	184	62	61	35	4	2	0	5		2	0	1.00	7	.271	.466	.330	62	7–4	.611	8
1962	86	232	52	8	0	10	(4	6)	90	25	35	24	4	2	0	5		0	1	.00	7	.224	.388	.297	26	3–4	.386	3
1963	64	147	43	6	0	8	(3	5)	73	20	28	15	2	1	0	1		1	0	1.00	4	.293	.497	.360	26	3–1	.731	3
1965	4	9	2	0	0	0	(0	0)	2	1	0	0	0	0	0			0	0	.00		.222	.222	.222	0	0–0	.166	0
13.1 yrs	2120	7555	2150	321	49	358	(210	148)	3643	1175	1430	704	49	49	9	44		30	26	.54	146	.285	.482	.347	1280	134–74	.643	182
	577	164		25	4	27			278	90	109	54		4	1			2	2		11	.285	.482	.347				

Teams: New York, A.L. 1946–1963, (N) 1965.

Points in MVP Voting: 1946, 0; 1947, 18 (.05); 1948, 13 (.01); 1949, 9 (.03); 1950, 146 (3rd, .45); 1951, 184 (1st, .55); 1952, 104 (4th, .31); 1953, 167 (2nd, .50); 1954, 230 (1st, .68); 1955, 218 (1st, .65); 1956, 186 (2nd, .55); 1958, 6 (.02); 1959, 26 (.08); 1960, 21 (.06); 1961, 2 (.01); 1962, 0; 1963, 0; 1965, 0. TOTAL: 3.95 Award Shares.

Other Notes: 1952: 11 HR vs. LHP, 19 off RHP.

Selected as catcher on *The Sporting News* post-season league All-Star team in 1950, 1952, 1954, 1956, and 1957.

FIELDING CATCHER

Year	G	PO	AS	Err	DP	PB	Pct.
1946	6	28	6	0	2	0	1.000
1947	51	259	18	8	5	3	.972
1948	71	297	36	7	5	8	.979
1949	109	544	60	7	18	4	.989
1950	148	777	64	13	16	7	.985
1951	141	693	82	13	25	3	.984
1952	140	700	73	6	10	5	.992
1953	133	566	64	9	9	8	.986
1954	149	717	63	8	14	5	.990
1955	145	721	54	13	10	3	.984
1956	135	732	55	11	15	7	.986
1957	121	704	61	4	12	9	.995
1958	88	509	41	0	8	5	1.000
1959	116	698	61	2	3	3	.997
1960	63	256	22	3	6	1	.989
1961	15	76	8	0	0	3	1.000
1962	31	175	16	2	6	1	.990
1963	35	244	13	3	5	1	.988
1965	2	15	1	1	0	0	.941
	1699	8711	798	110	175	76	.989

Assists per 154 Games: 72

PLAYER: ROY CAMPANELLA

						BATTING												BASERUNNING				PERCENTAGES			VALUES			
Year	G	AB	H	2B	3B	HR	(Hm	Rd)	TB	R	RBI	BB	IBB	HBP	SH	SF		SB	CS	SB%	GIDP	Avg.	Slug	On Base	Runs	Win–Loss	Pct.	AV
1948	83	279	72	11	3	9	(5	4)	116	32	45	36			1	5		3			3	.258	.416	.340	42	5–3	.577	6
1949	130	436	125	22	2	22	(15	7)	217	65	82	67			3	1		3			11	.287	.498	.385	86	8–4	.680	14
1950	126	437	123	19	3	31	(18	13)	241	70	89	55			2	0		1			17	.281	.551	.364	84	8–4	.649	13
1951	143	505	164	33	1	33	(21	12)	298	90	108	53			4	0		1	2	.33	19	.325	.590	.393	112	10–3	.748	17
1952	128	468	126	18	1	22	(7	15)	212	73	97	57			3	5		8	4	.67	22	.269	.453	.349	70	8–6	.568	11
1953	144	519	162	26	3	41	(22	19)	317	103	142	67			4	0		4	2	.67	13	.312	.611	.395	125	10–4	.744	20
1954	111	397	82	14	3	19	(9	10)	159	43	51	42		2	4	1		1	4	.20	13	.207	.401	.283	42	4–8	.322	9
1955	123	446	142	20	1	32	(21	11)	260	81	107	56	9	6	5	9		2	3	.40	14	.318	.583	.391	101	9–3	.735	15
1956	124	388	85	6	1	20	(12	8)	153	39	73	66	15	1	4	2		1	0	1.00	20	.219	.394	.330	49	6–7	.465	10
1957	103	330	80	9	0	13	(10	3)	128	31	62	34	6	4	6	6		1	0	1.00	11	.242	.388	.311	40	5–5	.479	7
	1215	4205	1161	178	18	242	(140	102)	2101	627	856	533			30	30		25	15	.54	143	.276	.500	.358	751	72–48	.602	122
7.5 yrs		561	155	24	2	32			280	84	114	71			4	4		3			19	.276	.500	.358				

Teams: Brooklyn, 1948–1957

Points in MVP Voting: 1948, 8 (.02); 1949, 22 (.06); 1950, 29 (.09); 1951, 243 (1st, .72); 1952, 25 (10th, .07); 1953, 297 (1st, .88); 1954, 0; 1955, 226 (1st, .67); 1956–57, 0. TOTAL: 2.51 Award Shares.

Reported Salaries: 1948, $6,500; 1949, $9,500; 1950, $12,500; 1952, $23,000; 1953, $30,000; 1954, $40,000; 1956, $50,000.

Explanation for Gaps in Career or Sudden Changes in Productivity:
1954—Fragment chipped off bone in heel of left hand after he caught his spikes while trying to break up double play in exhibition game against Yankees, March 21. He tried to play with it and the chip damaged the nerves in his hand. Operation that winter eased the problem, but it returned in 1956, and his hitting was never the same.

Other Notes: Won MVP award in 1955 despite missing almost a month with his knee in a cast.

FIELDING CATCHER

Year	G	PO	AS	Err	DP	PB	Pct.
1948	78	413	45	9	12	4	.981
1949	127	684	55	11	5	7	.985
1950	123	683	54	11	14	6	.985
1951	140	722	72	11	12	4	.986
1952	122	662	55	4	7	9	.994
1953	140	807	57	10	9	3	.989
1954	111	600	58	7	7	4	.989
1955	121	672	54	6	8	4	.992
1956	121	659	49	11	3	8	.985
1957	100	618	51	5	7	5	.993
	1183	6520	550	85	84	54	.988

Assists per 154 Games: 72

PLAYER: BILL FREEHAN

				BATTING														BASERUNNING				PERCENTAGES			VALUES			
Year	G	AB	H	2B	3B	HR	(Hm	Rd)	TB	R	RBI	BB	IBB	HBP	SH	SF	SB	CS	SB%	GIDP	Avg.	Slug	On Base	Runs	Win–Loss	Pct.	AV
1961	4	10	4	0	0	0	(0	0)	4	1	4	1	0	0	0	0	0	0	.00	0	.400	.400	.455	2	0–0	.779	0
1963	100	300	73	12	2	9	(3	6)	116	37	36	39	4	2	1	3	2	0	1.00	8	.243	.387	.330	40	5–4	.516	5
1964	144	520	156	14	8	18	(9	9)	240	69	80	36	3	8	1	7	5	1	.83	8	.300	.462	.350	86	10–5	.675	13
1965	130	431	101	15	0	10	(7	3)	146	45	43	39	15	7	5	3	4	2	.67	10	.234	.339	.303	45	6–7	.431	7
1966	136	492	115	22	0	12	(6	6)	173	47	46	40	9	3	7	2	5	2	.71	11	.234	.352	.290	50	6–9	.378	8
1967	155	517	146	23	1	20	(8	12)	231	66	74	73	15	20	3	5	1	2	.33	9	.282	.447	.387	94	11–4	.738	13
1968	155	540	142	24	2	25	(14	11)	245	73	84	65	4	24	3	3	0	1	.00	9	.263	.454	.364	94	11–4	.750	13
1969	143	489	128	16	3	16	(7	9)	198	61	49	53	3	8	2	3	1	2	.33	15	.262	.405	.341	67	8–6	.580	13
1970	117	395	95	17	3	16	(10	6)	166	44	52	52	5	4	3	4	0	3	.00	11	.241	.420	.330	55	6–6	.533	8
1971	148	516	143	26	4	21	(8	13)	240	57	71	54	9	9	3	4	2	7	.22	13	.277	.465	.352	82	9–5	.640	13
1972	111	374	98	18	2	10	(6	4)	150	51	56	48	0	6	1	1	0	1	.00	7	.262	.401	.353	55	7–3	.698	9
1973	110	380	89	10	1	6	(4	2)	119	33	29	40	2	11	1	3	0	0	.00	13	.234	.313	.322	39	5–7	.416	6
1974	130	445	132	17	5	18	(10	8)	213	58	60	42	2	5	6	4	2	0	1.00	12	.297	.479	.357	77	8–4	.676	10
1975	120	427	105	17	3	14	(6	8)	170	42	47	32	3	6	1	2	2	0	1.00	11	.246	.398	.306	51	6–6	.483	7
1976	71	237	64	10	1	5	(2	3)	91	22	27	12	0	1	1	4	0	0	.00	4	.270	.384	.302	28	3–3	.503	3
	1774	6073	1591	241	35	200	(100	100)	2502	706	758	626	74	114	38	48	24	21	.53	141	.262	.412	.338	865	102–74	.580	128
11.0 yrs		555	145	22	3	18			228	64	69	57	7	10	3	4	2	2		13	.262	.412	.338				

Teams: Detroit, 1961; Detroit 1963–1976.

Points in MVP Voting: 1961, 0; 1963, 0; 1964, 44 (7th, .16); 1965, 0; 1966, 0; 1967, 137 (3rd, .49); 1968, 161 (2nd, .58); 1969, 3 (.01); 1970, 0; 1971 0; 1972, 3 (.01); 1973, 0; 1974, 0; 1975, 0; 1976, 0. TOTAL: 1.25 Award Shares.

Reported Salaries: 1968—$37,000; 1969—about $52,000. Received $125,000 bonus to sign with Tigers in 1961.

Explanation for Gaps in Career or Sudden Changes in Productivity:
1965—Series of minor injuries.
1973—Must have been playing hurt but didn't report anything.

Other Notes: Freehan wrote a baseball diary, *Behind the Mask,* the same year that Bouton wrote his (1969). Much of the book is dated and embarrassing. He wrote about Mayo Smith: "I've played for a lot of managers, and Mayo, I guess, is the smartest at understanding personalities. He treats us like men, not children. I only wish we could all live up to that." In Bouton's book, Norm Cash is quoted as saying that Mayo Smith is the dumbest manager in baseball. The most durable part of Freehan's book are his numerous comments on Denny McLain, whom he couldn't stand but was fascinated with. His portrayal of McLain is basically that of a self-destructive egomaniac, desperately in need of a discipline that baseball did not provide him.

Selected as outstanding American League catcher by *The Sporting News,* 1967, 1968, 1969, 1971; also won Gold Glove Award, 1965 through 1969.

FIELDING CATCHER

Year	G	PO	AS	Err	DP	PB	Pct.
1961	3	14	4	0	0	0	1.000
1963	73	407	22	2	5	5	.995
1964	141	923	61	7	7	10	.993
1965	129	865	57	4	4	20	.996
1966	132	898	56	4	11	3	.996
1967	147	950	63	8	9	16	.992
1968	138	971	73	6	15	7	.994
1969	120	821	49	7	7	9	.992
1970	114	742	42	2	6	8	.997
1971	144	912	50	4	6	7	.996
1972	105	648	57	8	9	7	.989
1973	98	584	50	3	3	3	.995
1974	63	312	45	5	6	5	.986
1975	113	582	64	6	8	4	.991
1976	61	312	28	6	2	2	.983
	1581	9941	721	72	98	106	.993

Assists per 154 Games: 70

PLAYER: JOHNNY BENCH

	BATTING											BASERUNNING									PERCENTAGES			VALUES			
Year	G	AB	H	2B	3B	HR	(Hm	Rd)	TB	R	RBI	BB	IBB	HBP	SH	SF	SB	CS	SB%	GIDP	Avg.	Slug	On Base	Runs	Win–Loss	Pct.	AV
1967	26	86	14	3	1	1	(0	1)	22	7	6	5	0	0	1	1	0	1	.00	4	.163	.256	.204	4	0–3	.108	1
1968	154	564	155	40	2	15	(10	5)	244	67	82	31	8	2	2	8	1	5	.17	14	.275	.433	.310	71	9–8	.525	14
1969	148	532	156	23	1	26	(16	10)	259	83	90	49	7	4	0	7	6	6	.50	7	.293	.487	.353	92	9–5	.630	13
1970	158	605	177	35	4	45	(30	15)	355	97	148	54	9	0	1	11	5	2	.71	12	.293	.587	.344	121	12–5	.721	16
1971	149	562	134	19	2	27	(14	13)	238	80	61	49	7	0	0	2	2	1	.67	20	.238	.423	.299	66	9–8	.549	10
1972	147	538	145	22	2	40	(16	24)	291	87	125	100	23	2	0	12	6	6	.50	18	.270	.541	.379	110	12–4	.739	16
1973	152	557	141	17	3	25	(7	18)	239	83	104	83	14	0	1	10	4	1	.80	22	.253	.429	.344	82	10–7	.576	14
1974	160	621	174	38	2	33	(17	16)	315	108	129	80	15	3	0	4	5	4	.56	13	.280	.507	.363	114	12–5	.700	17
1975	142	530	150	39	1	28	(15	13)	275	83	110	65	12	2	0	8	11	0	1.00	12	.283	.519	.359	101	10–4	.707	16
1976	135	465	109	24	1	16	(12	4)	183	62	74	81	6	2	0	4	13	2	.87	9	.234	.394	.348	69	8–6	.547	12
1977	142	494	136	34	2	31	(16	15)	267	67	109	58	8	1	0	7	2	4	.33	10	.275	.540	.348	92	9–5	.660	15
1978	120	393	102	17	1	23	(11	12)	190	52	73	50	10	1	1	6	4	2	.67	9	.260	.483	.339	65	7–4	.631	10
1979	130	464	128	19	0	22	(7	15)	213	73	80	67	8	0	3	4	4	2	.67	11	.276	.459	.362	79	9–4	.664	13
1980	114	360	90	12	0	24	(9	15)	174	52	68	41	2	2	0	4	4	2	.67	9	.250	.483	.327	57	7–4	.617	9
1981	52	178	55	8	0	8	(5	3)	87	14	25	17	3	0	1	0	0	2	.00	4	.309	.489	.367	31	3–1	.699	3
1982	119	399	103	16	0	13	(5	8)	158	44	38	37	2	0	1	2	1	2	.33	14	.258	.396	.319	48	6–5	.548	6
1983	110	310	79	15	2	12	(5	7)	134	32	54	24	1	0	0	0	0	1	.00	13	.255	.432	.308	37	5–5	.500	5
	2158	7658	2048	381	24	389	(195	194)	3644	1091	1376	891	135	19	11	90	68	43	.61	201	.267	.476	.341	1240	137–84	.621	190
13.3 yrs		575	154	29	2	29			274	82	103	67	10	1	1	7	5	3		15	.267	.476	.341				

Teams: Cincinnati, 1967–1983

Points in MVP Voting: 1967, 0; 1968, 11 (.04); 1969, 12 (.04); 1970, 326 (1st, .97); 1971, 0; 1972, 263, (1st, .78); 1973, 41 (10th, .12); 1974, 141 (4th, .42); 1975, 117 (4th, .35); 1976, 0; 1977, 3 (.01); 1978, 0; 1979, 7 (.02); 1980, 7 (.02); 1981, 0; 1982, 0; 1983, 0. TOTAL: 2.77 Award Shares.

Reported Salaries: No information available.

Other Notes: Selected as outstanding catcher in the National League by *The Sporting News,* 1968, 1969, 1970, 1972, 1973, 1974, 1975.

FIELDING CATCHER

Year	G	PO	AS	Err	DP	PB	Pct.
1967	26	175	16	1	0	2	.995
1968	154	942	102	9	10	18	.991
1969	147	793	76	7	10	14	.992
1970	140	759	73	12	12	9	.986
1971	141	687	59	9	9	6	.988
1972	130	742	56	6	9	2	.993
1973	134	693	61	4	7	8	.995
1974	137	757	68	6	16	3	.993
1975	121	568	51	7	9	0	.989
1976	128	651	60	2	11	5	.997
1977	135	705	66	10	10	3	.987
1978	107	605	48	7	6	12	.989
1979	126	619	68	10	5	11	.986
1980	105	505	39	5	7	6	.991
1981	7	41	5	1	0	1	.979
1982	1	1	0	0	0	0	1.000
1983	5	17	2	1	0	0	.950
	1744	9260	850	97	121	100	.990

Assists per 154 Games: 75

First Base

Frank Chance
George Sisler
Jim Bottomley
Bill Terry
Lou Gehrig
Jimmie Foxx
Hank Greenberg
Johnny Mize
Gil Hodges
Ted Kluszewski
Norm Cash
Willie McCovey

PLAYER: FRANK CHANCE

BATTING / BASERUNNING / PERCENTAGES / VALUES

Year	G	AB	H	2B	3B	HR	Hm	Rd	TB	R	RBI	BB	IBB	HBP	SH	SF	SB	CS	SB%	GIDP	Avg.	Slug	On Base	Runs	Win–Loss	Pct.	AV
1898	53	147	42	4	3	1			55	32	14	7		6	2		7				.286	.374	.340	20	2–2	.491	2
1899	64	192	55	6	2	1			68	37	22	15		4	2		10				.286	.354	.347	27	3–3	.476	3
1900	56	151	46	8	4	0			62	26	13	15		14	8		8				.305	.411	.399	27	3–2	.614	3
1901	69	241	67	12	4	0			87	38	36	29		6	4		30				.278	.361	.364	43	5–2	.647	4
1902	75	240	69	9	4	1			89	39	31	35		8	2		28				.288	.371	.393	46	5–2	.772	4
1903	125	441	144	24	10	2			194	83	81	78			2		67				.327	.440	.426	115	10–2	.816	11
1904	124	451	140	16	10	6			194	89	49	36			11		42				.310	.430	.353	88	10–3	.794	10
1905	118	392	124	16	12	2			170	92	70	78			15		38				.316	.434	.416	93	9–2	.847	9
1906	136	474	151	24	10	3			204	103	71	70			18		57				.319	.430	.393	111	11–2	.846	13
1907	110	382	112	19	2	1			138	58	49	51			5		35				.293	.361	.372	67	9–2	.805	7
1908	129	452	123	27	4	2			164	65	55	37			16		27				.272	.363	.317	62	9–5	.643	6
1909	93	324	88	16	4	0			112	53	46	30		4	12		29				.272	.346	.330	48	7–3	.697	5
1910	88	295	88	12	8	0			116	54	36	37		10	6		16				.298	.393	.388	52	6–2	.715	4
1911	31	88	21	6	3	1			36	23	17	25		5	6		9				.239	.409	.411	20	2–1	.723	1
1912	2	5	1	0	0	0			1	2	0	3		0	1		1				.200	.200	.500	1	0–0	.650	0
1913	11	24	5	0	0	0			5	3	6	8		0	0		1				.208	.208	.406	2	0–0	.381	0
1914	1	0	0	0	0	0			0	0	0	0		0	0		0				.000			0	0–0	.000	0
7.9 yrs	1285	4299	1276	199	80	20			1695	797	596	554		57	110		405				.297	.394	.376	823	90–33	.733	82
		542	161	25	10	3			214	100	75	70			14		51				.297	.394	.376				

Runs created estimates prior to 1900 are of indeterminate accuracy

Teams: Chicago, N.L. 1898–1912; New York, A.L. 1913–1914.
Points in MVP Voting: 1911, 0; 1913, 0; 1914, 0.

FIELDING FIRST BASE

Year	G	PO	AS	Err	DP	Pct.
1898	3	18	0	2	0	.900
1899	1	2	0	0	0	1.000
1900	1	5	1	1	0	.857
1901	6	27	3	4	1	.882
1902	38	391	20	13	21	.969
1903	121	1204	68	36	49	.972
1904	123	1205	106	13	48	.990
1905	115	1165	75	13	54	.990
1906	136	1376	83	8	61	.995
1907	108	1126	80	10	64	.992
1908	126	1291	86	15	56	.989
1909	92	901	40	6	43	.994
1910	87	773	38	3	48	.996
1911	29	289	11	3		.990
1912	2	22	0	0		1.000
1913	8	88	4	0		1.000
1914	1	1	0	0		1.000
	997	9884	615	127	445	.988

Assists per 154 Games: 95

PLAYER: GEORGE SISLER

				BATTING													BASERUNNING				PERCENTAGES			VALUES			
Year	G	AB	H	2B	3B	HR	(Hm Rd)	TB	R	RBI	BB	IBB	HBP	SH	SF	SB	CS	SB%	GIDP	Avg.	Slug	On Base	Runs	Win−Loss	Pct.	AV
1915	81	274	78	10	2	3	(2 1)	101	28	29	7			2	12		10	9	.53		.285	.369	.295	33	4−4	.530	3
1916	151	580	177	21	11	3	(2 2)	229	83	76	40			5	19		34	26	.57		.305	.395	.345	94	12−5	.699	10
1917	135	539	190	30	9	2	(1 1)	244	60	52	30			3	15		37				.353	.453	.380	104	11−3	.788	13
1918	114	452	154	21	9	2	(1 1)	199	69	41	40			5	9		45				.341	.440	.393	92	10−2	.828	10
1919	132	511	180	31	15	10	(7 3)	271	96	83	27			5	18		28				.352	.530	.378	112	11−2	.817	15
1920	154	631	257	49	18	19	(15 4)	399	136	122	46			2	13		42	17	.71		.407	.632	.441	186	13−2	.848	19
1921	138	582	216	38	18	11	(7 5)	323	125	104	34			5	14		35	11	.76		.371	.555	.402	138	11−4	.739	16
1922	142	586	246	42	18	8	(4 4)	348	134	105	49			3	16		51	19	.73		.420	.594	.456	173	12−2	.857	18
1924	151	636	194	27	10	9	(3 6)	268	94	74	31			3	14		19	17	.53		.305	.421	.333	94	9−9	.506	10
1925	150	649	224	21	15	12	(10 2)	311	100	105	27			0	12		11	12	.48		.345	.479	.365	115	10−8	.565	13
1926	150	613	178	21	12	7	(4 3)	244	78	71	30			3	16		12	8	.60		.290	.398	.319	82	8−9	.468	8
1927	149	614	201	32	8	5	(5 0)	264	87	97	24			4	19		27				.327	.430	.346	90	9−8	.517	13
1928	138	540	179	27	4	4	(1 3)	226	72	70	31			2	15		11				.331	.419	.361	81	8−6	.568	11
1929	154	629	205	40	9	1	(0 1)	266	67	79	33			4	20		6				.326	.423	.353	93	9−8	.547	12
1930	116	431	133	15	7	3	(0 3)	171	54	67	23			2	14		7				.309	.397	.336	58	6−6	.483	6
2055	8267	2812	425	165	99	(62 39)	3864	1283	1175	472		48	226		375	119	.64		.340	.467	.370	1546	144−79	.646	177	
12.7 yrs	652	222	34	13	8		305	101	93	37		4	18		30				.340	.467	.370					

Teams: St. Louis, A.L. 1915–1927; Washington/Boston, A.L./N.L. 1928; Boston, 1929–1930.

Points in MVP Voting: 1922, 59 (1st, .92). TOTAL: .92 Award Shares.
A.L. players were not eligible for the award after having won it once.

Explanation for Gaps in Career or Sudden Changes in Productivity: Developed sinus condition, during 1922 season, which led to infection affecting optic nerve; had double vision in 1923 and could not play.

HOME AND ROAD DATA FOR 1920 SEASON

	G	AB	R	H	2B	3B	HR	RBI	BB	Avg.
HOME	78	317	90	150	24	11	15	87	29	.473
ROAD	76	314	46	107	25	7	4	35	17	.341

Source: Pete Palmer

FIELDING FIRST BASE

Year	G	PO	AS	Err	DP	Pct.
1915	37	358	19	4	20*	.990
1916	139	1507	83	24	85	.985
1917	133	1384	101	22	97	.985
1918	114	1244	95	13	64	.990
1919	131	1249	120	13	62	.991
1920	154	1477	140	16	87	.990
1921	138	1267	108	10	86	.993
1922	141	1293	125	17	116	.988
1924	151	1319	111	23	114	.984
1925	150	1330	131	26	120	.983
1926	149	1467	87	21	141	.987
1927	149	1374	131	24	138	.984
1928	123	1233	86	15	103*	.989
1929	154	1398	111	28	131	.982
1930	107	915	81	13	103	.987
	1970	18815	1529	269	1467	.987

Assists per 154 Games: 120
*Estimated.

PLAYER: JIM BOTTOMLEY

BATTING / BASERUNNING / PERCENTAGES / VALUES

Year	G	AB	H	2B	3B	HR	Hm	Rd	TB	R	RBI	BB	IBB	HBP	SH	SF	SB	CS	SB%	GIDP	Avg.	Slug	On Base	Runs	Win–Loss	Pct.	AV
1922	37	151	49	8	5	5			82	29	35	6		2	2		3	1	.75		.325	.543	.354	29	3–1	.632	3
1923	134	523	194	34	14	8			280	79	94	45		4	15		4	6	.40		.371	.535	.414	117	10–3	.767	12
1924	137	528	167	31	12	14			264	87	111	35		3	17		5	4	.56		.316	.500	.352	94	9–5	.638	11
1925	153	619	227	44	12	21			358	92	128	47		2	13		3	4	.43		.367	.578	.405	145	12–4	.759	14
1926	154	603	180	40	14	19			305	98	120	58		4	19		4				.299	.506	.354	109	11–6	.640	11
1927	152	574	174	31	15	19			292	95	124	74		5	26		8				.303	.509	.373	112	11–5	.687	12
1928	149	576	187	42	20	31			362	123	136	71		3	17		10				.325	.628	.391	142	12–3	.789	16
1929	146	560	176	31	12	29			318	108	137	70		1	17		3				.314	.568	.381	122	11–5	.689	14
1930	131	487	148	33	7	15			240	92	97	44		5	24		5				.304	.493	.352	86	7–7	.531	11
1931	108	382	133	34	5	9			204	73	75	34		1	2		3				.348	.534	.401	82	7–2	.768	8
1932	91	311	92	16	3	11			147	45	48	25		1	2		2				.296	.473	.348	51	5–3	.637	5
1933	145	549	137	23	9	13	1	12	217	57	83	42		7	11		3			13	.250	.395	.305	68	9–7	.564	7
1934	142	556	158	31	11	11			244	72	78	33		0	3		1			9	.284	.439	.323	80	9–6	.574	8
1935	107	399	103	21	1	1			129	44	49	18		2	4		3			11	.258	.323	.291	37	4–8	.327	5
1936	140	544	162	39	11	12	9	3	259	72	95	44		3	5		0	0	.00		.298	.476	.351	92	8–7	.514	8
1937	65	109	26	7	0	1			36	11	12	18		0	0		1	0	1.00		.239	.330	.346	14	1–2	.373	1
	1991	7471	2313	465	151	219			3737	1177	1422	664		43	177		58	15	.52	33	.310	.500	.361	1381	130–75	.633	146
12.3 yrs		608	188	38	12	18			304	96	116	54		3	14		5				.310	.500	.361				

Teams: St. Louis, N.L. 1922–1932; Cincinnati 1933–1935; St. Louis, A.L. 1936–1937.
Points in MVP Voting: 1927, 6 (.08); 1931, 7 (.11); 1932, 0; 1933, 6 (.08); 1934, 0; 1935, 0; 1936, 0; 1937, 0. TOTAL: .27 Award Shares.

FIELDING FIRST BASE

Year	G	PO	AS	Err	DP	Pct.
1922	34	346	12	5	20	.986
1923	130	1264	43	18	95	.986
1924	133	1297	48	24	110	.982
1925	153	1466	74	21	133	.987
1926	154	1607	54	19	118	.989
1927	152	1656	70	20	149	.989
1928	148	1454	52	20	113	.987
1929	145	1347	75	13	122	.991
1930	124	1164	41	12	127	.990
1931	93	897	43	12	95	.987
1932	74	662	41	10	67	.986
1933	145	1511	72	15	112	.991
1934	139	1303	77	15	106	.989
1935	97	934	53	8	74	.992
1936	140	1250	47	10	103	.992
1937	24	179	12	1	16	.995
	1885	18337	814	223	1560	.988

Assists per 154 Games: 67

PLAYER: BILL TERRY

Year	G	AB	H	2B	3B	HR	(Hm	Rd)	TB	R	RBI	BB	IBB	HBP	SH	SF	SB	CS	SB%	GIDP	Avg.	Slug	On Base	Runs	Win—Loss	Pct.	AV
																		BASERUNNING				**PERCENTAGES**			**VALUES**			
1923	3	7	1	0	0	0	(	)	1	1	0	2		0	0		0	0	.00		.143	.143	.333	0	0—0	.150	0
1924	77	163	39	7	2	5	(	)	65	26	24	17		0	0		1	1	.50		.239	.399	.311	21	2—3	.435	2
1925	133	489	156	31	6	11	(	)	232	75	70	42		1	4		4	5	.44		.319	.474	.371	86	9—5	.656	10
1926	98	225	65	12	5	5	(	)	102	26	43	22		0	8		3				.289	.453	.341	35	4—3	.606	3
1927	150	580	189	32	13	20	(	)	307	101	121	46		2	19		1				.326	.529	.366	112	11—5	.672	14
1928	149	568	185	36	11	17	(	)	294	100	101	64		0	17		7				.326	.518	.384	114	11—4	.711	14
1929	150	607	226	39	5	14	(	)	317	103	117	48		0	18		10				.372	.522	.407	128	11—4	.719	15
1930	154	633	254	39	15	23	(	)	392	139	129	57		1	19		8				.401	.619	.439	170	12—3	.788	18
1931	153	611	213	43	20	9	(	)	323	121	112	47		2	2		8				.349	.529	.396	127	12—4	.772	14
1932	154	643	225	42	11	28	(	)	373	124	117	32		1	1		4				.350	.580	.381	138	12—4	.766	16
1933	123	475	153	20	5	6	(5	1)	201	68	58	40		0	9		3			10	.322	.423	.368	77	9—3	.733	9
1934	153	602	213	30	6	8	(	)	279	109	83	60		2	19		0			8	.354	.463	.403	122	12—4	.765	16
1935	145	596	203	32	8	6	(	)	269	91	64	41		0	16		7			13	.341	.451	.374	104	11—5	.675	12
1936	79	229	71	10	5	2	(	)	97	36	39	19		0	5		0			7	.310	.424	.356	35	4—2	.613	4
	1721	6428	2193	373	112	154	(	)	3252	1120	1078	537		9	137		56	6	.45	38	.341	.506	.385	1269	119—49	.708	147
10.6 yrs		605	206	35	11	14			306	105	101	51		1	13		5				.341	.506	.385				

Teams: New York, N.L. 1923–1936.

Points in MVP Voting: 1926, 0; 1927, 6 (.08); 1930, 47 (1st, .54); 1931, 23 (3rd, .36); 1932, 19 (4th, .22); 1933, 35 (4th, .44); 1934, 30 (7th, .38); 1935, 20 (6th, .25). TOTAL: 2.27 Award Shares. Also finished third in BBWAA MVP vote for 1930, with 58/80 points, or .73.

Explanation for Gaps in Career or Sudden Changes in Productivity:

1926—Played regularly in 1925 when Frankie Frisch was hurt and being used at other positions, and George Kelly (the Giants' regular first baseman) played second base. In 1926, he was the odd man out in an infield of five Hall of Famers—Terry, Kelly, Frisch, Jackson, and Lindstrom.

1933—Suffered broken wrist in late April.

FIELDING FIRST BASE

Year	G	PO	AS	Err	DP	Pct.
1923	2	22	1	0	1	1.000
1924	42	325	14	4	30	.988
1925	126	1270	77	14	83	.990
1926	38	391	31	9	36	.979
1927	150	1621	105	12	135	.993
1928	149	1584	78	12	148	.993
1929	149	1575	111	11	146	.994
1930	154	1538	128	17	128	.990
1931	153	1411	105	16	108	.990
1932	154	1493	137	14	125	.991
1933	117	1246	76	11	103	.992
1934	153	1592	105	10	131	.994
1935	143	1379	99	6	105	.996
1936	56	525	41	2	55	.996
	1586	15972	1108	138	1334	.992

Assists per 154 Games: 108

PLAYER: LOU GEHRIG

Year	G	AB	H	2B	3B	HR	(Hm	Rd)	TB	R	RBI	BB	IBB	HBP	SH	SF	SB	CS	SB%	GIDP	Avg.	Slug	On Base	Runs	Win—Loss	Pct.	AV
1923	13	26	11	4	1	1	(0	1)	20	6	9	2		0	1		0	0	.00		.423	.769	.448	9	1—0	.905	1
1924	10	12	6	1	0	0	(0	0)	7	2	6	1		0	0		0	0	.00		.500	.583	.538	4	0—0	.920	0
1925	126	437	129	23	10	20	(11	9)	232	73	68	46		2	12		6	3	.67		.295	.531	.356	85	8—4	.677	10
1926	155	572	179	47	20	16	(4	12)	314	135	107	105		1	18		6	5	.55		.313	.549	.409	137	12—4	.742	13
1927	155	584	218	52	18	47	(24	23)	447	149	175	109		3	21		10				.373	.765	.460	208	13—2	.883	21
1928	154	562	210	47	13	27	(12	15)	364	139	142	95		4	16		4	11	.27		.374	.648	.456	169	12—2	.836	17
1929	154	553	166	33	9	35	(21	14)	322	127	126	122		5	12		4	4	.50		.300	.582	.423	140	12—5	.704	15
1930	154	581	220	42	17	41	(14	27)	419	143	174	101		3	18		12	14	.46		.379	.721	.461	195	12—3	.805	20
1931	155	619	211	31	15	46	(24	22)	410	163	184	117		0	2		17	12	.59		.341	.662	.444	185	13—3	.789	17
1932	156	596	208	42	9	34	(12	22)	370	138	151	108		3	1		4	11	.27		.349	.621	.451	168	12—3	.795	16
1933	152	593	198	41	12	32	(17	15)	359	138	139	92		1	1		9	13	.41		.334	.605	.424	151	12—4	.747	16
1934	154	579	210	40	6	49	(30	19)	409	128	165	109		2	0		9	5	.64		.363	.706	.465	195	13—2	.884	21
1935	149	535	176	26	10	30	(15	15)	312	125	119	132		5	0		8	7	.53		.329	.583	.466	154	12—2	.834	15
1936	155	579	205	37	7	49	(27	22)	403	167	152	130		7	3		3	4	.43		.354	.696	.476	199	12—2	.847	20
1937	157	569	200	37	9	37	(24	13)	366	138	159	127		4	0		4	3	.57		.351	.643	.473	181	12—2	.853	18
1938	157	576	170	32	6	29	(16	13)	301	115	114	107		5	1		6	1	.86		.295	.523	.409	131	11—5	.709	13
1939	8	28	4	0	0	0	(0	0)	4	2	1	5		0	0		0	0	.00	2	.143	.143	.273	1	0—1	.048	0
	2164	8001	2721	535	162	493	(251	242)	5059	1888	1991	1508		45	106		102	93	.49		.340	.632	.442	2311	167—44	.789	233
13.4 yrs		599	204	40	12	37			379	141	149	113		3	8		8				.340	.632	.442				

Teams: New York, A.L., 1923–1939.

Points in MVP Voting: 1923, 0; 1926, 7 (10th, .11); 1927, 56 (1st, .88); 1931, 40 (1st, .63); 1932, 47 (2nd, .53); 1933, 39 (4th, .49); 1934, 54 (5th, .68); 1935, 29 (5th, .36); 1936, 73 (1st, .91); 1937, 42 (4th, .53); 1938, 11 (.03). TOTAL: 5.15 Award Shares.

Reported Salaries: 1927—$8,000; 1934—$23,000; 1935—$23,000; 1938—$41,000

Other Notes: 1934–10 HR vs. LHP, 39 vs. RHP.

1936–13 HR vs. LHP, 36 vs. RHP.

Named outstanding major league first baseman for 1927, 1928, 1931, 1934, 1936, 1937 by *The Sporting News*.

FIELDING FIRST BASE

Year	G	PO	AS	Err	DP	Pct.
1923	9	53	4	4	4	.933
1924	2	10	1	0	0	1.000
1925	114	1126	53	13	72	.989
1926	155	1566	73	15	87	.991
1927	155	1662	88	15	108	.992
1928	154	1488	79	18	112	.989
1929	154	1458	82	9	134	.994
1930	153	1298	89	15	109	.989
1931	154	1352	58	13	120	.991
1932	155	1293	75	18	101	.987
1933	152	1290	64	9	102	.993
1934	153	1284	80	8	126	.994
1935	149	1337	82	15	96	.990
1936	155	1377	82	9	128	.994
1937	157	1370	74	16	113	.989
1938	157	1483	100	14	157	.991
1939	8	64	4	2	5	.971
	2136	19511	1087	193	1574	.991

Assists per 154 Games: 78

PLAYER: JIMMIE FOXX

							BATTING											BASERUNNING				PERCENTAGES			VALUES			
Year	G	AB	H	2B	3B	HR	(Hm	Rd)	TB	R	RBI	BB	IBB	HBP	SH	SF		SB	CS	SB%	GIDP	Avg.	Slug	On Base	Runs	Win–Loss	Pct.	AV
1925	10	9	6	1	0	0	(0	0)	7	2	0	0		0	0			0	0	.00		.667	.778	.667	4	0–0	.983	0
1926	26	32	10	2	1	0	(0	0)	14	8	5	1		0	2			1	0	1.00		.313	.438	.314	5	1–0	.607	1
1927	61	130	42	6	5	3	(3	0)	67	23	20	14		1	1			2				.323	.515	.390	26	2–1	.692	2
1928	118	400	131	29	10	13	(7	6)	219	85	79	60		1	12			3	8	.27		.328	.548	.406	91	8–3	.749	11
1929	149	517	183	23	9	33	(18	15)	323	123	118	103		2	16			10	7	.59		.354	.625	.451	154	11–2	.833	17
1930	153	562	188	33	13	37	(22	15)	358	127	156	93		0	18			7	7	.50		.335	.637	.418	154	12–4	.768	16
1931	139	515	150	32	10	30	(18	12)	292	93	120	73		1	4			4	3	.57		.291	.567	.378	113	10–4	.726	13
1932	154	585	213	33	9	58	(31	27)	438	151	169	116		0	0			3	7	.30		.364	.749	.469	207	13–2	.865	21
1933	149	573	204	37	9	48	(31	17)	403	125	163	96		1	0			2	2	.50		.356	.703	.449	184	12–2	.837	20
1934	150	539	180	28	6	44	(22	22)	352	120	130	111		1	1			11	2	.85		.334	.653	.448	165	12–2	.837	18
1935	147	535	185	33	7	36	(17	19)	340	118	115	114		0	0			6	4	.60		.346	.636	.461	163	11–2	.836	17
1936	155	585	198	32	8	41	(21	20)	369	130	143	105		1	2			13	4	.76		.338	.631	.439	168	13–3	.834	15
1937	150	569	162	24	6	36	(18	18)	306	111	127	99		1	4			10	8	.56		.285	.538	.389	123	11–5	.684	14
1938	149	565	197	33	9	50	(35	15)	398	139	175	119		0	1			5	4	.56		.349	.704	.461	189	12–2	.851	20
1939	124	467	168	31	10	35	(17	18)	324	130	105	89		2	5			4	3	.57	17	.360	.694	.460	144	10–2	.812	15
1940	144	515	153	30	4	36	(19	17)	299	106	119	101		0	2			4	7	.36	18	.297	.581	.411	122	10–5	.685	13
1941	135	487	146	27	8	19	(12	7)	246	87	105	93		0	2			2	5	.29	21	.300	.505	.411	100	9–5	.662	14
1942	100	305	69	12	0	8	(5	3)	105	43	33	40		2	0			1			10	.226	.344	.320	34	4–5	.441	4
1944	15	20	1	1	0	0	(0	0)	2	0	2	2		0	0			0			0	.050	.100	.136	0	0–1	.012	0
1945	89	224	60	11	1	7	(3	4)	94	30	38	23		0	1			0			3	.268	.420	.335	32	4–3	.563	3
	2317	8134	2646	458	125	534	(299	235)	4956	1751	1922	1452		13	71			88	71	.55	59	.325	.609	.425	2177	165–53	.758	234
14.3 yrs		569	185	32	9	37			347	122	134	102		1	5			6				.325	.609	.425				

Teams: Philadelphia, A.L. 1925–1935; Boston, A.L. 1936–1942; Chicago, N.L. 1942, 1944; Philadelphia, N.L. 1945

Points in MVP Voting: 1926, 0; 1927, 0; 1931, 0; 1932, 56 (1st, .64); 1933, 74 (1st, .93); 1934, 11 (10th, .14); 1935, 11 (.14); 1936, 16 (.20); 1937, 0; 1938, 305 (1st, .91); 1939, 170 (2nd, .51); 1940, 110 (6th, .33); 1941, 0; 1942, 0; 1944, 0. TOTAL: 3.80 Award Shares.

Explanation for Gaps in Career or Sudden Changes in Productivity: Had attack of appendicitis, had appendix removed late in the season, 1939. Had it not been for this he might have become the only player ever to win four MVP awards; however, since DiMaggio (who won the award) also missed about the same number of games, it was a fair fight.

Other Notes: 1936: 7 HR vs. LHP, 34 vs. RHP
1938: 7 HR vs. LHP, 43 vs. RHP
1939: 3 HR vs. LHP, 32 vs. RHP

Named outstanding major league first baseman in 1929, 1932, 1933, 1938, and 1939 by *The Sporting News*.

FIELDING FIRST BASE

Year	G	PO	AS	Err	DP	Pct.
1927	32	258	15	7	10	.975
1928	30	273	6	2	19	.993
1929	142	1226	74	6	98	.995
1930	153	1362	79	14	101	.990
1931	112	964	49	7	89	.993
1932	141	1328	79	9	115	.994
1933	149	1402	93	15	98	.990
1934	149	1378	85	10	133	.993
1935	121	1109	77	3	107	.997
1936	139	1226	76	12	108	.991
1937	150	1287	106	8	122	.994
1938	149	1282	116	19	153	.987
1939	123	1101	91	10	104	.992
1940	95	844	79	9	87	.990
1941	124	1155	112	10	105	.992
1942	79	720	58	10	60	.987
1945	40	292	27	4	19	.988
	1919	17207	1222	155	1528	.992

Assists per 154 Games: 98

PLAYER: HANK GREENBERG

				BATTING											BASERUNNING				PERCENTAGES			VALUES			
Year	G	AB	H	2B	3B	HR	(Hm Rd)	TB	R	RBI	BB	IBB	HBP	SH	SB	CS	SB%	GIDP	Avg.	Slug	On Base	Runs	Win–Loss	Pct.	AV
1930	1	1	0	0	0	0	(0 0)	0	0	0	0				0	0	.00		0	0	0	0	0–0	.000	0
1933	117	449	135	33	3	12	(9 3)	210	59	87	46	1		2	6	2	.75		.301	.468	.365	79	8–4	.652	9
1934	153	593	201	63	7	26	(15 11)	356	118	139	63	2		9	9	5	.64		.339	.600	.399	144	12–4	.743	15
1935	152	619	203	46	16	36	(18 18)	389	121	170	87	0		4	4	3	.57		.328	.628	.408	161	13–4	.784	18
1936	12	46	16	6	2	1	(0 1)	29	10	16	9	0		0	1	0	1.00		.348	.630	.455	14	1–0	.811	1
1937	154	594	200	49	14	40	(25 15)	397	137	183	102	3		2	8	3	.73		.337	.668	.435	178	12–3	.803	19
1938	155	556	175	23	4	58	(39 19)	380	144	146	119	3		3	7	5	.58		.315	.683	.436	172	12–3	.822	19
1939	138	500	156	42	7	33	(16 17)	311	112	112	91	2		11	8	3	.73	8	.312	.622	.412	136	11–3	.788	15
1940	148	573	195	50	8	41	(27 14)	384	129	150	93	1		3	6	3	.67	15	.340	.670	.431	171	12–2	.833	17
1941	19	67	18	5	1	2	(2 0)	31	12	12	16	0		0	1	0	1.00	1	.269	.463	.410	14	1–0	.742	1
1945	78	270	84	20	2	13	(7 6)	147	47	60	42	0		0	3	1	.75	9	.311	.544	.404	61	6–1	.824	6
1946	142	523	145	29	5	44	(29 15)	316	91	127	80	0		1	5	1	.83	17	.277	.604	.373	119	12–3	.796	15
1947	125	402	100	13	2	25	(18 7)	192	71	74	104	4		0	0			16	.249	.478	.408	83	8–4	.664	8
	1394	5193	1628	379	71	331	(205 126)	3142	1051	1276	852	16		35	58	26	.69	66	.313	.605	.409	1331	108–32	.772	143
8.6 yrs		603	189	44	8	38		365	122	148	99	2		4	7				.313	.605	.409	7			

Teams: Detroit, A.L. 1930, 1933–1941, 1945–1946; Pittsburgh, 1947.

Points in MVP Voting: 1933, 0; 1934, 29 (6th, .36); 1935, 80 (1st, 1.00); 1937, 48 (3rd, .60); 1938, 162 (3rd, .48); 1939, 12 (.04); 1940, 292 (1st, .87); 1941, 0; 1945, 25 (.07); 1946, 91 (8th, .27); 1947, 0. TOTAL: 3.69 Award Shares.

Reported Salaries: 1941 salary called for $55,000, but of course he was drafted early in the season. When he came out in 1945 he resumed at the same salary, which was raised to $75,000 in 1946. In 1947 he and the Tiger management could not see eye to eye about his value, and the Tigers asked waivers on him. Reportedly asking to be traded to the Yankees, Greenberg was sent to Pittsburgh on waivers, which required a $20,000 payment from the Tigers under a clause in his contract. He talked about retiring then, but was disuaded from doing so for $100,000, plus (reportedly) a yearling from John Galbreath's Darby Dan farms.

Other Notes: Named as outstanding major league first baseman in 1935 and as the outstanding left fielder in 1940 by *The Sporting News*.

1938—10 HR vs. LHP, 48 vs. RHP.

1939—2 HR vs. LHP, 31 vs. RHP.

Mr. Greenberg noted that there were few left-handed pitchers in the American League in his time.

FIELDING FIRST BASE

Year	G	PO	AS	Err	DP	Pct.
1933	117	1133	63	14	111	.988
1934	153	1454	84	16	124	.990
1935	152	1437	99	13	142	.992
1936	12	119	9	1	14	.992
1937	154	1477	102	13	133	.992
1938	155	1484	120	14	146	.991
1939	136	1205	75	9	108	.993
1946	140	1272	93	15	110	.989
1947	119	983	79	9	85	.992
	1138	10564	724	104	973	.991

Assists per 154 Games: 98

PLAYER: JOHNNY MIZE

Year	G	AB	H	2B	3B	HR	(Hm	Rd)	TB	R	RBI	BB	IBB	HBP	SH	SF	SB	CS	SB%	GIDP	Avg.	Slug	On Base	Runs	Win—Loss	Pct.	AV
1936	126	414	136	30	8	19	(	)	239	76	93	50		1	4		1			4	.329	.577	.399	102	8—2	.778	11
1937	145	560	204	40	7	25	(	)	333	103	113	56		5	0		2			5	.364	.595	.427	150	12—2	.840	15
1938	149	531	179	34	16	27	(	)	326	85	102	74		4	0		0			14	.337	.614	.422	141	12—2	.835	15
1939	153	564	197	44	14	28	(	)	353	104	108	92		4	10		0			9	.349	.626	.437	162	12—2	.862	14
1940	155	579	182	31	13	43	(25	18)	368	111	137	82		5	0		7			10	.314	.636	.404	152	12—3	.825	15
1941	126	473	150	39	8	16	(	)	253	67	100	70		1	3		4			8	.317	.535	.404	106	10—2	.802	12
1942	142	541	165	25	7	26	(	)	282	97	110	60		5	1		3			8	.305	.521	.379	110	11—3	.775	14
1946	101	377	127	18	2	22	(	)	215	70	70	62		5	1		3			5	.337	.570	.436	99	8—1	.860	10
1947	154	586	177	26	2	51	(29	22)	360	137	138	74		4	0		2			6	.302	.614	.384	143	12—4	.768	18
1948	152	560	162	26	4	40	(	)	316	110	125	94		4	0		4			7	.289	.564	.395	131	12—3	.770	14
1949	119	411	108	16	0	19	(	)	181	63	64	54		4	1		1			5	.263	.440	.353	67	7—4	.621	8
1950	90	274	76	12	0	25	(14	11)	163	43	72	29		2	0		0	1	.00	4	.277	.595	.351	59	5—2	.694	7
1951	113	332	86	14	1	10	(7	3)	132	37	49	36		4	0		1	0	1.00	7	.259	.398	.339	47	5—4	.540	5
1952	78	137	36	9	0	4	(2	2)	57	9	29	11		2	0		0	0	.00	6	.263	.416	.327	20	2—2	.589	2
1953	81	104	26	3	0	4	(2	2)	41	6	27	12		2	0		0	0	.00	1	.250	.394	.339	15	2—1	.556	1
	1884	6443	2011	367	82	359	(79	58)	3619	1118	1337	856		52	20		28	1		99	.312	.562	.396	1503	130—40	.767	161
11.6 yrs		554	173	32	7	31			311	96	115	74		4	2		2			9	.312	.562	.396				

Column group headers: BATTING | BASERUNNING | PERCENTAGES | VALUES

Teams: St. Louis, N.L. 1936–1941; New York, N.L. 1942, 1946–1949; New York, A.L. 1949–1953.

Points in MVP Voting: 1937, 18 (10th, .23); 1938, 28 (.08); 1939, 178 (2nd, .53); 1940, 209 (2nd, .62); 1941, 48 (9th, .14); 1942, 97 (5th, .29); 1946, 14 (.04); 1947, 144 (3rd, .43); 1948, 22 (.07); 1949, 0; 1950, 11 (.03); 1951, 2 (.01); 1952, 0; 1953, 0. TOTAL: 2.47 Award Shares.

Explanation for Gaps in Career or Sudden Changes in Productivity: 1946—Broken hand.

Other Notes: Named outstanding major league first baseman in 1942, 1947, 1948, by *The Sporting News.*

FIELDING FIRST BASE

Year	G	PO	AS	Err	DP	Pct.
1936	97	897	66	6	63	.994
1937	144	1308	67	17	104	.988
1938	140	1297	93	15	117	.989
1939	152	1348	90	19	123	.987
1940	153	1376	80	14	105	.990
1941	122	1157	82	8	104	.994
1942	138	1393	74	8	98	.995
1946	101	928	83	11	80	.989
1947	154	1381	118	6	120	.996
1948	152	1359	111	13	114	.991
1949	107	953	68	7	82	.993
1950	72	490	31	2	73	.996
1951	93	632	44	4	86	.994
1952	27	218	18	3	32	.987
1953	15	113	7	0	19	1.000
	1667	14850	1032	133	1320	.992

Assists per 154 Games: 95

PLAYER: GIL HODGES

BATTING / BASERUNNING / PERCENTAGES / VALUES

Year	G	AB	H	2B	3B	HR	(Hm	Rd)	TB	R	RBI	BB	IBB	HBP	SH	SF	SB	CS	SB%	GIDP	Avg.	Slug	On Base	Runs	Win–Loss	Pct.	AV
1943	1	2	0	0	0	0	(0	0)	0	0	0	1		0	0		1			0	.000	.000	.333	0	0–0	.065	0
1947	28	77	12	3	1	1	(0	1)	20	9	7	14		0	0					3	.156	.260	.286	6	1–2	.206	0
1948	134	481	120	18	5	11	(9	2)	181	48	70	43		0	4		7			11	.249	.376	.309	56	6–8	.438	6
1949	156	596	170	23	4	23	(15	8)	270	94	115	66		4	10		10			13	.285	.453	.355	99	10–7	.593	12
1950	153	561	159	26	2	32	(19	13)	285	98	113	73		1	11		6			14	.283	.508	.361	105	10–6	.632	14
1951	158	582	156	25	3	40	(16	24)	307	118	103	93		5	1		9	7	.56	13	.268	.527	.373	119	11–5	.688	13
1952	153	508	129	27	1	32	(18	14)	254	87	102	107		2	2		2	4	.33	9	.254	.500	.384	106	11–4	.726	14
1953	141	520	157	22	7	31	(18	13)	286	101	122	75		3	0		1	4	.20	4	.302	.550	.393	119	10–4	.728	13
1954	154	579	176	23	5	42	(25	17)	335	106	130	74		1	5	19	3	3	.50	13	.304	.579	.370	128	12–5	.714	16
1955	150	546	158	24	5	27	(18	9)	273	75	102	80	3	3	3	10	2	1	.67	16	.289	.500	.375	100	10–6	.620	13
1956	153	550	146	29	4	32	(18	14)	279	86	87	76	10	0	5	2	3	3	.50	16	.265	.507	.351	109	11–4	.745	13
1957	150	579	173	28	7	27	(16	11)	296	94	98	63	6	2	4	6	5	3	.62	11	.299	.511	.364	109	12–4	.731	12
1958	141	475	123	15	1	22	(13	9)	206	68	64	52	3	0	2	3	8	2	.80	15	.259	.434	.329	67	7–7	.521	9
1959	124	413	114	19	2	25	(12	13)	212	57	80	58	6	3	3	3	3	2	.60	13	.276	.513	.365	77	8–4	.685	10
1960	101	197	39	8	1	8	(3	5)	73	22	30	26	1	1	4	3	0	1	.00	5	.198	.371	.286	22	3–4	.413	3
1961	109	215	52	4	0	8	(3	5)	80	25	31	24	1	0	2	4	3	1	.75	5	.242	.372	.310	26	3–4	.425	3
1962	54	127	32	1	0	9	(7	2)	60	15	17	15	1	0	0	0	0	0	.00	4	.252	.472	.331	19	2–2	.539	2
1963	11	22	5	0	0	0	(0	0)	5	2	3	3	0	0	0	0	0	0	.00		.227	.227	.320	2	0–0	.358	0
	2071	7030	1921	295	48	370	(210	160)	3422	1105	1274	943	31	25	56	50	63	31	.56	165	.273	.487	.356	1268	126–74	.629	153
12.8 yrs		550	150	23	4	29	(	)	268	86	100	74	2	4			5			13	.273	.487	.356				

Teams: Brooklyn, 1943–1957; Los Angeles, 1958–1961; New York, N.L. 1962–1963.
Points in MVP Voting: 1947, 0; 1948, 1 (.00); 1949, 29 (.09); 1950, 55 (8th, .16); 1951, 10 (.03); 1952, 15 (.04); 1953, 13 (.04); 1954, 40 (10th, .12); 1955, 0; 1956, 0; 1957, 54 (7th, .16); 1958, 0; 1959, 4 (.01); 1960, 0; 1961, 0; 1962, 0; 1963, 0. TOTAL: .65 Award Shares.
Explanation for Gaps in Career or Sudden Changes in Productivity: None. Doesn't seem to have been hurt in 1960, just lost his job when Norm Larker got hot.
Other Notes: Gold Glove: 1957, 1958, 1959.

FIELDING FIRST BASE

Year	G	PO	AS	Err	DP	Pct.
1948	96	830	60	13	85	.986
1949	156	1336	80	7	142	.995
1950	153	1273	100	8	159	.994
1951	158	1365	126	12	171	.992
1952	153	1322	116	11	152	.992
1953	127	1025	99	8	105	.993
1954	154	1381	132	7	129	.995
1955	139	1274	105	12	126	.991
1956	138	1190	103	10	105	.992
1957	150	1317	115	14	115	.990
1958	122	907	69	8	134	.992
1959	113	891	66	8	77	.992
1960	92	403	33	2	40	.995
1961	100	454	37	1	44	.998
1962	47	315	32	5	23	.986
1963	10	61	8	0	7	1.000
	1908	15344	1281	126	1614	.992

Assists per 154 Games: 103

PLAYER: TED KLUSZEWSKI

Year	G	AB	H	2B	3B	HR	(Hm	Rd)	TB	R	RBI	BB	IBB	HBP	SH	SF	SB	CS	SB%	GIDP	Avg.	Slug	On Base	Runs	Win—Loss	Pct.	AV
1947	9	10	1	0	0	0	(0	0)	1	1	2	1		0	0		0			0	.100	.100	.182	0	0—0	.021	0
1948	113	379	104	23	4	12	(	)	171	49	57	18		0	0		1			14	.274	.451	.307	48	5—5	.510	5
1949	136	531	164	26	2	8	(	)	218	63	68	19		0	0		3			10	.309	.411	.333	70	8—6	.557	9
1950	134	538	165	37	0	25	(14	11)	277	76	111	33		1	0		3			20	.307	.515	.348	89	9—5	.647	11
1951	154	607	157	35	2	13	(8	5)	235	74	77	35		2	0		6	2	.75	16	.259	.387	.301	69	9—9	.506	8
1952	135	497	159	24	11	16	(4	12)	253	62	86	47		4	1		3	3	.50	13	.320	.509	.383	97	10—3	.761	12
1953	149	570	180	25	0	40	(23	17)	325	97	108	55		4	0		2	0	1.00	13	.316	.570	.380	126	11—4	.751	13
1954	149	573	187	28	3	49	(34	15)	368	104	141	78		3	0	5	0	2	.00	12	.326	.642	.407	151	12—3	.812	19
1955	153	612	192	25	0	47	(22	25)	358	116	113	66	25	4	0	4	1	1	.50	10	.314	.585	.382	136	12—4	.765	15
1956	138	517	156	14	1	35	(23	12)	277	91	102	49	22	3	0	5	1	0	1.00	11	.302	.536	.362	99	10—4	.701	12
1957	69	127	34	7	0	6	(3	3)	59	12	21	5	3	1	0	0	0	0	.00	2	.268	.465	.301	18	2—2	.515	2
1958	100	301	88	13	4	4	(2	2)	121	29	37	26	6	1	1	2	0	0	.00	8	.292	.402	.347	41	5—3	.594	5
1959	91	223	62	12	2	4	(4	0)	90	22	27	14	4	0	1	1	0	1	.00	7	.278	.404	.318	27	3—3	.498	4
1960	81	181	53	9	0	5	(2	3)	77	20	39	22	5	0	0	3	0	1	.00	3	.293	.425	.364	29	3—2	.627	3
1961	107	263	64	12	0	15	(9	6)	121	32	39	24	5	0	0	3	0	0	.00	4	.243	.460	.303	37	4—4	.513	4
10.6 yrs	1718	5929	1766	290	29	279	(148	111)	2951	848	1028	492	70	23	3	23	20	10	.57	143	.298	.498	.353	1037	104—57	.646	122
		559	167	27	3	26			278	80	97	46		2				2			13	.298	.498	.353				

Teams: Cincinnati, 1947–1957; Pittsburgh, 1958–1959; Chicago, A.L. 1959–1960; Los Angeles, A. L. 1961.

Points in MVP Voting: 1947, 0; 1948, 0; 1949, 0; 1950, 14 (.04); 1951, 0; 1952, 16 (.05); 1953, 69 (7th, .21); 1954, 217 (2nd, .65); 1955, 111 (6th, .33); 1956, 18 (.05); 1957, 0; 1958, 0; 1959, 0; 1960, 0; 1961, 0. TOTAL: 1.33 Award Shares.

Reported Salaries: Received $15,000 signing bonus in 1945.

Explanation for Gaps in Career or Sudden Changes in Productivity:

1953—The increase in power occurred when GM Gabe Paul shortened the right field foul line from 366 feet to 342. Kluszewski's HR at home jumped from 4 to 23 (on the road he increased from 12 to 17).

1956—The April 15, 1957 edition of *Sports Illustrated* said that in 1956 "he was overweight and suffered pinched sciatic nerve."

1957—*TSN Guide* says he suffered "chronic hip and back problems."

Other Notes: Drove in only 433 runs with his 279 home runs, or 1.55 RBI per HR, the lowest ratio of any player with 250 or more career HR.

Named outstanding major league first baseman for 1954, 1955, and 1956 by *The Sporting News*.

FIELDING FIRST BASE

Year	G	PO	AS	Err	DP	Pct.
1947	2	10	0	0	1	1.000
1948	98	833	65	9	60	.990
1949	134	1140	65	14	109	.989
1950	131	1123	61	15	101	.987
1951	154	1381	88	5	115	.997
1952	133	1121	66	8	116	.993
1953	147	1285	58	7	149	.995
1954	149	1237	101	5	166	.996
1955	153	1388	86	8	153	.995
1956	131	1166	89	13	110	.990
1957	23	161	15	2	11	.989
1958	72	591	36	4	62	.994
1959	49	371	22	0	27	1.000
1960	39	325	19	1	38	.997
1961	66	520	28	6	51	.989
	1481	12652	799	97	1269	.993

Assists per 154 Games: 83

PLAYER: NORM CASH

				BATTING												BASERUNNING				PERCENTAGES			VALUES			
Year	G	AB	H	2B	3B	HR	(Hm Rd)	TB	R	RBI	BB	IBB	HBP	SH	SF	SB	CS	SB%	GIDP	Avg.	Slug	On Base	Runs	Win—Loss	Pct	AV
1958	13	8	2	0	0	0	(0 0)	2	2	0	0	0	0	0	0	0	0	.00	0	.250	.250	.250	0	0—0	.235	0
1959	58	104	25	0	1	4	(3 1)	39	16	16	18	3	5	1	2	1	1	.50		.240	.375	.372	17	2—1	.640	1
1960	121	353	101	16	3	18	(13 5)	177	64	63	65	1	6	0	4	4	2	.67	0	.286	.501	.402	79	8—2	.800	8
1961	159	535	193	22	8	41	(21 20)	354	119	132	124	19	9	2	2	11	5	.69	16	.361	.662	.487	178	12—2	.887	20
1962	148	507	123	16	2	39	(25 14)	260	94	89	104	12	13	0	5	6	3	.67	13	.243	.513	.382	104	11—4	.707	13
1963	147	493	133	19	1	26	(19 7)	232	67	79	89	8	6	2	3	2	3	.40	9	.270	.471	.386	94	10—4	.708	11
1964	144	479	123	15	5	23	(14 9)	217	63	83	70	4	3	0	7	2	1	.67	12	.257	.453	.351	78	9—5	.637	10
1965	142	467	124	23	1	30	(17 13)	239	79	82	77	5	4	1	4	6	6	.50	9	.266	.512	.371	91	10—3	.745	12
1966	160	603	168	18	3	32	(18 14)	288	98	93	66	4	4	1	5	2	1	.67	15	.279	.478	.351	101	11—6	.651	12
1967	152	488	118	16	5	22	(10 12)	210	64	72	81	9	4	1	3	3	2	.60	7	.242	.430	.352	78	9—5	.666	10
1968	127	411	108	15	1	25	(19 6)	200	50	63	39	7	3	2	3	1	1	.50	12	.263	.487	.329	63	8—4	.689	7
1969	142	483	135	15	4	22	(11 11)	224	81	74	63	5	6	1	3	2	1	.67	9	.280	.464	.368	85	10—4	.714	11
1970	130	370	96	18	2	15	(7 8)	163	58	53	72	6	5	0	5	0	1	.00	16	.259	.441	.383	64	7—4	.644	7
1971	135	452	128	10	3	32	(14 18)	240	72	91	59	7	7	1	4	1	0	1.00	5	.283	.531	.372	93	9—3	.768	12
1972	137	440	114	16	0	22	(11 11)	196	51	61	50	13	4	4	3	0	2	.00	9	.259	.445	.338	66	9—4	.694	10
1973	121	363	95	19	0	19	(8 11)	171	51	40	47	7	8	0	2	1	0	1.00	6	.262	.471	.357	63	7—3	.700	7
1974	53	149	34	3	2	7	(4 3)	62	17	12	19	2	3	1	0	1	1	.50	1	.228	.416	.327	21	2—2	.567	2
	2089	6705	1820	241	41	377	(214 163)	3274	1046	1103	1043	112	90	17	55	43	30	.59	139	.271	.488	.374	1278	134—56	.708	153
12.9 yrs		520	141	19	3	29		254	81	86	81	9	7	1	4	3	2		11	.271	.488	.374				

Teams: Chicago, A.L., 1958–1959, Detroit, 1960–1974.

Points in MVP Voting: 1958, 0; 1959, 0; 1960, 0; 1961, 151 (4th, .54); 1962, 3 (.01); 1963, 0; 1964, 0; 1965, 1 (.00); 1966, 23 (.08); 1967, 0; 1968, 3 (.01); 1969, 0; 1970, 0; 1971, 21 (.06); 1972, 0; 1973, 0; 1974, 0. Total: .70 Award Shares.

Other Notes: Named outstanding American League first baseman by *The Sporting News,* 1961, 1971.

FIELDING FIRST BASE

Year	G	PO	AS	Err	DP	Pct.
1959	31	231	14	4	19	.984
1960	99	739	59	7	68	.991
1961	157	1231	127	11	121	.992
1962	146	1081	116	10	94	.992
1963	142	1161	99	7	93	.994
1964	137	1105	92	4	97	.997
1965	139	1091	97	9	96	.992
1966	158	1271	114	17	118	.988
1967	146	1135	112	6	89	.995
1968	117	924	88	8	66	.992
1969	134	1016	96	7	99	.994
1970	114	868	70	10	76	.989
1971	131	1020	75	9	105	.992
1972	134	1060	70	8	102	.993
1973	114	856	64	8	72	.991
1974	44	368	24	6	32	.985
	1943	15157	1317	131	1347	.992

Assists per 154 Games: 104

PLAYER: WILLIE McCOVEY

						BATTING												BASERUNNING				PERCENTAGES			VALUES			
Year	G	AB	H	2B	3B	HR	(Hm	Rd)	TB	R	RBI	BB	IBB	HBP	SH	SF	SB	CS	SB%	GIDP	Avg.	Slug	On Base	Runs	Win–Loss	Pct.	AV
1959	52	192	68	9	5	13	(8	5)	126	32	38	22	1	4	0	1	2	0	1.00	7	.354	.656	.429	56	4–1	.883	5
1960	101	260	62	15	3	13	(4	9)	122	37	51	45	4	0	0	2	1	1	.50	3	.238	.469	.349	43	5–3	.644	4
1961	106	328	89	12	3	18	(9	9)	161	59	50	37	3	5	0	4	1	2	.33	8	.271	.491	.350	56	6–3	.629	6
1962	91	229	67	6	1	20	(12	8)	135	41	54	29	1	0	0	3	3	3	.50	6	.293	.590	.368	48	5–2	.715	5
1963	152	564	158	19	5	44	(26	18)	319	103	102	50	5	11	1	1	1	1	.50	.10	.280	.566	.349	111	12–4	.743	12
1964	130	364	80	14	1	18	(8	10)	150	55	54	61	5	5	0	4	2	1	.67	9	.220	.412	.336	53	7–4	.610	6
1965	160	540	149	17	4	39	(22	17)	291	93	92	88	5	6	2	3	0	4	.00	8	.276	.539	.380	115	12–3	.790	13
1966	150	502	148	26	6	36	(22	14)	294	85	96	76	10	6	0	4	2	1	.67	8	.295	.586	.391	119	11–2	.825	12
1967	135	456	126	17	4	31	(13	18)	244	73	91	71	17	6	2	4	3	3	.50	8	.276	.535	.377	94	10–3	.795	12
1968	148	523	153	16	4	36	(20	16)	285	81	105	72	20	5	0	8	4	2	.67	10	.293	.545	.378	110	12–3	.826	14
1969	149	491	157	26	2	45	(22	23)	322	101	126	121	45	4	0	7	0	0	.00	11	.320	.656	.453	151	12–1	.885	17
1970	152	495	143	39	2	39	(16	23)	303	98	126	137	40	3	0	3	0	0	.00	13	.289	.612	.444	140	11–3	.799	16
1971	105	329	91	13	0	18	(9	9)	158	45	70	64	21	4	0	5	0	2	.00	6	.277	.480	.396	65	7–2	.737	7
1972	81	263	56	8	0	14	(8	6)	106	30	35	38	5	2	0	1	0	0	.00	3	.213	.403	.316	35	4–4	.537	4
1973	130	383	102	14	3	29	(21	8)	209	52	75	105	25	1	0	6	1	0	1.00	6	.266	.546	.402	95	9–2	.796	12
1974	128	344	87	19	1	22	(10	12)	174	53	63	96	9	1	0	1	1	0	1.00	8	.253	.506	.416	79	8–2	.781	9
1975	122	413	104	17	0	23	(11	12)	190	43	68	57	8	3	0	2	1	0	1.00	10	.252	.460	.345	66	8–4	.683	8
1976	82	226	46	9	0	7	(4	3)	76	20	36	24	8	1	0	0	0	0	.00		.204	.336	.283	21	3–4	.404	2
1977	141	478	134	21	0	28	(6	22)	239	54	86	67	16	0	0	3	3	0	1.00	16	.280	.500	.367	86	9–4	.693	12
1978	108	351	80	19	2	12	(4	8)	139	32	64	36	8	0	0	2	1	0	1.00	12	.228	.396	.298	40	5–5	.503	4
1979	117	353	88	9	0	15	(9	6)	142	34	57	36	2	1	0	3	0	2	.00	7	.249	.402	.318	45	5–5	.500	5
1980	48	113	23	8	0	1	(0	1)	34	8	16	13	2	1	0	3	0	0	.00	3	.204	.301	.285	10	1–2	.366	1
	2588	8197	2211	353	46	521	(264	257)	4219	1229	1555	1345	260	69	5	70	26	22	.54	176	.270	.515	.374	1639	165–67	.712	186
16.0 yrs		513	138	22	3	33			264	77	97	84	16	4	0	4	2	1		11	.270	.515	.374				

Teams: San Francisco, 1959–1973; San Diego, 1974–1976; Oakland, 1976; San Francisco, 1977–1980

Points in MVP Voting: 1959, 1 (.00); 1960, 0; 1961, 0; 1962, 0; 1963, 9 (.03); 1964, 0; 1965, 25 (10th, .09); 1966, 12 (.04); 1967, 2 (.01); 1968, 135 (3rd, .48); 1969, 265 (1st, .79); 1970, 47 (9th, .14); 1971, 15 (.04); 1972, 0; 1973, 0; 1974, 0; 1975, 0; 1976, 0; 1977, 5 (.01); 1978, 0; 1979, 0; 1980, 0. TOTAL: 1.63 Award Shares.

Reported Salaries: 1970—$100,000; 1972—$115,000; 1973—$125,000

Explanation for Gaps in Career or Sudden Changes in Productivity:

1960—After sensational beginning in 1959, McCovey hit seven home runs in the first fifteen games in 1960, but then tailed off so severely that he was sent down in mid-July. He was then platooned for two years.

1964—Suffered from cracked ribs, bad knees and pulled groin muscles.

1971—Tore cartilage in left knee in spring training, plus nine games missed with severe sprain of left hand.

1972—Right arm broken in collision with John Jeter, April 18.

Other Notes: 1963—6 HR vs. LHP, 38 vs. RHP

Named outstanding National League first baseman in 1965, 1968, 1969 and 1970 by *The Sporting News*.

FIELDING FIRST BASE						
Year	G	PO	AS	Err	DP	Pct.
1959	51	424	29	5	29	.989
1960	71	557	39	9	42	.985
1961	84	669	55	11	55	.985
1962	17	105	7	1	12	.991
1963	23	143	14	1	5	.994
1964	26	177	14	7	19	.965
1965	156	1310	87	13	93	.991
1966	145	1287	81	22	91	.984
1967	127	1221	81	15	102	.989
1968	146	1305	103	21	91	.985
1969	148	1392	79	12	116	.992
1970	146	1217	134	15	117	.989
1971	95	828	63	15	80	.983
1972	74	617	32	9	52	.986
1973	117	930	76	12	89	.988
1974	104	815	47	11	59	.987
1975	115	979	73	15	94	.986
1976	51	420	44	4	39	.991
1977	136	1072	60	13	93	.989
1978	97	721	44	10	49	.987
1979	89	740	48	10	60	.987
1980	27	241	12	2	18	.992
	2045	17170	1222	233	1405	.987

Assists per 154 Games: 92

Second Base

Nap Lajoie
Johnny Evers
Miller Huggins
Eddie Collins
Larry Doyle
Del Pratt
Rogers Hornsby
Frankie Frisch
Charlie Gehringer
Tony Lazzeri
Billy Herman
Bobby Doerr
Joe Gordon
Red Schoendienst
Jackie Robinson
Nellie Fox
Bill Mazeroski
Joe Morgan
Rod Carew
Bobby Grich

PLAYER: NAP LAJOIE

					BATTING												BASERUNNING				PERCENTAGES			VALUES			
Year	G	AB	H	2B	3B	HR	(Hm Rd)	TB	R	RBI	BB	IBB	HBP	SH	SF	SB	CS	SB%	GIDP	Avg.	Slug	On Base	Runs	Win–Loss	Pct.	AV
1896	39	175	57	12	7	4	(3 1)	95	36	42	1		0	2		7				.326	.543	.326	35	3–2	.542	3
1897	127	545	197	40	23	9	(2 7)	310	107	127	15			5		20				.361	.569	.375	128	10–4	.721	13
1898	147	610	200	43	11	6	(2 4)	283	113	127	21			5		25				.328	.464	.347	111	10–6	.622	17
1899	77	312	118	19	9	6	(3 3)	173	70	70	12			2		13				.378	.554	.399	77	6–2	.774	9
1900	102	451	152	33	12	7	(4 3)	230	95	92	10			2		22				.337	.510	.350	91	8–4	.644	13
1901	131	543	229	48	14	14	(5 9)	347	145	125	24			1		27				.422	.639	.445	171	11–2	.855	22
1902	87	352	133	35	5	7	(5 2)	199	81	65	19			8		20				.378	.565	.401	92	7–2	.816	11
1903	126	488	173	41	11	7	(1 6)	257	90	93	24			13		21				.355	.527	.375	111	10–3	.796	15
1904	140	559	211	49	15	5	(4 1)	305	92	102	27			6		29				.377	.546	.402	139	12–2	.882	19
1905	65	249	82	12	2	2	(2 0)	104	29	41	17			3		11				.329	.418	.368	44	5–2	.762	5
1906	152	602	214	48	9	0	(0 0)	280	88	91	30			17		20				.355	.465	.376	120	13–3	.812	16
1907	137	509	152	30	6	2	(2 0)	200	53	63	30			13		24				.299	.393	.330	76	10–4	.714	11
1908	157	581	168	32	6	2	(1 1)	218	77	74	47			30		15				.289	.375	.327	82	12–6	.670	11
1909	128	469	152	33	7	1	(0 1)	202	56	47	35		6	11		13				.324	.431	.370	81	10–3	.770	9
1910	159	591	227	51	7	4	(2 2)	304	92	76	60		5	21		26				.384	.514	.431	145	13–2	.871	19
1911	90	315	115	20	1	2	(0 2)	143	36	60	26		4	8		13				.365	.454	.411	65	6–2	.758	7
1912	117	448	165	34	4	0	(0 0)	207	66	90	28		7	17		18				.368	.462	.400	95	9–3	.773	12
1913	137	465	156	25	2	1	(0 1)	188	67	68	33		15	12		17				.335	.404	.389	81	9–3	.748	12
1914	121	419	108	14	2	1	(1)	129	37	50	32		2	15		14				.258	.308	.303	46	6–7	.449	6
1915	129	490	137	24	5	1	(0 1)	174	40	61	11		4	15		10				.280	.355	.292	56	6–9	.408	8
1916	113	426	105	14	4	2	(2 0)	133	33	35	14		1	14		15				.246	.312	.264	41	5–8	.387	6
	2481	9599	3251	657	162	83	(38 44)	4481	1503	1599	516		44	220		380				.339	.467	.367	1887	181–76	.703	244
15.3 yrs		627	212	43	11	5		293	98	104	34		7	14		25				.339	.467	.367	Runs created estimates prior to 1901 of indeterminate accuracy			

Teams: Philadelphia, N.L., 1896–1900; Philadelphia, A.L., 1901–1902; Cleveland, A.L., 1902–1914; Philadelphia, A.L., 1915–1916.

Points in MVP Voting: 1911, 5 (.08); 1913, 7 (.11); 1914, 0.

Reported Salaries: 1901—$8,000; 1902—$8,000; 1903—$8,000.

Explanation for Gaps in Career or Sudden Changes in Productivity:

1899—Knee problem.

1901—The 85-point jump in his batting average is a result of moving from an extraordinarily strong league, the N.L. in 1900, to a very weak league, the A.L. in 1901, which really was no more than a marginal major league.

1902—Upon the emergence of the American League, Lajoie jumped from one Philadelphia team to the other, and in so doing became the epicenter of the legal dispute over baseball's reserve arrangement. He was eventually ordered by the Supreme Court of Pennsylvania (in April 1902) to play for the National League team, but American League president Ban Johnson got around the rule by transferring Lajoie from Philadelphia to Cleveland, and keeping him out of Pennsylvania, where he could have been arrested.

1909—Wrist injury.

1911—Injury described in *Reach Guide* as "ruptured muscle."

1912—Back problem.

FIELDING SECOND BASE

Year	G	PO	AS	E	DP	Pct.	Range
1898	146	442	406	46	59	.949	5.81
1899	67	224	231	22	39	.954	6.79
1900	102	287	341	30	69	.954	6.16
1901	119	395	381	32	60	.960	6.52
1902	87	272	286	15	49	.974	6.41
1903	123	366	402	36	61	.955	6.24
1904	95	272	255	21	42	.962	5.55
1905	59	148	177	3	25	.991	5.51
1906	130	354	415	21	76	.973	5.92
1907	128	314	461	25	86	.969	6.05
1908	156	450	538	37	78	.964	6.33
1909	120	193	370	28	55	.953	4.69
1910	149	387	419	28	60	.966	5.41
1911	37	91	93	10	16	.948	4.97
1912	97	241	244	21	49	.959	5.05
1913	126	279	363	20	59	.970	5.10
1914	80	187	215	17	45	.959	5.02
1915	110	251	332	23	61	.962	5.92
1916	105	254	325	16	61	.973	5.51
	2036	5407	6259	451	1050	.963	5.73

Assists per 154 Games: 473

PLAYER: JOHNNY EVERS

								BATTING											BASERUNNING				PERCENTAGES			VALUES			
Year	G	AB	H	2B	3B	HR	(Hm	Rd)	TB	R	RBI	BB	IBB	HBP	SH	SF	SB	CS	SB%	GIDP	Avg.	Slug	On Base	Runs	Win–Loss	Pct.	AV
1902	26	90	20	0	0	0	(	)	20	7	2	3			3		1				.222	.222	.240	6	1–2	.229	1
1903	124	464	136	27	7	0	(	)	177	70	52	19			11		25				.293	.381	.314	68	7–6	.546	8
1904	152	532	141	14	7	0	(	)	169	49	47	28			23		26				.265	.318	.290	63	9–7	.541	9
1905	99	340	94	11	2	1	(	)	112	44	37	27			20		19				.276	.329	.313	47	6–4	.610	5
1906	154	533	136	17	6	1	(	)	168	65	51	36			24		49				.255	.315	.290	70	10–7	.590	9
1907	150	507	127	18	4	2	(	)	159	66	51	38			14		46				.250	.314	.295	65	10–5	.650	10
1908	126	416	125	19	6	0	(	)	156	83	37	66			22		36				.300	.375	.379	81	10–3	.786	8
1909	127	463	122	19	6	1	(	)	156	88	24	73	4		12		28				.263	.337	.361	70	10–4	.707	7
1910	125	433	114	11	7	0	(	)	139	87	28	108	1		13		28				.263	.321	.402	72	9–4	.663	10
1911	46	155	35	4	3	0	(	)	45	29	7	34	2		4		6				.226	.290	.364	19	2–3	.460	2
1912	143	478	163	23	11	1	(	)	211	73	63	74	2		14		16				.341	.441	.421	101	10–3	.736	13
1913	135	444	126	20	5	3	(	)	165	81	49	50	3		24		11				.284	.372	.344	66	7–6	.552	10
1914	139	491	137	20	3	1	(	)	166	81	40	87	2		31		12				.279	.338	.370	74	9–6	.622	10
1915	83	278	73	4	1	1	(	)	82	38	22	50	0		21		7	8	.47		.263	.295	.352	36	5–4	.566	4
1916	71	241	52	4	1	0	(	)	58	33	15	40	1		12		5				.216	.241	.316	22	4–4	.455	2
1917	80	266	57	5	1	1	(	)	67	25	12	43	0		8		9				.214	.252	.315	25	4–5	.433	3
1922	1	3	0	0	0	0	(	)	0	0	1	2	0		0		0	0	.00		.000	.000	.400	0	0–0	.000	0
1929	1	0	0	0	0	0	(	)	0	0	0	0	0		0		0				.000	.000	.000	0	0–0	.000	0
11.0 yrs	1782	6134	1658	216	70	12	(	)	2050	919	538	778	15		256		324	8	.47		.270	.334	.341	884	112–74	.602	113
	558	151		20	6	1			186	84	49	71			23		29				.270	.334	.341				

Teams: Chicago, N.L., 1902–13; Boston, N.L., 1914–16; Boston/Philadelphia, N.L., 1917; Chicago, A.L., 1922; Boston, N.L., 1929.

Points in MVP Voting: 1911, 0; 1913, 10, (10th, .16); 1914, 50 (1st, .78).

Reported Salaries: 1902—$60 per month while with Troy, raised to $100 per month when joined Cubs; 1906—$225 per month.

Explanation for Gaps in Career or Sudden Changes in Productivity:

1905—Injured in collision at first base; out more than a month.

1909—Held out until late April.

1911—Nervous breakdown.

1915—Suffered an ankle injury while running the bases; out several weeks.

FIELDING SECOND BASE

Year	G	PO	AS	Err	DP	Pct.	Range
1902	18	38	58	1	5	.990	5.33
1903	110	245	306	37	39	.937	5.01
1904	152	381	518	54	53	.943	5.91
1905	99	249	290	36	38	.937	5.44
1906	153	344	441	44	51	.947	5.13
1907	150	346	499	32	58	.964	5.63
1908	123	237	361	25	39	.960	4.86
1909	126	262	354	38	29	.942	4.89
1910	125	282	347	33	55	.950	5.03
1911	33	66	90	4	17	.975	4.73
1912	143	319	439	32	71	.959	5.30
1913	135	303	423	30	70	.960	5.38
1914	139	301	397	17	73	.976	5.02
1915	83	170	209	16	33	.959	4.57
1916	71	98	175	14	29	.951	3.85
1917	73	114	210	9	15	.973	4.44
1922	1	3	3	0	0	1.000	6.00
1929	1	0	0	1	0	0	0
	1735	3758	5120	423	675	.955	5.12

Assists per 154 Games: 454

PLAYER: MILLER HUGGINS

				BATTING													BASERUNNING				PERCENTAGES			VALUES			
Year	G	AB	H	2B	3B	HR	(Hm Rd)	TB	R	RBI	BB	IBB	HBP	SH	SF	SB	CS	SB%	GIDP	Avg.	Slug	On Base	Runs	Win—Loss	Pct.	AV
1904	140	491	129	12	7	2	( )	161	96	30	88			15		13				.263	.328	.365	69	9—6	.585	9
1905	149	564	154	11	8	1	( )	184	117	38	103			9		27				.273	.326	.380	85	9—7	.557	10
1906	146	545	159	11	7	0	( )	184	81	26	71			21		41				.292	.338	.361	89	11—5	.707	12
1907	156	561	139	12	4	1	( )	162	64	41	83			27		28				.248	.289	.331	71	10—7	.596	8
1908	135	498	119	14	5	0	( )	143	65	23	58			28		30				.239	.287	.303	57	9—7	.534	7
1909	57	159	34	3	1	0	( )	39	18	6	28		0	8		11				.214	.245	.318	17	2—3	.419	2
1910	151	547	145	15	6	1	( )	175	101	36	116		6	19		34				.265	.320	.388	85	9—7	.575	12
1911	138	509	133	19	2	1	( )	159	106	24	96		0	15		37				.261	.312	.369	75	8—7	.543	11
1912	120	431	131	15	4	0	( )	154	82	29	87		1	11		35				.304	.357	.413	80	8—4	.662	11
1913	120	382	109	12	0	0	( )	121	74	27	91		7	14		23				.285	.317	.419	62	7—4	.628	10
1914	148	509	134	17	4	1	( )	162	85	24	105		7	14		32	36	.47		.263	.318	.387	75	10—6	.633	12
1915	107	353	85	5	2	2	( )	100	57	24	74		3	8		13	12	.52		.241	.283	.370	42	5—5	.508	6
1916	18	9	3	0	0	0	( )	3	2	0	2		0	2		0				.333	.333	.385	2	0—0	.721	0
	1585	5558	1474	146	50	9	( )	1747	948	328	1002		24	191		324	48	.48		.265	.314	.369	808	99—69	.588	110
9.8 yrs		568	151	15	5	1		179	97	34	102			20		33				.265	.314	.369				

Teams: Cincinnati, N.L., 1904–1909; St. Louis, N.L., 1910–1916.

Points in MVP Voting: 1911, 21 (6th, .33); 1913, 0; 1914, 0.

Explanation for Gaps in Career or Sudden Changes in Productivity:
1909—Seems to have just been benched; no injury.

FIELDING SECOND BASE

Year	G	PO	AS	E	DP	Pct.	Range
1904	140	337	448	46	32	.945	5.61
1905	149	346	525	51	55	.945	5.85
1906	146	341	458	44	62	.948	5.47
1907	156	353	443	32	73	.961	5.10
1908	135	302	406	30	45	.959	5.24
1909	31	70	97	12		.933	5.39
1910	151	325	452	30	58	.963	5.15
1911	136	281	439	29	62	.961	5.29
1912	114	272	337	37	50	.943	5.34
1913	112	265	339	14	44	.977	5.39
1914	147	328	428	28	58	.964	5.14
1915	107	194	315	23	44	.957	4.76
1916	7	10	10	0	0	1.000	2.86
	1531	3424	4697	376	583	.956	5.30

Assists per 154 Games: 472

PLAYER: EDDIE COLLINS

	BATTING																BASERUNNING				PERCENTAGES			VALUES			
Year	G	AB	H	2B	3B	HR	(Hm	Rd)	TB	R	RBI	BB	IBB	HBP	SH	SF	SB	CS	SB%	GIDP	Avg.	Slug	On Base	Runs	Win–Loss	Pct.	AV
1906	6	17	4	0	0	0	(0	0)	4	1	0	0		0*	1		1				.235	.235	.222	1	0–0	.294	0
1907	14	20	5	0	1	0	(0	0)	7	0	2	0		0*	1		0				.250	.350	.238	2	0–0	.406	0
1908	102	330	90	18	7	1	(1	0)	125	39	40	16		3	15		8				.273	.379	.299	42	6–4	.611	4
1909	153	572	198	30	10	3	(2	1)	257	104	56	62		6	21		67				.346	.449	.402	134	14–2	.872	16
1910	153	583	188	16	15	3	(1	2)	243	81	81	49		6	22		81				.322	.417	.368	122	13–3	.813	15
1911	132	493	180	22	13	3	(0	3)	237	92	73	62		15	18		38				.365	.481	.437	124	10–3	.798	16
1912	153	543	189	25	11	0	(0	0)	236	137	64	101		0	29		63				.348	.435	.431	136	12–3	.789	16
1913	148	534	184	23	13	3	(2	1)	242	125	73	85		7	26		55				.345	.453	.423	132	12–3	.795	16
1914	152	526	181	23	14	2	(2	0)	238	122	85	97		6	28		58	30	.66		.344	.452	.432	135	12–2	.839	15
1915	155	521	173	22	10	4	(1	3)	227	118	77	119		5	35		46	30	.61		.332	.436	.437	134	13–2	.835	16
1916	155	545	168	14	17	0	(0	0)	216	87	52	86		3	39		40	21	.66		.308	.396	.382	104	13–4	.751	12
1917	156	564	163	18	12	0	(0	0)	205	91	67	89		3	33		53				.289	.363	.370	102	12–4	.744	12
1918	97	330	91	8	2	2	(1	1)	109	51	30	73		0	22		22				.276	.330	.386	56	7–3	.701	9
1919	140	518	165	19	7	4	(1	3)	210	87	80	68		2	40		33				.319	.405	.374	100	11–4	.703	13
1920	153	601	222	37	13	3	(2	1)	294	115	75	69		2	34		19	8	.70		.369	.489	.415	132	12–4	.746	16
1921	139	526	177	20	10	2	(0	2)	223	79	58	66		2	13		12	10	.55		.337	.424	.404	94	9–5	.634	14
1922	154	598	194	20	12	1	(0	1)	241	92	69	73		3	27		20	12	.62		.324	.403	.385	101	11–4	.637	14
1923	145	505	182	22	5	5	(0	5)	229	89	67	84		4	39		47	29	.62		.360	.453	.427	108	11–4	.711	15
1924	152	556	194	27	7	6	(2	4)	253	108	86	89		3	28		42	17	.71		.349	.455	.423	119	10–5	.669	14
1925	118	425	147	26	3	3	(1	2)	188	80	80	87		4	17		19	6	.76		.346	.442	.447	96	8–3	.723	12
1926	106	375	129	32	4	1	(0	1)	172	66	62	62		3	15		13	8	.62		.344	.459	.426	80	8–3	.746	10
1927	95	225	76	12	1	1	(0	1)	93	50	15	60		0	8		6				.338	.413	.464	48	4–2	.716	6
1928	36	33	10	3	0	0	(0	0)	13	3	7	4		0	0		0	0	.00		.303	.394	.378	5	1–0	.599	1
1929	9	7	0	0	0	0	(0	0)	0	0	0	2		0	0		0	0	.00		.000	.000	.222	0	0–0	.007	0
1930	3	2	1	0	0	0	(0	0)	1	1	0	0		0	0		0	0	.00		.500	.500	.500	0	0–0	.836	0
	2826	9949	3311	437	187	47	(16	31)	4263	1818	1299	1503		77	511		743	171	.65		.333	.428	.406	2107	209–73	.742	262
17.4 yrs		570	190	25	11	3			244	104	74	86		4	29		43				.333	.428	.406				

*Estimated.

Teams: Philadelphia, A.L., 1906–1914; Chicago, A.L., 1915–1926; Philadelphia, A.L., 1927–1930.

Points in MVP Voting: 1911, 32 (3rd, .50); 1913, 30 (3rd, .47); 1914, 63 (1st, .98); 1922, 18 (5th, .28); 1923, 37 (2nd, .58); 1924, 49 (2nd, .77); 1926, 0; 1927, 0. TOTAL: 3.58 Award Shares.

Reported Salaries: 1915—$14,500.

Explanation for Gaps in Career or Sudden Changes in Productivity: 1925—Injured leg.

FIELDING SECOND BASE

Year	G	PO	AS	E	DP	Pct.	Range
1906	1	0	0	0	0	0	0
1907	0	0	0	0	0	0	0
1908	47	111	127	14	5	.944	5.06
1909	152	373	406	27	55	.967	5.12
1910	153	402	451	25	67	.972	5.58
1911	132	348	349	24	49	.967	5.28
1912	153	387	426	38	63	.955	5.31
1913	148	314	449	28	54	.965	5.16
1914	152	354	387	23	55	.970	4.87
1915	155	344	487	22	54	.974	5.36
1916	155	346	415	19	75	.976	4.91
1917	156	353	388	24	68	.969	4.75
1918	96	231	285	14	53	.974	5.37
1919	140	347	401	20	66	.974	5.34
1920	153	449	471	23	76	.976	6.01
1921	136	376	458	28	84	.968	6.13
1922	154	406	451	21	73	.976	5.56
1923	142	347	430	20	77	.975	5.47
1924	150	396	446	20	83	.977	5.61
1925	116	290	346	20	74	.970	5.48
1926	101	228	307	15	53	.973	5.30
1927	56	124	150	10	31	.965	4.89
1928	2	0	2	0	0	1.000	1.00
	2650	6526	7632	435	1215	.970	5.34

Assists per 154 Games: 443

PLAYER: LARRY DOYLE

			BATTING															BASERUNNING				PERCENTAGES			VALUES			
Year	G	AB	H	2B	3B	HR	(Hm	Rd)	TB	R	RBI	BB	IBB	HBP	SH	SF		SB	CS	SB%	GIDP	Avg.	Slug	On Base	Runs	Win−Loss	Pct.	AV
1907	69	227	59	3	0	0	(	)	62	16	16	20			4			3				.260	.273	.315	22	3−4	.463	2
1908	104	377	116	16	9	0	(	)	150	65	33	22			25			17				.308	.398	.325	58	8−4	.685	6
1909	146	568	171	27	11	6	(	)	238	86	49	45		7	12			30				.301	.419	.353	95	12−5	.718	11
1910	151	575	164	21	14	8	(	)	237	97	69	71		5	19			39				.285	.412	.358	101	12−5	.686	11
1911	143	526	163	25	25	13	(	)	277	102	77	71		5	20			38				.310	.527	.384	124	12−3	.794	13
1912	143	558	184	33	8	10	(	)	263	98	90	56		2	13			36				.330	.471	.385	116	11−4	.741	13
1913	132	482	135	25	6	5	(	)	187	67	73	59		4	12			38				.280	.388	.355	78	10−5	.678	11
1914	145	539	140	19	8	5	(	)	190	87	63	58		10	16			17				.260	.353	.334	69	9−8	.529	9
1915	150	591	189	40	10	4	(	)	261	86	70	32		3	15			22	18	.55		.320	.442	.349	97	11−5	.697	11
1916	122	479	133	29	11	3	(	)	193	61	54	28		4	16			19				.278	.403	.313	66	9−5	.639	10
1917	135	476	121	19	5	6	(	)	168	48	61	48		0	26			5				.254	.353	.307	56	8−7	.544	8
1918	75	257	67	7	4	3	(	)	91	38	36	37		0	4			10				.261	.354	.349	34	5−3	.612	4
1919	113	381	110	14	10	7	(	)	165	61	52	31		5	3			12				.289	.433	.348	59	7−3	.677	6
1920	137	471	134	21	2	4	(	)	171	48	50	47			2	10			11	9	.55		.285	.363	.345	61	8−6	.562	8
	1765	6507	1886	299	123	74	(	)	2653	960	793	625		47	195			297	27	.55		.290	.408	.347	1036	123−65	.653	123
10.9 yrs		597	173	27	11	7	(	)	244	88	73	57			18			27				.290	.408	.347				

Teams: New York, N.L. 1907–1916; Chicago, N.L. 1916–1917; New York, N.L. 1918–1920.

Points in MVP Voting: 1911, 23 (3rd, .36); 1912, Won Chalmers Award (Credited with .80 Award Share); 1913, 5 (.08); 1914, 0. TOTAL: 1.24 Award Shares.

Explanation for Gaps in Career or Sudden Changes in Productivity: 1918 *Reach Guide* says he suffered "an accident" in 1917.

FIELDING SECOND BASE

Year	G	PO	AS	Err	DP	Pct.	Range
1907	69	128	158	26	7	.917	4.14
1908	102	180	291	33	28	.935	4.62
1909	143	292	322	39	51	.940	4.29
1910	151	313	388	53	62	.930	4.64
1911	141	272	340	36	46	.944	4.34
1912	143	313	379	38	68	.948	4.84
1913	130	313	345	31	55	.955	5.06
1914	145	307	379	29	61	.959	4.73
1915	150	313	396	40	66	.947	4.73
1916	122	289	387	27	53	.962	5.54
1917	128	300	348	33	54	.952	5.06
1918	73	121	221	11	24	.969	4.68
1919	100	214	311	24	48	.956	5.25
1920	133	278	389	23	61	.967	5.02
	1730	3633	4654	443	684	.949	4.79

Assists per 154 Games: 414

PLAYER: DEL PRATT

Year	G	AB	H	2B	3B	HR	(Hm	Rd)	TB	R	RBI	BB	IBB	HBP	SH	SF	SB	CS	SB%	GIDP	Avg.	Slug	On Base	Runs	Win–Loss	Pct.	AV
1912	151	570	172	26	15	5	(	)	243	76	69	36		4	12		24				.302	.426	.341	91	10–6	.636	11
1913	155	592	175	31	13	2			238	60	87	40		1	18		37				.296	.402	.332	89	11–6	.658	11
1914	158	584	165	34	13	5			240	85	65	50		2	18		37	28	.57		.283	.411	.332	90	12–5	.683	11
1915	159	602	175	31	11	3			237	61	78	26		3	32		32	23	.58		.291	.394	.308	84	11–7	.601	12
1916	158	596	159	35	12	5			233	64	103	54		3	16		26	17	.61		.267	.391	.323	80	11–7	.602	11
1917	123	450	111	22	8	1			152	40	53	33		2	14		18				.247	.338	.293	49	6–7	.468	6
1918	126	477	131	19	7	2			170	65	55	35		2	23		12				.275	.356	.313	59	8–7	.540	9
1919	140	527	154	27	7	4			207	69	56	36		4	16		22				.292	.393	.333	75	9–6	.626	10
1920	154	574	180	37	8	4			245	84	97	50		3	27		12	10	.55		.314	.427	.356	91	9–7	.571	11
1921	135	521	169	36	10	5			240	80	100	44		1	8		8	10	.44		.324	.461	.373	89	9–5	.664	13
1922	154	607	183	44	7	6			259	73	86	53		4	9		7	10	.41		.301	.427	.357	93	10–7	.599	10
1923	101	297	92	18	3	0			116	43	40	25		6	14		5	1	.83		.310	.391	.360	46	5–4	.533	5
1924	121	429	130	32	3	1			171	56	77	31		2	26		6	9	.40		.303	.399	.334	59	6–7	.434	8
11.3 yrs	1835	6826	1996	392	117	43	(	)	2751	856	966	513		37	233		246	108	.55		.292	.403	.335	996	117–81	.593	128
	603	176		35	10	4			243	76	85	45		3	21		22				.292	.403	.335				

Teams: St. Louis, A.L. 1912–1917; New York, A.L. 1918–1920; Boston, A.L. 1921–1922; Detroit, A.L. 1923–1924.

Points in MVP Voting: 1913, 0; 1914, 0; 1922, 7 (.11); 1923, 0; 1924, 0. TOTAL: .11 Award Shares.

Explanation for Gaps in Career or Sudden Changes in Productivity:
1917—Did not play much in September after suing owner for slanderous remarks (see 1918, Section I).

FIELDING SECOND BASE

Year	G	PO	AS	Err	DP	Pct.	Range
1912	121	273	326	36	49	.943	4.95
1913	146	364	425	41	56	.951	5.40
1914	152	358	423	46	48	.944	5.14
1915	158	417	441	31	82	.965	5.43
1916	158	438	491	33	74	.966	5.88
1917	119	324	353	29	64	.959	5.69
1918	126	340	386	23	82	.969	5.76
1919	140	315	491	26	64	.969	5.76
1920	154	354	515	26	77	.971	5.64
1921	134	283	408	28	90	.961	5.16
1922	154	362	484	30	80	.966	5.49
1923	60	108	140	14	21	.947	4.13
1924	63	133	192	18	38	.948	5.16
	1685	4069	5075	381	825	.960	5.43

Assists per 154 Games: 464

PLAYER: ROGERS HORNSBY

Year	G	AB	H	2B	3B	HR	(Hm	Rd)	TB	R	RBI	BB	IBB	HBP	SH	SF	SB	CS	SB%	GIDP	Avg.	Slug	On Base	Runs	Win–Loss	Pct.	AV
1915	18	57	14	2	0	0			16	5	4	2		0	2		0	2	.00		.246	.281	.262	4	1–1	.285	0
1916	139	495	155	17	15	6			220	63	65	40		4	11		17				.313	.444	.362	80	10–3	.739	11
1917	145	523	171	24	17	8			253	86	66	45		4	17		17				.327	.484	.374	95	11–3	.779	14
1918	115	416	117	19	11	5			173	51	60	40		3	7		8				.281	.416	.343	59	8–4	.640	9
1919	138	512	163	15	9	8			220	68	71	48		7	10		17				.318	.430	.378	84	10–4	.731	10
1920	149	589	218	44	20	9			329	96	94	60		3	8		12	15	.44		.370	.559	.426	138	12–3	.811	17
1921	154	592	235	44	18	21			378	131	126	60		7	15		13	13	.50		.397	.639	.448	169	13–2	.847	19
1922	154	623	250	46	14	42	24	18	450	141	152	65		1	15		17	12	.59		.401	.722	.449	200	13–2	.851	24
1923	107	424	163	32	10	17			266	89	83	55		3	5		3	7	.30		.384	.627	.454	120	9–2	.851	14
1924	143	536	227	43	14	25			373	121	94	89		2	13		5	12	.29		.424	.696	.497	186	12–1	.900	21
1925	138	504	203	41	10	39			381	133	143	83		2	16		5	3	.62		.403	.756	.476	187	11–1	.895	24
1926	134	527	167	34	5	11			244	96	93	61		0	16		3				.317	.463	.377	94	9–5	.647	11
1927	155	568	205	32	9	26			333	133	125	86		4	26		9				.361	.586	.431	148	12–3	.799	18
1928	140	486	188	42	7	21			307	99	94	107		1	25		5				.387	.632	.478	154	11–2	.865	19
1929	156	602	229	47	8	39	24	15	409	156	149	87		1	22		2				.380	.681	.445	183	13–3	.824	21
1930	42	104	32	5	1	2			45	15	18	12		1	3		0				.308	.433	.375	17	1–1	.502	2
1931	100	357	118	37	1	16			205	64	90	56		0	5		1				.331	.574	.416	88	7–2	.783	10
1932	19	58	13	2	0	1			18	10	7	10		2	0		0				.224	.310	.357	7	1–1	.470	0
1933	57	92	30	7	0	3	1	2	46	11	23	14		2	0		1	0	.00	0	.326	.500	.426	22	2–0	.817	2
1934	24	23	7	2	0	1			12	2	11	7		1	0		0	0	.00		.304	.522	.484	7	1–0	.831	1
1935	10	24	5	3	0	0			8	1	3	3		0	0		0	0	.00		.208	.333	.296	2	0–1	.292	0
1936	2	5	2	0	0	0			2	1	2	1		0	0		0	0	.00		.400	.400	.500	1	0–0	.709	0
1937	20	56	18	3	0	1			24	7	11	7		0	0		0	0	.00		.321	.429	.397	10	1–1	.593	1
Total	2259	8173	2930	541	169	301	49	35	4712	1579	1584	1038		48	216		135	64	.46		.358	.577	.424	2056	166–46	.784	248
13.9 yrs		586	210	39	12	22			338	113	114	74		3	15		10				.358	.577	.424				

Teams: St. Louis, N.L. 1915–1926; New York, N.L. 1927; Boston, N.L., 1928; Chicago, N.L., 1929–1932; St. Louis, N.L. and A.L. 1933; St. Louis, A.L. 1934–1937.

Points in MVP Voting: 1924, 62 (2nd, .78); 1925, 1st; 1926, 7 (.09); 1927, 66 (2nd, .83); 1929, 1st; 1931, 5 (.08); 1932, 0; 1933, 0; 1934, 0; 1935, 0; 1937, 0. TOTAL: 3.38 Award Shares. (Hornsby was voted the N.L. MVP in both 1925 and 1929, but I do not have vote totals for either year. I credited him with .80 Award Shares each year.)

Reported Salaries: 1916—$2,000; 1917—$3,000; 1918—$3,000; 1919—$3,000; 1920—$4,000; 1923-24-25—$18,000 a year; 1925 purchased stock in Cardinals team, which he sold for a substantial profit in the winter of 1925–1926. 1926 salary reported at $30,000.

Explanation for Gaps in Career or Sudden Changes in Productivity:
1930—Operation performed to remove a bone growth from his right heel in November 1929. The heel would trouble him the rest of his career. In addition, Hornsby broke his left ankle in the first game of a Memorial Day, 1930, double header and missed most of the season.

Other Notes: Named outstanding major league second baseman by *The Sporting News* in 1925, 1926, 1927, 1928, and 1929.

FIELDING SECOND BASE

Year	G	PO	AS	Err	DP	Pct.	Range
1916		3	4	1	0	.875	7.00
1919	25	46	101	5	13	.967	5.88
1920	149	343	524	34	76	.962	5.82
1921	142	305	477	25	59	.969	5.51
1922	154	398	473	30	81	.967	5.66
1923	96	192	283	19	47	.962	4.95
1924	143	301	517	30	102	.965	5.72
1925	136	287	416	34	95	.954	5.17
1926	134	245	433	27	73	.962	5.06
1927	155	299	582	25	98	.972	5.68
1928	140	295	450	21	85	.973	5.32
1929	156	286	547	23	106	.973	5.34
1930	25	44	76	11	16	.916	4.80
1931	69	107	205	16	24	.951	4.52
1933	17	24	35	2	7	.967	3.47
1935	2	1	2	0	0	1.000	1.50
1937	17	30	41	4	10	.947	4.18
	1561	3206	5166	307	892	.965	5.36

Assists per 154 Games: 510

HOME AND ROAD DATA FOR 1922 SEASON

	G	AB	R	H	2B	3B	HR	RBI	Avg.
HOME	77	313	65	126	22	6	24	82	.403
ROAD	77	310	76	124	24	8	18	70	.400

HOME AND ROAD DATA FOR 1929 SEASON

	G	AB	R	H	2B	3B	HR	RBI	Avg.
HOME	77	294	82	118	25	2	24	79	.401
ROAD	79	308	74	111	22	6	15	70	.360

Data courtesy of Gordon L. Herman

PLAYER: FRANKIE FRISCH

				BATTING													BASERUNNING				PERCENTAGES			VALUES			
Year	G	AB	H	2B	3B	HR	(Hm Rd)	TB	R	RBI	BB	IBB	HBP	SH	SF	SB	CS	SB%	GIDP	Avg.	Slug	On Base	Runs	Win–Loss	Pct.	AV
1919	54	190	43	3	2	2	( )	56	21	24	4		0	3		15				.226	.295	.239	16	2–4	.333	2
1920	110	440	123	10	10	4	( )	165	57	77	20		0	13		34	11	.76		.280	.375	.302	52	7–7	.502	9
1921	153	618	211	31	17	8	( )	300	121	100	42		1	26		49	13	.79		.341	.485	.370	118	11–6	.669	15
1922	132	514	168	16	13	5	( )	225	101	51	47		3	18		31	17	.65		.327	.438	.375	87	9–6	.602	12
1923	151	641	223	32	10	12	( )	311	116	111	46		4	11		29	12	.71		.348	.485	.389	123	11–5	.677	15
1924	145	603	198	33	15	7	( )	282	121	69	56		2	14		22	9	.71		.328	.468	.379	111	11–6	.657	15
1925	120	502	166	26	6	11	( )	237	89	48	32		3	5		21	12	.64		.331	.472	.371	87	9–5	.646	12
1926	135	545	171	29	4	5	( )	223	75	44	33		0	11		23				.314	.409	.346	76	9–6	.577	12
1927	153	617	208	31	11	10	( )	291	112	78	43		7	26		48				.337	.472	.372	109	11–6	.665	16
1928	141	547	164	29	9	10	( )	241	107	86	64		1	19		29				.300	.441	.363	95	10–6	.634	14
1929	138	527	176	40	12	5	( )	255	93	74	53		2	17		24				.334	.484	.386	99	9–5	.636	15
1930	133	540	187	46	9	10	( )	281	121	114	55		0	16		15				.346	.520	.396	111	9–5	.647	16
1931	131	518	161	24	4	4	( )	205	96	82	45		2	5		28				.311	.396	.365	76	8–6	.582	14
1932	115	486	142	26	2	3	( )	181	59	60	25		0	2		18				.292	.372	.326	58	6–7	.481	9
1933	147	585	177	32	6	4	( )	233	74	66	48		3	10		18			20	.303	.398	.353	83	10–7	.596	11
1934	140	550	168	30	6	3	( )	219	74	75	45		1	10		11			17	.305	.398	.353	79	8–7	.546	11
1935	103	354	104	16	2	1	( )	127	52	55	33		1	14		2			7	.294	.359	.343	48	5–5	.503	6
1936	93	303	83	10	0	1	( )	96	40	26	36		1	8		2			9	.274	.317	.345	36	3–5	.390	4
1937	17	32	7	2	0	0	( )	9	3	4	1		0	1		0			2	.219	.281	.235	2	0–1	.109	0
	2311	9112	2880	466	138	105	( )	3937	1532	1244	728		31	229		419	74	.72	55	.316	.432	.360	1466	149–103	.591	207
14.3 yrs		639	202	33	10	7	( )	276	107	87	51		2	16		29				.316	.432	.360				

Teams: New York, N.L. 1919–1926; St. Louis, N.L. 1927–1937.
Points in MVP Voting: 1924, 43 (3rd, .54); 1926, 0; 1927, 54 (3rd, .68); 1930 BBWA, 64 (2nd, .80); 1931, 65 (1st, .81); 1932, 13 (9th, .15); 1933, 7 (.09); 1934, 4 (.05); 1935, 7 (.09); 1937, 0. TOTAL: 3.21 Award Shares.
1931—Finished fourth in voting for *Sporting News* MVP Award, but won the first BBWAA award.
Explanation for Gaps in Career or Sudden Changes in Productivity:
1925—Ankle injury.
Other Notes: Macmillan contains error in games in field, 1937.
Named outstanding major league second baseman in 1930, 1931 by *The Sporting News*.

FIELDING SECOND BASE

Year	G	PO	AS	Err	DP	Pct.	Range
1919	29	82	92	5	7	.972	6.00
1920	0	0	0	0	0	0	0
1921	61	147	218	14	36	.963	5.98
1922	85	176	288	12	40	.975	5.46
1923	135	307	451	21	79	.973	5.61
1924	143	391	537	27	100	.972	6.49
1925	42	105	162	12	20	.957	6.36
1926	127	261	471	19	69	.975	5.76
1927	153	396	641	22	104	.979	6.78
1928	139	383	474	21	80	.976	6.17
1929	121	295	374	21	66	.970	5.53
1930	123	307	473	25	93	.969	6.34
1931	129	290	424	19	93	.974	5.53
1932	75	214	250	14	53	.971	6.19
1933	132	371	378	14	71	.982	5.67
1934	115	294	351	15	74	.977	5.61
1935	88	193	252	8	48	.982	5.06
1936	61	124	176	11	27	.965	4.92
1937	17	12	14	0	0	1.000	1.53
	1775	4348	6026	280	1060	.974	5.84

Assists per 154 Games: 523

PLAYER: CHARLIE GEHRINGER

				BATTING													BASERUNNING				PERCENTAGES			VALUES			
Year	G	AB	H	2B	3B	HR	(Hm Rd)	TB	R	RBI	BB	IBB	HBP	SH	SF	SB	CS	SB%	GIDP	Avg.	Slug	On Base	Runs	Win–Loss	Pct.	AV
1924	5	13	6	0	0	0	(0 0)	6	2	1	0		1	0		1	1	.50		.462	.462	.500	3	0–0	.747	0
1925	8	18	3	0	0	0	(0 0)	3	3	0	2		0	0		0	1	.00		.167	.167	.250	1	0–1	.038	0
1926	123	459	127	19	17	1	(0 1)	183	62	48	30		1	27		9	7	.56		.277	.399	.306	59	6–9	.394	7
1927	133	508	161	29	11	4	(1 3)	224	110	61	52		2	9		17				.317	.441	.377	85	8–6	.578	12
1928	154	603	193	29	16	6	(4 2)	272	108	74	69		6	13		15	9	.62		.320	.451	.382	110	11–6	.640	13
1929	155	634	215	45	19	13	(7 6)	337	131	106	64		6	11		27	9	.75		.339	.532	.399	139	11–6	.654	18
1930	154	610	201	47	15	16	(7 9)	326	144	98	69		7	13		19	15	.56		.330	.534	.396	130	10–6	.624	18
1931	101	383	119	24	5	4	(0 4)	165	67	53	29		0	2		13	4	.76		.311	.431	.357	60	6–4	.591	8
1932	152	618	184	44	11	19	(6 13)	307	112	107	68		3	3		9	8	.53		.298	.497	.368	114	11–6	.621	14
1933	155	628	204	42	6	12	(8 4)	294	103	105	68		3	6		5	4	.56		.325	.468	.390	117	12–5	.692	16
1934	154	601	214	50	7	11	(2 9)	311	134	127	99		3	5		11	8	.58		.356	.517	.446	144	12–4	.751	17
1935	150	610	201	32	8	19	(11 8)	306	123	108	79		3	17		11	4	.73		.330	.502	.399	129	11–5	.692	17
1936	154	641	227	60	12	15	(7 8)	356	144	116	83		4	3		4	1	.80		.354	.555	.430	157	12–4	.738	18
1937	144	564	209	40	1	14	(10 4)	293	133	96	90		1	5		11	4	.73		.371	.520	.455	140	11–3	.753	18
1938	152	568	174	32	5	20	(12 8)	276	133	107	112		4	3		14	1	.93		.306	.486	.422	127	11–4	.707	16
1939	118	406	132	29	6	16	(9 7)	221	86	86	68		1	11		4	3	.57	7	.325	.544	.414	97	8–3	.743	12
1940	139	515	161	33	3	10	(5 5)	230	108	81	101		3	10		10	0	1.00	9	.313	.447	.421	109	10–4	.698	11
1941	127	436	96	19	4	3	(2 1)	132	65	46	95		3	3		1	2	.33	11	.220	.303	.361	54	6–7	.438	8
1942	45	45	12	0	0	1	(1 0)	15	6	7	7		0	0		0	0	.00	0	.267	.333	.365	6	1–0	.640	1
	2323	8860	2839	574	146	184	(92 92)	4257	1774	1427	1185		45	141		181	81	.67	27	.320	.480	.398	1781	155–85	.646	224
14.3 yrs		618	198	40	10	13		297	124	100	83		3	10		13			10	.320	.480	.398				

Teams: Detroit, A.L. 1924–1942.

Points in MVP Voting: 1924, 0; 1926, 0; 1927, 0; 1931, 0; 1932, 20 (4th, .23); 1933, 32 (6th, .40); 1934, 65 (2nd, .81); 1935, 26 (6th, .33); 1936, 39 (4th, .49); 1937, 78 (1st, .98); 1938, 27 (10th, .08); 1939, 21 (.06); 1940, 3 (.01); 1941, 0; 1942, 0. TOTAL: 3.39 Award Shares.

Explanation for Gaps in Career or Sudden Changes in Productivity:
1931—Arm Injury.
1939—1940 *Guide* says that he missed thirty-seven games with injuries, but doesn't say what they were.

Other Notes: Named to the major league All-Star team in 1933, 1934, 1935, 1936, 1937, 1938 by *The Sporting News*.

FIELDING SECOND BASE

Year	G	PO	AS	Err	DP	Pct.	Range
1924	5	12	17	1	2	.967	5.80
1925	6	8	20	0	5	1.000	4.67
1926	112	255	323	16	56	.973	5.16
1927	121	304	438	27	84	.965	6.13
1928	154	377	507	35	101	.962	5.74
1929	154	404	501	23	93	.975	5.88
1930	154	399	501	19	97	.979	5.84
1931	78	224	236	10	54	.979	5.90
1932	152	396	495	30	110	.967	5.86
1933	155	358	542	17	111	.981	5.81
1934	154	355	516	17	100	.981	5.66
1935	149	349	489	13	99	.985	5.62
1936	154	397	524	25	116	.974	5.58
1937	142	331	485	12	102	.986	5.75
1938	152	393	455	21	115	.976	5.58
1939	107	245	312	13	67	.977	5.21
1940	138	276	374	19	72	.972	4.71
1941	116	279	324	11	59	.982	5.58
1942	3	7	9	0	1	1.000	5.33
	2206	5369	7068	309	1444	.976	5.64

Assists per 154 Games: 493

PLAYER: TONY LAZZERI

Year	G	AB	H	2B	3B	HR	(Hm	Rd)	TB	R	RBI	BB	IBB	HBP	SH	SF	SB	CS	SB%	GIDP	Avg.	Slug	On Base	Runs	Win–Loss	Pct.	AV
						BATTING											BASERUNNING				PERCENTAGES			VALUES			
1926	155	589	162	28	14	18	(9	9)	272	79	114	54		2	20		16	7	.70		.275	.462	.328	93	9–8	.528	11
1927	153	570	176	29	8	18	(11	7)	275	92	102	69		0	21		22				.309	.482	.371	104	10–6	.624	15
1928	116	404	134	30	11	10	(5	5)	216	62	82	43		1	15		15	5	.75		.332	.535	.384	87	8–3	.699	10
1929	147	545	193	37	11	18	(5	13)	306	101	106	69		4	18		9	10	.47		.354	.561	.418	131	11–4	.731	16
1930	143	571	173	34	15	9	(4	5)	264	109	121	60		3	16		4	4	.50		.303	.462	.363	100	8–8	.486	13
1931	135	484	129	27	7	8	(4	4)	194	67	83	79		1	7		18	9	.67		.267	.401	.368	76	6–8	.457	9
1932	141	510	153	28	16	15	(11	4)	258	79	113	82		2	7		11	11	.50		.300	.506	.394	104	9–5	.631	14
1933	139	523	154	22	12	18	(7	11)	254	94	104	73		2	4		15	7	.68		.294	.486	.380	100	9–6	.602	12
1934	123	438	117	24	6	14	(7	7)	195	59	67	71		0	5		11	1	.92		.267	.445	.366	77	8–5	.612	9
1935	130	477	130	18	6	13	(6	7)	199	72	83	63		3	1		11	5	.69		.273	.417	.360	75	8–6	.563	11
1936	150	537	154	29	6	14	(3	11)	237	82	109	97		1	3		8	5	.62		.287	.441	.395	100	9–7	.567	12
1937	126	446	109	21	3	14	(8	6)	178	56	70	71		0	1		7	1	.87		.244	.399	.347	67	6–7	.485	8
1938	54	120	32	5	0	5	(2	3)	52	21	23	22		0	1		0			5	.267	.433	.378	20	2–1	.628	2
1939	27	83	24	2	0	4	(3	1)	38	13	14	17		2	0		1			3	.289	.458	.422	17	2–1	.749	2
10.7 yrs	1739	6297	1840	334	115	178	(85	93)	2938	986	1194	870		21	116		148	65	.66		.292	.467	.374	1152	104–75	.582	144
	587		171	31	11	17			274	92	111	81		2	11		14				.292	.467	.374				

Teams: New York, A.L. 1926–37; Chicago, N.L. 1938; Brooklyn, N.L./New York, N.L. 1939.

Points in MVP Voting: 1926, 7 (10th, .11); 1927, 8 (.13); 1931, 0; 1932, 8 (.09); 1933, 6 (.08); 1934, 0; 1935, 0; 1937, 0; 1938, 0; 1939, 0. TOTAL: .30 Award Shares.

Reported Salaries: 1927—$8,000.

Explanation for Gaps in Career or Sudden Changes in Productivity:
1928—Shoulder separation.
1934—No report of injuries. Started season as third baseman with Rolfe at second; for a time battled Saltzgaver and Rolfe for playing time.

Other Notes: After the 1937 season, Jake Ruppert was reportedly offered cash for Lazzeri by a couple of teams, but rather than accepting it gave Lazzeri his release to allow him to make his own deal—a class gesture of the kind that baseball has had few enough of.

Named outstanding major league second baseman in 1932 by *The Sporting News*.

FIELDING SECOND BASE

Year	G	PO	AS	Err	DP	Pct.	Range
1926	149	298	461	31	72	.961	5.09
1927	113	213	398	18	60	.971	5.41
1928	116	236	331	26	56	.956	4.89
1929	147	368	467	27	101	.969	5.68
1930	77	184	245	13	39	.971	5.57
1931	90	216	288	22	52	.958	5.60
1932	133	362	405	17	70	.978	5.77
1933	138	338	407	25	71	.968	5.40
1934	92	218	265	12	52	.976	5.25
1935	118	285	329	19	72	.970	5.20
1936	148	346	414	25	88	.968	5.14
1937	125	251	382	22	64	.966	5.06
1938	4	8	17	0	1	1.000	6.25
1939	11	28	36	6	9	.914	5.82
	1461	3351	4445	263	807	.967	5.34

Assists per 154 Games: 468

PLAYER: BILLY HERMAN

							BATTING										BASERUNNING				PERCENTAGES			VALUES			
Year	G	AB	H	2B	3B	HR	(Hm Rd)	TB	R	RBI	BB	IBB	HBP	SH	SF	SB	CS	SB%	GIDP	Avg.	Slug	On Base	Runs	Win—Loss	Pct.	AV
1931	25	98	32	7	0	0	( )	39	14	16	13		0	4		2				.327	.398	.391	17	2—1	.608	2
1932	154	656	206	42	7	1	( )	265	102	51	40		5	22		14				.314	.404	.347	95	11—8	.587	13
1933	153	619	173	35	2	0	( )	212	82	44	45		4	13		5			21	.279	.342	.326	70	9—9	.512	10
1934	113	456	138	21	6	3	( )	180	79	42	34		3	8		6			8	.303	.395	.349	66	7—5	.594	9
1935	154	666	227	57	6	7	( )	317	113	83	42		3	24		6			17	.341	.476	.370	121	12—6	.679	15
1936	153	632	211	57	7	5	( )	297	101	93	59		1	17		5			16	.334	.470	.382	118	12—5	.718	15
1937	138	564	189	35	11	8	( )	270	106	65	56		1	11		2			7	.335	.479	.389	112	10—4	.713	13
1938	152	624	173	34	7	1	( )	224	86	56	59		2	11		3			24	.277	.359	.336	76	9—9	.495	11
1939	156	623	191	34	18	7	( )	282	111	70	66		5	19		9			24	.307	.453	.367	106	11—6	.642	12
1940	135	558	163	24	4	5	( )	210	77	57	47		0	11		1			16	.292	.376	.341	72	8—7	.536	11
1941	144	572	163	30	5	3	(1 2)	212	81	41	67		1	9		1			13	.285	.371	.356	79	9—7	.558	10
1942	155	571	146	34	2	2	(0 2)	190	76	65	72		0	4		6			9	.256	.333	.337	68	8—8	.519	10
1943	153	585	193	41	2	2	(2 0)	244	76	100	66		0	12		4			19	.330	.417	.391	97	10—5	.649	14
1946	122	436	130	31	5	3	(1 2)	180	56	50	69		1	6		3			14	.298	.413	.391	73	8—4	.696	8
1947	15	47	10	4	0	0	(0 0)	14	3	6	2		0	0		0			3	.213	.298	.245	3	0—1	.115	0
	1922	7707	2345	486	82	47	( )	3136	1163	839	737	26	171			67			191	.304	.407	.360	1172	128—85	.601	153
11.9 yrs		650	198	41	7	4		264	98	71	62	2	14			6				.304	.407	.360				

Teams: Chicago, N.L. 1931–1941; Brooklyn, N.L. 1941–1943; Brooklyn/Boston, N.L. 1946; Pittsburgh, 1947.

Points in MVP Voting: 1931, 0; 1932, 14 (6th, .16); 1933, 0; 1934, 4 (.05); 1935, 38 (4th, .48); 1936, 37 (3rd, .62); 1937, 19 (9th, .24); 1938, 0; 1940, 0; 1941, 27 (.08); 1942, 0; 1943, 140 (4th, .42); 1946, 0; 1947, 0. TOTAL: 2.05 Award Shares.

Other Notes: Named as outstanding major league second baseman in 1943 by *The Sporting News*.

Macmillan contains error on games played at second base in 1947. Sixty (60) is the correct figure, not 76.

FIELDING SECOND BASE

Year	G	PO	AS	Err	DP	Pct.	Range
1931	25	76	79	10	17	.939	6.20
1932	154	401	527	38	102	.961	6.03
1933	153	466	512	45	114	.956	6.39
1934	111	278	385	17	64	.975	5.97
1935	154	416	520	35	109	.964	6.08
1936	153	457	492	24	110	.975	6.20
1937	137	384	468	41	97	.954	6.22
1938	151	404	517	18	111	.981	6.10
1939	156	377	485	29	95	.967	5.53
1940	135	366	448	22	94	.974	6.03
1941	144	330	374	26	69	.964	4.89
1942	153	383	402	22	97	.973	5.13
1943	117	291	322	18	69	.971	5.24
1946	60	137	137	9	27	.968	4.57
1947	10	14	13	0	2	1.000	2.70
	1813	4780	5681	354	1177	.967	5.77

Assists per 154 Games: 483

PLAYER: BOBBY DOERR

	BATTING																	BASERUNNING				PERCENTAGES			VALUES			
Year	G	AB	H	2B	3B	HR	(Hm	Rd)	TB	R	RBI	BB	IBB	HBP	SH	SF	SB	CS	SB%	GIDP	Avg.	Slug	On Base	Runs	Win–Loss	Pct.	AV
1937	55	147	33	5	1	2	(2	0)	46	22	14	18		1	4		2	4	.33		.224	.313	.306	15	1–3	.266	2
1938	145	509	147	26	7	5	(5	0)	202	70	80	59	0		22		5	10	.33		.289	.397	.349	74	7–9	.439	12
1939	127	525	167	28	2	12	(7	5)	235	75	73	38	1		10		1	10	.09	17	.318	.448	.359	78	7–8	.482	12
1940	151	595	173	37	10	22	(16	6)	296	87	105	57	0		6		10	5	.67	16	.291	.497	.350	104	9–7	.562	14
1941	132	500	141	28	4	16	(11	5)	225	74	93	43	0		6		1	3	.25	6	.282	.450	.335	78	7–6	.540	11
1942	144	545	158	35	5	15	(8	7)	248	71	102	67	1		12		4	4	.50	11	.290	.455	.362	95	10–5	.657	15
1943	155	604	163	32	3	16	(9	7)	249	78	75	62	1		9		8	8	.50	11	.270	.412	.334	86	11–6	.632	14
1944	125	468	152	30	10	15	(11	4)	247	95	81	58	0		10		5	2	.71	3	.325	.528	.392	106	10–3	.783	15
1946	151	583	158	34	9	18	(13	5)	264	95	116	66	1		6		5	6	.45	18	.271	.453	.341	90	10–7	.588	15
1947	146	561	145	23	10	17	(12	5)	239	79	95	59	0		4		3	3	.50	25	.258	.426	.327	74	8–8	.507	13
1948	140	527	150	23	6	27	(19	8)	266	94	111	83	4		4		3	2	.60	13	.285	.505	.383	107	10–5	.661	16
1949	139	541	167	30	9	18	(9	9)	269	91	109	75	0		7		2	2	.50	31	.309	.497	.388	101	10–6	.629	17
1950	149	586	172	29	11	27	(18	9)	304	103	120	67	1		9		3	4	.43	21	.294	.519	.362	109	9–7	.549	15
1951	106	402	116	21	2	13	(5	8)	180	60	73	57	1		3		2	1	.67	10	.289	.448	.376	71	7–4	.625	11
	1865	7093	2042	381	89	223	(145	78)	3270	1094	1247	809	11		115		54	64	.46	182	.288	.461	.357	1187	116–85	.578	182
11.5 yrs		616	177	33	8	19			284	95	108	70	1		10		5	6		18	.288	.461	.357				

Teams: Boston, A.L. 1937–1951.

Points in MVP Voting: 1937, 0; 1938, 0; 1939, 0; 1940, 0; 1941, 0; 1942, 24 (.07); 1943, 21 (.06); 1944, 75 (7th, .22); 1946, 0; 1947, 6 (.02); 1948, 10 (.03); 1949, 7 (.02); 1950, 15 (.05); 1951, 0. TOTAL: .47 Award Shares.

Explanation for Gaps in Career or Sudden Changes in Productivity:
1945—In the army.
1951—Stopped by severe sacroiliac attack, August 7; this ended his career.

Other Notes: Named as the outstanding major league second baseman in 1944 and 1946 by *The Sporting News*.

FIELDING SECOND BASE

Year	G	PO	AS	Err	DP	Pct.	Range
1937	47	94	124	6	29	.973	4.64
1938	145	372	420	26	118	.968	5.46
1939	126	336	431	19	95	.976	6.09
1940	151	401	480	21	118	.977	5.83
1941	132	290	389	20	85	.971	5.14
1942	142	376	453	21	105	.975	5.84
1943	155	415	490	9	132	.990	5.84
1944	125	341	363	17	96	.976	5.63
1946	151	420	483	13	129	.986	5.98
1947	146	376	466	16	118	.981	5.77
1948	138	366	430	6	119	.993	5.77
1949	139	395	439	17	134	.980	6.00
1950	149	443	431	11	130	.988	5.87
1951	106	303	311	12	99	.981	5.79
	1852	4928	5710	214	1507	.980	5.74

Assists per 154 Games: 475

PLAYER: JOE GORDON

Year	G	AB	H	2B	3B	HR	(Hm	Rd)	TB	R	RBI	BB	IBB	HBP	SH	SF	SB	CS	SB%	GIDP	Avg.	Slug	On Base	Runs	Win–Loss	Pct.	AV
				BATTING													**BASERUNNING**				**PERCENTAGES**			**VALUES**			
1938	127	458	117	24	7	25	(13	12)	230	83	97	56		3	3		11	3	.79		.255	.502	.338	81	7–6	.562	12
1939	151	567	161	32	5	28	(11	17)	287	92	111	75		2	4		11	10	.52	15	.284	.506	.367	103	10–6	.622	14
1940	155	616	173	32	10	30	(15	15)	315	112	103	52		3	6		18	8	.69	12	.281	.511	.337	107	11–7	.624	14
1941	156	588	162	26	7	24	(8	16)	274	104	87	72		4	1		10	9	.53	16	.276	.466	.358	98	10–7	.610	13
1942	147	538	173	29	4	18	(7	11)	264	88	103	79		1	7		12	6	.67	22	.322	.491	.405	108	11–4	.748	15
1943	152	543	135	28	5	17	(11	6)	224	82	69	98		2	7		4	7	.36	18	.249	.413	.362	84	10–6	.638	11
1946	112	376	79	15	0	11	(4	7)	127	35	47	49		4	2		2	5	.29	14	.210	.338	.306	38	5–7	.398	8
1947	155	562	153	27	6	29	(12	17)	279	89	93	62		1	1		7	3	.70	16	.272	.496	.345	96	11–5	.691	12
1948	144	550	154	21	4	32	(17	15)	279	96	124	77		3	3		5	2	.71	16	.280	.507	.370	106	11–5	.699	14
1949	148	541	136	18	3	20	(11	9)	220	74	84	83		4	4		5	6	.45	.20	.251	.407	.353	79	10–7	.593	13
1950	119	368	87	12	1	19	(10	9)	158	59	57	56		2	3		4	1	.80	10	.236	.429	.338	56	6–5	.546	7
	1566	5707	1530	264	52	253	(119	134)	2657	914	975	759		29	41		89	60	.60	159	.268	.466	.355	959	102–63	.619	133
9.7 yrs		590	158	27	5	26			275	95	101	79		3	4		9	6		18	.268	.466	.355				

Teams: New York, A.L. 1938–1943, 1946; Cleveland, A.L. 1947–1950.

Points in MVP Voting: 1938, 23 (.07); 1939, 43 (9th, .13); 1940, 3 (.01); 1941, 60 (7th, 18); 1942, 270 (1st, .80); 1943, 4 (.01); 1946, 0; 1947, 59 (7th, .18); 1948, 63 (6th, .19); 1949, 0; 1950, 0. TOTAL: 1.57 Award Shares.

Explanation for Gaps in Career or Sudden Changes in Productivity: In the army, 1944 and 1945. My memory is that he had some sort of back problem, but I can't find a reference for that, so I could be wrong.

Other Notes: Named as outstanding major league second baseman in 1939, 1940, 1941, 1942, 1947, and 1948 by *The Sporting News*. Cited by Pete Palmer as one of the players whose statistics were most hurt by the parks in which he played.

FIELDING SECOND BASE

Year	G	PO	AS	Err	DP	Pct.	Range
1938	126	290	450	31	98	.960	5.87
1939	151	370	461	28	116	.967	5.50
1940	155	374	505	23	116	.975	5.67
1941	131	332	397	32	109	.958	5.56
1942	147	354	442	28	121	.966	5.41
1943	152	407	490	29	114	.969	5.90
1946	108	281	346	17	87	.974	5.81
1947	155	341	466	18	110	.978	5.21
1948	144	330	436	23	97	.971	5.32
1949	145	297	430	15	123	.980	5.01
1950	105	224	283	16	69	.969	4.83
	1519	3600	4706	260	1160	.970	5.47

Assists per 154 Games: 477

PLAYER: RED SCHOENDIENST

Year	G	AB	H	2B	3B	HR	(Hm	Rd)	TB	R	RBI	BB	IBB	HBP	SH	SF	SB	CS	SB%	GIDP	Avg.	Slug	On Base	Runs	Win–Loss	Pct.	AV
1945	137	565	157	22	6	1	(	)	194	89	47	21		1	10		26			6	.278	.343	.300	59	7–9	.434	10
1946	142	606	170	28	5	0	(	)	208	94	34	37		0	7		12			11	.281	.343	.318	67	8–9	.492	10
1947	151	659	167	25	9	3	(	)	219	91	48	48		0	3		6			16	.253	.332	.303	65	7–12	.367	8
1948	119	408	111	21	4	4	(	)	152	64	36	28		0	2		1			6	.272	.373	.317	49	5–6	.481	7
1949	151	640	190	25	2	3	(	)	228	102	54	51		2	9		8			10	.297	.356	.346	82	9–8	.534	11
1950	153	642	177	43	9	7	(4	3)	259	81	63	33		2	16		3			15	.276	.403	.306	79	9–10	.480	13
1951	135	553	160	32	7	6	(1	5)	224	88	54	35		3	11		0	1	.00	13	.289	.405	.329	75	9–7	.551	12
1952	152	620	188	40	7	7	(6	1)	263	91	67	42		0	11		9	6	.60	17	.303	.424	.342	89	10–7	.599	13
1953	146	564	193	35	5	15	(9	6)	283	107	79	60		0	3		3	3	.50	19	.342	.502	.404	114	11–4	.730	17
1954	148	610	192	38	8	5	(1	4)	261	98	79	54		1	5	9	4	2	.67	17	.315	.428	.364	96	9–7	.555	14
1955	145	553	148	21	3	11	(9	2)	208	68	51	54	5	4	0	4	7	7	.50	9	.268	.376	.335	70	8–8	.487	10
1956	132	487	147	21	3	2	(2	0)	180	61	29	41	1	2	3	3	1	3	.25	13	.302	.370	.354	63	8–6	.577	10
1957	150	648	200	31	8	15	(10	5)	292	91	65	33	1	3	8	2	4	4	.50	10	.309	.451	.340	99	11–7	.619	14
1958	106	427	112	23	1	1	(1	0)	140	47	24	31	0	1	5	1	3	1	.75	8	.262	.328	.310	44	6–7	.459	7
1959	5	3	0	0	0	0	(0	0)	0	0	0	0	0	0	0	0	0	0	.00	0	.000	.000	.000	0	0–0	.000	0
1960	68	226	58	9	1	1	(1	0)	72	21	19	17	4	1	2	0	1	0	1.00	3	.257	.319	.309	23	2–4	.388	2
1961	72	120	36	9	0	1	(0	1)	48	9	12	12	2	0	1	0	1	0	1.00	1	.300	.400	.361	18	2–1	.627	2
1962	98	143	43	4	0	2	(0	2)	53	21	12	9	2	1	0	0	0	0	.00	6	.301	.371	.346	17	2–2	.488	3
1963	6	5	0	0	0	0	(0	0)	0	0	0	0	0	0	1	0	0	0	.00	0	.000	.000	.000	0	0–0	.000	0
	2216	8479	2449	427	78	84	(44	29)	3284	1223	773	606	15	21	97	19	93	27	.55	180	.289	.387	.334	1109	123–113	.521	163
13.7 yrs		620	179	31	6	6			240	89	57	44		2	7		7			13	.289	.387	.334				

Teams: St. Louis, N.L., 1945–1956; New York, N.L., 1956–1957; Milwaukee, N.L., 1957–1960; St. Louis, N.L., 1961–1963.

Points in MVP Voting: 1946, 6 (.02); 1947, 0; 1948, 0; 1949, 30 (10th, .09); 1950, 0; 1951, 0; 1952, 25 (10th, .07); 1953, 155 (4th, .46); 1954, 24 (.07); 1956, 0; 1957, 221 (3rd, .66); 1958, 0; 1959, 0; 1960, 0; 1962, 0; 1963, 0. TOTAL: 1.83 Award Shares.

Explanation for Gaps in Career or Sudden Changes in Productivity:
1948—Right shoulder popped out of its socket several times.
1958—Had pleurisy and fractured a finger, July 4.
1959—Hospitalized shortly after 1958 World Series with tuberculosis; missed almost all of 1959 season.

Other Notes: Named as outstanding major league second baseman in 1953 and 1957 by *The Sporting News.*

FIELDING SECOND BASE

Year	G	PO	AS	Err	DP	Pct.	Range
1945	1	0	1	0	0	1.000	1.00
1946	128	340	354	11	87	.984	5.42
1947	142	357	404	19	109	.976	5.36
1948	96	230	269	10	57	.980	5.20
1949	138	399	424	11	105	.987	5.96
1950	143	393	403	12	124	.985	5.57
1951	124	339	386	7	113	.990	5.85
1952	142	399	424	19	108	.977	5.80
1953	140	365	430	14	109	.983	5.68
1954	144	394	477	18	137	.980	6.05
1955	142	296	381	10	96	.985	4.77
1956	121	298	308	4	79	.993	5.01
1957	149	379	448	12	113	.986	5.55
1958	105	233	301	7	77	.987	5.09
1959	4	1	1	1	0	.667	0.50
1960	62	120	148	10	34	.964	4.32
1961	32	43	42	4	10	.955	2.66
1962	21	30	42	1	10	.986	3.43
1963	0	0	0	0	0	0	0
	1834	4616	5243	170	1368	.983	5.38

Assists per 154 Games: 440

PLAYER: JACKIE ROBINSON

Year	G	AB	H	2B	3B	HR	(Hm	Rd)	TB	R	RBI	BB	IBB	HBP	SH	SF	SB	CS	SB%	GIDP	Avg.	Slug	On Base	Runs	Win—Loss	Pct.	AV
1947	151	590	175	31	5	12	(6	6)	252	125	48	74		9	28		29			5	.297	.427	.368	104	11—6	.645	10
1948	147	574	170	38	8	12	(7	5)	260	108	85	57		7	8		22			7	.296	.453	.362	99	10—5	.661	12
1949	156	593	203	38	12	16	(8	8)	313	122	124	86		8	17		37			22	.342	.528	.422	135	12—4	.751	18
1950	141	518	170	39	4	14	(7	7)	259	99	81	80		5	10		12			11	.328	.500	.416	114	10—4	.730	17
1951	153	548	185	33	7	19	(8	11)	289	106	88	79		9	6		25	8	.76	10	.338	.527	.425	133	11—3	.787	18
1952	149	510	157	17	3	19	(10	9)	237	104	75	106		14	6		24	7	.77	16	.308	.465	.436	116	11—3	.772	16
1953	136	484	159	34	7	12	(7	5)	243	109	95	74		7	9		17	4	.81	12	.329	.502	.418	111	9—4	.722	14
1954	124	386	120	22	4	15	(12	3)	195	62	59	63		7	5	4	7	3	.70	13	.311	.505	.409	84	8—3	.714	9
1955	105	317	81	6	2	8	(6	2)	115	51	36	61	5	3	6	3	12	3	.80	8	.256	.363	.372	49	5—5	.523	6
1956	117	357	98	15	2	10	(7	3)	147	61	43	60	2	3	9	2	12	5	.71	9	.275	.412	.374	60	7—4	.636	7
	1379	4877	1518	273	54	137	(78	59)	2310	947	734	740		72	104		197	30	.76	113	.311	.474	.402	1004	94—40	.700	127
8.5 yrs		573	178	32	6	16	(	)	271	111	86	87		8	12		23			13	.311	.474	.402				

Teams: Brooklyn, N.L. 1947–1956.

Points in MVP Voting: 1947, 106 (5th, .32); 1948, 30 (.09); 1949, 264 (1st, .79); 1950, 23 (.07); 1951, 92 (6th, .27); 1952, 31 (7th, .09); 1953, 19 (.06); 1954, 0; 1955, 0; 1956, 17 (.05). TOTAL: 1.83 Award Shares. Every writer placed Robinson on his ballot in 1949.

Reported Salaries: 1950—$35,000.

Other Notes: Named outstanding major league second baseman in 1949, 1950, 1951, 1952 by *The Sporting News*.

Hit only 1 HR vs. LHP, 1952.

FIELDING SECOND BASE

Year	G	PO	AS	Err	DP	Pct.	Range
1948	116	308	315	13	80	.980	5.37
1949	156	395	421	16	119	.981	5.23
1950	144	359	390	11	133	.986	5.20
1951	150	390	435	7	137	.992	5.50
1952	146	353	400	20	113	.974	5.16
1953	9	16	25	0	7	1.000	4.56
1954	4	13	10	0	0	1.000	5.75
1955	1	4	2	0	1	1.000	6.00
1956	22	39	49	1	17	.989	4.00
	748	1877	2047	68	607	.983	5.25

Assists per 154 Games: 421

PLAYER: NELLIE FOX

							BATTING											BASERUNNING				PERCENTAGES			VALUES			
Year	G	AB	H	2B	3B	HR	(Hm	Rd)	TB	R	RBI	BB	IBB	HBP	SH	SF		SB	CS	SB%	GIDP	Avg.	Slug	On Base	Runs	Win–Loss	Pct.	AV
1947	7	3	0	0	0	0	(0	0)	0	2	0	1		0	0			0	0	.00	0	0	0	.250	0	0–0	.021	0
1948	3	13	2	0	0	0	(0	0)	2	0	0	1		0	0			0	1	1.00	0	.154	.154	.214	1	0–0	.086	0
1949	88	247	63	6	2	0	(0	0)	73	42	21	32		6	11			2	2	.50	10	.255	.296	.341	27	3–5	.358	3
1950	130	457	113	12	7	0	(0	0)	139	45	30	35		2	10			4	3	.57	6	.247	.304	.298	44	5–9	.352	6
1951	147	604	189	32	12	4	(0	4)	257	93	55	43		14	20			9	12	.43	7	.313	.425	.361	96	11–6	.628	13
1952	152	648	192	25	10	0	(0	0)	237	76	39	34		3	15			5	5	.50	11	.296	.366	.327	78	10–8	.569	11
1953	154	624	178	31	8	3	(0	3)	234	92	72	49		7	12			4	5	.44	15	.285	.375	.338	79	9–8	.534	12
1954	155	631	201	24	8	2	(0	2)	247	111	47	51		5	15	4		16	9	.64	13	.319	.391	.364	93	11–6	.643	13
1955	154	636	198	28	7	6	(2	4)	258	100	59	38	1	17	14	4		7	9	.44	8	.311	.406	.357	95	11–6	.632	12
1956	154	649	192	20	10	4	(0	4)	244	109	52	44	1	10	13	5		8	4	.67	19	.296	.376	.341	84	9–9	.497	12
1957	155	619	196	27	8	6	(0	6)	257	110	61	75	2	16	5	3		5	6	.45	7	.317	.415	.400	109	12–5	.724	15
1958	155	623	187	21	6	0	(0	0)	220	82	49	47	5	11	12	5		5	6	.45	13	.300	.353	.351	79	10–8	.560	11
1959	156	624	191	34	6	2	(0	2)	243	84	70	71	8	7	9	5		5	6	.45	6	.306	.389	.376	97	11–5	.669	14
1960	150	605	175	24	10	2	(1	1)	225	85	59	50	2	10	14	5		2	4	.33	11	.289	.372	.344	81	9–8	.532	12
1961	159	606	152	11	5	2	(1	1)	179	67	51	59	3	9	15	7		2	3	.40	17	.251	.295	.316	60	6–12	.337	9
1962	157	621	166	27	7	2	(1	1)	213	79	54	38	0	7	13	5		1	2	.33	13	.267	.343	.308	67	8–10	.438	10
1963	137	539	140	19	0	2	(0	2)	165	54	42	24	1	7	10	2		0	2	.00	10	.260	.306	.294	49	6–9	.405	8
1964	133	442	117	12	6	0	(0	0)	141	45	28	27	1	10	20	3		0	2	.00	8	.265	.319	.307	47	7–7	.507	6
1965	21	41	11	2	0	0	(0	0)	13	3	1	0	0	1	0	0		0	0	.00	1	.268	.317	.286	3	0–1	.370	0
	2367	9232	2663	355	112	35	(5	30)	3347	1279	790	719	24	142	208	48		76	80	.49	175	.288	.363	.341	1189	139–123	.531	167
14.6 yrs		632	182	24	8	2			229	88	54	49		10	14			5	5		12	.288	.363	.341				

Teams: Philadelphia, A.L. 1947–1949; Chicago, A.L. 1950–1963; Houston N.L. 1964–1965.

Points in MVP Voting: 1947, 0; 1948, 0; 1949, 0; 1950, 0; 1951, 25 (.07); 1952, 59 (7th, .18); 1953, 0; 1954, 30 (9th, .09); 1955, 84 (7th, .25); 1957, 193 (4th, .57); 1958, 88 (8th, .26); 1959, 295 (1st, .88); 1960, 11 (.03); 1961, 0; 1962, 0; 1963, 2 (.01); 1964, 0; 1965, 0. TOTAL: 2.34 Award Shares.

Other Notes: Named outstanding major league second baseman for 1955, 1956, 1958, and 1959 by *The Sporting News*.

Gold Gloves: 1957, 1959, 1960.

FIELDING SECOND BASE

Year	G	PO	AS	Err	DP	Pct.	Range
1947	1	1	0	0	0	1.000	1.00
1948	3	13	6	1	1	.950	6.33
1949	77	191	196	7	68	.982	5.03
1950	121	340	344	18	100	.974	5.65
1951	147	413	449	17	112	.981	5.86
1952	151	406	433	13	111	.985	5.56
1953	154	451	426	15	101	.983	5.69
1954	155	400	392	9	103	.989	5.11
1955	154	399	483	24	110	.974	5.73
1956	154	478	396	12	124	.986	5.68
1957	155	453	453	13	141	.986	5.85
1958	155	444	399	13	117	.985	5.44
1959	156	364	453	10	93	.988	5.24
1960	149	412	447	13	126	.985	5.77
1961	159	413	407	15	97	.982	5.16
1962	154	376	428	8	93	.990	5.22
1963	134	305	342	8	71	.988	4.83
1964	115	231	317	13	51	.977	4.77
1965	1	0	2	0	0	1.000	2.00
	2295	6090	6373	209	1619	.984	5.43

Assists per 154 Games: 428

PLAYER: BILL MAZEROSKI

	BATTING																	BASERUNNING					PERCENTAGES				VALUES			
Year	G	AB	H	2B	3B	HR	(Hm	Rd)	TB	R	RBI	BB	IBB	HBP	SH	SF		SB	CS	SB%	GIDP		Avg.	Slug	On Base		Runs	Win—Loss	Pct.	AV
1956	81	255	62	8	1	3	(1	2)	81	30	14	18	1	0	4	0		0	0	.00	4		.243	.318	.289		24	3—4	.400	3
1957	148	526	149	27	7	8	(0	8)	214	59	54	27	2	1	11	3		3	3	.50	6		.283	.407	.312		68	8—7	.551	10
1958	152	567	156	24	6	19	(8	11)	249	69	68	25	3	3	9	3		1	1	.50	15		.275	.439	.303		73	9—7	.540	13
1959	135	493	119	15	6	7	(2	5)	167	50	59	29	1	1	10	4		1	3	.25	16		.241	.339	.277		44	5—10	.317	8
1960	151	538	147	21	5	11	(5	6)	211	58	64	40	15	1	4	8		4	0	1.00	9		.273	.392	.318		68	8—7	.524	11
1961	152	558	148	21	2	13	(4	9)	212	71	59	26	10	3	2	6		2	1	.67	9		.265	.380	.297		62	7—9	.439	11
1962	159	572	155	24	9	14	(4	10)	239	55	81	37	16	2	2	4		0	3	.00	15		.271	.418	.314		71	9—8	.523	12
1963	142	534	131	22	3	8	(2	6)	183	43	52	32	6	0	7	3		2	0	1.00	15		.245	.343	.283		50	7—9	.440	10
1964	162	601	161	22	8	10	(5	5)	229	66	64	29	11	0	10	4		1	1	.50	21		.268	.381	.295		63	8—10	.443	10
1965	130	494	134	17	1	6	(1	5)	171	52	54	18	5	2	4	9		2	1	.67	16		.271	.346	.292		47	6—8	.422	10
1966	162	621	163	22	7	16	(6	10)	247	56	82	31	9	1	2	5		4	3	.57	16		.262	.398	.295		69	8—10	.442	14
1967	163	639	167	25	3	9	(3	6)	225	62	77	30	7	0	5	5		1	2	.33	17		.261	.352	.290		62	7—11	.387	12
1968	143	506	127	18	2	3	(2	1)	158	36	42	38	10	2	6	4		3	4	.43	18		.251	.312	.300		45	7—9	.428	10
1969	67	227	52	7	1	3	(1	2)	70	13	25	22	3	2	1	4		1	1	.50	6		.229	.308	.297		21	2—5	.341	2
1970	112	367	84	14	0	7	(1	6)	119	29	39	27	9	2	5	3		2	0	1.00	6		.229	.324	.280		34	4—7	.344	5
1971	70	193	49	3	1	1	(0	1)	57	17	16	15	1	0	2	3		0	0	.00	3		.254	.295	.300		18	2—4	.361	2
1972	34	64	12	4	0	0	(0	0)	16	3	3	3	1	0	3	2		0	0	.00	2		.188	.250	.208		3	0—2	.142	0
	2163	7755	2016	294	62	138	(45	93)	2848	769	851	447	110	20	87	70		27	23	.54	194		.260	.367	.296		824	99—127	.439	143
13.4 yrs		581	151	22	5	10			213	58	64	33	8	1	7	5		2	2		15		.260	.367	.296					

Teams: Pittsburgh, N.L. 1956–1972.

Points in MVP Voting: 1956, 0; 1957, 0; 1958, 61 (8th, .18); 1959, 0; 1960, 0; 1962, 0; 1963, 0; 1964, 0; 1965, 0; 1966, 3 (.01); 1967, 0; 1968, 0; 1969, 0; 1970, 0; 1971, 0; 1972, 0; TOTAL: .19 Award Shares.

Explanation for Gaps in Career or Sudden Changes in Productivity:

1965—Broke a bone in his right foot during spring training.

1969—Suffered pulled muscles in both legs early in the season.

Other Notes: Named outstanding major league second baseman in 1960 and outstanding National League second baseman in 1962 and 1967 by *The Sporting News*.

Gold Gloves: 1958, 1960, 1961, 1963, 1964, 1965, 1966, 1967.

FIELDING SECOND BASE

Year	G	PO	AS	Err	DP	Pct.	Range
1956	81	163	242	8	56	.981	5.00
1957	144	308	443	17	96	.978	5.22
1958	152	344	496	17	118	.980	5.53
1959	133	303	373	13	100	.981	5.08
1960	151	413	449	10	127	.989	5.71
1961	152	410	505	23	144	.975	6.02
1962	159	425	509	14	138	.985	5.87
1963	138	340	506	14	131	.984	6.13
1964	162	346	543	23	122	.975	5.49
1965	127	290	439	9	113	.988	5.74
1966	162	411	538	8	161	.992	5.86
1967	163	417	498	18	131	.981	5.61
1968	142	319	467	15	107	.981	5.54
1969	65	134	192	4	46	.988	5.02
1970	102	227	325	7	87	.987	5.41
1971	46	95	121	3	22	.986	4.70
1972	15	29	39	1	7	.986	4.53
	2094	4974	6685	204	1706	.983	5.57

Assists per 154 Games: 492

PLAYER: JOE MORGAN

Year	G	AB	H	2B	3B	HR	(Hm	Rd)	TB	R	RBI	BB	IBB	HBP	SH	SF	SB	CS	SB%	GIDP	Avg.	Slug	On Base	Runs	Win–Loss	Pct.	AV
							BATTING											**BASERUNNING**				**PERCENTAGES**			**VALUES**			
1963	8	25	6	0	1	0	(0	0)	8	5	3	5	0	0	0	0	1	0	1.00	0	.240	.320	.367	4	0–0	.693	0
1964	10	37	7	0	0	0	(0	0)	7	4	0	6	0	0	0	0	0	1	.00	0	.189	.189	.302	2	0–1	.265	0
1965	157	601	163	22	12	14	(4	10)	251	100	40	97	1	3	3	4	20	9	.69	4	.271	.418	.371	103	12–5	.701	11
1966	122	425	121	14	8	5	(3	2)	166	60	42	89	3	3	9	2	11	8	.58	2	.285	.391	.403	77	9–3	.719	8
1967	133	494	136	27	11	6	(2	4)	203	73	42	81	5	2	1	2	29	5	.85	2	.275	.411	.378	88	10–4	.699	13
1968	10	20	5	0	1	0	(0	0)	7	6	0	7	0	0	0	0	3	0	1.00	0	.250	.350	.444	5	0–0	.857	0
1969	147	535	126	18	5	15	(7	8)	199	94	43	110	1	1	7	4	49	14	.78	5	.236	.372	.361	86	10–6	.618	10
1970	144	548	147	28	9	8	(4	4)	217	102	52	102	3	1	5	2	42	13	.76	11	.268	.396	.380	92	10–6	.606	11
1971	160	583	149	27	11	13	(4	9)	237	87	56	88	2	1	10	7	40	8	.83	4	.256	.407	.345	95	12–5	.708	13
1972	149	552	161	23	4	16	(9	7)	240	122	73	115	1	6	3	4	58	17	.77	5	.292	.435	.415	117	12–4	.769	17
1973	157	576	167	35	2	26	(9	17)	284	116	82	111	3	4	3	4	67	15	.82	12	.290	.493	.404	128	13–4	.776	16
1974	149	512	150	31	3	22	(13	9)	253	107	67	120	8	3	1	5	58	12	.83	7	.293	.494	.426	125	12–3	.804	16
1975	146	498	163	27	6	17	(10	7)	253	107	94	132	3	3	0	6	67	10	.87	3	.327	.508	.466	145	11–2	.863	20
1976	141	472	151	30	5	27	(13	14)	272	113	111	114	8	1	0	12	60	9	.87	2	.320	.576	.444	144	11–2	.857	18
1977	153	521	150	21	6	22	(11	11)	249	113	78	117	2	2	0	5	49	10	.83	5	.288	.478	.417	121	11–3	.759	15
1978	132	441	104	27	0	13	(6	7)	170	68	75	79	3	2	0	11	19	5	.79	6	.236	.385	.347	67	8–6	.575	9
1979	127	436	109	26	1	9	(4	5)	164	70	32	93	11	1	3	5	28	6	.82	8	.250	.376	.377	72	8–5	.628	10
1980	141	461	112	17	5	11	(2	9)	172	66	49	93	6	0	3	3	24	6	.80	4	.243	.373	.365	73	9–4	.673	10
1981	90	308	74	16	1	8	(4	4)	116	47	31	66	7	0	1	3	14	5	.74	3	.240	.377	.370	49	6–3	.670	6
1982	134	463	134	19	4	14	(6	8)	203	68	61	85	4	2	1	3	24	4	.86	3	.289	.438	.399	92	9–3	.753	14
1983	123	404	93	20	1	16	(9	7)	163	72	59	89	1	4	1	6	18	2	.90	13	.230	.403	.369	68	8–4	.645	8
1984	116	365	89	21	0	6	(2	4)	128	50	43	66	3	1	0	8	8	3	.73	6	.244	.351	.356	54	5–5	.500	5
	2649	9277	2517	449	96	268	(122	146)	3962	1650	1133	1865	75	40	51	96	689	162	.81	105	.271	.427	.390	1804	186–79	.701	230
16.4 yrs		567	154	27	6	16			242	101	69	114	5	2	3	6	42	10	.81	6	.271	.427	.390				

Teams: Houston, 1963–1971; Cincinnati, 1972–1979; Houston, 1980; San Francisco, 1981–1982; Philadelphia, 1983; Oakland, 1984.

Points in MVP Voting: 1963, 0; 1964, 0; 1965, 1 (.00); 1966, 0; 1967, 0; 1968, 0; 1970, 0; 1971, 0; 1972, 197 (4th, .59); 1973, 102 (8th, .21); 1975, 321.5 (1st, .96); 1976, 311 (1st, .93); 1977, 0; 1978, 0; 1979, 0; 1980, 0; 1981, 0; 1982, 17 (.05); 1983, 0. TOTAL: 3.14 Award Shares.

Explanation for Gaps in Career or Sudden Changes in Productivity:

1966—June 25, knee cap fractured when struck by line drive during batting practice (Astros, in fourth place at that time, collapsed immediately thereafter, losing 28 of 31 games at one point. Morgan did not return until August 5.)

1968—Acquired severely torn ligaments in his knee when hit by sliding Tommy Agee in fifth game of season. Surgery was required. (Astros, 4–0 at the time of the injury, finished last.)

1972—Increase in offense due primarily to getting out of the Astrodome.

Other Notes: Named outstanding National League second baseman in 1972, 1974, 1975, 1976, 1977 by *The Sporting News*.

Gold Gloves: 1973, 1974, 1975, 1976, 1977.

FIELDING SECOND BASE

Year	G	PO	AS	Err	DP	Pct.	Range
1963	7	15	15	3	2	.909	4.29
1964	10	31	25	3	4	.949	5.60
1965	157	348	492	27	82	.969	5.35
1966	117	256	316	21	61	.965	4.89
1967	130	297	344	14	67	.979	4.93
1968	5	9	6	2	2	.882	3.00
1969	132	303	328	18	79	.972	4.78
1970	142	349	430	17	98	.979	5.49
1971	157	336	482	12	93	.986	5.21
1972	149	370	436	8	92	.990	5.41
1973	154	417	440	9	106	.990	5.56
1974	142	344	385	13	92	.982	5.13
1975	142	356	425	11	96	.986	5.50
1976	133	342	335	13	85	.981	5.09
1977	151	351	359	5	100	.993	4.70
1978	124	252	290	11	49	.980	4.37
1979	121	259	329	12	74	.980	4.86
1980	130	244	348	7	68	.988	4.55
1981	87	177	258	4	61	.991	5.00
1982	120	254	364	7	69	.989	5.15
1983	117	231	331	17	63	.971	4.80
	100	201	229	10	62	.990	4.30
	2527	5742	6967	244	1505	.981	5.03

Assists per 154 Games: 424

PLAYER: ROD CAREW

	BATTING																	BASERUNNING				PERCENTAGES			VALUES			
Year	G	AB	H	2B	3B	HR	(Hm	Rd)	TB	R	RBI	BB	IBB	HBP	SH	SF		SB	CS	SB%	GIDP	Avg.	Slug	On Base	Runs	Win–Loss	Pct.	AV
1967	137	514	150	22	7	8	1	7	210	66	51	37	4	2	7	1		5	9	.36	12	.292	.409	.337	68	9–6	.594	10
1968	127	461	126	27	2	1	1	0	160	46	42	26	1	1	2	2		12	4	.75	11	.273	.347	.311	49	7–6	.545	6
1969	123	458	152	30	4	8	4	4	214	79	56	37	0	3	6	0		19	8	.70	7	.332	.467	.381	83	9–3	.715	9
1970	51	191	70	12	3	4	0	4	100	27	28	11	0	2	0	0		4	6	.40	1	.366	.524	.407	39	4–1	.798	4
1971	147	577	177	16	10	2	1	1	219	88	48	45	1	1	6	3		6	7	.46	23	.307	.380	.353	73	9–7	.540	9
1972	142	535	170	21	6	0	0	0	203	61	51	43	9	2	9	2		12	6	.67	11	.318	.379	.364	75	10–5	.688	11
1973	149	580	203	30	11	6	3	3	273	98	62	62	9	2	7	6		41	16	.72	16	.350	.471	.406	113	11–4	.728	18
1974	153	599	218	30	5	3	2	1	267	86	55	74	9	1	13	3		38	16	.70	17	.364	.446	.425	118	12–4	.763	17
1975	143	535	192	24	4	14	10	4	266	89	80	64	18	1	7	10		35	9	.80	10	.359	.497	.417	118	11–3	.769	16
1976	156	605	200	29	12	9	4	5	280	97	90	67	14	1	8	6		49	22	.69	12	.331	.463	.390	111	12–5	.688	14
1977	155	616	239	38	16	14	8	6	351	128	100	69	15	3	1	5		23	13	.64	6	.388	.570	.448	160	12–3	.817	18
1978	152	564	188	26	10	5	1	4	249	85	70	78	19	1	2	6		27	7	.79	18	.333	.441	.410	105	11–4	.737	13
1979	110	409	130	15	3	3	1	2	160	78	44	73	7	0	8	3		18	8	.69	9	.318	.391	.412	73	7–4	.615	7
1980	144	540	179	34	7	3	2	1	236	74	59	59	7	1	9	3		23	15	.61	15	.331	.437	.391	92	9–5	.633	13
1981	93	364	111	17	1	2	0	2	136	57	21	45	7	0	10	2		16	9	.64	8	.305	.374	.371	53	6–4	.591	7
1982	138	523	167	25	5	3	1	2	211	88	44	67	5	2	16	4		10	17	.37	9	.319	.403	.386	83	9–6	.600	11
1983	129	472	160	24	2	2	1	1	194	66	44	57	9	1	3	3		6	7	.46	15	.339	.411	.407	78	8–5	.641	11
1984	93	329	97	8	1	3	3	0	116	42	31	40	1	0	5	4		4	3	.57	7	.295	.353	.367	45	5–4	.555	5
1985	127	443	124	17	3	2	1	1	153	69	39	64	9	1	9	1		5	5	.50	8	.280	.345	.371	60	7–6	.547	7
	2469	9315	3053	445	112	92	44	48	3998	1424	1015	1018	144	25	128	64		353	187	.65	215	.328	.429	.388	1596	168–86	.661	206
15.24 yrs		611	200	29	7	6			262	93	67	67	9	2	8	4		23	12		14	.328	.429	.388				

Teams: Minnesota, 1967–1978; California, 1980–present.

Points in MVP Voting: 1967, 0; 1968, 0; 1969, 30 (10th, .09); 1970, 0; 1971, 0; 1972, 16 (.05); 1973, 83 (4th, .25); 1974, 70 (7th, .21); 1975, 54.5 (9th, .16); 1976, 71 (6th, .21); 1977, 273 (1st, .70); 1978, 46 (.12); 1979, 0; 1980, 0; 1981, 0; 1982, 5 (.01); 1983, 0. TOTAL: 1.80 Award Shares.

Reported Salaries: $5,000 signing bonus plus $7,500 when made majors. 1964 in minors, $400/month; 1967, $7,000; 1975, $120,000.

Explanation for Gaps in Career or Sudden Changes in Productivity:

1968–69—Required to attend week-end meetings and two weeks summer camp as part of military reserve commitment.

1970—Required knee surgery after being hit while pivoting on double play, June 22.

1979—Thumb injury.

Other Notes: Named outstanding American League second baseman 1967, 1968, 1969, 1972, 1973, 1974, and 1975 by *The Sporting News*.

Named outstanding American League first baseman in 1977 and 1978 by *The Sporting News*.

FIELDING SECOND BASE

Year	G	PO	AS	Err	DP	Pct.	Range
1967	134	289	314	15	60	.976	4.50
1968	117	262	280	18	48	.968	4.63
1969	118	244	302	17	80	.970	4.63
1970	45	73	122	8	26	.961	4.33
1971	142	321	329	16	76	.976	4.58
1972	139	331	378	16	85	.978	5.10
1973	147	383	413	13	96	.984	5.41
1974	148	375	416	33	114	.960	5.34
1975	123	285	369	18	79	.973	5.32
1976	7	4	2	0	0	1.000	0.86
1977	4	4	3	0	0	1.000	1.75
1978	4	1	0	0	0	1.000	0.25
	1128	2572	2928	154	664	.973	4.88

Assists per 154 Games: 351

PLAYER: BOBBY GRICH

Year	G	AB	H	2B	3B	HR	(Hm	Rd)	TB	R	RBI	BB	IBB	HBP	SH	SF	SB	CS	SB%	GIDP	Avg.	Slug	On Base	Runs	Win-Loss		Pct.	AV
1970	30	95	20	1	3	0	(0	0)	27	11	8	9	0	0	0	0	1	1	.50	2	.211	.284	.279	7	1-2		.273	1
1971	7	30	9	0	0	1	(0	1)	12	7	6	5	0	0	0	0	1	0	1.00	0	.300	.400	.400	6	1-0		.757	1
1972	133	460	128	21	3	12	(6	6)	191	66	50	53	3	7	3	5	13	6	.68	8	.278	.415	.356	71	10-3		.758	12
1973	162	581	146	29	7	12	(7	5)	225	82	50	107	3	7	3	2	17	9	.65	7	.251	.387	.371	92	11-6		.645	12
1974	160	582	153	29	6	19	(11	8)	251	92	82	90	6	20	7	8	17	11	.61	15	.263	.431	.372	99	12-6		.677	14
1975	150	524	136	26	4	13	(5	8)	209	81	57	107	4	8	9	7	14	10	.58	9	.260	.399	.383	90	11-5		.685	13
1976	144	518	138	31	4	13	(8	5)	216	93	54	86	1	3	7	1	14	6	.70	8	.266	.417	.369	87	11-4		.706	13
1977	52	181	44	6	0	7	(4	3)	71	24	23	37	4	1	3	3	6	6	.50	5	.243	.392	.364	27	3-3		.559	4
1978	144	487	122	16	2	6	(4	2)	160	68	42	75	1	7	19	3	4	3	.57	6	.251	.329	.345	64	8-7		.522	10
1979	153	534	157	30	5	30	(15	15)	287	78	101	59	10	2	12	2	1	0	1.00	14	.294	.537	.358	103	10-5		.650	16
1980	150	498	135	22	2	14	(7	7)	203	60	62	84	2	4	5	5	3	7	.30	16	.271	.408	.374	78	8-6		.564	13
1981	100	352	107	14	2	22	(7	15)	191	56	61	40	4	4	5	3	2	4	.33	5	.304	.543	.374	73	7-2		.758	11
1982	145	506	132	28	5	19	(8	11)	227	74	65	82	3	8	6	3	3	3	.50	13	.261	.449	.367	87	9-6		.624	13
1983	120	387	113	17	0	16	(8	8)	178	65	62	76	2	7	4	3	2	4	.33	11	.292	.460	.411	77	8-3		.699	10
1984	116	363	93	15	1	18	(9	9)	164	60	58	57	3	2	6	4	2	5	.29	10	.256	.452	.357	59	7-4		.608	8
1985	144	479	116	17	3	13	(7	6)	178	74	53	81	3	3	8	0	3	5	.38	18	.242	.372	.355	63	7	7	.491	13
1986	98	313	84	18	0	9	(5	4)	129	42	30	39	1	3	10	1	1	3	.25	9	.268	.412	.354	45	5	4	.535	6
	2008	6890	1833	320	47	224	(109	115)	2919	1034	864	1087	50	86	107	50	104	83	.56	157	.266	.424	.371	1127	127-75		.628	170
12.40 yrs		556	148	26	4	18			235	83	70	88	4	7	9	4	8	7	.56	13	.266	.424	.371					

Teams: Baltimore, 1970–1976; California, 1977–1984.

Points in MVP Voting: 1970, 0; 1971, 0; 1972, 16 (.05); 1973, 9 (.03); 1974, 49 (9th, .15); 1975, 0; 1976, 0; 1977, 0; 1978, 0; 1979, 58 (8th, .15); 1980, 0; 1981, 19 (.05); 1982, 0; 1983, 0. TOTAL: .43 Award Shares.

Reported Salaries: Free agent contract in 1977 reportedly five years, $1.75 million.

Explanation for Gaps in Career or Sudden Changes in Productivity: 1977—Strained back while carrying an air conditioner.

Other Notes: Named as the outstanding American League second baseman in 1976, 1979, and 1981 by *The Sporting News.* Gold Glove: 1973, 1974, 1975, 1976.

FIELDING SECOND BASE

Year	G	PO	AS	Err	DP	Pct.	Range
1970	9	28	31	0	5	1.000	6.56
1971	2	5	7	0	2	1.000	6.00
1972	45	95	113	3	27	.986	4.62
1973	162	431	509	5	130	.995	5.80
1974	160	484	453	20	132	.979	5.86
1975	150	423	484	21	122	.977	6.05
1976	140	389	400	12	91	.985	5.64
1978	144	325	419	13	77	.983	5.17
1979	153	340	438	13	111	.984	5.08
1980	146	326	463	9	101	.989	5.40
1981	100	230	349	10	85	.983	5.79
1982	142	338	450	11	112	.986	5.55
1983	118	270	415	22	94	.969	5.81
1984	91	182	249	8	65	.982	4.74
1985	116	224	380	2	99	.997	5.21
1986	87	127	221	7	49	.980	4.00
	1765	4217	5381	156	1302	.984	5.44

Assists per 154 Games: 470

Third Base

Jimmy Collins
Tommy Leach
Home Run Baker
Larry Gardner
Heine Groh
Pie Traynor
Stan Hack
Harlond Clift
Ed Yost
Al Rosen
Eddie Mathews
Harmon Killebrew
Ken Boyer
Brooks Robinson
Ron Santo
Richie Allen
Mike Schmidt
George Brett

PLAYER: JIMMY COLLINS

	BATTING															BASERUNNING				PERCENTAGES			VALUES			
Year	G	AB	H	2B	3B	HR	(Hm	Rd)	TB	R	RBI	BB	IBB	HBP	SH	SF	SB	CS	SB%	GIDP	Avg.	Slug	On Base	Runs	Win–Loss	Pct.	AV
1895	107	411	112	20	5	7	(	)	163	75	57	37			4		12				.273	.397	.333	60	4–8	.355	6
1896	84	304	90	10	9	1	(	)	121	48	46	30			8		10				.296	.398	.359	49	4–5	.437	4
1897	134	529	183	28	13	6	(	)	255	103	132	41			8		14				.346	.482	.393	109	8–6	.601	13
1898	152	597	196	35	5	15	(	)	286	107	111	40			13		12				.328	.479	.370	114	11–5	.666	15
1899	151	599	166	28	11	4	(	)	228	98	91	40			9		12				.277	.381	.322	80	8–9	.468	11
1900	142	586	178	25	5	6	(	)	231	104	95	34			9		23				.304	.394	.342	90	8–8	.501	13
1901	138	564	187	42	16	6	(	)	279	109	94	34			12		19				.332	.495	.370	114	10–5	.688	12
1902	108	429	138	21	10	6	(	)	197	71	61	24			19		18				.322	.459	.358	81	8–4	.673	9
1903	130	540	160	33	17	5	(	)	242	87	72	24			13		23				.296	.448	.326	90	10–6	.637	12
1904	156	631	168	33	13	3	(	)	236	85	67	27			16		19				.266	.374	.296	79	11–8	.593	9
1905	131	508	140	25	5	4	(	)	187	66	65	37			9		18				.276	.368	.325	69	9–6	.610	10
1906	37	142	39	8	4	1	(	)	58	17	16	4			2		1				.275	.408	.295	18	2–2	.569	2
1907	143	523	146	30	0	0	(	)	176	51	45	34			12		8				.279	.337	.323	63	8–7	.543	8
1908	115	433	94	14	3	0	(	)	114	34	30	20			13		5				.217	.263	.252	30	4–10	.279	4
	1728	6796	1997	352	116	64	(	)	2773	1055	982	426			147		194				.294	.408	.336	1046	107–88	.549	128
10.7 yrs		637	187	33	11	6	(	)	260	99	92	40			14		18				.294	.408	.336				

Teams: Boston and Louisville, N.L., 1895, Boston N.L., 1896–1900, Boston, A.L., 1901–1907, Philadelphia, A.L., 1907–1908.

Explanation for Gaps in Career or Sudden Changes in Productivity:

1896—Injury to ankle

1906—Knee injury

FIELDING THIRD BASE

Year	G	PO	AS	Err	DP	Pct.	Range
1895	77	128	185	30	12	.913	4.06
1896	80	134	207	34	16	.909	4.26
1897	134	214	303	47	20	.917	3.86
1898	152	243	332	42	20	.932	3.78
1899	151	217	376	36	23	.943	3.93
1900	141	251	329	40	21	.935	4.11
1901	138	203	328	50	24	.914	3.85
1902	107	143	255	19	14	.954	3.72
1903	130	178	260	22	19	.952	3.37
1904	156	191	320	30	15	.945	3.28
1905	132	164	268	36	12	.923	3.27
1906	32	43	70	11		.911	3.53
1907	141	143	257	47	13	.895	2.84
1908	115	117	216	26	14	.928	2.90
	1686	2369	3706	470	223	.928	3.60

Assists per 154 games: 339

PLAYER: TOMMY LEACH

Year	G	AB	H	2B	3B	HR	(Hm	Rd)	TB	R	RBI	BB	IBB	HBP	SH	SF	SB	CS	SB%	GIDP	Avg.	Slug	On Base	Runs	Win–Loss	Pct.	AV
1898	3	10	3	0	0	0	(	)	3	0	0	0			0		0				.300	.300	.300	1	0–0	.303	0
1899	106	406	117	10	6	5	(	)	154	75	57	37			10		19				.288	.379	.340	63	6–6	.515	7
1900	51	160	34	1	2	1	(	)	42	20	16	21			5		8				.213	.263	.296	16	2–4	.306	1
1901	98	374	112	12	13	1	(	)	153	64	44	20			10		16				.299	.409	.327	59	6–4	.583	7
1902	135	514	144	21	22	6	(	)	227	97	85	45			13		25				.280	.442	.330	89	10–5	.655	12
1903	127	507	151	16	17	7	(	)	222	97	87	40			12		22				.298	.438	.342	89	9–6	.603	10
1904	146	579	149	15	12	2	(	)	194	92	56	45			4		23				.257	.335	.309	70	9–8	.506	9
1905	131	499	128	10	14	2	(	)	172	71	53	37			17		17				.257	.345	.298	62	8–8	.498	8
1906	133	476	136	10	7	1	(	)	163	66	39	33			16		21				.286	.342	.322	65	9–5	.632	9
1907	149	547	166	19	12	4	(	)	221	102	43	40			29		43				.303	.404	.334	98	12–4	.737	14
1908	152	583	151	24	16	5	(	)	222	93	41	54			27		24				.259	.381	.309	79	11–7	.625	9
1909	151	587	153	29	8	6	(	)	216	126	43	66	2		27		27				.261	.368	.324	83	11–7	.600	12
1910	135	529	143	24	5	4	(	)	189	83	52	38	0		20		18				.270	.357	.308	66	8–8	.518	10
1911	108	386	92	12	6	3	(	)	125	60	43	46	2		12		19				.238	.324	.314	46	6–6	.458	6
1912	110	362	93	14	5	2	(	)	123	74	51	67	3		7		20				.257	.340	.371	54	6–5	.541	9
1913	130	454	131	23	10	6	(	)	192	99	32	77	1		6		21				.289	.423	.388	80	9–4	.663	13
1914	153	577	152	24	9	7	(	)	215	80	46	79	1		19		16				.263	.373	.343	80	10–7	.570	10
1915	107	335	75	7	5	0	(	)	92	42	17	56	2		3		20	14	.59		.224	.275	.336	36	5–5	.501	2
1918	30	72	14	2	3	0	(	)	22	14	5	19			3		2				.194	.306	.351	9	1–1	.538	1
	2155	7957	2144	273	172	62	(	)	2947	1355	810	820	11		240		361	14	.59		.269	.370	.330	1142	136–101	.574	151
13.3 yrs		598	161	21	13	5			222	102	61	62			18		27				.269	.370	.330				

Teams: Louisville, N.L., 1898–1899; Pittsburgh, 1900–1911; Pittsburgh/Chicago, N.L., 1912; Chicago, N.L., 1913; Cincinnati, 1915; Pittsburgh, 1918.

Points in MVP Voting: 1911, 0; 1913, 0; 1914, 0.

Explanation for Gaps in Career or Sudden Changes in Productivity:
1900—Loaned to Wooster (league unknown) to get some playing time.
1916–1918—Played for Rochester, Kansas City, and Chattanooga. When he was recalled by Pittsburgh during the first World War, Edward L. Wolfe wrote a poem called "The Old Guys" that read, in part,

> —"Youth will be served," the expert cried,
> In tones that would not be denied.
> "Ball players mostly all are through
> Before the age of thirty-two.
> This work-or-fight rule wrecks the game;
> The players left are old and lame.
> We'll have to close the gates and quit;
> The old boys neither field nor hit."
> Then Tom Leach tottered down the years
> And played a game that 'roused fans' cheers.

Other Notes: 1912–1913 defensive lines figured by Neil Munro.

FIELDING THIRD BASE

Year	G	PO	AS	Err	DP	Pct.	Range
1898	3	2	7	7	0	.750	3.00
1899	80	135	200	34	13	.908	4.19
1900	31	45	69	18	4	.864	3.68
1901	92	122	196	34	9	.903	3.46
1902	164	170	316	39	10	.926	2.96
1903	127	178	292	65	16	.879	3.70
1904	146	212	371	60	18	.907	3.99
1905	58	80	123	14		.935	3.50
1906	65	73	135	16		.929	3.20
1907	33	39	65	15		.874	3.15
1908	150	199	293	33	19	.937	3.28
1909	13					0	
1911	1					0	
1912	4	9	7	1	0	.938	4.00
1913	2	6	2	3	0	.727	4.00
1914	16	25	26	7		.879	3.19
	985	1295	2103	343	89	.908	3.46

Assists per 154 Games: 329

PLAYER: HOME RUN BAKER

	BATTING																	BASERUNNING				PERCENTAGES			VALUES			
Year	G	AB	H	2B	3B	HR	(Hm	Rd)	TB	R	RBI	BB	IBB	HBP	SH	SF		SB	CS	SB%	GIDP	Avg.	Slug	On Base	Runs	WinLoss	Pct.	AV
1908	9	31	9	3	0	0	(0	0)	12	5	4	0			2			0				.290	.387	.273	4	1—0	.558	0
1909	148	541	165	27	19	4	(2	2)	242	73	89	26		5	34			20				.305	.447	.323	90	12—4	.740	11
1910	146	561	159	25	15	2	(1	1)	220	83	73	34		4	21			21				.283	.392	.318	79	11—6	.637	11
1911	148	592	198	40	14	9	(7	2)	293	96	115	40		2	25			38				.334	.495	.364	124	12—5	.711	14
1912	149	577	200	40	21	10	(7	3)	312	116	133	50		6	11			40				.347	.541	.398	141	12—3	.797	18
1913	149	565	190	34	9	12	(7	5)	278	116	126	63		10	7			34				.336	.492	.408	122	11—4	.764	16
1914	150	570	182	23	10	8	(5	4)	249	84	97	53		3	8			19	20	.49		.319	.437	.375	97	11—5	.706	12
1916	100	360	97	23	2	10	(6	4)	154	46	52	36		5	1			15				.269	.428	.343	55	7—3	.685	7
1917	146	553	156	24	2	6	(5	1)	202	57	70	48		5	7			18				.282	.365	.341	72	10—6	.638	11
1918	126	504	154	24	5	6	(5	1)	206	65	68	28		2	12			8				.306	.409	.337	74	9—5	.657	11
1919	141	567	166	22	1	10	(8	2)	220	70	78	44		2	9			13				.293	.388	.341	77	10—6	.612	10
1921	94	330	97	16	2	9	(9	0)	144	46	71	26		4	9			8	4	.67		.294	.436	.344	51	5—5	.501	7
1922	69	234	65	12	3	7	(7	0)	104	30	36	15		2	7			1	3	.25		.278	.444	.318	33	4—3	.536	4
	1575	5985	1838	313	103	93	(69	25)	2636	887	1012	463		50	153			235	27	.51		.307	.440	.353	1018	113—54	.676	132
9.7 yrs		616	189	32	11	10			271	91	104	48			16			24	7			.307	.440	.353				

Teams: Philadelphia, A.L. 1908–1915; New York, A.L., 1916–1922.

Points in MVP Voting: 1911, 8 (.13), 1913, 21 (5th, .33); 1914, 17 (4th, .27); 1922, 0. TOTAL: .73 Award Shares.

Explanation for Gaps in Career or Sudden Changes in Productivity:

1915—After teammates Eddie Collins and Jack Barry were sold, Baker refused to report, and sat out the season (playing semi-pro baseball in Upland, N.Y.).

1916—Broken ribs.

1920—Announced his retirement following the death of his wife in the winter of 1919. Was reinstated by Commissioner Landis in 1921.

1922—Macmillan says he was "injured," without specifying, but 1923 *Spalding Guide* gives the impression that Dugan simply took the job away from him.

FIELDING THIRD BASE

Year	G	PO	AS	Err	DP	Pct.	Range
1908	9	12	22	0		1.000	3.78
1909	146	209	277	42	16	.920	3.33
1910	146	207	313	45	35	.920	3.56
1911	148	217	274	30	26	.942	3.32
1912	149	217	321	34	25	.941	3.61
1913	149	233	280	44	19	.921	3.44
1914	149	221	292	24	20	.955	3.44
1916	96	133	210	22	16	.940	3.57
1917	146	202	317	28	21	.949	3.55
1918	126	175	282	13	30	.972	3.63
1919	141	176	286	22	28	.955	3.28
1921	83	84	173	11	16	.959	3.10
1922	60	68	108	7	7	.962	2.93
	1548	2154	3155	322	259	.943	3.43

Assists per 154 Games: 314

PLAYER: LARRY GARDNER

Year	BATTING																BASERUNNING				PERCENTAGES			VALUES			
	G	AB	H	2B	3B	HR	(Hm	Rd)	TB	R	RBI	BB	IBB	HBP	SH	SF	SB	CS	SB%	GIDP	Avg.	Slug	On Base	Runs	Win—Loss	Pct.	AV
1908	2	6	3	0	0	0	(	)	3	0	1	0		0	0		0				.500	.500	.500	1	0—0	.929	0
1909	19	37	11	1	2	0	(	)	16	8	5	4		1	3		1				.297	.432	.356	7	1—0	.706	1
1910	113	413	117	12	10	2	(	)	155	55	36	41		4	17		8				.283	.375	.341	58	7—5	.609	7
1911	138	492	140	17	8	4	(	)	185	80	44	64		5	32		27				.285	.376	.352	81	9—6	.606	12
1912	143	517	163	24	18	3	(	)	232	88	86	56		1	16		25				.315	.449	.373	98	10—4	.705	13
1913	131	473	133	17	10	0	(	)	170	64	63	47		1	14		18				.281	.359	.338	63	8—6	.553	9
1914	155	553	143	23	19	3	(	)	213	50	68	35		0	11		16	23	.41		.259	.385	.297	66	9—7	.574	8
1915	127	430	111	14	6	1	(	)	140	51	55	39		5	26		11	12	.48		.258	.326	.310	50	7—7	.493	5
1916	148	493	152	19	7	2	(	)	191	47	62	48		2	23		12				.308	.387	.357	75	10—3	.725	10
1917	146	501	133	23	7	1	(	)	173	53	61	54		3	40		16				.265	.345	.318	66	10—6	.634	8
1918	127	463	132	22	6	1	(	)	169	50	52	43		0	16		9				.285	.365	.335	60	8—5	.593	8
1919	139	524	157	29	7	2	(	)	206	67	79	39		3	31		7				.300	.393	.333	75	9—6	.577	10
1920	154	597	185	31	11	3	(	)	247	72	118	53		1	32		3	20	.13		.310	.414	.350	86	9—9	.494	12
1921	153	586	187	32	14	3	(	)	256	101	115	65		4	31		3	3	.50		.319	.437	.373	103	10—7	.576	13
1922	137	470	134	31	3	2	(	)	177	74	68	49		2	17		9	8	.53		.285	.377	.344	64	6—8	.451	8
1923	52	79	20	5	1	0	(	)	27	4	12	12		0	2		0	1	.00		.253	.342	.344	10	1—1	.380	1
1924	38	50	10	0	0	0	(	)	10	3	4	5		0	0		0	2	.00		.200	.200	.273	3	0—1	.087	0
11.9 yrs	1922	6684	1931	300	129	27	(	)	2570	867	929	654		32	311		165	69	.38		.289	.385	.341	967	114—83	.579	125
		563	163	25	11	2			217	73	78	55			26		14				.289	.385	.341				

Teams: Boston, AL 1908–17; Philadelphia, A.L. 1918; Cleveland, 1919–24
Points in MVP Voting: 1911, 0; 1913, 0; 1914, 0; 1922, 0; 1923, 0; 1924, 0.
Reported Salaries: 1913—$6,000.

FIELDING THIRD BASE

Year	G	PO	AS	E	DP	Pct.	Range
1908	2	1	0	2	0	.333	0.50
1909	8	4	12	4	0	.800	2.00
1910	0	0	0	0	0		
1911	72	92	161	10	3	.962	3.51
1912	143	167	296	35	16	.930	3.24
1913	130	126	220	21	13	.943	2.66
1914	153	187	312	31	18	.942	3.26
1915	127	134	227	26	16	.933	2.84
1916	147	149	278	21	24	.953	2.90
1917	146	148	315	31	18	.937	3.17
1918	127	158	291	17	33	.964	3.54
1919	139	143	291	25	23	.946	3.12
1920	154	156	362	13	32	.976	3.36
1921	152	179	335	27	23	.950	3.38
1922	128	133	259	20	24	.951	3.06
1923	19	10	41	2	2	.962	2.68
1924	8	1	6	1	1	.875	0.87
	1655	1788	3406	286	246	.948	3.15

Assists per 154 Games: 317

PLAYER: HEINE GROH

	BATTING																BASERUNNING				PERCENTAGES			VALUES			
Year	G	AB	H	2B	3B	HR	(Hm	Rd)	TB	R	RBI	BB	IBB	HBP	SH	SF	SB	CS	SB%	GIDP	Avg.	Slug	On Base	Runs	Win–Loss	Pct.	AV
1912	27	48	13	2	1	0	(	)	17	8	3	8			0	0	6				.271	.354	.375	8	1–0	.648	1
1913	121	399	112	19	5	3	(	)	150	51	48	38			4	19	24				.281	.376	.335	59	7–5	.578	8
1914	139	455	131	18	4	2	(	)	163	59	32	64		13	17		24				.288	.358	.379	72	9–5	.663	9
1915	160	587	170	32	9	3	(	)	229	72	50	50		9	31		12	17	.41		.290	.390	.338	85	12–6	.665	10
1916	149	553	149	24	14	2	(	)	207	85	28	84		4	11		13				.269	.374	.363	79	10–6	.648	10
1917	156	599	182	39	11	1	(	)	246	91	53	71		8	7		15				.304	.411	.381	96	11–5	.700	13
1918	126	493	158	28	3	1	(	)	195	88	37	54		7	13		11				.320	.396	.386	79	9–4	.687	11
1919	122	448	139	17	11	5	(	)	193	79	63	56		4	15		21				.310	.431	.380	81	10–3	.776	12
1920	145	550	164	28	12	0	(	)	216	86	49	60		8	14		16	19	.46		.298	.393	.367	81	10–6	.619	10
1921	97	357	118	19	6	0	(	)	149	54	48	36		4	19		22	14	.61		.331	.417	.380	60	7–4	.657	10
1922	115	426	113	21	3	3	(	)	149	63	51	53		5	13		5	6	.45		.265	.350	.344	55	6–7	.444	7
1923	123	465	135	22	5	4	(	)	179	91	48	60		6	9		3	4	.43		.290	.385	.372	71	7–6	.535	9
1924	145	559	157	32	3	2	(	)	201	82	46	52		11	13		8	6	.57		.281	.360	.346	74	8–9	.468	9
1925	25	65	15	4	0	0	(	)	19	7	4	6		0	1		0				.231	.292	.292	6	1–1	.274	0
1926	12	35	8	2	0	0	(	)	10	2	3	2		0	0		0				.229	.286	.270	3	0–1	.250	0
1927	14	35	10	1	0	0	(	)	11	2	3	2		0	0		0				.286	.314	.324	3	0–1	.368	0
	1676	6074	1774	308	87	26	(	)	2334	920	566	696		83	182		180	66	.50		.292	.384	.363	912	107–68	.613	119
10.3 yrs		587	171	30	8	3			226	89	55	67		8	18		17				.292	.384	.363				

Teams: New York, N.L. 1912; New York/Cincinnati, 1913; Cincinnati, 1914–1921; New York, N.L., 1922–1926; Pittsburgh, 1927.

Points in MVP Voting: 1913, 0; 1914, 2 (.03); 1927, 0.

Explanation for Gaps in Career or Sudden Changes in Productivity:

1918–1919—Seasons shortened by war.

1921—In 1921, Groh was one of several Cincinnati players to hold out, but was the most persistent, holding out even into the season. He was asking $15,000; what he got is not on record. Cincinnati placed him on the ineligible list, meaning that only Judge Landis could let him back in baseball, and then sold his release to New York. Groh applied to Judge Landis for reinstatement, and the Judge agreed, but to the surprise and consternation of all parties ruled that Groh must play for Cincinnati, not New York. No one liked this solution, but all accepted it, and the deal was repeated after the season.

1925—Tore up his knee late in the 1924 season, and it never really did come back.

FIELDING THIRD BASE

Year	G	PO	AS	Err	DP	Pct.	Range
1912	6					0	0
1913	2					0	0
1915	131	153	280	14	34	.969	3.31
1916	110	123	252	17	32	.957	3.41
1917	154	178	331	18	28	.966	3.31
1918	126	180	253	14	37	.969	3.44
1919	121	171	226	12	22	.971	3.28
1920	144	179	252	14	30	.969	2.99
1921	97	97	188	15	27	.950	2.94
1922	110	100	207	11	25	.965	2.79
1923	118	117	233	9	18	.975	2.97
1924	145	121	286	7	13	.983	2.81
1925	16	14	16	3	1	.909	1.87
1926	7	6	12	1	1	.947	2.57
1927	12	9	14	1	0	.958	1.92
	1299	1448	2550	136	268	.967	3.10

Assists per 154 Games: 304

PLAYER: PIE TRAYNOR

				BATTING													BASERUNNING				PERCENTAGES			VALUES			
Year	G	AB	H	2B	3B	HR	(Hm	Rd)	TB	R	RBI	BB	IBB	HBP	SH	SF	SB	CS	SB%	GIDP	Avg.	Slug	On Base	Runs	Win—Loss	Pct.	AV
1920	17	52	11	3	1	0	(	)	16	6	2	3		1	0		1	0	1.00		.212	.308	.268	5	1—1	.402	0
1921	7	19	5	0	0	0	(	)	5	0	2	1		0	0		0	0	.00		.263	.263	.300	2	0—0	.312	0
1922	142	571	161	17	12	4	(	)	214	89	81	27		4	13		17	3	.85		.282	.375	.312	70	7—10	.406	9
1923	153	616	208	19	19	12	(	)	301	108	101	34		5	6		28	13	.68		.338	.489	.374	112	11—5	.666	15
1924	142	545	160	26	13	5	(	)	227	86	82	37		1	13		24	18	.57		.294	.417	.332	74	9—7	.539	12
1925	150	591	189	39	14	6	(	)	274	114	106	52		2	13		15	9	.62		.320	.464	.369	103	10—7	.586	11
1926	152	574	182	25	17	3	(	)	250	83	92	38		1	26		8				.317	.436	.346	88	9—7	.579	11
1927	149	573	196	32	9	5	(	)	261	93	106	22		3	35		11				.342	.455	.349	92	10—6	.601	14
1928	144	569	192	38	12	3	(	)	263	91	124	28		1	42		12				.337	.462	.345	96	9—7	.579	13
1929	130	540	192	27	12	4	(	)	255	94	108	30		3	24		13				.356	.472	.377	96	9—6	.602	14
1930	130	497	182	22	11	9	(	)	253	90	119	48		1	23		7				.366	.509	.406	104	8—5	.649	14
1931	155	615	183	37	15	2	(	)	256	81	103	54		0	8		6				.298	.416	.350	91	10—7	.613	11
1932	135	513	169	27	10	2	(	)	222	74	68	32		4	7		6				.329	.433	.369	82	9—5	.639	12
1933	154	624	190	27	6	1	(	)	232	85	82	35		1	16		5			14	.304	.372	.334	80	10—8	.555	11
1934	119	444	137	22	10	1	(	)	182	62	61	21		1	2		3			23	.309	.410	.340	56	6—6	.476	9
1935	57	204	57	10	3	1	(	)	76	24	36	10		3	3		2			9	.279	.373	.318	23	2—3	.424	3
1937	5	12	2	0	0	0	(	)	2	3	0	0		0	0		0			1	.167	.167	.167	0	0—0	.009	0
	1941	7559	2416	371	164	58	(	)	3289	1183	1273	472		31	231		158	43	.66	47	.320	.435	.352	1174	119—89		.570	161
12.0 yrs		631	202	31	14	5	(	)	275	99	106	39		3	19		13				.320	.435	.352				

Teams: Pittsburgh, 1920–1937.

Points in MVP Voting: 1926, 14 (.18); 1927, 18 (7th, .23); 1931, 17 (6th, .27); 1932, 31 (3rd, .35); 1933, 20 (8th, .25); 1934, 0; 1935, 0; 1937, 0. TOTAL: 1.28 Award Shares.

Other Notes: Named outstanding major league third baseman for 1925, 1926, 1927, 1929, 1931, 1933 by *The Sporting News*.

FIELDING THIRD BASE

Year	G	PO	AS	Err	DP	Pct.	Range
1921	3	3	8	1	0	.917	3.67
1922	124	147	216	21	19	.945	2.93
1923	153	191	310	26	30	.951	3.27
1924	141	179	268	15	31	.968	3.17
1925	150	226	303	24	41	.957	3.53
1926	148	182	279	23	39	.952	3.11
1927	143	212	265	19	23	.962	3.34
1928	144	175	296	27	15	.946	3.27
1929	130	148	238	20	23	.951	2.97
1930	130	130	268	25	18	.941	3.06
1931	155	172	284	37	21	.925	2.94
1932	127	173	222	27	14	.936	3.11
1933	154	176	300	27	16	.946	3.09
1934	110	116	176	14	16	.954	2.65
1935	49	59	84	18	2	.888	2.92
1937	3	2	8	0	0	1.000	3.33
	1864	2291	3525	324	308	.947	3.12

Assists per 154 Games: 291

PLAYER: STAN HACK

			BATTING													BASERUNNING				PERCENTAGES			VALUES			
Year	G	AB	H	2B	3B	HR	(Hm Rd)	TB	R	RBI	BB	IBB	HBP	SH	SF	SB	CS	SB%	GIDP	Avg.	Slug	On Base	Runs	Win–Loss	Pct.	AV
1932	72	178	42	5	6	2	( )	65	32	19	17		1	2		5				.236	.365	.303	20	2–3	.433	1
1933	20	60	21	3	1	1	( )	29	10	2	8		3	0		4			0	.350	.483	.451	15	1–0	.875	1
1934	111	402	116	16	6	1	( )	147	54	21	45		2	9		11			8	.289	.366	.356	57	6–5	.566	8
1935	124	427	133	23	9	4	( )	186	75	64	65		3	9		14			5	.311	.436	.399	83	8–3	.706	10
1936	149	561	167	27	4	6	( )	220	102	78	89		2	14		17			14	.298	.392	.387	94	10–5	.650	10
1937	154	582	173	27	6	2	( )	218	106	63	83		3	10		16			6	.297	.375	.382	94	9–6	.596	10
1938	152	609	195	34	11	4	( )	263	109	67	94		0	4		16			6	.320	.432	.409	119	12–4	.759	12
1939	156	641	191	28	6	8	( )	255	112	56	65		2	15		17			7	.298	.398	.357	99	11–7	.616	11
1940	149	603	191	38	6	8	( )	265	101	40	75		3	5		21			3	.317	.439	.392	112	11–4	.738	14
1941	151	586	186	33	5	7	( )	250	111	45	99		1	8		10			3	.317	.427	.412	114	11–4	.752	11
1942	140	553	166	36	3	6	( )	226	91	39	94		0	10		9			2	.300	.409	.396	100	11–4	.738	12
1943	144	533	154	24	4	3	( )	195	78	35	82		0	15		5			3	.289	.366	.375	83	10–5	.665	10
1944	98	383	108	16	1	3	( )	135	65	32	53		0	4		5			7	.282	.352	.366	53	6–5	.566	7
1945	150	597	193	29	7	2	( )	242	110	43	99		1	5		12			4	.323	.405	.417	111	12–4	.760	13
1946	92	323	92	13	4	0	( )	113	55	26	83		0	3		3			6	.285	.350	.428	56	6–2	.725	7
1947	76	240	65	11	2	0	( )	80	28	12	41		0	2		0			4	.271	.333	.375	33	4–3	.584	4
1938	7278	2193	363	81	57		( )	2889	1239	642	1092		21	115		165			78	.301	.397	.389	1243	132–64	.674	141
12.0 yrs	608	183	30	7	5			241	104	54	91		2	10		14				.301	.397	.389				

Teams: Chicago, N.L. 1932–1947.

Points in MVP Voting: 1932, 0; 1933, 0; 1934, 0; 1935, 0; 1937, 0; 1938, 87 (7th, .26); 1939, 17 (.05); 1940, 61 (8th, .18); 1941, 26 (.08); 1942, 11 (.03); 1943, 10 (.03); 1944, 2 (.01); 1945, 42 (.13); 1946, 0; 1947, 0. TOTAL: .77 Award Shares.

Explanation for Gaps in Career or Sudden Changes in Productivity:

1933—Returned to minors.

1946—Broken finger.

Other Notes: Named outstanding major league third baseman for 1940, 1941, 1942 by *The Sporting News.*

FIELDING THIRD BASE

Year	G	PO	AS	Err	DP	Pct.	Range
1932	51	36	90	12	5	.913	2.47
1933	17	19	40	1	8	.983	3.47
1934	109	102	198	16	10	.949	2.75
1935	111	87	237	20	21	.942	2.92
1936	140	121	202	17	13	.950	2.31
1937	150	151	247	13	25	.968	2.65
1938	152	178	300	23	26	.954	3.14
1939	156	177	278	21	15	.956	2.92
1940	148	175	302	23	27	.954	3.22
1941	150	138	295	21	22	.954	2.89
1942	139	154	261	15	21	.965	2.99
1943	136	149	264	17	11	.960	3.04
1944	75	96	164	17	7	.939	3.47
1945	146	195	312	13	27	.975	3.47
1946	90	102	168	9	6	.968	3.00
1947	66	64	136	8	11	.962	3.03
	1836	1944	3494	246	255	.957	2.96

Assists per 154 Games: 293

PLAYER: HARLOND CLIFT

							BATTING												BASERUNNING				PERCENTAGES			VALUES			
Year	G	AB	H	2B	3B	HR	(Hm	Rd)	TB	R	RBI	BB	IBB	HBP	SH	SF		SB	CS	SB%	GIDP	Avg.	Slug	On Base	Runs	Win–Loss	Pct.	AV
1934	147	572	149	30	10	14	(8	6)	241	104	56	84		2	6			7	2	.78		.260	.421	.354	91	9–7	.568	9
1935	137	475	140	26	4	11	(4	7)	207	101	69	83		6	5			0	3	.00		.295	.436	.402	89	8–5	.616	10
1936	152	576	174	40	11	20	(12	8)	296	145	73	115		7	3			12	4	.75		.302	.514	.422	134	10–5	.667	15
1937	155	571	175	36	7	29	(14	15)	312	103	118	98		6	4			8	5	.62		.306	.546	.411	134	11–5	.704	15
1938	149	534	155	25	7	34	(20	14)	296	119	118	118		5	1			10	5	.67		.290	.554	.422	133	11–4	.727	16
1939	151	526	142	25	2	15	(6	9)	216	90	84	111		5	11			4	3	.57	6	.270	.411	.395	97	8–6	.566	13
1940	150	523	143	29	5	20	(12	8)	242	92	87	104		2	2			9	8	.53	9	.273	.463	.395	103	9–5	.640	12
1941	154	584	149	33	9	17	(8	9)	251	108	84	113		0	6			6	4	.60	12	.255	.430	.373	102	10–7	.589	12
1942	143	541	148	39	4	7	(3	4)	216	108	55	106		2	7			6	4	.60	9	.274	.399	.390	95	10–5	.653	10
1943	113	409	97	11	3	3	(1	2)	123	47	29	59		2	7			5	4	.56	11	.237	.301	.331	44	6–7	.454	7
1944	12	44	7	3	0	0	(0	0)	10	4	3	3		0	0			0	0	.00	1	.159	.227	.213	2	0–1	.119	
1945	119	375	79	12	0	8	(0	8)	115	49	53	76		4	1			2	1	.67	3	.211	.307	.349	48	6–5	.559	6
9.8 yrs	1582	5730	1558	309	62	178	(88	90)	2525	1070	829	1070		41	53			69	43	.62	51	.272	.441	.387	1072	100–63	.612	125
		587	160	32	6	18			259	110	85	110		4	5			7	4		10	.272	.441	.387				

Teams: St. Louis, A.L. 1934–1942; St. Louis/ Washington, 1943; Washington, 1944–1945

Points in MVP Voting: 1934, 0; 1935, 0; 1937, 11 (.14); 1938, 11 (.03); 1940, 0; 1941, 0; 1942, 0; 1943, 0; 1944, 0. TOTAL: .17 Award Shares.

Explanation for Gaps in Career or Sudden Changes in Productivity:

1943—Mumps.

1944—Shoulder injury when thrown from horse.

Other Notes: 1936—5 HR vs. LHP, 15 vs. RHP.

1938—8 HR vs. LHP; 26 vs. RHP.

1939—2 HR vs. LHP; 13 vs. RHP.

FIELDING THIRD BASE

Year	G	PO	AS	Err	DP	Pct.	Range
1934	141	150	245	30	28	.929	2.80
1935	127	130	240	26	12	.934	2.91
1936	152	158	310	24	27	.951	3.08
1937	155	198	405	34	50	.947	3.89
1938	149	176	306	19	31	.962	3.23
1939	149	184	324	25	34	.953	3.41
1940	147	161	329	21	32	.959	3.33
1941	154	195	316	22	27	.959	3.32
1942	141	160	287	28	28	.941	3.17
1943	112	144	264	21	20	.951	3.64
1944	12	10	22	6	2	.842	2.67
1945	111	111	218	23	18	.935	2.96
	1550	1777	3266	279	309	.948	3.25

Assists per 154 Games: 324

PLAYER: ED YOST

						BATTING												BASERUNNING				PERCENTAGES			VALUES			
Year	G	AB	H	2B	3B	HR	(Hm	Rd)	TB	R	RBI	BB	IBB	HBP	SH	SF	SB	CS	SB%	GIDP	Avg.	Slug	On Base	Runs	Win—Loss	Pct	AV
1944	7	14	2	0	0	0	(0	0)	2	3	0	1		0	1		0	0	.00	0	.143	.143	.200	1	0—0	.068	0
1946	8	25	2	1	0	0	(0	0)	3	2	1	5		0	1		2	1	.67	1	.080	.120	.233	1	0—1	.051	0
1947	115	428	102	17	3	0	(0	0)	125	52	14	45		2	10		3	5	.37	8	.238	.292	.314	41	5—8	.413	4
1948	145	555	138	32	11	2	(0	2)	198	74	50	82		4	7		4	3	.57	15	.249	.357	.349	73	8—8	.500	7
1949	124	435	110	19	7	9	(0	9)	170	57	45	91		1	4		3	3	.50	11	.253	.391	.383	71	7—5	.587	9
1950	155	573	169	26	2	11	(1	10)	232	114	58	141		8	9		6	6	.50	13	.295	.405	.440	116	11—5	.689	12
1951	154	568	161	36	4	12	(1	11)	241	109	65	126		11	11		6	4	.60	7	.283	.424	.423	117	11—5	.713	11
1952	157	587	137	32	3	12	(0	12)	211	92	49	129		8	10		4	3	.57	9	.233	.359	.378	93	11—6	.646	8
1953	152	577	137	30	7	9	(1	8)	228	107	45	123		4	9		7	3	.70	5	.272	.395	.403	103	11—5	.682	10
1954	155	539	138	26	4	11	(4	7)	205	101	47	131		5	11	1	7	3	.70	5	.256	.380	.405	97	11—5	.680	11
1955	122	375	91	17	5	7	(0	7)	139	64	48	95		11	6	3	4	3	.57	7	.243	.371	.407	66	7—4	.631	6
1956	152	515	119	17	2	11	(9	2)	173	94	53	151	0	8	9	1	8	5	.62	8	.231	.336	.412	87	8—7	.544	10
1957	110	414	104	13	5	9	(2	7)	154	47	38	73	9	5	0	0	1	11	.08	6	.251	.372	.370	58	6—6	.521	6
1958	134	406	91	16	0	8	(5	3)	131	55	37	81	2	9	1	6	3	6	.33	9	.224	.323	.361	52	6—6	.498	7
1959	148	521	145	19	0	21	(12	9)	227	115	61	135	2	12	4	3	9	2	.82	6	.278	.436	.435	115	11—4	.741	13
1960	143	497	129	23	2	14	(7	7)	198	78	47	125	1	8	3	3	4	4	.56	11	.260	.398	.414	92	10—4	.705	10
1961	76	213	43	4	0	3	(2	1)	56	29	15	50	1	2	2	0	0	1	.00	2	.202	.263	.358	24	2—4	.383	1
1962	52	104	25	9	1	0	(0	0)	36	22	10	30	0	1	1	1	0	2	.00	3	.240	.346	.412	17	2—1	.593	1
13.0 yrs	2109	7346	1863	337	56	139	(44	95)	2729	1215	683	1614	15	99	98	18	72	66	.52	133	.254	.371	.394	1225	130—85	.605	128
		564	143	26	4	11			210	93	52	124	3	8	8	3	6	5	.52	10	.254	.371	.394				

Teams: Washington, 1944–1958; Detroit, 1959–1960; Los Angeles Angels, 1961–1962.

Points in MVP Voting: 1944, 0; 1945, 0; 1947, 0; 1948, 0; 1949, 0; 1950, 8 (.02); 1951, 2 (.01); 1952, 0; 1953, 3 (.01); 1958, 0; 1959, 0; 1960, 0; 1961, 0; 1962, 0. TOTAL: .04 Award Shares.

Explanation for Gaps in Career or Sudden Changes in Productivity:

1945–1946 Military service

1957 Groin injury

1961 Broken hand

Other Notes: I am not, by including Ed Yost and not George Kell, making any argument about their relative merits as players.

FIELDING THIRD BASE

Year	G	PO	AS	Err	DP	Pct.	Range
1944	3	6	5	1	0	.917	3.67
1946	7	7	17	0	1	1.000	3.43
1947	114	125	198	14	11	.958	2.83
1948	145	189	240	15	21	.966	2.96
1949	122	158	232	19	23	.954	3.20
1950	155	205	307	30	45	.945	3.30
1951	152	203	234	21	22	.954	2.87
1952	157	212	249	18	26	.962	2.94
1953	152	190	300	18	31	.965	3.22
1954	155	170	347	17	29	.968	3.34
1955	107	100	217	19	22	.943	2.96
1956	135	164	303	18	31	.963	3.46
1957	107	109	207	16	18	.952	2.95
1958	114	109	186	11	20	.964	2.59
1959	146	168	259	17	21	.962	2.92
1960	142	155	208	26	18	.933	2.56
1961	67	57	103	6	4	.964	2.39
1962	28	29	47	4	2	.950	2.71
	2008	2356	3659	270	345	.957	3.00

Assists per 154 games: 281

PLAYER: AL ROSEN

Year	G	AB	H	2B	3B	HR	(Hm	Rd)	TB	R	RBI	BB	IBB	HBP	SH	SF	SB	CS	SB%	GIDP	Avg.	Slug	On Base	Runs	Win–Loss	Pct.	AV
1947	7	9	1	0	0	0	(0	0)	1	1	0	0		0	0		0	0	.00	0	.111	.111	.111	0	0–0	.009	0
1948	5	5	1	0	0	0	(0	0)	1	0	0	0		0	0		0	0	.00	1	.200	.200	.200	0	0–0	.000	0
1949	23	44	7	2	0	0	(0	0)	9	3	5	7		0	0		0	1	.00	1	.159	.205	.275	3	0–1	.164	0
1950	155	554	159	23	4	37	(21	16)	301	100	116	100		10	4		5	7	.42	27	.287	.543	.403	120	11–5	.717	14
1951	154	573	152	30	1	24	(13	11)	256	82	102	85		2	1		7	5	.58	14	.265	.447	.362	96	11–5	.667	12
1952	148	567	171	32	5	28	(11	17)	297	101	105	75		4	3		8	6	.57	18	.302	.524	.385	115	12–4	.735	14
1953	155	599	201	27	5	43	(25	18)	367	115	145	85		4	0		8	7	.53	19	.336	.613	.422	155	13–3	.827	20
1954	137	466	140	20	2	24	(14	10)	236	76	102	85		3	1	11	6	2	.75	14	.300	.506	.403	101	10–3	.786	14
1955	139	492	120	13	1	21	(13	8)	198	61	81	92	5	4	0	8	4	2	.67	14	.244	.402	.362	76	9–6	.605	11
1956	121	416	111	18	2	15	(6	9)	178	64	61	58	4	0	0	7	1	3	.25	13	.267	.428	.351	62	7–5	.603	8
6.4 yrs	1044	3725	1063	165	20	192	(103	89)	1844	603	717	587	9	27	9	26	39	33	.54	121	.285	.495	.383	729	74–32	.697	93
		578	165	26	3	30			286	94	111	91	6	4	1	11	6	5		19	.285	.495	.383				

Header groups: BATTING | BASERUNNING | PERCENTAGES | VALUES

Teams: Cleveland, 1947–1956.

Points in MVP Voting: 1947, 0; 1948, 0; 1949, 0; 1950, 11 (.03); 1951, 0; 1952, 51 (10th, .15); 1953, 336 (1st, 1.00). TOTAL: 1.18 Award Shares.

Explanation for Gaps in Career or Sudden Changes in Productivity: Career got a very late start because he was owned by Cleveland and blocked behind Ken Keltner.

1955—Productivity cut by ailing finger and back trouble that forced his retirement.

Other Notes: 1952—12 HR vs. LHP, 16 vs. RHP.

Named outstanding major league third baseman in 1953 and 1954 by *The Sporting News*.

FIELDING THIRD BASE

Year	G	PO	AS	Err	DP	Pct.	Range
1947	2	0	0	0	0		
1948	2	1	1	0	0	1.000	1.00
1949	10	10	16	0	1	1.000	2.60
1950	154	151	322	15	24	.969	3.07
1951	154	157	277	19	20	.958	2.82
1952	147	159	256	18	25	.958	2.82
1953	154	174	338	19	38	.964	3.32
1954	87	110	149	11	14	.959	2.98
1955	106	119	195	12	17	.963	2.96
1956	116	89	219	18	20	.945	2.66
	932	970	1773	112	159	.961	2.94

Assists per 154 Games: 293

PLAYER: EDDIE MATHEWS

						BATTING													BASERUNNING				PERCENTAGES			VALUES			
Year	G	AB	H	2B	3B	HR	(Hm	Rd)	TB	R	RBI	BB	IBB	HBP	SH	SF	SB	CS	SB%	GIDP	Avg.	Slug	On Base	Runs	Win–Loss	Pct.	AV
1952	145	528	128	23	5	25	(11	14)	236	80	58	59			1	5	6	4	.60	9	.242	.447	.317	78	10–6	.619	10
1953	157	579	175	31	8	47	(17	30)	363	110	135	99			2	1	1	3	.25	6	.302	.627	.405	157	13–2	.854	17
1954	138	476	138	21	4	40	(16	24)	287	96	103	113		2	3	7	10	3	.77	9	.290	.603	.421	133	11–2	.862	17
1955	141	499	144	23	5	41	(20	21)	300	108	101	109	20	1	1	6	3	4	.43	5	.289	.601	.412	131	11–3	.812	17
1956	151	552	150	21	2	37	(15	22)	286	103	95	91	17	1	3	4	6	0	1.00	4	.272	.518	.372	114	12–4	.766	13
1957	148	572	167	28	9	32	(13	19)	309	109	94	90	5	0	2	2	3	1	.75	6	.292	.540	.386	126	12–4	.769	14
1958	149	546	137	18	1	31	(17	14)	250	97	77	85	5	2	8	8	5	0	1.00	9	.251	.458	.345	94	11–5	.685	12
1959	148	594	182	16	8	46	(20	26)	352	118	114	80	2	3	3	2	2	1	.67	6	.306	.593	.389	143	13–3	.817	17
1960	153	548	152	19	7	39	(23	16)	302	108	124	111	3	2	4	6	7	3	.70	8	.277	.551	.395	128	12–3	.775	15
1961	152	572	175	23	6	32	(14	18)	306	103	91	93	3	2	1	4	12	7	.63	10	.306	.535	.402	128	12–3	.776	15
1962	152	536	142	25	6	29	(18	11)	266	106	90	101	7	2	0	4	4	2	.67	11	.265	.496	.381	106	11–4	.725	13
1963	158	547	144	27	4	23	(11	12)	248	82	84	124	14	1	0	2	3	4	.43	9	.263	.453	.399	106	12–4	.752	13
1964	141	502	117	19	1	23	(10	13)	207	83	74	85	5	1	0	2	2	2	.50	8	.233	.412	.344	75	8–7	.535	11
1965	156	546	137	23	0	32	(17	15)	256	77	95	73	7	3	1	3	1	0	1.00	11	.251	.469	.340	89	10–5	.653	11
1966	134	452	113	21	4	16	(8	8)	190	72	53	63	6	0	1	1	1	1	.50	6	.250	.420	.340	67	7–5	.576	9
1967	137	436	103	16	2	16	(6	10)	171	53	57	63	12	3	3	6	2	4	.33	6	.236	.392	.331	59	7–6	.548	6
1968	31	52	11	0	0	3	(1	2)	20	4	8	5	1	0	0	0	0	0	.00		.212	.385	.281	6	1–1	.546	1
	2391	8537	2315	354	72	512	(237	275)	4349	1509	1453	1444	107	26	36	58	68	39	.64	123	.271	.509	.375	1739	173–67	.721	211
14.8 yrs		578	157	24	5	35			295	102	98	98		2	2		5	3		8	.271	.509	.375				

Teams: Boston (N) 1952; Milwaukee, 1953–1965; Atlanta, 1966; Houston/Detroit, 1967; Detroit, 1968

Points in MVP Voting: 1953, 216 (2nd, .64); 1954, 5 (.02); 1955, 6 (.02); 1956, 0; 1957, 45 (8th, .13); 1958, 0; 1959, 189.5 (2nd, .62); 1960, 52 (10th, .15); 1962, 1 (.00); 1963, 0; 1964, 0; 1965, 8 (.03); 1966, 0; 1967, 0; 1968, 0. TOTAL: 1.61 Award Shares.

Explanation for Gaps in Career or Sudden Changes in Productivity: 1966—Had some disagreements with Bobby Bragan and was benched.

Other Notes: Named outstanding major league third baseman for 1955, 1957, 1959, and 1960 by *The Sporting News*.

FIELDING THIRD BASE

Year	G	PO	AS	Err	DP	Pct.	Range
1952	142	160	259	19	21	.957	2.95
1953	157	154	311	30	33	.939	2.96
1954	127	112	254	13	28	.966	2.88
1955	137	140	280	21	23	.952	3.07
1956	150	133	287	25	22	.944	2.80
1957	147	131	299	16	27	.964	2.93
1958	149	116	351	22	24	.955	3.13
1959	148	144	305	18	21	.961	3.03
1960	153	141	280	22	23	.950	2.75
1961	151	168	281	18	30	.961	2.97
1962	140	141	283	16	22	.964	3.03
1963	121	113	276	13	23	.968	3.21
1964	128	130	247	15	19	.962	2.95
1965	153	113	301	19	19	.956	2.71
1966	127	114	237	20	31	.946	2.76
1967	45	36	61	6	3	.942	2.16
1968	6	3	10	0	0	1.000	2.17
	2181	2049	4322	293	369	.956	2.92

Assists per 154 Games: 305

PLAYER: HARMON KILLEBREW

						BATTING												BASERUNNING				PERCENTAGES			VALUES			
Year	G	AB	H	2B	3B	HR	(Hm	Rd)	TB	R	RBI	BB	IBB	HBP	SH	SF	SB	CS	SB%	GIDP	Avg.	Slug	On Base	Runs	Win–Loss	Pct.	AV
1954	9	13	4	1	0	0	(0	0)	5	1	3	2		0	0	0	0	0	.00	1	.308	.385	.400	2	0–0	.579	0
1955	38	80	16	1	0	4	(3	1)	29	12	7	9	0	0	0	0	0	0	.00	3	.200	.363	.281	8	1–2	.325	1
1956	44	99	22	2	0	5	(0	5)	39	10	13	10	0	0	0	1	0	0	.00	2	.222	.394	.291	11	1–2	.368	1
1957	9	31	9	2	0	2	(2	0)	17	4	5	2	0	0	0	0	0	0	.00	0	.290	.548	.333	6	1–0	.710	0
1958	13	31	6	0	0	0	(0	0)	6	2	2	0	0	1	0	1	0	0	.00	0	.194	.194	.212	1	0–1	.114	0
1959	153	546	132	20	2	42	(22	20)	282	98	105	90	1	7	0	4	3	2	.60	12	.242	.516	.354	103	11–5	.694	13
1960	124	442	122	19	1	31	(12	19)	236	84	80	71	3	1	0	3	1	0	1.00	10	.276	.534	.375	91	9–3	.735	10
1961	150	541	156	20	7	46	(29	17)	328	94	122	107	6	3	0	5	1	2	.33	11	.288	.606	.405	138	12–3	.801	14
1962	155	552	134	21	1	48	(20	28)	301	85	126	106	6	4	0	4	1	2	.33	14	.243	.545	.366	113	11–5	.694	12
1963	142	515	133	18	0	45	(26	19)	286	88	96	72	4	3	0	6	0	0	.00	16	.258	.555	.349	99	11–4	.708	13
1964	158	577	156	11	1	49	(26	23)	316	95	111	93	5	8	0	4	0	0	.00	15	.270	.548	.377	122	12–4	.748	12
1965	113	401	108	16	1	25	(11	14)	201	78	75	72	12	4	0	2	0	0	.00	10	.269	.501	.384	79	8–3	.733	9
1966	162	569	160	27	1	39	(24	15)	306	89	110	103	18	2	0	3	0	2	.00	12	.281	.538	.391	122	13–3	.803	13
1967	163	547	147	24	1	44	(21	23)	305	105	113	131	15	3	0	8	1	0	1.00	16	.269	.558	.408	131	13–3	.825	15
1968	100	295	62	7	2	17	(5	12)	124	40	40	70	9	2	0	4	0	0	.00	13	.210	.420	.361	46	6–3	.683	6
1969	162	555	153	20	2	49	(28	21)	324	106	140	145	20	5	0	4	8	2	.80	16	.276	.584	.427	146	13–3	.821	17
1970	157	527	143	20	1	41	(16	25)	288	96	113	128	23	2	0	8	0	3	.00	28	.271	.546	.411	116	12–4	.761	14
1971	147	500	127	19	1	28	(15	13)	232	61	119	114	14	0	0	10	3	2	.60	21	.254	.464	.386	92	10–5	.689	13
1972	139	433	100	13	2	26	(12	14)	195	53	74	94	12	1	0	4	0	1	.00	16	.231	.450	.367	73	9–4	.720	11
1973	69	248	60	9	1	5	(2	3)	86	29	32	41	2	1	0	0	0	0	.00	10	.242	.347	.352	31	3–4	.472	3
1974	122	333	74	7	0	13	(9	4)	120	28	54	45	6	0	0	4	0	0	.00	12	.222	.360	.312	37	4–6	.438	5
1975	106	312	62	13	0	14	(8	6)	117	25	44	54	4	1	0	2	1	2	.33	16	.199	.375	.317	39	5–5	.488	4
	2435	8147	2086	290	24	573	(291	282)	4143	1283	1584	1559	160	48	0	77	19	18	.51	243	.256	.509	.376	1609	166–71	.702	186
15.0 yrs		542	139	19	2	38			276	85	105	104	11	3	0	5	1	1		16	.256	.509	.376				

Teams: Washington, A.L. 1954–1960; Minnesota, 1961–1974; Kansas City, 1975.

Points in MVP Voting: 1958, 0; 1959, 21 (.06); 1960, 0; 1961, 29 (.10); 1962, 99 (3rd, .35); 1963, 85 (4th, .30); 1964, 31 (10th, .11); 1965, 15 (.05); 1966, 96 (4th, .34); 1967, 161 (2nd, .58); 1968, 0; 1969, 294 (1st, .88); 1970, 152 (3rd, .45); 1971, 5 (.01); 1972, 0; 1973, 0; 1974, 0; 1975, 0. TOTAL: 3.23 Award Shares.

Reported Salaries: 1971—$100,000

1972—$125,000

1973—$125,000

Explanation for Gaps in Career or Sudden Changes in Productivity:

1957–1958—Harmon was a bonus baby, and thus had to spend two years in the major leagues under the rules then in force. After that, he spent parts of three seasons in the minor leagues.

1965—Suffered dislocated elbow, August 2, when hit by Russ Snyder on a play at first base. At the time, he led the league in home runs (22) and RBI (70).

1968—Ruptured a hamstring muscle in right leg stretching for a throw during the All-Star game, July 9.

1973—Underwent knee surgury in mid-season.

Other Notes: Named outstanding American League left fielder for 1964 by *The Sporting News*. Named outstanding American League first baseman by *The Sporting News* for 1967. Named outstanding American League third baseman for 1969, 1970 by *The Sporting News*.

FIELDING THIRD BASE

Year	G	PO	AS	Err	DP	Pct.	Range
1955	23	23	49	5	3	.935	3.13
1956	20	18	40	3	3	.951	2.90
1957	7	2	16	1	2	.947	2.57
1958	9	8	13	0	1	1.000	2.33
1959	150	129	325	30	18	.938	3.03
1960	65	45	103	9	7	.943	2.28
1961	45	28	75	9	10	.920	2.29
1965	44	37	78	4	3	.966	2.61
1966	107	83	190	14	11	.951	2.55
1967	3	2	3	1	0	.833	1.67
1968	11	7	15	3	1	.880	2.00
1969	105	75	185	20	12	.929	2.48
1970	138	108	203	17	14	.948	2.25
1971	64	42	93	11	3	.925	2.11
	791	607	1388	127	88	.940	2.52

Assists per 154 Games: 270

PLAYER: KEN BOYER

				BATTING												BASERUNNING				PERCENTAGES			VALUES			
Year	G	AB	H	2B	3B	HR	(Hm | Rd)	TB	R	RBI	BB	IBB	HBP	SH	SF	SB	CS	SB%	GIDP	Avg.	Slug	On Base	Runs	Win–Loss	Pct.	AV
1955	147	530	140	27	2	18	(7 | 11)	225	78	62	37	5	1	1	5	22	17	.56	6	.264	.425	.310	67	7–8	.470	10
1956	150	595	182	30	2	26	(12 | 14)	294	91	98	38	7	1	2	3	8	3	.73	18	.306	.494	.346	97	10–6	.645	12
1957	142	544	144	18	3	19	(10 | 9)	225	79	62	44	8	1	4	5	12	8	.60	11	.265	.414	.316	70	8–8	.483	10
1958	150	570	175	21	9	23	(14 | 9)	283	101	90	49	8	3	1	8	11	6	.65	15	.307	.496	.360	100	11–5	.684	13
1959	149	563	174	18	5	28	(14 | 14)	286	86	94	67	7	2	0	1	12	6	.67	7	.309	.508	.384	112	11–4	.742	14
1960	151	552	168	26	10	32	(16 | 16)	310	95	97	56	10	4	0	4	8	7	.53	13	.304	.562	.370	111	12–4	.768	16
1961	153	589	194	26	11	24	(11 | 13)	314	109	95	68	9	1	0	5	6	3	.67	11	.329	.533	.397	126	12–3	.775	15
1962	160	611	178	27	5	24	(10 | 14)	287	92	98	75	7	1	2	2	12	7	.63	15	.291	.470	.368	105	11–6	.663	13
1963	159	617	176	28	2	24	(15 | 9)	280	86	111	70	10	2	0	4	1	0	1.00	20	.285	.454	.358	98	11–6	.644	12
1964	162	628	185	30	10	24	(12 | 12)	307	100	119	70	12	2	0	4	3	5	.37	22	.295	.489	.365	107	12–6	.674	14
1965	144	535	139	18	2	13	(9 | 4)	200	71	75	57	3	1	4	7	2	7	.22	16	.260	.374	.326	64	7–8	.468	10
1966	136	496	132	28	2	14	(10 | 4)	206	62	61	30	5	0	1	7	4	3	.57	15	.266	.415	.303	59	7–7	.488	10
1967	113	346	86	12	3	7	(4 | 3)	125	34	34	33	3	0	2	3	2	3	.40	10	.249	.361	.310	38	6–5	.539	3
1968	93	245	63	7	2	6	(4 | 2)	92	20	41	17	3	1	0	5	2	2	.50	4	.257	.376	.302	28	4–3	.625	3
1969	25	34	7	2	0	0	(0 | 0)	9	0	4	2	0	0	0	0	0	0	.00	2	.206	.265	.250	2	0–1	.177	0
	2034	7455	2143	318	68	282	(148 | 134)	3443	1104	1141	713	97	20	17	63	105	77	.58	185	.287	.462	.348	1182	130–80	.619	155
12.6 yrs	594	171	25	5	22				274	88	91	57	8	2	1	5	8	6		15	.287	.462	.348				

Teams: St. Louis, 1955–1965; New York, N.L. 1966; New York, N.L./Chicago, A.L. 1967; Chicago/Los Angeles, 1968; Los Angeles, 1969.

Points in MVP Voting: 1955, 0; 1956, 2 (.01); 1957, 0; 1958, 31 (.09); 1959, 37 (10th, .12); 1960, 80 (6th, .24); 1961, 43 (7th, .19); 1962, 5 (.02); 1963, 19 (.07); 1964, 243 (1st, .87); 1965, 0; 1966, 0; 1967, 0; 1968, 0; 1969, 0. TOTAL: 1.61 Award Shares.

Explanation for Gaps in Career or Sudden Changes in Productivity:
1965—Bothered most of the season by hip and back problems.

Other Notes: Named outstanding major league third baseman for 1956 by *The Sporting News.* Named outstanding National League third baseman for 1961, 1962, 1963, 1964, by *The Sporting News.*

Gold Glove: 1958, 1959, 1960, 1961, 1963.

FIELDING THIRD BASE

Year	G	PO	AS	E	DP	Pct.	Range
1955	139	124	253	19	24	.952	2.71
1956	149	130	309	18	37	.961	2.95
1957	41	41	93	13	7	.912	3.27
1958	144	156	350	20	41	.962	3.51
1959	143	134	300	20	32	.956	3.03
1960	146	140	300	19	37	.959	3.01
1961	153	117	346	24	23	.951	3.03
1962	160	158	318	22	34	.956	2.97
1963	159	129	293	34	23	.925	2.65
1964	162	131	337	24	30	.951	2.89
1965	143	113	250	12	18	.968	2.54
1966	130	113	292	21	33	.951	3.12
1967	77	49	151	10	11	.952	2.60
1968	39	32	60	8	5	.920	2.36
	1785	1567	3652	264	355	.952	2.92

Assists per 154 Games: 315

PLAYER: BROOKS ROBINSON

Year	G	AB	H	2B	3B	HR	(Hm	Rd)	TB	R	RBI	BB	IBB	HBP	SH	SF	SB	CS	SB%	GIDP	Avg.	Slug	On Base	Runs	Win–Loss	Pct.	AV
1955	6	22	2	0	0	0	(0	0)	2	0	1	0	0	0	0	0	0	0	.00	0	.091	.091	.091	0	0–1	.003	0
1956	15	44	10	4	0	1	(0	1)	17	5	1	1	0	0	0	0	0	0	.00	0	.227	.386	.244	4	0–1	.395	0
1957	50	117	28	6	1	2	(0	2)	42	13	14	7	0	1	0	1	1	0	1.00	4	.239	.359	.286	11	1–2	.423	1
1958	145	463	110	16	3	3	(2	1)	141	31	32	31	1	5	7	1	1	2	.33	19	.238	.305	.288	38	5–9	.365	4
1959	88	313	89	15	2	4	(3	1)	120	29	24	17	5	2	1	0	2	2	.50	5	.284	.383	.324	38	5–4	.577	5
1960	152	595	175	27	9	14	(7	7)	262	74	88	35	0	0	13	8	2	2	.50	29	.294	.440	.323	78	9–8	.531	11
1961	163	668	192	38	7	7	(5	2)	265	89	61	47	2	4	8	9	1	3	.25	21	.287	.397	.330	85	11–8	.564	9
1962	162	634	192	29	9	23	(13	10)	308	77	86	42	3	1	10	10	3	1	.75	18	.303	.486	.337	102	12–6	.661	13
1963	161	589	148	26	4	11	(5	6)	215	67	67	46	4	1	8	4	2	3	.40	8	.251	.365	.301	66	8–9	.494	8
1964	163	612	194	35	3	28	(12	16)	319	82	118	51	10	4	8	10	1	0	1.00	17	.317	.521	.364	115	13–4	.764	15
1965	144	559	166	25	2	18	(10	8)	249	81	80	47	9	2	4	4	3	0	1.00	15	.297	.445	.349	86	11–5	.688	11
1966	157	620	167	35	2	23	(13	10)	275	91	100	56	11	5	1	4	2	3	.40	18	.269	.444	.332	88	10–7	.578	12
1967	158	610	164	25	5	22	(10	12)	269	88	77	54	9	4	5	8	1	3	.25	21	.269	.434	.326	83	11–7	.589	11
1968	162	608	154	36	6	17	(8	9)	253	65	75	44	11	4	3	8	1	1	.50	12	.253	.416	.303	76	11–7	.627	11
1969	156	598	140	21	3	23	(10	13)	236	73	84	56	10	3	3	10	2	1	.67	19	.234	.395	.297	69	9–10	.470	10
1970	158	608	168	31	4	18	(9	9)	261	84	94	53	5	4	1	7	1	1	.50	18	.276	.429	.334	85	10–7	.579	12
1971	156	589	160	21	1	20	(16	4)	243	67	92	63	8	3	1	7	0	0	.00	15	.272	.413	.341	83	10–7	.605	12
1972	153	556	139	23	2	8	(3	5)	190	48	64	43	4	2	4	7	1	0	1.00	12	.250	.342	.301	58	9–7	.573	8
1973	155	549	141	17	2	9	(5	4)	189	53	72	55	5	3	8	4	2	0	1.00	19	.257	.344	.321	61	8–9	.461	10
1974	153	553	159	27	0	7	(2	5)	207	46	59	56	13	3	5	5	2	0	1.00	14	.288	.374	.350	74	9–6	.597	11
1975	144	482	97	15	1	6	(1	5)	132	50	53	44	10	1	8	4	0	0	.00	6	.201	.274	.263	37	4–11	.291	6
1976	71	218	46	8	2	3	(2	1)	67	16	11	8	0	1	3	2	0	0	.00	5	.211	.307	.237	16	2–5	.273	2
1977	24	47	7	2	0	1	(1	0)	12	3	4	4	0	0	0	1	0	0	.00	2	.149	.255	.212	2	0–1	.107	0
	2896	10654	2848	482	68	268	(137	131)	4270	1232	1357	860	120	53	101	114	28	22	.56	297	.267	.401	.319	1358	169–140	.547	185
17.9 yrs		596	159	27	4	15			239	69	76	48	7	3	6	6	2	1		17	.267	.401	.319				

Teams: Baltimore, 1955–1977.

Points in MVP Voting: 1958, 0; 1959, 0; 1960, 211 (3rd, .63); 1961, 4 (.01); 1962, 41 (9th, .15); 1963, 0; 1964, 269 (1st, .96); 1965, 150 (3rd, .54); 1966, 153 (2nd, .55); 1967, 0; 1968, 8 (.03); 1969, 5 (.01); 1970, 75 (7th, .22); 1971, 163 (4th, .49); 1972, 3 (.01); 1973, 0; 1974, 30 (.09); 1975, 0; 1976, 0; 1977, 0. TOTAL: 3.69 Award Shares.

Reported Salaries: 1961—$20,000; 1963—$35,000; 1972—$110,000; 1973—$110,000. $4,000 signing bonus, 1955.

Explanation for Gaps in Career or Sudden Changes in Productivity:
1959—Sent back down.
1963—No known reason for the year. Any injuries he had, he never told anybody about.
1965—Missed sixteen games in May with a cracked bone in his right thumb and a pulled shoulder muscle.

Other Notes: Named outstanding American League third baseman for 1961, 1962, 1964, 1965, 1966, 1967, 1968, 1971, 1972 by *The Sporting News.*
Gold Glove: 1960, 1961, 1962, 1963, 1964, 1965, 1966, 1967, 1968, 1969, 1970, 1971, 1972, 1973, 1974, 1975.

FIELDING THIRD BASE

Year	G	PO	AS	E	DP	Pct.	Range
1955	6	2	8	2	1	.833	1.67
1956	14	9	25	2	3	.944	2.43
1957	47	34	66	3	5	.971	2.13
1958	140	151	275	21	30	.953	3.04
1959	87	92	187	13	25	.955	3.21
1960	152	171	328	12	34	.977	3.28
1961	163	151	331	14	34	.972	2.96
1962	162	163	339	11	32	.979	3.10
1963	160	153	330	12	43	.976	3.02
1964	163	153	327	14	40	.972	2.94
1965	143	144	296	15	36	.967	3.08
1966	157	174	313	12	26	.976	3.10
1967	158	147	405	11	37	.980	3.49
1968	162	168	353	16	31	.970	3.22
1969	156	163	370	13	37	.976	3.42
1970	156	157	321	17	30	.966	3.06
1971	156	131	354	16	35	.968	3.11
1972	152	129	333	11	27	.977	3.04
1973	154	129	354	15	25	.970	3.14
1974	153	115	410	18	44	.967	3.43
1975	143	96	326	9	30	.979	2.95
1976	71	59	126	6	11	.969	2.61
1977	15	6	28	0	2	1.000	2.27
	2870	2697	6205	263	618	.971	3.10

Assists per 154 Games: 333

PLAYER: RON SANTO

Year	G	AB	H	2B	3B	HR	(Hm	Rd)	TB	R	RBI	BB	IBB	HBP	SH	SF	SB	CS	SB%	GIDP	Avg.	Slug	On Base	Runs	Win–Loss	Pct.	AV
1960	95	347	87	24	2	9	(7	2)	142	44	44	31	5	0	2	2	0	3	.00	9	.251	.409	.309	42	5–6	.451	6
1961	154	578	164	32	6	23	(15	8)	277	84	83	73	7	0	1	3	2	3	.40	25	.284	.479	.362	95	10–7	.591	12
1962	162	604	137	20	4	17	(12	5)	216	44	83	65	5	2	3	5	4	1	.80	17	.227	.358	.300	65	7–11	.387	9
1963	162	630	187	29	6	25	(13	12)	303	79	99	42	7	4	0	11	6	4	.60	17	.297	.481	.339	99	13–5	.718	12
1964	161	592	185	33	13	30	(16	14)	334	94	114	86	5	2	0	6	3	4	.43	11	.313	.564	.398	135	13–3	.803	16
1965	164	608	173	30	4	33	(20	13)	310	88	101	88	7	5	0	3	3	1	.75	12	.285	.510	.378	121	13–4	.752	15
1966	155	561	175	21	8	30	(17	13)	302	93	94	95	7	6	2	8	4	5	.44	16	.312	.538	.411	127	12–4	.770	15
1967	161	586	176	23	4	31	(21	10)	300	107	98	96	9	3	0	12	1	5	.17	17	.300	.512	.395	120	13–4	.760	16
1968	162	577	142	17	3	26	(21	5)	243	86	98	96	7	3	1	5	3	4	.43	18	.246	.421	.353	87	11–6	.648	11
1969	160	575	166	18	4	29	(18	11)	279	97	123	96	7	2	0	14	1	3	.25	21	.289	.485	.384	108	12–5	.720	15
1970	154	555	148	30	4	26	(16	10)	264	83	114	92	6	1	1	6	2	0	1.00	17	.267	.476	.368	100	10–6	.650	12
1971	154	555	148	22	1	21	(13	8)	235	77	88	79	8	0	1	7	4	0	1.00	20	.267	.423	.354	84	10–6	.632	11
1972	133	464	140	25	5	17	(10	7)	226	68	74	69	5	4	2	8	1	4	.20	13	.302	.487	.389	89	10–3	.746	13
1973	149	536	143	29	2	20	(13	7)	236	65	77	63	8	4	0	1	1	2	.33	27	.267	.440	.348	76	9–6	.600	10
1974	117	375	83	12	1	5	(4	1)	112	29	41	37	1	2	0	3	0	2	.00	16	.221	.299	.293	31	3–8	.275	3
	2243	8143	2254	365	67	342	(216	126)	3779	1138	1331	1108	94	38	13	94	35	41	.46	256	.277	.464	.362	1379	150–83	.642	176
13.8 yrs		588	163	26	5	25			273	82	96	80	7	3	1	7	3	3	.46	18	.277	.464	.362				

Teams: Chicago, N.L. 1960–1973; Chicago, A.L. 1974.

Points in MVP Voting: 1960, 0; 1962, 0; 1963, 41 (8th, .15); 1964, 59 (8th, .21); 1965, 11 (.04); 1966, 23 (.08); 1967, 103 (4th, .37); 1968, 2 (.01); 1969, 124 (5th, .37); 1970, 0; 1971, 0; 1972, 0; 1973, 0; 1974, 0. TOTAL: 1.23 Award Shares.

Reported Salaries: 1973—$110,000; 1974—$117,000.

Explanation for Gaps in Career or Sudden Changes in Productivity:
1972—Missed a month with a wrist injury.
1974—A lot of the difference in his batting is due to the extreme difference between Wrigley Field (1973) and Comiskey Park (1974), but he was also trying to play a strange position (2B).

Other Notes: Named outstanding National League third baseman for 1966, 1967, 1968, 1969, 1972 by *The Sporting News*.
Gold Glove: 1964, 1965, 1966, 1967, 1968.

FIELDING THIRD BASE

Year	G	PO	AS	E	DP	Pct.	Range
1960	94	78	144	16	6	.933	2.36
1961	153	157	307	31	41	.937	3.03
1962	157	161	332	23	33	.955	3.14
1963	162	136	374	26	25	.951	3.15
1964	161	156	367	20	31	.963	3.25
1965	164	155	373	24	27	.957	3.22
1966	152	150	391	25	36	.956	3.56
1967	161	187	393	26	33	.957	3.60
1968	162	130	378	15	33	.971	3.14
1969	160	144	334	27	23	.947	2.99
1970	152	143	320	27	36	.945	3.05
1971	149	118	274	17	29	.958	2.63
1972	129	108	274	21	19	.948	2.96
1973	146	107	271	20	17	.950	2.59
1974	28	25	49	2	6	.974	2.64
	2130	1955	4581	320	395	.953	3.07

Assists per 154 Games: 331

PLAYER: RICHIE ALLEN

Year	G	AB	H	2B	3B	HR	(Hm	Rd)	TB	R	RBI	BB	IBB	HBP	SH	SF	SB	CS	SB%	GIDP	Avg.	Slug	On Base	Runs	Win–Loss	Pct.	AV
1963	10	24	7	2	1	0	(0	0)	11	6	2	0	0	0	0	1	0	0	.00	2	.292	.458	.280	2	0–0	.406	0
1964	162	632	201	38	13	29	(14	15)	352	125	91	67	13	0	6	3	3	4	.43	8	.318	.557	.379	135	13–3	.794	14
1965	161	619	187	31	14	20	(9	11)	306	93	85	74	6	2	6	6	15	2	.88	13	.302	.494	.372	119	13–4	.746	13
1966	141	524	166	25	10	40	(17	23)	331	112	110	68	13	3	0	4	10	6	.62	9	.317	.632	.396	131	12–2	.838	18
1967	122	463	142	31	10	23	(9	14)	262	89	77	75	18	1	1	0	20	5	.80	9	.307	.566	.404	109	11–2	.849	14
1968	152	521	137	17	9	33	(17	16)	271	87	90	74	15	1	2	7	7	7	.50	7	.263	.520	.350	97	11–4	.762	11
1969	118	438	126	23	3	32	(21	11)	251	79	89	64	10	0	0	4	9	3	.75	10	.288	.573	.375	95	9–3	.768	10
1970	122	459	128	17	5	34	(17	17)	257	88	101	71	16	2	0	1	5	4	.56	9	.279	.560	.377	97	10–3	.749	12
1971	155	549	162	24	1	23	(11	12)	257	82	90	93	13	1	1	5	8	1	.89	23	.295	.468	.394	102	12–4	.746	11
1972	148	506	156	28	5	37	(27	10)	305	90	113	99	16	1	0	3	19	8	.70	13	.308	.603	.420	131	12–2	.874	16
1973	72	250	79	20	3	16	(7	9)	153	39	41	33	3	1	1	3	7	2	.78	9	.316	.612	.392	59	6–1	.807	7
1974	128	462	139	23	1	32	(15	17)	260	84	88	57	9	1	0	5	7	1	.87	16	.301	.563	.375	96	10–3	.751	11
1975	119	416	97	21	3	12	(6	6)	160	54	62	58	4	2	1	4	11	2	.85	19	.233	.385	.326	52	6–7	.457	5
1976	85	298	80	16	1	15	(9	6)	143	52	49	37	2	0	1	3	11	4	.73	13	.268	.480	.345	47	6–3	.629	5
1977	54	171	41	4	0	5	(4	1)	60	19	31	24	0	1	0	4	1	3	.25	4	.240	.351	.330	20	3–3	.489	2
	1749	6332	1848	320	79	351	(183	168)	3379	1099	1119	894	138	16	19	53	133	52	.72	164	.292	.534	.377	1290	132–45	.745	149
10.8 yrs		586	171	30	7	33			313	102	104	83	13	1	2	5	12	5		15	.292	.534	.377				

Teams: Philadelphia, 1963–1969; St. Louis, 1970; Los Angeles, 1971; Chicago, A.L., 1972–1974; Philadelphia, 1975–1976; Oakland, 1977.

Points in MVP Voting: 1963, 0; 1964, 63 (7th, .23); 1965, 2 (.01); 1966, 107 (4th, .38); 1967, 9 (.03); 1968, 0; 1969, 0; 1970, 0; 1971, 0; 1972, 321 (1st, .96); 1973, 1 (.00); 1974, 8 (.02); 1975, 0; 1976, 0; 1977, 0. TOTAL: 1.63 Award Shares.

Reported Salaries: 1967—$82,000; 1970—$90,000; 1972—$125,000.

Explanation for Gaps in Career or Sudden Changes in Productivity:

1966—Dislocated right shoulder while sliding, April 29. Phillies lost 13 of 24 games while he was out of lineup.

1967—While pushing an old automobile, August 24, Allen put his hand on a headlight and broke through it, severely cutting his right hand. He was out the rest of the way, and the Phillies were 14–21 in that period, and lost six 1–0 games.

1968—Sidelined by groin injury. Benched briefly by Gene Mauch. Also may have been hampered by hand injury suffered in 1967.

1969—Suspended, June 24 through July 20, after failing to show up at Shea Stadium for a scheduled double-header. Had been fined $1,000 in May after reporting to the ballpark after the game had started two straight days. Team played very well during his absence.

1970—Had problem with Achilles tendon, pulled muscles.

1973—June 28, Mike Epstein stepped on his leg after he dove for a throw wide of the bag. Allen suffered broken bone on the back of lower leg and batted only five times the rest of the season. The White Sox, in first place at the time of the injury, finished fifth in the division.

1974—Had sore shoulder much of season plus some back trouble; announced his retirement September 13 and was placed on the disabled list.

1975—Quiet season; cause of poor performance unknown.

1976—Was on disabled list several times for a variety of injuries.

1977—Released in mid-season after confrontation with Charles O. Finley.

Other Notes: Named outstanding American League first baseman for 1972, 1974, by *The Sporting News*.

FIELDING THIRD BASE

Year	G	PO	AS	Err	DP	Pct.	Range
1963	1	0	0	0	0	0	0
1964	162	154	325	41	30	.921	2.96
1965	160	129	305	26	29	.943	2.71
1966	91	81	180	9	15	.967	2.87
1967	121	95	249	35	23	.908	2.84
1968	10	7	15	6	4	.786	2.20
1970	38	27	67	11	3	.895	2.47
1971	67	36	133	15	12	.918	2.52
1972	2	1	2	0	0	1.000	1.50
	652	530	1276	143	116	.927	2.77

Assists per 154 Games: 301

PLAYER: MIKE SCHMIDT

Year	G	AB	H	2B	3B	HR	(Hm	Rd)	TB	R	RBI	BB	IBB	HBP	SH	SF	SB	CS	SB%	GIDP	Avg.	Slug	On Base	Runs	Win–Loss	Pct.	AV
1972	13	34	7	0	0	1	(1	0)	10	2	3	5	0	1	0	0	0	0	.00	0	.206	.294	.325	4	1–0	.515	0
1973	132	367	72	11	0	18	(9	9)	137	43	52	62	3	9	1	4	8	2	.80	8	.196	.373	.323	48	6–6	.503	8
1974	162	568	160	28	7	36	(19	17)	310	108	116	106	14	4	3	5	23	12	.66	4	.282	.546	.394	130	13–3	.785	15
1975	158	562	140	34	3	38	(22	16)	294	93	95	101	10	4	6	1	29	12	.71	7	.249	.523	.364	113	12–5	.705	14
1976	160	584	153	31	4	38	(17	21)	306	112	107	100	8	11	3	7	14	9	.61	7	.262	.524	.374	121	13–4	.754	14
1977	154	544	149	27	11	38	(17	21)	312	114	101	104	4	9	1	9	15	8	.65	10	.274	.574	.393	129	12–4	.758	14
1978	145	513	129	27	2	21	(13	8)	223	93	78	91	12	4	0	8	19	6	.76	4	.251	.435	.364	90	10–5	.695	12
1979	160	541	137	25	4	45	(16	29)	305	109	114	120	12	3	2	9	9	5	.64	13	.253	.564	.385	123	12–4	.762	16
1980	150	548	157	25	8	48	(25	23)	342	104	121	89	10	2	0	13	12	5	.71	6	.286	.624	.380	137	13–3	.816	17
1981	102	354	112	19	2	31	(17	14)	228	78	91	73	18	4	0	3	12	4	.75	9	.316	.644	.435	102	8–1	.849	14
1982	148	514	144	26	3	35	(17	18)	281	108	87	107	17	3	0	7	14	7	.67	11	.280	.547	.403	118	12–3	.798	15
1983	154	534	136	16	4	40	(19	21)	280	104	109	128	17	3	0	4	7	8	.47	10	.255	.524	.399	117	12–4	.770	15
1984	151	528	146	23	3	36	(16	20)	283	93	106	92	14	4	0	8	5	7	.42	15	.277	.536	.383	109	11–4	.730	15
1985	158	549	152	31	5	33	(14	19)	292	89	93	87	8	3	0	6	1	3	.25	10	.277	.532	.375	113	12–4	.757	13
1986	160	552	160	29	1	37	(20	17)	302	97	119	89	25	7	0	9	1	2	.33	8	.290	.547	.390	122	12–4	.759	15
	2107	7292	1954	352	57	495	(242	253)	3905	1347	1392	1354	172	71	16	93	169	90	.65	122	.268	.536	.384	1570	156–53	.745	197
13.0 yrs		561	150	27	4	38			300	104	107	104	13	5	1	7	13	7	.65	9	.268	.536	.384	13	7		

Teams: Philadelphia, 1972–present.

Points in MVP Voting: 1972, 0; 1973, 0; 1974, 136 (6th, .40); 1975, 0; 1976, 179 (3rd, .53); 1977, 48 (10th, .14); 1978, 0; 1979, 32 (.10); 1980, 336 (1st, 1.00); 1981, 321 (1st, .96); 1982, 54 (6th, .16); 1983, 191 (3rd, .57); 1984, 55½ (7th, .17); 1985, 0; 1986, 287 (1st, .85). TOTAL: 4.88 Award Shares.

Reported Salaries: 1977–1982, $560,000/year; 1984, $2,023,000.

Other Notes: Named outstanding National League third baseman for 1974, 1976, 1977, 1979, 1980, 1981, 1982, 1983, 1984, 1986 by *The Sporting News*
Gold Glove: 1976, 1977, 1978, 1979, 1980, 1981, 1982, 1983, 1984, 1986.
Values presented here go only through 1986. Those given in Section II include estimated data for the 1987 season.

FIELDING THIRD BASE

Year	G	PO	AS	E	DP	Pct.	Range
1972	11	6	21	1	3	.964	2.45
1973	125	101	251	17	30	.954	2.82
1974	162	134	404	26	40	.954	3.32
1975	151	132	368	24	30	.954	3.31
1976	160	139	377	21	29	.961	3.22
1977	149	106	396	19	33	.964	3.37
1978	139	98	324	16	34	.963	3.04
1979	157	114	361	23	36	.954	3.03
1980	149	98	372	27	31	.946	3.15
1981	101	74	249	15	20	.956	3.20
1982	148	110	324	23	28	.950	2.93
1983	153	107	332	19	29	.959	2.87
1984	145	85	329	26	19	.941	2.86
1985	54	31	109	11	8	.927	2.59
1986	124	78	220	6	27	.980	2.40
	1928	1413	4437	274	397	.955	3.03

Assists per 154 Games: 354

PLAYER: GEORGE BRETT

Year	G	AB	H	2B	3B	HR	(Hm	Rd)	TB	R	RBI	BB	IBB	HBP	SH	SF	SB	CS	SB%	GIDP	Avg	Slug	On Base	Runs	Win-Loss	Pct.	AV
1973	13	40	5	2	0	0	(0	0)	7	2	0	0	0	0	0	1	0	0	.00	0	.125	.175	.122	1	0–1	.021	0
1974	133	457	129	21	5	2	(0	2)	166	49	47	21	3	0	6	2	8	5	.62	9	.282	.363	.309	67	8–5	.611	7
1975	159	634	195	35	13	11	(2	9)	289	84	89	46	6	2	9	6	13	10	.57	8	.308	.456	.349	94	11–7	.622	11
1976	159	645	215	34	14	7	(6	1)	298	94	67	49	4	1	2	8	21	11	.66	8	.333	.462	.376	117	13–4	.740	14
1977	139	564	176	32	13	22	(9	13)	300	105	88	55	9	2	3	3	14	12	.54	12	.312	.532	.372	106	11–5	.694	13
1978	128	510	150	45	8	9	(4	5)	238	79	62	39	6	1	3	5	23	7	.77	6	.294	.467	.341	83	9–5	.659	10
1979	154	645	212	42	20	23	(11	12)	363	119	107	51	14	0	1	4	17	10	.63	8	.329	.563	.375	136	12–5	.710	15
1980	117	449	175	33	9	24	(13	11)	298	87	118	58	16	1	0	7	15	6	.71	11	.390	.664	.454	131	10–1	.867	17
1981	89	347	109	27	7	6	(2	4)	168	42	43	27	7	1	0	4	14	6	.70	7	.314	.484	.361	67	7–2	.771	6
1982	144	552	166	32	9	21	(9	12)	279	101	82	71	14	1	0	5	6	1	.86	12	.301	.505	.378	87	9–6	.610	14
1983	123	464	144	38	2	25	(7	18)	261	90	93	57	13	1	0	3	0	1	.00	9	.310	.563	.385	75	8–4	.646	12
1984	104	377	107	21	3	13	(6	7)	173	42	69	38	6	0	0	7	0	1	.00	11	.284	.459	.344	58	7–4	.628	8
1985	155	550	184	38	5	30	(15	15)	322	108	112	103	31	3	0	9	9	1	.90	12	.335	.585	.436	149	12–2	.869	16
1986	124	442	128	28	4	16	(8	8)	212	70	73	80	18	4	0	4	1	2	.33	6	.290	.481	.401	89	9–3	.767	9
10.7 yrs	1741	6675	2095	428	112	209	(92	117)	3374	1072	1050	695	147	17	25	67	141	73	.66	113	.314	.505	.377	1277	126–54	.699	152
		621	195	40	10	19			314	100	98	65	14	2	2	6	13	7		11	.314	.505	.377				

Teams: Kansas City, 1973–Present

Points in MVP Voting: 1973, 0; 1974, 0; 1975, 37.5 (.11); 1976, 217 (2nd, .65); 1977, 51 (.13); 1978, 14 (.04); 1979, 226 (3rd, .58); 1980, 336 (1st, .85); 1981, 1 (.00); 1982, 9 (.02); 1983, 0; 1984,0; 1985, 274 (2nd, .70); 1986, 0. TOTAL: 3.08 Award Shares.

Reported Salaries: 1979, $140,000; 1980, $140,000; 1981, $190,000; 1982–1986, $1,000,000/year ($900,000/year plus $500,000 signing bonus).

Explanation for Gaps in Career or Sudden Changes in Productivity:

1977—Missed twelve games with elbow injury, five with infection of some kind. 1978—Out April 28 to May 19 with a shoulder problem. Out July 26 to August 14 with a chipped bone in his right thumb. After he returned to the lineup in August, his hand was still hurting him a lot, and he hit just .179 (12 for 67) the rest of that month, which is wholly responsible for his failure to hit .300 that year.

1980—Damaged ligament in right ankle while stealing a base, June 10; out June 10–July 10. Out September 7 through 16 with tendinitis in his right wrist.

1981—Missed playing time with hemorrhoids and an ankle injury, plus the strike.

1983—Broke a toe when going through a doorway.

Other Notes: Named outstanding American League third baseman for 1976, 1979, 1980, by *The Sporting News*. Gold Glove: 1985. Values presented here go only through 1986. Those given in Section II include estimated data for the 1987 season.

The Sporting News names three teams after each season, a Gold Glove team of the best fielders, a Silver Slugger team of the best hitters and an All-Star team of the best all-around players. In 1985 they named George Brett the best hitter and the best fielder, but did not name him the best all-around player. You figure it out.

FIELDING THIRD BASE

Year	G	PO	AS	Err	DP	Pct.	Range
1973	13	9	28	1	2	.974	2.85
1974	132	102	279	21	16	.948	2.89
1975	159	131	355	26	27	.949	3.06
1976	157	140	355	26	22	.950	3.15
1977	135	115	325	20	33	.957	3.26
1978	128	104	289	16	25	.961	3.07
1979	149	129	373	30	28	.944	3.37
1980	112	103	256	17	28	.955	3.21
1981	88	74	170	14	7	.946	2.77
1982	134	107	294	17	22	.959	2.99
1983	102	85	188	24	25	.919	2.68
1984	101	59	201	14	18	.949	2.57
1985	152	107	339	15	33	.967	2.93
1986	115	97	218	16	17	.952	2.74
	1677	1362	3670	257	303	.951	3.00

Assists per 154 Games: 337

Shortstop

Bobby Wallace
Honus Wagner
Joe Tinker
Art Fletcher
Ray Chapman
Rabbit Maranville
Dave Bancroft
Joe Sewell
Travis Jackson
Joe Cronin
Dick Bartell
Luke Appling
Arky Vaughan
Lou Boudreau
Pee Wee Reese
Phil Rizzuto
Ernie Banks
Luis Aparicio
Maury Wills

PLAYER: BOBBY WALLACE

					BATTING													BASERUNNING				PERCENTAGES			VALUES			
Year	G	AB	H	2B	3B	HR	(Hm	Rd)	TB	R	RBI	BB	IBB	HBP	SH	SF	SB	CS	SB%	GIDP	Avg.	Slug	On Base	Runs	Win−Loss	Pct.	AV
1894	4	13	2	1	0	0	(	)	3	0	1	0		0	0		0				.154	.231	.154	0	0−0	.024	0
1895	30	98	21	2	3	0	(	)	29	16	10	6		2	6		0				.214	.296	.264	8	0−3	.148	8
1896	45	149	35	6	3	1	(	)	50	19	17	11		0	4		2				.235	.336	.280	16	1−3	.262	7
1897	131	522	177	35	21	4	(	)	266	99	112	48			14		14				.339	.510	.385	115	10−4	.690	14
1898	154	593	160	25	13	3	(	)	220	81	99	63			11		7				.270	.371	.334	81	9−9	.494	10
1899	151	577	174	28	14	12	(	)	266	91	108	54			5		17				.302	.461	.358	105	10−6	.626	14
1900	129	489	133	25	9	4	(	)	188	70	70	40			4		7				.272	.384	.325	69	7−8	.463	10
1901	135	556	179	34	15	2	(	)	249	69	91	20			10		15				.322	.448	.340	94	9−6	.587	14
1902	133	495	142	32	9	1	(	)	195	71	63	45			6		18				.287	.394	.342	76	9−6	.605	11
1903	136	519	127	21	17	1	(	)	185	63	54	28			9		10				.245	.356	.279	58	8−8	.497	9
1904	139	550	150	29	4	2	(	)	193	57	69	42			8		20				.273	.351	.320	72	10−6	.625	11
1905	156	587	159	25	9	1	(	)	205	67	59	45			8		13				.271	.349	.319	73	10−7	.589	10
1906	139	476	123	21	7	2	(	)	164	64	67	58			13		24				.258	.345	.331	67	9−5	.645	12
1907	147	538	138	20	7	0	(	)	172	56	70	54			9		16				.257	.320	.319	64	9−7	.557	12
1908	137	487	123	24	4	1	(	)	158	59	60	52			19		5				.253	.324	.314	54	8−7	.541	11
1909	116	403	96	12	2	1	(	)	115	36	35	38		4	6		7				.238	.285	.306	37	5−7	.448	6
1910	138	508	131	19	7	0	(	)	164	47	37	49		1	10		12				.258	.323	.308	56	7−8	.472	10
1911	125	410	95	12	2	0	(	)	111	35	31	46		2	6		8				.232	.271	.308	36	4−9	.289	7
1912	99	323	78	14	5	0	(	)	102	39	31	43		1	5		3				.241	.316	.328	34	4−6	.401	5
1913	53	147	31	5	0	0	(	)	36	11	21	14		3	8		1				.211	.245	.279	11	1−4	.262	2
1914	26	73	16	2	1	0	(	)	20	3	5	5		0	4		1				.219	.274	.256	6	1−2	.318	1
1915	9	13	3	0	1	0	(	)	5	1	4	5		0	0		0				.231	.385	.444	2	0−0	.684	0
1916	14	18	5	0	0	0	(	)	5	0	1	2		0	2		0				.278	.278	.318	2	0−0	.472	0
1917	8	10	1	0	0	0	(	)	1	0	2	0		0	2		0				.100	.100	.083	0	0−0	.012	0
1918	32	98	15	1	0	0	(	)	16	3	4	6		0	4		1				.153	.163	.194	4	0−3	.073	1
	2386	8652	2314	393	153	35	(	)	3118	1057	1121	774		15	173		201				.267	.360	.323	1140	131−124	.514	185
14.7 yrs		587	157	27	10	2			212	72	76	53			12		14				.267	.360	.323				

Teams: Cleveland, N.L., 1894–1898; St. Louis, N.L. 1899–1901; St. Louis, A.L., 1902–1916; St. Louis, N.L. 1917–1918.

Reported Salaries: 1906, $6,500.

Explanation for Gaps in Career or Sudden Changes in Productivity:

1913—Broken hand.

1914—Badly burned.

FIELDING SHORTSTOP

Year	G	PO	AS	Err	DP	Pct.	Range
1899	100	238	386	55	40	.919	6.24
1900	126	327	447	55	31	.934	6.14
1901	134	326	542	66	67	.929	6.48
1902	131	299	474	42	64	.948	5.90
1903	135	282	468	62	53	.924	5.56
1904	139	303	482	44	37	.947	5.65
1905	156	385	506	62	40	.935	5.71
1906	138	309	461	41	47	.949	5.58
1907	147	338	517	54	54	.941	5.82
1908	137	286	510	41	45	.951	5.81
1909	87	193	279	27	34	.946	5.43
1910	98	258	344	33	37	.948	6.14
1911	124	280	417	42	47	.943	5.62
1912	86	185	271	28	29	.942	5.30
1913	38	67	96	12	8	.931	4.29
1914	19	26	46	9		.889	3.79
1915	9	11	17	5		.848	3.11
1916	5	8	27	2		.946	7.00
1917	2	4	6	1	0	.909	5.00
1918	12	20	27	5	5	.904	3.92
	1823	4145	6323	686	638	.938	5.74

Assists per 154 Games: 534

PLAYER: HONUS WAGNER

	BATTING														BASERUNNING				PERCENTAGES			VALUES			
Year	G	AB	H	2B	3B	HR	(Hm | Rd)	TB	R	RBI	BB	IBB	HBP	SH	SF	SB	CS	SB%	GIDP	Avg.	Slug	On Base	Runs	Win—Loss	Pct.	AV
1897	61	241	83	17	4	2	(	)	114	38	39	15			5		19				.344	.473	.375	53	4—2	.669	4
1898	151	591	180	31	4	10	(	)	249	80	105	31			10		27				.305	.421	.334	97	9—7	.570	12
1899	147	571	197	47	13	7	(	)	291	102	113	40			4		37				.345	.510	.385	131	11—4	.742	13
1900	135	528	201	45	22	4	(	)	302	107	100	41			4		38				.381	.572	.422	148	11—2	.852	17
1901	141	556	196	39	10	6	(	)	273	100	126	53			10		49				.353	.491	.402	136	12—3	.800	17
1902	137	538	177	33	16	3	(	)	251	105	91	43			8		42				.329	.467	.374	114	11—3	.774	15
1903	129	512	182	30	19	5	(	)	265	97	101	44			8		46				.355	.518	.401	130	11—3	.795	16
1904	132	490	171	44	14	4	(	)	255	97	75	59			5		53				.349	.520	.415	133	11—2	.870	17
1905	147	548	199	32	14	6	(	)	277	114	101	54			7		57				.363	.505	.415	144	12—2	.866	17
1906	142	516	175	38	9	2	(	)	237	103	71	58			6		53				.339	.459	.402	121	12—2	.865	17
1907	142	515	180	38	14	6	(	)	264	98	82	46			14		61				.350	.513	.393	135	12—2	.881	16
1908	151	568	201	39	19	10	(	)	308	100	109	54			14		53				.354	.542	.401	146	13—2	.891	20
1909	137	495	168	39	10	5	(	)	242	92	100	66		3	27		35				.339	.489	.401	117	12—2	.836	18
1910	150	556	178	34	8	4	(	)	240	90	81	59		5	20		24				.320	.432	.378	103	11—4	.732	14
1911	130	473	158	23	16	9	(	)	240	87	89	67		6	12		20				.334	.507	.414	109	10—3	.804	17
1912	145	558	181	35	20	7	(	)	277	91	102	59		6	11		26				.324	.496	.388	118	12—4	.763	17
1913	114	413	124	18	4	3	(	)	159	51	56	26		5	10		21				.300	.385	.341	60	7—5	.613	10
1914	150	552	139	15	9	1	(	)	175	60	50	51		2	11		23				.252	.317	.312	60	9—8	.544	11
1915	151	566	155	32	17	6	(	)	239	68	78	39		4	16		22	15	.60		.274	.422	.317	81	11—6	.663	11
1916	123	432	124	15	9	1	(	)	160	45	39	34		8	10		11				.287	.370	.343	58	8—4	.658	8
1917	74	230	61	7	1	0	(	)	70	15	24	24		1	9		5				.265	.304	.326	25	4—3	.536	2
17.2 yrs	2789 607	10449	3430 199	651 38	252 15	101 6	(	)	4888 284	1740 101	1732 101	963 56		40	221 13		722 42	15	.60		.328 .328	.468 .468	.380 .380	2219	213—70	.752	289

Runs created estimates prior to 1900 are of indeterminate accuracy.

Teams: Louisville, N.L. 1897–1899; Pittsburgh, 1900–1917
Points in MVP Voting: 1911, 23 (4th, .36); 1913, 11 (9th, .17); 1914, 0. TOTAL: .53 Award Shares.
Reported Salaries: Signed at Patterson, 1897, for $562.50 for the season. Went to Louisville same year for $250/month; 1900, $2,100; 1908, $10,000. One report says he then signed for $10,000 each year for rest of career.

FIELDING SHORTSTOP

Year	G	PO	AS	Err	DP	Pct.	Range
1901	61	177	226	35	31	.920	6.61
1902	45	89	146	29	12	.890	5.22
1903	111	303	397	50	51	.933	6.31
1904	121	274	367	49	46	.929	5.30
1905	145	353	517	60	64	.935	6.00
1906	137	334	473	51	57	.941	5.89
1907	138	314	428	49	32	.938	5.38
1908	151	354	469	50	47	.943	5.45
1909	136	344	430	49	58	.940	5.69
1910	138	337	413	51	62	.936	5.43
1911	101	221	312	39	55	.932	5.28
1912	143	341	462	32	74	.962	5.62
1913	105	289	323	24	47	.962	5.83
1914	132	322	424	39	45	.950	5.65
1915	131	298	395	38	53	.948	5.29
1916	92	226	261	30	32	.942	5.29
1917	1	0	2	0	0	1.000	2.00
	1888	4576	6045	675	766	.940	5.63

Assists per 154 Games: 493

PLAYER: JOE TINKER

Year	G	AB	H	2B	3B	HR	(Hm	Rd)	TB	R	RBI	BB	IBB	HBP	SH	SF	SB	CS	SB%	GIDP	Avg.	Slug	On Base	Runs	WinLoss	Pct.	AV
1902	133	501	137	19	5	2	(	)	172	55	54	26			18		27				.273	.343	.299	65	9–6	.585	10
1903	124	460	134	21	7	2	(	)	175	67	70	37			13		27				.291	.380	.335	73	8–6	.582	10
1904	141	488	108	12	13	3	(	)	155	55	41	29			12		41				.221	.318	.259	54	8–8	.495	9
1905	149	547	135	18	8	2	(	)	175	70	66	34			29		31				.247	.320	.277	65	9–8	.521	10
1906	148	523	122	18	4	1	(	)	151	75	64	43			36		30				.233	.289	.274	58	8–9	.482	8
1907	116	400	88	11	3	1	(	)	108	36	36	25			16		20				.220	.270	.256	37	6–7	.462	6
1908	157	548	146	23	14	6	(	)	215	67	68	32			29	8	30				.266	.392	.292	75	11–6	.626	11
1909	143	516	132	26	11	4	(	)	192	56	57	17	0		22		23				.256	.372	.268	59	9–7	.567	11
1910	133	473	136	25	9	3	(	)	188	48	69	24	0		18		20				.288	.397	.311	66	8–6	.596	10
1911	144	536	149	24	12	4	(	)	209	61	69	39	0		18		30				.278	.390	.317	77	9–7	.556	12
1912	142	550	155	24	7	0	(	)	193	80	75	38	2		34		25				.282	.351	.313	73	8–9	.465	13
1913	110	382	121	20	13	1	(	)	170	47	57	20	1		15		10				.317	.445	.340	61	7–4	.643	8
1914	126	438	112	21	7	2	(	)	153	50	46	38					19				.256	.349	.315	53	7–6	.537	9
1915	31	67	18	2	1	0	(	)	22	7	9	13					3				.269	.328	.388	9	1–1	.609	1
1916	7	10	1	0	0	0	(	)	1	0	1	1		0	0		0				.100	.100	.182	0	0–0	.019	0
11.1 yrs	1804	6439	1694	264	114	31	(	)	2279	774	782	416		3	260		336				.263	.354	.297	827	107–90	.545	128
		578	152	24	10	3			205	70	70	37			26		30				.263	.354	.297				

Teams: Chicago, N.L. 1902–1912; Cincinnati, 1913; Chicago, F.L. 1914–1915; Chicago, N.L., 1916.

Points in MVP Voting: 1911, 11 (10th, .17); 1913, 0; 1914, 0.

Reported Salaries: Denver, 1900—$75/month; 1902—$1,500; 1913—$10,000; 1914 —$12,000; 1915—$12,000.

Explanation for Gaps in Career or Sudden Changes in Productivity:
1907—Operation for appendicitis at beginning of season.

Other Notes: The 1909 *Spalding Guide,* on a whim, listed the three National League players having the most fly ball sacrifice hits in 1908, although these were not officially separated from other sacrifices anywhere else. Tinker was one of the three, with eight; these are counted here as both sacrifice hits (SH) and sacrifice flies (SF).

FIELDING SHORTSTOP

Year	G	PO	AS	E	DP	Pct.	Range
1902	124	243	453	72	47	.906	5.61
1903	107	229	362	61	37	.906	5.52
1904	140	327	465	64	54	.925	5.66
1905	149	345	527	56	67	.940	5.85
1906	147	288	472	45	55	.944	5.17
1907	112	215	388	39	45	.939	5.38
1908	157	314	570	39	48	.958	5.63
1909	143	320	470	50	49	.940	5.52
1910	131	277	411	42	54	.942	5.25
1911	143	333	486	55	56	.937	5.73
1912	142	354	470	50	73	.943	5.80
1913	101	223	320	18	34	.968	5.38
1916	4	3	7	1	0	.909	2.50
	1600	3471	5401	592	619	.937	5.54

Assists per 154 Games: 520

PLAYER: ART FLETCHER

			BATTING														BASERUNNING				PERCENTAGES			VALUES			
Year	G	AB	H	2B	3B	HR	(Hm Rd)	TB	R	RBI	BB	IBB	HBP	SH	SF	SB	CS	SB%	GIDP	Avg.	Slug	On Base	Runs	Win–Loss	Pct.	AV
1909	29	98	21	0	1	0	( )	23	7	6	1		2	0		0				.214	.235	.238	5	1–2	.174	1
1910	51	125	28	2	1	0	( )	32	12	13	4		0	3		9				.224	.256	.242	10	1–3	.278	1
1911	112	326	104	17	8	1	( )	140	73	37	30		14	7		20				.319	.429	.393	64	7–2	.738	6
1912	129	419	118	17	8	2	( )	157	64	57	16		14	14		16				.282	.375	.320	57	6–6	.506	8
1913	136	538	160	20	9	4	( )	210	76	71	24		15	17		32				.297	.390	.335	80	10–5	.647	11
1914	135	514	147	26	8	2	( )	195	62	79	22		13	20		15				.286	.379	.320	68	8–7	.555	11
1915	149	562	143	17	7	3	( )	183	59	74	6		14	17		12	18	.40		.254	.326	.272	53	6–11	.383	11
1916	133	500	143	23	8	3	( )	191	53	66	13		14	15		15				.286	.382	.314	64	9–6	.613	11
1917	151	557	145	24	5	4	( )	191	70	56	23		19	9		12				.260	.343	.308	60	9–7	.538	10
1918	124	468	123	20	2	0	( )	147	51	47	18		15	12		12				.263	.314	.304	48	7–7	.478	8
1919	127	488	135	20	5	3	( )	174	54	54	9		7	12		6				.277	.357	.293	52	7–7	.480	10
1920	143	550	156	32	9	4	( )	218	57	62	16		9	19		7	8	.47		.284	.396	.305	66	7–9	.479	10
1922	110	396	111	20	5	7	( )	162	46	53	21		5	9		3	2	.60		.280	.409	.318	53	5–7	.424	7
1529	5541	1534	238	76	33	( )		2023	684	675	203		141	154		159	28	.44		.277	.365	.311	678	82–80	.504	105
9.4 yrs		587	163	25	8	3			214	72	72	22		15	16		17				.277	.365	.311				

Teams: New York, N.L. 1909–1920; Philadelphia, 1920, 1922.

Points in MVP Voting: 1911, 0; 1913, 7 (.11); 1914, 5 (.08). TOTAL: .19 Award Shares.

Explanation for Gaps in Career or Sudden Changes in Productivity:
1921—Following the death of his father in 1920, Fletcher retired to run the family business.

FIELDING SHORTSTOP

Year	G	PO	AS	E	DP	Pct.	Range
1909	19	40	52	11		.893	4.84
1910	22	31	37	8		.895	3.09
1911	74	116	224	27		.926	4.59
1912	126	237	428	52	60	.927	5.28
1913	136	245	435	50	42	.932	5.00
1914	135	299	446	63		.922	5.52
1915	149	302	544	58	76	.936	5.68
1916	133	253	497	48	56	.940	5.64
1917	151	276	565	39	71	.956	5.57
1918	124	268	484	32	54	.959	6.06
1919	127	265	521	47	49	.944	6.19
1920	142	302	522	48	63	.945	5.80
1922	106	202	379	38	63	.939	5.48
	1444	2836	5134	521	534	.939	5.52

Assists per 154 Games: 548

PLAYER: RAY CHAPMAN

				BATTING											BASERUNNING				PERCENTAGES			VALUES		
Year	G	AB	H	2B	3B	HR	(Hm	Rd)	TB	R	RBI	BB	IBB	HBP	SH	SF	SB	CS	SB%	GIDP	Avg.	Slug	On Base	Runs	Win–Loss	Pct.	AV
1912	31	109	34	6	3	0	(0	0)	46	29	19	10		1	12		10				.312	.422	.341	22	2–1	.674	2
1913	140	508	131	19	7	3	(1	2)	173	78	39	46		2	48		29				.258	.341	.296	67	9–8	.533	9
1914	106	375	103	16	10	2	(0	2)	145	59	42	48		1	18		24	9	.73		.275	.387	.344	59	7–4	.631	8
1915	154	570	154	14	17	3	(2	1)	211	101	67	70		3	29		36	15	.71		.270	.370	.338	85	11–7	.609	12
1916	109	346	80	10	5	0	(0	0)	100	50	27	50		1	40		21	14	.60		.231	.289	.300	41	5–7	.407	6
1917	156	563	170	28	12	3	(2	0)	231	98	36	61		0	67		52				.302	.410	.334	106	13–5	.732	16
1918	128	446	119	19	8	1	(0	1)	157	84	32	84		6	35		30				.267	.352	.366	74	9–5	.675	10
1919	115	433	130	23	10	3	(2	1)	182	75	53	31		3	50		18				.300	.420	.317	72	8–5	.614	10
1920	111	435	132	27	8	3	(1	2)	184	97	49	52		2	41		13	9	.59		.303	.423	.351	72	7–6	.545	12
	1050	3785	1053	162	80	18	(8	9)	1429	671	364	452		19	340		233	47	.67		.278	.378	.332	598	72–48	.601	85
6.5 yrs		584	162	25	12	3			220	104	56	70		3	52		36				.278	.378	.332				

Teams: Cleveland, 1912–1920.

Explanation for Gaps in Career or Sudden Changes in Productivity:

1914—Ankle injury.

1916—Injury described by 1917 *Reach Guide* as "broken bone," by 1969 Macmillan as "knee injury." The Indians were in first place at the time of the injury but fell apart following injuries to Chapman and two pitchers and finished sixth.

1920—Killed by pitch.

FIELDING SHORTSTOP

Year	G	PO	AS	E	DP	Pct.	Range
1912	31	70	72	15	10	.904	4.58
1913	138	299	408	48	59	.936	5.12
1914	72	161	187	33	24	.913	4.83
1915	154	378	469	50	38	.944	5.50
1916	52	117	170	20	20	.935	5.52
1917	156	360	528	59	71	.938	5.69
1918	128	321	398	49	42	.936	5.62
1919	115	255	347	36	44	.944	5.23
1920	111	243	371	26	43	.959	5.53
	957	2204	2950	336	351	.939	5.39

Assists per 154 games: 475

PLAYER: RABBIT MARANVILLE

Year	G	AB	H	2B	3B	HR	(Hm RD)	TB	R	RBI	BB	IBB	HBP	SH	SF	SB	CS	SB%	GIDP	Avg.	Slug	On Base	Runs	Win–Loss	Pct.	AV
1912	26	86	18	2	0	0	( )	20	8	8	9			1	5	1				.209	.233	.277	7	0–2	.168	1
1913	143	571	141	13	8	2	( )	176	68	48	68			3	17	25				.247	.308	.322	64	7–10	.420	11
1914	156	586	144	23	6	4	( )	191	74	78	45			6	27	28				.246	.326	.294	66	9–10	.467	12
1915	149	509	124	23	6	2	( )	165	51	43	45			2	23	18	12	.60		.244	.324	.295	56	8–8	.483	9
1916	155	604	142	16	13	4	( )	196	79	38	50			2	24	32	15	.68		.235	.325	.285	65	10–9	.536	10
1917	142	561	146	19	13	3	( )	200	69	43	40			2	10	27				.260	.357	.307	67	9–7	.579	11
1918	11	38	12	0	1	0	( )	14	3	3	4			0	0	0				.316	.368	.381	5	1–0	.674	1
1919	131	480	128	18	10	5	( )	181	44	43	36			1	12	12				.267	.377	.312	59	9–7	.570	9
1920	134	493	131	19	15	1	( )	183	48	43	28			0	13	14	11	.56		.266	.371	.298	55	7–8	.477	10
1921	153	612	180	25	12	1	( )	232	90	70	47			3	23	25	12	.68		.294	.379	.336	82	10–8	.546	12
1922	155	672	198	26	15	0	( )	254	115	63	61			2	12	24	13	.65		.295	.378	.349	92	9–10	.463	12
1923	141	581	161	19	9	1	( )	201	78	41	42			1	9	14	11	.56		.277	.346	.322	66	7–10	.393	12
1924	152	594	158	33	20	2	( )	237	62	71	35			0	11	18	14	.56		.266	.399	.302	70	8–10	.459	11
1925	75	266	62	10	3	0	( )	78	37	23	29			0	10	6	5	.55		.233	.293	.298	25	2–6	.272	4
1926	78	234	55	8	5	0	( )	73	32	24	26			0	6	7				.235	.312	.305	23	3–4	.370	3
1927	9	29	7	1	0	0	( )	8	0	0	2			0	0	0				.241	.276	.290	2	0–1	.256	0
1928	112	366	88	14	10	1	( )	125	40	34	36			1	9	3				.240	.342	.303	39	4–7	.364	5
1929	146	560	159	26	10	0	( )	205	87	55	47			4	23	13				.284	.366	.331	70	7–9	.430	12
1930	142	558	157	26	8	2	( )	205	85	43	48			5	17	9				.281	.367	.334	70	7–9	.438	11
1931	145	562	146	22	5	0	( )	178	69	33	56			2	16	9				.260	.317	.321	61	8–9	.474	9
1932	149	571	134	20	4	0	( )	162	67	37	46			3	15	4				.235	.284	.288	50	6–12	.318	8
1933	143	478	104	15	4	0	( )	127	46	38	36			1	17	2			17	.218	.266	.265	35	5–11	.304	5
1935	23	67	10	2	0	0	( )	12	3	5	3			0	1				4	.149	.179	.183	2	0–2	.025	0
16.5 yrs	2670	10078	2605	380	177	28	( )	3423	1255	884	839		39	300		291	93	.62		.258	.340	.309	1132	134–169	.443	178
	611	158	23	11	2			208	76	54	51		2	18		18				.258	.340	.309				

Teams: Boston, N.L. 1912–1920; Pittsburgh, 1921–1924; Chicago, N.L. 1925; Brooklyn, 1926; St. Louis, N.L., 1927–1928; Boston, N.L. 1932, 1933, 1935.

Points in MVP Voting: 1913, 23 (3rd, .36); 1914, 44 (2nd, .69); 1924, 33 (7th, .41); 1926, 0; 1931, 11 (.17); 1932, 13 (8th, .15); 1933, 11 (.14); 1935, 0. TOTAL: 1.92 Award Shares.

Reported Salaries: 1912, $200/month; 1914, $3,500.

Explanation for Gaps in Career or Sudden Changes in Productivity:
1918—Volunteered for U.S. Navy early in season.
1925—Broken leg.
1926—Unconditionally released halfway through the season.
1927—Played at Rochester in International League (135 games).
1934—Broke leg in spring training—out for season.

FIELDING SHORTSTOP

Year	G	PO	AS	Err	DP	Pct.	Range
1912	26	46	97	11	8*	.929	5.50
1913	143	317	475	43	49	.949	5.54
1914	154	407	574	65	92	.938	6.37
1915	149	391	486	55	63	.941	5.89
1916	155	386	515	50	79	.947	5.81
1917	142	341	474	46	67	.947	5.74
1918	11	34	34	5	5*	.932	6.18
1919	131	361	488	53	74	.941	6.48
1920	133	354	462	45	62	.948	6.14
1921	153	325	529	34	72	.962	5.58
1922	138	359	453	33	81	.961	5.88
1923	141	332	505	30	94	.965	5.94
1925	74	162	261	20	51	.955	5.72
1926	60	138	192	18	28	.948	5.50
1927	9	17	34	2	6	.962	5.67
1928	112	236	362	19	57	.969	5.34
1929	146	319	536	35	104	.961	5.86
1930	138	343	445	29	98	.965	5.71
1931	137	271	432	38	93	.949	5.13
	2152	5139	7354	631	1183	.952	5.81

Assists per 154 Games: 526
*Estimated.

PLAYER: DAVE BANCROFT

							BATTING										BASERUNNING				PERCENTAGES			VALUES			
Year	G	AB	H	2B	3B	HR	(Hm Rd)	TB	R	RBI	BB	IBB	HBP	SH	SF	SB	CS	SB%	GIDP	Avg.	Slug	On Base	Runs	Win–Loss	Pct.	AV
1915	153	563	143	18	2	7	( )	186	85	30	77		2	23		15	27	.36		.254	.330	.334	69	10–7	.573	10
1916	142	477	101	10	0	3	( )	120	53	33	74		4	16		15				.212	.252	.313	46	7–9	.434	9
1917	127	478	116	22	5	4	( )	160	56	43	44		0	18		14				.243	.335	.296	52	7–7	.509	7
1918	125	499	132	19	4	0	( )	159	69	26	54		1	7		11				.265	.319	.333	58	8–7	.541	9
1919	92	335	91	13	7	0	( )	118	45	25	31		0	9		8				.272	.352	.325	41	5–4	.563	5
1920	150	613	183	36	9	0	( )	237	102	36	42		2	16		8	12	.40		.299	.387	.337	80	10–8	.561	12
1921	153	606	193	26	15	6	( )	267	121	67	66		4	22		17	10	.63		.318	.441	.377	106	11–6	.623	15
1922	156	651	209	41	5	4	( )	272	117	60	79		3	12		16	11	.59		.321	.418	.391	111	11–7	.622	15
1923	107	444	135	33	3	1	( )	177	80	31	62		1	6		8	7	.53		.304	.399	.386	72	7–5	.572	10
1924	79	319	89	11	1	2	( )	108	49	21	37		1	5		4	4	.50		.279	.339	.351	40	5–5	.507	5
1925	128	479	153	29	8	2	( )	204	75	49	64		0	17		7	4	.64		.319	.426	.388	85	8–5	.625	13
1926	127	453	141	18	6	1	( )	174	70	44	64		2	22		3				.311	.384	.383	72	8–5	.617	11
1927	111	375	91	13	4	1	( )	115	44	31	43		1	8		5				.243	.307	.316	38	4–7	.355	6
1928	149	515	127	19	5	0	( )	156	47	51	59		2	15		7				.247	.303	.318	54	6–9	.408	10
1929	104	358	99	11	3	1	( )	119	35	44	29		0	16		7				.277	.332	.318	40	3–7	.327	6
1930	10	17	1	1	0	0	( )	2	0	0	2		0	0		0				.059	.118	.158	0	0–1	.011	0
	1913	7182	2004	320	77	32	( )	2574	1048	591	827		23	212		145	75	.50		.279	.358	.346	964	111–99	.529	143
11.8 yrs		608	170	27	7	3	( )	218	89	50	70		2	18		12				.279	.358	.346				

Teams: Philadelphia, N.L. 1915–1919; Philadelphia, N.L./New York, N.L. 1920; New York, N.L. 1921–1923; Boston, N.L. 1924–1927; Brooklyn, 1928–1929; New York, N.L. 1930.

Points in MVP Voting: 1926, 17 (10th, .21); 1927, 0.

Explanation for Gaps in Career or Sudden Changes in Productivity:

1923—Caught a cold while riding in a Pullman sleeper with the window open on a trip back from St. Louis in mid-June. Cold developed into a serious dose of pneumonia, and Bancroft was out about two months.

1924—Appendix ruptured, July 1; out until September 10.

FIELDING SHORTSTOP

Year	G	PO	AS	Err	DP	Pct.	Range
1915	153	336	492	64	60	.928	5.41
1916	142	326	510	60	64	.933	5.89
1917	120	274	439	49	56	.936	5.94
1918	125	371	457	64	57	.928	6.62
1919	88	242	306	28	43	.951	6.23
1920	150	362	598	45	95	.955	6.40
1921	153	396	546	39	105	.960	6.16
1922	156	405	579	62	93	.941	6.31
1923	96	246	381	43	53	.936	6.53
1924	79	186	259	18	57	.961	5.63
1925	125	300	459	44	81	.945	6.07
1926	123	317	398	33	75	.956	5.81
1927	104	275	329	39	66	.939	5.81
1928	149	350	484	46	66	.948	5.60
1929	102	224	309	25	45	.955	5.23
1930	8	13	15	1	2	.966	3.50
	1873	4623	6561	660	1018	.944	5.97

Assists per 154 Games: 539

PLAYER: JOE SEWELL

	BATTING													BASERUNNING				PERCENTAGES			VALUES			
Year	G	AB	H	2B	3B	HR	(Hm	Rd)	TB	R	RBI	BB	IBB	HBP	SH	SF	SB	CS	SB%	GIDP	Avg.	Slug	On Base	Runs	Win–Loss	Pct.	AV
1920	22	70	23	4	1	0	(0	0)	29	14	12	9			1	3	1	0	1.00		.329	.414	.398	13	1–1	.653	1
1921	154	572	182	36	12	4	(1	3)	254	101	91	80		11	20		7	6	.54		.318	.444	.400	109	10–6	.623	12
1922	153	558	167	28	7	2	(1	1)	215	80	83	73		6	19		10	12	.45		.299	.385	.375	86	8–8	.516	12
1923	153	553	195	41	10	3	(1	2)	265	98	109	98		7	24		9	6	.60		.353	.479	.440	128	11–4	.720	16
1924	153	594	188	45	5	4	(4	0)	255	99	104	67		2	22		3	2	.60		.316	.429	.375	102	10–7	.592	15
1925	155	608	204	37	7	1	(0	1)	258	78	98	64		4	23		7	6	.54		.336	.424	.389	106	10–7	.607	16
1926	154	578	187	41	5	4	(1	3)	250	91	85	65		8	21		17	7	.71		.324	.433	.387	104	11–5	.685	14
1927	153	569	180	48	5	1	(0	1)	241	83	92	51		9	23		3				.316	.424	.368	91	10–6	.605	13
1928	155	588	190	40	2	4	(1	3)	246	79	70	58		7	25		7	1	.87		.323	.418	.376	100	10–6	.617	14
1929	152	578	182	38	3	7	(2	5)	247	90	73	48		5	41		6	6	.50		.315	.427	.350	93	10–7	.567	12
1930	109	353	102	17	6	0	(0	0)	131	44	48	42		6	13		1	4	.20		.289	.371	.355	49	4–6	.401	6
1931	130	484	146	22	1	6	(4	2)	188	102	64	62		9	17		1	1	.50		.302	.388	.379	78	7–7	.485	11
1932	124	503	137	21	3	11	(11	0)	197	95	68	56		3	14		0	2	.00		.272	.392	.340	71	6–8	.433	8
1933	135	524	143	18	1	2	(2	0)	169	87	54	71		1	10		2	2	.50		.273	.323	.355	65	6–9	.376	9
	1902	7132	2226	436	68	49	(28	21)	2945	1141	1051	844		79	275		74	55	.56		.312	.413	.378	1198	113–88	.563	159
11.7 yrs		607	190	37	6	4			251	97	90	72		6	23		6				.312	.413	.378				

Teams: Cleveland, 1920–1930; New York, A.L. 1931–1933.
Points in MVP Voting: 1922, 0; 1923, 20 (4th, .31); 1924, 9 (9th, .14); 1926, 0; 1927, 9 (10th, .14); 1931, 0; 1932, 0; 1933, 0. TOTAL: .59 Award Shares.
Other Notes: Named outstanding major league shortstop in 1926 by *The Sporting News*.

FIELDING SHORTSTOP

Year	G	PO	AS	Err	DP	Pct.	Range
1920	22	44	70	15	14	.884	5.18
1921	154	319	480	47	75	.944	5.19
1922	139	295	462	49	72	.939	5.45
1923	151	286	497	59	82	.930	5.19
1924	153	349	514	36	76	.960	5.64
1925	153	314	529	29	80	.967	5.51
1926	154	326	463	37	86	.955	5.12
1927	153	361	480	33	80	.962	5.50
1928	137	297	438	28	103	.963	5.36
	1216	2591	3933	333	668	.951	5.37

Assists per 154 Games: 498

PLAYER: TRAVIS JACKSON

	BATTING																BASERUNNING				PERCENTAGES			VALUES			
Year	G	AB	H	2B	3B	HR	(Hm Rd)	TB	R	RBI	BB	IBB	HBP	SH	SF	SB	CS	SB%	GIDP	Avg.	Slug	On Base	Runs	Win—Loss	Pct.	AV
1922	3	8	0	0	0	0	( )	0	1	0	0		0	0		0	0	.00		.000	.000	.000	0	0—0	.000	
1923	96	327	90	12	7	4	( )	128	45	37	22		0	2		3	3	.50		.275	.391	.319	41	4—5	.432	6
1924	151	596	180	26	8	11	( )	255	81	76	21		0	16		6	7	.46		.302	.428	.318	80	8—9	.487	12
1925	112	411	117	15	2	9	( )	163	51	59	24		2	7		8	3	.73		.285	.397	.322	54	6—6	.485	7
1926	111	385	126	24	8	8	( )	190	64	51	20		1	14		2				.327	.494	.350	66	7—3	.669	9
1927	127	469	149	29	4	14	( )	228	67	98	32		1	15		8				.318	.486	.352	80	8—5	.609	12
1928	150	537	145	35	6	14	( )	234	73	77	56		0	33		8				.270	.436	.321	79	8—8	.511	14
1929	149	551	162	21	12	21	( )	270	92	94	64		0	19		10				.294	.490	.356	98	9—6	.589	15
1930	116	431	146	27	8	13	( )	228	70	82	32		1	17		6				.339	.529	.372	85	7—4	.615	13
1931	145	555	172	26	10	5	( )	233	65	71	36		1	2		13				.310	.420	.352	81	9—6	.603	12
1932	52	195	50	17	1	4	( )	81	23	38	13		2	1		1				.256	.415	.308	25	3—3	.468	3
1933	53	122	30	5	0	0	( )	35	11	12	8		0	4		2			3	.246	.287	.284	10	1—2	.374	1
1934	137	523	140	26	7	16	( )	228	75	101	37		0	14		1			15	.268	.436	.308	71	8—7	.527	12
1935	128	511	154	20	12	9	( )	225	74	80	29		1	15		3			12	.301	.440	.331	76	8—6	.572	9
1936	126	465	107	8	1	7	( )	138	41	53	18		1	12		0			9	.230	.297	.254	36	4—11	.251	5
	1656	6086	1768	291	86	135	( )	2636	833	929	412		10	171		71	13	.57	39	.291	.433	.328	881	90—83	.522	130
10.2 yrs		595	173	28	8	13		258	81	91	40		1	17		7				.291	.433	.328				

Teams: New York, N.L. 1922–1936.

Points in MVP Voting: 1926, 0; 1927, 42 (5th, .53); 1931, 15 (10th, .17); 1932, 0; 1933, 0; 1934, 39 (4th, .49); 1935, 1 (.01). TOTAL: 1.20 Award Shares.

Explanation for Gaps in Career or Sudden Changes in Productivity:

1925—Unknown injuries.

1932—Broken knee; out last half of season.

1933—Knees still bothering him a lot; lost job and did not play well until September, when Vergez was lost to appendicitis, and Jackson took his job.

Other Notes: Named outstanding major league shortstop for 1927, 1928, and 1929 by *The Sporting News*.

FIELDING SHORTSTOP

Year	G	PO	AS	Err	DP	Pct.	Range
1922	3	3	7	1	1	.909	3.33
1923	60	86	210	18	26	.943	4.93
1924	151	332	534	58	101	.937	5.74
1925	110	277	366	40	64	.941	5.85
1926	108	256	351	24	71	.962	5.62
1927	124	287	444	37	85	.952	5.90
1928	149	354	547	45	112	.952	6.05
1929	149	329	552	28	110	.969	5.91
1930	115	218	441	30	72	.956	5.73
1931	145	303	496	25	79	.970	5.51
1932	52	106	166	22	31	.925	5.23
1933	21	32	41	9	13	.890	3.48
1934	130	283	458	43	60	.945	5.70
1936	9	11	22	1	2	.971	3.67
	1326	2877	4635	381	827	.952	5.66

Assists per 154 Games: 538

PLAYER: JOE CRONIN

				BATTING														BASERUNNING				PERCENTAGES			VALUES			
Year	G	AB	H	2B	3B	HR	(Hm	Rd)	TB	R	RBI	BB	IBB	HBP	SH	SF	SB	CS	SB%	GIDP	Avg.	Slug	On Base	Runs	Win–Loss	Pct.	AV
1926	38	83	22	2	2	0	(0	0)	28	9	11	6			0	3	0				.265	.337	.304	9	1–2	.370	1
1927	12	22	5	1	0	0	(0	0)	6	2	3	2			0	0	0				.227	.273	.292	2	0–0	.246	0
1928	63	227	55	10	4	0	(0	0)	73	23	25	22			0	10	4	0	1.00		.242	.322	.297	25	3–4	.368	3
1929	145	494	139	29	8	8	(0	8)	208	72	61	85		1	21		5	9	.36		.281	.421	.374	84	8–6	.571	13
1930	154	587	203	41	9	13	(2	11)	301	127	126	72		5	22		17	10	.63		.346	.513	.408	129	11–5	.711	18
1931	156	611	187	44	13	12	(3	9)	293	103	126	81		4	4		10	9	.53		.306	.480	.389	116	11–6	.664	16
1932	143	557	177	43	18	6	(2	4)	274	95	116	66		3	3		7	5	.58		.318	.492	.391	109	10–5	.678	16
1933	152	602	186	45	11	5	(1	4)	268	89	118	87		2	5		5	4	.56		.309	.445	.395	111	11–5	.669	16
1934	127	504	143	30	9	7	(4	3)	212	68	101	53		1	9		8	0	1.00		.284	.421	.347	78	8–6	.571	12
1935	144	556	164	37	14	9	(6	3)	256	70	95	63		3	8		3	3	.50		.295	.460	.365	96	10–5	.653	11
1936	81	295	83	22	4	2	(1	1)	119	36	43	32		1	6		1	3	.25		.281	.403	.347	43	4–4	.524	6
1937	148	570	175	40	4	18	(11	7)	277	102	110	84		6	11		5	3	.62		.307	.486	.395	116	10–5	.685	15
1938	143	530	172	51	5	17	(12	5)	284	98	94	91		5	11		7	5	.58		.325	.536	.421	126	10–4	.732	18
1939	143	520	160	33	3	19	(12	7)	256	97	107	87		0	20		6	6	.50	18	.308	.492	.394	108	9–6	.628	17
1940	149	548	156	35	6	24	(14	10)	275	104	111	83		1	13		7	5	.58	6	.285	.502	.372	109	10–6	.623	14
1941	143	518	161	38	8	16	(9	7)	263	98	95	82		1	14		1	4	.20	20	.311	.508	.397	105	10–5	.653	15
1942	45	79	24	3	0	4	(2	2)	39	7	24	15		0	1		0	1	.00	3	.304	.494	.411	16	2–1	.723	2
1943	59	77	24	4	0	5	(3	2)	43	8	29	11		0	0		0	0	.00	3	.312	.558	.398	17	2–0	.819	2
1944	76	191	46	7	0	5	(4	1)	68	24	28	34		1	5		1	4	.20	7	.241	.356	.351	24	3–3	.447	2
1945	3	8	3	0	0	0	(0	0)	3	1	3	1		3	0	0	0	0	.00	0	.375	.375	.545	2	0–0	.883	0
	2124	7579	2285	515	118	170	(86	84)	3546	1233	1424	1059		34	166		87	71	.55	57	.301	.468	.382	1424	132–77	.631	197
13.1 yrs		578	174	39	9	13			270	94	109	81		3	13		7	6	.55	15	.301	.468	.382				

Teams: Pittsburgh, 1926–1927; Washington, 1928–1934; Boston, A, 1935–1945

Points in MVP Voting: 1926, 0; 1931, 37 (2nd, .58); 1932, 11 (9th, .13); 1933, 62 (2nd. .78); 1934, 0; 1935, 0; 1937, 19 (7th, .24); 1938, 92 (6th, .27); 1939, 15 (.04); 1940, 3 (.01); 1941, 26 (.08); 1942, 0; 1943, 3 (.01); 1944, 0. TOTAL: 2.94 Award Shares.

Explanation for Gaps in Career or Sudden Changes in Productivity:

1927—Sat on bench almost entire season; released to minors (Kansas City) after the year.

1936—Broken finger.

1945—Fractured his right leg, April 19; retired.

Other Notes: Named outstanding major league shortstop 1930, 1931, 1932, 1933, 1934, 1938, 1939, by *The Sporting News*.

Selected as American League Most Valuable Player by *The Sporting News,* 1930 (credited with .80 award share for this).

FIELDING SHORTSTOP

Year	G	PO	AS	Err	DP	Pct.	Range
1926	7	20	18	3	1	.927	5.43
1927	4	8	12	0	0	1.000	5.00
1928	63	133	190	16	42	.953	5.13
1929	143	285	459	62	92	.923	5.20
1930	154	336	509	35	95	.960	5.49
1931	155	323	488	43	94	.950	5.23
1932	141	306	448	32	95	.959	5.35
1933	152	297	528	34	95	.960	5.43
1934	127	246	486	38	86	.951	5.76
1935	139	264	431	37	86	.949	5.00
1936	60	115	191	23	34	.930	5.10
1937	148	300	414	31	89	.958	4.82
1938	142	304	449	36	110	.954	5.30
1939	142	306	437	32	93	.959	5.23
1940	146	252	443	38	89	.948	4.76
1941	119	225	324	24	64	.958	4.61
1942	1	1	2	0	0	1.000	3.00
	1843	3721	5829	484	1165	.952	5.18

Assists per 154 Games: 487

PLAYER: DICK BARTELL

Year	G	AB	H	2B	3B	HR	(Hm	Rd)	TB	R	RBI	BB	IBB	HBP	SH	SF	SB	CS	SB%	GIDP	Avg.	Slug	On Base	Runs	Win—Loss	Pct.	AV
1927	1	2	0	0	0	0	(	)	0	0	0	2		0	0		0				0	0	.500	0	0—0	.306	0
1928	72	233	71	8	4	1	(	)	90	27	36	21		6	11		4				.305	.386	.362	34	3—3	.509	4
1929	143	610	184	40	13	2	(	)	256	101	57	40		2	22		11				.302	.420	.335	86	8—9	.457	11
1930	129	475	152	32	13	4	(	)	222	69	75	39		5	22		8				.320	.467	.362	82	7—6	.523	11
1931	135	554	160	43	7	0	(	)	217	88	34	27		3	30		6				.289	.392	.309	71	7—9	.441	11
1932	154	614	189	48	7	1	(	)	254	118	53	64		6	35		8				.308	.414	.360	99	9—8	.527	14
1933	152	587	159	25	5	1	(	)	197	78	37	56		5	37		6			8	.271	.336	.321	73	8—9	.464	11
1934	146	604	187	30	4	0	(	)	225	102	37	64		9	9		13			11	.310	.373	.379	92	9—7	.572	12
1935	137	539	141	28	4	14	(	)	219	60	53	37		6	21		5			9	.262	.406	.305	72	8—8	.487	12
1936	145	510	152	31	3	8	(	)	213	71	42	40		5	18		6			9	.298	.418	.344	79	9—6	.608	13
1937	128	516	158	38	2	14	(	)	242	91	62	40		10	14		5			9	.306	.469	.359	92	10—4	.689	14
1938	127	481	126	26	1	9	(	)	181	67	49	55		8	9		4			10	.262	.376	.342	67	8—6	.545	10
1939	105	336	80	24	2	3	(	)	117	37	34	42		7	10		6			10	.238	.348	.327	42	5—6	.450	5
1940	139	528	123	24	3	7	(	)	174	76	53	76		5	11		12	2	.86	11	.233	.330	.329	64	6—10	.375	10
1941	109	385	115	21	0	5	(	)	151	44	36	54		4	10		6			11	.299	.392	.382	63	7—4	.634	7
1942	90	316	77	10	3	5	(	)	108	53	24	44		8	5		4			6	.244	.342	.346	42	5—4	.543	5
1943	99	337	91	14	0	5	(	)	120	48	28	47		7	5		5			8	.270	.356	.366	48	6—4	.604	6
1946	5	2	0	0	0	0	(	)	0	0	0	0		0	0												
	2016	7629	2165	442	71	79	(	)	2986	1130	710	748		96	269		109	2		102	.284	.391	.344	1106	114—105	.521	158
12.4 yrs		613	174	36	6	6			240	91	57	60		8	22		9				.284	.391	.344				

Teams: Pittsburgh, 1927–1930; Philadelphia, 1931–1934; New York, N.L. 1935–1938; Chicago, N.L. 1939; Detroit, 1940; Detroit/New York, N.L. 1941; New York, N.L. 1942–1943, 1946.

Points in MVP Voting: 1931, 0; 1932, 0; 1933, 3 (.04); 1934, 0; 1935, 0; 1936, 2 (.03); 1937, 26 (6th, .33); 1938, 0; 1940, 26 (.08); 1941, 0; 1942, 0; 1943, 5 (.01); 1946, 0. TOTAL: .48 Award Shares.

Reported Salaries: 1927, $2,750 in minors; 1928, $2,750 in majors; 1934, $10,500; 1935, $12,500; 1936, $12,500.

Explanation for Gaps in Career or Sudden Changes in Productivity:
1938—Broken little finger on right hand
1944–1945—Served in Navy

Other Notes: Named outstanding major league shortstop in 1937 by *The Sporting News*.

FIELDING SHORTSTOP

Year	G	PO	AS	Err	DP	Pct.	Range
1927	1	3	2	0	1	1.000	5.00
1928	27	52	81	10	14	.930	4.93
1929	97	179	246	21	21	.953	4.38
1930	126	304	458	48	111	.941	6.05
1931	133	315	432	41	96	.948	5.62
1932	154	359	529	34	83	.963	5.77
1933	152	381	493	45	100	.951	5.75
1934	146	350	483	40	93	.954	5.71
1935	137	339	424	37	71	.954	5.57
1936	144	317	559	40	106	.956	6.08
1937	128	281	476	33	96	.958	5.91
1938	127	288	447	37	85	.952	5.79
1939	101	241	307	33	62	.943	5.43
1940	139	295	394	34	74	.953	4.96
1941	26	43	56	4	7	.961	3.81
1942	31	59	76	7	14	.951	4.35
1943	33	66	127	7	17	.965	5.85
	1702	3872	5590	471	1051	.953	5.56

Assists per 154 Games: 506

PLAYER: LUKE APPLING

Section groups — BATTING: G through SF · BASERUNNING: SB, CS, SB%, GIDP · PERCENTAGES: Avg, Slug, On Base · VALUES: Runs, Win–Loss, Pct, AV

Year	G	AB	H	2B	3B	HR	Hm	Rd	TB	R	RBI	BB	IBB	HBP	SH	SF	SB	CS	SB%	GIDP	Avg	Slug	On Base	Runs	Win–Loss	Pct	AV
1930	6	26	8	2	0	0	0	0	10	2	2	0			0		2	0	1.00		.308	.385	.308	3	0–0	.469	0
1931	96	297	69	13	4	1	1	0	93	36	28	29		1	3		9	2	.82		.232	.313	.300	31	3–6	.297	4
1932	139	489	134	20	10	3	0	3	183	66	63	40			3		9	8	.53		.274	.374	.327	60	6–8	.405	9
1933	151	612	197	36	10	6	4	2	271	90	85	56			2		6	11	.35		.322	.443	.378	102	10–6	.612	13
1934	118	452	137	28	6	2	1	1	183	75	61	59			5		3	1	.75		.303	.405	.380	78	7–5	.579	11
1935	153	525	161	28	6	1	1	0	204	94	71	122			7		12	6	.67		.307	.389	.433	98	10–5	.657	15
1936	138	526	204	31	7	6	2	4	267	111	128	85			6		10	6	.62		.388	.508	.468	130	10–3	.749	19
1937	154	574	182	42	8	4	2	2	252	98	77	86		1	4		18	10	.64		.317	.439	.405	105	10–5	.653	14
1938	81	294	89	14	0	0	0	0	103	41	44	42		1	1		1	3	.25		.303	.350	.391	44	4–4	.554	5
1939	148	516	162	16	6	0	0	0	190	82	56	105			9		16	9	.64	11	.314	.368	.424	88	9–5	.627	14
1940	150	566	197	27	13	0	0	0	250	96	79	69		1	3		3	5	.37	11	.348	.442	.418	110	11–4	.738	15
1941	154	592	186	26	8	1	1	0	231	93	57	82		1	2		12	8	.60	10	.314	.390	.397	101	11–5	.705	13
1942	142	543	142	26	4	3	1	2	185	78	53	63		3	4		17	5	.77	7	.262	.341	.339	72	9–6	.593	9
1943	155	585	192	33	2	3	2	1	238	63	80	90		1	1		27	8	.77	13	.328	.407	.418	114	12–3	.796	17
1945	18	58	21	2	2	1	0	1	30	12	10	12		0	1		1	0	1.00	0	.362	.517	.465	16	1–0	.891	2
1946	149	582	180	27	5	1	0	1	220	59	55	71		0	6		8	6	.60	15	.309	.378	.381	89	11–5	.695	13
1947	139	503	154	29	0	8	4	4	207	67	49	64		1	4		8	6	.57	15	.306	.412	.383	83	10–4	.700	12
1948	139	497	156	16	2	0	0	0	156	63	47	94		0	3		10	4	.71	17	.314	.354	.421	83	9–5	.657	11
1949	142	492	148	21	5	5	3	2	194	82	58	121		0	6		7	12	.37	23	.301	.394	.435	91	10–5	.668	13
1950	50	128	30	3	4	0	0	0	41	11	13	12		0	4		2	0	1.00	7	.234	.320	.292	12	1–3	.312	2
	2422	8857	2749	440	102	45	22	23	3528	1319	1116	1302	10		74		179	108	.62	129	.310	.398	.396	1511	153–88	.635	211
15.0 yrs		592	184	29	7	3			236	88	75	87		1	5		12	7	.62	15	.310	.398	.396				

Teams: Chicago, A.L. 1930–1950.

Points in MVP Voting: 1931, 0; 1932, 2 (.03); 1933, 1 (.01); 1934, 0; 1935, 7 (.09); 1936, 65 (2nd, .81); 1937, 5 (.06); 1938, 0; 1940, 54 (10th, .16); 1941, 0; 1942, 0; 1943, 215 (2nd, .64); 1946, 26 (.08); 1947, 43 (10th, .13); 1948, 8 (.02); 1949, 3 (.01); 1950, 0. TOTAL: 2.04 Award Shares.

Explanation for Gaps in Career or Sudden Changes in Productivity:
1938—Fractured an ankle during spring training.
1944–1945—In the Army.

Other Notes: Named outstanding major league shortstop for 1936, 1940, and 1943 by *The Sporting News*.

FIELDING SHORTSTOP

Year	G	PO	AS	Err	DP	Pct.	Range
1930	6	12	17	4	1	.879	4.83
1931	76	147	232	42	37	.900	4.99
1932	85	195	287	37	66	.929	5.67
1933	151	314	534	55	107	.939	5.62
1934	110	243	341	34	55	.945	5.31
1935	153	335	556	39	93	.958	5.82
1936	137	320	471	41	119	.951	5.77
1937	154	280	541	49	111	.944	5.33
1938	78	149	258	20	37	.953	5.22
1939	148	289	461	39	78	.951	5.07
1940	150	307	436	37	83	.953	4.95
1941	154	294	473	42	95	.948	4.98
1942	141	269	418	38	77	.948	4.87
1943	155	300	500	36	115	.957	5.16
1945	17	37	56	7	7	.930	5.47
1946	149	252	505	39	99	.951	5.08
1947	129	232	422	35	86	.949	5.07
1948	64	133	210	20	50	.945	5.36
1949	141	253	450	26	95	.964	4.99
1950	20	37	50	3	13	.967	4.35
	2218	4398	7218	643	1424	.948	5.24

Assists per 154 Games: 501

PLAYER: ARKY VAUGHAN

	BATTING																BASERUNNING				PERCENTAGES			VALUES			
Year	G	AB	H	2B	3B	HR	(Hm	Rd)	TB	R	RBI	BB	IBB	HBP	SH	SF	SB	CS	SB%	GIDP	Avg.	Slug	On Base	Runs	Win−Loss	Pct.	AV
1932	129	497	158	15	10	4	(	)	205	71	61	39		6	13		10				.318	.412	.366	78	8−5	.610	10
1933	152	573	180	29	19	9	(3	6)	274	85	97	64		5	13		3			9	.314	.478	.380	112	12−4	.753	13
1934	149	558	186	41	11	12	(	)	285	115	94	94		2	6		10			3	.333	.511	.427	135	11−3	.800	14
1935	137	499	192	34	10	19	(	)	303	108	99	97		7	7		4			5	.385	.607	.485	163	11−1	.902	19
1936	156	568	190	30	11	9	(	)	269	122	78	118		5	10		6			7	.335	.474	.447	137	11−3	.779	15
1937	126	469	151	17	17	5	(	)	217	71	72	54		2	6		7			6	.322	.463	.390	91	9−3	.742	11
1938	148	541	174	35	5	7	(	)	240	88	68	104		2	3		14			8	.322	.444	.431	115	11−3	.778	15
1939	152	595	182	30	11	6	(	)	252	94	62	70		6	22		12			5	.306	.424	.372	106	11−5	.672	15
1940	156	594	178	40	15	7	(	)	269	113	95	88		3	4		12			5	.300	.453	.390	113	10−5	.664	14
1941	106	374	118	20	7	6	(	)	170	69	38	50		2	11		8			3	.316	.455	.389	72	7−3	.741	9
1942	128	495	137	18	4	2	(1	1)	169	82	49	51		3	9		8			4	.277	.341	.342	63	8−6	.562	9
1943	149	610	186	39	6	5	(1	4)	252	112	66	60		3	12		20			9	.305	.413	.364	96	10−6	.623	13
1947	64	126	41	5	2	2	(1	1)	56	24	25	27		0	0		4			2	.325	.444	.444	27	2−1	.767	3
1948	65	123	30	3	0	3	(1	2)	42	19	22	21		0	0		0			4	.244	.341	.354	15	2−2	.473	1
	1817	6622	2103	356	128	96	(	)	3003	1173	926	937		46	116		118			70	.318	.453	.400	1323	124−51	.710	161
11.2 yrs		590	187	32	11	9			268	105	83	84		4	10		11				.318	.453	.400				

Teams: Pittsburgh, 1932–1941; Brooklyn, 1942–1943, 1947–1948.

Points in MVP Voting: 1932, 0; 1933, 2 (.03); 1934, 1 (.01); 1935, 45 (3rd, .56); 1937, 0; 1938, 163 (3rd, .49); 1940, 27 (.08); 1941, 2 (.01); 1942, 0; 1943, 15 (.04); 1947, 0; 1948, 0. TOTAL: 1.22 Award Shares.

Explanation for Gaps in Career or Sudden Changes in Productivity:
1944–46—Voluntarily retired because of personality conflicts with Leo Durocher (see Section II).

Other Notes: Named outstanding major league shortstop for 1935 by *The Sporting News*.

Although Vaughan finished third in the voting for the BBWAA MVP award in 1935, he won *The Sporting News* selection for the same honor.

FIELDING SHORTSTOP

Year	G	PO	AS	Err	DP	Pct.	Range
1932	128	247	403	46	74	.934	5.08
1933	152	310	487	46	95	.945	5.24
1934	149	329	480	41	77	.952	5.43
1935	137	249	422	35	55	.950	4.90
1936	156	327	477	47	86	.945	5.15
1937	108	231	335	26	58	.956	5.24
1938	147	306	507	33	107	.961	5.53
1939	152	330	531	34	103	.962	5.66
1940	155	308	542	52	94	.942	5.48
1941	97	172	289	20	42	.958	4.75
1942	5	11	16	0	4	1.000	5.40
1943	99	175	291	17	55	.965	4.71
	1485	2995	4780	397	850	.951	5.24

Assists per 154 Games: 496

PLAYER: LOU BOUDREAU

Year	G	AB	H	2B	3B	HR	(Hm	Rd)	TB	R	RBI	BB	IBB	HBP	SH	SF	SB	CS	SB%	GIDP	Avg.	Slug	On Base	Runs	Win–Loss	Pct.	AV
																			BATTING				BASERUNNING		PERCENTAGES	VALUES		
1938	1	1	0	0	0	0	(0	0)	0	0	0	1		0	0		0	0	.00	0	.000	.000	.500	0	0–0	.271	0
1939	53	225	58	15	4	0	(0	0)	81	42	19	28		0	3		2	1	.67	5	.258	.360	.336	28	3–4	.446	4
1940	155	627	185	46	10	9	(1	8)	278	97	101	73		2	4		6	3	.67	23	.295	.443	.368	103	11–6	.646	14
1941	148	579	149	45	8	10	(2	8)	240	95	56	85		3	14		9	4	.69	11	.257	.415	.348	92	10–7	.606	13
1942	147	506	143	18	10	2	(0	2)	187	57	58	75		4	19		7	16	.30	12	.283	.370	.368	73	9–6	.587	12
1943	152	539	154	32	7	3	(1	2)	209	69	67	90		0	20		4	7	.36	12	.286	.388	.376	87	11–5	.673	14
1944	150	584	191	45	5	3	(0	3)	255	91	67	73		5	19		11	3	.79	10	.327	.437	.395	112	12–4	.735	17
1945	97	346	106	24	1	3	(1	2)	141	50	48	35		2	20		0	4	.00	9	.306	.408	.355	53	7–3	.661	8
1946	140	515	151	30	6	6	(0	6)	211	51	62	40		1	15		6	7	.46	11	.293	.410	.336	72	9–5	.632	12
1947	150	538	165	45	3	4	(2	2)	228	79	67	67		4	14		1	0	1.00	9	.307	.424	.379	95	11–4	.717	16
1948	152	560	199	34	6	18	(6	12)	299	116	106	98		2	16		3	2	.60	15	.355	.534	.442	143	12–3	.825	19
1949	134	475	135	20	3	4	(2	2)	173	53	60	70		4	12		0	1	.00	19	.284	.364	.373	68	8–6	.599	11
1950	81	260	70	13	2	1	(1	0)	90	23	29	31		1	3		1	2	.33	9	.269	.346	.346	32	3–4	.442	4
1951	82	273	73	18	1	5	(2	3)	108	37	47	30		6	1		1	0	1.00	10	.267	.396	.348	39	4–4	.493	4
1952	4	2	0	0	0	0	(0	0)	0	1	2	0		0	1		0	0	.00	0	.000	.000	.000	0	0–0	.000	0
	1646	6030	1779	385	66	68	(18	50)	2500	861	789	796		34	164		51	50	.50	155	.295	.415	.371	996	110–61	.641	148
10.2 yrs		593	175	38	6	7			246	85	78	78		3	16		5	5		15	.295	.415	.371				

Teams: Cleveland, 1938–1950; Boston (A), 1951–1952.

Points in MVP Voting: 1938, 0; 1940, 119 (5th, .35); 1941, 10 (.03); 1942, 34 (10th, .10); 1943, 40 (10th, .12); 1944, 84 (6th, .25); 1945, 70 (8th, .21); 1946, 37 (10th, .11); 1947, 168 (3rd, .50); 1948, 324 (1st, .96); 1949, 10 (.03); 1950, 0; 1951, 0; 1952, 0. TOTAL: 2.66 Award Shares.

Reported Salaries: 1950—$65,000.

Explanation for Gaps in Career or Sudden Changes in Productivity:

1945—Fractured an ankle in August, missed rest of the season.

1951—Bone in left hand broken by pitch from Dizzy Trout, August 5; missed almost all of rest of season.

Other Notes: Named outstanding major league shortstop for 1947 and 1948 by *The Sporting News.*

FIELDING SHORTSTOP

Year	G	PO	AS	Err	DP	Pct.	Range
1939	53	103	184	14	31	.953	5.42
1940	155	277	454	24	116	.968	4.72
1941	147	296	444	26	97	.966	5.03
1942	146	281	426	26	107	.965	4.84
1943	152	328	488	25	122	.970	5.37
1944	149	339	516	19	134	.978	5.74
1945	97	217	289	9	73	.983	5.22
1946	139	315	405	22	94	.970	5.18
1947	148	305	475	14	120	.982	5.27
1948	151	297	483	20	119	.975	5.17
1949	88	176	272	8	78	.982	5.09
1950	61	118	170	4	44	.986	4.72
1951	52	80	153	12	45	.951	4.48
1952	1	0	1	0	0	1.000	1.00
	1539	3132	4760	223	1180	.973	5.13

Assists per 154 Games: 476

HOME AND ROAD DATA FOR 1948 SEASON

	G	AB	R	H	2B	3B	HR	RBI	BB	Avg.
HOME	76	265	42	80	13	0	6	44	49	.302
ROAD	76	295	74	119	21	6	12	62	49	.403

Source: Pete Palmer

PLAYER: PEE WEE REESE

Year	G	AB	H	2B	3B	HR	(Hm	Rd)	TB	R	RBI	BB	IBB	HBP	SH	SF	SB	CS	SB%	GIDP	Avg.	Slug	On Base	Runs	Win–Loss	Pct.	AV
1940	84	312	85	8	4	5	(2	3)	116	58	28	45		1	3		15			1	.272	.372	.363	47	5–3	.625	5
1941	152	595	136	23	5	2	(0	2)	175	76	46	68		3	8		10			6	.229	.294	.307	59	6–11	.369	8
1942	151	564	144	24	5	3	(1	2)	187	87	53	82		0	9		15			8	.255	.332	.345	71	9–7	.540	12
1946	152	542	154	16	10	5	(1	4)	205	79	60	87		1	14		10			10	.284	.378	.376	85	10–5	.653	11
1947	142	476	135	24	4	12	(6	6)	203	81	73	104		2	8		7			7	.284	.426	.408	93	9–4	.697	15
1948	151	566	155	31	4	9	(4	5)	221	96	75	79		0	9		25			16	.274	.390	.358	82	9–7	.555	13
1949	155	617	172	27	3	16	(8	8)	253	132	73	116		4	6		26			5	.279	.410	.393	111	11–6	.642	15
1950	141	531	138	21	5	11	(6	5)	202	97	52	91		1	10		17			7	.260	.380	.363	81	8–7	.528	11
1951	154	616	176	20	8	10	(6	4)	242	94	84	81		2	12		20	14	.59	19	.286	.393	.364	91	9–9	.524	13
1952	149	559	152	18	8	6	(3	3)	204	94	58	86		0	15		30	5	.86	16	.272	.365	.361	84	9–7	.569	11
1953	140	524	142	25	7	13	(8	5)	220	108	61	82		4	15		22	6	.79	15	.271	.420	.365	88	8–7	.537	12
1954	141	554	171	35	8	10	(3	7)	252	98	69	90		3	8	6	8	5	.62	20	.309	.455	.399	105	10–5	.651	13
1955	145	553	156	29	4	10	(7	3)	223	99	61	78	1	3	13	5	8	7	.53	22	.282	.403	.363	82	8–8	.510	11
1956	147	572	147	19	2	9	(5	4)	197	85	46	56	1	1	15	4	13	4	.76	14	.257	.344	.315	66	8–10	.443	9
1957	103	330	74	3	1	1	(0	1)	82	33	29	39	1	1	6	2	5	2	.71	7	.224	.248	.302	27	3–7	.299	3
1958	59	147	33	7	2	4	(3	1)	56	21	17	26	0	0	6	2	1	2	.33	3	.224	.381	.326	20	2–3	.459	2
	2166	8058	2170	330	80	126	(63	63)	3038	1338	885	1210	3	26	157	19	232	45	.70	176	.269	.377	.360	1192	126–107	.541	164
13.4 yrs		603	162	25	6	9			227	100	66	90		2	12		17			13	.269	.377	.360				

Teams: Brooklyn, 1940–1942, 1946–1957; Los Angeles, 1958.

Points in MVP Voting: 1940, 0; 1942, 6 (.02); 1946, 79 (6th, .24); 1947, 80 (8th, .24); 1948, 60 (6th, .18); 1949, 118 (5th, .35); 1950, 8 (.02); 1951, 15 (.04); 1952, 30 (8th, .09); 1953, 27 (.08); 1954, 53 (9th, .16); 1955, 36 (9th, .11); 1956, 71 (8th, .21); 1957, 0; 1958, 0. TOTAL: 1.74 Award Shares.

Reported Salaries: 1950—$35,000.

Explanation for Gaps in Career or Sudden Changes in Productivity: In the Navy, 1943–1945

Other Notes: Named outstanding major league shortstop for 1953 by *The Sporting News*.

Finished fifth to ninth in MVP voting eight times.

FIELDING SHORTSTOP

Year	G	PO	AS	Err	DP	Pct.	Range
1940	83	190	238	18	41	.960	5.16
1941	151	346	473	47	76	.946	5.42
1942	151	337	482	35	99	.959	5.42
1946	152	285	463	26	104	.966	4.92
1947	142	266	441	25	99	.966	4.98
1948	149	335	453	31	93	.962	5.29
1949	155	316	454	18	93	.977	4.97
1950	134	282	398	26	94	.963	5.07
1951	154	292	422	35	106	.953	4.64
1952	145	282	376	21	89	.969	4.54
1953	135	265	380	23	83	.966	4.78
1954	140	270	426	25	74	.965	4.97
1955	142	239	404	23	86	.965	4.53
1956	136	263	367	23	79	.965	4.63
1957	23	46	62	6	16	.947	4.70
1958	22	26	52	6	14	.929	3.55
	2014	4040	5891	388	1246	.962	4.93

Assists per 154 Games: 450

PLAYER: PHIL RIZZUTO

	BATTING															BASERUNNING				PERCENTAGES			VALUES			
Year	G	AB	H	2B	3B	HR	(Hm	Rd)	TB	R	RBI	BB	IBB	HBP	SH	SF	SB	CS	SB%	GIDP	Avg.	Slug	On Base	Runs	Win−Loss	Pct.	AV
1941	133	515	158	20	9	3	(	)	205	65	46	27		1	5		14	5	.74	13	.307	.398	.339	70	7−7	.528	13
1942	144	553	157	24	7	4	(	)	207	79	68	44		6	10		22	6	.79	13	.284	.374	.338	71	8−7	.525	13
1946	126	471	121	17	1	2	(	)	146	53	38	34		6	7		14	7	.67	10	.257	.310	.311	48	6−8	.424	9
1947	153	549	150	26	9	2	(	)	200	78	60	57		8	9		11	6	.65	6	.273	.364	.345	76	9−7	.551	11
1948	128	464	117	13	2	6	(	)	152	65	50	60		2	13		6	5	.55	6	.252	.328	.332	57	6−8	.421	9
1949	153	614	169	22	7	5	(	)	220	110	65	72		1	25		18	6	.75	18	.275	.358	.340	82	9−10	.471	12
1950	155	617	200	36	7	7	(4	3)	271	125	66	91		7	19		12	8	.60	6	.324	.439	.406	124	11−5	.672	16
1951	144	540	148	21	6	2	(2	0)	187	87	43	58		5	26		18	3	.86	10	.274	.346	.335	73	8−8	.494	12
1952	152	578	147	24	10	2	(0	2)	197	89	43	67		5	23		17	6	.74	9	.254	.341	.325	73	9−9	.505	12
1953	134	413	112	21	3	2	(0	2)	145	54	54	71		4	18		4	3	.57	6	.271	.351	.370	63	7−5	.576	9
1954	127	307	60	11	0	2	(1	1)	77	47	15	41		1	18	2	3	2	.60	7	.195	.251	.276	25	2−8	.241	4
1955	81	143	37	4	1	1	(0	1)	46	19	9	22	0	3	13	0	7	1	.87	2	.259	.322	.343	21	2−2	.524	2
1956	31	52	12	0	0	0	(0	0)	12	6	6	6	0	0	7	0	3	0	1.00	1	.231	.231	.277	5	0−1	.246	0
	1661	5816	1588	239	62	38	(7	9)	2065	877	563	650		49	193		149	58	.72	107	.273	.355	.341	786	85−85	.500	122
10.3 yrs		567	155	23	6	4			201	86	55	63		5	19		15	6		10	.273	.355	.341				

Teams: New York, A.L. 1941–1942, 1946–1956.

Points in MVP Voting: 1941, 0; 1942, 9 (.03); 1946, 0; 1947, 0; 1948, 1 (.00); 1949, 0; 1950, 284 (1st, .88); 1951, 47 (.14); 1952, 33 (.10); 1953, 76 (6th, 23). TOTAL: 1.28 Award Shares.

Explanation for Gaps in Career or Sudden Changes in Productivity: In the Navy, 1943–45.

Other Notes: Named outstanding major league shortstop in 1949, 1950, 1951, and 1952 by *The Sporting News*.

FIELDING SHORTSTOP

Year	G	PO	AS	Err	DP	Pct.	Range
1941	128	252	399	29	109	.957	5.09
1942	144	324	445	30	114	.962	5.34
1946	125	267	378	26	97	.961	5.16
1947	151	340	450	25	111	.969	5.23
1948	128	259	348	17	85	.973	4.74
1949	152	329	440	23	118	.971	5.06
1950	155	301	452	14	123	.982	4.86
1951	144	317	407	24	113	.968	5.03
1952	152	308	458	19	116	.976	5.04
1953	133	214	409	24	100	.963	4.68
1954	126	184	294	16	84	.968	3.79
1955	79	93	132	10	30	.957	2.85
1956	30	31	54	6	17	.934	2.83
	1647	3219	4666	263	1217	.968	4.79

Assists per 154 Games: 436

PLAYER: ERNIE BANKS

							BATTING											BASERUNNING				PERCENTAGES			VALUES			
Year	G	AB	H	2B	3B	HR	(Hm Rd)	TB	R	RBI	BB	IBB	HBP	SH	SF	SB	CS	SB%	GIDP	Avg.	Slug	On Base	Runs	Win–Loss	Pct.	AV
1953	10	35	11	1	1	2	(1 1)	20	3	6	4		0	0		0	0	.00	0	.314	.571	.385	8	1–0	.795	1
1954	154	593	163	19	7	19	(11 8)	253	70	79	40		7	5	4	6	10	.37	11	.275	.427	.324	81	8–9	.498	13
1955	154	596	176	29	9	44	(26 18)	355	98	117	45	6	2	0	3	9	3	.75	16	.295	.596	.345	117	12–4	.731	16
1956	139	538	160	25	8	28	(16 12)	285	82	85	52	18	0	0	3	6	9	.40	7	.297	.530	.358	99	11–4	.723	14
1957	156	594	169	34	6	43	(25 18)	344	113	102	70	11	3	2	5	8	4	.67	12	.285	.579	.359	123	12–4	.747	15
1958	154	617	193	23	11	47	(30 17)	379	119	129	52	12	4	1	8	4	4	.50	14	.313	.614	.365	135	13–4	.750	18
1959	155	589	179	25	6	45	(24 21)	351	97	143	64	20	7	2	9	2	4	.33	18	.304	.596	.373	126	12–4	.754	20
1960	156	597	162	32	7	41	(18 23)	331	94	117	71	28	4	0	6	1	3	.25	14	.271	.554	.350	113	12–5	.683	16
1961	138	511	142	22	4	29	(19 10)	259	75	80	54	21	2	0	6	1	2	.33	11	.278	.507	.346	88	9–5	.621	16
1962	154	610	164	20	6	37	(19 18)	307	87	104	30	3	7	0	10	5	1	.83	19	.269	.503	.306	89	10–8	.558	12
1963	130	432	98	20	1	18	(10 8)	174	41	64	39	16	4	1	8	0	3	.00	7	.227	.403	.291	50	7–6	.541	7
1964	157	591	156	29	6	23	(12 11)	266	67	95	36	11	3	1	6	1	2	.33	16	.264	.450	.306	77	9–8	.533	10
1965	163	612	162	25	3	28	(14 14)	277	79	106	55	19	6	0	7	3	5	.37	16	.265	.453	.328	87	10–7	.585	10
1966	141	511	139	23	7	15	(6 9)	221	52	75	29	10	3	4	5	0	1	.00	15	.272	.432	.310	66	7–7	.498	9
1967	151	573	158	26	4	23	(14 9)	261	68	95	27	8	3	8	4	2	2	.50	20	.276	.455	.306	74	9–8	.541	10
1968	150	552	136	27	0	32	(21 11)	259	71	83	27	4	5	9	2	2	0	1.00	12	.246	.469	.282	72	9–7	.579	9
1969	155	565	143	19	2	23	(15 8)	235	60	106	42	7	7	8	7	0	0	.00	15	.253	.416	.305	71	9–8	.522	10
1970	72	222	56	6	2	12	(7 5)	102	25	44	20	3	3	1	3	0	0	.00	5	.252	.459	.317	32	3–3	.532	4
1971	39	83	16	2	0	3	(2 1)	27	4	6	6	1	0	3	0	0	0	.00	1	.193	.325	.239	14	2–1	.632	1
	2528	9421	2583	407	90	512	(290 222)	4706	1305	1636	763	198	70	45	96	50	53	.49	229	.274	.500	.329	1521	166–103	.615	211
15.6 yrs		604	166	26	6	33		302	84	105	49		4	3		3	3	.49	15	.274	.500	.329				

Teams: Chicago, N.L. 1953–1971.

Points in MVP Voting: 1953, 0; 1954, 14 (.04); 1955, 195 (3rd, .58); 1956, 2 (.01); 1957, 60 (6th, .18); 1958, 283 (1st, .84); 1959, 232.5 (1st, .75); 1960, 100 (4th, .30); 1962, 5 (.02); 1963, 0; 1964, 0; 1965, 0; 1966, 0; 1967, 22 (.08); 1968, 14 (.05); 1969, 15 (.04); 1970, 0; 1971, 0. TOTAL: 2.89 Award Shares.

Explanation for Gaps in Career or Sudden Changes in Productivity:

1961—Four-year streak of playing every game ended by knee problem, June 23; later had some trouble with depth perception in left eye.

1963—Had fifteen HR by June 19, hit only three thereafter. Diagnosed as suffering from subclinical mumps, which means that instead of breaking out, they just stay in your blood and make you sick.

1970—Knees gave out. Spent twenty-nine days on disabled list.

Other Notes: Named outstanding major league shortstop for 1955, 1958, 1959, 1960 by *The Sporting News*. Gold Glove: 1960.

FIELDING SHORTSTOP

Year	G	PO	AS	Err	DP	Pct.	Range
1953	10	19	33	1	9	.981	5.20
1954	154	312	475	34	105	.959	5.11
1955	154	290	482	22	102	.972	5.01
1956	139	279	357	25	92	.962	4.58
1957	100	168	261	11	59	.975	4.29
1958	154	292	468	32	100	.960	4.94
1959	154	271	519	12	95	.985	5.13
1960	156	283	488	18	94	.977	4.94
1961	104	173	358	19	68	.965	5.11
	1125	2087	3441	174	724	.969	4.91

Assists per 154 Games: 471

PLAYER: LUIS APARICIO

Year	G	AB	H	2B	3B	HR	(Hm	Rd)	TB	R	RBI	BB	IBB	HBP	SH	SF	SB	CS	SB%	GIDP	Avg.	Slug	On Base	Runs	Win–Loss	Pct.	AV
							BATTING											**BASERUNNING**				**PERCENTAGES**				**VALUES**		
1956	152	533	142	19	6	3	(1	2)	182	69	56	34	2	1	14	1	21	4	.84	9	.266	.341	.304	59	6–9	.407	12
1957	143	575	148	22	6	3	(2	1)	191	82	41	52	1	0	9	4	28	8	.78	7	.257	.332	.313	65	8–9	.470	11
1958	145	557	148	20	9	2	(1	1)	192	76	40	35	2	1	8	3	29	6	.83	8	.266	.345	.305	62	8–8	.481	12
1959	152	612	157	18	5	6	(2	4)	203	98	51	53	1	3	11	7	56	13	.81	11	.257	.332	.310	70	9–10	.475	12
1960	153	600	166	20	7	2	(2	0)	206	86	61	43	3	1	20	6	51	8	.86	12	.277	.343	.313	73	8–10	.463	14
1961	156	625	170	24	4	6	(4	2)	220	90	45	38	0	1	4	4	53	13	.80	12	.272	.352	.311	72	8–10	.429	12
1962	153	581	140	23	5	7	(4	3)	194	72	40	32	1	1	4	4	31	12	.72	11	.241	.334	.278	54	6–11	.347	11
1963	146	601	150	18	8	5	(2	3)	199	73	45	36	2	2	6	6	40	6	.87	10	.250	.331	.289	62	8–10	.446	10
1964	146	578	154	20	3	10	(5	5)	210	93	37	49	0	3	7	5	57	17	.77	13	.266	.363	.321	71	9–8	.537	13
1965	144	564	127	20	10	8	(4	4)	191	67	40	46	0	3	14	2	26	7	.79	11	.225	.339	.280	57	7–10	.427	10
1966	151	659	182	25	8	6	(3	3)	241	97	41	33	2	1	12	2	25	11	.69	10	.276	.366	.306	74	9–10	.461	13
1967	134	546	127	22	5	4	(1	3)	171	55	31	29	2	1	6	5	18	5	.78	8	.233	.313	.267	47	6–11	.358	7
1968	155	622	164	24	4	4	(1	3)	208	55	36	33	3	2	5	2	17	11	.61	10	.264	.334	.300	61	10–8	.554	11
1969	156	599	168	24	5	5	(3	2)	217	77	51	66	1	2	10	4	24	4	.86	14	.280	.362	.347	81	10–7	.565	14
1970	146	552	173	29	3	5	(4	1)	223	86	43	53	1	1	5	5	8	3	.73	11	.313	.404	.369	85	9–6	.617	14
1971	125	491	114	23	0	4	(1	3)	149	56	45	35	0	2	9	4	6	4	.60	7	.232	.303	.279	44	5–10	.329	7
1972	110	436	112	26	3	3	(1	2)	153	47	39	26	0	2	5	5	3	3	.50	8	.257	.351	.295	45	6–7	.434	7
1973	132	499	135	17	1	0	(0	0)	154	56	49	41	0	1	12	7	13	1	.93	12	.271	.309	.317	53	6–9	.420	8
16.0 yrs	2599	10230	2677	394	92	83	(41	42)	3504	1335	791	736	22	27	161	76	506	136	.79	184	.262	.343	.306	1137	138–163	.458	198
		638	167	25	6	5			218	83	49	46	1	2	10	5	32	8	.79	11	.262	.343	.306				

Teams: Chicago, A.L. 1956–1962; Baltimore, 1963–1967; Chicago, A.L. 1968–1970; Boston, 1971–1973.

Points in MVP Voting: 1958, 0; 1959, 255 (2nd, .76); 1960, 6 (.02); 1961, 16 (.06); 1962, 0; 1963, 3 (.01); 1964, 3.5 (.01); 1965, 0; 1966, 51 (9th, .18); 1967, 0; 1968, 13 (.05); 1969, 0; 1970, 35 (.10); 1971, 0; 1972, 9.5 (.03); 1973, 0. TOTAL: 1.22 Award Shares.

Reported Salaries: 1972—$100,000; 1973—$100,000.

Explanation for Gaps in Career or Sudden Changes in Productivity:
1972—Missed a month in mid-season (including All-Star Game) because of broken and dislocated finger.

Other Notes: Named outstanding American League shortstop for 1963, 1966, 1968, 1970, 1972 by *The Sporting News.*
Gold Glove: 1958, 1959, 1960, 1961, 1962, 1964, 1966, 1968, 1970.

FIELDING SHORTSTOP

Year	G	PO	AS	Err	DP	Pct.	Range
1956	152	250	474	35	91	.954	4.76
1957	142	246	449	20	85	.972	4.89
1958	145	289	463	21	90	.973	5.19
1959	152	282	460	23	87	.970	4.88
1960	153	305	551	18	117	.979	5.59
1961	156	264	487	30	86	.962	4.81
1962	152	280	452	20	102	.973	4.82
1963	145	275	403	12	76	.983	4.68
1964	145	260	437	15	98	.979	4.81
1965	141	238	439	20	87	.971	4.80
1966	151	303	441	17	104	.978	4.93
1967	131	221	333	25	67	.957	4.23
1968	154	269	535	19	92	.977	5.22
1969	154	248	563	20	94	.976	5.27
1970	146	251	483	18	99	.976	5.03
1971	121	194	338	16	56	.971	4.40
1972	109	183	304	16	54	.968	4.47
1973	132	190	404	21	68	.966	4.50
	2581	4548	8016	366	1553	.972	4.87

Assists per 154 Games: 478

PLAYER: MAURY WILLS

						BATTING												BASERUNNING				PERCENTAGES			VALUES			
Year	G	AB	H	2B	3B	HR	(Hm	Rd)	TB	R	RBI	BB	IBB	HBP	SH	SF	SB	CS	SB%	GIDP	Avg.	Slug	On Base	Runs	Win—Loss	Pct.	AV
1959	83	242	63	5	2	0	(0	0)	72	27	7	13	5	0	3	0	7	3	.70	3	.260	.298	.295	22	2—5	.329	2
1960	148	516	152	15	2	0	(0	0)	171	75	27	35	8	3	3	2	50	12	.81	11	.295	.331	.340	62	8—7	.523	12
1961	148	613	173	12	10	1	(1	0)	208	105	31	59	2	1	13	1	35	15	.70	6	.282	.339	.339	77	8—9	.468	11
1962	165	695	208	13	10	6	(0	6)	259	130	48	51	1	2	7	4	104	13	.89	7	.299	.373	.344	106	11—8	.582	14
1963	134	527	159	19	3	0	(0	0)	184	83	34	44	0	1	5	3	40	19	.68	3	.302	.349	.352	69	9—6	.623	12
1964	158	630	173	15	5	2	(0	2)	204	81	34	41	0	0	11	3	53	17	.76	6	.275	.324	.312	70	10—9	.525	11
1965	158	650	186	14	7	0	(0	0)	214	92	33	40	2	4	14	2	94	31	.75	6	.286	.329	.324	77	11—8	.569	14
1966	143	594	162	14	2	1	(0	1)	183	60	39	34	0	2	13	0	38	24	.61	6	.273	.308	.308	57	8—9	.480	11
1967	149	616	186	12	9	3	(2	1)	225	92	45	31	1	1	12	4	29	10	.74	6	.302	.365	.328	78	9—8	.540	11
1968	153	627	174	12	6	0	(0	0)	198	76	31	45	1	1	11	1	52	21	.71	10	.278	.316	.321	67	10—9	.532	11
1969	151	623	171	10	8	4	(1	3)	209	80	47	59	2	1	5	2	40	21	.66	7	.274	.335	.335	73	9—9	.522	11
1970	132	522	141	19	3	0	(0	0)	166	77	34	50	2	0	5	1	28	13	.68	10	.270	.318	.330	57	6—9	.416	9
1971	149	601	169	14	3	3	(2	1)	198	73	44	40	2	0	7	6	15	8	.65	8	.281	.329	.320	66	9—9	.498	10
1972	71	132	17	3	1	0	(0	0)	22	16	4	10	0	0	10	0	1	1	.50	3	.129	.167	.178	5	0—4	.067	1
	1942	7588	2134	177	71	20	(6	14)	2513	1067	458	552	26	16	119	29	586	208	.74	92	.281	.331	.325	884	111—108	.508	140
12.0 yrs		633	178	15	6	2			210	89	38	46	2	1	10	2	49	17		8	.281	.331	.325				

Teams: Los Angeles, 1959–1966; Pittsburgh, 1967–1968; Montreal/Los Angeles, 1969; Los Angeles, 1970–1972.

Points in MVP Voting: 1959, 0; 1960, 7 (.02); 1961, 36 (9th, .16); 1962, 209 (1st, .75); 1963, 9 (.03); 1964, 0; 1965, 164 (3rd, .59); 1966, 5 (.02); 1967, 0; 1968, 0; 1969, 17 (.05); 1970, 0; 1971, 74 (6th, .22); 1972, 0. TOTAL: 1.84 Award Shares.

Reported Salaries: 1951, $135/month in minors; 1952, $200/month in minors; 1972, $100,000.

Explanation for Gaps in Career or Sudden Changes in Productivity: 1963—Suffered foot injury on opening day.

Other Notes: Hit four home runs in the Polo Grounds in 1962.
Named outstanding National League shortstop in 1961, 1962, 1965 by *The Sporting News.*
Gold Glove: 1961, 1962.

FIELDING SHORTSTOP

Year	G	PO	AS	E	DP	Pct.	Range
1959	82	121	220	12	39	.966	4.16
1960	145	260	431	40	78	.945	4.77
1961	148	253	428	29	104	.959	4.60
1962	165	295	493	36	86	.956	4.78
1963	109	171	322	21	47	.959	4.52
1964	149	273	422	27	77	.963	4.66
1965	155	267	535	25	89	.970	5.17
1966	139	227	453	23	79	.967	4.89
1967	2	4	3	0	1	1.000	3.50
1968	10	10	32	1	5	.977	4.20
1969	150	240	496	28	92	.963	4.91
1970	126	171	396	24	58	.959	4.50
1971	144	220	484	16	86	.978	4.89
1972	31	38	89	2	18	.984	4.10
	1555	2550	4804	284	859	.963	4.73

Assists per 154 Games: 476

Left Field

Fred Clarke
Sherry Magee
Joe Jackson
Zack Wheat
Harry Heilmann
Ken Williams
Goose Goslin
Joe Medwick
Bob Johnson
Ted Williams
Stan Musial
Ralph Kiner
Frank Howard
Billy Williams
Carl Yastrzemski
Lou Brock
Willie Stargell
Jim Rice

PLAYER: FRED CLARKE

Year	G	AB	H	2B	3B	HR	(Hm	Rd)	TB	R	RBI	BB	IBB	HBP	SH	SF	SB	CS	SB%	GIDP	Avg.	Slug	On Base	Runs	Win−Loss	Pct.	AV
1894	76	316	87	11	7	7	(	)	133	55	48	25		4	1		25				.275	.421	.335	53	4−5	.459	6
1895	132	556	197	21	5	4	(	)	240	96	82	34		10	3		40				.354	.432	.400	113	8−6	.582	14
1896	131	517	169	15	18	9	(	)	247	96	79	43		14	7		34				.327	.478	.389	110	9−5	.617	13
1897	129	525	213	30	13	6	(	)	287	120	67	45			3		57				.406	.547	.450	160	10−2	.833	17
1898	149	599	190	23	12	3	(	)	246	116	47	48			5		40				.317	.411	.365	108	10−6	.631	13
1899	148	601	209	21	11	5	(	)	267	124	70	49			10		49				.348	.444	.391	130	11−4	.717	15
1900	106	399	112	15	12	3	(	)	160	85	32	51			9		21				.281	.401	.355	68	7−5	.603	9
1901	129	527	171	24	15	6	(	)	243	118	60	51			13		23				.324	.461	.376	106	10−4	.711	12
1902	114	461	148	27	14	2	(	)	209	104	53	51			6		29				.321	.453	.384	95	10−3	.761	11
1903	104	427	150	32	15	5	(	)	227	88	70	41			13		21				.351	.532	.397	105	9−3	.774	12
1904	72	278	85	7	11	0	(	)	114	51	25	22			8		11				.306	.410	.347	47	5−3	.681	5
1905	141	525	157	18	15	2	(	)	211	95	51	55			22		24				.299	.402	.352	91	10−5	.680	13
1906	118	417	129	14	13	1	(	)	172	69	39	40			20		18				.309	.412	.354	74	9−3	.753	9
1907	148	501	145	18	13	2	(	)	195	97	59	68			16		37				.289	.389	.364	91	11−4	.746	12
1908	151	551	146	18	15	2	(	)	200	83	53	65			22		24				.265	.363	.331	77	11−6	.645	11
1909	152	550	158	16	11	3	(	)	205	97	68	80		6	24		31				.287	.373	.370	92	11−5	.694	12
1910	123	429	113	23	9	2	(	)	160	57	63	53		4	29		12				.263	.373	.330	62	8−6	.569	9
1911	110	392	127	25	13	5	(	)	193	73	49	53		2	13		10				.324	.492	.396	82	8−3	.764	9
1913	9	13	1	1	0	0	(	)	2	0	0	0		0	1		0				.077	.154	.071	0	0−0	.004	0
1914	2	2	0	0	0	0	(	)	0	0	0	0	0	0	0		0				.000	.000	.000	0	0−0	.000	0
1915	1	2	1	0	0	0	(	)	1	0	0	0	0	0	0		0				.500	.500	.500	0	0−0	.926	0
13.9 yrs	2245	8588	2708	359	222	67	(	)	3712	1624	1015	874		40	225		506				.315	.432	.372	1664	162−77	.678	201
		620	195	26	16	5			268	117	73	63			16		37				.315	.432	.372				

Runs created estimates prior to 1900 are of indeterminate accuracy.

Teams: Louisville, 1894–1899; Pittsburgh, 1900–1915.
Points in MVP Voting: 1911, 0; 1913, 0; 1914, 0.
Explanation for Gaps in Career or Sudden Changes in Productivity:
1902—Foot injury.
1904—Leg injury.

FIELDING LEFT FIELD

Year	G	PO	AS	E	DP	Pct.	Range
1894	76	162	15	23	2	.885	2.33
1895	132	344	20	49	4	.881	2.76
1896	131	277	18	30	2	.908	2.25
1897	128	282	18	24	0	.926	2.34
1898	149	344	19	23	3	.940	2.44
1899	144	327	20	13	2	.964	2.41
1900	104	263	8	16	2	.944	2.61
1901	127	282	13	9	0	.970	2.32
1902	113	215	13	10	2	.958	2.02
1903	101	168	10	7	3	.962	1.76
1904	70	135	4	3	2	.979	1.99
1905	137	270	16	7	4	.976	2.09
1906	110	209	15	6	3	.974	2.04
1907	144	298	15	4	2	.987	2.17
1908	151	350	15	10	2	.973	2.42
1909	152	362	17	5	2	.987	2.49
1910	118	284	10	10	4	.967	2.49
1911	101	216	8	7	3	.970	2.22
1913	2	2	0	0	0	1.000	1.00
1915	1	0	0	0	0	0	0
	2191	4790	254	256	42	.952	2.30

Assists per 154 Games: 17.9

PLAYER: SHERRY MAGEE

					BATTING													BASERUNNING				PERCENTAGES			VALUES			
Year	G	AB	H	2B	3B	HR	(Hm	Rd)	TB	R	RBI	BB	IBB	HBP	SH	SF	SB	CS	SB%	GIDP	Avg.	Slug	On Base	Runs	Win–Loss	Pct.	AV
1904	95	364	101	15	12	3	(	)	149	51	57	14				7	11				.277	.409	.299	51	6–5	.545	7
1905	155	603	180	24	17	5	(	)	253	100	98	44				14	48				.299	.420	.339	108	12–5	.690	11
1906	154	563	159	36	8	6	(	)	229	77	67	52				10	55				.282	.407	.338	101	12–4	.752	13
1907	140	503	165	28	12	4	(	)	229	75	85	53				8	46				.328	.455	.387	111	12–2	.858	16
1908	143	508	144	30	16	2	(	)	212	79	62	49				19	40				.283	.417	.335	87	12–3	.780	11
1909	142	522	141	33	14	2	(	)	208	60	66	43	11		27		38				.270	.398	.323	83	11–5	.707	9
1910	154	519	172	39	17	6	(	)	263	110	123	94	12		22		49				.331	.507	.430	139	12–2	.832	15
1911	121	445	128	32	5	15	(	)	215	79	94	49	6		14		22				.288	.483	.356	86	9–4	.698	11
1912	132	464	142	25	9	6	(	)	203	79	72	55	7		29		30				.306	.438	.368	91	9–4	.688	11
1913	138	470	144	36	6	11	(	)	225	92	70	38	9		21		23				.306	.479	.355	89	10–4	.708	10
1914	146	544	171	39	11	15	(	)	277	96	103	55	3		14		25				.314	.509	.372	110	11–4	.739	15
1915	156	571	160	34	12	2	(	)	224	72	87	54	7		23		15	12	.56		.280	.392	.337	82	11–6	.643	12
1916	120	419	101	17	5	3	(	)	137	44	54	44	6		16		10				.241	.327	.311	47	7–5	.572	5
1917	117	383	107	16	8	1	(	)	142	41	52	29	5		18		11				.279	.371	.324	51	7–4	.608	6
1918	115	400	119	15	13	2	(	)	166	46	76	37	9		10		14				.298	.415	.362	64	8–4	.672	6
1919	56	163	35	6	1	0	(	)	43	11	21	26	4		8		4				.215	.264	.323	16	2–3	.443	1
	2084	7441	2169	425	166	83	(	)	3175	1112	1187	736	79		260		441	12	.56		.291	.427	.350	1316	151–65	.698	159
12.9 yrs		578	169	33	13	6			247	86	92	57			20		34				.291	.427	.350				

Teams: Philadelphia, 1904–1914; Boston, 1915–1916; Boston/Cincinnati, 1917; Cincinnati, 1918–1919.

Points in MVP Voting: 1911, 0; 1913, 0; 1914, 14 (8th, .22).

Explanation for Gaps in Career or Sudden Changes in Productivity:
1911—In a game in July, Magee slugged an umpire named Finneran and knocked him to the ground near home plate. It was described as a "brutal and unprovoked assault," though Magee had already been ejected from the game. He was suspended for the balance of the season and fined $200, but the league president lifted the suspension after 36 days.

Other Notes: The 1969 Macmillan *Encyclopedia* says that Magee was declared ineligible in 1920, but this was a typographical error, a confusion of Sherry Magee with Lee Magee, another National League outfielder who was suspended.

FIELDING LEFT FIELD

Year	G	PO	AS	Err	DP	Pct.	Range
1904	94	146	19	14	3	.922	1.76
1905	155	341	19	14	6	.963	2.32
1906	154	316	18	6	2	.982	2.17
1907	139	297	13	7	7	.978	2.23
1908	142	279	15	9	5	.970	2.07
1909	142	282	11	9	0	.970	2.06
1910	154	285	9	8	2	.974	1.91
1911	120	248	14	5	3	.981	2.18
1912	124	251	8	10	2	.963	2.09
1913	123	236	7	8	2	.968	1.98
1914	67	137	3	9		.940	2.09
1915	134	346	16	7	4	.981	2.70
1916	120	220	6	5	0	.978	1.88
1917	106	220	14	8	4	.967	2.21
1918	38	87	3	2		.978	2.37
1919	47	98	2	1	0	.990	2.13
	1859	3789	177	122	40	.970	2.13

Assists per 154 Games: 14.7

PLAYER: JOE JACKSON

Year	G	AB	H	2B	3B	HR	(Hm	Rd)	TB	R	RBI	BB	IBB	HBP	SH	SF	SB	CS	SB%	GIDP	Avg.	Slug	On Base	Runs	Win–Loss	Pct.	AV
1908	5	23	3	0	0	0	(0	0)	3	0	3	0		0	0	0	0				.130	.130	.130	0	0–1	.016	0
1909	5	17	5	0	0	0	(0	0)	5	3	3	1		0	0	0	0				.294	.294	.333	2	0–0	.523	0
1910	20	75	29	2	5	1	(1	0)	44	15	11	8		0	3		4				.387	.587	.430	21	2–0	.888	2
1911	147	571	233	45	19	7	(2	5)	337	126	83	56		8	6		41				.408	.590	.463	175	12–1	.895	19
1912	152	572	226	44	26	3	(1	2)	331	121	90	54		12	15		35				.395	.579	.447	166	12–2	.874	18
1913	148	528	197	39	17	7	(3	4)	291	109	71	80		5	10		26				.373	.551	.453	140	12–2	.886	15
1914	122	453	153	22	13	3	(1	2)	210	61	53	41		5	13		22	15	.60		.338	.464	.389	89	9–3	.758	12
1915	128	461	142	20	14	5	(1	4)	205	63	81	52		6	11		16	20	.44		.308	.445	.377	82	9–4	.722	10
1916	155	592	202	40	21	3	(1	2)	293	91	78	46		5	16		24	14	.63		.341	.495	.384	119	13–3	.810	14
1917	146	538	162	20	17	5	(2	3)	231	91	75	57		7	19		13				.301	.429	.364	89	11–4	.729	13
1918	17	65	23	2	2	1	(0	1)	32	9	20	8		0	5		3				.354	.492	.397	15	2–0	.835	2
1919	139	516	181	31	14	7	(1	6)	261	79	96	60		4	17		9				.351	.506	.410	111	11–3	.786	14
1920	146	570	218	42	20	12	(5	7)	336	105	121	56		7	16		9	12	.43		.382	.589	.433	145	12–3	.815	16
	1330	4981	1774	307	168	54	(18	36)	2579	873	785	519		59	131		202	61	.54		.356	.518	.413	1154	105–26	.804	135
8.2 yrs		607	216	37	20	7			314	106	96	63		7	16		25	18			.356	.518	.413				

Teams: Philadelphia, 1908–1909; Cleveland, 1910–1914; Cleveland/Chicago, A.L. 1915; Chicago, 1916–1920.
Points in MVP Voting: 1911, 28 (4th, .44); 1913, 43 (2nd, .67); 1914, 15 (5th, .23). TOTAL: 1.34 Award Shares.
Reported Salaries: 1919, less than $6,000.
Explanation for Gaps in Career or Sudden Changes in Productivity:
1918—Left team early in season.
1920—Banned for life.

FIELDING LEFT FIELD

Year	G	PO	AS	Err	DP	Pct.	Range
1908	5	6	1	1	0	.875	1.40
1909	4	10	0	2	0	.833	2.50
1910	20	40	2	1	0	.977	2.10
1911	147	242	32	12	8	.958	1.86
1912	150	273	30	16	2	.950	2.02
1913	148	211	28	18	5	.930	1.61
1914	119	195	13	7	4	.967	1.75
1915	95	152	12	8	3	.953	1.73
1916	155	290	17	8	5	.975	1.98
1917	145	341	18	6	4	.984	2.48
1918	17	36	1	0	0	1.000	2.18
1919	139	252	15	9	4	.967	1.92
1920	145	314	14	12	2	.965	2.26
	1289	2362	183	100	37	.962	1.97

Assists per 154 Games: 21.9

PLAYER: ZACK WHEAT

	BATTING															BASERUNNING				PERCENTAGES			VALUES			
Year	G	AB	H	2B	3B	HR	(Hm	Rd)	TB	R	RBI	BB	IBB	HBP	SH	SF	SB	CS	SB%	GIDP	Avg.	Slug	On Base	Runs	Win−Loss	Pct.	AV
1909	26	102	31	7	3	0	(	)	44	15	4	6		0	5		1				.304	.431	.327	15	2−1	.693	1
1910	156	606	172	36	15	2	(	)	244	78	55	47		6	11		16				.284	.403	.336	87	12−6	.660	10
1911	140	534	153	26	13	5	(	)	220	55	76	29		7	18		21				.287	.412	.321	79	10−6	.628	11
1912	123	453	138	28	7	8	(	)	204	70	65	39		6	7		16				.305	.450	.362	79	8−4	.655	9
1913	138	535	161	28	10	7	(	)	230	64	71	25		2	11		19				.301	.430	.328	79	10−6	.635	12
1914	145	533	170	26	9	9	(	)	241	66	89	47		3	19		20				.319	.452	.365	95	11−4	.716	13
1915	146	528	136	15	12	5	(	)	190	64	66	52		5	10		21	14	.60		.258	.360	.324	66	9−7	.583	9
1916	149	568	177	32	13	9	(	)	262	76	73	43		6	9		19				.312	.461	.361	98	12−3	.781	12
1917	109	362	113	15	11	1	(	)	153	38	41	20		2	3		5				.312	.423	.349	53	7−3	.713	7
1918	105	409	137	15	3	0	(	)	158	39	51	16		3	5		9				.335	.386	.360	59	8−3	.742	9
1919	137	536	159	23	11	5	(	)	219	70	62	33		6	6		15				.297	.409	.341	76	10−5	.665	10
1920	148	583	191	26	13	9	(	)	270	89	73	48		6	6		8	10	.44		.328	.463	.381	102	12−4	.743	12
1921	148	568	182	31	10	14	(	)	275	91	85	44		3	9		11	8	.58		.320	.484	.367	101	11−5	.684	10
1922	152	600	201	29	12	16	(	)	302	92	112	45		7	8		9	6	.60		.335	.503	.383	116	11−5	.697	15
1923	98	349	131	13	5	8	(	)	178	63	65	23		2	4		3	3	.50		.375	.510	.413	73	7−2	.754	8
1924	141	566	212	41	8	14	(	)	311	92	97	49		4	5		3	4	.43		.375	.549	.425	132	11−3	.814	14
1925	150	616	221	42	14	14	(	)	333	125	103	45		1	8		3	1	.75		.359	.541	.399	129	11−5	.702	14
1926	111	411	119	31	2	5	(	)	169	68	35	21		1	12		4				.290	.411	.317	53	6−3	.529	7
1927	88	247	80	12	1	1	(	)	97	34	38	18		4	7		2				.324	.393	.370	36	4−3	.537	3
2410	9106	2884	476	172	132	(	)	4100	1289	1261	650		74	163		205	46	.56			.317	.450	.361	1531	170−79	.682	186
14.9 yrs		612	194	32	12	9			276	87	85	44		5	11		14				.317	.450	.361				

Teams: Brooklyn, 1909–1926; Philadelphia, 1927.

Points in MVP Voting: 1911, 0; 1913, 0; 1914, 10 (9th, .16); 1924, 40 (4th, .50); 1926, 0; 1927, 0. TOTAL: .66 Award Shares.

Explanation for Gaps in Career or Sudden Changes in Productivity:

1917—*Reach Guide* mentions injury but does not specify.

1923—Held out well into season.

FIELDING LEFT FIELD

Year	G	PO	AS	E	DP	Pct.	Range
1909	26	54	5	3	1	.952	2.27
1910	156	354	21	15	6	.962	2.40
1911	136	287	12	14	0	.955	2.20
1912	122	285	13	10	2	.968	2.44
1913	135	338	13	8	7	.978	2.60
1914	144	331	21	14	5	.962	2.44
1915	144	345	18	18	4	.953	2.52
1916	149	333	14	9	0	.975	2.33
1917	109	216	12	5	5	.979	2.09
1918	105	219	11	5	2	.979	2.19
1919	137	297	9	9	5	.971	2.23
1920	148	287	10	9	5	.971	2.01
1921	148	283	18	11	3	.965	2.03
1922	152	317	17	3	1	.991	2.20
1923	87	135	4	14	1	.908	1.60
1924	139	288	13	11	4	.965	2.17
1925	149	320	7	13	2	.962	2.19
1926	102	202	9	10	3	.955	2.07
1927	62	105	8	2	1	.983	1.82
	2350	4996	235	183	54	.966	2.23

Assists per 154 Games: 15.4

PLAYER: HARRY HEILMANN

Year	G	AB	H	2B	3B	HR	(Hm	Rd)	TB	R	RBI	BB	IBB	HBP	SH	SF	SB	CS	SB%	GIDP	Avg.	Slug	On Base	Runs	Win—Loss	Pct.	AV
1914	67	182	41	8	1	2	(2	0)	57	25	22	22			2	12	1	8	.11		.225	.313	.298	19	2—4	.398	1
1916	136	451	127	30	11	2	(1	1)	185	57	76	42			5	15	9				.282	.410	.339	70	8—5	.639	7
1917	150	556	156	22	11	5	(1	4)	215	57	86	41			3	19	11				.281	.387	.323	73	9—7	.571	9
1918	79	286	79	10	6	5	(2	3)	116	34	44	35			2	8	13				.276	.406	.350	47	6—3	.666	4
1919	140	537	172	30	15	8	(3	5)	256	74	95	37			2	18	7				.320	.477	.355	93	10—5	.686	9
1920	145	543	168	28	5	9	(5	4)	233	66	89	39			2	18	3	7	.30		.309	.429	.347	82	9—7	.553	10
1921	149	602	237	43	14	19	(7	12)	365	114	139	53			2	15	2	6	.25		.394	.606	.435	159	12—3	.782	17
1922	118	455	162	27	10	21	(8	13)	272	92	92	58			3	11	8	4	.67		.356	.598	.423	119	9—3	.786	9
1923	144	524	211	44	11	18	(11	7)	331	121	115	74			5	23	8	7	.53		.403	.632	.463	159	11—2	.850	19
1924	153	570	197	45	16	10	(5	5)	304	107	113	78			4	26	13	5	.72		.346	.533	.412	134	11—4	.728	15
1925	150	573	225	40	11	13	(6	7)	326	97	133	67			1	23	6	6	.50		.393	.569	.441	149	11—3	.773	16
1926	141	502	184	41	8	9	(4	5)	268	90	103	67			4	25	6	7	.46		.367	.534	.426	120	10—3	.749	15
1927	141	505	201	50	9	14	(10	4)	311	106	120	72			2	17	11				.398	.616	.461	145	10—2	.832	19
1928	151	558	183	38	10	14	(10	4)	283	83	107	57			0	18	7	3	.70		.328	.507	.379	112	10—5	.680	14
1929	125	453	156	41	7	15	(9	6)	256	86	120	50			2	14	5	6	.45		.344	.565	.401	104	8—4	.672	11
1930	142	459	153	43	6	19	(4	15)	265	79	91	64			1	15	2				.333	.577	.404	109	9—3	.760	14
1932	15	31	8	2	0	0	(0	0)	10	3	6	0			0	0	0				.258	.323	.258	2	0—1	.305	0
	2146	7787	2660	542	151	183	(88	95)	4053	1291	1551	856		40	277		112	59	.50		.342	.520	.397	1696	147—63	.702	192
13.2 yrs		588	201	41	11	14			306	97	117	65		3	21		8				.342	.520	.397				

Teams: Detroit, 1914–1929; Cincinnati, 1930, 1932.
Points in MVP Voting: 1914, 0; 1922, 8 (.13); 1923, 31 (3rd, .48); 1924, 9 (9th, .14); 1926, 16 (5th, .25); 1927, 35 (2nd, .55); 1932, 0. TOTAL: 1.55 Award Shares.
Reported Salaries: 1921, $7,500; 1922, $12,500.
Explanation for Gaps in Career or Sudden Changes in Productivity:
1918—In the military.
1922—Broke collarbone late in season.
1931—Unknown illness.

FIELDING LEFT FIELD

Year	G	PO	AS	Err	DP	Pct.	Range
1914	29	35	5	6	1	.870	1.38
1916	77	110	10	6	0	.952	1.56
1917	123	200	17	9	4	.960	1.76
1918	40	60	6	3	1	.957	1.65
1920	21	27	6	0	0	1.000	1.57
1921	143	233	10	10	1	.960	1.70
1922	115	175	6	10	2	.948	1.57
1923	130	272	13	12	2	.960	2.19
1924	147	263	31	9	6	.970	2.00
1925	148	278	9	9	1	.970	1.94
1926	134	228	18	7	4	.972	1.84
1927	135	218	11	8	5	.966	1.70
1928	126	215	17	7	2	.971	1.84
1929	113	193	8	7	3	.966	1.78
1930	106	279	16	14	5	.955	2.78
	1587	2786	183	117	37	.962	1.87

Assists per 154 Games: 17.8

PLAYER: KEN WILLIAMS

							BATTING												BASERUNNING				PERCENTAGES			VALUES			
Year	G	AB	H	2B	3B	HR	(Hm	Rd)	TB	R	RBI	BB	IBB	HBP	SH	SF		SB	CS	SB%	GIDP	Avg.	Slug	On Base	Runs	Win–Loss	Pct.	AV
1915	71	219	53	10	4	0	(0	0)	71	22	16	15		2	7			4	3	.57		.242	.324	.288	22	3–4	.464	2
1916	10	27	3	0	0	0	(0	0)	3	1	1	2		0	0			1				.111	.111	.172	1	0–1	.030	0
1918	2	1	0	0	0	0	(0	0)	0	0	1	1		0	0			0				.000		.500	0	0–0	.000	0
1919	65	227	68	10	5	6	(5	1)	106	32	35	26		2	11			7				.300	.467	.361	42	5–2	.724	5
1920	141	521	160	34	13	10	(9	1)	250	90	72	41		4	26			18	8	.69		.307	.480	.346	91	9–6	.581	11
1921	146	547	190	31	7	24	(15	9)	307	115	117	74		4	21			20	17	.54		.347	.561	.415	130	11–4	.711	16
1922	153	585	194	34	11	39	(32	7)	367	128	155	74		7	12			37	19	.66		.332	.627	.406	150	13–4	.780	20
1923	147	555	198	37	12	29	(18	11)	346	106	91	79		2	10			18	17	.51		.357	.623	.432	148	12–3	.829	19
1924	114	398	129	21	4	18	(14	4)	212	78	84	69		1	11			20	11	.65		.324	.533	.415	93	8–3	.725	12
1925	102	411	136	31	5	25	(17	8)	252	83	105	37		3	11			10	5	.67		.331	.613	.381	97	8–4	.686	12
1926	108	347	97	15	7	17	(13	4)	177	55	74	39		1	14			5	4	.56		.280	.510	.342	63	6–4	.604	8
1927	131	421	136	23	6	17	(14	3)	222	70	74	57		1	15			9				.323	.527	.393	89	8–4	.684	13
1928	133	462	140	25	1	8	(4	4)	191	59	67	37		1	15			4	9	.31		.303	.413	.346	66	7–6	.561	8
1929	74	139	48	14	2	3	(1	2)	75	21	21	15		0	7			1	5	.17		.345	.540	.391	29	3–1	.718	3
	1397	4860	1552	285	77	196	(142	54)	2579	860	913	566		28	160			154	98	.58		.319	.531	.382	1019	93–45	.675	129
8.6 yrs		564	180	33	9	23			299	100	106	66		3	19			18				.319	.531	.382				

Teams: Cincinnati, 1915–1916; St. Louis, 1918–1927; Boston, 1928–1929.
Points in MVP Voting: 1922, 0; 1923, 4 (.06); 1924, 1 (.02); 1926, 0; 1927, 0.
Explanation for Gaps in Career or Sudden Changes in Productivity:
1916–1918—Played at Spokane and Portland, was also in military.
1924—Fractured ankle in July, out five weeks.
1925—Injured by pitch, hit in head.

FIELDING LEFT FIELD

Year	G	PO	AS	Err	DP	Pct.	Range
1915	62	117	11	7	4	.948	2.06
1916	10	19	2	1	0	.955	2.10
1919	63	168	10	12	3	.937	2.83
1920	138	331	17	14	6	.961	2.52
1921	145	331	24	26	3	.932	2.45
1922	153	372	16	12	4	.970	2.54
1923	145	333	23	12	5	.967	2.46
1924	109	257	13	9	2	.968	2.48
1925	102	242	11	12	4	.955	2.48
1926	91	189	12	11	2	.948	2.21
1927	113	260	15	10	4	.965	2.43
1928	127	253	10	8	0	.970	2.07
1929	36	75	3	3	2	.963	2.17
	1294	2947	167	137	39	.958	2.41

Assists per 154 Games: 19.8

HOME AND ROAD DATA FOR 1922 SEASON

	G	AB	R	H	2B	3B	HR	RBI	BB	Avg.
HOME	77	295	80	110	14	8	32	103	30	.373
ROAD	76	290	48	84	20	3	7	53	44	.290

Source: Pete Palmer

PLAYER: GOOSE GOSLIN

				BATTING													BASERUNNING				PERCENTAGES			VALUES			
Year	G	AB	H	2B	3B	HR	(Hm	Rd)	TB	R	RBI	BB	IBB	HBP	SH	SF	SB	CS	SB%	GIDP	Avg.	Slug	On Base	Runs	Win—Loss	Pct.	AV
1921	14	50	13	1	1	1	(1	0)	19	8	6	6		1	1		0	0	.00		.260	.380	.345	7	1—1	.516	1
1922	101	358	116	19	7	3	(1	2)	158	44	53	25		3	8		4	4	.50		.324	.441	.365	58	6—3	.649	6
1923	150	600	180	29	18	9	(1	8)	272	86	99	40		3	13		7	2	.78		.300	.453	.340	95	10—7	.590	11
1924	154	579	199	30	17	12	(1	11)	299	100	129	68		9	17		16	14	.53		.344	.516	.410	126	12—4	.766	15
1925	150	601	201	34	20	18	(6	12)	329	116	113	53		6	10		26	8	.76		.334	.547	.388	131	12—4	.732	17
1926	147	567	201	26	15	17	(0	17)	308	105	108	63		7	18		8	8	.50		.354	.543	.414	131	11—4	.740	18
1927	148	581	194	37	15	13	(7	6)	300	96	120	50		5	23		21				.334	.516	.378	114	11—5	.693	13
1928	135	456	173	36	10	17	(4	13)	280	80	102	48		4	20		16	3	.84		.379	.614	.426	126	10—2	.844	16
1929	145	553	159	28	7	18	(3	15)	255	82	91	66		2	18		10	3	.77		.288	.461	.355	97	10—6	.602	10
1930	148	584	180	36	12	37	(17	20)	351	115	138	67		3	14		17	11	.61		.308	.601	.374	132	12—5	.699	16
1931	151	591	194	42	10	24	(15	9)	328	114	105	80		4	0		9	6	.60		.328	.555	.412	137	12—4	.746	15
1932	150	572	171	28	9	17	(12	5)	268	88	104	92		2	1		12	9	.57		.299	.469	.397	110	10—6	.633	13
1933	132	549	163	35	10	10	(4	6)	248	97	64	42		1	7		5	2	.71		.297	.452	.344	87	9—7	.571	10
1934	151	614	187	38	7	13	(4	9)	278	106	100	65		2	5		5	4	.56		.305	.453	.370	105	10—7	.573	12
1935	147	590	172	34	6	9	(1	8)	245	88	109	56		2	3		5	4	.56		.292	.415	.353	88	8—7	.517	9
1936	147	572	180	33	8	24	(12	12)	301	122	125	85		0	5		14	4	.78		.315	.526	.402	126	10—5	.666	13
1937	79	181	43	11	1	4	(3	1)	68	30	35	35		2	1		0	1	.00		.238	.376	.365	27	2—3	.435	1
1938	38	57	9	3	0	2	(0	2)	18	6	8	8		0	0		0		.00		.158	.316	.262	5	0—1	.195	0
	2287	8655	2735	500	173	248	(92	156)	4325	1483	1609	949		56	162		175	83	.68		.316	.500	.381	1702	155—82	.655	196
14.1 yrs		613	194	35	12	18			306	105	114	67		4	11		12				.316	.500	.381				

Teams: Washington, 1921–1929; Washington/St. Louis, 1930; St. Louis, 1931–1932; Washington, 1933; Detroit, 1934–1937; Washington, 1938.

Points in MVP Voting: 1922, 0; 1923, 0; 1924, 0; 1926, 9 (9th, .14); 1927, 15 (6th, .23); 1931, 6 (.09); 1932, 3 (.03); 1933, 0; 1934, 6 (.08); 1935, 0. TOTAL: .57 Award Shares.

Explanation for Gaps in Career or Sudden Changes in Productivity:
1922—Broken wrist.

The increase in power in 1930 is largely a result of escaping from Griffith Stadium in Washington, the worst home run park in baseball for a left-handed batter. Note that in the years 1921–1929 he hit only 24 home runs at home, whereas he hit 84 on the road. In almost any other park, he would have been hitting 30 to 40 home runs a year.

Other Notes: 1936—Only 1 HR vs. LHP, 23 vs. RHP.

Named to *The Sporting News* major league All-Star team in 1925 and 1926.

FIELDING LEFT FIELD

Year	G	PO	AS	Err	DP	Pct.	Range
1921	14	30	1	0	0	1.000	2.21
1922	93	197	8	15	1	.932	2.21
1923	149	310	26	15	5	.957	2.26
1924	154	369	12	16	4	.960	2.47
1925	150	385	24	12	1	.971	2.73
1926	147	373	25	15	8	.964	2.71
1927	148	356	8	17	3	.955	2.46
1928	125	266	14	11	4	.962	2.24
1929	142	299	7	10	1	.968	2.15
1930	148	309	15	12	1	.964	2.19
1931	151	319	14	14	1	.960	2.21
1932	149	330	16	18	5	.951	2.24
1933	128	261	17	10	7	.965	2.17
1934	149	290	15	15	2	.953	2.05
1935	144	326	6	12	2	.965	2.31
1936	144	266	11	13	1	.955	1.92
1937	40	81	2	4	1	.954	2.07
1938	13	25	0	0	0	1.000	1.92
	2188	4792	221	209	47	.960	2.29

Assists per 154 Games: 15.6

PLAYER: JOE MEDWICK

Year	G	AB	H	2B	3B	HR	(Hm	Rd)	TB	R	RBI	BB	IBB	HBP	SH	SF	SB	CS	SB%	GIDP	Avg.	Slug	On Base	Runs	Win–Loss	Pct.	AV
							BATTING										BASERUNNING				PERCENTAGES			VALUES			
1932	26	106	37	12	1	2	(	)	57	13	12	2		1	0		3				.349	.538	.367	20	2–1	.736	2
1933	148	595	182	40	10	18	(7	11)	296	92	98	26		2	3		5			15	.306	.497	.335	97	11–5	.677	13
1934	149	620	198	40	18	18	(	)	328	110	106	21		1	4		3			15	.319	.529	.341	109	11–5	.667	12
1935	154	634	224	46	13	23	(	)	365	132	126	30		4	2		4			15	.353	.576	.385	139	12–4	.777	15
1936	155	636	223	64	13	18	(	)	367	115	138	34		4	3		3			14	.351	.577	.386	141	12–4	.750	19
1937	156	633	237	56	10	31	(	)	406	111	154	41		2	1		4			11	.374	.641	.414	170	13–2	.842	18
1938	146	590	190	47	8	21	(	)	316	100	122	42		2	0		0			21	.322	.536	.369	113	11–5	.708	14
1939	150	606	201	48	8	14	(	)	307	98	117	45		2	14		6			15	.332	.507	.372	117	12–5	.718	15
1940	143	581	175	30	12	17	(5	12)	280	83	86	32		3	0		2			19	.301	.482	.341	90	10–6	.630	12
1941	133	538	171	33	10	18	(12	6)	278	100	88	38		1	2		2			20	.318	.517	.363	95	10–4	.692	13
1942	142	553	166	37	4	4	(2	2)	223	69	96	32		0	2		2			15	.300	.403	.337	72	9–6	.590	10
1943	126	497	138	30	3	5	(	)	189	54	70	19		1	3		1			17	.278	.380	.304	53	6–8	.451	8
1944	128	490	165	24	3	7	(	)	216	64	85	38		1	6		2			12	.337	.441	.381	82	8–4	.656	11
1945	92	310	90	17	0	3	(	)	116	31	37	14		1	3		5			9	.290	.374	.320	36	4–5	.444	4
1946	41	77	24	4	0	2	(2	0)	34	7	18	6		1	1		0			1	.312	.442	.365	13	1–1	.708	1
1947	75	150	46	12	0	4	(	)	70	19	28	16		0	0		0			3	.307	.467	.373	26	3–1	.683	3
1948	20	19	4	0	0	0	(	)	4	0	2	1		0	0		0			1	.211	.211	.250	1	0–1	.093	0
	1984	7635	2471	540	113	205	(	)	3852	1198	1383	437		26	44		42			203	.324	.505	.360	1375	135–66	.671	170
12.2 yrs		623	202	44	9	17			315	98	113	36		2	4		3			17	.324	.505	.360				

Teams: St. Louis, 1932–1939; St. Louis/Brooklyn, 1940; Brooklyn, 1941–1942; Brooklyn/New York, 1943; New York, N.L. 1944; New York/Boston, 1945; Brooklyn, 1946; St. Louis, 1947–1948.

Points in MVP Voting: 1932, 0; 1933, 5 (.06); 1934, 0; 1935, 37 (5th, .46); 1937, 70 (1st, .88); 1938, 55 (.16); 1939, 81 (7th, .24); 1940, 0; 1941, 0; 1942, 20 (.06); 1943, 0; 1944, 9 (.03); 1946, 0; 1947, 0; 1948, 0. TOTAL: 1.89 Award Shares.

Other Notes: Named to *The Sporting News* major league All-Star team in 1935, 1936, 1937, 1938, 1939.

FIELDING LEFT FIELD

Year	G	PO	AS	Err	DP	Pct.	Range
1932	26	63	2	2	1	.970	2.50
1933	147	318	17	7	2	.980	2.28
1934	149	322	10	14	1	.960	2.23
1935	154	352	8	13	0	.965	2.34
1936	155	367	16	6	4	.985	2.47
1937	156	329	9	4	1	.988	2.17
1938	144	330	12	9	6	.974	2.37
1939	149	313	10	8	1	.976	2.17
1940	140	321	8	6	0	.982	2.35
1941	131	270	11	5	2	.983	2.15
1942	140	287	5	3	1	.990	2.09
1943	117	195	11	7	2	.967	1.76
1944	122	290	8	2	2	.993	2.44
1945	61	124	8	1	2	.992	2.16
1946	18	30	0	0	0	1.000	1.67
1947	43	56	3	0	2	1.000	1.37
1948	1	0	0	0	0	.000	0
	1853	3967	138	87	27	.979	2.22

Assists per 154 Games: 11.5

PLAYER: BOB JOHNSON

			BATTING														BASERUNNING				PERCENTAGES			VALUES			
Year	G	AB	H	2B	3B	HR	(Hm Rd)	TB	R	RBI	BB	IBB	HBP	SH	SF	SB	CS	SB%	GIDP	Avg.	Slug	On Base	Runs	Win–Loss	Pct.	AV
1933	142	535	155	44	4	21	(10 11)	270	103	93	85		0	5		8	3	.73		.290	.505	.384	109	9–6	.622	12
1934	141	547	168	26	6	34	(22 12)	308	111	92	58		1	3		12	8	.60		.307	.563	.373	114	10–5	.679	15
1935	147	582	174	29	5	28	(16 12)	297	103	109	78		2	2		2	4	.33		.299	.510	.383	116	10–6	.653	13
1936	153	566	165	29	14	25	(16 9)	297	91	121	88		2	1		6	6	.50		.292	.525	.388	118	10–6	.634	13
1937	138	477	146	32	6	25	(14 11)	265	91	108	98		1	0		9	7	.56		.306	.556	.425	117	10–3	.762	17
1938	152	563	176	27	9	30	(21 9)	311	114	113	87		2	0		9	8	.53		.313	.552	.406	128	11–4	.705	16
1939	150	544	184	30	9	23	(13 10)	301	115	114	99		4	10		15	5	.75	12	.338	.553	.433	138	11–4	.744	16
1940	138	512	137	25	4	31	(15 16)	263	93	103	83		4	1		8	2	.80	20	.268	.514	.373	100	9–6	.620	13
1941	149	552	152	30	8	22	(10 12)	264	98	107	95		3	3		6	4	.60	16	.275	.478	.383	106	10–6	.643	14
1942	149	550	160	35	7	13	(8 5)	248	78	80	82		1	1		3	2	.60	16	.291	.451	.383	99	10–5	.688	10
1943	117	438	116	22	8	7	(2 5)	175	65	63	62		3	0		11	5	.69	11	.265	.400	.360	66	8–5	.623	9
1944	144	525	170	40	8	17	(14 3)	277	106	106	95		4	2		2	6	.25	14	.324	.528	.430	124	11–3	.793	14
1945	143	529	148	27	7	12	(7 5)	225	71	74	63		1	0		5	3	.62	13	.280	.425	.358	83	10–5	.657	12
	1863	6920	2051	396	95	288	(168 120)	3501	1239	1283	1073		24	28		96	63	.60	102	.296	.506	.391	1418	129–62	.677	174
11.5 yrs		602	178	34	8	25		304	108	112	93		2	2		8	5	.60	17	.296	.506	.391				

Teams: Philadelphia, AL, 1933–1942; Washington, 1943; Boston, AL, 1944–1945.
Points in MVP Voting: 1933, 5 (.06); 1934, 0; 1935, 0; 1937, 0; 1938, 13 (.04); 1939, 52 (.15); 1940, 0; 1941, 0; 1942, 0; 1943, 116 (5th, .35); 1944, 51 (10th, .15); 1945, 6 (.02). TOTAL: .77 Award Shares.
Other Notes: 1936—4 HR vs. LHP, 21 vs. RHP.
1938—4 HR vs. LHP, 26 vs. RHP.
1939—3 HR vs. LHP, 20 vs. RHP.

FIELDING LEFT FIELD

Year	G	PO	AS	Err	DP	Pct.	Range
1933	142	298	16	16	3	.952	2.21
1934	139	304	17	11	3	.967	2.31
1935	147	337	13	20	4	.946	2.38
1936	131	289	13	12	3	.962	2.31
1937	133	313	14	8	3	.976	2.46
1938	150	400	21	16	3	.963	2.81
1939	150	369	15	13	3	.967	2.56
1940	136	310	15	13	4	.962	2.39
1941	122	287	17	3	0	.990	2.49
1942	149	318	18	13	1	.963	2.26
1943	88	212	11	1	1	.996	2.53
1944	142	270	23	7	3	.977	2.06
1945	140	296	15	8	4	.975	2.22
	1769	4003	208	141	35	.968	2.38

Assists per 154 Games: 18.1

PLAYER: TED WILLIAMS

	BATTING																BASERUNNING				PERCENTAGES			VALUES			
Year	G	AB	H	2B	3B	HR	(Hm	Rd)	TB	R	RBI	BB	IBB	HBP	SH	SF	SB	CS	SB%	GIDP	Avg.	Slug	On Base	Runs	Win–Loss	Pct.	AV
1939	149	565	185	44	11	31	(14	17)	344	131	145	107		2	0	3	2	1	.67	10	.327	.609	.434	157	12–3	.790	18
1940	144	561	193	43	14	23	(9	14)	333	134	113	96		3	1		4	4	.50	13	.344	.594	.442	154	11–3	.792	15
1941	143	456	185	33	3	37	(19	18)	335	135	120	145		3	0		2	4	.33	10	.406	.735	.551	202	10–1	.931	23
1942	150	522	186	34	5	36	(16	20)	338	141	137	145		4	0		3	2	.60	12	.356	.648	.499	185	12–1	.911	20
1946	150	514	176	37	8	38	(18	20)	343	142	123	156		2	0		0	0	.00	12	.342	.667	.497	188	12–1	.914	19
1947	156	528	181	40	9	32	(16	16)	335	125	114	162		2	1		0	1	.00	10	.343	.634	.498	186	12–1	.909	20
1948	137	509	188	44	3	25	(9	16)	313	124	127	126		3	0		4	0	1.00	10	.369	.615	.497	172	11–2	.877	18
1949	155	566	194	39	3	43	(23	20)	368	150	159	162		2	0		1	1	.50	22	.343	.650	.490	193	13–2	.872	20
1950	89	334	106	24	1	28	(16	12)	216	82	97	82		0	0		3	0	1.00	12	.317	.647	.452	103	7–2	.793	11
1951	148	531	169	28	4	30	(18	12)	295	109	126	144		0	0		1	1	.50	10	.318	.556	.464	152	11–2	.831	17
1952	6	10	4	0	1	1	(1	0)	9	2	3	2		0	0		0	0	.00	0	.400	.900	.500	5	0–0	.963	0
1953	37	91	37	6	0	13	(8	5)	82	17	34	19		0	0		0	1	.00	1	.407	.901	.509	44	2–0	.962	4
1954	117	386	133	23	1	29	(16	13)	245	93	89	136		5	0	3	0	0	.00	10	.345	.635	.517	142	9–1	.908	16
1955	98	320	114	21	3	28	(15	13)	225	77	83	91	17	2	0	4	2	0	1.00	8	.356	.703	.496	118	7–1	.911	14
1956	136	400	138	28	2	24	(10	14)	242	71	82	102	11	1	0	0	0	0	.00	13	.345	.605	.479	121	9–2	.852	15
1957	132	420	163	28	1	38	(12	26)	307	96	87	119	33	5	0	2	0	0	.00	11	.388	.731	.526	167	9–1	.932	21
1958	129	411	135	23	2	26	(10	16)	240	81	85	98	12	0	0	4	1	0	1.00	19	.328	.584	.454	112	9–2	.837	13
1959	103	272	69	15	0	10	(3	7)	114	32	43	52	6	2	0	5	0	0	.00	7	.254	.419	.372	45	5–3	.602	5
1960	113	310	98	15	0	29	(15	14)	200	56	72	75	7	3	0	2	1	1	.50	7	.316	.645	.451	95	7–1	.861	11
	2292	7706	2654	525	71	521	(248	273)	4884	1798	1839	2019	86	39	2	23	24	17	.59	197	.344	.634	.481	2541	168–28	.858	280
14.1 yrs		545	188	37	5	37			345	127	130	143	20	3	0	4	2	1		14	.344	.634	.481	127			14

Teams: Boston, 1939–1942, 1946–1960.

Points in MVP Voting: 1939, 126 (4th, .38); 1940, 16 (.05); 1941, 254 (2nd, .76); 1942, 249 (2nd, .74); 1946, 224 (1st, .67); 1947, 201 (2nd, .60); 1948, 171 (3rd, .51); 1949, 272 (1st, .81); 1950, 7 (.02); 1951, 35 (.10); 1952, 0; 1953, 0; 1954, 65 (7th, .19); 1955, 143 (4th, .43); 1956, 70 (6th, .21); 1957, 209 (2nd, .62); 1958, 89 (7th, .26); 1959, 0; 1960, 25 (.07). TOTAL: 6.42 Award Shares.

Reported Salaries: 1939, $4,500; 1940, $10,000; 1942, $30,000; 1946, $40,000 + $10,000 bonus for not playing in some exhibitions; 1947, $70,000; 1950, $100,000; 1955, $98,000; 1959, $125,000; 1960, $95,000.

Explanation for Gaps in Career or Sudden Changes in Productivity:

1943–45—Marines.

1950—Crashed into wall at Comiskey Park during All-Star Game; damaged elbow. Surgery required—thirteen chips removed from elbow. Ralph Kiner hit the fly.

1952–53—Back in marines.

1954—First day of spring training fell and broke his collarbone. Patched together with stainless steel pin, which Williams still has in him. Did not play first thirty-six games of season.

1955—Slowed by bad back, pneumonia, lumbago and injury to arch of foot caused when he slipped in the shower.

1959—Operated on for pinched nerve in neck.

Other Notes: Named to *The Sporting News* major league All-Star team in 1939, 1940, 1941, 1942, 1946, 1947, 1948, 1949, 1951, 1955, 1956, 1957.

In 1939 SF were counted as sacrifice hits. Pete Palmer has determined that all three of Williams' recorded SH for 1939 were run scoring flies.

FIELDING LEFT FIELD

Year	G	PO	AS	Err	DP	Pct.	Range
1939	149	318	11	19	3	.945	2.21
1940	143	302	13	13	2	.960	2.20
1941	133	262	11	11	2	.961	2.05
1942	150	313	15	4	4	.988	2.19
1946	150	325	7	10	2	.971	2.21
1947	156	347	10	9	2	.975	2.29
1948	134	289	9	5	2	.983	2.22
1949	155	337	12	6	3	.983	2.25
1950	86	165	7	8	0	.956	2.00
1951	147	315	12	4	6	.988	2.22
1952	2	4	0	0	0	1.000	2.00
1953	26	31	1	1	1	.970	1.23
1954	115	213	5	4	0	.982	1.90
1955	93	170	5	2	0	.989	1.88
1956	110	174	7	5	2	.973	1.65
1957	125	215	2	1	0	.995	1.74
1958	114	154	3	7	0	.957	1.38
1959	76	94	4	3	0	.970	1.29
1960	87	131	6	1	1	.993	1.57
	2151	4159	140	113	30	.974	2.00

Assists per 154 Games: 10.0

PLAYER: STAN MUSIAL

						BATTING											BASERUNNING				PERCENTAGES			VALUES			
Year	G	AB	H	2B	3B	HR	(Hm	Rd)	TB	R	RBI	BB	IBB	HBP	SH	SF	SB	CS	SB%	GIDP	Avg.	Slug	On Base	Runs	Win–Loss	Pct.	AV
1941	12	47	20	4	0	1	(0	1)	27	8	7	2		0	0		1			0	.426	.574	.449	12	1–0	.893	1
1942	140	467	147	32	10	10	(8	2)	229	87	72	62		2	5		6			3	.315	.490	.394	96	10–2	.800	12
1943	157	617	220	48	20	13	(7	6)	347	108	81	72		2	10		9			17	.357	.562	.419	147	14–2	.866	17
1944	146	568	197	51	14	12	(5	7)	312	112	94	90		5	4		7			7	.347	.549	.438	145	12–2	.866	15
1946	156	624	228	50	20	16	(10	6)	366	124	103	73		3	2		7			7	.365	.587	.433	164	13–2	.880	15
1947	149	587	183	30	13	19	(5	14)	296	113	95	80		4	6		4			18	.312	.504	.394	118	12–4	.730	13
1948	155	611	230	46	18	39	(16	23)	429	135	131	79		3	1		7			18	.376	.702	.450	191	13–2	.892	23
1949	157	612	207	41	13	36	(13	23)	382	128	123	107		2	0		3			12	.338	.624	.438	173	13–2	.866	18
1950	146	555	192	41	7	28	(15	13)	331	105	109	87		3	0		5			11	.346	.596	.437	149	12–2	.853	15
1951	152	578	205	30	12	32	(19	13)	355	124	108	98		1	1		4	5	.44	6	.355	.614	.448	169	13–2	.881	19
1952	154	578	194	42	6	21	(10	11)	311	105	91	96		2	0		7	7	.50	11	.336	.538	.432	141	12–2	.833	15
1953	157	593	200	53	9	30	(15	15)	361	127	113	105		0	0		3	4	.43	10	.337	.609	.437	166	13–2	.845	17
1954	153	591	195	41	9	35	(19	16)	359	120	126	103		4	0	7	1	7	.12	20	.330	.607	.428	155	12–4	.780	17
1955	154	562	179	30	5	33	(22	11)	318	97	108	80	19	8	2	4	5	4	.56	12	.319	.566	.407	131	12–3	.784	14
1956	156	594	184	33	6	27	(14	13)	310	87	109	75	15	3	3	7	2	0	1.00	19	.310	.522	.384	119	12–4	.732	14
1957	134	502	176	38	3	29	(12	17)	307	82	102	66	19	2	1	8	1	1	.50	13	.351	.612	.421	129	11–2	.828	17
1958	135	472	159	35	2	17	(13	4)	249	64	62	72	26	1	0	4	0	0	.00	19	.337	.528	.423	102	10–3	.785	14
1959	115	341	87	13	2	14	(10	4)	146	37	44	60	11	0	0	3	2	0	.00	12	.255	.428	.364	53	6–4	.584	7
1960	116	331	91	17	1	17	(10	7)	161	49	63	41	7	2	0	4	1	1	.50	5	.275	.486	.354	59	7–3	.709	7
1961	123	372	107	22	4	15	(11	4)	182	46	70	52	17	1	0	6	0	0	.00	7	.288	.489	.371	69	7–3	.697	8
1962	135	433	143	18	1	19	(10	9)	220	57	82	64	4	3	0	5	3	0	1.00	13	.330	.508	.416	94	9–3	.777	12
1963	124	337	86	10	2	12	(8	4)	136	34	58	35	9	2	0	5	2	0	1.00	3	.255	.404	.325	47	5–4	.566	5
	3026	10972	3630	725	177	475	(252	223)	6134	1949	1951	1599	127	53	35	53	78	31	.48	243	.331	.559	.416	2627	228–58	.798	295
18.7 yrs		587	194	39	9	25			328	104	104	86		3	2		4			13	.331	.559	.416				

Teams: St. Louis, 1941–1963.

Points in MVP Voting: 1941, 0; 1942, 26 (.08); 1943, 267 (1st, .79); 1944, 136 (4th, .40); 1946, 319 (1st, .95); 1947, 12 (.04); 1948, 303 (1st, .90); 1949, 226 (2nd, .79); 1950, 158 (2nd, .85); 1951, 191 (2nd, .57); 1952, 127 (5th, .38); 1953, 62 (8th, .18); 1954, 97 (6th, .29); 1955, 46 (8th, .14); 1956, 62 (9th, .18); 1957, 230 (2nd, .68); 1958, 39 (.12); 1959, 0; 1960, 18 (.06); 1962, 19 (10th, .07). TOTAL: 7.47 Award Shares.

Reported Salaries: 1938, $65/month in minors; 1940, $100/month in minors; 1941, $100/month raised to $150 and then $350 when promoted in minors; 1941, $400/month in majors; 1942, $400/month raised to $4,500; 1943, $6,250; 1944, $10,000; 1946, $13,500; 1947, $31,000; 1948, $31,000 raised to $36,000; 1949, $55,000; 1950, $55,000; 1951, $80,000 (not paid until February 1952 due to regulations of Wage Stabilization Board); 1952 and for several season thereafter, $80,000; 1958, $91,000.

Explanation for Gaps in Career of Sudden Changes in Productivity:
1945—Navy service
1947—Acute appendicitis (onset in April; hit .146 in April, .227 in May.)
1950—Late April: strained ligament in left knee, bothered him all year
   Early June: suffered hand injury on wild throw from pitcher while playing first base. Was hitting .440 at the time.
1957—League-record consecutive game streak ended when he took a terrible swing at a pitch, threw left arm out of joint, fractured bone in shoulder socket and tore muscles in shoulder and around shoulder blade.
1959—Reported at 187, well over normal weight; also had a baby who cried a lot and caused him to lose some sleep during the summer.
Other Notes: Nine seasons in top five in MVP voting.
Named to *The Sporting News* major league All-Star team in 1943, 1944, 1946, 1948, 1949, 1950, 1951, 1952, 1953, 1954, 1957, 1958.

		FIELDING LEFT FIELD					
Year	G	PO	AS	Err	DP	Pct.	Range
1941	11	20	1	0	0	1.000	1.91
1942	135	296	6	5	0	.984	2.24
1943	155	376	15	7	4	.982	2.52
1944	146	353	16	5	2	.987	2.53
1946	42	110	4	2	0	.983	2.71
1948	155	347	10	7	3	.981	2.30
1949	156	326	10	3	5	.991	2.15
1950	77	132	2	5	1	.964	1.74
1951	91	216	13	6	4	.974	2.52
1952	135	298	6	4	2	.987	2.25
1953	157	294	9	5	1	.984	1.93
1954	152	271	13	3	4	.990	1.87
1955	51	75	2	1	0	.987	1.51
1956	53	84	5	1	0	.989	1.68
1959	3	1	0	0	0	1.000	0.33
1960	59	97	2	1	0	.990	1.68
1961	103	149	9	1	0	.994	1.53
1962	119	164	6	4	1	.977	1.43
1963	96	121	4	4	0	.969	1.30
	1896	3730	133	64	27	.984	2.04

Assists per 154 Games: 10.8

PLAYER: RALPH KINER

				BATTING														BASERUNNING				PERCENTAGES			VALUES			
Year	G	AB	H	2B	3B	HR	(Hm	Rd)	TB	R	RBI	BB	IBB	HBP	SH	SF	SB	CS	SB%	GIDP	Avg.	Slug	On Base	Runs	Win–Loss	Pct.	AV
1946	144	502	124	17	3	23	(8	15)	216	63	81	74			1	2	3			15	.247	.430	.344	75	9–5	.630	9
1947	152	565	177	23	4	51	(28	23)	361	118	127	98			2	1	1			12	.313	.639	.416	154	12–3	.812	17
1948	156	555	147	19	5	40	(31	9)	296	104	123	112			3	0	1			15	.265	.533	.391	120	12–4	.744	14
1949	152	549	170	19	5	54	(29	25)	361	116	127	117			1	0	6			10	.310	.658	.432	163	12–2	.854	18
1950	150	547	149	21	6	47	(27	20)	323	112	118	122			3	0	2			22	.272	.590	.408	133	12–4	.747	14
1951	151	531	164	31	6	42	(26	16)	333	124	109	137			2	0	2	1	.67	10	.309	.627	.452	165	12–2	.850	16
1952	149	516	126	17	2	37	(22	15)	258	90	87	110			7	0	3	0	1.00	6	.244	.500	.384	111	11–3	.763	11
1953	158	562	157	20	3	35	(19	16)	288	100	116	100			3	1	2	1	.67	11	.279	.512	.390	120	11–4	.726	13
1954	147	557	159	36	5	22	(9	13)	271	88	73	76			2	5	3	2	0	1.00	17	.285	.487	.369	103	10–5	.657	10
1955	113	321	78	13	0	18	(11	7)	145	56	54	65	1		0	0	4	0	0	.00	8	.243	.452	.367	57	6–3	.669	7
9.1 yrs	1472	5205	1451	216	39	369	(210	159)	2852	971	1015	1011	1		24	9	7	22	2	.82	126	.279	.548	.397	1202	108–37	.747	129
		573	160	24	4	41			314	107	112	111			3	1		2			14	.279	.548	.397				

Teams: Pittsburgh, 1946–1952; Pittsburgh/Chicago, N.L. 1953; Chicago, 1954; Cleveland, 1955

Points in MVP Voting: 1946, 2 (.01); 1947, 101 (6th, .30); 1948, 55 (7th, .16); 1949, 133 (4th, .40); 1950, 91 (5th, .27); 1951, 49 (10th, .15); 1952, 8 (.02); 1953, 0; 1954, 0; 1955, 0. TOTAL: 1.31 Award Shares.

Reported Salaries: 1950, $65,000; 1952, $90,000.

Explanation for Gaps in Career or Sudden Changes in Productivity:
1947—Pittsburgh LF fence moved in to normal distance (335 feet; was 365 feet prior to 1947).
1952, 1955—Productivity curtailed by back problems.

Other Notes: Named to *The Sporting News* major league All-Star team in 1947, 1949, 1950, 1951.
Only 3 HR vs. LHP, 34 vs. RHP, 1952.
7 HR vs. LHP, 47 vs. RHP, 1949
Tied N.L. record for home runs on the road (23) in 1947; broke it in '49 with 25. Record now held by George Foster.

FIELDING LEFT FIELD

Year	G	PO	AS	Err	DP	Pct.	Range
1946	140	339	6	11	0	.969	2.46
1947	152	390	8	7	1	.983	2.62
1948	154	382	6	10	1	.975	2.52
1949	152	311	12	7	3	.979	2.12
1950	150	287	13	11	2	.965	2.00
1951	94	195	7	7	1	.967	2.15
1952	149	250	9	8	0	.970	1.74
1953	157	282	11	8	3	.973	1.87
1954	147	298	6	9	1	.971	2.07
1955	87	141	2	2	0	.986	1.64
	1382	2875	80	80	12	.974	2.14

Assists per 154 Games: 8.9

PLAYER: FRANK HOWARD

Year	G	AB	H	2B	3B	HR	(Hm	Rd)	TB	R	RBI	BB	IBB	HBP	SH	SF	SB	CS	SB%	GIDP	Avg.	Slug	On Base	Runs	Win—Loss	Pct	AV
1958	8	29	7	1	0	1	(0	1)	11	3	2	1	0	0	0	0	0	0	.00	1	.241	.379	.267	3	0–1	.306	0
1959	9	21	3	0	1	1	(0	1)	8	2	6	2	0	0	0	0	0	0	.00	0	.143	.381	.217	2	0–0	.294	0
1960	117	448	120	15	2	23	(14	9)	208	54	77	32	1	3	2	2	0	1	.00	8	.268	.464	.320	67	8–5	.631	8
1961	92	267	79	10	2	15	(4	11)	138	36	45	21	3	1	1	2	0	1	.00	12	.296	.517	.347	45	5–3	.619	5
1962	141	493	146	25	6	31	(13	18)	276	80	119	39	10	1	1	4	1	0	1.00	18	.296	.560	.346	93	9–4	.677	12
1963	123	417	114	16	1	28	(13	15)	216	58	64	33	4	4	2	3	1	2	.33	7	.273	.518	.330	72	9–3	.738	8
1964	134	433	98	13	2	24	(11	13)	187	60	69	51	10	0	1	7	1	0	1.00	14	.226	.432	.303	58	8–5	.585	8
1965	149	516	149	22	6	21	(5	16)	246	53	84	55	2	2	0	2	0	0	.00	9	.289	.477	.358	92	10–4	.724	11
1966	146	493	137	19	4	18	(13	5)	218	52	71	53	6	1	0	2	1	1	.50	14	.278	.442	.348	77	9–4	.678	11
1967	149	519	133	20	2	36	(19	17)	265	71	89	60	7	5	0	1	0	1	.00	14	.256	.511	.338	88	11–4	.719	12
1968	158	598	164	28	3	44	(18	26)	330	79	106	54	12	6	0	5	0	0	.00	13	.274	.552	.338	110	13–4	.759	12
1969	161	592	175	17	2	48	(27	21)	340	111	111	102	19	5	0	3	1	0	1.00	29	.296	.574	.402	132	13–4	.786	13
1970	161	566	160	15	1	44	(24	20)	309	90	126	132	29	2	0	6	1	2	.33	23	.283	.546	.416	130	13–3	.795	15
1971	153	549	153	25	2	26	(10	16)	260	60	83	77	20	2	0	5	1	0	1.00	29	.279	.474	.367	89	11–5	.689	11
1972	109	320	78	10	0	10	(9	1)	118	29	38	46	8	1	0	1	1	0	1.00	16	.244	.369	.340	38	5–4	.560	4
1973	85	227	58	9	1	12	(6	6)	105	26	29	24	4	0	0	0	0	1	1.00	12	.256	.463	.327	30	4–3	.550	4
	1895	6488	1774	245	35	382	(186	196)	3235	864	1119	782	135	33	7	43	8	9	.47	219	.273	.499	.352	1124	128–57	.691	134
11.7 yrs		555	152	21	3	33			277	74	96	67	12	3	1	4	1	1		19	.273	.499	.352				

Teams: Los Angeles Dodgers, 1958–1964; Washington Senators, 1965–1971; Texas Rangers, 1972; Detroit Tigers, 1972–1973.

Points in MVP Voting: 1958–1961, 0; 1962, 32 (9th, .11); 1963–1964, 0; 1965, 2 (.01); 1966–1967, 0; 1968, 63 (8th, .23); 1969, 115 (4th, .34); 1970, 91 (5th, .27); 1971–1973, 0. TOTAL: .96 Award Shares.

FIELDING LEFT FIELD

Year	G	PO	AS	Err	DP	Pct.	Range
1958	8	12	1	0	0	1.000	1.62
1959	6	10	0	0	0	1.000	1.67
1960	115	177	8	3	1	.984	1.61
1961	65	79	6	6	0	.934	1.31
1962	131	187	19	6	4	.972	1.57
1963	111	190	4	8	0	.960	1.75
1964	122	183	2	4	0	.979	1.52
1965	138	204	5	4	0	.981	1.51
1966	135	216	5	4	1	.982	1.64
1967	141	210	5	3	1	.986	1.52
1968	107	160	11	8	1	.955	1.60
1969	114	147	3	4	0	.974	1.32
1970	120	172	6	5	4	.973	1.48
1971	100	141	7	1	0	.993	1.48
1972	22	26	0	1	0	.963	1.18
	1435	2114	82	57	12	.975	1.53

Assists per 154 Games: 8.8

PLAYER: BILLY WILLIAMS

Year	G	AB	H	2B	3B	HR	(Hm	Rd)	TB	R	RBI	BB	IBB	HBP	SH	SF	SB	CS	SB%	GIDP	Avg.	Slug	On Base	Runs	Win−Loss	Pct.	AV
1959	18	33	5	0	1	0	(0	0)	7	0	2	1	0	0	0	0	0	0	.00	2	.152	.212	.176	1	0−1	.030	0
1960	12	47	13	0	2	2	(0	2)	23	4	7	5	0	0	0	0	0	0	.00	1	.277	.489	.346	8	1−0	.648	1
1961	146	529	147	20	7	25	(17	8)	256	75	86	45	11	5	1	4	6	0	1.00	11	.278	.484	.337	87	9−6	.602	10
1962	159	618	184	22	8	22	(12	10)	288	94	92	70	3	4	0	7	9	9	.50	11	.298	.466	.369	107	11−6	.660	12
1963	161	612	175	36	9	25	(16	9)	304	87	95	68	9	2	2	3	7	6	.54	12	.286	.497	.357	108	13−4	.761	13
1964	162	645	201	39	2	33	(20	13)	343	100	98	59	8	2	0	3	10	7	.59	11	.312	.532	.370	125	13−4	.746	15
1965	164	645	203	39	6	34	(20	14)	356	115	108	65	7	3	1	5	10	1	.91	20	.315	.552	.377	132	13−4	.772	15
1966	162	648	179	23	5	29	(16	13)	299	100	91	69	16	4	0	6	6	3	.67	12	.276	.461	.347	104	11−7	.622	12
1967	162	634	176	21	12	28	(12	16)	305	92	84	68	8	2	2	6	6	3	.67	13	.278	.481	.346	106	12−6	.678	11
1968	163	642	185	30	8	30	(16	14)	321	91	98	48	10	2	0	7	4	1	.80	13	.288	.500	.336	107	13−5	.720	11
1969	163	642	188	33	10	21	(14	7)	304	103	95	59	15	4	0	3	3	2	.60	15	.293	.474	.355	106	12−6	.685	10
1970	161	636	205	34	4	42	(28	14)	373	137	129	72	9	2	0	4	7	1	.87	13	.322	.586	.391	147	13−4	.788	16
1971	157	594	179	27	5	28	(16	12)	300	86	93	77	18	3	0	3	7	5	.58	17	.301	.505	.383	112	12−4	.752	14
1972	150	574	191	34	6	37	(24	13)	348	95	122	62	20	6	0	8	3	1	.75	14	.333	.606	.398	137	13−2	.838	16
1973	156	576	166	22	2	20	(10	10)	252	72	86	76	14	1	0	6	4	3	.57	13	.288	.438	.369	94	11−5	.691	13
1974	117	404	113	22	0	16	(10	6)	183	55	68	67	12	1	0	2	4	5	.44	9	.280	.453	.382	71	7−4	.645	8
1975	155	520	127	20	1	23	(8	15)	218	68	81	76	7	2	1	3	0	0	.00	9	.244	.419	.341	78	8−7	.542	8
1976	120	351	74	12	0	11	(6	5)	119	36	41	58	15	0	1	3	4	2	.67	4	.211	.339	.320	41	5−6	.465	4
	2488	9350	2711	434	88	426	(245	181)	4599	1410	1476	1045	182	43	8	73	90	49	.65	200	.290	.492	.361	1671	178−80	.689	189
15.4 yrs		609	177	28	6	28			299	92	96	68	12	3	1	5	6	3		13	.290	.492	.361				

Teams: Chicago, N.L. 1959–1974; Oakland, 1975–1976.

Points in MVP Voting: 1959, 0; 1960, 0; 1962, 0; 1963, 0; 1964, 6 (.02); 1965, 21 (.08); 1966, 0; 1967, 0; 1968, 48 (8th, .17); 1969, 6 (.02); 1970, 218 (2nd, .65); 1971, 10 (.03); 1972, 211 (2nd, .63); 1973, 2 (.01); 1974, 0; 1975, 0; 1976, 0. TOTAL: 1.61 Award Shares.

Reported Salaries: 1972, $115,000.

Explanation for Gaps in Career or Sudden Changes in Productivity:
1974—Attempting to play first base, spiked himself in the ankle, August 19, and was out for a month.

Other Notes: Named to *The Sporting News* National League All-Star team in 1964, 1968, 1970, 1972.

FIELDING LEFT FIELD

Year	G	PO	AS	E	DP	Pct.	Range
1959	10	18	0	0	0	1.000	1.80
1960	12	25	0	1	0	.962	2.08
1961	135	220	9	11	3	.954	1.70
1962	159	273	18	10	4	.967	1.83
1963	160	298	13	4	2	.987	1.94
1964	162	233	14	13	0	.950	1.52
1965	164	296	10	10	2	.968	1.87
1966	162	319	9	8	3	.976	2.02
1967	162	271	3	3	1	.989	1.69
1968	163	261	4	9	0	.967	1.63
1969	159	250	15	12	2	.957	1.67
1970	160	259	13	3	1	.989	1.70
1971	154	284	8	7	3	.977	1.90
1972	144	233	9	4	0	.984	1.68
1973	138	253	14	4	1	.985	1.93
1974	43	69	4	2	2	.973	1.70
1976	1	0	0	0	0	0	0
	2088	3562	143	101	24	.973	1.77

Assists per 154 Games: 10.5

PLAYER: CARL YASTRZEMSKI

Year	G	AB	H	2B	3B	HR	(Hm	Rd)	TB	R	RBI	BB	IBB	HBP	SH	SF	SB	CS	SB%	GIDP	Avg.	Slug	On Base	Runs	Win–Loss	Pct.	AV
1961	148	583	155	31	6	11	(6	5)	231	71	80	50	3	3	2	5	6	5	.55	19	.266	.396	.323	72	8–9	.450	8
1962	160	646	191	43	6	19	(11	8)	303	99	94	66	7	3	2	2	7	4	.64	27	.296	.469	.362	103	11–7	.609	12
1963	151	570	183	40	3	14	(6	8)	271	91	68	95	6	1	1	1	8	5	.62	12	.321	.475	.418	118	12–3	.771	13
1964	151	567	164	29	9	15	(6	9)	256	77	67	75	6	2	1	1	6	5	.55	30	.289	.451	.373	89	10–7	.587	13
1965	133	494	154	45	3	20	(16	4)	265	78	72	70	8	1	2	4	7	6	.54	16	.312	.536	.394	102	10–4	.736	14
1966	160	594	165	39	2	16	(11	5)	256	81	80	84	10	1	0	1	8	9	.47	17	.278	.431	.368	92	10–6	.620	13
1967	161	579	189	31	4	44	(27	17)	360	112	121	91	11	4	1	5	10	8	.56	5	.326	.622	.418	155	13–2	.861	19
1968	157	539	162	32	2	23	(11	12)	267	90	74	119	13	2	0	4	13	6	.68	12	.301	.495	.426	121	12–3	.825	15
1969	162	603	154	28	2	40	(21	19)	306	96	111	101	9	1	0	2	15	7	.68	14	.255	.507	.362	113	12–6	.666	13
1970	161	566	186	29	0	40	(22	18)	335	125	102	128	12	1	0	2	23	13	.64	12	.329	.592	.452	157	13–2	.834	17
1971	148	508	129	21	2	15	(7	8)	199	75	70	106	12	1	0	5	8	7	.53	10	.254	.392	.381	80	9–6	.618	12
1972	125	455	120	18	2	12	(5	7)	178	70	68	67	3	4	0	9	5	4	.56	13	.264	.391	.357	66	8–5	.596	9
1973	152	540	160	25	4	19	(8	11)	250	82	95	105	13	0	1	6	9	7	.56	19	.296	.463	.406	103	11–4	.715	11
1974	148	515	155	25	2	15	(5	10)	229	93	79	104	16	3	0	11	12	7	.63	12	.301	.445	.414	102	11–4	.738	13
1975	149	543	146	30	1	14	(8	6)	220	91	60	87	12	2	0	2	8	4	.67	14	.269	.405	.371	84	9–7	.572	10
1976	155	546	146	23	2	21	(10	11)	236	71	102	80	6	1	1	8	5	6	.45	12	.267	.432	.357	86	10–6	.623	11
1977	150	558	165	27	3	28	(14	14)	282	99	102	73	6	1	0	11	11	1	.92	10	.296	.505	.372	110	11–5	.684	15
1978	144	523	145	21	2	17	(7	10)	221	70	81	76	8	3	1	8	4	5	.44	9	.277	.423	.367	85	9–6	.620	11
1979	147	518	140	28	1	21	(15	6)	233	69	87	62	8	2	0	8	3	3	.50	12	.270	.450	.346	81	8–7	.559	10
1980	105	364	100	21	1	15	(5	10)	168	49	50	44	5	0	1	3	0	2	.00	9	.275	.462	.350	58	6–4	.583	7
1981	91	338	83	14	1	7	(3	4)	120	36	53	49	4	0	0	3	0	1	.00	10	.246	.355	.338	41	4–6	.446	4
1982	131	459	126	22	1	16	(7	9)	198	53	72	59	1	2	0	3	0	1	.00	12	.275	.431	.358	72	8–5	.600	10
1983	119	380	101	24	0	10	(6	4)	155	38	56	54	11	2	0	1	0	0	.00	13	.266	.408	.359	55	6–5	.547	6
20.4 yrs	3308	11988	3419	646	59	452	(237	215)	5539	1816	1844	1845	190	40	13	105	168	116	.59	323	.285	.462	.379	2147	220–118	.650	266
		587	167	32	3	22			271	89	90	90	9	2	1	5	8	6		16	.285	.462	.379				

Teams: Boston, 1961–1983.

Points in MVP Voting: 1961, 0; 1962, 9 (.03); 1963, 81 (6th, .29); 1964, 0; 1965, 22 (10th, .08); 1966, 0; 1967, 275 (1st, .98); 1968, 50 (9th, .18); 1969, 8 (.02); 1970, 136 (4th, .40); 1971, 0; 1972, 0; 1973, 9 (.03); 1974, 14 (.04); 1975, 1 (.00); 1976, 26 (.08); 1977, 25 (.06); 1978, 17 (.04); 1979, 0; 1980, 0; 1981, 0; 1982, 0; 1983, 0. TOTAL: 2.23 Award Shares.

Reported Salaries: 1970—approximately $125,000; 1972—$167,000.

Explanation for Gaps in Career or Sudden Changes in Productivity:
1965—Suffered rib and kidney injuries in collision on basepaths, May 16. Out 27 games.
1972—Missed a month with a knee injury.
1980—August 30, out for season when ran into Monster (wall) in left field, making catch.
1981—Strike.

Other Notes: Named to *The Sporting News* American League All-Star team in 1963, 1965, 1967.

FIELDING LEFT FIELD

Year	G	PO	AS	E	DP	Pct.	Range
1961	147	248	12	10	1	.963	1.77
1962	160	329	15	11	3	.969	2.15
1963	151	283	18	6	3	.980	1.99
1964	148	372	19	11	3	.973	2.64
1965	130	222	11	3	2	.987	1.79
1966	158	310	15	5	2	.985	2.06
1967	161	297	13	7	1	.978	1.93
1968	155	301	12	3	3	.991	2.02
1969	143	246	17	4	2	.985	1.84
1970	69	120	3	6	0	.953	1.78
1971	146	281	16	2	4	.993	2.03
1972	83	141	10	4	1	.974	1.82
1973	14	30	0	0	0	1.000	2.14
1974	63	99	2	4	1	.962	1.60
1975	8	15	1	0	0	1.000	2.00
1976	51	93	3	2	0	.980	1.88
1977	140	287	16	0	1	1.000	2.16
1978	71	136	8	2	2	.986	2.03
1979	36	63	1	2	0	.970	1.78
1980	39	65	3	0	1	1.000	1.74
1982	2	3	0	0	0	1.000	1.50
1983	1	0	0	0	0	0	0
	2076	3941	195	82	30	.981	1.99

Assists per 154 Games: 14.5

PLAYER: LOU BROCK

Year	G	AB	H	2B	3B	HR	(Hm	Rd)	TB	R	RBI	BB	IBB	HBP	SH	SF	SB	CS	SB%	GiDP	Avg.	Slug	On Base	Runs	Win–Loss	Pct	AV
1961	4	11	1	0	0	0	(0	0)	1	1	0	1	0	0	0	0	0	0	.00	0	.091	.091	.167	0	0–0	.014	0
1962	123	434	114	24	7	9	(5	4)	179	73	35	35	4	3	0	5	16	7	.70	5	.263	.412	.319	58	6–6	.519	7
1963	148	547	141	19	11	9	(4	5)	209	79	37	31	2	4	2	4	24	12	.67	2	.258	.382	.300	64	9–7	.569	9
1964	155	634	200	30	11	14	(6	8)	294	111	58	40	0	4	13	4	43	18	.70	5	.315	.464	.358	107	12–6	.676	13
1965	155	631	182	35	8	16	(10	6)	281	107	69	45	6	10	11	0	63	27	.70	2	.288	.445	.345	99	11–7	.623	13
1966	156	643	183	24	12	15	(6	9)	276	94	46	31	6	3	0	1	74	18	.80	7	.285	.429	.320	91	12–6	.672	11
1967	159	689	206	32	12	21	(13	8)	325	113	76	24	6	6	2	3	52	18	.74	6	.299	.472	.327	106	13–6	.673	14
1968	159	660	184	46	14	6	(2	4)	276	92	51	46	7	3	1	2	62	12	.84	4	.279	.418	.328	98	13–5	.728	11
1969	157	655	195	33	10	12	(6	6)	284	97	47	50	15	2	2	1	53	14	.79	2	.298	.434	.349	105	13–5	.741	11
1970	155	664	202	29	5	13	(7	6)	280	114	57	60	12	1	1	3	51	15	.77	10	.304	.422	.361	105	11–7	.611	12
1971	157	640	200	37	7	7	(3	4)	272	126	61	76	5	1	1	2	64	19	.77	5	.312	.425	.385	114	12–5	.690	13
1972	153	621	193	26	8	3	(2	1)	244	81	42	47	12	1	3	3	63	18	.78	6	.311	.393	.359	93	12–5	.682	10
1973	160	650	193	29	8	7	(4	3)	259	110	63	71	15	0	1	5	70	20	.78	9	.297	.398	.364	101	12–6	.676	10
1974	153	635	194	25	7	3	(1	2)	242	105	48	61	16	2	2	1	118	33	.78	8	.306	.381	.368	98	11–7	.638	12
1975	136	528	163	27	6	3	(1	2)	211	78	47	38	6	3	3	0	56	16	.78	7	.309	.400	.359	79	9–5	.633	11
1976	133	498	150	24	5	4	(2	2)	196	73	67	35	7	1	4	6	56	19	.75	19	.301	.394	.344	65	8–7	.547	11
1977	141	489	133	22	6	2	(0	2)	173	69	46	30	2	2	0	0	35	24	.59	6	.272	.354	.317	52	6–9	.402	7
1978	92	298	66	9	0	0	(0	0)	75	31	12	17	2	0	1	1	17	5	.77	4	.221	.252	.263	21	2–7	.261	2
1979	120	405	123	15	4	5	(2	3)	161	56	38	23	1	3	0	5	21	12	.64	7	.304	.398	.342	54	6–5	.540	6
16.1 yrs	2616	10332	3023	486	141	149	(74	75)	4238	1610	900	761	124	49	47	46	938	307	.75	114	.293	.410	.343	1456	180–110	.620	183
		640	187	30	9	9			262	100	56	47	8	3	3	3	58	19		7	.293	.410	.343				

Teams: Chicago Cubs, 1961–1964; St. Louis Cardinals, 1964 through 1979.
Points in MVP Voting: 1962–1963, 0; 1964, 40 (10th, .14); 1965, 0; 1966, 2 (.01); 1967, 49 (7th, .18); 1968, 73 (6th, 26); 1969–1970, 0; 1971, 20 (.06); 1972, 13 (.04); 1973, 65 (6th, .19); 1974, 233 (2nd, .69); 1975, 6 (.02); 1976, 3 (.01); 1977–1979, 0. TOTAL: 1.60 Award Shares.

FIELDING LEFT FIELD

Year	G	PO	AS	Err	DP	Pct	Range
1961	3	6	0	2	0	.750	2.00
1962	106	243	7	9	2	.965	2.36
1963	140	269	17	8	7	.973	2.04
1964	154	266	15	14	1	.953	1.82
1965	153	272	11	12	1	.959	1.85
1966	154	269	9	19	1	.936	1.81
1967	157	272	12	13	2	.956	1.81
1968	156	269	9	14	1	.952	1.78
1969	157	255	7	14	2	.949	1.67
1970	152	247	9	10	2	.962	1.68
1971	157	262	7	14	3	.951	1.71
1972	149	253	6	13	1	.952	1.74
1973	159	310	3	12	1	.963	1.97
1974	152	283	8	10	2	.967	1.91
1975	128	247	5	9	0	.966	1.97
1976	123	221	6	4	0	.983	1.85
1977	130	184	2	9	1	.954	1.43
1978	79	114	2	3	0	.975	1.47
1979	98	152	7	7	2	.958	1.62
	2507	4394	142	196	29	.959	1.81

Assists per 154 Games: 8.7

PLAYER: WILLIE STARGELL

				BATTING													BASERUNNING				PERCENTAGES			VALUES			
Year	G	AB	H	2B	3B	HR	(Hm	Rd)	TB	R	RBI	BB	IBB	HBP	SH	SF	SB	CS	SB%	GIDP	Avg.	Slug	On Base	Runs	Win–Loss	Pct.	AV
1962	10	31	9	3	1	0	(0	0)	14	1	4	3	1	0	0	0	0	1	.00	0	.290	.452	.353	5	1–0	.640	0
1963	108	304	74	11	6	11	(3	8)	130	34	47	19	0	2	0	3	0	2	.00	6	.243	.428	.290	36	5–4	.563	4
1964	117	421	115	19	7	21	(12	9)	211	53	78	17	2	2	1	1	1	1	.50	7	.273	.501	.303	62	7–4	.635	8
1965	144	533	145	25	8	27	(8	19)	267	68	107	39	13	7	0	3	1	1	.50	8	.272	.501	.328	87	10–4	.699	11
1966	140	485	153	30	0	33	(11	22)	282	84	102	48	16	6	5	5	2	3	.40	7	.315	.581	.377	107	10–3	.783	12
1967	134	462	125	18	6	20	(11	9)	215	54	73	67	25	3	2	2	1	0	1.00	12	.271	.465	.364	78	9–4	.669	10
1968	128	435	103	15	1	24	(11	13)	192	57	67	47	11	6	1	7	5	0	1.00	12	.237	.441	.315	61	8–5	.651	8
1969	145	522	160	31	6	29	(14	15)	290	89	92	61	14	6	0	5	1	0	1.00	10	.307	.556	.382	112	11–3	.781	13
1970	136	474	125	18	3	31	(13	18)	242	70	85	44	11	5	0	6	0	1	.00	14	.264	.511	.329	77	9–5	.629	10
1971	141	511	151	26	0	48	(21	27)	321	104	125	83	20	7	0	5	0	0	.00	8	.295	.628	.398	131	11–2	.832	16
1972	138	495	145	28	2	33	(16	17)	276	75	112	65	15	2	0	7	1	1	.50	7	.293	.558	.373	105	11–3	.801	12
1973	148	522	156	43	3	44	(24	20)	337	106	119	80	22	3	0	4	0	0	.00	6	.299	.646	.392	136	12–2	.836	15
1974	140	508	153	37	4	25	(8	17)	273	90	96	87	21	6	0	4	0	2	.00	8	.301	.537	.407	115	11–3	.788	12
1975	124	461	136	32	2	22	(12	10)	238	71	90	58	6	3	0	4	0	0	.00	9	.295	.516	.375	91	10–3	.770	10
1976	117	428	110	20	3	20	(11	9)	196	54	65	50	6	5	0	4	2	0	1.00	4	.257	.458	.339	70	8–4	.664	7
1977	63	186	51	12	0	13	(7	6)	102	29	35	31	10	3	0	2	1	0	1.00	4	.274	.548	.383	39	4–1	.753	4
1978	122	390	115	18	2	28	(15	13)	221	60	97	50	10	7	0	3	3	2	.60	8	.295	.567	.382	85	8–2	.791	12
1979	126	424	119	19	0	32	(16	16)	234	60	82	47	12	3	0	6	0	1	.00	10	.281	.552	.352	81	8–3	.711	12
1980	67	202	53	10	1	11	(7	4)	98	28	38	26	10	2	0	1	0	0	.00	2	.262	.485	.351	35	4–2	.706	4
1981	38	60	17	4	0	0	(0	0)	21	2	9	5	1	0	0	1	0	0	.00	8	.283	.350	.333	8	1–1	.566	1
1982	74	73	17	4	0	3	(1	2)	30	6	17	10	1	0	0	2	0	0	.00	1	.233	.411	.318	10	1–1	.532	1
	2360	7927	2232	423	55	475	(221	254)	4190	1195	1540	937	227	78	9	75	17	16	.52	143	.282	.529	.360	1531	160–60	.726	180
14.6 yrs		544	153	29	4	33			288	82	106	64	16	5	1	5	1	1		10	.282	.529	.360				

Teams: Pittsburgh, 1962–1982.

Points in MVP Voting: 1962, 0; 1963, 0; 1964, 0; 1965, 15 (.05); 1966, 19 (.07); 1967, 0; 1968, 0; 1969, 7 (.02); 1970, 20 (.06); 1971, 222 (2nd, .66); 1972, 201 (3rd, .60); 1973, 250 (2nd, .74); 1974, 43 (10th, .13); 1975, 69 (7th, .21); 1976, 0; 1977, 0; 1978, 39 (9th, .12); 1979, 216 (1st, .64); 1980, 0; 1981, 0; 1982, 0. TOTAL: 3.30 Award Shares.

Reported Salaries: *The Sporting News* guides carry lists of $100,000-a-year players in the early 1970s. Although Stargell was one of the greatest stars in the game in those years, his name never appears on those lists.

Explanation for Gaps in Career or Sudden Changes in Productivity:

1967—Had two injuries to left thigh muscle, but played with them and diminished effectiveness.

1975—Out four weeks with broken rib.

1976—Stargell's wife, Delores, developed a blood clot in her brain in May. Stargell's concern over her health, plus nagging injuries, ruined that season.

1977—Season ended in mid-July by pinched nerve in left elbow.

1980—Injured left knee in July, and later found out that he had arthritis in the knee.

Other Notes: 1979—9 HR vs. LHP, 23 vs. RHP.

Named outstanding National League left fielder in 1965, 1966, and 1971 and the outstanding first baseman in 1972 by *The Sporting News*.

FIELDING LEFT FIELD

Year	G	PO	AS	Err	DP	Pct.	Range
1962	9	12	1	1	0	.929	1.44
1963	65	78	3	4	0	.953	1.25
1964	59	79	2	9	0	.900	1.37
1965	137	208	12	8	3	.965	1.61
1966	127	180	9	11	0	.945	1.49
1967	98	140	12	10	1	.938	1.55
1968	113	144	12	9	0	.945	1.38
1969	116	159	4	5	1	.970	1.41
1970	125	184	16	5	1	.976	1.60
1971	135	237	8	4	4	.984	1.81
1972	32	50	1	2	0	.962	1.59
1973	142	261	14	7	1	.975	1.94
1974	135	253	8	9	1	.967	1.93
	1293	1985	102	84	12	.961	1.61

Assists per 154 Games: 12.1

PLAYER: JIM RICE

					BATTING													BASERUNNING				PERCENTAGES			VALUES			
Year	G	AB	H	2B	3B	HR	(Hm	Rd)	TB	R	RBI	BB	IBB	HBP	SH	SF		SB	CS	SB%	GIDP	Avg.	Slug	On Base	Runs	Win—Loss	Pct.	AV
1974	24	67	18	2	1	1	(1	0)	25	6	13	4	0	1	0	3		0	0	.00	2	.269	.373	.307	8	1—1	.464	0
1975	144	564	174	29	4	22	(12	10)	277	92	102	36	7	4	1	8		10	5	.67	19	.309	.491	.349	92	10—6	.607	12
1976	153	581	164	25	8	25	(12	13)	280	75	85	28	2	4	2	9		8	5	.62	18	.282	.482	.314	83	10—7	.575	9
1977	160	644	206	29	15	39	(27	12)	382	104	114	53	10	8	0	5		5	4	.56	21	.320	.593	.376	136	13—5	.723	13
1978	163	677	213	25	15	46	(28	18)	406	121	139	58	7	5	1	5		7	5	.58	15	.315	.600	.370	147	14—4	.767	18
1979	158	619	201	39	6	39	(27	12)	369	117	130	57	4	4	0	8		9	4	.69	16	.325	.596	.381	138	12—4	.748	16
1980	124	504	148	22	6	24	(11	13)	254	81	86	30	5	4	1	3		8	3	.73	16	.294	.504	.336	81	8—6	.592	12
1981	108	451	128	18	1	17	(10	7)	199	51	62	34	3	3	0	7		2	2	.50	14	.284	.441	.333	64	7—6	.538	9
1982	145	573	177	24	5	24	(9	15)	283	86	97	55	6	7	0	3		0	1	.00	29	.309	.494	.375	98	10—6	.650	12
1983	155	626	191	34	1	39	(16	23)	344	90	126	52	10	6	0	5		0	2	.00	31	.305	.550	.361	113	12—6	.659	16
1984	159	657	184	25	7	28	(17	11)	307	98	122	44	8	1	0	6		4	0	1.00	36	.280	.467	.323	88	9—10	.473	13
1985	140	546	159	20	3	27	(10	17)	266	85	103	51	5	2	0	9		2	0	1.00	35	.291	.487	.349	83	9—7	.553	10
1986	157	618	200	39	2	20	(10	10)	303	98	110	62	5	4	0	9		0	1	.00	19	.324	.490	.384	115	11—5	.692	15
11.0 yrs	1790	7127	2163	331	74	351	(190	161)	3695	1104	1259	564	72	53	5	80		55	32	.63	271	.303	.518	.355	1243	125—73	.631	155
		645	196	30	7	32			334	100	114	51	7	5	0	7		5	3		25	.303	.518	.355				

Teams: Boston, 1974–present

Points in MVP Voting: 1974, 0; 1975, 154 (3rd, .46); 1976, 0; 1977, 163 (4th, .42); 1978, 352 (1st, .90); 1979, 124 (5th, .32); 1980, 0; 1981, 0; 1982, 10 (.03); 1983, 150 (4th, .38); 1984, 10 (.03); 1985,0; 1986, 241 (3rd, .72). TOTAL: 3.26 Award Shares.

Reported Salaries: 1978, $125,000; 1979, $500,000; 1980, $500,000; 1981–1985, $640,000/year plus $700,000 signing bonus.

Explanation for Gaps in Career or Sudden Changes in Productivity:
1980—Out thirty-one games with broken wrist.
1981—Strike.

Other Notes: Named to *Sporting News* American League All-Star team in 1975, 1977, 1978, 1979, 1983, 1986.

Values presented here go only through 1986. Those given in Section II include estimated data for the 1987 season.

FIELDING LEFT FIELD

Year	G	PO	AS	E	DP	Pct.	Range
1974	3	4	0	1	0	.800	1.33
1975	90	162	6	0	0	1.000	1.87
1976	98	199	8	7	0	.967	2.11
1977	44	83	4	4	1	.956	1.98
1978	114	245	13	3	1	.989	2.26
1979	125	241	8	4	1	.984	1.99
1980	109	233	10	3	2	.988	2.23
1981	108	237	9	3	0	.988	2.28
1982	145	273	10	9	3	.969	1.95
1983	151	339	21	6	5	.984	2.38
1984	157	336	12	4	3	.989	2.22
1985	130	236	8	9	3	.964	1.88
1986	156	330	16	8	0	.977	2.22
	1430	2918	125	61	17	.980	2.13

Assists per 154 Games: 13.5

Center Field

Roy Thomas
Ty Cobb
Tris Speaker
Max Carey
Edd Roush
Kiki Cuyler
Hack Wilson
Al Simmons
Sam West
Earl Averill
Doc Cramer
Joe DiMaggio
Larry Doby
Duke Snider
Richie Ashburn
Mickey Mantle
Willie Mays
Vada Pinson
Amos Otis

PLAYER: ROY THOMAS

				BATTING													BASERUNNING				PERCENTAGES			VALUES			
Year	G	AB	H	2B	3B	HR	(Hm Rd)	TB	R	RBI	BB	IBB	HBP	SH	SF	SB	CS	SB%	GIDP	Avg.	Slug	On Base	Runs	Win−Loss	Pct.	AV
1899	150	547	178	12	4	0	( )	198	137	47	115			23		42				.325	.362	.428	113	10−5	.649	15
1900	140	531	168	4	3	0	( )	178	132	33	115			14		37				.316	.335	.429	99	9−6	.578	14
1901	129	479	148	5	2	1	( )	160	102	28	100			15		27				.309	.334	.418	85	9−4	.676	12
1902	138	500	143	4	7	0	( )	161	89	24	107			17		17				.286	.322	.401	78	9−5	.628	12
1903	130	477	156	11	2	1	( )	174	88	27	107			20		17				.327	.365	.435	92	9−5	.660	15
1904	139	496	144	6	6	3	( )	171	92	29	102			7		28				.290	.345	.407	85	9−5	.657	14
1905	147	562	178	11	6	0	( )	201	118	31	93			16		23				.317	.358	.404	98	11−5	.684	14
1906	142	493	125	10	7	0	( )	149	81	16	107			14		22				.254	.302	.378	70	9−5	.633	13
1907	121	419	102	15	3	1	( )	126	70	23	83			15		11				.243	.301	.358	54	8−5	.609	8
1908	108	410	103	11	10	1	( )	137	54	24	51			8		11				.251	.334	.328	49	7−5	.578	8
1909	83	281	74	9	1	0	( )	85	36	11	47	0		11		5				.263	.302	.357	34	5−4	.556	4
1910	23	71	13	0	2	0	( )	17	7	4	7	1		2		4				.183	.239	.259	6	1−2	.231	0
1911	21	30	5	2	0	0	( )	7	5	2	8	0		4		0				.167	.233	.310	2	0−1	.232	0
9.1 yrs	1471	5296	1537	100	53	7	( )	1764	1011	299	1042	1		166		244				.290	.333	.397	865	96−58	.623	129
		583	169	11	6	1		194	111	33	115					27				.290	.333	.397				

Teams: Philadelphia, 1899–1907; Philadelphia/Pittsburgh, 1908; Boston, 1909; Philadelphia, 1910–1911.
Points in MVP Voting: 1911, 0.

FIELDING CENTER FIELD

Year	G	PO	AS	Err	DP	Pct.	Range
1899	135	313	22	17	8	.952	2.48
1900	139	303	19	14	6	.958	2.32
1901	129	283	9	10	2	.967	2.26
1902	138	277	23	8	3	.974	2.17
1903	130	318	19	13	3	.963	2.59
1904	139	321	21	9	4	.974	2.46
1905	147	373	27	7	6	.983	2.72
1906	142	340	12	5	5	.986	2.48
1907	121	274	15	6	4	.980	2.39
1908	107	282	7	7	4	.976	2.70
1909	71	155	9	4	1	.976	2.31
1910	20	38	2	2		.952	2.00
1911	11	14	3	0		1.000	1.55
	1429	3291	188	102	46	.972	2.43

Assists per 154 Games: 20.3

PLAYER: TY COBB

			BATTING															BASERUNNING				PERCENTAGES			VALUES			
Year	G	AB	H	2B	3B	HR	(Hm	Rd)	TB	R	RBI	BB	IBB	HBP	SH	SF	SB	CS	SB%	GIDP	Avg.	Slug	On Base	Runs	Win-Loss	Pct.	AV
1905	41	150	36	6	0	1	(0	1)	45	19	15	10		0	4		2				.240	.300	.280	14	2–3	.418	1
1906	98	358	113	13	7	1	(0	1)	143	45	41	19		2	14		23				.316	.399	.341	62	7–3	.730	7
1907	150	605	212	29	15	5	(1	4)	286	97	116	24		3	12		49				.350	.473	.371	131	13–3	.811	17
1908	150	581	188	36	20	4	(0	4)	276	88	101	34		7	14		39				.324	.475	.360	114	12–4	.769	14
1909	156	573	216	33	10	9	(6	3)	296	116	115	48		6	24		76				.377	.517	.415	159	13–2	.893	19
1910	140	508	194	35	13	8	(4	4)	279	106	88	64		4	17		65				.382	.549	.442	155	12–1	.897	19
1911	146	591	248	47	24	8	(5	3)	367	147	144	44		8	11		83				.420	.621	.459	207	12–2	.891	23
1912	140	553	227	30	23	7	(1	6)	324	119	90	43		5	8		61	34	.64		.410	.586	.452	174	12–2	.883	20
1913	122	428	167	18	16	4	(0	4)	229	70	67	58		4	11		52				.390	.535	.457	124	9–1	.876	17
1914	97	345	127	22	11	2	(1	1)	177	69	57	57		6	6		35	17	.67		.368	.513	.459	94	8–1	.881	10
1915	156	563	208	31	13	3	(1	2)	274	144	99	118		10	9		96	38	.72		.369	.487	.480	155	13–3	.837	19
1916	145	542	201	31	10	5	(2	3)	267	113	68	78		2	14		68	24	.74		.371	.493	.442	136	12–2	.844	17
1917	152	588	225	44	23	7	(1	5)	336	107	102	61		4	16		55				.383	.571	.433	165	13–2	.891	21
1918	111	421	161	19	14	3	(0	3)	217	83	64	41		2	9		34				.382	.515	.431	105	9–1	.864	13
1919	124	497	191	36	13	1	(0	1)	256	92	70	38		1	9		28				.384	.515	.422	116	10–2	.833	16
1920	112	428	143	28	8	2	(1	1)	193	86	63	58		2	7		14	10	.58		.334	.451	.410	82	8–4	.686	10
1921	128	507	197	37	16	12	(5	7)	302	124	101	56		3	15		22	15	.59		.389	.596	.441	134	10–3	.768	18
1922	137	526	211	42	16	4	(1	3)	297	99	99	55		4	27		9	13	.41		.401	.565	.441	133	11–3	.778	19
1923	145	556	189	40	7	6	(2	4)	261	103	88	66		3	22		9	10	.47		.340	.469	.399	108	10–5	.660	14
1924	155	625	211	38	10	4	(0	4)	281	115	74	85		1	15		23	14	.62		.338	.450	.409	121	11–6	.644	17
1925	121	415	157	31	12	12	(2	10)	248	97	102	65		5	5		13	9	.59		.378	.598	.463	118	8–2	.804	14
1926	79	233	79	18	5	4	(0	4)	119	48	62	26		1	13		9	4	.69		.339	.511	.388	49	4–2	.677	5
1927	133	490	175	32	7	5	(2	3)	236	104	93	67		5	12		22				.357	.482	.430	104	9–3	.729	15
1928	95	353	114	27	4	1	(1	0)	152	54	40	34		4	2		5	8	.38		.323	.431	.387	58	6–4	.624	6
	3033	11436	4190	723	297	118	(36	81)	5861	2245	1959	1249		92	296		892	196	.65		.366	.513	.423	2817	236–63	.790	351
18.7 yrs		611	224	39	16	6			313	120	105	67		5	16		48	21			.366	.513	.423				

Teams: Detroit, 1905–1926; Philadelphia, 1927–1928

Points in MVP Voting: 1911, 64 (1st, 1.00); 1913, 3 (.05); 1914, 7 (.11); 1922, 0; 1923, 0; 1924, 0; 1926, 0; 1927, 0. TOTAL: 1.16 Award Shares. (Note that Cobb drew MVP votes in 1913 and 1914 although as a previous winner he was ineligible for the award.)

Reported Salaries: 1904, $50/month in minors; 1905, $90/month in minors; 1905, $250 after joining Tigers; 1906, $1500; 1907, $2400; 1908 and 1909, $4,000 plus $800 bonus for hitting .300; 1910–1912, $9,000/year; 1913, $11,332.55 ($12,000 pro-rated for time missed holding out); 1914, $15,000; 1915–1917, $20,000; 1918 through 1920, $20,000 each year; 1921, $35,000; 1924, $38,000; 1925, $50,000; 1927 estimated $70,000–$80,000; 1928 estimated $35,000.

As is well known, Cobb engaged in an endless variety of off-field money-making enterprises—playing exhibition games, appearing in vaudeville and movies, doing radio reports of World Series, selling automobiles, bottling soda, building tract houses and apartments, endorsing everything including beer, overcoats and several brands of cigarettes. He invested wisely, including an early investment in Coca Cola. His wealth at the time of his death was reported as at least $11.8 million.

Explanation for Gaps in Career or Sudden Changes in Productivity:

1912—Suspended ten days following May 15 attack on umpire

1913—Held out into season, June 22 injured in collision with Doc Johnston Cleveland, spiked by Buck Weaver (wound became infected), also called home by illness of his wife

1914—Suffered cracked rib on HBP from Rube Foster, out June 20–August 13 with broken thumb suffered in fight with butcher's clerk.

1918—Fell on right shoulder May 25, out until June 5; late July hurt left shoulder sliding; end of season became Captain in Chemical Warfare Service, United States Army

1919—Out thirteen games June/July with boil on his leg

1920—Wrenched left knee July 14, out two weeks

1921—Spiked himself while sliding; required five stitches and injury became infected (out almost a month). Also had to leave team for sick wife, suspended for fighting with umpire

1922—Caught spikes while sliding in spring training

1925—Surgery on eyes before season

1927—Suspended for five days for bumping umpire

FIELDING CENTER FIELD

Year	G	PO	AS	E	DP	Pct.	Range
1905	41	85	6	4	1	.958	2.22
1906	96	209	14	9	4	.961	2.32
1907	150	238	30	11	12	.961	1.79
1908	150	212	23	14	5	.944	1.57
1909	156	222	24	14	7	.946	1.58
1910	137	305	18	14	4	.958	2.36
1911	146	376	24	18	10	.957	2.74
1912	140	324	21	22	5	.940	2.46
1913	118	262	22	16	8	.947	2.41
1914	96	177	8	10	0	.949	1.93
1915	156	328	22	18	7	.951	2.24
1916	143	325	18	17	9	.953	2.40
1917	152	373	27	11	9	.973	2.63
1918	95	225	12	6	1	.975	2.49
1919	123	272	19	8	3	.973	2.37
1920	112	246	8	9	2	.966	2.27
1921	121	301	27	10	2	.970	2.71
1922	134	330	14	7	3	.980	2.57
1923	141	362	14	12	2	.969	2.67
1924	155	417	12	6	8	.986	2.77
1925	105	267	9	15	1	.948	2.63
1926	55	109	4	6	2	.950	2.05
1927	126	243	9	8	2	.969	2.00
1928	95	154	7	6	0	.964	1.69
	2943	6362	392	271	107	.961	2.29

Assists per 154 Games: 20.5

PLAYER: TRIS SPEAKER

Year	G	AB	H	2B	3B	HR	(Hm	Rd)	TB	R	RBI	BB	IBB	HBP	SH	SF	SB	CS	SB%	GIDP	Avg.	Slug	On Base	Runs	Win–Loss	Pct.	AV
1907	7	19	3	0	0	0	(0	0)	3	0	1	1		0	0		0				.158	.158	.200	1	0–1	.081	0
1908	31	118	26	2	3	0	(0	0)	34	12	9	4		1	3		2				.220	.288	.246	9	1–3	.321	1
1909	143	544	168	26	13	7	(6	1)	241	73	77	38		7	17		35				.309	.443	.351	99	11–4	.741	14
1910	141	538	183	20	14	7	(4	3)	252	92	65	52		6	12		35				.340	.468	.396	115	12–3	.815	14
1911	141	510	167	34	13	8	(5	3)	251	88	80	59	13	1	17		25				.327	.492	.399	113	11–3	.773	14
1912	153	580	222	53	13	9	(4	6)	328	136	98	82		6	7		52				.383	.566	.459	175	13–2	.886	21
1913	141	520	190	35	22	3	(0	3)	278	94	81	65		7	16		46				.365	.535	.431	137	12–2	.858	17
1914	158	571	193	46	18	4	(0	4)	287	100	90	77		7	13		42	29	.59		.338	.503	.415	133	13–2	.864	17
1915	150	547	176	25	12	0	(0	0)	225	108	69	81		7	17		29	25	.54		.322	.411	.405	103	12–4	.762	15
1916	151	546	211	41	8	2	(0	2)	274	102	83	82		4	15		35	27	.56		.386	.502	.459	132	12–2	.839	20
1917	142	523	184	42	11	2	(1	1)	254	90	60	67		7	15		30				.352	.486	.422	118	12–2	.852	17
1918	127	471	150	33	11	0	(0	0)	205	73	61	64		3	11		27				.318	.435	.395	90	10–3	.782	14
1919	134	494	146	38	12	2	(1	1)	214	83	63	73		8	20		15				.296	.433	.382	89	10–4	.691	13
1920	150	552	214	50	11	8	(6	2)	310	137	107	97		5	20		10	13	.43		.388	.562	.469	152	12–2	.827	19
1921	132	506	183	52	14	3	(2	1)	272	107	74	68		2	12		2	4	.33		.362	.538	.430	121	10–3	.753	17
1922	131	426	161	48	8	11	(5	6)	258	85	71	77		1	12		8	3	.73		.378	.606	.463	127	9–2	.841	18
1923	150	574	218	59	11	17	(10	7)	350	133	130	93		4	22		10	9	.53		.380	.610	.455	166	12–3	.813	19
1924	135	486	167	36	9	9	(3	6)	248	94	65	72		4	13		5	7	.42		.344	.510	.423	109	9–4	.727	15
1925	117	429	167	35	5	12	(6	6)	248	79	87	70		4	15		5	2	.71		.389	.578	.465	123	9–2	.833	15
1926	150	540	164	52	8	7	(3	4)	253	96	86	94		0	28		6	1	.86		.304	.469	.390	110	11–4	.721	14
1927	141	523	171	43	6	2	(0	2)	232	71	73	55		4	15		9				.327	.444	.385	91	9–5	.642	13
1928	64	191	51	23	2	3	(3	0)	87	28	29	10		2	9		5	1	.83		.267	.455	.297	27	3–3	.501	2
	2789	10208	3515	793	224	116	(59	58)	5104	1881	1559	1381		102	309		433	121	.57		.344	.500	.417	2337	212–62	.775	309
17.2 yrs		593	204	46	13	7			296	109	91	80		6	18		25	13			.344	.500	.417				

Teams: Boston, 1907–1915; Cleveland, 1916–1926; Washington, 1927; Philadelphia, 1928.

Points in MVP Voting: 1911, 16 (7th, .25); 1913, 26 (4th, .41); 1914, 9 (.14); 1922, 0; 1923, 0; 1924, 0; 1926, 0; 1927, 0. TOTAL: .80 Award Shares.

Reported Salaries: 1913—$9,000; 1915—$17,500; 1916–1918—$15,000 a year; 1919 —$18,000.

Other Notes: Was remarkably healthy.

FIELDING CENTER FIELD

Year	G	PO	AS	E	DP	Pct.	Range
1907	4	4	2	0	1	1.000	1.50
1908	31	37	8	0	3	1.000	1.45
1909	142	319	35	10	12	.973	2.49
1910	140	337	20	16	7	.957	2.55
1911	138	297	26	15	5	.956	2.34
1912	153	372	35	18	9	.958	2.66
1913	139	374	30	25	7	.942	2.91
1914	156	423	29	15	12	.968	2.90
1915	150	378	21	10	8	.976	2.66
1916	151	359	25	10	10	.975	2.54
1917	142	365	23	8	5	.980	2.73
1918	127	352	15	10	6	.973	2.89
1919	134	375	25	7	6	.983	2.99
1920	149	363	24	9	8	.977	2.60
1921	128	345	15	6	2	.984	2.81
1922	110	285	13	5	6	.983	2.71
1923	150	369	26	13	7	.968	2.63
1924	128	323	20	13	3	.963	2.68
1925	109	311	16	11	9	.967	3.00
1926	149	394	20	8	7	.981	2.78
1927	120	278	12	10	5	.967	2.42
1928	50	111	8	3	1	.975	2.38
	2700	6771	448	222	139	.970	2.67

Assists per 154 Games: 25.6

PLAYER: MAX CAREY

				BATTING										BASERUNNING				PERCENTAGES			VALUES			
Year	G	AB	H	2B	3B	HR	(Hm Rd)	TB	R	RBI	BB	IBB	HBP	SH	SF	SB	CS	SB%	GIDP	Avg.	Slug	On Base	Runs	Win—Loss	Pct.	AV
1910	2	6	3	0	1	0	( )	5	2	2	2			0	0	0				.500	.833	.625	3	0—0	.978	0
1911	129	427	110	15	10	5	( )	160	77	43	44			7	25		27				.258	.375	.320	64	8—6	.561	9
1912	150	587	177	23	8	5	( )	231	114	66	61			5	37		45				.302	.394	.352	104	11—6	.653	13
1913	154	620	172	23	10	5	( )	230	99	49	55			3	14		61	17	.78		.277	.371	.332	92	11—7	.612	11
1914	156	593	144	25	17	1	( )	206	76	31	59			2	10		38				.243	.347	.309	72	11—7	.594	9
1915	140	564	143	26	5	3	( )	188	76	27	57			4	5		36	17	.68		.254	.333	.324	68	10—7	.583	11
1916	154	599	158	23	11	7	( )	224	90	42	59			7	14		63	19	.77		.264	.374	.330	87	12—6	.664	12
1917	155	588	174	21	12	1	( )	222	82	51	58			10	12		46	14	.77		.296	.378	.362	94	12—4	.742	12
1918	126	468	128	14	6	3	( )	163	70	48	62			4	15		58	15	.79		.274	.348	.353	73	10—4	.687	11
1919	66	244	75	10	2	0	( )	89	41	9	25			2	4		18	9	.67		.307	.365	.371	38	5—2	.742	4
1920	130	485	140	18	4	1	( )	169	74	35	59			3	20		52	10	.84		.289	.348	.356	72	10—5	.672	13
1921	140	521	161	34	4	7	( )	224	85	56	70			4	30		37	12	.76		.309	.430	.376	95	11—5	.684	14
1922	155	629	207	28	12	10	( )	289	140	70	80			4	19		51	2	.96		.329	.459	.398	131	12—5	.690	17
1923	153	610	188	32	19	6	( )	276	120	63	73			7	9		51	8	.86		.308	.452	.383	117	11—5	.674	15
1924	149	599	178	30	9	7	( )	247	113	55	58			7	19		49	13	.79		.297	.412	.356	97	11—7	.625	12
1925	133	542	186	39	13	5	( )	266	109	44	66			4	8		46	11	.81		.343	.491	.413	106	9—5	.656	15
1926	113	424	98	17	6	0	( )	127	64	35	38			0	21		10				.231	.300	.282	38	4—10	.285	7
1927	144	538	143	30	10	1	( )	196	70	54	64			1	20		32				.266	.364	.334	69	9—7	.568	11
1928	108	296	73	11	0	2	( )	90	41	19	47			2	8		18				.247	.304	.346	34	4—5	.455	4
1929	19	23	7	0	0	0	( )	7	2	1	3			1	0						.304	.304	.407	3	0—0	.475	0
	2476	9363	2665	419	159	69	( )	3609	1545	800	1040		77	290			738	147	.79		.285	.385	.351	1458	171—103	.623	198
15.3 yrs		613	174	27	10	5		236	101	52	68		5	19			48				.285	.385	.351				

Teams: Pittsburgh, 1910–1925; Pittsburgh/Brooklyn, 1926; Brooklyn, 1927–1929
Points in MVP Voting: 1911, 0; 1913, 0; 1914, 0.
Explanation for Gaps in Career or Sudden Changes in Productivity:
1919—Unknown illness.
Other Notes: Named to *The Sporting News* major league All-Star Team in 1925.

FIELDING CENTER FIELD

Year	G	PO	AS	E	DP	Pct.	Range
1910	2	10	1	0	0	1.000	5.50
1911	122	304	11	8	5	.975	2.58
1912	150	369	19	13	10	.968	2.59
1913	154	363	28	16	6	.961	2.54
1914	154	318	23	12	3	.966	2.21
1915	140	307	21	6	5	.982	2.34
1916	154	419	32	8	10	.983	2.93
1917	153	440	28	10	8	.979	3.06
1918	126	359	25	17	9	.958	3.05
1919	63	173	5	10	1	.947	2.83
1920	129	345	10	12	0	.967	2.75
1921	139	431	15	20	6	.957	3.21
1922	155	449	22	15	4	.969	3.04
1923	153	450	28	19	4	.962	3.12
1924	149	428	16	16	3	.965	2.98
1925	130	363	20	20	2	.950	2.95
1926	109	295	8	19	3	.941	2.78
1927	141	331	19	11	6	.970	2.48
1928	95	202	8	3	1	.986	2.21
1929	4	7	0	0	0	1.000	1.75
	2422	6363	339	235	86	.966	2.77

Assists per 154 Games: 21.6

PLAYER: EDD ROUSH

Year	G	AB	H	2B	3B	HR	(Hm Rd)	TB	R	RBI	BB	IBB	HBP	SH	SF	SB	CS	SB%	GIDP	Avg.	Slug	On Base	Runs	Win–Loss	Pct.	AV
1913	9	10	1	0	0	0	( )	1	2	0	0			0	2	0				.100	.100	.083	0	0–0	.017	0
1914	74	166	54	8	4	1	( )	73	26	30	6					12				.325	.440	.349	28	3–1	.691	3
1915	145	551	164	20	11	3	( )	215	73	60	38					28				.298	.390	.343	78	10–5	.657	12
1916	108	341	91	7	15	0	( )	128	38	20	14		7	9		19				.267	.375	.302	46	6–4	.619	5
1917	136	522	178	19	14	4	( )	237	82	67	27		5	13		21				.341	.454	.370	94	10–3	.757	14
1918	113	435	145	18	10	5	( )	198	61	62	22		2	33		24				.333	.455	.343	85	9–3	.743	12
1919	133	504	162	19	13	3	( )	216	73	71	42		6	20		20				.321	.429	.367	87	11–3	.763	13
1920	149	579	196	22	16	4	( )	262	81	90	42		3	26		36	24	.60		.339	.453	.371	98	12–5	.692	15
1921	112	418	147	27	12	4	( )	210	68	71	31		5	9		19	17	.53		.352	.502	.395	80	8–3	.743	12
1922	49	165	58	7	4	1	( )	76	29	24	19		3	2		5	3	.62		.352	.461	.423	33	3–1	.737	4
1923	138	527	185	41	18	6	( )	280	88	88	46		3	16		10	15	.40		.351	.531	.395	109	11–4	.753	14
1924	121	483	168	23	21	3	( )	242	67	72	22		0	14		17	13	.57		.348	.501	.366	86	10–4	.728	12
1925	134	540	183	28	16	8	( )	267	91	83	35		4	11		22	20	.52		.339	.494	.376	90	10–5	.656	14
1926	144	563	182	37	10	7	( )	260	95	79	38		0	30		8				.323	.462	.349	92	10–6	.631	11
1927	140	570	173	27	4	7	( )	229	83	58	26		1	17		18				.304	.402	.326	74	7–8	.467	11
1928	46	163	41	5	3	2	( )	58	20	13	14		1	2		1				.252	.356	.311	18	2–3	.396	2
1929	115	450	146	19	7	8	( )	203	76	52	45		3	11		6				.324	.451	.381	78	7–5	.599	11
1931	101	376	102	12	5	1	( )	127	46	41	17		3	4		2				.271	.338	.305	39	4–6	.414	5
	1967	7363	2376	339	183	67	( )	3282	1099	981	484		46	219		268	92	.54		.323	.446	.358	1215	134–70	.655	170
12.1 yrs		606	196	28	15	6		270	91	81	40					22				.323	.446	.358				

Teams: Chicago, A.L. 1913; Indianapolis, F.L. 1914; Newark, F.L. 1915; New York /Cincinnati, 1916; Cincinnati, 1917–1926; New York, N.L. 1927–1929; Cincinnati, 1931.

Points in MVP Voting: 1926, 0; 1931, 0.

Reported Salaries: 1927–29—three-year contract for $70,000.

Explanation for Gaps in Career or Sudden Changes in Productivity:

1918—Unknown injuries; 1918 and 1919 seasons shortened.

1921—Held out; how long and whether there were subsequent injuries is not known.

1922—Held out into season; also had unknown injuries.

1927—Held out.

1928—Unknown illness.

1930—Sat out season in salary dispute.

FIELDING CENTER FIELD

Year	G	PO	AS	Err	DP	Pct.	Range
1913	2	3	0	0	0	1.000	1.50
1914	43	85	5	1	1	.989	2.09
1915	144	331	20	10	3	.972	2.44
1916	84	210	9	7	1	.969	2.61
1917	134	335	15	14	0	.962	2.61
1918	113	320	13	14	2	.960	2.95
1919	133	335	22	4	5	.989	2.68
1920	139	410	18	11	6	.975	3.08
1921	108	286	9	6	0	.980	2.73
1922	43	96	8	1	0	.990	2.42
1923	137	337	14	11	3	.970	2.56
1924	119	270	10	12	4	.959	2.35
1925	134	343	15	8	3	.978	2.67
1926	144	304	12	15	2	.955	2.19
1927	138	327	19	9	4	.975	2.51
1928	39	100	7	5	0	.955	2.74
1929	107	248	18	5	5	.982	2.49
1931	88	197	5	4	1	.981	2.30
	1849	4537	219	137	40	.972	2.57

Assists per 154 Games: 18.2

PLAYER: KIKI CUYLER

BATTING / BASERUNNING / PERCENTAGES / VALUES

Year	G	AB	H	2B	3B	HR	Hm	Rd	TB	R	RBI	BB	IBB	HBP	SH	SF	SB	CS	SB%	GIDP	Avg.	Slug	On Base	Runs	Win–Loss	Pct.	AV
1921	1	3	0	0	0	0			0	0	0	0		0	0		0	0	.00		.000	.000	.000	0	0–0	.000	0
1922	1	0	0	0	0	0			0	0	0	0		0	0		0	0	.00		.000	.000	.000	0	0–0	.000	0
1923	11	40	10	1	2	0			15	4	2	5		1	0		2	3	.40		.250	.375	.348	5	0–1	.379	0
1924	117	466	165	27	16	9			251	94	85	30		7	12		32	11	.74		.354	.539	.392	101	10–3	.781	13
1925	153	617	220	43	26	17			366	144	102	58		13	12		41	13	.76		.357	.593	.416	157	12–4	.768	17
1926	157	614	197	31	15	8			282	113	92	50		9	21		35				.321	.459	.369	105	11–6	.644	13
1927	85	285	88	13	7	3			124	60	31	37		3	5		20				.309	.435	.388	49	5–3	.643	6
1928	133	499	142	25	9	17			236	92	79	51		7	24		37				.285	.473	.344	84	9–5	.638	14
1929	139	509	183	29	7	15			271	111	102	66		5	16		43				.360	.532	.426	118	9–4	.720	17
1930	156	642	228	50	17	13			351	155	134	72		10	17		37				.355	.547	.418	148	11–5	.690	19
1931	154	613	202	37	12	9			290	110	61	72		5	20		13				.330	.473	.393	120	12–4	.734	15
1932	110	446	130	19	9	10			197	58	77	29		4	10		9				.291	.442	.333	67	7–5	.595	7
1933	70	262	83	13	3	5	2	3	117	37	35	21		4	7		4			10	.317	.447	.367	43	5–2	.708	4
1934	142	559	189	42	8	6			265	80	69	31		4	13		15			10	.338	.474	.369	101	10–4	.713	12
1935	107	380	98	13	4	6			137	58	40	37		7	6		8			5	.258	.361	.330	49	5–6	.490	6
1936	144	567	185	29	11	7			257	96	74	47		2	7		16			7	.326	.453	.376	102	10–5	.676	12
1937	117	406	110	12	4	0			130	48	32	36		2	5		10			15	.271	.320	.330	43	5–7	.429	7
1938	82	253	69	10	8	2			101	45	23	34		2	1		6			6	.273	.399	.362	39	4–3	.577	3
11.6 yrs	1879	7161	2299	394	158	127			3390	1305	1038	676		85	176		328	27	.74	53	.321	.473	.378	1331	128–66	.660	162
		617	198	34	14	11			292	113	89	58		7	15		28				.321	.473	.378				

Teams: Pittsburgh, 1921–1927; Chicago, N.L. 1928–1934; Chicago/Cincinnati, 1935; Cincinnati, 1936–1937; Brooklyn, 1938.

Points in MVP Voting: 1924, 25 (8th, .31); 1926, 0; 1931, 16 (7th, .25); 1932, 7 (.08); 1933, 0; 1934, 4 (.05); 1935, 0; 1937, 0; 1938, 0. TOTAL: .69 Award Shares.

Explanation for Gaps in Career or Sudden Changes in Productivity:

1927—Benched in mid-season for not hustling.

1932—Broken foot.

1933—Broken ankle.

1935—Just didn't hit.

Other Notes: Named to *The Sporting News* major league All-Star team in 1925.

FIELDING CENTER FIELD

Year	G	PO	AS	Err	DP	Pct.	Range
1921	1	1	0	0	0	1.000	1.00
1923	11	26	1	2	0	.931	2.45
1924	114	246	19	16	4	.943	2.32
1925	153	362	21	13	4	.967	2.50
1926	157	405	19	14	4	.968	2.70
1927	73	195	6	4	0	.980	2.75
1928	127	257	18	5	3	.982	2.17
1929	129	288	15	8	6	.974	2.35
1930	156	377	21	8	7	.980	2.55
1931	153	347	11	11	4	.970	2.34
1932	109	239	7	8	1	.969	2.26
1933	69	130	2	3	0	.978	1.91
1934	142	319	15	10	3	.971	2.35
1935	99	221	10	4	2	.983	2.33
1936	140	322	9	9	3	.974	2.36
1937	106	174	8	5	1	.973	1.72
1938	68	125	9	1	1	.993	1.97
	1807	4034	191	121	43	.972	2.34

Assists per 154 Games: 16.3

PLAYER: HACK WILSON

				BATTING														BASERUNNING				PERCENTAGES			VALUES			
Year	G	AB	H	2B	3B	HR	(Hm	Rd)	TB	R	RBI	BB	IBB	HBP	SH	SF	SB	CS	SB%	GIDP	Avg.	Slug	On Base	Runs	Win–Loss	Pct.	AV
1923	3	10	2	0	0	0	(	)	2	0	0	0		0		0	0	0	.00		.200	.200	.200	0	0–0	.058	0
1924	107	383	113	19	12	10	(	)	186	62	57	44		1		6	4	3	.57		.295	.486	.364	70	7–4	.640	9
1925	62	180	43	7	4	6	(	)	76	28	30	21		1		4	5	2	.71		.239	.422	.316	25	3–3	.487	3
1926	142	529	170	36	8	21	(	)	285	97	109	69		6		9	10				.321	.539	.400	115	11–3	.793	15
1927	146	551	175	30	12	30	(	)	319	119	129	71		6		18	13				.318	.579	.390	126	12–4	.765	15
1928	145	520	163	32	9	31	(	)	306	89	120	77		2		24	4				.313	.588	.388	122	12–3	.788	15
1929	150	574	198	30	5	39	(25	14)	355	135	159	78		2		16	3				.345	.618	.415	148	11–4	.756	18
1930	155	585	208	35	6	56	(33	23)	423	146	190	105		1		18	3				.356	.723	.443	189	12–3	.812	21
1931	112	395	103	22	4	13	(	)	172	66	61	63		0		0	1				.261	.435	.362	65	6–5	.579	8
1932	135	481	143	37	5	23	(	)	259	77	123	51		1		6	2				.297	.538	.362	95	9–4	.684	12
1933	117	360	96	13	2	9	(5	4)	140	41	54	52		0		1	7			8	.267	.389	.358	53	6–4	.615	5
1934	74	192	47	5	0	6	(	)	70	24	30	43		0		0	0			7	.245	.365	.383	29	3–3	.517	3
	1348	4760	1461	266	67	244	(63	41)	2593	884	1062	674		20		102	52	5	.64		.307	.545	.388	1037	92–39	.705	124
8.3 yrs		572	176	32	8	29			312	106	128	81		2		12	6				.307	.545	.388				

Teams: New York, N.L. 1923–1925; Chicago, N.L. 1926–1931; Brooklyn, 1932–1933; Brooklyn/Philadelphia, 1934.

Points in MVP Voting: 1926, 25 (5th, .31); 1927, 9 (.11); 1930 BBWAA, 70 (1st, .88); 1931, 0; 1932, 4 (.05); 1933, 0; 1934, 0. TOTAL: .47 Award Shares.

Reported Salaries: 1931—$33,000; 1932—$16,500.

Explanation for Gaps in Career or Sudden Changes in Productivity:
1925—Returned to minors.
1931—Wilson said in a 1948 interview, "I began to spend the winter in taprooms. When spring training rolled around, I was twenty pounds overweight. I couldn't stop drinking . . . I was suspended before the season was over." (Quoted from *Hack,* his biography with Robert S. Boone and Gerald Grunska.)

Other Notes: Named to *The Sporting News* major league All-Star team in 1929 and 1930. Also see material supplied by Gordon Herman in essay "Honors," page 167.

FIELDING CENTER FIELD

Year	G	PO	AS	Err	DP	Pct.	Range
1923	3	6	0	0	6	1.000	2.00
1924	103	230	8	2	238	.992	2.31
1925	50	75	3	2	78	.975	1.56
1926	140	348	11	5	359	.986	2.56
1927	146	400	13	3	413	.993	2.83
1928	143	321	11	2	332	.994	2.32
1929	150	380	14	4	394	.990	2.63
1930	155	357	9	2	366	.995	2.36
1931	103	210	9	1	219	.995	2.13
1932	125	220	14	4	234	.983	1.87
1933	90	181	3	0	184	1.000	2.04
1934	49	82	3	3	85	.966	1.73
	1257	2810	98	28	2908	.990	2.31

Assists per 154 Games: 12.0

HOME AND ROAD DATA FOR 1930 SEASON

	G	AB	R	H	2B	3B	HR	RBI	Avg.
HOME	78	286	77	110	13	3	33	113	.385
ROAD	77	299	69	98	22	3	23	77	.328

Data courtesy of Gordon L. Herman of Spokane

PLAYER: AL SIMMONS

						BATTING												BASERUNNING				PERCENTAGES			VALUES			
Year	G	AB	H	2B	3B	HR	(Hm	Rd)	TB	R	RBI	BB	IBB	HBP	SH	SF		SB	CS	SB%	GIDP	Avg.	Slug	On Base	Runs	Win−Loss	Pct.	AV
1924	152	594	183	31	9	8	(6	2)	256	69	102	30		2	18			16	15	.52		.308	.431	.334	84	9−8	.511	12
1925	153	658	253	43	12	24	(11	13)	392	122	129	35		1	6			7	14	.33		.384	.596	.413	154	13−4	.777	17
1926	147	581	199	53	10	19	(9	10)	329	90	109	48		1	10			10	3	.77		.343	.566	.388	129	12−3	.807	15
1927	106	406	159	36	11	15	(6	9)	262	86	108	31		1	20			10				.392	.645	.417	108	8−2	.813	14
1928	119	464	163	33	9	15	(9	6)	259	78	107	31		3	11			1	4	.20		.351	.558	.387	100	9−3	.751	13
1929	143	581	212	41	9	34	(16	18)	373	114	157	31		1	16			4	2	.67		.365	.642	.388	145	12−3	.789	20
1930	138	554	211	41	16	36	(25	11)	392	152	165	39		1	17			9	2	.82		.381	.708	.411	163	11−3	.817	19
1931	128	513	200	37	13	22	(10	12)	329	105	128	47		3	0			3	3	.50		.390	.641	.444	145	10−2	.858	17
1932	154	670	216	28	9	35	(22	13)	367	144	151	47		1	0			4	2	.67		.322	.548	.368	134	10−6	.647	16
1933	146	605	200	29	10	14	(7	7)	291	85	119	39		2	2			5	1	.83		.331	.481	.372	109	10−5	.661	15
1934	138	558	192	36	7	18	(8	10)	296	102	104	53		2	0			3	2	.60		.344	.530	.403	120	10−4	.711	15
1935	128	525	140	22	7	16	(11	5)	224	68	79	33		2	1			4	6	.40		.267	.427	.312	68	6−9	.413	10
1936	143	568	186	38	6	13	(10	3)	275	96	112	49		2	1			6	4	.60		.327	.484	.382	105	9−6	.597	13
1937	103	419	117	21	10	8	(3	5)	182	60	84	27		4	3			3	2	.60		.279	.434	.327	60	6−6	.500	8
1938	125	470	142	23	6	21	(7	14)	240	79	95	38		2	2			2	1	.67		.302	.511	.355	86	8−5	.595	10
1939	102	351	96	17	5	7	(2	5)	144	39	44	24		2	4			0			13	.274	.410	.320	47	6−4	.567	5
1940	37	81	25	4	0	1	(0	1)	32	7	19	4		0	1			0	0	.00	4	.309	.395	.337	10	1−1	.398	1
1941	9	24	3	1	0	0	(0	0)	4	1	1	1		0	0			0	0	.00		.125	.167	.160	0	0−1	.006	0
1943	40	133	27	5	0	1	(0	1)	35	9	12	8		0	0			0	1	.00	3	.203	.263	.248	8	1−3	.249	1
1944	4	6	3	0	0	0	(0	0)	3	1	2	0		0	0			0	0	.00		.500	.500	.500	1	0−0	.778	0
	2215	8761	2927	539	149	307	(162	145)	4685	1507	1827	615		30	112			87	62	.55	23	.334	.535	.375	1774	153−78	.661	221
13.7 yrs		641	214	39	11	22			343	110	134	45		2	8			6			19	.334	.535	.375				

Teams: Philadelphia, 1924–1932; Chicago, A.L. 1933–1935; Detroit, 1936; Washington, 1937–1938; Boston/Cincinnati 1939; Philadelphia, 1940–1941; Boston, 1943; Philadelphia, 1944.

Points in MVP Voting: 1924, 7 (.11); 1926, 16 (5th, .25); 1927, 18 (4th, .28); 1929, 40 (1st, .61); 1931, 16 (7th, .25); 1932, 0; 1933, 19 (8th, .24); 1934, 9 (.11); 1935, 0; 1937, 0; 1938, 0; 1940,0; 1941, 0; 1943, 0; 1944, 0. TOTAL: 1.85 Award Shares.

Reported Salaries: 1931–1933, $100,000 for three seasons.

Explanation for Gaps in Career or Sudden Changes in Productivity: 1927—Groin injury.

Other Notes: Named to *The Sporting News* major league All-Star team in 1927, 1929, 1930, 1931, 1933, 1934.

FIELDING CENTER FIELD

Year	G	PO	AS	Err	DP	Pct.	Range
1924	152	390	17	10	4	.976	2.68
1925	153	447	8	16	2	.966	2.97
1926	147	333	11	9	5	.975	2.34
1927	105	247	10	4	2	.985	2.45
1928	114	231	10	3	2	.988	2.11
1929	142	349	19	4	2	.989	2.59
1930	136	275	10	3	1	.990	2.10
1931	128	287	10	4	0	.987	2.32
1932	154	290	9	6	4	.980	1.94
1933	145	372	15	4	1	.990	2.67
1934	138	286	14	4	3	.987	2.17
1935	126	349	5	7	1	.981	2.61
1936	138	352	8	5	1	.986	2.61
1937	102	240	7	4	5	.984	2.42
1938	117	232	4	4	1	.983	2.02
1939	87	172	8	4	2	.978	2.07
1940	18	51	1	2	0	.963	2.89
1941	5	16	0	0	0	1.000	3.20
1943	33	66	3	1	1	.986	2.09
1944	2	3	0	0	0	1.000	1.50
	2142	4988	169	94	37	.982	2.41

Assists per 154 Games: 12.2

PLAYER: SAM WEST

Year	G	AB	H	2B	3B	HR	(Hm	Rd)	TB	R	RBI	BB	IBB	HBP	SH	SF	SB	CS	SB%	GIDP	Avg.	Slug	On Base	Runs	Win—Loss	Pct	AV
1927	38	67	16	4	1	0	(	)	22	9	6	8		0	0		1				.239	.328	.320	7	1—1	.359	0
1928	125	378	114	30	7	3	(	)	167	59	40	20		1	6		5	6	.45		.302	.442	.338	54	6—5	.531	8
1929	142	510	136	16	8	3	(	)	177	60	75	45		0	22		9	8	.53		.267	.347	.326	59	6—9	.379	11
1930	120	411	135	22	10	6	(	)	195	75	67	37		1	9		5	5	.50		.328	.474	.385	75	7—4	.637	9
1931	132	526	175	43	13	3	(	)	253	77	91	30		0	3		6	8	.43		.333	.481	.369	90	9—5	.634	14
1932	146	554	159	27	12	6	(	)	228	88	83	48		1	9		4	5	.44		.287	.412	.345	79	8—8	.505	11
1933	133	517	155	25	12	11	(	)	237	93	48	59		1	5		10	8	.56		.300	.458	.373	89	9—5	.617	14
1934	122	482	157	22	10	9	(	)	226	90	55	62		0	10		3	5	.37		.326	.469	.403	92	9—4	.685	13
1935	138	527	158	37	4	10	(	)	233	93	70	75		1	12		1	6	.14		.300	.442	.388	92	8—6	.574	13
1936	152	533	148	26	4	7	(	)	203	78	70	94		0	10		2	0	1.00		.278	.381	.386	85	7—8	.461	13
1937	122	457	150	37	4	7	(	)	216	68	58	46		0	3		1	1	.50		.328	.473	.390	85	7—4	.620	13
1938	136	509	155	27	7	6	(	)	214	68	74	47		0	11		2	1	.67		.305	.420	.363	79	7—7	.512	11
1939	115	390	110	20	8	3	(	)	155	52	52	67		0	14		1	1	.50	5	.282	.397	.387	65	7—5	.588	7
1940	57	99	25	6	1	1	(	)	36	7	18	16		0	2		0	2	.00	0	.253	.364	.357	14	1—1	.496	1
1941	26	37	10	0	0	0	(	)	10	3	6	11		0	1		1	0	1.00	0	.270	.270	.437	6	1—0	.573	1
1942	49	151	35	5	0	0	(	)	40	14	25	31		0	6		2	0	1.00	1	.232	.265	.363	18	2—3	.399	2
	1753	6148	1838	347	101	75			2612	934	838	696		5	123		53	56	.48		.299	.425	.371	990	93—77	.549	141
10.8 yrs		568	170	32	9	7			241	86	77	64		0	11		5	5			.299	.425	.371				

Teams: Washington, 1927–1932; St. Louis Browns, 1933–1938; Washington, 1938–1941; White Sox, 1942.

Points in MVP Voting: 1927, 0; 1931, 6 (.09); 1932 TSN, 0; 1933, 11 (.14); 1934, 5 (.06); 1935, 0; 1936, 2 (.03); 1937–1942, 0. TOTAL: .32 Award Shares.

FIELDING CENTER FIELD

Year	G	PO	AS	Err	DP	Pct.	Range
1927	18	28	3	2	0	.939	1.72
1928	116	210	13	1	0	.996	1.92
1929	139	376	25	9	8	.978	2.88
1930	118	310	8	9	1	.972	2.69
1931	127	402	13	4	3	.990	3.27
1932	143	450	15	10	7	.979	3.25
1933	127	329	14	4	3	.988	2.70
1934	120	303	14	9	3	.972	2.64
1935	135	449	7	5	2	.989	3.38
1936	148	442	10	8	2	.983	3.05
1937	105	298	17	4	6	.987	3.00
1938	126	322	4	7	3	.979	2.59
1939	89	232	7	2	3	.992	2.69
1940	9	18	0	0	0	1.000	2.00
1941	8	19	0	0	0	1.000	2.37
1942	45	112	1	2	1	.983	2.51
	1573	4300	151	76	42	.983	2.83

Assists per 154 Games: 14.8

PLAYER: EARL AVERILL

Year	G	AB	H	2B	3B	HR	(Hm	Rd)	TB	R	RBI	BB	IBB	HBP	SH	SF	SB	CS	SB%	GIDP	Avg.	Slug	On Base	Runs	Win—Loss	Pct.	AV
1929	152	602	199	43	13	18	(10	8)	322	110	97	64		3	17		13	13	.50		.331	.535	.388	124	12 – 5	.708	15
1930	139	534	181	33	8	19	(13	6)	287	102	119	56		2	13		10	7	.59		.339	.537	.395	114	9 – 5	.646	15
1931	155	627	209	36	10	32	(20	12)	361	140	143	68		6	0		9	9	.50		.333	.576	.404	143	12 – 5	.711	19
1932	153	631	198	37	14	32	(16	16)	359	116	124	75		6	0		5	8	.38		.314	.569	.392	139	12 – 5	.712	16
1933	151	599	180	39	16	11	(6	5)	284	83	92	54		5	0		3	1	.75		.301	.474	.363	104	11 – 5	.683	12
1934	154	598	187	48	6	31	(17	14)	340	128	113	99		4	1		4	3	.57		.313	.569	.413	144	12 – 4	.757	16
1935	140	563	162	34	13	19	(12	7)	279	109	79	70		1	4		8	4	.67		.288	.496	.365	103	10 – 6	.646	13
1936	152	614	232	39	15	28	(19	9)	385	136	126	65		1	2		3	3	.50		.378	.627	.437	167	12 – 3	.797	19
1937	156	609	182	33	11	21	(15	6)	300	121	92	88		0	5		5	4	.56		.299	.493	.385	118	11 – 6	.659	13
1938	134	482	159	27	15	14	(8	6)	258	101	93	81		3	1		5	2	.71		.330	.535	.429	114	9 – 3	.746	15
1939	111	364	96	28	6	11	(8	3)	169	66	65	49		1	11		4	3	.57	4	.264	.464	.344	61	6 – 5	.573	7
1940	64	118	33	4	1	2	(0	2)	45	10	20	5		0	1		0	0	.00	3	.280	.381	.306	14	1 – 2	.386	1
1941	8	17	2	0	0	0	(0	0)	2	2	2	1		1	0		0	0	.00	0	.118	.118	.211	1	0 – 1	.051	0
	1669	6358	2020	401	128	238	(144	94)	3391	1224	1165	775		33	55		69	57	.55	7	.318	.533	.392	1346	118 – 53	.689	161
10.3 yrs		617	196	39	12	23			329	119	113	75		3	5		7	6		6	.318	.533	.392				

Column groupings: BATTING — BASERUNNING — PERCENTAGES (Avg. / Slug / On Base) — VALUES (Runs / Win—Loss / Pct. / AV)

Teams: Cleveland, 1929–1938; Cleveland/Detroit, 1939; Detroit, 1940; Boston, 1941.

Points in MVP Voting: 1931, 27 (4th, .42); 1932, 29 (3rd, .33); 1933, 5 (.06); 1934, 3 (.04); 1935, 0; 1936, 43 (3rd, .54); 1937, 4 (.05); 1938, 34 (8th, .10); 1940, 0; 1941, 0. TOTAL: 1.54 Award Shares.

Other Notes: Named to *The Sporting News* major league All-Star team in 1931, 1932, 1934, 1936.

13 HR vs. LHP, 15 vs. RHP, 1936

FIELDING CENTER FIELD

Year	G	PO	AS	E	DP	Pct.	Range
1929	152	388	14	14	3	.966	2.64
1930	134	345	11	19	5	.949	2.66
1931	155	398	9	10	3	.976	2.63
1932	153	412	12	16	3	.964	2.77
1933	149	390	8	12	3	.971	2.67
1934	154	410	12	13	3	.970	2.74
1935	139	371	6	7	2	.982	2.71
1936	150	369	11	12	2	.969	2.53
1937	156	362	11	9	3	.976	2.39
1938	131	331	14	9	2	.975	2.63
1939	91	169	3	4	0	.977	1.89
1940	22	23	2	1	0	.962	1.14
1941	4	5	2	0	0	1.000	1.75
	1590	3973	115	126	29	.970	2.57

Assists per 154 Games: 11.1

PLAYER: DOC CRAMER

				BATTING														BASERUNNING				PERCENTAGES			VALUES			
Year	G	AB	H	2B	3B	HR	(Hm	Rd)	TB	R	RBI	BB	IBB	HBP	SH	SF	SB	CS	SB%	GIDP	Avg.	Slug	On Base	Runs	Win—Loss	Pct	AV
1929	2	6	0	0	0	0	(	)	0	0	0	0		0	0	0	0	0	.00		.000	.000	.000	0	0—0	.000	0
1930	30	82	19	1	1	0	(	)	22	12	6	2		0	1		0	0	.00		.232	.268	.250	5	0—2	.145	0
1931	65	223	58	8	2	2	(	)	76	37	20	11		2	6		2	1	.67		.260	.341	.301	23	2—4	.353	3
1932	92	384	129	27	6	3	(	)	177	73	46	17		2	4		3	1	.75		.336	.461	.367	64	6—4	.574	8
1933	152	661	195	27	8	8	(	)	262	109	75	36		0	21		5	4	.56		.295	.396	.331	86	8—11	.406	9
1934	153	649	202	29	9	6	(	)	267	99	46	40		2	12		1	5	.17		.311	.411	.353	93	9—9	.506	13
1935	149	644	214	37	4	3	(	)	268	96	70	37		5	15		6	7	.46		.332	.416	.373	99	9—8	.550	13
1936	154	643	188	31	7	0	(	)	233	99	41	49		5	16		4	6	.40		.292	.362	.347	82	8—10	.452	11
1937	133	560	171	22	11	0	(	)	215	90	51	35		4	17		8	6	.57		.305	.384	.351	76	7—8	.465	11
1938	148	658	198	36	8	0	(	)	250	116	71	51		3	5		4	9	.31		.301	.380	.354	87	8—10	.446	13
1939	137	589	183	30	6	0	(	)	225	110	56	36		2	15		3	3	.50	16	.311	.382	.352	79	7—9	.434	12
1940	150	661	200	27	12	1	(	)	254	94	51	36		1	14		3	5	.37	13	.303	.384	.340	84	7—11	.410	11
1941	154	660	180	25	6	2	(	)	223	93	66	37		6	4		4	1	.80	16	.273	.338	.317	69	7—12	.363	8
1942	151	630	166	26	4	0	(	)	200	71	43	43		3	6		4	4	.50	15	.263	.317	.314	61	8—10	.441	9
1943	140	606	182	18	4	1	(	)	211	79	43	31		1	13		4	3	.57	8	.300	.348	.335	71	9—7	.551	11
1944	143	578	169	20	9	2	(	)	213	69	42	37		2	9		6	5	.55	7	.292	.369	.337	72	9—7	.560	10
1945	141	541	149	22	8	6	(	)	205	62	58	35		3	15		2	9	.18	9	.275	.379	.323	64	8—8	.516	9
1946	68	204	60	8	2	1	(	)	75	26	26	15		0	5		3	0	1.00	6	.294	.368	.342	26	3—3	.538	2
1947	73	157	42	2	2	2	(	)	54	21	30	20		0	2		0	4	.00	9	.268	.344	.350	16	2—3	.377	2
1948	4	4	0	0	0	0	(	)	0	1	1	3		0	0		0	0	.00	0	.000	.000	.429	0	0—0	.192	0
	2239	9140	2705	396	109	37	(	)	3430	1357	842	571		41	180		62	73	.46	99	.296	.375	.340	1159	118—136	.465	155
13.8 yrs		661	196	29	8	3			249	116	61	41		3	13		4	5			.296	.375	.340				

Teams: 1929–1935, Philadelphia Athletics; 1936–1940, Red Sox; 1941, Washington; 1942–1948, Detroit.

Points in MVP Voting: 1931, 0; 1932 TSN, 0; 1933, 0; 1934, 0; 1935, 18 (8th, .23); 1936, 0; 1937, 0; 1938, 1 (.00); 1940, 0; 1941, 0; 1942, 0; 1943, 8 (.02); 1944, 14 (.04); 1945, 4 (.01); 1946–1948, 0. TOTAL: .30 Award Shares.

Explanation for Gaps in Career or Sudden Changes in Productivity:
1931—Broken finger
1932—Cracked collarbone, missed most of second half of season

FIELDING CENTER FIELD

Year	G	PO	AS	Err	DP	Pct.	Range
1929	1	6	0	0	0	1.000	6.00
1930	21	37	1	3	0	.927	1.81
1931	55	133	5	3	1	.979	2.51
1932	86	233	7	6	2	.976	2.79
1933	152	387	13	12	2	.971	2.63
1934	152	385	12	6	0	.985	2.61
1935	149	429	6	11	1	.975	2.92
1936	154	443	20	12	6	.975	3.01
1937	133	365	12	12	4	.969	2.83
1938	148	417	15	6	3	.986	2.92
1939	135	356	12	6	0	.984	2.73
1940	149	333	11	11	2	.969	2.31
1941	152	369	9	6	1	.984	2.49
1942	150	352	15	7	6	.981	2.45
1943	138	346	9	4	3	.989	2.57
1944	141	337	13	7	2	.980	2.48
1945	140	314	7	3	4	.991	2.29
1946	50	89	2	0	0	1.000	1.82
1947	35	79	3	3	0	.965	2.34
1948	1	2	0	0	0	1.000	2.00
	2142	5412	172	118	37	.979	2.61

Assists per 154 Games: 12.4

PLAYER: JOE DiMAGGIO

				BATTING													BASERUNNING				PERCENTAGES			VALUES			
Year	G	AB	H	2B	3B	HR	(Hm	Rd)	TB	R	RBI	BB	IBB	HBP	SH	SF	SB	CS	SB%	GIDP	Avg.	Slug	On Base	Runs	Win–Loss	Pct.	AV
1936	138	637	206	44	15	29	(8	21)	367	132	125	24		4	3		4	0	1.00		.323	.576	.350	127	11–6	.633	15
1937	151	621	215	35	15	46	(19	27)	418	151	167	64		5	2		3	0	1.00		.346	.673	.410	173	13–3	.814	19
1938	145	599	194	32	13	32	(15	17)	348	129	140	59		2	0		6	1	.86		.324	.581	.386	136	11–4	.726	16
1939	120	462	176	32	6	30	(12	18)	310	108	126	52		4	6		3	0	1.00	11	.381	.671	.443	139	10–2	.859	19
1940	132	508	179	28	9	31	(16	15)	318	93	133	61		3	0		1	2	.33	16	.352	.626	.425	135	11–2	.827	19
1941	139	541	193	43	11	30	(16	14)	348	122	125	76		4	0		4	2	.67	6	.357	.643	.440	162	12–2	.873	20
1942	154	610	186	29	13	21	(8	13)	304	123	114	68		2	0		4	2	.67	9	.305	.498	.376	120	12–4	.753	14
1946	132	503	146	20	8	25	(8	17)	257	81	95	59		2	3		1	0	1.00	13	.290	.511	.365	94	10–4	.705	14
1947	141	534	168	31	10	20	(9	11)	279	97	97	64		3	0		3	0	1.00	14	.315	.522	.391	109	10–4	.719	14
1948	153	594	190	26	11	39	(15	24)	355	110	155	67		8	0		1	1	.50	20	.320	.598	.396	137	12–4	.772	17
1949	76	272	94	14	6	14	(5	9)	162	58	67	55		2	0		0	1	.00	11	.346	.596	.459	75	6–1	.824	9
1950	139	525	158	33	10	32	(9	23)	307	114	122	80		1	0		0	0	.00	14	.301	.585	.394	122	10–4	.735	15
1951	116	415	109	22	4	12	(8	4)	175	72	71	61		6	0		0	0	.00	16	.263	.422	.365	65	7–5	.586	10
	1736	6821	2214	389	131	361	(148	213)	3948	1390	1537	790		46	14		30	9	.77	130	.325	.579	.398	1593	134–44	.751	201
10.7 yrs		637	207	36	12	34			368	130	143	74		4	1		3	1		16	.325	.579	.398				

Teams: New York, A.L. 1936–1942, 1946–1951.

Points in MVP Voting: 1936, 26 (8th, .33); 1937, 74 (2nd, .93); 1938, 106 (5th, .32); 1939, 280 (1st, .83); 1940, 151 (3rd, .45); 1941, 291 (1st, .87); 1942, 86 (7th, .26); 1946, 6 (.02); 1947, 202 (1st, .60); 1948, 213 (2nd, .63); 1949, 18 (.05); 1950, 54 (9th, .17); 1951, 0. TOTAL: 5.46 Award Shares.

Reported Salaries: 1936—$8.500; 1937—$15,000; 1938—$25,000 (held out until late April); 1940—$32,500; 1941—$37.500; 1942—$42,500; 1950—$100,000; 1951—$100,000. Was reportedly offered $100,000 to play just half the games (the home games) in 1952, but declined.

Explanation for Gaps in Career or Sudden Changes in Productivity:

1938—Held out, missed first two weeks of season.

1939—Trying to make hairpin turn in Yankees tenth game of season, tore muscles in right leg above the ankle. Out 33 games.

1941—August 19, jammed his spikes into second base sliding in on a double; badly sprained ankle. Out until September 9.

1943–45—In the army.

1949—Operation in off-season to remove bone spur from right heel. Did not play until June 27.

1950—Benched briefly in August for not hitting.

1951—Slowed by leg and ankle injuries.

Other Notes: Named to *The Sporting News* major league All-Star team in 1937, 1938, 1939, 1940, 1941, 1942, 1947, 1948.

FIELDING CENTER FIELD

Year	G	PO	AS	Err	DP	Pct.	Range
1936	138	339	22	8	2	.978	2.62
1937	150	413	21	17	4	.962	2.89
1938	145	366	20	15	4	.963	2.66
1939	117	328	13	5	2	.986	2.91
1940	130	359	5	8	2	.978	2.80
1941	139	385	16	9	5	.978	2.88
1942	154	409	10	8	3	.981	2.72
1946	131	314	15	6	3	.982	2.51
1947	139	316	2	1	0	.997	2.29
1948	152	441	8	13	1	.972	2.95
1949	76	195	1	3	0	.985	2.58
1950	137	363	9	9	1	.976	2.72
1951	113	288	11	3	3	.990	2.65
	1721	4516	153	105	30	.978	2.71

Assists per 154 Games: 13.7

PLAYER: LARRY DOBY

Year	G	AB	H	2B	3B	HR	(Hm	Rd)	TB	R	RBI	BB	IBB	HBP	SH	SF	SB	CS	SB%	GIDP	Avg.	Slug	On Base	Runs	Win–Loss	Pct.	AV
1947	29	32	5	1	0	0	(0	0)	6	3	2	1			0	0	0	0	.00	2	.156	.188	.182	1	0–1	.031	0
1948	121	439	132	23	9	14	(4	10)	215	83	66	54			5	2	9	9	.50	8	.301	.490	.382	84	8–4	.704	11
1949	147	547	153	25	3	24	(9	15)	256	106	85	91			7	5	10	9	.53	14	.280	.468	.386	104	11–4	.728	11
1950	142	503	164	25	5	25	(16	9)	274	110	102	98			6	2	8	6	.57	9	.326	.545	.440	130	11–2	.814	15
1951	134	447	132	27	5	20	(8	12)	229	84	69	101			3	0	4	1	.80	10	.295	.512	.428	108	10–2	.821	14
1952	140	519	143	26	8	32	(15	17)	281	104	104	90		0	2		5	2	.71	6	.276	.541	.381	116	11–3	.772	16
1953	149	513	135	18	5	29	(13	16)	250	92	102	96		6	2		3	2	.60	7	.263	.487	.384	105	10–4	.725	13
1954	153	577	157	18	4	32	(16	16)	279	94	126	85		3	1	9	3	1	.75	7	.272	.484	.363	109	12–4	.738	16
1955	131	491	143	17	5	26	(16	10)	248	91	75	61	8	2	2	4	2	0	1.00	6	.291	.505	.368	95	10–3	.741	14
1956	140	504	135	22	3	24	(15	9)	235	89	102	102	6	4	4	5	0	1	.00	7	.268	.466	.389	100	10–4	.700	13
1957	119	416	120	27	2	14	(3	11)	193	57	79	56	3	2	0	3	2	3	.40	13	.288	.464	.373	71	8–4	.689	9
1958	89	247	70	10	1	13	(6	7)	121	41	45	26	2	0	0	3	0	2	.00	7	.283	.490	.348	41	4–3	.641	5
1959	39	113	26	4	2	0	(0	0)	34	6	13	10	0	0	0	1	1	0	1.00	1	.230	.301	.290	11	1–2	.356	0
	1533	5348	1515	243	52	253	(121	132)	2621	960	970	871	19	38	20	25	47	36	.57	97	.283	.490	.385	1075	108–41	.724	137
9.5 yrs		565	160	26	5	27			277	101	103	92		4	2		5	4	.57	10	.283	.490	.385				

Teams: Cleveland, 1947–1955; Chicago, A.L. 1956–1957; Cleveland, 1958; Detroit/Chicago, 1959.

Points in MVP Voting: 1947, 0; 1948, 3 (.01); 1949, 0; 1950, 57 (8th, .18); 1951, 0; 1952, 46 (.14); 1954, 210 (2nd, .63); 1958, 0; 1959, 0. TOTAL: .96 Award Shares.

Explanation for Gaps in Career or Sudden Changes in Productivity: Career got late start because of color line.

Other Notes: 1952–13 HR vs. LHP, 19 vs. RHP.

Named to *The Sporting News* major league All-Star team in 1950.

FIELDING CENTER FIELD

Year	G	PO	AS	Err	DP	Pct.	Range
1948	114	287	12	14	3	.955	2.62
1949	147	355	7	9	2	.976	2.46
1950	140	367	2	5	1	.987	2.64
1951	132	321	12	8	3	.977	2.52
1952	136	398	11	6	3	.986	3.01
1953	146	354	10	6	3	.984	2.49
1954	153	411	14	2	6	.995	2.78
1955	129	313	6	2	1	.994	2.47
1956	137	371	4	5	2	.987	2.74
1957	110	255	3	4	0	.985	2.35
1958	68	141	5	0	0	1.000	2.15
1959	28	43	2	2	0	.957	1.61
	1440	3616	88	63	26	.983	2.57

Assists per 154 Games: 9.4

PLAYER: DUKE SNIDER

Year	G	AB	H	2B	3B	HR	(Hm	Rd)	TB	R	RBI	BB	IBB	HBP	SH	SF	SB	CS	SB%	GIDP	Avg.	Slug	On Base	Runs	Win—Loss	Pct.	AV
1947	40	83	20	3	1	0	(0	0)	25	6	5	3		1	2		2			0	.241	.301	.270	7	1–2	.298	0
1948	53	160	39	6	6	5	(1	4)	72	22	21	12		0	0		4			4	.244	.450	.297	21	2–2	.487	2
1949	146	552	161	28	7	23	(8	15)	272	100	92	56		4	3		12			8	.292	.493	.359	100	10–5	.653	13
1950	152	620	199	31	10	31	(18	13)	343	109	107	58		0	6		16			9	.321	.553	.376	131	12–5	.719	14
1951	150	606	168	26	6	29	(21	8)	293	96	101	62		0	4		14	10	.58	23	.277	.483	.342	96	10–8	.558	13
1952	144	534	162	25	7	21	(12	9)	264	80	92	55		0	9		7	4	.64	17	.303	.494	.363	96	10–5	.678	14
1953	153	590	198	38	4	42	(23	19)	370	132	126	82		3	5		16	7	.70	10	.336	.627	.416	161	12–3	.797	17
1954	149	584	199	39	10	40	(23	17)	378	120	130	84		4	1	6	6	6	.50	12	.341	.647	.423	164	13–3	.828	16
1955	148	538	166	34	6	42	(23	19)	338	126	134	104	19	1	4	6	9	7	.56	9	.309	.628	.415	145	12–3	.801	18
1956	151	542	158	33	2	43	(25	18)	324	112	101	99	26	1	6	4	3	3	.50	16	.292	.598	.396	128	12–3	.793	16
1957	139	508	139	25	7	40	(23	17)	298	91	92	77	12	1	3	3	3	4	.43	17	.274	.587	.367	106	11–4	.751	14
1958	106	327	102	12	3	15	(6	9)	165	45	58	32	4	1	1	4	2	2	.50	11	.312	.505	.370	59	6–3	.665	8
1959	126	370	114	11	2	23	(13	10)	198	59	88	58	13	0	5	2	1	5	.17	8	.308	.535	.395	78	8–3	.751	10
1960	101	235	57	13	5	14	(11	3)	122	38	36	46	8	1	1	2	1	0	1.00	7	.243	.519	.365	46	5–2	.722	5
1961	85	233	69	8	3	16	(8	8)	131	35	56	29	3	1	2	1	1	1	.50	6	.296	.562	.372	48	5–2	.743	5
1962	80	158	44	11	3	5	(1	4)	76	28	30	36	6	2	0	0	2	0	1.00	5	.278	.481	.418	34	3–1	.727	3
1963	129	354	86	8	3	14	(7	7)	142	44	45	56	9	1	0	4	0	1	.00	2	.243	.401	.345	53	6–4	.635	6
1964	91	167	35	7	0	4	(1	3)	54	16	17	22	4	0	0	0	0	0	.00	2	.210	.323	.302	17	2–3	.446	2
	2143	7161	2116	358	85	407	(224	183)	3865	1259	1331	971	104	21	52	32	99	50	.57	166	.295	.540	.377	1489	139–59	.704	176
13.2 yrs		541	160	27	6	31			292	95	101	73		2	4		7			13	.295	.540	.377				

Teams: Brooklyn, 1947–57; Los Angeles, 1958–62; New York, N.L., 1963; San Francisco, 1964.

Points in MVP Voting: 1947, 0; 1948, 0; 1949, 0; 1950, 53? (9th, .16); 1951, 0?; 1952, 30 (8th, .09); 1953, 157 (3rd, .47); 1954, 125 (4th, .37); 1955, 221 (2nd, .66); 1956, 55 (10th, .16); 1957, 10 (?, .03); 1958, 0; 1959, 1 (.00); 1960, 0; 1962, 0; 1963, 0; 1964, 0. TOTAL: 1.94 Award Shares.

Reported Salaries: 1959—$50,000.

Explanation for Gaps in Career or Sudden Changes in Productivity:
1958—Productivity curtailed by back trouble and move to Los Angeles Coliseum.
1960—Strained knee in 1959 World Series.
1961—Broken elbow.

Other Notes: Named to *The Sporting News* major league All-Star team, 1953, 1954, 1955.

FIELDING CENTER FIELD

Year	G	PO	AS	Err	DP	Pct.	Range
1947	25	48	0	1	0	.980	1.92
1948	47	87	5	1	0	.989	1.96
1949	145	355	12	6	2	.984	2.53
1950	151	378	15	7	1	.982	2.60
1951	150	382	12	5	1	.987	2.63
1952	141	341	13	3	3	.992	2.51
1953	151	370	7	5	3	.987	2.50
1954	148	360	8	7	1	.981	2.49
1955	146	348	9	4	0	.989	2.45
1956	150	358	11	6	1	.984	2.46
1957	136	304	6	3	1	.990	2.28
1958	92	151	4	2	0	.987	1.68
1959	107	157	2	4	1	.975	1.49
1960	75	108	3	4	1	.965	1.48
1961	66	113	6	3	3	.975	1.48
1962	39	56	3	2	0	.967	1.51
1963	106	139	5	2	0	.986	1.36
1964	43	44	2	1	0	.979	1.07
	1918	4099	123	66	18	.985	2.20

Assists per 154 Games: 9.9

PLAYER: RICHIE ASHBURN

Year	G	AB	H	2B	3B	HR	(Hm	Rd)	TB	R	RBI	BB	IBB	HBP	SH	SF	SB	CS	SB%	GIDP	Avg.	Slug	On Base	Runs	Win—Loss	Pct.	AV
1948	117	463	154	17	4	2	(	)	185	78	40	60		1	6		32			1	.333	.400	.406	91	9–3	.769	15
1949	154	662	188	18	11	1	(	)	231	84	37	58		1	7		9			7	.284	.349	.339	86	10–8	.548	11
1950	151	594	180	25	14	2	(0	2)	239	84	41	63		2	11		14			11	.303	.402	.366	96	11–6	.658	13
1951	154	643	221	31	5	4	(1	3)	274	92	63	50		2	17		29	6	.83	4	.344	.426	.383	118	12–4	.740	16
1952	154	613	173	31	6	1	(1	0)	219	93	42	75		2	11		16	11	.59	7	.282	.357	.357	86	11–7	.612	11
1953	156	622	205	25	9	2	(0	2)	254	110	57	61		5	14		14	6	.70	3	.330	.408	.386	109	11–5	.695	15
1954	153	559	175	16	8	1	(0	1)	210	111	41	125		4	14	1	11	8	.58	3	.313	.376	.432	109	11–4	.751	13
1955	140	533	180	32	9	3	(0	3)	239	91	42	105	5	3	2	1	12	10	.55	3	.338	.448	.447	117	11–3	.794	14
1956	154	628	190	26	8	3	(0	3)	241	94	50	79	3	5	6	1	10	1	.91	4	.303	.384	.381	101	11–6	.643	12
1957	156	626	186	26	8	0	(0	0)	228	93	33	94	1	4	1	4	13	10	.57	10	.297	.364	.390	95	11–6	.645	11
1958	152	615	215	24	13	2	(1	1)	271	98	33	97	7	4	7	2	30	12	.71	8	.350	.441	.436	129	12–4	.754	16
1959	153	564	150	16	2	1	(1	0)	173	86	20	79	4	6	7	4	9	11	.45	10	.266	.307	.356	66	8–9	.469	9
1960	151	547	159	16	5	0	(0	0)	185	99	40	116	1	1	7	1	16	4	.80	4	.291	.338	.411	91	10–5	.643	11
1961	109	307	79	7	4	0	(0	0)	94	49	19	55	2	3	1	2	7	6	.54	4	.257	.306	.372	39	4–5	.459	4
1962	135	389	119	7	3	7	(6	1)	153	60	28	81	2	0	1	2	12	7	.63	4	.306	.393	.423	72	7–3	.668	9
	2189	8365	2574	317	109	29	(10	16)	3196	1322	586	1198	25	43	112	18	234	92	.66	83	.308	.382	.392	1405	148–77	.657	180
13.5 yrs		619	190	23	8	2			237	98	43	89	3	8			17			6	.308	.382	.392				

(Header grouping: BATTING — G, AB, H, 2B, 3B, HR, (Hm, Rd), TB, R, RBI, BB, IBB, HBP, SH, SF; BASERUNNING — SB, CS, SB%, GIDP; PERCENTAGES — Avg., Slug, On Base; VALUES — Runs, Win—Loss, Pct., AV)

Teams: Philadelphia, 1948–59; Chicago, N.L. 1960–61; New York, N.L., 1962.
Points in MVP Voting: 1948, 48 (.14); 1949, 6 (.02); 1950, 0; 1951, 69 (7th, .21); 1952, 0; 1953, 5 (.01); 1954, 5 (.01); 1955, 17 (.05); 1956, 1 (.00); 1957, 0; 1958, 62 (7th, .18); 1959, 0; 1960, 0; 1962, 0. TOTAL: .60 Award Shares.

FIELDING CENTER FIELD

Year	G	PO	AS	Err	DP	Pct.	Range
1948	116	344	14	7	2	.981	3.09
1949	154	514	13	11	3	.980	3.42
1950	147	405	8	5	2	.988	2.81
1951	154	538	15	7	6	.987	3.59
1952	154	428	23	9	5	.980	2.93
1953	156	496	18	5	4	.990	3.29
1954	153	483	12	8	2	.984	3.24
1955	140	387	10	7	3	.983	2.84
1956	154	503	11	9	3	.983	3.34
1957	156	502	18	7	7	.987	3.33
1958	152	495	8	8	2	.984	3.31
1959	149	359	4	11	1	.971	2.44
1960	146	317	11	8	2	.976	2.25
1961	76	131	4	3	0	.978	1.78
1962	97	187	9	5	1	.975	2.02
	2104	6089	178	110	43	.983	2.98

Assists per 154 Games: 13.0

PLAYER: MICKEY MANTLE

				BATTING													BASERUNNING				PERCENTAGES			VALUES			
Year	G	AB	H	2B	3B	HR	(Hm	Rd)	TB	R	RBI	BB	IBB	HBP	SH	SF	SB	CS	SB%	GIDP	Avg.	Slug	On Base	Runs	Win–Loss	Pct.	AV
1951	96	341	91	11	5	13	(7	6)	151	61	65	43		0	2		8	7	.53	3	.267	.443	.347	55	6–4	.602	5
1952	142	549	171	37	7	23	(11	12)	291	94	87	75		0	2		4	1	.80	5	.311	.530	.393	123	12–3	.810	14
1953	127	461	136	24	3	21	(8	13)	229	105	92	79		0	0		8	4	.67	2	.295	.497	.398	100	9–3	.771	13
1954	146	543	163	17	12	27	(14	13)	285	129	102	102		0	2	4	5	2	.71	3	.300	.525	.407	129	12–3	.802	15
1955	147	517	158	25	11	37	(19	18)	316	121	99	113	6	3	2	3	8	1	.89	4	.306	.611	.429	148	12–2	.863	19
1956	150	533	188	22	5	52	(27	25)	376	132	130	112	6	2	1	4	10	1	.91	4	.353	.705	.463	188	12–1	.897	24
1957	144	474	173	28	6	34	(14	20)	315	121	94	146	23	0	0	3	16	3	.84	5	.365	.665	.512	178	11–1	.935	19
1958	150	519	158	21	1	42	(21	21)	307	127	97	129	13	2	2	2	18	3	.86	11	.304	.592	.442	147	12–2	.855	16
1959	144	541	154	23	4	31	(18	13)	278	104	75	94	6	2	1	2	21	3	.87	7	.285	.514	.391	118	11–3	.773	16
1960	153	527	145	17	6	40	(23	17)	294	119	94	111	6	1	0	5	14	3	.82	11	.275	.558	.399	125	12–3	.783	16
1961	153	514	163	16	6	54	(24	30)	353	132	128	126	9	0	1	5	12	1	.92	2	.317	.687	.447	174	12–1	.897	19
1962	123	377	121	15	1	30	(16	14)	228	96	89	122	9	1	0	2	9	0	1.00	4	.321	.605	.486	126	9–1	.887	15
1963	65	172	54	8	0	15	(8	7)	107	40	35	40	4	0	0	1	2	1	.67	5	.314	.622	.441	49	4–1	.878	6
1964	143	465	141	25	2	35	(16	19)	275	92	111	99	18	0	0	3	6	3	.67	9	.303	.591	.423	121	11–2	.854	16
1965	122	361	92	12	1	19	(9	10)	163	44	46	73	7	0	0	1	4	1	.80	11	.255	.452	.379	64	8–3	.728	8
1966	108	333	96	12	1	23	(11	12)	179	40	56	57	5	0	0	3	1	1	.50	9	.288	.538	.389	71	7–2	.800	9
1967	144	440	108	17	0	22	(10	12)	191	63	55	107	7	1	0	5	1	1	.50	9	.245	.434	.391	82	10–3	.768	11
1968	144	435	103	14	1	18	(10	8)	173	57	54	106	7	1	1	4	6	2	.75	9	.237	.398	.384	74	10–3	.759	8
	2401	8102	2415	344	72	536	(266	270)	4511	1677	1509	1734	126	13	14	47	153	38	.80	113	.298	.557	.420	2072	178–40	.815	249
14.8 yrs		547	163	23	5	36			304	113	102	117		1	1		10	3	.80	8	.298	.557	.420				

FIELDING CENTER FIELD

Year	G	PO	AS	Err	DP	Pct.	Range
1951	86	135	4	6	1	.959	1.62
1952	141	347	15	12	5	.968	2.57
1953	121	322	10	6	2	.982	2.74
1954	144	327	20	9	5	.975	2.41
1955	145	372	11	2	2	.995	2.64
1956	144	370	10	4	3	.990	2.64
1957	139	324	6	7	1	.979	2.37
1958	150	331	5	8	2	.977	2.24
1959	143	366	7	2	3	.995	2.61
1960	150	326	9	3	1	.991	2.23
1961	150	351	6	6	0	.983	2.38
1962	117	214	4	5	1	.978	1.86
1963	52	99	2	1	0	.990	1.94
1964	132	217	3	5	1	.978	1.67
1965	108	165	3	6	0	.966	1.56
1966	97	172	2	0	0	1.000	1.79
	2019	4438	117	82	27	.982	2.26

Assists per 154 Games: 9.0

Teams: New York, A.L. 1951–1968.

Points in MVP Voting: 1951, 0; 1952, 143 (3rd, .43); 1953, 4 (.01); 1955, 113 (5th, .34); 1956, 336 (1st, 1.00); 1957, 233 (1st, .69); 1958, 127 (5th, .38); 1959, 13 (.04); 1960, 222 (2nd, .66); 1961, 198 (2nd, .71); 1962, 234 (1st, .84); 1963, 0; 1964, 171 (2nd, .61); 1965, 3 (.01); 1966, 0; 1967, 0; 1968, 0. TOTAL: 5.72 Award Shares. Note: 1954, not in top 10.

Reported Salaries: 1950—$225/month in minors; 1951—$7,500; 1953—$10,000; 1954—$12,500; 1955—$17,000; 1956—$32,500; 1957—$65,000; 1958—$70,000; 1959—$77,000; 1960—$67,000; 1961—$75,000; 1962—$90,000; 1963—$100,000.

Explanation for Gaps in Career or Sudden Changes in Productivity:
1953—Tore cartilage in left knee chasing ball hit by Willie Mays, during 1951 World Series; afterward developed osteomyelitis in the knee.
1957—Hospitalized with shin splints in early September.
1962—Tore thigh muscle in right leg running out ground ball, May 18; pulled muscle in his side, September 4.
1963—Broke a bone in his left foot when he got it entangled in a wire fence during game in Baltimore, June 5.
1965—Pulled leg muscles; pinched nerve in neck.

Other Notes: Named to *The Sporting News* major league All-Star team in 1952, 1956, 1957. Named to *The Sporting News* American League All-Star team in 1961, 1962, 1964.
Gold Glove—1962.

PLAYER: WILLIE MAYS

Year	G	AB	H	2B	3B	HR	(Hm	Rd)	TB	R	RBI	BB	IBB	HBP	SH	SF	SB	CS	SB%	GIDP	Avg.	Slug	On Base	Runs	Win–Loss	Pct.	AV
1951	121	464	127	22	5	20	(13	7)	219	59	68	56		2	1		7	4	.64	11	.274	.472	.354	79	8–5	.642	10
1952	34	127	30	2	4	4	(2	2)	52	17	23	16		1	0		4	1	.80	2	.236	.409	.326	18	2–2	.555	2
1954	151	565	195	33	13	41	(20	21)	377	119	110	66		2	0	7	8	5	.62	12	.345	.667	.411	157	13–2	.870	19
1955	152	580	185	18	13	51	(22	29)	382	123	127	79	13	4	0	7	24	4	.86	12	.319	.659	.400	157	13–3	.837	20
1956	152	578	171	27	8	36	(20	16)	322	101	84	68	20	1	0	3	40	10	.80	16	.296	.557	.369	118	13–4	.780	16
1957	152	585	195	26	20	35	(17	18)	366	112	97	76	15	1	0	6	38	19	.67	14	.333	.626	.407	145	13–3	.814	19
1958	152	600	208	33	11	29	(16	13)	350	121	96	78	12	1	0	6	31	6	.84	11	.347	.583	.419	152	13–3	.821	18
1959	151	575	180	43	5	34	(16	18)	335	125	104	65	9	2	0	6	27	4	.87	11	.313	.583	.381	131	12–3	.799	17
1960	153	595	190	29	12	29	(12	17)	330	107	103	61	11	4	0	9	25	10	.71	15	.319	.555	.381	124	13–4	.771	17
1961	154	572	176	32	3	40	(21	19)	334	129	123	81	15	2	0	4	18	9	.67	14	.308	.584	.393	130	12–4	.765	15
1962	162	621	189	36	5	49	(28	21)	382	130	141	78	11	4	0	3	18	2	.90	19	.304	.615	.384	146	13–4	.767	18
1963	157	596	187	32	7	38	(20	18)	347	115	103	66	5	2	0	7	8	3	.73	15	.314	.582	.380	131	13–3	.789	16
1964	157	578	171	21	9	47	(25	22)	351	121	111	82	13	1	1	3	19	5	.79	11	.296	.607	.382	136	13–3	.835	18
1965	157	558	177	21	3	52	(24	28)	360	118	112	76	16	0	2	2	9	4	.69	11	.317	.645	.397	143	13–2	.858	19
1966	152	552	159	29	4	37	(16	21)	307	99	103	70	11	2	1	4	5	1	.83	13	.288	.556	.367	113	12–3	.771	15
1967	141	486	128	22	2	22	(13	9)	220	83	70	51	7	2	2	3	6	0	1.00	12	.263	.453	.333	74	9–5	.672	10
1968	148	498	144	20	5	23	(12	11)	243	84	79	67	7	2	0	6	12	6	.67	13	.289	.488	.372	91	11–3	.778	11
1969	117	403	114	17	3	13	(7	6)	176	64	58	49	7	3	0	4	6	2	.75	8	.283	.437	.362	66	7–4	.663	8
1970	139	478	139	15	2	28	(15	13)	242	94	83	79	3	3	0	6	5	0	1.00	7	.291	.506	.390	101	9–4	.698	13
1971	136	417	113	24	5	18	(9	9)	201	82	61	112	11	3	1	4	23	3	.88	8	.271	.482	.425	98	9–2	.798	12
1972	88	244	61	11	1	8	(3	5)	98	35	22	60	6	1	4	0	4	5	.44	9	.250	.402	.395	41	5–2	.685	5
1973	66	209	44	10	0	6	(4	2)	72	24	25	27	0	1	1	1	3	3	.50	3	.211	.344	.301	22	3–3	.458	3
18.5 yrs	2992	10881	3283	523	140	660	(335	325)	6066	2062	1903	1463	192	44	13	91	338	103	.77	251	.302	.557	.383	2373	229–70	.766	301
		589	178	28	8	36			328	112	103	79		2	1		18	6		14	.302	.557	.383				

Teams: New York, N.L. 1951–1957; San Francisco, 1958–1971; San Francisco/New York, 1972; New York, N.L. 1973.

Points in MVP Voting: 1951, 0; 1952, 0; 1954, 283 (1st, .84); 1955, 165 (4th, .49); 1956, 14 (.04); 1957, 174 (4th, .52); 1958, 185 (2nd, .55); 1959, 85 (6th, .28); 1960, 115 (3rd, .34); 1961, 70 (6th, .31); 1962, 202 (2nd, .72); 1963, 102 (5th, .36); 1964, 66 (6th, .24); 1965, 224 (1st, .80); 1966, 111 (3rd, .40); 1967, 0; 1968, 14 (.05); 1969, 0; 1970, 0; 1971, 11 (.03); 1972, 0; 1973, 0. TOTAL: 5.97 Award Shares.

Reported Salaries: 1951—$5,000; 1960—$75,000; 1961—$85,000; 1962—$90,000; 1963—$105,000; 1970—approx. $125,000; 1971—$150,000; 1972—$165,000.

Explanation for Gaps in Career or Sudden Changes in Productivity: 1952–53—In military service.

Other Notes: Named to *The Sporting News* major league All-Star team in 1954, 1957, 1958, 1959, 1960.

Named to *The Sporting News* National League All-Star team in 1961, 1962, 1963, 1964, 1965, 1966.

Gold Glove—1957, 1958, 1959, 1960, 1961, 1962, 1963, 1964, 1965, 1966, 1967, 1968.

FIELDING CENTER FIELD

Year	G	PO	AS	Err	DP	Pct.	Range
1951	121	353	12	9	2	.976	3.02
1952	34	109	6	1	2	.991	3.38
1954	151	448	13	7	9	.985	3.05
1955	152	407	23	8	8	.982	2.83
1956	152	415	14	9	6	.979	2.82
1957	150	422	14	9	5	.980	2.91
1958	151	429	17	9	2	.980	2.95
1959	147	353	6	6	2	.984	2.44
1960	152	392	12	8	3	.981	2.66
1961	153	385	7	8	3	.980	2.56
1962	161	429	6	4	1	.991	2.70
1963	157	397	7	8	3	.981	2.57
1964	155	370	10	6	4	.984	2.45
1965	151	337	13	6	4	.983	2.32
1966	150	370	8	7	2	.982	2.52
1967	134	277	3	7	0	.976	2.09
1968	142	301	7	7	2	.978	2.17
1969	109	199	4	5	0	.976	1.86
1970	129	269	6	7	3	.975	2.13
1971	84	192	2	6	1	.970	2.31
1972	63	138	3	3	1	.979	2.24
1973	45	103	2	1	0	.991	2.33
	2843	7095	195	141	62	.981	2.56

Assists per 154 Games: 10.6

PLAYER: VADA PINSON

								BATTING										BASERUNNING				PERCENTAGES			VALUES			
Year	G	AB	H	2B	3B	HR	(Hm	Rd)	TB	R	RBI	BB	IBB	HBP	SH	SF		SB	CS	SB%	GIDP	Avg.	Slug	On Base	Runs	Win—Loss	Pct	AV
1958	27	96	26	7	0	1	(0	1)	36	20	8	11	0	1	2	0		2	1	.67	1	.271	.375	.352	13	2–1	.570	1
1959	154	648	205	47	9	20	(13	7)	330	131	84	55	3	1	2	0		21	6	.78	9	.316	.509	.371	124	12–5	.690	17
1960	154	652	187	37	12	20	(11	9)	308	107	61	47	3	5	1	1		32	12	.73	11	.287	.472	.339	104	12–7	.635	14
1961	154	607	208	34	8	16	(9	7)	306	101	87	39	1	1	4	8		23	10	.70	9	.343	.504	.379	116	12–4	.731	17
1962	155	619	181	31	7	23	(14	9)	295	107	100	45	7	4	0	7		26	8	.76	12	.292	.477	.341	101	11–7	.618	14
1963	162	652	204	37	14	22	(14	8)	335	96	106	36	3	1	0	6		27	8	.77	16	.313	.514	.347	113	13–5	.734	14
1964	156	625	166	23	11	23	(11	12)	280	99	84	42	2	5	1	3		8	2	.80	9	.266	.448	.316	89	11–6	.642	10
1965	159	669	204	34	10	22	(16	6)	324	97	94	43	3	7	6	3		21	8	.72	14	.305	.484	.352	112	11–7	.626	15
1966	156	618	178	35	6	16	(9	7)	273	70	76	33	6	5	7	6		18	10	.64	10	.288	.442	.326	87	10–8	.566	11
1967	158	650	187	28	13	18	(9	9)	295	90	66	26	1	3	4	1		26	8	.76	6	.288	.454	.318	94	12–6	.681	12
1968	130	499	135	29	6	5	(4	1)	191	60	48	32	8	0	5	6		17	11	.61	5	.271	.383	.311	59	7–7	.484	7
1969	132	495	126	22	6	10	(4	6)	190	58	70	35	2	3	1	9		4	4	.50	12	.255	.384	.303	56	8–7	.547	8
1970	148	574	164	28	6	24	(19	5)	276	74	82	28	7	3	0	6		7	6	.54	12	.286	.481	.319	84	10–6	.619	11
1971	146	566	149	23	4	11	(8	3)	213	60	35	21	0	6	3	3		25	6	.81	9	.263	.376	.295	63	8–8	.491	9
1972	136	484	133	24	2	7	(1	6)	182	56	49	30	12	5	4	4		17	6	.74	7	.275	.376	.321	59	9–5	.645	9
1973	124	466	121	14	6	8	(5	3)	171	56	57	20	3	0	8	7		5	5	.50	11	.260	.367	.286	46	6–8	.413	6
1974	115	406	112	18	2	6	(3	3)	152	46	41	21	4	2	3	4		21	5	.81	6	.276	.374	.312	49	6–6	.514	6
1975	103	319	71	14	5	4	(1	3)	107	38	22	10	4	2	1	4		5	6	.45	5	.223	.335	.248	24	3–7	.263	3
	2469	9645	2757	485	127	256	(151	105)	4264	1366	1170	574	69	54	52	78		305	122	.71	164	.286	.442	.327	1394	161–109	.595	184
15.2 yrs		633	181	32	8	17			280	90	77	38	5	4	3	5		20	8	.71	11	.286	.442	.327				

Teams: Cincinnati, 1958–1968; St. Louis Cardinals, 1969; Cleveland, 1970–1971; California, 1972–1973; Kansas City Royals, 1974–1975.

Points in MVP Voting: 1958, 0; 1959, 11 (.04); 1960, 6 (.02); 1961, 104 (3rd, .46); 1962, 0; 1963, 32 (10th, .11); 1964, 6 (.02); 1965–1975, 0. TOTAL: .65 Award Shares.

FIELDING CENTER FIELD

Year	G	PO	AS	Err	DP	Pct.	Range
1958	27	50	4	0	1	1.000	2.00
1959	154	423	11	7	4	.984	2.82
1960	154	401	11	8	1	.981	2.68
1961	153	391	19	10	4	.976	2.68
1962	152	344	13	4	1	.989	2.35
1963	162	357	9	8	0	.979	2.26
1964	156	299	14	9	1	.972	2.01
1965	159	354	9	3	1	.992	2.28
1966	154	344	9	13	1	.964	2.29
1967	157	341	4	5	1	.986	2.20
1968	123	258	7	6	0	.978	2.15
1969	124	218	6	1	2	.996	1.81
1970	141	265	8	5	3	.982	1.94
1971	141	305	11	7	2	.978	2.24
1972	134	205	11	2	3	.991	1.61
1973	120	210	11	8	2	.965	1.84
1974	110	188	9	4	2	.980	1.79
1975	82	144	6	1	0	.993	1.83
	2403	5097	172	101	29	.981	2.19

Assists per 154 Games: 11.0

PLAYER: AMOS OTIS

Year	G	AB	H	2B	3B	HR	(Hm	Rd)	TB	R	RBI	BB	IBB	HBP	SH	SF	SB	CS	SB%	GIDP	Avg.	Slug	On Base	Runs	Win–Loss	Pct.	AV
						BATTING											BASERUNNING				PERCENTAGES			VALUES			
1967	19	59	13	2	0	0	(0	0)	15	6	1	5	0	1	1	0	0	4	.00	0	.220	.254	.288	4	0–1	.245	0
1969	48	93	14	3	1	0	(0	0)	19	6	4	6	1	0	3	0	1	0	1.00	0	.151	.204	.196	4	0–3	.120	1
1970	159	620	176	36	9	11	(6	5)	263	91	58	68	3	1	6	5	33	2	.94	8	.284	.424	.350	102	12–6	.679	14
1971	147	555	167	26	4	15	(3	12)	246	80	79	40	2	2	2	8	52	8	.87	18	.301	.443	.344	87	11–5	.700	16
1972	143	540	158	28	2	11	(2	9)	223	75	54	50	3	3	6	6	28	12	.70	6	.293	.413	.349	82	10–5	.684	13
1973	148	583	175	21	4	26	(11	15)	282	89	93	63	5	1	1	3	13	9	.59	10	.300	.484	.367	103	11–5	.660	14
1974	146	552	157	31	9	12	(3	9)	242	87	73	58	4	2	8	12	18	5	.78	16	.284	.438	.343	86	10–6	.626	12
1975	132	470	116	26	6	9	(6	3)	181	87	46	66	1	4	4	4	39	11	.78	14	.247	.385	.339	68	8–6	.569	11
1976	153	592	165	40	2	18	(10	8)	263	93	86	55	7	5	5	8	26	7	.79	13	.279	.444	.338	92	11–6	.634	12
1977	142	478	120	20	8	17	(7	10)	207	85	78	71	5	0	3	9	23	7	.77	13	.251	.433	.340	74	8–6	.559	12
1978	141	486	145	30	7	22	(11	11)	255	74	96	66	7	4	1	10	32	8	.80	10	.298	.525	.379	102	10–3	.754	15
1979	151	577	170	28	2	18	(10	8)	256	100	90	68	8	3	7	5	30	5	.86	12	.295	.444	.365	100	10–7	.591	14
1980	107	394	99	16	3	10	(4	6)	151	56	53	39	0	3	2	10	16	1	.94	9	.251	.383	.315	52	6–6	.473	7
1981	99	372	100	22	3	9	(4	5)	155	49	57	31	1	2	3	9	16	7	.70	7	.269	.417	.319	51	6–5	.583	7
1982	125	475	136	25	3	11	(5	6)	200	73	88	37	3	2	1	9	9	5	.64	17	.286	.421	.334	64	7–7	.503	9
1983	98	356	93	16	3	4	(3	1)	127	35	41	27	3	0	0	1	5	2	.71	7	.261	.357	.313	39	4–6	.430	5
1984	40	97	16	4	0	0	(0	0)	20	6	10	7	0	0	0	4	0	0	.00	4	.165	.206	.213	4	0–3	.110	0
	1998	7299	2020	374	66	193	(85	108)	3105	1092	1007	757	53	33	54	103	341	93	.79	158	.277	.425	.341	1113	125–86	.593	162
12.3 yrs		592	164	30	5	16			252	89	82	61	4	3	4	8	28	8		13	.277	.425	.341				

Teams: New York, N.L. 1967, 1969; Kansas City, 1970–1983; Pittsburgh, 1984.

Points in MVP Voting: 1967, 0; 1969, 0; 1970, 0; 1971, 67 (8th, .20); 1972, 1 (.00); 1973, 112 (3rd, .33); 1974, 0; 1975, 0; 1976, 58 (7th, .17); 1977, 0; 1978, 90 (4th, .23); 1979, 0; 1980, 0; 1981, 0; 1982, 0; 1983, 0. TOTAL: .93 Award Shares.

Explanation for Gaps in Career or Sudden Changes in Productivity:

1980—Ruptured tendon in finger when hit by pitch from batting practice machine while working out during spring training lockout.

1981—Strike season.

1983—Released, August 25.

1984—Released, August 5.

Other Notes: Named to *The Sporting News* American League All-Star team for 1971, 1973, 1974

Gold Glove—1971, 1973, 1974.

FIELDING CENTER FIELD

Year	G	PO	AS	E	DP	Pct.	Range
1967	16	22	2	0	1	1.000	1.50
1969	35	46	3	0	0	1.000	1.40
1970	159	388	15	4	6	.990	2.53
1971	144	404	10	4	4	.990	2.87
1972	137	351	6	3	8	.992	2.61
1973	135	330	10	5	4	.986	2.52
1974	143	425	8	6	3	.986	3.03
1975	130	310	9	4	3	.988	2.45
1976	152	373	5	3	1	.992	2.49
1977	140	326	10	3	0	.991	2.40
1978	136	382	9	2	1	.995	2.87
1979	146	385	11	3	5	.992	2.71
1980	105	310	6	4	1	.987	3.01
1981	97	294	6	2	1	.993	3.09
1982	125	310	5	1	1	.997	2.52
1983	96	233	6	1	1	.996	2.49
1984	32	49	5	2	0	.964	1.69
	1928	4938	126	47	35	.990	2.61

Assists per 154 Games: 9.9

Right Field

Jimmy Sheckard
Elmer Flick
Sam Crawford
Wildfire Schulte
Babe Ruth
Babe Herman
Paul Waner
Mel Ott
Chuck Klein
Enos Slaughter
Charlie Keller
Carl Furillo
Al Kaline
Hank Aaron
Roberto Clemente
Frank Robinson
Tony Oliva
Pete Rose
Reggie Jackson
Bobby Bonds

PLAYER: JIMMY SHECKARD

							BATTING										BASERUNNING				PERCENTAGES			VALUES			
Year	G	AB	H	2B	3B	HR	(Hm	Rd)	TB	R	RBI	BB	IBB	HBP	SH	SF	SB	CS	SB%	GIDP	Avg.	Slug	On Base	Runs	Win–Loss	Pct.	AV
1897	13	49	16	3	2	3	(	)	32	12	14	6			0		5				.327	.653	.400	15	1–0	.784	1
1898	105	409	119	17	9	4	(	)	166	51	64	37			6		8				.291	.406	.345	63	6–5	.549	7
1899	147	536	158	18	10	3	(	)	205	104	75	56			6		77				.295	.382	.358	105	10–5	.655	13
1900	85	273	82	19	10	1	(	)	124	74	39	42			4		30				.300	.454	.389	63	5–2	.683	6
1901	133	558	197	30	21	11	(	)	302	116	104	47			3		35				.353	.541	.401	140	11–3	.799	16
1902	127	501	133	21	10	4	(	)	186	89	37	58			8		25				.265	.371	.337	75	9–5	.630	10
1903	139	515	171	29	9	9	(	)	245	99	75	75			20		67				.332	.476	.403	135	11–3	.794	15
1904	143	507	121	23	6	1	(	)	159	70	46	56			18		21				.239	.314	.305	60	8–7	.527	10
1905	130	480	140	20	11	3	(	)	191	58	41	61			15		23				.292	.398	.362	83	9–5	.667	11
1906	149	549	144	27	10	1	(	)	194	90	45	67			40		30				.262	.353	.322	83	11–6	.636	10
1907	142	482	127	22	1	1	(	)	154	75	36	76			35		31				.263	.320	.342	74	11–4	.711	10
1908	115	403	93	18	3	2	(	)	123	54	22	62			21		18				.231	.305	.319	48	7–6	.543	5
1909	148	525	134	29	5	1	(	)	176	81	43	72	1		46		15				.255	.335	.321	70	11–7	.614	9
1910	144	507	130	27	6	5	(	)	184	82	51	83	5		31		22				.256	.363	.348	78	10–6	.606	10
1911	156	539	149	26	11	4	(	)	209	121	50	147	3		15		32				.276	.388	.425	106	11–5	.701	13
1912	146	523	128	22	10	3	(	)	179	85	47	122	5		10		15				.245	.342	.386	76	8–8	.514	8
1913	99	252	49	3	4	0	(	)	60	34	24	68	1		9		11				.194	.238	.358	26	3–5	.342	3
	2121	7608	2091	354	138	56	(	)	2889	1295	813	1135	15		287		465				.275	.380	.358	1301	144–84	.631	157
13.1 yrs		581	160	27	11	4			221	99	62	87			22		36				.275	.380	.358				

Teams: Brooklyn, 1897–1898; Baltimore, 1899; Brooklyn, 1900–1901; Baltimore/Brooklyn, 1902; Brooklyn, 1903–1905; Chicago, N.L., 1906–1912; St. Louis/Cincinnati, 1913.

Points in MVP Voting: 1911, 9 (.14).

Reported Salaries: 1912—$4,250.

FIELDING RIGHT FIELD

Year	G	PO	AS	E	DP	Pct.	Range
1897	2	4	0	1	0	.800	2.00
1898	105	213	12	18	2	.926	2.14
1899	146	298	33	20	14	.943	2.27
1900	78	171	13	15	3	.925	2.36
1901	121	287	15	18	5	.944	2.50
1902	127	289	12	11	6	.965	2.37
1903	139	314	36	18	7	.951	2.52
1904	141	291	16	14	5	.956	2.18
1905	129	266	24	10	6	.967	2.25
1906	149	264	13	4	1	.986	1.86
1907	141	222	13	6	2	.975	1.67
1908	115	201	13	10	3	.955	1.86
1909	148	277	18	10	5	.967	1.99
1910	143	308	21	8	3	.976	2.30
1911	156	332	32	14	12	.963	2.33
1912	146	332	26	14	4	.962	2.45
1913	84	134	10	6	3	.960	1.71
	2070	4203	307	196	81	.958	2.18

Assists per 154 Games: 22.9

PLAYER: ELMER FLICK

	BATTING															BASERUNNING				PERCENTAGES			VALUES			
Year	G	AB	H	2B	3B	HR	(Hm Rd)	TB	R	RBI	BB	IBB	HBP	SH	SF	SB	CS	SB%	GIDP	Avg.	Slug	On Base	Runs	Win–Loss	Pct.	AV
1898	134	453	142	16	14	7	( )	207	84	81	86			11		23				.313	.457	.415	100	9–4	.702	12
1899	127	485	166	22	14	2	( )	222	98	98	42			8		31				.342	.458	.389	102	9–4	.698	10
1900	138	547	207	33	16	11	( )	305	106	110	56			6		35				.378	.558	.432	152	11–3	.794	17
1901	138	542	182	32	17	8	( )	272	112	88	52			13		30				.336	.502	.386	122	11–3	.800	12
1902	121	461	137	21	12	2	( )	188	85	64	53	6		10		24				.297	.408	.370	80	8–5	.620	8
1903	140	523	155	23	16	2	( )	216	81	51	51			11		24				.296	.413	.352	88	10–5	.665	10
1904	150	579	177	31	18	5	( )	259	97	56	51			20		38				.306	.447	.351	112	13–4	.773	11
1905	131	496	152	29	19	4	( )	231	71	64	53			12		35				.306	.466	.365	103	11–3	.798	11
1906	157	624	194	34	22	1	( )	275	98	62	54			15		39				.311	.441	.358	119	14–4	.778	12
1907	147	549	166	15	18	3	( )	226	78	58	64			13		41				.302	.412	.367	101	12–3	.792	11
1908	9	35	8	1	1	0	( )	11	4	2	3			1		0				.229	.314	.282	3	0–1	.431	0
1909	66	235	60	10	2	0	( )	74	28	15	22	1		1		9				.255	.315	.320	26	4–3	.542	3
1910	24	68	18	2	1	1	( )	25	5	7	10	0		0		1				.265	.368	.359	9	1–1	.611	1
9.1 yrs	1482	5597	1764	269	170	46	( )	2511	947	756	597	1		121		330				.315	.449	.375	1118	112–41	.733	118
	612		193	29	19	5		274	104	83	65			13		36				.315	.449	.375				

Teams: Philadelphia, N.L. 1898–1902; Cleveland, A.L./Philadelphia, A.L. 1902; Cleveland, A.L., 1903–1910.

Points in MVP Voting: No award during his career.

Explanation for Gaps in Career or Sudden Changes in Productivity:

1908—Unknown illness.

1909—Macmillan *Encyclopedia* says he was injured; *Reach Guide* says he "proved unequal to the task of playing regularly."

FIELDING RIGHT FIELD

Year	G	PO	AS	Err	DP	Pct.	Range
1898	133	242	25	13	4	.954	2.01
1899	125	234	21	14	7	.948	2.04
1900	138	237	19	23	6	.918	1.86
1901	138	275	22	12	7	.961	2.15
1902	121	171	16	13	2	.935	1.55
1903	140	216	14	11	3	.954	1.64
1904	144	231	18	10	5	.961	1.73
1905	130	177	18	13	3	.937	1.50
1906	150	248	13	5	4	.981	1.74
1907	147	219	22	11	7	.956	1.64
1908	9	10	1	0	0	1.000	1.22
1909	61	87	4	4	1	.958	1.49
1910	18	21	0	1	0	.955	1.17
	1454	2368	193	130	49	.952	1.76

Assists per 154 Games: 20.4

PLAYER: SAM CRAWFORD

Year	G	AB	H	2B	3B	HR	(Hm	Rd)	TB	R	RBI	BB	IBB	HBP	SH	SF	SB	CS	SB%	GIDP	Avg.	Slug	On Base	Runs	Win−Loss	Pct.	AV
1899	31	127	39	2	8	1	(0	1)	60	25	20	2			4		6				.307	.472	.308	22	2−2	.560	2
1900	101	389	104	14	15	7	(4	3)	169	68	59	28			4		14				.267	.434	.314	60	6−6	.513	6
1901	131	515	170	20	16	16	(8	8)	270	91	104	37			14		13				.330	.524	.372	109	10−4	.729	13
1902	140	555	185	16	23	3	(0	3)	256	94	78	47			6		16				.333	.461	.382	108	11−4	.749	12
1903	137	550	184	23	25	4	(1	3)	269	88	89	25			25		18				.335	.489	.348	109	12−4	.756	13
1904	150	571	143	21	17	2	(0	2)	204	49	73	44			11		20				.250	.357	.299	71	10−7	.583	10
1905	154	575	171	40	10	6	(2	4)	249	73	75	50	1		3		22				.297	.433	.353	99	12−4	.741	12
1906	145	563	166	25	16	2	(1	1)	229	65	72	38	0		8		24				.295	.407	.335	89	11−5	.697	12
1907	144	582	188	34	17	4	(0	4)	268	102	81	37	1		11		18				.323	.460	.358	108	12−4	.746	12
1908	152	591	184	33	16	7	(2	5)	270	102	80	37	3		23		15				.311	.457	.343	100	12−5	.698	11
1909	156	589	185	35	14	6	(3	3)	266	83	97	47	1		25		30				.314	.452	.352	108	13−4	.753	13
1910	154	588	170	26	19	5	(4	1)	249	83	120	37	1		24		20				.289	.423	.320	89	11−7	.613	13
1911	146	574	217	36	14	7	(4	3)	302	109	115	61	0		13		37				.378	.526	.429	147	11−3	.790	18
1912	149	581	189	30	21	4	(2	2)	273	81	109	42	2		19		41				.325	.470	.362	116	11−5	.688	14
1913	153	609	193	32	23	9	(5	4)	298	78	83	52	0		11		13				.317	.489	.365	110	12−5	.692	11
1914	157	582	183	22	26	8	(3	5)	281	74	104	69	1		22		25	16	.61		.314	.483	.375	115	13−4	.759	15
1915	156	612	183	31	19	4	(3	2)	264	81	112	66	0		16		24	14	.63		.299	.431	.359	102	11−6	.644	13
1916	100	322	92	11	13	0	(0	0)	129	41	42	37	0		9		10				.286	.401	.351	48	6−3	.631	6
1917	61	104	18	4	0	2	(0	2)	28	6	12	4	0		4		0				.173	.269	.196	6	0−3	.143	0
15.5 yrs	2517	9579	2964	455	312	97	(42	56)	4334	1393	1525	760		10	252		366	30	.62		.309	.452	.353	1714	185−84	.687	206
		617	191	29	20	6			279	90	98	49			16		24				.309	.452	.353				

Runs created estimates prior to 1900 are of indeterminate accuracy

Teams: Cincinnati, 1899–1902; Detroit, 1903–1917.

Points in MVP Voting: 1911, 4 (.06); 1913, 5 (.08); 1914, 35 (2nd, .55). TOTAL: .63 Award Shares.

Reported Salaries: 1899—$150/month; 1905—$2,700; 1908—$4,000; 1912—$5,000; 1913—$5,000; 1915–1917—$7,500/year.

Other Notes: Played good baseball in the Coast League for 3½ years after being released by Tigers.

FIELDING RIGHT FIELD

Year	G	PO	AS	Err	DP	Pct.	Range
1899	31	56	9	2	2	.970	2.10
1900	94	237	18	14	2	.948	2.71
1901	126	209	20	19	6	.923	1.82
1902	140	208	24	17	5	.932	1.66
1903	137	225	16	10	3	.960	1.76
1904	150	220	18	7	8	.971	1.59
1905	103	152	18	2	3	.988	1.65
1906	116	171	19	3	2	.984	1.64
1907	144	311	22	12	2	.965	2.31
1908	134	252	9	8	2	.970	1.95
1909	139	297	7	11	2	.965	2.19
1910	153	223	10	9	2	.963	1.52
1911	146	181	16	5	3	.975	1.35
1912	149	169	16	3	5	.984	1.24
1913	140	201	14	8	5	.964	1.54
1914	157	193	15	5	4	.977	1.32
1915	156	219	8	6	1	.974	1.46
1916	79	85	6	2	2	.978	1.15
1917	3	7	0	0	0	1.000	2.33
	2297	3616	265	143	59	.964	1.69

Assists per 154 Games: 17.8

PLAYER: WILDFIRE SCHULTE

						BATTING												BASERUNNING				PERCENTAGES			VALUES			
Year	G	AB	H	2B	3B	HR	(Hm	Rd)	TB	R	RBI	BB	IBB	HBP	SH	SF		SB	CS	SB%	GIDP	Avg.	Slug	On Base	Runs	Win—Loss	Pct	AV
1904	20	84	24	4	3	2	(	)	40	16	13	2			0			1				.286	.476	.302	13	2—1	.687	1
1905	123	493	135	15	14	1	(	)	181	67	47	32			18			16				.274	.367	.318	66	9—6	.606	7
1906	146	563	158	18	13	7	(	)	223	77	60	31			31			25				.281	.396	.318	84	11—6	.654	10
1907	97	342	98	14	7	2	(	)	132	44	32	22			20			7				.287	.386	.330	49	7—3	.694	5
1908	102	386	91	20	2	1	(	)	118	42	43	29			25			15				.236	.306	.289	40	6—7	.434	4
1909	140	538	142	16	11	4	(	)	192	57	60	24	2		27			23				.264	.357	.298	64	10—7	.570	9
1910	151	559	168	29	15	10	(	)	257	93	68	39	3		27			22				.301	.460	.349	97	12—5	.688	12
1911	154	577	173	30	21	21	(	)	308	105	121	76	3		31			23				.300	.534	.384	127	13—5	.732	15
1912	139	553	146	27	11	13	(	)	234	90	70	53	7		19			17				.264	.423	.336	85	9—8	.529	8
1913	132	495	138	28	6	9	(	)	205	85	72	39	5		17			21				.279	.414	.338	74	8—7	.557	11
1914	137	465	112	22	7	5	(	)	163	54	61	39	5		18			16				.241	.351	.306	54	7—8	.452	5
1915	151	550	137	20	6	12	(	)	205	66	69	49	2		27			19				.249	.373	.313	69	9—9	.504	7
1916	127	407	113	16	4	5	(	)	152	43	41	37	1		5			14				.278	.373	.339	54	7—5	.625	6
1917	94	252	54	15	1	1	(	)	74	32	22	26	2		5			9				.214	.294	.293	23	3—5	.399	2
1918	93	267	77	14	3	0	(	)	97	35	44	47	6		9			5				.288	.363	.406	42	6—2	.725	4
	1806	6531	1766	288	124	93	(	)	2581	906	823	545	36		279			233				.270	.395	.330	941	117—83	.586	106
11.1 yrs.		586	158	26	11	8			232	81	74	49	4		25			21				.270	.395	.330				

Teams: Chicago Cubs, 1904–1916; Pittsburgh Pirates, 1916–1917; Philadelphia Phillies, 1917; Washington, 1918.

Points in MVP Voting: 1911, 29 (1st, .45). Shulte won the only MVP award for which he was eligible during his career.

Explanation for Gaps in Career or Sudden Changes in Productivity: 1907—Out with groin injury

FIELDING RIGHT FIELD

Year	G	PO	AS	Err	DP	Pct.	Range
1904	20	34	3	2		.949	1.85
1905	123	189	14	4	0	.981	1.65
1906	146	218	18	6	7	.975	1.62
1907	91	130	11	4	1	.972	1.55
1908	102	145	8	1	2	.994	1.50
1909	140	169	14	6	1	.968	1.31
1910	150	221	18	8	5	.968	1.59
1911	154	246	19	8	8	.971	1.72
1912	139	219	19	12	6	.952	1.71
1913	129	180	13	9	2	.955	1.50
1914	134	217	9	11	2	.954	1.69
1915	147	280	24	12	3	.962	2.07
1916	113	197	10	9	0	.958	1.83
1917	70	96	4	6		.943	1.43
1918	75	145	10	5	4	.969	2.07
	1733	2686	194	103	41	.965	1.66

Assists per 154 Games: 17.2

PLAYER: BABE RUTH

Year	G	AB	H	2B	3B	HR	(Hm	Rd)	TB	R	RBI	BB	IBB	HBP	SH	SF	SB	CS	SB%	GIDP	Avg.	Slug	On Base	Runs	Win–Loss	Pct.	AV
1914	5	10	2	1	0	0	(0	0)	3	1	0	0		0	0		0	0	.00		.200	.300	.200	1	0–0	.201	0
1915	42	92	29	10	1	4	(1	3)	53	16	20	9		0	2		0	0	.00		.315	.576	.369	19	2–1	.800	12
1916	67	136	37	5	3	3	(0	3)	57	18	16	10		0	4		0				.272	.419	.313	19	3–1	.678	19
1917	52	123	40	6	3	2	(1	1)	58	14	10	12		0	7		0				.325	.472	.366	22	3–1	.801	17
1918	95	317	95	26	11	11	(0	11)	176	50	64	57		2	3		6				.300	.555	.406	75	7–1	.866	15
1919	130	432	139	34	12	29	(9	20)	284	103	112	101		6	3		7				.322	.657	.454	128	10–1	.885	22
1920	142	458	172	36	9	54	(29	25)	388	158	137	148		3	5		14	14	.50		.376	.847	.526	211	11–1	.934	26
1921	152	540	204	44	16	59	(32	27)	457	177	171	144		4	4		17	13	.57		.378	.846	.509	238	12–1	.913	27
1922	110	406	128	24	8	35	(14	21)	273	94	99	84		1	4		2	6	.25		.315	.672	.430	120	9–2	.854	14
1923	152	522	205	45	13	41	(19	22)	399	151	131	170		4	3		17	21	.45		.393	.764	.542	223	12–1	.928	26
1924	153	529	200	39	7	46	(24	22)	391	143	121	142		4	6		9	13	.41		.378	.739	.508	205	12–1	.911	23
1925	98	359	104	12	2	25	(11	14)	195	61	66	59		2	6		2	4	.33		.290	.543	.387	78	7–3	.722	11
1926	152	495	184	30	5	47	(23	24)	365	139	145	144		3	10		11	9	.55		.372	.737	.508	196	11–1	.904	23
1927	151	540	192	29	8	60	(28	32)	417	158	164	138		0	14		7				.356	.772	.477	204	12–1	.893	23
1928	154	536	173	29	8	54	(29	25)	380	163	142	135		3	8		4	5	.44		.323	.709	.456	182	12–2	.857	21
1929	135	499	172	26	6	46	(21	25)	348	121	154	72		3	13		5	3	.62		.345	.697	.421	150	11–2	.815	17
1930	145	518	186	28	9	49	(26	23)	379	150	153	136		1	21		10	10	.50		.359	.732	.478	191	11–2	.823	21
1931	145	534	199	31	3	46	(24	22)	374	149	163	128		0	0		5	4	.56		.373	.700	.494	192	11–2	.862	20
1932	133	457	156	13	5	41	(19	22)	302	120	137	130		2	0		2	2	.50		.341	.661	.489	157	10–2	.856	18
1933	137	459	138	21	3	34	(22	12)	267	97	103	114		2	0		4	5	.44		.301	.582	.442	124	10–3	.760	16
1934	125	365	105	17	4	22	(13	9)	196	78	84	103		2	0		1	3	.25		.288	.537	.447	95	8–2	.784	10
1935	28	72	13	0	0	6	(2	4)	31	13	12	20		0	0		2			2	.181	.431	.359	12	1–1	.583	1
	2503	8399	2873	506	136	714	(347	367)	5793	2174	2204	2056		42	113		123	112	.48		.342	.690	.469	2843	188–33	.851	382
15.5 yrs		544	186	33	9	46			375	141	143	133		3	7		8				.342	.690	.469				

(Batting · Baserunning · Percentages · Values)

Teams: Boston, 1914–19; New York, A.L., 1920–34; Boston, 1935.

Points in MVP Voting: 1922, 0; 1923, 64 (1st, 1.00); 1931, 13 (9th, .20); 1932, 7 (.08); 1933, 0; 1934, 0; 1935, 0.

Reported Salaries: 1914—in minors, started at rate of $600/year, raised to $1,200 after a month, $1,800 later in summer and $2,500 (yearly rate) when sold to majors; 1915—$3,500; 1916—$3,500; 1917—$5,000; 1918—$7,000; 1919—$10,000; 1920—$20,000; 1921—$30,000; 1922–1926—five-year contract at $52,000/year; 1927—$70,000; 1928—$70,000; 1929—$70,000; 1930—$80,000; 1931—$80,000; 1932—$75,000; 1933—$52,000; 1934—$35,000; 1935—rate of $35,000/year.

Explanation for Gaps in Career or Sudden Changes in Productivity:
1922—Suspended until May 20 for violation of commissioner's orders on barnstorming.
1925—Keeled over April 8, required surgery to remove abdominal abscess; out until early June; suspended by Miller Huggins, August 29.

Other Notes: Named to *The Sporting News* major league All-Star team in 1926, 1927, 1928, 1929, 1930, and 1931.
1919—7 HR vs. LHP, 22 vs. RHP.
1927—17 HR vs. LHP, 43 vs. RHP.
1934—7 HR vs. LHP, 15 vs. RHP.

FIELDING RIGHT FIELD

Year	G	PO	AS	Err	DP	Pct.	Range
1918	59	121	8	7	3	.949	2.19
1919	111	230	16	2	6	.992	2.22
1920	139	259	21	19	3	.936	2.01
1921	152	348	17	13	6	.966	2.40
1922	110	225	14	9	3	.964	2.17
1923	148	378	20	11	2	.973	2.69
1924	152	340	18	14	4	.962	2.36
1925	98	207	15	6	3	.974	2.27
1926	149	308	11	7	5	.979	2.14
1927	151	328	14	13	4	.963	2.26
1928	154	304	9	8	0	.975	2.03
1929	133	240	5	4	2	.984	1.84
1930	144	266	10	10	0	.965	1.92
1931	142	237	5	7	2	.972	1.70
1932	127	209	10	9	1	.961	1.72
1933	132	215	9	7	4	.970	1.70
1934	111	197	3	8	0	.962	1.80
1935	26	39	1	2	0	.952	1.54
	2238	4451	206	156	48	.968	2.08

Assists per 154 Games: 14.2

PLAYER: BABE HERMAN

	BATTING															BASERUNNING				PERCENTAGES			VALUES			
Year	G	AB	H	2B	3B	HR	(Hm | Rd)	TB	R	RBI	BB	IBB	HBP	SH	SF	SB	CS	SB%	GIDP	Avg.	Slug	On Base	Runs	Win–Loss	Pct.	AV
1926	137	496	158	35	11	11	(	)	248	64	81	44		1	13		8				.319	.500	.366	91	10–4	.710	10
1927	130	412	112	26	9	14	(	)	198	65	73	39		1	14		4				.272	.481	.326	65	8–4	.673	7
1928	134	486	165	37	6	12	(	)	250	64	91	38		2	16		1				.340	.514	.378	94	10–3	.749	12
1929	146	569	217	42	13	21	(	)	348	105	113	55		0	13		21				.381	.612	.427	146	11–3	.790	18
1930	153	614	241	48	11	35	(	)	416	143	130	66		4	15		18				.393	.678	.445	183	13–2	.846	19
1931	151	610	191	43	16	18	(	)	320	93	97	50		0	1		17				.313	.525	.365	116	12–4	.723	12
1932	148	577	188	38	19	16	(	)	312	87	87	60		0	5		7				.326	.541	.386	124	12–3	.795	16
1933	137	508	147	36	12	16	(10 | 6)	255	77	93	50		0	7		6			15	.289	.502	.349	90	10–4	.730	11
1934	125	467	142	34	5	14	(	)	228	65	84	35		0	5		1			9	.304	.488	.349	81	9–4	.682	8
1935	118	430	136	31	6	10	(	)	209	52	65	38		1	2		5			7	.316	.486	.372	80	8–3	.709	8
1936	119	380	106	25	2	13	(	)	174	59	71	39		1	1		4	0	1.00	11	.279	.458	.347	61	6–4	.586	7
1937	17	20	6	3	0	0	(	)	9	2	3	1		1	0		2	0	1.00		.300	.450	.364	4	0–0	.588	0
1945	37	34	9	1	0	1	(	)	13	6	9	5		0	0		0			1	.265	.382	.359	5	1–0	.552	0
	1552	5603	1818	399	110	181	(	)	2980	882	997	520		11	92		94			43	.324	.532	.377	1139	109–40	.731	128
9.6 yrs		585	190	42	11	19			311	92	104	54		1	10		10				.324	.532	.377				

Teams: Brooklyn, 1926–1931; Cincinnati, 1932; Chicago, N.L., 1933–1934; Pittsburgh/Cincinnati, 1935; Cincinnati, 1936; Detroit, 1937; Brooklyn, 1945.

Points in MVP Voting: 1926, 8 (.10); 1931, 7 (.11); 1932, 0; 1933, 0; 1934, 0; 1935, 0; 1937, 0. TOTAL: .21 Award Shares.

Explanation for Gaps in Career or Sudden Changes in Productivity:

1932—Missed several games after suffering an iodine burn.

Played at Toledo most of 1937, Jersey City 1938, Hollywood 1939–1944.

FIELDING OUTFIELD

Year	G	PO	AS	Err	DP	Pct.	Range
1926	35	61	4	3	0	.956	1.86
1927	1	0	0	0	0	0	0
1928	127	225	12	16	2	.937	1.87
1929	141	244	10	16	2	.941	1.80
1930	153	260	10	6	1	.978	1.76
1931	150	287	24	13	7	.960	2.07
1932	146	392	18	13	6	.969	2.81
1933	131	252	12	12	1	.957	2.02
1934	113	192	7	6	2	.971	1.76
1935	91	178	6	5	0	.974	2.02
1936	92	175	3	6	0	.967	1.93
1937	2	3	0	0	0	1.000	1.50
1945	3	0	0	0	0	0	0
	1185	2269	106	96	21	.961	2.00

Assists per 154 Games: 13.8

PLAYER: PAUL WANER

Year	G	AB	H	2B	3B	HR	(Hm	Rd)	TB	R	RBI	BB	IBB	HBP	SH	SF	SB	CS	SB%	GIDP	Avg.	Slug	On Base	Runs	Win–Loss	Pct.	AV
1926	144	536	180	35	22	8	(	)	283	101	79	66		4	12		11				.336	.528	.405	115	11–3	.755	15
1927	155	623	237	40	17	9	(	)	338	113	131	60		3	23		5				.380	.543	.423	144	12–3	.788	19
1928	152	602	223	50	19	6	(	)	329	142	86	77		5	13		6				.370	.547	.438	145	12–3	.783	17
1929	151	596	200	43	15	15	(	)	318	131	100	89		3	15		15				.336	.534	.415	135	11–5	.709	17
1930	145	589	217	32	18	8	(	)	309	117	77	57		4	15		18				.368	.525	.418	129	10–5	.683	15
1931	150	559	180	35	10	6	(	)	253	88	70	73		4	10		6				.322	.453	.398	105	11–4	.729	13
1932	154	630	215	62	10	7	(	)	318	107	82	56		2	9		13				.341	.505	.392	126	12–4	.739	15
1933	154	618	191	38	16	7	(4	3)	282	101	70	60		2	14		3			10	.309	.456	.365	109	12–5	.711	12
1934	146	599	217	32	16	14	(	)	323	122	90	68		2	8		8			15	.362	.539	.424	142	12–3	.796	17
1935	139	549	176	29	12	11	(	)	262	98	78	61		3	10		2			15	.321	.477	.385	105	10–4	.710	12
1936	148	585	218	53	9	5	(	)	304	107	94	74		3	4		7			15	.373	.520	.443	140	11–3	.802	16
1937	154	619	219	30	9	2	(	)	273	94	74	63		0	8		4			11	.354	.441	.409	118	12–4	.750	14
1938	148	625	175	31	6	6	(	)	236	77	69	47		1	7		2			16	.280	.378	.328	79	9–9	.510	9
1939	125	461	151	30	6	3	(	)	202	62	45	35		0	10		0			12	.328	.438	.368	76	8–4	.651	11
1940	89	238	69	16	1	1	(	)	90	32	32	23		0	0		0			4	.290	.378	.352	32	3–3	.495	3
1941	106	329	88	10	2	2	(	)	108	45	50	55		0	1		1			10	.267	.328	.371	43	5–4	.547	4
1942	114	333	86	17	1	1	(	)	108	43	39	62		1	8		2			7	.258	.324	.369	46	6–4	.602	4
1943	82	225	70	16	0	1	(	)	89	29	26	35		1	6		0			9	.311	.396	.397	38	4–2	.634	4
1944	92	143	40	4	1	0	(	)	46	17	17	29		0	1		1			3	.280	.322	.399	21	2–2	.547	3
1945	1	0	0	0	0	0	(	)	0	0	0	1		0	0		0						1.000	0	0–0	1.000	0
	2549	9459	3152	603	190	112	(	)	4471	1626	1309	1091	38	174			104			127	.333	.473	.398	1849	174–75	.699	220
15.7 yrs		601	200	38	12	7			284	103	83	69	2	11			7				.333	.473	.398				

Teams: Pittsburgh, 1926–1940; Brooklyn/Boston, 1941; Boston, 1942; Brooklyn, 1943; Brooklyn/New York, A.L. 1944; New York, A.L. 1945.

Points in MVP Voting: 1926, 15 (.19); 1927, 72 (1st, .90); 1931, 0; 1932, 10 (.11); 1933, 0; 1934, 50 (2nd, .63); 1935, 1 (.01); 1936, 29 (5th, .48); 1937, 21 (8th, .26); 1938, 0; 1939, 0; 1940, 0; 1941, 0; 1942, 0; 1943, 0; 1944, 0. TOTAL: 2.58 Award Shares.

Other Notes: Named to *The Sporting News* major league All-Star team in 1927, 1928, 1937.

FIELDING RIGHT FIELD

Year	G	PO	AS	Err	DP	Pct.	Range
1926	139	307	21	8	3	.976	2.36
1927	143	326	20	7	4	.980	2.42
1928	131	299	14	8	0	.975	2.39
1929	143	328	15	5	5	.986	2.40
1930	143	344	9	15	4	.959	2.47
1931	138	342	28	9	8	.976	2.68
1932	154	367	13	10	3	.974	2.47
1933	154	346	16	7	2	.981	2.35
1934	145	323	15	5	1	.985	2.33
1935	136	283	13	5	2	.983	2.18
1936	145	323	15	14	7	.960	2.33
1937	150	271	16	9	3	.970	1.91
1938	147	284	11	7	0	.977	2.01
1939	106	206	12	5	4	.978	2.06
1940	45	62	3	1	0	.985	1.44
1941	86	141	7	6	3	.961	1.72
1942	94	150	6	5	3	.969	1.66
1943	57	116	4	5	1	.960	2.11
1944	32	54	3	1	0	.983	1.78
	2288	4872	241	132	53	.975	2.23

Assists per 154 Games: 16.2

PLAYER: MEL OTT

							BATTING										BASERUNNING				PERCENTAGES			VALUES			
Year	G	AB	H	2B	3B	HR	(Hm	Rd)	TB	R	RBI	BB	IBB	HBP	SH	SF	SB	CS	SB%	GIDP	Avg	Slug	On Base	Runs	Win−Loss	Pct.	AV
1926	35	60	23	2	0	0	0	0	25	7	4	1		0	0		1				.383	.417	.393	9	1−0	.685	1
1927	82	163	46	7	3	1	1	0	62	23	19	13		0	4		2				.282	.380	.328	20	2−3	.441	2
1928	124	435	140	26	4	18	9	9	228	69	77	52		2	10		3				.322	.524	.389	89	8−3	.723	12
1929	150	545	179	37	2	42	20	22	346	138	151	113		6	10		6				.328	.635	.442	157	12−3	.812	20
1930	148	521	182	34	5	25	21	4	301	122	119	103		2	20		9				.349	.578	.444	139	10−3	.755	15
1931	138	497	145	23	8	29	20	9	271	104	115	80		2	1		10				.292	.545	.391	109	10−3	.763	15
1932	154	566	180	30	8	38	24	14	340	119	123	100		4	3		6				.318	.601	.422	148	12−3	.813	17
1933	152	580	164	36	1	23	13	10	271	98	103	75		2	4		1			10	.283	.467	.365	105	12−4	.761	13
1934	153	582	190	29	10	35	17	18	344	119	135	85		3	1		0			10	.326	.591	.414	150	13−2	.840	18
1935	152	593	191	33	6	31	19	12	329	113	114	82		3	5		7			4	.322	.555	.404	144	12−3	.807	16
1936	150	534	175	28	6	33	18	15	314	120	135	111		5	10		6			8	.328	.588	.441	153	12−2	.860	18
1937	151	545	160	28	2	31	15	16	285	99	95	102		3	4		7			4	.294	.523	.405	128	12−3	.801	14
1938	152	527	164	23	6	36	20	16	307	116	116	118		5	2		2			8	.311	.583	.440	149	12−2	.856	16
1939	125	396	122	23	2	27	15	12	230	85	80	100		1	11		2			5	.308	.581	.439	115	9−2	.844	12
1940	151	536	155	27	3	19	12	7	245	89	79	100		6	5		6			9	.289	.457	.403	107	11−4	.739	11
1941	148	525	150	29	0	27	19	8	260	89	90	100		3	6		5			2	.286	.495	.399	117	11−3	.779	12
1942	152	549	162	21	0	30	23	7	273	118	93	109		3	3		6			3	.295	.497	.413	124	12−3	.806	13
1943	125	380	89	12	2	18	18	0	159	65	47	95		3	4		7			4	.234	.418	.388	72	8−3	.720	9
1944	120	399	115	16	4	26	21	5	217	91	82	90		3	2		2				.288	.544	.421	103	9−2	.807	12
1945	135	451	139	23	0	21	18	3	225	73	79	71		8	2		1			6	.308	.499	.410	101	9−3	.785	12
1946	31	68	5	1	0	1	1	0	9	2	4	8		0	2		0			1	.074	.132	.167	2	0−2	.033	0
1947	4	4	0	0	0	0	0	0	0	0	0	0		0	0		0			0	.000	.000	.000	0	0−0	.000	0
	2732	9456	2876	488	72	511	324	187	5041	1859	1860	1708		64	109		89			82	.304	.533	.410	2243	197−56	.779	258
16.9 yrs		561	171	29	4	30			299	110	110	101		4	6		5				.304	.533	.410				

Teams: New York, N.L. 1926–1947

Points in MVP Voting: 1926, 0; 1931, 15 (8th, .23); 1932, 1 (.01); 1933, 0; 1934, 37 (5th, .46); 1935, 3 (.04); 1936, 28 (6th, .47); 1937, 24 (7th, .30); 1938, 132 (4th, .39); 1939, 21 (.06); 1940, 0; 1941, 12 (.04); 1942, 190 (.57); 1943, 9 (.03); 1944, 20 (.06); 1945, 22 (.07); 1946, 0. TOTAL: 2.73 Award Shares.

Explanation for Gaps in Career or Sudden Changes in Productivity:
1939—Missed the last month with "severe Charleyhorses."

Other Notes: Named to *The Sporting News* major league All-Star team in 1934, 1935, 1936, and 1938.

Also hit 40 HR in Baker Bowl (1928–1938); hit only 13 career HR in Cincinnati.

FIELDING RIGHT FIELD

Year	G	PO	AS	Err	DP	Pct.	Range
1926	10	18	3	2	0	.913	2.10
1927	32	52	2	1	1	.982	1.69
1928	115	214	14	7	4	.970	1.98
1929	149	335	26	10	12	.973	2.42
1930	146	320	23	11	6	.969	2.35
1931	137	332	20	7	4	.981	2.57
1932	154	347	11	6	5	.984	2.32
1933	152	283	12	5	3	.983	1.94
1934	153	286	12	8	1	.974	1.95
1935	137	285	17	3	7	.990	2.20
1936	148	250	20	4	3	.985	1.82
1937	91	156	13	0	1	1.000	1.86
1938	37	65	3	0	0	1.000	1.84
1939	96	175	6	5	2	.973	1.89
1940	111	210	9	4	2	.982	1.97
1941	145	256	19	9	3	.968	1.90
1942	152	269	15	3	3	.990	1.87
1943	111	219	12	6	1	.975	2.08
1944	103	199	6	3	0	.986	1.99
1945	118	217	11	4	1	.983	1.93
1946	16	23	2	0	1	1.000	1.56
	2313	4511	256	98	60	.980	2.06

Assists per 154 Games: 17.0

PLAYER: CHUCK KLEIN

BATTING

Year	G	AB	H	2B	3B	HR	(Hm	Rd)	TB	R	RBI	BB	IBB	HBP	SH	SF	SB	CS	SB%	GIDP	Avg.	Slug	On Base	Runs	Win–Loss	Pct.	AV
1928	64	253	91	14	4	11	(	)	146	41	34	14		1	7		0				.360	.577	.385	55	5–2	.716	6
1929	149	616	219	45	6	43	(25	18)	405	126	145	54			9		5				.356	.657	.402	158	11–4	.724	17
1930	156	648	250	59	8	40	(26	14)	445	158	170	54		4	13		4				.386	.687	.428	186	12–4	.745	19
1931	148	594	200	34	10	31	(	)	347	121	121	59		1	2		7				.337	.584	.396	137	12–3	.773	17
1932	154	650	226	50	15	38	(	)	420	152	137	60		1	0		20				.348	.646	.404	167	13–3	.787	18
1933	152	606	223	44	7	28	(20	8)	365	101	120	56		1	4		15			3	.368	.602	.420	162	12–2	.862	19
1934	115	435	131	27	2	20	(	)	222	78	80	47	2	1			3			6	.301	.510	.371	86	9–3	.742	10
1935	119	434	127	14	4	21	(	)	212	71	73	41		1	9		4			10	.293	.488	.348	76	8–4	.645	8
1936	146	601	184	35	7	25	(	)	308	102	104	49		0	6		6			8	.306	.512	.355	114	11–5	.666	12
1937	115	406	132	20	2	15	(	)	201	74	57	39		1	3		3			6	.325	.495	.383	81	7–3	.688	9
1938	129	458	113	22	2	8	(	)	163	53	61	38		0	4		7			7	.247	.356	.302	52	6–8	.419	4
1939	110	317	90	18	5	12	(	)	154	45	56	36		0	8		2			4	.284	.486	.349	58	6–3	.673	6
1940	116	354	77	16	2	7	(	)	118	39	37	44		0	2		2			8	.218	.333	.303	38	5–6	.432	4
1941	50	73	9	0	0	1	(	)	12	6	3	10		0	1		0			2	.123	.164	.226	3	0–2	.083	0
1942	14	14	1	0	0	0	(	)	1	0	0	0		0	0		0			1	.071	.071	.071	0	0–1	.000	0
1943	12	20	2	0	0	0	(	2)	2	0	3	0		0	0		1			0	.100	.100	.100	0	0–1	.006	0
1944	4	7	1	0	0	0	(	1)	1	1	0	0		0	0		0			0	.143	.143	.143	0	0–0	.028	0
10.8 yrs	1753	6486	2076	398	74	300	(71	40)	3522	1168	1201	601	12		69		79			55	.320	.543	.375	1373	115–55	.676	149
		599	192	37	7	28			325	108	111	56	1		6		7				.320	.543	.375				7

Teams: Philadelphia, 1928–1933; Chicago, N.L. 1934–1935; Chicago, N.L./Philadelphia, 1936; Philadelphia, 1937–1938; Philadelphia/Pittsburgh, 1939; Philadelphia, 1940–1944.

Points in MVP Voting: 1931, 40 (1st, .63); 1932, 46 (1st, .52); 1933, 48 (2nd, .60); 1934, 0; 1935, 0; 1937, 0; 1938, 0; 1940, 0; 1941, 0; 1942, 0; 1943, 0; 1944, 0. TOTAL: 1.75 Award Shares.

Explanation for Gaps in Career or Sudden Changes in Productivity:
1934—Bothered much of season by what was called a charley horse—probably a pulled hamstring.
1935—Did not play regularly after mid-July.
1937—Unknown injuries.

Other Notes: Named to *The Sporting News* major league All-Star team of 1932 and 1933.

FIELDING RIGHT FIELD

Year	G	PO	AS	Err	DP	Pct.	Range
1928	63	128	7	3	0	.978	2.14
1929	149	321	18	12	3	.966	2.28
1930	156	362	44	17	10	.960	2.60
1931	148	292	13	9	0	.971	2.06
1932	154	331	29	15	3	.960	2.34
1933	152	339	21	5	5	.986	2.37
1934	110	222	6	9	2	.962	2.07
1935	111	215	11	10	7	.958	2.04
1936	146	276	16	23	2	.927	2.00
1937	102	175	11	10	3	.949	1.82
1938	119	229	8	10	1	.960	1.99
1939	77	153	5	7	1	.958	2.05
1940	116	180	4	3	2	.984	1.59
1941	14	22	1	1	0	.958	1.64
1943	2	0	0	1	0	0	0
1944	1	5	0	0	0	1.000	5.00
	1620	3250	194	135	39	.962	2.13

Assists per 154 Games: 18.4

HOME AND ROAD DATA FOR 1930 SEASON

	G	AB	R	H	2B	3B	HR	RBI	Avg.
HOME	77	323	88	143	31	3	26	109	.443
ROAD	79	325	70	107	28	5	14	61	.329

Data courtesy of Gordon L. Herman of Spokane

PLAYER: ENOS SLAUGHTER

	BATTING																BASERUNNING				PERCENTAGES			VALUES			
Year	G	AB	H	2B	3B	HR	(Hm Rd)	TB	R	RBI	BB	IBB	HBP	SH	SF	SB	CS	SB%	GIDP	Avg.	Slug	On Base	Runs	Win–Loss	Pct.	AV
1938	112	395	109	20	10	8	( )	173	59	58	32		0	4		1			0	.276	.438	.327	61	7–5	.585	6
1939	149	604	193	52	5	12	( )	291	95	86	44		5	11		2			11	.320	.482	.364	108	11–5	.685	11
1940	140	516	158	25	13	17	( )	260	96	73	50		2	1		8			4	.306	.504	.369	99	10–4	.717	14
1941	113	425	132	22	9	13	( )	211	71	76	53		2	4		4			5	.311	.496	.386	86	9–3	.762	9
1942	152	591	188	31	17	13	( )	292	100	98	88		6	2		9			6	.318	.494	.410	128	12–3	.817	12
1946	156	609	183	30	8	18	( )	283	100	130	69		2	5		9			7	.300	.465	.371	110	12–4	.738	15
1947	147	551	162	31	13	10	( )	249	100	86	59		4	5		4			10	.294	.452	.363	93	10–5	.653	12
1948	146	549	176	27	11	11	( )	258	91	90	81		1	6		4			11	.321	.470	.405	110	11–4	.741	11
1949	151	568	191	34	13	13	( )	290	92	96	79		1	6		3			7	.336	.511	.414	127	12–3	.799	14
1950	148	556	161	26	7	10	(4 6)	231	82	101	66		2	8		3			12	.290	.415	.362	87	9–6	.617	10
1951	123	409	115	17	8	4	(3 1)	160	48	64	67		3	4		7	2	.78	10	.281	.391	.383	67	7–4	.643	9
1952	140	510	153	17	12	11	(5 6)	227	73	101	70		1	6		6	1	.86	11	.300	.445	.382	93	10–4	.713	13
1953	143	492	143	34	9	6	(4 2)	213	64	89	80		5	1	0	4	4	.50	10	.291	.433	.394	90	9–4	.667	10
1954	69	125	31	4	2	1	(1 0)	42	19	19	28	0	1	0		0	2	.00	0	.248	.336	.383	18	2–2	.575	1
1955	118	276	87	12	4	5	(3 2)	122	50	35	41	4	2	1	5	2	3	.40	8	.315	.442	.400	50	5–3	.637	6
1956	115	306	86	18	5	2	(2 0)	120	52	27	34	1	1	2	1	2	1	.67	6	.281	.392	.352	44	5–4	.538	5
1957	96	209	53	7	1	5	(3 2)	77	24	34	40	5	0	4	3	0	2	.00	5	.254	.368	.363	30	4–3	.579	3
1958	77	138	42	4	1	4	(1 3)	60	21	19	21	0	0	1	0	2	0	1.00	3	.304	.435	.394	25	3–1	.713	3
1959	85	117	20	2	0	6	(4 2)	40	10	22	16	1	0	1	1	1	0	1.00	2	.171	.342	.267	11	1–2	.336	1
	2380	7946	2383	413	148	169	( )	3599	1247	1304	1018	11	37	73	10	71	15	.62	128	.300	.453	.378	1436	147–68	.684	165
14.7 yrs		541	162	28	10	12		245	85	89	69		3	5		5			9	.300	.453	.378				

Teams: St. Louis, 1938–1942, 1946–1953; New York, A.L. 1954; New York/Kansas City, 1955; Kansas City/New York, A.L. 1956; New York, A.L. 1957–1958; New York/Milwaukee, 1959.

Points in MVP Voting: 1938, 0; 1940, 0; 1941, 12 (.04); 1942, 200 (2nd, .60); 1946, 144 (3rd, .43); 1947, 12 (.04); 1948, 55 (.16); 1949, 181 (3rd, .54); 1950, 0; 1951, 0; 1952, 92 (6th, 27); 1953, 0; 1954, 0. TOTAL: 2.08 Award Shares.

Reported Salaries: 1938—$2,200; 1939—$3,300; 1940—$4,125; 1942—$9,000; 1950—$25,000; 1951—$22,500; 1954—$28,000; 1955—$18,000; 1956—$18,000.

Explanation for Gaps in Career or Sudden Changes in Productivity:
1954—Platooned.
1959—Attempted to play with broken foot.

Other Notes: Named to *The Sporting News* major league All-Star team in 1942 and 1946.

FIELDING RIGHT FIELD

Year	G	PO	AS	Err	DP	Pct.	Range
1938	92	189	7	6	0	.970	2.13
1939	149	348	18	12	5	.968	2.46
1940	132	267	8	3	5	.989	2.08
1941	108	173	5	10	1	.947	1.65
1942	151	287	15	4	2	.987	2.00
1946	156	284	23	6	6	.981	1.97
1947	142	306	15	6	5	.982	2.26
1948	146	330	9	10	1	.971	2.32
1949	150	330	10	6	1	.983	2.27
1950	145	260	9	6	1	.978	1.86
1951	106	198	10	1	3	.995	1.97
1952	137	250	11	3	3	.989	1.91
1953	137	235	2	1	0	.996	1.73
1954	30	37	0	1	0	.974	1.23
1955	77	126	5	2	2	.985	1.70
1956	76	133	2	2	0	.985	1.78
1957	64	97	2	0	0	1.000	1.55
1958	35	43	1	2	0	.957	1.26
1959	32	32	0	1	0	.970	1.00
	2065	3925	152	82	35	.980	1.97

Assists per 154 Games: 11.3

PLAYER: CHARLIE KELLER

					BATTING												BASERUNNING				PERCENTAGES			VALUES			
Year	G	AB	H	2B	3B	HR	(Hm	Rd)	TB	R	RBI	BB	IBB	HBP	SH	SF	SB	CS	SB%	GIDP	Avg.	Slug	On Base	Runs	Win—Loss	Pct.	AV
1939	111	398	133	21	6	11	(5	6)	199	87	83	81		0	11		6	3	.67	4	.334	.500	.437	97	8—2	.772	11
1940	138	500	143	18	15	21	(7	14)	254	102	93	106		0	3		6	2	.80	11	.286	.508	.409	114	10—4	.746	13
1941	140	507	151	24	10	33	(17	16)	294	102	122	102		1	0		6	4	.60	3	.298	.580	.416	134	11—2	.819	15
1942	152	544	159	24	9	26	(13	13)	279	106	108	114		2	1		14	2	.87	5	.292	.513	.416	131	12—3	.819	13
1943	141	512	139	15	11	31	(21	10)	269	97	86	106		0	2		7	5	.58	7	.271	.525	.395	116	12—3	.810	14
1945	44	163	49	7	4	10	(8	2)	94	26	34	31		0	0		0	2	.00	2	.301	.577	.412	41	4—1	.846	4
1946	150	538	148	29	10	30	(18	12)	287	98	101	113		1	0		1	4	.20	5	.275	.533	.405	127	12—3	.793	14
1947	45	151	36	6	1	13	(8	5)	83	36	36	41		1	0		0	0	.00	0	.238	.550	.404	37	4—3	.757	3
1948	83	247	66	15	2	6	(3	3)	103	41	44	41		0	1		1	1	.50	7	.267	.417	.370	40	4—3	.593	3
1949	60	116	29	4	1	3	(2	1)	44	17	16	25		2	1		2	0	1.00	3	.250	.379	.389	20	2—1	.585	2
1950	50	51	16	1	3	2	(2	0)	29	7	16	13		0	0		0	0	.00	0	.314	.569	.453	15	1—0	.862	1
1951	54	62	16	2	0	3	(3	0)	27	6	21	11		0	1		0	0	.00	0	.258	.435	.365	11	1—1	.709	1
1952	2	1	0	0	0	0	(0	0)	0	0	0	0		0	0		0	0	.00	0	0	0	0	0	0—0	.000	0
	1170	3790	1085	166	72	189	(107	82)	1962	725	760	784		10	20		45	23	.66	50	.286	.518	.408	883	80—23	.774	94
7.2 yrs		525	150	23	10	26			272	100	105	109		1	3		6	3			.286	.518	.408				

Teams: New York, A.L. 1939–1949; Detroit, 1950–1951; New York, A.L. 1952.

Points in MVP Voting: 1939, 0; 1940, 0; 1941, 0; 1942, 15 (.04); 1943, 31 (.09); 1946, 17 (.05); 1947, 0; 1948, 0; 1949, 0; 1950, 0; 1951, 0; 1952, 0. TOTAL: .19 Award Shares.

Explanation for Gaps in Career or Sudden Changes in Productivity:

1944—In merchant marines.

1946—Career curtailed by chronic back trouble beginning in 1946.

1948—Broken hand.

FIELDING OUTFIELD

Year	G	PO	AS	Err	DP	Pct.	Range
1939	105	213	5	7	1	.969	2.08
1940	136	317	5	11	2	.967	2.37
1941	137	328	7	7	2	.980	2.45
1942	152	321	10	5	1	.985	2.18
1943	141	338	8	2	0	.994	2.45
1945	44	110	4	0	0	1.000	2.59
1946	149	324	4	7	0	.979	2.20
1947	43	85	2	3	0	.967	2.02
1948	66	126	1	3	0	.977	1.92
1949	31	41	0	1	0	.976	1.32
1950	6	10	0	0	0	1.000	1.67
1951	8	22	0	0	0	1.000	2.75
1952	1	0	0	0	0		0
	1019	2235	46	46	6	.980	2.24

Assists per 154 Games: 7.0

PLAYER: CARL FURILLO

Year	G	AB	H	2B	3B	HR	(Hm	Rd)	TB	R	RBI	BB	IBB	HBP	SH	SF	SB	CS	SB%	GIDP	Avg.	Slug	On Base	Runs	Win—Loss	Pct	AV
1946	117	335	95	18	6	3			134	29	35	31		1	12		6			10	.284	.400	.346	46	6–4	.574	7
1947	124	437	129	24	7	8			191	61	88	34		1	4		7			17	.295	.437	.347	62	7–6	.545	8
1948	108	364	108	20	4	4			148	55	44	43		2	5		6			7	.297	.407	.374	57	6–4	.613	9
1949	142	549	177	27	10	18			278	95	106	37		3	7		4			16	.322	.506	.368	98	9–5	.647	12
1950	153	620	189	30	6	18	11	7	285	99	106	41		5	3		8			19	.305	.460	.353	96	9–7	.559	12
1951	158	667	197	32	4	16	12	4	285	93	91	43		7	7		8	7	.53	15	.295	.427	.344	97	10–9	.539	10
1952	134	425	105	18	1	8	3	5	149	52	59	31		4	2		1	4	.20	16	.247	.351	.304	42	5–8	.356	8
1953	132	479	165	38	6	21	9	12	278	82	92	34		4	1		1	1	.50	15	.344	.580	.393	107	9–3	.727	13
1954	150	547	161	23	1	19	12	7	243	56	96	49		5	3	3	2	4	.33	17	.294	.444	.356	83	8–7	.551	11
1955	140	523	164	24	3	26	17	9	272	83	95	43	5	7	1	4	4	5	.44	15	.314	.520	.371	97	9–5	.656	13
1956	149	523	151	30	0	21	12	9	244	66	83	57	15	1	2	4	1	1	.50	27	.289	.467	.357	80	9–6	.605	12
1957	119	395	121	17	4	12	7	5	182	61	66	29	4	5	7	4	0	2	.00	13	.306	.461	.358	62	7–4	.644	8
1958	122	411	119	19	3	18	11	7	198	54	83	35	2	2	4	7	0	2	.00	15	.290	.482	.343	64	7–5	.579	7
1959	50	93	27	4	0	0	0	0	31	8	13	7	2	0	1	2	0	0	.00	5	.290	.333	.333	10	1–2	.384	1
1960	8	10	1	0	1	0	0	0	3	1	1	0	0	0	0	0	0	0	.00	0	.100	.300	.100	0	0–0	.048	0
	1806	6378	1909	324	56	192	(94	65)	2921	895	1058	514	28	47	59	24	48	26	.40	207	.299	.458	.355	1003	102–75	.578	131
11.1 yrs		572	171	29	5	17			262	80	95	46		4	5		4			19	.299	.458	.355				

Teams: Dodgers, 1946–1960
Points in MVP Voting: 1946, 1 (.00); 1947–1948, 0; 1949, 68 (6th, .20); 1950, 4 (.01); 1951, 6 (.02); 1952, 0; 1953, 54 (9th, .16); 1954, 0; 1955, 2 (.01); 1956, 9 (.03); 1957, 0; 1958, 1 (.00); 1959, 0; 1960, 0. TOTAL: .43 Award Shares.

FIELDING OUTFIELD

Year	G	PO	AS	Err	DP	Pct.	Range
1946	112	292	9	5	4	.984	2.69
1947	121	287	9	7	3	.977	2.45
1948	104	274	13	5	2	.983	2.76
1949	142	286	13	11	2	.965	2.11
1950	153	246	18	8	2	.971	1.73
1951	157	330	24	5	6	.986	2.25
1952	131	225	12	3	2	.987	1.81
1953	131	232	11	3	3	.988	1.85
1954	149	306	10	9	3	.972	2.12
1955	140	249	10	5	4	.981	1.85
1956	146	230	10	4	2	.984	1.64
1957	107	153	7	2	1	.988	1.50
1958	119	187	5	5	0	.975	1.61
1959	25	23	0	2	0	.920	0.92
1960	2	2	0	0	0	1.000	1.00
	1739	3322	151	74	34	.979	2.00

Assists per 154 Games: 13.4

PLAYER: AL KALINE

Year	G	AB	H	2B	3B	HR	(Hm	Rd)	TB	R	RBI	BB	IBB	HBP	SH	SF	SB	CS	SB%	GIDP	Avg.	Slug	On Base	Runs	Win–Loss	Pct.	AV
1953	30	28	7	0	0	1	(0	1)	10	9	2	1		1	0		1	0	1.00	1	.250	.357	.300	3	0–1	.342	0
1954	138	504	139	18	3	4	(1	3)	175	42	43	22		0	7	2	9	5	.64	21	.276	.347	.301	49	6–9	.401	9
1955	152	588	200	24	8	27	(16	11)	321	121	102	82	12	5	0	6	6	8	.50	13	.340	.546	.421	136	12–3	.786	16
1956	153	617	194	32	10	27	(13	14)	327	96	128	70	4	1	1	4	7	1	.87	10	.314	.530	.382	129	12–4	.731	15
1957	149	577	170	29	4	23	(10	13)	276	83	90	43	7	3	6	7	11	9	.55	10	.295	.478	.340	92	11–5	.671	12
1958	146	543	170	34	7	16	(11	5)	266	84	85	54	6	2	3	5	7	4	.64	18	.313	.490	.372	96	11–4	.712	13
1959	136	511	167	19	2	27	(16	11)	271	86	94	72	12	4	2	6	10	4	.71	11	.327	.530	.408	114	10–3	.761	17
1960	147	551	153	29	4	15	(7	8)	235	77	68	65	3	3	5	5	19	4	.83	18	.278	.426	.351	84	10–6	.621	12
1961	153	586	190	41	7	19	(8	11)	302	116	82	66	2	4	4	5	14	1	.93	16	.324	.515	.391	121	12–4	.736	15
1962	100	398	121	16	6	29	(16	13)	236	78	94	47	3	1	2	4	4	0	1.00	17	.304	.593	.374	85	8–3	.743	11
1963	145	551	172	24	3	27	(22	5)	283	89	101	54	12	4	3	4	6	4	.60	12	.312	.514	.373	105	11–4	.726	12
1964	146	525	154	31	5	17	(9	8)	246	77	68	75	6	3	2	3	4	1	.80	12	.293	.469	.382	97	10–4	.718	12
1965	125	399	112	18	2	18	(8	10)	188	72	72	72	11	0	0	3	6	0	1.00	9	.281	.471	.388	77	8–3	.755	9
1966	142	479	138	29	1	29	(18	11)	256	85	88	81	7	5	1	6	5	5	.50	7	.288	.534	.392	105	10–3	.768	14
1967	131	458	141	28	2	25	(15	10)	248	94	78	83	10	1	2	6	8	2	.80	16	.308	.541	.409	104	10–2	.815	15
1968	102	327	94	14	1	10	(4	6)	140	49	53	49	6	2	3	3	6	4	.60	4	.287	.428	.391	59	7–2	.772	6
1969	131	456	124	17	0	21	(13	8)	204	74	69	54	4	1	0	7	1	2	.33	11	.272	.447	.346	71	8–5	.647	9
1970	131	467	130	24	4	16	(9	7)	210	64	71	77	5	1	3	7	2	2	.50	20	.278	.450	.375	79	9–5	.642	11
1971	133	405	119	19	2	15	(11	4)	187	69	54	82	9	7	1	6	4	6	.40	12	.294	.462	.415	81	9–3	.741	11
1972	106	278	87	12	2	10	(6	4)	133	46	32	28	5	2	1	5	1	0	1.00	11	.313	.478	.373	48	6–2	.769	6
1973	91	310	79	13	0	10	(6	4)	122	40	45	29	4	3	0	5	4	1	.80	10	.255	.394	.320	39	5–4	.519	4
1974	147	558	146	28	2	13	(7	6)	217	71	64	65	2	1	1	5	2	2	.50	12	.262	.389	.337	75	9–7	.543	7
	2834	10116	3007	499	75	399	(226	173)	4853	1622	1583	1277	131	55	45	104	137	65	.68	271	.297	.480	.374	1848	194–87	.691	236
17.5 yrs		578	172	29	4	23			277	93	90	73	8	3	3	6	8	4		15	.297	.480	.374				

Teams: Detroit, 1953–1974.

Points in MVP Voting: 1953, 0; 1955, 201 (2nd, .60); 1956, 142 (3rd, .42); 1957, 40 (10th, .12); 1958, 5 (.01); 1959, 84 (6th, .25); 1960, 0; 1961, 35 (9th, .13); 1962, 58 (6th, .21); 1963, 148 (2nd, .53); 1964, 17 (.06); 1965, 9 (.03); 1966, 66 (7th, .24); 1967, 88 (5th, .31); 1968, 0; 1969, 0; 1970, 0; 1971, 0; 1972, 4 (.01); 1973, 0; 1974, 0. TOTAL: 2.92 Award Shares.

Reported Salaries: 1972—$100,000.

Explanation for Gaps in Career or Sudden Changes in Productivity:

1959—Fractured jaw, June 18.

1962—Out 61 games with badly broken right collarbone, broke it making diving catch, May 26; out until June 23.

1965—Out 18 games, pulled rib cartilage, August 19.,

1967—Broken a hand slamming a bat into a bat rack (a most un-Kaline-like thing to do), June 27.

1968—Broken arm.

1972—Bothered most of season by sore left leg.

Other Notes: Named to *The Sporting News* American League All-Star team in 1955, 1962, 1963, 1966, and 1967. Gold Glove—1957, 1958, 1959, 1961, 1962, 1963, 1964, 1965, 1966, 1967.

FIELDING RIGHT FIELD

Year	G	PO	AS	Err	DP	Pct.	Range
1953	20	11		1	0	1.000	0.60
1954	135	283	16	9	0	.971	2.21
1955	152	306	14	7	4	.979	2.11
1956	153	343	18	6	4	.984	2.36
1957	145	319	13	5	2	.985	2.29
1958	145	316	23	2	4	.994	2.34
1959	136	364	4	4	0	.989	2.71
1960	142	367	5	5	1	.987	2.62
1961	147	378	9	4	3	.990	2.63
1962	100	225	8	4	1	.983	2.33
1963	140	257	5	2	0	.992	1.87
1964	136	278	6	3	2	.990	2.09
1965	112	193	2	3	0	.985	1.74
1966	136	279	7	2	1	.993	2.10
1967	130	217	14	4	2	.983	1.78
1968	74	131	1	3	0	.978	1.78
1969	118	192	9	7	4	.966	1.70
1970	91	156	3	2	1	.988	1.75
1971	129	207	6	0	0	1.000	1.65
1972	84	111	5	1	0	.991	1.38
1973	63	102	1	0	0	1.000	1.63
	2488	5035	170	73	29	.986	2.09

Assists per 154 Games: 10.5

PLAYER: HANK AARON

	BATTING																BASERUNNING				PERCENTAGES			VALUES			
Year	G	AB	H	2B	3B	HR	(Hm	Rd)	TB	R	RBI	BB	IBB	HBP	SH	SF	SB	CS	SB%	GIDP	Avg.	Slug	On Base	Runs	Win−Loss	Pct.	AV
1954	122	468	131	27	6	13	(1	12)	209	58	69	28		3	6	4	2	2	.50	13	.280	.447	.318	64	8−5	.594	7
1955	153	602	189	37	9	27	(14	13)	325	105	106	49	5	3	7	4	3	1	.75	20	.314	.540	.362	114	11−5	.695	12
1956	153	609	200	34	14	26	(15	11)	340	106	92	37	6	2	5	7	2	4	.33	21	.328	.558	.362	115	12−4	.742	15
1957	151	615	198	27	6	44	(18	26)	369	118	132	57	15	0	0	3	1	1	.50	13	.322	.600	.378	136	13−3	.783	16
1958	153	601	196	34	4	30	(10	20)	328	109	95	59	16	1	0	3	4	1	.80	21	.326	.546	.386	121	13−3	.787	15
1959	154	629	223	46	7	39	(20	19)	400	116	123	51	17	4	0	9	8	0	1.00	19	.355	.636	.401	156	13−3	.837	18
1960	153	590	172	20	11	40	(21	19)	334	102	126	60	13	2	0	12	16	7	.70	8	.292	.566	.352	119	12−5	.722	16
1961	155	603	197	39	10	34	(19	15)	358	115	120	56	20	2	1	9	21	9	.70	16	.327	.594	.380	132	13−4	.769	18
1962	156	592	191	28	6	45	(18	27)	366	127	128	66	14	3	0	6	15	7	.68	14	.323	.618	.390	140	13−3	.808	17
1963	161	631	201	29	4	44	(19	25)	370	121	130	78	18	0	0	5	31	5	.86	11	.319	.586	.391	149	14−3	.838	18
1964	145	570	187	30	2	24	(11	13)	293	103	95	62	9	0	0	2	22	4	.85	22	.328	.514	.393	112	11−4	.705	16
1965	150	570	181	40	1	32	(19	13)	319	109	89	60	10	1	0	8	24	4	.86	15	.318	.560	.379	122	12−3	.785	16
1966	158	603	168	23	1	44	(21	23)	325	117	127	76	15	1	0	8	21	3	.87	14	.279	.539	.356	118	12−5	.704	17
1967	155	600	184	37	3	39	(23	16)	344	113	109	63	19	0	0	6	17	6	.74	11	.307	.573	.369	126	13−3	.797	15
1968	160	606	174	33	4	29	(17	12)	302	84	86	64	23	1	0	5	28	5	.85	21	.287	.498	.354	104	13−4	.776	14
1969	147	547	164	30	3	44	(21	23)	332	100	97	87	19	2	0	3	9	10	.47	14	.300	.607	.396	128	12−3	.810	17
1970	150	516	154	26	1	38	(23	15)	296	103	118	74	15	2	0	6	9	0	1.00	6	.298	.574	.385	116	11−3	.757	13
1971	139	495	162	22	3	47	(31	16)	331	95	118	71	21	2	0	5	1	1	.50	9	.327	.669	.410	137	11−2	.867	17
1972	129	449	119	10	0	34	(19	15)	231	75	77	92	15	1	0	2	4	0	1.00	17	.265	.514	.390	91	9−4	.722	12
1973	120	392	118	12	1	40	(24	16)	252	84	96	68	13	1	0	4	1	1	.50	7	.301	.643	.402	104	8−2	.802	13
1974	112	340	91	16	0	20	(11	9)	167	47	69	39	6	0	1	2	1	0	1.00	6	.268	.491	.340	58	7−3	.721	7
1975	137	465	109	16	2	12	(4	8)	165	45	60	70	3	1	1	6	0	1	.00	15	.234	.355	.331	56	6−8	.439	7
1976	85	271	62	8	0	10	(6	4)	100	22	35	35	1	0	0	2	0	1	.00	16	.229	.369	.315	31	4−4	.506	3
20.4 yrs	3298	12364	3771	624	98	755	(385	370)	6856	2174	2297	1402	293	32	21	121	240	73	.77	328	.305	.555	.373	2550	252−87	.744	319
		607	185	31	5	37			337	107	113	69		2	1	6	12	4		16	.305	.555	.373				

Teams: Milwaukee, 1954–1965; Atlanta, 1966–1974; Milwaukee, 1975–1976.

Points in MVP Voting: 1954, 0 (?); 1955, 36 (9th, .11); 1956, 146 (3rd, .43); 1957, 239 (1st, .71); 1958, 166 (3rd, .49); 1959, 174 (3rd, .56); 1960, 49 (.16); 1961, 39 (8th, .17); 1962, 72 (6th, .26); 1963, 135 (3rd, .48); 1964, 22 (.08); 1965, 58 (7th, .21); 1966, 57 (8th, .20); 1967, 79 (5th, .28); 1968, 19 (.07); 1969, 188 (3rd, .56); 1970, 16 (.05); 1971, 180 (3rd, .54); 1972, 12 (.04); 1973, 35 (.10). TOTAL: 5.50 Award Shares.

Reported Salaries: 1970— approx. $125,000; 1972—$165,000.

Explanation for Gaps in Career or Sudden Changes in Productivity:
1954—Broke ankle while sliding late in season.

Other Notes: Named to *The Sporting News* major league All-Star team in 1956, 1958, and 1959.
Named to *The Sporting News* National League All-Star team in 1963, 1965, 1967, 1969, 1970, and 1971.
Gold Glove—1958, 1959, 1960.

In 1954 Henry Aaron hit at least as many home runs in every National League park as he did in his own park in Milwaukee. He hit 3 home runs that year in Chicago and 3 in St. Louis, 2 in Brooklyn, and 1 each in Cincinnati, New York, Philadelphia, Pittsburgh, and Milwaukee.

FIELDING RIGHT FIELD

Year	G	PO	AS	E	DP	Pct.	Range
1954	116	223	5	7	0	.970	1.97
1955	126	254	9	9	2	.967	2.09
1956	152	316	17	13	4	.962	2.19
1957	150	346	9	6	0	.983	2.37
1958	153	305	12	5	0	.984	2.07
1959	152	261	12	5	3	.982	1.80
1960	153	320	13	6	6	.982	2.18
1961	154	377	13	7	3	.982	2.53
1962	153	340	11	7	1	.980	2.29
1963	161	267	10	6	1	.979	1.72
1964	139	270	13	5	5	.983	2.04
1965	148	298	9	4	2	.987	2.07
1966	158	315	12	4	5	.988	2.07
1967	152	321	12	7	3	.979	2.19
1968	151	330	13	3	2	.991	2.27
1969	144	267	11	5	3	.982	1.93
1970	125	246	6	6	1	.977	2.02
1971	60	104	2	2	0	.981	1.77
1972	15	28	4	3	0	.914	2.13
1973	105	206	5	5	0	.977	2.01
1974	89	142	3	2	0	.986	1.63
1975	3	2	0	0	0	1.000	0.67
1976	1	1	0	0	0	1.000	1.00
	2760	5539	201	117	41	.980	2.08

Assists per 154 Games: 11.2

PLAYER: ROBERTO CLEMENTE

				BATTING														BASERUNNING				PERCENTAGES			VALUES			
Year	G	AB	H	2B	3B	HR	(Hm	Rd)	TB	R	RBI	BB	IBB	HBP	SH	SF	SB	CS	SB%	GIDP	Avg.	Slug	On Base	Runs	Win−Loss	Pct.	AV
1955	124	474	121	23	11	5	(3	2)	181	48	47	18	3	2	4	3	2	5	.29	14	.255	.382	.281	46	5−9	.369	7
1956	147	543	169	30	7	7	(4	3)	234	66	60	13	2	4	8	4	6	6	.50	14	.311	.431	.325	72	9−6	.593	11
1957	111	451	114	17	7	4	(2	2)	157	42	30	23	1	0	0	1	0	4	.00	13	.253	.348	.288	41	5−8	.365	5
1958	140	519	150	24	10	6	(1	5)	212	69	50	31	1	0	3	3	8	2	.80	15	.289	.408	.326	67	8−6	.556	11
1959	105	432	128	17	7	4	(1	3)	171	60	50	15	2	3	3	3	2	3	.40	10	.296	.396	.320	52	6−6	.509	6
1960	144	570	179	22	6	16	(5	11)	261	89	94	39	4	2	4	5	4	5	.44	21	.314	.458	.355	87	10−6	.623	11
1961	146	572	201	30	10	23	(10	13)	320	100	89	35	10	3	1	3	4	1	.80	18	.351	.559	.389	119	11−3	.770	16
1962	144	538	168	28	9	10	(6	4)	244	95	74	35	9	1	1	6	6	4	.60	18	.312	.454	.351	81	9−5	.636	11
1963	152	600	192	23	8	17	(5	12)	282	77	76	31	6	4	4	3	12	2	.86	24	.320	.470	.354	94	12−5	.719	11
1964	155	622	211	40	7	12	(4	8)	301	95	87	51	16	2	3	5	5	2	.71	9	.339	.484	.387	118	12−4	.772	13
1965	152	589	194	21	14	10	(5	5)	273	91	65	43	14	5	2	3	8	0	1.00	17	.329	.463	.377	101	11−4	.743	12
1966	154	638	202	31	11	29	(16	13)	342	105	119	46	13	0	1	5	7	5	.58	14	.317	.536	.359	119	12−5	.721	14
1967	147	585	209	26	10	23	(9	14)	324	103	110	41	17	3	0	3	9	1	.90	15	.357	.554	.400	126	12−3	.808	16
1968	132	502	146	18	12	18	(6	12)	242	74	57	51	27	1	0	3	2	3	.40	13	.291	.482	.355	82	10−3	.749	12
1969	138	507	175	20	12	19	(6	13)	276	87	91	56	16	3	0	4	4	1	.80	19	.345	.544	.411	109	10−3	.792	14
1970	108	412	145	22	10	14	(6	8)	229	65	60	38	14	2	1	2	3	0	1.00	7	.352	.556	.407	93	8−2	.818	12
1971	132	522	178	29	8	13	(7	6)	262	82	86	26	5	0	1	4	1	2	.33	19	.341	.502	.369	90	10−4	.700	14
1972	102	378	118	19	7	10	(6	4)	181	68	60	29	7	0	0	6	0	0	.00	15	.312	.479	.356	61	7−3	.693	8
	2433	9454	3000	440	166	240	(102	138)	4492	1416	1305	621	167	35	36	66	83	46	.64	275	.317	.475	.358	1557	169−85	.664	204
15.0 yrs		629	200	29	11	16			299	94	87	41	11	2	2	4	6	3		18	.317	.475	.358				

Teams: Pittsburgh, N.L. 1955–1972.

Points in MVP Voting: 1955, 0; 1956, 0; 1957, 0; 1958, 0; 1959, 0; 1960, 62 (8th, .18); 1961, 81 (4th, .36); 1962, 6 (.02); 1963, 12 (.04); 1964, 56 (9th, .20); 1965, 56 (8th, .20); 1966, 218 (1st, .78); 1967, 129 (3rd, .46); 1968, 0; 1969, 51 (8th, .15); 1970, 33 (.10); 1971, 87 (5th, .26); 1972, 16 (.05). TOTAL: 2.80 Award Shares.

Reported Salaries: Received $10,000 signing bonus; in 1954. 1970—approx. $100,-000; 1972—$150,000; 1971—over $100,000.

Explanation for Gaps in Career or Sudden Changes in Productivity:

1957—Began having back trouble, a recurrence of an injury suffered in an automobile accident in 1954.

1959—Surgery for bone chips in his elbow.

1960 through 1962—Still troubled by bone chips in his elbow.

1963—Suspended for five days after incident May 28, 1963, in which he brushed or slapped umpire Bill Jackowski. Also missed a few games after food poisoning incident.

1968—Injured shoulder in household accident, off season (iron bar on his porch collapsed when he was swinging himself up on it and he fell and rolled downhill 75 to 100 feet). Shoulder bothered him all year.

1969—Shoulder problem and torn thigh muscle.

1970—Given quite a bit of rest by Larry Shepard; sprained a muscle in his back while swinging, September 4, and missed most of rest of year.

1972—Started only one game in 40-game stretch in July and August due to what is coded by the *Sports Encyclopedia: Baseball* as an ankle injury, but described in *Roberto Clemente* (Tempo Books, 1973) as a badly bruised left knee suffered in last game before All-Star break.

Other Notes: 1961—Hit .411 in sixty-eight day games.

Named to *The Sporting News* National League All-Star team in 1961, 1964, 1966, 1967.

Gold Glove—1961, 1962, 1963, 1964, 1965, 1966, 1967, 1968, 1969, 1970, 1971, 1972.

FIELDING RIGHT FIELD

Year	G	PO	AS	E	DP	Pct.	Range
1955	118	253	18	6	5	.978	2.30
1956	139	274	17	13	2	.957	2.09
1957	109	272	9	6	1	.979	2.58
1958	135	312	22	6	3	.982	2.47
1959	104	229	10	13	1	.948	2.30
1960	142	246	19	8	2	.971	1.87
1961	144	256	27	9	5	.969	1.97
1962	142	269	19	8	1	.973	2.03
1963	151	239	11	11	2	.958	1.66
1964	154	289	13	10	2	.968	1.96
1965	145	288	16	10	1	.968	2.10
1966	154	318	17	12	3	.965	2.18
1967	145	273	17	9	4	.970	2.00
1968	131	297	9	5	1	.984	2.34
1969	135	226	14	5	1	.980	1.78
1970	104	189	12	7	2	.966	1.93
1971	124	267	11	2	4	.993	2.24
1972	94	199	5	0	2	1.000	2.17
	2370	4696	266	140	42	.973	2.09

Assists per 154 Games: 17.3

PLAYER: FRANK ROBINSON

							BATTING										BASERUNNING				PERCENTAGES			VALUES			
Year	G	AB	H	2B	3B	HR	(Hm	Rd)	TB	R	RBI	BB	IBB	HBP	SH	SF	SB	CS	SB%	GIDP	Avg.	Slug	On Base	Runs	Win—Loss	Pct.	AV
1956	152	572	166	27	6	38	(22	16)	319	122	83	64	7	20	8	4	8	4	.67	14	.290	.558	.374	121	12—4	.726	13
1957	150	611	197	29	5	29	(14	15)	323	97	75	44	5	12	5	5	10	2	.83	13	.322	.529	.374	122	11—5	.695	14
1958	148	554	149	25	6	31	(18	13)	279	90	83	62	5	7	0	0	10	1	.91	13	.269	.504	.350	99	11—5	.688	14
1959	146	540	168	31	4	36	(26	10)	315	106	125	69	9	8	0	9	18	8	.69	16	.311	.583	.391	122	11—4	.737	14
1960	139	464	138	33	6	31	(16	15)	276	86	83	82	6	9	0	7	13	6	.68	18	.297	.595	.407	113	11—3	.795	13
1961	153	545	176	32	7	37	(17	20)	333	117	124	71	23	10	0	10	22	3	.88	15	.323	.611	.404	137	12—3	.816	18
1962	162	609	208	51	2	39	(24	15)	380	134	136	76	16	11	0	5	18	9	.67	13	.342	.624	.421	160	13—3	.828	19
1963	140	482	125	19	3	21	(10	11)	213	79	91	81	20	14	0	3	26	10	.72	7	.259	.442	.379	87	10—4	.724	12
1964	156	568	174	38	6	29	(11	18)	311	103	96	79	20	9	0	6	23	5	.82	13	.306	.548	.396	127	13—3	.826	15
1965	156	582	172	33	5	33	(18	15)	314	109	113	70	18	18	0	4	13	9	.59	14	.296	.540	.386	120	12—5	.711	14
1966	155	576	182	34	2	49	(27	22)	367	122	122	87	11	10	0	7	8	5	.62	24	.316	.637	.410	146	13—3	.824	17
1967	129	479	149	23	7	30	(19	11)	276	83	94	71	14	7	0	6	2	3	.40	10	.311	.576	.403	113	11—2	.836	13
1968	130	421	113	27	1	15	(7	8)	187	69	52	73	4	12	0	2	11	2	.85	15	.268	.444	.390	77	9—3	.784	8
1969	148	539	166	19	5	32	(20	12)	291	111	100	88	11	13	0	3	9	3	.75	12	.308	.540	.415	126	12—3	.824	14
1970	132	471	144	24	1	25	(12	13)	245	88	78	69	9	7	0	6	2	1	.67	13	.306	.520	.398	99	10—3	.771	15
1971	133	455	128	16	2	28	(17	11)	232	82	99	72	11	9	1	8	3	0	1.00	21	.281	.510	.383	88	10—4	.734	12
1972	103	342	86	6	1	19	(10	9)	151	41	59	55	0	2	0	6	2	3	.40	9	.251	.442	.353	55	7—3	.696	5
1973	147	534	142	29	0	30	(16	14)	261	85	97	82	12	10	1	3	1	1	.50	13	.266	.489	.371	99	11—4	.731	10
1974	144	477	117	27	3	22	(8	14)	216	81	68	85	14	10	1	6	5	2	.71	11	.245	.453	.366	84	10—4	.695	8
1975	49	118	28	5	0	9	(8	1)	60	19	24	29	3	0	1	1	0	0	.00	2	.237	.508	.383	25	3—1	.730	2
1976	36	67	15	0	0	3	(1	2)	24	5	10	11	0	0	0	1	0	0	.00	3	.224	.358	.329	8	1—1	.497	1
	2808	10006	2943	528	72	586	(321	265)	5373	1829	1812	1420	218	198	17	102	204	77	.73	269	.294	.537	.388	2127	211—68	.758	252
17.3 yrs		577	170	30	4	34			310	106	105	82	13	11	1	6	12	4		16	.294	.537	.388				

Teams: Cincinnati, N.L. 1956–1965; Baltimore, A.L. 1966–1971; Los Angeles, 1972; California, 1973; California/Cleveland, 1974; Cleveland, 1975–1976.

Points in MVP Voting: 1956, 79 (7th, .24); 1957, 42 (8th, .13); 1958, 4 (.01); 1959, 52 (9th, 17); 1960, 2 (.01); 1961, 219 (1st, .98); 1962, 164 (4th, .59); 1963, 0; 1964, 98 (4th, .35); 1965, 11 (.04); 1966, 280 (1st, 1.00); 1967, 31 (.11); 1968, 0; 1969, 162 (3rd, .48); 1970, 60 (10th, .18); 1971, 170 (3rd, .51); 1972, 0; 1973, 21 (.06); 1974, 0; 1975, 0; 1976, 0. TOTAL: 4.86 Award Shares.

Reported Salaries: 1970—approx. $125,000; 1972—$140,000.

Explanation for Gaps in Career or Sudden Changes in Productivity:

1960—Shoulder or elbow problem.

1963—Required thirty stitches in left arm to close spike wound, September 7.

1967—Suffered concussion, blurred vision following collision at second base; out a month.

1968—Had the mumps, a sore arm, and still had vision problems from previous season's collision.

1970—Shoulder injury after running into a wall early in season.

1972—Early-season injury; unknown.

Other Notes: Named to *The Sporting News* National League All-Star team in 1961 and 1962. Named to *The Sporting News* American League All-Star team in 1966 and 1967. Gold Glove—1958.

FIELDING RIGHT FIELD

Year	G	PO	AS	E	DP	Pct.	Range
1956	152	323	5	8	1	.976	2.16
1957	136	336	11	4	3	.989	2.55
1958	138	310	12	3	1	.991	2.33
1959	40	51	3	1	0	.982	1.35
1960	51	112	8	5	1	.960	2.35
1961	150	284	15	3	3	.990	1.99
1962	161	315	10	2	2	.994	2.02
1963	139	237	13	4	1	.984	1.80
1964	156	279	7	4	3	.986	1.83
1965	155	282	5	3	1	.990	1.85
1966	151	254	4	4	0	.985	1.71
1967	126	191	7	2	2	.990	1.57
1968	117	173	5	7	0	.962	1.52
1969	134	226	9	3	2	.987	1.75
1970	120	221	9	3	3	.987	1.92
1971	92	177	3	5	0	.973	1.96
1972	95	168	6	6	2	.967	1.83
1973	17	38	3	1	1	.976	2.41
1974	1	0	0	0	0	0	0
1976	1	1	0	0	0	1.000	1.00
	2132	3978	135	68	26	.984	1.93

Assists per 154 Games: 9.8

PLAYER: TONY OLIVA

	BATTING															BASERUNNING				PERCENTAGES			VALUES			
Year	G	AB	H	2B	3B	HR	(Hm | Rd)	TB	R	RBI	BB	IBB	HBP	SH	SF	SB	CS	SB%	GiDP	Avg.	Slug	On Base	Runs	Win–Loss	Pct.	AV
1962	9	9	4	1	0	0	(0 | 0)	5	3	3	3	0	0	0	0	0	0	.00	0	.444	.556	.583	3	0–0	.939	0
1963	7	7	3	0	0	0	(0 | 0)	3	0	1	0	0	0	0	0	0	0	.00	0	.429	.429	.429	1	0–0	.806	0
1964	161	672	217	43	9	32	(17 | 15)	374	109	94	34	8	6	3	3	12	6	.67	9	.323	.557	.358	132	13–4	.749	13
1965	149	576	185	40	5	16	(5 | 11)	283	107	98	55	12	4	2	10	19	9	.68	8	.321	.491	.377	109	11–4	.733	12
1966	159	622	191	32	7	25	(18 | 7)	312	99	87	42	10	5	2	6	13	7	.65	16	.307	.502	.352	106	12–5	.721	13
1967	146	557	161	34	6	17	(9 | 8)	258	76	83	44	12	8	1	5	11	3	.79	9	.289	.463	.346	91	11–5	.703	11
1968	128	470	136	24	5	18	(7 | 11)	224	54	68	45	16	7	1	5	10	9	.53	10	.289	.477	.356	77	10–3	.743	8
1969	153	637	197	39	4	24	(11 | 13)	316	97	101	45	12	3	2	5	10	13	.43	10	.309	.496	.354	107	12–6	.668	14
1970	157	628	204	36	7	23	(6 | 17)	323	96	107	38	12	3	1	4	5	4	.56	16	.325	.514	.364	112	12–5	.724	15
1971	126	487	164	30	3	22	(9 | 13)	266	73	81	25	8	2	0	4	4	1	.80	21	.337	.546	.369	90	10–3	.738	11
1972	10	28	9	1	2	0	(0 | 0)	10	1	1	2	0	0	0	0	0	0	.00	1	.321	.357	.367	4	0–0	.649	0
1973	146	571	166	20	0	16	(5 | 11)	234	63	92	45	14	4	0	4	2	1	.67	13	.291	.410	.345	79	9–7	.568	9
1974	127	459	131	16	2	13	(4 | 9)	190	43	57	27	11	2	2	4	0	1	.00	14	.285	.414	.324	58	7–6	.543	7
1975	131	455	123	10	0	13	(4 | 9)	172	46	58	41	15	13	0	6	0	1	.00	10	.270	.378	.344	60	7–6	.503	6
1976	67	123	26	3	0	1	(0 | 1)	32	3	16	2	1	2	0	1	0	0	.00	2	.211	.260	.234	7	1–3	.162	0
	1676	6301	1917	329	50	220	(95 | 125)	3002	870	947	448	131	59	14	57	86	55	.61	139	.304	.476	.352	1036	115–58	.665	119
10.3 yrs		609	185	32	5	21			290	84	92	43	13	6	1	6	8	5		13	.304	.476	.352				

Teams: Minnesota, 1962–1976.

Points in MVP Voting: 1962, 0; 1963, 0; 1964, 99 (4th, .35); 1965, 174 (2nd, .62); 1966, 71 (6th, .25); 1967, 6 (.02); 1968, 5 (.02); 1969, 21 (.06); 1970, 157 (2nd, .47); 1971, 36 (10th, .11); 1972, 0; 1973, 0; 1974, 0; 1975, 0; 1976, 0. TOTAL: 1.90 Award Shares.

Reported Salaries: 1961—in minors, $300/month plus $10 for signing contract; 1962—$550/month, in minors; 1963—$6,000, in minors; 1964, $7,500; 1965, $19,000; 1966, $32,000; 1967, $43,000; 1968, $52,000; 1969, $62,000; 1970, $78,000; 1971, $98,000; 1972, $105,000.

Explanation for Gaps in Career or Sudden Changes in Productivity:

1968—Missed nine games with pulled leg muscle, late July; season ended by shoulder separation, August 31.

1972—Right knee operated on in June, unable to walk much of season; Tony had a long series of operations on his knees, which probably prevented him from being one of the game's greatest stars.

Other Notes: Named to *The Sporting News* American League All-Star team in 1964, 1965, 1966, 1970, and 1971. Gold Glove—1966.

FIELDING RIGHT FIELD

Year	G	PO	AS	Err	DP	Pct.	Range
1962	2	3	0	0	0	1.000	1.50
1964	159	313	5	6	0	.981	2.00
1965	147	284	10	11	3	.964	2.00
1966	159	335	9	10	3	.972	2.16
1967	146	286	8	4	2	.987	2.01
1968	126	227	7	4	1	.983	1.86
1969	152	311	14	6	3	.982	2.14
1970	157	351	12	12	4	.968	2.31
1971	121	216	6	7	3	.969	1.83
1972	9	6	0	1	0	.857	0.67
	1178	2332	71	61	19	.975	2.04

Assists per 154 Games: 9.3

PLAYER: PETE ROSE

				BATTING														BASERUNNING				PERCENTAGES			VALUES			
Year	G	AB	H	2B	3B	HR	(Hm	Rd)	TB	R	RBI	BB	IBB	HBP	SH	SF	SB	CS	SB%	GIDP	Avg.	Slug	On Base	Runs	Win−Loss	Pct.	AV
1963	157	623	170	25	9	6	(2	4)	231	101	41	55	0	5	6	6	13	15	.46	8	.273	.371	.331	77	10−8	.555	8
1964	136	516	139	13	2	4	(3	1)	168	64	34	36	0	2	3	1	4	10	.29	6	.269	.326	.317	53	7−8	.474	7
1965	162	670	209	35	11	11	(7	4)	299	117	81	69	2	8	8	2	8	3	.73	10	.312	.446	.378	118	12−6	.661	13
1966	156	654	205	38	5	16	(11	5)	301	97	70	37	3	1	7	1	4	9	.31	12	.313	.460	.347	100	11−7	.629	12
1967	148	585	176	32	8	12	(7	5)	260	86	76	56	9	3	1	2	11	6	.65	9	.301	.444	.363	95	12−4	.737	10
1968	149	626	210	42	6	10	(6	4)	294	94	49	56	15	4	2	4	3	7	.30	11	.335	.470	.390	113	12−4	.733	13
1969	156	627	218	33	11	16	(10	6)	321	120	82	88	18	5	2	6	7	10	.41	13	.348	.512	.427	138	12−4	.756	17
1970	159	649	205	37	9	15	(7	8)	305	120	52	73	10	2	0	4	12	7	.63	7	.316	.470	.385	121	12−5	.711	13
1971	160	632	192	27	4	13	(8	5)	266	86	44	68	15	3	1	3	13	9	.59	9	.304	.421	.372	100	12−5	.726	13
1972	154	645	198	31	11	6	(1	5)	269	107	57	73	4	7	2	2	10	3	.77	7	.307	.417	.381	109	12−5	.707	13
1973	160	680	230	36	8	5	(3	2)	297	115	64	65	6	6	1	0	10	7	.59	14	.338	.437	.400	119	13−5	.724	14
1974	163	652	185	45	7	3	(2	1)	253	110	51	106	14	5	1	6	2	4	.33	9	.284	.388	.384	104	12−6	.641	11
1975	162	662	210	47	4	7	(3	4)	286	112	74	89	8	11	1	1	0	1	.00	13	.317	.432	.406	120	12−5	.714	13
1976	162	665	215	42	6	10	(7	3)	299	130	63	86	7	6	0	2	9	5	.64	17	.323	.450	.404	123	12−5	.698	13
1977	162	655	204	38	7	9	(3	6)	283	95	64	66	7	5	1	4	16	4	.80	9	.311	.432	.376	111	11−6	.649	13
1978	159	655	198	51	3	7	(2	5)	276	103	52	62	6	3	2	7	13	9	.59	8	.302	.421	.361	102	11−7	.634	11
1979	163	628	208	40	5	4	(1	3)	270	90	59	95	10	2	0	5	20	11	.65	18	.331	.430	.418	116	12−5	.719	15
1980	162	655	185	42	1	1	(0	1)	232	95	64	66	5	6	4	4	12	8	.60	13	.282	.354	.350	83	10−9	.534	10
1981	107	431	140	18	5	0	(0	0)	168	73	33	46	5	3	1	3	4	4	.50	8	.325	.390	.390	67	7−4	.633	9
1982	162	634	172	25	4	3	(2	1)	214	80	54	66	9	7	8	3	8	8	.50	11	.271	.338	.341	75	9−9	.507	9
1983	151	493	121	14	3	0	(0	0)	141	52	45	52	5	2	1	7	7	7	.50	11	.245	.286	.315	46	5−9	.361	5
1984	121	374	107	15	2	0	(0	0)	126	43	34	40	4	3	3	1	1	1	.50	11	.286	.337	.359	47	6−4	.589	5
	3371	13411	4097	726	131	158	(85	73)	5559	2090	1243	1450	162	99	55	74	187	148	.56	235	.305	.415	.374	2138	234−130	.642	247
20.8 yrs		644	197	35	6	8			267	100	60	70	8	5	3	4	9	7	.56	11	.305	.415	.374				

Teams: Cincinnati, 1963–1978; Philadelphia, 1979–1983; Montreal/Cincinnati, 1984.

Points in MVP Voting: 1963, 0; 1964, 0; 1965, 67 (6th, .24); 1966, 31 (10th, .11); 1967, 40 (10th, .14); 1968, 205 (2nd, .73); 1969, 127 (4th, .38); 1970, 54 (7th, .16); 1971, 1 (.00); 1972, 19 (.06); 1973, 274 (1st, .82); 1974, 0; 1975, 114 (5th, .34); 1976, 131 (4th, .39); 1977, 15 (.04); 1978, 35 (.10); 1979, 23 (.07); 1980, 0; 1981, 35 (.10); 1982, 0; 1983, 0. TOTAL: 3.68 Award Shares.

Reported Salaries: 1970—approximately $100,000; 1972—$107,000.

Explanation for Gaps in Career or Sudden Changes in Productivity: 1981—Strike.

Other Notes: Named to *The Sporting News* All-Star team, 1965, 1966, 1968, 1969, 1973, 1978, 1981.

Gold Glove—1969, 1970.

FIELDING OUTFIELD

Year	G	PO	AS	Err	DP	Pct.	Range
1963	1	0	0	0	0	0	0
1967	123	211	5	4	0	.982	1.76
1968	148	268	20	3	4	.990	1.95
1969	156	316	10	4	3	.988	2.09
1970	159	309	8	1	2	.997	1.99
1971	158	306	13	2	1	.994	2.02
1972	154	330	15	2	2	.994	2.24
1973	159	343	15	3	0	.992	2.25
1974	163	346	11	1	3	.997	2.19
1975	35	55	0	1	0	.982	1.57
1976	1	0	0	0	0	0	0
1978	7	3	0	0	0	1.000	0.43
1983	35	41	0	1	0	.976	1.17
1984	28	51	2	2	0	.964	1.89
	1327	2579	99	24	15	.991	2.02

Assists per 154 Games: 11.5

PLAYER: REGGIE JACKSON

Year	G	AB	H	2B	3B	HR	(Hm	Rd)	TB	R	RBI	BB	IBB	HBP	SH	SF	SB	CS	SB%	GIDP	Avg.	Slug	On Base	Runs	Win−Loss	Pct.	AV
1967	35	118	21	4	4	1	(0	1)	36	13	6	10	0	5	1	1	1	1	.50	1	.178	.305	.267	10	1−2	.362	0
1968	154	553	138	13	6	29	(9	20)	250	82	74	50	5	5	4	2	14	4	.78	3	.250	.452	.314	83	11−5	.701	11
1969	152	549	151	36	3	47	(26	21)	334	123	118	114	20	12	1	1	13	5	.72	8	.275	.608	.409	144	13−3	.822	17
1970	149	426	101	21	2	23	(8	15)	195	57	66	75	11	8	2	3	26	17	.60	10	.237	.458	.358	70	9−5	.647	9
1971	150	567	157	29	3	32	(17	15)	288	87	80	63	5	6	0	6	16	10	.62	7	.277	.508	.352	103	12−4	.730	14
1972	135	499	132	25	2	25	(16	9)	236	72	75	59	7	8	4	2	9	8	.53	5	.265	.473	.348	84	11−4	.748	11
1973	151	539	158	28	2	32	(18	14)	286	99	117	76	11	7	0	7	22	8	.73	13	.293	.531	.383	112	11−4	.752	15
1974	148	506	146	25	1	29	(14	15)	260	90	93	86	20	4	0	8	25	5	.83	8	.289	.514	.391	109	11−3	.803	14
1975	157	593	150	39	3	36	(18	18)	303	91	104	67	5	3	0	6	17	8	.68	10	.253	.511	.329	100	11−6	.654	13
1976	134	498	138	27	2	27	(12	15)	250	84	91	54	7	4	0	2	28	7	.80	17	.277	.502	.351	86	10−4	.719	14
1977	146	525	150	39	2	32	(11	21)	289	93	110	75	4	3	0	4	17	3	.85	3	.286	.550	.376	117	11−3	.762	13
1978	139	511	140	13	5	27	(17	10)	244	82	97	58	2	9	0	3	14	11	.56	8	.274	.477	.356	87	10−5	.688	12
1979	131	465	138	24	2	29	(15	14)	253	78	89	65	3	2	0	5	9	8	.53	17	.297	.544	.382	93	10−4	.719	14
1980	143	514	154	22	4	41	(16	25)	307	94	111	83	15	2	0	2	1	2	.33	7	.300	.597	.398	125	11−3	.798	14
1981	94	334	79	17	1	15	(7	8)	143	33	54	46	2	1	0	1	0	3	.00	8	.237	.428	.330	47	6−4	.637	5
1982	153	530	146	17	1	39	(21	18)	282	92	101	85	12	2	0	4	4	5	.44	10	.275	.532	.375	107	11−4	.711	12
1983	116	397	77	14	1	14	(7	7)	135	43	49	52	5	4	0	5	0	2	.00	5	.194	.340	.290	42	4−8	.347	6
1984	143	525	117	17	2	25	(15	10)	213	67	81	55	7	3	1	0	8	4	.67	10	.223	.406	.300	64	7−8	.476	8
1985	143	460	116	27	0	27	(15	12)	224	64	85	78	12	1	0	2	1	2	.33	16	.252	.487	.360	79	9−5	.639	10
1986	132	419	101	12	2	18	(11	7)	171	65	58	92	11	3	0	3	1	1	.50	14	.241	.408	.379	68	7−5	.591	8
	2705	9528	2510	449	48	548	(273	275)	4699	1509	1659	1343	164	92	13	67	226	114	.66	180	.263	.493	.358	1698	186−87	.680	220
16.7 yrs		571	150	27	3	33			281	90	99	80	10	6	1	4	14	7		11	.263	.493	.358				

(Column groups: BATTING | BASERUNNING | PERCENTAGES | VALUES)

Teams: Kansas City, 1967; Oakland, 1968–1975; Baltimore, 1976; New York, 1977–1981; California, 1982–1986; Oakland, 1987.

Points in MVP Voting: 1967, 0; 1968, 8 (.03); 1969, 110 (5th, .33); 1970, 0; 1971, 15 (.04); 1972, 9 (.03); 1973, 336 (1st, 1.00); 1974, 119 (4th, .35); 1975, 118 (5th, .35); 1976, 17 (.05); 1977, 67 (8th, .17); 1978, 18 (.05); 1979, 3 (.01); 1980, 234 (2nd, .60); 1981, 0; 1982, 107 (6th, .27); 1983–1986, 0. TOTAL: 3.28 Award Shares.

Reported Salaries: 1969—$20,000; 1970—$45,000 plus $2,000 (rent)
1971—$40,000; 1972—$55,000; 1973—$75,000; 1974—$135,000
1975—$137,000; 1976—$190,000;
1977–1981 5-year contract totals $2.96 million
1982–1985 $900,000 a year plus attendance bonuses

Explanation for Gaps in Career or Sudden Changes in Productivity:
1970—Held out first month of spring training; feuded with Finley much of season and was benched a few times, reportedly on Finley's orders.
1972—Pulled hamstring muscle shortly after All-Star Game; missed World Series with leg injury suffered in fifth game of play-off.
1974—Hurt his shoulder in fight with Bill North, June 5.
1976—Held out until May 2.
1977—Suspended briefly following a fight in the dugout with Billy Martin, June 18.
1978—Suspended for five days following incident in which he bunted after being ordered not to, July 17; pulled groin muscle about May 23, out about ten days. Martin also platooned him some in June and July.
1979—Calf muscle popped while jogging off the field, June 2, missed almost a month.
1981—Strike, minor injuries.
1983—Severely bruised ribs early in season.

Other Notes: Named to *The Sporting News* American League All-Star team in 1969, 1973, 1975, 1976, 1980.
Values presented here go only through 1986. Those presented in Section II may include estimated data for 1987.

FIELDING RIGHT FIELD

Year	G	PO	AS	E	DP	Pct.	Range
1967	34	55	1	4	0	.933	1.65
1968	151	269	14	12	5	.959	1.87
1969	150	278	14	11	2	.964	1.95
1970	142	251	8	12	0	.956	1.82
1971	145	285	15	7	3	.977	2.07
1972	135	301	5	9	5	.971	2.27
1973	145	302	4	9	0	.971	2.11
1974	127	296	8	10	2	.968	2.39
1975	147	315	13	12	5	.965	2.23
1976	121	284	8	11	3	.964	2.41
1977	127	236	7	13	0	.949	1.91
1978	104	212	6	3	1	.986	2.10
1979	125	274	7	4	2	.986	2.25
1980	94	174	3	7	0	.962	1.88
1981	61	111	3	3	0	.974	1.87
1982	140	200	6	6	1	.972	1.47
1983	47	66	4	1	1	.986	1.49
1984	3	7	0	0	0	1.000	2.33
1985	81	112	6	7	1	.944	1.46
1986	4	4	1	1	0	.833	1.25
	2083	4032	133	142	31	.967	2.00

Assists per 154 Games: 9.8

PLAYER: BOBBY BONDS

							BATTING											BASERUNNING				PERCENTAGES			VALUES			
Year	G	AB	H	2B	3B	HR	(Hm	Rd)	TB	R	RBI	BB	IBB	HBP	SH	SF	SB	CS	SB%	GIDP	Avg.	Slug	On Base	Runs	Win–Loss	Pct.	AV
1968	81	307	78	10	5	9	(8	1)	125	55	35	38	0	1	1	2	16	7	.70	0	.254	.407	.335	46	6–3	.690	5
1969	158	622	161	25	6	32	(23	9)	294	120	90	81	3	10	3	4	45	4	.92	9	.259	.473	.350	114	13–5	.703	12
1970	157	663	200	36	10	26	(14	12)	334	134	78	77	7	2	1	2	48	10	.83	6	.302	.504	.374	134	12–6	.683	16
1971	155	619	178	32	4	33	(17	16)	317	110	102	62	6	5	0	5	26	8	.76	10	.288	.512	.355	115	12–5	.719	15
1972	153	626	162	29	5	26	(14	12)	279	118	80	60	4	5	1	5	44	6	.88	13	.259	.446	.326	96	11–7	.604	10
1973	160	643	182	34	4	39	(19	20)	341	131	96	87	9	4	0	4	43	17	.72	8	.283	.530	.370	130	13–5	.722	15
1974	150	567	145	22	8	21	(8	13)	246	97	71	95	8	4	0	4	41	11	.79	4	.256	.434	.364	100	11–5	.682	12
1975	145	529	143	26	3	32	(9	23)	271	93	85	89	8	3	0	5	30	17	.64	10	.270	.512	.375	103	11–4	.739	15
1976	99	378	100	10	3	10	(6	4)	146	48	54	41	6	3	0	5	30	15	.67	7	.265	.386	.337	50	7–5	.593	8
1977	158	592	156	23	9	37	(18	19)	308	103	115	74	5	2	1	10	41	18	.69	9	.264	.520	.342	107	12–6	.674	13
1978	156	565	151	19	4	31	(15	16)	271	93	90	79	7	2	3	8	43	22	.66	14	.267	.480	.353	95	11–6	.647	12
1979	146	538	148	24	1	25	(19	6)	249	93	85	74	4	8	4	7	34	23	.60	9	.275	.463	.365	92	9–7	.581	12
1980	86	231	47	5	3	5	(1	4)	73	37	24	33	3	2	1	3	15	5	.75	4	.203	.316	.304	25	3–5	.364	2
1981	45	163	35	7	1	6	(2	4)	62	26	19	24	5	2	1	0	5	6	.45	4	.215	.380	.321	19	2–3	.430	2
	1849	7043	1886	302	66	332	(173	159)	3316	1258	1024	914	75	53	16	64	461	169	.73	107	.268	.471	.353	1224	134–71	.654	149
11.4 yrs		617	165	26	6	29			291	110	90	80	7	5	1	6	40	15	.73		9	.268	.471	.353				

Teams: San Francisco, N.L. 1968–1974; New York, A.L., 1975; California, A.L. 1976–1977; Chicago/Texas, 1978; Cleveland, 1979; St. Louis, 1980; Chicago, N.L., 1981.

Points in MVP Voting: 1968, 0; 1969, 2 (.01); 1970, 0; 1971, 139 (4th, .41); 1972, 0; 1973, 174 (3rd, .52); 1974, 0; 1975, 1 (.00); 1976, 0; 1977, 28 (.07); 1978, 0; 1979, 0; 1980, 0; 1981, 0. TOTAL: 1.01 Award Shares.

Other Notes: Named to *The Sporting News* National League All-Star team in 1973. Named to *The Sporting News* American League All-Star team in 1977. Gold Glove—1971, 1973, 1974.

FIELDING RIGHT FIELD

Year	G	PO	AS	E	DP	Pct.	Range
1968	80	169	6	4	1	.978	2.19
1969	155	339	9	8	2	.978	2.25
1970	157	326	14	11	7	.969	2.17
1971	154	329	10	2	1	.994	2.20
1972	153	345	8	8	3	.978	2.31
1973	158	346	12	11	5	.970	2.27
1974	148	305	11	11	3	.966	2.14
1975	129	287	12	4	6	.987	2.32
1976	98	199	9	5	3	.977	2.12
1977	140	272	5	4	0	.986	1.98
1978	133	253	16	9	6	.968	2.02
1979	116	267	9	6	1	.979	2.38
1980	70	114	5	4	2	.967	1.70
1981	45	108	2	2	0	.982	2.44
	1736	3659	128	89	40	.977	2.18

Assists per 154 Games: 11.4

Pitcher

Cy Young
Rube Waddell
Jack Chesbro
Joe McGinnity
Christy Mathewson
Eddie Plank
Addie Joss
Three Finger Brown
Chief Bender
Ed Walsh
Ed Reulbach
Eddie Cicotte
Walter Johnson
Hippo Vaughn
Rube Marquard
Grover Cleveland
  (Pete) Alexander
Wilbur Cooper
Eppa Rixey

Stan Coveleski
Bob Shawkey
Red Faber
Dolph Luque
Carl Mays
Dazzy Vance
Urban Shocker
Burleigh Grimes
Waite Hoyt
Eddie Rommel
Firpo Marberry
Ted Lyons
Red Ruffing
Lefty Grove
Freddie Fitzsimmons
Wes Ferrell
Carl Hubbell
Larry French

Lefty Gomez
Tommy Bridges
Dizzy Dean
Paul Derringer
Thornton Lee
Bucky Walters
Bob Feller
Mort Cooper
Hal Newhouser
Dizzy Trout
Early Wynn
Harry Brecheen
Warren Spahn
Billy Pierce
Bob Lemon
Robin Roberts
Whitey Ford
Hoyt Wilhelm

Elroy Face
Sandy Koufax
Jim Bunning
Don Drysdale
Bob Gibson
Jim Kaat
Juan Marichal
Gaylord Perry
Tommy John
Luis Tiant
Phil Niekro
Catfish Hunter
Jim Palmer
Ferguson Jenkins
Steve Carlton
Nolan Ryan
Tom Seaver
Rollie Fingers
Bert Blyleven

PLAYER: CY YOUNG

	HOW MUCH HE PITCHED							WHAT HE GAVE UP									WHAT THE RESULTS WERE						
Year	G	GS	CG	GF	ShO	IP	BFP	H	R	ER	HR	HB	TBB	SO	WP	Bk	W	L	Pct.	Rest of Team	Above Team	Runs per Game	Percentage of League
1890	17	16	16		0	148		145	83	57	5	5	30	39	7	0	9	7	.563	.302	4.2	5.05	.89
1891	55	46	43		0	424		431	239	134	6		140	147	9		27	20	.574	.413	7.6	5.07	.88
1892	53	49	48		9	453		363	159	97	8		118	168	13		36	11	.766	.559	9.7	3.16	.60
1893	53	46	42		1	423		442	229	158	10		103	102	16		32	16	.667	.513	7.4	4.87	.73
1894	52	47	44		2	409		488	266	179	18		106	108			25	22	.532	.524	.4	5.85	.78
1895	47	40	36		4	370		363	176	134	10		75	121			35	10	.778	.576	9.1	4.28	.64
1896	51	46	42		5	414		477	212	149	7		62	140			29	16	.644	.614	1.3	4.61	.75
1897	46	38	35		2	335		391	195	141	7	8	49	88			21	18	.538	.522	.7	5.24	.87
1898	46	41	40		1	378		387	174	106	6	9	41	101			25	14	.641	.509	5.1	4.14	.81
1899	44	42	40		4	369		368	170	106	9	6	44	111			26	15	.634	.527	4.4	4.15	.78
1900	41	35	32		4	321		337	146	107	8	2	36	115			20	18	.526	.441	3.2	4.09	.76
1901	43	41	38		5	371		324	113	67	6		37	158			33	10	.767	.495	11.7	2.74	.51
1902	45	43	41		3	385		350	137	92	6	14	53	160			32	10	.762	.474	12.1	3.20	.65
1903	40	35	34		7	342		294	116	79	6		37	176	5		28	10	.737	.630	4.1	3.05	.74
1904	43	41	40		10	380		327	104	83	6		29	200			26	16	.619	.616	.1	2.46	.70
1905	38	34	32		5	321		248	98	65	10		30	210			18	19	.486	.522	−1.3	2.75	.75
1906	39	34	28		0	288		288	135	102	7		25	140	5	1	13	21	.382	.300	2.8	4.22	1.15
1907	43	37	33		6	343		286	101	76	7		51	147			22	15	.595	.330	9.8	2.65	.73
1908	36	33	30	3	3	299	1116	230	68	42	1		37	150	4	0	21	11	.656	.443	6.8	2.05	.59
1909	35	34	30	0	3	295	1137	267	110	74	8		59	109	6	0	19	15	.559	.437	4.1	3.36	.97
1910	21	20	14	0	1	163	622	149	62	46	3		27	58	2	0	7	10	.412	.474	−1.1	3.42	.94
1911	18	18	12	0	2	126	523	137	75	53	4		28	55	6	0	7	9	.438	.385	.8	5.36	1.19
	906	816	750		77	7357		7092	3168	2147			1217	2803			511	313	.620	.495	103.1	3.88	.78
21.75 Years	42	38	34		4	338		326	146	99			56	129									

Teams: Cleveland, N.L. 1890–1898; St. Louis, N.L. 1899–1900; Boston, 1901–1908; Cleveland, 1909–1910; Cleveland/Boston, N.L. 1911.

Points in MVP Voting: 1911, 0.

Notes: Home run totals figured by Neil Munro at the Hall of Fame library. Munro also observes that Young was charged with 146 errors in his career. No record book lists a career record for errors by a pitcher, but that figure is the highest that we know of. We suspect that some other pitcher may have more.

PLAYER: RUBE WADDELL

	HOW MUCH HE PITCHED							WHAT HE GAVE UP										WHAT THE RESULTS WERE						
Year	G	GS	CG	GF	ShO	IP	BFP	H	R	ER	HR	SH	HB	TBB	SO	WP	Bk	W	L	Pct.	Rest of Team	Above Team	Runs per Game	Percentage of League
1897	2	1	1		0	14		17	7	5	0			6	5			0	1	.000	.403	−.4	4.50	.74
1899	10	9	9		1	79		69	38	27	4			14	44			7	2	.778	.476	2.7	4.33	.81
1900	29	22	16		2	209		176	101	55	3		13	55	130			8	13	.381	.602	−4.6	4.35	.81
1901	31	30	26		0	251		249	136	84	5			75	172			13	17	.433	.385	1.4	4.88	1.05
1902	33	27	26		3	276		224	89	63	7			64	210			25	7	.781	.558	7.2	2.90	.59
1903	39	38	34		4	324		274	112	88	3			85	302			21	16	.568	.551	.6	3.11	.76
1904	46	46	39		8	383		307	111	69	5			91	349			25	18	.581	.519	2.7	2.61	.74
1905	46	34	27		7	329		231	86	54			10	90	287			26	11	.703	.595	4.0	2.35	.64
1906	43	34	22		8	273		221	89	67			10	92	196	10	1	15	16	.484	.553	−2.1	2.93	.80
1907	44	33	20		7	285		234	120	68			14	73	232			19	13	.594	.611	−.5	3.79	1.04
1908	43	36	25	5	5	286	1143	223	93	60			8	90	232	7	0	19	14	.576	.538	1.3	2.93	.85
1909	31	28	16	2	5	220	829	204	78	58			7	57	141	3	0	12	13	.480	.392	2.2	3.19	.92
1910	10	2	0		0	33	140	31	19	13			1	11	16	0	0	3	1	.750	.293	1.8	5.18	1.42
9.51 Years	407	340	261		50	2962		2460	1079	711			803		2316			193	142	.576	.528	16.2	3.28	.77
	43	36	27		5	312		259	114	75			84	244										

Teams: Louisville, N.L. 1897, 1899; Pittsburgh, 1900; Pittsburgh/Chicago, N.L. 1901; Philadelphia, A.L. 1902–1907; St. Louis, A.L. 1908–1910.

Note: The listed record for errors by an American League pitcher is 55, by Ed Walsh. According to Neil Munro, however, Walsh was charged with 79 errors in American League games, far more than the record. Walsh was charged with 89 errors in this century, possibly the "modern" (post-1900) record, and with 91 errors in his career.

PLAYER: JACK CHESBRO

	HOW MUCH HE PITCHED							WHAT HE GAVE UP									WHAT THE RESULTS WERE						
Year	G	GS	CG	GF	ShO	IP	BFP	H	R	ER	HR	HB	TBB	SO	WP	Bk	W	L	Pct.	Rest of Team	Above Team	Runs per Game	Percentage of League
1899	19	17	15		0	149		165	98	68	3	11	59	28			6	10	.375	.526	-2.4	5.92	1.11
1900	32	26	14		3	216		220	125	88	4	11	79	56			14	13	.519	.580	-1.7	5.21	.97
1901	36	28	26		6	288		261	101	76	4		52	129			21	9	.700	.633	2.0	3.16	.68
1902	35	33	31		8	286		242	81	69	1	21	62	136			28	6	.824	.714	3.7	2.55	.64
1903	40	36	33		1	325		300	137	100	7		74	147			21	15	.583	.520	2.3	3.79	.93
1904	55	51	48		6	455		338	128	92	4		88	239			41	12	.774	.520	13.4	2.53	.72
1905	41	38	19		3	303		262	121	74			71	156			19	13	.594	.444	4.8	3.59	.98
1906	49	42	24		4	325		314	142	107			75	152			24	16	.600	.595	.2	3.93	1.07
1907	30	25	7		1	206		192	85	58			46	78			9	10	.474	.465	.2	3.71	1.02
1908	45	31	14	8	3	289		271	133	94			67	124			14	20	.412	.308	3.5	4.14	1.20
1909	10	5	2		0	56	242	77	51	38		3	17	20	0	0	0	4	.000	.510	-2.0	8.20	2.37
9.20 Years	392	332	233		35	2898		2642	1202	864			690	1265			197	128	.606	.532	23.9	3.73	.92
	43	36	25		4	315		287	131	94			75	137			22	14	.606	.532	2.5	3.73	.92

Teams: Pittsburgh, N.L., 1899–1902; New York, A.L., 1903–1909.

PLAYER: JOE McGINNITY

	HOW MUCH HE PITCHED						WHAT HE GAVE UP										WHAT THE RESULTS WERE						
Year	G	GS	CG	ShO	IP	BFP	H	R	ER	HR	SH	HB	TBB	SO	WP	Bk	W	L	Pct.	Rest of Team	Above Team	Runs per Game	Percentage of League
1899	48	41	38	4	366		358	168	105	3		28	93	74			28	17	.622	.563	2.7	4.13	.77
1900	44	37	32	1	343		350	184	111	5		41	113	93			29	9	.763	.541	8.4	4.83	.90
1901	48	43	39	1	382		412	219	151	6			96	75			26	21	.553	.488	3.0	5.16	1.12
1902	44	39	35	1	352		341	149	111	4			78	106			21	18	.538	.286	9.9	3.81	.90
1903	55	48	44	3	434	1807	391	162	117				109	171			31	20	.608	.602	.3	3.36	.70
1904	51	44	38	0	408		307	103	73				86	144			35	8	.814	.645	7.2	2.27	.58
1905	46	38	26	2	320		289	131	102			14	71	125	3		21	15	.583	.718	−4.8	3.68	.90
1906	45	37	32	3	340		316	127	85			7	71	105	0		27	12	.692	.611	3.2	3.36	.94
1907	47	34	23	3	310		320	126	109			15	58	120	3		18	18	.500	.547	−1.7	3.66	1.08
1908	37	20	7	5	186		192	73	47			7	37	55	3		11	7	.611	.640	−0.5	3.53	1.06
	465	381	314	23	3441		3276	1442	1011				812	1068			247	145	.630	.560	27.7	3.77	.89
10.79 Years	43	35	29	2	319		304	134	94				75	99			23	13	.630	.560	2.6	3.77	.89

Teams: Baltimore, N.L. 1899; Brooklyn, 1900; Baltimore, A.L. 1901; Baltimore, A.L. New York, N.L. 1902; New York, N.L. 1903–1908.

PLAYER: CHRISTY MATHEWSON

	HOW MUCH HE PITCHED						WHAT HE GAVE UP										WHAT THE RESULTS WERE						
Year	G	GS	CG	ShO	IP	BFP	H	R	ER	HR	SH	HB	TBB	SO	WP	Bk	W	L	Pct.	Rest of Team	Above Team	Runs per Game	Percentage of League
1900	5	1	1	0	30	133	35	32	18	1		3	14	15	1	0	0	3	.000	.444	−1.3	9.60	1.79
1901	40	38	36	5	336	1259	288	131	90	3		12	97	221	23	1	20	17	.541	.320	8.2	3.51	.76
1902	34	32	29	8	277	1038	241	114	65	3		9	73	159	14	1	14	17	.452	.324	4.0	3.70	.93
1903	45	42	37	3	366	1392	321	136	92	4		10	100	267	18	0	30	13	.698	.563	5.8	3.34	.70
1904	48	46	33	4	368	1384	306	120	83	7		4	78	212	10	1	33	12	.733	.676	2.6	2.93	.75
1905	43	37	32	8	339	1229	252	85	48	4		1	64	206	6	2	31	8	.795	.649	5.7	2.26	.55
1906	38	35	22	5	267	1012	262	100	88	3		3	77	128	4	0	22	12	.647	.627	.7	3.37	.94
1907	41	36	31	8	315	1180	250	88	70	6		2	53	178	5	0	24	13	.649	.500	5.5	2.51	.74
1908	56	44	34	11	391	1424	285	85	62	5		3	42	259	2	0	37	11	.771	.575	9.4	1.96	.59
1909	37	33	26	8	275	962	192	57	35	2		0	36	149	4	0	25	6	.806	.549	8.0	1.87	.51
1910	38	35	27	1	318	1242	292	98	67	5		3	60	184	8	0	27	9	.750	.542	7.5	2.77	.69
1911	45	37	29	5	307	1208	303	102	68	5		1	38	141	2	0	26	13	.667	.640	1.0	2.99	.68
1912	43	34	27	0	310	1236	311	107	73	6		2	34	134	3	0	23	12	.657	.690	−1.1	3.11	.67
1913	40	35	25	4	306	1195	291	93	70	8		0	21	93	3	0	25	11	.694	.655	1.4	2.74	.66
1914	41	35	29	5	312	1251	314	133	104	16		2	23	80	7	0	24	13	.649	.513	5.0	3.84	1.00
1915	27	24	11	1	186	768	199	97	74	9		1	20	57	1	0	8	14	.364	.469	−2.3	4.69	1.30
1916	13	7	5	1	75	299	74	35	25	4	7	0	8	19	1	0	4	4	.500	.549	−.4	4.20	1.22
	634	551	434	77	4778	18212	4216	1613	1132	91		56	838	2502	112	5	373	188	.665	.559	59.5	3.04	.75
15.02 Years	42	37	29	5	318		281	107	75			4	56	167	7		25	13	.665	.559	4.0	3.04	.75

Teams: New York, N.L., 1900–1915; New York, N.L./Cincinnati, 1916.
Points in MVP Voting: 1911, 25 (2nd, .39); 1913, 21 (3rd, .33); 1914, 4, (.06). TOTAL: .78 Award Shares.
Reported Salaries: 1899—in minors, $80 a month.

PLAYER: EDDIE PLANK

	HOW MUCH HE PITCHED							WHAT HE GAVE UP								WHAT THE RESULTS WERE						
Year	G	GS	CG	GF	ShO	IP	BFP	H	R	ER	HB	TBB	SO	WP	Bk	W	L	Pct.	Rest of Team	Above Team	Runs per Game	Percentage of League
1901	33	32	28		1	261	972	254	121	96	3	68	90	13		17	11	.607	.528	2.2	4.17	.78
1902	36	32	31		1	300	1039	319	139	110	14	61	107	4		20	15	.571	.624	−1.8	4.17	.85
1903	43	40	33		3	336	1291	317	139	89	23	65	176	8		23	16	.590	.542	1.9	3.72	.91
1904	43	43	37		7	357	1419	309	112	85	10	86	201	6		26	17	.605	.509	4.1	2.82	.80
1905	41	41	35		4	347	1268	287	111	87	22	75	210	5		26	12	.684	.600	3.2	2.88	.78
1906	26	25	21		5	212	845	173	53	53	15	51	108	2	0	19	6	.760	.492	6.7	2.25	.61
1907	43	40	33		8	344	1311	282	114	84	15	85	183	6		24	16	.600	.610	−.4	2.98	.82
1908	34	28	21	1	4	245	956	202	71	59	9	46	135	7	0	14	16	.467	.439	.8	2.61	.76
1909	34	33	24	0	3	275	1028	215	74	52	8	62	132	4	1	19	10	.655	.613	1.2	2.42	.70
1910	38	32	22	5	1	250	982	218	89	56	8	56	123	5	0	16	10	.615	.694	−2.0	3.20	.88
1911	40	30	24	5	6	257	1020	237	85	60	14	77	149	5	0	22	8	.733	.653	2.4	2.98	.65
1912	37	30	24	6	3	260	1044	234	90	64	6	83	110	5	1	26	6	.813	.533	8.9	3.12	.70
1913	41	29	18		7	243	963	211	87	70	6	57	151	4	0	18	10	.643	.624	.5	3.22	.82
1914	34	22	11		4	185	717	178	68	59	6	42	110	4	0	15	7	.682	.646	.8	3.31	.91
1915	42	31	23		6	268	1031	212	75	62	2	54	147	4		21	11	.656	.541	3.7	2.52	.70
1916	37	26	17		3	236	930	203	78	61	6	67	88	2	0	16	15	.516	.512	.1	2.97	.81
1917	20	13	8		1	131	506	105	39	26	2	38	26	1	0	5	6	.455	.364	1.0	2.68	.73
	622	527	410		67	4507	17322	3956	1545	1173	169	1072	2246	85		327	192	.630	.566	33.4	3.09	.78
14.60 Years	43	36	28		5	309		271	106	80	12	73	154	6		22	13	.630	.566	2.3	3.09	.78

Teams: Philadelphia, A.L. 1901–1914; St. Louis, F.L. 1915; St. Louis, A.L. 1916–1917.
Points in MVP Voting: 1911, 0; 1913, 0; 1914, 5 (.08).
Reported Salaries: 1901—$1,000; 1914—$5,000.
Note: Neil Munro has pointed out that there is probably an error in Plank's earned run data in 1906. Both figures are shown as 53, but it would have been nearly impossible for a pitcher in that era to have worked 212 innings without allowing an unearned run. Plank's team committed 267 errors that year. If 18 of the 53 runs were in fact unearned (that is, if the correct figure were 35, rather than 53) then Plank would be the ERA leader for the 1906 season, at 1.42.

PLAYER: ADDIE JOSS

	HOW MUCH HE PITCHED							WHAT HE GAVE UP								WHAT THE RESULTS WERE						
Year	G	GS	CG	GF	ShO	IP	BFP	H	R	ER	HB	TBB	SO	WP	BK	W	L	Pct.	Rest of Team	Above Team	Runs per Game	Percentage of League
1902	32	29	28		5	269		225	120	83		75	106			17	13	.567	.491	2.3	4.01	.82
1903	33	32	32		3	293		239	105	70		43	126	5		19	13	.594	.537	1.8	3.23	.79
1904	25	24	20		5	192		160	50	34		30	83			14	9	.609	.563	1.1	2.34	.66
1905	33	32	31		3	286		246	90	64	12	46	132			20	12	.625	.459	5.3	2.83	.77
1906	34	31	28		9	282		220	81	54	3	43	106	2	0	21	9	.700	.553	4.4	2.59	.70
1907	42	38	34		6	339		279	101	69	7	54	127			27	10	.730	.504	8.3	2.68	.73
1908	42	35	29	4	9	325	1209	232	77	42	2	30	130	6	0	24	12	.667	.559	3.9	2.13	.62
1909	33	28	24	4	4	243	912	198	71	46	4	31	67	3	0	13	14	.481	.460	.6	2.63	.76
1910	13	12	9	0	1	107	412	96	35	27	2	18	49	0	0	5	5	.500	.465	.4	2.94	.81
6.92 Years	287	261	235		45	2336		1895	730	489		370	926			160	97	.623	.514	28.0	2.81	.74
	42	38	34		7	338		274	106	71		54	134			23	14	.623	.514	4.1	2.81	.74

Teams: Cleveland, 1902–1910.

PLAYER: THREE FINGER BROWN

	HOW MUCH HE PITCHED							WHAT HE GAVE UP									WHAT THE RESULTS WERE						
Year	G	GS	CG	GF	ShO	IP	BFP	H	R	ER	SH	HB	TBB	SO	WP	Bk	W	L	Pct.	Rest of Team	Above Team	Runs per Game	Percentage of League
1903	26	24	19		1	201		231	105	58			59	83			9	13	.409	.296	2.5	4.70	.99
1904	26	23	21		4	212		155	74	44			50	81			15	10	.600	.609	−.2	3.14	.80
1905	30	24	24		4	249	930	219	89	60		1	44	89	2		18	12	.600	.602	−.0	3.22	.78
1906	36	32	27		9	277		198	56	32		4	61	144	2		26	6	.813	.750	2.0	1.82	.51
1907	34	27	20		6	233		180	51	36		6	40	107	4		20	6	.769	.690	2.0	1.97	.58
1908	44	31	27		9	312		214	64	51		5	49	123	6		29	9	.763	.603	6.1	1.85	.56
1909	50	34	32		8	343		246	78	50		7	53	172	9		27	9	.750	.658	3.3	2.05	.56
1910	46	31	27		7	295	1170	256	95	61		4	64	143	6	0	25	14	.641	.687	−1.8	2.90	.72
1911	53	27	21		0	270	1082	267	110	85		6	55	129	5		21	11	.656	.582	2.4	3.67	.83
1912	15	8	5		2	89	366	92	35	26		1	20	34	0		5	6	.455	.619	−1.8	3.54	.77
1913	39	16	11		1	176	702	174	79	56		1	44	41	1		11	12	.478	.408	1.6	4.04	.97
1914	35	26	18	8	2	233	968	235	106	91		3	61	113	7	1	14	11	.560	.421	3.5	4.09	1.00
1915	35	25	17		3	236		189	75	55			64	95			17	8	.680	.543	3.4	2.86	.74
1916	12	4	2		0	48	203	52	27	21	10	4	9	21	2	0	2	3	.400	.392	0.0	5.06	1.47
	481	332	271	56	56	3174		2708	1044	726			673	1375			239	130	.648	.585	23.0	2.96	.75
10.54 Years	46	32	26	5	5	301		257	99	69			64	131			23	12	.648	.585	2.2	2.96	.75

Teams: St. Louis, 1903; Chicago, N.L. 1904–1912; Cincinnati, 1913; St. Louis, F.L./Brooklyn, F.L., 1914; Chicago, F.L. 1915; Chicago, N.L. 1916.
Points in MVP Voting: 1911, 4 (.06); 1913, 1 (.02); 1914, 0.
Reported Salaries: 1903—$2,400.

PLAYER: CHIEF BENDER

	HOW MUCH HE PITCHED							WHAT HE GAVE UP									WHAT THE RESULTS WERE						
Year	G	GS	CG	GF	ShO	IP	BFP	H	R	ER	SH	HB	TBB	SO	WP	Bk	W	L	Pct.	Rest of Team	Above Team	Runs per Game	Percentage of League
1903	36	33	30		2	270		239	116	92			65	127			17	15	.531	.563	−1.0	3.87	.94
1904	29	20	18		4	204		167	66	65			59	149			10	11	.476	.546	−1.5	2.91	.82
1905	35	23	19		4	240		193	105	72			90	142			16	11	.593	.628	−1.0	3.94	1.07
1906	36	27	24		0	238		208	96	67			48	159			15	10	.600	.525	1.9	3.63	.99
1907	33	24	20		4	219		185	72	50			34	112			16	8	.667	.595	1.7	2.96	.81
1908	18	17	15	1	2	139		121	48	27			21	85			8	9	.471	.441	.5	3.11	.90
1909	34	29	24	5	5	250	968	196	68	46		5	45	161	5	1	18	8	.692	.606	2.2	2.45	.71
1910	30	28	25	1	3	250	936	182	63	44		10	47	155	7	0	23	5	.821	.648	4.9	2.27	.62
1911	31	24	16	3	3	216	846	198	66	52		4	58	114	4	0	17	5	.773	.651	2.7	2.75	.60
1912	27	19	12	6	1	171	675	169	63	52		1	33	90	2	0	13	8	.619	.588	.7	3.32	.75
1913	48	22	16		2	237	970	208	78	58		3	59	135	7	0	21	10	.677	.615	1.9	2.96	.76
1914	28	23	15		7	179	718	159	49	45		1	55	107	3	0	17	3	.850	.621	4.6	2.46	.67
1915	26	23	15		0	178		198	101	85			37	89			4	16	.200	.321	−2.4	5.11	1.33
1916	27	13	4		0	123	539	137	71	51	17	10	34	43	5		7	7	.500	.604	−1.5	5.20	1.51
1917	20	10	8		4	113	469	84	24	21		7	26	43	3		8	2	.800	.556	2.4	1.91	.54
1925	1	0	0	1	0	1	5	1	2	2	1	0	1	0	0	0	0	0	.000	.513	.0	18.00	3.47
	459	335	261		41	3028		2645	1088	829			712	1711			210	128	.621	.573	16.2	3.23	.84
10.24 Years	45	33	26		4	296		258	106	81			70	167			21	13	.621	.573	1.6	3.23	.84

Teams: Philadelphia, A.L. 1903–1914; Baltimore, F.L. 1915; Philadelphia, N.L. 1916–1917; Chicago, A.L. 1925.
Points in MVP Voting: 1911, 0; 1913, 2 (.03); 1914, 0.

PLAYER: ED WALSH

	HOW MUCH HE PITCHED							WHAT HE GAVE UP								WHAT THE RESULTS WERE						
Year	G	GS	CG	GF	ShO	IP	BFP	H	R	ER	HB	TBB	SO	WP	Bk	W	L	Pct.	Rest of Team	Above Team	Runs per Game	Percentage of League
1904	18	8	6		1	111		90	37	32		32	57			6	3	.667	.572	.8	3.00	.85
1905	22	13	9		1	137		121	56	33		29	71			8	3	.727	.596	1.4	3.68	1.00
1906	41	31	24		10	278		215	90	58	4	58	171	11		17	13	.567	.628	−1.8	2.91	.79
1907	56	46	37		5	422		341	123	75	7	87	206			24	18	.571	.578	−.3	2.62	.72
1908	66	49	42	9	11	464	1755	343	111	73	9	56	269	10	2	40	15	.727	.495	12.8	2.15	.63
1909	31	28	20	2	8	230	817	166	52	36	4	50	127	4	3	15	11	.577	.500	2.0	2.03	.59
1910	45	36	33	5	7	370	1359	242	90	52	4	61	258	6	2	18	20	.474	.435	1.5	2.19	.60
1911	56	37	33	6	5	369	1449	327	125	91	7	72	255	8	1	27	18	.600	.472	5.8	3.05	.66
1912	62	41	32	18	6	393	1533	332	125	94	2	94	254	10	5	27	17	.614	.464	6.6	2.86	.64
1913	16	14	7	2	1	98	418	91	37	28	4	39	34	7	0	8	3	.727	.496	2.5	3.40	.87
1914	8	5	3	1	1	45	177	33	19	14	1	20	15	1	0	2	3	.400	.456	−.3	3.80	1.04
1915	3	3	3	0	1	27	101	19	4	4	0	7	12	0	0	3	0	1.000	.596	1.2	1.33	.34
1916	2	1	0	1	0	3	17	4	3	1	0	3	3	0	0	0	1	.000	.582	−.6	9.00	2.45
1917	4	3	1	1	0	18	82	22	9	7	1	9	4	1	1	0	1	.000	.474	−.5	4.50	1.28
9.60 Years	430	315	250		57	2965		2346	881	598	50	617	1736	57		195	126	.607	.510	31.2	2.67	.71
	45	33	26		6	309		244	92	62		64	181			20	13	.607	.510	3.3	2.67	.71

Teams: Chicago, A.L., 1904–1916; Boston, N.L., 1917.
Points in MVP Voting: 1911, 35 (2nd, .55); 1913, 0; 1914, 0.
Reported Salaries: 1904, $1,800; 1905, $1,800; 1906, $1,800; 1908, $7,000 ($3,500 contract plus $3,500 given him after season when he won 40 games).
Note: Walsh faced 1,755 plus batters in 1908, 1,755 plus those who had sacrifice hits, the total of which we do not know. This is an American League record, though the record is not listed.

PLAYER: ED REULBACH

	HOW MUCH HE PITCHED						WHAT HE GAVE UP									WHAT THE RESULTS WERE						
Year	G	GS	CG	ShO	IP	BFP	H	R	ER	SH	HB	TBB	SO	WP	Bk	W	L	Pct.	Rest of Team	Above Team	Runs per Game	Percentage of League
1905	34	29	28	5	292		208	71	46		18	73	152	5		18	13	.581	.607	−.8	2.19	.53
1906	33	24	20	6	218		129	51	40		13	92	94	3		20	4	.833	.750	2.0	2.11	.59
1907	27	22	16	4	192		147	48	36		9	64	96	2		17	4	.810	.687	2.6	2.25	.66
1908	46	35	25	7	298		227	81	67		12	106	133	5		24	7	.774	.610	5.1	2.45	.74
1909	35	32	23	6	263		194	69	52		11	82	105	4		19	9	.679	.680	−.0	2.36	.65
1910	24	23	13	1	173	703	161	76	60		9	49	55	4		14	8	.636	.682	−1.0	3.95	.98
1911	33	29	15	2	222	916	191	97	73		4	103	79	4		16	9	.640	.589	1.3	3.93	.89
1912	39	19	8	0	169	708	161	86	71		8	60	75	1		11	6	.647	.602	.8	4.58	.99
1913	25	14	9	2	149	610	118	61	44		5	55	56	3		8	9	.471	.470	.0	3.68	.89
1914	44	29	14	3	256	1066	228	108	75		10	83	119	6		11	18	.379	.512	−3.8	3.80	.99
1915	33	30	23	4	270		233	89	67			69	117			20	10	.667	.492	5.2	2.97	.76
1916	21	11	6	0	109	450	99	38	30	11	4	41	47	4		7	6	.538	.590	−.7	3.14	.91
1917	5	2	0	0	22		21	7	7			15	9			0	1	.000	.474	−.5	2.86	.82
8.98 Years	399	299	200	40	2633		2117	882	668	103		892	1137	41		185	104	.640	.605	10.1	3.01	.79
	44	33	22	4	293		236	98	74			99	127			21	12	.640	.605	1.1	3.01	.79

Teams: Chicago, N.L. 1905–1912; Chicago/Brooklyn, 1913; Brooklyn, 1914; Newark, F.L. 1915; Boston, N.L. 1916–1917.
Points in MVP Voting: 1911, 0; 1913, 0; 1914, 0.

PLAYER: EDDIE CICOTTE

	HOW MUCH HE PITCHED							WHAT HE GAVE UP									WHAT THE RESULTS WERE						
Year	G	GS	CG	GF	ShO	IP	BFP	H	R	ER	SH	HB	TBB	SO	WP	Bk	W	L	Pct.	Rest of Team	Above Team	Runs per Game	Percentage of League
1905	3	1	1		0	18		25	8	7			5	6			1	1	.500	.517	−0.0	4.00	1.09
1908	39	24	17	10	2	207		198	73	56			59	95			11	12	.478	.489	−0.2	3.17	.91
1909	27	15	10	4	1	160	596	117	58	35	1		56	82	3	0	13	5	.722	.564	2.8	3.27	.94
1910	36	30	20	3	4	250	1012	213	94	76		13	86	104	8	0	15	11	.577	.520	1.5	3.38	.91
1911	35	25	16	3	1	221	910	236	118	69		4	73	106	4	0	11	15	.423	.528	−2.7	4.81	1.05
1912	29	24	15	4	1	198	810	217	97	77	4		52	90	5	1	10	10	.500	.549	−1.0	4.41	.99
1913	41	30	18		3	268	1053	224	77	47	2		73	121	5	0	18	12	.600	.492	3.2	2.59	.66
1914	45	29	15		4	269	1023	220	96	61	3		72	122	6	0	11	16	.407	.465	−1.5	3.21	.86
1915	39	26	15		1	223	881	216	89	75	6		48	106	4	2	13	12	.520	.620	−2.5	3.59	.90
1916	44	19	11		2	187	705	138	56	37	1		70	91	2	0	15	7	.682	.561	2.7	2.70	.72
1917	49	35	29		7	347	1288	246	76	59	3		70	150	1	2	28	12	.700	.632	2.7	1.97	.54
1918	38	30	24		1	266	1023	275	98	78	2		40	104	2	0	12	19	.387	.484	−3.0	3.32	.90
1919	40	35	30		5	307	1176	256	77	62	2		49	110	1	0	29	7	.806	.567	8.6	2.26	.55
1920	37	35	28	2	4	303	1236	316	128	109	2		74	87	3	0	21	10	.677	.610	2.1	3.80	.80
11.11 Years	502	358	249	26	36	3224	11713	2897	1145	848	43		827	1374	44	5	208	149	.583	.547	12.6	3.20	.80
	45	32	22		3	290		261	103	76			74	124			19	13	.583	.547	1.1	3.20	.80

Teams: Detroit, 1905; Boston Red Sox, 1908–1912; White Sox, 1912–1920. Also played for Beelzebub, 1919. Cicotte was a teammate of Ty Cobb at Augusta in 1905.
Points in MVP Voting: 1911, 0; 1913, 0; 1914, 1 (.02).

PLAYER: WALTER JOHNSON

	HOW MUCH HE PITCHED							WHAT HE GAVE UP										WHAT THE RESULTS WERE						
Year	G	GS	CG	GF	ShO	IP	BFP	H	R	ER	HR	SH	HB	TBB	SO	WP	Bk	W	L	Pct.	Rest of Team	Above Team	Runs per Game	Percentage of League
1907	14	12	11	2	2	111	424	98	35	23	1		3	17	70	4	0	5	9	.357	.321	.5	2.84	.82
1908	36	29	23	5	6	257	985	194	75	47	0		11	53	160	13	1	14	14	.500	.427	2.0	2.63	.76
1909	40	36	27	4	4	297	1219	247	112	73	1		15	84	164	12	0	13	25	.342	.254	3.3	3.39	.93
1910	45	42	38	3	8	373	1367	269	92	56	1		13	76	313	21	0	25	17	.595	.376	9.2	2.22	.48
1911	40	37	36	3	6	323	1306	292	119	68	8		8	70	207	17	0	25	13	.658	.336	12.2	3.32	.75
1912	50	37	34	9	7	368	1413	259	89	57	2		16	76	303	11	0	32	12	.727	.546	8.0	2.18	.55
1913	47	36	30	10	12	346	1289	230	56	44	9		9	38	243	3	0	36	7	.837	.486	15.1	1.46	.40
1914	51	40	33	10	10	372	1406	287	88	71	3		11	74	225	14	1	28	18	.609	.491	5.4	2.13	.54
1915	47	39	35	7	8	337	1280	258	83	58	1		19	56	203	7	0	27	13	.675	.513	6.5	2.22	.60
1916	48	38	36	10	3	371	1460	290	105	78	0		9	82	228	9	0	25	20	.556	.472	3.8	2.55	.70
1917	47	34	30	12	8	328	1253	259	105	83	3		14	67	188	8	0	23	16	.590	.447	5.6	2.88	.79
1918	39	29	29	10	8	325	1261	241	71	46	2	34	8	70	162	8	0	23	13	.639	.533	3.8	1.97	.48
1919	39	29	27	10	7	290	1124	235	73	48	0		7	51	147	4	1	20	14	.588	.340	8.5	2.27	.48
1920	21	15	12	6	4	144	584	135	68	50	5		5	27	78	5	1	8	10	.444	.448	−.1	4.25	.83
1921	35	32	25	2	1	264	1119	265	122	103	7	18	2	92	143	7	0	17	14	.548	.516	1.0	4.16	.88
1922	41	31	23	9	4	280	1177	283	115	93	8	29	7	99	105	3	0	15	16	.484	.439	1.4	3.70	.77
1923	43	35	18	8	3	262	1098	267	112	101	9	27	20	69	130	2	0	17	12	.586	.468	3.4	3.85	.78
1924	38	38	20	0	6	278	1154	233	97	84	10	20	10	77	158	4	0	23	7	.767	.556	6.3	3.14	.60
1925	30	29	16	1	3	229	967	211	95	78	7	15	7	78	108	1	0	20	7	.741	.613	3.5	3.73	.79
1926	33	33	22	0	2	262	1101	259	120	105	13	37	5	73	125	2	0	15	16	.484	.555	−2.2	4.12	.84
1927	18	15	7	2	1	108	460	113	70	61	7	20	7	26	48	1	0	5	6	.455	.559	−1.2	5.83	1.22
	802	666	532	123	113	5925	23413	4925	1902	1427	97		206	1355	3508	156	4	416	279	.599	.460	96.0	2.89	.67
18.69 Years	43	36	28		6	317		264	102	76			11	72	188		0	22	15	.599	.460	5.1	2.89	.67

Teams: Washington, A.L. 1907–1927.

Points in MVP Voting: 1911, 19 (5th, .30); 1913, 54 (1st, .84); 1922, 5 (.08); 1923, 0; 1924, 55 (1st, .86); 1925, 0. TOTAL: 2.08 Award Shares.

Reported Salaries: 1907—$1,050; 1908—$2,700; 1914—$10,000; 1915—$12,500.

Other Notes: Named to *The Sporting News* major league All-Star team in 1925.

Opposition Stolen Bases: 1920, 11; 1921, 19; 1922, 11; 1923, 9; 1924, 10. TOTAL: 60/1228 innings, 0.44 per nine innings.

Note: 21 Wild Pitches in 1910 are 7 more than #2 man in league.

PLAYER: HIPPO VAUGHN

	HOW MUCH HE PITCHED							WHAT HE GAVE UP									WHAT THE RESULTS WERE						
Year	G	GS	CG	GF	ShO	IP	BFP	H	R	ER	SH	HB	TBB	SO	WP	Bk	W	L	Pct.	Rest of Team	Above Team	Runs per Game	Percentage of League
1908	2	0	0		0	2		1	1	1			4	2			0	0	.000	.331	.0	4.50	1.31
1910	29	25	18	1	5	222	869	190	76	45		10	58	107	7	0	12	11	.522	.594	−1.7	3.08	.85
1911	26	18	11	3	0	146	618	158	92	71		7	54	74	4	1	8	11	.421	.511	−1.7	5.67	1.23
1912	27	18	10	7	0	144	631	141	81	62		5	80	95	11	0	6	11	.353	.452	−1.7	5.06	1.14
1913	7	6	5		2	56		37	13	9			27	36			5	1	.833	.565	1.6	2.09	.50
1914	42	35	23		4	294	1209	236	119	67		8	109	165	13		21	13	.618	.475	4.9	3.64	.95
1915	41	34	18		4	270	1121	240	105	86		11	77	148	5		19	12	.613	.443	5.3	3.50	.97
1916	44	35	21		4	294	1191	269	94	72	41	7	67	144	6		17	14	.548	.410	4.3	2.88	.83
1917	41	39	27		5	296	1216	255	97	66	31	9	91	195	2		23	13	.639	.432	7.4	2.95	.84
1918	35	33	27		8	290	1146	216	75	56	24	7	76	148	4		22	10	.688	.639	1.5	2.33	.64
1919	38	37	25	1	4	307	1224	264	83	61	29	6	62	141	5	0	21	14	.600	.514	3.0	2.43	.67
1920	40	38	24	2	4	301	1255	301	113	85	28	8	81	131	3	1	19	16	.543	.471	2.5	3.38	.85
1921	17	14	7	2	0	109	500	153	90	73	15	5	31	30	1	1	3	11	.214	.439	−3.1	7.43	1.62
9.16 Years	389	332	216		40	2731		2461	1039	754		75	817	1416			176	137	.562	.491	22.4	3.42	.88
	42	36	24		4	298		269	113	82		8	89	155			19	15	.562	.491	2.4	3.42	.88

Teams: New York, A.L., 1908, 1910–1911; New York/Washington, 1912; Chicago, N.L., 1913–1921.
Points in MVP Voting: 1911, 0; 1913, 0; 1914, 0.

PLAYER: RUBE MARQUARD

	HOW MUCH HE PITCHED								WHAT HE GAVE UP										WHAT THE RESULTS WERE						
Year	G	GS	CG	GF	ShO	IP	BFP		H	R	ER	SH	HB	TBB	SO	WP	BK		W	L	Pct.	Rest of Team	Above Team	Runs per Game	Percentage of League
1908	1	1	0		0	5			6	5	2			2	2				0	1	.000	.641	−.6	9.00	2.71
1909	29	22	8		0	173			155	81	50		9	73	109	8			5	13	.278	.644	−6.6	4.21	1.16
1910	13	8	2		0	71			65	35	35			40	52				4	4	.500	.596	−.8	4.44	1.10
1911	45	33	22		5	278	1117		221	98	77		4	106	237	10			24	7	.774	.615	4.9	3.17	.72
1912	43	38	22		1	295	1230		286	112	84		3	80	175	8			26	11	.703	.675	1.0	3.42	.74
1913	42	33	20		4	288	1122		248	100	80		3	49	151	3			23	10	.697	.655	1.4	3.13	.75
1914	39	33	15		4	268	1086		261	117	91		2	47	92	12			12	22	.353	.600	−8.4	3.93	1.02
1915	33	23	10		2	194	813		207	102	87		1	38	92	6			11	10	.524	.458	1.4	4.73	1.31
1916	36	20	15		2	205	793		169	54	36	18	0	38	107	3			13	6	.684	.600	1.6	2.37	.69
1917	37	29	14		2	233	942		200	84	66	19	0	60	117	4			19	12	.613	.425	5.8	3.24	.92
1918	34	29	19	0	4	239	980		231	97	70	32	1	59	89	3	0		9	18	.333	.485	−4.1	3.65	1.01
1919	8	7	3	0	0	59	238		54	17	15	7	0	10	29	3	0		3	3	.500	.493	−.0	2.59	.71
1920	28	26	10	1	1	190	779		181	83	68	22	1	35	89	5			10	7	.588	.606	−.3	3.93	.99
1921	39	35	18	1	2	266	1116		291	123	100	37	7	50	88	5	1		17	14	.548	.434	3.5	4.16	.91
1922	39	24	7	10	0	198	884		255	131	112	26	0	66	57	3	1		11	15	.423	.331	2.4	5.95	1.19
1923	38	29	11	6	3	239	1015		265	127	99	29	2	65	78	1	0		11	14	.440	.333	2.7	4.78	.99
1924	6	6	1	0	0	36	150		33	17	12	6	1	13	10	1	0		1	2	.333	.347	−.0	4.25	.94
1925	26	8	0	0	0	72	347		105	60	46	12	0	27	19	1	0		2	8	.200	.476	−2.8	7.50	1.48
	536	404	197		30	3309			3233	1443	1130		34	858	1593	76			201	177	.532	.529	1.2	3.92	.96
12.08 Years	44	33	16		2	274			268	119	94			71	132				17	15	.532	.529	.1	3.92	.96

Teams: New York, N.L., 1908–1914; New York/Brooklyn, 1915; Brooklyn, 1916–1920; Cincinnati, 1921; Boston, N.L., 1922–1925.

Points in MVP Voting: 1911, 19 (7th, .30); 1913, 0; 1914, 0; 1925, 0.

PLAYER: GROVER CLEVELAND (PETE) ALEXANDER

	HOW MUCH HE PITCHED							WHAT HE GAVE UP									WHAT THE RESULTS WERE						
Year	G	GS	CG	GF	ShO	IP	BFP	H	R	ER	SH	HB	TBB	SO	WP	BK	W	L	Pct.	Rest of Team	Above Team	Runs per Game	Percentage of League
1911	48	37	31	9	7	367	1440	285	133	105		8	129	227	4	1	28	13	.683	.504	7.3	3.26	.74
1912	46	34	26	9	3	310	1290	289	133	97		6	105	195	5	0	19	17	.528	.466	2.2	3.86	.84
1913	47	35	23	9	9	306	1234	288	106	96		3	75	159	3	0	22	8	.733	.545	5.6	3.12	.75
1914	46	39	32	6	6	355	1459	327	133	94		11	76	214	1	0	27	15	.643	.420	9.4	3.37	.88
1915	49	42	36	6	12	376	1435	253	86	51	35	10	64	241	2	0	31	10	.756	.532	9.2	2.06	.57
1916	48	45	38	3	16	389	1500	323	90	67	37	10	50	167	3	0	33	12	.733	.537	8.8	2.08	.60
1917	45	44	35	1	8	388	1531	336	107	79	32	6	58	201	2	0	30	13	.698	.523	7.5	2.48	.70
1918	3	3	3	0	0	26	98	19	7	2	2	1	3	15	0	0	2	1	.667	.651	.0	2.42	.67
1919	30	27	20	3	9	235	906	180	51	45	16	0	38	121	1	0	16	11	.593	.522	1.9	1.95	.54
1920	46	40	33	6	7	363	1447	335	96	77	26	1	69	173	3	0	27	14	.659	.425	9.6	2.38	.60
1921	31	29	21	1	3	252	1033	286	110	95	33	1	33	77	1	0	15	13	.536	.392	4.0	3.93	.86
1922	33	31	20	2	1	246	1014	283	111	99	18	3	34	48	4	0	6	13	.552	.512	1.2	4.06	.81
1923	39	36	26	1	3	305	1246	308	128	108	25	0	30	72	2	0	22	12	.647	.508	4.7	3.78	.78
1924	21	20	12	0	0	169	708	183	82	57	10	1	25	33	1	0	12	5	.706	.507	3.4	4.37	.96
1925	32	30	20	1	1	236	977	270	106	89	9	3	29	63	1	0	15	11	.577	.414	4.2	4.04	.80
1926	30	23	15	7	2	200	815	191	83	68	17	2	31	47	0	0	12	10	.545	.568	-.5	3.74	.82
1927	37	30	22	4	2	268	1082	261	94	75	32	1	38	48	1	0	21	10	.677	.582	3.0	3.16	.69
1928	34	31	18	2	1	244	1009	262	106	91	25	2	37	59	3	0	16	9	.640	.612	.7	3.91	.83
1929	22	19	8	3	0	132	562	149	65	57	16	1	23	33	2	0	9	6	.589	.511	.3	4.43	.83
1930	9	3	0	2	0	22	109	40	24	22	2	0	6	6	0	0	0	3	.000	.344	-1.0	9.82	1.73
	696	598	439	75	90	5189	20895	4868	1851	1474		70	953	2199	39	1	373	208	.642	.502	81.6	3.21	.73
16.42 Years	42	36	27		5	316		296	113	90		4	58	134	2		23	13	.642	.502	5.0	3.21	.73

Teams: Philadelphia, N.L., 1911–1917; Chicago, N.L., 1918–1925; Chicago, N.L./St. Louis, N.L., 1926; St. Louis, N.L., 1927–1929; Philadelphia, N.L., 1930.

Points in MVP Voting: 1911, 23 (5th, .36); 1913, 0; 1914, 9 (10th, .14); 1926, 5 (.06).

Reported Salaries: 1914, $10,000; 1915, $10,000; 1918, $8,000.

Other Notes: Named to *The Sporting News* major league All-Star team in 1926.

Early Games Finished totals figured from box scores by Neil Munro.

PLAYER: WILBUR COOPER

	HOW MUCH HE PITCHED							WHAT HE GAVE UP									WHAT THE RESULTS WERE						
Year	G	GS	CG	GF	ShO	IP	BFP	H	R	ER	SH	HB	TBB	SO	WP	BK	W	L	Pct.	Rest of Team	Above Team	Runs per Game	Percentage of League
1912	6	4	3		2	38	158	32	7	7		0	15	30	1	0	3	0	1.000	.608	1.2	1.66	.36
1913	30	9	3		1	93	414	98	52	34		2	45	39	4		5	3	.625	.518	.9	5.03	1.21
1914	40	34	19		0	267	1097	246	99	63		5	79	102	4		16	15	.516	.431	2.6	3.34	.87
1915	38	21	11		1	186	778	180	92	38		9	52	71	8		5	16	.238	.511	-5.7	4.45	1.23
1916	42	23	16		2	246	984	189	72	51	28	4	74	111	3		12	11	.522	.405	2.7	2.63	.76
1917	40	34	23		7	298	1159	276	96	78	33	4	54	99	1		17	11	.607	.270	9.4	2.90	.82
1918	38	29	26		3	273	1078	219	86	64	23	10	65	117	4		19	14	.576	.500	2.5	2.84	.78
1919	35	32	27	3	4	287	1147	229	97	85	40	15	74	106	5	0	19	13	.594	.486	3.4	3.04	.83
1920	44	37	28	6	3	327	1312	307	113	87	35	11	52	114	1	0	24	15	.615	.478	5.3	3.11	.78
1921	38	38	29	0	2	327	1377	341	145	118	32	10	80	134	4	0	22	14	.611	.581	1.1	3.99	.87
1922	41	37	27	3	4	295	1251	330	130	104	31	7	61	129	4	0	23	14	.622	.530	3.4	3.97	.79
1923	39	38	26	1	1	295	1259	331	136	117	26	11	71	77	2	0	17	19	.472	.593	-4.4	4.15	.86
1924	38	35	25	3	4	269	1109	296	116	98	18	5	40	62	2	0	20	14	.588	.588	-.0	3.88	.85
1925	32	26	13	5	0	212	936	249	115	101	16	4	61	41	1	0	12	14	.462	.547	-2.2	4.88	.96
1926	16	11	3		2	69	318	92	50	44	15	3	30	20	0	0	2	5	.286	.545	-1.8	6.52	1.41
	517	408	279		36	3482	14377	3415	1406	1089		100	853	1252	44		216	178	.548	.502	18.5	3.63	.86
11.84 Years	44	34	24			294		289	119	92			72	106			19	15	.548	.502	1.7	3.63	.86

Teams: Pittsburgh, N.L. 1912–1924; Chicago, N.L. 1925; Chicago, N.L./Detroit, 1926.
Points in MVP Voting: 1913, 0; 1914, 0; 1926, 0.

PLAYER: EPPA RIXEY

	HOW MUCH HE PITCHED							WHAT HE GAVE UP									WHAT THE RESULTS WERE						
Year	G	GS	CG	GF	ShO	IP	BFP	H	R	ER	SH	HB	TBB	SO	WP	Bk	W	L	Pct.	Rest of Team	Above Team	Runs per Game	Percentage of League
1912	23	20	10		3	162	650	147	57	45		2	54	59	8		10	10	.500	.477	.5	3.17	.68
1913	35	19	9		2	156	659	148	67	54		6	56	75	3		9	5	.643	.577	.9	3.87	.93
1914	24	15	2		0	103	461	124	73	50		3	45	41	7		2	11	.154	.511	−4.6	6.38	1.66
1915	29	22	10		2	177	735	163	67	47		2	64	88	8		11	12	.478	.612	−3.1	3.41	.94
1916	38	33	20		3	287	1155	239	91	59	29	7	74	134	13		22	10	.688	.570	3.8	2.85	.83
1917	39	36	23		4	281	1140	249	102	71	35	5	67	121	6		16	21	.432	.617	−6.8	3.27	.93
1919	23	18	11	4	1	154	652	160	88	68	23	3	50	63	5	0	6	12	.333	.345	−.2	5.14	1.41
1920	41	33	25	4	1	284	1175	288	137	110	49	4	69	109	8	0	11	22	.333	.425	−3.0	4.34	1.09
1921	40	36	21	3	2	301	1260	324	128	93	41	5	66	76	6	0	19	18	.514	.440	2.7	3.83	.83
1922	40	38	26	2	2	313	1303	337	146	123	27	4	45	80	3	1	25	13	.658	.526	5.0	4.20	.84
1923	42	37	23	4	3	309	1294	334	124	96	34	4	65	97	6	0	20	15	.571	.597	−.9	3.61	.74
1924	35	29	15	6	4	238	966	219	86	73	27	2	47	57	3	0	15	14	.517	.548	−.9	3.25	.72
1925	39	36	22	3	2	287	1186	302	109	92	26	7	47	69	1	0	21	11	.656	.488	5.4	3.42	.68
1926	37	29	14	4	3	233	959	231	104	88	28	2	58	61	2	0	14	8	.636	.553	1.8	4.02	.88
1927	34	29	11	5	1	220	913	240	106	85	32	3	43	42	6	0	12	10	.545	.481	1.4	4.34	.95
1928	43	37	17	6	3	291	1219	317	127	111	48	3	67	58	2	0	19	18	.514	.513	.0	3.93	.84
1929	35	24	11	8	0	201	875	235	102	93	19	8	60	37	1	0	10	13	.435	.427	.2	4.57	.85
1930	32	21	5	9	0	164	735	207	103	93	29	7	47	37	2	0	9	13	.409	.379	.7	5.65	1.00
1931	22	17	4	3	0	127	542	143	71	55	21	0	30	22	3	1	4	7	.364	.378	−.2	5.03	1.12
1932	25	11	6	9	2	112	458	108	50	33	13	4	16	14	3	1	5	5	.500	.382	1.2	4.02	.87
1933	16	12	5	3	1	94	417	118	48	33	9	0	12	10	1	0	6	3	.667	.364	2.7	4.60	1.16
15.90 Years	692	552	290		39	4494	18754	4633	1986	1572	490	76	1082	1350	97	3	266	251	.515	.502	6.6	3.98	.90
	44	35	18		2	283		291	125	99		5	68	85	6		17	16	.515	.502	.4	3.98	.90

Teams: Philadelphia, 1912–1920; Cincinnati, 1921–1933.
Points in MVP Voting: 1913, 0; 1914, 0; 1924, 0; 1926, 0; 1927, 0; 1931, 0; 1932, 0; 1933, 0.

PLAYER: STAN COVELESKI

	HOW MUCH HE PITCHED							WHAT HE GAVE UP									WHAT THE RESULTS WERE						
Year	G	GS	CG	GF	ShO	IP	BFP	H	R	ER	SH	HB	TBB	SO	WP	Bk	W	L	Pct.	Rest of Team	Above Team	Runs per Game	Percentage of League
1912	5	2	2	2	1	21	83	18	9	8		1	4	9	1	0	2	1	.667	.591	.2	3.86	.87
1916	45	27	11	12	1	232	946	247	100	88		1	58	76	3	1	15	12	.556	.488	1.8	3.88	1.05
1917	45	36	25	8	9	298	1142	202	78	60		1	94	133	3	0	19	14	.576	.570	.2	2.36	.65
1918	38	33	25	5	2	311	1222	261	90	63		4	76	87	2	0	22	13	.629	.543	3.0	2.60	.71
1919	43	34	24	9	4	296	1138	286	99	83		5	60	118	5	0	23	12	.657	.587	2.5	3.01	.73
1920	41	37	26	3	3	315	1247	284	110	87		4	65	133	1	0	24	14	.632	.638	-.2	3.14	.66
1921	43	40	29	3	2	316	1360	341	137	118	54	4	84	99	5	0	23	13	.639	.602	1.3	3.90	.76
1922	35	33	21	2	3	277	1163	292	120	102	31	2	64	98	4	0	17	14	.548	.496	1.6	3.90	.82
1923	33	31	17	2	5	228	957	251	98	70	24	2	42	54	1	0	13	14	.481	.492	-.3	3.87	.81
1924	37	33	18	3	2	240	1077	286	140	108	26	4	73	58	5	0	15	16	.484	.426	1.8	5.25	1.06
1925	32	32	15	0	3	241	994	230	86	76	17	2	73	58	2	0	20	5	.800	.603	4.9	3.21	.62
1926	36	34	11	1	3	245	1066	272	122	85	34	0	81	50	3	0	14	11	.560	.536	.6	4.48	.95
1927	5	4	0	0	0	14	63	13	7	5	3	0	8	3	0	0	2	1	.667	.550	.4	4.50	.91
1928	12	8	2	2	0	58	257	72	41	37	14	0	20	5	0	0	5	1	.833	.649	1.1	6.36	1.34
10.59 Years	450	384	226	52	38	3092	12715	3055	1237	990		30	802	981	35	1	214	141	.603	.550	18.9	3.60	.79
	42	36	21	5	4	292	1201	288	117	93		3	76	93	3	0	20	13	.603	.550	1.8	3.60	.79

Teams: Philadelphia, A.L., 1912; Cleveland, A.L., 1916–1924; Washington, A.L., 1925–1927; New York, A.L., 1928.
Points in MVP Voting: 1922, 0; 1923, 0; 1924, 0; 1926, 0; 1927, 0.
Opposition Stolen Bases: 1920, 14; 1921, 19; 1922, 16; 1923, 8; 1924, 15. TOTAL: 72/1376 Innings, 0.47 per nine innings.

PLAYER: BOB SHAWKEY

	HOW MUCH HE PITCHED							WHAT HE GAVE UP									WHAT THE RESULTS WERE						
Year	G	GS	CG	GF	ShO	IP	BFP	H	R	ER	SH	HB	TBB	SO	WP	Bk	W	L	Pct.	Rest of Team	Above Team	Runs per Game	Percentage of League
1913	18	15	8	1	1	111	498	92	41	29		3	50	52	2	0	8	5	.615	.629	−.2	3.32	.85
1914	38	31	18	5	5	237	925	223	88	72		2	75	89	0	0	16	8	.667	.648	.4	3.34	.91
1915	33	22	12	7	2	186	741	181	95	76		3	73	87	3	0	10	13	.435	.349	2.0	4.60	1.16
1916	53	27	21	23	4	277	1064	204	78	68		6	81	122	2	0	23	14	.622	.487	5.0	2.53	.69
1917	32	26	16	5	2	236	930	207	81	64		6	72	97	4	0	14	15	.483	.460	.7	3.09	.85
1918	3	2	1	1	1	16	60	7	2	2	1	0	10	3	0	0	1	1	.500	.488	.0	1.13	.31
1919	41	27	22	9	3	261	1041	218	94	79		5	92	122	1	0	20	11	.645	.556	2.8	3.24	.79
1920	38	31	20	5	5	268	1104	246	88	73		1	85	126	3	0	20	13	.606	.620	−.5	2.96	.62
1921	38	31	18	6	3	245	1053	245	131	111	27	7	86	126	2	1	18	12	.600	.650	−1.5	4.81	.94
1922	39	33	19	4	3	300	1253	286	112	97	37	0	98	130	3	0	20	12	.625	.607	.6	3.36	.71
1923	36	31	17	3	1	259	1076	232	114	101	27	4	102	125	8	0	16	11	.593	.656	−1.7	3.96	.83
1924	38	25	10	9	1	208	862	226	107	95	22	3	74	114	5	0	16	11	.593	.584	.2	4.63	.93
1925	33	20	9	8	1	186	802	209	101	85	20	5	67	81	4	0	6	14	.300	.470	−3.4	4.89	.94
1926	29	10	3	14	1	104	445	102	49	42	18	2	37	63	0	0	8	7	.533	.597	−1.0	4.24	.90
1927	19	2	0	11	0	44	190	44	19	14	5	1	16	23	3	0	2	3	.400	.725	−1.6	3.89	.79
10.65 Years	488	333	194	111	33	2938	12074	2722	1200	1008		48	1018	1360	40	1	198	150	.569	.564	1.8	3.68	.84
	46	31	18		3	276		256	113	95		5	96	128	4		19	14	.569	.564	.2	3.68	.84

Teams: Philadelphia, A.L. 1913–1914; Philadelphia/New York, A.L. 1915; New York, A.L. 1916–1927.
Points in MVP Voting: 1922, 0; 1923, 0; 1924, 0; 1926, 0.
Reported Salaries: 1927—$10,500.
Opposition Stolen Bases: 1920, 6; 1921, 8; 1922, 9; 1923, 8; 1924, 9. TOTAL: 40/1280 innings, 0.28 per nine innings.

PLAYER: RED FABER

	HOW MUCH HE PITCHED							WHAT HE GAVE UP									WHAT THE RESULTS WERE					
Year	G	GS	CG	GF	ShO	IP	BFP	H	R	ER	SH	HB	TBB	SO	WP	Bk	W	L	Pct.	Rest of Team	Above Team	Runs Per Game	Percentage of League
1914	40	20	11	17	2	181	721	154	77	54		12	64	88	8	0	10	9	.526	.444	1.6	3.83	1.05
1915	50	32	22	14	3	300	1212	264	118	85		11	99	182	4	0	24	14	.632	.595	1.4	3.54	.89
1916	35	25	15	7	3	205	798	167	67	46		5	61	87	0	1	17	9	.654	.563	2.4	2.94	.80
1917	41	29	17	10	3	248	1010	224	92	53		10	85	84	1	1	16	13	.552	.672	−3.5	3.34	.91
1918	11	9	5	1	1	81	309	70	23	11		0	23	26	2	0	4	1	.800	.445	1.8	2.56	.70
1919	25	20	9	3	0	162	698	185	92	69		8	45	45	2	0	11	9	.550	.642	−1.8	5.11	1.25
1920	40	39	28	1	2	319	1298	332	136	106		4	88	108	4	0	23	13	.639	.619	.7	3.84	.81
1921	43	39	32	4	4	331	1350	293	107	91	45	7	87	124	5	0	25	15	.625	.325	12.0	2.91	.57
1922	43	38	31	5	4	353	1464	334	128	110	51	6	83	148	2	0	21	17	.553	.483	2.7	3.26	.69
1923	32	31	15	1	2	232	1000	233	114	88	33	6	62	91	5	0	14	11	.560	.426	3.3	4.42	.93
1924	21	20	9	1	0	161	717	173	78	69	24	2	58	47	4	0	9	11	.450	.429	.4	4.36	.88
1925	34	32	16	1	1	238	1009	266	117	100	26	2	59	71	0	0	12	11	.522	.511	.2	4.42	.85
1926	27	25	13	0	1	185	798	203	84	73	17	2	57	65	1	0	15	8	.652	.508	3.3	4.09	.86
1927	18	15	6	1	0	111	488	131	64	56	22	5	41	39	3	0	4	7	.364	.465	−1.1	5.19	1.05
1928	27	27	16	0	2	201	918	223	98	84	25	4	68	43	1	0	13	9	.591	.447	3.2	4.39	.92
1929	31	31	15	0	1	234	984	241	119	101	32	9	61	68	3	0	13	13	.500	.365	3.5	4.58	.91
1930	29	26	10	2	0	169	742	188	101	79	24	5	49	62	3	0	8	13	.381	.406	−.5	5.38	.99
1931	44	19	5	14	1	184	807	210	96	78	10	3	57	49	0	0	10	14	.417	.357	1.4	4.70	.91
1932	42	5	0	28	0	106	472	123	61	44	9	1	38	26	1	0	2	11	.154	.341	−2.4	5.18	.99
1933	36	2	0	24	0	86	376	92	41	33	12	1	28	18	3	0	3	4	.429	.448	−.1	4.29	.87
	669	484	275	134	30	4087	17171	4106	1813	1430		103	1213	1471	52	2	254	212	.545	.484	28.4	3.99	.86
14.88 Years	45	33	18		2	275		276	122	96		7	82	99	4		17	14	.545	.484	1.9	3.99	.86

Teams: Chicago, A.L., 1914–1933.
Points in MVP Voting: 1922, 0; 1923, 0; 1924, 0; 1926, 0; 1927, 0; 1931, 0; 1932, 0; 1933, 0.
Reported Salaries: 1914, $1,200.
Opposition Stolen Bases: 1920, 13; 1921, 17; 1922, 13; 1923, 24; 1924, 15. TOTAL: 82/1396 innings, 0.53 per nine innings.

PLAYER: DOLPH LUQUE

	HOW MUCH HE PITCHED							WHAT HE GAVE UP									WHAT THE RESULTS WERE						
Year	G	GS	CG	GF	ShO	IP	BFP	H	R	ER	SH	HB	TBB	SO	WP	Bk	W	L	Pct.	Rest of Team	Above Team	Runs per Game	Percentage of League
1914	2	1	1	0	0	9	35	15	5	4	1	0	4	1	1	0	0	1	.000	.618	-.6	5.00	1.28
1915	2	1	0	1	0	5	25	6	3	2	0	0	4	3	1	0	0	0	.000	.546	.0	5.40	1.32
1918	12	10	9	2	1	83	349	84	44	35	13	1	32	26	4	1	6	3	.667	.521	1.3	4.77	1.43
1919	30	9	6	1	2	106	429	89	35	31	16	2	36	40	0	0	10	3	.769	.677	1.2	2.97	.82
1920	37	23	10	11	1	208	825	168	65	58	13	4	60	72	2	0	13	9	.591	.527	1.4	2.81	.70
1921	41	36	25	5	3	304	1259	318	132	114	31	1	64	102	2	0	17	19	.472	.453	.7	3.91	.88
1922	39	32	18	5	0	261	1093	266	123	96	27	1	72	79	4	2	13	23	.361	.619	-9.3	4.24	.92
1923	41	37	28	4	6	322	1301	279	90	69	21	5	88	151	4	1	27	8	.771	.538	8.2	2.52	.61
1924	31	28	13	3	2	219	924	229	99	77	25	2	53	86	1	1	10	15	.400	.570	-4.3	4.07	1.06
1925	36	36	22	0	4	291	1196	263	109	85	17	2	78	140	8	0	16	18	.471	.538	-2.3	3.37	.93
1926	34	30	16	1	1	234	993	231	123	89	27	2	77	83	3	0	13	16	.448	.592	-4.2	4.73	1.37
1927	29	27	17	1	2	231	949	225	103	82	29	0	56	76	6	0	13	12	.520	.484	.9	4.01	1.14
1928	33	29	11	4	1	234	1010	254	112	93	29	2	84	72	3	0	11	10	.524	.511	.3	4.31	1.19
1929	32	22	8	4	1	176	771	213	103	88	26	2	56	43	2	0	5	16	.238	.459	-4.6	5.27	1.13
1930	31	24	16	5	2	199	849	221	107	95	22	0	58	62	5	0	14	8	.636	.545	2.0	4.84	1.22
1931	19	15	5	2	0	103	443	122	59	52	4	1	27	25	0	0	7	6	.538	.518	.3	5.16	1.12
1932	38	5	1	22	0	110	483	128	53	49	9	0	32	32	2	0	6	7	.462	.468	-.1	4.34	.87
1933	35	0	0	22	0	80	327	75	27	24	9	0	19	23	0	0	8	2	.800	.585	2.2	3.04	.63
1934	26	0	0	19	0	42	195	54	20	18	6	1	17	12	2	0	4	3	.571	.610	-.3	4.29	.94
1935	2	0	0	0	0	3	14	1	0	0	2	0	1	2	0	0	1	0	1.000	.592	.4	0	0
11.90 Years	550 46	365 31	206 17	128	26 2	3220 271	13470	3241 272	1412 119	1161 98	327	26	918 77	1130 95	50	5	194 16	179 15	.520 .520	.538 .538	-6.8 -.6	3.95 3.95	.95 .95

Teams: Boston, N.L. 1914–1915; Cincinnati, 1918–1929; Brooklyn, N.L. 1930–1931; New York, N.L. 1932–1935.
Points in MVP Voting: 1926, 0; 1927, 0; 1931, 0; 1932, 0; 1933, 1 (.01).
Reported Salaries: 1914—$250 per month.

PLAYER: CARL MAYS

	HOW MUCH HE PITCHED							WHAT HE GAVE UP									WHAT THE RESULTS WERE					
Year	G	GS	CG	GF	ShO	IP	BFP	H	R	ER	SH	HB	TBB	SO	WP	Bk	W	L	Pct.	Rest of Team	Above Team	Runs per Game	Percentage of League
1915	38	6	2	27	0	132	514	119	54	38		5	21	65	3	0	5	5	.500	.681	−1.8	3.68	.93
1916	44	25	14	13	2	245	972	208	79	65		9	74	76	2	1	19	13	.594	.590	.1	2.90	.79
1917	35	33	27	2	2	289	1129	230	81	56		14	74	91	6	0	22	9	.710	.562	4.6	2.52	.69
1918	35	33	30	1	8	293	1135	230	94	72		11	81	114	6	0	21	13	.618	.587	1.0	2.89	.79
1919	34	29	23	6	3	265	1063	227	91	62		10	77	107	4	0	14	14	.500	.527	−.8	3.09	.75
1920	45	37	26	8	6	312	1301	310	127	106	7	9	84	92	2	0	26	11	.703	.590	4.2	3.66	.77
1921	49	38	30	10	1	337	1400	332	145	114	22	9	76	70	2	0	27	9	.750	.607	5.2	3.87	.76
1922	34	29	21	4	1	240	988	257	111	96	28	7	50	41	1	0	13	14	.481	.638	−4.2	4.16	.88
1923	23	7	2	11	0	81	383	119	59	56	14	4	32	16	1	0	5	2	.714	.641	.5	6.56	1.37
1924	37	27	15	10	2	226	940	238	97	79	19	4	36	63	1	0	20	9	.690	.508	5.3	3.86	.85
1925	12	5	3	5	0	52	225	60	22	19	6	2	13	10	0	0	3	5	.375	.531	−1.2	3.81	.75
1926	39	33	24	2	3	281	1158	286	112	98	37	4	53	58	2	0	19	12	.613	.553	1.9	3.59	.79
1927	14	9	6	4	0	82	343	89	39	32	10	1	10	17	1	0	3	7	.300	.503	−2.0	4.28	.93
1928	14	7	4	4	1	63	269	67	33	27	3	0	22	10	0	0	4	1	.800	.503	1.5	4.71	1.00
1929	37	8	1	19	0	123	538	140	67	59	18	2	31	32	3	0	7	2	.778	.542	2.1	4.90	.91
	490	326	228	126	29	3021	12358	2912	1211	979		89	734	862	34	1	208	126	.623	.574	16.2	3.61	.81
10.61 Years	46	31	21		3	285		274	114	92		8	69	81	3	0	20	12	.623	.574	1.5	3.61	.81

Teams: Boston, 1915–1918; Boston/New York, A.L., 1919; New York, A.L., 1920–1923; Cincinnati, 1924–1928; New York, N.L., 1929.

Points in MVP Voting: 1922, 0; 1923, 0; 1926, 4 (.05); 1927, 0.

Opposition Stolen Bases: 1920, 18; 1921, 13; 1922, 11; 1923, 6. TOTAL: 48/970 innings, 0.45 per nine innings.

PLAYER: DAZZY VANCE

	HOW MUCH HE PITCHED							WHAT HE GAVE UP									WHAT THE RESULTS WERE						
Year	G	GS	CG	GF	ShO	IP	BFP	H	R	ER	SH	HB	TBB	SO	WP	Bk	W	L	Pct.	Rest of Team	Above Team	Runs per Game	Percentage of League
1915	9	4	1	4	0	31	131	26	17	14		3	21	18	1	0	0	4	.000	.473	−1.9	4.94	1.23
1918	2	0	0	1	0	2	15	9	5	4	0		2	0	0	0	0	0	.000	.488	.0	22.50	6.17
1922	36	30	16	4	5	246	1069	259	122	101	28	8	94	134	5	0	18	12	.600	.468	4.0	4.46	.89
1923	37	35	21	2	3	280	1187	263	127	109	26	11	100	197	5	0	18	15	.545	.479	2.2	4.08	.84
1924	35	34	30	1	3	309	1221	238	89	74	17	9	77	262	4	0	28	6	.824	.533	9.9	2.59	.57
1925	31	31	26	0	4	265	1089	247	115	104	25	10	66	221	3	0	22	9	.710	.377	10.3	3.91	.77
1926	24	22	12	2	1	169	713	172	80	73	20	1	58	140	1	1	9	10	.474	.463	.2	4.26	.94
1927	34	32	25	2	2	273	1123	242	98	82	35	6	69	184	2	0	16	15	.516	.402	3.5	3.23	.71
1928	38	32	24	5	4	280	1126	226	79	65	26	7	72	200	1	0	22	10	.688	.455	7.5	2.54	.54
1929	31	26	17	3	1	231	978	244	110	100	30	9	47	126	3	0	14	13	.519	.444	2.0	4.29	.80
1930	35	31	20	3	4	259	1061	241	97	75	21	5	55	173	4	1	17	15	.531	.566	−1.1	3.37	.59
1931	30	29	12	1	2	219	918	221	99	82	17	0	53	150	1	0	11	13	.458	.531	−1.7	4.07	.91
1932	27	24	9	2	1	176	742	171	90	82	16	1	57	103	2	0	12	11	.522	.527	−0.1	4.60	1.00
1933	28	11	2	8	0	99	427	105	42	39	5	1	28	67	3	0	6	2	.750	.524	1.8	3.82	.96
1934	25	6	1	4	0	77	341	90	47	39	4	3	25	42	1	0	1	3	.250	.487	−.9	5.49	1.17
1935	20	0	0	11	0	51	225	55	29	25	1	3	16	28	1	0	3	2	.600	.453	.7	5.12	1.09
	442	347	216	53	30	2967	12366	2809	1246	1068	271	77	840	2045	37	2	197	140	.585	.477	36.3	3.78	.81
10.10 Years	44	34	21	5	3	294		278	123	106			83	202		0	20	14	.585	.477	3.6	3.78	.81

Teams: Pittsburgh, N.L./New York, A.L. 1915; New York, A.L. 1918; Brooklyn, 1922–1932; St. Louis, 1933; St. Louis/Cincinnati, 1934; Brooklyn, N.L. 1935.

Points in MVP Voting: 1924, 74 (1st, .93); 1926, 0; 1927, 0; 1931, 0; 1932, 0; 1933, 0; 1934, 0; 1935, 0.

Other Notes: Named to *The Sporting News* major league All-Star team in 1925.

PLAYER: URBAN SHOCKER

	HOW MUCH HE PITCHED							WHAT HE GAVE UP									WHAT THE RESULTS WERE					
Year	G	GS	CG	GF	ShO	IP	BFP	H	R	ER	SH	HB	TBB	SO	WP	Bk	W	L	Pct.	Rest of Team	Above Team	Runs per Game	Percentage of League
1916	12	9	4	3	1	82	329	67	25	24		6	32	43	2	0	5	3	.625	.514	.9	2.74	.75
1917	26	13	7	5	0	145	564	124	59	42		0	46	68	4	1	8	5	.615	.450	2.2	3.66	1.00
1918	14	9	7	5	0	95	371	69	26	19		1	40	33	2	0	6	5	.545	.478	.7	2.46	.68
1919	30	25	13	5	5	211	850	193	75	63		4	55	86	2	0	13	11	.542	.470	1.7	3.20	.78
1920	38	28	22	10	5	246	981	224	97	74		4	70	107	0	0	20	10	.667	.455	6.3	3.55	.75
1921	47	39	31	7	4	327	1401	345	151	129	31	6	86	132	3	0	27	12	.692	.470	8.7	4.16	.81
1922	48	38	29	8	2	348	1443	365	141	115	38	4	59	149	2	2	24	17	.585	.611	−1.0	3.65	.77
1923	43	35	24	7	3	277	1154	292	122	105	29	3	49	109	2	0	20	12	.625	.450	5.6	3.96	.83
1924	39	32	17	3	4	239	1032	262	124	111	28	3	49	84	0	0	16	13	.552	.593	−1.2	4.67	.94
1925	41	30	15	7	2	244	1032	278	108	99	24	3	58	74	1	0	12	12	.500	.438	1.5	3.98	.77
1926	41	33	19	6	0	258	1108	272	113	97	22	2	71	59	0		19	11	.633	.581	1.6	3.94	.83
1927	31	27	13	1	2	200	839	207	86	63	25	1	41	35	1		18	6	.750	.708	1.0	3.87	.79
1928	1	0	0	1	0	2	7	3	0	0	0	0	0	0	0	0	0	0	.000	.604	.0	0	0
	411	318	201	68	28	2674	11111	2701	1127	941		37	656	979	19	3	188	117	.616	.525	28.0	3.79	.84
9.35 Years	44	34	22		3	286		278	121	101		3	70	105	2		20	13	.616	.525	3.0	3.79	.84

Teams: New York, A.L. 1916–1917; St. Louis, 1918–1924; New York, A.L. 1925–1928.

Points in MVP Voting: 1922, 5 (.08); 1923, 5 (.08); 1924, 0; 1926, 0; 1927, 0. TOTAL: .16 Award Shares.

Reported Salaries: 1927—$13,500.

Opposition Stolen Bases: 1920, 14; 1921, 12; 1922, 14; 1923, 11; 1924, 12. TOTAL: 63/1388 innings, 0.41 per nine innings.

PLAYER: BURLEIGH GRIMES

	HOW MUCH HE PITCHED							WHAT HE GAVE UP									WHAT THE RESULTS WERE						
Year	G	GS	CG	GF	ShO	IP	BFP	H	R	ER	SH	HB	TBB	SO	WP	Bk	W	L	Pct.	Rest of Team	Above Team	Runs per Game	Percentage of League
1916	6	5	4	1	0	46	182	40	19	12	6	0	10	20	1	0	2	3	.400	.423	−.1	3.72	1.08
1917	37	17	8	15	1	194	824	186	101	76	33	6	70	72	5	2	3	16	.158	.356	−3.8	4.69	1.33
1918	41	28	19	10	7	270	1078	210	94	64	27	4	76	113	11	2	19	9	.679	.388	8.1	3.13	.86
1919	25	21	13	4	1	181	791	179	97	70	24	3	60	82	7	3	10	11	.476	.496	−.4	4.82	1.32
1920	40	33	25	6	5	304	1246	271	101	75	34	4	67	131	9	0	23	11	.676	.583	3.2	2.99	.75
1921	37	35	30	1	2	302	1253	313	120	95	31	5	76	136	6	0	22	13	.629	.470	5.5	3.58	.78
1922	36	34	18	1	1	259	1153	324	157	135	24	7	84	99	6	1	17	14	.548	.480	2.1	5.46	1.09
1923	39	38	33	1	2	327	1418	356	165	130	37	11	100	119	6	0	21	18	.538	.478	2.3	4.54	.94
1924	38	36	30	1	1	311	1345	351	161	132	23	6	91	135	5	0	22	13	.629	.588	1.4	4.66	1.03
1925	33	31	19	2	0	247	1129	305	164	138	32	7	102	73	8	0	12	19	.387	.459	−2.2	5.98	1.18
1926	30	29	18	1	1	225	996	238	114	93	40	5	88	64	4	1	12	13	.480	.461	.5	4.56	1.00
1927	39	34	15	4	2	260	1103	274	116	102	20	4	87	102	4	0	19	8	.704	.575	3.5	4.02	.88
1928	48	37	28	9	4	331	1377	311	146	110	39	9	77	97	3	1	25	14	.641	.531	4.3	3.97	.84
1929	33	29	18	4	2	233	1004	245	108	81	20	4	70	62	0	0	17	7	.708	.550	3.8	4.17	.78
1930	33	28	11	5	1	201	896	246	119	91	26	7	65	73	7	0	16	11	.593	.567	.7	5.33	.94
1931	29	28	17	1	3	212	914	240	97	86	6	10	59	67	2	1	17	9	.654	.656	−.1	4.12	.92
1932	30	18	5	5	1	141	642	174	89	75	6	1	50	36	2	1	6	11	.353	.613	−4.4	5.68	1.24
1933	21	10	3	7	1	83	363	86	42	35	11	2	37	16	4	0	3	7	.300	.576	−2.8	4.55	1.15
1934	22	4	0	14	0	53	245	63	38	36	4	2	26	15	2	0	4	5	.444	.583	−1.3	6.45	1.34
14.19 Years	616	495	314	92	35	4180	17959	4412	2048	1636	443	97	1295	1512	92	12	270	212	.560	.518	20.5	4.41	.99
	43	35	22		2	295		311	144	115			91	107			19	15	.560	.518	1.4	4.41	.99

Teams: Pittsburgh, 1916–1917; Brooklyn, 1918–1926; New York, N.L., 1927; Pittsburgh, N.L. 1928–1929; Boston, N.L./St. Louis, 1930; St. Louis, 1931; Chicago, N.L., 1932; Chicago/St. Louis, 1933; St. Louis/Pittsburgh, 1934.

Points in MVP Voting: 1926, 0; 1927, 4 (.05); 1931, 0; 1932, 0; 1933, 0; 1934, 0.

Other Notes: Named to *The Sporting News* major league All-Star team in 1929.

PLAYER: WAITE HOYT

	HOW MUCH HE PITCHED							WHAT HE GAVE UP									WHAT THE RESULTS WERE						
Year	G	GS	CG	GF	ShO	IP	BFP	H	R	ER	SH	HB	TBB	SO	WP	Bk	W	L	Pct.	Rest of Team	Above Team	Runs per Game	Percentage of League
1918	1	0	0	1	0	1	3	0	0	0	0	0	0	2	0	0	0	0	.000	.573	.0	0	0
1919	13	11	6	2	1	105	400	99	42	38		0	22	28	1	0	4	6	.400	.488	−.9	3.60	.88
1920	22	11	6	9	2	121	530	123	72	59		1	47	45	3	0	6	6	.500	.468	.4	5.36	1.13
1921	43	32	21	7	1	282	1201	301	121	97	25	5	81	102	3	1	19	13	.594	.653	−1.9	3.86	.75
1922	37	31	17	3	3	265	1117	271	114	101	25	9	76	95	5	0	19	12	.613	.610	.1	3.87	.82
1923	37	28	19	7	1	239	993	227	97	80	25	4	66	60	1	0	17	9	.654	.643	.3	3.65	.76
1924	46	32	14	13	2	247	1098	295	117	104	26	3	76	71	0	0	18	13	.581	.587	−.2	4.26	.86
1925	46	30	17	14	1	243	1074	283	124	108	27	1	78	86	5	0	11	14	.440	.450	−.2	4.59	.88
1926	40	27	12	8	1	218	941	224	112	93	29	2	62	79	2	0	16	12	.571	.595	−.7	4.62	.98
1927	36	32	23	4	3	256	1045	242	90	75	23	4	54	86	1	0	22	7	.759	.704	1.6	3.16	.64
1928	42	31	19	11	3	273	1153	279	118	102	31	1	60	67	2	0	23	7	.767	.629	4.1	3.89	.82
1929	30	25	12	3	0	202	884	219	115	95	26	3	69	57	2	0	10	9	.526	.578	−1.0	5.12	1.02
1930	34	27	10	5	1	183	841	240	116	96	19	2	56	35	5	2	11	10	.524	.795	−5.7	5.70	1.05
1931	32	26	14	4	2	203	908	254	130	112	12	2	69	40	1	0	13	13	.500	.586	−2.2	5.76	1.12
1932	26	16	3	4	0	124	548	141	70	60	20	5	37	36	1	0	6	10	.375	.493	−1.9	5.08	1.11
1933	36	8	4	14	1	117	478	118	45	38	7	1	19	44	1	1	5	7	.417	.577	−1.9	3.46	.87
1934	48	15	6	20	3	191	785	184	75	62	11	2	43	105	1	0	15	6	.714	.457	5.4	3.53	.75
1935	39	11	5	19	0	164	694	187	72	62	11	1	27	63	2	1	7	11	.389	.585	−3.5	3.95	.84
1936	22	9	6	10	0	117	483	115	44	35	9	3	20	37	0	0	7	5	.583	.542	.5	3.38	.72
1937	38	19	10	10	1	195	828	211	97	74	10	0	36	65	2	0	8	9	.471	.460	.2	4.48	.99
1938	6	1	0	3	0	16	78	24	9	9	1	0	5	3	0	0	0	3	.000	.473	−1.4	5.06	1.15
14.33 Years	674	422	224	171	26	3762	16082	4037	1780	1500		49	1003	1206	39	5	237	182	.566	.587	−9.0	4.26	.89
	47	29	16		2	263		282	124	105		3	70	84	3		17	13	.566	.587	−.6	4.26	.89

Teams: New York, N.L., 1918; Boston, 1919–20; New York, A.L. 1921–29; New York, A.L./Detroit, 1930; Detroit/Philadelphia, A.L. 1931; Brooklyn/New York, 1932; Pittsburgh, 1933–1936; Pittsburgh/Brooklyn, 1937; Brooklyn, 1938.
Points in MVP Voting: 1922, 0; 1923, 0; 1924, 0; 1926, 0; 1927, 0; 1931, 0; 1932, 0; 1933, 0; 1934, 2 (.03); 1935, 0; 1937, 0; 1938, 0.
Reported Salaries: 1927—$11,000.
Other Notes: Named to *The Sporting News* major league All-Star team in 1928.
Opposition Stolen Bases: 1920, 14; 1921, 11; 1922, 17; 1923, 12; 1924, 13. TOTAL: 67/1154 innings, 0.52 per nine innings.

PLAYER: EDDIE ROMMEL

	HOW MUCH HE PITCHED							WHAT HE GAVE UP									WHAT THE RESULTS WERE						
Year	G	GS	CG	GF	ShO	IP	BFP	H	R	ER	SH	HB	TBB	SO	WP	Bk	W	L	Pct.	Rest of Team	Above Team	Runs per Game	Percentage of League
1920	33	12	8	16	2	174	685	165	68	55		4	43	43	1	1	7	7	.500	.293	2.9	3.52	.74
1921	46	32	20	14	0	285	1230	312	155	125	42	1	87	71	4	2	16	23	.410	.325	3.3	4.89	.96
1922	51	33	22	16	3	294	1203	294	128	107	33	5	63	54	3	0	27	13	.675	.333	13.7	3.92	.83
1923	56	31	19	20	3	298	1292	306	141	108	54	1	108	76	6	0	18	19	.486	.443	1.6	4.26	.89
1924	43	34	21	6	3	278	1164	302	139	122	24	3	94	72	2	0	18	15	.545	.445	3.3	4.50	.91
1925	52	28	14	20	1	261	1154	285	127	107	37	7	95	67	5	0	21	10	.677	.554	3.8	4.38	.85
1926	37	26	12	7	3	219	926	225	91	75	30	2	54	52	3	0	11	11	.500	.563	−1.4	3.74	.78
1927	30	17	8	4	2	147	642	166	83	71	10	3	48	33	2	1	11	3	.786	.571	3.0	5.08	1.03
1928	43	11	6	18	0	174	711	177	70	59	15	2	26	37	2	0	13	5	.722	.630	1.7	3.62	.76
1929	32	6	4	16	0	114	503	135	52	36	9	1	34	25	1	1	12	2	.857	.676	2.5	4.11	.82
1930	35	9	5	20	0	130	550	142	66	62	10	1	27	35	0	0	9	4	.692	.660	.4	4.57	.84
1931	25	10	8	10	1	118	498	136	50	39	2	1	27	18	2	0	7	5	.583	.714	−1.6	3.81	.74
1932	17	0	0	15	0	65	292	84	43	40	7	0	18	16	3	0	1	2	.333	.510	−.5	5.95	1.14
	500	249	147	182	18	2557	10850	2729	1213	1006		31	724	599	34	5	171	119	.590	.477	32.8	4.27	.86
9.99 Years	50	25	15		2	256		273	121	101		3	72	60	3		17	12	.590	.477	3.3	4.27	.86

Teams: Philadelphia, A.L., 1920–1932.
Points in MVP Voting: 1922, 31 (2nd, .48); 1923, 0; 1924, 0; 1926, 0; 1927, 0; 1931, 0; 1932, 0.
Other Notes: Named to *The Sporting News* major league All-Star team in 1925.
Opposition Stolen Bases: 1920, 11; 1921, 10; 1922, 10; 1923, 10; 1924, 11. TOTAL: 52/1329 innings, .35 per nine innings.

PLAYER: FIRPO MARBERRY

	HOW MUCH HE PITCHED							WHAT HE GAVE UP									WHAT THE RESULTS WERE						
Year	G	GS	CG	GF	ShO	IP	BFP	H	R	ER	SH	HB	TBB	SO	WP	Bk	W	L	Pct.	Rest of Team	Above Team	Runs per Game	Percentage of League
1923	11	4	2	5	0	45	190	42	16	14	7	3	17	18	0	0	4	0	1.000	.477	2.1	3.20	.67
1924	50	15	6	30	0	195	838	190	88	67	32	9	70	68	2	0	11	12	.478	.618	−3.2	4.06	.82
1925	55	0	0	39	0	93	400	84	47	36	10	4	45	53	0	0	8	6	.571	.642	−1.0	4.55	.88
1926	64	5	3	47	0	138	588	120	50	46	25	3	66	43	0	0	12	7	.632	.527	2.0	3.26	.69
1927	56	10	2	30	0	155	694	177	92	80	26	3	68	74	2	0	10	7	.588	.547	.7	5.34	1.09
1928	48	11	7	26	1	161	675	160	79	69	25	3	42	76	0	0	13	13	.500	.484	.4	4.42	.93
1929	49	26	16	21	0	250	1028	233	100	85	27	6	69	121	2	1	19	12	.613	.430	5.7	3.60	.72
1930	33	22	9	9	2	185	774	190	92	84	17	0	53	56	0	0	15	5	.750	.590	3.2	4.48	.83
1931	45	25	11	14	1	219	913	211	92	84	10	3	63	88	3	0	16	4	.800	.567	4.7	3.78	.74
1932	54	15	8	26	1	198	846	202	98	88	18	2	72	66	1	2	8	4	.667	.599	.8	4.45	.85
1933	37	32	15	5	1	238	990	232	98	87	16	1	61	84	1	1	16	11	.593	.465	3.5	3.71	.75
1934	38	19	6	14	1	156	683	174	92	79	5	0	48	64	2	0	15	5	.750	.642	2.2	5.31	1.04
1935	5	2	1	2	0	19	89	22	11	9	4	0	9	7	1	0	0	1	.000	.620	−.6	5.21	1.02
1936	6	1	0	3	0	14	61	12	7	6	2	1	3	4	0	0	0	2	.000	.543	−1.1	4.50	.79
	551	187	86	271	7	2066	8769	2049	962	834	224	38	686	822	14	4	147	89	.623	.541	19.2	4.19	.83
10.14 Years	54	18	8	27	1	204		202	95	82			68	81			15	9	.623	.541	1.9	4.19	.83

Teams: Washington, A.L., 1923–1932; Detroit, 1933–35; New York, N.L./Washington, 1936.
Points in MVP Voting: 1923, 0; 1924, 0; 1926, 0; 1927, 0; 1931, 0; 1932, 0; 1933, 0; 1934, 0; 1935, 0.
Opposition Stolen Bases: 1923, 3; 1924, 18. TOTAL: 21/240 innings, .79 per nine innings.

PLAYER: TED LYONS

	HOW MUCH HE PITCHED							WHAT HE GAVE UP									WHAT THE RESULTS WERE						
Year	G	GS	CG	GF	ShO	IP	BFP	H	R	ER	SH	HB	TBB	SO	WP	Bk	W	L	Pct.	Rest of Team	Above Team	Runs per Game	Percentage of League
1923	9	1	0	5	0	23	113	30	21	16	4	1	15	6	3	1	2	1	.667	.444	.7	8.22	1.72
1924	41	22	12	15	0	216	987	279	143	117	39	2	72	52	4	0	12	11	.522	.415	2.4	5.96	1.20
1925	43	32	19	8	5	263	1110	274	111	95	38	2	83	45	5	0	21	11	.656	.475	5.8	3.80	.73
1926	39	31	24	8	3	284	1208	268	108	95	37	1	106	51	1	0	18	16	.529	.529	-.0	3.42	.72
1927	39	34	30	4	2	308	1262	291	125	97	34	0	67	71	2	0	22	14	.611	.410	7.2	3.65	.74
1928	39	27	21	12	0	240	1093	276	133	106	36	2	68	60	2	0	15	14	.517	.456	1.8	4.99	1.05
1929	37	31	21	6	1	259	1102	276	136	118	31	2	76	57	3	0	14	20	.412	.381	1.0	4.73	.94
1930	42	36	29	6	1	298	1258	331	160	125	36	2	57	69	2	1	22	15	.595	.342	9.4	4.83	.89
1931	22	12	7	8	0	101	435	117	50	45	7	0	33	16	1	1	4	6	.400	.364	.4	4.46	.87
1932	33	26	19	4	1	231	979	243	104	84	11	3	71	58	1	0	10	15	.400	.310	2.3	4.05	.77
1933	36	27	14	9	2	228	1016	260	142	111	12	0	74	74	10	0	10	21	.323	.479	-4.8	5.61	1.13
1934	30	24	21	4	0	205	928	249	138	111	10	2	66	53	2	1	11	13	.458	.328	3.1	6.06	1.18
1935	23	22	19	1	3	191	811	194	79	64	12	3	56	54	4	0	15	8	.652	.457	4.5	3.72	.73
1936	26	24	15	2	1	182	804	227	115	104	11	3	45	48	1	0	10	13	.435	.555	-2.8	5.69	1.00
1937	22	22	11	0	0	169	706	182	86	78	6	1	45	45	2	0	12	7	.632	.548	1.6	4.58	.88
1938	23	23	17	0	1	195	862	238	93	80	15	0	52	54	1	1	9	11	.450	.438	.3	4.29	.80
1939	21	21	16	0	0	173	702	162	71	53	18	1	26	65	0	0	14	6	.700	.530	3.4	3.69	.71
1940	22	22	17	0	4	186	789	188	85	67	5	0	37	72	6	0	12	8	.600	.522	1.6	4.11	.83
1941	22	22	19	0	2	187	795	199	87	77	15	4	37	63	2	0	12	10	.545	.492	1.2	4.19	.88
1942	20	20	20	0	1	180	720	167	52	42	11	2	26	50	3	0	14	6	.700	.406	5.9	2.60	.61
1946	5	5	5	0	0	43	174	38	17	11	3	0	9	10	0	0	1	4	.200	.490	-1.4	3.56	.88
	594	484	356	92	27	4162	17854	4489	2056	1696	391	31	1121	1073	55	5	260	230	.531	.442	43.3	4.45	.89
13.75 Years	43	35	26	7	2	303		326	150	123	28	2	82	78	4	0	19	17	.531	.442	3.1	4.45	.89

Teams: Chicago, A.L. 1923–1942, 1946.

Points in MVP Voting: 1923, 0; 1924, 0; 1926, 0; 1927, 34 (3rd, .53); 1931, 0; 1932, 3 (.03); 1933, 0; 1934, 0; 1935, 10 (.13); 1937, 0; 1938, 0; 1939, 13 (.04); 1940, 2 (.01); 1941, 12 (.04); 1942, 23 (.07); 1946, 0. TOTAL: .85 Award Shares.

Other Notes: Named to *The Sporting News* major league All-Star team in 1927.

Opposition Stolen Bases: 1924, 17. TOTAL: 17/216 innings, 0.71 per nine innings.

PLAYER: RED RUFFING

	HOW MUCH HE PITCHED							WHAT HE GAVE UP									WHAT THE RESULTS WERE					
Year	G	GS	CG	GF	ShO	IP	BFP	H	R	ER	SH	HB	TBB	SO	WP	Bk	W	L	Pct.	Rest of Team	Above Team	Runs per Game	Percentage of League
1924	8	2	0	3	0	23	108	29	17	17	3	3	9	10	1	0	0	0	.000	.435	.0	6.65	1.34
1925	37	27	13	6	3	217	957	253	135	121	33	2	75	64	1	1	9	18	.333	.304	.8	5.60	1.08
1926	37	22	6	11	0	166	724	169	98	81	34	5	68	58	0	0	6	15	.286	.303	−.4	5.31	1.12
1927	26	18	10	7	0	158	703	160	94	82	34	4	87	77	5	1	5	13	.278	.338	−1.1	5.35	1.09
1928	42	34	25	8	1	289	1273	303	147	125	38	10	96	118	4	0	10	25	.286	.398	−3.9	4.58	.96
1929	35	30	18	5	2	244	1112	280	162	132	48	2	118	109	6	0	9	22	.290	.398	−3.3	5.98	1.19
1930	38	28	13	9	2	222	960	242	125	108	22	3	68	131	4	2	15	8	.652	.511	3.2	5.07	.94
1931	37	30	19	5	1	237	1042	240	130	116	11	6	87	132	1	0	16	14	.533	.643	−3.3	4.94	.96
1932	35	29	22	6	3	259	1098	219	102	89	13	3	115	190	5	0	18	7	.720	.690	.8	3.54	.68
1933	35	28	18	7	0	235	1006	230	118	102	16	4	93	122	0	0	9	14	.391	.646	−5.9	4.52	.91
1934	36	31	19	3	5	256	1100	232	134	112	13	1	104	149	1	0	19	11	.633	.605	.9	4.71	.92
1935	30	29	19	1	2	222	925	201	88	77	6	1	76	81	1	1	16	11	.593	.598	−.2	3.57	.70
1936	33	33	25	0	3	271	1151	274	133	116	15	3	90	102	7	0	20	12	.625	.678	−1.7	4.42	.78
1937	31	31	22	0	5	256	1058	242	101	85	9	1	68	131	1	1	20	7	.741	.646	2.6	3.55	.68
1938	31	31	22	0	4	247	1043	246	104	91	11	0	82	127	1	1	21	7	.750	.629	3.4	3.79	.71
1939	28	28	22	0	5	233	968	211	88	76	9	2	75	95	3	0	21	7	.750	.691	1.7	3.40	.65
1940	30	30	20	0	3	226	954	218	98	85	9	3	76	97	1	0	15	12	.556	.575	−.5	3.90	.79
1941	23	23	13	0	2	186	771	177	87	73	13	1	54	60	1	0	15	6	.714	.647	1.4	4.21	.89
1942	24	24	16	0	4	194	784	183	72	69	7	3	41	80	0	0	14	7	.667	.669	−.1	3.34	.78
1945	11	11	8	0	1	87	364	85	32	28	4	1	20	24	0	0	7	3	.700	.521	1.8	3.31	.85
1946	8	8	4	0	2	61	243	37	13	12	4	0	23	19	0	0	5	1	.833	.554	1.7	1.92	.47
1947	9	9	1	0	0	53	235	63	39	36	2	0	16	11	3	0	3	5	.375	.459	−.7	6.62	1.60
	624	536	335	71	48	4342	18579	4294	2117	1833	354	58	1541	1987	46	7	273	225	.548	.554	−2.8	4.39	.89
14.72 Years	42	36	23	5	3	295		292	144	125	24	4	105	135	3	0	19	15	.548	.554	−.2	4.39	.89

Teams: Boston, 1924–1929; Boston/New York, A.L. 1930; New York, A.L. 1931–1946; Chicago, A.L. 1947.

Points in MVP Voting: 1924, 0; 1926, 0; 1927, 0; 1931, 0; 1932, 0; 1933, 0; 1934, 0; 1935, 0; 1937, 18 (8th, .23); 1938, 146 (4th, .43); 1939, 116 (5th, .35); 1940, 0; 1941, 2 (.01); 1942, 0; 1945, 1 (.00); 1946, 0; 1947, 0. TOTAL: 1.02 Award Shares.

Other Notes: Named to *The Sporting News* major league All-Star team in 1937, 1938, and 1939.

PLAYER: LEFTY GROVE

	HOW MUCH HE PITCHED							WHAT HE GAVE UP									WHAT THE RESULTS WERE						
Year	G	GS	CG	GF	ShO	IP	BFP	H	R	ER	SH	HB	TBB	SO	WP	Bk	W	L	Pct.	Rest of Team	Above Team	Runs per Game	Percentage of League
1925	45	18	5	12	0	197	908	207	120	104	28	5	131	116	9	0	10	13	.435	.605	−3.9	5.48	1.06
1926	45	33	20	9	1	258	1072	227	97	72	35	6	101	184	5	0	13	13	.500	.565	−1.7	3.38	.71
1927	51	28	14	18	1	262	1106	251	116	93	30	2	79	174	5	1	20	12	.625	.582	1.4	3.98	.81
1928	39	31	24	6	4	262	1075	228	93	75	5	1	64	183	4	0	24	8	.750	.612	4.4	3.19	.67
1929	42	37	21	5	2	275	1168	278	104	86	22	3	81	170	8	0	20	6	.769	.677	2.4	3.40	.68
1930	50	32	22	17	2	291	1191	273	101	82	19	5	60	209	2	0	28	5	.848	.612	7.8	3.12	.58
1931	41	30	27	10	4	289	1160	249	84	66	9	1	62	175	2	0	31	4	.886	.650	8.3	2.62	.51
1932	44	30	27	13	4	292	1207	269	101	92	10	1	79	188	0	0	25	10	.714	.580	4.7	3.11	.59
1933	45	28	21	16	2	275	1173	280	113	98	12	4	83	114	1	0	24	8	.750	.462	9.2	3.70	.75
1934	22	11	5	6	0	109	506	149	84	79	7	1	32	43	1	0	8	8	.500	.500	0	6.94	1.35
1935	35	30	23	4	2	273	1137	269	105	82	21	3	65	121	2	0	20	12	.625	.479	4.7	3.46	.68
1936	35	30	22	3	6	253	1049	237	90	79	17	4	65	130	0	0	17	12	.586	.456	3.8	3.20	.56
1937	32	32	21	0	3	262	1127	269	101	88	12	1	83	153	5	0	17	9	.654	.500	4.0	3.47	.66
1938	24	21	12	3	1	164	706	169	65	56	11	1	52	99	3	0	14	4	.778	.565	3.8	3.57	.66
1939	23	23	17	0	2	191	798	180	63	54	15	1	58	81	0	0	15	4	.789	.561	4.3	2.97	.57
1940	22	21	9	1	1	153	652	159	73	68	11	1	50	62	1	0	7	6	.538	.532	.1	4.29	.86
1941	21	21	10	0	0	134	598	155	84	65	13	2	42	54	3	0	7	7	.500	.550	−.7	5.64	1.19
	616	456	300	123	35	3940	16633	3849	1594	1339	277	42	1187	2256	51	1	300	141	.680	.561	52.6	3.64	.71
13.80 Years	45	33	22	9	3	286		279	116	97	20	3	86	163	4		22	10	.680	.561	3.8	3.64	.71

Teams: Philadelphia, A.L., 1925–1933; Boston, A.L., 1934–1941.
Points in MVP Voting: 1926, 12 (8th, .19); 1927, 0; 1931, 78 (1st, .98); 1932, 0; 1933, 35 (5th, .44); 1934, 0; 1935, 8 (.10); 1936, 5 (.06); 1937, 0; 1938, 7 (.02); 1939, 17 (.05); 1940, 0; 1941, 0. TOTAL: 1.84 Award Shares.
Finished third in voting for TSN MVP award in 1931, but won BBWAA vote.
Reported Salaries: 1924, $17,500 (with Baltimore); 1931, $31,000 ($20,000 contract plus $1,000 for each win over 20).
Other Notes: Named to *The Sporting News* major league All-Star team in 1928, 1929, 1930, 1931, and 1932.

PLAYER: FREDDIE FITZSIMMONS

	HOW MUCH HE PITCHED							WHAT HE GAVE UP									WHAT THE RESULTS WERE						
Year	G	GS	CG	GF	ShO	IP	BFP	H	R	ER	SH	HB	TBB	SO	WP	Bk	W	L	Pct.	Rest of Team	Above Team	Runs per Game	Percentage of League
1925	10	8	6	2	1	75	304	70	25	22	4	0	18	17	0	0	6	3	.667	.559	1.0	3.00	.59
1926	37	26	12	7	0	219	907	224	90	70	20	4	58	48	3	0	14	10	.583	.472	2.7	3.70	.81
1927	42	31	14	7	1	245	1043	260	127	101	26	4	67	78	3	0	17	10	.630	.591	1.1	4.67	1.02
1928	40	32	16	7	1	261	1084	264	119	107	31	4	65	67	6	0	20	9	.690	.584	3.1	4.10	.87
1929	37	31	14	3	4	222	950	242	122	101	33	2	66	55	4	1	15	11	.577	.552	.6	4.95	.92
1930	41	29	17	9	1	224	946	230	125	106	21	1	59	76	6	0	19	7	.731	.531	5.2	5.02	.88
1931	35	33	19	1	4	254	1045	242	111	86	18	0	62	78	5	0	18	11	.621	.561	1.7	3.93	.88
1932	35	31	11	3	0	238	1060	287	132	117	13	3	83	65	7	0	11	11	.500	.462	.8	4.99	1.09
1933	36	35	13	1	1	252	895	243	106	81	14	2	72	65	2	0	16	11	.593	.600	−.2	3.79	.95
1934	38	37	14	1	3	263	1082	266	114	89	10	1	51	73	9	0	18	14	.563	.620	−1.8	3.90	.83
1935	18	15	6	3	4	94	399	104	43	42	6	1	22	23	3	0	4	8	.333	.617	−3.4	4.12	.88
1936	28	17	7	9	0	141	587	147	58	52	11	0	39	35	1	0	10	7	.588	.599	−.2	3.70	.79
1937	19	17	5	1	1	118	501	119	61	57	11	1	40	42	4	0	6	10	.375	.467	−1.5	4.65	1.03
1938	27	26	12	1	3	203	842	205	83	68	12	3	43	38	3	1	11	8	.579	.446	2.5	3.68	.83
1939	27	20	5	4	0	151	654	178	79	65	15	3	28	44	0	0	7	9	.438	.562	−2.0	4.71	1.06
1940	20	18	11	2	4	134	543	120	43	42	1	1	25	35	2	0	16	2	.889	.533	6.4	2.89	.66
1941	13	12	3	1	1	83	351	78	33	19	4	2	26	19	0	1	6	1	.857	.639	1.5	3.58	.85
1942	1	1	0	0	0	3	16	6	5	5	0	0	1	0	0	0	0	0	.000	.675	.0	15.00	3.84
1943	9	7	0	2	0	45	201	50	29	27	1	1	21	12	0	1	3	4	.429	.534	−.7	5.80	1.45
11.96 Years	513	426	185	64	29	3225	13410	3335	1505	1257	251	33	846	870	58	4	217	146	.598	.552	16.8	4.20	.92
	43	36	15	5	3	270		279	126	105	21	3	71	73	5	0	18	12	.598	.552	1.4	4.20	.92

Teams: New York, N.L., 1925–1936; New York/Brooklyn, 1937; Brooklyn, 1938–1943.
Points in MVP Voting: 1926, 0; 1927, 0; 1931, 0; 1932, 0; 1933, 0; 1934, 0; 1935, 0; 1937, 0; 1938, 1 (.00); 1940, 84 (5th, .25); 1941, 0; 1942, 0; 1943, 0. TOTAL: .25 Award Shares.

PLAYER: WES FERRELL

	HOW MUCH HE PITCHED							WHAT HE GAVE UP									WHAT THE RESULTS WERE					
Year	G	GS	CG	GF	ShO	IP	BFP	H	R	ER	SH	HB	TBB	SO	WP	Bk	W	L	Pct.	Rest of Team	Above Team	Runs per Game	Percentage of League
1927	1	0	0	1	0	1	8	3	3	3	1	0	2	0	0	0	0	0	.000	.431	.0	27.00	5.49
1928	2	2	1	0	0	16	67	15	5	4	0	0	5	4	0	0	0	2	.000	.408	−.8	2.81	.59
1929	43	25	18	12	1	243	1061	256	112	97	33	3	109	100	2	3	21	10	.677	.496	5.6	4.15	.83
1930	43	35	25	8	1	297	1274	299	141	109	27	0	106	143	5	1	25	13	.658	.483	6.7	4.27	.79
1931	40	35	27	4	2	276	1227	276	134	115	11	3	130	123	3	0	22	12	.647	.467	6.1	4.37	.85
1932	38	34	26	3	3	288	1244	299	141	117	9	0	104	105	4	1	23	13	.639	.552	3.1	4.41	.84
1933	28	26	16	2	1	201	886	225	108	94	16	2	70	41	1	0	11	12	.478	.500	−.5	4.84	.98
1934	26	23	17	3	3	181	785	205	87	73	8	0	49	67	3	0	14	5	.737	.466	5.1	4.33	.84
1935	41	38	31	3	3	322	1391	336	149	126	20	3	108	110	5	0	25	14	.641	.465	6.9	4.16	.82
1936	39	38	28	1	3	301	1341	330	160	140	13	6	119	106	3	0	20	15	.571	.454	4.1	4.78	.84
1937	37	35	26	2	0	281	1266	325	177	153	15	3	122	123	2	0	14	19	.424	.504	−2.6	5.67	1.08
1938	28	26	10	2	0	179	848	245	144	125	6	1	86	43	5	1	15	10	.600	.508	2.3	7.24	1.35
1939	3	3	1	0	0	19	85	14	10	10	4	0	17	6	1	0	1	2	.333	.709	−1.1	4.74	.91
1940	1	0	0	1	0	4	21	4	3	3	0	1	4	4	0	0	0	0	.000	.575	.0	6.75	1.54
1941	4	3	1	1	0	14	64	13	8	8	0	1	9	10	1	0	2	1	.667	.649	.1	5.14	1.21
8.84 Years	374	323	227	43	17	2623	11568	2845	1382	1177	163	23	1040	985	35	6	193	128	.601	.492	35.0	4.74	.94
	42	37	26	5	2	297		322	156	133	18	3	118	111	4	1	22	14	.601	.492	4.0	4.74	.94

Teams: Cleveland, 1927–1933; Boston, 1934–1936; Boston/Washington, 1937; Washington/New York, A.L., 1938; New York, A.L., 1939; Brooklyn, 1940; Boston, 1941.

Points in MVP Voting: 1927, 0; 1931, 10 (.16); 1932, 0; 1933, 0; 1934, 16 (8th, .20); 1935, 62 (2nd, .78); 1937, 0; 1938, 0; 1939, 0; 1940, 0. TOTAL: 1.14 Award Shares.

Other Notes: Named to *The Sporting News* major league All-Star team in 1930.

PLAYER: CARL HUBBELL

	HOW MUCH HE PITCHED							WHAT HE GAVE UP									WHAT THE RESULTS WERE						
Year	G	GS	CG	GF	ShO	IP	BFP	H	R	ER	SH	HB	TBB	SO	WP	Bk	W	L	Pct.	Rest of Team	Above Team	Runs per Game	Percentage of League
1928	20	14	8	5	1	124	511	117	49	39	15	3	21	37	1	0	10	6	.625	.601	.4	3.56	.76
1929	39	35	19	3	1	268	1130	273	128	110	26	6	67	106	5	0	18	11	.621	.541	2.3	4.30	.80
1930	37	32	17	4	3	242	1037	263	120	104	21	11	58	117	3	0	17	12	.586	.560	.8	4.46	.79
1931	36	30	21	5	4	247	1010	213	88	73	10	4	66	156	3	0	14	12	.538	.579	−1.1	3.21	.72
1932	40	32	22	7	0	284	1151	260	96	79	15	4	40	137	3	1	18	11	.621	.432	5.5	3.04	.66
1933	45	33	22	11	10	309	1206	256	69	57	30	3	47	156	3	0	23	12	.657	.581	2.7	2.01	.51
1934	49	34	23	11	5	313	1255	286	100	80	19	2	37	118	2	0	21	12	.636	.600	1.2	2.88	.61
1935	42	35	24	6	1	303	1265	314	125	110	21	3	49	150	7	0	23	12	.657	.576	2.8	3.71	.79
1936	42	34	25	6	3	304	1202	265	81	78	16	5	57	123	3	0	26	6	.813	.541	8.7	2.40	.51
1937	39	32	18	6	4	262	1087	261	108	93	15	3	55	159	7	0	22	8	.733	.598	4.0	3.71	.82
1938	24	22	13	2	1	179	732	171	70	61	10	2	33	104	1	0	13	10	.565	.551	.3	3.52	.80
1939	29	18	10	8	0	154	639	150	60	47	10	2	24	62	2	0	11	9	.550	.504	.9	3.51	.79
1940	31	28	11	3	2	214	916	220	102	87	6	2	59	86	3	0	11	12	.478	.473	.1	4.29	.98
1941	26	22	11	4	1	164	705	169	73	65	15	2	53	75	4	0	11	9	.550	.474	1.5	4.01	.95
1942	24	20	11	1	0	157	660	158	75	69	15	1	34	61	2	0	11	8	.579	.556	.4	4.30	1.10
1943	12	11	3	0	0	66	299	87	36	36	5	0	24	31	4	0	4	4	.500	.352	1.2	4.91	1.23
	535	432	258	82	36	3590	14805	3463	1380	1188	249	53	724	1678	53	1	253	154	.622	.544	31.8	3.46	.76
12.35 Years	43	35	21	7	3	291		281	112	96	20	4	59	136	4	0	20	12	.622	.544	2.6	3.46	.76

Teams: New York, N.L. 1928–1943.

Points in MVP Voting: 1931, 0; 1932, 6 (.07); 1933, 77 (1st, .96); 1934, 16 (10th, .20); 1935, 20 (6th, .25); 1936, 60 (1st, 1.00); 1937, 52 (3rd, .65); 1938, 0; 1940, 0; 1941, 0; 1942, 0; 1943, 0. TOTAL: 3.13 Award Shares.

Other Notes: Named to *The Sporting News* major league All-Star team in 1933, 1935, 1936, and 1937.

PLAYER: LARRY FRENCH

	HOW MUCH HE PITCHED								WHAT HE GAVE UP										WHAT THE RESULTS WERE						
Year	G	GS	CG	GF	ShO	IP	BFP		H	R	ER	SH	HB	TBB	SO	WP	Bk		W	L	Pct.	Rest of Team	Above Team	Runs per Game	Percentage of League
1929	30	13	6	10	0	123	552		130	78	67	16	3	62	49	3	0		7	5	.583	.574	.1	5.71	1.06
1930	42	35	21	5	3	275	1232		325	163	133	34	6	89	90	3	0		17	18	.486	.529	−1.5	5.33	.94
1931	39	35	20	4	1	276	1170		301	127	100	15	1	70	73	5	1		15	13	.536	.476	1.7	4.14	.92
1932	47	33	20	11	3	274	1167		301	127	92	15	1	62	72	1	0		18	16	.529	.567	−1.3	4.17	.91
1933	47	35	21	10	5	291	1209		290	106	88	19	5	55	88	1	0		18	13	.581	.561	.6	3.28	.83
1934	49	35	16	7	3	264	1141		299	135	105	15	3	59	103	4	0		12	18	.400	.517	−3.5	4.60	.98
1935	42	30	16	6	4	246	1039		279	94	81	16	2	44	90	0	1		17	10	.630	.654	−.6	3.44	.73
1936	43	28	16	8	4	252	1055		262	103	95	9	6	54	104	1	0		18	9	.667	.543	3.3	3.68	.78
1937	42	28	11	5	4	208	911		229	106	92	8	1	65	100	5	0		16	10	.615	.602	.4	4.59	1.01
1938	43	27	10	11	3	201	853		210	95	85	15	1	62	83	4	0		10	19	.345	.642	−8.6	4.25	.96
1939	36	21	10	11	2	194	828		205	80	71	14	1	50	98	5	0		15	8	.652	.527	2.9	3.71	.84
1940	40	33	18	6	3	246	1024		240	93	90	18	4	64	107	0	0		14	14	.500	.484	.4	3.40	.77
1941	32	19	6	5	1	154	688		177	94	77	13	3	47	68	1	0		5	14	.263	.481	−4.1	5.49	1.30
1942	38	14	8	10	4	149	596		127	39	30	10	5	36	62	1	0		15	4	.789	.659	2.5	2.36	.60
12.41 Years	570 46	386 31	199 16	109 9	40 3	3153 254	13465		3375 272	1440 116	1206 97	217 17	42 3	819 66	1187 96	34 3	2 0		197 16	171 14	.535 .535	.557 .557	−7.8 −.6	4.11 4.11	.90 .90

Teams: Pittsburgh, 1929–1934; Chicago, N.L., 1935–1940; Chicago, N.L./Brooklyn, 1941; Brooklyn, 1942.
Points in MVP Voting: 1931, 0; 1932, 0; 1933, 10 (.13); 1934, 0; 1935, 0; 1937, 0; 1938, 0; 1939, 0; 1940, 0; 1941, 0; 1942, 7 (.02). TOTAL: .15 Award Shares.

PLAYER: LEFTY GOMEZ

	HOW MUCH HE PITCHED							WHAT HE GAVE UP									WHAT THE RESULTS WERE						
Year	G	GS	CG	GF	ShO	IP	BFP	H	R	ER	SH	HB	TBB	SO	WP	Bk	W	L	Pct.	Rest of Team	Above Team	Runs per Game	Percentage of League
1930	15	6	2	3	0	60	273	66	41	37	8	1	28	22	0	0	2	5	.286	.571	−2.0	6.15	1.14
1931	40	26	17	10	1	243	1013	206	88	72	13	4	85	150	1	0	21	9	.700	.593	3.2	3.26	.63
1932	37	31	21	3	1	265	1149	266	140	124	16	2	105	176	0	0	24	7	.774	.675	3.1	4.75	.91
1933	35	30	14	3	4	235	1027	218	108	83	11	0	106	163	6	0	16	10	.615	.605	.3	4.14	.83
1934	38	33	25	5	6	282	1142	223	86	73	11	0	96	158	3	0	26	5	.839	.553	8.9	2.74	.54
1935	34	30	15	3	2	246	1030	223	104	87	22	2	86	138	8	0	12	15	.444	.631	−5.0	3.80	.75
1936	31	30	10	1	0	189	858	184	104	92	11	1	122	105	2	0	13	7	.650	.669	−.4	4.95	.87
1937	34	34	25	0	6	278	1148	233	88	72	10	1	93	194	2	0	21	11	.656	.664	−.2	2.85	.55
1938	32	32	20	0	4	239	1034	239	110	89	13	1	99	129	5	0	18	12	.600	.664	−1.9	4.14	.77
1939	26	26	14	0	2	198	831	173	80	75	9	3	84	102	3	0	12	8	.600	.718	−2.4	3.64	.70
1940	9	5	0	3	0	27	134	37	20	20	1	1	18	14	3	0	3	3	.500	.574	−.4	6.67	1.34
1941	23	23	8	0	2	156	712	151	76	65	4	1	103	76	5	0	15	5	.750	.642	2.2	4.38	.92
1942	13	13	2	0	0	80	355	67	42	38	5	2	65	41	1	0	6	4	.600	.674	−.7	4.73	1.11
1943	1	1	0	0	0	5	23	4	4	3	2	0	5	0	0	0	0	1	.000	.553	−.6	7.20	1.85
8.72 Years	368	320	173	31	28	2503	10729	2290	1091	930	136	19	1095	1468	39	0	189	102	.649	.636	3.9	3.92	.78
	42	37	20	4	3	287		263	125	107	16	2	126	168	4	0	22	12	.649	.636	.4	3.92	.78

Teams: New York, A.L., 1930–1942; Washington, 1943.
Points in MVP Voting: 1931, 0; 1932, 0; 1933, 0; 1934, 0; 1935, 0; 1937, 14 (9th, .18); 1938, 1 (.00); 1940, 0; 1941, 0; 1942, 0; 1943, 0.
Other Notes: Named to *The Sporting News* major league All-Star team in 1934 and 1938.

PLAYER: TOMMY BRIDGES

	HOW MUCH HE PITCHED							WHAT HE GAVE UP									WHAT THE RESULTS WERE						
Year	G	GS	CG	GF	ShO	IP	BFP	H	R	ER	SH	HB	TBB	SO	WP	Bk	W	L	Pct.	Rest of Team	Above Team	Runs per Game	Percentage of League
1930	8	5	2	2	0	38	158	28	18	17	5	0	23	17	0	0	3	2	.600	.483	.6	4.26	.79
1931	35	23	8	8	2	173	809	182	120	96	10	0	108	105	9	1	8	16	.333	.408	−1.8	6.24	1.21
1932	34	26	10	7	4	201	881	174	95	75	15	1	119	108	6	1	14	12	.538	.496	1.1	4.25	.81
1933	33	28	17	4	2	233	984	192	102	80	19	6	110	120	2	1	14	12	.538	.477	1.6	3.94	.79
1934	36	35	23	1	3	275	1153	249	117	112	11	3	104	151	3	0	22	11	.667	.653	.5	3.83	.75
1935	36	34	23	1	4	274	1195	277	129	107	10	3	113	163	5	1	21	10	.677	.600	2.4	4.24	.83
1936	39	38	26	1	5	295	1272	289	141	118	17	5	115	175	6	1	23	11	.676	.500	6.0	4.30	.76
1937	34	31	18	2	3	245	1076	267	129	111	9	3	91	138	4	1	15	12	.556	.583	−.7	4.74	.91
1938	25	20	13	4	0	151	665	171	83	77	10	2	58	101	2	0	13	9	.591	.538	1.2	4.95	.92
1939	29	26	16	2	2	198	840	186	87	77	7	6	61	129	4	0	17	7	.708	.492	5.2	3.95	.76
1940	29	28	12	1	2	198	843	171	89	74	9	0	88	133	5	0	12	9	.571	.586	−.3	4.05	.81
1941	25	22	10	2	1	148	630	128	66	56	9	1	70	90	2	1	9	12	.429	.496	−1.4	4.01	.85
1942	23	22	11	1	2	174	742	164	66	53	10	4	61	97	5	0	9	7	.563	.464	1.6	3.41	.80
1943	25	22	11	3	3	192	774	159	57	51	8	0	61	124	3	0	12	7	.632	.489	2.7	2.67	.69
1945	4	1	0	2	0	11	48	14	6	4	1	0	2	6	2	0	1	0	1.000	.572	.4	4.91	1.26
1946	9	1	0	6	0	22	95	24	16	14	0	1	8	17	1	1	1	1	.500	.599	−.2	6.55	1.61
	424	362	200	47	33	2828	12165	2675	1321	1122	150	35	1192	1674	59	8	194	138	.584	.528	18.8	4.20	.86
9.98 Years	42	36	20	5	3	283		268	132	112	15	4	119	168	6	1	19	14	.584	.528	1.9	4.20	.86

Teams: Detroit, 1930–1946.
Points in MVP Voting: 1931, 0; 1932, 0; 1933, 0; 1934, 0; 1935, 11 (.14); 1936, 25 (9th, .31); 1937, 0; 1938, 0; 1940, 0; 1941, 0; 1942, 0; 1943, 0; 1946, 0. TOTAL: .45 Award Shares.
Note: Macmillan erroneously lists Bridges with 15 complete games in 1931. Eight (8) is the correct figure.

PLAYER: DIZZY DEAN

	HOW MUCH HE PITCHED							WHAT HE GAVE UP									WHAT THE RESULTS WERE						
Year	G	GS	CG	GF	ShO	IP	BFP	H	R	ER	SH	HB	TBB	SO	WP	Bk	W	L	Pct.	Rest of Team	Above Team	Runs per Game	Percentage of League
1930	1	1	1	0	0	9	33	3	1	1	1	0	3	5	0	0	1	0	1.000	.595	.4	1.00	.18
1932	46	33	16	10	4	286	1203	280	122	105	18	5	102	191	2	2	18	15	.545	.446	3.3	3.84	.84
1933	48	34	26	11	3	293	1202	279	113	99	15	5	64	199	2	0	20	18	.526	.539	−.5	3.47	.87
1934	50	33	24	14	7	312	1291	288	110	92	16	6	75	195	2	0	30	7	.811	.560	9.3	3.17	.68
1935	50	36	29	14	3	324	1365	326	128	112	16	4	82	182	1	0	28	12	.700	.596	4.1	3.56	.76
1936	51	34	28	17	2	315	1303	310	128	111	20	3	53	195	4	0	24	13	.649	.538	4.1	3.66	.78
1937	27	25	17	2	4	197	818	206	76	59	11	2	33	120	1	3	13	10	.565	.519	1.1	3.47	.77
1938	13	10	3	2	1	75	288	63	20	15	0	1	8	22	0	0	7	1	.875	.569	2.4	2.40	.54
1939	19	13	7	5	2	96	403	98	40	36	9	1	17	27	0	0	6	4	.600	.542	.6	3.75	.84
1940	10	9	3	1	0	54	247	68	35	31	5	0	20	18	0	0	3	3	.500	.486	.1	5.83	1.33
1941	1	1	0	0	0	1	7	3	3	2	0	0	0	1	0	0	0	0	.000	.455	.0	27.00	6.38
1947	1	1	0	0	0	4	14	3	3	0	0	0	1	0	0	0	0	0	.000	.383	.0	0	0
	317	230	154	76	26	1966	8174	1927	776	663	111	27	458	1155	12	5	150	83	.644	.537	24.8	3.55	.78
7.06 Years	45	33	22	11	4	279		273	110	94	16	4	65	164	2	1	21	12	.644	.537	3.5	3.55	.78

Teams: St. Louis, 1930, 1932–1937; Chicago, N.L., 1938–1941; St. Louis, A.L., 1947.
Points in MVP Voting: 1932, 6 (.07); 1933, 23 (7th, .29); 1934, 78 (1st, .98); 1935, 66 (2nd, .83); 1936, 53 (2nd, .88); 1937, 0; 1938, 0; 1940, 0; 1941, 0; 1947, 0. TOTAL: 3.05 Award Shares.

PLAYER: PAUL DERRINGER

	HOW MUCH HE PITCHED							WHAT HE GAVE UP									WHAT THE RESULTS WERE						
Year	G	GS	CG	GF	ShO	IP	BFP	H	R	ER	SH	HB	TBB	SO	WP	Bk	W	L	Pct.	Rest of Team	Above Team	Runs per Game	Percentage of League
1931	35	23	15	10	4	212	901	225	88	79	11	4	65	134	6	0	18	8	.692	.648	1.1	3.74	.83
1932	39	30	14	4	1	233	1043	296	133	105	18	2	67	78	9	0	11	14	.440	.473	−.8	5.14	1.12
1933	36	33	17	3	2	248	1045	264	117	91	26	6	60	89	7	0	7	27	.206	.445	−8.1	4.25	1.07
1934	47	31	18	15	1	261	1128	297	129	104	14	4	59	122	7	0	15	21	.417	.322	3.4	4.45	.95
1935	45	33	20	9	3	277	1153	295	132	108	13	4	49	120	2	0	22	13	.629	.390	8.4	4.29	.91
1936	51	37	13	10	2	282	1207	331	147	126	14	4	42	121	6	2	19	19	.500	.474	1.0	4.69	1.00
1937	43	26	12	12	1	223	963	240	112	100	22	0	55	94	0	0	10	14	.417	.354	1.5	4.52	1.00
1938	41	37	26	4	4	307	1263	315	110	100	11	0	49	132	1	0	21	14	.600	.530	2.4	3.22	.73
1939	38	35	28	1	5	301	1245	321	115	98	29	3	35	128	2	0	25	7	.781	.590	6.1	3.44	.77
1940	37	37	26	0	3	297	1205	280	110	101	18	0	48	115	1	0	20	12	.625	.661	−1.2	3.33	.76
1941	29	28	17	4	2	228	950	233	91	84	20	0	54	76	2	0	12	14	.462	.594	−3.4	3.59	.85
1942	29	27	13	0	1	209	872	203	83	71	8	4	49	68	0	0	10	11	.476	.436	.8	3.57	.92
1943	32	22	10	7	2	174	743	184	90	69	8	0	39	75	3	0	10	14	.417	.496	−1.9	4.66	1.17
1944	42	16	7	17	0	180	772	205	96	83	11	0	39	69	2	0	7	13	.350	.507	−3.1	4.80	1.08
1945	35	30	15	5	1	214	901	223	99	82	9	1	51	86	2	0	16	11	.593	.646	−1.4	4.16	.93
	579	445	251	91	32	3646	15391	3912	1652	1401	232	32	761	1507	50	2	223	212	.513	.502	4.7	4.08	.93
13.14 Years	44	34	19	7	2	278		298	126	107	18	2	58	115	4	0	17	16	.513	.502	.4	4.08	.93

Teams: St. Louis, 1931–1932; St. Louis/Cincinnati, 1933; Cincinnati, 1934–1942; Chicago, N.L. 1943–1945.
Points in MVP Voting: 1931, 18 (5th, .28); 1932, 0; 1933, 0; 1934, 0; 1935, 4 (.05); 1936, 6 (.10); 1937, 0; 1938, 70 (8th, .21); 1939, 174 (3rd, .52); 1940, 121 (4th, .36); 1941, 0; 1942, 0; 1943, 0; 1944, 0. TOTAL: 1.52 Award Shares.
Other Notes: Named to *The Sporting News* major league All-Star team in 1940.

PLAYER: THORNTON LEE

	HOW MUCH HE PITCHED							WHAT HE GAVE UP										WHAT THE RESULTS WERE					
Year	G	GS	CG	GF	ShO	IP	BFP	H	R	ER	HR	SH	HB	TBB	SO	WP	Bk	W	L	Pct.	Rest of Team	Above Team	Runs per Game	Percentage of League
1933	3	2	2	0	0	17	75	13	9	8	0	0	0	11	7	0	0	1	1	.500	.500	0	4.76	.95
1934	24	6	0	6	0	86	400	105	57	48	12	3	3	44	41	1	1	1	1	.500	.553	−.1	5.97	1.16
1935	32	20	8	9	1	181	783	179	90	81	16	4	1	71	81	1	1	7	10	.412	.551	−2.4	4.48	.88
1936	43	8	2	13	0	127	584	138	86	69	5	2	2	67	49	3	2	3	5	.375	.527	−1.2	6.09	1.07
1937	30	25	13	4	2	205	876	209	91	80	10	1	1	60	80	1	0	12	10	.545	.561	−.3	4.00	.76
1938	33	30	18	3	1	245	1074	252	123	95	20	3	3	94	77	2	0	13	12	.520	.423	2.4	4.52	.84
1939	33	29	15	4	2	235	1006	260	121	110	23	3	3	70	81	2	1	15	11	.577	.547	.8	4.63	.89
1940	28	27	24	0	1	228	948	223	100	88	12	2	2	56	87	4	1	12	13	.480	.543	−1.6	3.95	.78
1941	35	34	30	1	3	300	1224	258	98	79	15	4	2	92	130	2	0	22	11	.667	.455	7.0	2.94	.62
1942	11	8	6	3	1	76	334	82	38	28	6	2	1	31	25	2	0	2	6	.250	.457	−1.7	4.50	1.06
1943	19	19	7	0	1	127	550	129	66	59	11	4	1	50	35	0	0	5	9	.357	.550	−2.7	4.68	1.20
1944	15	14	6	1	0	113	461	105	51	38	9	1	1	25	39	2	0	3	9	.250	.479	−2.7	4.06	.99
1945	29	28	19	1	1	228	951	208	81	62	15	10	1	76	108	1	1	15	12	.556	.532	.6	3.20	.82
1946	7	7	2	0	0	43	187	39	24	17	3	1	1	23	23	2	0	2	4	.333	.486	−.9	5.02	1.24
1947	21	11	2	5	1	87	394	86	50	43	7	2	1	56	57	1	0	3	7	.300	.465	−1.7	5.17	1.25
1948	11	4	1	0	0	33	150	41	20	16	3	2	1	12	17	0	0	1	3	.250	.513	−1.1	5.45	1.15
	374	272	155	55	14	2331	9999	2327	1105	921	166	43		838	937	24	7	117	124	.485	.508	−5.5	4.27	.89
8.33 Years	45	33	19	6	2	280		279	133	111	20	5		101	112	3	1	14	15	.485	.508	−.7	4.27	.89

Teams: Cleveland, 1933–1936; Chicago, A.L., 1937–1947; New York, N.L., 1948.

Points in MVP Voting: 1933, 0; 1934, 0; 1935, 0; 1936, 0; 1937, 0; 1938, 0; 1940, 0; 1941, 144 (4th, .43); 1942, 0; 1943, 0; 1944, 0; 1946, 0; 1947, 0; 1948, 0.

Other Notes: Named to *The Sporting News* major league All-Star team in 1941.

PLAYER: BUCKY WALTERS

	HOW MUCH HE PITCHED							WHAT HE GAVE UP										WHAT THE RESULTS WERE						
Year	G	GS	CG	GF	ShO	IP	BFP	H	R	ER	HR	SH	HB	TBB	SO	WP	Bk	W	L	Pct.	Rest of Team	Above Team	Runs per Game	Percentage of League
1934	2	1	0	1	0	7	30	8	3	1	0	1		2	7	0	0	0	0	.000	.500	.0	3.86	.82
1935	24	22	8	2	2	151	666	168	86	70	9	7		68	40	4	0	9	9	.500	.407	1.7	5.13	1.09
1936	40	33	15	3	4	258	1159	284	146	122	15	5		115	66	7	0	11	21	.344	.352	−.3	5.09	1.08
1937	37	34	15	1	3	246	1094	292	148	130	14	3		86	87	4	0	14	15	.483	.379	3.0	5.41	1.20
1938	39	34	20	3	3	251	1111	259	134	117	8	5		108	93	11	0	15	14	.517	.426	2.6	4.80	1.09
1939	39	36	31	2	2	319	1283	250	98	81	18	6		109	137	8	3	27	11	.711	.603	4.1	2.76	.62
1940	36	36	29	0	3	305	1207	241	95	84	14	5		92	115	3	0	22	10	.688	.645	1.4	2.80	.64
1941	37	35	27	2	5	302	1252	292	108	95	15	2		88	129	7	0	19	15	.559	.575	−.5	3.22	.76
1942	34	32	21	1	2	254	1054	223	101	75	12	5		73	109	2	0	15	14	.517	.504	.4	3.58	.92
1943	34	34	21	0	5	246	1054	244	105	97	19	1		109	80	8	1	15	15	.500	.581	−2.4	3.84	.96
1944	34	32	27	2	6	285	1162	233	92	76	7	4		87	77	2	0	23	8	.742	.537	6.4	2.91	.66
1945	22	22	12	0	3	168	706	166	62	50	12	2		51	45	3	0	10	10	.500	.381	2.4	3.32	.74
1946	22	22	10	0	2	151	636	146	55	43	9	2		64	60	2	1	10	7	.588	.416	2.9	3.28	.83
1947	20	20	5	0	2	122	550	137	83	78	15	6		49	43	0	1	8	8	.500	.471	.5	6.12	1.34
1948	7	5	1	1	0	35	157	42	25	18	6	6	0	18	19	1	0	0	3	.000	.427	−1.3	6.43	1.45
1950	1	0	0	0	0	4	19	5	2	2	0	1	0	2	0	1	0	0	0	.000	.539	.0	4.50	.97
	428	398	242	18	42	3104	13140	2990	1343	1139	173	51		1121	1107	63	6	198	160	.553	.495	20.8	3.89	.88
10.40 Years	41	38	23	2	4	298		287	129	110	17	5		108	106	6	1	19	15	.553	.495	2.0	3.89	.88

Teams: Boston A, 1934; Philadelphia, 1935–1937; Philadelphia/Cincinnati, 1938; Cincinnati, 1939–1948; Boston, 1950.
Points in MVP Voting: 1934, 0; 1935, 0; 1937, 0; 1938, 0; 1939, 303 (1st, .90); 1940, 146 (3rd, .43); 1941, 6 (.02); 1942, 0; 1943, 1 (.00); 1944, 107 (5th, .32); 1945, 0; 1947, 0; 1948, 0; 1950, 0. TOTAL: 1.67 Award Shares.
Other Notes: Named to *The Sporting News* major league All-Star team in 1939 and 1940.

PLAYER: BOB FELLER

	HOW MUCH HE PITCHED							WHAT HE GAVE UP												WHAT THE RESULTS WERE						
Year	G	GS	CG	GF	ShO	IP	BFP	H	R	ER	HR	SH	SF	HB	TBB	IBB	SO	WP	Bk	W	L	Pct.	Rest of Team	Above Team	Runs per Game	Percentage of League
1936	14	8	5	5	0	62	279	52	29	23		1		4	47		76	8	3	5	3	.625	.514	.9	4.21	.74
1937	26	19	9	4	0	149	651	116	68	56		12		2	106		150	5	2	9	7	.563	.536	.4	4.11	.79
1938	39	36	20	3	2	278	1248	225	136	126		11		7	208		240	5	1	17	11	.607	.556	1.4	4.40	.82
1939	39	35	24	3	4	297	1243	227	105	94		17		3	142		246	14	1	24	9	.727	.521	6.8	3.18	.61
1940	43	37	31	5	4	320	1304	245	102	93		13		5	118		261	8	0	27	11	.711	.534	6.7	2.87	.58
1941	44	40	28	4	6	343	1466	284	129	120		13		5	194		260	6	0	25	13	.658	.431	8.6	3.38	.71
1945	9	9	7	0	1	72	300	50	21	20		3		2	35		59	1	0	5	3	.625	.496	1.0	2.63	.67
1946	48	42	36	5	10	371	1512	277	101	90		25		3	153		348	3	0	26	15	.634	.372	10.8	2.45	.60
1947	42	37	20	4	5	299	1218	230	97	89		15		4	127		196	7	2	20	11	.645	.488	4.9	2.92	.70
1948	44	38	18	3	3	280	1186	255	123	111		11		2	116		164	2	0	19	15	.559	.645	-2.9	3.95	.84
1949	36	28	15	6	0	211	894	198	104	88		9		1	84		108	9	1	15	14	.517	.592	-2.2	4.44	.95
1950	35	34	16	0	3	247	1055	230	105	94	20	14		5	103		119	3	0	16	11	.593	.598	-.2	3.83	.76
1951	33	32	16	1	4	250	1061	239	105	97	22	13		7	95		111	2	0	22	8	.733	.573	4.8	3.78	.81
1952	30	30	11	0	1	192	869	219	124	101	13	22		3	83		81	1	1	9	13	.409	.636	-5.0	5.81	1.39
1953	25	25	10	0	1	176	721	163	78	70	16	8		3	60		60	1	1	10	7	.588	.599	-.2	3.99	.89
1954	19	19	9	0	1	140	580	127	53	48	13	6		3	39		59	0	0	13	3	.813	.710	1.6	3.41	.81
1955	25	11	2	4	1	83	340	71	43	32	7	2	4	1	31	2	25	0	1	4	4	.500	.610	-.9	4.66	1.05
1956	19	4	2	5	0	58	253	63	34	32	7	3	2	0	23	4	18	0	1	0	4	.000	.587	-2.3	5.28	1.13
13.39 Years	570	484	279	52	46	3828	16180	3271	1557	1384	98	198		60	1764		2581	75	13	266	162	.621	.541	34.3	3.66	.78
	43	36	21	4	3	286		244	116	103		14		4	132		193	6	1	20	12	.621	.541	2.6	3.66	.78

Teams: Cleveland, 1936–41, 1945–1956.

Points in MVP Voting: 1937, 0; 1938, 0; 1939, 155 (3rd, .46); 1940, 222 (2nd, .66); 1941, 174 (3rd, .52); 1946, 105 (6th, .31); 1947, 58 (8th, .17); 1948, 6 (.02); 1949, 0; 1950, 0; 1951, 118 (5th, .35); 1952, 0; 1953, 0. TOTAL: 2.49 Award Shares.

Reported Salaries: 1940, $50,000. Reportedly had attendance clause in contract in late forties. When Cleveland attendance went over two million in 1948, Feller reportedly cleared over $100,000, a record to that point.

Other Notes: Named to *The Sporting News* major league All-Star team in 1939, 1940, 1941, 1946, 1947.

PLAYER: MORT COOPER

	HOW MUCH HE PITCHED							WHAT HE GAVE UP										WHAT THE RESULTS WERE						
Year	G	GS	CG	GF	ShO	IP	BFP	H	R	ER	HR	SH	HB	TBB	SO	WP	Bk	W	L	Pct.	Rest of Team	Above Team	Runs per Game	Percentage of League
1938	4	3	1	1	0	24	102	17	11	8		2	1	12	11	0	0	2	1	.667	.466	.6	4.12	.93
1939	45	26	7	12	2	211	919	208	94	76	21	2	97	130	4	1	12	6	.667	.593	1.3	4.01	.90
1940	38	29	16	6	3	231	992	225	103	93	14	3	86	95	5	2	11	12	.478	.562	−1.9	4.01	.91
1941	29	25	12	2	0	187	800	175	88	81	11	3	69	118	7	0	13	9	.591	.641	−1.1	4.24	1.00
1942	37	35	22	1	10	279	1100	207	73	55	14	5	68	152	5	0	22	7	.759	.672	2.5	2.35	.60
1943	37	32	24	5	6	274	1109	228	81	70	17	5	79	141	4	2	21	8	.724	.672	1.5	2.66	.67
1944	34	33	22	1	7	252	1023	227	74	69	9	5	60	97	0	1	22	7	.759	.664	2.7	2.64	.60
1945	24	14	5	9	1	102	426	97	42	33	2	2	34	59	0	0	9	4	.692	.446	3.2	3.71	.83
1946	28	27	15	1	4	199	805	181	76	69	16	9	39	83	2	1	13	11	.542	.700	−3.8	3.44	.87
1947	18	15	4	1	0	83	369	99	58	50	9	6	26	27	0	0	3	10	.231	.574	−4.5	6.29	1.38
1949	1	0	0	0	0	0	3	2	3	3	1	0	0	1	0	1	0	0	0	.000	.396	.0	INF	INF
6.82 Years	295	239	128	39	33	1842	7648	1666	703	607	105	28	571	913	28	7	128	75	.631	.628	.6	3.43	.80
	43	35	19	6	5	270		244	103	89	15	4	84	134	4	1	19	11	.631	.628	.1	3.43	.80

Teams: St. Louis, N.L., 1938–1944; St. Louis, N.L./Boston, 1945; Boston, 1946; Boston/New York, N.L., 1947; Chicago, N.L., 1949.

Points in MVP Voting: 1938, 0; 1940, 0; 1941, 8 (.02); 1942, 263 (1st, .78); 1943, 130 (5th, .39); 1944, 63 (9th, .19); 1946, 0; 1947, 0; 1949, 0. TOTAL: 1.38 Award Shares.

Reported Salaries: 1944—$15,000.

Other Notes: Named to *The Sporting News* major league All-Star team in 1942, 1943, and 1944.

PLAYER: HAL NEWHOUSER

	HOW MUCH HE PITCHED							WHAT HE GAVE UP												WHAT THE RESULTS WERE						
Year	G	GS	CG	GF	ShO	IP	BFP	H	R	ER	HR	SH	SF	HB	TBB	IBB	SO	WP	Bk	W	L	Pct.	Rest of Team	Above Team	Runs per Game	Percentage of League
1939	1	1	1	0	0	5	22	3	3	3	2			0	4		4	3	0	0	1	.000	.529	−.5	5.40	1.04
1940	28	20	7	3	0	133	613	149	81	72	6			2	76		89	1	1	9	9	.500	.596	−1.7	5.48	1.10
1941	33	27	5	5	1	173	810	166	109	92	5			1	137		106	5	0	9	11	.450	.493	−.9	5.67	1.20
1942	38	23	11	14	1	184	789	137	73	50	10			2	114		103	2	0	8	14	.364	.492	−2.8	3.57	.84
1943	37	25	10	9	1	196	850	163	88	66	12			0	111		144	3	1	8	17	.320	.543	−5.6	4.04	1.04
1944	47	34	25	10	6	312	1271	264	94	77	18			1	102		187	4	2	29	9	.763	.509	9.7	2.71	.66
1945	40	36	29	2	8	313	1261	239	73	63	19			0	110		212	10	2	25	9	.735	.529	7.0	2.10	.54
1946	37	34	29	2	6	292	1176	215	77	63	9			1	98		275	8	0	26	9	.743	.555	6.6	2.37	.59
1947	40	36	24	4	3	285	1216	268	105	91	27			2	110		176	11	0	17	17	.500	.567	−2.3	3.32	.80
1948	39	35	19	4	2	272	1146	249	109	91	15			1	99		143	5	0	21	12	.636	.471	5.5	3.61	.76
1949	38	35	22	3	3	292	1228	277	118	109	12			0	111		144	3	0	18	11	.621	.552	2.0	3.64	.78
1950	35	30	15	5	1	214	929	232	110	103	23	12		4	81		87	4	0	15	13	.536	.635	−2.8	4.63	.92
1951	15	14	7	0	1	96	393	98	47	42	10	6		3	19		37	1	1	6	6	.500	.472	.3	4.41	.95
1952	25	19	8	2	0	154	643	148	72	64	13	13		0	47		57	3	0	9	9	.500	.301	3.6	4.21	1.01
1953	7	4	0	1	0	22	102	31	22	17	4	3		2	8		6	1	0	0	1	.000	.392	−.4	9.00	2.02
1954	26	1	0	15	0	47	187	34	16	13	3	6	0	0	18	1	25	0	0	7	2	.778	.717	.5	3.06	.73
1955	2	0	0	0	0	2	12	1	0	0	0	0	0	0	4	1	1	1	0	0	0	.000	.604	.0	0	0
	488	374	212	79	33	2992	12648	2674	1197	1016	53	175		19	1249		1796	65	7	207	150	.580	.529	18.2	3.60	.81
11.06 Years	44	34	19	7	3	271		242	108	92	16			2	113		162	6	1	19	14	.580	.529	1.6	3.60	.81

Teams: Detroit, 1939–1953; Cleveland, 1954–1955.

Points in MVP Voting: 1940, 0; 1941, 0; 1942, 0; 1943, 0; 1944, 236 (1st, .70); 1945, 236 (1st, .70); 1946, 197 (2nd, .59); 1947, 0; 1948, 43 (.13); 1949, 0; 1950, 0; 1951, 0; 1952, 0; 1953, 0. TOTAL: 2.12 Award Shares.

Other Notes: Named to the major league All-Star team in 1944, 1945, 1946 by *The Sporting News*.

PLAYER: DIZZY TROUT

	HOW MUCH HE PITCHED							WHAT HE GAVE UP												WHAT THE RESULTS WERE						
Year	G	GS	CG	GF	ShO	IP	BFP	H	R	ER	HR	SH	SF	HB	TBB	IBB	SO	WP	Bk	W	L	Pct.	Rest of Team	Above Team	Runs per Game	Percentage of League
1939	33	22	6	6	0	162	716	168	82	65		15		4	74		72	5	1	9	10	.474	.533	−1.1	4.56	.87
1940	33	10	1	6	0	101	469	125	60	50		5		3	54		64	3	0	3	7	.300	.604	−3.0	5.35	1.06
1941	37	18	6	11	1	152	671	144	76	63		13		2	84		88	4	1	9	9	.500	.485	.3	4.50	.95
1942	35	29	13	5	1	223	965	214	98	85		13		4	89		91	8	1	12	18	.400	.492	−2.8	3.96	.93
1943	44	30	18	14	5	247	1019	204	83	68		18		0	101		111	6	0	20	12	.625	.475	4.8	3.02	.78
1944	49	40	33	6	7	352	1421	314	104	83		11		4	83		144	2	0	27	14	.659	.540	4.9	2.66	.65
1945	41	31	18	9	4	246	1041	252	108	86		19		0	79		97	5	1	18	15	.545	.583	−1.2	3.95	1.01
1946	38	32	23	6	5	276	1142	244	85	72		17		3	97		151	2	1	17	13	.567	.605	−1.1	2.77	.68
1947	32	26	9	6	2	186	795	186	85	72		13		3	65		74	2	1	10	11	.476	.564	−1.8	4.11	.99
1948	32	23	11	6	2	184	803	193	87	70		10		2	73		91	3	1	10	14	.417	.523	−2.6	4.26	.90
1949	33	0	0	24	0	59	261	68	35	29		7		0	21		19	1	0	3	6	.333	.579	−2.2	5.34	1.14
1950	34	20	11	6	1	185	791	190	84	77	13	10		5	64		88	0	0	13	5	.722	.603	2.1	4.09	.81
1951	42	22	7	17	0	192	797	172	98	86	13	3		1	75		89	4	0	9	14	.391	.489	−2.2	4.59	.99
1952	36	19	2	11	0	161	719	163	78	70	7	18		3	87		77	5	0	10	13	.435	.450	−.4	4.36	1.04
1957	2	0	0	1	0	1	5	4	3	3	0	0	0	0	0	0	0	0	0	0	0	.000	.549	.0	27.00	6.38
	521	322	158	134	28	2727	11615	2641	1166	979	33	172		34	1046		1256	50	7	170	161	.514	.533	−6.5	3.85	.88
11.04 Years	47	29	14	12	3	247		239	106	89	3	16		3	95		114	5	1	15	15	.514	.533	−.6	3.85	.88

Teams: Detroit, 1939–1951; Detroit/Boston, 1952; Baltimore, 1957.

Points in MVP Voting: 1940, 0; 1941, 0; 1942, 0; 1943, 38 (.11); 1944, 232 (2nd, .69); 1946, 0; 1947, 0; 1948, 0; 1949, 0; 1950, 21 (.06); 1951, 0; 1952, 0. TOTAL: .86 Award Shares.

Other Notes: Named to *The Sporting News* major league All-Star team in 1944.

PLAYER: EARLY WYNN

	HOW MUCH HE PITCHED							WHAT HE GAVE UP											WHAT THE RESULTS WERE						
Year	G	GS	CG	GF	ShO	IP	BFP	H	R	ER	HR	SH	SF	HB	TBB	IBB	SO	WP	Bk	W	L	Pct.	Rest of Team	Above Team	Runs per Game	Percentage of League
1939	3	3	1	0	0	20	97	26	15	13	4			0	10		1	2	0	0	2	.000	.433	−.9	6.75	1.30
1941	5	5	4	0	0	40	167	35	14	7	2			0	10		15	0	0	3	1	.750	.450	1.2	3.15	.66
1942	30	28	10	2	1	190	870	246	129	108	10			3	73		58	3	1	10	16	.385	.416	−.8	6.11	1.43
1943	37	33	12	4	3	257	1067	232	97	83	17			1	83		89	2	0	18	12	.600	.537	1.9	3.40	.87
1944	33	25	19	7	2	208	883	221	97	78	15			2	67		65	2	0	8	17	.320	.434	−2.9	4.20	1.03
1946	17	12	9	5	0	107	460	112	45	37		5		3	33		36	3	0	8	5	.615	.482	1.7	3.79	.93
1947	33	31	22	2	2	247	1058	251	114	100		5		5	90		73	4	0	17	15	.531	.385	4.7	4.15	1.00
1948	33	31	15	1	1	198	912	236	144	128		18		1	94		49	2	0	8	19	.296	.381	−2.3	6.55	1.38
1949	26	23	6	2	0	165	724	186	84	76		6		1	57		62	0	0	11	7	.611	.574	.7	4.58	.98
1950	32	28	14	4	2	214	903	166	88	76	20	14		4	101		143	0	1	18	8	.692	.578	3.0	3.70	.73
1951	37	34	21	3	3	274	1138	227	102	92	18	20		3	107		133	1	0	20	13	.606	.603	.1	3.35	.72
1952	42	33	19	9	4	286	1190	239	103	92	23	22		1	132		153	5	0	23	12	.657	.588	2.4	3.24	.78
1953	36	34	16	2	1	252	1077	234	121	110	19	11		4	107		138	5	0	17	12	.586	.600	−.4	4.32	.97
1954	40	36	20	4	3	271	1102	225	93	82	21	18		0	83		155	2	0	23	11	.676	.733	−1.9	3.09	.74
1955	32	31	16	1	6	230	964	207	86	72	19	11	7	3	80	3	122	3	0	17	11	.607	.603	.1	3.37	.76
1956	38	35	18	2	4	278	1144	233	93	84	19	12	12	5	91	7	158	5	0	20	9	.690	.544	4.2	3.01	.65
1957	40	37	13	2	1	263	1146	270	139	126	32	13	5	5	104	7	184	0	0	14	17	.452	.508	−1.8	4.76	1.12
1958	40	34	11	6	4	240	1016	214	115	110	27	14	6	6	104	3	179	3	0	14	16	.467	.548	−2.5	4.31	1.03
1959	37	37	14	0	5	256	1076	202	106	90	20	6	6	9	119	5	179	5	0	22	10	.688	.590	3.1	3.73	.85
1960	36	35	13	1	4	237	1024	220	105	92	20	13	6	4	112	2	158	1	0	13	12	.520	.574	−1.3	3.99	.91
1961	17	16	5	1	0	110	457	88	43	43	11	6	3	1	47	0	64	1	0	8	2	.800	.513	2.9	3.52	.78
1962	27	26	11	1	3	168	710	171	90	83	15	2	2	3	56	6	91	2	0	7	15	.318	.557	−5.3	4.82	1.09
1963	20	5	1	7	0	55	223	50	14	14	2	6	2	0	15	3	29	0	0	1	2	.333	.491	−.5	2.29	.56
16.49 Years	691	612	290	66	49	4566	19408	4291	2037	1796	266	249	49	64	1775	36	2334	51	2	300	244	.551	.541	5.5	4.02	.91
	42	37	18	4	3	277		260	124	109		15		4	108		142	3	0	18	15	.551	.541	.3	4.02	.91

Teams: Washington, 1939, 1941–1944, 1946–1948; Cleveland, 1949–1957; Chicago, A.L., 1958–1962, Cleveland, 1963.
Points in MVP Voting: 1940, 0; 1941, 0; 1942, 0; 1943, 13 (.04); 1944, 0; 1946, 0; 1947, 7 (.02); 1948, 0; 1949, 0; 1950, 0; 1951, 29 (.09); 1952, 99 (5th, .29); 1953, 0; 1954, 74 (6th, .21); 1958, 0; 1959, 123 (3rd, .37); 1960, 0; 1961, 0; 1962, 0; 1963, 0. TOTAL: 1.02 Award Shares.
Reported Salaries: 1960, $40,000.
Other Notes: Named to *The Sporting News* major league All-Star team in 1959.

PLAYER: HARRY BRECHEEN

	HOW MUCH HE PITCHED							WHAT HE GAVE UP										WHAT THE RESULTS WERE						
Year	G	GS	CG	GF	ShO	IP	BFP	H	R	ER	HR	SH	HB	TBB	SO	WP	Bk	W	L	Pct.	Rest of Team	Above Team	Runs per Game	Percentage of League
1940	3	0	0	3	0	3	14	2	0	0		0	0	2	4	0	0	0	0	.000	.549	.0	.00	.00
1943	29	13	8	12	1	135	527	98	41	34		9	3	39	68	2	0	9	6	.600	.691	−1.4	2.73	.68
1944	30	22	13	4	3	189	774	174	67	60		6	3	46	88	3	2	16	5	.762	.669	1.9	3.19	.72
1945	24	18	13	6	3	157	629	136	48	44		8	5	44	63	0	0	14	4	.778	.596	3.3	2.75	.62
1946	36	30	14	3	5	231	954	212	73	64	8	13	4	67	117	1	0	15	15	.500	.659	−4.8	2.84	.72
1947	29	28	18	1	1	223	927	220	92	82	19	11	3	66	89	3	0	16	11	.593	.575	.5	3.71	.81
1948	33	30	21	1	7	233	931	193	62	58	6	11	2	49	149	2	1	20	7	.741	.512	6.2	2.39	.54
1949	32	31	14	1	2	215	906	207	96	80	17	12	7	65	88	3	0	14	11	.560	.636	−1.9	4.02	.88
1950	27	23	12	3	2	163	675	151	77	69	18	7	3	45	80	2	0	8	11	.421	.522	−1.9	4.25	.91
1951	24	16	5	7	0	139	582	134	54	50	11	4	1	54	57	0	1	8	4	.667	.514	1.8	3.50	.78
1952	25	13	4	5	1	100	408	82	39	37	12	9	3	28	54	1	0	7	5	.583	.570	.2	3.51	.84
1953	26	16	3	7	0	117	494	122	51	40	7	7	3	31	44	1	1	5	13	.278	.360	−1.5	3.92	.88
7.17 Years	318	240	125	53	25	1905	7821	1731	700	618		97	37	536	901	18	5	132	92	.589	.578	2.5	3.31	.76
	44	33	17	7	3	266		241	98	86		14	5	75	126	3	1	18	13	.589	.578	.3	3.31	.76

Teams: St. Louis, N.L., 1940, 1943–1952; St. Louis, A.L., 1953.
Points in MVP Voting: 1940, 0; 1943, 0; 1944, 0; 1945, 31 (.09); 1946, 14 (.04); 1947, 0; 1948, 61 (5th, .18); 1949, 0; 1950, 0; 1951, 0; 1952, 0; 1953, 0. TOTAL: .31 Award Shares.
Other Notes: Named to *The Sporting News* major league All-Star team in 1948.

PLAYER: WARREN SPAHN

	HOW MUCH HE PITCHED							WHAT HE GAVE UP												WHAT THE RESULTS WERE						
Year	G	GS	CG	GF	ShO	IP	BFP	H	R	ER	HR	SH	SF	HB	TBB	IBB	SO	WP	Bk	W	L	Pct.	Rest of Team	Above Team	Runs per Game	Percentage of League
1942	4	2	1	0	0	16	79	25	15	10	0	0		0	11		7	0	0	0	0	.000	.399	.0	8.44	2.16
1946	24	16	8	7	0	126	514	107	46	41	6	8		1	36		67	4	0	8	5	.615	.521	1.2	3.29	.83
1947	40	35	22	4	7	290	1174	245	87	75	15	7		1	84		123	5	0	21	10	.677	.528	4.6	2.70	.59
1948	36	35	16	1	3	257	1064	237	115	106	19	8		1	77		114	4	0	15	12	.556	.603	−1.3	4.03	.91
1949	38	38	25	0	4	302	1258	283	125	103	27	12		3	86		151	4	0	21	14	.600	.454	5.1	3.73	.82
1950	41	39	25	2	1	293	1217	248	123	103	22	14		1	111		191	8	0	21	17	.553	.534	.7	3.78	.81
1951	39	36	26	3	7	311	1289	278	111	103	20	11		1	109		164	7	1	22	14	.611	.458	5.5	3.21	.72
1952	40	35	19	5	5	290	1190	263	109	96	19	15		6	73		183	5	0	14	19	.424	.417	.2	3.38	.81
1953	35	32	24	3	5	266	1055	211	75	62	14	12		1	70		148	3	2	23	7	.767	.556	6.3	2.54	.53
1954	39	34	23	2	1	283	1175	262	107	99	24	11	8	1	86		136	3	1	21	12	.636	.562	2.5	3.40	.75
1955	39	32	16	7	1	246	1025	249	99	89	25	11	8	2	65	4	110	4	0	17	14	.548	.553	−.1	3.62	.80
1956	39	35	20	3	3	281	1113	249	92	87	25	7	5	3	52	12	128	7	0	20	11	.645	.585	1.9	2.95	.69
1957	39	35	18	4	4	271	1111	241	94	81	23	9	6	2	78	4	111	2	0	21	11	.656	.607	1.6	3.12	.71
1958	38	36	23	1	2	290	1176	257	106	99	29	9	4	2	76	7	150	2	1	22	11	.667	.579	2.9	3.29	.75
1959	40	36	21	3	4	292	1203	282	106	96	21	13	4	1	70	9	143	2	0	21	15	.583	.542	1.5	3.27	.74
1960	40	33	18	5	4	268	1110	254	114	104	24	10	4	4	74	9	154	1	0	21	10	.677	.545	4.1	3.83	.90
1961	38	34	21	3	4	263	1064	236	96	88	24	20	6	4	64	1	115	4	0	21	13	.618	.517	3.4	3.29	.73
1962	34	34	22	0	0	269	1088	248	97	91	25	11	10	3	55	4	118	4	0	18	14	.563	.523	1.3	3.25	.72
1963	33	33	22	0	7	260	1037	241	85	75	23	10	5	0	49	4	102	4	0	23	7	.767	.462	9.1	2.94	.77
1964	38	25	4	11	1	174	759	204	110	102	23	11	7	2	52	4	78	6	0	6	13	.316	.573	−4.9	5.69	1.42
1965	36	30	8	3	0	198	846	210	104	88	26	9	7	3	56	2	90	2	0	7	16	.304	.410	−2.4	4.73	1.17
	750	665	382	67	63	5246	21547	4830	2016	1798	434	218	74	42	1434	60	2583	81	5	363	245	.597	.526	43.2	3.46	.80
17.90 Years	42	37	21	3	4	293		270	113	100	24	12		2	80		144	5	0	20	14	.597	.526	2.4	3.46	.80

Teams: Boston, 1942, 1946–1952; Milwaukee, 1953–1964; New York, N.L./San Francisco, 1965.
Points in MVP Voting: 1942, 0; 1946, 0; 1947, 26 (.08); 1948, 31 (.09); 1949, 60 (.18); 1950, 14 (.04); 1951, 45 (.13); 1952, 8 (.02); 1953, 120 (5th, .36); 1954, 38 (.11); 1955, 0; 1956, 126 (4th, .38); 1957, 131 (5th, .39); 1958, 108 (5th, .32); 1959, 3 (.01); 1960, 0; 1961, 31 (.14); 1962, 0; 1963, 30 (.11); 1964, 0; 1965, 0. TOTAL: 2.36 Award Shares.
Other Notes: Named to *The Sporting News* major league All-Star team in 1953, 1957, 1958, 1960, and 1961.

PLAYER: BILLY PIERCE

	HOW MUCH HE PITCHED							WHAT HE GAVE UP												WHAT THE RESULTS WERE						
Year	G	GS	CG	GF	ShO	IP	BFP	H	R	ER	HR	SH	SF	HB	TBB	IBB	SO	WP	Bk	W	L	Pct.	Rest of Team	Above Team	Runs per Game	Percentage of League
1945	5	0	0	4	0	10	45	6	2	2		1		1	10		10	0	0	0	0	.000	.575	.0	1.80	.46
1948	22	5	0	9	0	55	258	47	40	39		5		1	51		36	1	0	3	0	1.000	.497	1.5	6.55	1.38
1949	32	26	8	4	0	172	761	145	89	74	14			0	112		95	5	2	7	15	.318	.424	−2.3	4.66	1.00
1950	33	29	15	3	1	219	978	189	112	97	11	11		2	137		118	4	0	12	16	.429	.381	1.3	4.60	.91
1951	37	28	18	6	1	240	1008	237	93	81	14	14		1	73		113	1	0	15	14	.517	.528	−.3	3.49	.75
1952	33	32	14	1	4	255	1042	214	76	73	12	17		3	79		144	3	0	15	12	.556	.520	1.0	2.68	.64
1953	40	33	19	6	7	271	1113	216	94	82	20	15		3	102		186	5	0	18	12	.600	.573	.8	3.12	.70
1954	36	26	12	4	4	189	818	179	86	73	15	11		3	86		148	3	1	9	10	.474	.630	−3.0	4.10	.98
1955	33	26	16	5	6	206	836	162	50	45	16	8	1	3	64	5	157	4	1	15	10	.600	.589	.3	2.18	.49
1956	35	33	21	2	1	276	1166	261	108	102	24	14	1	3	100	7	192	6	1	20	9	.690	.520	4.9	3.52	.76
1957	37	34	16	2	4	257	1062	228	98	93	18	16	1	1	71	9	171	3	1	20	12	.625	.574	1.6	3.43	.81
1958	35	32	19	3	3	245	983	204	83	73	33	12	4	1	66	2	144	1	0	17	11	.607	.516	2.6	3.05	.73
1959	34	33	12	0	2	224	934	217	98	90	26	8	3	3	62	4	114	2	1	14	15	.483	.640	−4.6	3.94	.90
1960	32	30	8	1	1	196	813	201	81	79	24	8	2	0	46	1	108	2	0	14	7	.667	.549	2.5	3.72	.85
1961	39	28	5	5	1	180	764	190	85	76	17	13	5	1	54	3	106	2	0	10	9	.526	.531	−.1	4.25	.94
1962	30	23	7	2	2	162	657	147	67	63	19	4	1	3	35	2	76	2	1	16	6	.727	.608	2.6	3.72	.83
1963	38	13	3	13	1	99	420	106	49	47	12	8	1	1	20	1	52	3	2	3	11	.214	.574	−5.0	4.45	1.17
1964	34	1	0	14	0	49	195	40	14	12	6	3	2	0	10	1	29	1	0	3	0	1.000	.547	1.4	2.57	.64
13.10 Years	585	432	193	84	38	3305	13853	2989	1325	1201	267	182	21	30	1178	35	1999	48	10	211	169	.555	.542	5.2	3.61	.82
	45	33	15	6	3	252		228	101	92		14		2	90		153	4	1	16	13	.555	.542	.4	3.61	.82

Teams: Detroit, 1945, 1948; Chicago, A.L., 1949–1961; San Francisco, 1962–1964.

Points in MVP Voting: 1948, 0; 1949, 0; 1950, 0; 1951, 0; 1952, 3 (.01); 1953, 55 (10th, .16); 1956, 75 (5th, .22); 1958, 0; 1959, 0; 1960, 0; 1961, 0; 1962, 0; 1963, 0; 1964, 0. TOTAL: .39 Award Shares.

Other Notes: Named to *The Sporting News* major league All-Star team in 1956 and 1957.

PLAYER: BOB LEMON

	HOW MUCH HE PITCHED							WHAT HE GAVE UP												WHAT THE RESULTS WERE						
Year	G	GS	CG	GF	ShO	IP	BFP	H	R	ER	HR	SH	SF	HB	TBB	IBB	SO	WP	Bk	W	L	Pct.	Rest of Team	Above Team	Runs per Game	Percentage of League
1946	32	5	1	17	0	94	412	77	40	26		8		0	68		39	5	0	4	5	.444	.441	.0	3.83	.94
1947	37	15	6	15	1	167	725	150	68	64		4		4	97		65	6	0	11	5	.688	.500	3.0	3.66	.88
1948	43	37	20	2	10	294	1214	231	104	92		13		3	129		147	3	0	20	14	.588	.636	−1.6	3.18	.67
1949	37	33	22	4	2	280	1159	211	101	93		14		6	137		138	1	0	22	10	.688	.549	4.4	3.25	.69
1950	44	37	22	5	3	288	1254	281	144	123	28	11		2	146		170	5	0	23	11	.676	.575	3.5	4.50	.89
1951	42	34	17	7	1	263	1139	244	119	103	19	12		2	124		132	4	1	17	14	.548	.618	−2.2	4.07	.88
1952	42	36	28	6	5	310	1252	236	104	86	15	9		6	105		131	8	0	22	11	.667	.587	2.6	3.02	.72
1953	41	36	23	4	5	287	1216	283	119	107	16	14		11	110		98	9	0	21	15	.583	.602	−.7	3.73	.84
1954	36	33	21	1	2	258	1077	228	95	78	12	21		4	92		110	6	1	23	7	.767	.710	1.7	3.31	.79
1955	35	31	5	3	0	211	909	218	103	91	17	7	3	5	74	3	100	8	0	18	10	.643	.595	1.3	4.39	.99
1956	39	35	21	3	2	255	1074	230	103	86	23	10	7	6	89	2	94	4	0	20	14	.588	.567	.7	3.64	.78
1957	21	17	2	2	0	117	540	129	70	60	9	12	8	7	64	6	45	3	0	6	11	.353	.515	−2.7	5.38	1.27
1958	11	1	0	4	0	25	128	41	15	15	3	1	1	1	16	2	8	1	0	0	1	.000	.507	−.5	5.40	1.30
10.40 Years	460	350	188	73	31	2849	12099	2559	1185	1024	142	136	19	57	1251	13	1277	63	2	207	128	.618	.589	9.6	3.74	.84
	44	34	18	7	3	274		246	114	98		13		5	120		123	6	0	20	12	.618	.589	.9	3.74	.84

Teams: Cleveland, 1946–1958
Points in MVP Voting: 1946, 0; 1947, 0; 1948, 101 (5th, .30); 1949, 57 (9th, .17); 1950, 102 (5th, .32); 1951, 0; 1952, 58 (8th, .17); 1953, 22 (.07); 1954, 179 (5th, .53); 1956, 40 (10th, .12); 1958, 0. TOTAL: 1.68 Award Shares.
Other Notes: Named to *The Sporting News* major league All-Star team in 1948, 1950, and 1954.

PLAYER: ROBIN ROBERTS

	HOW MUCH HE PITCHED							WHAT HE GAVE UP												WHAT THE RESULTS WERE						
Year	G	GS	CG	GF	ShO	IP	BFP	H	R	ER	HR	SH	SF	HB	TBB	IBB	SO	WP	Bk	W	L	Pct.	Rest of Team	Above Team	Runs per Game	Percentage of League
1948	20	20	9	0	0	147	604	148	63	52	10	6		4	61		84	1	0	7	9	.438	.428	.2	3.86	.87
1949	43	31	11	9	3	227	933	229	101	93	15	15		5	75		95	1	0	15	15	.500	.532	-1.0	4.00	.88
1950	40	39	21	1	5	304	1228	282	112	102	29	13		2	77		146	2	0	20	11	.645	.577	2.1	3.32	.71
1951	44	39	22	4	6	315	1274	284	115	106	20	10		3	64		127	4	0	21	15	.583	.441	5.1	3.29	.74
1952	39	37	30	2	3	330	1310	292	104	95	22	11		5	45		148	3	0	28	7	.800	.496	10.6	2.84	.68
1953	44	41	33	2	5	347	1412	324	119	106	30	12		2	61		198	3	0	23	16	.590	.522	2.7	3.09	.65
1954	45	38	29	6	4	337	1331	289	116	111	35	14	7	5	56		185	2	0	23	15	.605	.448	6.0	3.10	.68
1955	41	38	26	3	1	305	1256	292	137	111	41	11	5	2	53	3	160	3	0	23	14	.622	.462	5.9	4.04	.89
1956	43	37	22	6	1	297	1228	328	155	147	46	14	10	2	40	3	157	2	0	19	18	.514	.444	2.6	4.70	1.11
1957	39	32	14	5	2	250	1033	246	122	113	40	8	3	1	43	16	128	0	0	10	22	.313	.549	-7.6	4.39	1.00
1958	35	34	21	0	1	270	1116	270	112	97	30	10	9	2	51	5	130	2	0	17	14	.548	.423	3.9	3.73	.85
1959	35	35	19	0	2	257	1075	267	137	122	34	15	5	5	35	4	137	1	1	15	17	.469	.402	2.1	4.80	1.09
1960	35	33	13	2	2	237	982	256	113	106	31	9	7	2	34	7	122	0	0	12	16	.429	.373	1.6	4.29	1.01
1961	26	18	2	3	0	117	512	154	85	76	27	6	9	2	23	6	54	1	0	1	10	.091	.322	-2.5	6.54	1.45
1962	27	25	6	1	0	191	774	176	63	59	17	7	2	4	41	7	102	2	0	10	9	.526	.469	1.1	2.97	.67
1963	35	35	9	0	2	251	1014	230	100	93	35	9	2	3	40	8	124	0	0	14	13	.519	.533	-.4	3.59	.88
1964	31	31	8	0	4	204	846	203	69	66	18	9	4	3	52	6	109	2	1	13	7	.650	.592	1.2	3.04	.75
1965	30	25	8	2	3	191	762	171	73	59	18	6	6	1	30	4	97	1	1	10	9	.526	.510	.3	3.44	.86
1966	24	21	2	3	1	112	484	141	66	60	15	3	4	1	21	0	54	2	0	5	8	.385	.416	-.4	5.30	1.30
16.23 Years	676	609	305	49	45	4689	19174	4582	1962	1774	505	188	73	54	902	69	2357	32	3	286	245	.539	.476	33.4	3.77	.86
	42	38	19	3	3	289		282	121	109	31	12		3	56		145	2	0	18	15	.539	.476	2.1	3.77	.86

Teams: Philadelphia, N.L. 1948–1961; Baltimore, 1962–1964; Baltimore/Houston, 1965; Houston/Chicago, N.L. 1966.
Points in MVP Voting: 1948, 0; 1949, 0; 1950, 68 (7th, .20); 1951, 27 (.08); 1952, 211 (2nd, .67); 1953, 106 (6th, .32); 1954, 70 (7th, .21); 1955, 159 (5th, .47); 1956, 7 (.02); 1957, 0; 1958, 0; 1959, 0; 1960, 0; 1961, 0; 1962, 0; 1963, 0; 1964, 0; 1965, 0; 1966, 0. TOTAL: 1.97 Award Shares.
Other Notes: Named to *The Sporting News* major league All-Star team in 1952, 1953, 1954, and 1955.

PLAYER: WHITEY FORD

	HOW MUCH HE PITCHED							WHAT HE GAVE UP												WHAT THE RESULTS WERE					
Year	G	GS	CG	GF	ShO	IP	BFP	H	R	ER	HR	SH	SF	HB	TBB	IBB	SO	WP	Bk	W	L	Pct.	Rest of Team	Above Team	Runs per Game	Percentage of League
1950	20	12	7	5	2	112	465	87	39	35	7	8		2	52		59	3	0	9	1	.900	.618	2.8	3.13	.62
1953	32	30	11	2	3	207	881	187	77	69	13	6		4	110		110	3	0	18	6	.750	.638	2.7	3.35	.75
1954	34	28	11	4	3	211	862	170	72	66	10	21		1	101		125	1	0	16	8	.667	.669	−.1	3.07	.73
1955	39	33	18	4	5	254	1027	188	83	74	20	7	2	1	113	7	137	7	1	18	7	.720	.605	2.9	2.94	.66
1956	31	30	18	1	2	226	920	187	70	62	13	7	5	4	84	3	141	6	0	19	6	.760	.605	3.9	2.79	.60
1957	24	17	5	2	0	129	539	114	46	37	10	2	1	1	53	3	84	2	2	11	5	.688	.630	.9	3.21	.76
1958	30	29	15	1	7	219	872	174	62	49	14	5	1	3	62	3	145	5	0	14	7	.667	.586	1.7	2.55	.61
1959	35	29	9	4	2	204	877	194	82	69	13	9	3	1	89	5	114	5	1	16	10	.615	.492	3.2	3.62	.83
1960	33	29	8	1	4	193	797	168	76	66	15	10	5	1	65	5	85	5	0	12	9	.571	.639	−1.4	3.54	.81
1961	39	39	11	0	3	283	1159	242	108	101	23	7	3	1	92	3	209	8	0	25	4	.862	.632	6.7	3.43	.76
1962	38	37	7	0	0	258	1070	243	90	83	22	4	5	4	69	1	160	5	0	17	8	.680	.577	2.6	3.14	.71
1963	38	37	13	1	3	269	1068	240	94	82	26	6	8	2	56	3	189	9	0	24	7	.774	.615	4.9	3.14	.77
1964	39	36	12	2	8	245	996	212	67	58	10	13	2	2	57	3	172	6	0	17	6	.739	.590	3.4	2.46	.61
1965	37	36	9	1	2	244	1000	241	97	88	22	12	4	1	50	1	162	7	0	16	13	.552	.459	3.58	.91	
1966	22	9	0	7	0	73	318	79	33	20	8	6	3	0	24	6	43	1	0	2	5	.286	.447	−1.1	4.07	1.05
1967	7	7	2	0	1	44	173	40	11	8	2	1	1	0	9	0	21	2	0	2	4	.333	.449	−.7	2.25	.61
11.85 Years	498	438	156	35	45	3171	13024	2766	1107	967	228	124	43	28	1086	43	1956	75	4	236	106	.690	.587	35.1	3.14	.73
	42	37	13	3	4	268		233	93	82	19	10		2	92		165	6	0	20	9	.690	.587	3.0	3.14	.73

Teams: New York, A.L., 1950, 1953–1967.

Points in MVP Voting: 1950, 0; 1958, 0; 1959, 0; 1960, 0; 1961, 102 (5th, .36); 1962, 6 (.02); 1963, 125 (3rd, .45); 1964, 7 (.03); 1965, 0; 1966, 0; 1967, 0. TOTAL: .86 Award Shares.

Reported Salaries: Signing bonus of $7,000; 1953, $8,000; 1964, $76,000; 1965, $76,000; 1966, $76,000; 1967, $76,000.

Other Notes: Named to *The Sporting News* major league All-Star team in 1955 and 1956.
Named to *The Sporting News* American League All-Star team in 1961 and 1963.

PLAYER: HOYT WILHELM

	HOW MUCH HE PITCHED							WHAT HE GAVE UP												WHAT THE RESULTS WERE						
Year	G	GS	CG	GF	SV	IP	BFP	H	R	ER	HR	SH	SF	HB	TBB	IBB	SO	WP	Bk	W	L	Pct.	Rest of Team	Above Team	Runs per Game	Percentage of League
1952	71	0	0	32	11	159	646	127	60	43	12	7		5	57		108	3	0	15	3	.833	.566	4.8	3.40	.81
1953	68	0	0	39	15	145	628	127	61	49	13	14		4	77		71	9	0	7	8	.467	.453	.2	3.79	.80
1954	57	0	0	30	7	111	456	77	32	26	5	7	3	5	52		64	2	1	12	4	.750	.616	2.1	2.59	.57
1955	59	0	0	14	0	103	449	104	53	45	10	10	6	2	40	5	71	6	0	4	1	.800	.510	1.4	4.63	1.02
1956	64	0	0	38	8	89	403	97	45	38	7	10	1	2	43	10	71	6	0	4	9	.308	.447	-1.8	4.55	1.07
1957	42	0	0	32	12	59	246	54	29	27	8	0	0	4	22	1	29	0	0	2	4	.333	.568	-1.4	4.42	1.01
1958	39	10	4	17	5	131	525	95	41	34	6	11	3	2	45	4	92	2	2	3	10	.231	.521	-3.8	2.82	.68
1959	32	27	13	2	0	226	902	178	64	55	13	17	4	10	77	3	139	5	0	15	11	.577	.461	3.0	2.55	.58
1960	41	11	3	24	7	147	599	125	69	54	13	8	2	1	39	0	107	6	1	11	8	.579	.578	.0	4.22	.96
1961	51	1	0	43	18	110	458	89	35	28	5	6	0	4	41	5	87	3	0	9	7	.563	.589	-.4	2.86	.63
1962	52	0	0	44	15	93	371	64	28	20	5	5	4	3	34	2	90	11	0	7	10	.412	.483	-1.2	2.71	.61
1963	55	3	0	40	21	136	545	106	47	40	8	12	5	4	30	1	111	4	0	5	8	.385	.597	-2.8	3.11	.76
1964	73	0	0	55	27	131	507	94	35	29	7	10	3	2	30	1	95	3	0	12	9	.571	.610	-.8	2.40	.59
1965	66	0	0	45	20	144	545	88	34	29	11	8	5	2	32	7	106	10	0	7	7	.500	.595	-1.3	2.13	.54
1966	46	0	0	30	6	81	308	50	21	15	6	7	2	1	17	2	61	3	0	5	2	.714	.503	1.5	2.33	.60
1967	49	0	0	30	12	89	360	58	21	13	2	4	1	4	34	4	76	2	0	8	3	.727	.536	2.1	2.12	.57
1968	72	0	0	39	12	94	368	69	20	18	4	4	2	2	24	5	72	1	0	4	4	.500	.409	.7	1.91	.56
1969	52	0	0	42	14	78	303	50	22	19	4	2	1	4	22	4	67	6	0	7	7	.500	.453	.7	2.54	.63
1970	53	0	0	39	13	82	357	73	33	31	8	3	2	1	42	7	68	4	0	6	5	.545	.470	.8	3.62	.81
1971	12	0	0	7	3	20	72	12	7	6	3	0	1	0	5	0	16	0	0	0	1	.000	.553	-.6	3.15	.82
1972	16	0	0	9	1	25	112	20	16	13	0	1	4	0	15	0	9	4	0	0	1	.000	.552	-.6	5.76	1.47
	1070	52	20	651	227	2253	9160	1757	773	632	150	146	49	62	778	61	1610	90	4	143	122	.540	.529	2.8	3.09	.74
16.57 Years	65	3	1	39	14	136		106	47	38	9	9		4	47		97	5	0	9	7	.540	.529	.2	3.09	.74

Teams: New York, N.L., 1952–1956; St. Louis/Cleveland, 1957; Cleveland/Baltimore, 1958; Baltimore, 1959–1962; Chicago, A.L., 1963–1968; California/Atlanta, 1969; Atlanta/Los Angeles, 1971; Los Angeles, 1972.

Points in MVP Voting: 1952, 143 (4th, .43); 1953, 0; 1954, 17 (.05); 1955, 0; 1956, 0; 1957, 0; 1958, 0; 1959, 0; 1960, 0; 1961, 1 (.00); 1962, 0; 1963, 0; 1964, 8 (.03); 1965, 0; 1966, 0; 1967, 0; 1968, 0; 1969, 0; 1970, 0; 1971, 0; 1972, 0. TOTAL: .51 Award Shares.

PLAYER: ELROY FACE

	HOW MUCH HE PITCHED							WHAT HE GAVE UP											WHAT THE RESULTS WERE					
Year	G	GS	CG	GF	SV	IP	BFP	H	R	ER	HR	SH	SF	HB	TBB	IBB	SO	WP	Bk	W	L	Pct.	Rest of Team	Above Team	Runs per Game	Percentage of League
1953	41	13	2	13	0	119	524	145	90	87	19	3		2	30		56	3	1	6	8	.429	.314	1.6	6.81	1.43
1955	42	10	4	21	5	126	524	128	58	50	10	4	3	0	40	4	84	3	0	5	7	.417	.387	.4	4.14	.91
1956	68	3	0	34	6	135	569	131	57	53	16	13	1	1	42	15	96	1	0	12	13	.480	.419	1.5	3.80	.89
1957	59	1	0	32	10	94	395	97	41	32	9	3	8	1	24	5	53	2	0	4	6	.400	.403	−.0	3.93	.90
1958	57	0	0	40	20	84	341	77	30	27	6	3	0	0	22	6	47	2	0	5	2	.714	.537	1.2	3.21	.73
1959	57	0	0	47	10	93	380	91	29	28	5	9	3	1	25	8	69	4	0	18	1	.947	.444	9.6	2.81	.64
1960	68	0	0	61	24	115	454	93	39	37	11	9	4	0	29	9	72	2	0	10	8	.556	.625	−1.2	3.05	.72
1961	62	0	0	47	17	92	373	94	44	39	12	7	3	1	10	4	55	5	0	6	12	.333	.507	−3.1	4.30	.95
1962	63	0	0	57	28	91	348	74	23	19	7	4	5	1	18	7	45	0	0	8	7	.533	.582	−.7	2.27	.51
1963	56	0	0	38	16	70	298	75	33	25	6	11	2	3	19	11	41	1	0	3	9	.250	.473	−2.7	4.24	1.11
1964	55	0	0	25	4	80	343	82	48	46	11	4	6	1	27	10	63	3	0	3	3	.500	.494	.0	5.40	1.35
1965	16	0	0	12	0	20	85	20	6	6	1	1	1	0	7	5	19	2	0	5	2	.714	.548	1.2	2.70	.67
1966	54	0	0	42	18	70	295	68	24	21	9	9	1	1	24	5	67	2	0	6	6	.500	.573	−.9	3.09	.75
1967	61	0	0	45	17	74	298	62	23	20	5	4	2	0	22	11	41	2	0	7	5	.583	.493	1.1	2.80	.73
1968	45	0	0	33	13	53	211	48	17	15	3	3	1	2	8	3	35	0	0	2	4	.333	.500	−1.0	2.89	.84
1969	44	0	0	27	5	59	253	62	29	26	11	2	0	0	15	3	34	0	1	4	2	.667	.308	2.2	4.42	1.10
	848	27	6	574	193	1375	5691	1347	591	531	141	89	40	14	362	106	877	32	2	104	95	.523	.477	9.0	3.87	.92
12.99 Years	65	2	0	44	15	106		104	45	41	11	7		1	28		68	2	0	8	7	.523	.477	.7	3.87	.92

Teams: Pittsburgh, 1953, 1955–1967; Pittsburgh/Detroit, 1968; Montreal, 1969.
Points in MVP Voting: 1953, 0; 1955, 0; 1956, 0; 1957, 0; 1958, 8 (.02); 1959, 67 (7th, .22); 1960, 47 (.15); 1962, 0; 1963, 0; 1964, 0; 1965, 0; 1966, 0; 1967, 0; 1968, 0; 1969, 0. TOTAL: .39 Award Shares.

PLAYER: SANDY KOUFAX

	HOW MUCH HE PITCHED							WHAT HE GAVE UP												WHAT THE RESULTS WERE						
Year	G	GS	CG	GF	ShO	IP	BFP	H	R	ER	HR	SH	SF	HB	TBB	IBB	SO	WP	Bk	W	L	Pct.	Rest of Team	Above Team	Runs per Game	Percentage of League
1955	12	5	2	4	2	42	183	33	15	14	2	1	0	1	28	1	30	2	1	2	2	.500	.644	−.6	3.21	.71
1956	16	10	0	1	0	59	261	66	37	32	10	1	0	0	29	0	30	1	2	2	4	.333	.615	−1.7	5.64	1.33
1957	34	13	2	12	0	104	444	83	49	45	14	4	2	2	51	1	122	5	0	5	4	.556	.545	.1	4.24	.97
1958	40	26	5	7	0	159	714	132	89	79	19	4	4	1	105	6	131	17	0	11	11	.500	.455	1.0	5.04	1.15
1959	35	23	6	6	1	153	679	136	74	69	23	4	4	0	92	4	173	5	1	8	6	.571	.563	.1	4.35	.99
1960	37	26	7	7	2	175	753	133	83	76	20	8	3	1	100	6	197	9	0	8	13	.381	.556	−3.7	4.27	1.01
1961	42	35	15	2	2	256	1068	212	117	100	27	12	3	3	96	6	269	12	2	18	13	.581	.577	.1	4.11	.91
1962	28	26	11	2	2	184	744	134	61	52	13	4	1	2	57	4	216	3	0	14	7	.667	.611	1.2	2.98	.67
1963	40	40	20	0	11	311	1210	214	68	65	13	13	1	3	58	7	306	6	0	25	5	.833	.561	8.2	1.97	.52
1964	29	28	15	1	7	223	870	154	49	43	13	8	3	0	53	5	223	9	0	19	5	.792	.442	8.4	1.98	.49
1965	43	41	27	2	8	336	1297	216	90	76	26	13	3	5	71	4	382	11	0	26	8	.765	.555	7.1	2.41	.60
1966	41	41	27	0	5	323	1274	241	74	62	19	11	8	0	77	4	317	7	0	27	9	.750	.540	7.6	2.06	.50
9.10 Years	397	314	137	44	40	2325	9497	1754	806	713	199	83	32	18	817	48	2396	87	6	165	87	.655	.544	27.8	3.12	.73
	44	35	15	5	4	256		193	89	78	22	9	4	2	90	5	263	10	1	18	10	.655	.544	3.1	3.12	.73

Teams: Brooklyn, 1955–1957; Los Angeles, 1958–1966.

Points in MVP Voting: 1955, 0; 1956, 0; 1957, 0; 1958, 0; 1959, 0; 1960, 0; 1962, 3 (.01); 1963, 237 (1st, .85); 1964, 7.5 (.03); 1965, 177 (2nd, .63); 1966, 201 (2nd, .74). TOTAL: 2.26 Award Shares.

Reported Salaries: 1955, $6,000; 1956, $6,000; 1959, $14,000; 1960, $19,000; 1961, $18,500; 1962, $27,500; 1963, $35,000; 1964, $70,000; 1965, $110,000; 1966, $125,000.

Other Notes: Named to the National League All-Star team in 1963, 1964, 1965, 1966 by *The Sporting News*.

PLAYER: JIM BUNNING

	HOW MUCH HE PITCHED							WHAT HE GAVE UP												WHAT THE RESULTS WERE						
Year	G	GS	CG	GF	ShO	IP	BFP	H	R	ER	HR	SH	SF	HB	TBB	IBB	SO	WP	Bk	W	L	Pct.	Rest of Team	Above Team	Runs per Game	Percentage of League
1955	15	8	0	3	0	51	241	59	38	36	8	3	0	3	32	2	37	1	0	3	5	.375	.521	−1.2	6.71	1.51
1956	15	3	0	5	0	53	245	55	24	22	6	0	3	0	28	4	34	3	0	5	1	.833	.520	1.9	4.08	.88
1957	45	30	14	4	1	267	1081	214	91	80	33	10	8	11	72	5	182	4	1	20	8	.714	.460	7.1	3.07	.73
1958	35	34	10	0	3	220	923	188	96	86	28	7	4	10	79	4	177	5	3	14	12	.538	.492	1.2	3.93	.94
1959	40	35	14	4	1	250	1037	220	111	108	37	6	3	11	75	0	201	1	1	19	13	.594	.467	4.0	4.00	.92
1960	36	34	10	1	3	252	1024	217	92	78	20	23	6	11	64	7	201	2	0	11	14	.440	.465	−.6	3.29	.75
1961	38	37	12	1	4	268	1110	232	113	95	25	12	4	9	71	3	194	2	0	17	11	.607	.627	−.6	3.79	.84
1962	41	35	12	6	2	258	1103	262	112	103	28	8	6	13	74	3	184	4	0	19	10	.655	.500	4.5	3.91	.88
1963	39	35	6	3	2	248	1051	245	119	107	38	9	4	5	69	3	196	4	0	12	13	.480	.489	−.2	4.32	1.06
1964	41	39	13	2	5	284	1145	248	99	83	23	19	2	14	46	3	219	2	0	19	8	.704	.541	4.4	3.14	.78
1965	39	39	15	0	7	291	1191	253	92	84	23	21	5	12	62	10	268	1	0	19	9	.679	.496	5.1	2.85	.70
1966	43	41	16	2	5	314	1254	260	91	84	26	10	5	19	55	8	252	5	1	19	14	.576	.527	1.6	2.61	.64
1967	40	40	16	0	6	302	1216	241	94	77	13	9	8	13	73	20	253	4	1	17	15	.531	.500	1.0	2.80	.73
1968	27	26	3	0	1	160	684	168	75	69	18	9	2	8	48	6	95	3	0	4	14	.222	.528	−5.5	4.22	1.23
1969	34	34	5	0	0	212	892	212	97	87	15	6	3	7	59	4	157	4	1	13	10	.565	.540	.6	4.12	1.03
1970	34	33	4	0	0	219	937	233	111	100	19	12	11	8	56	9	147	1	0	10	15	.400	.463	−1.6	4.56	1.02
1971	29	16	1	8	0	110	484	126	72	67	11	12	5	6	37	7	58	1	0	5	12	.294	.428	−2.3	5.89	1.53
	591	519	151	39	40	3759	15618	3433	1527	1366	371	176	79	160	1000	98	2855	47	8	226	184	.551	.504	19.5	3.66	.87
14.06 Years	42	37	11	3	3	267		244	109	97	26	13	6	11	71	7	203	3	1	16	13	.551	.504	1.4	3.66	.87

Teams: Detroit, 1955–1963; Philadelphia, 1964–1967; Pittsburgh, 1968; Pittsburgh/Los Angeles, 1969; Philadelphia, 1970–1971.

Points in MVP Voting: 1957, 46 (9th, .14); 1958, 0; 1959, 0; 1960, 3 (.01); 1961, 0; 1962, 8 (.03); 1963, 0; 1964, 23 (.08); 1965, 0; 1966, 0; 1967, 5 (.02); 1968, 0; 1969, 0; 1970, 0; 1971, 0. TOTAL: .28 Award Shares.

Reported Salaries: Signing bonus of $4,000; 1950, $150/month in minors; 1954, $500/month in minors; 1956, $7,500; 1957, $11,500; 1958, $20,000; 1959, $25,000.

Other Notes: Named to *The Sporting News* major league All-Star team in 1957.
Named to *The Sporting News* National League All-Star team in 1964.

PLAYER: DON DRYSDALE

	HOW MUCH HE PITCHED							WHAT HE GAVE UP												WHAT THE RESULTS WERE						
Year	G	GS	CG	GF	ShO	IP	BFP	H	R	ER	HR	SH	SF	HB	TBB	IBB	SO	WP	Bk	W	L	Pct.	Rest of Team	Above Team	Runs per Game	Percentage of League
1956	25	12	2	6	0	99	413	95	35	29	9	4	2	3	31	3	55	3	0	5	5	.500	.611	−1.1	3.18	.75
1957	34	29	9	4	4	221	911	197	76	66	17	6	3	7	61	3	148	3	0	17	9	.654	.523	3.4	3.10	.71
1958	44	29	6	7	1	212	913	214	107	98	21	6	6	14	72	6	131	8	2	12	13	.480	.457	.6	4.54	1.03
1959	44	36	15	7	4	271	1142	237	113	104	26	12	0	18	93	9	242	4	2	17	13	.567	.563	.1	3.75	.85
1960	41	36	15	5	5	269	1083	214	93	85	27	3	3	10	72	5	246	6	0	15	14	.517	.536	−.5	3.11	.73
1961	40	37	10	2	3	244	1047	236	111	100	29	8	8	20	83	15	182	7	1	13	10	.565	.580	−.3	4.09	.91
1962	43	41	19	2	2	314	1289	272	122	99	21	9	6	11	78	12	232	8	0	25	9	.735	.588	5.0	3.50	.78
1963	42	42	17	0	3	315	1266	287	114	92	25	10	5	10	57	13	251	4	0	19	17	.528	.635	−3.9	3.26	.85
1964	40	40	21	0	5	321	1264	242	91	78	15	11	4	10	68	9	237	11	1	18	16	.529	.484	1.5	2.55	.64
1965	44	42	20	1	7	308	1262	270	113	95	30	16	4	12	66	11	210	11	0	23	12	.657	.583	2.6	3.30	.82
1966	40	40	11	0	3	274	1135	279	114	104	21	12	8	17	45	8	177	7	1	13	16	.448	.617	−4.9	3.74	.91
1967	38	38	9	0	3	282	1151	269	101	86	19	9	4	8	60	19	196	5	2	13	16	.448	.451	−.1	3.22	.84
1968	31	31	12	0	8	239	954	201	68	57	11	6	9	2	56	10	155	4	0	14	12	.538	.456	2.1	2.56	.75
1969	12	12	1	0	1	63	267	71	34	31	9	4	4	2	13	0	24	1	0	5	4	.556	.523	.3	4.86	1.21
12.42 Years	518	465	167	34	49	3432	14097	3084	1292	1124	280	116	66	154	855	123	2486	82	9	209	166	.557	.544	4.8	3.39	.82
	42	37	13	3	4	276		248	104	90	23	9	5	12	69	10	200	7	1	17	13	.557	.544	.4	3.39	.82

Teams: Brooklyn, 1956–1957; Los Angeles, 1958–1969.
Points in MVP Voting: 1956, 0; 1957, 8 (.02); 1958, 0; 1959, 0; 1960, 0; 1962, 85 (5th, .30); 1963, 3 (.01); 1964, 0; 1965, 77 (5th, .28); 1966, 0; 1967, 0; 1968, 0; 1969, 0. TOTAL: .61 Award Shares.
Reported Salaries: 1962, $35,000; 1964, $70,000; 1966, $110,000.
Other Notes: Named to *The Sporting News* National League All-Star team in 1962.

PLAYER: BOB GIBSON

	HOW MUCH HE PITCHED							WHAT HE GAVE UP												WHAT THE RESULTS WERE						
Year	G	GS	CG	GF	ShO	IP	BFP	H	R	ER	HR	SH	SF	HB	TBB	IBB	SO	WP	Bk	W	L	Pct.	Rest of Team	Above Team	Runs per Game	Percentage of League
1959	13	9	2	3	1	76	333	77	35	28	4	8	3	1	39	2	48	4	0	3	5	.375	.466	−.7	4.14	.94
1960	27	12	2	3	0	87	399	97	61	54	7	5	4	1	48	6	69	3	0	3	6	.333	.572	−2.2	6.31	1.49
1961	35	27	10	3	2	211	916	186	91	76	13	6	7	6	119	7	166	8	1	13	12	.520	.519	.0	3.88	.86
1962	32	30	15	2	5	234	967	174	84	74	15	8	1	10	95	9	208	11	0	15	13	.536	.515	.6	3.23	.72
1963	36	33	14	2	2	255	1088	224	110	96	19	10	7	13	96	1	204	6	1	18	9	.667	.556	3.0	3.88	1.02
1964	40	36	17	3	2	287	1191	250	106	96	25	12	5	9	86	9	245	6	0	19	12	.613	.565	1.5	3.32	.83
1965	38	36	20	1	6	299	1233	243	110	102	34	14	9	11	103	6	270	8	1	20	12	.625	.465	5.1	3.31	.82
1966	35	35	20	0	5	280	1119	210	90	76	20	15	5	5	78	5	225	12	0	21	12	.636	.481	5.1	2.89	.71
1967	24	24	10	0	2	175	703	151	62	58	10	4	2	3	40	3	147	3	1	13	7	.650	.624	.5	3.19	.83
1968	34	34	28	0	13	305	1161	198	49	38	11	15	2	7	62	6	268	4	0	22	9	.710	.573	4.3	1.45	.42
1969	35	35	28	0	4	314	1270	251	84	76	12	12	7	10	95	7	269	4	2	20	13	.606	.519	2.9	2.41	.60
1970	34	34	23	0	3	294	1213	262	111	102	13	6	10	4	88	9	274	5	1	23	7	.767	.402	11.0	3.40	.76
1971	31	31	20	0	5	246	1026	215	96	83	14	12	6	7	76	11	185	10	0	16	13	.552	.556	−.1	3.51	.91
1972	34	34	23	0	4	278	1119	226	83	76	14	10	7	3	88	11	208	10	2	19	11	.633	.444	5.7	2.69	.69
1973	25	25	13	0	1	195	790	159	71	60	12	11	8	3	57	6	142	6	1	12	10	.545	.493	1.2	3.28	.80
1974	33	33	9	0	1	240	1041	236	111	102	24	11	9	5	104	14	129	2	3	11	13	.458	.547	−2.1	4.16	1.01
1975	22	14	1	4	0	109	499	120	66	61	10	12	3	4	62	6	60	6	0	3	10	.231	.530	−3.9	5.45	1.34
12.64 Years	528	482	255	21	56	3885	16068	3279	1420	1258	257	171	95	102	1336	118	3117	108	13	251	174	.591	.516	31.7	3.29	.81
	42	37	20	2	4	307		259	112	100	20	14	8	8	106	9	247	9	1	20	14	.591	.516	2.5	3.29	.81

Teams: St. Louis, N.L., 1959–1975.

Points in MVP Voting: 1959, 9; 1960, 0; 1962, 0; 1963, 0; 1964, 2 (.01); 1965, 0; 1966, 0; 1967, 5 (.02); 1968, 242 (1st, .86); 1969, 2 (.01); 1970, 110 (4th, .33); 1971, 3 (.01); 1972, 0; 1973, 0; 1974, 0; 1975, 0. TOTAL: 1.24 Award Shares.

Reported Salaries: Signing bonus of $1,000; 1957, $3,000 in minors; 1970, $125,000; 1971, $150,000; 1972, $150,000.

Other Notes: Named to *The Sporting News* National League All-Star team in 1968 and 1970.

Gold Glove: 1965, 1966, 1967, 1968, 1969, 1970, 1971, 1972, 1973.

PLAYER: JIM KAAT

	HOW MUCH HE PITCHED							WHAT HE GAVE UP												WHAT THE RESULTS WERE						
Year	G	GS	CG	GF	ShO	IP	BFP	H	R	ER	HR	SH	SF	HB	TBB	IBB	SO	WP	Bk	W	L	Pct.	Rest of Team	Above Team	Runs per Game	Percentage of League
1959	3	2	0	0	0	5	29	7	9	7	1	2	1	2	4	0	2	2	0	0	2	.000	.414	−.8	16.20	3.71
1960	13	9	0	2	0	50	228	48	39	31	8	1	3	5	31	2	25	2	0	1	5	.167	.486	−1.9	7.02	1.60
1961	36	29	8	3	1	201	865	188	105	87	12	10	15	11	82	1	122	10	1	9	17	.346	.455	−2.8	4.70	1.04
1962	39	35	16	2	5	268	1112	243	106	94	23	11	6	18	75	5	173	13	0	18	14	.563	.562	.0	3.56	.80
1963	31	27	7	1	1	178	764	195	96	83	24	2	3	9	38	1	105	6	0	10	10	.500	.574	−1.5	4.85	1.19
1964	36	34	13	1	0	243	1009	231	100	87	23	13	8	9	60	5	171	13	1	17	11	.607	.463	4.0	3.70	.91
1965	45	42	7	2	2	264	1115	267	121	83	25	7	6	5	63	6	154	3	0	18	11	.621	.632	−.3	4.13	1.05
1966	41	41	19	0	3	305	1227	271	114	93	29	9	6	3	55	4	205	12	0	25	13	.658	.516	5.4	3.36	.86
1967	42	38	13	1	2	263	1100	269	110	89	21	11	3	9	42	2	211	9	1	16	13	.552	.564	−.4	3.76	1.02
1968	30	29	9	0	2	208	854	192	78	68	16	10	10	3	40	0	130	5	0	14	12	.538	.478	1.6	3.38	.99
1969	40	32	10	4	0	242	1048	252	114	94	23	4	10	9	75	15	139	9	0	14	13	.519	.615	−2.6	4.24	1.05
1970	45	34	4	3	1	230	972	244	110	91	26	7	9	3	58	8	120	11	0	14	10	.583	.609	−.6	4.30	1.05
1971	39	38	15	0	4	260	1098	275	104	96	16	13	6	6	47	9	137	8	0	13	14	.481	.459	.6	3.60	.94
1972	15	15	5	0	0	113	443	94	36	26	6	5	4	0	20	2	64	2	0	10	2	.833	.472	4.3	2.87	.83
1973	36	35	10	1	3	224	951	250	124	109	30	2	3	4	43	1	109	3	0	15	13	.536	.485	1.4	4.98	1.18
1974	42	39	15	0	3	277	1137	263	106	90	18	6	10	6	63	3	142	4	0	21	13	.618	.468	5.1	3.44	.85
1975	43	41	12	1	1	304	1297	321	121	105	20	11	10	9	77	0	142	0	2	20	14	.588	.433	5.3	3.58	.84
1976	38	35	7	1	1	228	924	241	95	88	21	8	6	10	32	3	83	1	0	12	14	.462	.654	−5.0	3.75	.94
1977	35	27	2	3	0	160	709	211	100	76	20	6	2	2	40	6	55	2	0	6	11	.353	.655	−5.1	5.63	1.28
1978	26	24	2	0	1	140	586	150	67	64	9	6	7	5	32	6	48	5	0	8	5	.615	.550		4.31	1.08
1979	43	2	0	15	0	66	286	73	33	29	5	0	0	2	19	4	25	2	0	3	3	.500	.552	−.3	4.50	.98
1980	53	14	6	22	1	135	573	148	66	59	6	9	7	0	37	13	37	4	1	8	8	.500	.466	.5	4.40	1.09
1981	41	1	0	16	0	53	229	60	25	20	2	6	5	0	17	8	8	2	0	6	6	.500	.589	−1.1	4.25	1.09
1982	62	2	0	12	0	75	321	79	40	34	6	4	6	2	23	9	35	2	0	5	3	.625	.565	.5	4.80	1.17
1983	24	0	0	9	0	35	162	48	19	15	5	4	1	0	10	3	19	0	0	0	0	.000	.488	−.0	4.89	1.19
19.72 Years	898	625	180	99	31	4527	19039	4620	2038	1718	395	167	147	122	1083	116	2461	130	6	283	237	.544	.530	7.2	4.05	.99
	46	32	9	5	2	230		234	103	87	23	8	7	6	55	7	125	7	0	14	12	.544	.530	.4	4.05	.99

Teams: Washington, A.L., 1959–1960; Minnesota, A.L., 1961–1972; Minnesota/Chicago, A.L., 1973; Chicago, A.L., 1974–1975; Philadelphia, N.L., 1976–1978; Philadelphia/New York, A.L. 1979; New York, A.L./St. Louis, N.L., 1980; St. Louis, 1981–1983.

Points in MVP Voting: 1959, 0; 1960, 0; 1961, 0; 1962, 0; 1963, 0; 1964, 0; 1965, 0; 1966, 84 (5th, .30); 1967, 4 (.01); 1968, 0; 1969, 0; 1970, 0; 1971, 0; 1972, 0; 1973, 0; 1974, 0; 1975, 2 (.01); 1976, 0; 1977, 0; 1978, 0; 1979, 0; 1980, 0; 1981, 0; 1982, 0; 1983, 0. TOTAL: .32 Award Shares.

Reported Salaries: 1980, $150,000; 1981, $150,000 plus $22,253 bonus earned; 1982, $200,000.

Other Notes: Named to *The Sporting News* American League All-Star team in 1966 and 1975.

Gold Glove: 1962, 1963, 1964, 1965, 1966, 1967, 1968, 1969, 1970, 1972, 1973, 1974, 1975, 1976, 1977.

PLAYER: JUAN MARICHAL

	HOW MUCH HE PITCHED							WHAT HE GAVE UP											WHAT THE RESULTS WERE						
Year	G	GS	CG	GF	ShO	IP	BFP	H	R	ER	HR	SH	SF	HB	TBB	IBB	SO	WP	Bk	W	L	Pct.	Rest of Team	Above Team	Runs per Game	Percentage of League
1960	11	11	6	0	1	81	328	59	29	24	5	4	1	0	28	1	58	3	2	6	2	.750	.500	2.0	3.22	.76
1961	29	27	9	2	3	185	769	183	88	80	24	4	4	2	48	5	124	7	1	13	10	.565	.550	.4	4.28	.95
1962	37	36	18	1	3	263	1101	233	112	98	34	9	5	3	90	5	153	3	1	18	11	.621	.625	−.1	3.83	.86
1963	41	40	18	1	5	321	1270	259	102	86	27	7	3	2	61	6	248	2	3	25	8	.758	.488	8.9	2.86	.75
1964	33	33	22	0	4	269	1089	241	89	74	18	10	4	1	52	8	206	4	2	21	8	.724	.519	6.0	2.98	.74
1965	39	37	24	2	10	295	1153	224	78	70	27	6	4	4	46	4	240	2	0	22	13	.629	.575	1.9	2.38	.59
1966	37	36	25	1	4	307	1180	228	88	76	32	8	3	5	36	3	222	3	0	25	6	.806	.523	8.8	2.58	.63
1967	26	26	18	0	2	202	839	195	79	62	20	9	3	1	42	9	166	0	0	14	10	.583	.558	.6	3.52	.92
1968	38	38	30	0	5	326	1307	295	106	88	21	12	6	6	46	9	218	8	2	26	9	.743	.488	8.9	2.93	.85
1969	37	36	27	1	8	300	1176	244	90	70	15	12	6	6	54	7	205	5	2	21	11	.656	.531	4.0	2.70	.67
1970	34	33	14	0	1	243	1035	269	128	111	28	6	9	1	48	3	123	4	0	12	10	.545	.529	.4	4.74	1.06
1971	37	37	18	0	4	279	1124	244	113	91	27	13	6	3	56	6	159	6	1	18	11	.621	.541	2.3	3.65	.94
1972	25	24	6	1	0	165	699	176	82	68	15	11	4	3	46	7	72	2	0	6	16	.273	.474	−4.4	4.47	1.15
1973	34	32	9	1	2	209	888	231	104	88	22	11	6	1	37	7	87	2	3	11	15	.423	.566	−3.7	4.48	1.09
1974	11	9	0	1	0	57	244	61	32	31	3	1	1	2	14	1	21	0	2	5	1	.833	.506	2.0	5.05	1.25
1975	2	2	0	0	0	6	34	11	9	9	2	2	0	0	5	1	1	0	1	0	1	.000	.547	−.5	13.50	3.31
	471	457	244	11	52	3508	14236	3153	1329	1126	320	125	65	40	709	82	2303	51	20	243	142	.631	.536	36.7	3.41	.84
11.64 Years	40	39	21	1	4	302		271	114	97	28	11	6	3	61	7	198	4	2	21	12	.631	.536	3.2	3.41	.84

Teams: San Francisco, N.L., 1960–1973; Boston, A.L., 1974; Los Angeles, N.L., 1975.

Points in MVP Voting: 1960, 0; 1962, 4 (.01); 1963, 31 (.11); 1964, 14 (.05); 1965, 26 (9th, .09); 1966, 74 (6th, .26); 1967, 0; 1968, 93 (5th, .33); 1969, 6 (.02); 1970, 0; 1971, 0; 1972, 0; 1973, 0; 1974, 0; 1975, 0. TOTAL: .87 Award Shares.

Reported Salaries: 1958 in minors, $250/month; 1961, $12,000; 1962, $14,500; 1963, $24,000; 1964, $40,000; 1965, $60,000; 1966, $75,000; 1967, $100,000; 1972, $140,000.

Other Notes: Named to *The Sporting News* National League All-Star team in 1963, 1965, 1966, and 1968.

PLAYER: GAYLORD PERRY

	HOW MUCH HE PITCHED							WHAT HE GAVE UP												WHAT THE RESULTS WERE						
Year	G	GS	CG	GF	ShO	IP	BFP	H	R	ER	HR	SH	SF	HB	TBB	IBB	SO	WP	Bk	W	L	Pct.	Rest of Team	Above Team	Runs per Game	Percentage of League
1962	13	7	1	1	0	43	195	54	29	25	3	3	4	0	14	2	20	3	0	3	1	.750	.621	.5	6.07	1.35
1963	31	4	0	6	0	76	340	84	41	34	10	7	1	2	29	7	52	4	1	1	6	.143	.561	−2.9	4.86	1.27
1964	44	19	5	11	2	206	832	179	65	63	16	8	6	5	43	6	155	5	0	12	11	.522	.561	−.9	2.84	.71
1965	47	26	6	8	0	196	848	194	105	91	21	9	5	6	70	16	170	12	0	8	12	.400	.613	−4.3	4.82	1.19
1966	36	35	13	0	3	256	1035	242	92	85	15	8	2	5	40	3	201	7	0	21	8	.724	.545	5.2	3.23	.79
1967	39	37	18	2	3	293	1178	231	98	85	20	11	2	4	84	17	230	13	1	15	17	.469	.585	−3.7	3.01	.78
1968	39	38	19	1	3	291	1159	240	93	79	10	11	3	4	59	12	173	6	0	16	15	.516	.550	−1.0	2.88	.84
1969	40	39	26	1	3	325	1345	290	115	90	23	14	4	11	91	14	233	12	0	19	14	.576	.550	.8	3.18	.80
1970	41	41	23	0	5	329	1336	292	138	117	27	7	7	8	84	8	214	11	0	23	13	.639	.500	5.0	3.78	.85
1971	37	37	14	0	2	280	1149	255	116	86	20	9	13	5	67	4	158	8	0	16	12	.571	.552	.5	3.73	.97
1972	41	40	29	1	5	343	1345	253	79	73	17	15	1	12	82	16	234	11	0	24	16	.600	.414	7.4	2.07	.60
1973	41	41	29	0	7	344	1410	315	143	129	34	8	3	5	115	9	238	17	0	19	19	.500	.419	3.1	3.74	.89
1974	37	37	28	0	4	322	1262	230	98	90	25	19	12	6	99	7	216	2	0	21	13	.618	.438	6.1	2.74	.68
1975	37	37	25	0	5	306	1248	277	127	110	28	11	3	4	70	6	233	5	0	18	17	.514	.484	1.1	3.74	.88
1976	32	32	21	0	2	250	1005	232	93	90	14	8	6	0	52	3	143	1	0	15	14	.517	.459	1.7	3.35	.84
1977	34	34	13	0	4	238	986	239	108	89	21	8	5	5	56	4	177	3	0	15	12	.556	.585	−.8	4.08	.90
1978	37	37	5	0	2	261	1055	241	96	79	9	8	9	2	66	8	154	4	3	21	6	.778	.504	7.4	3.31	.83
1979	32	32	10	0	0	233	963	225	90	79	12	14	2	4	67	10	140	6	0	12	11	.522	.406	2.7	3.48	.82
1980	34	32	6	2	2	206	884	224	107	84	14	9	7	8	64	3	135	9	0	10	13	.435	.543	−2.5	4.67	1.04
1981	23	23	3	0	0	151	644	182	70	66	9	12	6	4	24	1	60	3	1	8	9	.471	.472	−.0	4.17	1.07
1982	32	32	6	0	0	217	923	245	117	106	27	7	4	4	54	4	116	13	0	10	12	.455	.471	−.4	4.85	1.08
1983	30	30	3	0	1	186	811	214	108	96	24	11	6	4	49	4	82	5	0	7	14	.333	.426	−1.9	5.23	1.17
	777	690	303	33	53	5352	21953	4938	2128	1846	399	217	111	108	1379	164	3534	160	6	314	265	.542	.498	23.1	3.58	.87
18.56 Years	42	37	16	2	3	288		266	114	99	22	12	6	6	74	9	190	9	0	17	14	.542	.498	1.2	3.58	.87

Teams: San Francisco, 1962–1971; Cleveland, 1972–1974; Cleveland/Texas, 1975; Texas, 1976–1977; San Diego, N.L., 1978–1979; Texas/New York, A.L. 1980, Atlanta, N.L., 1981; Seattle, A.L., 1982; Seattle/Kansas City, A.L., 1983.

Points in MVP Voting: 1962, 0; 1963, 0; 1964, 0; 1965, 0; 1966, 8 (.03); 1967, 0; 1968, 0; 1969, 0; 1970, 24 (.07); 1971, 0; 1972, 88 (6th, .26); 1973, 4 (.01); 1974, 18 (.05); 1975, 0; 1976, 0; 1977, 0; 1978, 45 (8th, .13); 1979, 0; 1980, 0; 1981, 0; 1982, 0; 1983, 0. TOTAL: .55 Award Shares.

Reported Salaries: Signing Bonus—$73,500. 1962, $7,000; 1963, $8,000; 1964, $9,000; 1965, $15,000; 1966, $15,000, raised to $20,000 during season; 1967, $35,000; 1968, $45,000; 1969, $60,000; 1970, $75,000; 1971, $75,000; 1972, $100,000; 1973, $100,000; 1974, $100,000; 1980, $200,000; 1981, $300,000; 1982, $150,000.

Other Notes: Named to *The Sporting News* American League post-season All-Star team in 1972.

PLAYER: TOMMY JOHN

	HOW MUCH HE PITCHED							WHAT HE GAVE UP												WHAT THE RESULTS WERE						
Year	G	GS	CG	GF	ShO	IP	BFP	H	R	ER	HR	SH	SF	HB	TBB	IBB	SO	WP	Bk	W	L	Pct.	Rest of Team	Above Team	Runs per Game	Percentage of League
1963	6	3	0	1	0	20	91	23	10	5	1	3	1	0	6	1	9	1	0	0	2	.000	.494	−1.0	4.50	1.10
1964	25	14	2	0	1	94	402	97	53	41	10	5	2	0	35	4	65	5	1	2	9	.182	.510	−3.6	5.07	1.25
1965	39	27	6	4	1	183	752	162	67	63	12	7	1	2	58	6	126	8	0	14	7	.667	.574	1.9	3.30	.84
1966	39	33	10	0	5	223	904	195	76	65	13	7	4	7	57	4	138	10	1	14	11	.560	.504	1.4	3.07	.79
1967	31	29	9	1	6	178	715	143	62	49	12	5	5	5	47	7	110	5	0	10	13	.435	.568	−3.1	3.13	.85
1968	25	25	5	0	1	177	705	135	45	39	10	5	1	12	49	4	117	2	1	10	5	.667	.388	4.2	2.29	.67
1969	33	33	6	0	2	232	984	230	91	84	16	8	4	1	90	10	128	15	1	9	11	.450	.415	.7	3.53	.87
1970	37	37	10	0	3	269	1133	253	117	98	19	9	5	9	101	16	138	17	0	12	17	.414	.331	2.4	3.91	.95
1971	38	35	10	0	3	229	975	244	115	92	17	10	10	5	58	5	131	10	0	13	16	.448	.496	−1.4	4.52	1.18
1972	29	29	4	0	1	187	766	172	68	60	14	13	4	3	40	1	117	10	0	11	5	.688	.532	2.5	3.27	.84
1973	36	31	4	3	2	218	888	202	88	75	16	9	4	4	50	2	116	3	0	16	7	.696	.572	2.8	3.63	.89
1974	22	22	5	0	3	153	616	133	51	44	4	3	3	1	42	0	78	5	0	13	3	.813	.610	3.2	3.00	.73
1976	31	31	6	0	2	207	868	207	76	71	7	10	5	0	61	4	91	7	1	10	10	.500	.577	−1.5	3.30	.87
1977	31	31	11	0	3	220	906	225	82	68	12	10	1	3	50	3	123	6	0	20	7	.741	.578	4.4	3.35	.76
1978	33	30	7	3	0	213	912	230	95	78	11	4	2	5	53	7	124	6	1	17	10	.630	.578	1.4	4.01	1.01
1979	37	36	17	1	3	276	1116	268	109	91	9	11	5	4	65	1	111	11	1	21	9	.700	.523	5.3	3.55	.76
1980	36	36	16	0	6	265	1089	270	115	101	13	15	5	6	56	1	78	5	0	22	9	.710	.618	2.8	3.91	.87
1981	20	20	7	0	0	140	580	135	50	41	10	8	2	3	39	2	50	6	2	9	8	.529	.556	−.4	3.21	.79
1982	37	33	10	2	2	222	918	239	102	91	15	8	7	3	39	1	68	7	2	14	12	.538	.478	1.6	4.14	.92
1983	34	34	9	0	0	235	1010	287	126	113	20	8	7	2	49	5	65	11	0	11	13	.458	.580	−2.9	4.83	1.08
1984	32	29	4	1	1	181	796	223	97	91	15	2	6	4	56	3	47	11	0	7	13	.350	.521	−3.4	4.82	1.09
1985	23	17	0	2	0	86	397	117	59	53	9	9	4	2	28	1	25	7	0	4	10	.286	.531	−3.4	6.15	1.34
1986	13	10	1	2	0	71	290	73	27	23	8	5	3	2	15	1	28	2	0	5	3	.625	.552	.6	3.44	.74
	682	625	159	20	45	4279	17813	4263	1781	1536	273	174	91	83	1144	89	2083	170	11	264	210	.557	.526	14.5	3.75	.95
16.56 Years	41	38	10	1	3	258		258	108	93	16	11	5	5	69	5	126	10	1	16	13	.557	.526	.9	3.75	.95

Teams: Cleveland, 1963–1964; Chicago, A.L. 1965–1971; Los Angeles, 1972–1974, 1976–1978; New York, A.L., 1979–1982; California, 1982–1985; Oakland, 1986; Yankees, 1986.

Points in MVP Voting: 1963, 0; 1964, 0; 1965, 0; 1966, 0; 1967, 0; 1968, 0; 1969, 0; 1970, 0; 1971, 0; 1972, 0; 1973, 0; 1974, 0; 1976, 0; 1977, 33 (.10); 1978, 0; 1979, 0; 1980, 0; 1981, 0; 1982, 0; 1983–1986, 0. TOTAL: .10 Award Shares.

Reported Salaries: 1980, $461,667; 1981, $461,667; 1982–1983 contract, $500,000 for 1982, $700,000 for 1983, $305,000 signing bonus, modest performance bonuses.

Other Notes: Named to *The Sporting News* American League All-Star team in 1980.

Performance summaries in Section II may differ from the above because of the use of 1987 data in Section II.

PLAYER: LUIS TIANT

	HOW MUCH HE PITCHED							WHAT HE GAVE UP												WHAT THE RESULTS WERE						
Year	G	GS	CG	GF	ShO	IP	BFP	H	R	ER	HR	SH	SF	HB	TBB	IBB	SO	WP	Bk	W	L	Pct.	Rest of Team	Above Team	Runs per Game	Percentage of League
1964	19	16	9	3	3	127	512	94	41	40	13	6	2	2	47	2	105	4	0	10	4	.714	.466	3.5	2.91	.72
1965	41	30	10	4	2	196	812	166	88	77	20	11	4	3	66	3	152	2	0	11	11	.500	.543	−.9	4.04	1.02
1966	46	16	7	22	5	155	628	121	50	48	16	7	1	2	50	4	145	3	0	12	11	.522	.496	.6	2.90	.75
1967	33	29	9	4	1	214	872	177	76	65	24	4	0	1	67	2	219	1	1	12	9	.571	.447	2.6	3.20	.86
1968	34	32	19	0	9	258	987	152	53	46	16	5	0	4	73	4	264	3	0	21	9	.700	.496	6.1	1.85	.54
1969	38	37	9	0	1	250	1091	229	123	103	37	14	9	8	129	11	156	0	1	9	20	.310	.402	−2.6	4.43	1.10
1970	18	17	2	1	1	93	390	84	36	35	12	3	2	2	41	0	50	2	0	7	3	.700	.599	1.0	3.48	.85
1971	21	10	1	4	0	72	321	73	42	39	8	3	3	1	32	1	59	4	0	1	7	.125	.545	−3.4	5.25	1.37
1972	43	19	12	12	6	179	713	128	45	38	7	12	3	0	65	5	123	0	0	15	6	.714	.522	4.0	2.26	.65
1973	35	35	23	0	0	272	1096	217	105	101	32	11	9	7	78	3	206	2	0	20	13	.606	.535	2.3	3.47	.82
1974	36	38	25	0	7	311	1266	281	106	101	21	6	8	4	82	3	176	1	0	22	13	.629	.488	4.9	3.07	.76
1975	35	35	18	0	2	260	1080	262	126	116	25	7	5	4	72	0	142	2	0	18	14	.563	.602	−1.3	4.36	1.03
1976	38	38	19	0	3	279	1136	274	107	95	25	10	5	3	64	2	131	1	0	21	12	.636	.481	5.1	3.45	.86
1977	32	32	3	0	3	189	814	210	98	95	26	4	5	2	51	3	124	0	0	12	8	.600	.603	−.1	4.67	1.03
1978	32	31	12	1	5	212	863	185	80	78	26	7	3	5	57	4	114	0	2	13	8	.619	.606	.3	3.40	.81
1979	30	30	5	0	1	196	819	190	94	85	22	5	5	0	53	1	104	0	0	13	8	.619	.547	1.5	4.32	.92
1980	25	25	3	0	0	136	588	139	79	74	10	6	7	1	50	3	84	2	0	8	9	.471	.655	−3.1	5.23	1.16
1981	9	9	1	0	0	57	242	54	31	25	3	1	0	0	19	2	32	0	0	2	5	.286	.463	−1.2	4.89	1.25
1982	6	5	0	0	0	30	135	39	20	19	3	1	0	0	8	0	30	0	0	2	2	.500	.576	−.3	6.07	1.35
	571	484	187	51	49	3486	14365	3075	1400	1280	346	123	71	49	1104	53	2416	27	4	229	172	.571	.523	19.1	3.61	.89
13.40 Years	43	36	14	4	4	260		229	104	95	26	9	5	4	82	4	180	2	0	17	13	.571	.523	1.4	3.61	.89

Teams: Cleveland, 1964–1969; Minnesota, 1970; Boston, 1971–1978; New York, A.L. 1979–1980; Pittsburgh, 1981; California, 1982.

Points in MVP Voting: 1964, 0; 1965, 0; 1966, 0; 1967, 0; 1968, 78 (5th, .28); 1969, 0; 1970, 0; 1971, 0; 1972, 70.5 (8th, .21); 1973, 0; 1974, 41 (.12); 1975, 0; 1976, 3 (.01); 1977, 0; 1978, 0; 1979, 0; 1980, 0; 1981, 0; 1982, 0. TOTAL: .62 Award Shares.

Reported Salaries: 1980, $370,000; 1981, $197,500; 1982, $185,000.

PLAYER: PHIL NIEKRO

	HOW MUCH HE PITCHED							WHAT HE GAVE UP												WHAT THE RESULTS WERE						
Year	G	GS	CG	GF	ShO	IP	BFP	H	R	ER	HR	SH	SF	HB	TBB	IBB	SO	WP	Bk	W	L	Pct.	Rest of Team	Above Team	Runs per Game	Percentage of League
1964	10	0	0	2	0	15	66	15	10	8	1	3	0	1	7	0	8	1	0	0	0	.000	.543	-.0	6.00	1.50
1965	41	1	0	21	0	75	324	73	32	24	5	8	4	3	26	3	49	9	0	2	3	.400	.535	-.7	5.84	.95
1966	28	0	0	10	0	50	224	48	32	23	4	6	0	2	23	5	17	3	0	4	3	.571	.523	.3	5.76	1.41
1967	46	20	10	20	1	207	827	164	64	43	9	6	6	7	55	3	129	19	1	11	9	.550	.465	1.7	2.78	.73
1968	37	34	15	3	5	257	1019	228	83	74	16	10	5	5	45	3	140	16	3	14	12	.538	.493	1.2	2.91	.85
1969	40	35	21	4	4	284	1143	235	93	81	21	19	0	5	57	7	193	15	0	23	13	.639	.556	3.0	2.95	.74
1970	34	32	10	1	3	230	980	222	124	109	40	6	5	6	68	2	168	6	2	12	18	.400	.485	-2.5	4.85	1.09
1971	42	36	18	4	4	269	1101	248	112	89	27	11	4	3	70	6	173	8	1	15	14	.517	.504	.4	3.75	.97
1972	38	36	17	1	1	282	1150	254	112	96	22	13	3	5	53	3	164	10	3	16	12	.571	.429	4.0	3.57	.92
1973	42	30	9	7	1	245	1023	214	103	90	21	13	2	5	89	4	131	11	0	13	10	.565	.457	2.5	3.78	.92
1974	41	39	18	1	6	302	1219	249	91	80	19	10	8	6	88	3	195	6	4	20	13	.606	.527	2.6	2.71	.66
1975	39	37	13	2	1	276	1160	285	115	98	29	14	3	11	72	3	144	15	2	15	15	.500	.397	3.1	3.75	.92
1976	38	37	10	1	2	271	1157	249	116	99	18	14	5	8	101	7	173	14	4	17	11	.607	.396	5.9	3.85	.97
1977	44	43	20	1	2	330	1428	315	166	148	26	11	8	8	164	12	262	17	3	16	20	.444	.357	3.1	4.53	1.03
1978	44	42	22	1	4	334	1389	295	129	107	16	13	6	13	102	5	248	11	3	19	18	.514	.400	4.2	3.48	.87
1979	44	44	23	0	1	342	1436	311	160	129	41	14	7	11	113	8	208	18	4	21	20	.512	.378	5.5	4.21	1.00
1980	40	38	11	2	3	275	1137	256	119	111	30	14	5	3	85	3	176	9	1	15	18	.455	.516	-2.0	3.89	.97
1981	22	22	3	0	3	139	578	120	56	48	6	5	2	1	62	2	62	2	0	7	7	.500	.467	.5	3.63	.93
1982	35	35	4	0	2	234	969	225	106	94	23	7	3	3	73	1	144	4	1	17	4	.810	.511	6.3	4.08	1.00
1983	34	33	2	0	0	202	888	212	94	89	18	7	5	2	105	3	128	6	3	11	10	.524	.546	-.5	4.19	1.02
1984	32	31	5	1	1	216	916	219	85	74	15	5	11	3	76	0	136	2	0	16	8	.667	.514	3.7	3.55	.80
1985	33	33	7	0	1	220	955	203	110	100	29	1	3	2	120	1	149	5	2	16	12	.571	.609	-1.1	4.50	.98
1986	34	32	5	1	0	210	951	241	126	101	24	7	2	6	95	1	81	9	2	11	11	.500	.521	-.5	6.02	1.29
19.47 Years	838	690	243	83	45	5265	22040	4881	2238	1915	460	217	97	119	1743	85	3278	216	39	311	261	.544	.472	40.7	3.81	.94
	43	35	12	4	2	270		251	114	98	24	11	5	6	90	4	168	11	2	16	13	.544	.472	2.1	3.81	.94

Teams: Milwaukee, N.L., 1964–1965; Atlanta, N.L., 1966–1983; New York, A.L., 1984–1985; Cleveland, 1986.

Points in MVP Voting: 1964, 0; 1965, 0; 1966, 0; 1967, 0; 1968, 0; 1969, 47 (.14); 1970, 0; 1971, 0; 1972, 0; 1973, 0; 1974, 0; 1975, 0; 1976, 0; 1977, 0; 1978, 8 (.02); 1979, 11.5 (.03); 1980, 0; 1981, 0; 1982, 0; 1983–1986, 0. TOTAL: .19 Award Shares

Reported Salaries: 1980–1982 contract, 1980, $866,000; 1981, $1,148,700; 1982, $1,082,500 plus $500,000 deferred plus a new car each year.

Other Notes: Gold Glove: 1978, 1979, 1980, 1982, 1983.

Performance summaries in Section II may differ from the above because of the use of 1987 data in Section II.

PLAYER: CATFISH HUNTER

	HOW MUCH HE PITCHED							WHAT HE GAVE UP												WHAT THE RESULTS WERE						
Year	G	GS	CG	GF	ShO	IP	BFP	H	R	ER	HR	SH	SF	HB	TBB	IBB	SO	WP	BK	W	L	PCT	Rest of Team	Above Team	Runs Per Game	Percentage of League
1965	32	20	3	2	2	133	567	124	68	63	21	11	3	2	46	5	82	2	1	8	8	.500	.349	2.4	4.60	1.17
1966	30	25	4	0	0	177	740	158	87	79	17	8	4	2	64	4	103	2	2	9	11	.450	.464	−0.3	4.43	1.14
1967	35	35	13	0	5	260	1053	209	91	81	16	11	3	2	84	6	196	4	1	13	17	.433	.374	1.8	3.15	0.85
1968	36	34	11	2	2	234	968	210	99	87	29	9	3	4	69	10	172	0	1	13	13	.500	.507	−0.2	3.81	1.12
1969	38	35	10	0	3	247	1002	210	99	92	34	7	7	5	85	1	150	8	0	12	15	.444	.563	−3.2	3.61	0.88
1970	40	40	9	0	1	262	1116	253	124	111	32	12	8	9	74	3	178	6	1	18	14	.563	.546	0.5	4.26	1.10
1971	37	37	16	0	4	274	1109	225	103	90	27	9	6	4	80	7	181	2	0	21	11	.656	.620	1.2	3.38	0.81
1972	38	37	16	1	5	295	1148	200	74	67	21	15	4	3	70	6	191	3	0	21	7	.750	.567	5.1	2.26	0.65
1973	36	36	11	0	3	256	1240	222	105	95	25	9	10	4	69	2	124	1	0	21	5	.808	.537	7.0	3.69	0.86
1974	41	41	23	0	6	318	1010	268	97	88	39	3	9	1	46	1	143	2	0	25	12	.676	.520	5.8	2.75	0.67
1975	39	39	30	0	7	328	1294	248	107	94	25	7	8	5	83	4	177	7	0	23	14	.622	.488	5.0	2.94	0.68
1976	36	36	21	0	2	299	1210	268	126	117	28	13	13	3	68	5	173	6	0	17	15	.531	.630	−3.2	3.80	0.95
1977	22	22	8	0	1	143	608	137	83	75	29	5	5	3	47	3	52	2	1	9	9	.500	.632	−2.4	5.22	1.15
1978	21	20	5	1	1	118	477	98	49	47	16	4	4	1	35	0	56	2	0	12	6	.667	.607	1.1	3.74	0.89
1979	19	19	1	0	0	105	460	128	68	62	15	9	6	1	34	0	34	2	0	2	9	.182	.584	−4.4	5.83	1.25
12.26 yrs	500	476	181	6	42	3448	14002	2958	1380	1248	374	132	93	49	954	57	2012	49	7	224	166	.574	.533	16.2	3.60	0.90
	41	39	15	0	3	281	1142	241	113	102	31	11	8	4	78	5	164	4	1	18	14	.574	.533	1.3	3.60	0.90

Teams: Kansas City A's, 1965–1967; Oakland, 1968–1974; Yankees, 1975–1979.
Points in MVP Voting: 1965–1970, 0; 1971, 1 (.00); 1972, 57 (.17); 1973, 0; 1974, 107 (6th, .32); 1975, 31 (.09); 1976–1979, 0. TOTAL: .58 Award Shares.
Reported Salaries: 1975–1979, paid a reported $3.2 million for five years by Yankees as the first major free agent.

PLAYER: JIM PALMER

	HOW MUCH HE PITCHED							WHAT HE GAVE UP												WHAT THE RESULTS WERE						
Year	G	GS	CG	GF	ShO	IP	BFP	H	R	ER	HR	SH	SF	HB	TBB	IBB	SO	WP	Bk	W	L	Pct.	Rest of Team	Above Team	Runs per Game	Percentage of League
1965	27	6	0	7	0	92	394	75	49	38	6	5	4	2	56	1	75	4	0	5	4	.556	.582	−.2	4.79	1.22
1966	30	30	6	0	0	208	867	176	83	80	21	9	4	0	91	1	147	7	0	15	10	.600	.607	−.2	3.59	.92
1967	9	9	2	0	1	49	194	34	18	16	6	2	1	0	20	0	23	2	0	3	1	.750	.465	1.1	3.31	.89
1969	26	23	11	1	6	181	722	131	48	47	11	2	0	1	64	1	123	7	1	16	4	.800	.655	2.9	2.39	.59
1970	39	39	17	0	5	305	1257	263	98	92	21	14	3	1	100	4	199	10	3	20	10	.667	.667	−.0	2.89	.70
1971	37	37	20	0	3	282	1165	231	94	84	19	6	5	4	106	6	184	8	2	20	9	.690	.628	1.8	3.00	.79
1972	36	36	18	0	3	274	1094	219	73	63	21	10	4	1	70	1	184	4	1	21	10	.677	.480	6.1	2.40	.69
1973	38	37	19	1	6	296	1235	225	86	79	16	5	5	3	113	5	158	7	0	22	9	.710	.573	4.3	2.61	.62
1974	26	26	5	0	2	179	770	176	78	65	12	10	3	3	69	4	84	4	0	7	12	.368	.587	−4.2	3.92	.97
1975	39	38	25	1	10	323	1268	253	87	75	20	10	4	2	80	4	193	4	0	23	11	.676	.536	4.8	2.42	.57
1976	40	40	23	0	6	315	1256	255	101	88	20	10	14	8	84	5	159	5	0	22	13	.629	.520	3.8	2.89	.72
1977	39	39	22	0	3	319	1269	263	106	103	24	10	9	3	99	1	193	7	0	20	11	.645	.592	1.6	2.99	.66
1978	38	38	19	0	6	296	1197	246	94	81	19	10	4	1	97	1	138	5	1	21	12	.636	.539	3.2	2.86	.68
1979	23	22	7	1	0	156	639	144	66	57	12	5	5	0	43	0	67	1	0	10	6	.625	.643	−.3	3.81	.82
1980	34	33	4	0	0	224	959	238	108	99	26	11	5	3	74	0	109	2	0	16	10	.615	.618	−.1	4.34	.96
1981	22	22	5	0	0	127	532	117	60	53	14	4	6	2	46	1	35	3	1	7	8	.467	.578	−1.7	4.25	1.04
1982	36	32	8	1	2	227	920	195	85	78	22	5	3	4	63	1	103	2	1	15	5	.750	.556	3.9	3.37	.75
1983	14	11	0	1	0	77	330	86	42	36	11	4	3	0	19	0	34	1	1	5	4	.556	.608	−.5	4.91	1.10
1984	5	3	0	2	0	18	89	22	19	18	2	1	2	0	17	1	4	2	0	0	3	.000	.535	−1.6	9.68	2.19
13.58 Years	558	521	211	15	53	3948	16157	3349	1395	1252	303	133	84	38	1311	37	2212	85	11	268	152	.638	.579	24.9	3.18	.77
	41	38	16	1	4	291		247	103	92	22	10	6	3	97	3	163	6	1	20	11	.638	.579	1.8	3.18	.77

Teams: Baltimore, A.L., 1965–1967, 1969–1984.

Points in MVP Voting: 1965, 0; 1966, 0; 1967, 0; 1969, 0; 1970, 4 (.01); 1971, 5 (.01); 1972, 21 (.06); 1973, 172 (2nd, .51); 1974, 0; 1975, 82 (5th, .24); 1976, 47 (10th, .14); 1977, 9 (.02); 1978, 0; 1979, 0; 1980, 0; 1981, 0; 1982, 5 (.01); 1983, 0. TOTAL: 1.00 Award Shares.

Other Notes: Named to *The Sporting News* American League post-season All-Star team in 1971, 1973, 1975, 1976, and 1978.

Gold Glove: 1976, 1977, 1978, 1979.

PLAYER: FERGUSON JENKINS

	HOW MUCH HE PITCHED							WHAT HE GAVE UP												WHAT THE RESULTS WERE						
Year	G	GS	CG	GF	ShO	IP	BFP	H	R	ER	HR	SH	SF	HB	TBB	IBB	SO	WP	Bk	W	L	Pct.	Rest of Team	Above Team	Runs per Game	Percentage of League
1965	7	0	0	6	0	12	46	7	3	3	2	0	0	0	2	0	10	0	0	2	1	.667	.525	.4	2.25	.56
1966	61	12	2	22	1	184	752	150	77	68	24	10	4	3	52	12	150	1	1	6	8	.429	.358	1.0	3.77	.92
1967	38	38	20	0	3	289	1156	230	101	90	30	7	3	4	83	8	236	2	0	20	13	.606	.523	2.7	3.15	.82
1968	40	40	20	0	3	308	1231	255	96	90	26	11	1	3	65	7	260	6	1	20	15	.571	.504	2.4	2.81	.82
1969	43	42	23	1	7	311	1275	284	122	111	27	17	7	8	71	15	273	7	1	21	15	.583	.563	.7	3.53	.88
1970	40	39	24	1	3	313	1265	265	128	118	30	6	7	7	60	6	274	9	0	22	16	.579	.500	3.0	3.68	.83
1971	39	39	30	0	3	325	1299	304	114	100	29	11	10	5	37	6	263	3	4	24	13	.649	.472	6.5	3.16	.82
1972	36	36	23	0	5	289	1176	253	111	103	32	17	9	7	62	7	184	3	1	20	12	.625	.528	3.1	3.46	.88
1973	38	38	7	0	2	271	1119	267	133	117	35	17	11	4	57	10	170	1	0	14	16	.467	.481	-.4	4.42	1.08
1974	41	41	29	0	6	328	1305	286	117	103	27	9	12	8	45	3	225	4	2	25	12	.676	.480	7.3	3.21	.79
1975	37	37	22	0	4	270	1119	261	130	118	37	9	4	9	56	7	157	3	0	17	18	.486	.488	-.1	4.33	1.02
1976	30	29	12	1	2	209	857	201	85	76	20	5	10	5	43	6	142	3	1	12	11	.522	.511	.3	3.66	.91
1977	28	28	11	0	1	193	790	190	91	79	30	10	4	0	36	2	105	2	0	10	10	.500	.617	-2.3	4.24	.94
1978	34	30	16	3	4	249	990	228	92	84	21	10	6	3	41	2	157	2	1	18	8	.692	.507	4.8	3.33	.79
1979	37	37	10	0	3	259	1089	252	127	117	40	10	9	3	81	6	164	4	0	16	14	.533	.508	.8	4.41	.94
1980	29	29	12	0	0	198	827	190	90	83	22	5	5	4	52	8	129	5	0	12	12	.500	.467	.8	4.09	.91
1981	19	16	1	2	0	106	467	122	55	53	14	5	1	0	40	4	63	2	0	5	8	.385	.565	-2.3	4.67	1.15
1982	34	34	4	0	1	217	932	221	92	76	19	10	13	5	68	2	134	3	3	14	15	.483	.444	1.1	3.82	.93
1983	33	29	1	1	1	167	705	176	89	80	19	7	5	6	46	5	96	2	3	6	6	.500	.433	.8	4.80	1.17
15.90 Years	664	594	267	37	49	4498	18400	4142	1853	1669	484	176	124	84	997	116	3192	62	18	284	223	.560	.500	30.4	3.71	.90
	42	37	17	2	3	283		261	117	105	30	11	8	5	63	7	201	4	1	18	14	.560	.500	1.9	3.71	.90

Teams: Philadelphia, 1965; Philadelphia/Chicago, N.L., 1966; Chicago, N.L., 1967–1973; Texas, 1974–1975, Boston, 1976–1977; Texas, 1978–1981; Chicago, N.L., 1982–1983.

Points in MVP Voting: 1965, 0; 1966, 0; 1967, 26 (.09); 1968, 6 (.02); 1969, 0; 1970, 8 (.02); 1971, 71 (7th, .21); 1972, 1 (.00); 1973, 0; 1974, 118 (5th, .35); 1975, 0; 1976, 0; 1977, 0; 1978, 0; 1979, 0; 1980, 0; 1981, 0; 1982, 0; 1983, 0. TOTAL: .69 Award Shares.

Reported Salaries: 1972—$125,000.

Other Notes: Named to *The Sporting News* National League All-Star team in 1967, 1971 and 1972.

PLAYER: STEVE CARLTON

	HOW MUCH HE PITCHED							WHAT HE GAVE UP												WHAT THE RESULTS WERE						
Year	G	GS	CG	GF	ShO	IP	BFP	H	R	ER	HR	SH	SF	HB	TBB	IBB	SO	WP	Bk	W	L	Pct.	Rest of Team	Above Team	Runs per Game	Percentage of League
1965	15	2	0	5	0	25	104	27	7	7	3	1	0	1	8	1	21	5	0	0	0	.000	.497	−.0	2.52	.62
1966	9	9	2	0	1	52	223	56	22	18	2	2	3	0	18	1	25	2	1	3	3	.500	.513	−.1	3.81	.93
1967	30	28	11	1	2	193	802	173	71	64	10	9	3	2	62	1	168	6	0	14	9	.609	.630	−.5	3.31	.86
1968	34	33	10	1	5	232	954	214	87	77	11	11	9	3	61	4	162	6	0	13	11	.542	.609	−1.6	3.38	.98
1969	31	31	12	0	2	236	968	185	66	57	15	9	4	4	93	6	210	7	0	17	11	.607	.522	2.4	2.52	.63
1970	34	33	13	0	2	254	1086	239	123	105	25	14	7	2	109	16	193	14	1	10	19	.345	.496	−4.4	4.36	.98
1971	37	36	18	0	4	273	1171	275	120	108	23	10	8	5	98	11	172	12	0	20	9	.690	.526	4.7	3.96	1.02
1972	41	41	30	0	8	346	1351	257	84	76	17	9	9	1	87	8	310	8	2	27	10	.730	.269	17.1	2.18	.56
1973	40	40	18	0	3	293	1262	293	146	127	29	17	3	3	113	12	223	7	0	13	20	.394	.450	−1.8	4.48	1.09
1974	39	39	17	0	1	291	1227	249	118	104	21	13	8	5	136	8	240	11	4	16	13	.552	.481	2.0	3.65	.89
1975	37	37	14	0	3	255	1063	217	116	101	24	15	12	2	104	5	192	5	7	15	14	.517	.534	−.5	4.09	1.00
1976	35	35	13	0	2	253	1031	224	94	88	19	8	4	1	72	4	195	8	3	20	7	.741	.600	3.8	3.34	.84
1977	36	36	17	0	2	283	1135	229	99	83	25	9	4	4	89	5	198	3	7	23	10	.697	.605	3.0	3.15	.72
1978	34	34	12	0	3	247	1006	228	91	78	30	10	5	3	63	7	161	3	7	16	13	.552	.556	−.1	3.32	.83
1979	35	35	13	0	4	251	1029	202	112	101	25	9	5	5	89	11	213	10	11	18	11	.621	.496	3.6	4.02	.95
1980	38	38	13	0	3	304	1228	243	87	79	14	8	2	2	90	12	286	17	7	24	9	.727	.519	6.9	2.58	.64
1981	24	24	10	0	1	190	763	152	59	51	9	12	4	1	62	3	179	9	4	13	4	.765	.511	4.3	2.79	.71
1982	38	38	19	0	6	296	1193	253	114	102	17	11	5	1	86	5	286	9	9	23	11	.676	.511	5.5	3.47	.85
1983	37	37	8	0	3	284	1183	277	117	98	20	20	4	3	84	10	275	13	9	15	16	.484	.573	−2.7	3.71	.90
1984	33	33	1	0	0	229	964	214	104	91	14	8	7	0	79	7	163	11	7	13	7	.650	.479	3.4	4.09	1.01
1985	16	16	0	0	0	92	401	84	43	34	6	9	1	0	53	4	48	3	2	1	8	.111	.484	−3.4	4.21	1.03
1986	32	32	0	0	0	176	792	196	120	100	25	8	5	1	86	4	120	7	2	9	14	.391	.511	−2.8	6.14	1.41
17.44 Years	705	687	251	7	55	5055	20936	4487	2000	1749	386	228	118	49	1742	145	4040	176	83	323	229	.585	.515	38.7	3.56	.88
	40	39	14	0	3	290		257	115	100	22	13	7	3	100	8	232	10	5	19	13	.585	.515	2.2	3.56	.88

Teams: St. Louis, N.L. 1965–1971; Philadelphia, N.L. 1972–1986; San Francisco, 1986; White Sox, 1986.

Points in MVP Voting: 1965, 0; 1966, 0; 1967, 0; 1968, 0; 1969, 0; 1970, 0; 1971, 0; 1972, 124 (5th, .37); 1973, 0; 1974, 0; 1975, 0; 1976, 16 (.05); 1977, 100 (5th, .30); 1978, 0; 1979, 0; 1980, 134 (.40); 1981, 41 (8th, 12); 1982, 41 (9th, .12); 1983–1986, 0. TOTAL: 1.36 Award Shares.

Reported Salaries: 1970, $32,000; 1971, $40,000; 1981–1984 contract, 1981, $600,000; 1982, $700,000; 1983, $700,000; 1984, $700,000 plus $100,000 bonus for signing contract plus performance bonuses of $100,000 to $200,000/season.

Other Notes: Named to *The Sporting News* National League post-season All-Star team in 1969, 1971, 1972, 1977, 1979, 1980, and 1982.

Gold Glove—1981.

Performance summaries in Section II may differ from the above because of the use of 1987 data in Section II.

PLAYER: NOLAN RYAN

	HOW MUCH HE PITCHED							WHAT HE GAVE UP												WHAT THE RESULTS WERE						
Year	G	GS	CG	GF	ShO	IP	BFP	H	R	ER	HR	SH	SF	HB	TBB	IBB	SO	WP	Bk	W	L	Pct.	Rest of Team	Above Team	Runs per Game	Percentage of League
1966	2	1	0	0	0	3	17	5	5	5	1	0	0	0	3	1	6	1	0	0	1	.000	.413	−.4	15.00	3.66
1968	21	18	3	1	0	134	559	93	50	46	12	12	4	4	75	4	133	7	0	6	9	.400	.456	−.8	3.36	.98
1969	25	10	2	4	0	89	375	60	38	35	3	2	2	1	53	3	92	1	3	6	3	.667	.614	.5	3.84	.96
1970	27	19	5	4	2	132	570	86	59	50	10	8	4	4	97	2	125	8	0	7	11	.389	.528	−2.5	4.02	.90
1971	30	26	3	1	0	152	705	125	78	67	8	3	0	15	116	4	137	6	1	10	14	.417	.529	−2.7	4.62	1.20
1972	39	39	20	0	9	284	1154	166	80	72	14	11	3	10	157	4	329	18	0	19	16	.543	.467	2.7	2.54	.73
1973	41	39	26	2	4	326	1355	238	113	104	18	7	7	7	162	2	383	15	0	21	16	.568	.464	3.8	3.12	.74
1974	42	41	26	1	3	333	1392	221	127	107	18	12	4	9	202	3	367	9	0	22	16	.579	.371	7.9	3.43	.85
1975	28	28	10	0	5	198	864	152	90	76	13	6	7	7	132	0	186	12	0	14	12	.538	.430	2.8	4.09	.96
1976	39	39	21	0	7	284	1196	193	117	106	13	13	4	5	183	2	327	5	2	17	18	.486	.465	.7	3.71	.92
1977	37	37	22	0	4	299	1272	198	110	92	12	22	10	9	204	7	341	21	3	19	16	.543	.433	3.8	3.31	.73
1978	31	31	14	0	3	235	1008	183	106	97	12	11	14	3	148	7	260	13	2	10	13	.435	.554	−2.7	4.06	.97
1979	34	34	17	0	5	223	937	169	104	89	15	8	10	6	114	3	223	9	0	16	14	.533	.545	−.4	4.20	.90
1980	35	35	4	0	2	234	982	205	100	87	10	7	7	3	98	1	200	10	1	11	10	.524	.577	−1.1	3.85	.95
1981	21	21	5	0	3	149	605	99	34	28	2	5	3	1	68	1	140	16	2	11	5	.688	.532	2.5	2.05	.53
1982	35	35	10	0	3	250	1050	196	100	88	20	9	3	8	109	3	245	18	2	16	12	.571	.455	3.3	3.60	.88
1983	29	29	5	0	2	196	804	134	74	65	9	7	5	4	101	3	183	5	1	14	9	.609	.511	2.3	3.40	.83
1984	30	30	5	0	2	184	760	143	78	62	12	4	6	4	69	2	197	6	3	12	11	.522	.489	.7	3.82	.94
1985	35	35	4	0	0	232	983	205	108	98	12	11	12	9	95	8	209	14	2	10	12	.455	.521	−1.5	4.19	1.03
1986	30	30	1	0	0	178	729	119	72	66	14	5	4	4	82	5	194	15	0	12	8	.600	.592	.2	3.64	.87
	611	577	203	13	54	4115	17317	2990	1643	1440	228	163	109	113	2268	65	4277	209	22	253	226	.528	.489	19.0	3.59	.88
14.94 Years	41	39	14	1	4	276		200	110	96	15	11	7	8	152	4	286	14	1	17	15	.528	.489	1.3	3.59	.88

Teams: New York, N.L., 1966, 1968–1971; California, A.L., 1972–1979; Houston, 1980–1987.

Points in MVP Voting: 1966, 0; 1968, 0; 1969, 0; 1970, 0; 1971, 0; 1972, 2 (.01); 1973, 20 (.06); 1974, 24 (.07); 1975, 0; 1976, 0; 1977, 3 (.01); 1978, 0; 1979, 0; 1980, 0; 1981, 0; 1982, 0; 1983–1986, 0. TOTAL: .15 Award Shares.

Reported Salaries: 1980–1983, $1,125,000/year ($1,000,000/year plus $500,000 bonuses guaranteed in contract.

Other Notes: Named to *The Sporting News* American League All-Star team in 1977.

Performance summaries in Section II may differ from the above because of the use of 1987 data in Section II.

PLAYER: TOM SEAVER

	HOW MUCH HE PITCHED							WHAT HE GAVE UP												WHAT THE RESULTS WERE						
Year	G	GS	CG	GF	ShO	IP	BFP	H	R	ER	HR	SH	SF	HB	TBB	IBB	SO	WP	Bk	W	L	Pct.	Rest of Team	Above Team	Runs per Game	Percentage of League
1967	35	34	18	1	2	251	1029	224	85	77	19	10	5	5	78	6	170	5	0	16	13	.552	.338	6.2	3.05	.79
1968	36	35	14	1	5	278	1088	224	73	68	15	16	5	8	48	5	205	8	1	16	12	.571	.425	4.1	2.36	.69
1969	36	35	18	1	5	273	1089	202	75	67	24	20	5	7	82	9	208	8	1	25	7	.781	.577	6.5	2.47	.62
1970	37	36	19	1	2	291	1173	230	103	91	21	9	4	4	83	8	283	6	0	18	12	.600	.492	3.2	3.19	.71
1971	36	35	21	1	4	286	1103	210	61	56	18	11	6	4	61	2	289	5	1	20	10	.667	.477	5.7	1.92	.50
1972	35	35	13	0	3	262	1060	215	92	85	23	13	5	5	77	2	249	8	0	21	12	.636	.504	4.4	3.16	.81
1973	36	36	18	0	3	290	1147	219	74	67	23	10	5	4	64	5	251	5	0	19	10	.655	.477	5.2	2.30	.56
1974	32	32	12	0	5	236	956	199	89	84	19	10	2	3	75	10	201	4	2	11	11	.500	.429	1.6	3.39	.83
1975	36	36	15	0	5	280	1115	217	81	74	11	9	2	4	88	6	243	7	1	22	9	.710	.458	7.8	2.60	.64
1976	35	34	13	0	5	271	1079	211	83	78	14	7	2	4	77	9	235	12	0	14	11	.560	.526	.9	2.76	.69
1977	33	33	19	0	7	261	1031	199	78	75	19	5	6	0	66	6	196	7	1	21	6	.778	.430	9.4	2.69	.61
1978	36	36	8	0	1	260	1975	218	97	83	26	13	12	0	89	11	226	6	1	16	14	.533	.580	−1.4	3.36	.84
1979	32	32	9	0	5	215	868	187	85	75	16	10	6	0	61	6	131	4	0	16	6	.727	.532	4.3	3.56	.84
1980	26	26	5	0	1	168	692	140	74	68	24	2	8	1	59	3	101	4	0	10	8	.556	.549	.1	3.96	.98
1981	23	23	6	0	1	166	671	120	51	47	10	9	8	3	66	8	87	5	0	14	2	.875	.565	5.0	2.77	.71
1982	21	21	0	0	0	111	501	136	75	68	14	2	2	3	44	4	62	3	0	5	13	.278	.389	−2.0	6.08	1.49
1983	34	34	5	0	2	231	962	201	104	91	18	9	7	4	86	5	135	10	0	9	14	.391	.468	−1.8	4.05	.99
1984	34	33	10	1	4	237	978	216	108	104	27	8	7	2	61	3	131	5	0	15	11	.577	.434	3.7	4.11	.93
1985	35	33	6	1	0	239	993	223	103	84	22	7	8	6	69	6	134	10	0	16	11	.593	.511	2.2	3.88	.84
1986	28	28	2	0	0	176	759	180	83	79	17	7	6	7	56	2	103	4	0	7	13	.350	.544	−3.9	4.24	.91
16.31 Years	656	647	231	7	60	4782	19369	3971	1674	1521	380	187	111	76	1390	116	3640	126	8	311	205	.603	.484	61.1	3.15	.77
	40	40	14	0	4	293		243	103	93	23	11	8	5	85	7	223	8	0	19	13	.603	.484	3.7	3.15	.77

Teams: New York, N.L., 1967–1976; New York, N.L./Cincinnati, N.L., 1977; Cincinnati, N.L., 1978–1982; New York, N.L., 1983; Chicago, A.L., 1984–1986; Boston Red Sox, 1986.

Points in MVP Voting: 1967, 5 (.02); 1968, 0; 1969, 243 (2nd, .72); 1970, 2 (.01); 1971, 46 (.14); 1972, 2 (.01); 1973, 57 (.17); 1974, 0; 1975, 65 (9th, .19); 1976, 0; 1977, 1 (.00); 1978, 0; 1979, 9 (.03); 1980, 0; 1981, 35 (10th, .10); 1982, 0; 1983–1986, 0. TOTAL: 1.39 Award Shares.

Reported Salaries: 1972, $120,000; 1979–1983 contract, $250,000 signing bonus plus $275,000/year plus performance bonuses between $20,000–$60,000/year.

Other Notes: Named to *The Sporting News* National League All-Star team in 1969, 1973, 1975, and 1981.

Performance summaries in Section II may differ from the above because of the use of 1987 data in Section II.

PLAYER: ROLLIE FINGERS

	HOW MUCH HE PITCHED							WHAT HE GAVE UP												WHAT THE RESULTS WERE						
Year	G	GS	CG	GF	SV	IP	BFP	H	R	ER	HR	SH	SF	HB	TBB	IBB	SO	WP	Bk	W	L	Pct.	Rest of Team	Above Team	Runs per Game	Percentage of League
1968	1	0	0	0	0	1	9	4	4	4	1	0	0	1	1	0	0	1	0	0	0	.000	.506	-.0	36.00	10.57
1969	60	8	1	30	12	119	503	116	60	49	13	5	2	4	41	5	61	1	1	6	7	.462	.550	-1.2	4.54	1.12
1970	45	19	1	9	2	148	608	137	65	60	13	5	4	2	48	5	79	5	0	7	9	.438	.562	-2.0	3.95	.96
1971	48	8	2	28	17	129	503	94	46	43	14	7	3	8	30	3	98	1	0	4	6	.400	.642	-2.4	3.21	.84
1972	65	0	0	41	21	111	437	85	35	31	8	2	1	1	32	7	113	2	1	11	9	.550	.607	-1.1	2.84	.82
1973	62	2	0	49	22	127	521	107	41	27	5	1	3	4	39	6	110	2	0	7	8	.467	.592	-1.9	2.91	.69
1974	76	0	0	60	18	119	483	104	41	35	5	8	12	1	29	6	95	1	1	9	5	.643	.550	1.3	3.10	.77
1975	75	0	0	59	24	127	493	95	43	42	13	4	4	6	33	5	115	6	0	10	6	.625	.603	.4	3.05	.72
1976	70	0	0	62	20	135	559	118	40	37	3	16	11	7	40	10	113	2	0	13	11	.542	.540	.0	2.67	.67
1977	78	0	0	69	35	132	543	123	47	44	12	6	4	1	36	12	113	2	1	8	9	.471	.421	.8	3.20	.73
1978	67	0	0	62	37	107	434	84	33	30	4	4	3	1	29	12	72	2	0	6	13	.316	.545	-4.4	2.78	.70
1979	54	0	0	41	13	84	372	91	47	42	7	5	5	1	37	8	65	2	2	9	9	.500	.413	1.6	5.04	1.19
1980	66	0	0	46	23	103	428	101	35	32	3	6	6	0	32	13	69	5	1	11	9	.550	.437	2.3	3.06	.76
1981	47	0	0	41	28	78	297	55	9	9	3	4	1	1	13	5	61	1	0	6	3	.667	.560	1.0	1.04	.25
1982	50	0	0	45	29	80	318	63	23	23	5	4	6	1	20	5	71	4	0	5	6	.455	.596	-1.6	2.59	.58
1984	33	0	0	30	23	46	193	38	13	10	5	2	0	0	13	2	40	2	0	1	2	.333	.418	-.3	2.54	.58
1985	47	0	0	37	17	55	241	59	33	31	9	4	1	0	19	5	24	1	0	1	6	.143	.455	-2.2	5.37	1.17
14.53 Years	944	37	4	709	341	1701	6942	1474	615	549	123	83	66	39	492	109	1299	40	7	114	118	.491	.533	-9.7	3.25	.79
	65	3	0	49	23	117		101	42	38	8	6	5	3	34	8	89	3	0	8	8	.491	.533	-.7	3.25	.79

Teams: Oakland, A.L., 1968–1976; San Diego, N.L., 1977–1980; Milwaukee, A.L., 1981–1985.

Points in MVP Voting: 1968, 0; 1969, 0; 1970, 0; 1971, 0; 1972, 0; 1973, 0; 1974, 21 (.06); 1975, 129 (4th, .38); 1976, 12 (.04); 1977, 17 (.05); 1978, 16 (.05); 1979, 0; 1980, 0; 1981, 319 (1st, .82); 1982, 12 (.03); 1983–1985, 0. TOTAL: 1.43 Award Shares.

Reported Salaries: 1980–1981, $215,000 plus pro-rated share of signing bonus; 1982–1985, $2.4 million ($800,000/year average) plus performance bonuses.

PLAYER: BERT BLYLEVEN

	HOW MUCH HE PITCHED							WHAT HE GAVE UP												WHAT THE RESULTS WERE						
Year	G	GS	CG	GF	ShO	IP	BFP	H	R	ER	HR	SH	SF	HB	TBB	IBB	SO	WP	Bk	W	L	Pct.	Rest of Team	Above Team	Runs per Game	Percentage of League
1970	27	25	5	1	1	164	675	143	66	58	17	8	2	2	47	6	135	2	3	10	9	.526	.615	-1.7	3.62	.88
1971	38	38	7	0	5	278	1126	267	95	87	21	12	3	5	59	1	224	5	1	16	15	.516	.450	2.1	3.08	.81
1972	39	37	11	1	3	287	1158	247	93	87	22	14	6	10	69	7	228	7	1	17	17	.500	.500	0	2.92	.84
1973	40	40	25	0	9	325	1321	296	109	91	16	11	13	9	67	4	258	7	2	20	17	.541	.488	1.9	3.02	.71
1974	37	37	19	0	3	281	1149	244	99	83	14	13	5	9	77	3	249	3	0	17	17	.500	.508	-.3	3.17	.78
1975	35	35	20	0	3	276	1104	219	104	92	24	10	8	4	84	2	233	7	0	15	10	.600	.445	3.9	3.39	.80
1976	36	36	18	0	6	298	1225	283	106	95	14	18	6	12	81	6	219	7	2	13	16	.448	.496	-1.4	3.20	.80
1977	30	30	15	0	5	235	935	181	81	71	20	10	5	7	69	1	182	8	0	14	12	.538	.588	-1.3	3.10	.68
1978	34	34	11	0	4	244	1011	217	94	82	17	13	2	6	66	5	182	6	2	14	10	.583	.540	1.0	3.47	.87
1979	37	37	4	0	0	237	1018	238	102	95	21	14	9	6	92	8	172	9	0	12	5	.706	.593	1.9	3.87	.92
1980	34	32	5	1	2	217	907	219	102	92	20	10	2	0	59	5	168	2	1	8	13	.381	.532	-3.2	4.23	1.05
1981	20	20	9	0	1	159	644	145	52	51	9	3	3	5	40	1	107	3	1	11	7	.611	.482	2.3	2.94	.77
1982	4	4	0	0	0	20	89	16	14	11	2	0	2	0	11	0	19	0	0	2	2	.500	.481	-.1	6.30	1.82
1983	24	24	5	0	0	156	660	160	74	68	8	2	5	10	44	4	123	5	1	7	10	.412	.429	-.3	4.27	1.01
1984	33	32	12	0	4	245	1004	204	86	78	19	6	8	6	74	4	170	6	0	19	7	.731	.412	8.3	3.16	.71
1985	37	37	24	0	5	294	1203	264	121	103	23	5	8	9	75	1	206	4	1	17	16	.515	.400	3.8	3.71	.81
1986	36	36	16	0	3	272	1126	262	134	121	50	5	4	10	58	4	215	4	0	17	14	.548	.412	4.2	4.43	.95
	541	534	206	3	54	3988	16355	3605	1532	1365	317	154	91	110	1072	62	3090	85	15	229	197	.538	.487	21.4	3.46	.84
13.46 Years	40	40	15	0	4	296		268	114	101	24	11	7	8	80	5	230	6	1	17	15	.538	.487	1.6	3.46	.84

Teams: Minnesota, 1970–1975; Minnesota/Texas, 1976; Texas, 1977; Pittsburgh, 1978–1980; Cleveland, 1981–1985; Minnesota, 1985–present.

Points in MVP Voting: 1970, 0; 1971, 0; 1972, 0; 1973, 4 (.01); 1974, 0; 1975, 0; 1976, 0; 1977, 0; 1978, 0; 1979, 0; 1980, 0; 1981, 0; 1982, 0; 1983–1986, 0. TOTAL: .01 Award Shares.

Reported Salaries: 1980, $300,000; 1981–1986, $650,000/year.

Other Notes: Performance summaries in Section II may differ from the above because of the use of 1987 data in Section II.

NOTES ON THE SECOND EDITION

The first edition of this book, published in the spring of 1985, contained the usual collection of errors, typos, misleading generalizations, oversights, stupid comments and other bumbles. The following people are among the many who set me straight on some issue or another, and whose guidance is appreciated:

Jack Carlson sent a list of thirty corrections and recommendations for reconsideration, many of which were adopted. His comments about 19th-century ball were particularly valuable.

Charles Dineen, the son of Bill Dineen, very properly objected to my characterizing Cy Young as the hero of the 1903 World Series, when it was Dineen who pitched shutouts in games two and eight to lead the Sox to victory.

Dan Whitney convinced me not to describe Hal Chase as a "borderline psychotic."

Among those who corrected specific errors or suggested small changes were Fritz Ankerman, Ronald Bower, Ev Cope, Gary Edmondson, Charlie Harville, Scott Johnson, David A. Lawrence, Thomas D. Lightfoot, Robert McConnell, James F. Maxfield, William B. Mead, A. Miles, Leonard Newman, Robert Robinson, Steve Shabad, Bert Sugar, Gregory Thomajan, Bernard Waltzer and Ross Wetzsteon.

Gordon Herman has peppered my mail box with statistical research, great bundles of which are quoted here. Mr. Herman contributed home/road home run totals for Rogers Hornsby and Chuck Klein, other information about Mr. Hornsby, and many other notable items about baseball circa 1930, some of which are attributed where used.

Joseph Overfield, one of the game's distinguished researchers, gave me a few additional details about the early history of baseball in the Buffalo area, including the death of Ed Delahanty.

Tot Holmes provided information about the early use of numbers on uniforms, and also filled in the home/road home run totals for several players.

Bob Hoie, the author of an important article about Hal Chase that was quoted in the original edition of this book, sent me a very nice letter later which contained additional information about Chase, which is also quoted.

Philip E. Von Borries corrected an error concerning Pete Browning and another about Bob Carruthers, and also provided material about baseball movies as well as other comments.

David Ball sent me several pages of notes concerning 19th-century baseball, including the quoted material about Indianapolis platooning in 1887.

When I said I didn't know anything about Johnny Bassler, John R. Schmidt sent me an article about something Bassler once did, which is quoted in this edition.

Jack Kavanagh educated me about Frank Shellenback, stirrups on uniforms and Joe Medwick, and several of his recommended changes are included in this volume.

Patrick Walsh corrected several statistical errors.

In the first edition of the book I mentioned some gaps in the records available to me about Most Valuable Player voting. Many people helped to fill these gaps. Among the people who sent me copies of missing MVP votes are Ray Andreotti, Frank B. Gerheim, Charlie Harville, Gordon L. Herman, Angelo Louisa and Mike Sparrow. Mr. Louisa, I think, put forth particular efforts to make these records available to me.

Adie Suehsdorf sent me a clipping explaining Dave Bancroft's illness in 1923.

Cappy Gagnon is a frequent correspondent of mine, and one from whom I learn much. He has sent me many clips, photocopies, etc., which have influenced what appears in these pages. Hank Greenberg himself, by way of Cappy Gagnon, corrected the information concerning Hank Greenberg's salaries.

The original version of this book contained two notes entitled "Gruesome, Ain't It?" and "Yes, Hasn't It?" (pages 28 and 29). The first note said that Jack Glasscock and Bill Gleason, rival shortstops in St. Louis in the 1880s, had both been killed in car accidents on December 21, 1917. The second note said that the first note apparently was not true, but it had been reported that way and I didn't know why.

A gentleman named Joe Simenic wrote to straighten it out. It turns out that the Glasscock who was killed in an accident that day was a different man (reporter's error), and that Gleason, while seriously injured by a passing fire truck, was not killed. I decided not to use the items in this edition of the book, but I appreciate Mr. Simenic's generosity in providing the information.

Philip Lowry has advanced the state of knowledge about ballparks to such an extent that in some future edition I may take my poor ballpark material clean out of the book, but while it is here his help in clarifying the record is much appreciated.

Richard Lindberg, author of *Who's on Third* (a history of the White Sox) wrote to explain his comments about Judge Landis's treatment of the Sox. While we reached no agreement, I appreciate the kind approach, and on that basis edited my mention of his work, which was a little harsh.

Richard Malatzky wrote to me concerning the fate of Terry Larkin, and is quoted there.

Craig Wright suggested comments about Buck Ewing and Mel Ott and provided additional information about Dick Allen. Craig also wrote several times debating debatable points, some of which must surely have sunk in on me despite one's natural reluctance to accept guidance from friends as one would from strangers.

Arthur Kimes sent me a chart with which to adjust dollar values over time —quite a useful tool in the present context as well as in others.

Ed Tassinari sent along the list of players who were from towns with the same name, which is acknowledged where it is used. Peter LeClair contributed to the same list, and also spotted several typos and oversights.

Eddie Epstein talked to Phil Wood about Mickey Vernon's career and then sent me the resulting article, which is how I wound up with the new Mickey Vernon comment.

Gene Hasson was a young first baseman for the Philadelphia A's in 1938. Milt Litvin swears that one day a ball was hit to the A's third baseman, who sailed a throw over Hasson's head. As Hasson ran after the ball his hat fell off, and Hasson, with the ball still in play, stopped to retrieve his hat, then went after the ball. He was on a train to the Reading that night.

I have absolutely no documentation for that story, but I wanted to thank Milt Litvin for sending it along anyway, and I included it here as a bonus for the people who actually bother to read the acknowledgments. It is true, by the way, that Gene Hasson played 47 major league games by the age of twenty-two, hitting .293 and slugging .497, but never batted again in the major leagues, which I suppose lends the story at least a smidgen of support.

Pete Palmer called my attention to several errors and explained some little mysteries that I had commented on—the discrepancy in Rube Parnham's stats mentioned in the first edition, the exact dates during which the American League maintained counts of earned runs scored, etc. Pete also furnished some fresh information, including the note about Malzone also leading the league in fielding percentage and errors.

Bob McDowell, a devotee of the Burt Standish books, corrected the information relating to these books.

Among all individuals, however, the most assistance in clarifying the record came from the estimable Canadian baseball researcher, Neil Munro. If you study this edition of the book carefully enough, you can find several thousand bits of data about pitchers which did not appear in the first edition of the book. Neil Munro is the primary source of that new data.

You know, when I as a writer look at my books two or three years later I am often amazed at the mistakes that I made. I suspect that this is true of almost every writer. I mean by this not only that we are chagrined to discover that we have warped a few tales and fumbled a few hundred facts, but that we—I, at least—look at the manuscript and say "What the hell is that sentence doing with its arm twisted behind its knee that way, and why is that useless adjective there and couldn't I have found some more graceful way to convey that impression and what was I thinking of when I wrote this piece of crap and this thing is a good idea but I must have just come from one of Ginsburg's parties or something." It is a rare treat for me to be able to go back into the manuscript and make even more mistakes, mess the thing up so throroughly that in reading it again in a few years I am sure I shall pass away from raw embarrassment.

No, seriously, I appreciated the opportunity. It has always been my intention to write a book that would go through several editions, and with that in mind I set up several sorts of dust bins of history, figuring that if the book survived, if it were reissued a few times, the material could collect. The reported salaries, for example—I had maybe three hundred of them in the first edition, and maybe three hundred random salaries from baseball history aren't of much use in reconstructing the economic history of the game, but maybe there are five hundred in this edition and maybe there will be twelve hundred in the next edition, and maybe eventually we will reach the point at which anybody who is curious about a good player's salary history will have a reliable place to go to look it up. In the first edition of the book I did a history of MVP voting, but I was missing data from quite a few votes. With the help of readers, we cut the number of missing votes in half or thereabouts, and maybe, if you keep writing, in the next edition I can publish a complete history of MVP voting, and maybe then in the edition after that I'll just jerk that stuff out and replace it with something else.

In essence, I see this work as a living book. It was my thinking that I wanted to change it enough that, if it were to go through three or four more editions, then at the end of that process it would be an essentially new book, a book that a person who had the first edition could purchase and feel that he was getting something entirely different.

I still have a lot of things I want to do. I didn't do much with statistics for active players in this edition because of the publication of *The Great American Baseball Stat Book,* which provides a source for that data. I was trying to cover things in this book that aren't covered anywhere else, so I eliminated the stats for a few active players, like Carlton Fisk, and did not add any other recent players. When I read the article on platooning, I can't for the life of me figure out why I decided to start the subject in the middle and walk backwards, but to get rid of this contrivance the article would have to be completely rewritten, and that takes a lot of time. It's a project for the next edition.

In making these revisions, I much appreciate all the help from readers. If there are still errors here, please knock. If you think I chose the wrong player as the fastest runner of the 1940s, feel free to argue; facts are much more appreciated than opinions, but opinions will be dealt with with whatever good grace I can muster at the moment. I ain't the kind of guy who could write books and put them in a drawer and be happy to have written them. I need readers. I am grateful for every one of you.

Glossary of Terms
in Use in Sabermetrics

approximate value: A crude integer estimate of the value of a given season, ranging from 0 for ineffective, part-time play up to an average of 9 or 10 for a regular player, 16 to 20 for an MVP-type season.

award share: The total MVP award vote drawn by a player over the course of his career, stated in constant terms with 1.00 representing the potential vote for one season. (Award Shares could also be calculated for a few other awards, such as the Cy Young.)

base-out percentage: A method developed by Barry Codell for the evaluation of offensive statistics; quite similar to total average.

Brock2 system: A complex set of several hundred interlocking formulas, designed to project a player's final career totals on the basis of his performance up to a given point in time.

career value: The value of a player to his team over the course of his entire career.

defensive efficiency record: A mathematical attempt to answer this question: Of all balls put into play against this team, what percentage did the defense succeed in turning into outs?

defensive spectrum: An arrangement of defensive positions according to raw abilities needed to learn to play each. The spectrum has shifted at times throughout history, but generally reads "designated hitter, first base, left field, right field, third base, center field, second base, shortstop." Catcher is not a part of the spectrum.

definition A: Definition A of a potential Hall of Famer is "A player who could reasonably be argued to be the greatest ever at the position he plays."

definition B: Definition B of a potential Hall of Famer is "A player who is one of the greatest players ever at the position that he plays, and (ordinarily) the dominant player of his time at the position."

definition C: "A player who is consistently among the best at his position."

definition D: "A player who rises well above the level of the average player, and who would be capable of contributing to a pennant-winning team."

expected remaining future value: See Trade Value.

the favorite toy: A method used to estimate the chance that a player, at a given point in his career, will reach some standard of career excellence (such as 3,000 hits, 500 home runs).

isolated power: The difference between batting average and slugging percentage.

Johnson effect: The tendency of teams which exceed their Pythagorean projection for wins in one season to relapse in the following season.

linear weights: A common mathematical tool used to derive the value of each element within a data set, and thus produce formulas that can combine those values. Commonly used by Pete Palmer in analyzing baseball.

offensive earned run average: A method developed by Thomas Cover to estimate the number of earned runs created by each player per 27 outs.

offensive losses: An estimate of the number of team losses that would result from a player's offensive production.

offensive winning percentage: A mathematical answer to this question: If every player on a team hit the same way this player hits, and the team allowed an average number of runs to score, what would the team's winning percentage be?

offensive wins: An estimate of the number of team wins that would result from a player's offensive production.

on-base percentage: If you don't know what on-base percentage is you shouldn't be reading this book.

Palmer method: The collective analytical procedures developed by Pete Palmer. (Has nothing to do with either childbirth or penmanship.)

park adjustment: Any of a number of methods used to adjust offensive or defensive statistics for park illusions.

park illusion: The distortion of offensive or defensive abilities as reflected in statistics due to the characteristics of a given park.

peak value: The value of a player to his team at his highest clearly established level of performance.

project scoresheet: A volunteer effort currently in progress to make scoresheets of all major league games available to the public.

pythagorean method: The practical application of the Pythagorean theory to derive conclusions or state relationships.

pythagorean theory: The name given to a known property of any baseball team, that being that the ratio between their wins and their losses will be similar to the relationship between the square of their runs scored and the square of their runs allowed.

range factor: The average number of plays per game successfully made by a fielder (that is, total chances per game minus errors per game).

RBI importance: That portion of a player's runs batted which are counted as victory-important.

reservoir estimation technique: The process of comparing a team's talent resources by figuring the "trade value" of all players on the roster.

runs created: An estimate of the number of team runs that would result from a player's offensive statistics; can be derived by any of a number of formulas.

sabermetrics: The search for objective knowledge about baseball.

SABR: The Society for American Baseball Research.

secondary average: The sum of a player's extra bases on hits, his walks and his stolen bases expressed per at bat. The unique feature of secondary averages is that overall league secondary averages tend to be almost exactly the same as league batting averages, immediately creating meaningful standards of reference for the category.

total average: A method developed by Thomas Boswell for the evaluation of offensive statistics.

trade value: An estimate of the approximate value that a player will have in the rest of his career.

victory-important RBI (VI-RBI): An attempt to measure the number of a player's runs batted in that are contributions to eventual victory.

Bibliography

Allen, Lee. *The Cincinnati Reds.* New York: G. P. Putnam's Sons, 1948.

Allen, Lee, and Meany, Tom. *Kings of the Diamond.* New York: G. P. Putnam's Sons, 1965.

Allen, Maury. *Baseball's 100.* New York: A & W Visual Library, 1981.

———. *Damn Yankee: The Billy Martin Story.* New York: Times Books, 1980.

Alexander, Charles C. *Ty Cobb.* New York: Oxford University Press, 1984.

Angell, Roger. *The Summer Game.* New York: Popular Library, 1962.

Asinof, Eliot. *Eight Men Out.* New York: Holt, Rinehart and Winston, 1963.

Bartell, Richard, and Norman L. Macht. *Rowdy Richard.* Berkeley, California: North Atlantic Books, 1987.

The Baseball Encyclopedia. New York: Macmillan, 1969, 1982.

Baseball Digest magazine. Evanston, Illinois, issue of October 1955.

Baseball Historical Review. Cooperstown, N.Y.: The Society for American Baseball Research, 1981.

Baseball Research Journal. Cooperstown, N.Y.: The Society for American Baseball Research, 1975, 1976, 1977, 1978, 1979, 1980, 1981, 1982, 1983, 1984, 1985, 1986.

Beverage, Richard E. *The Angels.* Placentia, Calif.: The Deacon Press, 1981.

Boone, Robert S. and Gerald Grunska. *Hack.* Highland Park, Illinois: Highland Press, 1978.

Boswell, Thomas. *Why Time Begins on Opening Day.* Garden City, N.Y.: Doubleday and Company, 1984.

Bouton, Bobbie, and Marshall, Nancy. *Home Games.* New York: St. Martin's/Marek, 1983.

Bouton, Jim. *Ball Four.* New York: Dell, 1970.

———. *I'm Glad You Didn't Take It Personally.* New York: Dell, 1971.

Bouton, Jim, ed. *I Managed Good, But Boy Did They Play Bad.* New York: Dell, 1973.

Brosnan, Jim. *The Long Season.* New York: Grosset and Dunlap, 1960.

———. *Pennant Race.* New York: Dell, 1962.

Brown, Warren. *The Chicago White Sox.* New York: G. P. Putnam's Sons, 1952.

Burdette, Lew, with Gene Schoor. *Lew Burdette of the Braves.* New York: G. P. Putnam and Sons, 1960.

Bunning, Jim, with Ralph Bernstein. *The Story of Jim Bunning.* Philadelphia and New York: J. B. Lippincott Company, 1965.

Campanella, Roy. *It's Good to Be Alive.* New York: Signet, 1959.

Carew, Rod with Ira Berkow. *Carew.* New York: Simon and Schuster, 1979.

Cohen, Joel H. *Inside Corner—Talks with Tom Seaver.* New York: Atheneum, 1974.

Cohen, Richard M.; Deutsch, Jordan A.; and Neft, Davis S. *The Sports Encyclopedia: Baseball.* New York: St. Martin's/Marek, 1985.

Coleman, Jerry; Harwell, Ernie; Kiner, Ralph; McCarver, Tim; Martin, Ned; and Robinson, Brooks. *The Scouting Report: 1983.* New York: Harper and Row, 1983.

Connor, Anthony J. *Voices from Cooperstown.* New York: Collier Books, 1982.

Creamer, Robert L. *Stengel—His Life and Times.* New York: Simon and Schuster, 1984.

Daley, Arthur. *Inside Baseball.* New York: Grosset and Dunlap, 1950.

Davids, L. Robert, ed. *Insider's Baseball, by the Society for American Baseball Research,* New York: Charles Scribners' Sons, 1983.

Deutsch, Jordan A., Cohen, Richard M., Johnson, Roland T., and Neft, David S. *The Scrapbook History of Baseball.* Indianapolis/New York: Bobbs-Merrill, 1975.

Durocher, Leo. *Nice Guys Finish Last.* New York: Simon and Schuster, 1975.

Einstein, Charles. *The Fireside Book of Baseball.* New York: Simon and Schuster, 1956. (See article by Bill Corum.)

———. *Willie's Time: A Memoir of Another America.* New York: J. B. Lippincott Company, 1979.

Faber, Charles F. *Baseball Ratings.* Jefferson, North Carolina: McFarland & Company, 1985.

Flood, Curt. *The Way It Is.* New York: Trident Press, 1970.

Ford, Whitey, with Phil Pepe. *Slick: My Life in and Around Baseball.* New York: William Morrow and Company, Inc., 1987.

Freehan, Bill. *Behind the Mask.* New York and Cleveland: World Publishing Company, 1970.

Gallico, Paul. *Lou Gehrig.* New York: Grosset and Dunlap, 1942.

Garagiola, Joe. *Baseball Is a Funny Game.* New York: Bantam Books, 1960.

Gibson, Bob, with Phil Pepe. *From Ghetto to Glory: The Story of Bob Gibson.* Englewood Cliffs, New Jersey: Prentice-Hall, Inc., 1968.

Graham, Frank. *Lou Gehrig.* New York: G. P. Putnam's Sons, 1942.

———. *The New York Giants.* New York: G. P. Putnam's Sons, 1952.

Higbe, Kirby and Quigley, Martin. *The High Hard One.* New York: Viking Press, 1967.

Hill, Art. *I Don't Care If I Never Come Back.* New York: Simon and Schuster, 1980.

Holtzman, Jerome. *No Cheering in the Press Box.* New York: Holt, Rinehart and Winston, 1973, 1974.

Honig, Donald. *The Man in the Dugout.* Chicago: Follett Publishing Co., 1977.

Hornsby, Rogers with Bill Surface. *My War with Baseball.* New York: Coward-McCann, Inc., 1962.

Jackson, Reggie. *Reggie.* Chicago: Playboy Press, 1975.

———. *Reggie.* New York: Villard Books, 1984.

Kahn, Roger. *The Boys of Summer.* New York: New American Library, 1971.

Kerrane, Kevin and Grossinger, Richard. *Baseball I Gave You All the Best Years of My Life.* Richmond, California: North Atlantic Books, 1976.

Koufax, Sandy with Linn, Ed. *Koufax.* New York: Viking Press, 1966.

Leitner, Irving A. *Baseball—Diamond in the Rough.* New York: Criterion Books, 1972.

Lewine, Harris; Okrent, Daniel; and Nemec, David. *The Ultimate Baseball Book.* Boston: Houghton Mifflin Co., 1981.

Libby, Bill. *Thurman Munson.* New York: G. P. Putnam's Son, 1978.

Lieb, Frederick. *The St. Louis Cardinals, the Story of a Great Baseball Club.* New York: G. P. Putnam's Sons, 1944–45.

———. *Baseball As I Have Known It.* New York: Coward, McCann, 1977.

———. *Connie Mack.* New York: G. P. Putnam's Sons, 1945.

Lieb, Frederick, and Baumgartner, Stan. *The Philadelphia Phillies.* New York: G. P. Putnam's Sons, 1953.

Lindberg, Richard. *Who's on Third.* South Bend, Ind.: Icarus Press, 1983.

Lowenfish, Lee, and Lupien, Tony. *The Imperfect Diamond.* New York: Stein and Day, 1980.

Lowrey, Philip J. *Green Cathedrals.* Cooperstown, New York: Society for American Baseball Research, 1986.

Lyle, Sparky, and Golenbock, Peter. *The Bronx Zoo.* New York: Dell, 1979.

MacFarlane, Paul, ed. *Daguerreotypes.* St. Louis: The Sporting News, 1981.

Mantle, Mickey with Herb Gluck. *The Mick.* New York: Doubleday and Company, Inc., 1985.

Marichal, Juan, with Charles Einstein. *A Pitcher's Story.* Garden City, New York: Doubleday, 1967.

Mathewson, Christy. *Pitching in a Pinch.* New York: Stein and Day, 1977.

Mayer, Ronald A. *The 1937 Newark Bears.* Union City, N.J.: William H. Wise and Co., 1980.

McCaffrey, Eugene V. and McCaffrey, Roger A. *Players' Choice.* New York: Facts on File Publications.

Mead, William B. *Even the Browns.* Chicago: Contemporary Books, 1978.

Meany, Tom. *Baseball's Greatest Players.* New York: Grosset and Dunlap, 1953.

Mehl, Ernest. *The Kansas City Athletics.* New York: Henry Holt and Company, Inc., 1956.

Minor League Baseball Stars. Cooperstown, N.Y.: The Society for American Baseball Research, 1978.

Munson, Thurman, and Appel, Martin. *Thurman Munson.* New York: Coward, McCann, 1978.

Murray, Tom, ed. *Sport Magazine's All-Time All-Stars.* New York: Signet, 1948.

Musial, Stanley as told to Bob Broeg. *Stan Musial: The Man's Own Story.* Garden City, New York: Doubleday and Company, Inc., 1964.

The National Pastime. Cooperstown, New York: Society for American Baseball Research. (Reference Volume 4, No. 1, article by Frederick Ivor-Campbell.)

Obojski, Robert. *Bush League.* New York: Macmillan, 1975.

———. *All-Star Baseball.* New York: Stein and Day, 1980.

Official Baseball Dope Book, 1983. St. Louis: The Sporting News, 1983.

Official Baseball Guide. St. Louis: The Sporting News, 1942, 1943, 1945, 1946, 1947, 1948, 1950, 1951, 1952, 1953, 1954, 1955, 1956, 1957, 1958, 1959, 1960, 1961, 1962, 1963, 1964, 1965, 1966, 1967, 1968, 1969, 1970, 1971, 1972, 1973, 1974, 1975, 1976, 1977, 1978, 1979, 1980, 1981, 1983, 1984.

Official Baseball Record Book. St. Louis: The Sporting News, 1983.

Official Baseball Register. St. Louis: The Sporting News, 1962, 1984.

Official Major League Baseball Record Book. New York: Fawcett, Gold Medal, 1971.

Official World Series Records, 1903–1976, 1978. St. Louis: The Sporting News, 1976, 1978.

Oliva, Tony, with Bob Fowler. *Tony O!* New York: Hawthorn Books, Inc., 1973.

Pepe, Phil. *The Wit and Wisdom of Yogi Berra. New York:* Hawthorn Books, Inc. 1974.

Pepe, Phil, and Hollander, Zander. *The Baseball Book of Lists.* New York: Associated Features, 1983.

Pepitone, Joe. *Joe, You Coulda Made Us Proud.* Chicago: Playboy Press, 1975.

Perry, Gaylord. *Me and the Spitter.* New York: New American Library, 1974.

Peterson, Robert. *Only the Ball Was White.* Englewood Cliffs, N.J., Prentice Hall, 1970.

Piersall, Jim, and Hirshberg, Al. *Fear Strikes Out.* Boston: Little, Brown and Co., 1955.

Polner, Murray. *Branch Rickey.* New York: Signet, 1982.

Quigley, Martin. *The Crooked Pitch.* Chapel Hill, N.C.: Algonquin Books, 1984.

The Reach Official Base Ball Guide, Philadelphia: A. J. Reach Company, 1909, 1911, 1912, 1915, 1917, 1918, 1919, 1922, 1925, 1928, 1932, 1933, 1934, 1937, 1939.

Reidenbaugh, Lowell, and Carter, Craig, eds. *Take Me Out to the Ballpark.* St. Louis: The Sporting News, 1983.

Rice, Grantland. *The Tumult and the Shouting.* New York: A. S. Barnes and Co., 1954.

Ritter, Lawrence S. *The Glory of Their Times.* New York: Collier Books, 1966.

Ritter, Lawrence S., and Honig, Donald. *The 100 Greatest Baseball Players of All Times.* New York: Crown Publishers, Inc., 1981.

Rubin, Robert. *Ty Cobb: The Greatest.* New York: G. P. Putnam and Sons, 1978.

Ruth, Babe with Considine, Bob, *The Babe Ruth Story.* New York: E. P. Dutton and Company, Inc., 1948.

Schlossberg, Dan. *The Baseball Catalog.* Middle Village, N.Y., Jonathan David Publishers, Inc., 1980.

Selzer, Jack, *Baseball in the Nineteenth Century: An Overview.* Cooperstown, New York: Society for American Baseball Research, 1986.

Seymour, Harold. *Baseball—The Early Years.* New York: Oxford University Press, 1960.

Smith, Curt. *Voices of the Game.* South Bend, Indiana: Diamond Communications, Inc., 1987.

Smith, Red. *Press Box.* New York: Avon Books, Discus, 1976.

———. *To Absent Friends from Red Smith.* New York: Atheneum, 1982.

Smith, Robert. *Baseball in America.* New York: Holt, Rinehart and Winston, 1961.

Spalding's Official Base Ball Guide. New York: American Sports Publishing Co., 1907, 1908, 1909, 1910, 1911, 1912, 1916, 1921, 1923, 1924, 1926, 1935, 1936, 1938.

Spink, J. G. Taylor. *Judge Landis and Twenty-Five Years of Baseball.* New York: Thomas Y. Crowell Co., 1947. (Note: Book probably written by Fred Lieb.)

Spink, J. G. Taylor; Richart, Paul A.; and Nemec, Ray. *Daguerreotypes.* St. Louis: The Sporting News, 1961.

The Sporting News. St. Louis, Missouri, issue of June 5, 1976.

Stein, Fred. *Under Coogan's Bluff.* Glenshaw, Pa.: Chapter and Task, 1978.

Stengel, Casey. *Casey at the Bat.* New York: Random House, 1962.

Stockton, J. Roy. *The Gashouse Gang.* New York: A. S. Barnes and Co., 1945.

Stokes, Geoffrey. *Pinstripe Pandemonium.* New York: Harper and Row, 1984.

Thorn, John. *A Century of Baseball Lore.* New York: Galahad Books, 1974.

———, ed. *The National Pastime.* Cooperstown, N.Y.: The Society for American Baseball Research, 1983.

Thorn, John, and Palmer, Pete. *The Hidden Game of Baseball.* Garden City, N.Y.: Doubleday and Co., 1984.

Thorn, John, and Rucker, Mark, eds., *The National Pastime—Special Pictorial Issue: The Nineteenth Century.* Cooperstown, N.Y.: The Society for American Baseball Research, 1984.

Miller, Ira, *Roberto Clemente,* New York, Grosset and Dunlap, 1973.

Voigt, David Quentin. *American Baseball.* Norman, Okla.: University of Oklahoma Press, 1966.

Walton, Ed. *Red Sox, Triumphs and Tragedies.* New York: Stein and Day, 1980.

Weaver, Earl. *It's What You Learn After You Know It All That Counts.* New York: Simon and Schuster, 1982.

Williams, Ted. *My Turn at Bat—the Story of My Life.* New York: Pocket Books, 1969.

Wills, Maury with Steve Gardner. *It Pays to Steal.* Englewood Cliffs, New Jersey: Prentice-Hall, Inc., 1963.

Index

Page numbers in italics denote illustrations.

ABOUT THE AUTHOR

BILL JAMES was born in Kansas and graduated from the University of Kansas. He is the author of the annual *Bill James Baseball Abstract* and coauthor of *Bill James Presents the Great American Baseball Stat Book.* James currently lives in Winchester, Kansas, with his wife, Susan McCarthy, their daughter, and the new baby that should be arriving any day now.